Lecture Notes in Computer Science 8642

Commenced Publication in 1973
Founding and Former Series Editors:
Gerhard Goos, Juris Hartmanis, and Jan van Leeuwen

Michel Abdalla   Roberto De Prisco (Eds.)

Security and Cryptography for Networks

9th International Conference, SCN 2014
Amalfi, Italy, September 3-5, 2014
Proceedings

 Springer

Volume Editors

Michel Abdalla
École Normale Supérieure & CNRS
45 rue d'Ulm
75005 Paris, France
E-mail: michel.abdalla@ens.fr

Roberto De Prisco
Università di Salerno
Dipartimento di Informatica
via Ponte don Melillo
84084 Fisciano, Italy
E-mail: robdep@dia.unisa.it

ISSN 0302-9743   e-ISSN 1611-3349
ISBN 978-3-319-10878-0   e-ISBN 978-3-319-10879-7
DOI 10.1007/978-3-319-10879-7
Springer Cham Heidelberg New York Dordrecht London

Library of Congress Control Number: 2014946896

LNCS Sublibrary: SL 4 – Security and Cryptology

Typesetting: Camera-ready by author, data conversion by Scientific Publishing Services, Chennai, India

Printed on acid-free paper

Springer is part of Springer Science+Business Media (www.springer.com)

Preface

The 9th Conference on Security and Cryptography for Networks (SCN 2014) was held in Amalfi, Italy, during September 3-5, 2014. The conference has traditionally been held in Amalfi, with the exception of the fifth edition which was held in the nearby Maiori. The first three editions of the conference were held in 1996, 1999, and 2002. Since 2002, the conference has been held biannually.

Modern information infrastructures rely heavily on computer networks with the Internet being the one that is most used. Implementing secure distributed transactions for such networks poses new challenges. The SCN conference is an international meeting that focuses on cryptographic and information security tools, both from a theoretical and from a practical perspective, that are needed to face the above challenges. SCN gives to researchers, practitioners, developers, and users interested in the security of communication networks, the possibility to foster cooperation and to exchange techniques, tools, experiences, and ideas in the stunning Amalfi Coast setting.

The conference received 95 submissions in a broad range of cryptography and security areas, setting a new record number of submissions for SCN. The selection of the papers was a difficult task. Amongst the many high-quality submissions, 31 were accepted for publication in these proceedings on the basis of quality, originality, and relevance to the conference's scope.

The international Program Committee (PC) consisted of 33 members who are top experts in the conference fields. At least three PC members reviewed each submitted paper, while submissions co-authored by a PC member were subjected to the more stringent evaluation of four PC members. In addition to the PC members, many external reviewers joined the review process in their particular areas of expertise. We were fortunate to have this knowledgeable and energetic team of experts, and are deeply grateful to all of them for their hard and thorough work, which included a very active discussion phase. Special thanks to Brett Hemenway, Giuseppe Persiano, and Ivan Visconti, for their extra work as shepherds.

Given the perceived quality of the submissions, the PC also decided to give a best paper award, both to promote outstanding work in the fields of cryptography and information security and to keep encouraging high-quality submissions to SCN. This award was given to the paper "On the Classification of Finite Boolean Functions up to Fairness" by Nikolaos Makriyannis.

The paper submission, review, and discussion processes were effectively and efficiently made possible by the Web Submission and Review software, written by Shai Halevi, and hosted at École Normale Supérieure. Many thanks to Shai for his assistance with the system's various features and constant availability.

The program was further enriched by the invited talks of Dario Catalano (University of Catania, Italy) Sanjam Garg (IBM T.J. Watson Research Center,

USA), and Hoeteck Wee (École Normale Supérieure, France), top experts on the subjects of the conference.

SCN 2014 was organized in cooperation with the International Association for Cryptologic Research (IACR).

We thank all the authors who submitted papers to this conference; the Organizing Committee members, colleagues, and student helpers for their valuable time and effort; and all the conference attendees who made this event a truly intellectually stimulating one through their active participation.

We finally thank the *Dipartimento di Informatica* of the University of Salerno, Italy, for the financial support.

September 2014   Michel Abdalla
                                                                 Roberto De Prisco

SCN 2014

The 9th Conference on
Security and Cryptography for Networks

Amalfi, Italy
September 3–5, 2014

Organized by

Dipartimento di Informatica
Università di Salerno

In Cooperation with
The International Association for Cryptologic Research (IACR)

Program Chair

Michel Abdalla   ENS and CNRS, France

General Chair

Roberto De Prisco   Università di Salerno, Italy

Organizing Committee

Aniello Castiglione   Università di Salerno, Italy
Luigi Catuogno   Università di Salerno, Italy
Paolo D'Arco   Università di Salerno, Italy

Steering Committee

Carlo Blundo   Università di Salerno, Italy
Alfredo De Santis   Università di Salerno, Italy
Ueli Maurer   ETH Zürich, Switzerland
Rafail Ostrovsky   University of California - Los Angeles, USA
Giuseppe Persiano   Università di Salerno, Italy
Jacques Stern   ENS, France
Douglas Stinson   University of Waterloo, Canada
Gene Tsudik   University of California - Irvine, USA
Moti Yung   Google, USA and Columbia University, USA

Program Committee

Masayuki Abe	NTT, Japan
Giuseppe Ateniese	Rome University, Italy
Nuttapong Attrapadung	AIST, Japan
Olivier Blazy	Ruhr-Universität Bochum, Germany
Carlo Blundo	Università di Salerno, Italy
Elette Boyle	Technion, Israel
Jean-Sébastien Coron	University of Luxembourg, Luxembourg
Stefan Dziembowski	University of Warsaw, Poland
Dario Fiore	IMDEA, Spain
Marc Fischlin	Darmstadt University of Technology, Germany
Pierre-Alain Fouque	University of Rennes, France
Brett Hemenway	University of Pennsylvania, USA
Stanislaw Jarecki	University of California - Irvine, USA
Gaëtan Leurent	Inria, France
Daniele Micciancio	University of California - San Diego, USA
Michael Naehrig	Microsoft Research, USA
Adam O'Neill	Georgetown University, USA
Claudio Orlandi	Aarhus University, Denmark
Carles Padró	Nanyang Technological University, Singapore
Christopher Peikert	Georgia Institute of Technology, USA
Giuseppe Persiano	Università di Salerno, Italy
Thomas Peyrin	Nanyang Technological University, Singapore
Emmanuel Prouff	ANSSI, France
Christian Rechberger	DTU, Denmark
Vincent Rijmen	K.U. Leuven, Belgium
Christian Schaffner	University of Amsterdam, The Netherlands
Thomas Shrimpton	Portland State University, USA
François-Xavier Standaert	Université catholique de Louvain, Belgium
Stefano Tessaro	University of California - Santa Barbara, USA
Mehdi Tibouchi	NTT, Japan
Damien Vergnaud	ENS, France
Ivan Visconti	University of Salerno, Italy
Bogdan Warinschi	University of Bristol, UK

External Reviewers

Mohamed Abdelraheem	Ilario Bonacina	Dario Catalano
Hoda A. Alkhzaimi	Joppe W. Bos	Nishanth Chandran
Jacob Alperin-Sheriff	Niek Bouman	Melissa Chase
Marcin Andrychowicz	Hank Carter	Jie Chen
Gilad Asharov	Henry Carter	Céline Chevalier
Abhishek Banerjee	Ignacio Cascudo	Craig Costello
Céline Blondeau	David Cash	Dana Dachman-Soled

Bernardo David
Léo Ducas
Keita Emura
Anna Lisa Ferrara
Nils Fleischhacker
Jean-Pierre Flori
Georg Fuchsbauer
Benjamin Fuller
Irene Giacomelli
Vincent Grosso
Dennis Hofheinz
Vincenzo Iovino
Ioana Ivan
Amandine Jambert
Abhishek Jain
Jérémy Jean
Hugo Jonker
Saqib A. Kakvi

Eike Kiltz
Taechan Kim
Susumu Kiyoshima
François Koeune
Hugo Krawczyk
Wang Lei
Patrick Longa
Vadim Lyubashevsky
Daniel Malinowski
Takahiro Matsuda
Sarah Meiklejohn
Diego Mirandola
Ivica Nikolic
Ryo Nishimaki
Miyako Ohkubo
Jiaxin Pan
Maura Paterson
Thomas Peters

Ananth Raghunathan
Samuel Ranellucci
Thomas Roche
Yusuke Sakai
Benedikt Schmidt
Dominique Schroder
Maciej Skórski
Gabriele Spini
Mario Strefler
Katsuyuki Takashima
Tyge Tiessen
Gaven Watson
Hoeteck Wee
Shota Yamada
Eugen Zalinescu
Bingsheng Zhang

Abstracts of Invited Talks

Program Obfuscation via Multilinear Maps

Sanjam Garg

IBM T.J. Watson
sanjamg@cs.ucla.edu

Abstract. Recent proposals for plausible candidate constructions of *multilinear maps* and *obfuscation* have radically transformed what we imagined to be possible in cryptography. For over a decade cryptographers had been very skeptical about the existence of such objects. In this article, we provide a very brief introduction to these results and some of their interesting consequences.

Functional Encryption and Its Impact on Cryptography

Hoeteck Wee[*]

ENS, Paris, France
wee@di.ens.fr

Abstract. Functional encryption is a novel paradigm for public-key encryption that enables both fine-grained access control and selective computation on encrypted data, as is necessary to protect big, complex data in the cloud. In this article, we provide a brief introduction to functional encryption, and an overview of its overarching impact on the field of cryptography.

[*] CNRS (UMR 8548) and INRIA. Supported in part by NSF Awards CNS-1237429 and CNS-1319021 and a fellowship from the Alexander von Humboldt Foundation.

Homomorphic Signatures and Message Authentication Codes

Dario Catalano

Università di Catania, Italy
catalano@dmi.unict.it

Abstract. Homomorphic message authenticators allow to validate computation on previously signed data. The holder of a dataset $\{m_1, \ldots, m_\ell\}$ uses her secret key sk to produce corresponding tags $(\sigma_1, \ldots, \sigma_\ell)$ and stores the authenticated dataset on a remote server. Later the server can (publicly) compute $m = f(m_1, \ldots, m_\ell)$ together with a succinct tag σ certifying that m is the correct output of the computation f. A nice feature of homomorphic authenticators is that the validity of this tag can be verified *without* having to know the original dataset. This latter property makes the primitive attractive in a variety of context and applications, including, for instance, verifiable delegation of computation on outsourced data.

In this short survey, I will give an overview of the state of the art in the areas of homomorphic signatures and message authentication codes. I will (briefly) describe some of the most recent results and provide an overview of the main challenges that remain to address.

Table of Contents

Network Security

Functional Encryption

Invited Talk II

Cryptanalysis

Secure Computation – Implementation

Zero Knowledge

Message Authentication

Invited Talk III

Proofs of Space and Erasure

Public-Key Encryption

Universally Composable
Non-Interactive Key Exchange

Eduarda S.V. Freire[1,*], Julia Hesse[2], and Dennis Hofheinz[2,**]

[1] Royal Holloway, University of London, United Kingdom
Eduarda.Freire.2009@live.rhul.ac.uk
[2] Karlsruhe Institute of Technology, Germany
{julia.hesse,dennis.hofheinz}@kit.edu

Abstract. We consider the notion of a *non-interactive key exchange* *(NIKE)*. A NIKE scheme allows a party A to compute a common shared key with another party B from B's public key and A's secret key alone. This computation requires no interaction between A and B, a feature which distinguishes NIKE from regular (i.e., interactive) key exchange not only quantitatively, but also qualitatively.

Our first contribution is a formalization of NIKE protocols as ideal functionalities in the Universal Composability (UC) framework. As we will argue, existing NIKE definitions (all of which are game-based) do not support a modular analysis either of NIKE schemes themselves, or of the use of NIKE schemes. We provide a simple and natural UC-based NIKE definition that allows for a modular analysis both of NIKE schemes and their use in larger protocols.

We investigate the properties of our new definition, and in particular its relation to existing game-based NIKE definitions. We find that
(a) game-based NIKE security is equivalent to UC-based NIKE security against *static* corruptions, and
(b) UC-NIKE security against adaptive corruptions *cannot* be achieved without additional assumptions (but *can* be achieved in the random oracle model).
Our results suggest that our UC-based NIKE definition is a useful and simple abstraction of non-interactive key exchange.

Keywords: non-interactive key exchange, universal composability.

1 Introduction

Non-interactive key exchange. In a non-interactive key exchange (NIKE) scheme, any two parties can compute a common shared key without any interaction. Concretely, a NIKE scheme enables a party A to compute a shared key $K_{A,B} = K_{B,A}$ with party B from A's secret key sk_A and B's public key pk_B. A very simple

* Supported by CAPES Foundation/Brazil on grant 0560/09-0 and Royal Holloway, University of London.
** Supported in part by DFG grant GZ HO 4534/4-1.

M. Abdalla and R. De Prisco (Eds.): SCN 2014, LNCS 8642, pp. 1–20, 2014.
© Springer International Publishing Switzerland 2014

(albeit only mildly secure) example of a NIKE scheme is the Diffie-Hellman key exchange protocol [10]. (Here, $K_{A,B} = g^{ab}$ can be computed from $\mathsf{sk}_A = a$ and $\mathsf{pk}_B = g^b$, or from $\mathsf{pk}_A = g^a$ and $\mathsf{sk}_B = b$.)

A NIKE scheme offers guarantees that are quite different from a regular (i.e., interactive) key exchange (KE) protocol: a NIKE scheme can only offer one session (i.e., shared key) per pair of public keys. On the other hand, in NIKE schemes, the notion of (specifically adversarial) key registrations plays a crucial role. Namely, while KE schemes use long-term public keys commonly only to achieve authentication properties (e.g., [7]), a NIKE scheme must completely rely on public and secret keys. In return, a NIKE scheme offers its functionality without any interaction – a feature that has found use, e.g., in constructions of PKE schemes [13], designated verifier signature schemes [16], deniable authentication [11], or in wireless and sensor networks [14]. To see how the latter could benefit from the non-interactivity we refer to [8], where it is shown that the energy costs of communication can be significantly reduced when using non-interactive key exchange schemes rather than interactive ones. Moreover, as a further application, NIKE can even be used as a basis for interactive key exchange [2]. We stress that in many of the above mentioned applications [13, 16, 11], non-interactivity is a crucial requirement, and not only an efficiency bonus. We believe that this justifies the investigation of NIKE schemes as such.

Previous NIKE definitions. Somewhat surprisingly, the syntax and security of NIKE schemes has been formalized only very recently, by Cash, Kiltz, and Shoup [9].[1] They also construct an efficient NIKE scheme in the random oracle model (ROM), based on the Computational Diffie-Hellman assumption. Further constructions and variants of the NIKE definition were given by Freire et al. [13]. All of the security definitions in [9, 13] are game-based and do not consider the registration process of public keys itself. This is a bit unfortunate, in particular since a factoring-based NIKE scheme from [13] explicitly requires a nontrivial key registration (and can thus not be completely modeled in the setting of [13]).

In fact, game-based security definitions (like those from [9, 13]) appear unsuitable to model an interactive key registration process for NIKE schemes. Namely, adding a (presumably adversarially controlled) interactive message scheduling would considerably complicate the clean and simple NIKE definitions of [9, 13]. Indeed, it seems more natural and modular to conceptually separate the interactive key registration process from the actual security of (non-interactive) NIKE sessions. However, it is not obvious how to achieve such a conceptual separation using a game-based security definition.

Our contribution. In this work, we devise a simple and intuitive NIKE definition that enables a modular analysis both of NIKE schemes themselves and their use in larger protocols. Our definition is set in the framework of Universal Composability (UC) [3], which allows for a convenient separation of the interactive key registration phase and the actual NIKE scheme. Specifically, we can analyze key

---

[1] A formalization of NIKE schemes as variants of interactive KE schemes (e.g., using the KE security model of [7]) seems possible; however, as argued above, a case-tailored NIKE definition would appear simpler and more useful.

registration and NIKE scheme (assuming correctly registered public keys) separately. Besides, a formalization as an ideal functionality in the UC framework yields a very natural and intuitive characterization of a NIKE scheme.

We demonstrate the usefulness of our definition by showing that our definition generalizes existing game-based NIKE definitions, and that the factoring-based NIKE scheme of [13] can be analyzed with respect to our NIKE definition. This in particular means that, while being conceptually simpler, our NIKE notion retains a form of backward compatibility with existing notions.

Why KE functionalities are not suitable for NIKE protocols. Existing KE functionalities (e.g., [7]) are designed for interactive key exchange protocols and allow multiple sessions per pair of public keys. In contrast, our NIKE functionality is non-interactive (i.e., immediate) and supports only one session per pair of public keys. As mentioned above, non-interactivity is crucial in certain applications (e.g., [13, 16, 14, 11]); however, currently no NIKE schemes that support multiple sessions per pair of public keys are known. (Hence we have restricted our functionality to one session per pair of public keys.)

One could of course modify existing KE functionalities by restricting them to one session, or by modifying the adversary to immediately deliver outputs. This would have essentially the same effect as our tailor-made NIKE functionality. We believe however that a specific NIKE functionality is simpler, and the conceptual differences between (interactive) KE and NIKE justify a separate functionality.

Some technical details. As already explained, we formalize a NIKE scheme itself and the key registration process separately. Concretely, we consider three ideal functionalities (in the sense of UC), $\mathcal{F}_{CRS}$, $\mathcal{F}_{NIKE}$ and $\mathcal{F}_{KR}$. $\mathcal{F}_{CRS}$ provides a common reference string (CRS), which abstracts the availability of public parameters for the NIKE scheme. $\mathcal{F}_{KR}$ abstracts the key registration process. We stress that, similar to [17], and unlike [1, 6], our $\mathcal{F}_{KR}$ functionality allows a party to register arbitrary public keys (that pass some – possibly interactive – validity check). In particular, $\mathcal{F}_{KR}$ does not choose key pairs for a party. This yields a weaker, but arguably more realistic abstraction of key registration. Indeed, we will not attempt to implement $\mathcal{F}_{KR}$ itself – rather, we view $\mathcal{F}_{KR}$ as an abstraction of an actual key registration authority.

$\mathcal{F}_{NIKE}$, on the other hand, completely abstracts a NIKE scheme. Hence, a NIKE scheme may (or may not) implement $\mathcal{F}_{NIKE}$ in the $(\mathcal{F}_{CRS}, \mathcal{F}_{KR})$-hybrid model (i.e., using an instance of $\mathcal{F}_{CRS}$ and $\mathcal{F}_{KR}$). In a nutshell, $\mathcal{F}_{NIKE}$ simply provides every pair of parties with a single, independently uniform shared key.

We first show that our formalization can be seen as a generalization of the previous game-based definitions of [9, 13]. Concretely, let us call a NIKE scheme NIKE *CKS-secure* if it achieves the game-based notion of [9]. We show that the *CKS* notion and the NIKE security notions from [13] are all polynomially equivalent even if we allow a re-registration of users that are not allowed in those models. Since [9, 13] do not model key registration, we must assume that NIKE runs with a trivial key registration in which parties simply send their public keys to $\mathcal{F}_{KR}$, and no validity check whatsoever is performed. We show that

(a) NIKE is *CKS*-secure if and only if NIKE securely realizes $\mathcal{F}_{NIKE}$ (with respect to the trivial key registration described above) against *static*[2] adversaries,
(b) $\mathcal{F}_{NIKE}$ cannot be realized without additional (e.g., set-up) assumptions against *adaptive* adversaries, but
(c) if NIKE is *CKS*-secure,[3] then a variant of NIKE with hashed shared keys securely realizes $\mathcal{F}_{NIKE}$ against adaptive adversaries in the ROM.

Results (b) and (c) resemble similar results by Nielsen [18] for the case of UC-secure public-key encryption. Specifically, to show (b), we show that a UC simulator $\mathcal{S}$ (as necessary to show UC security) attempting to emulate an adaptive attack on NIKE may run into a commitment problem. (We note, however, that the commitment problem we encounter for NIKE schemes is slightly different from the one for public-key encryption from [18]; see Section 4.2 for details.)

Secondly, we remark that $\mathcal{F}_{NIKE}$ and $\mathcal{F}_{KR}$ allow to model NIKE schemes that cannot be modeled using previous NIKE notions. Specifically, we observe that the key registration of the factoring-based NIKE scheme from [13] can be handled using $\mathcal{F}_{KR}$.

Further related work. We note that, apart from the mentioned works dealing with *public-key-based* NIKE schemes, the concept of NIKE has also been considered in the *identity-based* setting (e.g., [19, 12]).

Roadmap. We recall (and slightly adapt) previous NIKE definitions and security models in Section 2, and we present our UC-based NIKE definition in Section 3. We investigate the properties of our new definition in Section 4. Namely, Section 4.1 relates our definition (restricted to static corruptions) to existing (game-based) definitions. Section 4.2 and Section 4.4 contain our results for adaptive corruptions: Section 4.2 shows that adaptive UC-based NIKE security cannot be achieved without additional (e.g., setup) assumptions, and Section 4.4 describes a simple transformation that achieves adaptive UC-based NIKE security in the ROM. See the full version [20] for more detailed explanations, proofs and a complete modelling of the factoring-based NIKE scheme from [13].

2   Preliminaries

NIKE schemes. Following [9], and later [13], we formally define non-interactive key exchange in the *public key setting*. A non-interactive key exchange scheme NIKE in the public key setting consists of three algorithms: NIKE.CommonSetup, NIKE.KeyGen and NIKE.SharedKey. The first algorithm is run by a trusted authority, while the second and third algorithms can be run by any user.

- NIKE.CommonSetup(1^k): This algorithm is probabilistic and takes as input a security parameter k. It outputs a set of system parameters, *params*.

---

[2] However, our result hinges on the exact definition of "static corruptions" — see Section 4.1 for details.
[3] Actually we only need a weaker version of this notion, which is "search-based" instead of indistinguishability-based.

- NIKE.KeyGen($params$, ID): This is the key generation algorithm, a probabilistic algorithm that on inputs $params$ and a user identifier ID $\in \mathcal{IDS}$, where $\mathcal{IDS}$ is an identity space, outputs a public key/secret key pair (pk, sk).
- NIKE.SharedKey(ID_1, pk_1, ID_2, sk_2): On inputs a user identifier $ID_1 \in \mathcal{IDS}$ and a public key pk_1 along with another user identifier $ID_2 \in \mathcal{IDS}$ and a secret key sk_2, this deterministic algorithm outputs a shared key in $\mathcal{SHK}$, the shared key space, for the two users, or a failure symbol $\bot$. We assume that this algorithm outputs $\bot$ if $ID_1 = ID_2$ or if any of its input is missing or is not in the correct domain.

For correctness, for any pair of user identifiers ID_1, ID_2, and corresponding public key/secret key pairs (pk_1, sk_1), (pk_2, sk_2), NIKE.SharedKey satisfies

$$\text{NIKE.SharedKey}(ID_1, pk_1, ID_2, sk_2) = \text{NIKE.SharedKey}(ID_2, pk_2, ID_1, sk_1).$$

W.l.o.g., we will only consider a shared key space of $\mathcal{SHK} = \{0, 1\}^k$.

(Game-based) security of NIKE. Several game-based security notions for NIKE, where an adversary against a NIKE scheme is required to distinguish real from random keys, were presented in [13]. The security notions in [13] are denoted by *CKS-light*, *CKS*, *CKS-heavy* and *m-CKS-heavy*. In those notions, minimal assumptions are made about the Certificate Authority (CA) in the PKI supporting the non-interactive key exchange. The security models in [13] do not rely on the CA checking that a) a public key submitted for certification has not been submitted before, and b) the party submitting the public key knows the corresponding secret key. An adversary against a NIKE scheme in those models is thus allowed to introduce arbitrary public keys (for which it might not know the corresponding secret keys) into the system. However, the security models in [13] do not capture re-registration of (honest or corrupted) users, (i.e., when a user renews its public key).

In this paper, we make use of some of the security notions from [13], but in the more realistic scenario where users are allowed to re-register public keys with a CA, and an adversary against a NIKE scheme is allowed to re-register a user as corrupted even if it was registered as honest before. Also, for some cases we need weaker security notions, where an adversary instead of being required to distinguish real from random keys, it is required to actually output the shared key between two honest users.

We start with recalling the strongest model from [13], *m-CKS-heavy*, which is defined in terms of a game between an adversary $\mathcal{B}$ and a challenger $\mathcal{C}$. First, $\mathcal{B}$ obtains a set of system parameters, $params$, from $\mathcal{C}$, which is obtained by running $params \xleftarrow{\$} \text{NIKE.CommonSetup}(1^k)$. $\mathcal{C}$ then randomly chooses a bit b and answers the following oracle queries from $\mathcal{B}$:

(register honest user, ID). $\mathcal{C}$ runs (pk, sk) $\xleftarrow{\$}$ NIKE.KeyGen($params$, ID) to generate a keypair, records ($honest$, ID, pk, sk) and sends pk to $\mathcal{B}$.

(register corrupt user, ID, pk). $\mathcal{C}$ records ($corrupt$, ID, pk, $\bot$), thereby overwriting any existing entry for this ID.

(extract, ID). $\mathcal{C}$ returns all values sk that appear in stored entries of the form ($honest$, ID, pk, sk) for the given ID.

Table 1. Allowed number of queries for an adversary in the game-based security definitions for NIKE from [13]. * means that the adversary is allowed to make an arbitrary number of queries.

Security notion	reg.hon.	reg.corr.	extract	hon.rev.	corr.rev.	test
CKS-light	2	*	0	0	*	1
CKS	*	*	0	0	*	*
CKS-heavy	*	*	*	*	*	1
m-CKS-heavy	*	*	*	*	*	*

(honest reveal, $\mathsf{ID}_i, \mathsf{ID}_j$). Here $\mathcal{B}$ supplies two identities ID_i and ID_j, both registered as honest. $\mathcal{C}$ obtains the shared key between the identities ID_i and ID_j by running $K_{i,j} \leftarrow \mathtt{NIKE.SharedKey}(\mathsf{ID}_i, \mathsf{pk}_i, \mathsf{ID}_j, \mathsf{sk}_j)$ and returns $K_{i,j}$ to $\mathcal{B}$.

(corrupt reveal, $\mathsf{ID}_i, \mathsf{ID}_j$). Here $\mathcal{B}$ supplies one honest and one corrupt identity. $\mathcal{C}$ obtains the shared key between the identities ID_i and ID_j by running $K_{i,j} \leftarrow \mathtt{NIKE.SharedKey}(\mathsf{ID}_i, \mathsf{pk}_i, \mathsf{ID}_j, \mathsf{sk}_j)$ if ID_j is honest or $K_{i,j} \leftarrow \mathtt{NIKE.SharedKey}(\mathsf{ID}_j, \mathsf{pk}_j, \mathsf{ID}_i, \mathsf{sk}_i)$ if ID_i is honest. $\mathcal{C}$ returns $K_{i,j}$ to $\mathcal{B}$.

(test, $\mathsf{ID}_i, \mathsf{ID}_j$). $\mathcal{C}$ computes the corresponding shared key by running $K_{i,j} \leftarrow \mathtt{NIKE.SharedKey}(\mathsf{ID}_i, \mathsf{pk}_i, \mathsf{ID}_j, \mathsf{sk}_j)$ if $b = 0$, or draws $K_{i,j}$ uniformly random from $\mathcal{SHK}$ if $b = 1$ (note that both identities are honest). $\mathcal{C}$ returns $K_{i,j}$ to $\mathcal{B}$.

The identities $\mathsf{ID}_i, \mathsf{ID}_j$ belong to an identity space $\mathcal{IDS}$ and are merely used to track which public keys are associated with which users. Also, $\mathcal{B}$ is allowed to make an arbitrary number of queries. We assume that $\mathcal{C}$ maintains a list of shared keys and sends the same shared key for a pair of identities if $\mathcal{B}$ makes the same test query again. To avoid trivial wins, $\mathcal{B}$ is not allowed to issue an honest reveal query and a test query on the same pair of identities. For the same reason, $\mathcal{B}$ is not allowed to issue an extract query on any identity involved in a test query, and vice versa. $\mathcal{B}$ is also not allowed to make a register corrupt user query on an identity which has already been registered as honest. $\mathcal{B}$ wins the game if it outputs a bit $\hat{b} = b$. Now $\mathcal{B}$'s advantage in the m-CKS-heavy game is:

$$\mathrm{Adv}_{\mathcal{B}}^{m\text{-}CKS\text{-}heavy}(k, q_H, q_C, q_E, q_{HR}, q_{CR}, q_T) = \left| \Pr[\hat{b} = b] - 1/2 \right|,$$

where $q_H, q_C, q_E, q_{HR}, q_{CR}$ and q_T are the numbers of register honest user, register corrupt user, extract, honest reveal, corrupt reveal and test queries made by $\mathcal{B}$. Informally, a NIKE scheme is m-CKS-heavy-secure if there is no polynomial-time adversary that makes at most q_H register honest user queries, etc., having non-negligible advantage in k. In our proofs, we will w.l.o.g. restrict to adversaries that make exactly as many queries of each type as they are allowed. See Table 1 for a summary of the differences between the models from [13] in terms of allowed adversarial queries.

Throughout the paper, we add $^+$ to the notation of the security models from [13] to denote the augmented versions of those models when re-registration of honest users is allowed, and we add $^{++}$ to the notation to denote that both re-registration of honest users, as well as corrupt registration of previously registered honest users, are allowed. We show that our strongest security model, the m-CKS-heavy^{++} , is polynomially equivalent to the weakest notion from [13], the *CKS-light* model. Then it follows that all the above mentioned security models *with or without* re-registration of users are also polynomially equivalent. We start with a description of our augmented version of the *m-CKS-heavy* model.

The m-CKS-heavy^{++} *security model.* Our *m-CKS-heavy*$^{++}$ security model differs from the *CKS-heavy* model by allowing an adversary $\mathcal{A}$ to make multiple (`register honest user`, ID) queries for the same ID. Upon each such request, $\mathcal{C}$ runs (pk, sk) $\xleftarrow{\$}$ NIKE.KeyGen(*params*, ID) to obtain a new public key/secret key pair and returns pk to $\mathcal{A}$. $\mathcal{C}$ then overwrites any existing entry (*honest*, ID, pk, sk) for ID in its list. Additionally, $\mathcal{A}$ is allowed to register previously registered honest users as corrupt users by issuing a (`register corrupt user`, ID, pk) query to its challenger $\mathcal{C}$. The user will from then on be considered as corrupt. Here $\mathcal{C}$ deletes any existing entry for ID of the form (*honest*, ID, pk', sk') and adds a new entry (*corrupt*, ID, pk, $\perp$) to its list. We can loosen some restrictions on the adversary concerning trivial wins, e.g., allow `extract` queries on users involved in `test` queries as long as that user has been re-registered since the `test` query was issued. The adversary's goal in the *m-CKS-heavy*$^{++}$ game is the same as in the *m-CKS-heavy* game. The following theorem, the proof of which can be found in the full version [20], shows that the new strong security notion is equivalent to the weakest notion from [13].

Theorem 1 (*m-CKS-heavy*$^{++}$ $\Leftrightarrow$ *CKS-light*). *The* m-CKS-heavy^{++} *and CKS-light security models are polynomially equivalent.*

A strictly weaker notion: weakCKS^{++} *security.* We introduce a weaker notion, called *weakCKS*$^{++}$, where the adversary has to output a current shared key between two honest parties. The adversary is allowed to issue the following queries: (`register honest user`, ID), (`register corrupt user`, ID, pk), (`extract`, ID) and (`corrupt reveal`, ID$_i$, ID$_j$). We note that, similar to Theorem 1, it can be shown that the *weakCKS*$^{++}$ security model is polynomially equivalent to its version without the extra allowance of the above mentioned re-registration of users, which we denote by the *weakCKS* security model.

3   NIKE in the UC Model

NIKE in the UC model of protocol execution. In order to establish relationships between game-based NIKE security notions and UC notions, we first explain how parties behave in a real execution of a NIKE scheme NIKE with environment $\mathcal{Z}$ and adversary $\mathcal{A}$, in the hybrid-model with a key registration functionality $\mathcal{F}_{KR}^{f}$ (described below) and a common reference string functionality $\mathcal{F}_{CRS}$.

   A party P$_i$ proceeds as follows, running with $\mathcal{Z}$, $\mathcal{A}$, $\mathcal{F}_{KR}^{f}$ and $\mathcal{F}_{CRS}$:
- Upon receipt of (`register`, P$_i$) from $\mathcal{Z}$ for the first time, request *params* from the $\mathcal{F}_{CRS}$ functionality and run NIKE.KeyGen(*params*, P$_i$) to generate a public

key/secret key pair $(\mathsf{pk}_i, \mathsf{sk}_i)$. Register the public key pk_i with $\mathcal{F}_{KR}^f$ by sending $(\mathtt{register}, \mathsf{P}_i, \mathsf{pk}_i, \tau)$, where τ is a proof of validity of pk_i[4].

- On input $(\mathtt{init}, \mathsf{P}_i, \mathsf{P}_j)$ from $\mathcal{Z}$, request the public key corresponding to party P_j by sending $(\mathtt{lookup}, \mathsf{P}_j)$ to $\mathcal{F}_{KR}^f$. Compute the shared key $K_{i,j} \leftarrow$ NIKE.SharedKey$(\mathsf{P}_j, \mathsf{pk}_j, \mathsf{P}_i, \mathsf{sk}_i)$ and send $(\mathsf{P}_i, \mathsf{P}_j, K_{i,j})$ to $\mathcal{Z}$.

- On input $(\mathtt{renew}, \mathsf{P}_i)$ from $\mathcal{Z}$ compute $(\mathsf{pk}_i, \mathsf{sk}_i) \xleftarrow{\$}$ NIKE.KeyGen$(params, \mathsf{P}_i)$ to generate a new public key/secret key pair. Register pk_i with $\mathcal{F}_{KR}^f$ as before.

- Upon receipt of $(\mathtt{corrupt}, \mathsf{P}_i)$ from $\mathcal{A}$, send the entire current state to $\mathcal{A}$ and, from this point on, relay everything to or from $\mathcal{A}$.

Ideal functionalities for NIKE. We now introduce our ideal functionalities $\mathcal{F}_{NIKE}$ and $\mathcal{F}_{KR}^f$. $\mathcal{F}_{NIKE}$ abstracts the task of non-interactive key exchange. To enable a modular analysis of NIKE schemes we separate the process of key registration from the issuance of shared keys and, in addition to $\mathcal{F}_{NIKE}$, introduce a separate ideal functionality $\mathcal{F}_{KR}^f$ for the task of public key registration.

The key exchange functionality $\mathcal{F}_{NIKE}$. Our ideal functionality $\mathcal{F}_{NIKE}$ is suitable for non-interactive key exchange in the public key setting. $\mathcal{F}_{NIKE}$ handles the generation of shared keys between two parties, providing the security guararan-tees of non-interactive key exchange: if an honest party P_i obtained a key $K_{i,j}$ from a session with an honest party P_j, then $K_{i,j}$ is ideally random and unknown to the adversary. Also, $\mathcal{F}_{NIKE}$ requires the requesting party to know the iden-tity of the peer. We stress that $\mathcal{F}_{NIKE}$ can also handle issuance of new shared keys (e.g., after a party renews its public key in a real NIKE scheme). If one of the parties is corrupted by the time that a request was made, then there is no guarantee of security of the shared key.

We remark that, as standard in the GNUC model, $\mathcal{F}_{NIKE}$'s output towards the parties is scheduled *immediately*, i.e., without adversarial intervention. Even more, we model $\mathcal{F}_{NIKE}$ such that the computation of shared keys between honest parties is completely oblivious to the adversary. This models the fact that a party, when using a non-interactive key exchange scheme, needs to be able to perform this computation without the help of other parties. Modeling $\mathcal{F}_{NIKE}$ as immediate enforces this, because the execution of an interactive protocol can be delayed by the real-world adversary and is thus not simulatable in the ideal world, where the adversary has no ability to schedule $\mathcal{F}_{NIKE}$'s output. We note that even in this setting, during computation of a shared key, a real-world party is still able to use hybrid ideal functionalities that do not communicate with the adversary.

$\mathcal{F}_{NIKE}$ operates in two modes, depending on the kind of session for which it should output a key. We call a session honest if both parties are honest,

---

[4] How such a proof τ looks like depends on the concrete NIKE scheme. For instance, in most existing NIKE protocols, the proof will be trivial (i.e., empty), since the validity of public keys is publicly verifiable.

otherwise the session is called corrupted. We assume $\mathcal{F}_{NIKE}$ knows which parties are corrupted.[5] Additionally, $\mathcal{F}_{NIKE}$ maintains three lists:

- a list Λ_{renew} to store parties that want to renew their public key/secret key pair;
- a list Λ_{reg} to store parties that successfully registered a public key;
- a list Λ_{keys} to store shared keys for pairs of parties.

We note that technically, sessions with dishonest parties who still maintain an honestly registered key could alternatively be treated as honest. This yields an alternative ideal functionality that provides slightly better security guarantees than $\mathcal{F}_{NIKE}$ at the cost of a more complicated description. (Our proofs below carry over to such an alternative functionality.)

$\mathcal{F}_{NIKE}$ proceeds as follows, running on security parameter k, with parties $P_1, \ldots, P_n$ and an adversary.

- On input (register, P_i) from P_i forward (register, P_i) to the adversary.
- On input (P_i, registered) from the adversary, if $P_i \notin \Lambda_{reg}$, add P_i to Λ_{reg}. Else, if $P_i \in \Lambda_{renew}$, delete every existing entry ($\{P_i, \cdot\}, key$) from Λ_{keys} and delete P_i from Λ_{renew}. In any case, send (P_i, registered) back to the adversary.
- On input (init, P_i, P_j) from P_i, if $P_j \notin \Lambda_{reg}$, return ($P_i, P_j, \bot$) to P_i. If $P_j \in \Lambda_{reg}$, we consider two cases:
  - Corrupted session mode: if there exists an entry ($\{P_i, P_j\}, K_{i,j}$) in Λ_{keys}, set $key = K_{i,j}$. Else send (init, P_i, P_j) to the adversary. After receiving ($\{P_i, P_j\}, K_{i,j}$) from the adversary, set $key = K_{i,j}$ and add ($\{P_i, P_j\}, key$) to Λ_{keys}.
  - Honest session mode: if there exists an entry ($\{P_i, P_j\}, K_{i,j}$) in Λ_{keys}, set $key = K_{i,j}$, else choose $key \xleftarrow{\$} \{0,1\}^k$ and add ($\{P_i, P_j\}, key$) to Λ_{keys}.
  - Return (P_i, P_j, key) to P_i.
- On input (renew, P_i) from P_i, store P_i in Λ_{renew} and forward (renew, P_i) to the adversary.

Description of the ideal functionality $\mathcal{F}_{NIKE}$

On the immediateness of $\mathcal{F}_{NIKE}$. As specified above, $\mathcal{F}_{NIKE}$ does *not* guarantee immediate output upon an init query that refers to a corrupted session. Namely, in that case, the adversary is queried for a key $K_{i,j}$, and could potentially block $\mathcal{F}_{NIKE}$'s output by not sending that key. (We stress that the simulators we construct will never block immediate delivery of keys in this sense.) To avoid this possibility to block outputs, we could have let the adversary upload an algorithm AdvKey to $\mathcal{F}_{NIKE}$ that is used to immediately derive keys $K_{i,j} := \mathsf{AdvKey}(P_i, P_j)$

---

[5] This assumption is standard in UC (e.g., [7]) and implemented as part of the model of computation. However, since the corruption mechanism is not fully specified in GNUC (yet), we simply assume a mechanism. (For concreteness, we assume that ideal functionalities send any party a special "corrupted?" request that is automatically and directly answered with "yes" if and only if that party has been corrupted.)

without querying the adversary. (This is in analogy to similar algorithms in signature and encryption functionalities [4, 5].) While possible, this would entail technical complications (such as communicating code and an AdvKey function that will have to use a pseudorandom function to derive keys), so we keep the slightly simpler and more intuitive formulation from above.

The key registration functionality $\mathcal{F}_{KR}^f$. The ideal functionality for key registration is motivated by the key registration process in the real world, which is usually operated by a trusted authority, e.g., a CA. We can assume authenticated channels between each party and the CA (because usually a CA requires a proof of identity, e.g. possession of an identity card or, for remote use, a valid signature). Using standard techniques (e.g., public-key encryption), we can then establish secure channels between party and CA. Note that, even with secure channels, the adversary still learns about registrations taking place and is able to delay them. This leads to the following ideal functionality:

$\mathcal{F}_{KR}^f$ proceeds as follows, running with parties $P_1, \ldots, P_n$ and an adversary.

- On input $(\texttt{register}, P_i, \mathsf{pk}_i, \tau)$ from P_i send $(\texttt{register}, P_i)$ to the adversary.
- On input $(\texttt{output}, P_i)$ from the adversary, if $f(P_i, \mathsf{pk}_i, \tau) = 0$, send $\bot$ to P_i. Otherwise, store (P_i, pk_i) and send $(P_i, \mathsf{pk}_i, \texttt{registered})$ to P_i.
- On input $(\texttt{lookup}, P_i)$ return (P_i, pk_i). If this entry does not exist, return $\bot$.

Description of the ideal functionality $\mathcal{F}_{KR}^f$

$\mathcal{F}_{KR}^f$ is provided with an efficiently computable function f that takes as input a party identifier P_i, a public key pk_i and a proof of validity, τ, of the public key. f returns 1 if τ is a valid proof for pk_i, and 0 otherwise. The adversary obtains a notification from $\mathcal{F}_{KR}^f$ when a party tries to register and needs to send a notification back so that $\mathcal{F}_{KR}^f$ can proceed. This models the fact that the output of the functionality can be delayed by the adversary.

Note that the function f needs to be specified and can be used to obtain different ideal functionalities. For example, if we want $\mathcal{F}_{KR}^f$ to accept all public keys, we can set f to be constant, e.g. $f \equiv 1$. We denote this special functionality by $\mathcal{F}_{KR}^1$ and allow omitting τ in the inputs for $\mathcal{F}_{KR}^1$. We explicitly allow interactive key registrations (i.e., implementations of $\mathcal{F}_{KR}^f$) – only the ideal functionality $\mathcal{F}_{KR}^f$ uses f to (non-interactively) check validity of keys. (Hence, an interactive key registration protocol could enable a simulator to extract a witness for f).

Finally, we remark that we explicitly do not require proofs of possession (of secret keys), as popular in concrete public-key infrastructures. However, proofs of possession can be seen as a special case of $\mathcal{F}_{KR}^f$ (in which τ simply is the secret key for pk, which can be verified by a suitable f).

4   Results

4.1   Static Corruption

We show that any CKS^+-secure NIKE scheme NIKE emulates the functionality $\mathcal{F}_{NIKE}$ in a hybrid UC model, if and only if the environment $\mathcal{Z}$ is restricted to static corruptions. (With static corruptions, we mean that a party can only be corrupted before it obtains any protocol input from $\mathcal{Z}$. However, we point out that there is a subtlety regarding the precise definition of static corruptions – see the comment after the proof of Theorem 3.).

We remind the reader that the CKS^+ security notion is an augmented version of the CKS security notion from [13] including honest re-registration of parties (see Section 2 for definitions).

Theorem 2. *Let* NIKE *be a* CKS^+ *-secure NIKE scheme. Then* NIKE *realizes* $\mathcal{F}_{NIKE}$ *in the* $(\mathcal{F}_{CRS}, \mathcal{F}_{KR}^1)$*-hybrid model with respect to static corruptions.*

Proof. It suffices to show that there exists a simulator $\mathcal{S}$ for the dummy adversary $\mathcal{A}$. $\mathcal{S}$ interacts with an environment $\mathcal{Z}$ and $\mathcal{F}_{NIKE}$. $\mathcal{S}$ maintains a list of corrupted parties and a list Λ with entries of the form $(\mathsf{P}_i, \mathsf{pk}_i, \mathsf{sk}_i)$, containing party identifiers and their public key/secret key pairs. For every party only the newest entry is kept. Thus, there is at most one entry for each party identifier P_i. A party's entry contains a public key if and only if it successfully registered this key with $\mathcal{F}_{KR}^1$. We specify the reactions of $\mathcal{S}$ to invocations from $\mathcal{Z}$ and $\mathcal{F}_{NIKE}$:

(parameters) **from** $\mathcal{Z}$. The environment $\mathcal{Z}$ issues this request to the adversary because it cannot access $\mathcal{F}_{CRS}$ directly. $\mathcal{S}$ simulates $\mathcal{F}_{CRS}$ by obtaining $params \xleftarrow{\$} \mathtt{NIKE.CommonSetup}(1^k)$ once and, from then on, $\mathcal{S}$ always answers this request with $params$.

(register, P_i) **from** $\mathcal{F}_{NIKE}$. We may assume that $\mathcal{S}$ already computed the public parameters $params$. If the list Λ does not contain any entry $(\mathsf{P}_i, \cdot, \cdot)$, $\mathcal{S}$ obtains $(\mathsf{pk}_i, \mathsf{sk}_i) \xleftarrow{\$} \mathtt{NIKE.KeyGen}(params, \mathsf{P}_i)$ and stores $(\mathsf{P}_i, \mathsf{pk}_i, \mathsf{sk}_i)$ in Λ. $\mathcal{S}$ then sends a message $(\mathsf{P}_i, \mathtt{registered})$ to $\mathcal{F}_{NIKE}$, waits for $(\mathsf{P}_i, \mathtt{registered})$ from $\mathcal{F}_{NIKE}$ and sends (register, P_i) to $\mathcal{Z}$ (simulating that message from $\mathcal{F}_{KR}^1$ to the dummy adversary $\mathcal{A}$).

(init, $\mathsf{P}_i, \mathsf{P}_j$) **from** $\mathcal{F}_{NIKE}$. This input implies that $\mathsf{P}_i, \mathsf{P}_j$ are not both honest. We may assume P_j is corrupted, because $\mathcal{S}$ would not send (init, $\mathsf{P}_i, \mathsf{P}_j$) through a corrupted P_i. $\mathcal{S}$ returns $(\mathsf{P}_i, \mathsf{P}_j, \mathtt{NIKE.SharedKey}(\mathsf{P}_j, \mathsf{pk}_j, \mathsf{P}_i, \mathsf{sk}_i))$ to $\mathcal{F}_{NIKE}$ (note that the shared key could be $\perp$).

(renew, P_i) **from** $\mathcal{F}_{NIKE}$. $\mathcal{S}$ obtains $(\mathsf{pk}_i, \mathsf{sk}_i) \xleftarrow{\$} \mathtt{NIKE.KeyGen}(params, \mathsf{P}_i)$ and stores $(\mathsf{P}_i, \mathsf{pk}_i, \mathsf{sk}_i)$ in Λ, overwriting any existing entry for P_i if necessary. $\mathcal{S}$ then sends $(\mathsf{P}_i, \mathtt{registered})$ to $\mathcal{F}_{NIKE}$, waits for $(\mathsf{P}_i, \mathtt{registered})$ from $\mathcal{F}_{NIKE}$ and sends (register, P_i) to $\mathcal{Z}$.

(corrupt, P_i) **from** $\mathcal{Z}$. Again, $\mathcal{Z}$ will issue this request to the adversary. $\mathcal{S}$ corrupts P_i and adds P_i to its list of corrupted parties.

($\mathtt{register}, \mathsf{P}_i, \mathsf{pk}_i$) **from** $\mathcal{Z}$. Such a request will only be made by $\mathcal{Z}$ to the adversary, which is asked to let a corrupted party P_i register pk_i as its public key. $\mathcal{S}$ then stores ($\mathsf{P}_i, \mathsf{pk}_i, \perp$) in Λ, sends ($\mathsf{P}_i, \mathtt{registered}$) to $\mathcal{F}_{NIKE}$, waits for ($\mathsf{P}_i, \mathtt{registered}$) from $\mathcal{F}_{NIKE}$ and sends ($\mathtt{register}, \mathsf{P}_i$) to $\mathcal{Z}$. $\mathcal{S}$ then sends ($\mathtt{register}, \mathsf{P}_i$) to $\mathcal{Z}$, ($\mathsf{P}_i, \mathtt{registered}$) to $\mathcal{F}_{NIKE}$ and stores ($\mathsf{P}_i, \mathsf{pk}_i, \perp$) in Λ.

($\mathtt{lookup}, \mathsf{P}_i$) **from any entity.** If Λ contains an entry ($\mathsf{P}_i, \mathsf{pk}_i, \cdot$), then return ($\mathsf{P}_i, \mathsf{pk}_i$), else return $\perp$.

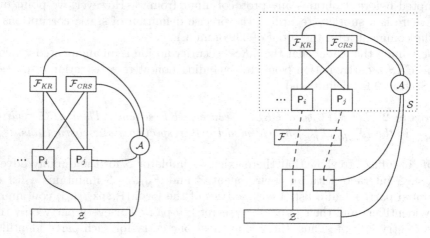

Fig. 1. Transition from G_0 (left) to G_1 (right)

Now let $\mathcal{A}$ be the dummy adversary and $\mathtt{NIKE}$ a CKS^+-secure NIKE scheme. We show that for every environment $\mathcal{Z}$

$$\mathrm{Exec}[\mathcal{F}_{NIKE}, \mathcal{S}, \mathcal{Z}] \approx \mathrm{Exec}[\mathtt{NIKE}, \mathcal{A}, \mathcal{Z}].$$

Here $\mathrm{Exec}[\mathtt{NIKE}, \mathcal{A}, \mathcal{Z}]$ (resp. $\mathrm{Exec}[\mathcal{F}_{NIKE}, \mathcal{S}, \mathcal{Z}]$) denotes the random variable describing the output of environment $\mathcal{Z}$ when interacting with adversary $\mathcal{A}$ (resp. $\mathcal{S}$) and protocol $\mathtt{NIKE}$ (resp. functionality $\mathcal{F}_{NIKE}$).[6]

Game G_0: Real protocol run. This is the real execution of $\mathtt{NIKE}$ with dummy adversary $\mathcal{A}$. A specific instance of this game is depicted on the left-hand side of Figure 1.

Game G_1: Regrouping of machines and addition of relays. We regroup every machine except for $\mathcal{Z}$ from game G_0 into one machine and call it $\mathcal{S}$. We add single relays for every party, outside of $\mathcal{S}$, and one relay called $\mathcal{F}$ covering all wires between the single relays and $\mathcal{S}$.

Obviously the view of $\mathcal{Z}$ is distributed exactly as in game G_0. Figure 1 shows the transformation from G_0 to G_1 in a situation with one honest and one corrupted party.

---

[6] Throughout the paper we assume $\mathcal{Z}$ to be uniform, i.e. $\mathcal{Z}$ gets no auxiliary input.

Game G_2: Merging wires. Merge all wires between $\mathcal{F}$ and $\mathcal{S}$ into one wire. Let $\mathcal{F}$ determine recipients of messages (consisting of a tuple) from $\mathcal{S}$ by choosing the first party that occurs in the tuple. $\mathcal{S}$ determines recipients in the same way.

Messages are delivered to the same recipients as in the previous game, hence, the view of $\mathcal{Z}$ is distributed exactly as before.

The main difference between G_2 and the ideal execution with $\mathcal{F}_{NIKE}$ is that in G_2 the keys of honest sessions are computed using NIKE.SharedKey, whereas in the ideal execution the keys are randomly chosen. This will change in the last game G_5. Next, in game G_3, we make a simple but slightly technical modification: we let $\mathcal{F}$ perform a check to determine whether it should forward a shared key coming from $\mathcal{S}$ to the requesting party. (Namely, if the other party involved in this session has not registered its public key yet, then $\mathcal{F}$ can answer this request with $\bot$ on its own.)

Game G_3: Allowing $\mathcal{F}$ to store information and make decisions. We let $\mathcal{S}$ send $(\mathsf{P}_i, \texttt{registered})$ to $\mathcal{F}$ whenever a party successfully registers a public key pk_i with $\mathcal{F}_{KR}^1$. We let $\mathcal{F}$ bounce the message back to $\mathcal{S}$ and additionally maintain a list Λ_{reg} with parties for which $\mathcal{F}$ already received such a message. Upon receiving $(\texttt{init}, \mathsf{P}_i, \mathsf{P}_j)$, if $\mathsf{P}_j \notin \Lambda_{reg}$, $\mathcal{F}$ sends $(\mathsf{P}_i, \mathsf{P}_j, \bot)$ to P_i. Else $\mathcal{F}$ relays $(\texttt{init}, \mathsf{P}_i, \mathsf{P}_j)$ to $\mathcal{S}$ and receives an answer $(\mathsf{P}_i, \mathsf{P}_j, K_{i,j})$. $\mathcal{F}$ relays $(\mathsf{P}_i, \mathsf{P}_j, K_{i,j})$ to P_i.

We have to check whether the output of P_i in G_2 is $(\mathsf{P}_i, \mathsf{P}_j, \bot)$ if and only if the output of P_i in G_3 is $(\mathsf{P}_i, \mathsf{P}_j, \bot)$. In G_2, P_i outputs $(\mathsf{P}_i, \mathsf{P}_j, \bot)$ if and only if $\bot \leftarrow$ NIKE.SharedKey$(\mathsf{P}_j, \mathsf{pk}_j, \mathsf{P}_i, \mathsf{sk}_i)$. By definition of $\mathcal{F}$ in G_3, the output of a party P_i is $(\mathsf{P}_i, \mathsf{P}_j, \bot)$ if and only if $\mathsf{P}_j \notin \Lambda_{reg}$ or $\mathcal{S}$ answered with $(\mathsf{P}_i, \mathsf{P}_j, \bot)$. A missing pk_j will cause NIKE.SharedKey$(\mathsf{P}_j, \mathsf{pk}_j, \mathsf{P}_i, \mathsf{sk}_i)$ to output $\bot$, hence, both events together are equivalent to $\bot \leftarrow$ NIKE.SharedKey$(\mathsf{P}_j, \mathsf{pk}_j, \mathsf{P}_i, \mathsf{sk}_i)$.

Game G_4: More lists and more decisions for $\mathcal{F}$. Here, we introduce two new lists, Λ_{keys} and Λ_{renew}, to $\mathcal{F}$. These lists resemble the lists used internally by $\mathcal{F}_{NIKE}$. Specifically, whenever $\mathcal{F}$ has to send a message $(\mathsf{P}_i, \mathsf{P}_j, key)$ to P_i where $key \neq \bot$, it also stores $(\{\mathsf{P}_i, \mathsf{P}_j\}, key)$ to Λ_{keys}. Whenever $\mathcal{F}$ receives a message $(\texttt{renew}, \mathsf{P}_i)$ from P_i, it adds P_i to Λ_{renew}. Whenever $\mathcal{F}$ receives a message $(\mathsf{P}_i, \texttt{registered})$ from $\mathcal{S}$, if $\mathsf{P}_i \in \Lambda_{renew}$, $\mathcal{F}$ deletes all entries $(\{\mathsf{P}_i, \cdot\}, key)$ from Λ_{keys} and removes P_i from Λ_{renew}. So far there were no modifications regarding $\mathcal{F}$'s outputs. Now upon receipt of $(\texttt{init}, \mathsf{P}_i, \mathsf{P}_j)$ with $\mathsf{P}_j \in \Lambda_{reg}$ we let $\mathcal{F}$ check the list Λ_{keys} for an entry $(\{\mathsf{P}_i, \mathsf{P}_j\}, key)$. If there is one, $\mathcal{F}$ does not relay $(\texttt{init}, \mathsf{P}_i, \mathsf{P}_j)$ to the adversary and instead returns $(\{\mathsf{P}_i, \mathsf{P}_j\}, key)$ to P_i right away.

The output of $\mathcal{F}$ is the same as in Game G_3, because any entry in Λ_{keys} was computed by $\mathcal{S}$ and therefore matches the answer of $\mathcal{S}$ to the init request in Game G_3.

Game G_5: Building the ideal functionality $\mathcal{F}_{NIKE}$. We now substitute all shared keys between two honest parties in Λ_{reg} (computed with NIKE.SharedKey) with random keys. Concretely, for every honest session $(\texttt{init}, \mathsf{P}_i, \mathsf{P}_j)$, for P_j in $\mathcal{F}$'s list Λ_{reg}, we let $\mathcal{F}$ determine the key for that session. First of all we prevent $\mathcal{F}$ from forwarding $(\texttt{init}, \mathsf{P}_i, \mathsf{P}_j)$ to the adversary. Next, if Λ_{keys} contains an

Table 2. Corresponding queries

UC requests	CKS^+ queries
(parameters)	(parameters)
$(\texttt{corrupt}, \mathsf{P}_i) + (\texttt{register}, \mathsf{P}_i, \mathsf{pk}_i)$	$(\texttt{register corrupt user}, \mathsf{P}_i, \mathsf{pk}_i)$
$(\texttt{register}, \mathsf{P}_i)$ or $(\texttt{renew}, \mathsf{P}_i)$	$(\texttt{register honest user}, \mathsf{P}_i)$
$(\texttt{init}, \mathsf{P}_i, \mathsf{P}_j)$, corrupt session	$(\texttt{corrupt reveal}, \mathsf{P}_i, \mathsf{P}_j)$
$(\texttt{init}, \mathsf{P}_i, \mathsf{P}_j)$, honest session	$(\texttt{test}, \mathsf{P}_i, \mathsf{P}_j)$

entry $(\{\mathsf{P}_i, \mathsf{P}_j\}, K_{i,j})$, $\mathcal{F}$ sets $key = K_{i,j}$. Else $\mathcal{F}$ chooses $key \xleftarrow{\$} \{0,1\}^k$, stores $(\{\mathsf{P}_i, \mathsf{P}_j\}, key)$ and sends $(\mathsf{P}_i, \mathsf{P}_j, key)$ to P_i.

Let $\mathcal{Z}$ be a distinguishing environment between games G_4 and G_5. We use $\mathcal{Z}$ to construct an adversary $\mathcal{B}$ against NIKE in the CKS^+ security game. Besides playing the CKS^+ security game with its challenger $\mathcal{C}$, $\mathcal{B}$ runs $\mathcal{Z}$ and acts as a mediator between $\mathcal{Z}$ and $\mathcal{C}$.

Table 2 shows requests of $\mathcal{Z}$ and the corresponding queries in the CKS^+ security game that $\mathcal{B}$ issues to get answers for $\mathcal{Z}$'s requests. Note that $\mathcal{B}$ can embed its own challenge into the UC execution with $\mathcal{Z}$ by answering initialization requests for honest sessions from $\mathcal{Z}$ with $\mathcal{C}$'s responses to $\texttt{test}$ queries. We omit a detailed description of $\mathcal{B}$ and briefly list what $\mathcal{B}$ has to do besides issuing the requests shown in Table 2.

- To be able to answer $\texttt{lookup}$ requests from $\mathcal{Z}$, $\mathcal{B}$ has to keep track of all public keys.
- When answering $(\texttt{init}, \mathsf{P}_i, \mathsf{P}_j)$ requests from $\mathcal{Z}$, $\mathcal{B}$ returns $\bot$ to $\mathcal{Z}$ if P_j has not been registered with $\mathcal{C}$ yet.

Note that according to Table 2 both $(\texttt{register}, \mathsf{P}_i)$ and $(\texttt{renew}, \mathsf{P}_i)$ requests from $\mathcal{Z}$ lead to the same request in the CKS^+ game. This is due to the fact that renewing a public key in the CKS^+ game is done by re-registering the user as honest. Let $\text{Adv}_{\mathcal{Z}}^{G_4, G_5} = |\Pr[1 \leftarrow \mathcal{Z}|\mathcal{Z} \text{ runs in } G_5] - \Pr[1 \leftarrow \mathcal{Z}|\mathcal{Z} \text{ runs in } G_4]|$ denote the advantage of $\mathcal{Z}$ in distinguishing G_4 and G_5. By assumption, $\text{Adv}_{\mathcal{Z}}^{G_4, G_5}$ is non-negligible. Let $\hat{b}$ denote the output bit of $\mathcal{Z}$ and b the bit chosen by the CKS^+ challenger $\mathcal{C}$. If $b = 0$, $\mathcal{C}$ answers $\texttt{test}$ queries with real shared keys, else the keys are randomly chosen from $\{0,1\}^k$. Thus if $b = 0$, $\mathcal{B}$ simulates G_4, and if $b = 1$, $\mathcal{B}$ simulates G_5. We let $\mathcal{B}$ output $\hat{b}$, i.e. the same bit as $\mathcal{Z}$. Hence, we have that $\text{Adv}_{\mathcal{B}}^{CKS^+} = \text{Adv}_{\mathcal{Z}}^{G_4, G_5}$. Clearly, as $\text{Adv}_{\mathcal{Z}}^{G_4, G_5}$ is non-negligible, $\text{Adv}_{\mathcal{B}}^{CKS^+}$ is non-negligible as well. This contradicts the CKS^+ security of NIKE and thus we conclude that $\text{Adv}_{\mathcal{Z}}^{G_4, G_5}$ is negligible.

It is easy to see that $\mathcal{F}$ in game G_5 behaves exactly like $\mathcal{F}_{NIKE}$, and game G_5 is equal to an ideal execution of NIKE with $\mathcal{F}_{NIKE}$ and $\mathcal{S}$. It follows that

$$\text{Exec}[\text{NIKE}, \mathcal{A}, \mathcal{Z}] = \text{GAME}_{\mathcal{Z}}^{G_0} \approx \text{GAME}_{\mathcal{Z}}^{G_5} = \text{Exec}[\mathcal{F}_{NIKE}, \mathcal{S}, \mathcal{Z}],$$

where $\text{GAME}_{\mathcal{Z}}^{G_0}$ (resp. $\text{GAME}_{\mathcal{Z}}^{G_5}$) denotes the output of $\mathcal{Z}$ when running in game G_0 (resp. G_5).

Remark. The hybrid functionality $\mathcal{F}_{CRS}$ is required to guarantee that the parameters for the NIKE scheme cannot be adversarially chosen. But since there is no need for the simulator to program the CRS, we can also assume $\mathcal{F}_{CRS}$ to be a *global functionality*. The global CRS functionality, denoted by $\bar{\mathcal{G}}_{CRS}$, can be directly accessed by $\mathcal{Z}$ and is a strictly weaker assumption than our functionality $\mathcal{F}_{CRS}$. A detailed description of $\bar{\mathcal{G}}_{CRS}$ can be found in [6].

Theorem 2 states that CKS^+ security (or any equivalent notion) of a NIKE scheme is sufficient for UC security of the scheme with respect to static adversaries. Next we show that CKS^+ security (or any equivalent notion) is also a requirement for UC-secure NIKE schemes. We recall that there is an equivalence between several flavours of game-based security notions for NIKE (see [13]) and it therefore suffices to show CKS-*light* security.

Theorem 3. *Let* NIKE *be a UC-secure NIKE scheme realizing* $\mathcal{F}_{NIKE}$ *in the* $(\mathcal{F}_{CRS}, \mathcal{F}^1_{KR})$-*hybrid model with respect to static corruptions. Then* NIKE *is CKS-light-secure.*

Proof sketch: We will first map any CKS-*light* adversary $\mathcal{B}$ to a suitable environment $\mathcal{Z}$ that simulates $\mathcal{B}$ and translates $\mathcal{B}$'s queries in a similar way as shown in Table 2.[7] Hence, running $\mathcal{Z}$ with NIKE provides $\mathcal{B}$ with a view as in the CKS-*light* game with $b = 0$ (i.e., with real keys). Now consider an environment $\tilde{\mathcal{Z}}$ that works like $\mathcal{Z}$, but substitutes all shared keys between honest parties provided by NIKE (or $\mathcal{F}_{NIKE}$) with random keys. Hence, running $\tilde{\mathcal{Z}}$ with NIKE provides $\mathcal{B}$ with a view as in the CKS-*light* game with $b = 1$ (i.e., with random keys). Intuitively, if $\mathcal{B}$ is a successful CKS-*light* distinguisher, then $\mathcal{B}$ can distinguish between running with $\mathcal{Z}$ or $\tilde{\mathcal{Z}}$ *in the real UC model*. However, in the ideal UC model, $\mathcal{Z}$ and $\tilde{\mathcal{Z}}$ provide $\mathcal{B}$ with identical views; hence, $\mathcal{B}$ will not be able to distinguish running with $\mathcal{Z}$ or $\tilde{\mathcal{Z}}$ in the ideal UC model. In this way, a successful $\mathcal{B}$ acts as a successful distinguisher between the real and the ideal UC model.

On the UC notion of static corruption. In the proof of Theorem 3, we use the relatively loose definition of static corruption in the UC model (cf. [5, Section 6.7]). In fact, Theorem 3 would not hold if we applied a stricter (with respect to adversarial constraints) definition of static corruption. For instance, we could require that no corruptions take place after *the first* honest party receives an input. (This is in fact the default notion of static corruptions in the GNUC model of security, at least since the December 2012 update of [15].) For this notion of static corruption, we can construct counterexamples to Theorem 3. On the other hand, once there is only a fixed polynomial number of parties whose identities are known in advance, the environment $\mathcal{Z}$ from the proof of Theorem 3 can guess the two honest parties that $\mathcal{B}$ chooses and corrupt all other parties in advance. Hence, Theorem 3 holds even with respect to stricter notions of static corruption, once the set of possible honest parties is polynomially small.

---

[7] Note, however, that the CKS-*light* game does not feature **renew** queries. Furthermore, the number of queries considered in the CKS-*light* game is in fact more restricted than in the CKS^+ game.

4.2   Adaptive Corruption

We consider adaptive corruption, where $\mathcal{Z}$ is now allowed to corrupt formerly honest protocol participants. To avoid trivial protocols, say that a function f (that recognize valid keys in $\mathcal{F}_{KR}^f$) is *nontrivial* for a given NIKE scheme iff $f(\mathsf{P}_i, \mathsf{pk}_i, \tau) = 1$ for all parameters *params* generated by NIKE.CommonSetup(1^k) and all public keys generated by NIKE.KeyGen(*params*, P_i) along with proofs τ.

Theorem 4. *There is no NIKE scheme NIKE and function f which is nontrivial for NIKE, such that NIKE realizes $\mathcal{F}_{NIKE}$ in the $(\mathcal{F}_{CRS}, \mathcal{F}_{KR}^f)$-hybrid model with respect to adaptive corruptions.*

Proof. We specify an adversary $\mathcal{A}$ and an environment $\mathcal{Z}$ and show that there is no simulator $\mathcal{S}$ for this setup.

Let NIKE be any non-interactive key exchange scheme. W.l.o.g we assume that all secret keys have the same bit length $l = l(k)$, where k denotes the security parameter. Let NIKE.SharedKey be the shared key algorithm of NIKE that takes as inputs $(\mathsf{P}_i, \mathsf{pk}_i, \mathsf{P}_j, \mathsf{sk}_j), i \neq j$, and outputs shared keys of length k. Let $n := \lceil \frac{l}{k} \rceil + 2$. For convenience we let $\mathcal{A}$ be the dummy adversary and let $\mathcal{Z}$ mount the attack on NIKE, which is described in five steps:

1. Send (**parameters**) to $\mathcal{A}$ to obtain *params*, a set of system parameters.
2. Send (**register**, P_i) to P_i, $i = 1, \ldots, n$ and (**init**, $\mathsf{P}_i, \mathsf{P}_1$) to P_i, $i = 2, \ldots, n$. Thus, $\mathcal{Z}$ obtains the shared keys $K_{1,i}$ between party P_1 and party P_i, $i = 2, \ldots, n$.
3. Obtain the public keys $\mathsf{pk}_1, \ldots, \mathsf{pk}_n$, corresponding to parties $\mathsf{P}_1, \ldots, \mathsf{P}_n$, from $\mathcal{A}$.
4. Send (**corrupt**, P_1) to $\mathcal{A}$ to learn sk_1. Abort if $\mathsf{sk}_1 \notin \{0,1\}^l$.
5. If $K_{1,i} = $ NIKE.SharedKey$(\mathsf{P}_i, \mathsf{pk}_i, \mathsf{P}_1, \mathsf{sk}_1) \; \forall i = 2, \ldots, n$, output 1, else output 0.

In the real world $\mathcal{Z}$ will always output 1 by the correctness of NIKE and the nontriviality of f. Now let $\mathcal{S}$ be any simulator. The ideal world execution with $\mathcal{S}$ will have to proceed as follows:

1. $\mathcal{S}$ arbitrarily chooses a set of system parameters *params* and sends *params* to $\mathcal{Z}$.
2. Here $\mathcal{S}$ cannot choose the shared keys $\tilde{K}_{1,i}$, $i = 2, \ldots, n$, between the honest parties, because these are chosen by $\mathcal{F}_{NIKE}$ (and in fact unknown to $\mathcal{S}$).
3. Now $\mathcal{S}$ arbitrarily chooses public keys $\mathsf{pk}_1, \ldots, \mathsf{pk}_n$, simulating $\mathcal{F}_{KR}^f$, and sends them to $\mathcal{Z}$.
4. $\mathcal{S}$ also corrupts P_1 and learns $\tilde{K}_{1,i}$, $i = 2, \ldots, n$. $\mathcal{S}$ chooses $\mathsf{sk}_1 \in \{0,1\}^l$ and sends it to $\mathcal{Z}$.

To see what happens in step 5 we define

$$F_{\vec{\mathsf{pk}}}(\mathsf{sk}_1) : \{0,1\}^l \longrightarrow \{0,1\}^{(n-1)k}$$

$$\mathsf{sk}_1 \longmapsto (\text{NIKE.SharedKey}(\mathsf{P}_2, \mathsf{pk}_2, \mathsf{P}_1, \mathsf{sk}_1), \ldots,$$

$$\text{NIKE.SharedKey}(\mathsf{P}_n, \mathsf{pk}_n, \mathsf{P}_1, \mathsf{sk}_1))$$

where $\vec{\mathsf{pk}} := (\mathsf{pk}_2, \ldots, \mathsf{pk}_n)$. $\mathcal{F}_{NIKE}$ chooses $(\tilde{K}_{1,2}, \ldots, \tilde{K}_{1,n})$ uniformly from $\{0,1\}^{(n-1)k}$, hence the probability that there exists sk_1 with

$$F_{\vec{\mathsf{pk}}}(\mathsf{sk}_1) = (\tilde{K}_{1,2}, .., \tilde{K}_{1,n})$$

is at most $\frac{2^l}{2^{(n-1)k}}$. As n was chosen such that $(n-1)k \geq l+k$, we have $\frac{2^l}{2^{(n-1)k}} \leq \frac{2^l}{2^{l+k}} \leq 2^{-k}$, which is negligible in k. It follows that $\mathcal{Z}$ will output 1 only with negligible probability.

Remarks. (1) If the secret key depends deterministically on the public key, the attack is simpler, because after the first step $\mathcal{S}$ is committed to secret keys. After receiving the public keys, $\mathcal{Z}$ initializes a key exchange session between two honest parties and later corrupts one of them. Due to the commitment in the first step, the probability that the secret key matches the uniformly chosen shared key is negligible in the size k of the shared key.

(2) In the security models from [13], adaptive corruption corresponds to an adversary which issues a test query for two honest identities and additionally uses an extract query to get one of the secret keys. This case is excluded as trivial win for the adversary.

Relation to a Similar Result of Nielsen in Secure Message Transfer
Nielsen's results. We have shown that security against adaptive corruptions is not possible without additional assumptions. Taking into account the results of Nielsen [18], this is not surprising. There, it is shown that there is no non-interactive protocol which realizes secure message transfer (SMT) without additional assumptions. Non-interactive SMT protocols (according to the definition of [18]) can essentially be viewed as a PKE scheme. The impossibility result is due to the fact that the simulator has to commit to a transcript of encryptions before knowing the underlying messages. Upon corruption, $\mathcal{S}$, now knowing the messages, can only hope to adjust the secret key to explain the transcript. Nielsen shows that a secret key of fixed length does not provide enough entropy to explain an unbounded number of encryptions.

Why his result does not imply ours. Regarding NIKE, a similar problem arises when formerly honest parties, when being corrupted, reveal an unbounded number of earlier computed shared keys. The simulator has to use the secret key to explain those shared keys. Analogous to [18] we can prove an impossibility result due to a lack of entropy in the secret key.

One could hope to conclude this directly from the result of [18] with the following argument: every NIKE can be used to realize SMT. Thus an impossibility result for the latter would imply Theorem 4. However, [18] crucially uses that the SMT protocol can transmit arbitrarily long messages between two parties. In contrast, a NIKE only creates fixed-length (i.e., k-bit) shared keys between each pair of parties. Such a short key cannot (in any obvious way) be used to transmit arbitrarily long messages *against adaptive corruptions.*

Therefore Nielsen's impossibility result for non-interactive SMT can not be used to directly conclude Theorem 4. Nevertheless our technique is strongly inspired by the idea of Nielsen, namely using an unbounded number of key exchange sessions instead of unbounded-length messages.

Generalizations of our negative result to other (non-programmable) functionalities. Theorem 4 shows that security against adaptive corruption is not achievable in the $(\mathcal{F}_{CRS}, \mathcal{F}_{KR}^{f})$-hybrid model. The result would be even stronger if we added more powerful hybrid functionalities. We find that, similar to another result from [18], even a global random oracle functionality to which $\mathcal{Z}$ has direct access does not facilitate security against adaptive corruption. (This notion of a globally accessible functionality has been formalized in [18], but can be cast more generally in the "GUC" variant of UC [6].)

Even more, (the proof of) Theorem 4 would still hold in any hybrid model that, in addition to $\mathcal{F}_{CRS}$ and $\mathcal{F}_{KR}^{f}$, provides only *non-programmable* hybrid functionalities. In this context, by non-programmable we mean that the input/output behaviour of the functionality is completely independent of the simulator (note that this also includes that the simulator is not able to program the output of the functionality via scheduling of messages). This observation points us to hybrid functionalities that actually facilitate adaptive corruption. And indeed, in Section 4.4 we will see that a programmable random oracle functionality is enough to achieve adaptive UC security.

4.3   Summary of Relations Established So Far

There is a strong relation between the game-based security notions from [9, 13] and UC security with respect to $\mathcal{F}_{NIKE}$, our functionality for non-interactive key exchange. In Section 4.1 we have shown equivalence of *CKS* security (or other equivalent notions from [13]) to static UC-NIKE security (w.r.t $\mathcal{F}_{NIKE}$ using $\mathcal{F}_{CRS}$ and $\mathcal{F}_{KR}$). Furthermore, Theorem 4 implies that *CKS* security is not enough to achieve adaptive UC-NIKE security (w.r.t $\mathcal{F}_{NIKE}$ using $\mathcal{F}_{CRS}$ and $\mathcal{F}_{KR}$). The relations between the security notions are depicted in Figure 2.

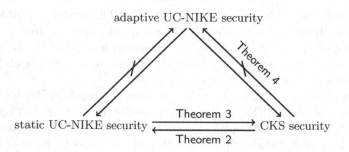

Fig. 2. Relations between *CKS* security models and UC-NIKE security

4.4 Transformation to Adaptively Secure NIKE in the ROM

In Section 4.2 we have proven that, without additional assumptions, $\mathcal{F}_{NIKE}$ cannot be realized in the $(\mathcal{F}_{CRS}, \mathcal{F}_{KR}^{f})$-hybrid model in the presence of adaptive adversaries. We now show how to achieve adaptive UC security if we assume the existence of a random oracle. More specifically, we show that if a NIKE scheme NIKE is secure in the sense of a strictly weaker ("search-based" instead of indistinguishability-based) notion of security than the notions presented in [13], and with additional allowance of re-registration of honest users and corrupt registration of previously registered honest users, then a hash variant of NIKE securely realizes our non-interactive key exchange functionality $\mathcal{F}_{NIKE}$ in the $\mathcal{F}_{RO}$-hybrid model. The security model used in our reduction is denoted by $weakCKS^{++}$ (see Section 2 for a definition).

Definition 1 (Transformation to the ROM). *Let NIKE be a non-interactive key exchange scheme with shared key algorithm NIKE.SharedKey and let $H : \{0,1\}^* \to \{0,1\}^{k'}$ be a hash function (viewed as a random oracle), where k' is a security parameter. Let NIKE' be a modification of the scheme NIKE such that its shared key algorithm, NIKE'.SharedKey', is defined as*

$$NIKE'.SharedKey'(\mathsf{P}_i, \mathsf{pk}_i, \mathsf{P}_j, \mathsf{sk}_j)$$
$$\text{if } \begin{cases} \mathsf{P}_i < \mathsf{P}_j \text{ return } H(\mathsf{P}_i, \mathsf{P}_j, NIKE.SharedKey(\mathsf{P}_i, \mathsf{pk}_i, \mathsf{P}_j, \mathsf{sk}_j)) \\ \mathsf{P}_j < \mathsf{P}_i \text{ return } H(\mathsf{P}_j, \mathsf{P}_i, NIKE.SharedKey(\mathsf{P}_i, \mathsf{pk}_i, \mathsf{P}_j, \mathsf{sk}_j)) \end{cases}$$

Here we are assuming that the party identifiers come from a space with a natural ordering and that the shared key space of NIKE' is $\{0,1\}^{k'}$.

Theorem 5. *Let NIKE be a $weakCKS^{++}$-secure non-interactive key exchange protocol. Then, in the presence of adaptive adversaries, the modification NIKE' of NIKE realizes $\mathcal{F}_{NIKE}$ in the $(\mathcal{F}_{CRS}, \mathcal{F}_{KR}^{1}, \mathcal{F}_{RO})$-hybrid model.*

Proof sketch: We show that $\mathcal{Z}$ cannot distinguish the real protocol run of NIKE' with the ideal functionalities $\mathcal{F}_{CRS}$, $\mathcal{F}_{KR}^{1}$ and $\mathcal{F}_{RO}$, and an adversary $\mathcal{A}$, from the ideal protocol run with $\mathcal{F}_{NIKE}$ and $\mathcal{S}$, unless $\mathcal{Z}$ makes a specific type of RO query. Then we show that if $\mathcal{Z}$ makes such a RO query, we can construct an adversary against NIKE in the $weakCKS^{++}$ security game. By our assumption, there is no such adversary with non-negligible advantage. Thus, the probability that $\mathcal{Z}$ makes that RO query is negligible and therefore the real and ideal execution (with our simulator $\mathcal{S}$) cannot be distinguished by any environment $\mathcal{Z}$.

References

[1] Barak, B., Canetti, R., Nielsen, J.B., Pass, R.: Universally composable protocols with relaxed set-up assumptions. In: 45th FOCS, pp. 186–195. IEEE Computer Society Press (2004)

[2] Barker, E., Johnson, D., Smid, M.: NIST special publication 800-56A: Recommendation for pair-wise key establishment schemes using discrete logarithm cryptography, revised (2007)

[3] Canetti, R.: Universally composable security: A new paradigm for cryptographic protocols. In: 42nd FOCS, pp. 136–145. IEEE Computer Society Press (2001)

[4] Canetti, R.: Universally composable signature, certification, and authentication. In: CSFW 2004, p. 219. IEEE Computer Society (2004)

[5] Canetti, R.: Universally composable security: A new paradigm for cryptographic protocols. Cryptology ePrint Archive (2005), http://eprint.iacr.org/2000/067

[6] Canetti, R., Dodis, Y., Pass, R., Walfish, S.: Universally composable security with global setup. In: Vadhan, S.P. (ed.) TCC 2007. LNCS, vol. 4392, pp. 61–85. Springer, Heidelberg (2007)

[7] Canetti, R., Krawczyk, H.: Universally composable notions of key exchange and secure channels. In: Knudsen, L.R. (ed.) EUROCRYPT 2002. LNCS, vol. 2332, pp. 337–351. Springer, Heidelberg (2002)

[8] Capar, C., Goeckel, D., Paterson, K.G., Quaglia, E.A., Towsley, D., Zafer, M.: Signal-flow-based analysis of wireless security protocols. Inf. Comput. 226, 37–56 (2013)

[9] Cash, D., Kiltz, E., Shoup, V.: The twin diffie-hellman problem and applications. In: Smart, N.P. (ed.) EUROCRYPT 2008. LNCS, vol. 4965, pp. 127–145. Springer, Heidelberg (2008)

[10] Diffie, W., Hellman, M.E.: New directions in cryptography. IEEE Transactions on Information Theory 22(6), 644–654 (1976)

[11] Dodis, Y., Katz, J., Smith, A., Walfish, S.: Composability and on-line deniability of authentication. In: Reingold, O. (ed.) TCC 2009. LNCS, vol. 5444, pp. 146–162. Springer, Heidelberg (2009)

[12] Freire, E.S.V., Hofheinz, D., Paterson, K.G., Striecks, C.: Programmable hash functions in the multilinear setting. In: Canetti, R., Garay, J.A. (eds.) CRYPTO 2013, Part I. LNCS, vol. 8042, pp. 513–530. Springer, Heidelberg (2013)

[13] Freire, E.S., Hofheinz, D., Kiltz, E., Paterson, K.G.: Non-interactive key exchange. In: Kurosawa, K., Hanaoka, G. (eds.) PKC 2013. LNCS, vol. 7778, pp. 254–271. Springer, Heidelberg (2013)

[14] Gennaro, R., Halevi, S., Krawczyk, H., Rabin, T., Reidt, S., Wolthusen, S.D.: Strongly-resilient and non-interactive hierarchical key-agreement in mANETs. In: Jajodia, S., Lopez, J. (eds.) ESORICS 2008. LNCS, vol. 5283, pp. 49–65. Springer, Heidelberg (2008)

[15] Hofheinz, D., Shoup, V.: GNUC: A new universal composability framework. Cryptology ePrint Archive (2011), http://eprint.iacr.org/2011/303

[16] Jakobsson, M., Sako, K., Impagliazzo, R.: Designated verifier proofs and their applications. In: Maurer, U.M. (ed.) EUROCRYPT 1996. LNCS, vol. 1070, pp. 143–154. Springer, Heidelberg (1996)

[17] Kidron, D., Lindell, Y.: Impossibility results for universal composability in public-key models and with fixed inputs. Journal of Cryptology 24(3), 517–544 (2011)

[18] Nielsen, J.B.: Separating random oracle proofs from complexity theoretic proofs: The non-committing encryption case. In: Yung, M. (ed.) CRYPTO 2002. LNCS, vol. 2442, pp. 111–126. Springer, Heidelberg (2002)

[19] Sakai, R., Ohgishi, K., Kasahara, M.: Cryptosystems based on pairing. In: SCIS 2000, Okinawa, Japan (2000)

[20] Freire, E.S.V., Hesse, J., Hofheinz, D.: Universally Composable Non-Interactive Key Exchange. Cryptology ePrint Archive (2014), http://eprint.iacr.org/2014/528

Forward Secure Non-Interactive Key Exchange

David Pointcheval[1] and Olivier Sanders[1,2]

[1] École normale supérieure, CNRS & INRIA, Paris, France
[2] Orange Labs, Applied Crypto Group, Caen, France

Abstract. Exposure of secret keys is a major concern when crypto-graphic protocols are implemented on weakly secure devices. Forward security is thus a way to mitigate damages when such an event occurs. In a forward-secure scheme, the public key is indeed fixed while the secret key is updated with a one-way process at regular time periods so that security of the scheme is ensured for any period prior to the exposure, since previous secret keys cannot be recovered from the corrupted one. Efficient constructions have been proposed for digital signatures or public-key encryption schemes, but none for non-interactive key exchange protocols, while the non-interactivity makes them quite vulnerable since the public information cannot evolve from an execution to another one.

In this paper we present a forward-secure non-interactive key exchange scheme with sub-linear complexity in the number of time periods. Our protocol is described using generic *leveled* multilinear maps, but we show that it is compatible with the recently introduced candidates for such maps. We also discuss various security models for this primitive and prove that our scheme fulfills them, under standard assumptions.

Keywords: forward security, non-interactive key exchange, multilinear map.

1 Introduction

1.1 Non-Interactive Key Exchange

The famous interactive key exchange protocol introduced in 1976 in the seminal paper [DH76] by Diffie and Hellman can be turned into a simple and quite efficient non-interactive key exchange (NIKE) scheme: it enables two parties, who have first agreed on some parameters, to share a common secret without exchanging any additional messages but just their public keys. More precisely, the parameters simply consist of a group $\mathbb{G}$ of prime order p along with a generator $g \in \mathbb{G}$. When Alice, whose secret/public keys pair is $(x, X = g^x)$ for some $x \in \mathbb{Z}_p$, wants to share a secret with Bob, whose public key is $Y = g^y$, she computes $K = Y^x$, which value can be recovered by Bob by computing X^y. However, eavesdroppers have no clue about this value, because of the intractability of the Diffie-Hellman problem. Hashing the resulting secret K along with both identities even leads to a provably secure scheme, according to the expected properties for a NIKE scheme, and this scheme is remarkably efficient. Indeed, both secret

M. Abdalla and R. De Prisco (Eds.): SCN 2014, LNCS 8642, pp. 21–39, 2014.

and public keys consist of one element and sharing a secret only requires one exponentiation from each user.

A first basic security model for NIKE has been provided by Bernstein [Ber06]. Thereafter, Cash, Kiltz and Shoup [CKS08] enhanced it, allowing dishonestly generated public keys. This models the real-life situation where public keys are published by users, without certification, or with a weak certification only (when the certification authority does not check the knowledge of the associated secret key, but just the identity of the owner of the public key). However, Freire *et al* [FHKP13] pointed out some weaknesses in their model such as the inability of the adversary to corrupt honest users, and thus get honestly generated secret keys or shared keys between two honest entities. They proposed the *dishonest-key registration model*, as the strongest security model, together with a scheme in a pairing-friendly setting, secure in the standard model.

Sakai, Oghishi and Kasahara [SOK00] proposed the first Identity-based NIKE (Id-NIKE) scheme, later formalized and proven secure by Dupont and Enge in an ad-hoc security model [DE06]. The above concerns about the Certification Authority, and dishonestly generated public keys, are irrelevant in the identity-based setting, however, again, the lack of oracle access to previous shared keys was noticed as a potential weakness by Paterson and Srinivasan [PS09]. They thus fixed the previous model and explored the relationships between Id-NIKE and Identity-Based Encryption (IBE). Moreover, they proposed constructions, using trapdoor discrete log groups, whose instantiations suffer from the high computational cost of the `Extract` algorithm (to get secret keys from identities), with security in the random oracle model. Recently, Freire *et al* [FHPS13] provided the first Id-NIKE and Hierarchical Id-NIKE schemes secure against corruptions in the standard model.

1.2   Forward Security

As for most of cryptographic protocols, the main threat against a NIKE scheme is exposure of users' secret keys since, contrarily to interactive key exchange protocols which can still provide some security in this case, all the session keys between the corrupted user and any other user get immediately leaked. Leakage of a secret key is therefore a major issue for all users, not only for the corrupted one. A classical solution to prevent leakage is to distribute the secret across multiple servers via secret sharing. However, this is not compatible with the goal of *non-interactive* key exchange which is to limit communications between the different parties. Anderson [And97] thus suggested *forward security* to mitigate damages caused by key exposure: the lifetime of a system is now divided into T time periods, the secret keys evolving with time. More precisely, at any time period i, each user owns a secret key sk_i which he can use as usual, but also to derive his secret key sk_{i+1}, for the next time period. However, forward security requires that an adversary being able to recover sk_i is unable to compromise the security of any previous time period: the evolving process from sk_i to sk_{i+1} has to be one-way. In his talk, Anderson proposed a non trivial solution, but constructing protocols whose parameters were sub-linear in the number of periods remained a challenge. The case of digital signatures was first addressed by Bellare and Miner [BM99] which provided a security model but also different constructions, one of them achieving constant key-size (*i.e.* independent of T). Then, many other papers followed [AR00, IR01, KR02, BSSW06, ABP13], most of them providing schemes in the RSA setting. The case of public-key encryption has later been addressed by Canetti, Halevi and Katz [CHK07] whose construction in a pairing-friendly setting has complexity logarithmic in T only.

Although the case of forward-secure NIKE was mentioned in [And97], the problem of constructing a scheme with sub-linear complexity has still remained open. One could think that the ideas used to construct forward-secure signature or encryption schemes can lead to forward-secure NIKE schemes, however, this does not seem to be the case for the reasons we describe below. We here make a distinction between constructions in the RSA setting [BM99, AR00, IR01, ABP13] and the ones in a pairing-friendly setting [BSSW06, CHK07].

The first forward-secure schemes were proposed in the RSA setting: the key evolving process relies on the fact that exponentiation is a one-way function, even with a public exponent. Informally, the underlying idea is to set the public key as $Z = S^{e_1 \cdots e_T}$ for T public exponents $e_1, ..., e_T$ (we may have $e_i = e_j$) and a secret element S. At each time period i, the user will prove knowledge of an $(e_i \cdots e_T)$-th root of Z (thus sk_i is $S^{e_1 \cdots e_{i-1}}$), such a proof leading to an efficient signature scheme by using the Fiat-Shamir heuristic [FS86]. Updating the secret key simply consists in computing $sk_i^{e_i}$ and so does not require any randomness which would be convenient for constructing a NIKE scheme. However, while assuming that Alice knows some n-th root of a public element Z_A and that Bob knows an m-th root of a public element Z_B, computing a common secret between Alice and Bob is far from being obvious. Therefore, the RSA setting unfortunately seems to be more suitable for signatures than for NIKE schemes.

Since the seminal paper from Joux [Jou00], pairings have been widely used in cryptography, their properties allowing to solve open problems such as to construct an efficient identity-based encryption scheme [BF01]. In [CHK07], Canetti, Katz and Halevi used them to propose a forward-secure encryption scheme with logarithmic complexity in the number of time periods. However, since the involved groups are of prime order, exponentiation with public exponent is no longer a one-way function. The update algorithm is then more complex and involves randomness which makes sharing a common secret more difficult since non-interactivity of the primitive implies that Bob cannot get information about the random values used by Alice. The signature scheme of Boyen *et al* [BSSW06] is quite similar, therefore the underlying idea of constructions in a pairing-friendly setting does not seem to suit the NIKE case either. However, we emphasize that the randomness used to update the secret key is not necessarily incompatible with NIKE but the protocol must ensure that the common secret shared by Alice and Bob is independent of it.

1.3 Achievements

The lack of forward-secure NIKE scheme with sub-linear complexity could be explained by the limitations of cryptographic tools known until recently. As with pairings a decade ago, the recent candidates for multilinear maps proposed by Garg, Gentry and Halevi [GGH13] and Coron, Lepoint and Tibouchi [CLT13] offer new functionalities allowing to achieve constructions previously impossible. An example is provided in [FHPS13] where the authors used them to propose the first Id-NIKE scheme secure in the standard model.

In this work we prove that constructing a forward-secure NIKE scheme is also possible by using multilinear maps. Our scheme shares some similarities with tree-based forward-secure schemes since we also associate time periods with all nodes of the tree. But the construction manages to handle both evolution of secret keys and key exchange with the tree. It also provides some flexibility with the number of levels of the multilinear map, since whatever the number of time periods a bilinear map can be enough, at the cost of a larger secret key, while a smaller secret key will require a multilinear map with a higher number of levels. In addition, our construction is compatible with multilinear maps from [GGH13] and [CLT13], but requires some modifications that we describe in this paper. We also formally define two security models for forward-secure NIKE and prove that our scheme achieves the strongest one under a conventional assumption in the standard model.

1.4 Organization

In the next section, we recall the definition of generic leveled-multilinear maps and some of the differences with their approximations proposed in [GGH13] and [CLT13]. Section 3 describes a security model for forward-secure NIKE. We present a protocol using binary tree in Section 4 and then discuss the necessary adjustments to suit existing implementations of multilinear maps. We then show how to generalize the underlying idea of the previous protocol to get a trade-off between the size of the secret key and the number of levels of the multilinear map.

2 Leveled Multilinear Maps

Boneh and Silverberg [BS03] defined n-linear maps as non-degenerate maps e from $\mathbb{G}_1^n$ to $\mathbb{G}_2$ (where $\mathbb{G}_1$ and $\mathbb{G}_2$ are groups of same order) such that, for all $g_1, ..., g_n \in \mathbb{G}_1$ and $a_1, ..., a_n \in \mathbb{Z}$, $e(g_1^{a_1}, ..., g_n^{a_n}) = e(g_1, ..., g_n)^{a_1 \cdots a_n}$. The candidate multilinear map proposed by Garg, Gentry and Halevi [GGH13] actually yields a richer structure since it is now possible to multiply any (bounded) subset of encodings instead of n at a time. As in [HSW13], such maps will be denoted *leveled* multilinear maps. We recall the formal definition of generic n-leveled multilinear groups.

Leveled Multilinear Maps. Generic n-leveled multilinear groups consist of n cyclic groups $\mathbb{G}_1, ..., \mathbb{G}_n$ of prime order p, along with bilinear maps $e_{i,j} : \mathbb{G}_i \times \mathbb{G}_j \to \mathbb{G}_{i+j}$ for $i, j \geq 1$ and $i+j \leq n$ such that, for all $g_i \in \mathbb{G}_i$, $g_j \in \mathbb{G}_j$ and $a, b \in \mathbb{Z}_p$, $e_{i,j}(g_i^a, g_j^b) = e_{i,j}(g_i, g_j)^{a \cdot b}$. In the following we will write e instead of $e_{i,j}$ when i and j are obvious and $e(g_1, g_2, ..., g_n)$ instead of $e(g_1, e(g_2, ... g_n) ...))$.

The *graded encoding schemes* proposed in [GGH13] and [CLT13] are only approximations of such leveled multilinear maps. One of the main differences is that group elements have many possible representations called *encodings*. An encoding can be re-randomized but at the cost of introducing some noise. Such a randomization, performed using the Rerand algorithm, is sometimes necessary to prevent recovering of secret values. Indeed, let c be a secret level-zero encoding and g a public level-1 encoding. The level-1 encoding $y = c \cdot g$ (which is the equivalent of g^c in conventional groups) cannot be directly published since anyone will be able to recover c by computing $y.g^{-1}$, it must first be re-randomized into a new level-1 encoding $y' \leftarrow \mathsf{Rerand}(y)$. All these randomizations could be an obstacle for sharing a common secret, however, it is possible to extract, using the Extract algorithm, a *canonical* bit string which depends on the group element and not on its encoding, meaning that two encodings of the same element will give the same extracted string. Then the security of our protocols relies on the following assumption.

The n-Multilinear Decisional Diffie-Hellman (n-MDDH) Assumption

Given $(g, g^{x_1}, ..., g^{x_{n+1}}, G) \in \mathbb{G}_1^{n+2} \times \mathbb{G}_n$, it is hard to decide whether $G = e(g^{x_1}, ..., g^{x_n})^{x_{n+1}}$ or not.

3 Forward-Secure Non-Interactive Key Exchange and Security Model

3.1 Syntax

Following [CKS08] and [FHKP13], a forward-secure non-interactive key-exchange is defined by the following algorithms along with an identity space $\mathcal{IDS}$ and a shared key space $\mathcal{SHK}$. Identities are used to track which public keys are associated with which users but we are not in the identity-based setting.

- $\mathsf{Setup}(1^k, T)$: On inputs a security parameter k and a number of time periods T, this probabilistic algorithm outputs *params*, a set of system parameters that are implicit to the other algorithms. The current time period t^* is initially set to 1;
- $\mathsf{Keygen}(ID)$: On input an identity $ID \in \mathcal{IDS}$ this probabilistic algorithm outputs a public key/secret key pair (pk, sk_{t^*}), for the current time period t^*. We assume that the secret keys implicitly contain the time periods, hence the subscripts;

- **Update**(sk_t): This algorithm takes as inputs the secret key sk_t at some period t (implicitly included in sk_t) and outputs the new secret key sk_{t+1} for the next time period, if $t < T$. If $t = T$ then the secret key is erased and there is no new key;
- **Sharekey**($ID_A, pk^{(A)}, ID_B, sk_t^{(B)}$): On inputs an identity ID_A, associated with a public key $pk^{(A)}$ and a secret key $sk_t^{(B)}$ with identity ID_B, outputs either a shared key $shk_t^{AB} \in \mathcal{SHK}$ or a failure symbol $\perp$. This algorithm outputs $\perp$ if $ID_A = ID_B$. Since the secret key sk_t contains the time period, the shared key shk_t^{AB} is also specific to that time period t.

Correctness requires that, for any pair (ID_A, ID_B), if the secret keys $sk_t^{(A)}$ and $sk_t^{(B)}$ indeed correspond to the same time period t:

$$\mathbf{Sharekey}(ID_A, pk^{(A)}, ID_B, sk_t^{(B)}) = \mathbf{Sharekey}(ID_B, pk^{(B)}, ID_A, sk_t^{(A)}).$$

As in most of the forward-secure primitives, we provide the number of time periods to the **Setup** algorithm, because the parameters depend on it. In practice, one can take T large enough. Note that $T = 2^{15}$ is enough to enumerate one-day time-periods for one century.

3.2 Security Model

We define the security of a forward-secure non-interactive key exchange through a game between an adversary $\mathcal{A}$ and a challenger $\mathcal{C}$. Our security model makes use of the following oracles:

- $\mathcal{O}\mathrm{RegHon}(ID)$ is an oracle used by $\mathcal{A}$ to register a new honest user ID at the initial time period. The challenger runs the **Keygen** algorithm with 1 as the current time period, returns the public key pk to $\mathcal{A}$ and records $(ID, sk_1, pk, \mathsf{honest})$. This implicitly defines all the secret keys $sk_2, \ldots, sk_T$;
- $\mathcal{O}\mathrm{RegCor}(ID, pk)$ is an oracle used by $\mathcal{A}$ to register a new corrupted user ID with public key pk. The challenger then records the tuple $(ID, -, pk, \mathsf{corrupted})$.
- $\mathcal{O}\mathrm{Breakin}(ID, t)$ is an oracle used by $\mathcal{A}$ to get the ID's secret key at the time period t. The challenger looks for a tuple $(ID, sk_1, pk, \mathsf{honest})$. If there is a match, then it returns sk_t. Else, it returns $\perp$.
- $\mathcal{O}\mathrm{Reveal}(ID_A, ID_B, t)$ is an oracle used by $\mathcal{A}$ to get the shared key $shk_t^{(AB)}$ between ID_A and ID_B for the time period t. If both ID_A and ID_B are corrupted then $\mathcal{C}$ returns $\perp$. Else, it runs the **Sharekey** algorithm with the secret key of one of the honest users for the appropriate time period and the public key of the other user and returns $shk_t^{(AB)}$.

A non-interactive key exchange is forward-secure if, for any adversary $\mathcal{A}$ and any security parameter k, the advantage $\Pr[\mathbf{Exp}_{\mathcal{A}}^{\mathsf{fs}}(k) = 1] - \frac{1}{2}$ is negligible in k, where $\mathbf{Exp}_{\mathcal{A}}^{\mathsf{fs}}(k)$ is defined as follows:

1. $params \leftarrow \mathsf{Setup}(1^k, T)$
2. $(ID_A, ID_B, t^*) \leftarrow \mathcal{A}^{\mathcal{O}\mathrm{RegHon}, \mathcal{O}\mathrm{RegCor}, \mathcal{O}\mathrm{Breakin}, \mathcal{O}\mathrm{Reveal}}(params)$
3. $b \overset{\$}{\leftarrow} \{0, 1\}$
4. If $b = 0$ then $shk_{t^*}^{(AB)} \leftarrow \mathsf{Sharekey}(ID_A, pk^{(A)}, ID_B, sk_{t^*}^{(B)})$
5. Else, $shk_{t^*}^{(AB)} \overset{\$}{\leftarrow} \mathcal{SHK}$
6. $b^* \leftarrow \mathcal{A}^{\mathcal{O}\mathrm{RegHon}, \mathcal{O}\mathrm{RegCor}, \mathcal{O}\mathrm{Breakin}, \mathcal{O}\mathrm{Reveal}}(shk_{t^*}^{(AB)})$
7. If ID_A or ID_B is corrupted then return 0
8. If an $\mathcal{O}\mathrm{Breakin}$-query has been asked on $ID \in \{ID_A, ID_B\}$ with $t \leq t^*$ then return 0
9. If an $\mathcal{O}\mathrm{Reveal}$-query has been asked on (ID_A, ID_B, t^*) then return 0
10. If $b^* = b$ then return 1
11. Else, return 0

The adversary succeeds if it is able to distinguish a valid shared key between two users from a random element of the shared key space $\mathcal{SHK}$. To avoid trivial cases, the adversary is not allowed to corrupt the targeted users at a time period prior to t^* or to get the shared key between them at this time period. We emphasize that the adversary may corrupt any user (including ID_A or ID_B) for time periods $t > t^*$, which models the forward security.

Registration. The use of a Certification Authority (CA) is inevitable for protocols which are not in the ID-based settings, in order to link ID's and pk's. However, the assumptions made about the procedures followed by this entity differ according to each model.

- In the *registered-key model*, when a user wants to get his pubic key certified, the CA verifies, using a proof of knowledge, that the user actually knows the associated secret key. This enables the challenger (the simulator in the security proof) to extract the secret key and thus to answer every $\mathcal{O}\mathrm{Reveal}$-queries involving corrupted users.
- Cash, Kiltz and Shoup [CKS08] considered a stronger model where the CA no longer requires such a proof of knowledge of the secret key. In [FHKP13], the authors named it the *dishonest-key registration model*, since the public keys are not checked anymore.

In the latter case, some $\mathcal{O}\mathrm{Reveal}$ queries are not easy to answer, since none of the secret keys are known to the challenger/simulator. Hence the use of the Twin Diffie-Hellman [CKS08] which allows the challenger to check some consistency, in the random oracle model, under the sole CDH assumption. The requirement of the random oracle model has been more recently removed [FHKP13], by using chameleon hash functions [KR00]. To this end, they actually add some elements to the public key which provide a way for the challenger to recover the Diffie-Hellman value without knowledge of the corresponding secret keys. However, consistency still has to be checked, which is possible in the pairing settings only.

We can use the same approach, but with generic leveled multilinear maps, which are not provided with the existing implementations [GGH13, CLT13] of such maps. We explain the reasons in the Section 4.4.

3.3 Forward Security with Linear Complexity

A trivial solution, secure in our model, is to generate T independent keys pair (pk'_i, sk'_i) for any NIKE scheme and to set pk as $(pk'_1, \ldots, pk'_T)$ and sk_1 as $(sk'_1, \ldots, sk'_T)$. Updating the secret key $sk_i = (sk'_i, \ldots, sk'_T)$ simply consists in erasing the value sk'_i. To avoid the linear complexity of the public key we may use the following idea, similar to the one from [And97]: Let $(\mathbb{G}_1, \mathbb{G}_2, \mathbb{G}_T, e, p)$ be a bilinear setting, with groups of prime order p, and $g_1, \ldots, g_T \xleftarrow{\$} \mathbb{G}_1$, $g \xleftarrow{\$} \mathbb{G}_2$. To generate his public/secret key pair, a user randomly selects $x \xleftarrow{\$} \mathbb{Z}_p$ and sets $pk \leftarrow g^x$ and $sk_1 \leftarrow (g_1^x, \ldots, g_T^x)$. To update his secret key a user proceeds as in the previous solution, and to share a session key, at time period t, with another user whose public key is g^y, he computes $e(g_t^x, g^y)$. This scheme is correct and secure in the *registered-key model*. We can also avoid the linear complexity of the public parameters by setting $g_i \leftarrow H(t_i)$ for some cryptographic hash function $H : \{0,1\}^* \to \mathbb{G}_1$. But the resulting scheme will now be secure in the *random oracle model* only, with both the public keys and public parameters of constant size, while the secret keys are linear in the number of time periods T. Our goal is now to achieve a sub-linear complexity for the secret keys too.

4   A Forward-Secure Non-Interactive Key Exchange Scheme

As in [HSW13], we first describe a version of our scheme, using generic leveled multilinear maps, that we prove secure in the *registered-key model*. We then explain how to achieve security in the *dishonest-key registration model* defined in [FHKP13] and discuss the necessary adjustments to suit existing multilinear maps [GGH13, CLT13].

4.1   The Protocol

Let $\mathcal{S}_n$ be the set of bitstrings of size smaller than n. We recall the lexicographic order on $\mathcal{S}_n$. Let $s = b_1 \cdots b_\ell$ and $s' = b'_1 \cdots b'_k$, with $\ell \le k \le n$, be two bitstrings, then:

- if $b_i = b'_i, \forall\, 1 \le i \le \ell$, then $s < s'$ if $\ell < k$, and $s = s'$ otherwise;
- else, let $j \le \ell$ be such that $b_i = b'_i, \forall\, 1 \le i < j$, but $b_j \ne b'_j$. If $b_j < b'_j$ then $s < s'$, else $s > s'$.

Each bitstring $s \in \mathcal{S}_n$ will now refer to a time period. Specifically, the i-th bitstring of $\mathcal{S}_n$ (considering that the empty string does not belong in the set) will refer to the i-th time period: the order is thus $0, 00, 000, \ldots, 0^n, 0^{n-1}1, 0^{n-2}1, 0^{n-2}10$,

$0^{n-2}11, \ldots, 1^n$, with $T = \#\mathcal{S}_n = 2^{n+1} - 2$ elements, and thus corresponding to $2^{n+1} - 2$ time periods.

Let $(\mathbb{G}_1, \ldots, \mathbb{G}_{n+1})$ be an $(n+1)$-leveled multilinear group setting of order p, the algorithms defining our forward-secure NIKE are described below:

- $\mathtt{Setup}(1^k, n)$: This algorithm outputs the parameters $(g, g_1, \ldots, g_n) \xleftarrow{\$} \mathbb{G}_1^{n+1}$ along with $h_s \xleftarrow{\$} \mathbb{G}_1$ for each bitsring $s \in \mathcal{S}_n$. The public parameters $params$ contain the $T + n + 1$ elements. In the following, for each $s = b_1 \cdots b_\ell \in \mathcal{S}_n$, we will denote $G_s = e(h_{b_1}, h_{b_1 b_2}, \ldots, h_{b_1 b_2 \cdots b_\ell}) \in \mathbb{G}_\ell$, where $e(h_b) = h_b \in \mathbb{G}_1$.
- $\mathtt{Keygen}(ID)$: The user ID first selects $x \xleftarrow{\$} \mathbb{Z}_p$ and then outputs $pk \leftarrow g^x$ and the secret key of ID at the first time period, for $s = 0$, is $sk_0 \leftarrow \{h_1^x, h_0^x\}$. In the following, for each $s = b_1 \cdots b_\ell \in \mathcal{S}_n$, we denote $z_s^{(ID)} = G_s^x \in \mathbb{G}_\ell$.
- $\mathtt{Update}(sk_s)$: Let ℓ be the length of $s = b_1 \cdots b_\ell$ and $\mathcal{I}_s$ be the set $\{1 \le i \le \ell : b_i = 0\}$. Then, sk_s can be parsed as $\cup_{i \in \mathcal{I}_s}\{z_{b_1 \cdots b_{i-1} 1}\} \cup \{z_s\}$ (see the Correctness paragraph below) and the algorithm proceeds as follows:
  - if $\ell < n$, then the next bitstring is $s\|0$, the algorithm computes $z_{s\|0} \leftarrow e(z_s, h_{s\|0})$, $z_{s\|1} \leftarrow e(z_s, h_{s\|1})$ and returns $sk_{s\|0} \leftarrow (sk_s \setminus \{z_s\}) \cup \{z_{s\|1}, z_{s\|0}\}$;
  - if $\ell = n$, then we have $s = b_1 \cdots b_n$. If $s = 1^n$, then we have reached the last time period and the algorithm returns $\perp$. Else, let j be the greatest index such that $b_j = 0$, the next time period s^* is then $b_1 \cdots b_{j-1} 1$. The algorithm then returns $sk_{s^*} \leftarrow \cup_{i \in \mathcal{I}_s, i \le j}\{z_{b_1 \cdots b_{i-1} 1}\} \subset sk_s$.
- $\mathtt{Sharekey}(ID_A, pk^{(A)}, ID_B, sk_s^{(B)})$: This algorithm returns $\perp$ if $ID_A = ID_B$. Else, it outputs $shk_s^{AB} \leftarrow e(z_s^{(B)}, g_{\ell+1}, \ldots, g_n, pk^{(A)})$ where ℓ is the length of s.

Correctness. We first prove by induction that, for each time period s, $sk_s = \cup_{i \in \mathcal{I}_s}\{z_{b_1 \cdots b_{i-1} 1}\} \cup \{z_s\}$.

- For $s = 0$ we have $\mathcal{I}_s = \{0\}$ and $sk_0 = \{z_1\} \cup \{z_0\}$.
- If $\ell < n$ then the length of the next time period, $s^* = s\|0$, is $\ell + 1$ and $\mathcal{I}_{s^*} = \mathcal{I}_s \cup \{\ell + 1\}$. The $\mathtt{Update}$ algorithm ensures that the next secret key sk_{s^*} is $\cup_{i \in \mathcal{I}_{s^*}}\{z_{b_1 \cdots b_{i-1} 1}\} \cup \{z_{s^*}\}$.
- If $\ell = n$, then the next time period is $s^* = b_1 \cdots b_{j-1} 1$, so $\mathcal{I}_{s^*} = \mathcal{I}_s \cap \{1, \ldots, j-1\}$. The new secret key $sk_{s^*} := \cup_{i \in \mathcal{I}_s, i \le j}\{z_{b_1 \cdots b_{i-1} 1}\} = \cup_{i \in \mathcal{I}_s, i < j}\{z_{b_1 \cdots b_{i-1} 1}\} \cup \{z_{s^*}\} = \cup_{i \in \mathcal{I}_{s^*}}\{z_{b_1 \cdots b_{i-1} 1}\} \cup \{z_{s^*}\}$ is then consistent.

Finally, our protocol is correct since:

$$\mathtt{Sharekey}(ID_A, pk^{(A)}, ID_B, sk_s^{(B)}) = e(z_s^{(B)}, g_{\ell+1}, \ldots, g_n, pk^{(A)})$$
$$= e(h_{b_1}^{x_B}, h_{b_1 b_2}, \ldots, h_{b_1 b_2 \cdots b_\ell}, g_{\ell+1}, \ldots, g_n, g^{x_A})$$
$$= e(h_{b_1}^{x_A}, h_{b_1 b_2}, \ldots, h_{b_1 b_2 \cdots b_\ell}, g_{\ell+1}, \ldots, g_n, g^{x_B})$$
$$= e(z_s^{(A)}, g_{\ell+1}, \ldots, g_n, pk^{(B)})$$
$$= \mathtt{Sharekey}(ID_B, pk^{(B)}, ID_A, sk_s^{(A)}).$$

Our Protocol in a Nutshell. The Update algorithm must be a one-way function to ensure the forward-security, but correctness requires keeping a relation between the secret key and the public key. Therefore we cannot use an arbitrary one-way function (such as, for example, hash functions). Our secret key sk_s at a time period $s = b_1 \cdots b_\ell$ can be divided into two parts: the element z_s used to share a secret key at the current time period, and the other ones $(\cup_{i \in \mathcal{I}_s}\{z_{b_1 \cdots b_{i-1}1}\})$ that will be used to update the key. Since, $\forall i \in \mathcal{I}_s$, the strings $b_1 \cdots b_{i-1}1$ are not a prefix of a previous time period s^*, no one can compute z_{s^*} from sk_s. Moreover, multilinearity of the map implies that z_s is an element A^x (if pk is g^x) with $A \in \mathbb{G}_\ell$, which ensures correctness of our scheme. The use of different parameters $(g_1, \ldots, g_n)$ and h_s, for $s \in \mathcal{S}_n$, offers an efficient way to answer the oracle queries while being able to introduce the challenge values at a selected period, as shown in section 4.2.

For example, assume that $n = 3$ and $s = 01$, then we have $sk_{01} = \{z_1\} \cup \{z_{01}\}$. Since the length of $s = 01$ is $2 < n = 3$, updating the secret key to the next time period $s' = 010$ consists of replacing z_{01} by $z_{010} \leftarrow e(z_{01}, h_{010})$ and $z_{011} \leftarrow e(z_{01}, h_{011})$, so the new secret key $sk_{s'}$ is $\{z_1, z_{011}\} \cup \{z_{010}\}$ (see Figure 1). Now, s' has reached the maximum length $n = 3$ so the Update algorithm will simply delete the element z_{010} to output the secret key of the following time period 011.

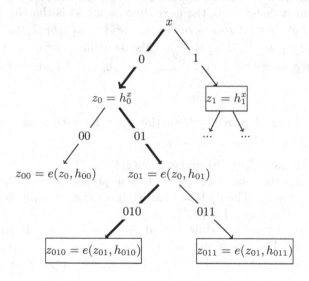

Fig. 1. Example for time period 010

4.2   Security Analysis

Theorem 1. *In the registered-key model, our forward-secure NIKE scheme with $2^{n+1} - 2$ time periods is secure under the $(n + 1)$-MDDH assumption.*

Proof. Let $\mathcal{A}$ be an adversary against our forward-secure NIKE scheme such that $\varepsilon = \Pr[\mathbf{Exp}_{\mathcal{A}}^{\text{fs}}(k) = 1] - 1/2$, then we construct $\mathcal{B}$, an adversary against the $(n+1)$-MDDH problem, as follows:

- $\mathcal{B}$ first makes a guess for the target time period $s^* = b_1^* \cdots b_{\ell^*}^* \xleftarrow{\$} \mathcal{S}_n$, of length ℓ^*, and the two distinct honest users involved in the target session, $i_0, i_1 \xleftarrow{\$} \{1, \dots, q_H\}$ where q_H is a bound on the number of $\mathcal{O}\text{RegHon}$-queries.
- On input an $(n+1)$-MDDH challenge $(g, g^{x_1}, \dots, g^{x_{n+2}}, G)$, $\mathcal{B}$ generates $(m_1, \dots, m_n) \xleftarrow{\$} \mathbb{Z}_p^n$ and $n_s \xleftarrow{\$} \mathbb{Z}_p$ for each $s \in \mathcal{S}_n$, then sets:
  - $\forall i \in \{1, \dots, n\} \backslash \{\ell^*\}$, $g_i \leftarrow (g^{x_i})^{m_i}$
  - $g_{\ell^*} \leftarrow g^{m_{\ell^*}}$
  - $\forall i \in \{1, \dots, \ell^*\}$, $h_{b_1^* \cdots b_i^*} \leftarrow g^{x_i \cdot n_{b_1^* \cdots b_i^*}}$
  - $\forall s \in \mathcal{S}_n \backslash \{b_1^*, b_1^* b_2^*, \dots, b_1^* \cdots b_{\ell^*}^*\}$, $h_s \leftarrow g^{n_s}$

This way, only elements h_t such that t is a prefix of s^* will be challenge elements. This enables $\mathcal{B}$ to handle any $\mathcal{O}\text{Breakin}$-query on time periods later than s^*. Similarly, setting g_{ℓ^*} as a non-challenge element allows $\mathcal{B}$ to answer any $\mathcal{O}\text{Reveal}$-query for time periods other than s^*. Now, $\mathcal{B}$ runs $\mathcal{A}$ with the above parameters and answers the different queries as follows:

- $\mathcal{O}\text{RegHon}(ID)$: Upon receiving an i-th register honest query, for a new identity ID, $\mathcal{B}$ acts as follows: If $i \neq i_0$ and $i \neq i_1$ then it runs the Keygen-algorithm on ID and returns the resulting public key to $\mathcal{A}$. Else, we have $i = i_b$ for $b \in \{0,1\}$ and ID will now be denoted ID_b. $\mathcal{B}$ will act as if $sk_0^{(b)} = \{h_1^{x_{n+1+b}}, h_0^{x_{n+1+b}}\}$ and then set $pk^{(b)} = g^{x_{n+1+b}}$, from the challenge input.
- $\mathcal{O}\text{RegCor}(ID, pk)$: Upon receiving a public key pk along with a new identity ID, $\mathcal{B}$ registers them. Since we first consider the *registered-key model*, we assume that $\mathcal{B}$ extracts the secret key $sk = x$ during the proof of knowledge of the secret key.
- $\mathcal{O}\text{Breakin}(ID, s)$: If $ID \neq ID_b$ for $b \in \{0,1\}$, then $\mathcal{B}$ returns $sk_s^{(ID)}$. Else, the behaviour of $\mathcal{B}$ depends on s. If $s \leq s^*$, then $\mathcal{B}$ aborts. Else, $\mathcal{B}$ parses s as $b_1 \cdots b_k$. The secret key of ID_b at this time period is $sk_s^{(b)} = \cup_{i \in \mathcal{I}_s} \{z_{b_1 \cdots b_{i-1}1}^{(b)}\} \cup \{z_s^{(b)}\}$. $\mathcal{B}$ proceeds as follows for each $i \in \mathcal{I}_s$:
  - If $i > \ell^*$, then $h_{b_1 \cdots b_{i-1}1} = g^{n_{b_1 \cdots b_{i-1}1}}$ and thus $z_{b_1 \cdots b_{i-1}1}^{(b)} = e(h_{b_1}^{x_{n+1+b}}, h_{b_1 b_2}, \dots, h_{b_1 \cdots b_{i-1}1})$ which $\mathcal{B}$ can compute as:
  $$e(h_{b_1}, h_{b_1 b_2}, \dots, (g^{x_{n+1+b}})^{n_{b_1 \cdots b_{i-1}1}})$$
  - If $i \leq \ell^*$, then $c_1 \cdots c_i := b_1 \cdots b_{i-1}1$ cannot be a prefix of s^*, otherwise we would have $s^* \geq b_1 \cdots b_{i-1}1 > s$ (since $b_i = 0$). So there is $j < i$ such that $b_j^* \neq c_j$ or $b_i^* = 0$ (which means that for $j = i$, $b_j^* \neq 1 = c_i$), implying that $\mathcal{B}$ is able to return $z_{b_1 \cdots b_{i-1}1}^{(b)} = z_{c_1 \cdots c_i}^{(b)} = e(h_{c_1}^{x_{n+1+b}}, h_{c_1 c_2}, \dots, h_{c_1 c_2 \cdots c_i})$ by computing:
  $$e(h_{c_1}, h_{c_1 c_2}, \dots, h_{c_1 \cdots c_{j-1}}, (g^{x_{n+1+b}})^{n_{c_1 \cdots c_j}}, h_{c_1 \cdots c_{j+1}}, \dots, h_{c_1 c_2 \cdots c_i})$$
  which is a valid value since $h_{c_1 \cdots c_j} = g^{n_{c_1 \cdots c_j}}$.

Similarly, $\mathcal{B}$ is able to return $z_s^{(b)}$, since s is not a prefix of s^*, and thus $h_s = g^{n_s}$, which means that $\mathcal{B}$ can answer every $\mathcal{O}$Breakin-query on ID_b for time periods $s > s^*$.

– $\mathcal{O}$Reveal(ID_A, ID_B, s): If at least one of the involved identity is honest and different from ID_0 and ID_1, then $\mathcal{B}$ runs the Sharekey algorithm. Else, we may assume (without loss of generality) that $ID_B = ID_b$ for some $b \in \{0, 1\}$. Since $\mathcal{B}$ is able to answer $\mathcal{O}$Breakin-queries involving ID_0 or ID_1 for time periods $s > s^*$, it is able to answer any $\mathcal{O}$Reveal-queries for these time periods. We then only consider time periods $s \le s^*$:

- $s < s^*$. We distinguish the two following cases.
  * If there is $t \in \mathcal{S}_n$ such that t is a prefix of s but not of s^*, then h_t is not a challenge element so $\mathcal{B}$ can compute z_t (and so z_s) in the same way as in $\mathcal{O}$Breakin-queries, and then return the valid shared key.
  * Else, $s = b_1^* \cdots b_k^*$ is a prefix of s^*, then $\mathcal{B}$ returns the valid shared key by computing:

$$e(h_{b_1^*}, \ldots, h_{b_1^* \cdots b_k^*}, g_{k+1}, \ldots, g_{\ell^*-1}, (g^{x_{n+1+b}})^{m_{\ell^*}}, g_{\ell^*+1}, \ldots, g_n, pk^{(A)}).$$

- $s = s^*$. If $\{ID_A, ID_B\} = \{ID_0, ID_1\}$ then $\mathcal{B}$ aborts. Else, ID_A is a corrupted user, and then $\mathcal{B}$ uses the extracted key x_{ID_A} to return the shared key between ID_A and ID_b.

– At the challenge phase, $\mathcal{A}$ outputs two identities ID_A and ID_B along with a time period s. If $s \ne s^*$ or $\{ID_A, ID_B\} \ne \{ID_0, ID_1\}$ then $\mathcal{B}$ aborts. Else, it returns $G^{\prod_{i=1}^{\ell^*} n_{b_1 \cdots b_i} \prod_{i=\ell^*+1}^{n} m_i}$ which is a valid shared key between ID_0 and ID_1 if $G = e(g^{x_1}, \ldots, g^{x_{n+1}})^{x_{n+2}}$ and a random element from the shared key space otherwise. $\mathcal{B}$ is then able, using the bit returned by $\mathcal{A}$, to distinguish the $(n+1)$-MDDH problem with an advantage greater than $\varepsilon / (T q_H^2)$.

$\square$

We stress that in order to have the $(n + 1)$-MDDH problem intractable, one needs to use an $(n+1)$-leveled multilinear map. With more levels, this problem because easy.

4.3   Dishonest-Key Registration Model

The simulator $\mathcal{B}$ above only needs the *registered-key* model to answer $\mathcal{O}$Reveal-queries involving a dishonest identity A and one of the target identity ID_b during the time period s^*. Indeed, the public elements $\{g_1, ..., g_n\}$ and $\{h_s\}_{s \in \mathcal{S}_n}$ are constructed in such a way that at least one of those involved in the shared keys does not depend on a challenge element when $s \ne s^*$. The simulator is then able to output $shk_{s \ne s^*}^{A, ID_b}$ by replacing this element by $(g^{x_{n+1+b}})^r$ where $r \in \{m_1, ..., m_n\} \cup \{n_s\}_{s \in \mathcal{S}_n}$. This is no longer true for the time period s^*, so $\mathcal{B}$ will use the secret key of A, extracted during the $\mathcal{O}$RegCor-queries, to output $shk_{s^*}^{A, ID_b}$.

In [FHKP13], the authors provide an efficient way to avoid the *registered-key model* by using a chameleon hash function [KR00] $\mathcal{H} : \{0,1\}^* \times \mathcal{R} \to \mathbb{Z}_p$, where $\mathcal{R}$ is the random space. The public parameters *params* now contain three additional elements u_0, u_1 and u_2 used to compute the public keys. Indeed, besides g^x, users now compute $t \leftarrow \mathcal{H}(g^x \| ID, r)$ for some random $r \in \mathcal{R}$ and $z \leftarrow (u_0 u_1^t u_2^{t^2})^x$, and set their public key as (g^x, z, r). Before sharing a key *shk*, correctness of the public key must be checked, which is possible in an n-linear setting (as long as $n > 1$).

To handle $\mathcal{O}\text{Reveal}$-queries involving a dishonest user, the reduction $\mathcal{B}$ will construct the parameters u_i as follows:

- $\mathcal{B}$ first selects at random $m_0, m_1 \xleftarrow{\$} \{0,1\}$ and $v_0, v_1 \xleftarrow{\$} \mathcal{R}$;
- $\mathcal{B}$ computes $t_0 \leftarrow \mathcal{H}(m_0, v_0)$, $t_1 \leftarrow \mathcal{H}(m_1, v_1)$ and a polynomial $p(t) = p_0 + p_1 \cdot t + p_2 \cdot t^2$ of degree 2 whose roots are t_0 and t_1;
- Now let b_1 be the prefix of length 1 of s^* in the security proof, then $\mathcal{B}$ sets $u_i \leftarrow h_{b_1}^{p_i} g^{q_i}$, for $i = 0, 1, 2$, where q_0, q_1, q_2 are the coefficients of another random polynomial of degree 2.

To register ID_0 or ID_1, $\mathcal{B}$ will use the secret key of the chameleon hash function to get r_0 or r_1 such that $\mathcal{H}(g^{x_{n+1+b}} \| ID_b, r_b) = t_b$ and outputs $(g^{x_{n+1+b}}, g^{x_{n+1+b} \cdot q(t_b)}, r_b)$ for $b \in \{0,1\}$. This is a valid public key because $p(t_b) = 0$.

To answer $\mathcal{O}\text{Reveal}$-queries involving a dishonest identity A during the time period s^*, correctness of the public key is first checked. So we may assume the public key $pk^{(A)}$ is well-formed: $pk^{(A)} = \{g^{x_A}, h_{b_1}^{p(t_A) \cdot x_A} g^{q(t_A) \cdot x_A}, r_A\}$, where $t_A \leftarrow \mathcal{H}(g^{x_A} \| ID_A, r_A)$. Let $pk^{(A)}[i]$ be the i-th element of $pk^{(A)}$, $\mathcal{B}$ is able to recover $h_{b_1}^{x_A}$ by computing $(pk^{(A)}[2]/(pk^{(A)}[1])^{q(t_A)})^{1/p(t_A)}$. Since b_1 is a prefix of s^*, $\mathcal{B}$ is able to recover $z_{s^*}^{(A)} = e(h_{b_1}^{x_A}, \ldots, h_{s^*})$, which is the secret element from $sk_{s^*}^{(A)}$ used by A to compute the shared key at the time period s^*.

The reduction $\mathcal{B}$ thus no longer needs the *registered-key model* to handle $\mathcal{O}\text{Reveal}$-queries. The resulting protocol is then secure even considering the *dishonest-key registration model*. However, as explained below, we can only use this idea with generic leveled multilinear groups, and this is not yet possible with the concrete constructions proposed by [GGH13] and [CLT13].

4.4 Adjustments to Existing Multilinear Maps

We currently do not have a concrete construction for leveled multilinear maps: Garg, Gentry and Halevi [GGH13], followed by Coron, Lepoint and Tibouchi [CLT13], have unfortunately just proposed approximations of such maps. Nevertheless, the differences between their schemes and generic leveled multilinear maps imply some changes in our protocol. The main drawback of these modifications is that our protocol does no longer support the *dishonest-key registration model* and thus requires a proof of knowledge of the secret key during the registration phase. This is due to the fact that we cannot select elements from the exponent group (called level-zero encoding in their paper), but only sample random ones. This is problematic because, in the previous security proof, simulations of answers to $\mathcal{O}\text{Reveal}$-queries involving a corrupted identity were possible due to the elements u_0, u_1 and u_2, constructed using some specific exponents, which were the coefficients of the polynomial $p(t)$. Moreover, in that security proof, there is a need for inverting the exponent $p(t_A)$. Using the terminology of [GGH13] and [CLT13], this means that, knowing a level-zero encoding of some c we have to compute a level-zero encoding of c^{-1} which is not known as possible. We thus cannot achieve security in the *dishonest-key registration model* and then only consider the *registered-key model*. The resulting scheme is then similar to the one described at the beginning of this section but requires the following adjustments:

- In the `Keygen` algorithm, the element x will now be a sampled level-0 encoding. The public key pk and the secret key sk_0 contain level-1 encodings which must be re-randomized (see Section 2) using the `Rerand` algorithm.
- Similarly, in the `Update` algorithm, the new values z_s must be randomized to prevent recovery of secret keys of previous time periods.
- In the `Sharekey` algorithm, the secret key cannot be $e(z_s^{(B)}, g_{\ell+1}, \ldots, g_n, pk^{(A)})$ since this value depends on the randomness used for randomizing encodings during previous steps. We then run the `Extract` algorithm on this value and define the shared secret key shk_s^{AB} as the output.

This instantiation of our protocol illustrates that randomness is compatible with NIKE schemes as long as the output of the `Sharekey` algorithm does not depend on it.

4.5   System Parameters

Our protocol requires $(n+1)$-leveled multilinear groups to handle $T = 2^{n+1} - 2$ time periods. The set of public parameters, consisting of $T + n + 1$ elements from $\mathbb{G}_1$, can be shorten using a hash function $\mathcal{H} : \{0,1\}^* \rightarrow \mathbb{G}_1$ (for example we may set $h_s \leftarrow \mathcal{H}(s)$), however, the security proof will require to model $\mathcal{H}$ as a random oracle.

The size of the secret key sk_s depends on the time period s, however, it never contains more than $n+1$ elements since $\#sk_s \leq \#\mathcal{I}_s + 1 \leq n+1$. Even if the number of levels only grows logarithmically *w.r.t.* the number of time periods, the dependence between the former and the parameters size remains a problem for the existing multilinear maps. In the next section we describe a generalization of our protocol which provides a trade-off between the number of levels and the size of the secret key.

5   A General Framework

A natural goal when designing a forward-secure NIKE is to make the parameters independent of the number of time periods. Compared to the protocol described in Section 3.3, our protocol has decreased the number of elements in the secret key but has increased the number of levels of the multilinear maps. It is possible to go further with this trade-off and thus achieve a protocol with only one element in the secret key (but with a larger number of levels). We show in this section that each protocol of this paper is actually a variant of a general framework allowing us to choose the number of elements in the secret keys or the number of levels (but not both of them). The idea is somewhat similar with the generic construction described in [BM99, Section 2] but with two major differences: First, Bellare and Miner considered certification chains where the secret key s_i at some time period i was used to certify the public key p_{i+1} of a new secret/public keys pair (s_{i+1}, p_{i+1}). Signatures issued at the time period i must then contain the full certification chain, namely $((\sigma_i, p_i), \ldots, (\sigma_2, p_2))$ where σ_i is the certificate on p_i w.r.t p_{i-1}. Using a binary tree, they reached a logarithmic number of elements in messages and in storage. However, this idea is suitable for signature schemes but not for NIKE, one reason being that the new public keys p_i will remain unknown to other parties unless one publishes them all at the beginning, which would correspond to the trivial solution. The second difference is that, with their solution, a signing key (the secret key along with the stored values (σ_i, p_i)) with constant size is unachievable whereas this is theoretically possible with our construction (see Section 5.2).

5.1 The Framework

In the previous section, we considered the set $\mathcal{S}_n$ of bitstrings of size smaller than n. In this section we rather consider the sets $\mathcal{S}_n^{(m)} := \{b_1 \cdots b_k : k \leq n \text{ and } 0 \leq b_i < m\}$ for any integer $m > 0$ (the previous section therefore corresponds to the particular case where $m = 2$). Each string still refers to a time period, a protocol using $(n+1)$-leveled multilinear groups then ensures $\frac{m}{m-1} \times (m^n - 1)$ time periods if $m > 1$ and n time periods if $m = 1^1$.

- Setup and Sharekey algorithms are the same as the ones described in Section 4.1.
- Keygen(*ID*): The user *ID* first selects $x \xleftarrow{\$} \mathbb{Z}_p$ and then outputs $pk \leftarrow g^x$ and the secret key of *ID* at the first time period, $sk_0 \leftarrow \{h_{m-1}^x, \ldots, h_1^x, h_0^x\}$. In the following, for each $s = b_1 \cdots b_\ell \in \mathcal{S}_n^{(m)}$, $z_s^{(ID)}$ will still denote the following element of $\mathbb{G}_\ell$: $e(h_{b_1}^x, h_{b_1 b_2}, \ldots, h_{b_1 b_2 \cdots b_\ell})$.
- Update(sk_s): Let ℓ be the length of $s = b_1 \cdots b_\ell$ and $\mathcal{I}_s$ be the set $\{1 \leq i \leq \ell : b_i < m - 1\}$. Then, $sk_s = \bigcup_{i \in \mathcal{I}_s} \bigcup_{b_i < b \leq m-1} \{z_{b_1 \cdots b_{i-1} b}\} \cup \{z_s\}$ and the algorithm proceeds as follows:
  - If $\ell < n$, then the next bitstring is $s \| 0$, the algorithm computes $z_{s\|0} \leftarrow e(z_s, h_{s\|0})$, $z_{s\|1} \leftarrow e(z_s, h_{s\|1})$, $\ldots$, $z_{s\|m-1} \leftarrow e(z_s, h_{s\|m-1})$, and returns $sk_{s\|0} \leftarrow (sk_s \setminus \{z_s\}) \cup \{z_{s\|m-1}, \ldots, z_{s\|1}, z_{s\|0}\}$.
  - If $\ell = n$, then we have $s = b_1 \cdots b_n$. If $b_i = m - 1$, for all i, then we have reached the last time period and the algorithm returns $\bot$. Else, let j be the greatest integer such that $b_j < m - 1$, the next time period s^* is then $b_1 \cdots b_{j-1}(b_j + 1)$. The algorithm then returns $sk_{s^*} \leftarrow \bigcup_{i \in \mathcal{I}_s, i \leq j} \bigcup_{b_i < b \leq m-1} \{z_{b_1 \cdots b_{i-1} b}\} \cup \{z_s\} \subset sk_s$.

---

[1] This comes from the fact that $p_n = \#\mathcal{S}_n^{(m)}$ follows an arithmetico-geometric progression $p_n = m(p_{n-1} + 1)$, with $p_0 = 0$.

The proof of correctness is similar to the case where $m = 2$: each time we move from a period s of length ℓ to a period $s||0$ of length $\ell + 1$, the Update algorithm simply stores the elements z_{s^*} for every strings s^* of length $\ell + 1$ whose prefix is s. Evolution of the secret key thus remains possible while recovery of elements z_t with $t \leq s$ is impossible. Adaptation of the security proof is straightforward.

5.2 System Parameters

The relation $T = \frac{m}{m-1} \cdot (m^n - 1)$ (or $T = n$ if $m = 1$) illustrates the trade-off between the number of levels $(n + 1)$ of the multilinear map and the parameter m affecting the size of the secret key. Indeed, our algorithms Keygen and Update lead to a secret key containing up to $n(m - 1) + 1$ elements. Let us focus on the two following particular cases:

Case 1: $n = 1$. Our protocol only requires two levels from the multilinear map so we can use conventional bilinear groups. The secret key at the first time period is $\{h_{m-1}^x, \ldots, h_0^x,\}$ (with $m = T$), the update algorithm is to simply delete the last element of the secret key. This protocol is then exactly the same as the one described in Section 3.3.

Case 2: $m = 1$. For convenience, we will denote in such a case the time periods by $\{1, \ldots, T\}$ rather than $\{0, 00, \ldots, 00 \cdots 000\}$. The secret key always contains one element $z_i = e(h_1^x, h_2, \ldots, h_i) \in \mathbb{G}_i$, updating it just consists in computing $z_{i+1} \leftarrow e(z_i, h_{i+1})$. Assuming, as Papamanthou $et\ al$ [PTT10], the existence of multilinear maps where the size of the different groups $\mathbb{G}_i$ is independent of the number of levels leads to a protocol where the sizes of the parameters and of the secret and public keys are independent of the number of time periods T. However, implementations of such a protocol with the maps from [GGH13] and [CLT13] will not achieve constant size since the size of the elements in the secret key will actually depend on the number of levels and so on the number of time periods.

Trade-off. Between these two extreme cases, one can choose suitable parameters according to the performance of the selected multilinear map. The maximal number of elements in the secret key is $N = n(m - 1) + 1$, and can be expressed as a function of m and T using the relation $T = \frac{m}{m-1} \cdot (m^n - 1)$ if $m > 1$. We then get:

$$N = 1 + \frac{m-1}{\log(m)} \cdot \log\left(\frac{m-1}{m} \times T + 1\right)$$

which is an increasing function of m in $]1; T]$. There is thus no *optimal* choice for the parameters (m, n). They have thus to be chosen according to some external constraints.

6   Conclusion

In this paper, we have first proposed two new security models for forward-secure non-interactive key exchange scheme, in order to limit damages in case of key exposure. In the first *registered-key* model, the certificate authority is assumed to strictly check the knowledge of the secret keys before certifying public keys together with an identity, whereas in the second *dishonest-key registration* model, the certificate authority just checks the identity but not the knowledge of the secret key associated to the public key. The latter model encompasses related-key attacks, where an adversary would try to generate public keys related to honest-user keys.

We then have proposed a construction that can be secure in the strongest security model using generic leveled multilinear maps. Unfortunately, concrete multilinear maps do not yet satisfy all the required properties, and thus our concrete construction just provides forward security in the registered-key model. We have thus pointed out a gap between generic leveled multilinear maps and concrete ones.

Of course, the efficiency of our construction depends to a large extent on the one of such maps. However, our construction can be made practical by tuning the number of levels of the multilinear map, impacting the size of the secret key but not the number of time periods.

Acknowledgments. This work was supported in part by the French ANR-12-INSE-0014 SIMPATIC Project and in part by the European Research Council under the European Community's Seventh Framework Programme (FP7/2007-2013 Grant Agreement no. 339563 – CryptoCloud).

References

[ABP13] Abdalla, M., Ben Hamouda, F., Pointcheval, D.: Tighter Reductions for Forward-Secure Signature Schemes. In: Kurosawa, K., Hanaoka, G. (eds.) PKC 2013. LNCS, vol. 7778, pp. 292–311. Springer, Heidelberg (2013)

[And97] Anderson, R.: Two remarks on public key cryptology (1997)

[AR00] Abdalla, M., Reyzin, L.: A New Forward-Secure Digital Signature Scheme. In: Okamoto, T. (ed.) ASIACRYPT 2000. LNCS, vol. 1976, pp. 116–129. Springer, Heidelberg (2000)

[Ber06] Bernstein, D.J.: Curve25519: New diffie-hellman speed records. In: Yung, M., Dodis, Y., Kiayias, A., Malkin, T. (eds.) PKC 2006. LNCS, vol. 3958, pp. 207–228. Springer, Heidelberg (2006)

[BF01] Boneh, D., Franklin, M.: Identity-Based Encryption from the Weil Pairing. In: Kilian, J. (ed.) CRYPTO 2001. LNCS, vol. 2139, pp. 213–229. Springer, Heidelberg (2001)

[BM99] Bellare, M., Miner, S.K.: A Forward-Secure Digital Signature Scheme. In: Wiener, M. (ed.) CRYPTO 1999. LNCS, vol. 1666, pp. 431–448. Springer, Heidelberg (1999)

[BS03] Boneh, D., Silverberg, A.: Applications of multilinear forms to cryptography. Contemporary Mathematics 324, 71–90 (2003)

[BSSW06] Boyen, X., Shacham, H., Shen, E., Waters, B.: Forward-secure signatures with untrusted update. In: Juels, A., Wright, R.N., De Capitani di Vimercati, S (eds.) ACM CCS 2006: 13th Conference on Computer and Communications Security, pp. 191–200. ACM Press (October/November 2006)

[CHK07]   Canetti, R., Halevi, S., Katz, J.: A forward-secure public-key encryption scheme. Journal of Cryptology 20(3), 265–294 (2007)

[CKS08]   Cash, D.M., Kiltz, E., Shoup, V.: The Twin Diffie-Hellman Problem and Applications. In: Smart, N.P. (ed.) EUROCRYPT 2008. LNCS, vol. 4965, pp. 127–145. Springer, Heidelberg (2008)

[CLT13]   Coron, J.-S., Lepoint, T., Tibouchi, M.: Practical Multilinear Maps over the Integers. In: Canetti, R., Garay, J.A. (eds.) CRYPTO 2013, Part I. LNCS, vol. 8042, pp. 476–493. Springer, Heidelberg (2013)

[DE06]   Dupont, R., Enge, A.: Provably secure non-interactive key distribution based on pairings. Discrete Applied Mathematics 154(2), 270–276 (2006)

[DH76]   Diffie, W., Hellman, M.E.: New directions in cryptography. IEEE Transactions on Information Theory 22(6), 644–654 (1976)

[FHKP13] Freire, E.S.V., Hofheinz, D., Kiltz, E., Paterson, K.G.: Non-Interactive Key Exchange. In: Kurosawa, K., Hanaoka, G. (eds.) PKC 2013. LNCS, vol. 7778, pp. 254–271. Springer, Heidelberg (2013)

[FHPS13] Freire, E.S.V., Hofheinz, D., Paterson, K.G., Striecks, C.: Programmable Hash Functions in the Multilinear Setting. In: Canetti, R., Garay, J.A. (eds.) CRYPTO 2013, Part I. LNCS, vol. 8042, pp. 513–530. Springer, Heidelberg (2013)

[FS86]   Fiat, A., Shamir, A.: How to Prove Yourself: Practical Solutions to Identification and Signature Problems. In: Odlyzko, A.M. (ed.) CRYPTO 1986. LNCS, vol. 263, pp. 186–194. Springer, Heidelberg (1987)

[GGH13]   Garg, S., Gentry, C., Halevi, S.: Candidate Multilinear Maps from Ideal Lattices. In: Johansson, T., Nguyen, P.Q. (eds.) EUROCRYPT 2013. LNCS, vol. 7881, pp. 1–17. Springer, Heidelberg (2013)

[HSW13]   Hohenberger, S., Sahai, A., Waters, B.: Full Domain Hash from (Leveled) Multilinear Maps and Identity-Based Aggregate Signatures. In: Canetti, R., Garay, J.A. (eds.) CRYPTO 2013, Part I. LNCS, vol. 8042, pp. 494–512. Springer, Heidelberg (2013)

[IR01]   Itkis, G., Reyzin, L.: Forward-Secure Signatures with Optimal Signing and Verifying. In: Kilian, J. (ed.) CRYPTO 2001. LNCS, vol. 2139, pp. 332–354. Springer, Heidelberg (2001)

[Jou00]   Joux, A.: A one round protocol for tripartite diffie-hellman. In: Bosma, W. (ed.) ANTS 2000. LNCS, vol. 1838, pp. 385–394. Springer, Heidelberg (2000)

[KR00]   Krawczyk, H., Rabin, T.: Chameleon signatures. In: ISOC Network and Distributed System Security Symposium – NDSS, The Internet Society (February 2000)

[KR02]   Kozlov, A., Reyzin, L.: Forward-Secure Signatures with Fast Key Update. In: Cimato, S., Galdi, C., Persiano, G. (eds.) SCN 2002. LNCS, vol. 2576, pp. 241–256. Springer, Heidelberg (2003)

[PS09]   Paterson, K.G., Srinivasan, S.: On the relations between non-interactive key distribution, identity-based encryption and trapdoor discrete log groups. Des. Codes Cryptography 52(2), 219–241 (2009)

[PTT10]   Papamanthou, C., Tamassia, R., Triandopoulos, N.: Optimal Authenticated
          Data Structures with Multilinear Forms. In: Joye, M., Miyaji, A., Otsuka,
          A. (eds.) Pairing 2010. LNCS, vol. 6487, pp. 246–264. Springer, Heidelberg
          (2010)
[SOK00]   Sakai, R., Ohgishi, K., Kasahara, M.: Cryptosystems based on pairing over
          elliptic curve. In: Symposium on Cryptography and Information Security
          (2000)

Secure Key Exchange and Sessions without Credentials

Ran Canetti[1,*], Vladimir Kolesnikov[2], Charles Rackoff[3], and Yevgeniy Vahlis[4]

[1] Boston University, Boston, USA and Tel-Aviv University, Tel-Aviv, Israel
canetti@tau.ac.il
[2] Bell Labs, Murray Hill, NJ, USA
kolesnikov@research.bell-labs.com
[3] University of Toronto, Toronto, Canada
rackoff@cs.toronto.edu
[4] Bionym Inc., Toronto, Canada
yvahlis@bionym.com

Abstract. Secure communication is a fundamental cryptographic primitive. Typically, security is achieved by relying on an existing credential infrastructure, such as a PKI or passwords, for identifying the end points to each other. But what can be obtained when no such credential infrastructure is available?

Clearly, when there is no pre-existing credential infrastructure, an adversary can mount successful "man in the middle" (MIM) attacks by modifying the communication between the legitimate endpoints. Still, we show that not all is lost, as long as the adversary's control over the communication is not complete: We present relatively efficient key exchange and secure session protocols that guarantee that any MIM adversary is immediately detected *as soon as he fails to intercept even a single message* between the legitimate endpoints.

To obtain this guarantee we strengthen the notion of key exchange to require that the keys exchanged in any two sessions are independent of each other as long as each session has at least one honest endpoint, *even if both sessions has an adversarial endpoint.* We call this notion **credential-free key exchange.** We then strengthen the existing notion of secure session protocols to provide the above guarantee given a CFKE (existing definitions and constructions are insufficient for this purpose). We provide two alternative definitions and constructions of CFKE, a game-based one with a (very efficient) construction in the RO model, and a UC one with a construction in the CRS model.

1 Introduction

Secure communication over adversary-controlled channels is one of the most widely and frequently used achievements of cryptography. The standard approach to secure communication involves two steps. First, the two conversing parties A and B securely establish a *session key*, and second, they use the key to encrypt and authenticate the exchanged messages. The first step, *key exchange* (KE), ensures that only authorized players are able to successfully compute the keys. This guarantee holds even if the

* Supported by the Check Point Institute for Information Security, an NSF EAGER grant, and NSF Algorithmic Foundations grant no. 1218461.

M. Abdalla and R. De Prisco (Eds.): SCN 2014, LNCS 8642, pp. 40–56, 2014.
© Springer International Publishing Switzerland 2014

adversary is capable of complete control of the channel, including arbitrary message observation, alteration and scheduling.

Traditionally, the ability of communicating parties to authenticate themselves almost always requires possession of secrets, and corresponding authorization architectures and protocols employ some kind of *infrastructure*, which manages these secrets. Common examples include Public Key Infrastructure (PKI), shared long term private keys, and human memorizable passwords.

In this work, we focus on efficiently achieving a strong security guarantee for the problems of key exchange and secure sessions in the credential-free setting.

Practical Need for Authentication without Credentials. While trusted infrastructure aids greatly in certifying the identities, capabilities or permissions of communicating parties, its heavy cost is not justified in many non-security-critical applications. In some cases, there may not be an authority who is qualified or trusted to operate the infrastructure and issue credentials. Some applications may use infrastructure opportunistically and use PKI when available, but may fall back on weak authentication without credentials. In yet other scenarios, such as ad-hoc peer-to-peer information sharing networks, it is not required to associate a network entity with a real-life entity, but rather there is a need to ensure the persistence of the connection.

The practical importance of the problem has led to a rich body of network security research. Several techniques of *weak authentication* have emerged, were standardized, and successfully widely deployed. For details, we refer the reader to the related research described in [CKR+13]. Our work is a more formal approach that achieves much stronger security.

1.1 The Setting and Our Contributions

In our setting, two parties A and B have decided to have a communication session over an insecure channel. A and B do not share any information other than which channel to use for communication, and possibly a global public reference string. The decision itself may have been made in an insecure way; for example, A may have really been invited by an adversary Adv rather than by B. As there is no infrastructure to support authentication, Adv may falsely claim any identity. The channel A and B will use for their session may also be controlled by Adv, who can read from it and write to it at will. Without credentials, we have no hope of preventing Adv falsely taking another player's identity or playing man-in-the-middle (MIM).

We are motivated by today's many networking architectures, where it is difficult for the adversary to always be an active MIM. Examples include LANs, wireless and cellular networks, ad-hoc networks, opportunistic routing, etc. We present a candidate for what we believe is the "next best" achievable security guarantee in this setting. Namely, we require that *the adversary must remain continuously active on the channel throughout the entire session to avoid detection*.

We formalize this by proposing new definitions of KE and secure sessions, which, when combined, guarantee the above property (see Sect. 5.1). Our definitional approach is as follows. In the KE preceeding the communication, either the exchanged key is hidden from Adv, or, if the adversary is playing MIM between A and B, then A and B will output keys that are random and independent from each other, and the adversary's view contains no secrets about these keys. We model this by requiring the view of the adversary to be simulatable given the outputs of the parties. We identify and formalize a security property of secure session protocols, which we call MIM-integrity, which ensures that the MIM-adversary must remain continuously active on the channel throughout the entire session to avoid detection. We show that combining above KE and secure sessions guarantees secure communication in the above sense. In this work we:

1. Present definitions of secure credential-free key exchange (CFKE) in the standalone and universally composable (UC) [Can00] settings. Our definitions guarantee that if two parties participate in a CFKE protocol, they either output the same key which is completely hidden from the adversary, or output two keys that are almost independent and uniformly random given the transcript of the view of the adversary.

2. Present simple definitions of secure credential-free secure sessions (CFSS), which, in addition to the standard security properties, guarantee that MIM must be continuously active to avoid detection.

3. We show that composing any CFKE and CFSS results in secure communication in the credential-free setting. We also show that, in contrast, session protocols, even those standardized by the Internet bodies, are *insecure* in our setting.

4. Describe a construction of a CFKE protocol in the standalone model with a global common reference string (CRS), and prove its security in the standard model. We then show how to construct a secure session with a new integrity property (MIM-integrity) that guarantees that an adversary must modify every message in transit from A to B or be detected.

5. Analyze two existing KE protocols: we show that the well known hashed Diffie-Hellman protocol satisfies a variant of our standalone definition in the random oracle model. We additionally compare our standalone protocol to the instantiation of our UC definition using the construction of [BCL$^+$05], and show that it provides a useful tradeoff in settings with high latency, where low round complexity is crucial.

1.2 Intuition for Our Constructions

CFKE. The key difference between a CFKE protocol and an unauthenticated key exchange (such as the basic Diffie-Hellman protocol) is that neither party should be able to influence the outcome too much. This is necessary to achieve independence of keys in the man-in-the-middle scenario.

A naive CFKE approach may be to use a coin toss protocol as a black box, and simply encrypt its messages. However, there is no key infrastructure that would allow A and B to encrypt! Indeed, the whole purpose of CFKE is to attempt to establish such an infrastructure. Moreover, simply exchanging public keys to be used for encryption won't work since the adversary may be able to replace (or modify) the public keys on the way, stripping the coin toss protocol from any privacy. This leads us to the following intuitive observation: any cryptographic keys that are sent across the channel and are

used for the security of KE, must be strongly tied to the randomness used to generate
the final key.

Overview of the construction. Our credential-free key exchange protocol is symmetric, and consists of two rounds where A and B simultaneously send messages to each
other. It proceeds as follows:

1. A and B generate and announce public keys, and commit to the public keys *together
   with* random nonces. Here the commitment must have strong non-malleability properties (which we identify and formally define).
2. Using the public keys announced in the first round, A and B send to each other
   encrypted decommitment strings for the commitments they announced in the first
   round.
3. A and B use the decommitment strings to obtain each other's nonces, and output
   their exclusive-OR.

Relying on the non-malleability property of the commitment scheme, we get that no
adversary can modify either A's public key or her nonce, without changing the other
(similarly for B). Moreover, since the nonce is hidden by the commitment, the adversary is unable to commit to a related nonce, if she decides to modify the public key. On
the other hand, if she leaves the public key untouched, she will not be able to learn B's
decommitment when he sends it in the next round.

Using CFKE for Communication. CFKE can be used to construct secure session protocols with security against MIM-adversaries. We show that the following is a secure
credential-free secure session (CFSS): a secure session protocol in the traditional sense,
where additionally the sender simply attaches to each message, in the clear, a dedicated
part of the secret key. That is, if A's key is $K_A = (K_{A,1}, K_{A,2})$, then $K_{A,1}$ is used
for the underlying secure session protocol, and $K_{A,2}$ is attached as an authenticator to
each message. Now, when B receives a message from A with an attached authenticator
$K_{A,2}$, he checks if $K_{A,2} = K_{B,2}$, and aborts if the check fails. It is easy to see that
any adversary that does not change the authenticator on each message will be caught as
soon as a single message is transmitted directly.

1.3 Discussion

Password-Authenticated Key Exchange (PAKE)   [BM92, KOY01, GL01],
[GL03, CHK+05, KV11, CDSVW12], when *executed with fixed publicly known password, say, the all-zero password*, can be viewed as a protocol in a credential-free setting.
In fact, such a PAKE achieves guarantees somewhat similar to those of CFKE, and at the
first glance may seem sufficient for our task. There are, however, important differences
between CFKE and PAKE, which render PAKE inapplicable to our setting.

Firstly, the definitional approach to PAKE fundamentally differs from our approach:
a successful Adv in PAKE may be able to fix the output key to an arbitrary value, which
would render such KE useless for CFSS (indeed, MIM Adv can set the two players' key
to be equal and known to him, and thus break the CFSS protection).

Beyond just definitions, many natural PAKE protocols in fact do allow a player to
set the session key (and, to our knowledge, no protocols prove otherwise). Indeed, such

a PAKE can be easily constructed from any secure PAKE by adding a round where the successfully authenticated players (now presumed honest by PAKE definitions) are allowed to set the session key to anything of their choice.

More importantly, many existing protocols from the literature, e.g., of Canetti et al. [CDSVW12] have the above feature. We stress that it is a natural property of their approach; provably avoiding it would complicate their construction and would require a new definition and a proof. In [CDSVW12], UC-secure PAKE is built from Oblivious Transfer (OT), roughly as follows: the two players run several OT instances, where the secrets are randomly chosen strings, and the password defines the selection bits. The session key of OT receiver is the XOR of the received secrets, and OT sender's key is the XOR of the secrets corresponding to his password. It is easy to see that in the above PAKE, the OT sender can set the session key to any string of his choice. We note that the above PAKE OT idea is the basis for two constructions of [CDSVW12], and in both of them the property of OT sender being able to set the key is preserved.

Practical Impact of MIM-integrity. Despite seeming simplicity, MIM-integrity is a subtle concept and can be violated by seemingly secure natural protocols. Consider a session protocol where players periodically refresh the session key. Typically, one player chooses a nonce n, and each player updates his key sk to $\text{PRF}_{sk}(n)$. One prominent example of such a protocol is in EAP-TLS [ALE09]. This refresh is a frequently employed "best security practice", which aims to limit the amount of ciphertext an adversary can collect to attack the underlying encryption. However, CFSS using the above security heuristic is completely insecure, as, since AES is invertible, MIM Adv can choose nonces n_A, n_B which would set the refreshed keys $K_A = K_B$, allowing the adversary to withdraw and only occasionally interfere with communication when needed.

Open Directions. The main open direction left by our work is to design new secure session protocols and notions of security against MIM adversaries that rely on other (possibly weaker or incomparable) properties of networks in practice. For example, one may be able to design secure sessions that always detect a MIM adversary assuming network delay, or that messages are sent in pieces and that an adversary is unable to predict future content (this idea was used in the Interlock protocol [RS84]). We believe that our notion (and constructions) of CFKE can be used as a formal basis for such future explorations.

1.4 Related Work

The problem of unauthenticated secure communication over insecure channels traces back to the work of Dolev, Dwork, and Naor in [DDN91]. They introduced the non-malleability guarantee: any adversary controlling the channel between two parties either remains essentially passive, or is forced to run two independent instances of the protocol, one with each honest party. The study of non-malleability has led to a rich body of research that can be roughly classified according to two types of constructions: constructions of specific non-malleable primitives such as encryption, zero-knowledge proof systems, commitments, etc; and non-malleable "meta-protocols" that are used to establish per-session infrastructures. These include non-malleable coin tossing [Bar02], establishing a public key infrastructure [BCL$^+$05], and a shared secret key infrastructure [CCGS10]. Such protocols can then provide setup for the protocols that need it.

Barak [Bar02] defines and constructs non-malleable coin tossing protocols, where two parties wish to agree on an almost unbiased *public* random string in the presence of MIM adversary. This coin tossing guarantees that an adversary must either allow the players to output the same random string, or cause them to output two separate and independently generated random strings. The protocols of [Bar02] work without *any* infrastructure, but provide no privacy guarantee (the outcome of the coin toss is always known to the adversary).

In [BCL$^+$05] Barak *et al.* define split functionalities – a variant of ideal functionalities of the UC framework. Split functionalities allow an adversary to partition the set of honest parties P into disjoint "authentication sets". The idea is that all parties within each set $H_i \subseteq P$ have successfully established an authenticated session. The adversary is then unable to impersonate any party in H_i to any other party in H_i, but can impersonate any party in $P \setminus H_i$ to any party in H_i. Since the adversary determines the authenticated sets, this allows her, for example, to set all authenticated sets to be singletons, in which case no authenticated communication between honest parties is possible. This indeed seems unavoidable since the adversary has complete control over the communication channels. Camenisch *et al.* [CCGS10] define, among other things, split key exchange and give a construction based on the decisional Diffie-Hellman assumption.

Our non-malleable KE can be built from split functionalities and coin toss. Indeed, coin-toss whose output is hidden from Adv is easily achieved assuming secure channels (e.g., Blum's protocol with a UC-commitment suffices). Then, applying the compilers of [BCL$^+$05] or [CCGS10] to such secret coin toss functionality guarantees that either key is hidden from Adv (Adv chose to interact with a single ideal functionality that issues keys secretly to the two honest parties), or that Adv knows both independent keys (Adv interacts with two separate functionalities, playing the role of an honest party in each one). Using the recent commitment protocol of Lindell [Lin11], the resulting KE protocol requires seven rounds of communication, and sending of a constant number of group elements.

2   Preliminaries

Notation. We write PPT to denote Probabilistic Polynomial Time. When we wish to fix the random bits of a PPT algorithm M to a particular value, we write $M(x;r)$ to denote running M on input x and randomness r. We write $time_n(M)$ to denote the running time of algorithm M on security parameter n. We use $x \in_R S$ to denote the fact that x is sampled according to a distribution S. Similarly, when describing an algorithm we may write $x \leftarrow_R S$ to denote the action of sampling an element from S and storing it in a variable x. We denote by $1_{\mathbb{G}}$ the unit element of a group.

Discrete Logarithm Assumption. Let $\mathcal{G}$ be a probabilistic group generator such that $\mathbb{G} \leftarrow_R \mathcal{G}(1^n)$ is a group of order p where p is a prime of length about n bits. The Discrete Logarithm assumption for $\mathcal{G}$ is that given $\mathbb{G}$, g, g^x, where $\mathbb{G} \leftarrow_R \mathcal{G}(1^n)$, $g \in_R \mathbb{G}$, $x \in_R \mathbb{Z}_p$, it is infeasible to find x.

Non-malleable Public Key Encryption (PKE). Let $\mathcal{PKE} = \langle \mathsf{KeyGen}, \mathsf{Enc}, \mathsf{Dec} \rangle$ be a public key encryption scheme. We say that $\mathcal{PKE}$ is non-malleable if no adversary can distinguish the encryptions of two messages of her choice, even if she is allowed to make a single decryption query after seeing the challenge ciphertext C_*. The decryption query is of course restricted to all strings that are not equal to C_*.

Target Collision Resistant Hash Functions. A family $\mathcal{H} = \{H_k\}_{k \in \{0,1\}^*}$ of hash functions is target collision resistant if no efficient adversary can win the following game: (i) the adversary selects a target input x; (ii) a random key $k \in_R \{0,1\}^n$ is chosen; (iii) the adversary is given k and must output another input y such that $H_k(x) = H_k(y)$.

3   Definition of Secure Key Exchange without Credentials

We start with a syntactic definition of a credential-free key exchange (CFKE) protocol. A CFKE protocol is a triple $\mathcal{CFKE} = \langle \mathsf{KEInit}, \mathsf{KE}_A, \mathsf{KE}_B \rangle$ where KEInit takes as input a security parameter 1^n and outputs a common reference string PUB. The protocol itself consists of the actions performed by a role-A party, specified by KE_A, and a role-B party whose actions are specified by KE_B (the roles are assigned to break the symmetry, e.g. to determine who moves first). The pair $\mathsf{KE} = \langle \mathsf{KE}_A, \mathsf{KE}_B \rangle$ is a two party protocol in the common reference string model. We shall use KE to discuss the protocol as a whole, and distinguish between KE_A and KE_B when such a distinction is warranted.

Adversary for a CFKE protocol is a triple of PPT algorithms $\mathsf{Adv} = (A_{ke}, A_{ind}, A_{mal})$. To define security of CFKE we describe three experiments where the first experiment models the interaction of Adv with the protocol KE, and the other experiments capture *privacy* and *non-malleability* properties.

Security Experiments. We start with the description of the experiment ExpCFKE which defines the interaction of the adversary with the protocol: let $\mathcal{KE}$ be a CFKE and let A_{ke} be a PPT algorithm.

Experiment. $\mathsf{ExpCFKE}(1^n, \mathcal{KE}, A_{ke})$

1. $\mathsf{KEInit}(1^n)$ is run to obtain public parameters PUB, which are given to A_{ke}.
2. The key exchange protocol is run between two parties A and B, where A acts according to KE_A and B acts according to KE_B. All the communication is routed through A_{ke}. During this process A_{ke} can inject, delete, and modify messages between the two parties at will.
3. After KE concludes, let K_A^{out} and K_B^{out} be the outputs of the protocol, and let $view(A_{ke})$ be the view of A_{ke} during its execution. The view consists of the randomness of A_{ke}, and all the (potentially modified) messages exchanged between A and B during the execution of the protocol.
4. The outcome of the experiment is the tuple $(K_A^{out}, K_B^{out}, view(A_{ke}))$.

Intuitively, we wish to achieve the following security guarantee: either the two parties agree on a key and the adversary knows nothing about it, or the adversary is forced to perform two independent key exchanges (one with each party) resulting in the parties outputting independently random keys. We capture this intuition by describing two security experiments for CFKE: privacy and non-malleability.

The first experiment ExpCFKEInd requires the adversary to distinguish a key agreed upon by the two parties in the protocol from a random key. If the two parties do not agree on a key (i.e. $K_A^{out} \neq K_B^{out}$) then the adversary automatically loses in the privacy experiment. This is enforced by setting the outcome of the experiment by flipping an unbiased coin. Let $b \in \{0, 1\}$, the privacy experiment is defined as follows:

Experiment. ExpCFKEInd($1^n, \mathcal{KE}, A_{ke}, A_{ind}, b$)

1. Run experiment ExpCFKE($1^n, \mathcal{KE}, A_{ke}$) to obtain ($K_A^{out}, K_B^{out}, view(A_{ke})$).
2. If $K_A^{out} \neq K_B^{out}$, flip an unbiased coin $b' \in_R \{0, 1\}$ and set the outcome of the experiment to b'.
3. Else, let $K_0 = K_A^{out}$, $K_1 \in_R \{0, 1\}^n$. Let $b' \leftarrow_R A_{ind}(view(A_{ke}), K_b)$. The outcome of the experiment is b'.

Definition 1. *Let* $\mathcal{KE} = $ (KEInit, KE) *be a credential-free key exchange. We say that* $\mathcal{KE}$ *is private if for every CFKE adversary* Adv $= (A_{ke}, A_{ind}, A_{mal})$, *there exists a negligible function* $neg(\cdot)$, *such that for all* $n \in \mathbb{N}$

$$|\Pr[\mathsf{ExpCFKEInd}(1^n, \mathcal{KE}, A_{ke}, A_{ind}, 0) = 1] -$$
$$\Pr[\mathsf{ExpCFKEInd}(1^n, \mathcal{KE}, A_{ke}, A_{ind}, 1) = 1]| \leq neg(n)$$

In the second experiment ExpCFKENMal the goal of the adversary is to make the two parties output different keys with some correlation that may depend on the adversary's view. We require that for every adversary there exists a simulator such that the view of the adversary in an interaction that causes the parties to output two different keys K_A, K_B is simulatable given random keys K_A, K_B. The simulated view should be indistinguishable from the real one even given K_A and K_B.

This captures the intuition that the only way the adversary can make the parties output different keys is by making them output independent random keys. As we discussed in the introduction, we cannot completely prevent the adversary from influencing the output of the parties since she always has the option to omit the message that determines that outcome, unless the outcome satisfies some property (e.g. the key K_A has zero as its first bit). We require that this is essentially the only way the adversary can influence the outputs of the parties. This is captured by allowing the simulator to sample polynomially many pairs of uniformly random keys, and pick one pair for the output. This essentially grants the simulator exactly the ability to try a new key unless the current key satisfies a relatively likely property. For $b \in \{0, 1\}$ and a simulator S the non-malleability experiment is:

Experiment. ExpCFKENMal($1^n, \mathcal{KE}, A_{ke}, A_{mal}, S, b$)

1. Run experiment ExpCFKE($1^n, \mathcal{KE}, A_{ke}$) to obtain ($K_A^{out}, K_B^{out}, view(A_{ke})$).
2. If $K_A^{out} = K_B^{out}$, flip an unbiased coin $b' \in_R \{0, 1\}$ and set the outcome of the experiment to b'.
3. Else, run simulator $S(1^n)$ and allow S to sample a polynomial number of uniformly random key pairs $(K_A, K_B) \in (\{0, 1\}^n)^2$. Let $view'$ be the output of the simulator and (K_A, K_B) be the last pair of keys sampled by S.
4. Set $Y_0 = (K_A^{out}, K_B^{out}, view(A_{ke}))$, and $Y_1 = (K_A, K_B, view')$, and let $b' \leftarrow_R A_{mal}(Y_b)$. The outcome of the experiment is b'.

Definition 2. *Let* $\mathcal{KE}$ = (KEInit, KE) *be a credential-free key exchange. We say that* $\mathcal{KE}$ *is* non-malleable *if for every CFKE adversary* Adv = $(A_{ke}, A_{ind}, A_{mal})$, *there exists an expected PPT simulator* S, *and a negligible function* $neg(\cdot)$, *such that for all* $n \in \mathbb{N}$

$$|\Pr[\mathsf{ExpCFKENMal}(1^n, \mathcal{KE}, A_{ke}, A_{mal}, S, 0) = 1]-$$
$$\Pr[\mathsf{ExpCFKENMal}(1^n, \mathcal{KE}, A_{ke}, A_{mal}, S, 1) = 1]| \le neg(n)$$

Finally, we say that a CFKE protocol is secure if it satisfies both properties described above.

Definition 3. *Let* $\mathcal{KE}$ = (KEInit, KE) *be a credential-free key exchange. We say that* $\mathcal{KE}$ *is* secure *if it satisfies* privacy, *and* non-malleability.

On Concurrent CFKE Executions. As in standard definitions of KE (e.g. [CK01]), it suffices to consider only the case where there is a single "test session" that the adversary tries to break. In addition, since the parties do not have initial credential or public keys, here there is no need to explicitly model additional parties other than the two parties performing the exchange. Indeed, consider an alternative definition based on Definition 3, where Adv is allowed to generate several instances of honest and dishonest players, with whom Adv interacts in a concurrent manner. At multiple points during the interaction, Adv adaptively selects a pair of players, requests and answers the challenge of the KE game. The adversary wins if it wins in any one of the selected challenge exchanges. It is easy to see that this stronger definition is equivalent to the current, single session one. Indeed, an adversary that breaks the multi-session definition can be turned into an adversary that wins the single session definition by choosing a single session at random and simulating all the other sessions and players internally. (Note that this simulation and the corresponding definitional simplification is only possible in the credential-free setting.)

Universally Composable CFKE. To allow for formal composability of CFKE protocols, we also provide a UC definition and construction of the CFKE notion. Due to limited space, this is presented in [CKR+13].

4   Two Credential-Free Key Exchange Protocols

We present two constructions of CFKE protocols. Our main protocol is shown to be secure in the standard model, and requires two simultaneous rounds of communication. The second protocol that we present is what is commonly known as "Hashed Diffie-Hellman". We show that HDH is *not* a secure CFKE protocol in the standard random oracle model. However, we show that if one is willing to assume that HDH uses its own random oracle, that is not later used by other protocols, it is a secure CFKE protocol.

4.1   Protocol 1: Standard Model

We now present our main protocol (see Section 1.2 for its intuition). For our construction, we rely on a non-interactive equivocal commitment scheme with a specialized non-malleability property. Commitments are discussed in detail in [CKR$^+$13]. We note that while our definition is specialized to allow us to prove the security of our CFKE protocol, it may be of independent interest as a property of non-interactive commitment schemes.

Let $\mathcal{COM} = \langle \mathsf{ComInit}, \mathsf{Commit}, \mathsf{Decommit} \rangle$ be a 2-strongly non-malleable commitment scheme [CKR$^+$13], and let $\mathcal{PKE} = \langle \mathsf{KeyGen}, \mathsf{Enc}, \mathsf{Dec} \rangle$ be a non-malleable public key encryption scheme. We construct a two-flow credential-less key exchange protocol $\mathcal{CFKE}_1 = \langle \mathsf{KEInit}, \mathsf{KE}_A, \mathsf{KE}_B \rangle$ based on $\mathcal{COM}$ and $\mathcal{PKE}$.

The public parameters generating algorithm KEInit on input security parameter 1^n runs $\mathsf{ComInit}(1^n)$ to obtain a common reference string PUB for $\mathcal{COM}$, and outputs PUB as the public parameters of the key exchange protocol. The protocol KE consists of two rounds where in each round Alice and Bob send a message to each other. In our protocol, the actions of the parties are symmetric, and so the messages at each round can be sent in parallel, without either side waiting for the other to send first. The complete description of the protocol is given in Figure 1.

Alice	Public	Bob
	PUB	
Run KeyGen(1^n) to obtain pub_A, pri_A		Run KeyGen(1^n) to obtain pub_B, pri_B
Choose a random key $K_A \in_R \{0,1\}^n$		Choose a random key $K_B \in_R \{0,1\}^n$
$(\alpha_A, \beta_A) \leftarrow_R \mathsf{Commit}_{PUB}(pub_A, K_A)$		$(\alpha_B, \beta_B) \leftarrow_R \mathsf{Commit}_{PUB}(pub_B, K_B)$
	$\xrightarrow{pub_A, \alpha_A}$	
	$\xleftarrow{pub_B, \alpha_B}$	
Compute $C_A \leftarrow_R \mathsf{Enc}_{pub_B}(\beta_A)$		Compute $C_B \leftarrow_R \mathsf{Enc}_{pub_A}(\beta_B)$
	$\xrightarrow{C_A}$	
	$\xleftarrow{C_B}$	
Compute $\beta'_B \leftarrow \mathsf{Dec}_{pri_A}(C_B)$		Compute $\beta'_A \leftarrow \mathsf{Dec}_{pri_B}(C_A)$
$(pub'_B, K'_B) \leftarrow \mathsf{Decommit}_{PUB}(\alpha_B, \beta'_B)$		$(pub'_A, K'_A) \leftarrow \mathsf{Decommit}_{PUB}(\alpha_A, \beta'_A)$
If $\bot \in \{\beta'_B, pub'_B, K'_B\}$ or $pub'_B \neq pub_B$		If $\bot \in \{\beta'_A, pub'_A, K'_A\}$ or $pub'_A \neq pub_A$
or $\alpha_B = \alpha_A$		or $\alpha_A = \alpha_B$
$\quad$ Output $\hat{K}_A \in_R \{0,1\}^n$		$\quad$ Output $\hat{K}_B \in_R \{0,1\}^n$
Else		Else
$\quad$ Output $K_A \oplus K'_B$		$\quad$ Output $K_B \oplus K'_A$

Fig. 1. The CFKE Protocol $\mathcal{CFKE}_1$

Privacy. To achieve privacy, the protocol must guarantee that if the two parties agree on a key (i.e. output the same string) then the adversary is unable to distinguish that key from a random one. we prove the following theorem:

Theorem 1. *If $\mathcal{PKE}$ is a non-malleable public key encryption scheme and $\mathcal{COM}$ is a computationally binding, 2-strongly non-malleable commitment scheme, then the protocol $\mathcal{CFKE}_1$ is private according to Definition 1.*

Intuitively, this follows from the following two facts: (i) if the adversary modifies A's a public key (the case of B is symmetric), then because of the strong non-malleability

Schedule E_A		Schedule E_B	
$\alpha_A \longrightarrow$	$\longleftarrow \alpha_B$	$\alpha_A \longrightarrow$	$\longleftarrow \alpha_B$
	$\alpha'_A \longrightarrow$	$\longleftarrow \alpha'_B$	
	$\longleftarrow \beta_B$	$\beta_A \longrightarrow$	
$\longleftarrow \alpha'_B$			$\alpha'_A \longrightarrow$
$\beta_A \longrightarrow$			$\longleftarrow \beta_B$
$\longleftarrow \beta'_B$	$\beta'_A \longrightarrow$	$\longleftarrow \beta'_B$	$\beta'_A \longrightarrow$

Fig. 2. Two possible schedules for adversarial commitments

of the commitment scheme, she must choose a new nonce to accompany the modified public key. However, if she does so, the probability that A and B output the same key is negligible. On the other hand, if she allows A and B to exchange public keys, then privacy follows from the semantic security of the encryption scheme. Due to limited space we present the details of the proof in [CKR+13].

Non-malleability. To show non-malleability, we must describe a simulator that can simulate the view of the adversary given a choice of one of polynomially many pairs of random outputs for the two parties. We prove the following theorem:

Theorem 2. *If $\mathcal{COM}$ is a 2-strongly non-malleable commitment scheme then the protocol $\mathcal{CFKE}_1$ is non-malleable according to Definition 2.*

Proof Sketch. We next present an overview of our proof. The complete details are given in [CKR+13]. Our proof is structured as follows. We first describe a simulator that achieves a weaker notion of security, where the simulator is allowed to lock an output for each party. That is, the simulator can sample pairs of output keys as before, but now it has the additional ability to lock one key in the pair, and continue randomizing the other key. Once a key is locked the simulator has committed to making that key the output of the corresponding party. Once we describe a simulator Sim in the weaker model, achieving simulation according to the actual notion of security is straightforward: sample a pair of random keys $\hat{K}_A$ and $\hat{K}_B$ and guess at which iteration Sim will lock each key. Then, generate the rest of the keys randomly. This procedure is repeated until the guess is correct.

The simulator Sim itself is described [CKR+13]. On a high level the simulator works as follows. Let us denote by E_A (E_B) the event that the adversary submits both α'_A and α'_B before seeing an encryption of β_A (β_B). Note that since each party outputs the encrypted decommitment after obtaining the commitment of the other party, at least one of these events must always occur (see Figure 2 for an illustration of the two possible schedules). Specifically, according to schedule E_A the adversary submits both α'_A and α'_B before seeing an encryption of β_A. Similarly, according to schedule E_B the adversary submits both commitments before obtaining β_B. The simulator first generates a tuple γ of the form $(PUB, pub_A, \alpha_A, pub_B, \alpha_B, r_{adv})$. This commits the adversary to one of the two schedules described in Figure 2. Assuming that E_A is the schedule that the adversary follows conditioned on γ, the simulator proceeds to extract a decommitment for α'_A by simulating the interaction of the adversary with the protocol to completion (the case when the schedule induced by γ is E_B is symmetric). Now, by making use of the strong non-malleability of the commitment scheme, and ignoring (for the moment) the possibility that the adversary chooses to provide an invalid decommitment for α'_A, we know that there is a unique value K'_A that α'_A will be decommitted to. Therefore, the decommitment β'_A obtained by the simulator, together with the commitment α'_A, allow the simulator to obtain K'_A.

At this point, the simulator fixes a key $\hat{K}_B$ to be output by Bob, and rewinds the adversary to the point where she submitted her commitment α'_A. The simulator then uses the equivocability of the commitment scheme to decommit α_B to $K_B \stackrel{def}{=} \hat{K}_B \oplus K'_A$. A similar extract-then-adjust procedure is repeated with the Alice side of the interaction: fixing $(\gamma, \alpha'_A, \beta_B)$ the simulator obtains a commitment α'_B from the adversary and simulates the protocol to completion to obtain a decommitment β'_B. Again, ignoring invalid commitments and applying the strong non-malleability property of the commitment scheme, there is only a single value to which the adversary can decommit α'_B. That value, K'_B, is obtained by the simulator from α'_B and β'_B. The simulator then rewinds the adversary to the point where $(\gamma, \alpha'_A, \beta_B, \alpha'_B)$ are fixed, fixes a key $\hat{K}_A$ to be output by Alice, and decommits α_A to $K_A \stackrel{def}{=} \hat{K}_A \oplus K'_B$. As a result, K_A and K_B are properly distributed in the transcript of the protocol – uniformly random, and the simulator successfully forces the correct outputs $\hat{K}_A$ and $\hat{K}_B$ for Alice and Bob respectively.

Under the simplifying assumptions that the adversary always decommits a given commitment α'_A or α'_B to a unique value, and that no invalid decommitments are ever generated, the simulator described above perfectly simulates the view of the adversary in the non-malleability experiment. The main technical difficulty is caused by the fact that after fixing the commitment α'_A or α'_B the adversary still has a choice whether to decommit to K'_A (K'_B) or to produce an invalid decommitment. To accommodate this possibility the actual simulator may rewind the adversary many times until the "right" kind of commitment is produced. For example, if the adversary first decommits α'_A to K'_A then after rewinding the simulator will keep trying new random keys $\hat{K}_B$ for Bob until the adversary decommits α'_A to K'_A again. This repeated rewinding is what causes the running time of our simulator to be expected rather than strict polynomial. The only computational part of our argument concerns the inability of the adversary to decommit a single commitment α'_A or α'_B to more than one non-$\perp$ value. If this were not the case then our simulator would potentially not be able to predict the value K'_A to which α'_A will be decommitted, and therefore fail to set β'_A appropriately. However, no efficient adversary can violate this requirement without breaking the strong non-malleability of the commitment scheme.

We give the complete details in Appendix [CKR$^+$13].

4.2   Protocol 2: Hashed Diffie-Hellman as CFKE

We next analyze the hashed Diffie-Hellman (HDH) [DH76] protocol (cf. Figure 3) in the context of CFKE. Note, HDH (and natural variants) are insecure in the sense of

Alice	Bob
Hash function H	
Generator $g \in \mathbb{G}$	
Choose $x \in_R \mathbb{Z}_p$	Choose $y \in_R \mathbb{Z}_p$
Compute $X \leftarrow g^x$	Compute $Y \leftarrow g^y$
$\xrightarrow{\quad X \quad}$	
$\xleftarrow{\quad Y \quad}$	
Reject if $Y = 1_\mathbb{G}$, otherwise	Reject if $X = 1_\mathbb{G}$, otherwise
compute $K_A = H(Y^x)$	compute $K_B = H(X^y)$

Fig. 3. The Hashed Diffie-Hellman protocol $\mathcal{CFKE}_2$

Definition 2. Indeed, a MIM adversary in HDH can learn the pre-images under the hash function H of the keys K_A and K_B by running a separate instance of the protocol with each party. This violates the non-malleability requirement of CFKE. One can then design (contrived) session protocols that become insecure when the adversary has this information. For example, a secure CFKE protocol can stop encrypting and authenticating messages if Alice receives a message containing the pre-image of her key under H. Additionally, HDH requires a slight tweak to meet the intuitive requirement of non-malleability. Namely, the parties must check that they do not receive $1_\mathbb{G}$ from the other party. Otherwise, the adversary can force the output to be the hash of $1_\mathbb{G}$.

HDH variants, such as the one described in Figure 3, can be natural and useful CFKE protocols, and should be allowed by the definition (especially since "incompatible" CFSS protocols can be naturally excluded – see below). A simple amendment to the definition of non-malleability resolves this. To accommodate protocols that output a hash of a value as the final key, we let the simulator in experiment ExpCFKENMal fix the output key pair to be the outcome of the last two queries that the simulator makes to the random oracle before terminating. More precisely, we modify step 3 in the experiment as follows:

3'. Run simulator $S(1^n)$ and allow S to query the random oracle H. Let $view'$ be the output of the simulator and (K_A, K_B) be the last two values returned by H as responses to queries made by S.

Definition 4. Let $\mathcal{KE} = (\mathsf{KEInit}, \mathsf{KE})$ be a credential-free key exchange in the random oracle model. We say that $\mathcal{KE}$ is secure if it satisfies privacy, and amended non-malleability.

We note that the original version of Step 3 can be simulated in the above variant simply by querying the random oracle on pairs of random inputs.

As discussed above, Definition 4 requires excluding "incompatible" CFSS protocols, namely those that may query the same RO used in CFKE. Hence, a simple way to ensure security of composed CFKE (Definition 4 version) and CFSS is to require that different RO are used for the two types of protocols. This is achieved in practice by using a protocol name as a prefix in all hash function calls.

Theorem 3. *Let $CFKE_2$ be the protocol of Figure 3. Let hash function H in the description of $CFKE_2$ is modeled as a random function. Then, $CFKE_2$ is a secure CFKE according to Definition 4.*

The proof of Theorem 3 is straightforward: privacy follows from the decisional Diffie-Hellman assumption (DDH), similarly to the standard Diffie-Hellman key exchange protocol. Non-malleability is shown by having the simulator query the random oracle on the two values queried last by the two parties.

5 Definition and Construction of Credential-Free Secure Sessions

The notion of secure session protocol (with a supposedly shared session key) appears intuitive, and is often omitted from formal discussion. However, existing formalizations of secure sessions and secure channels [Sho99, CK02] show that subtleties arise even in these "simple" settings. Further, as we pointed out in Section 1.3, standard definitions (and even constructions!) of secure sessions don't work in our credential-free scenario. In this section, we justify and formalize the new notion.

We simplify presentation by only considering one-way sessions where A communicates a long message to B. This message arrives in pieces to A, which are encrypted using (possibly randomized!) encryption function Enc and sent to B one at a time. The adversary sees the encryptions and chooses the pieces in a very adaptive manner: he chooses the first piece, sees its encryption, chooses the second piece, sees its encryption, etc. B decrypts the pieces one at a time (using Dec). Each such decryption will involve an integrity test; if any such test fails, we say that B outputs a special symbol FAIL for the piece, and for simplicity we will assume that B must then output FAIL for all succeeding pieces.

Formally, a session protocol is a tuple $\langle Enc, Dec \rangle$, which satisfies correctness in the absence of an adversary. That is, if Enc and Dec are given the same key K, and if Enc is given a sequence of message pieces $m_0, m_1, \ldots, m_w$, and if the resulting encryptions are fed into Dec, then Dec will output message pieces $m_0, m_1, \ldots, m_w$. A standard secure session must satisfy the standard notions of *integrity* and *privacy*.

Definition of Credential-Free Secure Sessions (CFSS). We say a session protocol is a CFSS, if it satisfies: *Integrity*, *Privacy*, and *MIM-Integrity*. We omit formalization of the first two standard properties.

Informally, MIM-integrity guarantees that as soon as Adv allows an unmodified message to pass through between the endpoints with unequal random keys, Adv is detected (player outputs FAIL). To define MIM-integrity (and hence CFSS), fix a session protocol (Enc,Dec).

MIM-Integrity: Consider an adversary Adv on input security parameter 1^n. Adv is a probabilistic algorithm that runs in time polynomial in n. We define an experiment that begins with two random n-bit strings K_A and K_B being chosen; Adv sees both K_A and K_B; K_A is given to A (who uses Enc) and K_B is given to B (who uses Dec).

Adv interactively chooses $m_0, m_1, \ldots, m_w$ while seeing $e_0, e_1, \ldots, e_w$. (Note that since A – that is Enc – is allowed to be probabilistic, Adv might not be able to compute $e_0, e_1, \ldots, e_w$ on his own.) Adv then computes and sends $e_0', e_1', \ldots, e_j'$ to B, where

$0 \leq j \leq w$ and $e'_j = e_i$ for some i, $0 \leq i \leq w$ (e'_i is an unmodified message that should trigger FAIL). If B doesn't output FAIL in response to e'_j, we say that Adv *wins*. Let $p_{Adv}(n)$ be the probability that Adv wins.

MIM-Integrity means that for every such Adv for every c, for sufficiently large n, $p_{Adv}(n) \leq 1/n^c$.

A number of works examine sessions and their underlying encryption schemes (e.g., [BKN02]), with some of the approaches somewhat similar to ours. MIM-integrity is a unique aspect of our work, and we are not aware of existing definitions which could be used in its place.

A CFSS Protocol. It is not hard to create a session protocol that satisfies these three concepts. It is straightforward to verify that the following construction is a CFSS.

Construction. Say that the session key consists of two parts: an n bit privacy key k_1 and an n bit integrity key k_2. Assume we have two pseudo-random function generators F and F', where $F_{k_1} : \{0,1\}^n \rightarrow \{0,1\}^n$ and $F'_{k_2} : \{0,1\}^{2n} \rightarrow \{0,1\}^n$. A encrypts the ith n-bit piece m_i, by computing $\alpha = F_{k_1}(\bar{i}) \oplus m_i$ and letting the encryption be $e_i = \alpha F'_{k_2}(\bar{i}\alpha)$. (Here, $\bar{i}$ denotes the n-bit representation of i.) B decrypts in the obvious way: given the i-th encryption $e'_i = \alpha' \beta'$, B FAILS if $\beta' \neq F'_{k_2}(\bar{i}\alpha')$, and otherwise outputs $F_{k_1}(\bar{i}) \oplus \alpha'$. It is easy to see that this satisfies integrity and privacy, but it does not necessarily satisfy MIM-integerity. In order to satisfy MIM-integrity, we add to e_i the string $F_{k_1}(1^n)$, and we add to B the additional stipulation that given $e'_i = \alpha' \beta' \gamma'$, B FAILs if $\gamma' \neq F_{k_1}(1^n)$. (Of course, we need to ensure that the counter never reaches the value 2^n. Alternatively, we could add a dedicated part k_3 of the key to each message, however, adding $F_{k_1}(1^n)$ allows for shorter keys.)

5.1 Composing CFKE and CFSS

In this section we informally argue that composing CFKE and CFSS provides the guarantee that the adversary must remain continuously active on the channel throughout the entire session to avoid detection.

This is indeed easy to see. In one case, CFSS (namely, its standard integrity and privacy properties) guarantees that if the keys are random and unknown to Adv, then channel is fully secure in the standard strong sense. In the other case, Adv knows the keys of the players, and the keys are random and independent of each other, the MIM-integrity property of CFSS guarantees that as soon as Adv allows an unmodified message to pass between the players, it is immediately detected. Finally, the CFKE definition is tailored to explicitly guarantee that the keys that the players output fall under one of the two of the above cases.

References

[ALE09]   Arkko, J., Lehtovirta, V., Eronen, P.: RFC 5448: Improved extensible authentication protocol method for 3rd generation authentication and key agreement, EAP-AKA' (May 2009), http://tools.ietf.org/html/rfc5448

[Bar02]   Barak, B.: Constant-round coin-tossing with a man in the middle or realizing the shared random string model. In: FOCS, pp. 345–355. IEEE Computer Society (2002)

[BCL$^+$05] Barak, B., Canetti, R., Lindell, Y., Pass, R., Rabin, T.: Secure Computation Without Authentication. In: Shoup, V. (ed.) CRYPTO 2005. LNCS, vol. 3621, pp. 361–377. Springer, Heidelberg (2005)

[BKN02]   Bellare, M., Kohno, T., Namprempre, C.: Authenticated encryption in SSH: Provably fixing the SSH binary packet protocol. In: Atluri, V. (ed.) ACM CCS 02: 9th Conference on Computer and Communications Security, November 18–22, pp. 1–11. ACM Press, New York (2002)

[BM92]   Bellovin, S.M., Merritt, M.: Encrypted key exchange: Password-based protocols secureagainst dictionary attacks. In: SP 1992: Proceedings of the 1992 IEEE Symposium on Security and Privacy, p. 72. IEEE Computer Society, Washington, DC (1992)

[Can00]   Canetti, R.: Universally composable security: A new paradigm for cryptographic protocols. Cryptology ePrint Archive, Report 2000/067 (2000), http://eprint.iacr.org/

[CCGS10]   Camenisch, J., Casati, N., Gross, T., Shoup, V.: Credential Authenticated Identification and Key Exchange. In: Rabin, T. (ed.) CRYPTO 2010. LNCS, vol. 6223, pp. 255–276. Springer, Heidelberg (2010)

[CDSVW12]   Canetti, R., Dachman-Soled, D., Vaikuntanathan, V., Wee, H.: Efficient password authenticated key exchange via oblivious transfer. In: Fischlin, M., Buchmann, J., Manulis, M. (eds.) PKC 2012. LNCS, vol. 7293, pp. 449–466. Springer, Heidelberg (2012)

[CF01]   Canetti, R., Fischlin, M.: Universally composable commitments. In: Kilian, J. (ed.) CRYPTO 2001. LNCS, vol. 2139, pp. 19–40. Springer, Heidelberg (2001)

[CHK$^+$05] Canetti, R., Halevi, S., Katz, J., Lindell, Y., MacKenzie, P.: Universally Composable Password-Based Key Exchange. In: Cramer, R. (ed.) EUROCRYPT 2005. LNCS, vol. 3494, pp. 404–421. Springer, Heidelberg (2005)

[CK01]   Canetti, R., Krawczyk, H.: Analysis of key-exchange protocols and their use for building secure channels. In: Pfitzmann, B. (ed.) EUROCRYPT 2001. LNCS, vol. 2045, pp. 453–474. Springer, Heidelberg (2001)

[CK02]   Canetti, R., Krawczyk, H.: Universally Composable Notions of Key Exchange and Secure Channels. In: Knudsen, L.R. (ed.) EUROCRYPT 2002. LNCS, vol. 2332, pp. 337–351. Springer, Heidelberg (2002)

[CKOS01]   Di Crescenzo, G., Katz, J., Ostrovsky, R., Smith, A.: Efficient and non-interactive non-malleable commitment. In: Pfitzmann, B. (ed.) EUROCRYPT 2001. LNCS, vol. 2045, p. 40. Springer, Heidelberg (2001)

[CKR$^+$13] Canetti, R., Kolesnikov, V., Rackoff, C., Vahlis, Y.: Secure key exchange and sessions without credentials. Cryptology ePrint Archive, Report 2013/693 (2013), http://eprint.iacr.org/

[DCIO98]   Di Crescenzo, G., Ishai, Y., Ostrovsky, R.: Non-interactive and non-malleable commitment. In: Proceedings of the Thirtieth Annual ACM Symposium on Theory of Computing, pp. 141–150. ACM (1998)

[DDN91]   Dolev, D., Dwork, C., Naor, M.: Non-malleable cryptography (extended abstract). In: STOC, pp. 542–552. ACM (1991)

[DG03]   Damgard, I., Groth, J.: Non-interactive and reusable non-malleable commitment schemes. In: Proceedings of the Thirty-Fifth Annual ACM Symposium on Theory of Computing, p. 437. ACM (2003)

[DH76]   Diffie, W., Hellman, M.E.: New directions in cryptography. IEEE Transactions on Information Theory IT-22(6), 644–654 (1976)

[FF00]   Fischlin, M., Fischlin, R.: Efficient non-malleable commitment schemes. In: CRYPTO, pp. 413–431 (2000)

[GL01]   Goldreich, O., Lindell, Y.: Session-Key Generation Using Human Passwords Only. In: Kilian, J. (ed.) CRYPTO 2001. LNCS, vol. 2139, pp. 408–432. Springer, Heidelberg (2001)

[GL03]   Gennaro, R., Lindel, Y.: A framework for password-based authenticated key exchange. In: Biham, E. (ed.) EUROCRYPT 2003. LNCS, vol. 2656, pp. 524–543. Springer, Heidelberg (2003)

[KOY01]   Katz, J., Ostrovsky, R., Yung, M.: Efficient Password-Authenticated Key Exchange Using Human-Memorable Passwords. In: Pfitzmann, B. (ed.) EUROCRYPT 2001. LNCS, vol. 2045, pp. 475–494. Springer, Heidelberg (2001)

[KV11]   Katz, J., Vaikuntanathan, V.: Round-Optimal Password-Based Authenticated Key Exchange. In: Ishai, Y. (ed.) TCC 2011. LNCS, vol. 6597, pp. 293–310. Springer, Heidelberg (2011)

[Lin11]   Lindell, Y.: Highly-efficient universally-composable commitments based on the DDH assumption. In: Paterson, K.G. (ed.) EUROCRYPT 2011. LNCS, vol. 6632, pp. 446–466. Springer, Heidelberg (2011)

[NT94]   Neuman, B.C., Ts'o, T.: Kerberos: an authentication service for computer networks. IEEE Communications Magazine 32(9), 33–38 (1994)

[PR05]   Pass, R., Rosen, A.: New and improved constructions of non-malleable cryptographic protocols. In: Proceedings of the Thirty-Seventh annual ACM Symposium on Theory of Computing, p. 542. ACM (2005)

[RS84]   Rivest, R.L., Shamir, A.: How to expose an eavesdropper. Commun. ACM 27, 393–394 (1984)

[Sho99]   Shoup, V.: On formal models for secure key exchange. Technical Report RZ 3120 (#93166), IBM (1999)

Relaxed Two-to-One Recoding Schemes

Omkant Pandey[1,*], Kim Ramchen[2], and Brent Waters[2,**]

[1] University of Illinois, Urbana-Champaign
omkant@uiuc.edu
[2] University of Texas, Austin
{kramchen,bwaters}@cs.utexas.edu

Abstract. A *two-to-one recoding* (TOR) scheme is a new cryptographic primitive, proposed in the recent work of Gorbunov, Vaikuntanathan, and Wee (GVW), as a means to construct attribute-based encryption (ABE) schemes for all boolean circuits. GVW show that TOR schemes can be constructed assuming the hardness of the learning-with-errors (LWE) problem.

We propose a slightly weaker variant of TOR schemes called *correlation-relaxed two-to-one recoding* (CR-TOR). Unlike the TOR schemes, our weaker variant does not require an encoding function to be pseudorandom on correlated inputs. We instead replace it with an indistinguishability property that states a ciphertext is hard to decrypt without access to a certain encoding. The primary benefit of this relaxation is that it allows the construction of ABE for circuits using the TOR paradigm from a broader class of cryptographic assumptions.

We show how to construct a CR-TOR scheme from the noisy cryptographic multilinear maps of Garg, Gentry, and Halevi as well as those of Coron, Lepoint, and Tibouchi. Our framework leads to an instantiation of ABE for circuits that is conceptually different from the existing constructions.

1 Introduction

Encrypting data using traditional public-key encryption results in a very coarse-grained access to the data, since only those who possess an appropriate secret-key can decrypt the resulting ciphertext. Attribute-based encryption (ABE), introduced by Sahai and Waters [26] is an emerging class of cryptosystems which allow for significantly more fine-grained access to data. There are two variants

---

* Part of this work was done while the author was at The University of Texas at Austin.
** Supported by NSF CNS-0915361 and CNS-0952692, CNS-1228599 DARPA through the U.S. Office of Naval Research under Contract N00014-11-1-0382, DARPA N11AP20006, Google Faculty Research award, the Alfred P. Sloan Fellowship, Microsoft Faculty Fellowship, and Packard Foundation Fellowship. Any opinions, findings, and conclusions or recommendations expressed in this material are those of the author(s) and do not necessarily reflect the views of the Department of Defense or the U.S. Government.

M. Abdalla and R. De Prisco (Eds.): SCN 2014, LNCS 8642, pp. 57–76, 2014.

of ABE cryptosystems [16]: Key-Policy ABE and Ciphertext-Policy ABE. In Key-Policy ABE, the secret-keys SK_f have an associated boolean-function f called the policy. The messages are encrypted under an assignment x of boolean variables called the attributes. A secret-key SK_f can decrypt a message M encrypted under assignment x if and only if $f(x) = 1$. In Ciphertext-Policy ABE, these roles are reversed: secret-keys are associated with assignments x and ciphertexts are associated with policies f.

Recently, two independent works due to Garg, Gentry, Halevi, Sahai, and Waters [13], and Gorbunov, Vaikuntanathan, and Wee [15] showed how to construct ABE schemes for general circuits. More specifically, these works show how to realize the class of access policies f that can be expressed as a boolean circuit of depth d and input length n; both d and n are fixed at the system setup and can be polynomial in the security parameter; the size of ciphertexts and public-parameters is at most polynomial in d and n but independent of the size of the circuits in the class. The construction of [13] uses noisy cryptographic multilinear maps of Garg, Gentry, and Halevi [12], and is based on a new assumption in ideal lattices. The construction of [15] is based on the (standard) learning-with-errors assumption [23]. Prior to these works, the construction of [16] supported the largest class of access policies until now; namely the policies corresponding to polynomial sized boolean formulas, or equivalently circuits in the complexity class $\mathbf{NC^1}$.

Two-to-one recoding schemes. The work of GVW on attribute-based encryption introduces an interesting new framework called *two-to-one recoding* (TOR) schemes. Roughly speaking, a TOR scheme resembles a proxy re-encryption scheme [4]: it has an "encoding" mechanism with the following functionality. Given the encodings of a message m under two different public-keys pk_1 and pk_2, and an appropriate trapdoor t, it is possible to obtain the encoding of m under a third public-key pk_3. The trapdoor t, called the recoding key, can be generated using any one of the secret-keys corresponding to pk_1 or pk_2. GVW show that if such a primitive satisfies several additional simulatability and indistinguishability properties (described later), then circuit ABE can be constructed in a black box manner.

TOR schemes are intriguing primitive that we find interesting at least for two reasons. First, because it immediately yields a (black-box) construction of circuit ABE. And second, *how* it yields ABE construction. Roughly speaking, the TOR encodings and recoding-keys are used imitate the circuit-computation along the lines of garbled-circuits [29]. This ability to execute a circuit computation "securely and in a tamper-proof manner" makes TOR a powerful primitive.

Relaxing the requirements of TOR schemes. In this work, we take a closer look at TOR as an independent primitive. In particular, we investigate the possibility of building TOR schemes from assumptions that are different from LWE.

Our focal point is the *correlated pseudorandomness* property [24] which states that "the output of the encoding function on several correlated inputs looks pseudorandom.' While this property follows naturally from the LWE construction of

GVW, it proves to be significantly more difficult to achieve in other contexts. For instance, we found that it was possible to achieve TOR in generic multilinear maps using a natural generalization of the "matrix DDH" assumption [21]. However, this assumption assumption is actually false in the framework of GGH [12]. In addition, while it remains plausible in the framework of CLT [11], the resulting construction encumbers significant additional overhead to the existing multilinear construction of Garg, Gentry, Halevi, Sahai, and Waters [13]. Ideally, we would like an abstraction that both leads to circuit ABE from a broader range of assumptions and one which naturally leads to competitive constructions.

With this goal in mind we reexamine how correlated pseudorandomness was used in the GVW construction. In the GVW Circuit ABE construction multiple TOR primitives for each input gate for each interior gate in a private key circuit for f. However, in their proof the correlated randomness property is actually not needed or used at any of these gates except the final output gate. This follows from the fact that in the circuit ABE construction there is no real reason to hide from an attacker that two encodings are generated from the same randomness — the attacker naturally knows this anyway for a well formed ciphertext. The correlated randomness property is used in combination with a one time encryption property at the output gate to show that if an attacker cannot derive the encoding, then he cannot decrypt a message.

Our goal is to present a relaxed formulation of two-to-one reencoding that more directly meets this intuitive security goal. We aim to replace correlated pseudorandomness with a security goal that more tightly meets what is needed to construct Circuit ABE systems.

Our contributions. We first present a relaxed formulation called *correlation-relaxed two-to-one recoding* (CR-TOR) schemes. In this framework the encodings are not required to be pseudorandom on correlated inputs. Rather, we capture the corresponding security requirement by an indistinguishability game which specifies only that there exists an encryption function producing an indistinguishable ciphertexts which can be decrypted by "appropriately computed" encodings. In terms of circuit ABE, an "appropriately computed" encoding will be the recoding corresponding to the output of the circuit. After presenting our formulation of CR-TOR, we show that it is sufficient to build circuit ABE in a black-box manner.

Next, we consider the question of constructing CR-TOR and TOR schemes from assumptions different from LWE. For this purpose, we turn to the framework of idealized multilinear maps [6,12,11,13], and show how to construct a:

- CR-TOR scheme based on a natural generalization of the DDH assumption;
- TOR scheme based on the "matrix DDH" assumption (in groups with multilinear maps)

We note that the construction of CR-TOR is much more efficient compared to the corresponding construction of TOR (which requires us to use matrix DDH assumption). This indicates that correlated pseudorandomness property of TOR comes at a price in efficiency.

As of today, no constructions of idealized multilinear maps are known. However, the breakthrough work of Garg, Gentry, and Halevi [12], as well as the recent followup work of Coron, Lepoint, and Tibouchi [11], constructs randomized encoding schemes which can be seen as candidate constructions for "approximate" multilinear maps. These constructions are based on new cryptographic assumptions on ideal lattices.

We show that our construction of CR-TOR scheme can be easily adapted to work in the framework of both GGH [12] and CLT [11]. Moreover, the performance of the resulting constructions is roughly on par with the GGHSW constructions [13].

However, our construction of the TOR scheme can only work with the framework of CLT. This is because the matrix DDH assumption does *not* hold in the GGH setting; but it remains plausible in the CLT setting. Furthermore, the overhead is significantly increased compared to the CR-TOR systems. The additional overhead can be directly attributed to achieving the stronger (and unused) correlation resistance property.

Finally, we note that since CR-TOR suffices to obtain circuit ABE in a black-box manner, we obtain a new construction of circuit ABE that is distinct from both GVW[15] and GGHSW [13]. At a conceptual level, this construction resembles the GVW construction since it is obtained from CR-TOR; on the other hand, it uses multilinear maps as its internal mechanism for computation, resulting in the same underlying assumption as the GGHSW construction. We remark that the construction of circuit ABE in all of these works, including ours, are in the selective-security model [5,16].

Goals and Non-goals. One of our main objectives in this work is to understand which properties of TOR are crucial to build circuit-ABE and eliminate the unnecessary ones. Specifically, we have investigated the correlated pseudorandomness property and find that it might be unwarranted for circuit-ABE, resulting in unnecessary inefficiencies. This argument is supported by constructing a circuit-ABE scheme which compares favourably to existing schemes [13,15] in terms of efficiency. However, *building a new and more efficient circuit-ABE scheme is* not *a goal* of this paper. We do so only to demonstrate that correlated pseudorandomness property is not required for circuit-ABE; relaxed-TOR is sufficient and enables a better construction.

Related works. After the introduction of ABE, while limited progress was made on expanding the class of access policies f, significant progress was made in many directions on ABE. New proof techniques were developed in [27,18,22,8,1,3,20,2] to diversify the underlying security assumptions based on both bilinear pairings as well as lattices. New constructions for decentralizing trust in the key-issuing authority were proposed in [9,10,19]. In addition, schemes supporting policies of different flavors were also developed such as: inner-product policy [17], regular languages [28], branching programs [7], and more expressive schemes in the (much weaker) "bounded collusion" model [25,14].

Paper organization. We will start by recalling the setting of idealized multilinear maps and attribute-based encryption in Section 2. We provide a definition of our correlation-relaxed TOR in the next section 3, followed by a black-box construction of ABE from CR-TOR in Section 4. We conclude by presenting a construction of our CR-TOR in Section 5. Due to space constraints, the construction of the original TOR (with strong correlation-psuedorandomness property) is given in appendix A. Finally, in Appendix B we describe how to translate our construction in the framework of graded encoding schemes of GGH.

2 Preliminaries

In this section we recall the setting of multilinear maps, hardness assumptions, and definitions for circuit ABE. We follow the conventions established in [15,13].

2.1 Multilinear Maps

We first recall the setting of ideal multilinear maps. Following [13], we assume the existence of a group generator $\mathcal{G}$, which takes as input a security parameter λ and a positive integer d to indicate the number of allowed pairing operations. $\mathcal{G}(1^\lambda, d)$ outputs a sequence of groups $\mathbb{G} = (\mathbb{G}_1, \ldots, \mathbb{G}_d)$ each of large prime order $p > 2^\lambda$. Let g_i be a canonical generator of $\mathbb{G}_i$ publicly known from group's description, and let $g = g_1$.

We assume the existence of a set of efficiently computable bilinear maps $\{e_{i,j} : \mathbb{G}_i \times \mathbb{G}_j \rightarrow \mathbb{G}_{i+j} | i, j \geq 1; i + j \leq d\}$. The map $e_{i,j}$ satisfies the following relation:

$$e_{i,j}(g_i^a, g_j^b) = g_{i+j}^{ab} : \forall a, b \in \mathbb{Z}_p.$$

A consequence of this is that $e_{i,j}(g_i, g_j) = g_{i+j}$. When the context is obvious, we will sometimes abuse notation and drop the subscripts i, j. For example, we may simply write:

$$e(g_i^a, g_j^b) = g_{i+j}^{ab}.$$

Assumption 1. (*d*-Multilinear Decisional Diffie-Hellman (*d*-MDDH) assumption) *Suppose that a challenger runs* $\mathcal{G}(1^\lambda, d)$ *and generates groups* $(\mathbb{G}_1, \ldots, \mathbb{G}_d)$ *of prime order* p *with generators* $(g_1, \ldots, g_d)$. *Then, the d-MDDH assumption states that the advantage* $Adv_\mathcal{A}(\lambda)$ *of every polynomial time adversary* $\mathcal{A}$, *defined below, is at most negligible in* λ:

$$|\Pr[\mathcal{A}(g, g^s, g^{c_1}, \ldots, g^{c_d}, g_d^{sc_1 \cdots c_d}) = 1] - \Pr[\mathcal{A}(g, g^s, g^{c_1}, \ldots, g^{c_d}, g_d^u) = 1]|$$

where $s, c_1, \ldots, c_k$ *and* u *are uniformly distributed in* $\mathbb{Z}_p$.

This is a natural generalization of the DDH assumption in the multilinear setting. Intuitively, this assumption is plausible because there are $d + 1$ element multiplications in the exponent, which cannot be computed using a d-linear map.

We will describe our constructions in this ideal setting first. However, later we will show how to adapt them to the noisy settings of GGH and CLT [12,11].

2.2 Attribute Based Encryption

The definition of ABE provided here is for the key-policy variant of ABE, where the secret-keys are generated for a circuit C, and the ciphertexts are encrypted under a "set of attributes" denoted by an *index* $\text{ind} \in \{0,1\}^l$.

ABE for circuits. An ABE scheme for a class of circuits $\mathcal{C}$ is a tuple of algorithms $\mathcal{ABE} = (\mathsf{Setup}, \mathsf{Enc}, \mathsf{KeyGen}, \mathsf{Dec})$ where:

- $\mathsf{Setup}(1^\lambda, l, n)$. The setup algorithm takes as input the security parameter λ, the length l of the index ind, and a bound n on circuit depth; it outputs public parameters pp and the master key msk.
- $\mathsf{Enc}(pp, \text{ind} \in \{0,1\}^l, m)$. The encryption algorithm takes as input the public parameters pp, a bit string $\text{ind} \in \{0,1\}^l$ representing the assignment of boolean variables (a.k.a. "attributes"), and a message m. It outputs a ciphertext ct.
- $\mathsf{KeyGen}(msk, C)$. The key generation algorithm takes as input the master key msk and the description of a circuit C of maximum depth n. It outputs a secret-key sk_C.
- $\mathsf{Decrypt}(sk_C, ct)$. The decryption algorithm takes as input a secret key sk_C and ciphertext ct. The algorithm attempts to decrypt and outputs a message m if successful; otherwise it outputs a special symbol $\bot$.

Correctness. It is required that for all pp and msk produced by algorithm Setup, for all $\text{ind} \in {0,1}^l$, all messages m, for all appropriate circuits C such that $C(\text{ind}) = 1$, if $\mathsf{KeyGen}(msk, C) \to sk_C$ and $\mathsf{Enc}(pp, \text{ind}, m) \to ct$ then: $\mathsf{Dec}(sk_C, ct) = m$.

Selective security game for ABE. The selective-security game [16,13,5] for ABE proceeds in following stages between an adversary $\mathcal{A}$ and a challenger:

- INIT The adversary declares an index ind^*
- SETUP The challenger runs the Setup algorithm and gives the public-parameters to the adversary.
- PHASE 1 The adversary adaptively makes secret-key queries for several circuit C_j such that $C_j(\text{ind}^*) = 0$ for every j. The challenger answers each query by running the KeyGen algorithm using the master secret-key.
- CHALLENGE The adversary submits two challenge messages m_0 and m_1 of equal length. The challenger flips a bit b and sends an encryption of m_b under the index ind^* to the adversary.
- PHASE 2 Phase 1 is repeated.
- GUESS The adversary outputs a guess b'.

The *advantage* of the adversary $\mathcal{A}$ in the selective-security game is defined as $\left| \Pr[b' = b] - \frac{1}{2} \right|$. We say that an ABE scheme is selectively-secure if the advantage of every polynomial time adversary $\mathcal{A}$ in the above game is at most negligible.

3 Correlation-Relaxed Two-to-One Recoding Schemes

In this section we will define our relaxation of the original TOR scheme of [15]. Let us first recall some salient features of the scheme. A TOR scheme defines a probabilistic algorithm $\mathsf{Encode}(\cdot, \cdot)$ whose first input is a public key, and whose second input is a tag, from some tag set $\mathcal{S}$. Additionally there is a "two-to-one" recoding algorithm with the following property: for any tuple of public keys (pk_0, pk_1, pk_{tgt}) and any $s \in \mathcal{S}$, there exists a recoding key rk such that the recoding algorithm performs the following transformation

$$(\mathsf{Encode}(pk_0, s), \mathsf{Encode}(pk_1, s)) \overset{rk}{\to} \mathsf{Encode}(pk_{tgt}, s)$$

There is an algorithm to generate the recoding key using either sk_0 or sk_1, such that the key has the same distribution in either case. Additionally there is an algorithm to simulate a fake recoding key/public key pair for any input keys pk_0 and pk_1. The fake pair (rk, pk_{tgt}) should be indistinguishable from that generated honestly by the recode key generation algorithm for a random pk_{tgt}. Finally "correlated pseudorandomness" states that given polynomially many encodings of tag s under distinct public keys, an encoding under a fresh public key is indistinguishable from random.

Our relaxation. We now describe the core features of our relaxation. Firstly we remove the requirement for "correlated pseudorandomness", paving the way for construction of secure ABE from new assumptions. In doing so we introduce a message encryption function whose random input is precisely the tag s, i.e. the function is deterministic once s is picked. Additionally our scheme also generates encodings deterministically.

Looking ahead to our ABE scheme in the next section, we will see that the encryption function only uses randomness when sampling a tag. Therefore ABE from correlation relaxed TOR can use a reduced entropy pool, which is useful when encryption is performed on embedded systems. However one consequence is that our key generation algorithm must generate "levelled" public keys. Intuitively the reason is that in the original TOR scheme, encodings under distinct public keys are unrelated, whereas in the relaxed scheme encodings at given level are all re-randomized versions of a specific encoding.

Finally, we capture security of correlation relaxed TOR by an indistinguishability experiment; *indistinguishability of encoding derived ciphertexts* (IND-EDC). The game specifies that the encrypted messages are indistinguishable given polynomially many encodings of the tag.

The definition. A *correlation-relaxed two-to-one recoding* (CR-TOR) scheme over an input space $\mathcal{S} = \mathcal{S}_\lambda$ is a tuple of eight polynomial time algorithms (Params, Keygen, Encode, ReKeyGen, SimReKeyGen, Recode, Encrypt, Decrypt). The first three algorithms define a mechanism for encoding the input as follows:

- Params$(1^\lambda, d)$ is a probabilistic algorithm that takes as input the security parameter λ and an upper bound d on the number of recoding operations; it outputs the global public parameters pp.

- Keygen(pp, i) is a probabilistic algorithm that takes as input the public parameters pp, an index i called the *level index*; it outputs a public/secret key pair (pk, sk). When $i = d$ only, the algorithm is deterministic and outputs a unique public/secret key pair.
- Encode(pk, s) is a deterministic algorithm that takes as input a public-key pk and an input $s \in \mathcal{S}_\lambda$ to be encoded; it outputs ψ which is called an encoding of s. Input s is sometimes referred to as the *tag* or the *secret*.

The next three algorithms provide two different mechanisms to generate recoding-keys, and a recoding mechanism as follows:

- ReKeyGen($pp, i, pk_0, pk_1, sk_0, pk_{tgt}$) is a probabilistic algorithm that takes as input the public parameters pp, a level index i, a key pair (pk_0, sk_0), another public key pk_1, and a "target" public key pk_{tgt}; it outputs a trapdoor rk called the *recoding key*.
- SimReKeyGen(pp, i, pk_0, pk_1) is a probabilistic algorithm that takes as input public parameters pp, a level index i, and two public-keys pk_0, pk_1; it outputs a recoding-key rk together with a "target" public key pk_{tgt}.
- Recode(rk, ψ_0, ψ_1) is a deterministic algorithm that takes as input a recoding key rk, and two encodings ψ_0, ψ_1; it outputs an encoding ψ_{tgt}.

Finally, the last two algorithms define a symmetric encryption scheme with the following properties:

- Encrypt($pp, m; s$) is a probabilistic algorithm which takes as input the public parameters pp, a message m (from a well-defined message space $\mathcal{M}$) and a tag $s \in \mathcal{S}$ as random coins; it outputs a ciphertext τ.
- Decrypt(pp, ψ_{out}, τ) is a deterministic algorithm which takes as input the public parameters pp, an encoding ψ_{out}, and a ciphertext τ; it produces a message $m \in \mathcal{M}$.

In addition, the following requirements must be satisfied.

Correctness. At a high level, correctness states that each properly generated recoding-key works correctly for input encodings ψ_0, ψ_1. Since encodings are generated under public-keys, and public-keys are generated for a given level-index i,[1] stating this requirement is somewhat notation-heavy. In addition, we will have the correctness requirement on the encrypt and decrypt algorithms.

Formally, the first requirement is stated as follows. For every λ, d, every $pp \leftarrow$ Params($1^\lambda, d$), and every pk generated for index $i < d$ (i.e. $(pk, sk) \leftarrow$ Keygen(pp, i)), and every tag $s \in \mathcal{S}$ there exists a set $\Psi_{pk,s}$ satisfying the following condition. Suppose that (pk_0, sk_0) and (pk_1, sk_1) are generated by Keygen(pp, i) for index i, and (pk_{tgt}, sk_{tgt}) by Keygen($pp, i+1$) for the index $i+1$. Then, for all $\psi_0 \in \Psi_{pk_0,s}, \psi_1 \in \Psi_{pk_1,s}$ and $rk \leftarrow$ ReKeyGen($pp, i, pk_0, pk_1, sk_0, pk_{tgt}$), it holds that Recode($rk, \psi_0, \psi_1$) $\in \Psi_{pk_{tgt},s}$.

---

[1] This is another minor deviation in our definition from original TOR; it can be seen as an additional weakening. We will avoid subscripting each pk with its level index i when clear from the context.

The second requirement is as follows. Let $(pk_{out}, sk_{out}) \leftarrow \mathsf{Keygen}(pp, i = d)$. Then, for all $m \in \mathcal{M}$, $s \in \mathcal{S}$, $\psi_{out} \in \Psi_{pk_{out},s}$, it holds that $\mathsf{Decrypt}(pp, \psi_{out}, \mathsf{Encrypt}(pp, m; s)) = m$.

Key indistinguishability. Let $i < d$, and $(pk_b, sk_b) \leftarrow \mathsf{Keygen}(pp, i)$, and $(pk_{tgt}, sk_{tgt}) \leftarrow \mathsf{Keygen}(pp, i + 1)$. Then, the following two ensembles must be statistically close:[2]

$$[Aux, \mathsf{ReKeyGen}(pp, i, pk_0, pk_1, sk_0, pk_{tgt})] \equiv_s$$
$$[Aux, \mathsf{ReKeyGen}(pp, i, pk_0, pk_1, sk_1, pk_{tgt})]$$

where $Aux = ((pk_0, sk_0), (pk_1, sk_1), (pk_{tgt}, sk_{tgt}))$.

Recoding Simulation. Let $i < d$. Let $(pk_b, sk_b) \leftarrow \mathsf{Keygen}(pp, i)$ for $b = 0, 1$. Then the following two ensembles are statistically close:

$$[Aux, pk_{tgt}, rk : (pk_{tgt}, sk_{tgt}) \leftarrow \mathsf{Keygen}(pp, i + 1),$$
$$rk \leftarrow \mathsf{ReKeyGen}(pp, i, pk_0, pk_1, sk_0, pk_{tgt})] \equiv_s$$
$$[Aux, pk_{tgt}, rk : (pk_{tgt}, rk) \leftarrow \mathsf{SimReKeyGen}(pp, i, pk_0, pk_1)]$$

where $Aux = ((pk_0, sk_0), (pk_1, sk_1))$.

The above two properties are statistical properties and identical to the properties of original TOR scheme. We now describe the third property called *indistinguishability of encoding derived ciphertexts* or IND-EDC. This is a computational property; recall that the original TOR formulation had *correlated pseudorandomness* which is stronger than IND-EDC.

Indistinguishability of Encoding Derived Ciphertexts (IND-EDC). We require that the advantage of every polynomial time adversary $\mathcal{A}$ in the IND-EDC game is at most negligible where the IND-EDC game proceeds as follows and the *advantage* of $\mathcal{A}$ is defined as $\left| \Pr[b' = b] - \frac{1}{2} \right|$ (see below):

- The challenger sends $(pp, pk_1, \ldots, pk_\ell)$ to the adversary where: $pp \leftarrow \mathsf{Params}(1^\lambda, d)$, $(pk_j, sk_j) \leftarrow \mathsf{Keygen}(pp, 1)$ for $j = 1, \ldots, \ell = \mathsf{poly}(\lambda)$
- Adversary sends two equal length messages m_0, m_1.
- Challenger samples a random bit b and secret tag $s \in \mathcal{S}$. It sends $(\psi_1, \ldots, \psi_\ell, \tau_b)$ where $\psi_j \leftarrow \mathsf{Encode}(pk_j, s)$ for every $j \in [\ell]$, and $\tau_b \leftarrow \mathsf{Encrypt}(pp, m_b; s)$.
- Adversary outputs a bit b' and halts.

4   Circuit ABE from Correlation-Relaxed TOR

In this section we construct ABE for circuits from correlation-relaxed TOR. The construction is very similar to the GVW construction of ABE from TOR [15]

---

[2] Computational indistinguishability may also be sufficient.

except that in proving security, instead of using correlation pseudorandomness, we will use IND-EDC property.

Circuits are described using the same convention as in [15], which as follows. Without loss of generality, we consider the class of circuits $\mathcal{C} = \{\mathbf{C}_\lambda\}_{\lambda \in \mathbb{N}}$ where each circuit $C \in \mathbf{C}_\lambda$ is a *layered* circuit consisting of input wires, gates, internal wires, and a single output wire. Recall that in a layered circuits gates are arranged in layers where every gate at a given layer has a pre-specified depth. The lowest row has depth 1 and depth increases by one as we go up. A gate at depth i receives both of its inputs from wires at depth $i - 1$. The circuit has $l = l(\lambda)$ input wires, numbered from 1 to l. The size of the circuit is denoted by $|C|$, and all internal wires are indexed from $l + 1, \ldots, |C| - 1$; the output wire has index $|C|$. Every gate is a boolean-gate with exactly two input wires and one output wire.

Our construction of ABE from a CR-TOR scheme follows.

The construction. Suppose that the algorithms of the given CR-TOR scheme are: (Params, Keygen, Encode, ReKeyGen, SimReKeyGen, Recode, Encrypt, Decrypt). The algorithms of our ABE scheme $\mathcal{ABE} = (\mathsf{Setup}, \mathsf{Enc}, \mathsf{KeyGen}, \mathsf{Dec})$ are as follows.

- $\mathsf{Setup}(1^\lambda, l, d)$: The setup algorithm for ABE first runs the parameter generation algorithm of CR-TOR to obtain global public-parameters: $pp \leftarrow$ Params$(1^\lambda, d)$. Then, for each input wire $i \in [l]$, it generates two fresh public and secret key pairs, and an additional pair for the output wire:

$$(pk_{i,b}, sk_{i,b}) \leftarrow \mathsf{Keygen}(pp, 1) \text{ for } i \in [l], b \in \{0, 1\}$$
$$(pk_{\mathrm{out}}, sk_{\mathrm{out}}) \leftarrow \mathsf{Keygen}(pp, d)$$

It outputs the master public-key and master secret-key pair (mpk, msk) as follows (note that secret-key sk_{out} is not used):

$$mpk := pp, pk_{\mathrm{out}}, \{pk_{i,b}\}_{i \in [l], b \in \{0,1\}}, msk := \{sk_{i,b}\}_{i \in [l], b \in \{0,1\}}.$$

- $\mathsf{Enc}(mpk, \mathbf{ind}, m)$: Let $\mathbf{ind} = (\mathbf{ind}_1, \ldots, \mathbf{ind}_l) = \in \{0, 1\}^l$. The algorithm chooses a uniform $s \xleftarrow{\$} S$, encodes it under the public-keys specified by the bits of $\mathbf{ind}$, and finally encrypts m under pp and s. That is,

$$\psi_i \leftarrow \mathsf{Encode}(pk_{i, \mathbf{ind}_i}, s), \forall i \in [l], \text{ and } \tau \leftarrow \mathsf{Encrypt}(pp, m; s),$$

The algorithm outputs $ct_{\mathbf{ind}} = (\mathbf{ind}, \psi_1, \ldots, \psi_l, \tau)$ as the ciphertext.
- $\mathsf{KeyGen}(msk, C)$: The algorithm proceeds in two steps:
  1. For every non-input wire $w \in \{l+1, \ldots, |C|\}$ of the circuit C, it generates two public-secret key pairs denoting two possible values $b \in \{0, 1\}$ for this wire. However, the public-key corresponding to the circuit-output 1 is (always) set to pk_{out}. That is, for every $w \in \{l + 1, \ldots, |C|\}$ and every $b \in \{0, 1\}$ such that $(w, b) \neq (|C|, 1)$, generate: $(pk_{w,b}, sk_{w,b}) \leftarrow \mathsf{Keygen}(pp, i)$, where i is the depth of wire w; then set $pk_{|C|,1} = pk_{\mathrm{out}}$.

2. For every gate $g := (u, v, w)$ at level i—where (u, v) are two incoming wires of g and w is its outgoing wire—compute four recoding-keys $rk_{b,c}^w$ for wire w as follows:

$$rk_{b,c}^w \leftarrow \mathsf{ReKeyGen}(pp, i, pk_{u,b}, pk_{v,c}, sk_{u,b}, pk_{w,g_w(b,c)})$$

where $g_w(b, c)$ denotes the output of g on input (b, c).

The algorithm outputs the secret key sk_C which is a collection of all $4(|C|-l)$ recoding keys it has computed (along with the circuit C).

$$sk_C := C, \left(rk_{b,c}^w : w \in [l+1, |C|], b \in \{0,1\}, c \in \{0,1\} \right).$$

- $\mathsf{Dec}(sk_C, ct_{\mathsf{ind}})$: If $C(\mathsf{ind}) = 0$, algorithm outputs $\bot$. Otherwise, $C(\mathsf{ind}) = 1$ defines a computation of the circuit where each wire carries a well defined value in $\{0,1\}$. In particular, an input wire $w \in \{1, \ldots, l\}$ carries the bit ind_w, and every other wire $w \in \{l+1, \ldots, |C|\}$ carries a bit as follows. Suppose w is the outgoing wire of (uniquely defined) gate $g := (u, v, w)$, and wires u and v carry values b^* and c^* respectively; then w carries the value $d^* = g_w(b^*, c^*)$. For every wire, the decryption algorithm computes:

$$\psi_{w,d^*} \leftarrow \mathsf{Recode}\left(rk_{b^*,c^*}^w, \psi_{u,b^*}, \psi_{v,c^*} \right)$$

using appropriate values from the ciphertext ct_{ind} and the key sk_C. Note that since $C(\mathsf{ind}) = 1$, the algorithm must have also computed an encoding $\psi_{\mathsf{out}} \in \Psi_{pk_{\mathsf{out}},s}$ corresponding to the output wire. The decrypted message is:
$m \leftarrow \mathsf{Decrypt}(pp, \psi_{\mathsf{out}}, \tau)$.

Theorem 1. *Scheme $\mathcal{ABE}$ described above is a selectively-secure ABE scheme for all polynomial size circuits as per the definition in section 2.*

Proof. To prove the theorem, we show that if there exists a PPT adversary $\mathcal{A}$ breaking the selective security of $\mathcal{ABE}$ with noticeable advantage, then there exists a PPT $\mathcal{B}$ winning the IND-EDC game with noticeable advantage (against the underlying CR-TOR scheme). The construction of $\mathcal{B}$, called the simulator, proceeds as follows.

Simulator $\mathcal{B}$. The simulator participates in the IND-EDC game with an outside challenger. At the same time, internally, it plays the selective-security game with $\mathcal{A}$ as follows. $\mathcal{B}$ runs $\mathcal{A}$ answering its queries in various stages as follows.

INIT. It receives an index ind^* from $\mathcal{A}$.

SETUP. In this phase, first the simulator $\mathcal{B}$ asks the challenger of IND-EDC game to send $(pp, pk_1, \ldots, pk_l, pk_{\mathsf{out}})$. Then, it prepares the parameters for $\mathcal{A}$ as follows. It defines $pk_{i,\mathsf{ind}_i^*} = pk_i$, and generates the remaining keys as: $(pk_{i,1-\mathsf{ind}_i^*}, sk_{i,1-\mathsf{ind}_i^*}) \leftarrow \mathsf{Keygen}(pp, 1)$. It sends mpk to $\mathcal{A}$ where:

$$mpk := pp, pk_{\mathsf{out}}, \{pk_{i,b}\}_{i \in [l], b \in \{0,1\}}.$$

Note that the mpk is well defined and distributed identically to the output of the actual setup algorithm of $\mathcal{ABE}$.

PHASE 1. In this phase $\mathcal{A}$ submits polynomially many secret-key queries for various circuits. Let C be one such query, then by definition of the game, $C(\text{ind}^*) = 0$. The computation $C(\text{ind}^*)$ defines a unique value carried by each wire of C. $\mathcal{B}$ generates the simulated-key for C as follows.

- For each wire $w \in [l+1, |C|-1]$ generate $(pk_{w,1-b^*}, sk_{w,1-b^*}) \leftarrow \text{Keygen}(pp, i)$, where i is the depth of w and b^* is the bit it carries in computation $C(\text{ind}^*)$. Define $pk_{|C|,1} = pk_{\text{out}}$.
- For every gate $g = (u, v, w)$ do the following (here i is the depth of g, and b^*, c^* are the bits carried by its incoming wires u, v in computation $C(\text{ind}^*)$):
    1. $pk_{w,g(b^*,c^*)}, rk^w_{b^*,c^*} \leftarrow \text{SimReKeyGen}(pp, i, pk_{u,b^*}, pk_{v,c^*})$. Note that at this point, two public-keys for each wire in C have been fixed including the output wire.[3] This step also fixes one recode-key for each wire corresponding to the computation $C(\text{ind}^*)$. The remaining 3 recode-keys for each wire are sampled in the next step.
    2. For $(b, c) \in \{0, 1\}^2 \setminus (b^*, c^*)$, sample:
    $$rk^w_{b,c} \leftarrow \text{ReKeyGen}(pp, i, sk^*, pk_{u,b}, pk_{v,c}, pk_{w,g(b,c)}),$$
    where sk^* is any one of the two secret-keys $sk_{u,b}$ or $sk_{v,c}$; note that at least one of them is always known.
- Output $sk_C =: \left(rk^w_{b,c} : w \in [l+1, |C|], b \in \{0, 1\}, c \in \{0, 1\} \right)$.

Observe that this indeed fixes all recode keys as desired, and that the distribution of sk_C is statistically close to the output of KeyGen of $\mathcal{ABE}$ due to the statistical properties of recoding simulation and key indistinguishability.

CHALLENGE. When $\mathcal{A}$ sends (m_0, m_1), the simulator forwards them to the outside challenger, and recieves $(\psi_1, \ldots, \psi_l, \tau_b)$ where $\psi_i = \text{Encode}(pk_i, s) : i \in [l]$ and $\tau_b = \text{Encrypt}(pp, m_b; s)$ for a random bit b. The simulator forwards this response to $\mathcal{A}$.

PHASE 2. $\mathcal{B}$ answers the queries of $\mathcal{A}$ as in phase 1.

GUESS. $\mathcal{A}$ outputs a guess bit b'. The simulator also outputs b' and halts.

By construction $(\psi_1, \ldots, \psi_l, \tau_b)$ is a correctly distributed $\mathcal{ABE}$ encryption of m_b. Therefore $\mathcal{B}$ wins the IND-EDC game if $\mathcal{A}$ wins the selective security game.

5   Correlation-Relaxed TOR from Multilinear Maps

In this section we provide an instantiation of our CR-TOR scheme. For convenience we first describe our construction using idealized multilinear maps under

---

[3] While $pk_{|C|,0}$ is obtained in this step, the key $pk_{|C|,1} = pk_{\text{out}}$, always (and hence never sampled once pk_{out} is fixed).

the d-MDDH assumption (see Section 2). We will then describe how to adapt this construction to the noisy multilinear maps of GGH in appendix B.

5.1 Overview

At a high level our construction works as follows. Let $\mathbb{G} = (\mathbb{G}_1, \ldots, \mathbb{G}_d)$ be a tuple of groups equipped with a multilinear map e (Section 2). Let $h_1, \ldots, h_d$ be random elements in $\mathbb{G}_1$, which will be public parameters. A public key at level $i < d$ is formed by powering h_i to a random exponent $z \overset{\$}{\leftarrow} \mathbb{Z}_q$. The corresponding public key/secret key pair is (h_i^z, z). The unique public key at level $i = d$ is simply h_d and we take the corresponding secret key[4] to be $z = 1$. Let $y_1 = h_1$ and define recursively $y_{i+1} = e(y_i, h_{i+1})$ for $i < d$. Note that y_i is an element in $\mathbb{G}_i$ for all $i \geq 1$.

Encoding and Recoding. We take $\mathcal{S} = \mathbb{Z}_q$ to be the set of tags. Let $pk = h_i^z$ be a level i public key. Then the set of encodings of a tag s under pk is simply the singleton set $\Psi_{pk,s} = \{y_i^{zs}\}$. Generating a recode key for a pair of public keys $(h_i^{z_0}, h_i^{z_1})$ to a target public key $h_{i+1}^{z_{\mathrm{tgt}}}$ consists of constructing a pair of elements (ρ_0, ρ_1) such that $\rho_0^{z_0} \cdot \rho_1^{z_1} = h_{i+1}^{z_{\mathrm{tgt}}}$. Given encodings $\psi_0 = y_i^{z_0 s}$, $\psi_1 = y_i^{z_1 s}$, one recodes by computing $e(\psi_0, \rho_0) \cdot e(\psi_1, \rho_1) = \psi_{\mathrm{tgt}}$; this calculation is detailed below.

The encoding produced under the output public key is indistinguishable from random if d-MDDH assumption holds. Therefore, we can use it encrypt/blind a message. These are the core ideas, the full scheme follows.

5.2 Construction

- Params($1^\lambda, d$): Output a description of a tuple of groups $\mathbb{G} = (\mathbb{G}_1, \ldots, \mathbb{G}_d)$ together with a multilinear map $e(\mathbb{G}_i, \mathbb{G}_1) \rightarrow \mathbb{G}_{i+1}$ for $i < d$. Each group has prime order q. Let $g = g_1$ be a canonical generator of $\mathbb{G}_1$. Choose $h_1, \ldots, h_d \overset{\$}{\leftarrow} \mathbb{G}_1$. Let $y_1 = h_1$ and define $y_{i+1} = e(y_i, h_{i+1})$ for $i < d$.
- Keygen(pp, i): If $i < d$ choose $z \overset{\$}{\leftarrow} \mathbb{Z}_q$, let $pk = h_i^z$ and let $sk = z$. If $i = d$, let $pk = h_d$ and let $sk = 1$. Output the pair (pk, sk).
- Encode(pk, s): Let $pk = h_1^z$ be a level one public key. Compute $\psi = (h_1^z)^s = h_1^{zs}$.
- ReKeyGen($pp, i, sk_0, pk_0, pk_1, pk_{\mathrm{tgt}}$): Let $pk_0 = h_i^{z_0}, pk_1 = h_i^{z_1}, sk_0 = z_0$. Compute $rk = (\rho_0, \rho_1)$ as follows:
  1. Choose $r_1 \overset{\$}{\leftarrow} \mathbb{Z}_q$ and let $\rho_1 = h_i^{r_1}$.
  2. Compute $\rho_0 = (pk_{\mathrm{tgt}}/(pk_1)^{r_1})^{z_0^{-1}}$.
  Note that the above samples (ρ_0, ρ_1) according to the relation $\rho_0^{z_0} \cdot \rho_1^{z_1} = h_{i+1}^{z_{\mathrm{tgt}}}$, but does so knowing only secret key z_0.

---

[4] Recall from the definition of correlation relaxed TOR that the secret key at level $i = d$ plays no role in the actual computation.

- Recode$(rk_{0,1}^{\text{tgt}}, \psi_0, \psi_1) = e(\psi_0, \rho_0) \cdot e(\psi_1, \rho_1) = e(y_i^{z_0 s}, \rho_0) \cdot e(y_i^{z_1 s}, \rho_1)$
$$= e(y_i^s, \rho_0^{z_0}) \cdot e(y_i^s, \rho_0^{z_1}) = e(y_i^s, \rho_0^{z_0} \cdot \rho_1^{z_1})$$
$$= e(y_i^s, pk_{\text{tgt}}) = e(y_i^s, h_{i+1}^{z_{\text{tgt}}})$$
$$= e(y_i, h_{i+1})^{z_{\text{tgt}} s} = y_{i+1}^{z_{\text{tgt}} s} = \psi_{i+1}^{\text{tgt}}.$$

- SimReKeyGen(pp, i, pk_0, pk_1): Let $pk_0 = h_i^{z_0}, pk_1 = h_i^{z_1}$.
  1. Choose $r_0, r_1 \xleftarrow{\$} \mathbb{Z}_q$, set $\rho_0 = h_i^{r_0}$ and $\rho_1 = h_i^{r_1}$. Output recode key $rk = (\rho_0, \rho_1)$.
  2. Let $pk_{\text{tgt}} = (pk_0)^{r_0} \cdot (pk_1)^{r_1}$. Output pk_{tgt}.
- Encrypt$(pp, m; s)$: We have $pp = (h_1, \ldots, h_d)$. Output $\tau = m \cdot e(\ldots e(e(h_1, h_2), h_3) \ldots, h_d)^s = m \cdot y_d^s$.
- Decrypt$(pp, \psi_{\text{out}}, \tau)$: Compute $m = \tau / \psi_{\text{out}}$.

The correctness properties are easy to verify. We now show that other properties hold as well if the d-MDDH assumption holds.

Key indistinguishability. Let $(pk_b, sk_b) \leftarrow$ Keygen(pp, i) for $b = 0, 1$ and $(pk_{\text{tgt}}, sk_{\text{tgt}}) \leftarrow$ Keygen$(pp, i + 1)$. Let $pk_b = h_i^{z_b}, sk_b = z_b$ and $pk_{\text{tgt}} = h_{i+1}^{z_{\text{tgt}}}$. The distributions

$$(\rho_0, \rho_1) : \rho_0 = h_i^{r_0}, \rho_1 = (pk_{\text{tgt}}/(pk_0)^{r_0})^{z_1^{-1}}, r_0 \xleftarrow{\$} \mathbb{Z}_q$$

$$(\rho_0, \rho_1) : \rho_1 = h_i^{r_1}, \rho_0 = (pk_{\text{tgt}}/(pk_1)^{r_1})^{z_0^{-1}}, r_1 \xleftarrow{\$} \mathbb{Z}_q$$

are statistically indstinguishable since both experiments sample uniformly from the set $S_{z_0, z_1, pk_{\text{tgt}}} = \{(\rho_0, \rho_1) : \rho_0^{z_0} \cdot \rho_1^{z_1} = pk_{\text{tgt}}\}$.

Recoding simulation. Let $(pk_b, sk_b) \leftarrow$ Keygen(pp, i) for $b = 0, 1$. Let $pk_b = h_i^{z_b}, sk_b = z_b$. The distributions:

$$pk_{\text{tgt}}, (\rho_0, \rho_1) : pk_{\text{tgt}} = h_{i+1}^{z_{\text{tgt}}}, \rho_0 = h_i^{r_0}, \rho_1 = (pk_{\text{tgt}}/(pk_0)^{r_0})^{z_1^{-1}}, z_{\text{tgt}}, r_0, r_1 \xleftarrow{\$} \mathbb{Z}_q$$

$$pk_{\text{tgt}}, (\rho_0, \rho_1) : pk_{\text{tgt}} = (pk_0)^{r_0} \cdot (pk_1)^{r_1}, \rho_0 = h_i^{r_0}, \rho_1 = h_i^{r_1}, r_0, r_1 \xleftarrow{\$} \mathbb{Z}_q$$

are statistically indistinguishable since in both experiments pk_{tgt} is uniform over $\mathbb{G}_1$ and (ρ_0, ρ_1) sampled uniformly from the set $S_{z_0, z_1, y_{\text{tgt}}}$ defined above.

Indistinguishability of Encoding Derived Ciphertexts. We prove the following claim.

Claim 1. *The above scheme is IND-EDC if the d-Multilinear Decisional Diffie-Hellman assumption holds.*

Proof. Suppose there exists an IND-EDC adversary $\mathcal{A}$ against the above scheme with advantage ϵ. Then there exists an adversary $\mathcal{B}$ which breaks the d-MDDH problem with the same advantage. $\mathcal{B}$ is passed an instance $(g^s, g^{c_1}, \ldots, g^{c_d}, T)$ and runs as follows:

1. Generates $x_1, \ldots x_l \xleftarrow{\$} \mathbb{Z}_q$. Lets $pp = (g^{c_1}, \ldots, g^{c_d})$. Lets $pk_j = g^{x_j}$ for $j \in [l]$. Lets $\psi_j = (g^s)^{x_j}$ for $j \in [l]$
2. Sends $(pp, pk_1, \ldots, pk_l)$ to $\mathcal{A}$.
3. Receives (m_0, m_1) from $\mathcal{A}$.
4. Chooses $b \xleftarrow{\$} 0, 1$ and sends $(\psi_1, \ldots, \psi_l, \tau_b = m_b \cdot T)$ to $\mathcal{A}$.
5. Receives guess b' from $\mathcal{A}$.
6. Outputs 1 if $b' = b$.

Let E_T be the event that T is a multilinear Diffie-Hellman element, while E_F be the event that T is a random element of $\mathbb{G}_d$. Note that $x_j \xleftarrow{\$} \mathbb{Z}_q$ has the same distribution as $c_1 \cdot z_j : z_j \xleftarrow{\$} \mathbb{Z}_q$, thus pk_j are simulated correctly. If E_T occurs, then τ_b is exactly equivalent to the output of $\mathsf{Encrypt}(pp, m_b; s)$, thus $b' = b$ holds exactly when $\mathcal{A}$ wins the IND-EDC game. But if E_F occurs, then τ_b is statistically independent of b, thus $b' = b$ with probability $1/2$. So $\mathcal{B}$ has advantage $|\Pr[b' = b|E_T] - \Pr[b' = b|E_F]| = 1/2 + \epsilon - 1/2 = \epsilon$.

Corollary 1. *Assume the existence of multilinear maps and the validity of d-MDDH assumption. Then, there exists a selectively-secure ABE scheme for all polynomial-size circuits of depth at most $d - 1$.*

References

1. Agrawal, S., Boneh, D., Boyen, X.: Efficient lattice (H)IBE in the standard model. In: Gilbert, H. (ed.) EUROCRYPT 2010. LNCS, vol. 6110, pp. 553–572. Springer, Heidelberg (2010)
2. Agrawal, S., Boyen, X., Vaikuntanathan, V., Voulgaris, P., Wee, H.: Functional encryption for threshold functions (or fuzzy IBE) from lattices. In: Fischlin, M., Buchmann, J., Manulis, M. (eds.) PKC 2012. LNCS, vol. 7293, pp. 280–297. Springer, Heidelberg (2012)
3. Agrawal, S., Freeman, D.M., Vaikuntanathan, V.: Functional encryption for inner product predicates from learning with errors. In: Lee, D.H., Wang, X. (eds.) ASIACRYPT 2011. LNCS, vol. 7073, pp. 21–40. Springer, Heidelberg (2011)
4. Blaze, M., Bleumer, G., Strauss, M.: Divertible protocols and atomic proxy cryptography. In: Nyberg, K. (ed.) EUROCRYPT 1998. LNCS, vol. 1403, pp. 127–144. Springer, Heidelberg (1998)
5. Boneh, D., Boyen, X.: Efficient selective-ID secure identity-based encryption without random oracles. In: Cachin, C., Camenisch, J.L. (eds.) EUROCRYPT 2004. LNCS, vol. 3027, pp. 223–238. Springer, Heidelberg (2004)
6. Boneh, D., Silverberg, A.: Applications of multilinear forms to cryptography. IACR Cryptology ePrint Archive 2002, 80 (2002)
7. Boyen, X.: Attribute-based functional encryption on lattices. In: Sahai, A. (ed.) TCC 2013. LNCS, vol. 7785, pp. 122–142. Springer, Heidelberg (2013)
8. Cash, D., Hofheinz, D., Kiltz, E., Peikert, C.: Bonsai trees, or how to delegate a lattice basis. In: Gilbert, H. (ed.) EUROCRYPT 2010. LNCS, vol. 6110, pp. 523–552. Springer, Heidelberg (2010)
9. Chase, M.: Multi-authority attribute based encryption. In: Vadhan, S.P. (ed.) TCC 2007. LNCS, vol. 4392, pp. 515–534. Springer, Heidelberg (2007)

10. Chase, M., Chow, S.S.M.: Improving privacy and security in multi-authority attribute-based encryption. In: ACM Conference on Computer and Communications Security, pp. 121–130 (2009)
11. Coron, J.-S., Lepoint, T., Tibouchi, M.: Practical multilinear maps over the integers. In: Canetti, R., Garay, J.A. (eds.) CRYPTO 2013, Part I. LNCS, vol. 8042, pp. 476–493. Springer, Heidelberg (2013)
12. Garg, S., Gentry, C., Halevi, S.: Candidate multilinear maps from ideal lattices. In: Johansson, T., Nguyen, P.Q. (eds.) EUROCRYPT 2013. LNCS, vol. 7881, pp. 1–17. Springer, Heidelberg (2013)
13. Garg, S., Gentry, C., Halevi, S., Sahai, A., Waters, B.: Attribute-based encryption for circuits from multilinear maps. In: Canetti, R., Garay, J.A. (eds.) CRYPTO 2013, Part II. LNCS, vol. 8043, pp. 479–499. Springer, Heidelberg (2013)
14. Gorbunov, S., Vaikuntanathan, V., Wee, H.: Functional encryption with bounded collusions via multi-party computation. In: Safavi-Naini, R., Canetti, R. (eds.) CRYPTO 2012. LNCS, vol. 7417, pp. 162–179. Springer, Heidelberg (2012)
15. Gorbunov, S., Vaikuntanathan, V., Wee, H.: Attribute-based encryption for circuits. In: Proceedings of the 45th Annual ACM Symposium on Symposium on Theory of Computing, STOC 2013, pp. 545–554. ACM, New York (2013)
16. Goyal, V., Pandey, O., Sahai, A., Waters, B.: Attribute-based encryption for fine-grained access control of encrypted data. In: Proceedings of the 13th ACM Conference on Computer and Communications Security, CCS 2006, pp. 89–98. ACM, New York (2006)
17. Katz, J., Sahai, A., Waters, B.: Predicate encryption supporting disjunctions, polynomial equations, and inner products. In: Smart, N.P. (ed.) EUROCRYPT 2008. LNCS, vol. 4965, pp. 146–162. Springer, Heidelberg (2008)
18. Lewko, A., Okamoto, T., Sahai, A., Takashima, K., Waters, B.: Fully secure functional encryption: Attribute-based encryption and (Hierarchical) inner product encryption. In: Gilbert, H. (ed.) EUROCRYPT 2010. LNCS, vol. 6110, pp. 62–91. Springer, Heidelberg (2010)
19. Lewko, A., Waters, B.: Decentralizing attribute-based encryption. In: Paterson, K.G. (ed.) EUROCRYPT 2011. LNCS, vol. 6632, pp. 568–588. Springer, Heidelberg (2011)
20. Lewko, A., Waters, B.: New proof methods for attribute-based encryption: Achieving full security through selective techniques. In: Safavi-Naini, R., Canetti, R. (eds.) CRYPTO 2012. LNCS, vol. 7417, pp. 180–198. Springer, Heidelberg (2012)
21. Naor, M., Segev, G.: Public-key cryptosystems resilient to key leakage. In: Halevi, S. (ed.) CRYPTO 2009. LNCS, vol. 5677, pp. 18–35. Springer, Heidelberg (2009)
22. Okamoto, T., Takashima, K.: Fully secure functional encryption with general relations from the decisional linear assumption. In: Rabin, T. (ed.) CRYPTO 2010. LNCS, vol. 6223, pp. 191–208. Springer, Heidelberg (2010)
23. Regev, O.: On lattices, learning with errors, random linear codes, and cryptography. In: STOC, pp. 84–93 (2005)
24. Rosen, A., Segev, G.: Chosen-ciphertext security via correlated products. In: Reingold, O. (ed.) TCC 2009. LNCS, vol. 5444, pp. 419–436. Springer, Heidelberg (2009)
25. Sahai, A., Seyalioglu, H.: Worry-free encryption: functional encryption with public keys. In: ACM Conference on Computer and Communications Security, pp. 463–472 (2010)
26. Sahai, A., Waters, B.: Fuzzy identity-based encryption. In: Cramer, R. (ed.) EUROCRYPT 2005. LNCS, vol. 3494, pp. 457–473. Springer, Heidelberg (2005)

27. Waters, B.: Dual system encryption: Realizing fully secure IBE and HIBE under simple assumptions. In: Halevi, S. (ed.) CRYPTO 2009. LNCS, vol. 5677, pp. 619–636. Springer, Heidelberg (2009)
28. Waters, B.: Functional encryption for regular languages. In: Safavi-Naini, R., Canetti, R. (eds.) CRYPTO 2012. LNCS, vol. 7417, pp. 218–235. Springer, Heidelberg (2012)
29. Yao, A.C.-C.: How to generate and exchange secrets (extended abstract). In: FOCS, pp. 162–167 (1986)

A   Construction of TOR

In this section we construct a TOR recoding [15] which is secure under the matrix d-linear assumption [21]. The construction is described in the ideal multilinear setting. By following the description in the next section, this construction is easily adapted to the setting of noisy multilinear maps of both GGH and CLT.

An important remark is that the matrix d-linear assumption cannot hold in the GGH framework [12]. Nevertheless, it remains plausible in the framework of CLT [11]. Therefore, the resulting instantiation of TOR scheme only makes sense in the CLT framework.

Notation. For matrices $M = (m_{ij}) \in \mathbb{Z}_q^{a \times b}, N = (n_{ij}) \in \mathbb{Z}_q^{b \times c}$ define $g^M \otimes N = (\prod_{k=1}^n (g^{m_{ik}})^{n_{kj}})_{ij} = (\prod_{k=1}^n g^{m_{ik} n_{kj}})_{ij} = g^{MN}$ and $M \otimes g^N = (\prod_{k=1}^n (g^{n_{kj}})^{m_{ik}}) = (\prod_{k=1}^n g^{m_{ik} n_{kj}})_{ij} = g^{MN}$.

Assumption 2 (Matrix d-linear assumption [21]). *For any integers a and b, and for any $d \le i < j \le \min(a, b)$ the ensembles $(g, g^R) : R \xleftarrow{\$} \mathsf{Rk}_i(\mathbb{Z}_q^{a \times b})$ and $(g, g^R) : R \xleftarrow{\$} \mathsf{Rk}_j(\mathbb{Z}_q^{a \times b})$ are computationally indistinguishable.*

A.1   TOR from Matrix Decision Linear Assumption

We now describe our construction. Recall that in the (original) TOR scheme, instead of IND-EDC game, one requires correlated pseudorandomness property. All other properties and algorithms remain the same as in the definition of CR-TOR (see section 3). The algorithms of the TOR scheme are as follows.

- Params$(1^\lambda, d)$: Output a description of a tuple of groups $\mathbb{G} = (\mathbb{G}_1, \ldots, \mathbb{G}_d)$ together with a multilinear map $e(\mathbb{G}_i, \mathbb{G}_1) \to \mathbb{G}_{i+1}$ for $i < d$. Each group has prime order q. Let g_i be a canonical generator of $\mathbb{G}_i$ and let $g = g_1$.
- Keygen(pp): Sample $A \xleftarrow{\$} \mathbb{Z}_q^{d \times d}$. Set $pk = g^A$.
- Encode$(pk, s) = pk \otimes s = (g^A)^s = g^{As}$.
- ReKeyGen$(pk_0, pk_1, sk_b, pk_{tgt})$: Let $pk_0 = g^{A_0}, pk_1 = g^{A_1}, pk_{tgt} = g^{A_{tgt}}$, so $sk_b = A_b$. Compute $rk = (\rho_0, \rho_1) = (g^{R_0}, g^{R_1})$ as follows:
    1. Sample $R_{1-b} \xleftarrow{\$} \mathbb{Z}_q^{d \times d}$ and let $\rho_{1-b} = g^{R_{1-b}}$.
    2. Compute $\rho_b = (g^{A_{tgt}}/(\rho_{1-b} \otimes A_{1-b})) \otimes A_b^{-1}$.

- Recode($rk_{0,1}^{tgt}, \psi_0, \psi_1$) = $e(\rho_0, g_i^{A_0 s}) \times e(\rho_1, g_i^{A_1 s}) = g_{i+1}^{R_0 A_0 s} \times g_{i+1}^{R_1 A_1 s} = g_{i+1}^{(R_0 A_0 + R_1 A_1)s} = g_{i+1}^{R_t s} = \psi_{tgt}$.
- SimReKeyGen(pk_0, pk_1): Let $pk_0 = g^{A_0}$ and $pk_1 = g^{A_1}$
  1. Sample $R_0, R_1 \xleftarrow{\$} \mathbb{Z}_q^{d \times d}$, set $\rho_0 = g^{R_0}, \rho_1 = g^{R_1}$ output $rk = (\rho_0, \rho_1)$.
  2. Let $pk = R_0 \otimes g^{A_0} \times R_1 \otimes g^{A_1} = g^{(R_0 A_0 + R_1 A_1)}$.

The correctness properties of our scheme are easy to verify. We show that it satisfies all other properties of TOR as well.

Key indistinguishability. We require that for all ($pk_0 = g^{A_0}, pk_1 = g^{A_1}, pk_{tgt} = g^{A_t}$) the following distributions are indistinguishable:

- Choose $R_0 \xleftarrow{\$} \mathbb{G}_1^{d \times d}$, compute $\rho_0 = g^{R_0}$ and compute $\rho_1 = (g^{A_t}/(R_0 \otimes g^{A_0})) \otimes A_1^{-1}$. Output ($\rho_0, \rho_1$).
- Choose $R_1 \xleftarrow{\$} \mathbb{G}_1^{d \times d}$, compute $\rho_1 = g^{R_1}$ and compute $\rho_0 = (g^{A_t}/(R_1 \otimes g^{A_1})) \otimes A_0^{-1}$. Output ($\rho_0, \rho_1$).

However this follows from the fact that $f : \mathbb{Z}_q^{d \times d} \to \mathbb{Z}_q^{d \times d}$ satisfying $f(X) = (g^{A_t}/(X \otimes g^{A_0})) \otimes A_1^{-1}$ is injective.

Recoding simulation. This follows from the fact that ($pk_{tgt} = R_0 \otimes g^{A_0} \times R_1 \otimes g^{A_1}, g^{R_0}, g^{R_1}$) : $A_0 \xleftarrow{\$} \mathbb{Z}_q^{d \times d}, A_1 \xleftarrow{\$} \mathbb{Z}_q^{d \times d}, R_0 \xleftarrow{\$} \mathbb{Z}_q^{d \times d}, R_1 \xleftarrow{\$} \mathbb{Z}_q^{d \times d}$ is statistically close to ($g^{A_{tgt}}, g^{R_0}, g^{R_1}$) : $A_{tgt} \xleftarrow{\$} \mathbb{Z}_q^{d \times d}, R_0 \xleftarrow{\$} \mathbb{Z}_q^{d \times d}, R_1 \xleftarrow{\$} \mathbb{Z}_q^{d \times d}$.

Correlated pseudorandomness. We defer the proof of this lemma to the full version.

Lemma 1. *The TOR construction achieves correlated pseudorandomness (Section 4.1 [15]) if the matrix d-linear assumption [21] holds.*

One-time semantic security. Let $\mathcal{M} = \mathbb{G}_d^d$, define

$$\mathsf{E}(\psi, \boldsymbol{\mu}) = \psi \odot \boldsymbol{\mu}$$

where $\odot$ denotes the component-wise product. One-time semantic security follows from the fact that ψ is computationally indistinguishable from a vector of random group elements.

B   Mapping Our Constructions to Graded Encoding Systems

In this section we describe how to translate our constructions using multilinear maps to the graded encoding system of Garg et al. [12]. For simplicity we focus on mapping our construction of CR-TOR from generic multilinear maps in Section 5.

B.1 Graded Encoding Systems

In the framework of Garg et al. [12] an element g_i^α in a mutlinear group family is an encoding of α at level i. The encoding permits the following operations: equality testing, addition and a bounded number of multiplications. At a high level a d-graded encoding system is a ring R and system of sets $\mathcal{S} = S_i^{(\alpha)} \subset \{0,1\}^* : \alpha \in R, 0 \le i \le d$ such that for every i, the sets $\{S_i^{(\alpha)} : \alpha \in R\}$ are disjoint and form a partition of $S_i = \cup_\alpha S_i^{(\alpha)}$.

The GGH system is equipped with the following additional procedures for manipulating encodings: InstGen, samp, enc, $+$, $\times$, reRand, isZero, ext. We defer definitions of these to the full version.

Graded Multilinear Decisonal Diffie Hellman Assumption. We will require the following analogue of the d-Multilinear Decision Diffie Hellman assumption for d-graded encoding systems.

Assumption 3. (d-Graded Multilinear Decisional Diffie-Hellman (d-GMDDH) assumption) *Suppose that a challenger runs* InstGen$(1^\lambda, 1^d)$ *generating* (params, $\mathbf{p}_{zt}$). *Let* $s, c_1, \ldots c_d \leftarrow$ samp(params). *Define* $\tilde{s} = $ cenc$_1$(params, $1, s$), $\tilde{c}_1 = $ cenc$_1$(params, $1, c_1$), $\ldots$, $\tilde{c}_d = $ cenc$_1$(params, $1, c_d$). *Then, the d-GMDDH assumption states that the advantage* $Adv_\mathcal{A}(\lambda)$ *of every polynomial time adversary* $\mathcal{A}$, *defined below, is at most negligible in* λ:

$$| \Pr[\mathcal{A}(\tilde{s}, \tilde{c}_1, \ldots, \tilde{c}_d, v) = 1] - \Pr[\mathcal{A}(\tilde{s}, \tilde{c}_1, \ldots, \tilde{c}_d, w) = 1]|$$

where $v = $ cenc$_1$(params, $d, s \cdot c_1 \ldots c_d$) *and* $w = $ cenc$_1$(params, d, samp(params)).

B.2 Our Correlation-Relaxed TOR Using Graded Encodings

The canonicalizing algorithm cenc$_l$(params, $i, \mathbf{u}$) defined in Remark 2 [12] takes an encoding $\mathbf{u}$ and produces another encoding $\mathbf{u}'$ which is equivalent to l re-randomizations of $\mathbf{u}$. For our purposes l will always be a small constant. For convenience we suppress the params argument when making repeated calls to samp and cenc$_l$.

- Params$(1^\lambda, d)$: Run InstGen$(1^\lambda, 1^d)$ to generate (params, $\mathbf{p}_{zt}$) where params is a description of a d-Graded Encoding System $\mathcal{S} = (S_1, \ldots, S_d)$. Let $c_1, \ldots, c_d \leftarrow$ samp(). Let $h_1 = $ cenc$_1(1, c_1), \ldots, h_d = $ cenc$_1(1, c_d)$. Define $y_i = \prod_{i=1}^i h_i \in S_i$ for $i = 1 \ldots d$.
- Keygen(pp, i): If $i < d$ sample $z \leftarrow$ samp(), let $pk = $ cenc$_2(1, h_i \cdot z)$ and let $sk = z$. If $i = d$, let $pk = h_d$ and $sk = 1$. Output the pair (pk, sk).
- Encode(pk, s): Let $pk = $ cenc$_2(1, h_1 \cdot z)$ be a level one public key. Compute $\psi = $ cenc$_3(1, pk \cdot s)$.
- ReKeyGen$(pp, i, sk_0, pk_0, pk_1, pk_{tgt})$: Let $pk_0 = $ cenc$_2(1, h_i \cdot z_0)$, $pk_1 = $ cenc$_2(1, h_i \cdot z_1)$, $sk_0 = z_0$. Compute $rk = (\rho_0, \rho_1)$ as follows:
  1. Sample $r_1 \leftarrow$ samp() and let $\rho_1 = $ cenc$_3(1, h_i \cdot r_1)$.

2. Compute $\rho_0 = \mathsf{cenc}_3(1, (pk_{tgt} - pk_1 \cdot r_1) \cdot z_0^{-1})$ where z_0^{-1} is computed over R_q.

Note that the above samples (ρ_0, ρ_1) according to the relation $\rho_0 \cdot z_0 + \rho_1 \cdot z_1 = h_{i+1} \cdot z_{tgt}$, but does so knowing only secret key z_0.

- $\mathsf{Recode}(rk_{0,1}^{tgt}, \psi_0, \psi_1) = \psi_0 \cdot \rho_0 + \psi_1 \cdot \rho_1 = (y_i \cdot (z_0 \cdot s)) \cdot \rho_0 + (y_i \cdot (z_1 \cdot s)) \cdot \rho_1$

$$= (y_i \cdot s) \cdot \rho_0 \cdot z_0 + (y_i \cdot s) \cdot \rho_0 \cdot z_1 = (y_i \cdot s) \cdot (\rho_0 \cdot z_0 + \rho_1 \cdot z_1)$$

$$= (y_i \cdot s) \cdot pk_{tgt} = (y_i \cdot s) \cdot (h_{i+1} \cdot z_{tgt})$$

$$= (y_i \cdot h_{i+1}) \cdot (z_{tgt} \cdot s) = y_{i+1} \cdot (z_{tgt} \cdot s) = \psi_{i+1}^{tgt}.$$

- $\mathsf{SimReKeyGen}(pp, i, pk_0, pk_1)$: Let $pk_0 = \mathsf{cenc}_2(1, h_i \cdot z_0)$, $pk_1 = \mathsf{cenc}_2(1, h_i \cdot z_1)$.

    1. Sample $r_0, r_1 \leftarrow \mathsf{samp}()$, set $\rho_0 = \mathsf{cenc}_3(1, h_i \cdot r_0)$ and $\rho_1 = \mathsf{cenc}_3(1, h_i \cdot r_1)$. Output recode key $rk = (\rho_0, \rho_1)$.
    2. Let $pk_{tgt} = \mathsf{cenc}_3(1, pk_0 \cdot r_0 + pk_1 \cdot r_1)$. Output pk_{tgt}.

- $\mathsf{Encrypt}(pp, m; s)$: We have $pp = (h_1, \ldots, h_d)$. Let $P = \mathsf{ext}(\mathbf{p}_{zt}, s \cdot \prod_{i=1}^{d} h_i)$. Output $\tau = m \oplus P$.

- $\mathsf{Decrypt}(pp, \psi_{out}, \tau)$: Compute $m = \tau \oplus \mathsf{ext}(\mathbf{p}_{zt}, \psi_{out})$.

Once again, correctness follows easily. We prove the other properties now.

Key indistinguishability. Let $(pk_b, sk_b) \leftarrow \mathsf{Keygen}(pp, i)$ for $b = 0, 1$ and $(pk_{tgt}, sk_{tgt}) \leftarrow \mathsf{Keygen}(pp, i + 1)$. Let $pk_b = \mathsf{cenc}_2(1, h_i \cdot z_b)$, $sk_b = z_b$ and $pk_{tgt} = \mathsf{cenc}_2(1, h_{i+1} \cdot z_{tgt})$. The distributions

$$(\rho_0, \rho_1) : \rho_0 = \mathsf{cenc}_3(1, h_i \cdot r_0), \rho_1 = \mathsf{cenc}_3(1, (pk_{tgt} - pk_0 \cdot r_0) \cdot z_1^{-1}), r_0 \leftarrow \mathsf{samp}()$$

$$(\rho_0, \rho_1) : \rho_1 = \mathsf{cenc}_3(1, h_i \cdot r_1), \rho_0 = \mathsf{cenc}_3(1, (pk_{tgt} - pk_1 \cdot r_1) \cdot z_0^{-1}), r_1 \leftarrow \mathsf{samp}()$$

are statistically indstinguishable since both experiments sample uniformly from the set $S_{z_0, z_1, pk_{tgt}} = \{(\rho_0, \rho_1) : \rho_0 \cdot z_0 + \rho_1 \cdot z_1 = pk_{tgt}\}$.

Recoding simulation. Let $(pk_b, sk_b) \leftarrow \mathsf{Keygen}(pp, i)$ for $b = 0, 1$. Let $pk_b = \mathsf{cenc}_2(1, h_i \cdot z_b)$, $sk_b = z_b$. The distributions:

$$pk_{tgt}, (\rho_0, \rho_1) : pk_{tgt} = \mathsf{cenc}_3(1, h_{i+1} \cdot z_{tgt})), \rho_0 = \mathsf{cenc}_3(1, h_i \cdot r_0),$$

$$\rho_1 = \mathsf{cenc}_3(1, (pk_{tgt} - (pk_0) \cdot r_0) \cdot z_1^{-1}), z_{tgt}, r_0, r_1 \leftarrow \mathsf{samp}()$$

$$pk_{tgt}, (\rho_0, \rho_1) : pk_{tgt} = \mathsf{cenc}_3(1, (pk_0) \cdot r_0 + (pk_1) \cdot r_1), \rho_0 = \mathsf{cenc}_3(1, h_i \cdot r_0),$$

$$\rho_1 = \mathsf{cenc}_3(1, h_i \cdot r_1), r_0, r_1 \leftarrow \mathsf{samp}()$$

are statistically indistinguishable since in both experiments pk_{tgt} is nearly uniform over S_1 and (ρ_0, ρ_1) sampled uniformly from the set $S_{z_0, z_1, pk_{tgt}}$ defined above.

Indistinguishability of Encoding Derived Ciphertexts. We defer the proof of this claim to the full version.

Claim 2. *The above scheme is IND-EDC if the d-GMDDH assumption holds.*

Obfuscation ⇒
(IND-CPA Security ⇏ Circular Security)

Antonio Marcedone[1],[*] and Claudio Orlandi[2]

[1] Cornell University, USA and Scuola Superiore di Catania,
University of Catania, Italy
a.marcedone@studium.unict.it
[2] Aarhus University, Denmark
orlandi@cs.au.dk

Abstract. *Circular security* is an important notion for public-key encryption schemes and is needed by several cryptographic protocols. In circular security the adversary is given an extra "hint" consisting of a *cycle* of encryption of secret keys i.e., $(E_{pk_1}(sk_2), \ldots, E_{pk_n}(sk_1))$. A natural question is whether every IND-CPA encryption scheme is also circular secure. It is trivial to see that this is not the case when $n = 1$. In 2010 a separation for $n = 2$ was shown by [ABBC10, GH10] under standard assumptions in bilinear groups.

In this paper we finally settle the question showing that for every n there exists an IND-CPA secure scheme which is not n-circular secure.

Our result relies on the recent progress in cryptographic obfuscation.

1 Introduction

Public-key encryption schemes allow anyone to take a plaintext and create a corresponding ciphertext that carries little or no information about the encrypted plaintext, in the eyes of everyone else but the owner of the secret key.

One might think that for an encryption scheme all plaintexts are equal, but it turns out that some plaintexts are more equal than others. In particular, secret-keys (or functions of them) are a very special kind of plaintexts.

But why would you want to encrypt a secret key? A prime example is fully-homomorphic encryption (FHE): At the heart of virtually every fully-homomorphic encryption scheme there is a technique called "bootstrapping" that requires users to publish, in their public key, an encryption of the secret key [Gen09]. For another example think of two cryptographers, Alice and Bob, who get married and decide they should not keep any secret from each other and therefore decide to share their secret keys with each other. To do so Alice sends an encryption of her secret key sk_A to Bob using his public key pk_B, while Bob sends an encryption of his secret key sk_B to Alice using her public key pk_A. This is not a far fetched example and there are applications where this is actually done, see [CL01].

---

[*] Most of the work done while visiting Aarhus University.

M. Abdalla and R. De Prisco (Eds.): SCN 2014, LNCS 8642, pp. 77–90, 2014.

Suppose now that the evil eavesdropper Eve gets to see these encryptions of secret keys: is the encryption scheme still secure, or can Eve use this extra information to break its security?

Circular Security. In the FHE example, a secret key was encrypted under its own public key and we call this a 1-cycle i.e., Eve learns $E_{pk}(sk)$. When Alice and Bob both encrypt their secret keys under the other party's public key, we get a 2-cycle i.e., Eve learns $E_{pk_A}(sk_B)$ and $E_{pk_B}(sk_A)$. In general, we are interested in what happens when Eve learns the encryptions of n secret keys $(sk_1, \ldots, sk_n)$ under public keys $(pk_2, \ldots, pk_n, pk_1)$ respectively. If an encryption scheme is still secure when the adversary is given such a cycle of encryptions of secret keys, we say that the scheme is n-circular secure[1]. This notion was first defined in [CL01, BRS02]. Since then it has been an open problem to understand the relationship between the standard definition of security for public key encryption schemes (namely *indistinguishability under chosen-plaintext-attack* or *IND-CPA* for short) and n-circular security.

IND-CPA Security $\not\Rightarrow$ 1-Circular Security. It is quite easy to show that IND-CPA security does not imply 1-circular security. Take any IND-CPA secure scheme (G, E, D) and construct (G, E', D) as follows: on input m, the modified encryption scheme $E'_{pk}(\cdot)$ first checks if $m \stackrel{?}{=} sk$.[2] If so, E' outputs m, else it outputs $E_{pk}(m)$. The modified scheme is still IND-CPA secure (as it behaves exactly like E for all $m \neq sk$), but since $E'_{pk}(sk) = sk$ it is clear that it would be a very bad idea to let Eve learn this value.

Pairing Assumptions $\Rightarrow$ (IND-CPA Security $\not\Rightarrow$ 2-Circular Security). Surprisingly, it was quite harder to show that there are IND-CPA schemes that are not 2-circular secure. The reason for this is that the secret keys are generated independently and therefore the encryption algorithm does not have a way of distinguishing a secret key from a message (in fact, every message could be a secret key). This problem had been open for about a decade until it was finally solved in 2010 by [ABBC10, GH10]. Both these results hold under the assumption that some problems are hard in bilinear groups. The counterexample is obtained by embedding some extra elements in the ciphertexts. These extra values do not help the adversary to break the IND-CPA game but, when combined together using a bilinear map, allow to effectively decrypt one of the two "circular" ciphertexts and recover a secret key.

---

[1] There are different ways of defining circular security. The interested reader can check [CGH12] and reference therein for a discussion on the definitions. In this paper we will show a scheme where the adversary (given a cycle of encryption of secret keys) can recover *all the secret keys*, thus breaking even the weakest notions of circular security. Therefore the actual definition used is irrelevant for us.

[2] Note that it is always possible to check if $m = sk$ by, for example, encrypting a bunch of random messages using $E_{pk}(\cdot)$ and decrypting them using m i.e., the encryption algorithm checks if $D_m(E_{pk}(r)) = r$ for enough random values r. If the results are all correct, one can assume whp that $m = sk$.

Obfuscation ⇒ (IND-CPA Security ⇏ Circular Security). In this paper, we show that IND-CPA security does not imply n-circular security *for any* n. More precisely, for every n, we can construct a scheme that is not n'-circular secure for every $n' < n$. We can show our result assuming that software obfuscation is possible, as defined by [BGI+01, BGI+12].

(False ⇒ True)? One might now object that our theorem is trivial: the same paper that defined obfuscation also proved that this notion is *impossible to achieve!* However [BGI+01, BGI+12] "only" proved that there exist no single obfuscator that can obfuscate every circuit under the strongest possible notion of obfuscation – namely "virtual black box" (VBB) obfuscation – and during the last decade obfuscators for limited class of circuits have been shown, such as [CD08, Wee05, CRV10, HRSV11].

In a surprising turn of event – and thanks to the recent breakthrough on a candidate for multilinear maps [GGH13a] – the first candidate cryptographic obfuscation was presented in [GGH+13b]. The obfuscation of [GGH+13b] does not contradict the impossibility result of [BGI+01, BGI+12], as it achieves a weaker notion called *indistinguishability obfuscation* (iO). Yet, this arguably very weak notion of obfuscation allows for a long list of unexpected applications [SW14, HSW14, GGHR14, BZ14, KNY14], and one could say that the result in [GGH+13b] is *"an impractical obfuscation for all practical purposes"*[3].

Following this result, even a candidate VBB obfuscator has been proposed in [BR14]. This result overcomes the impossibility result of [BGI+01, BGI+12], by proving the security of the scheme in the *generic graded encoding scheme model*: this can be thought as the analogue of the *generic group model* for *discrete logarithm*, extended to the case of multilinear maps.

In Section 2 we show how to separate IND-CPA and circular security using VBB obfuscation, as this powerful tool allows for very simple and intuitive constructions. Then, in Section 3 we show the same result using the weaker (and therefore more realistic) assumption that an iO obfuscator exists.

Relation to [KRW13]. In October 2013 Koppula, Ramchen and Waters [KRW13] posted on ePrint a similar result with a proof of security under indistinguishability obfuscation. On the same day, we posted a draft of our result which only showed a counterexample under the assumption of VBB obfuscation (Section 2). Subsequently, in February 2014 we updated our draft with Section 3, which is a simple application of the punctured programming technique from [SW14] to our construction of Section 2. Thus that addition achieves a counterexample based only on indistinguishability obfuscation. While recognizing that [KRW13] were first in showing the separation using iO only, we believe that our counterexample has some advantages.

Circular Security of Bit-Encryption. In the previous discussion on circular security, we made the implicit conjecture that the secret keys are element of

---

[3] Cit. Yuval Ishai.

the plain-text space (or how could it be possible to encrypt them?). It has been conjectured that every IND-CPA bit-encryption scheme (that is, an encryption scheme that can only encrypt messages in $\{0,1\}$) is also circular secure. Rothblum [Rot13] shows an IND-CPA bit encryption scheme which is not 1-circular secure assuming the existence of multilinear maps in which the SXDH assumption holds. Koppula, Ramchen and Waters [KRW13] give a different separation, based on the existence of iO obfuscation.

The Good News. While our work provides strong evidence for the fact that not all IND-CPA secure public key encryption schemes achieve circular security, there are a number of encryption schemes that can be proven secure even under these attacks. We refer the interested reader to [BHHO08,CGH12,Hof13,BGK11, BG10] and references therein.

1.1   Technical Overview

The simplest way of constructing a public-key encryption scheme in a world where obfuscation exists is probably the following: a secret key is just a random string s and a public key is a circuit P that outputs 1 on input s and $\perp$ otherwise. We write $s \xrightarrow{P} 1$ for compactness. We can think of a plaintext m as a circuit $1 \rightarrow m$. Now to encrypt m under public key P one can construct a ciphertext C with the functionality $s \xrightarrow{C} m$ by composing the two circuits $s \xrightarrow{P} 1 \rightarrow m$. Correctness is trivial to check and security follows from the fact that the circuits are obfuscated and can therefore only be used as "black-boxes".

To break the circular security of the scheme, we add another circuit to the ciphertexts that "recognizes" circular encryptions without otherwise affecting the security of our scheme. Using the public key P we define a new circuit Q which takes as input a string y and a program B: Q evaluates $B(y)$ and checks if the result is equal to s using P and, if so, outputs s. In other words, Q only outputs s to someone that already knows it.

When creating a ciphertext we append a circuit R to the ciphertext, where R is an obfuscation of Q with the first input fixed to m. Following the definition of Q, the circuit R provides the following functionality: On input a ciphertext C, the circuit R tries to decrypt C with m and, if the output is s, releases the secret key s. So, if Q_1 is the circuit made from public key P_1 and then its first input is fixed to s_2, the ciphertext will now contain a circuit $R_{1,2}$ that can recognize encryptions of s_1 under the key s_2. So, our new scheme is not 2-circular secure!

The next observation is that any two circuits $x \xrightarrow{A} y$ and $y \xrightarrow{B} z$ can be composed into a circuit $x \xrightarrow{C} z$. In particular, from a set of n encryptions $s_i \xrightarrow{C_i} s_{(i+1 \mod n)}$ for $i = 1, \ldots, n$ one can compute n circuits

$$s_{(i+1 \mod n)} \xrightarrow{C_i^*} s_i$$

Clearly the size of these circuits grows with n, but this is not a problem as long as we set the input size of Q to be big enough.

This concludes the intuitive description of our "attack". To see that the scheme is IND-CPA secure, consider an intermediate game where we replace the real public key P with a circuit that always outputs $\perp$. If this can be done in an indistinguishable way, then we are done: if P always outputs $\perp$, then also C, Q output $\perp$ on any input, and therefore contain no information whatsoever about m (at least in the ideal world where the simulator only has oracle access to the circuits).

Now it is easy to see that if VBB obfuscators exist, we can replace P with a circuit that always output $\perp$ and the adversary will only distinguish if he queries the oracles on the secret key s. However, iO obfuscation does not allow to perform this replacement, as it only guarantees that obfuscations of circuits computing the same functions are indistinguishable. To fix that, we replace the public key P with a a string $p = \mathrm{PRG}(s)$: this still allows the other circuits C, Q to check if their input is equal to the secret key by computing $p \overset{?}{=} \mathrm{PRG}(x)$, and at the same time it allows us to replace p with an indistinguishable uniform random string (for which no secret key exists) in the hybrid game. Then, when p is a uniform random string, C and Q always output $\perp$ and we can therefore use iO obfuscation to argue that encryptions of m_0 are indistinguishable from encryptions of m_1.

1.2   Preliminaries

In this section, we state the notation and conventions used in the rest of the work. To keep the paper self contained, we will also recall some relevant definitions and theorems.

Notation and Conventions. We use lowercase letters s, x, y for strings in $\{0,1\}^n$. We use uppercase letters P, C, Q, R for "plaintext" circuits and $\overline{P}, \overline{C}, \overline{Q}, \overline{R}$ for obfuscated circuits. We call $\mathcal{P}$ the set of all polynomial-size circuits. We use the notation $P(x \in X) \in Y$ when we want to say that a circuit P takes input from $X \cup \{\perp\}$ and returns a value in $Y \cup \{\perp\}$. We write $P_{a \to b}$ for a circuit P that outputs b if $x = a$ and $\perp$ otherwise, and $P_{* \to \perp}$ for the circuit that outputs $\perp$ on any input. For all circuits we define $P(\perp) = \perp$.

If S is a finite set, $s \leftarrow S$ is a uniformly random sample from S. If A is a randomized algorithm, $x \leftarrow A$ is the output of A on a uniformly random input tape.

Definition 1 (Pseudorandom generator). *We say that a function* PRG : $\{0,1\}^k \to \{0,1\}^y$ *(with $y > k$) is a secure pseudorandom generator if no PPT adversary $\mathcal{A}$ can distinguish between a random string $c \leftarrow \{0,1\}^y$ and the output of the* PRG(s) *on a uniformly random point $s \in \{0,1\}^k$.*

Definition 2 (IND-CPA). *Let $\Pi = (\mathsf{Gen}, \mathsf{Enc}, \mathsf{Dec})$ be a public key encryption scheme. Let us define the following experiment (parametrized by a bit b) between an adversary $\mathcal{A}$ and a challenger:*

IND-CPA$_\Pi^b(\mathcal{A}, k)$:

1. The challenger runs $(sk, pk) \leftarrow \mathsf{Gen}(1^k)$ and gives pk to $\mathcal{A}$.
2. $\mathcal{A}$ outputs two messages (m_0, m_1) of the same length.
3. The challenger computes $\mathsf{Enc}(pk, m_b)$ and gives it to $\mathcal{A}$
4. $\mathcal{A}$ outputs a bit b' (if it aborts without giving any output, we just set $b' \leftarrow 0$). The challenger returns b' as the output of the game.

We say that Π is secure against a chosen plaintext attack if for any k and any PPT adversary $\mathcal{A}$

$$\mathbf{Adv}(\mathcal{A}) \stackrel{\text{def}}{=} \left| \Pr\left[\mathbf{IND\text{-}CPA}_\Pi^1(\mathcal{A}, k) = 1 \right] - \Pr\left[\mathbf{IND\text{-}CPA}_\Pi^0(\mathcal{A}, k) = 1 \right] \right| \leq \mathrm{negl}(k).$$

Definition 3 (Virtual Black-Box Obfuscator [BGI$^+$01, BGI$^+$12]). Let $\mathcal{C} = \{\mathcal{C}_n\}_{n \in \mathbb{N}}$ be a family of polynomial-size circuits, where $\mathcal{C}_n$ is a set of boolean circuits operating on inputs of length n. And let $\mathcal{O}$ be a PPT algorithm, which takes as input an input a length $n \in \mathbb{N}$, a circuit $C \in \mathcal{C}_n$, a security parameter $k \in \mathbb{N}$, and outputs a boolean circuit $\mathcal{O}(C)$ (not necessarily in $\mathcal{C}$).

$\mathcal{O}$ is a (black-box) obfuscator for the circuit family $\mathcal{C}$ if it satisfies:

Preserving Functionality: For every $n \in \mathbb{N}$, every $C \in \mathcal{C}$ and every $x \in \{0,1\}^n$, with all but $\mathrm{negl}(k)$ probability over the coins of $\mathcal{O}$:

$$\left(\mathcal{O}(C, 1^n, 1^k) \right)(x) = C(x)$$

Polynomial Slowdown: For every $n, k \in \mathbb{N}$ and $C \in \mathcal{C}$, the circuit $\mathcal{O}(C, 1^n, 1^k)$ is of size at most $\mathrm{poly}(|C|, n, k)$.

Virtual Black-Box: For every (non-uniform) polynomial size adversary $\mathcal{A}$, there exists a (non-uniform) polynomial size simulator $\mathcal{S}$, such that for every $n \in \mathbb{N}$ and for every $C \in \mathcal{C}$:

$$\left| \Pr_{\mathcal{O}, \mathcal{A}}\left[\mathcal{A}\left(\mathcal{O}(C, 1^n, 1^k) \right) = 1 \right] - \Pr_{\mathcal{S}}\left[\mathcal{S}^C(1^{|C|}, 1^n, 1^k) = 1 \right] \right| \leq \mathrm{negl}(k)$$

Definition 4 (Indistinguishability Obfuscation [BGI$^+$01, BGI$^+$12]). Given a circuit class $\{\mathcal{C}_k\}$, a (uniform) PPT machine $\mathcal{O}$ is called an indistinguishability obfuscator (iO) for $\{\mathcal{C}_k\}$ if it satisfies:

Preserving Functionality: For every $k \in \mathbb{N}$ and $C \in \mathcal{C}_k$,

$$\Pr[C'(x) = C(x) | C' \leftarrow \mathcal{O}(k, C)] = 1 \quad \forall x$$

Indistinguishability: For any (non necessarily uniform) distinguisher $\mathcal{D}$, all security parameters k and all couples $C_0, C_1 \in \mathcal{C}_k$ such that $C_0(x) = C_1(x)$ for all inputs x, we have that

$$\left| \Pr[D(\mathcal{O}(k, C_0) = 1] - \Pr[D(\mathcal{O}(k, C_1)) = 1] \right| \leq \mathrm{negl}(k)$$

Recently candidate obfuscators for every circuits have been presented: [BR14] shows that VBB obfuscation is possible under appropriate assumptions in a "generic group model" while [GGH$^+$13b] shows that iO obfuscation is possible under strong (but falsifiable) assumptions.

2 Separation from Virtual Black-Box Obfuscation

2.1 PKE from Obfuscation

We start by constructing a very simple IND-CPA public-key encryption scheme Gen, Enc, Dec based on obfuscation, and show some of its interesting property. In the next subsection, we will modify it in order to render it insecure under n-circular security attacks.

Key Generation: The algorithm $\mathsf{Gen}(1^k)$ chooses a random secret key $s \leftarrow \{0,1\}^k$. The public key is an obfuscated circuit $\overline{P} \leftarrow \mathcal{O}(P)$ where P is defined as follows:

def $P(x \in \{0,1\}^k) \in \{0,1\}$:

  1. if $(x \overset{?}{=} s)$ output 1; else output $\perp$.

Encryption: The algorithm $\mathsf{Enc}(\overline{P}, m)$ on input a public key $\overline{P} \in \mathcal{P}$ and a message $m \in \{0,1\}^k$ outputs an obfuscated circuit $\overline{C} \leftarrow \mathcal{O}(C)$ where C is defined as follows:

def $C(x \in \{0,1\}^k) \in \{0,1\}^k$:

  1. if $(\overline{P}(x) \overset{?}{=} 1)$ output m; else output $\perp$.

Decryption: The algorithm $\mathsf{Dec}(s, \overline{C})$ on input a secret key $s \in \{0,1\}^k$ and a ciphertext $\overline{C} \in \mathcal{P}$ outputs $m' = \overline{C}(s)$.

It is easy to check that if $(s, \overline{P}) \leftarrow \mathsf{Gen}$, then:

$$\mathsf{Dec}(s, \mathsf{Enc}(\overline{P}, m)) = m$$

Theorem 1. *If $\mathcal{O}$ is a VBB obfuscator for $\mathcal{P}$ according to Definition 3, then the scheme* $(\mathsf{Gen}, \mathsf{Enc}, \mathsf{Dec})$ *described above is IND-CPA secure according to Definition 2.*

To see that the scheme is IND-CPA secure, notice that thanks to the VBB property one can replace the public key $\overline{P}$ with an obfuscated version of $P_{*\to\perp}$ without the adversary noticing. Then, for every m, $\mathsf{Enc}(pk, m) = P_{*\to\perp}$, so in the ideal world (where the simulator only has oracle access to the circuits) the ciphertexts contain no information at all about the messages. A formal argument follows.

Proof. We prove the theorem by an hybrid argument. Let us define the following games:

Game 0: this is the same as **IND-CPA**$^0(\mathcal{A}, k)$.

Game 1: this is the same as the previous one, but in step 1 we set the public key pk to be an obfuscation (of proper size) of $P_{*\to\perp}$.

Game 2: this is the same as the previous one, but in step 3 instead of an encryption of m_1 we give $\mathcal{A}$ an obfuscation of $P_{*\to\perp}$.

Game 3: this is the same as Game 4, but in step 1 we set the public key $pk \leftarrow \mathcal{O}(P_{*\to\perp})$.

Game 4: this is the same as **IND-CPA**$^1(\mathcal{A}, k)$.

Proving that no adversary can distinguish between two consecutive games with more than negligible probability implies the security of our scheme.

We first prove that Game 0 and Game 1 (and similarly Games 4 and 3) are indistinguishable assuming the VBB property of $\mathcal{O}$. Assume by contradiction that there exists an adversary $\mathcal{A}$ such that $|\text{Game0}(\mathcal{A}, k) - \text{Game1}(\mathcal{A}, k)|$ is greater than any negligible function of k. Then we can build an adversary $\mathcal{A}'$ against the VBB property of $\mathcal{O}$ for the class of circuits $\mathcal{P}_k = \{P_{s\to1}|s \in \{0,1\}^k\} \cup \{P_{*\to\perp}\}$ as follows. $\mathcal{A}'$ gets in input a circuit $pk \leftarrow \mathcal{P}_k$, and runs $\mathcal{A}$ simulating the **IND-CPA** game against it. Its goal is to distinguish whether $pk = P_{*\to\perp}$ (and output 1) or not (and output 0); it works as follows:

$\mathcal{A}'(pk, k)$:
  1. Runs $\mathcal{A}$ giving it pk as the public key.
  2. $\mathcal{A}$ outputs two messages (m_0, m_1) of the same length.
  3. $\mathcal{A}'$ computes $\text{Enc}(pk, m_0)$ and gives it to $\mathcal{A}$
  4. When $\mathcal{A}$ outputs a bit b', $\mathcal{A}'$ outputs 1 if $b' = 0$ and 0 otherwise.

It is easy to see that, from $\mathcal{A}$'s point of view, this game is exactly like Game 1 when $pk = P_{*\to\perp}$, and exactly like Game 0 in the other case. Therefore (by contradiction) $\mathcal{A}'$ can distinguish between $P_{*\to\perp}$ and any other circuit in $\mathcal{P}_k$ with more than negligible advantage. However, no simulator (in the ideal world) can do this given only oracle access to pk, as this would imply querying the oracle for pk on input the only *random* point x such that $pk(x) \neq 1$, which can only happen with probability $\frac{1}{2^k}$.

As a final step, we prove that no adversary can distinguish between Games 1 and 2 (2 and 3 respectively) with more than negligible probability. The distribution of the view of $\mathcal{A}$ is identical in both games up to step 3, where it receives a direct obfuscation of $P_{*\to\perp}$ in Game 2, and an encryption $\text{Enc}(pk, m_0)$ in Game 1. However, since we are using an obfuscation of $P_{*\to\perp}$ as a public key in both games, the ciphertexts given to the adversary are both functionally equivalent[4] to (obfuscations of) $P_{*\to\perp}$. Therefore, by the security property of the obfuscator (as in the ideal world we are giving the same oracle to the simulator in both cases), $\mathcal{A}$ cannot distinguish between the two distributions and therefore between the two games. □

2.2 Properties of Our Scheme

The scheme (Gen, Enc, Dec) defined in the previous section has an interesting property, namely that it is possible to combine ciphertexts together in order to

---

[4] This means that they have the same input/output behaviour on all inputs. We also note that by this property this part of the proof also works if we assume indistinguishability obfuscation instead of the VBB one.

achieve some flavour of *proxy re-encryption*: it is possible to delegate to someone the power to transform ciphertexts encrypted under a public key $\overline{P_1}$ into ciphertexts encrypted under a different public key $\overline{P_2}$ without having to release the corresponding secret key s_1. To see how this is possible, think of a proxy who is given two public keys $(\overline{P_1}, \overline{P_2})$ and

$$\overline{C_{1\rightarrow 2}} = \mathsf{Enc}(\overline{P_2}, s_1)$$

(i.e., an encryption of secret key 2 using public key 1). It will be convenient now to say that a circuit $\overline{C}$ (not necessarily an output of Enc) is an encryption of m under key i if $\mathsf{Dec}(s_i, \overline{C}) = m$.

Then the proxy, using $\overline{C_1}$ s.t. $\mathsf{Dec}(s_1, \overline{C_1}) = m$ and $\overline{C_{1\rightarrow 2}}$ s.t. $\mathsf{Dec}(s_2, \overline{C_{1\rightarrow 2}}) = s_1$, can compute an encryption of m under key $\overline{P_2}$ by creating an obfuscated circuit $\overline{C_2} \leftarrow \mathcal{O}(C_2)$ where C_2 is defined as follows:

def $C_2(x \in \{0,1\}^k) \in \{0,1\}^k$
  1. Output $\overline{C_1}(\overline{C_{1\rightarrow 2}}(x))$;

It is now easy to check that $\overline{C_2}(s_2) = m$ and that, due to the property of the VBB obfuscator $\mathcal{O}$, nothing else can be computed from $\overline{C_2}$.

2-Cycle from n-Cycle: Using this property, we can go from a cycle of n encryptions to $n - 1$ cycles of length 2. Namely, let $\overline{C_{i\rightarrow(i+1)}} = \mathsf{Enc}(\overline{P_i}, s_{i+1})$ for all $i \in \{1, \ldots, n\}$ (where all additions are modulo n). Then one can create circuits

$$C^*_{(i+1)\rightarrow i} = \overline{C}_{(i+1)\rightarrow(i+2)} \circ \cdots \circ \overline{C}_{(i-1)\rightarrow i}$$

Note that in this case we are not even interested in re-obfuscating the concatenation of the circuits (like in the proxy re-encryption application) and the circuit $C^*_{(i+1)\rightarrow i}$ is a "functional ciphertext" in the sense that it is a circuit which decrypts to s_i on input s_{i+1}. The only difference between C^* and a "regular" ciphertext is that the size of C^* grows with n. Given an obfuscator $\mathcal{O}$, it is possible to find an upper bound $\beta_n = \mathrm{poly}(k, n)$ s.t. the size of $C^*_{(i+1)\rightarrow i}$ is less than β_n.

2.3 A PKE That is Not n-Circular Secure

In this section, we add a new element to the ciphertexts to make the scheme from the previous section insecure under circular attacks. Let $\mathcal{B}$ be the set of circuits of size at most β_n defined above, then we define the following circuit (where P represents the public key circuit as defined below):

def $Q(y \in \{0,1\}^k, B \in \mathcal{B}) \in \{0,1\}^k$:
  1. If $(P(B(y)) = 1)$, output $B(y)$; else output $\perp$.

Key Generation: (Unchanged from Sec. 2.1) The algorithm $\mathsf{Gen}(1^k)$ chooses a random secret key $s \leftarrow \{0,1\}^k$. The public key is an obfuscated circuit $\overline{P} \leftarrow \mathcal{O}(P)$ where P is defined as follows:

def $P(x \in \{0,1\}^k) \in \{0,1\}$:

1. if $(x \overset{?}{=} s)$ output 1; else output $\perp$.

Encryption: An encryption of m now is a pair $(\overline{C}, \overline{R})$ where $\overline{R}(\cdot) \leftarrow \mathcal{O}(Q(m, \cdot))$ and $\overline{C}$ is an obfuscation of the circuit C defined as follows:

def $C(x \in \{0,1\}^k) \in \{0,1\}^k$:

1. if $(\overline{P}(x) \overset{?}{=} 1)$ output m; else output $\perp$.

Decryption: (Unchanged from Sec. 2.1) The algorithm $\mathsf{Dec}(s, \overline{C})$ on input a secret key $s \in \{0,1\}^k$ and a ciphertext $\overline{C} \in \mathcal{P}$ outputs $m' = \overline{C}(s)$.

Circular (in)Security of Our Scheme: In our new scheme an encryption contains a circuit R which "remembers" the message m and then, on any circuit B, it tests whether $B(m)$ is equal to the secret key and, if so, it outputs it.

It is easy to see that this new scheme is not 1-circular secure, as $\overline{R}(\overline{C}) = Q(s, \mathsf{Enc}(\overline{P}, s)) = s$. The scheme is also insecure under 2-circular attacks: let s_1, s_2 be two secret keys and $\overline{P}_1, \overline{P}_2$ their respective public keys. The output of $\mathsf{Enc}(\overline{P}_1, s_2)$ is $(\overline{C}_1, \overline{R}_{1,2})$. That is, $\overline{R}_{1,2}$ is a circuit that accepts as input any circuit C of size at most β_n, and if $C(s_2) = s_1$ it outputs s_1.

Therefore if the adversary is also given an encryption $(\overline{C}_2, \overline{R}_{2,1}) \leftarrow \mathsf{Enc}(\overline{P}_2, s_1)$, he can invoke $R_{1,2}(\overline{C}_1)$ and $R_{2,1}(\overline{C}_2)$ to recover s_1, s_2 respectively. As described in the previous section, from any longer cycle of size up to n one can compute a functionally working encryption of s_1 under key 2 i.e., a circuit that on input s_2 outputs s_1, that can be fed as well to R to recover the secret key. Therefore the attack generalizes to n-circularity (as long as the concatenation of n ciphertexts has length less than β_n).

IND-CPA Security of Our Scheme: The modified scheme is still IND-CPA secure: Unless one knows an encryption of the secret key, R cannot be exploited. More formally, we prove the following:

Theorem 2. *If $\mathcal{O}$ is a VBB obfuscator for $\mathcal{P}$ according to Definition 3, then the modified scheme* $(\mathsf{Gen}, \mathsf{Enc}, \mathsf{Dec})$ *described in this section is IND-CPA secure.*

Proof. The proof is very similar to the one of the corresponding Theorem 1, the main difference being that in this case we need to "substitute" the two parts of the challenge ciphertext separately (and thus we need two more hybrid games):

Game 0: this is the same as $\mathbf{IND\text{-}CPA}^0(\mathcal{A}, k)$.

Game 1: this is the same as the previous one, but in step 1 we set the public key $pk \leftarrow \mathcal{O}(P_{* \to \perp})$.

Game 1.5: this is the same as the previous one, but in step 3 instead of giving $\mathcal{A}$ a complete encryption $(\overline{C}, \overline{R})$ of m_0 we substitute $\overline{R}$ with an obfuscation (of proper size) of $P_{* \to \perp}$ and give him $(\overline{C}, \mathcal{O}(P_{* \to \perp}))$.

Game 2: this is the same as the previous one, but in step 3 instead of an encryption $(\overline{C}, \overline{R})$ of m_0 we give $\mathcal{A}$ two obfuscations $(\mathcal{O}(P_{*\to\perp}), \mathcal{O}(P_{*\to\perp}))$ (of proper size).

Game 2.5: this is the same as Game 3, but in step 3 instead of giving $\mathcal{A}$ a complete encryption $(\overline{C}, \overline{R})$ of m_1, we substitute $\overline{R}$ with an obfuscation (of proper size) of $P_{*\to\perp}$ and give him $(\overline{C}, \mathcal{O}(P_{*\to\perp}))$.

Game 3: this is the same as Game 4, but in step 1 we set the public key pk to be an obfuscation (of proper size) of $P_{*\to\perp}$.

Game 4: this is the same as $\mathbf{IND\text{-}CPA}^1(\mathcal{A}, k)$.

An adversary that distinguishes Game 1 and Game 1.5 (resp. Game 3 and game 2.5) can be used to break the indistinguishability between two different obfuscations of $P_{*\to\perp}$: in Game 1, the circuit R always outputs $\perp$ as $pk = P_{*\to\perp}$, while in Game 1.5 $P_{*\to\perp}$ is obfuscated directly. Indistinguishability between the other games follows from the same arguments as Theorem 1. $\square$

3   Separation from Indistinguishability Obfuscation

To prove that our simple encryption scheme is IND-CPA secure, we had to argue that an obfuscation of a real public key $P_{s\to1}$ is indistinguishable from an obfuscation of $P_{*\to\perp}$. However indistinguishability obfuscation only guarantees that an adversary cannot tell the difference between the obfuscation of two circuits computing the same function.

To fix this, change our simple scheme in the following way: let $\text{PRG} : \{0,1\}^k \to \{0,1\}^{2k}$ be a pseudorandom generator, then we compute the public key pk as $pk = \text{PRG}(s)$. Note that in the simple public key encryption scheme we only used the obfuscated program P to check if we had the right secret key. This can be done using the new public key as well, by evaluating the PRG. At the same time, this will allow us to replace a real public key with an (indistinguishable) uniformly random string for which (with very high probability) no secret key exists, and therefore all ciphertexts will be functionally equivalent to $P_{*\to\perp}$.

3.1   The Technical Details

Key Generation: The algorithm $\text{Gen}(1^k)$ chooses a random secret key $s \leftarrow \{0,1\}^k$ and computes a string $p = \text{PRG}(s) \in \{0,1\}^{2k}$.

Encryption: The algorithm $\text{Enc}(p, m)$ on input a public key $p \in \{0,1\}^{2k}$ and a message $m \in \{0,1\}^k$ outputs an obfuscated circuit $\overline{C} \leftarrow \mathcal{O}(C)$ and $\overline{R}(\cdot) \leftarrow \mathcal{O}(Q(m, \cdot))$. where C, R are defined as follows:
def $C(x \in \{0,1\}^k) \in \{0,1\}^k$:
  1. if $(\text{PRG}(x) \stackrel{?}{=} p)$ output m; else output $\perp$.

def $Q(y \in \{0,1\}^k, B \in \mathcal{B}) \in \{0,1\}^k$:
  1. If $(\text{PRG}(B(y)) = p)$, output $B(y)$; else output $\perp$.

Decryption: The algorithm $\mathsf{Dec}(s, \overline{C}, \overline{R})$ on input a secret key $s \in \{0,1\}^k$ and a ciphertext $(\overline{C}, \overline{R}) \in \mathcal{P}$ outputs $m' = \overline{C}(s)$ (and ignores $\overline{R}$).

It can be easily verified that this scheme is also not circular secure, and we can argue that it is still IND-CPA secure.

Theorem 3. *If $\mathcal{O}$ be a iO obfuscator and* PRG *a secure pseudorandom generator, then* $(\mathsf{Gen}, \mathsf{Enc}, \mathsf{Dec})$ *described in this section is IND-CPA secure.*

Proof. This proof is very similar to the one of Theorem 2. The only difference is that we use a uniformly random string (instead of an obfuscation of $P_{* \to \bot}$) as a fake public key. The hybrids are as follows:

Game 0: this is the same as **IND-CPA**$^0(\mathcal{A}, k)$.

Game 1: this is the same as the previous one, but in step 1 we set the public key $pk \leftarrow \{0,1\}^{2k}$.

Game 1.5: this is the same as the previous one, but in step 3 instead of giving $\mathcal{A}$ a complete encryption $(\overline{C}, \overline{R})$ of m_0 we substitute $\overline{R}$ with an obfuscation (of proper size) of $P_{* \to \bot}$ and give him $(\overline{C}, \mathcal{O}(P_{* \to \bot}))$.

Game 2: this is the same as the previous one, but in step 3 instead of an encryption $(\overline{C}, \overline{R})$ of m_0 we give $\mathcal{A}$ two obfuscations $(\mathcal{O}(P_{* \to \bot}), \mathcal{O}(P_{* \to \bot}))$ (of proper size).

Game 2.5: this is the same as Game 3, but in step 3 instead of giving $\mathcal{A}$ a complete encryption $(\overline{C}, \overline{R})$ of m_1, we substitute $\overline{R}$ with an obfuscation (of proper size) of $P_{* \to \bot}$ and give him $(\overline{C}, \mathcal{O}(P_{* \to \bot}))$.

Game 3: this is the same as Game 4, but in step 1 we set the public key $pk \leftarrow \{0,1\}^{2k}$.

Game 4: this is the same as **IND-CPA**$^1(\mathcal{A}, k)$.

An adversary $\mathcal{A}$ distinguishing between Games 0 and 1 could be used to build an adversary $\mathcal{A}'$ against the security of the PRG as follows:

$\mathcal{A}'(pk \in \{0,1\}^{2k}, 1^k)$:

1. Runs $\mathcal{A}$ giving it pk as the public key.
2. $\mathcal{A}$ outputs two messages (m_0, m_1) of the same length.
3. $\mathcal{A}'$ computes $\mathsf{Enc}(pk, m_0)$ and gives it to $\mathcal{A}$
4. When $\mathcal{A}$ outputs a bit b', $\mathcal{A}'$ outputs 1 if $b' = 0$ and 0 otherwise.

From $\mathcal{A}$'s point of view, this game is exactly the same as Game 0 in the case where pk is computed as $pk \leftarrow \mathrm{PRG}(s)$ from a uniformly random seed $s \leftarrow \{0,1\}^k$, while it is exactly like Game 1 if pk is uniformly random.

Note that, in the case where $pk \leftarrow \{0,1\}^{2k}$ is uniformly random, with all but negligible probability there exists no s such that $\mathrm{PRG}(s) = pk$, and therefore the circuits $\overline{C}, \overline{R}$ contained in the ciphertexts of all other hybrids are always functionally equivalent to $P_{* \to \bot}$. Therefore those hybrids are indistinguishable under the assumption that $\mathcal{O}$ is an indistinguishability obfuscator.   □

Acknowledgements. The authors would like to thank Amit Sahai for the mantra "When you cannot solve a problem, try obfuscation" and Matthew Green for helpful comments.

References

[ABBC10] Acar, T., Belenkiy, M., Bellare, M., Cash, D.: Cryptographic agility and its relation to circular encryption. In: Gilbert, H. (ed.) EUROCRYPT 2010. LNCS, vol. 6110, pp. 403–422. Springer, Heidelberg (2010)

[BG10] Brakerski, Z., Goldwasser, S.: Circular and leakage resilient public-key encryption under subgroup indistinguishability. In: Rabin, T. (ed.) CRYPTO 2010. LNCS, vol. 6223, pp. 1–20. Springer, Heidelberg (2010)

[BGI⁺01] Barak, B., Goldreich, O., Impagliazzo, R., Rudich, S., Sahai, A., Vadhan, S.P., Yang, K.: On the (Im)possibility of obfuscating programs. In: Kilian, J. (ed.) CRYPTO 2001. LNCS, vol. 2139, pp. 1–18. Springer, Heidelberg (2001)

[BGI⁺12] Barak, B., Goldreich, O., Impagliazzo, R., Rudich, S., Sahai, A., Vadhan, S.P., Yang, K.: On the (im)possibility of obfuscating programs. J. ACM 59(2), 6 (2012)

[BGK11] Brakerski, Z., Goldwasser, S., Kalai, Y.T.: Black-box circular-secure encryption beyond affine functions. In: Ishai, Y. (ed.) TCC 2011. LNCS, vol. 6597, pp. 201–218. Springer, Heidelberg (2011)

[BHHO08] Boneh, D., Halevi, S., Hamburg, M., Ostrovsky, R.: Circular-secure encryption from decision diffie-hellman. In: Wagner, D. (ed.) CRYPTO 2008. LNCS, vol. 5157, pp. 108–125. Springer, Heidelberg (2008)

[BR14] Brakerski, Z., Rothblum, G.N.: Virtual black-box obfuscation for all circuits via generic graded encoding. In: Lindell, Y. (ed.) TCC 2014. LNCS, vol. 8349, pp. 1–25. Springer, Heidelberg (2014)

[BRS02] Black, J., Rogaway, P., Shrimpton, T.: Encryption-scheme security in the presence of key-dependent messages. In: Nyberg, K., Heys, H.M. (eds.) SAC 2002. LNCS, vol. 2595, pp. 62–75. Springer, Heidelberg (2003)

[BZ14] Boneh, D., Zhandry, M.: Multiparty key exchange, efficient traitor tracing, and more from indistinguishability obfuscation. CRYPTO 2014. Cryptology ePrint Archive, Report 2013/642 (2014), http://eprint.iacr.org/

[CD08] Canetti, R., Dakdouk, R.R.: Obfuscating point functions with multibit output. In: Smart, N.P. (ed.) EUROCRYPT 2008. LNCS, vol. 4965, pp. 489–508. Springer, Heidelberg (2008)

[CGH12] Cash, D., Green, M., Hohenberger, S.: New definitions and separations for circular security. In: Fischlin, M., Buchmann, J., Manulis, M. (eds.) PKC 2012. LNCS, vol. 7293, pp. 540–557. Springer, Heidelberg (2012)

[CL01] Camenisch, J.L., Lysyanskaya, A.: An efficient system for non-transferable anonymous credentials with optional anonymity revocation. In: Pfitzmann, B. (ed.) EUROCRYPT 2001. LNCS, vol. 2045, pp. 93–118. Springer, Heidelberg (2001)

[CRV10] Canetti, R., Rothblum, G.N., Varia, M.: Obfuscation of hyperplane membership. In: Micciancio, D. (ed.) TCC 2010. LNCS, vol. 5978, pp. 72–89. Springer, Heidelberg (2010)

[Gen09] Gentry, C.: Fully homomorphic encryption using ideal lattices. In: STOC, pp. 169–178 (2009)

[GGH13a]   Garg, S., Gentry, C., Halevi, S.: Candidate multilinear maps from ideal lattices. In: Johansson, T., Nguyen, P.Q. (eds.) EUROCRYPT 2013. LNCS, vol. 7881, pp. 1–17. Springer, Heidelberg (2013)

[GGH+13b]   Garg, S., Gentry, C., Halevi, S., Raykova, M., Sahai, A., Waters, B.: Candidate indistinguishability obfuscation and functional encryption for all circuits. In: FOCS, pp. 40–49 (2013)

[GGHR14]   Garg, S., Gentry, C., Halevi, S., Raykova, M.: Two-round secure MPC from indistinguishability obfuscation. In: Lindell, Y. (ed.) TCC 2014. LNCS, vol. 8349, pp. 74–94. Springer, Heidelberg (2014)

[GH10]   Green, M., Hohenberger, S.: CPA and CCA-secure encryption systems that are not 2-circular secure. IACR Cryptology ePrint Archive 2010, 144 (2010)

[Hof13]   Hofheinz, D.: Circular chosen-ciphertext security with compact ciphertexts. In: Johansson, T., Nguyen, P.Q. (eds.) EUROCRYPT 2013. LNCS, vol. 7881, pp. 520–536. Springer, Heidelberg (2013)

[HRSV11]   Hohenberger, S., Rothblum, G.N., Shelat, A., Vaikuntanathan, V.: Securely obfuscating re-encryption. J. Cryptology 24(4), 694–719 (2011)

[HSW14]   Hohenberger, S., Sahai, A., Waters, B.: Replacing a random oracle: Full domain hash from indistinguishability obfuscation. In: Nguyen, P.Q., Oswald, E. (eds.) EUROCRYPT 2014. LNCS, vol. 8441, pp. 201–220. Springer, Heidelberg (2014)

[KNY14]   Komargodski, I., Naor, M., Yogev, E.: Secret-sharing for NP from indistinguishability obfuscation. Cryptology ePrint Archive, Report 2014/213 (2014), http://eprint.iacr.org/

[KRW13]   Koppula, V., Ramchen, K., Waters, B.: Separations in circular security for arbitrary length key cycles. Cryptology ePrint Archive, Report 2013/683 (2013), http://eprint.iacr.org/

[Rot13]   Rothblum, R.D.: On the circular security of bit-encryption. In: Sahai, A. (ed.) TCC 2013. LNCS, vol. 7785, pp. 579–598. Springer, Heidelberg (2013)

[SW14]   Sahai, A., Waters, B.: How to use indistinguishability obfuscation: Deniable encryption, and more. In: STOC (2014)

[Wee05]   Wee, H.: On obfuscating point functions. In: STOC, pp. 523–532 (2005)

Program Obfuscation via Multilinear Maps

Sanjam Garg

IBM T.J. Watson
sanjamg@cs.ucla.edu

Abstract. Recent proposals for plausible candidate constructions of *multilinear maps* and *obfuscation* have radically transformed what we imagined to be possible in cryptography. For over a decade cryptographers had been very skeptical about the existence of such objects. In this article, we provide a very brief introduction to these results and some of their interesting consequences.

The goal of software obfuscation, often viewed as a panacea in cryptography, is to make computer programs "unintelligible" while preserving their functionality. The need for software obfuscation to perform tasks such as protecting intellectual property is so immense that even the commercial use of *insecure* obfuscation tools and techniques is rampant. Obfuscation offers solutions to many security problems. Consider for example the task of releasing a patch to fix a zero-day exploit in a software package. Attackers could reverse engineer this patch in order to figure out the vulnerability, putting unpatched machines at risk. Obfuscation offers the only known solution to this problem: release an initial patch in an obfuscated form, and then later transition to a more efficient un-obfuscated patch once large-scale adoption of the initial patch has completed. As another example, consider the very basic task of constructing a public-key encryption scheme [DH76, RSA78] with the smallest possible ciphertext size; obfuscation enables a candidate that quantitatively beats all known constructions in the literature.

The formal study of program obfuscation was initiated by Hada [Had00] and Barak et al. [BGI+01]. Unfortunately, they showed that the most natural simulation-based formulation of program obfuscation (a.k.a. "black-box obfuscation") is impossible to achieve for general programs. Faced with this impossibility result, Barak et al. [BGI+01] suggested another notion of program obfuscation called indistinguishability obfuscation: An indistinguishability obfuscator $i\mathcal{O}$ for a class of circuits $\mathcal{C}$ guarantees that given two equivalent circuits C_1 and C_2 from the class, the two distribution of obfuscations $i\mathcal{O}(C_1)$ and $i\mathcal{O}(C_2)$ should be computationally indistinguishable. We note that if the circuit class $\mathcal{C}$ has efficiently computable canonical forms, then the computation of that canonical form would already be an indistinguishability obfuscator. In a recent work Garg et al. [GGH+13b] provide the first efficient indistingushability obfuscator for all polynomial-size circuits.

It is not immediately clear how this weaker notion of obfuscation can be useful for applications. Perhaps the strongest philosophical justification for

M. Abdalla and R. De Prisco (Eds.): SCN 2014, LNCS 8642, pp. 91–94, 2014.
© Springer International Publishing Switzerland 2014

indistinguishability obfuscators comes from the work of Goldwasser and Rothblum [GR07], who showed that (efficiently computable) indistinguishability obfuscators achieve the notion of *Best-Possible Obfuscation* [GR07]: Informally, a best-possible obfuscator guarantees that its output hides as much about the input circuit as any circuit of a certain size. Concretely Garg et al. [GGH+13b] showed usefulness of indistinguishability obfuscation by showing that it can be used to enable a construction of functional encryption (more on it later) for all polynomial-size circuits. Subsequently a number of different works (such as [SW14, GGHR14]) have shown other novel ways of making use of indistinguishability obfuscators.

Technically speaking, obfuscation entails the ability to perform arbitrary computation on encrypted data while obtaining only the resulting output in unencrypted form. Gentry's breakthrough result on fully-homomorphic encryption [Gen09] enabled the goal of arbitrary computation on encrypted data, however the output of the computation in his scheme remains encrypted. *Multilinear maps* first envisioned by Boneh and Silverberg [BS02] and realized by Garg et al. [GGH13a] are the key technical tool that enable this challenging task of arbitrary computation with limited decryption. Multilinear maps specifically provide the ability to perform "somewhat" arbitrary computation on encrypted data along with the ability to check if two encryptions encrypt the same message. Garg et al. [GGH+13b] show that this limited capability can actually be sculpted to enable obfuscation for all polynomial-size circuits.

Follow up works on multilinear maps [CLT13] and obfuscation [BR14, BGK+14] have helped strengthened our belief in the existence of these objects. Various other works have also provided some optimizations, e.g., recent works by Boyle et al. [BCP14] and Ananth et al. [ABG+13] provide an obfuscation method for Turing Machines instead of just for circuits.

Taken together, multilinear maps and obfuscation radically enhance our tool set and open a floodgate of applications, including:

1. *Functional Encryption.* In functional encryption [BSW11, O'N10], ciphertexts encrypt inputs x and keys are issued for circuits C. Using the key SK_C to decrypt a ciphertext $CT_x = \mathsf{enc}(x)$, yields the value $C(x)$ but does not reveal anything else about x. Furthermore, no collusion of secret key holders should be able to learn anything more than the union of what they can each learn individually. Obfuscation based solution by Garg et al. [GGH+13b] provides the the first construction that allows for secret keys with arbitrary circuits. Subsequently Goldwasser et al. [GGG+14] construct a functional encryption scheme for which a secret key can take multiple multiple ciphertexts as input. Another work of Goyal et al. [GJKS13] enables a functional encryption scheme with secret keys for randomized circuits. Prior to obfuscation based solutions, the realizations of functional encryption were limited to simplistic set of permissible operations such as inner product.

2. *Witness Encryption.* Encryption in all its myriad flavors has always been imagined with some known recipient in mind. But, what if the intended recipient of the message is not known and may never be known? For example,

consider the task of encrypting a message for someone who knows a solution to a crossword puzzle that appeared in the *The New York Times*. Or, in general, a solution to some NP search problem which he might know or might acquire over a period of time. This notion, called *witness encryption*, was first posed by Rudich in 1989 [Rud89] (see [Bei11]) but was realized only recently using multilinear maps by Garg et al. [GGSW13].

3. *Non-Interactive Multiparty Key Exchange*. In their seminal result, Diffie and Hellman [DH76] realized non-interactive key exchange in a setting with two parties. This result was generalized to the three party setting in a landmark result by Joux [Jou04]. Multilinear maps of Garg et al. [GGH13a] enable the first solution for a setting of arbitrary number of parties. Subsequent follow up works such as [BZ13, ABG+13] have used obfuscation in order to obtain various optimizations.

References

[ABG+13]   Ananth, P., Boneh, D., Garg, S., Sahai, A., Zhandry, M.: Differing-inputs obfuscation and applications. Cryptology ePrint Archive, Report 2013/689 (2013), http://eprint.iacr.org/2013/689

[BCP14]   Boyle, E., Chung, K.-M., Pass, R.: On Extractability Obfuscation. In: Lindell, Y. (ed.) TCC 2014. LNCS, vol. 8349, pp. 52–73. Springer, Heidelberg (2014)

[Bei11]   Beimel, A.: Secret-sharing schemes: A survey. In: Chee, Y.M., Guo, Z., Ling, S., Shao, F., Tang, Y., Wang, H., Xing, C. (eds.) IWCC 2011. LNCS, vol. 6639, pp. 11–46. Springer, Heidelberg (2011)

[BGI+01]   Barak, B., Goldreich, O., Impagliazzo, R., Rudich, S., Sahai, A., Vadhan, S.P., Yang, K.: On the (Im)possibility of Obfuscating Programs. In: Kilian, J. (ed.) CRYPTO 2001. LNCS, vol. 2139, pp. 1–18. Springer, Heidelberg (2001)

[BGK+14]   Barak, B., Garg, S., Kalai, Y.T., Paneth, O., Sahai, A.: Protecting Obfuscation against Algebraic Attacks. In: Nguyen, P.Q., Oswald, E. (eds.) EUROCRYPT 2014. LNCS, vol. 8441, pp. 221–238. Springer, Heidelberg (2014)

[BR14]   Brakerski, Z., Rothblum, G.N.: Virtual Black-Box Obfuscation for All Circuits via Generic Graded Encoding. In: Lindell, Y. (ed.) TCC 2014. LNCS, vol. 8349, pp. 1–25. Springer, Heidelberg (2014)

[BS02]   Boneh, D., Silverberg, A.: Applications of multilinear forms to cryptography. Cryptology ePrint Archive, Report 2002/080 (2002), http://eprint.iacr.org/2002/080

[BSW11]   Boneh, D., Sahai, A., Waters, B.: Functional Encryption: Definitions and Challenges. In: Ishai, Y. (ed.) TCC 2011. LNCS, vol. 6597, pp. 253–273. Springer, Heidelberg (2011)

[BZ13]   Boneh, D., Zhandry, M.: Multiparty key exchange, efficient traitor tracing, and more from indistinguishability obfuscation. Cryptology ePrint Archive, Report 2013/642 (2013), http://eprint.iacr.org/2013/642

[CLT13]   Coron, J.-S., Lepoint, T., Tibouchi, M.: Practical Multilinear Maps over the Integers. In: Canetti, R., Garay, J.A. (eds.) CRYPTO 2013, Part I. LNCS, vol. 8042, pp. 476–493. Springer, Heidelberg (2013)

[DH76]   Diffie, W., Hellman, M.E.: New directions in cryptography. IEEE Trans-
            actions on Information Theory 22(6), 644–654 (1976)
[Gen09]   Gentry, C.: Fully homomorphic encryption using ideal lattices. In Michael
            Mitzenmacher. In: 41st ACM STOC, pp. 169–178. ACM Press (May/June
            2009)
[GGG+14]   Goldwasser, S., Dov Gordon, S., Goyal, V., Jain, A., Katz, J., Liu, F.-H.,
            Sahai, A., Shi, E., Zhou, H.-S.: Multi-input Functional Encryption. In:
            Nguyen, P.Q., Oswald, E. (eds.) EUROCRYPT 2014. LNCS, vol. 8441,
            pp. 578–602. Springer, Heidelberg (2014)
[GGH13a]   Garg, S., Gentry, C., Halevi, S.: Candidate Multilinear Maps from Ideal
            Lattices. In: Johansson, T., Nguyen, P.Q. (eds.) EUROCRYPT 2013.
            LNCS, vol. 7881, pp. 1–17. Springer, Heidelberg (2013)
[GGH+13b]   Garg, S., Gentry, C., Halevi, S., Raykova, M., Sahai, A., Waters, B.:
            Candidate indistinguishability obfuscation and functional encryption for
            all circuits. In: 54th FOCS, pp. 40–49. IEEE Computer Society Press
            (October 2013)
[GGHR14]   Garg, S., Gentry, C., Halevi, S., Raykova, M.: Two-Round Secure MPC
            from Indistinguishability Obfuscation. In: Lindell, Y. (ed.) TCC 2014.
            LNCS, vol. 8349, pp. 74–94. Springer, Heidelberg (2014)
[GGSW13]   Garg, S., Gentry, C., Sahai, A., Waters, B.: Witness encryption and its
            applications. In Dan Boneh, Tim Roughgarden, and Joan Feigenbaum.
            In: 45th ACM STOC. ACM Press, pp. 467–476 (June 2013)
[GJKS13]   Goyal, V., Jain, A., Koppula, V., Sahai, A.: Functional encryption for
            randomized functionalities. Cryptology ePrint Archive, Report 2013/729
            (2013), http://eprint.iacr.org/2013/729
[GR07]   Goldwasser, S., Rothblum, G.N.: On Best-Possible Obfuscation. In: Vad-
            han, S.P. (ed.) TCC 2007. LNCS, vol. 4392, pp. 194–213. Springer, Hei-
            delberg (2007)
[Had00]   Hada, S.: Zero-knowledge and code obfuscation. In: Okamoto, T. (ed.)
            ASIACRYPT 2000. LNCS, vol. 1976, pp. 443–457. Springer, Heidelberg
            (2000)
[Jou04]   Joux, A.: A one round protocol for tripartite Diffie-Hellman. Journal of
            Cryptology 17(4), 263–276 (2004)
[O'N10]   O'Neill, A.: Definitional issues in functional encryption. Cryptology
            ePrint Archive, Report 2010/556 (2010),
            http://eprint.iacr.org/2010/556
[RSA78]   Rivest, R.L., Shamir, A., Adleman, L.M.: A method for obtaining digital
            signature and public-key cryptosystems. Communications of the Associ-
            ation for Computing Machinery 21(2), 120–126 (1978)
[Rud89]   Rudich, S.: Unpublished (1989)
[SW14]   Sahai, A., Waters, B.: How to use indistinguishability obfuscation: deni-
            able encryption, and more. In: Shmoys, D.B. (ed.) 46th ACM STOC, pp.
            475–484. ACM Press (May/June 2014)

Constrained Verifiable Random Functions

Georg Fuchsbauer*

Institute of Science and Technology Austria

Abstract. We extend the notion of verifiable random functions (VRF) to *constrained VRFs*, which generalize the concept of constrained pseudorandom functions, put forward by Boneh and Waters (Asiacrypt'13), and independently by Kiayias et al. (CCS'13) and Boyle et al. (PKC'14), who call them delegatable PRFs and functional PRFs, respectively. In a standard VRF the secret key sk allows one to evaluate a pseudorandom function at any point of its domain; in addition, it enables computation of a non-interactive proof that the function value was computed correctly. In a constrained VRF from the key sk one can derive constrained keys sk_S for subsets S of the domain, which allow computation of function values and proofs only at points in S.

After formally defining constrained VRFs, we derive instantiations from the multilinear-maps-based constrained PRFs by Boneh and Waters, yielding a VRF with constrained keys for any set that can be decided by a polynomial-size circuit. Our VRFs have the same function values as the Boneh-Waters PRFs and are proved secure under the same hardness assumption, showing that verifiability comes at no cost. Constrained (functional) VRFs were stated as an open problem by Boyle et al.

1 Introduction

Verifiable Random Functions. A pseudorandom function (PRF) [GGM86] is an efficiently computable keyed function $F: \mathcal{K} \times \mathcal{X} \to \mathcal{Y}$ for which, when the seed k is chosen at random, no efficient attacker should be able to distinguish $F(k, x)$ from a random value, even when given oracle access to $F(k, \cdot)$ at any other point. This fundamental primitive in cryptography was extended to verifiable random functions (VRF) by Micali, Rabin and Vadhan [MRV99]. In a VRF a secret key sk, which is set up together with a public key pk, allows evaluation of F and furthermore computation of a non-interactive proof that the computed value y matches $F(sk, x)$. Verification of the proof must be done with respect to the public key pk only; in particular, we cannot make use of a common reference string (CRS). The proofs should remain sound even when pk was computed maliciously and $F(sk, x)$ should remain pseudorandom even when an adversary can query values of F and proofs for them at any other point.

The first VRF schemes, such as [Lys02, Dod03, DY05], were based on bilinear maps. Efficient schemes have proved difficult to construct, in particular ones with large domains based on non-interactive assumptions, and were only proposed

---

* Supported by the European Research Council, ERC Starting Grant (259668-PSPC).

from 2010 on [HW10, BMR10, ACF13]. VRFs have turned out to be a useful building block, e.g. in the construction of zero-knowledge proofs and databases [MR01, Lis05] and electronic payment schemes [MR02, BCKL09], to name a few.

Constrained VRFs. Boneh and Waters [BW13] define a new notion of PRFs, which they call constrained PRFs and which was concurrently introduced as delegatable PRFs by Kiayias, Papadopoulos, Triandopoulos and Zacharias [KPTZ13], and as functional PRFs by Boyle, Goldwasser and Ivan [BGI14]. While a key k for a PRF enables evaluation of the function F at all points of its domain $\mathcal{X}$, a constrained PRF allows one to derive constrained keys from k. A constrained key k_S corresponds to a set $S \subseteq \mathcal{X}$ and allows computation of $F(k, x)$ only for $x \in S$.

Pseudorandomness requires that given an oracle for function values at points of the adversary's choice and an oracle for constrained keys for sets of its choice, values of $F(k, \cdot)$ at points outside the queried sets and different from the queried points should still be indistinguishable from random. That is, after querying keys for $S_1, \ldots, S_q$ and functions values at $x_1, \ldots, x_p$, the value $F(k, x)$ should be indistinguishable from random for all $x \notin \bigcup_{i=1}^q S_i \cup \{x_1, \ldots, x_p\}$. Constrained PRFs were used to construct broadcast encryption and identity-based non-interactive key exchange in [BW13]. In particular *punctured PRFs* have proved to be a powerful tool in combination with indistinguishability obfuscation [GGH+13b], leading to solutions of longstanding open problems, such as deniable encryption [CDNO97] in [SW14] and instantiating full-domain hash [BR93] in [HSW14].

We unify VRFs and constrained PRFs by adding the possibility to derive constrained keys to the notion of VRFs. We then construct constrained VRF schemes based on the Boneh-Waters constrained PRFs which are defined using multilinear maps [BS02, GGH13a, CLT13]. Our second scheme allows derivation of constrained keys for any subset of the domain that can be decided by a boolean circuit of polynomial size.

Verifiable random functions turned out a lot harder to construct than PRFs. While the Dodis-Yampolskiy VRF [DY05] only supports domains of polynomial size, it requires a q-type assumption (where the parameter q of the assumption upper-bounds how many queries an adversary can make). Hohenberger and Waters [HW10] proposed the first VRF for large domains, whose function values are defined analogously to those of the PRF by Naor and Reingold [NR97], but lifted to the target group of a bilinear map. These maps are then used to verify the proofs of correct function evaluation. Hohenberger and Waters prove their construction secure under a non-standard q-type assumption, while the Naor-Reingold PRF is proved secure under the decisional Diffie-Hellman (DDH) assumption.

Using multilinear maps, the situation is different: Our VRF constructions support large input spaces when using complexity leveraging (see below), and we prove their security under the same assumption on which pseudorandomness of the Boneh-Waters constrained PRFs rely: the DDH assumption adapted to the multilinear-map environment. We moreover show that we do not need to lift the function values "up one level": our VRF values are defined exactly as the Boneh-Waters PRF values. We thus show how to add verifiability to the constrained PRFs from [BW13] without changing the PRF itself, nor using a different assumption to prove pseudorandomness.

Our Contribution. We first formalize the notion of constrained VRFs by extending the model for standard VRFs. In addition to Setup, Prove and Verify, we define an algorithm Constrain, which allows to derive constrained keys. We adapt the security notions of *provability*, *uniqueness* and *pseudorandomness* to the constrained setting and define a new security notion. It requires that a proof produced by a constrained key should be distributed like proofs computed using the actual secret key. A constrained key sk_S behaves thus exactly like the key sk on the subset S of the domain.

We present two multilinear-maps-based instantiations of constrained VRFs with input space $\mathcal{X} := \{0,1\}^n$ for different systems of sets for which constrained keys can be derived:

- Bit-fixing VRF: Constrained keys can be derived for any set $S_{\mathbf{v}} \subseteq \{0,1\}^n$, described by a vector $\mathbf{v} \in \{0, 1, ?\}$ as the set of all strings which match $\mathbf{v}$ at all coordinates that are not '?'.
- Circuit-constrained VRF: In our second construction keys can be derived for any set that is decidable by a polynomial-size circuit C. More precisely, a key sk_C, derived from sk for a circuit C, enables computation of $F(sk, x)$ and a proof for all x for which $C(x) = 1$.

Both our schemes are directly derived from the constructions of constrained PRFs given by Boneh and Waters [BW13]. These are defined over a *leveled multilinear group*, which is a sequence of groups $\mathbb{G}_1, \ldots, \mathbb{G}_\kappa$, each $\mathbb{G}_i$ of prime order $p > 2^\lambda$ and generated by g_i, equipped with bilinear maps ("pairings") $e_{i,j} \colon \mathbb{G}_i \times \mathbb{G}_j \to \mathbb{G}_{i+j}$, for $i + j \leq \kappa$. The bit-fixing PRF from [BW13] maps inputs from $\{0,1\}^n$ to an element of $\mathbb{G}_\kappa$ where $\kappa = n + 1$. A key is a tuple $k = (\alpha, d_{1,0}, d_{1,1}, \ldots, d_{n,0}, d_{n,1}) \in \mathbb{Z}_p^{2n+1}$ and the PRF is defined as

$$P(sk, x) := (g_{n+1})^{\alpha \prod_{i=1}^n d_{i,x_i}} . \tag{1}$$

As noted in [BW13], the values $D_{i,j} := g_1^{d_{i,j}}$ could be made public, and inspection of the proof reveals that $A := g_2^\alpha$ could also be made public without affecting pseudorandomness. These values could be used to make the PRF output P publicly verifiable if we added one level in the group sequence, that is, set $\kappa := n + 2$. Then in order to verify that some $P \in \mathbb{G}_{n+1}$ equals $P(sk, x)$ as defined in (1), one could repeatedly apply the pairings to A and $D_{1,x_1}, \ldots, D_{n,x_n}$ to compute $(g_{n+2})^{\alpha \prod_{i=1}^n d_{i,x_i}} \in \mathbb{G}_\kappa$ and check whether this equals the pairing of P with g_1, which would lift P to $\mathbb{G}_{n+2}$.

Of course this shows that $P(sk, x)$ is not pseudorandom anymore after adding a level in the group hierarchy; however, it can serve as the proof for a related value in $\mathbb{G}_\kappa$. After adding an element $\gamma \in \mathbb{Z}_p$ to the secret key, we define the VRF value as $F(sk, x) := (g_\kappa)^{\gamma \cdot \alpha \prod_{i=1}^n d_{i,x_i}}$. The value $P(sk, x) = (g_{\kappa-1})^{\alpha \prod_{i=1}^n d_{i,x_i}}$ can now be used to check whether some $y \in \mathbb{G}_\kappa$ equals $F(sk, x)$: we add $C := g_1^\gamma$ to the public key and then have $e_{1,\kappa-1}(C, P(sk, x)) = (g_\kappa)^{\gamma \cdot \alpha \prod_{i=1}^{n} d_{i,x_i}} = F(sk, x)$. A nice side effect of this approach is that since our proof corresponds to the PRF value in [BW13], we can reuse their constrained keys to construct proofs. In particular for the circuit-constrained VRF this involves sophisticated techniques derived from [GGH⁺13c].

While this approach works for both the bit-fixing VRF and the circuit-constrained VRF, a drawback is that it requires an extra level in the group hierarchy. Somewhat surprisingly, we show that this is not necessary: we instantiate circuit-constrained VRFs using the same number of group levels as the Boneh-Waters circuit-constrained PRF and for the bit-fixing construction we even require one level less than [BW13].

The reason for this is that, as we show, the bit-fixing PRF can be constructed over a multilinear group with $\kappa = n - 1$ (rather than $\kappa = n + 1$ in [BW13]) and the circuit-constrained PRF can be constructed for $\kappa = n + \ell - 1$ (rather than $\kappa = n + \ell$ in [BW13]), where ℓ is the maximum depth of the circuits. This allows us to use the freed level for verification and preserve the function value of the PRF. We present these modified constrained PRFs and prove their security in the full version [Fuc14].

In [Fuc14] we also show that, as for the constrained PRFs in [BW13], our constructions can be transferred from leveled multilinear groups to *graded encodings*, constructed by Garg, Gentry and Halevi [GGH13a], which can be viewed as "approximate" multilinear groups.

Complexity Leveraging. Pseudorandomness of our VRFs can be reduced to the multilinear DDH assumption without any security loss when considering *selective* security. For this notion the adversary must decide on which value it wants to be challenged before receiving the public key. *Adaptive security* (where the adversary can make its challenge query at any point) can then be obtained generically via *complexity leveraging* [BB04a]: the reduction simply guesses beforehand which challenge value the adversary will query. This leads to a security loss that is exponential in the input length, which must be compensated by increasing the parameters of the scheme.

Together with Konstantinov, Pietrzak and Rao [FKPR14], we recently showed that any *simple* reduction (that is, one which runs an adversary once without rewinding) from pseudorandomness of the Boneh-Waters constrained PRF to a non-interactive hardness assumption must incur a security loss that is exponential in the input length. Since constrained VRFs imply constrained PRFs, this also holds for our construction, meaning that our proofs using complexity leveraging are in some sense optimal.

Related Work. VRFs have been constructed in bilinear groups by Lysyanskaya [Lys02] and Dodis [Dod03]. Based on Boneh-Boyen signatures [BB04b], Dodis and Yampolskiy [DY05] gave the first efficient scheme that is secure under a non-interactive assumption, but for small input spaces only. Hohenberger and Waters [HW10] proposed the first VRF for exponential-size domains without resorting to complexity leveraging or interactive assumptions. Boneh, Montgomery and

Raghunathan [BMR10] achieve a similar result basing their construction on the Dodis-Yampolskiy VRF. Abdalla, Catalano and Fiore [ACF13] show connections of VRFs to identity-based key encapsulation, and also present a VRF with large input spaces. Evidence why VRFs are hard to construct is given by Brakerski, Goldwasser, Rothblum and Vaikuntanathan [BGRV09], who show that there is no black-box construction from one-way permutations, and Fiore and Schröder [FS12], showing that there is also none from trapdoor permutations. Variants of VRFs include simulatable VRFs [CL07] (where CRSs are allowed) and weak VRFs [BGRV09].

The concept of restricting keys for PRFs to subsets of their domains was concurrently introduced as constrained PRFs by Boneh and Waters [BW13], as delegatable PRFs by Kiayias et al. [KPTZ13], and as functional PRFs by Boyle et al. [BGI14]. The latter mention functional VRFs as an open problem.

An analogous notion for digital signatures, namely deriving signing keys that can only sign subsets of the message space was concurrently introduced by Boyle et al. [BGI14] as functional signatures and by Bellare and the author as policy-based signatures [BF14]. Since VRFs satisfy the definition of digital signatures, constrained VRFs immediately yield policy-based signatures (PBS) for the same classes of policies describing the constrained input (message) space. We note however that constraint-hiding constrained VRFs, which we construct in this paper, cannot satisfy the stronger of the two security definitions for PBS proposed in [BF14], which requires that the policy (constraint) can be extracted from a signature.

2   Preliminaries

Notation. If S is a finite set then $|S|$ denotes its size and $s \leftarrow_{\$} S$ denotes picking an element uniformly from S and assigning it to s. For $n \in \mathbb{N}$ we let $[n] = \{1, \ldots, n\}$. We denote the security parameter by $\lambda \in \mathbb{N}$ and its unary representation by 1^{λ}. Algorithms are randomized unless otherwise indicated and "PT" stands for "polynomial-time" for both randomized and deterministic algorithms. We denote by $y := A(x_1, \ldots; \rho)$ the operation of running algorithm A on inputs $x_1, \ldots$ and coins ρ and assigning the output to y. By $y \leftarrow_{\$} A(x_1, \ldots)$, we denote the operation of letting $y := A(x_1, \ldots; \rho)$ with ρ chosen at random. We denote by $[A(x_1, \ldots)]$ the set of points that have positive probability of being output by A on inputs $x_1, \ldots$.

Multilinear Groups. The usefulness of groups with multilinear maps in which computing discrete logarithms is hard was first observed by Boneh and Silverberg [BS02]. It was only recently that candidates for leveled multilinear forms were proposed by Garg, Gentry and Halevi [GGH13a] and then by Coron, Lepoint and Tibouchi [CLT13]. Although these constructions implement *graded encodings*, which differ from multilinear groups, we present our results in the language of multilinear groups. These can then be transferred in a straightforward manner to graded encodings, as we show in the full version [Fuc14].

Leveled multilinear groups are generated by a group generator $\mathcal{G}$, which takes as input the security parameter 1^λ and $\kappa \in \mathbb{N}$, which determines the number of levels. $\mathcal{G}(1^\lambda, \kappa)$ outputs a sequence of groups $\mathbb{G} = (\mathbb{G}_1, \ldots, \mathbb{G}_\kappa)$ of prime order $p > 2^\lambda$. We assume that the description of each group contains a canonical generator g_i. For all $i, j \geq 1$ with $i+j \leq \kappa$, there exists a bilinear map $e_{i,j} : \mathbb{G}_i \times \mathbb{G}_j \to \mathbb{G}_{i+j}$, which satisfies:

$$\forall a, b \in \mathbb{Z}_p : e_{i,j}(g_i^a, g_j^b) = (g_{i+j})^{a \cdot b} .$$

(We omit the indices i, j of the maps if they can be deduced from the context.) The only hardness assumption we will make is the following:

Assumption 1. *The κ-Multilinear Decisional Diffie-Hellman (κ-MDDH) assumption states that, given $(\mathbb{G}_1 \ldots, \mathbb{G}_\kappa)$ obtained by running $\mathcal{G}(1^\lambda, \kappa)$ and $g = g_1, g^{c_1}, \ldots, g^{c_{\kappa+1}}$ for $c_1, \ldots, c_{\kappa+1} \leftarrow_\$ \mathbb{Z}_p$, it is hard to distinguish $g_\kappa^{\prod_{j \in [\kappa+1]} c_j} \in \mathbb{G}_\kappa$ from a random group element in $\mathbb{G}_\kappa$.*

Circuits. Our treatment of circuits follows that by Boneh and Waters [BW13], who adapt the model of Bellare et al. [BHR12]. They consider boolean circuits with a single output gate and require that circuits are *layered* (where a gate at level j receives its inputs from wires at level $j - 1$) and *monotonic* in that they only contain AND and OR gates. This is without loss of generality, since an arbitrary circuit can be transformed into a layered monotonic circuit of polynomially related size.

Definition 1. *A circuit is a 5-tuple $f = (n, q, A, B, \mathtt{GateType})$, where n is the number of inputs and q is the number of gates. Wires are associated with the set $[n + q] = \{1, \ldots, n + q\}$, where $\{1, \ldots, n\}$ are the input wires and $n + q$ is the output wire. Gates are labeled by the same index as their outgoing wire, we thus define $\mathtt{Gates} := \{n + 1, \ldots, n + q\}$.*

The function $A \colon \mathtt{Gates} \to [n + q]$ maps a gate w to its first incoming wire $A(w)$ and $B \colon \mathtt{Gates} \to [n + q]$ maps a gate w to its second incoming wire $B(w)$. We require $w > B(w) > A(w)$. The function $\mathtt{GateType} \colon \mathtt{Gates} \to \{\mathrm{AND}, \mathrm{OR}\}$ specifies whether a gate is an AND or an OR gate.

The function $\mathtt{depth}(w)$ maps a wire to the length of the shortest path to an input wire plus 1; in particular for $w \in [n]$ we have $\mathtt{depth}(w) = 1$. Moreover, a circuit is layered if for all $w \in \mathtt{Gates} : \mathtt{depth}(A(w)) = \mathtt{depth}(B(w)) = \mathtt{depth}(w) - 1$. We let $f(x)$ denote the evaluation of the circuit f on input $x \in \{0, 1\}^n$ and let $f_w(x)$ denote the value of wire w of the circuit on input x.

3   Constrained Verifiable Random Functions

We extend the definition of constrained pseudorandom functions (PRF), defined by Boneh and Waters [BW13] to constrained verifiable random functions (VRF). A constrained PRF allows one to evaluate a keyed function $F \colon \mathcal{K} \times \mathcal{X} \to \mathcal{Y}$ and defines an algorithm that given a key $k \in \mathcal{K}$ and a set $S \subseteq \mathcal{X}$ derives a key k_S

with which one can only evaluate F on points $x \in S$. It is set up w.r.t. a set system $\mathcal{S} \subseteq 2^{\mathcal{X}}$, defining the sets for which constrained keys can be derived.

For VRFs, in addition to a (secret) key, the setup algorithm outputs a public key pk. Given a constrained secret key sk_S derived from sk for a set $S \in \mathcal{S}$ and an input $x \in S$, the algorithm Prove computes the value $y = F(sk, x)$ (like the algorithm eval in [BW13]). It moreover outputs a proof π for the fact that $F(sk, x) = y$, which can be verified w.r.t. pk via an algorithm Verify.

A constrained VRF should satisfy the following properties: *Provability* ensures completeness of the scheme: running Prove on a constrained key outputs the correct function value and a proof that passes verification. *Uniqueness* guarantees soundness of the proofs: for any (possibly maliciously computed) value pk and every $x \in \mathcal{X}$ there exists at most one $y \in \mathcal{Y}$ for which $\mathsf{Verify}(pk, x, y, \pi) = 1$ for some π. Compared to PRFs, *pseudorandomness* should also hold against adversaries that obtain the public key and proofs for input points in addition to function values and constrained keys of their choice.

Finally, we consider an additional privacy or anonymity notion, which ensures that proofs do not reveal anything about the constrained key used to compute them: proofs computed with a constrained key should be distributed like proofs computed with the actual secret key. Note that this notion would not be meaningful for constrained PRFs or (standard) VRFs: a constrained key for a PRF is only used to evaluate F, so by definition, different constrained keys yield the same output; and for standard VRFs all proofs are computed with the same key.

Definition. Let $F \colon \mathcal{K} \times \mathcal{X} \to \mathcal{Y}$ be a function computable in polynomial time, where $\mathcal{K}$ is the key space, $\mathcal{X}$ is the domain and $\mathcal{Y}$ the range (which may all be parametrized by the security parameter λ). F is said to be a *constrained verifiable random function* w.r.t. a set system $\mathcal{S} \subseteq 2^{\mathcal{X}}$ if there exists a *constrained-key space* $\mathcal{K}'$, a *proof space* $\mathcal{P}$ and PT algorithms Setup, Constrain, Prove and Verify:

- Setup(1^{λ}) outputs a pair of keys (pk, sk).
- Constrain(sk, S), on input a secret key and a set $S \in \mathcal{S}$, outputs a constrained key $sk_S \in \mathcal{K}'$.
- Prove(sk_S, x) outputs a pair $(y, \pi) \in \mathcal{Y} \times \mathcal{P} \cup \{(\bot, \bot)\}$ of a function value and a proof.
- Verify(pk, x, y, π) verifies that $y = F(sk, x)$ using proof π, outputting a value in $\{0, 1\}$.

We require the following properties:

Provability. For all $\lambda \in \mathbb{N}$, all $(pk, sk) \in [\mathsf{Setup}(1^{\lambda})]$, all $S \in \mathcal{S}$, all $sk_S \in [\mathsf{Constrain}(sk, S)]$, all $x \in \mathcal{X}$ and $(y, \pi) \in [\mathsf{Prove}(sk_S, x)]$ it holds that:

- If $x \in S$ then $y = F(sk, x)$ and $\mathsf{Verify}(pk, x, y, \pi) = 1$
- If $x \notin S$ then $(y, \pi) = (\bot, \bot)$

Uniqueness. For all $\lambda \in \mathbb{N}$, all pk, all $x \in \mathcal{X}$, $y_0, y_1 \in \mathcal{Y}$ and $\pi_0, \pi_1 \in \mathcal{P}$ one of the following holds:

- $y_0 = y_1$,
- Verify$(pk, x, y_0, \pi_0) = 0$, or
- Verify$(pk, x, y_1, \pi_1) = 0$,

that is, for every x there is at most one value y for which there exists a proof that $F(sk, x) = y$.

Constraint-Hiding. This notion ensures that the proof does not reveal which key was used to create it. In particular, we require that there exist a PT algorithm $P \colon \mathcal{K} \times \mathcal{X} \to \mathcal{P}$, such that for all $\lambda \in \mathbb{N}$, all $(pk, sk) \in [\mathsf{Setup}(1^\lambda)]$, all $S \in \mathcal{S}$, all $sk_S \in [\mathsf{Constrain}(sk, S)]$ and all $x \in S$ the following holds: the second output, π, of $\mathsf{Prove}(sk_S, x)$ and the output of $P(sk, x)$ are distributed identically.

Pseudorandomness. Consider the following experiment $\mathbf{Exp}_b^{\mathrm{pr}}(\lambda)$ for $\lambda \in \mathbb{N}$ and $b \in \{0, 1\}$:

- Generate $(pk, sk) \leftarrow_{\$} \mathsf{Setup}(1^\lambda)$.
- Initialize sets C and V to $\emptyset$, where V will contain the points the adversary can evaluate and C records the points at which the adversary queried a challenge. Moreover, initialize an empty list R indexed by the set $\mathcal{X}$, used to store random values.
- Run the adversary on pk and provide the following oracles:
  CONSTRAIN: On input $S \in \mathcal{S}$, if $S \cap C = \emptyset$, return $sk_S \leftarrow_{\$} \mathsf{Constrain}(sk, S)$ and set $V := V \cup S$; else return $\bot$.
  PROVE: Given $x \in \mathcal{X}$, if $x \notin C$, return $F((sk, x), P(sk, x))$ and set $V := V \cup \{x\}$; else return $\bot$.
  CHALLENGE: On input $x \in \mathcal{X}$, if $x \in V$ then return $\bot$. Else set $C := C \cup \{x\}$ and do the following. If $b = 0$ then return $F(sk, x)$; if $b = 1$ then return a consistent random value from $\mathcal{Y}$, that is, return $R[x]$ if $x \in C$ and otherwise choose $y \leftarrow_{\$} \mathcal{Y}$, set $R[x] := y$ and return y.
- Let $b' \in \{0, 1\}$ be the adversary's final output, which we define as the output of the experiment.

A constrained VRF is *pseudorandom* if the function $\big| \Pr[\mathbf{Exp}_1^{\mathrm{pr}}(\lambda) = 1] - \Pr[\mathbf{Exp}_0^{\mathrm{pr}}(\lambda) = 1] \big|$ is negligible in λ for all PT adversaries $\mathcal{A}$.

Note that by the constraint-hiding property an oracle to obtain Prove evaluations under constrained keys unknown to the adversary would be redundant. In our security proofs we will only allow the adversary to query its challenge oracle once. This restricted notion however implies the notion defined above via a standard hybrid argument.

4   Bit-Fixing VRF

In our first construction constrained keys can be derived for any "bit-fixing" set. Such a set is defined by a value $\mathbf{v} \in \{0, 1, ?\}^n$ as the set of all $x \in \{0, 1\}^n$ that match $\mathbf{v}$ at all positions where $\mathbf{v}$ is different from '?':

$$S_\mathbf{v} := \big\{ x \in \{0, 1\}^n \mid \forall i \in [n] : x_i = \mathbf{v}_i \vee \mathbf{v}_i = ? \big\}$$

The set system for our constrained VRF is then defined as $\mathcal{S} := \{S_v \subseteq \{0,1\}^n \mid v \in \{0,1,?\}^n\}$.

We show how to add verifiability to the bit-fixing PRF by Boneh and Waters [BW13], which has domain $\mathcal{X} = \{0,1\}^n$ and where keys can be derived for S_v for every $v \in \{0,1,?\}^n$. As discussed in the introduction, the idea is to use one extra level of the group hierarchy for verification: the element that was the PRF value now serves as proof and the VRF value will live one group level above. Verification is done using the pairings to check consistency. For their bit-fixing PRF, Boneh and Waters define

$$F_{\mathrm{PRF}} : \mathcal{K} \times \{0,1\}^n \to \mathbb{G}_{n+1}$$

$$((\alpha, \{d_{i,\beta}\}_{i\in[n], \beta\in\{0,1\}}), x) \mapsto (g_{n+1})^{\alpha \prod_{i\in[n]} d_{i,x_i}}$$

In [Fuc14] we show that $n-1$ group levels suffice when one defines the PRF value as $F'_{\mathrm{PRF}}(sk, x) = (g_{n-1})^{\prod_{i\in[n]} d_{i,x_i}}$. We use this value as the proof in our VRF construction and the same constrained keys for both the modified PRF and the VRF. In order to provide verifiability, we add back one level; the last group in our hierarchy is thus $\mathbb{G}_n$, which is one level below the one of the Boneh-Waters PRF.[1]

4.1   Construction

Setup($1^\lambda, 1^n$): On input the security parameter λ and the input length n, the setup runs $\mathcal{G}(1^\lambda, n)$ to compute a sequence of groups $\mathbb{G} = (\mathbb{G}_1, \ldots, \mathbb{G}_n)$ of prime order p, with generators $g_1, \ldots, g_n$, of which we let $g := g_1$. It chooses $\gamma \leftarrow_\$ \mathbb{Z}_p$ and $(d_{1,0}, d_{1,1}), \ldots, (d_{n,0}, d_{n,1}) \leftarrow_\$ \mathbb{Z}_p^2$ uniformly at random and sets $C := g^\gamma$ and $D_{i,\beta} := g^{d_{i,\beta}}$ for $i \in [n]$ and $\beta \in \{0,1\}$. The VRF public and secret key are defined as

$$pk := \big(\mathbb{G} = (\mathbb{G}_1, \ldots, \mathbb{G}_n), C, \{D_{i,\beta}\}_{i\in[n], \beta\in\{0,1\}}\big)$$

$$sk := \big(pk, \gamma, \{d_{i,\beta}\}_{i\in[n], \beta\in\{0,1\}}\big)$$

The domain is $\mathcal{X} = \{0,1\}^n$, the range of the function is $\mathcal{Y} = \mathbb{G}_n$ and proofs are in $\mathbb{G}_{n-1}$. The function value and the proof for input $x = (x_1, \ldots, x_n) \in \{0,1\}^n$ are defined as

$$F(sk, x) := g_n^{\gamma \prod_{i\in[n]} d_{i,x_i}} \qquad\qquad P(sk, x) := (g_{n-1})^{\prod_{i\in[n]} d_{i,x_i}}$$

Verify(pk, x, y, π): To verify a tuple $(x, y, \pi) \in \{0,1\}^n \times \mathbb{G}_n \times \mathbb{G}_{n-1}$ w.r.t. public key $pk = (\mathbb{G}, C, \{D_{i,\beta}\})$, compute $D(x) := g_n^{\prod_{i\in[n]} d_{i,x_i}}$ by applying the bilinear maps to $(D_{1,x_1}, \ldots, D_{n,x_n})$ and output 1 if the following equations are satisfied:

$$e(g, \pi) = D(x) \qquad\qquad e(C, \pi) = y$$

---

[1] If we wanted a VRF with the same function values as the Boneh-Waters PRF, it would suffice to set up $\kappa = n+1$ group levels, lift the domain of F from $\mathbb{G}_n$ to $\mathbb{G}_{n+1}$, that of P from $\mathbb{G}_{n-1}$ to $\mathbb{G}_n$, and define the public-key element $C := g_2^\gamma$ (instead of g^γ). The secret key element γ would then correspond to α in [BW13].

Constrain(sk, $\mathbf{v}$): Note that from a proof $P(sk, x)$, by pairing it with the public-key element C, one can compute $F(sk, x) = e(C, P(sk, x))$. It suffices thus that a constrained key lets us construct $P(sk, x)$.

The algorithm takes as input sk and a vector $\mathbf{v} \in \{0, 1, ?\}^n$ describing the constrained domain $S_{\mathbf{v}} := \{x \in \{0,1\}^n \mid \forall i \in [n] : x_i = \mathbf{v}_i \vee \mathbf{v}_i = ?\}$. Let $V := \{i \in [n] \mid \mathbf{v}_i \neq ?\}$ be the set of indices for which the input bit is fixed to 0 or 1. Return $sk_{\mathbf{v}} := (pk, k_{\mathbf{v}})$, with $k_{\mathbf{v}}$ defined as follows:

- If $|V| > 1$ then compute $k_{\mathbf{v}} := (g_{|V|-1})^{\prod_{i \in V} d_{i, \mathbf{v}_i}}$.
- If $V = \{j\}$ then set $k_{\mathbf{v}} := d_{j, \mathbf{v}_j}$.

(If $V = \emptyset$ then return sk, from which Prove(sk, x) simply computes $F(sk, x)$ and $P(sk, x)$.)

Prove($sk_{\mathbf{v}}$, x): Again let $V := \{i \in [n] \mid \mathbf{v}_i \neq ?\}$ and let $\overline{V} := \{i \in [n] \mid \mathbf{v}_i = ?\}$ be its complement. If $x_i \neq \mathbf{v}_i$ for some $i \in V$ then return $(\bot, \bot)$; else apply the bilinear maps to $\{D_{i,x_i}\}_{i \in \overline{V}}$ to compute

$$D_{\overline{V}}(x) := (g_{|\overline{V}|})^{\prod_{i \in \overline{V}} d_{i, x_i}}.$$

- If $|V| > 1$, set $P(sk, x) := e(D_{\overline{V}}(x), k_{\mathbf{v}})$
$$= e\big((g_{|\overline{V}|})^{\prod_{i \in \overline{V}} d_{i, x_i}}, (g_{|V|-1})^{\prod_{i \in V} d_{i, \mathbf{v}_i}}\big) = (g_{n-1})^{\prod_{i \in [n]} d_{i, x_i}}.$$
- If $V = \{j\}$, set $P(sk, x) := D_{\overline{V}}(x)^{k_{\mathbf{v}}}$
$$= \big((g_{|\overline{V}|})^{\prod_{i \in \overline{V}} d_{i, x_i}}\big)^{d_{j, \mathbf{v}_j}} = (g_{n-1})^{\prod_{i \in [n]} d_{i, x_i}}.$$

Finally, compute $e\big(C, P(sk, x)\big) = e\big(g^{\gamma}, (g_{n-1})^{\prod_{i \in [n]} d_{i, x_i}}\big) = F(sk, x)$.

4.2 Properties

Provability. When $(pk = (\mathbb{G}, C, \{D_{i, \beta}\}), sk) \leftarrow_{\$} \mathsf{Setup}(1^{\lambda})$ then from the definition of F and P it follows immediately that for all $x \in \{0,1\}^n$: $e(g, P(sk, x)) = g_n^{\prod_{i \in [n]} d_{i, x_i}} = D(x)$ and $e(C, P(sk, x)) = g_n^{\gamma \prod_{i \in [n]} d_{i, x_i}} = F(sk, x)$. We have thus $\mathsf{Verify}(pk, x, F(sk, x), P(sk, x)) = 1$.

Moreover, given a constrained key $sk_{\mathbf{v}}$ derived for a vector $\mathbf{v} \in \{0, 1, ?\}^n$ and $x \in \{0,1\}^n$ with $x_i = \mathbf{v}_i$ or $\mathbf{v}_i = ?$ for all i, it follows by inspection that Prove($sk_{\mathbf{v}}$, x) computes $(F(sk, x), P(sk, x))$, which we showed satisfy the verification equations.

Uniqueness. Consider a public key $pk = (\mathbb{G}, C, \{D_{i, \beta}\}_{i \in [n], \beta \in \{0,1\}})$, with $C \in \mathbb{G}_1$ and $D_{i, \beta} \in \mathbb{G}_1$, a value $x \in \{0,1\}^n$ and values $(y_0, \pi_0), (y_1, \pi_1) \in \mathbb{G}_n \times \mathbb{G}_{n-1}$ that satisfy $\mathsf{Verify}(pk, x, y_\beta, \pi_\beta) = 1$, for $\beta \in \{0,1\}$. It suffices to show that $y_0 = y_1$.

Let $\gamma, d_{i, \beta} \in \mathbb{Z}_p$ be such that $C = g^{\gamma}$ and $D_{i, \beta} = g^{d_{i, \beta}}$ for all i, β. The fist verification equation yields $e(g, \pi_\beta) = g_n^{\prod_{i \in [n]} d_{i, x_i}}$, which by the properties of the bilinear map e implies that $\pi_\beta = (g_{n-1})^{\prod_{i \in [n]} d_{i, x_i}}$ for $\beta \in \{0,1\}$. The second equation yields $y_\beta = e(C, \pi_\beta) = e\big(g^{\gamma}, (g_{n-1})^{\prod_{i \in [n]} d_{i, x_i}}\big)$ for both $\beta \in \{0,1\}$, which implies $y_0 = g_n^{\gamma \prod_{i \in [n]} d_{i, x_i}} = y_1$.

Constraint-Hiding. The proof algorithm P maps $sk = (\gamma, \{d_{i,\beta}\}_{i \in [n], \beta \in \{0,1\}})$ and $x \in \{0,1\}^n$ to $P(sk, x) := (g_{n-1})^{\prod_{i \in [n]} d_{i,x_i}}$. Since by provability, this is precisely the value that $\mathsf{Prove}(sk_\mathbf{v}, x)$ outputs for any constraint $\mathbf{v}$ and any x satisfying $\mathbf{v}$, the constraint-hiding property follows immediately.

4.3 Proof of Pseudorandomness

Theorem 1. *If there exists a PT adversary $\mathcal{A}$ that makes one challenge query and breaks pseudorandomness of the above n-bit-input bit-fixing VRF with advantage $\epsilon(\lambda)$ then there exists a PT algorithm $\mathcal{B}$ that breaks the n-Multilinear Decisional Diffie-Hellman assumption with advantage $2^{-n} \cdot \epsilon(\lambda)$.*

Proof. Without loss of generality, we assume that when x^* is $\mathcal{A}$'s challenge query then $\mathcal{A}$ never queries constrained keys that could evaluate x^*, nor its PROVE oracle on x^*. We construct $\mathcal{B}$, which receives an n-MDDH challenge consisting of a group-sequence description $\mathbb{G}$ and elements $g = g_1, g^{c_1}, \ldots, g^{c_{n+1}}$ and T, which is either $g_n^{\prod_{i \in [n+1]} c_j}$ or a random element from $\mathbb{G}_n$. $\mathcal{B}$ picks a random value $x^* \leftarrow_\$ \{0,1\}^n$, which it hopes will be $\mathcal{A}$'s challenge query, and $z_1, \ldots, z_n \leftarrow_\$ \mathbb{Z}_p$ and sets

$$D_{i,\beta} := \begin{cases} g^{c_i} & \text{if } x_i^* = \beta \\ g^{z_i} & \text{if } x_i^* \neq \beta \end{cases} \qquad \text{for } i \in [n],\ \beta \in \{0,1\},$$

which implicitly defines $d_{i,x_i^*} := c_i$ and $d_{i,\overline{x}_i^*} := z_i$ (with $\overline{x}_i^*$ denoting $1 - x_i^*$). It also defines $\gamma := c_{n+1}$ by setting $C := g^{c_{n+1}}$. $\mathcal{B}$ then runs $\mathcal{A}$ on input the public key $(\mathbb{G}, C, \{D_{i,\beta}\}_{i \in [n], \beta \in \{0,1\}})$, which is distributed as in the real scheme.

Constrain Queries. Suppose $\mathcal{A}$ queries a secret key for $\mathbf{v} \in \{0, 1, ?\}^n$. Let $V := \{i \in [n] \mid \mathbf{v}_i \neq ?\}$ be the set of indices that $\mathbf{v}$ fixes. $\mathcal{B}$ selects $j \in V$ such that $\mathbf{v}_j \neq x_j^*$. If no such j exists then the key could be used to evaluate $F(sk, x^*)$, meaning $\mathcal{B}$'s guess was wrong, as we assumed $\mathcal{A}$ would not make such a query. In this case $\mathcal{B}$ aborts outputting a random guess $b' \leftarrow_\$ \{0,1\}$.

If $|V| = 1$ then $V = \{j\}$, thus $\mathcal{B}$ knows z_j with $D_{j,\mathbf{v}_j} = D_{j,\overline{x}_j^*} = g^{z_j}$ and sets $k_\mathbf{v} := z_j$. If $|V| > 1$ then by repeatedly applying the bilinear maps to the values $\{D_{i,\mathbf{v}_i}\}_{i \in V \setminus \{j\}}$, it computes $(g_{|V|-1})^{\prod_{i \in V \setminus \{j\}} d_{i,\mathbf{v}_i}}$ and raises this value to $z_j = d_{j,\mathbf{v}_j}$ to compute $k_\mathbf{v} := (g_{|V|-1})^{\prod_{i \in V} d_{i,\mathbf{v}_i}}$. $\mathcal{B}$ answers the query with $(pk, k_\mathbf{v})$.

Prove Queries. Since $P(sk, x)$ is identical to a key for $\mathbf{v} = x$, this value can be computed as for the constrained-key query above. $F(sk, x)$ is computed by pairing it with C.

Challenge Query. If $\mathcal{A}$'s challenge query is different from x^* then $\mathcal{B}$ aborts outputting a random guess $b' \leftarrow_\$ \{0,1\}$. Otherwise, it outputs T as a response to the query. If $T = g_n^{\prod_{i \in [n+1]} c_j}$ then $T = g_n^{\gamma \prod_{i \in [n]} d_{i,x_i^*}} = F(sk, x^*)$. When $\mathcal{A}$ outputs a guess b' then $\mathcal{B}$, if it has not aborted, outputs the same guess b'.

Success Probability. We analyze the probability that $\mathcal{B}$ wins the MDDH game. Let abort denote the event that $\mathcal{B}$ aborts during the simulation. $\mathcal{B}$ aborts if and only if $\mathcal{A}$ queries its CHALLENGE oracle on a value different from x^* (as $\mathcal{A}$ does not make any "illegal" queries, $\mathcal{B}$ only aborts during CONSTRAIN and PROVE queries if its guess of x^* was wrong). We therefore have $\Pr[\mathsf{abort}] = 1 - 2^{-n}$. Moreover, if $\mathcal{B}$ aborts then it outputs a random bit, thus yielding $\Pr[\mathcal{B} \text{ wins} \,|\, \mathsf{abort}] = \frac{1}{2}$. If $\mathcal{B}$ does not abort then it wins with the same probability as $\mathcal{A}$ (since $\mathcal{A}$'s success is independent of $\mathcal{B}$'s guess of x^*), whose advantage is $\epsilon(\lambda)$, thus $\Pr[\mathcal{B} \text{ wins} \,|\, \overline{\mathsf{abort}}] = \frac{1}{2} + \epsilon(\lambda)$. Together, we have

$$\Pr[\mathcal{B} \text{ wins}] = \Pr[\mathcal{B} \text{ wins} \,|\, \mathsf{abort}] \cdot \Pr[\mathsf{abort}] + \Pr[\mathcal{B} \text{ wins} \,|\, \overline{\mathsf{abort}}] \cdot \Pr[\overline{\mathsf{abort}}]$$
$$= \tfrac{1}{2} \cdot (1 - 2^{-n}) + \left(\tfrac{1}{2} + \epsilon(\lambda)\right) \cdot 2^{-n} \;=\; \tfrac{1}{2} + 2^{-n} \cdot \epsilon(\lambda) \ ,$$

which shows that $\mathcal{B}$'s advantage in breaking n-MDDH is $\epsilon'(\lambda) = 2^{-n} \cdot \epsilon(\lambda)$. □

5   Circuit-Constrained VRF

Consider a polynomial-size circuit f as in Definition 1. Our second VRF construction allows us to derive a constrained key sk_f enabling function evaluations and proof computations for exactly those values x, for which $f(x) = 1$. Letting $\mathcal{C}$ be the set of all polynomial-size circuits, we have

$$\mathcal{S} := \{S_f \subseteq \{0,1\}^n \,|\, f \in \mathcal{C}\} \ , \qquad \text{with } \; S_f := \{x \in \{0,1\}^n \,|\, f(x) = 1\} \ .$$

Our circuit-constrained VRF is derived from the Boneh-Waters PRF [BW13] for the same set system. Their PRF values are in $\mathbb{G}_\kappa$ with $\kappa = n + \ell$, where ℓ is the maximum depth of the supported circuits. In [Fuc14] we show that their PRF construction can be modified and defined over a group sequence with $\kappa = n + \ell - 1$, by shifting the PRF value and elements of the constrained key down by one level. Pseudorandomness then follows from $(n + \ell - 1)$-MDDH.

For our constrained VRF we define the proofs as the values of the modified PRF in $\mathbb{G}_{n+\ell-1}$ (so proofs can be constructed using the constrained keys of the modified PRF), then add back one level in the group hierarchy and define the function values in $\mathbb{G}_{n+\ell}$ as pairings of the proof with an additional public-key element g^γ. The Boneh-Waters PRF is defined as $F_{\mathrm{PRF}}(k, x) := g_\kappa^{\alpha' \, \prod_{i \in [n]} d_{i,x_i}}$, where the key k consists of α' and the elements $d_{i,\beta}$. Our VRF values can be seen as the same but with α' split into α and γ, thus $F(sk, x) := g_\kappa^{\alpha \cdot \gamma \, \prod_{i \in [n]} d_{i,x_i}}$. The proof is the same value without γ and lives one level below the function value: $P(sk, x) := (g_{\kappa-1})^{\alpha \, \prod_{i \in [n]} d_{i,x_i}}$.

5.1   Construction

Setup($1^\lambda, 1^n, 1^\ell$): On input the security parameter λ, the bit length n and the maximum depth ℓ of the circuits, Setup does the following: Run $\mathcal{G}(1^\lambda, \kappa)$ with $\kappa := n + \ell$ to obtain a sequence of groups $\mathbb{G} = (\mathbb{G}_1, \ldots, \mathbb{G}_\kappa)$ of prime order p, with generators $g = g_1, \ldots, g_\kappa$. Choose secret-key values $\alpha, \gamma \leftarrow\!\!\!{\scriptstyle\$}\; \mathbb{Z}_p$ and $(d_{1,0}, d_{1,1}), \ldots, (d_{n,0}, d_{n,1}) \leftarrow\!\!\!{\scriptstyle\$}\; \mathbb{Z}_p^2$ and set $A := g_\ell^\alpha$, $C := g^\gamma$ and $D_{i,\beta} := g^{d_{i,\beta}}$ for

$i \in [n]$ and $\beta \in \{0,1\}$. The VRF public key pk is defined as the group sequence $\mathbb{G}$ and $\left(A, C, \{D_{i,\beta}\}_{i\in[n], \beta\in\{0,1\}}\right)$. The secret key sk consists of the public key as well as $\left(\alpha, \gamma, \{d_{i,\beta}\}_{i\in[n], \beta\in\{0,1\}}\right)$.

We define the domain as $\mathcal{X} := \{0,1\}^n$, the range as $\mathcal{Y} := \mathbb{G}_\kappa$, and the proof space as $\mathcal{P} := \mathbb{G}_{\kappa-1}$. On input $x = (x_1, \ldots, x_n) \in \mathcal{X}$, the function value and the proof are defined as

$$F(sk, x) := g_\kappa^{\alpha \cdot \gamma \prod_{i\in[n]} d_{i,x_i}} \qquad P(sk, x) := (g_{\kappa-1})^{\alpha \prod_{i\in[n]} d_{i,x_i}}$$

Verify(pk, x, y, π): Given a public key $pk = (\mathbb{G}, A, C, \{D_{i,\beta}\}_{i,\beta})$ and $(x, y, \pi) \in \{0,1\}^n \times \mathbb{G}_\kappa \times \mathbb{G}_{\kappa-1}$, first compute $D(x) := g_n^{\prod_{i\in[n]} d_{i,x_i}}$ by applying the bilinear maps to $(D_{1,x_1}, \ldots, D_{n,x_n})$ and return 1 if the following equations hold (and return 0 otherwise):

$$e(g, \pi) = e(A, D) \qquad e(C, \pi) = y$$

Constrain($sk, f = (n, q, A, B, \texttt{GateType})$): On input the secret key and a circuit description f, with n input wires, q gates (labeled from $n+1$ to $n+q$), and the wire $n+q$ designated as output wire, the constrain algorithm does the following:

Choose $r_1, \ldots, r_{n+q-1} \leftarrow_{\$} \mathbb{Z}_p$ and set $r_{n+q} := \alpha$. For every wire w generate a key component K_w, whose structure depends on the type of the wire: input wire, OR gate, or AND gate.

Input wire: If $w \in [n]$, it corresponds to the w-th input and the key component is

$$K_w := g^{r_w \cdot d_{w,1}} .$$

OR gate: If $w \in \texttt{Gates}$ with $\texttt{GateType}(w) = \text{OR}$ and $\texttt{depth}(w) = j$ then choose $a_w, b_w \leftarrow_{\$} \mathbb{Z}_p$ and compute the following key components:

$$\begin{aligned} K_{w,1} &:= g^{a_w} & K_{w,3} &:= (g_{j-1})^{r_w - a_w \cdot r_{A(w)}} \\ K_{w,2} &:= g^{b_w} & K_{w,4} &:= (g_{j-1})^{r_w - b_w \cdot r_{B(w)}} \end{aligned}$$

AND gate: If $w \in \texttt{Gates}$ with $\texttt{GateType}(w) = \text{AND}$ and $\texttt{depth}(w) = j$ then choose $a_w, b_w \leftarrow_{\$} \mathbb{Z}_p$ and compute the following key components:

$$K_{w,1} := g^{a_w} \qquad K_{w,2} := g^{b_w} \qquad K_{w,3} := (g_{j-1})^{r_w - a_w \cdot r_{A(w)} - b_w \cdot r_{B(w)}}$$

The constrained key sk_f consists of these components for all $n+q$ wires together with the circuit description f and the public key pk.

Prove(sk_f, x): Given a constrained key sk_f for circuit $f = (n, q, A, B, \texttt{GateType})$ and input $x \in \{0,1\}^n$, if $f(x) = 0$, return $(\bot, \bot)$. Otherwise, evaluate the circuit level by level starting from the input wires. For every wire w that evaluates to 1, compute the value $P_w = (g_{n+j-1})^{r_w \prod_{i\in[n]} d_{i,x_i}}$, where $j = \texttt{depth}(w)$. Note that since $r_{n+q} = \alpha$, we have $P_{n+q} = P(sk, x)$, from which we can then compute $F(sk, x)$ by pairing it with C. For every wire we distinguish the following cases:

Input wire: For $w \in [n]$ we only consider those w for which $x_w = f_w(x) = 1$. Repeatedly apply the bilinear maps to the values $\{D_{i,x_i}\}_{i \neq w}$ to compute $(g_{n-1})^{\prod_{i \in [n] \setminus \{w\}} d_{i,x_i}}$ and pair it with $K_w = g^{r_w \cdot d_{w,1}}$ in order to obtain $P_w = g_n^{r_w \prod_{i \in [n]} d_{i,x_i}}$.

OR gate: Let $w \in$ Gates be such that $f_w(x) = 1$ and $\mathsf{GateType}(w) = \mathrm{OR}$ and let $j = \mathsf{depth}(w)$. Define $D(x) := g_n^{\prod_{i \in [n]} d_{i,x_i}}$, which can be computed from the set $\{D_{i,x_i}\}_{i \in [n]}$. If $f_{A(w)}(x) = 1$ then compute:

$$
\begin{aligned}
e(P_{A(w)}, K_{w,1}) \cdot e(K_{w,3}, D(x)) &= e\big((g_{n+j-2})^{r_{A(w)} \prod_i d_{i,x_i}}, g^{a_w}\big) \\
&\cdot e\big((g_{j-1})^{r_w - a_w \cdot r_{A(w)}}, g_n^{\prod_i d_{i,x_i}}\big) = (g_{j+n-1})^{r_w \prod_i d_{i,x_i}} = P_w .
\end{aligned}
$$

Otherwise, we must have $f_{B(w)}(x) = 1$, so compute:

$$
e(P_{B(w)}, K_{w,2}) \cdot e(K_{w,4}, D(x)) = (g_{j+n-1})^{r_w \prod_i d_{i,x_i}} = P_w .
$$

AND gate: Let $w \in$ Gates be such that $f_w(x) = 1$, $\mathsf{GateType}(w) = \mathrm{AND}$ and $\mathsf{depth}(w) = j$. We have $f_{A(w)} = f_{B(w)} = 1$ and with $D(x)$ as above we compute:

$$
\begin{aligned}
&e(P_{A(w)}, K_{w,1}) \cdot e(P_{B(w)}, K_{w,2}) \cdot e(K_{w,3}, D(x)) \\
&= e\big((g_{n+j-2})^{r_{A(w)} \prod_i d_{i,x_i}}, g^{a_w}\big) \cdot e\big((g_{n+j-2})^{r_{B(w)} \prod_i d_{i,x_i}}, g^{b_w}\big) \\
&\cdot e\big((g_{j-1})^{r_w - a_w \cdot r_{A(w)} - b_w \cdot r_{B(w)}}, g_n^{\prod_i d_{i,x_i}}\big) = (g_{j+n-1})^{r_w \prod_i d_{i,x_i}} = P_w .
\end{aligned}
$$

Evaluating level by level all wires w for which $f_w(x) = 1$, we arrive at $P_{n+q} = (g_{n+\ell-1})^{\alpha \prod_i d_{i,x_i}} = P(sk, x)$, from which we compute

$$
e(C, P(sk, x)) = e\big(g^{\gamma}, (g_{\kappa-1})^{\alpha \prod_i d_{i,x_i}}\big) = F(sk, x)
$$

and output $\big(F(sk, x), P(sk, x)\big)$.

5.2   Properties

Provability. When $\big(pk = (\mathbb{G}, A, C, \{D_{i,\beta}\}), sk\big) \leftarrow_\$ \mathsf{Setup}(1^\lambda, 1^n, 1^\ell)$ then from the definition of F and P it follows that for all $x \in \{0,1\}^n$: $e\big(g, P(sk, x)\big) = e\big(A, D(x)\big)$ and $e\big(C, P(sk, x)\big) = F(sk, x)$.

Moreover, given a constrained key sk_f derived from sk for a depth-ℓ circuit f and $x \in \{0,1\}^n$ with $f(x) = 1$, we see that when running the Prove algorithm, the value computed for every depth-j gate w for which $f_w(x) = 1$ is $P_w = (g_{n+j-1})^{r_w \prod_{i \in [n]} d_{i,x_i}}$. Since the value r_{n+q} for the output gate was defined as $r_{n+q} := \alpha$, Prove outputs $(g_{n+\ell-1})^{\alpha \prod_{i \in [n]} d_{i,x_i}} = P(sk, x)$ and $e(C, P(sk, x)) = F(sk, x)$, which are the values that satisfy verification.

Uniqueness. Consider a public key pk that consists of $\mathbb{G} = (\mathbb{G}_1, \dots, \mathbb{G}_{n+\ell})$, $A \in \mathbb{G}_\ell$, $C \in \mathbb{G}_1$ and $\{D_{i,\beta}\}_{i \in [n], \beta \in \{0,1\}} \in \mathbb{G}_1^{2n}$, a value $x \in \{0,1\}^n$ and values

$(y_0, \pi_0), (y_1, \pi_1) \in \mathbb{G}_{n+\ell} \times \mathbb{G}_{n+\ell-1}$ that satisfy $\mathsf{Verify}(pk, x, y_\beta, \pi_\beta) = 1$, for $\beta \in \{0, 1\}$. It suffices to show that $y_0 = y_1$.

Let $\alpha, \gamma, d_{i,\beta} \in \mathbb{Z}_p$ be such that $A = g_\ell^\alpha$, $C = g^\gamma$ and $D_{i,\beta} = g^{d_{i,\beta}}$ for $i \in [n]$, $\beta \in \{0, 1\}$. The first verification equation is $e(g, \pi) = e(A, D(x)) = e\left(g_\ell^\alpha, g_n^{\prod_{i \in [n]} d_{i,x_i}}\right) = (g_{n+\ell})^{\alpha \prod_{i \in [n]} d_{i,x_i}}$, which can only be satisfied by $\pi = (g_{n+\ell-1})^{\alpha \prod_{i \in [n]} d_{i,x_i}}$. We thus have $\pi_0 = \pi_1 = \pi$.

The second verification equation is $y = e(C, \pi)$; so we have $y_0 = e(C, \pi_0) = e(C, \pi_1) = y_1$, which proves uniqueness.

Constraint-Hiding. A secret key $sk = \left(\alpha, \gamma, \{d_{i,\beta}\}_{i \in [n], \beta \in \{0,1\}}\right) \in \mathbb{Z}_p^{2n+2}$ and $x \in \{0, 1\}^n$ are mapped by to $P(sk, x) := (g_{n+\ell-1})^{\alpha \prod_{i \in [n]} d_{i,x_i}}$. Since by provability, this is precisely the value that $\mathsf{Prove}(sk_f, x)$ outputs for any $x \in \{0, 1\}^n$ and any key $sk_f \in [\mathsf{Constrain}(sk, f)]$ for any ℓ-level circuit f with $f(x) = 1$, the constraint-hiding property follows.

5.3   Proof of Pseudorandomness

Theorem 2. *If there exists a PT adversary $\mathcal{A}$ that makes one challenge query and breaks pseudorandomness of the above n-bit depth-ℓ circuit-constrained VRF with advantage $\epsilon(\lambda)$ then there exists a PT algorithm $\mathcal{B}$ that breaks the $(n + \ell)$-Multilinear Decisional Diffie-Hellman assumption with advantage $2^{-n} \cdot \epsilon(\lambda)$.*

Proof. The proof follows that of [BW13] closely. Consider a PT algorithm $\mathcal{A}$ that wins the pseudorandomness game with advantage $\epsilon(\lambda)$. Without loss of generality, we assume that $\mathcal{A}$ never queries a key for a circuit f with $f(x^*) = 1$ and never queries its PROVE oracle on x^* (where x^* is the value queried to CHALLENGE). We construct an algorithm $\mathcal{B}$ that uses $\mathcal{A}$ to break $(n+\ell)$-MDDH.

Setup. $\mathcal{B}$ receives a challenge consisting of a group sequence $\mathbb{G}$ and values $g = g_1, g^{c_1}, \ldots, g^{c_{n+\ell+1}}$ and T, where T is either $(g_{n+\ell})^{\prod_{i \in [n+\ell+1]} c_i}$ or a random group element in $\mathbb{G}_{n+\ell}$. Using the challenge, $\mathcal{B}$ sets up the keys as follows. It chooses $x^* \leftarrow_\$ \{0, 1\}^n$ and $z_1, \ldots, z_n \leftarrow_\$ \mathbb{Z}_p$ and sets

$$D_{i,\beta} := \begin{cases} g^{c_i} & \text{if } x_i^* = \beta \\ g^{z_i} & \text{if } x_i^* \neq \beta \end{cases} \qquad \text{for } i \in [n], \ \beta \in \{0, 1\},$$

Repeatedly applying the bilinear maps, it computes $A := g_\ell^{c_{n+1} \cdots c_{n+\ell}}$ and sets $C := g^{c_{n+\ell+1}}$. Note that this defines $d_{i,x_i^*} = c_i$ and $d_{i,\overline{x}_i^*} = z_i$ (where $\overline{x}_i^*$ denotes $1 - x_i^*$), as well as $\alpha = c_{n+1} \cdots c_{n+\ell}$ and $\gamma = c_{n+\ell+1}$, which is distributed as in the real scheme. The parameters are set up so that we have $F(sk, x^*) = (g_{n+\ell})^{\alpha \cdot \gamma \prod_{i \in [n]} d_{i,x_i^*}} = (g_{n+\ell})^{\prod_{i \in [n+\ell+1]} c_i}$. $\mathcal{B}$ runs $\mathcal{A}$ on input $pk = (\mathbb{G}, A, C, \{D_{i,\beta}\}_{i \in [n], \beta \in \{0,1\}})$.

Constrain Queries. Suppose $\mathcal{A}$ queries a private key for a circuit f. If $f(x^*) = 1$ then $\mathcal{B}$ aborts and outputs a guess $b' \leftarrow \{0, 1\}$. Otherwise, it must compute the key component K_w for every wire w of f. The simulation follows [BW13], who base their technique on [GGH+13c].

For the final gate $w = n + q$ we have $r_w = \alpha$ and elements of K_{n+q} contain $(g_{\ell-1})^\alpha = (g_{\ell-1})^{c_{n+1}\cdots c_{n+\ell}}$, which $\mathcal{B}$ cannot compute. Simulating this is thus the tricky part and is done as follows. In order to compute e.g. $K_{n+q,4} = (g_{\ell-1})^{\alpha - b_{n+q} \cdot r_{B(n+q)}}$ (if the last gate is an OR gate), $\mathcal{B}$ sets $b_{n+q} := c_{n+\ell}$ and $r_{B(n+q)} := c_{n+1} \cdots c_{n+\ell-1}$ (and adds some known randomness to each), so α cancels out and $\mathcal{B}$ can compute K_{n+q}. Now $r_{B(n+q)}$ in level $\ell - 1$ contains $c_{n+1} \cdots c_{n+\ell-1}$, which has one fewer challenge value. Applying the trick again, $\mathcal{B}$ chooses the randomness of $B(n+q)$'s parent gates in level $\ell-2$ as $c_{n+1} \cdots c_{n+\ell-2}$, and so on.

Note that since $f_{n+q}(x^*) = f(x^*) = 0$, if gate $n + q$ is an OR gate then both its parents must satisfy $f_{A(n+q)}(x^*) = f_{B(n+q)}(x^*) = 0$ and we need to embed challenge elements in both $r_{B(n+q)}$ and $r_{A(n+q)}$ to simulate K_{n+q}. On the other hand, for an AND gate w with $f_w(x^*) = 0$, only one of its parent gates must evaluate x^* to 0, and for the cancellation trick to work, it suffices to embed $c_{n+1} \cdots c_{n+\mathrm{depth}(w)-1}$ in the randomness of that parent.

For every gate w at level j for which $f_w(x^*) = 0$, we thus set $r_w := c_{n+1} \cdots c_{n+j}$ (plus some $\eta_w \leftarrow\!\!{}_\$ \mathbb{Z}_p$ to make r_w uniform). For the input wires we have $r_w := c_{n+1} + \eta_w$, for which we can simulate $K_w = g^{r_w \cdot d_{w,1}}$, since $d_{w,1} = z_w$ when $f_w(x^*) = x_w^* = 0$. Note that this does not work for wires and gates w with $f_w(x^*) = 1$, for which it however suffices to compute the key elements K_w honestly.

Formalizing the above, $\mathcal{B}$ answers a CONSTRAIN query for $f = (n, q, A, B, \mathtt{GateType})$ by computing K_w for every gate starting from the input wires:

Input wire: Suppose $w \in [n]$. If $x_w^* = 1$ then choose $r_w \leftarrow\!\!{}_\$ \mathbb{Z}_p$ and compute the key component

$$K_w := (D_{w,1})^{r_w} = g^{r_w \cdot d_{w,1}} \ .$$

If $x_w^* = 0$ (in which case $d_{w,1} = z_w$), we choose $\eta_w \leftarrow\!\!{}_\$ \mathbb{Z}_p$, implicitly set $r_w := c_{n+1} + \eta_w$ and compute

$$K_w := \left(g^{c_{n+1}} \cdot g^{\eta_w}\right)^{z_w} = g^{r_w \cdot d_{w,1}} \ .$$

OR gate: If $\mathtt{GateType}(w) = \mathrm{OR}$, we let $j = \mathrm{depth}(w)$ and again distinguish two cases. If $f_w(x^*) = 1$, choose $a_w, b_w, r_w \leftarrow\!\!{}_\$ \mathbb{Z}_p$ and set K_w as specified by Constrain:

$$K_{w,1} := g^{a_w} \qquad\qquad K_{w,3} := (g_{j-1})^{r_w - a_w \cdot r_{A(w)}}$$
$$K_{w,2} := g^{b_w} \qquad\qquad K_{w,4} := (g_{j-1})^{r_w - b_w \cdot r_{B(w)}}$$

(Even when $r_{A(w)} = c_{n+1} \cdots c_{n+j-1} + \eta_{A(w)}$, one can compute $(g_{j-1})^{r_{A(w)}}$ using the pairings.)

If $f_w(x^*) = 0$, $\mathcal{B}$ chooses $\psi_w, \phi_w, \eta_w \leftarrow\!\!{}_\$ \mathbb{Z}_p$ and implicitly sets $a_w := c_{n+j} + \psi_w$, $b_w := c_{n+j} + \phi_w$ and $r_w := c_{n+1} \cdots c_{n+j} + \eta_w$. Since $f_w(x^*) = 0$ implies $f_{A(w)}(x^*) = f_{B(w)}(x^*) = 0$, we have $r_{A(w)} = c_{n+1} \cdots c_{n+j-1} + \eta_{A(w)}$ and $r_{B(w)} = c_{n+1} \cdots c_{n+j-1} + \eta_{B(w)}$. This enables $\mathcal{B}$ to create the key components as follows:

$$K_{w,1} := g^{c_{n+j}} \cdot g^{\psi_w} \qquad\qquad K_{w,2} := g^{c_{n+j}} \cdot g^{\phi_w}$$

$$K_{w,3} := (g_{j-1})^{\eta_w - c_{n+j} \cdot \eta_{A(w)} - \psi_w(c_{n+1}\cdots c_{n+j-1} + \eta_{A(w)})}$$
$$= (g_{j-1})^{c_{n+1}\cdots c_{n+j} + \eta_w - (c_{n+j} + \psi_w) \cdot (c_{n+1}\cdots c_{n+j-1} + \eta_{A(w)})}$$
$$= (g_{j-1})^{r_w - a_w \cdot r_{A(w)}}$$

$$K_{w,4} := (g_{j-1})^{\eta_w - c_{n+j} \cdot \eta_{B(w)} - \phi_w(c_{n+1}\cdots c_{n+j-1} + \eta_{B(w)})} = (g_{j-1})^{r_w - b_w \cdot r_{B(w)}}$$

(Again, $\mathcal{B}$ can compute $K_{w,3}$ and $K_{w,4}$ by computing $(g_{j-1})^{c_{n+1}\cdots c_{n+j-1}}$ via the pairings.)

AND gate: If $\texttt{GateType}(w) = \text{AND}$, we let $j = \texttt{depth}(w)$ and distinguish two cases. If $f_w(x^*) = 1$ then $\mathcal{B}$ chooses $a_w, b_w, r_w \leftarrow_{\$} \mathbb{Z}_p$ and defines K_w as specified by Constrain:

$$K_{w,1} := g^{a_w} \qquad K_{w,2} := g^{b_w} \qquad K_{w,3} := (g_{j-1})^{r_w - a_w \cdot r_{A(w)} - b_w \cdot r_{B(w)}}$$

Otherwise, choose $\psi_w, \phi_w, \eta_w \leftarrow_{\$} \mathbb{Z}_p$. Suppose $f_{A(w)}(x^*) = 0$. Then implicitly set $a_w := c_{n+j} + \psi_w$, $b_w := \phi_w$ and $r_w := c_{n+1}\cdots c_{n+j} + \eta_w$. Since we have $r_{A(w)} = c_{n+1}\cdots c_{n+j-1} + \eta_{A(w)}$, and since $(g_{j-1})^{r_{B(w)}}$ is computable via the pairings, $\mathcal{B}$ can compute the key components as follows:

$$K_{w,1} := g^{c_{n+j}} \cdot g^{\psi_w} \qquad\qquad K_{w,2} := g^{\phi_w}$$

$$K_{w,3} := (g_{j-1})^{\eta_w - \psi_w \cdot c_{n+1}\cdots c_{n+j-1} - (c_{n+j} + \psi_w)\eta_{A(w)} - \phi_w \cdot r_{B(w)}}$$
$$= (g_{j-1})^{c_{n+1}\cdots c_{n+j} + \eta_w - (c_{n+j} + \psi_w) \cdot (c_{n+1}\cdots c_{n+j-1} + \eta_{A(w)}) - \phi_w \cdot r_{B(w)}}$$
$$= (g_{j-1})^{r_w - a_w \cdot r_{A(w)} - b_w \cdot r_{B(w)}}$$

If $f_{A(w)}(x^*) = 1$ then we must have $f_{B(w)}(x^*) = 0$ and $\mathcal{B}$ can compute the key components as above with the roles of a_w and b_w swapped.

Prove Queries. Suppose $\mathcal{A}$ queries its PROVE oracle on x. If $x = x^*$ then $\mathcal{B}$ aborts and outputs $b' \leftarrow_{\$} \{0,1\}$. Otherwise, let j be such that $x_j \neq x_j^*$. Repeatedly applying the bilinear maps, $\mathcal{B}$ computes $(g_{n-1})^{\prod_{i \in [n] \setminus \{j\}} d_{i,x_i}}$, and by raising it to $z_i = d_{i,x_i}$, obtains $H = (g_{n-1})^{\prod_{i \in [n]} d_{i,x_i}}$. This suffices to compute

$$e(A, H) = e(g_\ell^\alpha, (g_{n-1})^{\prod_{i \in [n]} d_{i,x_i}}) = P(\text{sk}, x)$$
$$e(C, P(\text{sk}, x)) = e(g^\gamma, (g_{n+\ell-1})^{\alpha \prod_{i \in [n]} d_{i,x_i}}) = F(\text{sk}, x)$$

Challenge Query. When $\mathcal{A}$ queries the challenge oracle for a value different from x^*, $\mathcal{B}$ aborts and outputs a random bit $b' \leftarrow_{\$} \{0,1\}$. Otherwise it returns T, which is either $(g_{n+\ell})^{\prod_{i \in [n+\ell+1]} c_i} = (g_{n+\ell})^{\alpha \cdot \gamma \prod_{i \in [n]} d_{i,x_i^*}} = F(\text{sk}, x^*)$ or a random element from $\mathbb{G}_{n+\ell}$, thus perfectly simulating the experiment for pseudorandomness. When $\mathcal{A}$ outputs a bit b', $\mathcal{B}$ halts and returns b'.

Success Probability. The probability that $\mathcal{B}$ wins the MDDH game is analyzed as for the bit-fixing VRF. Let `abort` denote the event that $\mathcal{B}$ aborts during the simulation. Since $\mathcal{B}$ aborts if and only if $\mathcal{A}$ queries its CHALLENGE oracle on a value different from x^*, we have $\Pr[\texttt{abort}] = 1 - 2^{-n}$. Moreover, if $\mathcal{B}$ aborts then it outputs a random bit, thus we have $\Pr[\mathcal{B} \text{ wins} \mid \texttt{abort}] = \frac{1}{2}$. If $\mathcal{B}$ does not abort then it wins with the same probability as $\mathcal{A}$ (since $\mathcal{A}$'s success is independent of $\mathcal{B}$ guess of x^*), whose advantage is $\epsilon(\lambda)$. Thus $\Pr[\mathcal{B} \text{ wins} \mid \overline{\texttt{abort}}] = \frac{1}{2} + \epsilon(\lambda)$. Together, this yields

$$\Pr[\mathcal{B} \text{ wins}] = \Pr[\mathcal{B} \text{ wins} \mid \texttt{abort}] \cdot \Pr[\texttt{abort}] + \Pr[\mathcal{B} \text{ wins} \mid \overline{\texttt{abort}}] \cdot \Pr[\overline{\texttt{abort}}]$$
$$= \tfrac{1}{2} \cdot (1 - 2^{-n}) + \left(\tfrac{1}{2} + \epsilon(\lambda)\right) \cdot 2^{-n} = \tfrac{1}{2} + 2^{-n} \cdot \epsilon(\lambda) \ ,$$

which shows that $\mathcal{B}$'s advantage in breaking $(n + \ell)$-MDDH is $2^{-n} \cdot \epsilon(\lambda)$. $\qquad\square$

References

[ACF13]   Abdalla, M., Catalano, D., Fiore, D.: Verifiable random functions: Relations to identity-based key encapsulation and new constructions. Journal of Cryptology, 1–50 (2013)

[BB04a]   Boneh, D., Boyen, X.: Efficient Selective-ID Secure Identity-Based Encryption Without Random Oracles. In: Cachin, C., Camenisch, J.L. (eds.) EUROCRYPT 2004. LNCS, vol. 3027, pp. 223–238. Springer, Heidelberg (2004)

[BB04b]   Boneh, D., Boyen, X.: Short Signatures Without Random Oracles. In: Cachin, C., Camenisch, J.L. (eds.) EUROCRYPT 2004. LNCS, vol. 3027, pp. 56–73. Springer, Heidelberg (2004)

[BCKL09]   Belenkiy, M., Chase, M., Kohlweiss, M., Lysyanskaya, A.: Compact E-Cash and Simulatable VRFs Revisited. In: Shacham, H., Waters, B. (eds.) Pairing 2009. LNCS, vol. 5671, pp. 114–131. Springer, Heidelberg (2009)

[BF14]   Bellare, M., Fuchsbauer, G.: Policy-Based Signatures. In: Krawczyk, H. (ed.) PKC 2014. LNCS, vol. 8383, pp. 520–537. Springer, Heidelberg (2014)

[BGI14]   Boyle, E., Goldwasser, S., Ivan, I.: Functional Signatures and Pseudorandom Functions. In: Krawczyk, H. (ed.) PKC 2014. LNCS, vol. 8383, pp. 501–519. Springer, Heidelberg (2014)

[BGRV09]   Brakerski, Z., Goldwasser, S., Rothblum, G.N., Vaikuntanathan, V.: Weak Verifiable Random Functions. In: Reingold, O. (ed.) TCC 2009. LNCS, vol. 5444, pp. 558–576. Springer, Heidelberg (2009)

[BHR12]   Bellare, M., Hoang, V.T., Rogaway, P.: Foundations of garbled circuits. In: Yu, T., Danezis, G., Gligor, V.D. (eds.) ACM CCS 2012, pp. 784–796. ACM Press (October 2012)

[BMR10]   Boneh, D., Montgomery, H.W., Raghunathan, A.: Algebraic pseudorandom functions with improved efficiency from the augmented cascade. In: Al-Shaer, E., Keromytis, A.D., Shmatikov, V. (eds.) ACM CCS 2010, pp. 131–140. ACM Press (October 2010)

[BR93]   Bellare, M., Rogaway, P.: Random oracles are practical: A paradigm for designing efficient protocols. In: Ashby, V. (ed.) ACM CCS 1993, pp. 62–73. ACM Press (November 1993)

[BS02]   Boneh, D., Silverberg, A.: Applications of multilinear forms to cryptogra-
           phy. Contemporary Mathematics 324, 71–90 (2002),
           http://eprint.iacr.org/2002/080
[BW13]   Boneh, D., Waters, B.: Constrained Pseudorandom Functions and Their
           Applications. In: Sako, K., Sarkar, P. (eds.) ASIACRYPT 2013, Part II.
           LNCS, vol. 8270, pp. 280–300. Springer, Heidelberg (2013)
[CDNO97]   Canetti, R., Dwork, C., Naor, M., Ostrovsky, R.: Deniable Encryption.
           In: Kaliski Jr., B.S. (ed.) CRYPTO 1997. LNCS, vol. 1294, pp. 90–104.
           Springer, Heidelberg (1997)
[CL07]   Chase, M., Lysyanskaya, A.: Simulatable VRFs with Applications to
           Multi-theorem NIZK. In: Menezes, A. (ed.) CRYPTO 2007. LNCS,
           vol. 4622, pp. 303–322. Springer, Heidelberg (2007)
[CLT13]   Coron, J.-S., Lepoint, T., Tibouchi, M.: Practical Multilinear Maps over
           the Integers. In: Canetti, R., Garay, J.A. (eds.) CRYPTO 2013, Part I.
           LNCS, vol. 8042, pp. 476–493. Springer, Heidelberg (2013)
[Dod03]   Dodis, Y.: Efficient construction of (distributed) verifiable random func-
           tions. In: Desmedt, Y.G. (ed.) PKC 2003. LNCS, vol. 2567, pp. 1–17.
           Springer, Heidelberg (2002)
[DY05]   Dodis, Y., Yampolskiy, A.: A verifiable random function with short proofs
           and keys. In: Vaudenay, S. (ed.) PKC 2005. LNCS, vol. 3386, pp. 416–431.
           Springer, Heidelberg (2005)
[FKPR14]   Fuchsbauer, G., Konstantinov, M., Pietrzak, K., Rao, V.: Adaptive se-
           curity of constrained prfs. Cryptology ePrint Archive, Report 2014/416
           (2014), http://eprint.iacr.org/
[FS12]   Fiore, D., Schröder, D.: Uniqueness Is a Different Story: Impossibility of
           Verifiable Random Functions from Trapdoor Permutations. In: Cramer,
           R. (ed.) TCC 2012. LNCS, vol. 7194, pp. 636–653. Springer, Heidelberg
           (2012)
[Fuc14]   Fuchsbauer, G.: Constrained verifiable random functions. Cryptology
           ePrint Archive (2014), http://eprint.iacr.org/
[GGH13a]   Garg, S., Gentry, C., Halevi, S.: Candidate Multilinear Maps from Ideal
           Lattices. In: Johansson, T., Nguyen, P.Q. (eds.) EUROCRYPT 2013.
           LNCS, vol. 7881, pp. 1–17. Springer, Heidelberg (2013)
[GGH+13b] Garg, S., Gentry, C., Halevi, S., Raykova, M., Sahai, A., Waters, B.: Can-
           didate indistinguishability obfuscation and functional encryption for all
           circuits. In: 54th FOCS, pp. 40–49. IEEE Computer Society Press (Octo-
           ber 2013)
[GGH+13c] Garg, S., Gentry, C., Halevi, S., Sahai, A., Waters, B.: Attribute-Based En-
           cryption for Circuits from Multilinear Maps. In: Canetti, R., Garay, J.A.
           (eds.) CRYPTO 2013, Part II. LNCS, vol. 8043, pp. 479–499. Springer,
           Heidelberg (2013)
[GGM86]   Goldreich, O., Goldwasser, S., Micali, S.: How to construct random func-
           tions. J. ACM 33(4), 792–807 (1986)
[HSW14]   Hohenberger, S., Sahai, A., Waters, B.: Replacing a Random Oracle: Full
           Domain Hash from Indistinguishability Obfuscation. In: Nguyen, P.Q.,
           Oswald, E. (eds.) EUROCRYPT 2014. LNCS, vol. 8441, pp. 201–220.
           Springer, Heidelberg (2014)
[HW10]   Hohenberger, S., Waters, B.: Constructing Verifiable Random Functions
           with Large Input Spaces. In: Gilbert, H. (ed.) EUROCRYPT 2010. LNCS,
           vol. 6110, pp. 656–672. Springer, Heidelberg (2010)

[KPTZ13]   Kiayias, A., Papadopoulos, S., Triandopoulos, N., Zacharias, T.: Delegatable pseudorandom functions and applications. In: Sadeghi, A.-R., Gligor, V.D., Yung, M. (eds.) ACM CCS 2013, pp. 669–684. ACM Press (November 2013)

[Lis05]   Liskov, M.: Updatable Zero-Knowledge Databases. In: Roy, B. (ed.) ASIACRYPT 2005. LNCS, vol. 3788, pp. 174–198. Springer, Heidelberg (2005)

[Lys02]   Lysyanskaya, A.: Unique Signatures and Verifiable Random Functions from the DH-DDH Separation. In: Yung, M. (ed.) CRYPTO 2002. LNCS, vol. 2442, pp. 597–612. Springer, Heidelberg (2002)

[MR01]   Micali, S., Reyzin, L.: Soundness in the Public-Key Model. In: Kilian, J. (ed.) CRYPTO 2001. LNCS, vol. 2139, pp. 542–565. Springer, Heidelberg (2001)

[MR02]   Micali, S., Rivest, R.L.: Micropayments Revisited. In: Preneel, B. (ed.) CT-RSA 2002. LNCS, vol. 2271, pp. 149–163. Springer, Heidelberg (2002)

[MRV99]   Micali, S., Rabin, M.O., Vadhan, S.P.: Verifiable random functions. In: 40th FOCS, pp. 120–130. IEEE Computer Society Press (October 1999)

[NR97]   Naor, M., Reingold, O.: Number-theoretic constructions of efficient pseudo-random functions. In: 38th FOCS, pp. 458–467. IEEE Computer Society Press (October 1997)

[SW14]   Sahai, A., Waters, B.: How to use indistinguishability obfuscation: deniable encryption, and more. In: 46th ACM STOC, pp. 475–484. ACM Press (2014)

Publicly Evaluable Pseudorandom Functions and Their Applications

Yu Chen[1] and Zongyang Zhang[2,3,*]

[1] State Key Laboratory of Information Security (SKLOIS),
Institute of Information Engineering, Chinese Academy of Sciences, China
chenyu@iie.ac.cn
[2] National Institute of Advanced Industrial Science and Technology, Japan
[3] Shanghai Jiao Tong University, China
zongyang.zhang@aist.go.jp

Abstract. We put forth the notion of *publicly evaluable* pseudorandom functions (PEPRFs), which is a non-trivial extension of the standard pseudorandom functions (PRFs). Briefly, PEPRFs are defined over domain X containing an NP language L in which the witness is hard to extract on average, and each secret key sk is associated with a public key pk. For any $x \in L$, in addition to evaluate $\mathsf{F}_{sk}(x)$ using sk as in the standard PRFs, one is also able to evaluate $\mathsf{F}_{sk}(x)$ with pk, x and a witness w for $x \in L$. We conduct a formal study of PEPRFs, focusing on applications, constructions, and extensions. In more details:

- We show how to construct public-key encryption scheme (PKE) from PEPRFs. The construction is simple, black-box, and admits a direct proof of security. We provide evidence that PEPRFs exist by showing generic constructions from both hash proof systems and extractable hash proof systems.
- We introduce the notion of publicly samplable PRFs (PSPRFs), which is a relaxation of PEPRFs, but nonetheless implies PKE. We show PSPRFs are implied by trapdoor relations, yet the latter are further implied by trapdoor functions. This helps us to unify and clarify many PKE schemes from different paradigms and general assumptions under the notion of PSPRFs.
- We propose two variants of PEPRFs. One is publicly evaluable predicate PRFs, which admit a direct construction of predicate encryption. The other is publicly evaluable and verifiable functions (PEVFs), which admit a simple construction of "hash-and-sign" signatures.

1 Introduction

Pseudorandom functions (PRFs) [18] are a fundamental concept in modern cryptography. Loosely speaking, PRFs are a family of keyed functions $F = \{\mathsf{F}_{sk} : X \to Y\}_{sk \in SK}$ such that: (1) it is easy to sample the functions and compute their values, i.e., given a secret key (or seed) sk, one can efficiently evaluate $\mathsf{F}_{sk}(x)$ at

---

* Corresponding author.

M. Abdalla and R. De Prisco (Eds.): SCN 2014, LNCS 8642, pp. 115–134, 2014.
© Springer International Publishing Switzerland 2014

all points $x \in X$; (2) given only black-box access to the function, no probabilistic polynomial-time (PPT) algorithm can distinguish F_{sk} for a randomly chosen sk from a real random function, or equivalently, without sk no PPT algorithm can distinguish $F_{sk}(x)$ from random at all points $x \in X$.

In this work, we extend the standard PRFs to what we call *publicly evaluable PRFs*, which partially fill the gap between the evaluation power with and without secret key. In a publicly evaluable PRF, there exists an NP language $L \subseteq X$, and each secret key sk is associated with a public key pk. In addition, for any $x \in L$, except via private evaluation with sk, one can also efficiently compute the value of $F_{sk}(x)$ via public evaluation with the corresponding public key pk and a witness w for $x \in L$. Regarding the security requirement for PEPRFs, we require weak pseudorandomness which ensures that no PPT adversary can distinguish F_{sk} from a real random function on uniformly distributed challenge points in L (this differs from the full pseudorandomness for PRFs in which the challenge points are arbitrarily chosen by an adversary).

While PEPRFs are a conceptually simple extension of the standard PRFs, they have surprisingly powerful applications beyond what is possible with standard PRFs. Most notably, as we will see shortly, they admit a simple and black-box construction of PKE.

1.1 Motivation

PRFs have a wide range of applications in cryptography. Perhaps the most simple application is an elegant construction of private-key encryption as follows: the secret key sk of PRF serves as the private key; to encrypt a message m, the sender first chooses a random $x \in X$, and then outputs ciphertext $(x, m \oplus F_{sk}(x))$. It is tempting to think whether PRFs might also yield public-key encryption in the same way. However, such construction fails in the public-key setting when F is a standard PRF. This is because without sk no PPT algorithm can evaluate $F_{sk}(x)$ (otherwise this violates the pseudorandomness of PRFs) and thus encrypting publicly is impossible. Moreover, since PRFs and one-way functions (OWFs) imply each other [18, 22], the implications of PRFs are inherently confined in Minicrypt [26]. This result rules out the possibilities of constructing PKE from PRFs in a black-box manner.

Meanwhile, most existing PKE schemes based on various concrete hardness assumptions can be casted into several existing paradigms or general assumptions in the literature. In details, hash proof systems [12] encompass the PKE schemes [11,13,30,32], extractable hash proof systems [42] encompass the PKE schemes [6, 8, 21, 24, 28], one-way trapdoor permutations/functions encompass the PKE schemes [37–40].[1] However, the celebrated ElGamal encryption [16] does not fit into any known paradigms or general assumptions. Motivated by the above discussion, we find the following intriguing question:

---

[1] The references [38, 39] actually refer to the padded version of RSA encryption and Rabin encryption.

What kind of extension of PRFs can translate the above construction in the private-key setting into public-key setting? Can it be used to explain unclassified PKE schemes? Can it yield CCA-secure PKE schemes?

1.2 Our Contributions

We give positive answers to the above questions. Our main results (summarized in Figure 1) are as follows:

- In Section 3, we introduce the notion of publicly evaluable PRFs (PEPRFs), which contains several conceptually extensions of standard PRFs. In PEPRF, there is an NP language L over domain X and each secret key sk is associated with a public key pk. Moreover, for any $x \in L$, except via private evaluation with sk, one can efficiently evaluate $\mathsf{F}_{sk}(x)$ using pk and a witness w for $x \in L$. We also formalize security notions for PEPRFs, namely weak pseudorandomness and adaptively weak pseudorandomness.
- In Section 4, we demonstrate the power of PEPRFs by showing that they enable the construction of private-key encryption to work in the public-key setting, following the KEM-DEM methodology. In sketch, the public/secret key of PEPRF serves as the public/secret key for PKE. To encrypt a message m, a sender first samples a random $x \in L$ with a witness w, then publicly evaluates $\mathsf{F}_{sk}(x)$ from pk, x and w, and outputs a ciphertext $(x, m \oplus \mathsf{F}_{sk}(x))$. To decrypt, a receiver simply uses sk to compute $\mathsf{F}_{sk}(x)$ privately, then recovers m. Such construction is simple, black-box, and admits a direct proof of security.[2] In particular, in Example 1 we show that the well-known ElGamal PKE can be explained neatly by a weakly pseudorandom PEPRF based on the Diffie-Hellman assumption. Interestingly, the above KEM construction from PEPRFs is somewhat dual to that from trapdoor functions (TDFs). In the construction from TDFs, a sender first produces a DEM key by picking $x \xleftarrow{\mathrm{R}} X$,[3] then generates the associated ciphertext $\mathsf{TDF}_{ek}(x)$; while in the construction from PEPRFs, a sender first generates a ciphertext by picking $x \xleftarrow{\mathrm{R}} X$, then produces the associated DEM key $\mathsf{F}_{sk}(x)$.
- In Section 5 and Section 6, as our main result, we show that both smooth hash proof system (HPS) and extractable hash proof system (EHPS) yield weakly pseudorandom PEPRFs, while both smooth plus weakly universal$_2$ HPS and all-but-one EHPS yield adaptively weakly pseudorandom PEPRFs, respectively. This means that the works on HPS and EHPS implicitly constructed PEPRFs. Therefore, PEPRFs is an abstraction of the common aspect of the HPS and EHPS which are not formalized before. The existing

---

[2] For simplicity, we treat PKE schemes as key encapsulation mechanisms (KEM) in this work. It is well known that one can generically obtain a fully fledged CCA-secure PKE by combining a CCA-secure KEM (the requirement on KEM could be weaker [23]) and a data encapsulation mechanism (DEM) with appropriate security properties [31,32].

[3] To obtain semantic security, one should use $\mathsf{hc}(x)$ instead of x as the DEM key, where hc is a hardcore predicate for the TDF.

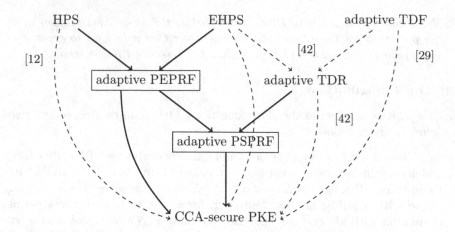

Fig. 1. Summary of CCA-secure PKEs from paradigms and general assumptions. Here, HPS refers to smooth plus universal$_2$ HPS, and EHPS refers to its all-but-one variant. The symbol $\rightarrow$ is an implication. The bold lines and rectangles denote our contributions, while the dashed lines denote those that are straight-forward or from previous work. All of the constructions from general assumptions are black-box.

constructions of HPS and EHPS imply that PEPRFs are achievable under a variety of number-theoretic assumptions.

- In Section 7, we introduce the notion of publicly samplable PRFs (PSPRFs), which is a relaxation of PEPRFs, but nonetheless imply PKE. Of independent interest, we redefine the notion of trapdoor relations (TDRs). We show that injective trapdoor functions (TDFs) imply "one-to-one" TDRs, while the latter further imply PSPRFs. This implication helps us to unify and clarify more PKE schemes based on different paradigms and general assumptions from a conceptual standpoint, and also suggests adaptive PSPRFs as a candidate of the weakest general assumption for CCA-secure PKE.

- In addition, we propose two variants of PEPRFs. One is publicly evaluable predicate PRFs, in which the secret key admits delegation for a set of predicates. We prove the usefulness of this notion by presenting a direct construction of predicate encryption from it. The other is publicly evaluable and verifiable functions (PEVFs), which enjoy an additional promising property named public verifiability while the best possible security degrades to being hard to compute on average. We justify the applicability of this notion by presenting a simple construction of "hash-and-sign" signatures from it. Due to space limitations, we include this part in the full version of this paper [9].

1.3 Related Work

CCA-Secure PKE from General Assumptions or Paradigms. Except the effort on constructing CCA-secure PKE from specific assumptions [20,34] or from encryption schemes satisfying some weak security notions [4,10,14,15,25,33,35], it is mostly of theoretical interest to build CCA-secure PKE from general assumptions and paradigms. Cramer and Shoup [12] generalized their CCA-secure PKE construction [11] to hash proof system (HPS) and used it as a paradigm to construct CCA-secure PKE from various decisional assumptions. Kurosawa and Desmedt [32] and Kiltz et al. [30] later improved upon the original HPS paradigm. Peikert and Waters [37] proposed lossy trapdoor functions (LTDFs) and showed a black-box construction of CCA-secure PKE from them. Rosen and Segev [40] introduced correlated-product secure trapdoor functions (CP-TDFs) and also showed a construction of CCA-secure PKE from them. Moreover, they showed that CP-TDFs are strictly weaker than LTDFs by giving a black-box separation between them. Kiltz et al. [29] introduced (injective) adaptive trapdoor functions (ATDFs) which are strictly weaker than both LTDFs and CP-TDFs but suffice to imply CCA-secure PKE. Wee [42] introduced extractable hash proof system (EHPS) and used it as a paradigm to construct CCA-secure PKE from a variety of search assumptions. Wee also showed that both EHPS and ATDFs imply (injective) adaptive trapdoor relations (ATDRs), which are sufficient to imply CCA-secure PKE. To the best of our knowledge, ATDR is the weakest general assumption that implies CCA-secure PKE. Very recently, Sahai and Waters [41] successfully translated the PRF-based private-key encryption to PKE by using punctured program technique in conjunction with indistinguishability obfuscation ($i\mathcal{O}$). Due to the use of obfuscation, their construction is inherently non-black-box.

Predicate PRFs. Very recently, predicate PRFs are studied in three concurrent and independent works, by Kiayias et al. [27] under the name of *delegatable PRFs*, by Boneh and Waters [5] under the name of *constrained PRFs*, and by Boyle, Goldwasser, and Ivan [7] under the name of *functional PRFs*. In predicate PRFs, one can derive a secret key sk_p for a predicate p from the master secret key msk. A secret key sk_p enables one to evaluate $\mathsf{F}_{msk}(x)$ at points x such that $p(x) = 1$. This natural extension turns out to be useful since it has powerful applications out of the scope of standard PRFs, such as identity-based key exchange, and optimal private broadcast encryption.

Witness PRFs. Independently and concurrently of our work, Zhandry [44] introduces the notion of *witness PRFs* (WPRFs), which is similar in concept to PEPRFs. In a nutshell, both WPRFs and PEPRFs are defined with respect to an NP language and extend the classical PRFs with the same extra functionality, i.e., one can publicly evaluate $\mathsf{F}_{sk}(x)$ for $x \in L$ with the knowledge of the corresponding witness w and public key pk. The main differences between WPRFs and our PEPRFs are as follows:

1. WPRFs can handle arbitrary NP languages, while PEPRFs are only for NP languages whose witness is hard to extract on average.
2. WPRFs require that $\mathsf{F}_{sk}(x)$ is pseudorandom for any adversarially chosen $x \in X \backslash L$, while PEPRFs only require that $\mathsf{F}_{sk}(x)$ is pseudorandom for randomly chosen $x \in L$.

WPRFs are introduced as a weaker primitive for several obfuscation-based applications. By utilizing the reduction from any NP language to the subset-sum problem, WPRFs can handle arbitrary NP languages. However, for applications of WPRFs whose functionalities rely on $F_{sk}(x)$ for $x \in L$, such as CCA-secure encryption, non-interactive key exchange, and hardcore functions for any one-way function, the underlying NP languages have to be at least hard-on-average. This is because these applications need the indistinguishability between $x \xleftarrow{R} L$ and $x \xleftarrow{R} X \backslash L$ to argue $F_{sk}(x)$ is computationally pseudorandom for $x \xleftarrow{R} L$.

2   Preliminaries and Definitions

Notations. For a distribution or random variable X, we write $x \xleftarrow{R} X$ to denote the operation of sampling a random x according to X. For a set X, we use $x \xleftarrow{R} X$ to denote the operation of sampling x uniformly at random from X, and use $|X|$ to denote its size. We write κ to denote the security parameter throughout this paper, and all algorithms (including the adversary) are implicitly given κ as input. We write $\mathsf{poly}(\kappa)$ to denote an arbitrary polynomial function in κ. We write $\mathsf{negl}(\kappa)$ to denote an arbitrary negligible function in κ, which vanishes faster than the inverse of any polynomial. We say a probability is overwhelming if it is $1 - \mathsf{negl}(\kappa)$, and said to be noticeable if it is $1/\mathsf{poly}(\kappa)$. A probabilistic polynomial-time (PPT) algorithm is a randomized algorithm that runs in time $\mathsf{poly}(\kappa)$. If $\mathcal{A}$ is a randomized algorithm, we write $z \leftarrow \mathcal{A}(x_1, \ldots, x_n; r)$ to indicate that $\mathcal{A}$ outputs z on inputs $(x_1, \ldots, x_n)$ and random coins r. We will omit r and simply write $z \leftarrow \mathcal{A}(x_1, \ldots, x_n)$ when it is clear from the context. For distributions X, Y, we write $X \approx_s Y$ to mean that they are statistically indistinguishable.

3   Publicly Evaluable PRFs

We now give a precise definition of PEPRFs. We begin with the syntax and then define the security.

Definition 1 (Publicly Evaluable PRFs). *PEPRFs consist of five polynomial-time algorithms as below:*

- Setup(κ): on input a security parameter κ, output public parameters pp which includes finite sets SK, PK, X, Y, a language $L \subseteq X$ (these sets may be parameterized by κ) and a witness set W, as well as a PEPRF family $F = \{F_{sk} : X \to Y \cup \bot\}_{sk \in SK}$.
- KeyGen(pp): on input pp, output a secret key sk and an associated public key pk.
- Sample(r): on input random coins r, output a random $x \in L$ along with a witness $w \in W$ for x. For simplicity and without loss of generality, we assume that x distributes uniformly over L conditioned on $r \xleftarrow{R} R$, where R is the randomness space.

- PubEval(pk, x, w): on input pk and $x \in L$ together with a witness $w \in W$ for x, output $y \in Y$.
- PrivEval(sk, x): on input sk and $x \in X$, output $y \in Y \cup \bot$.

Correctness: We require that for any $pp \leftarrow$ Setup(κ) and any $(pk, sk) \leftarrow$ KeyGen(pp), it holds that:

$$\forall x \in X : \qquad \mathsf{F}_{sk}(x) = \mathsf{PrivEval}(sk, x)$$
$$\forall x \in L \text{ with witness } w : \mathsf{F}_{sk}(x) = \mathsf{PubEval}(pk, x, w)$$

Security: Let $\mathcal{A} = (\mathcal{A}_1, \mathcal{A}_2)$ be an adversary against PEPRFs and define its advantage as:

$$\mathsf{Adv}_{\mathcal{A}}(\kappa) = \Pr\left[b = b' : \begin{array}{l} pp \leftarrow \mathsf{Setup}(\kappa); \\ (pk, sk) \leftarrow \mathsf{KeyGen}(pp); \\ state \leftarrow \mathcal{A}_1^{\mathcal{O}_{\mathsf{eval}}(\cdot)}(pp, pk); \\ \{(x_i^*, w_i^*) \leftarrow \mathsf{Sample}(r_i^*), r_i^* \xleftarrow{\mathrm{R}} R\}_{i=1}^{p(\kappa)}; \\ b \leftarrow \{0, 1\}; \\ b' \leftarrow \mathcal{A}_2^{\mathcal{O}_{\mathsf{eval}}(\cdot)}(state, \{x_i^*, \mathcal{O}_{\mathsf{ror}}(b, x_i^*)\}_{i=1}^{p(\kappa)}); \end{array} \right] - \frac{1}{2},$$

where $p(\kappa)$ is any polynomial, $\mathcal{O}_{\mathsf{eval}}(x) = \mathsf{F}_{sk}(x)$, $\mathcal{O}_{\mathsf{ror}}(0, x) = \mathsf{F}_{sk}(x)$, $\mathcal{O}_{\mathsf{ror}}(1, x) = \mathsf{H}(x)$ (here H is chosen uniformly at random from all the functions from X to Y)[4], and $\mathcal{A}_2$ is not allowed to query $\mathcal{O}_{\mathsf{eval}}(\cdot)$ with any x_i^*. We say that PEPRFs are adaptively weakly pseudorandom if for any PPT adversary $\mathcal{A}$ its advantage function $\mathsf{Adv}_{\mathcal{A}}(\kappa)$ is negligible in κ.[5]

The adaptively weak pseudorandomness captures the security against active adversaries, who are given adaptive access to oracle $\mathcal{O}_{\mathsf{eval}}(\cdot)$. We also consider weak pseudorandomness which captures the security against static adversaries, who is not given access to oracle $\mathcal{O}_{\mathsf{eval}}(\cdot)$.

Remark 1. Different from the standard PRFs, PEPRFs require the existence of an NP language $L \subseteq X$ and a public evaluation algorithm. Due to this strengthening on functionality, we cannot hope to achieve full PRF security, and hence settling for weak pseudorandomness is a natural choice.[6] Note that the weak pseudorandomness implicitly requires that in the NP language L the extraction of witness must be hard on average. This requirement is strictly weaker than the NP language L itself is hard on average.

---

[4] To efficiently simulate access to a uniformly random function H from X to Y, one may think of a process in which the adversary's queries to $\mathcal{O}_{\mathsf{ror}}(1, \cdot)$ are "lazily" answered with independently and randomly chosen elements in Y, while keeping track of the answers so that queries made repeatedly are answered consistently.

[5] The readers should not confuse with adaptive PRFs [3], where "adaptive" means that instead of deciding the queries in advance, an adversary can adaptively make queries to $\mathcal{O}_{\mathsf{ror}}(b, \cdot)$ based on previous queries.

[6] In the full PRF security experiment, the input x_i^* of $\mathcal{O}_{\mathsf{ror}}(b, \cdot)$ are chosen by the adversary, thus it may know the corresponding witness w_i^* and then evaluate $\mathsf{F}_{sk}(x_i^*)$ publicly.

Remark 2. In some scenarios, it is more convenient to work with a definition that slightly restricts an adversary's power, but is equivalent to Definition 1. That is, $p(\kappa)$ is fixed to 1. Due to the existence of oracle $\mathcal{O}_{\mathsf{eval}}(\cdot)$, a standard hybrid argument can show that PEPRFs secure under this restricted definition are also secure under Definition 1. In the remainder of this paper, we will work with this restricted definition.

Example 1. As a warm-up, we present an illustrative construction of PEPRF. Let $\mathbb{G}$ be a cyclic group of prime order p with canonical generator g, and define $\mathsf{F}_{sk} : \mathbb{G} \to \mathbb{G}$ as x^{sk}, where the secret key $sk \in \mathbb{Z}_p$ and the public key $pk = g^{sk} \in \mathbb{G}$. A natural NP language L defined over $\mathbb{G}$ is $\{x = g^w : w \in \mathbb{Z}_p\}$, where the exponent w serves as a witness for x. For any $x \in L$, one can publicly evaluate $\mathsf{F}_{sk}(x)$ via computing pk^w. It is easy to verify that this PEPRF is weakly pseudorandom assuming the DDH assumption holds in $\mathbb{G}$. Looking ahead, when applying the construction shown in Section 4 to this PEPRF, yields exactly the plain ElGamal PKE.

A Possible Relaxation. To be completely precise, we do not necessarily require the distribution of x induced by $\mathsf{Sample}(r)$ conditioned on $r \xleftarrow{\mathrm{R}} R$ is identical or statistically close to uniform. Instead, it could be some other prescribed distribution χ. In this case, weak pseudorandomness extends naturally to χ-weak pseudorandomness.

A Useful Generalization. In some scenarios, it is more convenient to work with a more generalized notion in which we consider a collection of languages $\{L_{pk}\}_{pk \in PK}$ indexed by public key rather than a fixed language L. Correspondingly, the sampling algorithm takes pk as an extra input to sample a random element from L_{pk}. We refer to such generalized notion as *PEPRFs for public-key dependent languages*, and we will work with it when constructing adaptive PEPRFs from hash proof system.

4   KEM from Publicly Evaluable PRFs

In this section, we present a simple and black-box construction of KEM from PEPRFs. For compactness, we refer the reader to Appendix A.1 for the definition and security notion of KEM.

- $\mathsf{Setup}(\kappa)$: run $\mathsf{PRF.Setup}(\kappa)$ to generate pp as public parameters.
- $\mathsf{KeyGen}(pp)$: run $\mathsf{PRF.KeyGen}(pp)$ to generate (pk, sk).
- $\mathsf{Encap}(pk; r)$: run $\mathsf{PRF.Sample}(r)$ to generate a random $x \in L$ with a witness $w \in W$ for x, set x as the ciphertext c and compute $\mathsf{PRF.PubEval}(pk, x, w)$ as the DEM key k, output (c, k).
- $\mathsf{Decap}(sk, c)$: output $\mathsf{PRF.PrivEval}(sk, c)$.

Correctness of the KEM follows directly from that of PEPRFs. For security, we have the following results:

Theorem 1. *The KEM is CPA-secure if the underlying PEPRFs are weakly pseudorandom.*

Proof. The proof is rather straightforward, which transforms an adversary $\mathcal{A}$ against the IND-CPA security of KEM to a distinguisher $\mathcal{B}$ against the weak pseudorandomness of PEPRFs. We proceed via a single game.

Game CPA: $\mathcal{B}$ receives (pp, pk) of PEPRFs, then simulates $\mathcal{A}$'s challenger in the IND-CPA experiment as follows:
Setup: $\mathcal{B}$ sends (pp, pk) to $\mathcal{A}$.
Challenge: Upon receiving the challenge instance (x^*, y^*) from its own challenger, where $(x^*, w^*) \leftarrow \mathsf{PRF.Sample}(r^*)$ and y^* is either $\mathsf{F}_{sk}(x^*)$ or randomly picked from Y, $\mathcal{B}$ sends (x^*, y^*) to $\mathcal{A}$ as the challenge.
Guess: $\mathcal{A}$ outputs its guess b' for b and $\mathcal{B}$ forwards b' to its own challenger.

Clearly, $\mathcal{A}$'s view in the above game is identical to that in the real IND-CPA experiment. Thus $\mathcal{B}$ can break the weak pseudorandomness with advantage at least $\mathsf{Adv}_{\mathcal{A}}^{\mathrm{CPA}}(\kappa)$. This concludes the proof.

Theorem 2. *The KEM is CCA-secure if the underlying PEPRFs are adaptively weakly pseudorandom.*

Proof. The proof is also straightforward, which transforms an adversary $\mathcal{A}$ against the IND-CCA security of KEM to a distinguisher $\mathcal{B}$ against the adaptively weak pseudorandomness of PEPRFs. We proceed via a single game.

Game CCA: $\mathcal{B}$ receives (pp, pk) of PEPRFs, then simulates $\mathcal{A}$'s challenger in the IND-CCA experiment as follows:
Setup: $\mathcal{B}$ sends (pp, pk) to $\mathcal{A}$.
Phase 1 - Decapsulation queries: on decapsulation query $\langle x \rangle$, $\mathcal{B}$ submits evaluation query on point x to its own challenger and forwards the reply to $\mathcal{A}$.
Challenge: Upon receiving the challenge instance (x^*, y^*) from its own challenger, where $(x^*, w^*) \leftarrow \mathsf{PRF.Sample}(r^*)$ and y^* is either $\mathsf{F}_{sk}(x^*)$ or randomly picked from Y, $\mathcal{B}$ sends (x^*, y^*) to $\mathcal{A}$ as the challenge.
Phase 2 - Decapsulation queries: same as in Phase 1 except that the decapsulation query $\langle x^* \rangle$ is not allowed.
Guess: $\mathcal{A}$ outputs its guess b' for b and $\mathcal{B}$ forwards b' to its own challenger.

Clearly, $\mathcal{A}$'s view in the above game is identical to that in the real IND-CCA experiment. Thus $\mathcal{B}$ can break the adaptively weak pseudorandomness with advantage at least $\mathsf{Adv}_{\mathcal{A}}^{\mathrm{CCA}}(\kappa)$. This concludes the proof.

We note that the above results also hold if the underlying PEPRFs are (adaptively) χ-weakly pseudorandom.

5 Connection to Hash Proof System

Hash proof system (HPS) was introduced by Cramer and Shoup [12] as a paradigm of constructing PKE from a category of decisional problems, named subset membership problems. As a warm up, we first recall the notion of HPS and then show how to construct PEPRFs from it.

HASH PROOF SYSTEM. HPS consists of the following algorithms:

- Setup(κ): on input a security parameter κ, output public parameters pp which include an HPS instance description $(H, SK, PK, X, L, W, \Pi, \alpha)$, where $H = \{H_{sk} : X \to \Pi\}_{sk \in SK}$ is a hash family indexed by SK, L is a language defined over X, W is the associated witness set, and α is a projection from SK to PK.
- KeyGen(pp): on input pp, pick $sk \xleftarrow{\text{R}} SK$, compute $pk \leftarrow \alpha(sk)$, output (pk, sk).
- Sample(r): on input random coins r, output a random $x \in L$ together with a witness w.
- Sample$'(r)$: on input random coins r, output a random $x \in X \backslash L$.
- Priv(sk, x): on input sk and x, output π such that $\pi = H_{sk}(x)$.
- Pub(pk, x, w): on input pk and $x \in L$ together with a witness w for x, output π such that $\pi = H_{sk}(x)$.

HPS satisfies the following basic property:

Definition 2 (sampling indistinguishable). *The two distributions induced by* Sample *and* Sample$'$ *are computationally indistinguishable based on the hardness of the underlying subset membership problem.*

The following notions capture a rich set of properties for H on inputs $x \in X \backslash L$.

Definition 3 (smooth). $(pk, H_{sk}(x)) \approx_s (pk, \pi)$, *where* $(pk, sk) \leftarrow$ KeyGen(pp), $x \leftarrow$ Sample$'(r)$, *and* $\pi \xleftarrow{\text{R}} \Pi$.

Definition 4 (universal$_1$). *For any* $x \in X \backslash L$, *and any* $\pi \in \Pi$, *it holds that:*

$$\Pr[H_{sk}(x) = \pi \mid \alpha(sk) = pk] \leq \epsilon$$

Definition 5 (universal$_2$). *For any* $x^* \in X \backslash L$, *any* $x \notin L \cup x^*$, *and any* $\pi \in \Pi$, *it holds that:*

$$\Pr[H_{sk}(x) = \pi \mid H_{sk}(x^*) = \pi^* \wedge \alpha(sk) = pk] \leq \epsilon$$

[12] indicated that universal$_2$ property implies universal$_1$ property, while [1] further showed that universal$_1$ property combining strong randomness extractor implies smoothness. The universal$_2$ property is much stronger than smoothness, since the former is defined for all points $x \in X \backslash L$ non-equal to x^*, where the latter is defined with respect to $x \xleftarrow{\text{R}} X \backslash L$. In the designing of CCA-secure PKE, the universal$_2$ property is necessary since the input x^* of universal$_2$ hash might be dependent on the target message choice of adversary. However, in the designing of KEM, x^* totally comes from the challenge instance of external decisional problem, therefore, it is possible to weaken the universal$_2$ property. Of independent interest, we formalize weak universal$_2$ property as follows:

Definition 6 (weak universal$_2$). *For $x^* \leftarrow$ Sample$'(r)$, any $x \notin L \cup x^*$, and any $\pi \in \Pi$, it holds that:*

$$\Pr[\mathsf{H}_{sk}(x) = \pi \mid \mathsf{H}_{sk}(x^*) = \pi^* \wedge \alpha(sk) = pk] \leq \epsilon$$

5.1 Construction from Smooth HPS

From smooth HPS, we construct weakly pseudorandom PEPRF as follows:

- Setup(κ): on input a security parameter κ, run HPS.Setup(κ) to generate an HPS instance $(H, PK, SK, X, L, \Pi, \alpha)$, then produces public parameters $pp = (F, PK, SK, X, L, Y)$ for PEPRFs from it, where $F = H$, $Y = \Pi$. We assume the public parameters pp of HPS and PEPRF contain essentially the same information.
- KeyGen(pp): on input pp, output $(pk, sk) \leftarrow$ HPS.KeyGen(pp).
- Sample(r): on input r, output $(x, w) \leftarrow$ HPS.Sample(r).
- PubEval(pk, x, w): on input pk and $x \in L$ together with a witness $w \in W$ for x, output $y \leftarrow$ HPS.Pub(pk, x, w).
- PrivEval(sk, x): on input sk and $x \in X$, output $y \leftarrow$ HPS.Priv(sk, x).

The algorithm HPS.Sample$'$ is not used in the construction, but it is crucial to establish the security. We have the following theorem of the above construction.

Theorem 3. *If the underlying subset membership problem is hard, then the PEPRFs from smooth HPS are weakly pseudorandom.*

Due to space limitations, we defer the proof to the full version of this paper [9].

5.2 Construction from Smooth and Weak Universal$_2$ HPS

From a smooth HPS and an associated weak universal$_2$ HPS, we construct adaptively weakly pseudorandom PEPRF as follows:

- Setup(κ): on input κ, run HPS$_1$.Setup(κ) to generate a smooth HPS instance $(\tilde{H}, PK_1, SK_1, \tilde{X}, \tilde{L}, W, \Pi_1, \alpha_1)$, run HPS$_2$.Setup($\kappa$) to generate a weak universal$_2$ HPS instance $(\hat{H}, PK_2, SK_2, \tilde{X}, \tilde{L}, W, \Pi_2, \alpha_2)$, then build $pp = (F, PK, SK, X, L, W, Y)$ for PEPRFs from them, where $X = \tilde{X} \times \Pi_2$, $Y = \Pi_1 \cup \bot$, $PK = PK_1 \times PK_2$, $SK = SK_1 \times SK_2$, and L will be defined later. We assume the two HPSs share the common sampling algorithm.
- KeyGen(pp): on input pp, run HPS$_1$.KeyGen(pp) and HPS$_2$.KeyGen(pp) to get (pk_1, sk_1) and (pk_2, sk_2) respectively, output $pk = (pk_1, pk_2)$, $sk = (sk_1, sk_2)$. We assume the public parameters pp of HPS and PEPRFs contain the same information.
- Sample($pk; r$): on input $pk = (pk_1, pk_2)$ and random coins r, pick $(\tilde{x}, w) \leftarrow$ HPS$_1$.Sample(r), compute $\pi_2 \leftarrow$ HPS$_2$.Pub($pk_2, \tilde{x}, w$). This sampling algorithm defines a collection of language $L = \{L_{pk}\}_{pk \in PK}$ over $X = \tilde{X} \times \Pi_2$ where each $L_{pk} = \{(\tilde{x}, \pi_2) : \tilde{x} \in \tilde{L} \wedge \pi_2 = \text{HPS}_2(pk_2, \tilde{x}, w)\}$. Note that a witness w for $\tilde{x} \in \tilde{L}$ is also a witness for $x = (\tilde{x}, \pi_2) \in L_{pk}$.

- PubEval(pk, x, w): on input $pk = (pk_1, pk_2)$ and an element $x = (\tilde{x}, \pi_2) \in L_{pk}$ together with a witness w, output $y \leftarrow \text{HPS}_1.\text{Pub}(pk_1, \tilde{x}, w)$.
- PrivEval(sk, x): on input $sk = (sk_1, sk_2)$ and $x = (\tilde{x}, \pi_2)$, output $y \leftarrow \text{HPS}_1.\text{Priv}(sk_1, \tilde{x})$ if $\pi_2 = \text{HPS}_2.\text{Priv}(sk_2, \tilde{x})$ and $\perp$ otherwise.

We have the following theorem of the above construction.

Theorem 4. *If the underlying subset membership problem is hard, then the PEPRFs from smooth and weak universal$_2$ HPSs are adaptively weakly pseudorandom.*

Due to space limitations, we defer the proof to the full version of this paper [9].

6   Connection to Extractable Hash Proof System

Extractable hash proof system (EHPS) was introduced by Wee [42] as a paradigm of constructing PKE from search problems. In the following, we recall the notion of EHPS and then show how to construct PEPRF from it.

EXTRACTABLE HASH PROOF SYSTEM. EHPS consists of a tuple of algorithms (Setup, KeyGen, KeyGen', Pub, Priv, Ext) as below:

- Setup(κ): on input a security parameter κ, output public parameters pp which include an EHPS instance (H, PK, SK, S, U, Π), where H is a hash family mapping U to Π indexed by PK. Let $\text{hc}(\cdot) : S \rightarrow \{0,1\}^l$ be a hardcore function for one-way binary relation R over $S \times U$.
- KeyGen(pp): on input public parameters pp, output a key pair (pk, sk).
- KeyGen'(pp): on input public parameters pp, output a key pair (pk, sk').
- Sample(r): on input random coins r, output a random tuple $(s, u) \in R$, where s can be viewed as pre-image of u. For our purpose, we further decompose algorithm Sample to SampLeft and SampRight. The former on input random coins r outputs $s \in S$, while the latter on input random coins r outputs $u \in U$. For all $r \in R$, we require that $(\text{SampLeft}(r), \text{SampRight}(r)) \in R$.
- Pub(pk, r): on input pk and r, output $\pi = H_{pk}(u)$ where $u = \text{SampRight}(r)$.
- Priv(sk', u): on input sk' and $u \in U$, output $\pi = H_{pk}(u)$.
- Ext(sk, u, π): on input sk, $u \in U$, and $\pi \in \Pi$, output $s \in S$ such that $(s, u) \in R$ if and only if $\pi = H_{pk}(u)$.

In EHPS, KeyGen' and Priv work in the hashing mode, which are only used to establish security. EHPS satisfies the following property:

Definition 7 (Indistinguishable). *The first outputs (namely pk) of KeyGen and KeyGen' are statistically indistinguishable.*

ALL-BUT-ONE EXTRACTABLE HASH PROOF SYSTEM. All-but-one (ABO) EHPS is a richer abstraction of EHPS, besides algorithms (Setup, KeyGen, KeyGen', Pub, Priv, Ext), it has an additional algorithm Ext'.

- KeyGen$'(pp, u^*)$: on input public parameter pp and an arbitrary $u^* \in U$, output a key pair (pk, sk').
- Ext$'(sk', u, \pi)$: on input sk', $u \in U$ such that $u \neq u^*$, and $\pi \in \Pi$, output $s \in S$ such that $(s, u) \in R$ if and only if $\pi = H_{pk}(u)$.

In ABO EHPS, KeyGen$'$, Priv, and Ext$'$ work in the ABO hashing mode, which are only used to establish security. ABO EHPS satisfies the following property:

Definition 8 (Indistinguishable). *For any $u^* \in U$, the first output (namely pk) of* KeyGen *and* KeyGen$'$ *are statistically indistinguishable.*

6.1   Construction from (All-But-One) EHPS

From (ABO) EHPS, we construct PEPRF as follows:

- Setup(κ): on input κ, run EHPS.Setup(κ) to generate an EHPS instance (H, PK, SK, S, U, Π), and build public parameters $pp = (F, PK, SK, X, L, W, Y)$ for PEPRF from it, where $X = U \times \Pi$, $Y = \{0, 1\}^l$, F, L, and W will be defined later. We assume the publicly parameters pp of PEPRF and EHPS essentially contain the same information.
- KeyGen(pp): on input pp, output $(pk, sk) \leftarrow$ EHPS.KeyGen(pp).
- Sample(r): on input random coins r, compute $u \leftarrow$ EHPS.SampRight(r), and $\pi \leftarrow$ EHPS.Pub(pk, r), output $x = (u, \pi)$ and $w = r$. This algorithm defines an NP language $L = \{(u, \pi) : u \in U \wedge \pi = H_{pk}(u)\}$ over X, where the random coins r used to sample u serves as a witness for $x = (u, \pi) \in L$. Note the witness set W is exactly the randomness space R used by EHPS.Sample.
- PubEval(pk, x, w): on input pk and $x \in L$ together with a witness $w \in W$ for x, compute $s \leftarrow$ EHPS.SampLeft(w), output $y \leftarrow$ hc(s).
- PrivEval(sk, x): on input secret key sk and parse x as (u, π), compute $s \leftarrow$ EHPS.Ext(sk, u, π), output $y \leftarrow$ hc(s). This algorithm defines $F_{sk}(x)$ as hc(EHPS.Ext(sk, x)).

We have the following two theorems about the above construction.

Theorem 5. *If the underlying binary relation* R *is one-way, then the PEPRFs from EHPS are weakly pseudorandom.*

Theorem 6. *If the underlying binary relation* R *is one-way, then the PEPRFs from all-but-one EHPS are adaptively weakly pseudorandom.*

Due to space limitations, we defer the proofs of the two theorems to the full version of this paper [9].

7   Publicly Samplable PRFs

In this section, we consider a functional relaxation for PEPRFs, that is, instead of requiring the existence of NP language L over X and the publicly evaluable property of $F_{sk}(x)$, we only require that the distribution $(x, F_{sk}(x))$ is efficiently samplable with pk. More precisely, algorithms Sample(r) and PubEval(pk, x, w) are replaced by algorithm PubSamp($pk; r$), which on input pk and random coins r outputs a random tuple $(x, y) \in X \times Y$ such that $y = F_{sk}(x)$. We refer to this relaxed notion as publicly samplable PRFs (PSPRFs). The (adaptively) weak pseudorandomness for PSPRFs can be defined analogously. It is easy to verify that PSPRF and KEM imply each other by viewing PSPRF.PubSamp (resp. PSPRF.PrivEval) as KEM.Encap (resp. KEM.Decap).[7] In light of this observation, we view PSPRFs as a high level interpretation of KEM, which allows significantly simpler and modular proof of security. In what follows, we revisit the notion of trapdoor one-way relations, and explore its relation to PSPRFs.

7.1 Trapdoor Relations

Before revisiting the notion of trapdoor relations, we first recall a closely related notion, namely trapdoor functions (TDFs) (c.f. Appendix A.2). Briefly, TDFs are a family of functions that are easy to compute, invert with trapdoor but hard to invert on average without trapdoor. Most attention in the literature has focus on injective (i.e. one-to-one) TDFs. It is well known that injective TDFs suffice for PKE [19, 43]. Bellare et al. [2] made a careful distinction for TDFs based on "the amount of non-injectivity", measured by pre-image size. A (trapdoor, one-way) function is said to have pre-image size $Q(\kappa)$ (where κ is the security parameter) if the number of pre-images of any range points is at most $Q(\kappa)$. They demonstrated that $Q(\kappa)$ is a crucial parameter with regarding to building PKE out of TDFs by showing two facts: (i) OWFs imply TDFs with super-polynomial pre-image size; (ii) TDFs with polynomial pre-image size is sufficient to imply PKE. Kiltz et al. [29] strengthened TDFs to adaptive TDFs (ATDFs), which remain one-way even the adversary can adaptively access an inversion oracle. They used injective ATDFs as a general assumption to construct CCA-secure PKE. Wee [42] introduced trapdoor relations (TDRs) as a functionality relaxation of injective TDFs, in which the "easy to compute" property is weakened to "easy to sample". Wee also showed how to construct such TDRs from EHPS. Note that the notion of TDRs defined in [42] is inherently to be "one-to-one", while the TDRs yielded from EHPS are potentially to be "one-to-many". Towards utmost generality, we redefine the notion of TDRs as follows:

Definition 9 (Trapdoor Relations). *Trapdoor relations are given by four polynomial-time algorithms as below.*

- Setup(κ): *on input security parameter κ, output public parameters pp which includes finite sets EK, TD, S, U, and a binary relation family $R : S \times U$ indexed by EK, which will be defined by PubSamp as below.*
- TrapGen(pp): *on input pp, output $(ek, td) \in EK \times TD$.*

---

[7] Without loss of generality, we assume KEM.Decap is deterministic. We note that there do exist probabilistic decapsulation algorithms which implement "implicit rejection" strategy [31]. In that case, we can view KEM.Decap as randomized PSPRFs.

- PubSamp$(ek; r)$: *on input ek and random coins r, output a tuple $(s, u) \in S \times U$. Implicitly, this gives us the relation $R_{ek} = \{(s, u) : \exists r \text{ s.t. } (s, u) = \text{PubSamp}(ek; r)\}$. We extend the distinction of non-injectivity for functions to the setting of binary relations. Hereafter, for every element $u \in U$ we define $S_u = \{s : (s, u) \in R_{ek}\}$; for every element $s \in S$ we define $U_s = \{u : (s, u) \in R_{ek}\}$. Let $Q(\kappa) = \max(|S_u|_{u \in U})$ and $P(\kappa) = \max(|U_s|_{s \in S})$. We say a binary relation $R : S \times U$ is "many-to-one" if $Q(\kappa) > 1$ and $P(\kappa) = 1$; say it is "one-to-many" if $P(\kappa) > 1$ and $Q(\kappa) = 1$; say it is "many-to-many" if $Q(\kappa) > 1$ and $P(\kappa) > 1$; say it is "one-to-one" if $Q(\kappa) = P(\kappa) = 1$.*
- TdInv(td, u): *on input td and $u \in U$, output $s \in S$ or a distinguished symbol $\perp$ indicating u is not well-defined with respect to td.*[8]

Correctness: We require that for any $pp \leftarrow \text{Setup}(\kappa)$ any $(ek, td) \leftarrow \text{KeyGen}(pp)$, and any $(s, u) \in R_{ek}$, it holds that: $\Pr[(\text{TdInv}(td, u), u) \in R_{ek}] = 1$.

Adaptive One-Wayness: Let $\mathcal{A} = (\mathcal{A}_1, \mathcal{A}_2)$ be an inverter against TDRs and define its advantage as:

$$\text{Adv}_{\mathcal{A}}(\kappa) = \Pr \left[(s, u^*) \in R_{ek} : \begin{array}{l} pp \leftarrow \text{Setup}(\kappa); \\ (ek, td) \leftarrow \text{TrapGen}(pp); \\ state \leftarrow \mathcal{A}_1^{\mathcal{O}_{\text{inv}}(\cdot)}(pp, ek); \\ (s^*, u^*) \leftarrow \text{PubSamp}(ek); \\ s \leftarrow \mathcal{A}_2^{\mathcal{O}_{\text{inv}}(\cdot)}(state, u^*) \end{array} \right],$$

where $\mathcal{O}_{\text{inv}}(y) = \text{TdInv}(td, y)$, and $\mathcal{A}_2$ is not allowed to query $\mathcal{O}_{\text{inv}}(\cdot)$ for the challenge u^*. We say TDRs are adaptively one-way (or simply adaptively) if for any PPT inverter its advantage is negligible in κ. The standard one-wayness can be defined similarly except that the adversary is not given access to $\mathcal{O}_{\text{inv}}(\cdot)$.

Construction from TDFs. It is easy to see that TDFs imply TDRs. TDRs can be constructed from TDFs as below:

- Setup(κ): run TDF.Setup(κ) to generate public parameters pp, set $S = X$, $U = Y$.
- KeyGen(κ): run TDF.TrapGen(pp) to generate (ek, td).
- PubSamp$(ek; r)$: run TDF.SampleDom(r) to sample a random element $s \in S$, compute $u \leftarrow \text{TDF.Eval}(ek, s)$, then output (s, u).
- TdInv(td, u): output TDF.TdInv(td, u).

The correctness and security of the above construction follows immediately from that of TDFs. We omit the details here for triviality. Obviously, the resulting TDR is "many-to-one" (resp. "one-to-one") if the underlying TDF is "many-to-one" (injective).

---

[8] We say u is well-defined with respect to td if there exists ek and random coins r_1, r_2 such that $(ek, td) = \text{KeyGen}(pp; r_1)$ and $(s, u) = \text{PubSamp}(ek; r_2)$.

7.2   Publicly Samplable PRFs from TDRs

Construction from TDRs. We show a simple construction of PSPRFs from "one-to-many" or "one-to-one" TDRs. Let $hc : S \rightarrow \{0,1\}^l$ be a hardcore function for TDRs, we construct PSPRFs from U to $\{0,1\}^l \cup \perp$ as follows:

- Setup(κ): on input a security parameter κ, run TDR.Setup(κ) to generate public parameters pp.
- KeyGen(pp): on input pp, compute $(ek, td) \leftarrow$ TDR.TrapGen(pp), set $pk = ek$ and $sk = td$, output (pk, sk).
- PubSamp($pk; r$): on input public key pk and random coins r, compute $(s, u) \leftarrow$ TDR.PubSamp($pk; r$), output $(u, hc(s))$.
- PrivEval(sk, u): on input sk and u, compute $s \leftarrow$ TDR.TdInv(sk, u), if $s = \perp$ output $\perp$, else output $hc(s)$.

The correctness of the above construction is easy to verify. For the security, we have the following result:

Theorem 7. *The resulting PSPRFs are (adaptively) weakly pseudorandom if the underlying TDRs are (adaptively) one-way.*

We omit the proof for its straightforwardness. The above result indicates that adaptive PSPRFs are implied by adaptive TDFs. By the separation result due to Gertner, Malkin, and Reingold [17] that it is impossible of basing TDFs on trapdoor predicates, as well as the equivalence among trapdoor predicates, CPA-secure PKEs and PSPRFs, we conclude that PSPRFs are strictly weaker than TDFs in a black-box sense. We conjecture that a similar separation result also exists between adaptive PSPRFs and ATDFs. Besides, whether adaptive PSPRFs are strictly weaker than general ATDRs is also unclear to us. We left this as an open problem.

Acknowledgment. We are grateful to Yi Deng, Qiong Huang, and Dennis Hofheinz for helpful discussions and advice. We also thank the SCN 2014 reviewers for many useful comments.

The first author is supported by the National Natural Science Foundation of China under Grant No. 61303257, No. 61379141, the IIE's Cryptography Research Project, the Strategic Priority Research Program of CAS under Grant No. XDA06010701, and the National 973 Program of China under Grant No. 2011CB302400. The second author is an International Research Fellow of JSPS and supported by the National Natural Science Foundation of China under Grant No. 61303201.

References

1. Alwen, J., Dodis, Y., Naor, M., Segev, G., Walfish, S., Wichs, D.: Public-key encryption in the bounded-retrieval model. In: Gilbert, H. (ed.) EUROCRYPT 2010. LNCS, vol. 6110, pp. 113–134. Springer, Heidelberg (2010)

2. Bellare, M., Halevi, S., Sahai, A., Vadhan, S.P.: Many-to-one trapdoor functions and their relation to public-key cryptosystems. In: Krawczyk, H. (ed.) CRYPTO 1998. LNCS, vol. 1462, pp. 283–298. Springer, Heidelberg (1998)
3. Berman, I., Haitner, I.: From non-adaptive to adaptive pseudorandom functions. In: Cramer, R. (ed.) TCC 2012. LNCS, vol. 7194, pp. 357–368. Springer, Heidelberg (2012)
4. Boneh, D., Canetti, R., Halevi, S., Katz, J.: Chosen-ciphertext security from identity-based encryption. SIAM Journal on Computation 36(5), 1301–1328 (2007)
5. Boneh, D., Waters, B.: Constrained pseudorandom functions and their applications. In: Sako, K., Sarkar, P. (eds.) ASIACRYPT 2013, Part II. LNCS, vol. 8270, pp. 280–300. Springer, Heidelberg (2013)
6. Boyen, X., Mei, Q., Waters, B.: Direct chosen ciphertext security from identity-based techniques. In: CCS 2005, pp. 320–329. ACM (2005)
7. Boyle, E., Goldwasser, S., Ivan, I.: Functional signatures and pseudorandom functions. In: Krawczyk, H. (ed.) PKC 2014. LNCS, vol. 8383, pp. 501–519. Springer, Heidelberg (2014)
8. Cash, D., Kiltz, E., Shoup, V.: The twin diffie-hellman problem and applications. J. Cryptology 22(4), 470–504 (2009)
9. Chen, Y., Zhang, Z.: Publicly evaluable pseudorandom functions and their applications. Cryptology ePrint Archive, Report 2014/306 (2014), http://eprint.iacr.org/2014/306
10. Cramer, R., Hofheinz, D., Kiltz, E.: A twist on the naor-yung paradigm and its application to efficient cca-secure encryption from hard search problems. In: Micciancio, D. (ed.) TCC 2010. LNCS, vol. 5978, pp. 146–164. Springer, Heidelberg (2010)
11. Cramer, R., Shoup, V.: A practical public key cryptosystem provably secure against adaptive chosen ciphertext attack. In: Krawczyk, H. (ed.) CRYPTO 1998. LNCS, vol. 1462, pp. 13–25. Springer, Heidelberg (1998)
12. Cramer, R., Shoup, V.: Universal hash proofs and a paradigm for adaptive chosen ciphertext secure public-key encryption. In: Knudsen, L.R. (ed.) EUROCRYPT 2002. LNCS, vol. 2332, pp. 45–64. Springer, Heidelberg (2002)
13. Cramer, R., Shoup, V.: Design and analysis of practical public-key encryption schemes secure against adaptive chosen ciphertext attack. SIAM Journal on Computing 33, 167–226 (2003)
14. Dachman-Soled, D.: A black-box construction of a cca2 encryption scheme from a plaintext aware encryption scheme. IACR Cryptology ePrint Archive 2013, 680 (2013)
15. Dolev, D., Dwork, C., Naor, M.: Nonmalleable cryptography. SIAM J. Comput. 30(2), 391–437 (2000)
16. ElGamal, T.: A public key cryptosystem and a signature scheme based on discrete logarithms. IEEE Transactions on Information Theory 31, 469–472 (1985)
17. Gertner, Y., Malkin, T., Reingold, O.: On the impossibility of basing trapdoor functions on trapdoor predicates. In: 42nd Annual Symposium on Foundations of Computer Science, FOCS 2001, pp. 126–135. IEEE Computer Society (2001)
18. Goldreich, O., Goldwasser, S., Micali, S.: How to construct random functions. J. ACM 33(4), 792–807 (1986)
19. Goldwasser, S., Micali, S.: Probabilistic encryption. J. Comput. Syst. Sci. 28(2), 270–299 (1984)
20. Hanaoka, G., Kurosawa, K.: Efficient chosen ciphertext secure public key encryption under the computational diffie-hellman assumption. In: Pieprzyk, J. (ed.) ASIACRYPT 2008. LNCS, vol. 5350, pp. 308–325. Springer, Heidelberg (2008)

21. Haralambiev, K., Jager, T., Kiltz, E., Shoup, V.: Simple and efficient public-key encryption from computational diffie-hellman in the standard model. In: Public Key Cryptography - PKC 2010. LNCS, vol. 6056, pp. 1–18. Springer (2010)
22. Håstad, J., Impagliazzo, R., Levin, L.A., Luby, M.: A pseudorandom generator from any one-way function. SIAM J. Comput. 28(4), 1364–1396 (1999)
23. Hofheinz, D., Kiltz, E.: Secure hybrid encryption from weakened key encapsulation. In: Menezes, A. (ed.) CRYPTO 2007. LNCS, vol. 4622, pp. 553–571. Springer, Heidelberg (2007)
24. Hofheinz, D., Kiltz, E.: Practical chosen ciphertext secure encryption from factoring. In: Joux, A. (ed.) EUROCRYPT 2009. LNCS, vol. 5479, pp. 313–332. Springer, Heidelberg (2009)
25. Hohenberger, S., Lewko, A.B., Waters, B.: Detecting dangerous queries: A new approach for chosen ciphertext security. In: Pointcheval, D., Johansson, T. (eds.) EUROCRYPT 2012. LNCS, vol. 7237, pp. 663–681. Springer, Heidelberg (2012)
26. Impagliazzo, R., Rudich, S.: Limits on the provable consequences of one-way permutations. In: Proceedings of the 21st Annual ACM Symposium on Theory of Computing, STOC 1989, pp. 44–61. ACM (1989)
27. Kiayias, A., Papadopoulos, S., Triandopoulos, N., Zacharias, T.: Delegatable pseudorandom functions and applications. In: 2013 ACM SIGSAC Conference on Computer and Communications Security, CCS 2013, pp. 669–684. ACM (2013)
28. Kiltz, E.: On the limitations of the spread of an ibe-to-pke transformation. In: Yung, M., Dodis, Y., Kiayias, A., Malkin, T. (eds.) PKC 2006. LNCS, vol. 3958, pp. 274–289. Springer, Heidelberg (2006)
29. Kiltz, E., Mohassel, P., O'Neill, A.: Adaptive trapdoor functions and chosen-ciphertext security. In: Gilbert, H. (ed.) EUROCRYPT 2010. LNCS, vol. 6110, pp. 673–692. Springer, Heidelberg (2010)
30. Kiltz, E., Pietrzak, K., Stam, M., Yung, M.: A new randomness extraction paradigm for hybrid encryption. In: Joux, A. (ed.) EUROCRYPT 2009. LNCS, vol. 5479, pp. 590–609. Springer, Heidelberg (2009)
31. Kiltz, E., Vahlis, Y.: Cca2 secure ibe: Standard model efficiency through authenticated symmetric encryption. In: Malkin, T. (ed.) CT-RSA 2008. LNCS, vol. 4964, pp. 221–238. Springer, Heidelberg (2008)
32. Kurosawa, K., Desmedt, Y.: A new paradigm of hybrid encryption scheme. In: Franklin, M. (ed.) CRYPTO 2004. LNCS, vol. 3152, pp. 426–442. Springer, Heidelberg (2004)
33. Lin, H., Tessaro, S.: Amplification of chosen-ciphertext security. In: Johansson, T., Nguyen, P.Q. (eds.) EUROCRYPT 2013. LNCS, vol. 7881, pp. 503–519. Springer, Heidelberg (2013)
34. Matsuda, T., Hanaoka, G.: Chosen ciphertext security via point obfuscation. In: Lindell, Y. (ed.) TCC 2014. LNCS, vol. 8349, pp. 95–120. Springer, Heidelberg (2014)
35. Naor, M., Yung, M.: Public-key cryptosystems provably secure against chosen ciphertext attacks. In: Proceedings of the 22th Annual ACM Symposium on Theory of Computing, STOC 1990, pp. 427–437. ACM (1990)
36. Peikert, C.: Lattice cryptography for the internet. IACR Cryptology ePrint Archive, Report 2014/070 (2014), http://eprint.iacr.org/2014/070
37. Peikert, C., Waters, B.: Lossy trapdoor functions and their applications. In: Proceedings of the 40th Annual ACM Symposium on Theory of Computing, STOC 2008, pp. 187–196. ACM (2008)
38. Rabin, M.: Probabilistic algorithms in finite fields. SIAM Journal on Computation 9, 273–280 (1981)

39. Rivest, R., Shamir, A., Adleman, L.: A method for obtaining digital signatures and public key cryptosystems. Communications of the ACM 21(2), 120–126 (1978)
40. Rosen, A., Segev, G.: Chosen-ciphertext security via correlated products. SIAM J. Comput. 39(7), 3058–3088 (2010)
41. Sahai, A., Waters, B.: How to use indistinguishability obfuscation: deniable encryption, and more. In: Symposium on Theory of Computing, STOC 2014, pp. 475–484. ACM Press, New York (2014)
42. Wee, H.: Efficient chosen-ciphertext security via extractable hash proofs. In: Rabin, T. (ed.) CRYPTO 2010. LNCS, vol. 6223, pp. 314–332. Springer, Heidelberg (2010)
43. Yao, A.C.C.: Theory and applications of trapdoor functions (extended abstract). In: FOCS, pp. 80–91. IEEE Computer Society Press (1982)
44. Zhandry, M.: How to avoid obfuscation using witness prfs. IACR Cryptology ePrint Archive, Report 2014/301 (2014), http://eprint.iacr.org/2014/301

A   Review of Standard Definitions

A.1   Key Encapsulation Mechanism

Following the treatment of [36], we equip key encapsulation mechanism (KEM) with an explicit setup algorithm run by a trusted party, which generates some global public parameters shared by all parties. If no trusted party is available, then the setup algorithm can be run by individual parties as part of key generation algorithm, and the public parameters are included in the resulting public key. Formally, a KEM consists of four polynomial-time algorithms:

- Setup(κ): on input security parameters κ, output public parameters pp. We assume that pp also includes the descriptions of ciphertext space C and DEM (data encapsulation mechanism) key space K. pp will be used as an implicit input for algorithms Encap and Decap.
- KeyGen(pp): on input pp, output a public/secret key pair (pk, sk).
- Encap(pk): on input public key pk, output a ciphertext c and a DEM key $k \in K$.
- Decap(sk, c): on input secret key sk and a ciphertext $c \in C$, output a DEM key k or a reject symbol $\perp$ indicating c is invalid.

Correctness: We require that for any $pp \leftarrow$ Setup(κ), any $(pk, sk) \leftarrow$ KeyGen(pp), and any $(c, k) \leftarrow$ Encap(pk), it holds that: $\Pr[\text{Decap}(sk, c) = k] = 1$.

Security: Let $\mathcal{A} = (\mathcal{A}_1, \mathcal{A}_2)$ be an adversary against KEM and define its advantage as:

$$\mathsf{Adv}_{\mathcal{A}}(\kappa) = \Pr \left[b = b' : \begin{array}{l} pp \leftarrow \mathsf{Setup}(\kappa); \\ (pk, sk) \leftarrow \mathsf{KeyGen}(pp); \\ state \leftarrow \mathcal{A}_1^{\mathcal{O}_{\mathsf{dec}}(\cdot)}(pp, pk); \\ (c^*, k_0^*) \leftarrow \mathsf{Encap}(pk), k_1^* \xleftarrow{\mathrm{R}} K; \\ b \xleftarrow{\mathrm{R}} \{0, 1\}; \\ b' \leftarrow \mathcal{A}_2^{\mathcal{O}_{\mathsf{dec}}(\cdot)}(state, c^*, k_b^*); \end{array} \right] - \frac{1}{2},$$

where $\mathcal{O}_{\text{dec}}(c) = \text{Decap}(sk, c)$, and $\mathcal{A}_2$ is not allowed to query $\mathcal{O}_{\text{dec}}(\cdot)$ for the challenge ciphertext c^*. A KEM is said to be IND-CCA secure if for any PPT adversary $\mathcal{A}$, its advantage defined as above is negligible in κ. The IND-CPA security for KEM can be defined similarly except that the adversary is not allowed to access $\mathcal{O}_{\text{dec}}(\cdot)$.

A.2   Trapdoor Functions

Trapdoor functions (TDFs) consists of five polynomial-time algorithms as below:

- Setup(κ): on input a security parameter κ, output public parameters pp which includes a TDF instance description (TDF, EK, TD, X, Y), where $TDF = \{\text{TDF}_{ek} : X \to Y\}_{ek \in EK}$.
- TrapGen(pp): on input pp, output $(ek, td) \in EK \times TD$.
- SampleDom(r): on input ek and random coins r, output a random $x \in X$.
- Eval(ek, x): on input ek and $x \in X$, output $\text{TDF}_{ek}(x)$.
- TdInv(td, y): on input td and $y \in Y$, output $x \in X$ or a distinguished symbol $\perp$ indicating y does not have pre-image.

Correctness: We require that for any $pp \leftarrow \text{Setup}(\kappa)$, any $(ek, td) \leftarrow \text{TrapGen}(pp)$, and any $y = \text{Eval}(ek, x)$, it holds that: $\Pr[\text{Eval}(ek, \text{TdInv}(td, y)) = y] = 1$.

Adaptive One-Wayness: Let $\mathcal{A} = (\mathcal{A}_1, \mathcal{A}_2)$ be an inverter against trapdoor functions and define its advantage as:

$$
\text{Adv}_{\mathcal{A}}(\kappa) = \Pr \left[x \in \text{TDF}_{ek}^{-1}(y^*) : \begin{array}{l} pp \leftarrow \text{Setup}(\kappa); \\ (ek, td) \leftarrow \text{TrapGen}(pp); \\ state \leftarrow \mathcal{A}_1^{\mathcal{O}_{\text{inv}}(\cdot)}(pp, ek); \\ y^* \leftarrow \text{Eval}(ek, x^*), x^* \leftarrow \text{SampleDom}(r^*); \\ x \leftarrow \mathcal{A}_2^{\mathcal{O}_{\text{inv}}(\cdot)}(state, y^*) \end{array} \right],
$$

where $\mathcal{O}_{\text{inv}}(y) = \text{TdInv}(td, y)$, and $\mathcal{A}_2$ is not allowed to query $\mathcal{O}_{\text{inv}}(\cdot)$ for the challenge y^*. We say TDFs are adaptively one-way (or simply adaptively) if for any PPT inverter its advantage is negligible in κ. The standard one-wayness can be defined similarly as above except that the adversary is not given access to the inversion oracle.

On the Classification of Finite Boolean Functions up to Fairness

Nikolaos Makriyannis

Departament de Tecnologies de la Informació i les Comunicacions
Universitat Pompeu Fabra, Spain
nikolaos.makriyannis@upf.edu

Abstract. Two parties, P_1 and P_2, wish to jointly compute some function $f(x,y)$ where P_1 only knows x, whereas P_2 only knows y. Furthermore, and most importantly, the parties wish to reveal only what the output suggests. Function f is said to be computable with *complete fairness* if there exists a protocol computing f such that whenever one of the parties obtains the correct output, then both of them do. The only protocol known to compute functions with complete fairness is the one of Gordon et al (STOC 2008). The functions in question are finite, Boolean, and the output is shared by both parties. The classification of such functions up to fairness may be a first step towards the classification of all functionalities up to fairness. Recently, Asharov (TCC 2014) identifies two families of functions that are computable with fairness using the protocol of Gordon et al and another family for which the protocol (potentially) falls short. Surprisingly, these families account for almost all finite Boolean functions. In this paper, we expand our understanding of what can be computed fairly with the protocol of Gordon et al. In particular, we fully describe which functions the protocol computes fairly and which it (potentially) does not. Furthermore, we present a new class of functions for which fair computation is outright impossible. Finally, we confirm and expand Asharov's observation regarding the fairness of finite Boolean functions: almost all functions $f : X \times Y \to \{0,1\}$ for which $|X| \neq |Y|$ are fair, whereas almost all functions for which $|X| = |Y|$ are not.

Keywords: Complete Fairness, Secure Two-Party Computation.

1 Introduction

Assume that k parties wish to jointly compute some functionality on k inputs where each party holds exactly one of the inputs. *Secure Multi-Party Computation* explains how, given certain security requirements and under certain assumptions, this task may be accomplished. For instance, using the standard convention, in the presence of an adversary that is malicious (may deviate from a protocol arbitrarily), computationally bounded, and only corrupts a strict minority of parties, it is well known [8] that for any functionality there exist protocols that guarantee at the same time, *privacy* - parties learn only what their

M. Abdalla and R. De Prisco (Eds.): SCN 2014, LNCS 8642, pp. 135–154, 2014.
© Springer International Publishing Switzerland 2014

(personal) inputs/outputs suggest, *correctness* - parties' outputs are distributed according to the prescribed functionality, *independence of inputs* - no party can choose his input as a function of another party's input, *complete fairness* - if a certain party learns the correct output then all of them do. On the other hand, if the adversary corrupts more than half of the parties, then protocols are known to exist that satisfy the first three requirements but not the last. Whether or not there exist protocols that guarantee complete fairness (*fairness* for short) is an open problem. In fact, the problem remains open even for the case where only two parties are involved and the functionality in question is finite, Boolean and deterministic. The aim of the present paper is to shed some light on this particular case: fairness of finite Boolean functions in 2PC.

It was long thought that non-trivial functions are *not* computable with fairness. Cleve's seminal paper [7], while not explicitly about fairness, has some clear implications regarding the topic in question. Loosely speaking, any function that can be used for coin-tossing is *not* computable with fairness. This includes, among others, the exclusive-or operation XOR : $(x, y) \mapsto x \oplus y$. Arguably, the implications of Cleve's paper may have deterred others from pursuing the question.

In a surprising turn of events, Gordon et al [9] showed that the folklore is false. In particular, all finite Boolean functions f that *do not* contain embedded XORs (i.e. $\exists x_1, y_1, x_2, y_2$ such that $f(x_1, y_1) = f(x_2, y_2) \neq f(x_1, y_2) = f(x_2, y_1)$) are computable with fairness. These functions roughly correspond to the Millionaire's Problem (i.e. $f(x, y) = 0 \Leftrightarrow x \geq y$). The authors also show that even certain XOR-embedded functions are fair. Using the real/ideal world paradigm, they design a protocol (that we henceforth refer to as the GHKL-protocol) and show that for certain functions, any real world adversary can be simulated in the ideal model. Thus proving that in an execution of the GHKL-protocol, the adversary cannot gain any advantage in learning the output over the honest party. On the other hand, in [4], Asharov et al give a complete characterization of finite Boolean functions that are not fair due to the coin-tossing criterion. In other words, there exists a class of functions (*strictly balanced* functions) that cannot be computed fairly, since the realisation of any such function yields a completely fair coin-toss. What's more, they show that functions that are not in that class *cannot* be reduced to the coin-tossing problem, meaning that any new negative results with respect to fairness must rely on different criteria.

Another major advancement towards characterizing all finite Boolean functions up to fairness appears recently in [2]. The author shows that there exists an extensive amount of functions that can be computed fairly using a slightly generalised version of the GHKL-protocol. Thus proving that these functions are inherently fair. Surprisingly, the author shows that taking a random function where players have input domains of different size will result, with overwhelming probability, in a fair function. On the flip side, Asharov shows that the GHKL-protocol does not account for all functions whose fairness remains unknown (In fact, almost all functions $f : X \times Y \to \{0, 1\}$ for which $|X| = |Y|$). These functions are not reducible to coin-tossing, nor are they computable with fairness using the GHKL-protocol, leaving the problem of determining whether they are fair or not wide open. Finally, the author also considers asymmetric and non-binary functions.

Preventing one party from gaining an advantage over the other seems like a desirable security requirement for 2PC. Fairness guarantees exactly that. In addition, apart from its obvious appeal as a security requirement, fairness is important to the theoretical foundation of Multi-Party Computation. The characterization of finite Boolean functions that are computable with fairness may be a first step towards the classification of all functionalities up to fairness.

Our Results. In the present paper, we take another step towards characterizing finite Boolean functions up to fairness. Ideally, we would like to find a universal criterion to determine whether a *deterministic single-output Boolean function* is computable with fairness. We remind the reader that certain functions are known to be fair (using the GHKL-protocol) and certain functions are not (due to the coin-tossing criterion). We contribute to both of these fronts. First, we give a definite answer to the following question: Given a finite Boolean function f : $X \times Y \to \{0, 1\}$, is f computable with fairness using the GHKL-protocol? In [2], Asharov answers the question for three particular families of functions. We settle the question using linear algebra. Next, we expand our knowledge of functions which are provably unfair. We show that certain functions are reducible to the sampling problem: P_1 and P_2 generate separate random bits according to some joint probability distribution. The sampling problem is a natural generalisation of coin-tossing and was shown *not* to be computable with fairness by Agrawal and Prabhakaran [1]. Finally, by using the same argument, we confirm and expand Asharov's observation regarding the fairness of finite Boolean functions: *almost all functions $f : X \times Y \to \{0, 1\}$ for which $|X| \neq |Y|$ are fair, whereas almost all functions for which $|X| = |Y|$ are not.*

Outline of the Paper. The next section contains notation and definitions. In particular, we introduce secure computation and the ideal model paradigm. In Section 3 we give an informal description of the GHKL-protocol (in its generalised version proposed by Asharov [2]) and a brief overview of the simulation strategy. We conclude with a sufficient criterion for fairness, as it appears in [9]. Our contributions begin in Section 4 where we find an equivalent criterion involving the linear dependence of the columns of a certain associated matrix. Section 5 contains the classification of all functions with respect to these criteria. Finally, the last section contains our negative result. We present a class of functions for which fair computation is impossible.

2 Preliminaries

We begin with notation and definitions. Throughout the paper we focus on functions of the form $f : X \times Y \to \{0, 1\}$, where X and Y are finite and ordered sets, that is $X = \{x_1, \ldots, x_\ell\}$ and $Y = \{y_1, \ldots, y_k\}$. To every such function we associate a matrix $M \in \mathbb{R}^{\ell \times k}$, where $M_{i,j} = f(x_i, y_j)$. The ith row and jth column of M will be denoted row_i and col_j, respectively. Thus,

$$M = \begin{pmatrix} \text{row}_1 \\ \vdots \\ \text{row}_\ell \end{pmatrix} = \begin{pmatrix} \text{col}_1 \mid \ldots \mid \text{col}_k \end{pmatrix}.$$

More generally, we use capital letters for matrices $(M, P, \ldots)$. We denote the kernel and image of M by $\ker(M)$ and $\text{im}(M)$ respectively, and its transpose by M^T. Vectors will be denoted by lower case letters $(u, v, \ldots)$ or bold letters $(\mathbf{p}, \mathbf{q}, \mathbf{x}, \ldots)$. In particular, $\mathbf{1}_\ell$ and $\mathbf{0}_\ell$ represent the all-1 and all-0 vector respectively, these elements will also be called monochromatic. We say that $\mathbf{p}^T = (p_1, \ldots, p_k)$ is a probability vector if $\sum_i p_i = 1$ and $p_j \geq 0$, for every j.

Let $\mathbb{R}^k$ denote the real vector space of dimension k and let $\langle u \mid v \rangle = u^T v$ denote the standard inner product. As usual, two vectors are orthogonal if their inner product is equal to 0. Similarly, two subsets of $\mathbb{R}^k$ are orthogonal if every element of the first is orthogonal to every element of the second. Recall the fundamental theorem of linear algebra: for a given matrix $M \in \mathbb{R}^{\ell \times k}$, $\ker(M)$ and $\text{im}(M^T)$ are orthogonal and their sum spans the entire space. Furthermore, let $I^{\ker(M)}$ denote the *orthogonal* projection of $\mathbb{R}^k$ onto $\ker(M)$ i.e. $I^{\ker(M)}$ is the unique linear map from $\mathbb{R}^k$ onto itself that annihilates the elements of $\text{im}(M^T)$ and corresponds to the identity when restricted to $\ker(M)$. Finally, given a vector space $\mathcal{V} \subseteq \mathbb{R}^k$ and a $k \times k$ matrix P, we say that P defines an endomorphism of $\mathcal{V}$ if $Pv \in \mathcal{V}$, for every $v \in \mathcal{V}$.

2.1 Two-Party Computation

Let $n \in \mathbb{N}$ denote the security parameter. A function $\mu(\cdot)$ is *negligible* if it vanishes faster than any (positive) inverse-polynomial. A distribution ensemble $X = \{X(a, n)\}_{a \in \Delta_n, n \in \mathbb{N}}$ is an infinite sequence of random variables indexed by Δ_n and $\mathbb{N}$. Two distribution ensembles, X and Y, are *computationally indistinguishable* if for every non-uniform polynomial-time algorithm D, there exists a negligible function μ such that for every a and n

$$|\Pr[D(X(a, n)) = 1] - \Pr[D(Y(a, n)) = 1]| \leq \mu(n).$$

Furthermore, we say that X and Y are *statistically close* if for all a and n, the following sum is upper-bounded by a negligible function in n:

$$\frac{1}{2} \cdot \sum_s |\Pr[X(a, n) = s] - \Pr[Y(a, n) = s]|,$$

where s ranges over the support of either $X(a, n)$ or $Y(a, n)$. We write $X \stackrel{c}{\equiv} Y$ when the ensembles are computationally indistinguishable and $X \stackrel{s}{\equiv} Y$ when they are statistically close.

Let P_1, P_2 denote the parties. A *two-party functionality* $\mathcal{F} = \{f_n\}_{n\in\mathbb{N}}$, is a sequence of random processes such that each f_n maps pairs of inputs (one for each party) to pairs of random variables (one for each party). The domain of f_n is denoted $X_n \times Y_n$ and the output (f_n^1, f_n^2). A *two-party protocol* π for computing a functionality $\mathcal{F}$, is a polynomial-time protocol such that on inputs $x \in X_n$ and $y \in Y_n$, the joint distribution of the outputs of any honest execution of π is statistically close to $f_n(x,y) = (f_n^1(x,y), f_n^2(x,y))$.

The Adversary. Following the usual convention, we introduce an adversary $\mathcal{A}$ given auxiliary input z corrupting one of the parties. The adversary is assumed to be malicious and computationally bounded. For a protocol π computing $\mathcal{F}$, let $(\text{Out}_{\mathcal{A}(z),\pi}^{\text{Real}}, \text{View}_{\mathcal{A}(z),\pi}^{\text{Real}})(x,y,n)$ denote the joint distribution of the honest party's output and the adversary's view during an execution of π, where x and y are the prescribed inputs and n is the security parameter.

2.2 The Ideal Model Paradigm

Let $\mathcal{F} = \{f_n\}_{n\in\mathbb{N}}$ be a two-party functionality and let π be a protocol for computing $\mathcal{F}$. Further assume that an adversary is corrupting one of the parties. Security in two-party computation is defined via an *ideal model*. Namely, we assume that parties have access to a trusted party that performs the computation for them, and we attempt to show that protocol π *emulates* this ideal scenario. We will now describe three ideal models and give definitions of security for each of them. The first corresponds to complete fairness which is the topic of the present paper. Our goal is to show there exist (or not) protocols which are secure with respect to this model. The other two are stepping stones which will help us achieve that goal. We now describe the *ideal model with complete fairness* (Figure 1).

Inputs: P_1 holds 1^n and $x \in X_n$, P_2 holds 1^n and $y \in Y_n$. The adversary is given an auxiliary input $z \in \{0,1\}^*$.

Parties send inputs: The honest party sends his input to $\mathcal{T}$, the corrupted party sends a value of the adversary's choice. Write (x',y') for the pair of inputs received by $\mathcal{T}$.

Trusted party performs computation: If either x' or y' are not in the appropriate domain, then $\mathcal{T}$ reassigns the aberrant input to some default value. Write (x',y') for the pair of inputs after (possible) reassignment. The trusted party then chooses a random string r and computes $(f_n^1, f_n^2) = f_n(x',y';r)$.

Trusted party sends outputs: Party P_1 receives f_n^1, P_2 receives f_n^2.

Outputs: The honest party outputs whatever $\mathcal{T}$ sent him, the corrupted party outputs nothing and the adversary outputs a probabilistic polynomial-time function of its view.

Fig. 1. Ideal model with complete fairness

Let $\mathcal{S}$ be an adversary given auxiliary input z corrupting one of the parties. Write $(\mathrm{Out}_{\mathcal{S}(z),f}^{\mathrm{IM\ fair}}, \mathrm{View}_{\mathcal{S}(z),f}^{\mathrm{IM\ fair}})(x,y,n)$ for the joint distribution of the honest party's output and the adversary's view, where x and y are the prescribed inputs and n is the security parameter. We now define security with respect to the ideal model with complete fairness.

Definition 2.1. *Let π be a protocol for computing $\mathcal{F}$. We say that π securely computes $\mathcal{F}$ with complete fairness (or $\mathcal{F}$ is fair for short) if for every non-uniform polynomial time adversary $\mathcal{A}$ in the real model, there exists a non-uniform polynomial time adversary $\mathcal{S}$ in the ideal model such that*

$$\left\{\left(\mathrm{Out}_{\mathcal{A}(z),\pi}^{\mathrm{Real}}, \mathrm{View}_{\mathcal{A}(z),\pi}^{\mathrm{Real}}\right)(x,y,n)\right\}_{\substack{(x,y)\in X_n\times Y_n,\\ z\in\{0,1\}^*, n\in\mathbb{N}}} \overset{c}{\equiv}$$

$$\left\{\left(\mathrm{Out}_{\mathcal{S}(z),\mathcal{F}}^{\mathrm{IM\ fair}}, \mathrm{View}_{\mathcal{S}(z),\mathcal{F}}^{\mathrm{IM\ fair}}\right)(x,y,n)\right\}_{\substack{(x,y)\in X_n\times Y_n,\\ z\in\{0,1\}^*, n\in\mathbb{N}}}.$$

In effect, showing that the above distribution ensembles are computationally indistinguishable implies that, in the plain model, the information acquired by the adversary together with his influence over the honest party's output is no worse than what can be achieved in an idealized situation. Moving on, we also define the *ideal model with abort* (Figure 2) and define security with respect to this model. We note that all functionalities are securely computable with abort (Definition 2.2). Once again, let $\mathcal{S}$ be an adversary given auxiliary input z corrupting one of the parties, and write $(\mathrm{Out}_{\mathcal{S}(z),f}^{\mathrm{IM\ abort}}, \mathrm{View}_{\mathcal{S}(z),f}^{\mathrm{IM\ abort}})(x,y,n)$ for the joint distribution of the honest party's output and the adversary's view, where x and y are the prescribed inputs and n is the security parameter.

Definition 2.2. *Let π be a protocol for computing $\mathcal{F}$. We say that π securely computes $\mathcal{F}$ with abort if for every non-uniform polynomial time adversary $\mathcal{A}$ in the real model, there exists a non-uniform polynomial time adversary $\mathcal{S}$ in the ideal model such that*

$$\left\{\left(\mathrm{Out}_{\mathcal{A}(z),\pi}^{\mathrm{Real}}, \mathrm{View}_{\mathcal{A}(z),\pi}^{\mathrm{Real}}\right)(x,y,n)\right\}_{\substack{(x,y)\in X_n\times Y_n,\\ z\in\{0,1\}^*, n\in\mathbb{N}}} \overset{c}{\equiv}$$

$$\left\{\left(\mathrm{Out}_{\mathcal{S}(z),\mathcal{F}}^{\mathrm{IM\ abort}}, \mathrm{View}_{\mathcal{S}(z),\mathcal{F}}^{\mathrm{IM\ abort}}\right)(x,y,n)\right\}_{\substack{(x,y)\in X_n\times Y_n,\\ z\in\{0,1\}^*, n\in\mathbb{N}}}.$$

The Hybrid Model. In secure computation, the hybrid model is a tool that allows us to break some cryptographic task into subtask and, assuming these subtasks can be implemented securely, prove the security of the overlying task.

Inputs: P_1 holds 1^n and $x \in X_n$, P_2 holds 1^n and $y \in Y_n$. The adversary is given an auxiliary input $z \in \{0,1\}^*$.

Parties send inputs: The honest party sends his input to $\mathcal{T}$, the corrupted party sends a value of the adversary's choice. Write (x', y') for the pair of inputs received by $\mathcal{T}$.

Trusted party performs computation: If either x' or y' are not in the appropriate domain, then $\mathcal{T}$ reassigns the aberrant input to some default value. Write (x', y') for the pair of inputs after (possible) reassignment. The trusted party then chooses a random string r and computes $(f_n^1, f_n^2) = f_n(x', y'; r)$.

Trusted party sends outputs: Corrupted party P_i receives f_n^i from the trusted party. The adversary then decides either to *abort* or *continue*. In the first case, $\mathcal{T}$ sends $\perp$ to the honest party. In the second case, P_{3-i} receives f_n^{3-i}.

Outputs: The honest party outputs whatever $\mathcal{T}$ sent him, the corrupted party outputs nothing and the adversary outputs a probabilistic polynomial-time function of its view.

Fig. 2. Ideal model with abort

Let $\mathcal{F}_1, \ldots, \mathcal{F}_m$ and $\mathcal{F}$ be two-party functionalities. A protocol π for computing $\mathcal{F}$ in the $(\mathcal{F}_1, \ldots, \mathcal{F}_m)$-hybrid model consists in an protocol computing $\mathcal{F}$ that proceed in rounds such that at any given round:

- Parties exchange information as in the real model *or*
- Parties invoke a trusted party computing $\mathcal{F}_i$ according to a specified ideal model.

We say that π computes $\mathcal{F}$ securely in the $(\mathcal{F}_1, \ldots, \mathcal{F}_m)$-hybrid model if for any adversary corrupting one of the parties in the hybrid model, there exists a simulator $\mathcal{S}$ in the ideal model such that the joint distribution of the adversary's view and honest party's output is indistinguishable in both worlds. Hence, applying the composition theorem of [6], and assuming there exists secure protocols $\rho_1, \ldots, \rho_m$ computing $\mathcal{F}_1, \ldots, \mathcal{F}_m$, protocol $\pi^{\rho_1 \cdots \rho_m}$ securely computes $\mathcal{F}$, where $\pi^{\rho_1 \cdots \rho_m}$ is obtained by replacing ideal calls to the trusted party with the appropriate protocols.

Reactive Functionalities. A reactive functionality $\mathcal{G}$ is a cryptographic task that proceeds in several phases, where the input of one phase may depend on the output of previous phases. With respect to the ideal model with abort, every reactive functionality can be computed securely. Let π be a protocol for computing $\mathcal{F}$ that does not involve any direct exchange of information between the parties. Rather, at any given round, parties make a single call to a trusted party computing $\mathcal{G}$ with abort. The composition theorem still holds, that is if the joint distribution of the adversary's view and honest party's output is indistinguishable in the $\mathcal{G}$-hybrid and ideal model *with complete fairness*, then protocol π^ρ securely computes $\mathcal{F}$ with complete fairness, where ρ securely computes $\mathcal{G}$ with abort. In fact, following Asharov [2], the GHKL-protocol in the next section is defined by means of a reactive functionality.

3   Computing Fair Functions

In this section, we focus on the GHKL-protocol [9], the only protocol that provably computes (certain) functions with complete fairness. We follow the description and generalisation proposed by Asharov in [2]. The protocol is defined in the hybrid model where parties have access to a trusted party computing a certain reactive functionality with abort. We give an informal description of the protocol and a brief overview of the simulation strategy. The complete description and simulation strategy can be found in [10] and [3], in their respective appendices.

3.1   Informal Description of the Generalised GHKL-Protocol

Let $f : X \times Y \to \{0, 1\}$ be a finite Boolean function, suppose that the prescribed inputs of P_1, P_2 are x and y respectively. The GHKL-protocol for computing f is parametrized by three values: a real number $\alpha \in (0, 1)$, a probability vector $\mathbf{p} \in \mathbb{R}^\ell$ and the security parameter n. Prior to the execution of the protocol, the number of rounds is fixed at $r = \alpha^{-1} \cdot \omega(\ln(n))$.

- **Compute Backup Outputs:** P_1 chooses $\widetilde{y} \in Y$ according to the uniform distribution and computes $a_0 = f(x_i, \widetilde{y})$, P_2 chooses $\widetilde{x} \in X$ according to distribution $\mathbf{p}$ and computes $b_0 = f(\widetilde{x}, y_j)$.
- **Preliminary Phase:** Parties are instructed to send their inputs to the trusted party. If either input is not in the correct domain, the trusted party responds with an abort symbol to both parties and halts. Otherwise, write (x', y') for the pair of inputs received by the trusted party. The trusted party is instructed to choose an integer i^* according to the geometric distribution with parameter α, and constructs the following bits:
  - For $i = 1 \ldots i^* - 1$, set $a_i = f(x', \widetilde{y}^{(i)})$ and $b_i = f(\widetilde{x}^{(i)}, y')$ where $\widetilde{y}^{(i)}$ and $\widetilde{x}^{(i)}$ are chosen according to the uniform distribution and distribution $\mathbf{p}$, respectively.
  - For $i = i^* \ldots r$, set $a_i = b_i = f(x', y')$.
- **Online Phase:** For $i = 1 \ldots r$
  1. P_2 sends proceed to the trusted party, P_1 then receives a_i.
  2. P_1 sends proceed to the trusted party, P_2 then receives b_i.
  If either party sends abort, then both receive $\perp$ and the trusted party halts.
- **Outputs:** Parties are instructed to output the last a_i/b_i they successfully constructed/received.

3.2   Security

In order to prove security, we need to show that any adversary in the hybrid model can be simulated in the ideal model with complete fairness. On an intuitive level, note that a corrupted P_2 cannot affect the protocol's fairness. No matter what, P_1 always receives the correct input first. In fact, a corrupted P_2 can be simulated regardless of the parameters, for *any* function (see [9] and [2]). On the other hand, precisely because P_1 receives the correct input first, an adversary

$\mathcal{A}$ controlling P_1 can potentially affect the protocol's fairness. We focus on the latter case and give an incomplete description of the simulator $\mathcal{S}$ *in the ideal model.*

Suppose that $\mathcal{A}$ hands $x \in X$ to $\mathcal{S}$ for the computation of f. The simulator chooses a value i^* according to the geometric distribution with parameter α. Now, for $i = 1 \ldots i^* - 1$, simulator $\mathcal{S}$ hands $a_i = f(x, \widetilde{y}^{(i)})$ to $\mathcal{A}$, where $\widetilde{y}^{(i)}$ is chosen according to the uniform distribution. If at any point the adversary decides to abort, $\mathcal{S}$ chooses x' according to probability distribution $\mathbf{x}_x^{(a_i)}$ (that we define below), sends x' to the trusted party, outputs whatever $\mathcal{A}$ outputs, and halts. Otherwise, at $i = i^*$, the simulator sends x to the trusted party and receives $a_{\text{out}} = f(x, y)$ which it hands to $\mathcal{A}$. If $\mathcal{A}$ aborts, then $\mathcal{S}$ outputs whatever $\mathcal{A}$ outputs, and halts. Finally, for $i = i^* + 1 \ldots r$, the simulator hands a_{out} to $\mathcal{A}$. Once again, if $\mathcal{A}$ aborts, then $\mathcal{S}$ outputs whatever $\mathcal{A}$ outputs, and halts.

Recall that the protocol is secure if the joint distributions of the adversary's view and the honest party output in the ideal and hybrid model are computationally indistinguishable. The simulation strategy boils down to the existence of $\mathbf{x}_x^{(a)}$ that will do the trick. Using the fact that i^* is chosen according to a geometric distribution, it can be shown that the above simulation works if for all $a \in \{0, 1\}$, for all $x \in \{x_1, \ldots, x_\ell\}$,

$$M^T \cdot \mathbf{x}_x^{(a)} = \mathbf{c}_x^{(a)},$$

where $M_{i,j} = f(x_i, y_j)$,

$$\mathbf{c}_x^{(0)}(j) \stackrel{\text{def}}{=} \begin{cases} p_{y_j} & \text{if } f(x, y_j) = 1 \\ \frac{\alpha \cdot p_{y_j}}{(1-\alpha) \cdot (1-p_x)} + p_{y_j} & \text{otherwise} \end{cases},$$

$$\mathbf{c}_x^{(1)}(j) \stackrel{\text{def}}{=} \begin{cases} \frac{\alpha \cdot (p_{y_j} - 1)}{(1-\alpha) \cdot p_x} + p_{y_j} & \text{if } f(x, y_j) = 1 \\ p_{y_j} & \text{otherwise} \end{cases},$$

and

$$(p_{y_1}, \ldots, p_{y_k}) \stackrel{\text{def}}{=} \mathbf{p}^T \cdot M, \qquad (p_{x_1}, \ldots, p_{x_\ell})^T \stackrel{\text{def}}{=} M \cdot (1/k, \ldots, 1/k)^T.$$

Theorem 3.1. *Using the notation above, if for some probability vector $\mathbf{p}$ and $\alpha \in (0, 1)$, and for all $i \in \{1, \ldots, \ell\}$, there exist probability vectors $\mathbf{x}_{x_i}^{(0)}, \mathbf{x}_{x_i}^{(1)} \in \mathbb{R}^\ell$ such that*

$$M^T \cdot \mathbf{x}_{x_i}^{(a)} = \mathbf{c}_{x_i}^{(a)},$$

then f is computable with complete fairness using the GHKL-protocol.

Arguably, a function that does not satisfy the criteria of the above theorem may still be computable with fairness using the GHKL-protocol. Of course, such a claim must be accompanied by a new valid simulation strategy, since the one described above will not work. With that in mind, and for the rest of the paper, a function will be said to be *GHKL-fair* if it satisfies the hypothesis of Theorem 3.1. In other words, a function is GHKL-fair if it is computable with fairness using the GHKL-protocol *and* the particular simulation strategy described above proves it.

4   Equivalent Conditions for GHKL-Fairness

The conditions of Theorem 3.1 depend heavily on parameters of the protocol, namely α, $\{p_{x_i}\}_i$ and $\{p_{y_j}\}_y$. A universal criterion for fairness would only depend on the function itself. Failing that, we aim to find equivalent conditions that are "easier" to verify. In this section, starting with the equations of Theorem 3.1, we present a new set of conditions that do not depend on α, nor $\{p_{x_i}\}_i$, but only $\{p_{y_j}\}_j$ and the function itself. Let f be a finite boolean function, and assume that f is GHKL-fair i.e. for some $\alpha \in (0,1)$ and probability vector $\mathbf{p}$, and all $i \in \{1,\ldots,\ell\}$, there exist probability vectors $\mathbf{x}_{x_i}^{(0)}, \mathbf{x}_{x_i}^{(1)} \in \mathbb{R}^\ell$ such that $M^T \cdot \mathbf{x}_{x_i}^{(a)} = \mathbf{c}_{x_i}^{(a)}$. Define

$$\widetilde{\mathbf{x}}_{x_i}^{(0)} \stackrel{\text{def}}{=} \frac{(1-\alpha)(1-p_{x_i})}{\alpha}\left(\mathbf{x}_{x_i}^{(0)} - \mathbf{p}\right) ,$$

$$\widetilde{\mathbf{x}}_{x_i}^{(1)} \stackrel{\text{def}}{=} \frac{(1-\alpha)p_{x_i}}{\alpha}\left(\mathbf{x}_{x_i}^{(1)} - \mathbf{p}\right) ,$$

and note that

$$M^T \cdot \widetilde{\mathbf{x}}_{x_i}^{(a)} = \widetilde{\mathbf{c}}_{x_i}^{(a)} , \tag{1}$$

where

$$\widetilde{\mathbf{c}}_{x_i}^{(0)}(j) = \begin{cases} 0 & \text{if } f(x_i, y_j) = 1 \\ p_{y_j} & \text{otherwise} \end{cases} , \qquad \widetilde{\mathbf{c}}_{x_i}^{(1)}(j) = \begin{cases} p_{y_j} - 1 & \text{if } f(x_i, y_j) = 1 \\ 0 & \text{otherwise} \end{cases} .$$

Furthermore,

$$\sum_j \widetilde{\mathbf{x}}_{x_i}^{(a)}(j) = 0 , \tag{2}$$

$$\forall j, \ \widetilde{\mathbf{x}}_{x_i}^{(0)}(j) \in \frac{(1-\alpha)(1-p_{x_i})}{\alpha} \cdot [-\mathbf{p}(j), 1 - \mathbf{p}(j)] , \tag{3}$$

$$\forall j, \ \widetilde{\mathbf{x}}_{x_i}^{(1)}(j) \in \frac{(1-\alpha)p_{x_i}}{\alpha} \cdot [-\mathbf{p}(j), 1 - \mathbf{p}(j)] . \tag{4}$$

Conversely, if for some probability vector $\mathbf{p}$ and $\alpha \in (0,1)$, and for all i, there exist $\widetilde{\mathbf{x}}_{x_i}^{(0)}$ and $\widetilde{\mathbf{x}}_{x_i}^{(1)}$ satisfying relations (1) to (4), then we can construct $\mathbf{x}_{x_i}^{(0)}$ and $\mathbf{x}_{x_i}^{(1)}$ satisfying Theorem 3.1. Specifically,

$$\mathbf{x}_{x_i}^{(0)} = \begin{cases} \frac{\alpha \cdot \widetilde{\mathbf{x}}_{x_i}^{(0)}}{(1-\alpha)(1-p_{x_i})} + \mathbf{p} & \text{if } p_{x_i} \neq 1 \\ \mathbf{p} & \text{otherwise} \end{cases} , \qquad \mathbf{x}_{x_i}^{(1)} = \begin{cases} \frac{\alpha \cdot \widetilde{\mathbf{x}}_{x_i}^{(1)}}{(1-\alpha)p_{x_i}} + \mathbf{p} & \text{if } p_{x_i} \neq 0 \\ \mathbf{p} & \text{otherwise} \end{cases} .$$

Simplifying Assumption. Probability vector $\mathbf{p}$ will be considered without zero-components i.e. $\forall j, \mathbf{p}(j) \neq 0$. Note that, in this case, the intervals defined in (3) and (4) grow arbitrarily as α tends to zero. Thus, we are only required to verify relations (1) and (2). On the other hand, we claim that this simplifying assumption does not incur any loss of generality: If there exists a "suitable" $\mathbf{p}$ with zero-entries, then we can construct another "suitable" probability vector that is strictly positive. For further details, see Appendix A. To sum up, we conclude with the following theorem.

Theorem 4.1. *Using the notation above, function f is GHKL-fair if and only if for some strictly positive $\mathbf{p}$, and all $i \in \{1, \ldots, \ell\}$, there exist $\widetilde{\mathbf{x}}_{x_i}^{(0)}$ and $\widetilde{\mathbf{x}}_{x_i}^{(1)}$ such that*

$$M^T \cdot \widetilde{\mathbf{x}}_{x_i}^{(a)} = \widetilde{\mathbf{c}}_{x_i}^{(a)} \qquad and \qquad \sum_j \widetilde{\mathbf{x}}_{x_i}^{(a)}(j) = 0 .$$

Recall that $\mathbf{p}^T M = (p_{y_1}, \ldots, p_{y_k})$. Define $P(M, \mathbf{p}) = \mathrm{diag}(p_{y_1}, \ldots, p_{y_k})$ i.e. the diagonal matrix whose components are the p_{y_i}. If no confusion arises, $P(M, \mathbf{p})$ will be denoted P. In Figure 3, we express the conditions of Theorem 4.1 with respect to matrix P.

For all $i \in \{1, \ldots, \ell\}$, for all $a \in \{0, 1\}$, there exists $(\mu_{i,1}^{(a)}, \ldots, \mu_{i,\ell}^{(a)})$ that satisfies

1. $\sum_j \mu_{i,j}^{(a)} = 0$,
2. $(\mu_{i,1}^{(0)}, \ldots, \mu_{i,\ell}^{(0)})M = (1_k^T - \mathrm{row}_i)P$,
3. $(\mu_{i,1}^{(1)}, \ldots, \mu_{i,\ell}^{(1)})M = \mathrm{row}_i(P - \mathrm{Id}_k)$.

Fig. 3. GHKL-fairness conditions

In effect, function f is GHKL-fair if $(1_k^T - \mathrm{row}_i)P$ and $\mathrm{row}_i(P - \mathrm{Id}_k)$ belong to the image of M^T and admit a suitable pre-image. Let $\mathcal{V} = \{v \in \mathbb{R}^\ell \mid \sum_i v_i = 0\}$. By considering an appropriate basis of $\mathcal{V}$, we note that the image of $\mathcal{V}$ by M^T corresponds exactly to the image of M'^T, where

$$M' = \begin{pmatrix} \mathrm{row}_1 \\ \mathrm{row}_1 \\ \vdots \\ \mathrm{row}_1 \end{pmatrix} - \begin{pmatrix} \mathrm{row}_2 \\ \mathrm{row}_3 \\ \vdots \\ \mathrm{row}_\ell \end{pmatrix} .$$

Furthermore, a quick analysis shows that $\ker(M') = \{v \in \mathbb{R}^k \mid Mv = (\delta, \ldots, \delta)^T\}$. Going back to the conditions of Figure 3, function f is GHKL-fair if $(1_k^T - \mathrm{row}_i)P$ and $\mathrm{row}_i(P - \mathrm{Id}_k)$ belong to the image of M'^T. By orthogonality,

$$\forall v \in \ker(M'), \quad \begin{cases} (1_k^T - \mathrm{row}_i)Pv = 0 \\ \mathrm{row}_i(P - \mathrm{Id}_k)v = 0 \end{cases} ,$$

both of which boil down to $\mathrm{row}_i Pv = \delta$. By letting i vary, we deduce the following Proposition.

Proposition 4.2. *Function f is GHKL-fair if and only if there exists $\mathbf{p}$ such that $Mv = MPv$, for every $v \in \ker(M')$.*

Already, we see that for a given $\mathbf{p}$, verifying that a function f is GHKL-fair is very easy. Take a basis of $\ker(M')$ and check that $M(\mathrm{Id}_k - P)v = \mathbf{0}_\ell$, for every element of the basis. Of course finding $\mathbf{p}$ is a non-trivial task, and we look into that later on. For the remainder of the section, we show that certain functions are not viable candidates for GHKL-fairness, regardless of the value of $\mathbf{p}$.

Lemma 4.3. *Assuming $Mv = MPv$, for every $v \in \ker(M')$, matrix P defines an endomorphism of $\ker(M)$ as well as $\mathrm{im}(M^T)$.*

Proof. First of all, if $v \in \ker(M)$, then $MPv = Mv = 0$ and thus $Pv \in \ker(M)$. On the other hand, let $u \in \mathrm{im}(M^T)$ and $v \in \ker(M)$. Since P is diagonal, we deduce that $\langle Pu \,|\, v \rangle = \langle u \,|\, Pv \rangle$, and thus $\langle Pu \,|\, v \rangle = 0$. Since v is arbitrary, $Pu \in \mathrm{im}(M^T)$. □

Lemma 4.4. *Suppose that $Mv = MPv$, for every $v \in \ker(M')$. Furthermore, assuming it exists, let $b \in \mathbb{R}^k$ denote the unique pre-image of $\mathbf{1}_\ell$ by M that is orthogonal to $\ker(M)$. Then, $b(j) \neq 0$ implies $\mathrm{col}_j = \mathbf{1}_\ell$.*

Proof. We know that $(\mathrm{Id}_k - P)b \in \ker(M)$. Now, since P is an endomorphism of $\mathrm{im}(M^T)$, and thus $(\mathrm{Id}_k - P)b \in \mathrm{im}(M^T)$, we deduce that $(\mathrm{Id}_k - P)b = 0$. Consequently $b(j) \neq 0$ implies $P_{j,j} = 1$, and since $P_{j,j} = \mathbf{p}^T \mathrm{col}_j$ and $\mathbf{p} > \mathbf{0}_\ell$, we conclude that $\mathrm{col}_j = \mathbf{1}_\ell$. □

Theorem 4.5. *Using the notation above, f is GHKL-fair if and only if*

1. *no linear combination of the non-monochromatic columns of M yields $\mathbf{1}_\ell$,*
2. *there exists a strictly positive $\mathbf{p}$ such that matrix P defines an endomorphism of $\ker(M)$.*

Proof. The second item is necessary because of Lemma 4.3. For the first item, suppose without loss of generality that the first k' columns contain $\mathbf{1}_\ell$ in their linear span, and none of them is monochromatic. We show that $b(j) \neq 0$, for some $j \in \{1, \ldots, k'\}$, in contradiction with Lemma 4.4. Let $v = (v_1, \ldots, v_{k'}, 0, \ldots, 0)$, such that $Mv = \mathbf{1}_\ell$. We know that $v = b + v'$, where $v' \in \ker(M)$. Consequently, $\langle v \,|\, b \rangle = \langle b \,|\, b \rangle > 0$, and we conclude that at least one of the first k' entries of b is non-zero.

Conversely, we show that the two conditions imply Proposition 4.2. First, since P is an endomorphism of $\ker(M)$, then $0 = Mv = MPv$, for all $v \in \ker(M)$. It remains to show that $Mb = MPb$. Since the non-monochromatic columns of M do not span the all-1 vector, we deduce that $b(j) \neq 0$ if and only if $\mathrm{col}_i = \mathbf{1}_\ell$, and thus $P_{i,i} = 1$. Consequently, $Pb = b$, and thus f is GHKL-fair. It can also be shown that neither condition is sufficient on its own. □

5 Classification of GHKL-Fair Functions

We now present a classification of finite Boolean functions with respect to GHKL-fairness. We subdivide functions into four families, three of which can be accounted for almost immediately. First, we prove a couple of claims.

Proposition 5.1. *If f is GHKL-fair, then the same is true of $1 - f$.*

Proof. We prove the claim by applying Proposition 4.2. Assuming that M is the associated matrix of f, write $\overline{M}$ for the associated matrix of $1 - f$. Using the same $\mathbf{p}$, assuming that $Mv = MPv$, for every $v \in \ker(M')$, and noting that $\ker(\overline{M}') = \ker(M')$, we conclude that $\overline{M}v = \overline{M} \cdot P(\overline{M}, \mathbf{p}) \cdot v$, for every $v \in \ker(\overline{M}')$. □

Corollary 5.2. *Suppose that f is GHKL-fair. Further assume that the first k' columns of M are non-monochromatic. Then, $\sum_{i=1}^{k'} v_i \mathrm{col}_i = \mathbf{0}_\ell$ implies $\sum_{i=1}^{k'} v_i = 0$.*

Proof. If not, we obtain a contradiction with the above proposition and the first item of Theorem 4.5. □

Define $M_{0/1} \in \{0,1\}^{\ell \times k'}$ obtained from M by deleting all monochromatic columns. We distinguish 4 types of functions depending on the following properties of their associated matrix:

(Type 1) $\mathbf{1}_\ell \in \mathrm{im}(M_{0/1})$.
(Type 2) $\mathbf{1}_\ell \notin \mathrm{im}(M_{0/1})$ and $\ker(M_{0/1}) = \{\mathbf{0}_{k'}\}$.
(Type 3) $\mathbf{1}_\ell \notin \mathrm{im}(M_{0/1})$ and $\ker(M_{0/1}) \neq \{\mathbf{0}_{k'}\}$ and $\ker(M_{0/1}) \subseteq \{v \mid \sum_i v_i = 0\}$.
(Type 4) $\mathbf{1}_\ell \notin \mathrm{im}(M_{0/1})$ and $\ker(M_{0/1}) \neq \{\mathbf{0}_{k'}\}$ and $\ker(M_{0/1}) \nsubseteq \{v \mid \sum_i v_i = 0\}$.

Theorem 5.3. *Let f be a finite Boolean function.*

- *If f is of type 1 or 4, then it is not GHKL-fair.*
- *If f is of type 2, then it is GHKL-fair.*

Proof. Functions of type 1 do not satisfy the first item of Theorem 4.5. Similarly, functions of type 4 are not in accordance with Corollary 5.2. On the other hand, and by applying Theorem 4.5, we note that functions of type 2 and 3 do not contain $\mathbf{1}_\ell$ in the linear span of the non-monochromatic columns. It remains to show that there exists a strictly positive $\mathbf{p}$ such that matrix P defines an endomorphism of the kernel. If f is of type 2, then columns of M that are linearly dependent are all monochromatic. Knowing that $(p_{y_1}, \ldots, p_{y_k}) = \mathbf{p}^T M$, a quick analysis shows that matrix P defines an endomorphism of $\ker(M)$, for any $\mathbf{p}$. Finally, for functions of type 3, the existence of $\mathbf{p}$ depends on the linearly dependent columns of $M_{0/1}$, and so a general rule cannot be extrapolated at this point. □

The theorem above confirms the findings of Asharov. Namely, in [2], the author identifies two families of GHKL-fair functions, both of which are of type 2. On the flip side, the author finds a family of functions for which the simulation strategy we consider falls short. Indeed, these are type 1 functions.

5.1   Finding the Probability Vector

Theorem 5.3 does not account for functions of type 3. Indeed, the existence of **p** depends on the linearly dependent columns of $M_{0/1}$. In the remainder of this section, we show that the existence of **p** is subject to the resolution of a linear program. We note that the program is defined in the broadest possible terms, meaning that it's a "one size fits all" way to find **p**. To illustrate, consider a matrix $M \in \{0,1\}^{\ell \times k}$ of type 2. Construct a new matrix by concatenating a column of M to itself. Now, M is of type 2 and thus GHKL-fair, whereas the other is of type 3. It is easy to see however that it is also GHKL-fair, for any **p**. Moving on, recall that $I^{\ker(M)}$ denotes the orthogonal projection onto the kernel of M. Furthermore, for all i, let I^{row_i} denote the diagonal matrix $I^{\mathrm{row}_i}_{j,j} = \mathrm{row}_i(j)$.

Theorem 5.4. *Let f be a finite Boolean function of type 3. Function f is GHKL-fair if and only if*

$$\begin{pmatrix} I^{\ker(M)} \cdot I^{\mathrm{row}_1} \\ \vdots \\ I^{\ker(M)} \cdot I^{\mathrm{row}_\ell} \end{pmatrix} M^T \begin{pmatrix} r_1 \\ \vdots \\ r_\ell \end{pmatrix} = \begin{pmatrix} 0 \\ \vdots \\ 0 \end{pmatrix} \tag{5}$$

admits a strictly positive solution.

Proof. Let $\mathbf{p} = (r_1, \ldots, r_\ell)^T$. First, note that $P = \sum_i r_i I^{\mathrm{row}_i}$, and that P defines an endomorphism of $\ker(M)$ if and only if

$$\forall j \in \{1, \ldots, \ell\}, \quad \left(\sum_i r_i I^{\mathrm{row}_i} \right) \mathrm{row}_j^T \in \mathrm{im}(M^T) . \tag{6}$$

Since the matrices are all diagonal, and thus commute, we deduce that

$$\left(\sum_i r_i I^{\mathrm{row}_i} \right) \mathrm{row}_j^T = \left(\sum_i r_i I^{\mathrm{row}_i} \right) I^{\mathrm{row}_j} \cdot 1_\ell = I^{\mathrm{row}_j} \left(\sum_i r_i \mathrm{row}_i^T \right)$$

$$= I^{\mathrm{row}_j} \left(\sum_i r_i \mathrm{row}_i^T \right) = I^{\mathrm{row}_j} \cdot M^T (r_1, \ldots, r_\ell)^T .$$

Consequently, (6) holds if and only if (5) admits a strictly positive solution, in which case the probability vector is obtained by normalisation. $\qquad\square$

5.2   Complete Fairness and GHKL-Fairness

We take a moment to discuss the relationship between complete and GHKL-fairness. Recall that the latter depends on a specific protocol (and simulation strategy), and constitutes a sufficient criterion for complete fairness. Let f be a finite Boolean function and define $f^T : (y, x) \mapsto f(x, y)$. It might be the case that f^T is GHKL-fair, while f is not. It is easy to see however that f is indeed computable with complete fairness, the protocol in question being the GHKL-protocol with the players' roles interchanged. We conclude that for any f, if either f or f^T are GHKL-fair, then f is computable with complete fairness.

Another possibility is to consider *computationally equivalent functions* [9] i.e. functions obtained by adding/deleting redundant inputs. By applying Theorem 4.5 however, one can show that GHKL-fairness is preserved. In particular, adding/deleting redundant inputs for P_2 has no effect, and with a straightforward modification of the probability vector, the same can be shown for P_1. In summary, assuming a given function f is fair, if neither f nor f^T is GHKL-fair then to the best of our knowledge, there is no immediate way to design a completely fair protocol computing f from the one of Gordon, Hazay, Katz and Lindell.

On the other hand, assume that fair computation is impossible for a given function f. Further assume that the function is not reducible to coin-tossing (not strictly balanced [4]). Then we need a new argument to prove that it is indeed unfair. In the next section, we do exactly that.

6   A Class of Unfair Functions

In this section, we present a new class of functions for which fair computation is impossible. We begin with an example. Let $f : \{x_1, \ldots, x_4\} \times \{y_1, \ldots, y_4\} \to \{0, 1\}$ be the function with associated matrix

$$M = \begin{pmatrix} 0 & 1 & 0 & 1 \\ 1 & 1 & 1 & 0 \\ 0 & 0 & 1 & 0 \\ 1 & 0 & 0 & 0 \end{pmatrix}.$$

First, note that neither f nor f^T are GHKL-fair, since both of them are of type 1. Assuming there exists a completely fair realization of function f, consider the following: P_1 chooses among $\{x_1, x_3, x_4\}$ with equal probability, P_2 chooses y_4 with probability $2/5$, or one of his other inputs with probability $1/5$. Players compute f on the chosen inputs and obtain b. Define

$$\text{Out}_1 = b, \qquad \text{Out}_2 = \begin{cases} 1 - b & \text{if } P_2 \text{ chose } y_2 \\ b & \text{otherwise} \end{cases}.$$

A quick analysis shows that $\Pr[\text{Out}_1 = 1] = 1/3$, $\Pr[\text{Out}_2 = 1] = 2/5$, and that the two are equal with probability $4/5$. If Out_1 and Out_2 were independent, they would be equal with probability $8/15$, which is not the case. Finally, it is not hard to see that any malicious behaviour by either party does not affect the probability distribution of the other party's output.

In fact, we have just described a non-trivial instance of the sampling problem: parties P_1 and P_2 generate bits b_1 and b_2, respectively, according to some *joint* probability distribution. Secure sampling is said to be non-trivial if the outputs are not independent. In [1], Agrawal and Prabhakaran show that this problem cannot be realised with complete fairness. In what follows, we demonstrate that there exists a large class of functions that are reducible to the sampling problem, and are thus unfair. Formally, let $\mathcal{F}_{SS}$ denote the following functionality:

- **Parameters.** $p, q \in [0,1]$ and $\chi \in [2\max(p+q-1,0)-2pq, \ 2\min(p,q)-2pq]$.
- **Inputs.** Empty for both parties.
- **Outputs.** P_1 and P_2 receive bits b_1 and $b_2 \in \{0,1\}$, respectively, such that
  1. $\Pr[b_1 = 1] = p$,
  2. $\Pr[b_2 = 1] = q$,
  3. $\Pr[b_1 = b_2] = pq + (1-p)(1-q) + \chi$.

Theorem 6.1. *Unless $\chi = 0$, functionality $\mathcal{F}_{SS}$ is not computable with complete fairness.*

Proof. The proof is a natural generalisation of Cleve's [7] original argument (where $p = q = 1/2$) and can be found in [1]. Note that if $\chi = 0$, then b_1 and b_2 are independent and $\mathcal{F}_{SS}$ is trivially fair. $\qquad\square$

In fact, $\mathcal{F}_{SS}$ is not computable with complete fairness even if we allow the adversary to learn the honest party's output. Formally, we augment the ideal model with complete fairness such that after sending the outputs, the trusted party divulges the honest party's output to the adversary. We claim that $\mathcal{F}_{SS}$ is not securely computable in this new augmented model. The claim is true because Cleve's argument makes no assumption regarding the privacy of the parties' outputs. As a corollary, we deduce that any finite Boolean function that can be reduced to an instance of the sampling problem is inherently unfair, even if the adversary learns the honest party's output.

6.1   Semi-balanced Functions

In [2], the author identifies a class of functions that are not GHKL-fair. Here, we go one step further and show that they are inherently unfair. In particular, they are all reducible to a (non-trivial) instance of the sampling problem.

Definition 6.2. *Let f be a finite boolean function with matrix representation M and write $\overline{M}$ for the matrix representation of $1 - f$. We say that f is right semi-balanced if*

$$\exists \mathbf{q} \in \mathbb{R}^k \text{ such that } \begin{cases} M\mathbf{q} = \mathbf{1}_\ell \\ \overline{M}\mathbf{q} \neq \mathbf{0}_\ell \end{cases}.$$

Similarly, f is left semi-balanced if

$$\exists \mathbf{p} \in \mathbb{R}^\ell \text{ such that } \begin{cases} M^T\mathbf{p} = \mathbf{1}_k \\ \overline{M}^T\mathbf{p} \neq \mathbf{0}_k \end{cases}.$$

Theorem 6.3. *If f is left and right semi-balanced, then f is not computable with complete fairness.*

We dedicate the rest of the section to the proof of Theorem 6.3. We show that any secure protocol computing f with respect to the ideal model with complete fairness, implies the existence of a secure protocol computing $\mathcal{F}_{SS}$ with respect to the augmented model where the adversary learns the honest party's output. Assuming f is left and right semi-balanced, fix $\mathbf{q} \in \mathbb{R}^k$, $\mathbf{p} \in \mathbb{R}^\ell$ such that

$$
\begin{cases}
\sum_i |p_i| = 1 \\
\mathbf{p}^T M = (\delta_1, \ldots, \delta_1), \quad \delta_1 > 0, \\
\mathbf{p}^T \overline{M} \neq (0, \ldots, 0)
\end{cases}
\qquad
\begin{cases}
\sum_i |q_i| = 1 \\
M\mathbf{q} = (\delta_2, \ldots, \delta_2)^T, \quad \delta_2 > 0 \\
\overline{M}\mathbf{q} \neq (0, \ldots, 0)^T
\end{cases}.
$$

Suppose that parties have access to a trusted party $\mathcal{T}$ computing f. Consider protocol π in the *f-hybrid* model:

- **Inputs:** On empty inputs, P_1 chooses x_i with probability $|p_i|$, P_2 chooses column y_j with probability $|q_j|$.
- **Invoke Trusted Party:** P_1, P_2 invoke the trusted party on inputs x_i and y_j respectively. As per the ideal model with complete fairness (Figure 1), $\mathcal{T}$ hands both parties a bit b.
- **Outputs:** If $p_i < 0$, then P_1 outputs $1 - b$. Similarly, if $q_j < 0$, then P_2 outputs $1 - b$. Otherwise, parties are instructed to output b.

Define p^+, q^+, p^-, q^- such that $p^- = 1 - p^+ = \sum_{p_i < 0} |p_i|$, and $q^- = 1 - q^+ = \sum_{q_j < 0} |q_j|$.

Lemma 6.4. $(p^+ - p^-)\delta_2 = (q^+ - q^-)\delta_1$.

Proof.

$$
\begin{aligned}
(p^+ - p^-)\delta_2 &= \mathbf{p}^T (\delta_2, \ldots, \delta_2)^T = \mathbf{p}^T M \mathbf{q} \\
&= (\delta_1, \ldots, \delta_1)\mathbf{q} = (q^+ - q^-)\delta_1.
\end{aligned}
$$

$\square$

Lemma 6.5. *An honest execution of π yields the following outputs:*

- $\Pr[\mathrm{Out}_1 = 1] = \delta_1 + p^-$,
- $\Pr[\mathrm{Out}_2 = 1] = \delta_2 + q^-$,
- Out_1 *and* Out_2 *are not independent random variables.*

Proof. Write $\mathrm{Out}_2^{(1)}(x_i)$ for $\Pr[\mathrm{Out}_2 = 1 \mid x = x_i]$, then

$$
\begin{aligned}
\left(\mathrm{Out}_2^{(1)}(x_1), \ldots, \mathrm{Out}_2^{(1)}(x_\ell) \right)^T &= \sum_{q_i < 0} |q_i|(\mathbf{1}_\ell - \mathrm{col}_i) + \sum_{q_i \geq 0} |q_i|\mathrm{col}_i \\
&= \sum_{q_i < 0} |q_i|\mathbf{1}_\ell + \sum_{i=1}^{k} q_i \mathrm{col}_i \\
&= q^- \mathbf{1}_\ell + M\mathbf{q} = (q^- + \delta_2, \ldots, q^- + \delta_2)^T.
\end{aligned}
$$

The output of P_1 is obtained in a similar fashion. Moving on, if Out_1 and Out_2 are independent, then they are equal with probability

$$(\delta_1 + p^-)(\delta_2 + q^-) + (-\delta_1 + p^+)(-\delta_2 + q^+) .$$

On the other hand, when the players execute π, they will agree on the output if and only if both players flip their bits, or both players do not. Thus, $\Pr[\text{Out}_1 = \text{Out}_2] = p^- q^- + p^+ q^+$. Consequently, if Out_1 and Out_2 are independent random variables, we deduce that

$$(\delta_1 + p^+)(\delta_2 + q^-) + (-\delta_1 + p^+)(-\delta_2 + q^+) = p^- q^- + p^+ q^+ ,$$

which boils down to $2\delta_1\delta_2 = \delta_1(q^+ - q^-) + \delta_2(p^+ - p^-)$. Now, by Lemma 6.4 and knowing that $\delta_1, \delta_2 \neq 0$, we deduce that that $\delta_2 = \sum_j q_j$ and $\delta_1 = \sum_{i=1}^{\ell} p_i$. These in turn are equivalent to $\overline{M}\mathbf{q} = \mathbf{0}_\ell$ and $\mathbf{p}^T \overline{M} = \mathbf{0}_k^T$, which we have ruled out by assumption. Hence, we conclude that

$$\Pr[\text{Out}_1 = \text{Out}_2] =$$
$$\Pr[\text{Out}_1 = 0]\Pr[\text{Out}_2 = 0] + \Pr[\text{Out}_1 = 1]\Pr[\text{Out}_2 = 1] + \chi ,$$

for some $\chi \neq 0$.   □

It remains to show that every adversary in the f-hybrid model can be simulated in the ideal model. We briefly describe the simulation strategy for a corrupted P_1, the other case being identical. First, construct $\ell \times k$ matrix $\widetilde{M}$ such that the j-th column of $\widetilde{M}$ is equal to col_j if $q_j > 0$, and $1 - \text{col}_j$ otherwise. Now, simulator $\mathcal{S}$ invokes $\mathcal{A}$ on the security parameter and auxiliary input z. The adversary hands x_i to $\mathcal{S}$ for the computation of f, and the simulator invokes the trusted party for computing $\mathcal{F}_{SS}$. As per the augmented model with complete fairness, the trusted party leaks the honest party's output, say Out_2, to $\mathcal{S}$. The simulator chooses y_j according to the prescribed distribution conditioned on $\widetilde{M}_{i,j} = \text{Out}_2$. If $q_j < 0$, the simulator hands $1 - \text{Out}_2$ to $\mathcal{A}$. Otherwise, $\mathcal{S}$ hands Out_2 to $\mathcal{A}$. In any case, the simulator outputs whatever $\mathcal{A}$ outputs, and halts. It is easy to see that the simulation strategy yields identical output distributions in the hybrid and ideal world.

7   Conclusion

To conclude, we make an observation regarding the number of functions that are either GHKL-fair or semi-balanced. A weaker version appears in [2] and the argument is based on [13]. Take a random function $f : X \times Y \to \{0,1\}$ such that $|X| > |Y|$. Then, with probability greater than $1 - \nu(|Y|)$, where $\nu(*)$ is some negligible function, f is GHKL-fair. Intuitively, this occurs because k random $0/1$-vectors of size ℓ (with $\ell > k$) will almost surely form a linearly independent set and yet their linear span will not contain the all-1 vector.

Similarly, take a random function $f : X \times Y \to \{0,1\}$ such that $|X| = |Y|$. Then, with probability greater than $1 - \nu(|Y|)$, where $\nu(*)$ is the same negligible function, f is (left *and* right) semi-balanced. The intuition now relies on the fact that for a random square matrix M, both M and $\overline{M}$ are non-singular with overwhelming probability. Putting everything together, we come to the following conclusion: Almost all functions for which $|X| \neq |Y|$ are computable with fairness, whereas almost all functions for which $|X| = |Y|$ are not.

References

[1] Agrawal, S., Prabhakaran, M.: On fair exchange, fair coins and fair sampling. In: Canetti, R., Garay, J.A. (eds.) CRYPTO 2013, Part I. LNCS, vol. 8042, pp. 259–276. Springer, Heidelberg (2013)

[2] Asharov, G.: Towards characterizing complete fairness in secure two-party computation. In: Lindell, Y. (ed.) TCC 2014. LNCS, vol. 8349, pp. 291–316. Springer, Heidelberg (2014)

[3] Asharov, G.: Towards characterizing complete fairness in secure two-party computation (extended version). Cryptology ePrint Archive, Report 2014/098 098 (2014), http://eprint.iacr.org/2014/098

[4] Asharov, G., Lindell, Y., Rabin, T.: A full characterization of functions that imply fair coin tossing and ramifications to fairness. In: Sahai, A. (ed.) TCC 2013. LNCS, vol. 7785, pp. 243–262. Springer, Heidelberg (2013)

[5] Blum, M.: Coin flipping by telephone a protocol for solving impossible problems. SIGACT News 15(1), 23–27 (1983)

[6] Canetti, R.: Security and composition of multiparty cryptographic protocols. J. Cryptology 13(1), 143–202 (2000)

[7] Cleve, R.: Limits on the security of coin flips when half the processors are faulty. In: STOC 1986, pp. 364–369. ACM (1986)

[8] Goldreich, O.: Foundations of Cryptography. Basic Applications, vol. 2. Cambridge University Press (2004)

[9] Gordon, D.S., Hazay, C., Katz, J., Lindell, Y.: Complete fairness in secure two-party computation. In: STOC 2008, pp. 413–422. ACM (2008)

[10] Gordon, S.D., Hazay, C., Katz, J., Lindell, Y.: Complete fairness in secure two-party computation (extended version). Cryptology ePrint Archive, Report 2008/303 (2008), http://eprint.iacr.org/2008/303

[11] Moran, T., Naor, M., Segev, G.: An optimally fair coin toss. In: Reingold, O. (ed.) TCC 2009. LNCS, vol. 5444, pp. 1–18. Springer, Heidelberg (2009)

[12] Yao, A.C.: Protocols for secure computations, pp. 160–164 (1982)

[13] Ziegler, G.M.: Lectures on 0/1-polytopes. In: Kalai, G., Ziegler, G.M. (eds.) Polytopes Combinatorics and Computation, DMV Seminar, pp. 1–41. Birkhauser, Basel (2000)

A   Considering Probability Vectors with Zero-Components

Let $f = \{x_1, \ldots, x_\ell\} \times \{y_1, \ldots, y_k\} \to \{0, 1\}$ and consider its associated matrix M. Furthermore, fix a probability vector $\mathbf{p} \in \mathbb{R}^\ell$ and define $k \times k$ matrix $P = \text{diag}(p_{y_1}, \ldots, p_{y_k})$ where

$$(p_{y_1}, \ldots, p_{y_k}) = \mathbf{p}^T M \ .$$

Recall the alternate GHKL-fairness conditions: for all $i \in \{1, \ldots, \ell\}$, for all $a \in \{0, 1\}$, there exists $(\mu_{i,1}^{(a)}, \ldots, \mu_{i,\ell}^{(a)})$ satisfying

1. $\sum_j \mu_{i,j}^{(a)} = 0$,
2. $(\mu_{i,1}^{(0)}, \ldots, \mu_{i,\ell}^{(0)})M = (\mathbf{1}_k^T - \text{row}_i)P$ with $\mu_{i,j}^{(0)} \geq 0$ if $\mathbf{p}(j) = 0$,
3. $(\mu_{i,1}^{(1)}, \ldots, \mu_{i,\ell}^{(1)})M = \text{row}_i(P - \text{Id}_k)$ with $\mu_{i,j}^{(1)} \geq 0$ if $\mathbf{p}(j) = 0$.

Without loss of generality, suppose that $\mathbf{p}(1) = 0$ and that the GHKL-fairness conditions are satisfied. Then

$$(\mu_{1,1}^{(0)}, \ldots, \mu_{1,\ell}^{(0)})M = (\mathbf{1}_k^T - \text{row}_1)P$$
$$(\mu_{1,1}^{(1)} + 1, \ldots, \mu_{1,\ell}^{(1)})M = \text{row}_1 P .$$

Add the two expressions together:

$$(\mu_{1,1}^{(0)} + \mu_{1,1}^{(1)} + 1, \ldots, \mu_{1,\ell}^{(0)} + \mu_{1,\ell}^{(1)})M = \mathbf{1}_k^T P = \mathbf{p}^T M .$$

Thus,

$$\left(\mu_{1,1}^{(0)} + \mu_{1,1}^{(1)} + 1 - \mathbf{p}(1), \ldots, \mu_{1,\ell}^{(0)} + \mu_{1,\ell}^{(1)} - \mathbf{p}(\ell)\right)M = 0 ,$$

and note that $\mu_{1,1}^{(0)} + \mu_{1,1}^{(1)} + 1 - \mathbf{p}(1) > 0$. Now, define $\mathcal{D} = \{j \mid \mathbf{p}(j) = 0\}$ and let $d = |\mathcal{D}|$. Using the same trick as above for every row indexed by $\mathcal{D}$, deduce that $(\nu_1, \ldots, \nu_\ell)M = 0$, where

- $\nu_i = 1 + \sum_{j \in \mathcal{D}}(\mu_{j,i}^{(0)} + \mu_{j,i}^{(1)}) > 0$ if $i \in \mathcal{D}$,
- $\nu_i = -d \cdot \mathbf{p}(i) + \sum_{j \in \mathcal{D}}(\mu_{j,i}^{(0)} + \mu_{j,i}^{(1)})$ if $i \notin \mathcal{D}$,
- $\sum_i \nu_i = 0$.

Next, choose $\gamma > 0$ such that

$$-\mathbf{p}(i) < \gamma \cdot \nu_i < 1 - \mathbf{p}(i) ,$$

for every $i \in \{1, \ldots, \ell\}$, and define probability vector $\widetilde{\mathbf{p}} = \mathbf{p} + \gamma \cdot \nu$. By noting that $\widetilde{\mathbf{p}}^T M = \mathbf{p}^T M = (p_{y_1}, \ldots, p_{y_k})$, we conclude that function f is GHKL-fair for a new probability vector without zero entries.

Communication-Efficient MPC for General Adversary Structures

Joshua Lampkins[1] and Rafail Ostrovsky[2]

[1] Department of Mathematics,
University of California, Los Angeles, CA 90095
jlampkins@math.ucla.edu
[2] Department of Computer Science and Department of Mathematics,
University of California, Los Angeles, CA 90095
rafail@cs.ucla.edu

Abstract. A multiparty computation (MPC) protocol allows a set of players to compute a function of their inputs while keeping the inputs private and at the same time securing the correctness of the output. Most MPC protocols assume that the adversary can corrupt up to a fixed fraction of the number of players. Hirt and Maurer initiated the study of MPC under more general corruption patterns, in which the adversary is allowed to corrupt any set of players in some pre-defined collection of sets [1]. In this paper we consider this important direction and present improved communication complexity of MPC protocols for general adversary structures. More specifically, ours is the first unconditionally secure protocol that achieves linear communication in the size of Monotone Span Program representing the adversary structure in the malicious setting against any $Q2$ adversary structure, whereas all previous protocols were at least cubic.

Keywords: Multiparty Computation, Secret Sharing, General Adversaries, $Q2$ Adversary Structures, Monotone Span Program.

1 Introduction

In a multiparty computation (MPC) protocol, it is assumed that some of the players might collude together to attempt to determine some other player's input or to alter the output of the function. This is generally modeled as a single adversary corrupting a subset of the players. In order for a protocol to have guaranteed termination for remaining honest (i.e., non-corrupted) players, one must assume that the adversary is limited in the number of players he can corrupt. Most MPC protocols have a simple threshold requirement on the adversary. For instance, if the total number of players is n and the number of players corrupted by the adversary is t, then a protocol might require $t < n/3$ or $t < n/2$.

In this paper, we consider requirements on the adversary which are more general than just threshold requirements. If $\mathcal{P}$ is the set of players, then the most general way of expressing the limitations of the adversary is to select a

M. Abdalla and R. De Prisco (Eds.): SCN 2014, LNCS 8642, pp. 155–174, 2014.
© Springer International Publishing Switzerland 2014

subset $\mathcal{A} \subset 2^{\mathcal{P}}$, called an adversary structure. The adversary is then allowed to corrupt any set of players in $\mathcal{A}$. This paper constructs a Multiparty Computation protocol that is secure against a malicious, adaptive adversary whose corruption pattern is specified by a general $Q2$ adversary structure[1] in the information theoretic setting with a broadcast channel.

1.1 Previous Work

The first MPC protocol for general adversaries was given in Hirt and Maurer [1]. The protocol was recursive, relying on the use of virtual processors/players and "nesting" the virtualization. The MPC protocol for malicious $Q2$ adversaries with a broadcast channel had communication complexity superpolynomial in the size of the description of the adversary structure; the protocol was slightly modified in Fitzi, Hirt and Maurer [2] to yield polynomial communication complexity. More explicit protocols were given in Cramer, Damgård and Maurer [3], Smith and Stiglic [4], and Cramer, Damgård, Dziembowski, Hirt and Rabin [5], each paper constructing an MPC protocol based on Monotone Span Program (MSP) secret sharing, initially developed by Karchmer and Wigderson [6]. An MPC protocol based on a different secret sharing scheme is given in Beaver and Wool [7], which deals with passive adversaries only.

This paper, along with [4] and [5], state the communication complexity in terms of the size d of the smallest multiplicative MSP[2] representing the adversary structure. A separate line of work (including [1] and [2] cited above) on MPC for general adversaries has stated the complexity in terms of the size of the set of maximal sets in the adversary structure, $|\overline{\mathcal{A}}|$. These works do not rely on MSPs, but construct fundamentally different secret sharing schemes. In [8] and [9], the authors achieve a protocol that is cubic in $|\overline{\mathcal{A}}|$; in [10], the authors present a protocol linear in $|\overline{\mathcal{A}}|$.

The two lines of work, those stating the complexity in terms of d and those stating the complexity in terms of $|\overline{\mathcal{A}}|$, are incomparable. It is shown in [11] how to construct an MSP with $d \leq n|\overline{\mathcal{A}}|$. However, this only provides an upper bound on d. In some instances, d can be as low as n. As a concrete example, suppose there is an MPC protocol being run by the U.S., China, and Russia. Each country has five servers running the protocol. We say that a country is corrupt if at least 3 out of the 5 servers in that country are corrupt. The MPC protocol tolerates an adversary that corrupts at most one country. In this case, $d = n = 15$, whereas $|\overline{\mathcal{A}}| = 3\binom{5}{2}^2 = 300$.

In [3], the authors show that a multiplicative MSP for a given adversary structure can be constructed from any MSP for that adversary structure; the size of the multiplicative MSP is at most twice the size of the original MSP. Thus requiring a multiplicative MSP instead of a general MSP makes no difference in terms of asymptotic complexity.

---

[1] $Q2$ adversary structures are defined in Sect. 3.

[2] The terms MSP and multiplicative MSP are defined in Sect. 3.

1.2   Our Contributions

This paper provides an MPC protocol in the setting of a malicious $Q2$ adversary with a broadcast channel. We improve upon the amortized efficiency of previous protocols for malicious, $Q2$ adversaries, as shown in Table 1. In examining the table note that d is the dominating term and can be exponential in n and is always at least n. So in addition to providing a strict improvement over previous protocols, our result is the first MPC protocol secure against malicious and adaptive $Q2$ adversaries that has communication complexity linear in d.

Table 1. Comparison of MPC protocols secure against malicious, $Q2$ adversaries with a broadcast channel. Here, d is the size of the smallest MSP representing adversary structure, n is the number of players, $\mathcal{C}$ is the size of the circuit, and κ is the security parameter. Bandwidth is measured in field elements, and counts both point-to-point communications and broadcasts.

Paper	[4]	[5]	This Paper
Bandwidth	$\Omega(\mathcal{C}\kappa n d^3)$	$\Omega(\mathcal{C}n d^3)$	$O(\mathcal{C}n^2 d + n^3 d + \kappa n^4 \log d)$

1.3   Techniques

One way of dealing with disputes is with a technique called Kudzu shares, as first defined by Beerliová-Trubíniová and Hirt [12]. When one player accuses another of lying (or other such misbehavior), they are said to be in dispute. When a dealer distributes a secret s, the shares sent to players in dispute with the dealer are defined to be zero. That is, instead of using a standard Shamir secret sharing, the dealer picks a random polynomial f such that $f(0) = s$ and $f(i) = 0$ for each P_i in dispute with the dealer. Then the shares $f(i)$ are sent to each player P_i. The shares of the players in dispute with the dealer are called Kudzu shares. Since the set of players in dispute with the dealer is public knowledge, *every* player will know the shares sent to players in dispute with the dealer. This prevents the recipients from lying about the shares they received later in the protocol. The secret sharing scheme from [3] can also be adapted to implement Kudzu shares; ours is the first MPC protocol to implement Kudzu shares with MSP secret sharing for general adversaries.

One common technique used in verifiable secret sharing (VSS) protocols is double sharing, in which the dealer shares the secret and then shares the shares. This allows the players to reconstruct the secret in the presence of corrupt players. Double sharing was used in both [4] and [5]. Since the size of an MSP sharing is d, the size of a double sharing is (at least) d^2. So to achieve communication complexity linear in d, we use another method for reconstructing. Throughout the protocol, each sharing is a linear combination of sharings generated by (possibly) multiple players during different executions of the VSS share protocol. So when an inconsistency is found during reconstruction in the protocol LC-Reconstruct, the players engage in a process similar to the bisection method to locate a *single* sharing for which there is an inconsistency. Then using the authentication/verification tags generated when sharing that value, the players can determine who the corrupt player is.

2   Protocol Overview

The general outline of our MPC protocol is much the same as the protocol in [12]. The MPC protocol is divided into a preparation phase (Sect. 4.7), an input phase (Sect. 4.8), and a computation phase (Sect. 4.9). In the preparation phase, random sharings are generated for random gates and multiplication triples are generated for multiplication gates (generation of multiplication triples is described in Sect. 4.6). In the input phase, players share their inputs. In the computation phase, the arithmetic gates are evaluated. Each phase is broken into (roughly) n^2 segments. All the gates in an individual segment are processed in parallel. If adversarial behavior causes the processing of a segment to fail, a new dispute is located, and the segment in repeated. Since there are n^2 segments, and since there can be no more than n^2 disputes, the asymptotic complexity of the protocol is not altered due to failed segments.

Our MPC protocol differs from that of [12] primarily in the underlying secret sharing schemes. Whereas [12] uses a threshold secret sharing scheme, ours uses a monotone span program secret sharing scheme for general adversaries (Sect. 4.1). In [12], a VSS scheme is constructed from the "basic" threshold scheme by constructing a bivariate polynomial and using information checking protocols [13]. Using a bivariate polynomial would not be suitable for our protocol, because it would add a d^2 factor to the communication complexity. Therefore we apply information checking techniques (Sect. 4.2) to the "basic" monotone span program secret sharing scheme to construct a VSS scheme (Sect. 4.3), which keeps the complexity linear in d. However, this prevents us from reconstructing as in [12]. Thus we use a reconstruction protocol (given in Sect. 4.4)that uses the bisection method (mentioned in Sect. 1.3) to locate a single sharing for which information tags can be used to locate a corrupt player.

3   Definitions and Assumptions

Our MPC protocol is designed for a synchronous network with secure point-to-point channels and an authenticated broadcast channel. The players are to compute an arithmetic circuit over a finite field $\mathbb{F}$ of size[3] $|\mathbb{F}| = 2^\kappa$. We let c_I, c_M, c_R, c_O denote the number of input, multiplication, random, and output gates (respectively) in the circuit. The total size of the circuit is $\mathcal{C} = c_I + c_M + c_R + c_O$. The multiplicative depth of the circuit is $\mathcal{D}$.

Let n represent the number of players. We denote the player set by $\mathcal{P} = \{P_1, \ldots, P_n\}$ and the adversary structure by $\mathcal{A} \subset 2^{\mathcal{P}}$. Adversary structures are

---

[3] We use a field of characteristic 2 because the information checking protocols require an extension field of size at least $d|\mathbb{F}|$, and using a base field of characteristic 2 ensures that the extension field is no more than twice the required size.

monotone, meaning that if $A \in \mathcal{A}$, then any subset of A is in $\mathcal{A}$. We denote by $\overline{\mathcal{A}}$ the set of maximal sets in $\mathcal{A}$ (i.e., the set of all sets in $\mathcal{A}$ that are not proper subsets of any other sets in $\mathcal{A}$). An adversary structure $\mathcal{A}$ is said to be $Q2$ if no two sets in the adversary structure cover the entire player set; that is, $\mathcal{A}$ is $Q2$ if $A, B \in \mathcal{A} \Rightarrow A \cup B \neq \mathcal{P}$. Note that for threshold adversaries, the requirement that $t < n/2$ is one example of a $Q2$ adversary structure. Our MPC protocol is able to tolerate a malicious, adaptive adversary whose corruption pattern is specified by a $Q2$ adversary structure.

We denote by $\mathcal{D}isp$ the set of pairs of players who are in dispute with one another. If at any time a dispute arises between player P_i and player P_j, (i.e., one of them says that the other is lying), the pair $\{P_i, P_j\}$ is added to $\mathcal{D}isp$. Since all disputes are handled over the broadcast channel, each player has the same record of which pairs of players are in $\mathcal{D}isp$. We define $\mathcal{D}isp_i = \{P_j \mid \{P_j, P_i\} \in \mathcal{D}isp\}$. If at any time the set $\mathcal{D}isp_i$ is no longer in $\mathcal{A}$, that means that at least one honest player has accused P_i, and therefore all players know that P_i must be corrupt. We use the set $\mathcal{C}orr$ to denote the set of players known by all players to be corrupt.

Most of the protocols in this paper use dispute control and will terminate when one or more pairs of players are added to $\mathcal{D}isp$. In this case, the protocol terminates unsuccessfully. We handle unsuccessful termination of protocols as in [12]. Namely, the circuit is divided into (roughly) n^2 segments, and if one of the sub-protocols terminates unsuccessfully during the computation for a segment, that segment is started over from the beginning. A new dispute is found at each unsuccessful termination, and since there can be at most n^2 disputes, this does not affect the asymptotic complexity of the protocol. Throughout this paper, we will assume (without explicitly stating it) that if a sub-protocol invoked by a parent protocol terminates unsuccessfully, then the parent protocol terminates unsuccessfully.

Let M be a $d \times e$ matrix over $\mathbb{F}$, and let $\mathbf{a} = (1, 0, 0, \cdots, 0)^\top \in \mathbb{F}^e$. The triple $(\mathbb{F}, M, \mathbf{a})$ is called a *monotone span program* (MSP).[4] Define $(x_1, x_2, \ldots, x_\ell)^\top *$ $(y_1, y_2, \ldots, y_\ell)^\top = (x_1 y_1, x_2 y_2, \ldots, x_\ell y_\ell)^\top$, and suppose $\boldsymbol{\lambda}$ is a vector in $\mathbb{F}^d$. We call $(\mathbb{F}, M, \mathbf{a}, \boldsymbol{\lambda})$ a *multiplicative MSP* if $(\mathbb{F}, M, \mathbf{a})$ is an MSP and if $\boldsymbol{\lambda}$ has the property that

$$\langle \boldsymbol{\lambda}, M\mathbf{b} * M\mathbf{b}' \rangle = \langle \mathbf{a}, \mathbf{b} \rangle \cdot \langle \mathbf{a}, \mathbf{b}' \rangle$$

for all $\mathbf{b}, \mathbf{b}' \in \mathbb{F}^e$. In this case, $\boldsymbol{\lambda}$ is called the *recombination vector*.

Each row of M will be labeled with an index i ($1 \leq i \leq n$), so that each row corresponds to some player. For any nonempty subset $A \subset \{1, 2, \ldots, n\}$, M_A denotes the matrix consisting of all rows whose index is in A. For a given adversary structure $\mathcal{A}$, we say that the MSP $(\mathbb{F}, M, \mathbf{a})$ *represents* $\mathcal{A}$ if

$$A \notin \mathcal{A} \iff \mathbf{a} \in \operatorname{Im} M_A^\top.$$

It is shown in Sect. 4.1 that the condition $\mathbf{a} \in \operatorname{Im} M_A^\top$ implies that a secret shared using M can be reconstructed from the shares of players in A.

---

[4] The definition of MSP in [3] allows $\mathbf{a}$ to be any fixed vector, but it is convenient to choose $\mathbf{a}$ as we have.

The size of the multiplicative MSP representing the adversary structure (measured as the number of rows in the matrix) is of prime importance in analyzing the communication complexity of the MPC protocol, because secrets are shared as a vector in the image of M. In [11], the authors show how to construct an MSP of size at most $n|\overline{\mathcal{A}}|$, and in [3] it is shown how to construct a multiplicative MSP from any given MSP such that the multiplicative MSP has size at most twice that of the original MSP.

A "basic" sharing of a value w created using the MSP (as generated by the protocol Share below) is denoted by $[w]$. The share of player P_i is denoted by w_i. Note that in general w_i will be a vector, since it represents a portion of a vector in the image of M, although it could be a single-element vector. This secret sharing scheme is linear in that each player can compute a sharing of an affine combination of already-shared secrets by performing local computations.

4   The Protocols

This section describes the MPC protocol and all sub-protocols. Due to space constraints, proofs are deferred to the full version [14].

4.1   Secret Sharing

Our MPC protocol uses a "basic" secret sharing protocol and constructs a verifiable secret sharing (VSS) protocol by combining the basic protocol with information checking [13]. The basic secret sharing protocol—which is described in this section—is essentially the secret sharing protocol of [3], except that it is implemented with Kudzu shares [12]. We first review the secret sharing protocol of [3] and then prove that this can be implemented with Kudzu shares.

Given an MSP with matrix M of size $d \times e$ as described in Sect. 3, the secret sharing protocol of [3] proceeds as follows: The dealer with secret s picks $e - 1$ random values $r_2, \ldots, r_e$, constructing a vector $\mathbf{s} = (s, r_2, r_3, \ldots, r_e)$. The dealer then computes $\mathbf{b} = M\mathbf{s} = [s]$ and sends some of the entries of the vector $\mathbf{b}$ to each player. It is shown in [3] how to construct multiplicative MSPs suitable for secret sharing for any given $Q2$ adversary structure. The multiplicative MSP can be constructed from any MSP for the given adversary structure, and the size of the multiplicative MSP will be at most twice the size of the original MSP.

To implement Kudzu shares with this secret sharing scheme, we note that the secret sharing scheme described above is perfectly private (proved in [3]). In other words, the adversary's view of the vector $\mathbf{b}$ is independent of the secret being shared. So for a sharing $\mathbf{b} = [s]$ and a set $A \in \mathcal{A}$, the dealer can construct a sharing of zero $[0]$ such that A's view of $[0]$ is the same as A's view of $[s]$. Then the sharing $[s] - [0]$ is a sharing of s with Kudzu shares, as the shares of all players in dispute with the dealer will be zero.

Protocol. Share(P_D, s)

The dealer P_D wants to share a secret $s \in \mathbb{F}$. He selects random values $r_2, r_3, \ldots$, $r_e \in \mathbb{F}$, constructing a vector $\mathbf{s} = (s, r_2, r_3, \ldots, r_e) \in \mathbb{F}^e$. The random values $r_2, r_3, \ldots, r_e$ are chosen subject to the constraint that the shares of players in dispute with P_D must be all-zero vectors. The dealer then computes $[s] = \mathbf{b} = M\mathbf{s}$, where M is the MSP corresponding to $\mathcal{A}$. The dealer sends $b_j = M_j\mathbf{s}$ to each $P_j \notin \mathcal{D}isp_D$ (where b_j is the vector of components of $\mathbf{b}$ corresponding to player P_j).

For a value $v \in \mathbb{F}$, we call the *canonical sharing* of v the sharing for which $r_2, r_3, \ldots, r_e$ are all zero.

In this paper, we will represent the complexity of each protocol in a table. The columns denote communication bandwidth, broadcast bandwidth, communication rounds, and broadcast rounds (abbreviated CB, BCB, CR, and BCR, respectively). The two rows represent the complexity in the absence of a dispute and the added complexity per dispute. It is assumed that the communication and broadcast bandwidths are stated asymptotically (i.e., the big-O is not written, but is assumed). Bandwidth is measured in field elements, so one would have to multiply by κ to compute the bandwidth in *bits*.

Share	CB	BCB	CR	BCR
$Without Dispute$	d	0	1	0
$Per Dispute$	0	0	0	0

Lemma 1. *The protocol* Share *is a secret sharing scheme secure against any malicious, adaptive adversary with Q2 adversary structure $\mathcal{A}$.*

We now show how reconstruction is performed on a sharing. Suppose we want to reconstruct a secret using the shares of some set A of players satisfying $A \notin \mathcal{A}$. Since the MSP represents $\mathcal{A}$, by definition this means that $\mathbf{a} \in \operatorname{Im} M_A^\top$. So there is some vector ω_A satisfying $M_A^\top \omega_A = \mathbf{a}$. If $[s]_A$ represents the shares of $[s]$ held by players in A and $\mathbf{s} = (s, r_2, \ldots, r_e)^\top$ represents the vector used in Share to generate the sharing $[s]$, then we can reconstruct the secret as

$$\langle \omega_A, [s]_A \rangle = \langle \omega_A, M_A \mathbf{s} \rangle = \langle M_A^\top \omega_A, \mathbf{s} \rangle = \langle \mathbf{a}, \mathbf{s} \rangle = s.$$

4.2 Information Checking

Information checking (IC) [13] is a scheme by which a sender can give a message to a receiver along with some auxiliary information (authentication tags); the sender also gives some auxiliary information (verification tags) to a verifier. This is done such that at a later time, if there is a disagreement about what the sender gave the receiver, the verifier can act as an "objective third party" to settle the dispute. Information checking is used for shares distributed in the VSS protocol so that incorrect shares can be identified during reconstruction. We ensure that the verifier does not find out any information about the message (until a dispute arises).

More specifically, an information checking scheme consists of two protocols, Distribute-Tags and Check-Message. In Distribute-Tags, the sender of the message gives authentication tags to the recipient of the message and verification tags to the verifier. The verifier randomly selects half the her tags to send to the recipient of the message, and the recipient checks that these correctly correspond with the authentication tags (otherwise dispute resolution occurs). In Check-Message, the recipient of the message forwards the message and the authentication tags to the verifier, who then checks these against the verification tags to determine if the message is valid.

The protocols Distribute-Tags and Check-Message that we use are variants of those used in [12], so their explicit description is deferred to the full version [14]. The main difference is that we use an extension field $\mathbb{G}$ of $\mathbb{F}$ to allow the sender to produce tags for messages of length at most d. Since d can be as much as exponential in n, this is a much larger message size than that allowed in [12].

Lemma 2. *The following four facts hold.*

1. *If* Distribute-Tags *succeeds and* P_V, P_R *are honest, then with overwhelming probability* P_V *accepts the linear combination of the messages in* Check-Message.

2. *If* Distribute-Tags *fails, then a new pair of players is added to* $\mathcal{D}isp$, *and at least one of the two players is corrupt.*

3. *If* P_S *and* P_V *are honest, then with overwhelming probability,* P_V *rejects any fake message* $\mathbf{m}' \neq \mathbf{m}$ *in* Check-Message.

4. *If* P_S *and* P_R *are honest, then* P_V *obtains no information about* $\mathbf{m}$ *during the execution of* Distribute-Tags *(even if it fails).*

The proof of this lemma and the complexities of the information checking protocols are given in the full version [14].

4.3 Verifiable Secret Sharing

A verifiable secret sharing (VSS) scheme consists of two protocols, VSS and VSS-Reconstruct. We use the following definition of secret sharing:

Definition 1. *Consider a protocol* VSS *for distributing shares of a secret* s *and a protocol* VSS-Reconstruct *for reconstructing* s *from the shares. We call this pair of protocols a VSS scheme if the following properties are satisfied (with overwhelming probability):*

1. **Termination:** *Either all honest players complete* VSS, *or a new dispute is found. All honest players will complete* VSS-Reconstruct.

2. **Privacy:** *If the dealer is honest, then before executing* VSS-Reconstruct, *the adversary has no information on the shared secret* s.

3. Correctness: *Once all honest players complete* VSS *there is a fixed value* r *such that:*

    3.1 If the dealer was honest throughout VSS, *then* $r = s$.

    3.2 Whether or not the dealer is honest, at the end of VSS-Reconstruct *the honest players will reconstruct* r.

The following protocol allows a dealer $P_D \in \mathcal{P} - Corr$ to verifiably share ℓ values. To verify correctness, each player acts as verifier and requests a random linear combination of these sharings (masked by a random sharing) to be opened. If the sharing is inconsistent (meaning that it is not in the span of M), then dispute resolution occurs. When P_D shares secrets, he utilizes information checking to produce authentication and verification tags in case a disagreement occurs later as to what was sent.

Protocol. $\mathrm{VSS}(P_D, \ell, s^{(1)}, \ldots, s^{(\ell)})$

We assume that $P_D \in \mathcal{P} - Corr$ wants to share $s^{(1)}, \ldots, s^{(\ell)}$. If $P_D \in Corr$, then all the sharings will be defined to be all-zero sharings.

1. *Distribution*

    1.1 P_D selects n extra random values $u^{(1)}, \ldots, u^{(n)}$, and then invokes Share to share $\{u^{(i)}\}_{i=1}^{n}$ and $\{s^{(i)}\}_{i=1}^{\ell}$.

    1.2 For each pair $P_R, P_V \notin \mathcal{D}isp_D$ such that $\{P_R, P_V\} \notin \mathcal{D}isp$, invoke Distribute-Tags$(P_D, P_R, P_V, \mathbf{s}_R)$, where

$$\mathbf{s}_R = (s_R^{(1)}, \ldots, s_R^{(\ell)}, u_R^{(1)}, \ldots, u_R^{(n)})$$

    (remember that each $s_R^{(k)}$ and $u_R^{(k)}$ is a vector).

2. *Verification*

    The following steps are performed in parallel for each $P_V \notin \mathcal{D}isp_D$, who acts as verifier.

    2.1 P_V choses a random vector $(r_1, \ldots, r_\ell) \in \mathbb{F}^\ell$ and broadcasts it.

    2.2 Each player $P_i \notin \mathcal{D}isp_D$ sends his share of $\sum_{k=1}^{\ell} r_k[s^{(k)}] + [u^{(V)}]$ to P_V.

    2.3 If P_V finds that the shares he received in the previous step (together with the Kudzu shares) form a consistent sharing, (i.e., it is a vector in the span of $M_{\mathcal{P}-Corr}$), then P_V broadcasts (accept, P_D), and the protocol terminates. Otherwise, P_V broadcasts (reject, P_D).

3. *Fault Localization*

    For the lowest player index V such that P_V that broadcast "(reject, P_D)" in the previous step, then the following steps are performed.

    3.1 P_D broadcasts each share of $\sum_{k=1}^{\ell} r_k[s^{(k)}] + [u^{(V)}]$. If this sharing is inconsistent, then P_D is added to $Corr$ and the protocol terminates.

    3.2 If the protocol did not terminate in the last step, then there is a share of some player $P_i \notin \mathcal{D}isp_D$ that broadcast a different share than P_D.

So P_V broadcasts $(\texttt{accuse}, P_i, P_D, v_i, v_D)$, where v_i is the value of the share sent by P_i and v_D the value sent by P_D.

3.3 If P_i disagrees with the value v_i broadcast by P_V, then P_i broadcasts $(\texttt{dispute}, P_i, P_V)$, the set $\{P_i, P_V\}$ is added to $\mathcal{D}isp$, and the protocol terminates.

3.4 If P_D disagrees with the value v_D broadcast by P_V, then P_D broadcasts $(\texttt{dispute}, P_D, P_V)$, the set $\{P_D, P_V\}$ is added to $\mathcal{D}isp$, and the protocol terminates.

3.5 If neither P_i nor P_D complained in the previous two steps, then $\{P_i, P_D\}$ is added to $\mathcal{D}isp$, and the protocol terminates.

VSS	CB	BCB	CR	BCR
$Without Dispute$	$\ell d + nd + n^2 \kappa \log d$	$n\ell + n^2$	4	3
$Per Dispute$	0	d	0	4

Note that this protocol can be easily modified to (verifiably) construct multiple sharings of $1 \in \mathbb{F}$, (i.e., the multiplicative identity). We simply require that all $s^{(k)} = 1$ for all $k = 1, \ldots, \ell$ and $u^{(k)} = 1$ for all $k = 1, \ldots, n$, and in step 2.3, P_V checks not only that the sharing is consistent, but that it is a sharing of $\sum_{k=1}^{\ell} r_k + 1$; step 3.1 is similarly altered. Furthermore, in the fault localization section, the players check not only that sharings are consistent, but that they are sharings of the correct values. We refer to this modified protocol by VSS-One.

Lemma 3. *The protocol* VSS *is statistically correct and perfectly private. More explicitly:*

1. *If* VSS *terminates successfully:*

   1.1 *With overwhelming probability, the* $s^{(1)}, \ldots, s^{(\ell)}$ *are correctly shared.*

   1.2 *With overwhelming probability, for each ordered triple of players* (P_i, P_j, P_k) *that are not in dispute with one another,[5] P_k has correct verification tags for the shares sent from P_i to P_j.*

2. *If the protocol terminates with a dispute, then the dispute is new.*

3. *Regardless of how the protocol terminates, the adversary gains no information on the* $s^{(1)}, \ldots, s^{(\ell)}$ *shared by honest players.*

The protocol VSS-Reconstruct, is used to reconstruct a sharing generated by a single player. The reconstruction protocol used in the main MPC protocol (called LC-Reconstruct) will be used to reconstruct linear combinations of sharings that were shared by multiple dealers. Since VSS-Reconstruct is largely the same as the reconstruction protocol in [12], using the authentication and verification tags generated in VSS-Share, it is deferred to the full version [14].

Lemma 4. *The pair* VSS *and* VSS-Reconstruct *described above constitute a VSS scheme.*

---

[5] That is, no pair of players in the triple are in dispute with each other.

4.4   Reconstructing Linear Combinations of Sharings

The following protocol is used to reconstruct linear combinations of sharings of secrets that have been shared using VSS. It assumes that each sharing $[w]$ is a sum of sharings $[w^{(1)}] + \cdots + [w^{(n)}]$, where $[w^{(i)}]$ is a linear combination of sharings shared by player P_i. Note that the protocol has some chance of failure. However, whenever the protocol fails, a new player is added to $Corr$, so it can fail only $O(n)$ times in the entire MPC protocol.

The technique for using information checking in LC-Reconstruct is non-standard, and deserves a bit of explanation. If the initial broadcasting of shares of $[w]$ is inconsistent, then the players open each $[w^{(j)}]$. If $[w^{(j)}]$ is the first such sharing that is inconsistent, then the players will want to use the verification tags to determine who is lying. However, $[w^{(j)}]$ is a *linear combination* of sharings that were generated with VSS. Each of these initial sharings has verification tags, but there is no means for combining the tags to get tags for $[w^{(j)}]$.

So the players need to localize which of the sharings in the linear combination $[w^{(j)}] = a_1[s^{(1)}] + \cdots + a_m[s^{(m)}]$ is inconsistent. One way to do this would be to have P_j state which player he accuses of lying and have that player broadcast shares of *each* $[s^{(k)}]$ (or if P_j is corrupt, all players broadcast their shares of each $[s^{(k)}]$). Once this is done, the players could use the tags for whichever share P_j claims is corrupt to determine who was lying. Although this approach would work, it would result in an enormous communication complexity. Therefore, instead of opening all of the $[s^{(k)}]$ all at once, the players use a "divide-and-conquer" technique: Break the sum into two halves, determine which sum has the inconsistency, break that sum in half, and so on until the players reach an individual sharing, at which point they can use the verification tags.

Although using this bisection technique allows the players to locate an individual incorrect sharing without substantially increasing the communication complexity, this technique adds a $\log C$ factor to the number of broadcast rounds. It is in interesting open question whether we can achieve the same communication complexity with a lower round complexity.

Protocol.   LC-Reconstruct($[w]$)

Throughout this protocol, if a player ever refuses to send or broadcast something that the protocol requires, that player is added to $Corr$, and the protocol terminates.

1. Each $P_i \notin Corr$ broadcasts his share w_i of $[w]$.

2. If the sharing broadcast in the previous step is consistent, then the players reconstruct w as described in Sect. 4.1, and the protocol terminates.

3. If the sharing was inconsistent, each $P_i \notin Corr$ broadcasts his share $w_i^{(j)}$ for each $P_j \in \mathcal{P}$.

4. If any player P_i broadcasted values such that his summands do not match his sum (i.e., if $w_i \neq \sum_{j=1}^{n} w_i^{(j)}$), then all such players are added to $Corr$, and the protocol terminates.

5. For the lowest j such that the shares of $w^{(j)}$ broadcast in step 3 are inconsistent, one of two steps is performed: If $P_j \notin Corr$ proceed to step 6. Otherwise, proceed to step 7.

6. $P_j \notin Corr$

   6.1 Since the shares of $w^{(j)}$ broadcast in step 3 are inconsistent, at least one player broadcast an incorrect share, so P_j broadcasts (accuse, i) for some player P_i that P_j accuses of sending an incorrect share.

   6.2 Since $[w^{(j)}]$ is a linear combination of sharings dealt by P_j, the players (internally) think of $[w^{(j)}]$ as $a_1[s^{(1)}] + \cdots + a_m[s^{(m)}]$, where each $[s^{(k)}]$ was generated with VSS and each a_k is non-zero. We arrange the $s^{(k)}$'s according to the order in which they were dealt.

   6.3 From the sharings $a_1[s^{(1)}], \ldots, a_m[s^{(m)}]$, define two sharings $a_1[s^{(1)}] + \cdots + a_{\lfloor m/2 \rfloor}[s^{(\lfloor m/2 \rfloor)}]$ and $a_{\lfloor m/2 \rfloor + 1}[s^{(\lfloor m/2 \rfloor + 1)}] + \cdots + a_m[s^{(m)}]$. The player P_i accused in step 6.1 broadcasts his share of each of these two sharings.

   6.4 If P_i broadcast shares of summands in the previous step that do not match up with the previously sent share of their sum, then P_i is added to $Corr$, and the protocol terminates.

   6.5 Player P_j broadcasts which of the sharings broadcast in step 6.3 he disagrees with. If this is a single sharing $a_k[s^{(k)}]$, then the players proceed to step 6.6. Otherwise, if the sharing is some sum $a_{k_1}[s^{(k_1)}] + \cdots + a_{k_2}[s^{(k_2)}]$, then the players return to step 6.3, but with $a_1[s^{(1)}], \ldots, a_m[s^{(m)}]$ replaced by $a_{k_1}[s^{(k_1)}], \ldots, a_{k_2}[s^{(k_2)}]$.

   6.6 At this point, P_i has broadcast his share of $a_k[s^{(k)}]$, and P_j has broadcast that he disagrees with this share. For each $P_V \notin Disp_j \cup Disp_i$, the players invoke Check-Message$(P_i, P_V, \mathbf{s}_i)$, where $\mathbf{s}_i$ is the vector defined in step 1.2 of the invocation of VSS in which $[s^{(k)}]$ was shared.

   6.7 If P_i sent shares to P_V in the invocation of Check-Message that do not match with the share of $a_k[s^{(k)}]$, then P_V broadcasts (accuse, i), and $\{P_i, P_V\}$ is added to $Disp$.

   6.8 For each $P_V \notin Disp_i$ that rejected the message sent by P_i in the invocation of Check-Message, $\{P_i, P_V\}$ is added to $Disp$. For each P_V that accepted the message, $\{P_j, P_V\}$ is added to $Disp$.

   6.9 At this point, all players are in dispute with either P_i or P_j. By the $Q2$ property of the adversary structure $\mathcal{A}$, this means that one of $Disp_i$ or $Disp_j$ is no longer in $\mathcal{A}$. If $Disp_i \notin \mathcal{A}$ then P_i is added to $Corr$, and if $Disp_j \notin \mathcal{A}$, then P_j is added to $Corr$. Then the protocol terminates.

7. $P_j \in Corr$

   7.1 Since $[w^{(j)}]$ is a linear combination of sharings dealt by P_j, the players (internally) think of $[w^{(j)}]$ as $a_1[s^{(1)}] + \cdots + a_m[s^{(m)}]$, where each $[s^{(k)}]$

was generated with VSS and each a_k is non-zero. We arrange the $s^{(k)}$'s according to the order in which they were dealt.

7.2 From the sharings $a_1[s^{(1)}], \ldots, a_m[s^{(m)}]$, define two sharings $a_1[s^{(1)}] + \cdots + a_{\lfloor m/2 \rfloor}[s^{(\lfloor m/2 \rfloor)}]$ and $a_{\lfloor m/2 \rfloor + 1}[s^{(\lfloor m/2 \rfloor + 1)}] + \cdots + a_m[s^{(m)}]$. Each player not in $Corr$ broadcasts his share of each of these two sharings.

7.3 Any player who broadcast shares of summands in the previous step that do not match up with the previously sent share of their sum is added to $Corr$, and the protocol terminates.

7.4 If the players reach this step, then one of the sharings broadcast in step 7.2 is inconsistent. If this is a single sharing $a_k[s^{(k)}]$, then the players proceed to step 7.5. Otherwise, if the sharing is some sum $a_{k_1}[s^{(k_1)}] + \cdots + a_{k_2}[s^{(k_2)}]$, then the players return to step 7.2, but with $a_1[s^{(1)}], \ldots, a_m[s^{(m)}]$ replaced by $a_{k_1}[s^{(k_1)}], \ldots, a_{k_2}[s^{(k_2)}]$.

7.5 The players invoke VSS-Reconstruct for the sharing $[s^{(k)}]$ decided upon in the last execution of step 7.4 (however, they skip the initial broadcasting of shares in VSS-Reconstruct, since shares of $a_k[s^{(k)}]$ have already been broadcast).

7.6 The invocation of VSS-Reconstruct in the previous step will have added a new player to $Corr$, so the protocol terminates.

LC-Reconstruct	CB	BCB	CR	BCR
$Without Dispute$	0	d	0	1
$Per Dispute$	$n^2\ell + n^2\kappa \log d$	$n^2 + nd + d\log C$	2	$6 + \log C$

Lemma 5. *If $[w]$ is a linear combination of sharings generated with* VSS, *then with overwhelming probability, an invocation of* LC-Reconstruct($[w]$) *will either reconstruct the correct value w or add a new player to Corr. Furthermore,* LC-Reconstruct *does not leak any information about any sharing other than $[w]$ to the adversary.*

4.5   Generating Random Values

The following protocol allows the players to generate a publicly known random vector $(s^{(1)}, \ldots, s^{(\ell)})$. If the protocol fails (which occurs if one of its sub-protocols fails), then a new dispute pair is found.

Protocol.   Generate-Randomness(ℓ)

---

1. Every player $P_i \notin Corr$ selects a random summand vector $s^{(1,i)}, \ldots, s^{(\ell,i)}$.
2. Call VSS($P_i, \ell, s^{(1,i)}, \ldots, s^{(\ell,i)}$) to let every $P_i \notin Corr$ verifiably share his summand vector.

3. Call LC-Reconstruct ℓ times in parallel to reconstruct the sum sharings $s^{(1)} = \sum_{P_i \notin Corr} s^{(1,i)}, \ldots, s^{(\ell)} = \sum_{P_i \notin Corr} s^{(\ell,i)}$.

Generate-Randomness	CB	BCB	CR	BCR
$Without Dispute$	$n\ell d + n^2 d + n^3 \kappa \log d$	$n^2 \ell + n^3 + d\ell$	4	4
$Per Dispute$	$n^2 \ell + n^2 \kappa \log d$	$n^2 + nd + d \log \mathcal{C}$	2	$6 + \log \mathcal{C}$

Lemma 6. *If* Generate-Randomness *terminates successfully, then the generated vector is random. If* Generate-Randomness *terminates unsuccessfully, then a new dispute is found.*

4.6 Generating Multiplication Triples

The following protocol allows the players to verifiably generate random sharings of triples (a, b, c) such that $ab = c$. The idea is that a random $a^{(k)}$ is generated, and then each P_i is "responsible for" creating a random triple $a^{(k)}b^{(i,k)} = c^{(i,k)}$. To verify correctness, the P_i also creates a triple $a^{(k)}\widetilde{b}^{(i,k)} = \widetilde{c}^{(i,k)}$, and this is used to mask an opening of $a^{(k)}b^{(i,k)} - c^{(i,k)}$. Once all these triples are checked, the final triple is defined to be $(a^{(k)}, \sum_{i=1}^{n} b^{(i,k)}, \sum_{i=1}^{n} c^{(i,k)})$.

Protocol.   Multiplication-Triple(ℓ)

---

1. *Generating Triples*

   1.1 Each $P_i \notin Corr$ invokes VSS($P_i, 2\ell n + 3\ell$) to generate uniformly random sharings and VSS-One($P_i, 2\ell n$) to generate sharings of $1 \in \mathbb{F}$; these invocations are done in parallel. Denote the random sharings of player P_i by $([a^{(i,1)}], \ldots, [a^{(i,\ell)}])$, $([b^{(i,1)}], \ldots, [b^{(i,\ell)}])$, $([\widetilde{b}^{(i,1)}], \ldots, [\widetilde{b}^{(i,\ell)}])$, and $\{([r^{(i,j,1)}], \ldots, [r^{(i,j,\ell)}]), ([\widetilde{r}^{(i,j,1)}], \ldots, [\widetilde{r}^{(i,j,\ell)}])\}_{j=1}^{n}$ and the sharings of ones by $\{([1^{(i,j,1)}], \ldots, [1^{(i,j,\ell)}]), ([\widetilde{1}^{(i,j,1)}], \ldots, [\widetilde{1}^{(i,j,\ell)}])\}_{j=1}^{n}$. The sharings of players in $Corr$ are defined to be all-zero sharings.

   1.2 For each $k = 1, \ldots, \ell$ and each i such that $P_i \notin Corr$, the players define and locally compute

$$[a^{(k)}] = \sum_{m=1}^{n} [a^{(m,k)}]$$

$$[r^{(i,k)}] = \sum_{m=1}^{n} [r^{(m,i,k)}]$$

$$[1^{(i,k)}] = \sum_{m=1}^{n} [1^{(m,i,k)}] + w[1^{(i,i,k)}],$$

   where $w \in \mathbb{F}$ is the unique element that makes $[1^{(i,k)}]$ a sharing of 1. The sharings $[\widetilde{r}^{(i,k)}]$ and $[\widetilde{1}^{(i,k)}]$ are similarly defined.

   1.3 Each $P_j \notin Corr$ sends his share of $[a^{(k)}][b^{(i,k)}] + [r^{(i,k)}][1^{(i,k)}]$ and $[a^{(k)}][\widetilde{b}^{(i,k)}] + [\widetilde{r}^{(i,k)}][\widetilde{1}^{(i,k)}]$ to $P_i \notin Corr$ for each $k = 1, \ldots, \ell$. (The shares of players in $Corr$ will be Kudzu shares, so P_i knows those shares as well.)

1.4 Each $P_i \notin Corr$ applies the recombination vector $\boldsymbol{\lambda}$ to the shares of $D^{(i,k)} = a^{(k)}b^{(i,k)} + r^{(i,k)}$ and $\widetilde{D}^{(i,k)} = a^{(k)}\widetilde{b}^{(i,k)} + \widetilde{r}^{(i,k)}$ received in the previous step to compute $D^{(i,k)}$ and $\widetilde{D}^{(i,k)}$ for each $k = 1, \ldots, \ell$.

1.5 Each P_i broadcasts $D^{(i,k)}$ and $\widetilde{D}^{(i,k)}$ for each $k = 1, \ldots, \ell$.

1.6 Each player locally computes $[c^{(i,k)}] = D^{(i,k)} - [r^{(i,k)}]$ and $[\widetilde{c}^{(i,k)}] = \widetilde{D}^{(i,k)} - [\widetilde{r}^{(i,k)}]$ (using the canonical sharings of $D^{(i,k)}$ and $\widetilde{D}^{(i,k)}$ as defined in Sect. 4.1).

2. *Error Detection*

2.1 The players invoke Generate-Randomness(ℓ) to generate a random vector $(s^{(1)}, \ldots, s^{(\ell)})$.

2.2 Each player not in $Disp_i$ broadcasts his share of $[\widehat{b}^{(i,k)}] = [\widetilde{b}^{(i,k)}] + s^{(k)}[b^{(i,k)}]$ for each $i = 1, \ldots, n$ and each $k = 1, \ldots, \ell$.

2.3 If the sharing of some $[\widehat{b}^{(i,k)}]$ broadcast in the previous step is inconsistent, P_i broadcasts (accuse, P_j) for some $P_j \notin Disp_i$ who broadcasted an incorrect share, then $\{P_i, P_j\}$ is added to $Disp$ and the protocol terminates.

2.4 The players invoke multiple instances of LC-Reconstruct in parallel to reconstruct $z^{(i,k)} = [a^{(k)}]\widehat{b}^{(i,k)} - [\widehat{c}^{(i,k)}] - s^{(k)}[c^{(i,k)}]$ for each $i = 1, \ldots, n$ and each $k = 1, \ldots, \ell$.

2.5 If all the $z^{(i,k)}$ reconstructed in the previous step are zero, then we define

$$[b^{(k)}] = \sum_{m=1}^{n}[b^{(m,k)}]$$

$$[c^{(k)}] = \sum_{m=1}^{n}[c^{(m,k)}],$$

and the protocol terminates successfully with the multiplication triples taken to be $(a^{(k)}, b^{(k)}, c^{(k)})$ for $k = 1, \ldots, \ell$.

3. *Fault Localization*

If any $z^{(i,k)}$ reconstructed in step 2.4 is not zero, the following is done for the lexicographically lowest pair (i, k) such that $z^{(i,k)} \neq 0$.

3.1 Each P_j broadcasts his share of $[a^{(m,k)}]$, $[\widetilde{r}^{(m,i,k)}]$, and $[r^{(m,i,k)}]$ for each $P_m \notin P_j$.

3.2 If P_i sees that the shares of some $P_j \notin Disp_i$ sent in the previous step are inconsistent with the share sent in step 1.3 or 2.4, then P_i broadcasts (accuse, P_j); then $\{P_j, P_i\}$ is added to $Disp$ and the protocol terminates.

3.3 Each P_m examines the shares broadcast in the previous step of all sharings that P_m generated. If P_m notices that some $P_j \notin Disp_m$ broadcast an incorrect share in the previous step, then P_m broadcasts (accuse, P_j); then $\{P_m, P_j\}$ is added to $Disp$ and the protocol terminates.

3.4 If no P_m broadcast an accusation in the previous step, then $\widetilde{P}_i$ is added to $Corr$ and the protocol terminates.

Multiplication-Triple	CB	BCB	CR	BCR
$Without Dispute$	$n^2\ell d + n^3\kappa\log d$	$n^3\ell + n\ell d$	9	11
$Per Dispute$	$n^2\ell + n^2\kappa\log d$	$n^2 + nd + d\log\mathcal{C}$	2	$6 + \log\mathcal{C}$

Lemma 7. *If* Multiplication-Triple *terminates unsuccessfully, then a new dispute is localized. If* Multiplication-Triple *succeeds, then it maintains statistical correctness and perfect privacy. That is, with overwhelming probability, at the end of the protocol the players hold sharings of ℓ multiplication triples (a, b, c) with $c = ab$; in addition, the adversary has no information on a, b, or c (other than that $c = ab$).*

4.7 Preparation Phase

The following protocol prepares the circuit for computation by generating the required sharings. The protocol generates multiplication triples for the multiplication gates and random sharings for random gates. The task is broken into n^2 segments. The number of multiplication triples and random sharings generated in each segment are denoted by L_M and L_R (respectively), and we require $L_M \le \lceil c_M/n^2\rceil$ and $L_R \le \lceil (c_R)/n^2\rceil$.

Protocol. Preparation-Phase

Initialize $\mathcal{Corr}$ and $\mathcal{Disp}$ to the empty set. For each segment handling L_M multiplication gates and L_R random gates, the following steps are performed. If any of the subprotocols fails, then the segment is repeated.

1. Invoke Multiplication-Triple(L_M). Assign one multiplication triple to each multiplication gate in this segment.
2. Each $P_i \notin \mathcal{Corr}$ invokes VSS($P_i, L_R, r^{(1,i)}, \ldots, r^{(L_R,i)}$), sharing uniformly random values. (The sharings of corrupt players are defined to be all-zero sharings.)
3. We define L_R random sharings by $[r^{(k)}] = \sum_{i=1}^{n}[r^{(k,i)}]$ for each $k = 1, \ldots, L_R$. Assign one random sharing to each random gate in this segment.

Preparation-Phase	CB	BCB	CR	BCR
$Without Dispute$	$n^2(c_M + c_R)d + n^5\kappa\log d$	$n^3(c_M + c_R) + n(c_M + c_R)d$	$13n^2$	$14n^2$
$Per Dispute$	$(c_M + c_R) + n^2\kappa\log d$	$n^2 + nd + d\log\mathcal{C}$	2	$6 + \log\mathcal{C}$

4.8 Input Phase

The goal of the input phase is to allow each player to share their inputs. We denote the number of inputs in a given segment by L. We require $L \leq \lceil c_I/n^2 \rceil$, and we also require that each segment contain inputs from only one player.

Protocol. Input-Phase

For each segment, the following steps are executed to let the dealer $P_D \notin Corr$ verifiably share L inputs $s^{(1)}, \ldots, s^{(L)}$. If some invocation of VSS fails, then the segment fails and is repeated.

1. Each $P_i \notin Corr$ invokes $\mathsf{VSS}(P_i, L, r^{(1,i)}, \ldots, r^{(L,i)})$, sharing uniformly random values. (The sharings of corrupt players are defined to be all-zero sharings.)

2. We define L random sharings by $[r^{(k)}] = \sum_{i=1}^{n} [r^{(k,i)}]$ for each $k = 1, \ldots, L$. Assign one random sharing to each input gate in this segment.

3. Each $P_i \notin Disp_D$ sends his share of each $[r^{(k)}]$ to P_D.

4. If P_D finds that one of the sharings was inconsistent, he broadcasts the index of this sharing, and the following steps are performed. If they are all consistent, then the players proceed to step 5.

   4.1 If P_D indicated that the random sharing $[r]$ was inconsistent, then each $P_i \notin Disp_D$ broadcasts their share of $[r]$.

   4.2 If P_D sees that some P_i broadcast a different share than was sent privately, then P_D broadcasts (accuse, i), $\{P_D, P_i\}$ is added to $Disp$, and the segment fails and is repeated.

   4.3 The players invoke LC-Reconstruct to reconstruct $[r]$ (but skipping the first step, because shares of $[r]$ have already been broadcast).

   4.4 Since the sharing $[r]$ was inconsistent, the invocation of LC-Reconstruct in the previous step will have located a new corrupt player, so the segment fails and is repeated.

5. Using the method for reconstructing secrets described in Sect. 4.1, P_D computes the random value r associated with each of his L input gates in this segment.

6. For each input gate with input s and random sharing $[r]$, P_D broadcasts $s - r$.

7. For each $s - r$ broadcast in the previous step, each player locally computes $s - r + [r]$ (using the canonical sharing of $s - r$ as defined in Sect. 4.1) as the sharing for that input gate. Since each player is storing each share as a sum of shares (one from each player), we update $[r]$ by adding the canonical sharing of $s - r$ to $[r^{(D)}]$ and leaving $[r^{(i)}]$ the same for $i \neq D$. In the dealer failed to broadcast a value for an input gate, or if the dealer was already in $Corr$, then the sharing for that gate is taken to be $[r]$.

Input-Phase	CB	BCB	CR	BCR
$Without Dispute$	$nc_I d + n^4 d + n^5 \kappa \log d$	$n^2 c_I + n^5$	$5n^2$	$4n^2$
$Per Dispute$	$c_I + n^2 \kappa \log d$	$n^2 + nd + d \log C$	2	$9 + \log C$

4.9   Computation Phase

After the circuit preparation has been done and after the inputs have been provided by the players, the computation phase is just a matter of opening linear combinations of sharings and possibly resolving disputes.

Each affine gate is computed by performing local computations. Each multiplication gate is computed by opening affine combinations of known sharings. Each output gate is computed by publicly opening it.[6] This means that the computation phase will consist of local operations and $c_M + c_O$ public openings.

The circuit will be divided into segments and evaluated one segment at a time. The segments will be constructed such that each segment has no more than $\lceil (c_M + c_O)/n^2 \rceil$ gates, and a single segment only contains gates from one multiplicative layer of the circuit. This means that if $\mathcal{D}$ is the multiplicative depth of the circuit, then there are at most $n^2 + \mathcal{D}$ segments. Each affine gate will be included in the first possible segment in which it can be evaluated.

If a fault occurs in some segment (which is to say that one of the opened sharings is inconsistent), then one or more new disputes are localized, and the segment is repeated.

It is important to remember that all sharings generated by VSS and Multiplication-Triple are sums of sharings such that one summand comes from each player. Since all sharings opened are affine combinations of these, this means that every sharing we will be opening in the computation phase is a sum of sharings with one summand coming from each player. Thus the protocol LC-Reconstruct can be performed.

Protocol.   Computation-Phase

For each segment with L reconstructions, the following steps are executed. If one of the reconstructions is inconsistent, then a new dispute is found, and the segment is repeated.

1. For each affine gate in the segment, the players evaluate the gate by local computations.

2. The players invoke LC-Reconstruct multiple times in parallel for each output gate in the segment.

---

[6] We assume that each player receives all the outputs, although the protocol could easily be modified to allow for private outputs.

3. For each multiplication gate in the segment with inputs $[x]$ and $[y]$ and associated multiplication triple $([a], [b], [c])$, the following steps are performed in parallel.

   3.1 In parallel with step 2, the players invoke LC-Reconstruct($[x - a]$) and LC-Reconstruct($[y - b]$).

   3.2 The players assign the sharing $(x - a)(y - b) - (x - a)[b] - (y - b)[a] + [c]$ as the output of the gate.

Computation-Phase	CB	BCB	CR	BCR
$Without Dispute$	0	Cd	0	$\mathcal{D}$
$Per Dispute$	$Cn + n^3 + n^2\kappa\log d$	$n^2 + nd + d\log C$	2	$6 + \log C$

4.10 Putting It All Together

We perform the MPC protocol by invoking Preparation-Phase, Input-Phase, and Computation-Phase in succession. Note that there is a term n added to the number of communication rounds to account for the fact that when a player is corrupted, all players will broadcast their shares sent by that player.

Theorem 1. *A set of n players communicating over a secure synchronous network can evaluate an agreed function of their inputs securely against a malicious, adaptive adversary with an arbitrary Q^2 adversary structure $\mathcal{A}$ with point-to-point communication bandwidth $O(n^2Cd + n^4d + n^5\kappa\log d)$ and broadcast bandwidth $O(n^3C + nCd + n^5 + n^3d + n^2d\log C)$, taking $20n^2$ communication rounds and $27n^2 + \mathcal{D} + n^2\log C$ broadcast rounds. Here, d is the number of rows in the smallest MSP representing $\mathcal{A}$, and κ is the size of an element of $\mathbb{F}$.*

Acknowledgments. Work is supported in part by NSF grants 09165174, 1065276, 1118126 and 1136174, US-Israel BSF grant 2008411, OKAWA Foundation Research Award, IBM Faculty Research Award, Xerox Faculty Research Award, B. John Garrick Foundation Award, Teradata Research Award, and Lockheed-Martin Corporation Research Award. This material is based upon work supported by the Defense Advanced Research Projects Agency through the U.S. Office of Naval Research under Contract N00014 -11 -1-0392. The views expressed are those of the author and do not reflect the official policy or position of the Department of Defense or the U.S. Government.

References

1. Hirt, M., Maurer, U.: Complete characterization of adversaries tolerable in general multiparty computations. In: Proc. PODC (1997)
2. Fitzi, M., Hirt, M., Maurer, U.M.: General adversaries in unconditional multiparty computation. In: Lam, K.-Y., Okamoto, E., Xing, C. (eds.) ASIACRYPT 1999. LNCS, vol. 1716, pp. 232–246. Springer, Heidelberg (1999)

3. Cramer, R., Damgård, I.B., Maurer, U.M.: General secure multi-party computation from any linear secret-sharing scheme. In: Preneel, B. (ed.) EUROCRYPT 2000. LNCS, vol. 1807, pp. 316–334. Springer, Heidelberg (2000)
4. Smith, A., Stiglic, A.: Multiparty computation unconditionally secure against Q^2 adversary structures. CoRR cs.CR/9902010 (1999)
5. Cramer, R., Damgård, I.B., Dziembowski, S., Hirt, M., Rabin, T.: Efficient multiparty computations secure against an adaptive adversary. In: Stern, J. (ed.) EUROCRYPT 1999. LNCS, vol. 1592, pp. 311–326. Springer, Heidelberg (1999)
6. Karchmer, M., Wigderson, A.: On span programs. In: Structure in Complexity Theory Conference, pp. 102–111 (1993)
7. Beaver, D., Wool, A.: Quorum-based secure multi-party computation. In: Nyberg, K. (ed.) EUROCRYPT 1998. LNCS, vol. 1403, pp. 375–390. Springer, Heidelberg (1998)
8. Maurer, U.: Secure multi-party computation made simple. Discrete Applied Mathematics 154(2), 370–381 (2006), Coding and Cryptography
9. Hirt, M., Maurer, U.M., Zikas, V.: MPC vs. SFE: Unconditional and computational security. In: Pieprzyk, J. (ed.) ASIACRYPT 2008. LNCS, vol. 5350, pp. 1–18. Springer, Heidelberg (2008)
10. Hirt, M., Tschudi, D.: Efficient general-adversary multi-party computation. In: Sako, K., Sarkar, P. (eds.) ASIACRYPT 2013, Part II. LNCS, vol. 8270, pp. 181–200. Springer, Heidelberg (2013)
11. Ito, M., Saito, A., Nishizeki, T.: Secret sharing scheme realizing general access structure. Electronics and Communications in Japan (Part III: Fundamental Electronic Science) 72(9), 56–64 (1989)
12. Beerliová-Trubíniová, Z., Hirt, M.: Efficient multi-party computation with dispute control. In: Halevi, S., Rabin, T. (eds.) TCC 2006. LNCS, vol. 3876, pp. 305–328. Springer, Heidelberg (2006)
13. Rabin, T., Ben-Or, M.: Verifiable secret sharing and multiparty protocols with honest majority (extended abstract). In: STOC, pp. 73–85 (1989)
14. Lampkins, J., Ostrovsky, R.: Communication-efficient mpc for general adversary structures. Cryptology ePrint Archive, Report 2013/640 (2013), http://eprint.iacr.org/

Publicly Auditable Secure Multi-Party Computation

Carsten Baum*, Ivan Damgård**, and Claudio Orlandi***

Aarhus University, Denmark
{cbaum,ivan,orlandi}@cs.au.dk

Abstract. In the last few years the efficiency of secure multi-party computation (MPC) increased in several orders of magnitudes. However, this alone might not be enough if we want MPC protocols to be used in practice. A crucial property that is needed in many applications is that everyone can check that a given (secure) computation was performed correctly – even in the extreme case where all the parties involved in the computation are corrupted, and even if the party who wants to verify the result was not participating. This is especially relevant in the *clients-servers* setting, where many clients provide input to a secure computation performed by a few servers. An obvious example of this is electronic voting, but also in many types of auctions one may want independent verification of the result. Traditionally, this is achieved by using non-interactive zero-knowledge proofs during the computation.

A recent trend in MPC protocols is to have a more expensive preprocessing phase followed by a very efficient online phase, e.g., the recent so-called SPDZ protocol by Damgård et al. Applications such as voting and some auctions are perfect use-case for these protocols, as the parties usually know well in advance when the computation will take place, and using those protocols allows us to use only cheap information-theoretic primitives in the actual computation. Unfortunately no protocol of the SPDZ type supports an audit phase.

In this paper, we show how to achieve efficient MPC with a public audit. We formalize the concept of *publicly auditable secure computation* and provide an enhanced version of the SPDZ protocol where, even if all the servers are corrupted, anyone with access to the transcript of the protocol can check that the output is indeed correct. Most importantly, we do so without significantly compromising the performance of SPDZ i.e. our online phase has complexity approximately twice that of SPDZ.

Keywords: Efficient Multi-Party Computation, Public Verifiability, Electronic Voting.

---

* Partially supported by the European Research Commission Starting Grant 279447.
** Supported by the Danish National Research Foundation, the National Science Foundation of China (under the grant 61061130540) and also from the CFEM research center within which part of this work was performed.
*** Supported by The Danish Council for Independent Research (DFF).

M. Abdalla and R. De Prisco (Eds.): SCN 2014, LNCS 8642, pp. 175–196, 2014.
© Springer International Publishing Switzerland 2014

1   Introduction

During the last few years MPC has evolved from a purely theoretical to a more practical tool. Several recent protocols (e.g. BeDOZa [6], TinyOT [24] and the celebrated SPDZ [14,12]) achieve incredible performance for the actual function evaluation, even if all but one player is actively corrupted. This is done by pushing all the expensive cryptographic work into an offline phase and using only simple arithmetic operations during the online phase[1]. Since these protocols allow the evaluation of an arbitrary circuit over a finite field or ring, one can in particular use these protocols to implement, for instance, a *shuffle-and-decrypt* operation for a voting application or the function that computes the winning bid in an auction. It is often the case that we know well in advance the time at which a computation is to take place, and in any such case, the aforementioned protocols offer very good performance. In fact the computational work per player in the SPDZ protocol is comparable to the work one has to perform to compute the desired function in the clear, with no security.

However, efficiency is not always enough: if the result we compute securely has large economic or political consequences, such as in voting or auction applications, it may be required that correctness of the result can be verified later. Ideally, we would want that this can done even if all parties involved in the computation are corrupted, and even if the party who wants to verify the result was not involved in the computation.

The traditional solution to this is to ask every player to commit to all his secret data and to prove in zero-knowledge for every message he sends, that this message was indeed computed according to the protocol. If a common reference string is available, we can use non-interactive zero-knowledge proofs, which allow anyone to verify the proofs and hence the result at any later time. However, this adds a very significant computational overhead, and would lead to a horribly inefficient protocol, compared to the online phase of SPDZ, for instance.

It is therefore natural to ask whether it is possible to achieve the best of both worlds and have *highly efficient MPC protocols with a high-speed online phase that are auditable*, in the sense that everyone who has access to the transcripts of the protocol can check if the result is correct *even when all the servers are corrupted*. In this paper we answer this question in the affirmative.

1.1   Contributions and Technical Overview

The model. In this work we will focus on client-server MPC protocols, where a set of parties (called the input parties) provide inputs to the actual working parties, who run the MPC protocol among themselves and make the output

---

[1] The offline phase is independent from the inputs and the circuit to be computed – only an upper bound on the number of multiplication gates is needed.

public[2]. We will focus on the setting of MPC protocols for dishonest majority (and static corruptions): as long as there is one honest party we can guarantee privacy of the inputs and correctness of the results, but we can neither guarantee termination nor fairness. We will enhance the standard network model with a *bulletin board* functionality. Parties are allowed to exchange messages privately, but our protocol will instruct them also to make part of their conversation public.

Auditable MPC. Our first contribution is to provide a formal definition of the notion of *publicly auditable MPC* as an extension of the classic formalization of secure function evaluation. We require correctness and privacy when there is at least one honest party, and in addition ask that anyone, having only access to the transcript of the computation published on the bulletin board, can check the correctness of the output. This is formalized by introducing an extra, non-corruptible party (the *auditor*) who can ask the functionality if the output was correct or not[3]. We stress that the auditor does not need to be involved (or even exist!) before and during the protocol. The role of the auditor is simply to check, once the computation is over, whether the output was computed correctly or not.[4]

SPDZ recap. Given the motivation of this work, we are only interested in the notion of auditable MPC if it can be achieved efficiently. Therefore our starting point is one of the most efficient MPC protocols for arithmetic circuits with a cheap, information-theoretic online phase, namely SPDZ.

In a nutshell SPDZ works as follows: At the end of the offline phase all parties hold additive shares of multiplicative triples (x, y, z) with $z = x \cdot y$. Now the players can use these preprocessed triples to perform multiplications using only linear operations over the finite field (plus some interaction). Moreover, these linear operations can now be performed locally and are therefore essentially for free. However an adversary could send the honest parties a share that is different from what he received at the end of the offline phase. To make sure this is not the case, SPDZ adds information-theoretic MACs of the form $\gamma = \alpha \cdot x$ to each shared value x, where both the MAC γ and the key α are shared among the parties. These MACs are trivially linear and can therefore *follow the computation*. Once the output is reconstructed, the MAC keys are also revealed and the MACs checked for correctness, and in the case the check goes through, the honest parties accept the output.

---

[2] Note that the sets need not be distinct, and using standard transformations we can make sure that the servers do not learn the inputs nor the output of the computation (think of the inputs/output being encrypted or secret shared).

[3] Of course, this only holds in the case where the computation did not abort.

[4] In terms of feasibility, auditable MPC can be achieved by compiling a strong semi-honest protocol with NIZKs – a semi-honest MPC protocol alone would not suffice as we cannot force the parties to sample uniform randomness, nor can we trust them to force each other to do so by secure coin-tossing when everyone is corrupted. However, this would not lead to a very practical solution.

Auditable SPDZ. In order to make SPDZ auditable, we enhance each shared value x with a Pedersen commitment $g^x h^r$ to x with randomness r. The commitment key (g, h) comes from a common reference string (CRS), such that even if all parties are corrupted, those commitments are still (computationally) binding. To allow the parties to open their commitments, we provide them also with a sharing of the randomness r (each party already knows a share of x). It is easy to see that this new *representation* of values is still linear and is therefore compatible with the existing SPDZ framework. During the computation phase, the parties ignore the commitments (they are created during the offline phase, and only the openings must be sent to $\mathcal{F}_{\text{BULLETIN}}$) and it will be the job of the auditor to use the linear properties of the commitments to verify that each step of the computation was carried out correctly. Clearly the *offline phase* of SPDZ needs to be modified, in order to produce the commitments to be used by the auditor. Moreover, we have to make this preprocessing step auditable as well. We refer to the full version for more details.

1.2   An Example Application: Low-latency Voting from MPC

Our work can be seen as a part of a recent trend in understanding how generic MPC protocols perform (in terms of efficiency) in comparison to special-purpose protocols (see [11,19] for a discussion on private-set intersection). A notable example of *special purpose* secure computation protocols are mixed-networks (mix-nets), first introduced by Chaum in 1981 [9]. Here we show how our publicly auditable version of SPDZ compares favorably with mix-nets in terms of latency.

In mix-nets a number of clients submit their encrypted inputs to some servers, who jointly shuffle and decrypt the inputs in such a way that no one should be able to link the input ciphertexts with the output plaintexts, if at least one of the shuffling servers is honest. Mix-nets are of prime importance in electronic voting (like e.g. the famous *Helios* [1] system). A disadvantage of mix-nets is that they are *inherently sequential*: server i cannot start shuffling before receiving the output of the shuffle performed by server $i-1$. Now, given that the voter's privacy depends on the assumption that there is at least 1 out of n uncorrupted server, it is desirable to increase the number of parties involved in the shuffle as much as possible. However, when using mix-nets the latency of the protocol is linear in n, and therefore increasing n has a very negative impact on the total efficiency of the protocol, here measured by the time between the last voter casts his vote and the output of the election is announced. We argue here that implementing a shuffle using a generic protocol like SPDZ makes the latency independent of the number of servers performing the shuffle.

More formally, let n be the number of servers, m the number of input ciphertexts, λ a computational security parameter and *sec* a statistical security parameter. The *computational latency* of mix-nets, here defined as the time we have to wait before all servers have done their computational work, will be at least $O(n \cdot m \cdot \lambda^3)$.[5] Using SPDZ, the computational latency is $O(m \cdot \log(m) \cdot sec^2)$,[6] since the *total* complexity of SPDZ is linear in n and the servers work in parallel (this was even verified experimentally). Therefore mix-nets are more expensive by a factor of $\left(\frac{n}{\log m} \cdot \frac{\lambda^3}{sec^2} \right)$: This is a significant speedup when n grows – note also that typical values of λ for public-key cryptography can be one or two orders of magnitudes greater than typical values for a statistical security parameter sec (only field operations are performed during the SPDZ online phase). Clearly, to verify the impact in practice one would have to implement both approaches and compare them. We leave this as an interesting future work.

The above comparison only considers the efficiency of the two approaches. However, as argued before, in applications like voting it is crucial to allow the voters to check that the outcome of the election is correct. Most mix-nets protocol already achieve public verifiability using non-interactive zero-knowledge proofs for the correctness of shuffles. This motivates our study of auditable generic protocols.

1.3 Related Work

For certain applications, there already exist *auditable protocols*. The idea is known in the context of e.g. electronic voting as *public verifiability*, and can also be found concerning online auctions and secret sharing. To the best of our knowledge, the term *public verifiability* was first used by Cohen and Fischer in [10]. Widely known publicly auditable voting protocols are those of Schoenmakers [28] and Chaum et al. [8] and the practical Helios [1]. Also stronger notions for voting protocols have been studied, see e.g. [27,22,30]. Verifiability also appeared for secret sharing schemes [28,17,29] and auctions [23,26]. We refer the reader to the mentioned papers and the references therein for more information on these subjects. It is crucial to point out that our suggested approach is not just another voting protocol – instead we lift verifiability to arbitrary secure computations. In this setting, the notion of public verifiability has not been studied, with the exception of [15], where the author presents a general transformation that turns *universally satisfiable* protocols into instances that are *auditable* in our sense. This transformation is general and slows down the computational phase of protocols, whereas our approach is tailored for fast computations.

In publicly verifiable delegation of computation (see e.g. [18,16] and references therein) a computationally limited device delegates a computation to the cloud and wants to check that the result is correct. Verifiable delegation is useless unless verification is more efficient than the evaluation. Note that in some sense our requirement is the opposite: We want our workers to work as little as possible, while we are fine with asking the auditor to perform more expensive computation.

External parties have been used before in cryptography to achieve otherwise impossible goals like fairness [20], but note that in our case *anyone can be the*

---

[5] The λ^3 factor is there because of the re-randomization step that is crucially done in every mix-net. Using "onions" of encryptions would not be more efficient.

[6] The $m \cdot \log m$ factor comes from the optimal shuffle of Ajtai et al. [2].

auditor and does not need to be online while the protocol is executed. This is a qualitative difference with most of the other semi-trusted parties that appear in the literature. A recent work [3] investigated an enhanced notion of covert security, that allows anyone to determine if a party cheated or not given the transcript of the protocol – note that the goal of our notion is different, as we are interested in what happens when *all* parties are corrupted.

2   Defining Auditable MPC

In this section, we formalize our notion of publicly auditable MPC. We add a new party to the standard formalization which *only performs the auditing* and does not need to participate during the offline or the online phase. This auditor does not even have to exist when the protocol is executed, but he can check the correctness of a result based on a protocol transcript. This *formal hack* makes it possible to guarantee correctness even if everyone participating in the computation is corrupted[7].

As mentioned, we put ourselves in the client-server model, so the parties involved in an auditable MPC protocols are:

The input parties: We consider m parties $\mathcal{I}_1, ..., \mathcal{I}_m$ with inputs $(x_1, ..., x_m)$.
The computing parties: We consider n parties $\mathcal{P}_1, ..., \mathcal{P}_n$ that participate in the computation phase. Given a set of inputs $x_1, ..., x_m$ they compute an output $y = C(x_1, ..., x_m)$ for some circuit C over a finite field. Note that $\{\mathcal{I}_1, ..., \mathcal{I}_m\}$ and $\{\mathcal{P}_1, ..., \mathcal{P}_n\}$ might not be distinct.
The auditor: After the protocol is executed, anyone acting as the auditor $\mathcal{T}_{\text{AUDIT}}$ can retrieve the transcript of the protocol τ from the bulletin board and (using only the circuit C and the output y) determine if the result is valid or not.

Our security notion is the standard one if there is at least one honest party (i.e. we guarantee privacy, correctness, etc.). However standard security notions do not give any guarantee in the *fully malicious* setting, i.e. when all parties are corrupted. We tweak the standard notions slightly and ask an additional property, called *auditable correctness*.

This notion captures the fact that in the fully malicious case, the input cannot be kept secret from the adversary $\mathcal{A}$. But we still want to prove that if the computing parties deviate from the protocol, this will be caught by $\mathcal{T}_{\text{AUDIT}}$, who has access to the transcript of the execution using a bulletin board $\mathcal{F}_{\text{BULLETIN}}$.

More formally, our definition for auditable correctness is as follows:

Definition 1 (Auditable Correctness). *Let C be a circuit, $x_1, ..., x_m$ be inputs to C, y be a potential output of C and τ be a protocol transcript for the*

---

[7] We are not adding a semi-trusted third party to the actual protocol: Our guarantee is that if there exist at least one honest party in the universe who cares about the output of the computation, that party can check at any time that the output is correct.

Functionality $\mathcal{F}_{\text{AuditMPC}}$

Initialize: On input (Init, C, p) from all parties (where C is a circuit with m inputs and one output, consisting of addition and multiplication gates over $\mathbb{Z}_p$):

   (1) Wait until $\mathcal{A}$ sends the sets $A_{BI} \subseteq \{1, \ldots, m\}$(corrupted input parties) and $A_{BP} \subseteq \{1, \ldots, n\}$(corrupted computing parties)

Input: On input $(\text{Input}, \mathcal{I}_i, \text{varid}_x, x)$ from $\mathcal{I}_i$ and $(\text{Input}, \mathcal{I}_i, \text{varid}_x, ?)$ from all parties $\mathcal{P}_j$, with varid_x a fresh identifier:

   (1) If $i \notin A_{BI}$ then store (varid_x, x). Else let $\mathcal{A}$ choose x' and store (varid_x, x').

   (2) If $|A_{BP}| = n$, send $(\text{Input}, \mathcal{I}_i, \text{varid}, x)$ to all $\mathcal{P}_j$.

Compute: On input (Compute) from all parties $\mathcal{P}_j$:

   (1) If an input gate of C has no value assigned, stop here.

   (2) Compute $y_c = C(x'_1, \ldots, x'_m)$

   (3) **if** $|A_{BP}| = 0$ set $y_o = y_c$.

      if $|A_{BP}| > 0$ output y_c to $\mathcal{A}$ and wait for y_o from $\mathcal{A}$. If $|A_{BP}| < n$, the functionality accepts only $y_o \in \{\bot, y_c\}$. If $|A_{BP}| = n$, any value $y_o \in \mathbb{Z}_p \cup \{\bot\}$ is accepted.

   (4) Send (output, y_o) to all parties $\mathcal{P}_j$.

Audit: On input (Audit, y) from $\mathcal{T}_{\text{AUDIT}}$ (where $y \in \mathbb{Z}_p$), and if **Compute** was executed, the functionality does the following:

   if $y_c = y_o = y$ then output ACCEPT y.

   if $y_o = \bot$ then output NO AUDIT POSSIBLE.

   if $y_c \neq y_o$ or $y \neq y_o$ then output REJECT.

Fig. 1. The ideal functionality that describes the online phase

evaluation of the circuit C. We say that an MPC protocol as satisfies Auditable Correctness *if the following holds: The auditor $\mathcal{T}_{\text{AUDIT}}$ with input τ outputs* ACCEPT y *with overwhelming probability if the circuit C on input $x_1, ..., x_m$ produces the output y. At the same time the auditor $\mathcal{T}_{\text{AUDIT}}$ will return* REJECT *(except with negligible probability) if τ is not a transcript of an evaluation of C or if $C(x_1, ..., x_m) \neq y$.*

In Figure 1 we present an ideal functionality that formalizes our notion of auditable MPC in the UC setting (where we use the same notation as before). We use this ideal world-real world paradigm, because it simplifies the proof, whereas the game-based definition gives a better intuition about auditability. The protocol/simulator transcript can then be used as in Definition 1, and a protocol that is secure in the ideal world-real world setting is also auditable correct according to the definition.

To simplify the exposition, $\mathcal{F}_{\text{AuditMPC}}$ is only defined for one output value y. This can easily be generalized.

Note that we only defined our $\mathcal{F}_{\text{AuditMPC}}$ for deterministic functionalities. The reason for this is that when all parties are corrupted even the auditor cannot check whether the players *followed the protocol correctly* in the sense of using real random tapes. This can be solved (using standard reductions) by letting the input parties contribute also random tapes and define the randomness used by the functionality as the XOR of those random tapes – but in the extreme case where all the input parties are corrupted this will not help us.

3   An Auditable MPC Protocol

We now present an MPC protocol that is an extension of [14,12]. We obtain a fast online phase, which almost only consists of opening shared values towards parties.

Our Setup. Let $p \in \mathbb{P}$ be a prime and G be some abelian group (in multiplicative notation) of order p where the *Discrete Logarithm Problem*(DLP) is hard to solve. The MPC protocol will evaluate a circuit C over $\mathbb{Z}_p$, whereas we use the group G to ensure auditability. Therefore, let $g, h \in G$ be two generators of the group G where h is chosen such that $\log_g(h)$ is not known (e.g. based on some CRS). For two values $x, r \in \mathbb{Z}_p$, we define $pc(x, r) := g^x h^r$.

We assume that a secure channel towards the input parties can be established, that a broadcast functionality is available and that we have access to a bulletin board $\mathcal{F}_{\text{BULLETIN}}$ (Fig. 2), a commitment functionality $\mathcal{F}_{\text{COMMIT}}$[8] (Fig. 3) and a procedure to jointly produce random values $\mathcal{P}_{\text{PROVIDERANDOM}}$ (Fig. 4)[9]. To implement $\mathcal{P}_{\text{PROVIDERANDOM}}$ let $\mathcal{U}_s(q, l)$ be a random oracle with seed $s \in \{0,1\}^*$ that outputs a uniformly random element from $\mathbb{Z}_q^l$. We use the bulletin board $\mathcal{F}_{\text{BULLETIN}}$ to keep track of all those values that are broadcasted. Observe that no information that was posted to $\mathcal{F}_{\text{BULLETIN}}$ can ever be changed or erased.

Sharing Values for the Online Phase. All computations during the online phase are done using additively-shared values. The parties are committed to each such shared value using a MAC key α and a commitment to the shared value. The key α is also additively-shared among the parties, where party $\mathcal{P}_i$ holds share α_i such that $\alpha = \sum_{i=1}^n \alpha_i$, and the commitments to each value are publicly known.

We define the $\langle \cdot \rangle$-representation of a shared value as follows:

Definition 2. *Let $r, s, e \in \mathbb{Z}_p$, then the $\langle r \rangle$-representation of r is defined as*

$$\langle r \rangle := ((r_1, ..., r_n), (\gamma(r)_1, ..., \gamma(r)_n))$$

where $r = \sum_{i=1}^n r_i$ and $\alpha \cdot r = \sum_{i=1}^n \gamma(r)_i$. Each player $\mathcal{P}_i$ will hold his shares $r_i, \gamma(r)_i$ of such a representation. Moreover, we define

---

[8] This other commitment functionality might be implemented by a hash function/random oracle, and is used whenever the linear operations of the commitment scheme are not necessary.

[9] Note that the random oracle model and $\mathcal{F}_{\text{COMMIT}}$ were already assumptions used in the original SPDZ protocol, our extra assumptions are the existence of $\mathcal{F}_{\text{BULLETIN}}$ and the DLP-hard group G.

The ideal functionality $\mathcal{F}_{\text{BULLETIN}}$

Store: On input $(\text{Store}, id, i, msg)$ from $\mathcal{P}_i$, where id was not assigned yet, the functionality stores (id, i, msg).

Reveal IDs: On input (All) from party $\mathcal{P}_i$ the functionality reveals all assigned id-values to $\mathcal{P}_i$

Reveal message: On input (Getmsg, id) from $\mathcal{P}_i$, the functionality checks whether id was assigned already. If so, then it returns (id, j, msg) to $\mathcal{P}_i$. Otherwise it returns $(id, \bot, \bot)$.

Fig. 2. The ideal Functionality for the Bulletin board

$$\langle r \rangle + \langle s \rangle := ((r_1 + s_1, ..., r_n + s_n), (\gamma(r)_1 + \gamma(s)_1, ..., \gamma(r)_n + \gamma(s)_n))$$
$$e \cdot \langle r \rangle := ((e \cdot r_1, ..., e \cdot r_n), (e \cdot \gamma(r)_1, ..., e \cdot \gamma(r)_n))$$
$$e + \langle r \rangle := ((r_1 + e, r_2, ..., r_n), (\gamma(r)_1 + e \cdot \alpha_1, ..., \gamma(r)_n + e \cdot \alpha_n))$$

This representation is closed under linear operations:

Remark 1. Let $r, s, e \in \mathbb{Z}_p$. We say that $\langle r \rangle \stackrel{\frown}{=} \langle s \rangle$ if both $\langle r \rangle, \langle s \rangle$ reconstruct to the same value. Then it holds that

$$\langle r \rangle + \langle s \rangle \stackrel{\frown}{=} \langle r + s \rangle, \ e \cdot \langle r \rangle \stackrel{\frown}{=} \langle e \cdot r \rangle, \ e + \langle r \rangle \stackrel{\frown}{=} \langle e + r \rangle$$

A value that is shared as above is reconstructed or *opened*[10] by summing up all shares. The correctness of this opening can be checked by checking the MAC(we will use a protocol where α will not be revealed). A value $\langle a \rangle$ can either be *publicly opened* if every player $\mathcal{P}_i$ broadcasts its share a_i, or *opened towards* $\mathcal{P}_i$ if every other party $\mathcal{P}_j, j \neq i$ sends its share a_j to $\mathcal{P}_i$. Similarly, if the players *open towards* $\mathcal{F}_{\text{BULLETIN}}$ this means that they send their shares of the particular value to the bulletin board.

During the online phase, the parties either open sharings (without revealing the MACs) or do the linear operations defined above. Together with the Beaver circuit randomization technique from [4] and a MAC checking procedure for the output phase, this already yields an actively secure MPC scheme that is secure against up to $n - 1$ corrupted players[11].

The $[\![\cdot]\!]$-representation. In order to make SPDZ auditable we enhance the way shared values are represented and stored. In a nutshell we force the computing parties to commit to the inputs, opened values and outputs of the computation. All intermediate steps can then be checked by performing the computation using the data on $\mathcal{F}_{\text{BULLETIN}}$. The commitment scheme is information-theoretically hiding, and we will carry both the actual value $\langle r \rangle$ as well as the randomness $\langle r_{rand} \rangle$ of the commitment through the whole computation.

---

[10] We use both terms for it in this paper.

[11] Provided that the offline phase generates valid multiplication triples and random values together with MACs.

The ideal functionality $\mathcal{F}_{\text{COMMIT}}$

Commit: On input (Commit, v, r, i, τ_v) by $\mathcal{P}_i$, where both v and r are either in $\mathbb{Z}_p$ or $\perp$, and τ_v is a unique identifier, it stores (v, r, i, τ_v) on a list and outputs (i, τ_v) to all players.

Open: On input (Open, i, τ_v) by $\mathcal{P}_i$, the ideal functionality outputs (v, r, i, τ_v) to all players. If (NoOpen, i, τ_v) is given by the adversary, and $\mathcal{P}_i$ is corrupt, the functionality outputs $(\perp, \perp, i, \tau_v)$ to all players.

Fig. 3. The Ideal Functionality for Commitments

Procedure $\mathcal{P}_{\text{PROVIDERANDOM}}$

Even though we do not mention minimum lengths of seeds here, they should be chosen according to a concrete security parameter.

ProvideRandom(q, l) On input (Urandomness, q, l) from each party $\mathcal{P}_i$:
   (1) Each party $\mathcal{P}_i$ commits to a seed $s_i \in \{0, 1\}^*$ using $\mathcal{F}_{\text{COMMIT}}$. It also sends the commitment to $\mathcal{F}_{\text{BULLETIN}}$.
   (2) Each party opens its commitment to all parties and $\mathcal{F}_{\text{BULLETIN}}$.
   (3) Each party locally computes $s = s_1 \oplus \cdots \oplus s_n$
   (4) Each party outputs $v \leftarrow \mathcal{U}_s(q, l)$.

Fig. 4. A protocol to jointly generate random values

Procedure $\mathcal{P}_{\text{MULT}}$

Multiply$([\![r]\!], [\![s]\!], [\![a]\!], [\![b]\!], [\![c]\!])$:
   (1) The players calculate $[\![\gamma]\!] = [\![r]\!] - [\![a]\!]$, $[\![\delta]\!] = [\![s]\!] - [\![b]\!]$
   (2) The players publicly reconstruct $\gamma, \delta, \gamma_{rand}, \delta_{rand}$ and send these values to $\mathcal{F}_{\text{BULLETIN}}$.
   (3) Each player locally calculates $[\![t]\!] = [\![c]\!] + \delta[\![a]\!] + \gamma[\![b]\!] + \gamma\delta$
   (4) Return $[\![t]\!]$ as the representation of the product.

Fig. 5. Protocol to generate the product of two $[\![\cdot]\!]$-shared values

The commitment to a value r will be a Pedersen commitment (see [25]) $pc(r, r_{rand})$. When we open a $[\![\cdot]\!]$-representation, we reconstruct both r and r_{rand}.[12] This way the commitment is also opened (it is already published on $\mathcal{F}_{\text{BULLETIN}}$) and everyone can check that it is correct (but the computing parties do not need to do so).

Definition 3. *Let $r, r_{rand} \in \mathbb{Z}_p$ and $g, h \in G$ where both g, h generate the group, then we define the $[\![r]\!]$-representation for r as*

$$[\![r]\!] := (\langle r \rangle, \langle r_{rand} \rangle, pc(r, r_{rand}))$$

---

[12] Our different flavours of opening for $\langle \cdot \rangle$-representations can be applied here as well.

where $\langle r \rangle, \langle r_{rand} \rangle$ are shared among the players as before.

We define linear operations on the representations as before:

Definition 4. *Let $a, b, a_{rand}, b_{rand}, e \in \mathbb{Z}_p$. We define the following linear operations on $[\![\cdot]\!]$-sharings:*

$$[\![a]\!] + [\![b]\!] := (\langle a \rangle + \langle b \rangle, \langle a_{rand} \rangle + \langle b_{rand} \rangle, pc(a, a_{rand}) \cdot pc(b, b_{rand}))$$

$$e \cdot [\![a]\!] := (e \cdot \langle a \rangle, e \cdot \langle a_{rand} \rangle, (pc(a, a_{rand}))^e)$$

$$e + [\![a]\!] := (e + \langle a \rangle, \langle a_{rand} \rangle, pc(e, 0) \cdot pc(a, a_{rand}))$$

With a slight abuse in notation, we see that

Remark 2. Let $r, s, e \in \mathbb{Z}_p$. It holds that

$$[\![r]\!] + [\![s]\!] \,\hat{=}\, [\![r + s]\!], \; e \cdot [\![r]\!] \,\hat{=}\, [\![e \cdot r]\!], \; e + [\![r]\!] \,\hat{=}\, [\![e + r]\!]$$

In order to multiply two representations, we rely on the protocol in Figure 5 (as in [4]): Let $[\![r]\!], [\![s]\!]$ be two values where we want to calculate a representation $[\![t]\!]$ such that $t = r \cdot s$. Assume the existence of a triple $([\![a]\!], [\![b]\!], [\![c]\!])$ such that a, b are uniformly random and $c = a \cdot b$. Then one can obtain $[\![t]\!]$ using $\mathcal{P}_{\mathrm{MULT}}$.

Most interestingly, one does not have to perform the computations on the commitments during the online phase. Instead, *only the $\langle \cdot \rangle$-representations are manipulated*!

Shared Randomness from an Offline Phase. Our online phase relies on the availability of $[\![\cdot]\!]$-representations of random values and multiplication triples. In Figure 6 and 8 we define the functionality $\mathcal{F}_{\mathrm{SETUP}}$ that describes our preprocessing protocol, which is essentially an *auditable* version of the SPDZ preprocessing functionality. If all parties are corrupted, the functionality might output an incorrect result – however this can be checked by the auditor. Since we assume that g, h come from a CRS, the audit is still correct in this setting.

The Online Phase. The online phase of our protocol is presented in Figure 9. To create the transcript, every party puts all values it ever *sends* or *receives* onto $\mathcal{F}_{\mathrm{BULLETIN}}$ (except for the private reconstruction of input values)[13]. The check of the MACs is done as in SPDZ using the protocol in Figure 11.

4 Security of the Online Phase

In this section, we will prove that for all poly-time adversaries $\mathcal{A}$ there exists a simulator $\mathcal{S}_{\mathrm{ONLINE}}$ such that Π_{AUDITMPC} is indistinguishable from $\mathcal{F}_{\mathrm{AUDITMPC}}$ to every poly-time environment $\mathcal{Z}$. As we argued before, this also implies that Π_{AUDITMPC} fulfills the *auditable correctness* requirement from Definition 1.

We start with the following Lemma from [12, Lemma 1] about correctness and soundness of the MAC check. We then prove the security of the online phase in Theorem 1.

---

[13] This does not break the security, because (informally speaking) this is the same information that an $\mathcal{A}$ receives if he corrupts $n - 1$ parties.

Functionality $\mathcal{F}_{\text{SETUP}}$, Part 1/3

$\odot$ denotes pointwise multiplication of vector entries and l is a fixed SIMD factor.

Initialize: On input (Init, p, l) from all players, the functionality stores the prime p and the SIMD factor l. $\mathcal{A}$ chooses the set of parties $A_{BP} \subseteq \{1, \ldots, n\}$ he corrupts.

(1) Choose a $g \in G$ and $s \in \mathbb{Z}_p^*$, set $h = g^s$. Send g, h to $\mathcal{A}$.

(2) For all $i \in A_{BP}$, $\mathcal{A}$ inputs $\alpha_i \in \mathbb{Z}_p$, while for all $i \notin A_{BP}$, the functionality chooses $\alpha_i \leftarrow \mathbb{Z}_p$ at random.

(3) Set they key $\alpha = \sum_{i=1}^{n} \alpha_i$ and send (α_i, g, h) to $\mathcal{P}_i, i \notin A_{BP}$.

(4) Set the flag $f = \top$.

Audit: On input (Audit), return REJECT if $f = \bot$ or if **Initialize** or **Compute** was not executed. Else return ACCEPT.

Fig. 6. The ideal functionality that describes the offline phase

Lemma 1. *Let $p \in \mathbb{P}$. On input $(a_1, \gamma(a_1), \ldots, a_t, \gamma(a_t), p)$ $\mathcal{P}_{\text{CHECKMAC}}$ is correct and sound:*

If $\forall i : \alpha \cdot a_i = \gamma(a_i)$ then it returns 1 with probability 1.

If $\exists i : \alpha \cdot a_i \neq \gamma(a_i)$ then it rejects except with probability $2/p$.

Theorem 1. *In the $\mathcal{F}_{\text{SETUP}}, \mathcal{F}_{\text{BULLETIN}}, \mathcal{F}_{\text{COMMIT}}$-hybrid model with a random oracle, the protocol Π_{AUDITMPC} implements $\mathcal{F}_{\text{AUDITMPC}}$ with computational security against any static adversary corrupting all parties if the DLP is hard in the group G.*

Proof. We prove the above statement by providing a simulator $\mathcal{S}_{\text{ONLINE}}$ (see Figure 12). The simulator is divided for two cases, for the honest minority ($\mathcal{S}_{\text{ONLINE,NORMAL}}$ in Figure 13) and the fully malicious setting ($\mathcal{S}_{\text{ONLINE,FULL}}$ in Figure 14).

At Least One Honest Party. The simulator runs an instance of Π_{AUDITMPC} with the players controlled by $\mathcal{Z}$ and simulated honest parties. For **Initialize, Input, Add, Multiply** it performs the same steps as in Π_{AUDITMPC}, only that it uses a fixed input 0 for the simulated honest parties during **Input**. Since every set of at most $n - 1$ shares of a value is uniformly random and does not reveal any information about the shared secret, this cannot be distinguished from a real execution.

During **Output**, we adjust the shares of one simulated honest party to agree with the correct output y from $\mathcal{F}_{\text{AUDITMPC}}$: The simulator obtained the result y' of the simulated computation, hence it can adjust the share of a simulated honest party. Moreover, it also adjusts the MAC share as depicted in $\mathcal{S}_{\text{ONLINE,NORMAL}}$ using the MAC key α provided by $\mathcal{F}_{\text{SETUP}}$. As argued in [14], the distribution of these shares of the simulated honest parties is the same as during a protocol execution.

Functionality $\mathcal{F}_{\text{SETUP}}$, Part 2/3

Compute: On input (GenerateData, T, ρ) from all players with T, ρ multiples of l:

(1) $RandomValues(T, l)$:
   (1.1) For each $i \notin A_{BP}$ choose uniformly random $r_i, s_i \leftarrow \mathbb{Z}_p^T$, send these to $\mathcal{P}_i$ and $pc(r_i, s_i)$ to $\mathcal{A}$.
   (1.2) For $i \in A_{BP}$, $\mathcal{A}$ inputs $r_i, s_i \in \mathbb{Z}_p^T$
   (1.3) Compute $[\![r]\!] \leftarrow \text{Bracket}(r_1, \ldots, r_n, s_1, \ldots, s_n, T)$.
   (1.4) Send the commitments of $[\![b]\!]$ to $\mathcal{F}_{\text{BULLETIN}}$.
   (1.5) Return $([\![r]\!])$.
(2) $Triples(\rho, l)$:
   (2.1) For $i \notin A_{BP}$, the functionality samples $a_i, a_{rand,i}, b_i, b_{rand,i} \in \mathbb{Z}_p^\rho$ at random, sends them to $\mathcal{P}_i$ and $pc(a_i, a_{rand,i}), pc(b_i, b_{rand,i})$ to $\mathcal{A}$.
   (2.2) For $i \in A_{BP}$, $\mathcal{A}$ inputs $a_i, a_{rand,i}, b_i, b_{rand,i} \in \mathbb{Z}_p^\rho$.
   (2.3) For each $i \notin A_{BP}$ sample uniformly random $o_i \in G^\rho$ and send them to $\mathcal{A}$.
   (2.4) For $i \in A_{BP}$ let $\mathcal{A}$ choose $c_i, c_{rand,i} \in \mathbb{Z}_p^\rho$.
   (2.5) Define $a = \sum_{j=1}^n a_j, b = \sum_{j=1}^n b_j$.
   (2.6) Let $j \notin A_{BP}$ be the smallest index of an honest player(if any). For all $i \notin A_{BP}, i \neq j$ choose $c_i \in \mathbb{Z}_p^\rho$ uniformly at random and $c_{rand,i} \in \mathbb{Z}_p^\rho$ subject to the constraint that $o_i = pc(c_i, c_{rand,i})$ using s. For $\mathcal{P}_j$ let $c_j = a \odot b - \sum_{i \in [n], i \neq j} c_i$ and $c_{rand,j} \in \mathbb{Z}_p^\rho$ such that $o_j = pc(c_j, c_{rand,j})$ using s. Send $c_i, c_{rand,i}$ to $\mathcal{P}_i$.
   (2.7) Let $c = \sum_{i=1}^n c_i$.
   (2.8) Run the macros $[\![a]\!] \leftarrow \text{Bracket}(a_1, \ldots, a_n, a_{rand,1}, \ldots, a_{rand,n}, \rho)$, $[\![b]\!] \leftarrow \text{Bracket}(b_1, \ldots, b_n, b_{rand,1}, \ldots, b_{rand,n}, \rho)$, $[\![c]\!] \leftarrow \text{Bracket}(c_1, \ldots, c_n, c_{rand,1}, \ldots, c_{rand,n}, \rho)$.
   (2.9) Let $L' = \{1, ..., \rho\}$
   (2.10) If $|A_{BP}| = n$ then let $\mathcal{A}$ input L, otherwise let $L = L'$. If $L \neq L'$ then set $f = \perp$.
   (2.11) Send the commitments of $([\![a[m]]\!], [\![b[m]]\!], [\![c[m]]\!])_{m \in L}$ to $\mathcal{F}_{\text{BULLETIN}}$
   (2.12) Return $([\![a[m]]\!], [\![b[m]]\!], [\![c[m]]\!])_{m \in L}$.

Fig. 7. The ideal functionality that describes the offline phase,continued

The commitment is information-theoretically hiding, and since the discrete logarithm $\log_g(h)$ is known to $\mathcal{S}_{\text{ONLINE,NORMAL}}$, it can compute a randomness value y_{rand} that correctly opens the commitment in $[\![y]\!]$ as posted on $\mathcal{F}_{\text{BULLETIN}}$ for the value y instead of y'. It then adjusts a share of y'_{rand} such that (y', y'_{rand}) open the commitment. Once again, the distribution of this share of $y_{rand'}$ agrees with the distribution in a real protocol execution.

If moreover $\mathcal{Z}$ decides to stop the execution, then $\mathcal{S}_{\text{ONLINE,NORMAL}}$ will forward this to the ideal functionality and $\mathcal{Z}$ will not receive any additional information, as in the real execution.

During the **Audit** phase, we also do exactly the same as in the protocol. Note that both **Output** and **Audit** will always reveal the correct values from

---

Functionality $\mathcal{F}_{\text{SETUP}}$, Part 3/3

Macro Bracket($r_1, \ldots, r_n, s_1, \ldots, s_n, d$): This macro will be run by the functionality to create $[\![\cdot]\!]$-representations.
  (1) Define $r = \sum_{i=1}^{n} r_i, s = \sum_{i=1}^{n} s_i$.
  (2) If $|A_{BP}| = n$, $\mathcal{A}$ inputs a vector $\boldsymbol{\Delta}_c \in G^d$.
      If $\boldsymbol{\Delta}_c$ is not the $(1, \ldots, 1)$ vector, set $f = \bot$. If $|A_{BP}| < n$ set $\boldsymbol{\Delta}_c$ to the all-ones vector.
  (3) Compute $\boldsymbol{com} = pc(\boldsymbol{r}, \boldsymbol{s}) \odot \boldsymbol{\Delta}_c$.
  (4) Run macro $\langle r \rangle \leftarrow$ Angle($r_1, \ldots, r_n, d$) and $\langle s \rangle \leftarrow$ Angle($s_1, \ldots, s_n, d$).
  (5) Define $[\![r]\!] = (\langle r \rangle, \langle s \rangle, \boldsymbol{com})$. Return $[\![r]\!]$.

Macro Angle($r_1, \ldots, r_n, d$): This macro will be run by the functionality to create $\langle \cdot \rangle$-representations.
  (1) Define $r = \sum_{i=1}^{n} r_i$
  (2) For $i \in A_{BP}$, $\mathcal{A}$ inputs $\gamma_i, \boldsymbol{\Delta}_\gamma \in \mathbb{Z}_p^d$, and for $i \notin A_{BP}$, choose $\gamma_i \in_R \mathbb{Z}_p^d$ at random except for γ_j, with j being the smallest index not in A_{BP} (if there exists one).
  (3) If $|A_{BP}| < n$ set $\gamma = \alpha \cdot r + \boldsymbol{\Delta}_\gamma$ and $\gamma_j = \gamma - \sum_{j \neq i=1}^{n} \gamma_i$, else set $\gamma = \sum_{i=1}^{n} \gamma_i$.
  (4) Define $\langle r \rangle = (r_1, \ldots, r_n, \gamma_1, \ldots, \gamma_n)$. Return $\langle r \rangle$.

Fig. 8. The ideal functionality that describes the output of the offline phase, continued

$\mathcal{F}_{\text{AUDITMPC}}$ in the simulated case. We have to show that in the real protocol, the probability that $\mathcal{A}$ can cheat is negligible.

Output: There are three ways how the output can be incorrect with respect to the inputs and the calculated function, which is if a multiplication triple was not correct even though it passed the check, or if a dishonest party successfully adjusted the MACs during the computation, or it successfully cheated during the output phase. As argued in [14], the first event only happens with probability $1/p$. If $\mathcal{A}$ can adjust the MACs correctly with non-negligible probability, then it can guess the secret MAC key α – which contradicts that it only holds at most $n-1$ shares of it which reveal no information. For the third case, Lemma 1 implies that this can only happen with probability $2/p$. Since we set p to be exponential in the security parameter, the distributions are statistically indistinguishable.

Audit: We focus on the two cases when $\mathcal{F}_{\text{AUDITMPC}}$ and Π_{AUDITMPC} disagree about the output of **Audit**. The conditions under which $\mathcal{S}_{\text{OFFLINE,NORMAL}}$ and Π_{AUDITMPC} output NO AUDIT POSSIBLE are the same.
  (1) $\mathcal{F}_{\text{AUDITMPC}}$ outputs ACCEPT y when Π_{AUDITMPC} outputs REJECT does not happen due to the construction of $\mathcal{S}_{\text{OFFLINE,NORMAL}}$.
  (2) $\mathcal{F}_{\text{AUDITMPC}}$ outputs REJECT when Π_{AUDITMPC} outputs ACCEPT y. $\mathcal{A}$ replaced the output with $\bot$, but $\mathcal{P}_{\text{CHECKMAC}}$ passed successfully. This happens with probability at most $2/p$ according to Lemma 1.

Protocol Π_{AuditMPC}, Part 1/2

Initialize: On input (Init, C, p) from all parties (where $p \in \mathbb{P}$ and C is a circuit over $\mathbb{Z}_p$, with ρ multiplication gates):

(1) The parties send (Init, p, l) to $\mathcal{F}_{\text{SETUP}}$ and obtain their shares α_i.

(2) The parties choose the smallest $\tau \geq \rho$ such that $l|\tau$ and send $(\text{GenerateData}, m + 2, \tau)$ to $\mathcal{F}_{\text{SETUP}}$. If they obtain $\rho' < \rho$ triples, they continue sending $(\text{GenerateData}, 0, \tau)$ until they obtained at least ρ triples in total.

Input: On input $(\text{Input}, \mathcal{I}_i, varid, x_i)$ by $\mathcal{I}_i$ and $(\text{Input}, \mathcal{I}_i, varid, ?)$ from all $\mathcal{P}_j$, the parties and $\mathcal{I}_i$ do the following (using a new random value $[\![r]\!]$):

(1) $[\![r]\!]$ is privately opened as r, r_{rand} to $\mathcal{I}_i$.

(2) Let c_r be the commitment of $[\![r]\!]$ on $\mathcal{F}_{\text{BULLETIN}}$. $\mathcal{I}_i$ checks that $c_r = pc(r, r_{rand})$. If not, the protocol is aborted.

(3) $\mathcal{I}_i$ broadcasts $\epsilon = x_i - r$ to all $\mathcal{P}_j$ and $\mathcal{F}_{\text{BULLETIN}}$.

(4) All players locally compute $[\![x_i]\!] = [\![r]\!] + \epsilon$

Compute: Upon input (Compute) from all $\mathcal{P}_i$, if **Initialize** has been executed and inputs for all input wires of C have been assigned, evaluate C gate per gate as follows:

Add: For two values $[\![r]\!], [\![s]\!]$ with IDs $varid_r, varid_s$:

(1) Let $varid_t$ be a fresh ID. Each party locally computes $[\![t]\!] = [\![r]\!] + [\![s]\!]$ and assigns $varid_t$ to it. The commitments are excluded from the computation.

Multiply: Multiply two values $[\![r]\!], [\![s]\!]$ with IDs $varid_r, varid_s$, using the multiplication triple $([\![a]\!], [\![b]\!], [\![c]\!])$.

(1) Let $varid_t$ be a fresh ID. The parties invoke $\mathcal{P}_{\text{MULT}}.Multiply([\![r]\!], [\![s]\!], [\![a]\!], [\![b]\!], [\![c]\!])$ to compute $[\![t]\!]$ and assign the ID $varid_t$. The commitments are excluded from the computation.

Output: The parties open the output $[\![y]\!]$. Let $a_1, ..., a_t$ be the values opened.

(1) All parties compute
$$r \leftarrow \mathcal{P}_{\text{CHECKMAC}}.CheckOutput(a_1, \gamma(a_1), \ldots, a_t, \gamma(a_t), p)$$
If $r \neq 0$ then stop.

(2) All parties open the output $[\![y]\!]$ towards $\mathcal{F}_{\text{BULLETIN}}$.

(3) All parties compute
$$s \leftarrow \mathcal{P}_{\text{CHECKMAC}}.CheckOutput(y, \gamma(y), y_{rand}, \gamma(y_{rand}), p)$$
If $s \neq 0$ then stop. Otherwise output y.

Fig. 9. The protocol for the online phase

Fully Malicious Setting. The intuition behind $\mathcal{S}_{\text{ONLINE,FULL}}$ is that we let $\mathcal{Z}$ send arbitrary messages during the online phase. But since all messages for $\mathcal{F}_{\text{SETUP}}$ go through $\mathcal{S}_{\text{ONLINE,FULL}}$, we extract the used inputs after the fact which we then can use with $\mathcal{F}_{\text{AuditMPC}}$. Observe that, since we cannot guarantee privacy, no inputs must be substituted. During the **Audit**, we run the protocol of Π_{AuditMPC} also in the simulator (but with different outputs, as we shall see). The difference between both again is the output of **Audit** in both worlds.

Protocol Π_{AuditMPC}, Part 2/2

Audit:
(1) If the **Output** step was not completed, output NO AUDIT POSSIBLE.
(2) Run **Audit** for $\mathcal{F}_{\text{Setup}}$. If it returns ACCEPT then continue, otherwise output NO AUDIT POSSIBLE.
(3) We follow the computation gates of the evaluated circuit C in the same order as they were computed. For the i-th gate, do the following:

  Input: Let $[\![r]\!]$ be the opened value and $varid_x$ be the ID of input x. Set $c_{varid_x} = pc(\epsilon, 0) \cdot c$, where c is the commitment in $[\![r]\!]$ and ϵ is the opened difference.

  Add: The parties added $[\![r]\!]$ with $varid_r$ and $[\![s]\!]$ with $varid_s$ to $[\![t]\!]$ with $varid_t$. Set $c_{varid_t} = c_{varid_r} \cdot c_{varid_s}$.

  Multiply: The parties multiplied $[\![r]\!]$ with $varid_r$ and $[\![s]\!]$ with $varid_s$ (using the auxiliary values $[\![a]\!], [\![b]\!], [\![c]\!], [\![\gamma]\!], [\![\delta]\!]$ with their respective IDs). The output has ID $varid_t$.

  (a) Set $c_{varid_t} = c_{varid_c} \cdot c_{varid_a}^{\delta} \cdot c_{varid_b}^{\gamma} \cdot pc(\gamma \cdot \delta, 0)$.

  (b) Check that $c_{varid_r} \cdot c_{varid_a}^{-1} \overset{?}{=} pc(\gamma, \gamma_{rand},)$ and

  $c_{varid_s} \cdot c_{varid_b}^{-1} \overset{?}{=} pc(\delta, \delta_{rand},)$. If not, output REJECT.

(4) Let y be the output of **Output** and c_y be the commitment for the output value $[\![y]\!]$.
  If $c_y = pc(y, y_{rand})$ then output ACCEPT y.
  If $c_y \neq pc(y, y_{rand})$ then output REJECT.

Fig. 10. The protocol for the online phase, continued

Procedure $\mathcal{P}_{\text{CheckMac}}$

$CheckOutput(v_1, \gamma(v_1), ..., v_t, \gamma(v_t), m)$ Here we check whether the MACs hold on t reconstructed values.
(1) Each $\mathcal{P}_i$ samples a value s_i and, to obtain the vector r, invokes $\mathcal{P}_{\text{ProvideRandom}}.ProvideRandom(m, t)$ with the seed s_i.
(2) Each $\mathcal{P}_i$ computes $v = \sum_{i=1}^{t} r[i] \cdot v_i$.
(3) Each $\mathcal{P}_i$ computes $\gamma_i = \sum_{j=1}^{t} r[j] \cdot \gamma(v_j)$ and $\sigma_i = \gamma_i - \alpha_i \cdot v$.
(4) Each $\mathcal{P}_i$ commits to σ_i using $\mathcal{F}_{\text{Commit}}$ as c_i'.
(5) Each c_i' is opened towards all players using $\mathcal{F}_{\text{Commit}}$.
(6) If $\sigma = \sum_{i=1}^{n} \sigma_i$ is 0 then return 1, otherwise return 0.

Fig. 11. Procedure to check validity of MACs

(1) $\mathcal{F}_{\text{AuditMPC}}$ outputs ACCEPT y when Π_{AuditMPC} outputs REJECT does not happen due to the construction of $\mathcal{S}_{\text{Offline,full}}$.
(2) $\mathcal{F}_{\text{AuditMPC}}$ outputs REJECT when Π_{AuditMPC} outputs ACCEPT y. $\mathcal{Z}$ replaced the output with another value y' (and also y'_{rand}) that open the commitment c_y. But in step (3) of **Compute**, the simulator already obtained y such that

---

Simulator $\mathcal{S}_{\text{ONLINE}}$

(1) Wait for the set A_{BP} of corrupted players from $\mathbf{Z}$.
(2) **If** $|A_{BP}| \neq n$ then forward all incoming messages that are not from $\mathcal{S}_{\text{ONLINE,NORMAL}}$ to $\mathcal{S}_{\text{ONLINE,NORMAL}}$, and forward all messages that come from $\mathcal{S}_{\text{ONLINE,NORMAL}}$ to the recipient.
If $|A_{BP}| = n$ then forward all incoming messages that are not from $\mathcal{S}_{\text{ONLINE,FULL}}$ to $\mathcal{S}_{\text{ONLINE,FULL}}$, and forward all messages that come from $\mathcal{S}_{\text{ONLINE,FULL}}$ to the recipient.

Fig. 12. Simulator for the online phase

$pc(y, y_{rand}) = pc(y', y'_{rand})$ for some y_{rand}.[14] This implies a solution of the DLP in poly-time, contradicting the assumption.

$\square$

5   On the Efficiency of Our Solution

In this section, we will outline why the practical efficiency of the offline and audit phase of our protocol crucially depends on how fast commitments can be computed and checked. We will moreover present a few optimizations for these tasks.

Asymptotic Efficiency. In terms of asymptotic efficiency, our suggested online phase is as efficient as the SPDZ protocol. Practically, the number of local field operations and sent values increases by a modest factor of two, plus some additional work for each input-providing party (to check whether the commitment is correct). It is an interesting open problem to see if one could get rid of even this minor slowdown.

To be more precise, we have to distinguish between the field operations in $\mathbb{Z}_p$ and the group operations in G. In the standard setting, where each party provides $O(1)$ inputs and $O(1)$ output values are jointly computed, and where the number of gates in our circuit is upper-bounded by $|C|$, all operations of the online phase (**Input, Add, Multiply, Output**) together can be performed by each player doing at most $O(n \cdot |C|)$ field operations. Assuming that we use Pedersen commitments to implement $\mathcal{F}_{\text{COMMIT}}$ in practice, we obtain an extra $O(n \cdot \log p)$ group operations during **Input** and **Output**. In terms of network load, each party sends or receives $O(n \cdot |C|)$ field elements over the network during the **Input** phase and while the computation is carried out, and $O(n)$ elements from $\mathbb{Z}_p$ and G during **Output**.

We moreover have to discuss our new **Audit** phase of the protocol (we exclude $\mathcal{F}_{\text{SETUP}}$ from the discussion). The strategy of **Audit** is to *follow the computation with the commitments*. Here, the number of operations in $\mathbb{Z}_p$ is $O(n \cdot |C|)$, which

---

[14] Computing y_{rand} from C and the randomization values of the inputs is straightforward. We omitted this computation here.

Simulator $\mathcal{S}_{\text{ONLINE,NORMAL}}$

The values g, h are provided as a CRS by this simulator, so $s = \log_g(h)$ is known as well as α.

Initialize: On input (Init, C, p) from $\boldsymbol{Z}$:
  (1) Set up $\mathcal{F}_{\text{BULLETIN}}$ and start a local instance Π of Π_{AUDITMPC} with the dishonest parties (and simulated honest parties).
  (2) Run a copy of $\mathcal{F}_{\text{SETUP}}$, with which $\boldsymbol{Z}$ and the simulated honest parties communicate through the simulator.
  (3) Run **Initialize** and **Compute** of $\mathcal{F}_{\text{SETUP}}$ as in Π_{AUDITMPC}.
Input: On input $(\mathsf{Input}, \boldsymbol{\mathcal{I}_i}, varid, \cdot)$ by $\boldsymbol{\mathcal{I}_i}$ and $(\mathsf{Input}, \boldsymbol{\mathcal{I}_i}, varid, ?)$ from and $\boldsymbol{Z}$:
  If $\boldsymbol{\mathcal{I}_i}$ is honest then follow Π_{AUDITMPC} for a fake input 0.
  If $\boldsymbol{\mathcal{I}_i}$ is dishonest then extract the input value x_i from Π and send it to $\mathcal{F}_{\text{AUDITMPC}}$. Execute this step with x_i in $\mathcal{F}_{\text{AUDITMPC}}$.
Compute: Upon input $(\mathsf{Compute})$ from $\boldsymbol{Z}$, if **Initialize** has been executed and inputs for all input gates of C have been provided, evaluate C gate per gate as follows:
  Add: Follow the steps of **Add** in Π_{AUDITMPC}.
  Multiply: Follow the steps of **Multiply** in Π_{AUDITMPC}.
  Output: Obtain the output y from $\mathcal{F}_{\text{AUDITMPC}}$ and simulate Π_{AUDITMPC} as follows:
    (1) Generate correct shares for the simulated honest parties for Π:
      (1.1) Let $\boldsymbol{\mathcal{P}_i}$ be a simulated honest party and y' be the output of Π with $\boldsymbol{Z}$ right now. Let $[\![y']\!] = (\langle y' \rangle, \langle y'_{rand} \rangle, c = pc(y', y'_{rand}))$, where $y' = \sum_k y'_{o,k}$ and $y'_{rand} = \sum_k y'_{rand,o,k}$. For all honest $\boldsymbol{\mathcal{P}_j}$ with $j \neq i$, let $y'_{q,j} = y'_{o,j}, y'_{rand,q,j} = y'_{rand,o,j}$. [a]
      (1.2) For $\boldsymbol{\mathcal{P}_i}$ set $y'_{q,i} = y'_{o,i} + (y - y')$ and $\gamma'_{q,i} = \gamma'_{o,i} + \alpha(y - y')$. We have $s \neq 0$, so $s^{-1} \bmod p$ exists. Set $y_{rand} = (y' - y + s \cdot y'_{rand})/s \bmod p$, and $y'_{rand,q,i} = y'_{rand,o,i} + (y_{rand} - y'_{rand})$, $\gamma'_{rand,q,i} = \gamma'_{rand,o,i} + \alpha \cdot (y_{rand} - y'_{rand})$.
      (1.3) Let $y' = \sum_k y_{q,k}, y'_{rand} = \sum_k y'_{rand,q,k}, \gamma' = \sum_k \gamma'_{q,k}$ and $\gamma'_{rand} = \sum_k \gamma'_{rand,q,k}$.
    (2) Follow the protocol Π_{AUDITMPC} to check the MACs according to step 1 of **Output**. If that step fails, let $\mathcal{F}_{\text{AUDITMPC}}$ deliver $\bot$ to the honest parties and stop.
    (3) Send the shares of the simulated honest parties of the output $[\![y]\!]$ to $\mathcal{F}_{\text{BULLETIN}}$. If $\boldsymbol{Z}$ does not provide shares of $[\![y]\!]$ for all dishonest parties, then let $\mathcal{F}_{\text{AUDITMPC}}$ set $y' = \bot$ and stop.
    (4) Run $\mathcal{P}_{\text{CHECKMAC}}$ as in Π_{AUDITMPC}. If the MAC on the output $[\![y]\!]$ is correct, let $\mathcal{F}_{\text{AUDITMPC}}$ set $y' = y$, otherwise $y' = \bot$.
Audit: Run **Audit** as in Π_{AUDITMPC} with the malicious players. Then invoke **Audit** in $\mathcal{F}_{\text{AUDITMPC}}$ and output REJECT if it is the output of $\mathcal{F}_{\text{AUDITMPC}}$. If not, reveal what $\mathcal{F}_{\text{AUDITMPC}}$ outputs.

---

[a] Similarly, the MAC keys $\gamma'_{o,j}, \gamma'_{rand,o,j}$ of those parties are not touched.

Fig. 13. Simulator for honest minority

Simulator $\mathcal{S}_{\text{ONLINE,FULL}}$

Initialize: On input (Init, C, p) from $\mathbf{Z}$:
  (1) Set up $\mathcal{F}_{\text{BULLETIN}}$ and start a local instance Π of Π_{AUDITMPC} with the dishonest parties.
  (2) Run a copy of $\mathcal{F}_{\text{SETUP}}$, with which $\mathbf{Z}$ communicates through the simulator.
  (3) Run **Initialize** and **Compute** of $\mathcal{F}_{\text{SETUP}}$ as in Π_{AUDITMPC}.

Input: On input $(\mathsf{Input}, \mathcal{I}_i, varid, \cdot)$ by $\mathcal{I}_i$ and $(\mathsf{Input}, \mathcal{I}_i, varid, ?)$ from $\mathbf{Z}$:
  If $\mathcal{I}_i$ is honest then ask $\mathcal{F}_{\text{AUDITMPC}}$ to reveal the input value x_i.
  If $\mathcal{I}_i$ is dishonest then extract the value x_i from Π and send it to $\mathcal{F}_{\text{AUDITMPC}}$.

Compute: Upon input $(\mathsf{Compute})$ from $\mathbf{Z}$, if **Initialize** has been executed and inputs for all input gates of C have been provided, evaluate C gate per gate as follows:
  Add: Follow the steps of **Add** in Π_{AUDITMPC}.
  Multiply: Follow the steps of **Multiply** in Π_{AUDITMPC}.
  Output:
    (1) Follow the protocol Π_{AUDITMPC} to check the MACs according to step 1 of **Output**. If that step fails, let $\mathcal{F}_{\text{AUDITMPC}}$ set $y' = \perp$ and stop.
    (2) If $\mathbf{Z}$ does not provide shares of $[\![y]\!]$ for all parties, then let $\mathcal{F}_{\text{AUDITMPC}}$ set $y' = \perp$ and stop.
    (3) Run $\mathcal{P}_{\text{CHECKMAC}}$ as in Π_{AUDITMPC}. If the MAC on the output $[\![y]\!]$ is correct, let $\mathcal{F}_{\text{AUDITMPC}}$ set $y' = y$, otherwise $y' = \perp$.

Audit: Run **Audit** as in Π_{AUDITMPC} with the malicious players. Then invoke **Audit** in $\mathcal{F}_{\text{AUDITMPC}}$ and output REJECT if it is the output of $\mathcal{F}_{\text{AUDITMPC}}$. If not, reveal what $\mathcal{F}_{\text{AUDITMPC}}$ outputs.

Fig. 14. Simulator for the fully malicious setting

is comparable to the online phase. In addition, the algorithm performs the gate operations on commitments and checks whether every opening of a commitment was correct – this in total requires $O((n + C) \cdot \log p)$ group operations.

To check whether the commitments are correctly opened, the audit process computes a random linear combination of the opened commitments (using coefficients from $\mathbb{Z}_p$) and the values which should open them (instead of checking all of them independently). This randomized check fails with probability $2^{-\log p}$. In practice, one would choose the coefficients of the random linear combination from the smaller interval $[0, ..., 2^k - 1]$ (where we can have $k \ll \log p$), thus saving operations in G.

Towards a Faster Offline Phase. Though the offline phase of [14] can directly be extended to support the computation of the commitments (as we describe in the full version), one can use different optimizations for it. First of all, computing the commitments can be made faster using preprocessing as in [7,21]. Moreover, it is possible to reduce the total number of commitments (introducing a moderate slowdown during the online phase) as follows:

Instead of computing *one commitment per value*, one can also use s pairwise distinct generators $g_1, ..., g_s \in \mathbb{Z}_p$ together with just one randomness parameter, where generator g_i is used to commit to the ith value.

A representation $(x_1, ..., x_t, r, g_1^{x_1} \cdots g_t^{x_t} h^r)$ of t values in parallel is componentwise linear, and multiplications can also be performed as before (now for multiple elements in parallel). We observe that the computation of a commitment with many generators can be substantially faster than computing all commitments individually. This optimization, similar to [13], works for a large class of circuits. We moreover note that, in order to use this optimization, one also has to precompute *permutations between the representations* which must then be used during the online phase. This leads to a moderate slowdown during the evaluation of the circuit.

Tweaks for the Audit Phase. The audit process, as explained in Figure 9, basically consists of (1) performing linear operations on commitments and (2) checking whether commitments open to the correct values. Whereas we see no approach to speed up the first part, we will address the second one using a well-known technique from [5].

Let $c_1, ..., c_n \in G$ be the commitments and let $x_1, ..., x_n, r_1, ..., r_n$ be the values that should open them. We want to establish that $\forall i \in \{1, ..., n\} : c_i = g^{x_i} h^{r_i}$.

The is to compute a random linear combination of all commitments, and thus check all of them at once. We choose the coefficients of the random combination from the interval $0, ..., 2^k - 1$.

Now computing such a random linear combination will yield a false positive with probability $\approx 2^{-k}$, but we can adjust the error probability here and make it independent of the field description size $\log p$ (remember that also G has to be a DLP-hard group of order p). This also yields less computational overhead, as we only have to raise group elements to at most 2^kth powers. The algorithm looks as follows:

(1) Choose $a \leftarrow \{0, ..., 2^k - 1\}^n$ uniformly at random.
(2) Check that $\prod_i c_i^{a[i]} = \prod_i (g^{x_i} h^{r_i})^{a[i]} = g^{\sum_i a[i] x_i} h^{\sum_i a[i] r_i}$.

Bellare et al. show in [5] that this algorithm indeed fails to correctly verify with probability 2^{-k}. Moreover, one can use a recursive approach to gain further speedup for a large number of commitments. We refer to [5] for more details.

6   Summary and Open Problems

In this paper, we described how to formally lift MPC into a setting where all servers are malicious. We outlined how this concept can then be securely realized on top of the SPDZ protocol. Though our approach can also be implemented for other MPC protocols, we focused on SPDZ since, even as an publicly auditable scheme, its online phase is very efficient. We note that our protocol would also work for Boolean circuits, but this would introduce a significant slowdown (since the MACs must then be defined as elements of an extension field over $\mathbb{F}_2$, which leads to a significant overhead). It is an interesting future direction to design an efficient auditable protocol optimized for Boolean circuits or circuits over fields with small characteristic.

With respect to online voting, there exist stronger degrees of auditability than we presented. An example is the notion of *universal verifiability* (see e.g. [27,22]) where the auditor must not know the output of the computation. We also do not provide *accountability* (see e.g. Küsters et al. [30]), and leave it as an open question whether similar, efficient protocols can be achieved in this setting.

We leave a working implementation of our scheme as a future work. As our protocol is very similar in structure to the original SPDZ, it should be possible to implement it easily on top of the existing codebase of [12].

Acknowledgements. We want to thank the anonymous reviewers for their helpful comments.

References

1. Helios, B.A.: Web-based open-audit voting. In: USENIX Security Symposium, vol. 17, pp. 335–348 (2008)
2. Ajtai, M., Komlós, J., Szemerédi, E.: An o(n log n) sorting network. In: STOC, pp. 1–9 (1983)
3. Asharov, G., Orlandi, C.: Calling out cheaters: Covert security with public verifiability. In: Wang, X., Sako, K. (eds.) ASIACRYPT 2012. LNCS, vol. 7658, pp. 681–698. Springer, Heidelberg (2012)
4. Beaver, D.: Efficient multiparty protocols using circuit randomization. In: Feigenbaum, J. (ed.) CRYPTO 1991. LNCS, vol. 576, pp. 420–432. Springer, Heidelberg (1992)
5. Bellare, M., Garay, J.A., Rabin, T.: Fast batch verification for modular exponentiation and digital signatures. In: Nyberg, K. (ed.) EUROCRYPT 1998. LNCS, vol. 1403, pp. 236–250. Springer, Heidelberg (1998)
6. Bendlin, R., Damgård, I., Orlandi, C., Zakarias, S.: Semi-homomorphic encryption and multiparty computation. In: Paterson, K.G. (ed.) EUROCRYPT 2011. LNCS, vol. 6632, pp. 169–188. Springer, Heidelberg (2011)
7. Brickell, E.F., Gordon, D.M., McCurley, K.S., Wilson, D.B.: Fast exponentiation with precomputation. In: Rueppel, R.A. (ed.) EUROCRYPT 1992. LNCS, vol. 658, pp. 200–207. Springer, Heidelberg (1993)
8. Chaum, D., Ryan, P.Y.A., Schneider, S.: A practical voter-verifiable election scheme. In: De Capitani di Vimercati, S., Syverson, P., Gollmann, D. (eds.) ESORICS 2005. LNCS, vol. 3679, pp. 118–139. Springer, Heidelberg (2005)
9. Chaum, D.L.: Untraceable electronic mail, return addresses, and digital pseudonyms. Communications of the ACM 24(2), 84–90 (1981)
10. Cohen, J.D., Fischer, M.J.: A robust and verifiable cryptographically secure election scheme. In: FOCS, vol. 85, pp. 372–382 (1985)
11. De Cristofaro, E., Tsudik, G.: Experimenting with fast private set intersection. In: Katzenbeisser, S., Weippl, E., Camp, L.J., Volkamer, M., Reiter, M., Zhang, X. (eds.) Trust 2012. LNCS, vol. 7344, pp. 55–73. Springer, Heidelberg (2012)
12. Damgård, I., Keller, M., Larraia, E., Pastro, V., Scholl, P., Smart, N.P.: Practical covertly secure mpc for dishonest majority - or: Breaking the spdz limits. In: Crampton, J., Jajodia, S., Mayes, K. (eds.) ESORICS 2013. LNCS, vol. 8134, pp. 1–18. Springer, Heidelberg (2013)

13. Damgård, I., Zakarias, S.: Constant-overhead secure computation of boolean circuits using preprocessing. In: Sahai, A. (ed.) TCC 2013. LNCS, vol. 7785, pp. 621–641. Springer, Heidelberg (2013)
14. Damgård, I., Pastro, V., Smart, N., Zakarias, S.: Multiparty computation from somewhat homomorphic encryption. In: Safavi-Naini, R., Canetti, R. (eds.) CRYPTO 2012. LNCS, vol. 7417, pp. 643–662. Springer, Heidelberg (2012)
15. Jacobus, S., de Hoogh, A.: Design of Large Scale Applications of Secure Multiparty Computation: Secure Linear Programming. PhD thesis, Technische Universiteit Eindhoven (2012)
16. Fiore, D., Gennaro, R.: Publicly verifiable delegation of large polynomials and matrix computations, with applications. In: ACM Conference on Computer and Communications Security, pp. 501–512 (2012)
17. Fujisaki, E., Okamoto, T.: A practical and provably secure scheme for publicly verifiable secret sharing and its applications. In: Nyberg, K. (ed.) EUROCRYPT 1998. LNCS, vol. 1403, pp. 32–46. Springer, Heidelberg (1998)
18. Gennaro, R., Gentry, C., Parno, B., Raykova, M.: Quadratic span programs and succinct nizks without pcps. In: Johansson, T., Nguyen, P.Q. (eds.) EUROCRYPT 2013. LNCS, vol. 7881, pp. 626–645. Springer, Heidelberg (2013)
19. Huang, Y., Evans, D., Katz, J.: Private set intersection: Are garbled circuits better than custom protocols? In: NDSS (2012)
20. Küpçü, A., Lysyanskaya, A.: Optimistic fair exchange with multiple arbiters. In: Gritzalis, D., Preneel, B., Theoharidou, M. (eds.) ESORICS 2010. LNCS, vol. 6345, pp. 488–507. Springer, Heidelberg (2010)
21. Lim, C.H., Lee, P.J.: More flexible exponentiation with precomputation. In: Desmedt, Y.G. (ed.) Advances in Cryptology - CRYPTO 1994. LNCS, vol. 839, pp. 95–107. Springer, Heidelberg (1994)
22. Moran, T., Naor, M.: Receipt-free universally-verifiable voting with everlasting privacy. In: Dwork, C. (ed.) CRYPTO 2006. LNCS, vol. 4117, pp. 373–392. Springer, Heidelberg (2006)
23. Naor, M., Pinkas, B., Sumner, R.: Privacy preserving auctions and mechanism design. In: Proceedings of the 1st ACM Conference on Electronic Commerce, pp. 129–139. ACM (1999)
24. Nielsen, J.B., Nordholt, P.S., Orlandi, C., Burra, S.S.: A new approach to practical active-secure two-party computation. In: Safavi-Naini, R., Canetti, R. (eds.) CRYPTO 2012. LNCS, vol. 7417, pp. 681–700. Springer, Heidelberg (2012)
25. Pedersen, T.P.: Non-interactive and information-theoretic secure verifiable secret sharing. In: Feigenbaum, J. (ed.) Advances in Cryptology - CRYPTO 1991. LNCS, vol. 576, pp. 129–140. Springer, Heidelberg (1992)
26. Sako, K.: An auction protocol which hides bids of losers. In: Imai, H., Zheng, Y. (eds.) PKC 2000. LNCS, vol. 1751, pp. 422–432. Springer, Heidelberg (2000)
27. Sako, K., Kilian, J.: Receipt-free mix-type voting scheme. In: Guillou, L.C., Quisquater, J.-J. (eds.) Advances in Cryptology - EUROCRYPT 1995. LNCS, vol. 921, pp. 393–403. Springer, Heidelberg (1995)
28. Schoenmakers, B.: A simple publicly verifiable secret sharing scheme and its application to electronic voting. In: Wiener, M. (ed.) CRYPTO 1999. LNCS, vol. 1666, pp. 148–164. Springer, Heidelberg (1999)
29. Stadler, M.A.: Publicly verifiable secret sharing. In: Maurer, U.M. (ed.) Advances in Cryptology - EUROCRYPT 1996. LNCS, vol. 1070, pp. 190–199. Springer, Heidelberg (1996)
30. Truderung, T., Vogt, A., Küsters, R.: Accountability: definition and relationship to verifiability. In: Proceedings of the 17th ACM Conference on Computer and Communications Security, pp. 526–535. ACM (2010)

Reducing the Overhead of MPC over a Large Population

Ashish Choudhury[1], Arpita Patra[2], and Nigel P. Smart[3]

[1] IIIT Bangalore, India
[2] Dept. of Computer Science & Automation, IISc Bangalore, India
[3] Dept. of Computer Science, Uni. Bristol, United Kingdom
partho31@gmail.com, arpita@csa.iisc.ernet.in,
nigel@cs.bris.ac.uk

Abstract. We present a secure honest majority MPC protocol, against a static adversary, which aims to reduce the communication cost in the situation where there are a large number of parties and the number of adversarially controlled parties is relatively small. Our goal is to reduce the usage of point-to-point channels among the parties, thus enabling them to run multiple different protocol executions. Our protocol has highly efficient theoretical communication cost when compared with other protocols in the literature; specifically the circuit-dependent communication cost, for circuits of suitably large depth, is $\mathcal{O}(|\mathsf{ckt}|\kappa^7)$, for security parameter κ and circuit size $|\mathsf{ckt}|$. Our protocol finds application in cloud computing scenario, where the fraction of corrupted parties is relatively small. By minimizing the usage of point-to-point channels, our protocol can enable a cloud service provider to run multiple MPC protocols.

1 Introduction

Threshold secure multi-party computation (MPC) is a fundamental problem in secure distributed computing. It allows a set of n mutually distrusting parties with private inputs to "securely" compute any publicly known function of their private inputs, even in the presence of a centralized adversary who can control any t out of the n parties and force them to behave in any arbitrary manner. Now consider a situation, where n is very large, say $n \geq 1000$ and the proportion of corrupted parties (namely the ratio t/n) is relatively small, say 5 percent. In such a scenario, involving all the n parties to perform an MPC calculation is wasteful, as typical (secret-sharing based) MPC protocols require all parties to simultaneously transmit data to all other parties. However, restricting to a small subset of parties may lead to security problems. In this paper we consider the above scenario and show how one can obtain a communication efficient, robust MPC protocol which is actively secure against a computationally bounded static adversary. In particular we present a protocol in which the main computation is performed by a "smallish" subset of the parties, with the whole set of parties used occasionally so as to "checkpoint" the computation. By not utilizing the entire set of parties all the time enables them to run many MPC calculations at once. The main result we obtain in the paper is as follows:

Main Result (Informal): Let $\epsilon = \frac{t}{n}$ with $0 \leq \epsilon < 1/2$ and let the t corrupted parties be under the control of a computationally bounded static adversary.

M. Abdalla and R. De Prisco (Eds.): SCN 2014, LNCS 8642, pp. 197–217, 2014.

Then for a security parameter κ (for example $\kappa = 80$ or $\kappa = 128$), there exists an MPC protocol with the following circuit-dependent communication complexity[1] to evaluate an arithmetic circuit ckt: **(a).** $\mathcal{O}(|\mathsf{ckt}| \cdot \kappa^7)$ for ckt with depth $\omega(t)$. **(b).** $\mathcal{O}(|\mathsf{ckt}| \cdot \kappa^4)$ for ckt with $d = \omega(t)$ and $w = \omega(\kappa^3)$ (i.e. $|\mathsf{ckt}| = \omega(\kappa^3 t)$).

Protocol Overview: We make use of two secret-sharing schemes. A secret-sharing scheme $[\cdot]$ which is an actively-secure variant of the Shamir secret-sharing scheme [22] with threshold t. This first secret-sharing scheme is used to share values amongst *all* of the n parties. The second secret-sharing scheme $\langle\cdot\rangle$ is an actively-secure variant of an additive secret-sharing scheme, amongst a well-defined subset $\mathcal{C}$ of the parties.

Assuming the inputs to the protocol are $[\cdot]$ shared amongst the parties at the start of the protocol, we proceed as follows. We first divide ckt into L levels, where each level consists of a sub-circuit. The computation now proceeds in L phases; we describe phase i. At the start of phase i we have that *all* n parties hold $[\cdot]$ sharings of the inputs to level i. The n parties then select (at random) a committee $\mathcal{C}$ of size c. If c is such that $\epsilon^{\mathsf{c}} < 2^{-\kappa}$ then statistically the committee $\mathcal{C}$ will contain at least one honest party, as the inequality implies that the probability that the committee contains no honest party is negligibly small. The n parties then engage in a "conversion" protocol so that the input values to level i are now $\langle\cdot\rangle$ shared amongst the committee. The committee $\mathcal{C}$ then engages in an actively-secure dishonest majority[2] MPC protocol to evaluate the sub-circuit at level i. If no abort occurs during the evaluation of the ith sub-circuit then the parties engage in another "conversion" protocol so that the output values of the sub-circuit are converted from a $\langle\cdot\rangle$ sharing amongst members in $\mathcal{C}$ to a $[\cdot]$ sharing amongst all n parties. This step amounts to check-pointing data. This ensures that the inputs to all the subsequent sub-circuits are saved in the form of $[\cdot]$ sharing which guarantees recoverability as long as $0 \leq \epsilon < \frac{1}{2}$. So the check-pointing prevents from re-evaluating the entire circuit from scratch after every abort of the dishonest-majority MPC protocol.

If however an abort occurs while evaluating the ith sub-circuit then we determine a pair of parties from the committee $\mathcal{C}$, one of whom is guaranteed to be corrupted and eliminate the pair from the set of active parties, and re-evaluate the sub-circuit again. In fact, cheating can also occur in the $\langle\cdot\rangle \leftrightarrow [\cdot]$ conversions and we need to deal with these as well. Thus if errors are detected we need to repeat the evaluation of the sub-circuit at level i. Since there are at most t bad parties, the total amount of backtracking (i.e. evaluating a sub-circuit already computed) that needs to be done is bounded by t. For large n and small t this provides an asymptotically efficient protocol.

The main technical difficulty is in providing actively-secure conversions between the two secret-sharing schemes, and providing a suitable party-elimination strategy for the dishonest majority MPC protocol. The party-elimination strategy we employ follows

---

[1] The communication complexity of an MPC protocol has two parts: a circuit-dependent part, dependent on the circuit size and a circuit-independent part. The focus is on the circuit-dependent communication, based on the assumption that the circuit is large enough so that the terms independent of the circuit-size can be ignored; see for example [10,4,11,5].

[2] In the dishonest-majority setting, the adversary may corrupt all but one parties. An MPC protocol in this setting aborts if a corrupted party misbehaves.

from standard techniques, as long as we can identify the pair of parties. This requirement, of a dishonest-majority MPC protocol which enables identification of cheaters, without sacrificing privacy, leads us to the utilization of the protocol in [11]. This results in us needing to use double-trapdoor homomorphic commitments as a basic building block. To ensure greater asymptotic efficiency we apply two techniques: **(a).** the checkpointing is done among a set of parties that assures honest majority with overwhelming probability **(b).** the packing technique from [16] to our Shamir based secret sharing.

To obtain an efficient protocol one needs to select L; if L is too small then the sub-circuits are large and so the cost of returning to a prior checkpoint will also be large. If however L is too large then we will need to checkpoint a lot, and hence involve all n parties in the computation at a lot of stages (and thus requiring all n parties to be communicating/computing). The optimal value of L for our protocol turns out to be t.

Related Work: The circuit-dependent communication complexity of the traditional MPC protocols in the honest-majority setting is $\mathcal{O}(|\mathsf{ckt}| \cdot \mathsf{Poly}(n, \kappa))$; this informally stems from the fact in these protocols we require all the n parties to communicate with each other for evaluating each gate of the circuit. Assuming $0 \leq \epsilon < 1/2$, [10] presents a computationally secure MPC protocol with communication complexity $\mathcal{O}(|\mathsf{ckt}| \cdot \mathsf{Poly}(\kappa, \log n, \log |\mathsf{ckt}|))$. The efficiency comes from the ability to pack and share several values simultaneously which in turn allow parallel evaluation of "several" gates simultaneously in a single round of communication. However, the protocol still requires communications between all the parties during each round of communication. Our protocol reduces the need for the parties to be communicating with all others at all stages in the protocol; moreover, asymptotically for large n it provides a better communication complexity over [10] (as there is no dependence on n), for circuits of suitably large depth as stated earlier. However, the protocol of [10] is secure against a more powerful adaptive adversary.

In the literature, another line of investigation has been carried out in [6,9,12,13] to beat the $\mathcal{O}(|\mathsf{ckt}| \cdot \mathsf{Poly}(n, \kappa))$ communication complexity bound of traditional MPC protocols, against a static adversary. The main idea behind all these works is similar to ours, which is to involve "small committees" of parties for evaluating each gate of the circuit, rather than involving all the n parties. The communication complexity of these protocols[3] is of the order $\mathcal{O}(|\mathsf{ckt}| \cdot \mathsf{Poly}(\log n, \kappa))$. Technically our protocol is different from these protocols in the following ways: **(a).** The committees in [6,9,12,13] are of size $\mathsf{Poly}(\log n)$, which ensures that with high probability the selected committees have honest majority. As a result, these protocols run any existing honest-majority MPC protocol among these small committees of $\mathsf{Poly}(\log n)$ size, which prevents the need to check-point the computation (as there will be no aborts). On the other hand, we only require committees with at least one honest party and our committee size is independent of n, thus providing better communication complexity. Indeed, asymptotically for large n, our protocol provides a better communication complexity over [6,9,12,13] (as there is no dependence on n), for circuits of suitably large depth. **(b).** Our protocol provides a

---

[3] Note, the protocol of [6] involves FHE to further achieve a communication complexity of $\mathcal{O}(\mathsf{Poly}(\log n))$.

better fault-tolerance. Specifically, [12,9,6] requires $\epsilon < 1/3$ and [13] requires $\epsilon < 1/8$; on the other hand we require $\epsilon < 1/2$.

We stress that the committee selection protocol in [6,9,12,13] is unconditionally secure and in the full-information model, where the corrupted parties can see all the messages communicated between the honest parties. On the other hand our implementation of the committee selection protocol is computationally secure. The committee election protocol in [6,9,12,13] is inherited from [14]. The committee selection protocol in these protocols are rather involved and not based on simply randomly selecting a subset of parties, possibly due to the challenges posed in the full information model with unconditional security; this causes their committee size to be logarithmic in n. However, if one is willing to relax at least one of the above two features (i.e. full information model and unconditional security), then it may be possible to select committees with honest majority in a simple way by randomly selecting committees, where the committee size may be independent of n. However investigating the same is out of the scope of this paper.

Finally we note that the idea of using small committees has been used earlier in the literature for various distributed computing tasks, such as the leader election [17,20], Byzantine agreement [18,19] and distributed key-generation [8].

On the Choice of ϵ: We select committees of size c satisfying $\epsilon^c < 2^{-\kappa}$. This implies that the selected committee has at least one honest participant with overwhelming probability. We note that it is possible to randomly select committees of "larger" size so that with overwhelming probability the selected committee will have honest majority. We label the protocol which samples a committee with honest majority and then runs an computationally secure honest majority MPC protocol (where we need not have to worry about aborts) as the "naive protocol". The naive protocol will have communication complexity $\mathcal{O}(|\mathsf{ckt}| \cdot \mathsf{Poly}(\kappa))$.

For "very small" values of ϵ, the committee size for the naive protocol is comparable to the committee size in our protocol. We demonstrate this with an example, with $n = 1000$ and security level $\kappa = 80$: The committee size we require to ensure both a single honest party in the committee and a committee with honest majority, with overwhelming probability of $(1 - 2^{-80})$ for various choices of ϵ, is given in the following table:

ϵ	c to obtain at least one honest party	c to obtain honest majority
$1/3$	48	448
$1/4$	39	250
$1/10$	23	84
$1/100$	11	20

From the table it is clear that when ϵ is closer to $1/2$, the difference in the committee size to obtain at least one honest party and to obtain honest majority is large. As a result, selecting committees with honest majority can be prohibitively expensive, thus our selection of small committees with dishonest majority provides significant improvements.

To see intuitively why our protocol selects smaller committees, consider the case when the security parameter κ tends to infinity: Our protocol will require a committee of size roughly $\epsilon \cdot n + 1$, whereas the naive protocol will require a committee of size roughly $2 \cdot \epsilon \cdot n + 1$. Thus the naive method will use a committee size of roughly twice that of our method. Hence, if small committees are what is required then our method improves on the naive method.

For fixed ϵ and increasing n, we can apply the binomial approximation to the hypergeometric distribution, and see that our protocol will require a committee of size $c \approx \kappa / \log_2(\frac{1}{\epsilon})$. To estimate the committee size for the naive protocol we use the cumulative distribution function for the binomial distribution, $F(b; c, \epsilon)$, which gives the probability that we select at least b corrupt parties in a committee of size c given the probability of a corrupt party being fixed at ϵ. To obtain an honest majority with probability less than $2^{-\kappa}$ we require $F(c/2; c, \epsilon) \approx 2^{-\kappa}$. By estimating $F(c/2; c, \epsilon)$ via Hoeffding's inequality we obtain

$$\exp\left(-2 \cdot \frac{(c \cdot \epsilon - c/2)^2}{c}\right) \approx 2^{-\kappa},$$

which implies

$$\kappa \approx \left(\frac{c \cdot (2 \cdot \epsilon - 1)^2}{2}\right) / \log_e 2.$$

Solving for c gives us

$$c \approx \frac{2 \cdot \kappa \cdot \log_e 2}{(2 \cdot \epsilon - 1)^2}.$$

Thus for fixed ϵ and large n the number of parties in a committee is $O(\kappa)$ for both our protocol, and the naive protocol. Thus the communication complexity of our protocol and the naive protocol is asymptotically the same. But, since the committees in our protocol are always smaller than those in the naive protocol, we will obtain an advantage when the ratio of the different committee size is large, i.e. when ϵ is larger.

The ratio between the committee size in the naive protocol and that of our protocol (assuming we are in a range when Hoeffding's inequality provides a good approximation) is roughly

$$\frac{-2 \cdot \log_e 2 \cdot \log_2 \epsilon}{(2 \cdot \epsilon - 1)^2}$$

So for large n the ratio between the committee sizes of the two protocols depends on ϵ alone (and is independent of κ). By way of example this ratio is approximately equal to 159 when $\epsilon = 0.45$, 19 when $\epsilon = 1/3$, 7 when $\epsilon = 1/10$ and 9.6 when $\epsilon = 1/100$; although the approximation via Hoeffding's inequality only really applies for ϵ close to $1/2$.

This implies that for values of ϵ close to $1/2$ our protocol will be an improvement on the naive protocol. However, the naive method does not have the extra cost of checkpointing which our method does; thus at some point the naive protocol will be more efficient. Thus our protocol is perhaps more interesting, when ϵ is not too small, say in the range of $[1/100, 1/2]$.

Possible Application of Our Protocol for Cloud-Computing. Consider the situation of an organization performing a multi-party computation on a cloud infrastructure, which involves a large number of machines, with the number of corrupted parties possibly high, but not exceeding one half of the parties, (which is exactly the situation considered in our MPC protocol). Using our MPC protocol, the whole computation can be then carried out by a small subset of machines, with the whole cloud infrastructure being used only for check-pointing the computation. By not utilizing the whole cloud infrastructure all the time, we enable the cloud provider to serve multiple MPC requests.

Our protocol is not adaptively secure. In fact, vulnerability to adaptive adversary is inherent to most of the committee-based protocols for several distributed computing tasks such as Leader Election [17,20], Byzantine Agreement [19,18], Distributed Key-generation [8] and MPC in [12,9]. Furthermore, We feel that adaptive security is not required in the cloud scenario. Any external attacker to the cloud data centre will have a problem determining which computers are being used in the committee, and an even greater problem in compromising them adaptively. The main threat model in such a situation is via co-tenants (other users processes) to be resident on the same physical machine. Since the precise machine upon which a cloud tenant sits is (essentially) randomly assigned, it is hard for a co-tenant adversary to mount a cross-Virtual Machine attack on a specific machine unless they are randomly assigned this machine by the cloud. Note, that co-tenants have more adversarial power than a completely external attacker. A more correct security model would be to have a form of adaptive security in which attackers pro-actively move from one machine to another, but in a random fashion. We leave analysing this complex situation to a future work.

2   Model, Notation and Preliminaries

We denote by $\mathcal{P} = \{P_1, \ldots, P_n\}$ the set of n parties who are connected by pair-wise private and authentic channels. We assume that there exists a PPT static adversary $\mathcal{A}$, who can maliciously corrupt any t parties from $\mathcal{P}$ at the beginning of the execution of a protocol, where $t = n \cdot \epsilon$ and $0 \le \epsilon < \frac{1}{2}$. There exists a publicly known randomized function $f : \mathbb{F}_p^n \to \mathbb{F}_p$, expressed as a publicly known arithmetic circuit ckt over the field $\mathbb{F}_p$ of prime order p (including random gates to enable the evaluation of randomized functions), with party P_i having a private input $x^{(i)} \in \mathbb{F}_p$ for the computation. We let d and w to denote the depth and (average) width of ckt respectively. The finite field $\mathbb{F}_p$ is assumed to be such that p is a prime, with $p > \max\{n, 2^\kappa\}$, where κ is the *computational security parameter*. Apart from κ, we also have an additional *statistical security parameter s* and the security offered by s (which is generally much smaller than κ) does not depend on the computational power of the adversary.

The security of our protocol(s) will be proved in the universal composability (UC) model. The UC framework allows for defining the security properties of cryptographic tasks so that security is maintained under general composition with an unbounded number of instances of arbitrary protocols running concurrently. In the framework, the security requirements of a given task are captured by specifying an ideal functionality run by a "trusted party" that obtains the inputs of the parties and provides them with the desired outputs. Informally, a protocol securely carries out a given task if running the protocol in the presence of a real-world adversary amounts to "emulating" the desired functionality. For more details, see the full version of this paper.

We do not assume a physical broadcast channel. Although our protocol uses an ideal broadcast functionality $\mathcal{F}_{\text{BC}}$ (Fig. 3), that allows a sender Sen $\in \mathcal{P}$ to reliably broadcast a message to a group of parties $\mathcal{X} \subseteq \mathcal{P}$, the functionality can be instantiated using point-to-point channels; see the full version of this paper for details.

The communication complexity of our protocols has two parts: the communication done over the point-to-point channels and the broadcast communication. The later is captured by $\mathcal{BC}(\ell, |\mathcal{X}|)$ to denote that in total, $\mathcal{O}(\ell)$ bits is broadcasted in the associated protocol to a set of parties of size $|\mathcal{X}|$.

Two different types of secret-sharing are employed in our protocols. The secret-sharings are inherently defined to include "verification information" of the individual shares in the form of publicly known commitments. We use a variant of the Pedersen homomorphic commitment scheme [21]. In our protocol, we require UC-secure commitments to ensure that a committer must know its committed value and just cannot manipulate a commitment produced by other committers to violate what we call "input independence". It has been shown in [7] that a UC secure commitment scheme is impossible to achieve without setup assumptions. The standard method to implement UC-secure commitments is in the Common Reference String (CRS) model where it is assumed that the parties are provided with a CRS that is set up by a "trusted third party" (TTP). We follow [11], where the authors show how to build a multiparty UC-secure homomorphic commitment scheme (where multiple parties can act as committer) based on any double-trapdoor homomorphic commitment scheme.

Definition 1 (Double-trapdoor Homomorphic Commitment for $\mathbb{F}_p$ [11]). *It is a collection of five PPT algorithms* (Gen, Comm, Open, Equivocate, TDExtract, $\odot$):

- Gen$(1^\kappa) \rightarrow (\mathsf{ck}, \tau_0, \tau_1)$: *the generation algorithm outputs a commitment key* ck, *along with trapdoors τ_0 and τ_1.*
- Comm$_{\mathsf{ck}}(x; r_0, r_1) \rightarrow \mathbf{C}_{x, r_0, r_1}$: *the commitment algorithm takes a message $x \in \mathbb{F}_p$ and randomness r_0, r_1 from the commitment randomness space $\mathcal{R}$ [4] and outputs a commitment $\mathbf{C}_{x; r_0, r_1}$ of x under the randomness r_0, r_1.*
- Open$_{\mathsf{ck}}(\mathbf{C}, (x; r_0, r_1)) \rightarrow \{0, 1\}$: *the opening algorithm takes a commitment $\mathbf{C}$, along with a message/randomness triplet (x, r_0, r_1) and outputs 1 if $\mathbf{C} = \mathsf{Comm}_{\mathsf{ck}}(x; r_0, r_1)$, else 0.*
- Equivocate$(\mathbf{C}_{x, r_0, r_1}, x, r_0, r_1, \overline{x}, \tau_i) \rightarrow (\overline{r}_0, \overline{r}_1) \in \mathcal{R}$: *using one of the trapdoors τ_i with $i \in \{0, 1\}$, the equivocation algorithm can open a commitment $\mathbf{C}_{x, r_0, r_1}$ with any message $\overline{x} \neq x$ with randomness $\overline{r}_0$ and $\overline{r}_1$ where $r_{1-i} = \overline{r}_{1-i}$.*
- TDExtract$(\mathbf{C}, x, r_0, r_1, \overline{x}, \overline{r}_0, \overline{r}_1, \tau_i) \rightarrow \tau_{1-i}$: *using one of the trapdoors τ_i with $i \in \{0, 1\}$ and two different sets of message/randomness triplet for the same commitment, namely x, r_0, r_1 and $\overline{x}, \overline{r}_0, \overline{r}_1$, the trapdoor extraction algorithm can find the other trapdoor τ_{1-i} if $r_{1-i} \neq \overline{r}_{1-i}$.*
  The commitments are homomorphic meaning that Comm$(x; r_0, r_1) \odot$ Comm$(y; s_0, s_1) =$ Comm$(x+y; r_0+s_0, r_1+s_1)$ *and* Comm$(x; r_0, r_1)^c =$ Comm$(c \cdot x; c \cdot r_0, c \cdot r_1)$ *for any publicly known constant c.*

We require the following properties to be satisfied:

- **Trapdoor Security:** *There exists no PPT algorithm A such that $A(1^\kappa, \mathsf{ck}, \tau_i) \rightarrow \tau_{1-i}$, for $i \in \{0, 1\}$.*

---

[4] For the ease of presentation, we assume $\mathcal{R}$ to be an additive group.

- **Computational Binding:** *There exists no PPT algorithm A with* $A(1^\kappa, \mathsf{ck}) \to (x,$ $r_0, r_1, \overline{x}, \overline{r}_0, \overline{r}_1)$ *and* $(x, r_0, r_1) \neq (\overline{x}, \overline{r}_0, \overline{r}_1)$, *but* $\mathsf{Comm}_{\mathsf{ck}}(x; r_0, r_1) = \mathsf{Comm}_{\mathsf{ck}}($ $\overline{x}; \overline{r}_0, \overline{r}_1).$
- **Statistical Hiding:** $\forall x, \overline{x} \in \mathbb{F}_p$ *and* $r_0, r_1 \in \mathcal{R}$, *let* $(\overline{r}_0, \overline{r}_1) = \mathsf{Equivocate}(\mathbf{C}_{x,r_0,r_1},$ $x, r_0, r_1, \overline{x}, \tau_i)$, *with* $i \in \{0, 1\}$. *Then* $\mathsf{Comm}_{\mathsf{ck}}(x; r_0, r_1) = \mathsf{Comm}_{\mathsf{ck}}(\overline{x}; \overline{r}_0, \overline{r}_1) =$ $\mathbf{C}_{x,r_0,r_1}$; *moreover the distribution of* (r_0, r_1) *and* $(\overline{r}_0, \overline{r}_1)$ *are statistically close.*

We will use the following instantiation of a double-trapdoor homomorphic commitment scheme which is a variant of the standard Pedersen commitment scheme over a group $\mathbb{G}$ in which discrete logarithms are hard [11]. The message space is $\mathbb{F}_p$ and the randomness space is $\mathcal{R} = \mathbb{F}_p^2$.

- $\mathsf{Gen}(1^\kappa) \to ((\mathbb{G}, p, g, h_0, h_1), \tau_0, \tau_1)$, where $\mathsf{ck} = (\mathbb{G}, p, g, h_0, h_1)$ such that $g, h_0,$ h_1 are generators of the group $\mathbb{G}$ of prime order p and $g^{\tau_i} = h_i$ for $i \in \{0, 1\}$.
- $\mathsf{Comm}_{\mathsf{ck}}(x; r_0, r_1) \to g^x h_0^{r_0} h_1^{r_1} = \mathbf{C}_{x,r_0,r_1}$, with $x, r_0, r_1 \in \mathbb{F}_p$.
- $\mathsf{Open}_{\mathsf{ck}}(\mathbf{C}, (x, r_0, r_1)) \to 1$, if $\mathbf{C} = g^x h_0^{r_0} h_1^{r_1}$, else $\mathsf{Open}_{\mathsf{ck}}(\mathbf{C}, (x, r_0, r_1)) \to 0$.
- $\mathsf{Equivocate}(\mathbf{C}_{x,r_0,r_1}, x, r_0, r_1, \overline{x}, \tau_i) \to (\overline{r}_0, \overline{r}_1)$ where $\overline{r}_{1-i} = r_{1-i}$ and $\overline{r}_i = \tau_i^{-1}(x - \overline{x}) + r_i$.
- $\mathsf{TDExtract}(\mathbf{C}, x, r_0, r_1, \overline{x}, \overline{r}_0, \overline{r}_1, \tau_i) \to \tau_{1-i}$, where if $\overline{r}_{1-i} \neq r_{1-i}$, then

$$\tau_{1-i} = \frac{\overline{x} - x + \tau_i(\overline{r}_i - r_i)}{r_{1-i} - \overline{r}_{1-i}}.$$

- The homomorphic operation $\odot$ is just the group operation i.e.

$$\begin{aligned}
\mathsf{Comm}(x; r_0, r_1) \odot \mathsf{Comm}(\overline{x}; \overline{r}_0, \overline{r}_1) &= g^x h_0^{r_0} h_1^{r_1} \cdot g^{\overline{x}} h_0^{\overline{r}_0} h_1^{\overline{r}_1} \\
&= g^{x+\overline{x}} \cdot h_0^{r_0+\overline{r}_0} \cdot h_1^{r_1+\overline{r}_1} \\
&= \mathsf{Comm}(x + \overline{x}; r_0 + \overline{r}_0, r_1 + \overline{r}_1).
\end{aligned}$$

We can now define the various types of secret-shared data used in our protocols. Let $\alpha_1, \ldots, \alpha_n \in \mathbb{F}_p$ be n publicly known non-zero, distinct values, where α_i is associated with P_i as the *evaluation point*. The $[\cdot]$ sharing is the standard Shamir-sharing [22], where the secret value will be shared among the set of parties $\mathcal{P}$ with threshold t. Additionally, a commitment of each individual share will be available publicly, with the corresponding share-holder possessing the randomness of the commitment.

Definition 2 (The $[\cdot]$ Sharing). *Let* $s \in \mathbb{F}_p$; *then* s *is said to be* $[\cdot]$-*shared among* $\mathcal{P}$ *if there exist polynomials, say* $f(\cdot), g(\cdot)$ *and* $h(\cdot)$, *of degree at most* t, *with* $f(0) = s$ *and every (honest) party* $P_i \in \mathcal{P}$ *holds a share* $f_i = f(\alpha_i)$ *of* s, *along with opening information* $g_i = g(\alpha_i)$ *and* $h_i = h(\alpha_i)$ *for the commitment* $\mathbf{C}_{f_i,g_i,h_i} = \mathsf{Comm}_{\mathsf{ck}}(f_i; g_i, h_i)$. *The information available to party* $P_i \in \mathcal{P}$ *as part of the* $[\cdot]$-*sharing of* s *is denoted by* $[s]_i = (f_i, g_i, h_i, \{\mathbf{C}_{f_j,g_j,h_j}\}_{P_j \in \mathcal{P}})$. *All parties will also have the access to* ck. *Moreover, the collection of* $[s]_i$'s, *corresponding to* $P_i \in \mathcal{P}$ *is denoted by* $[s]$.

The second type of secret-sharing (which is a variation of additive sharing), is used to perform computation via a dishonest majority MPC protocol amongst our committees.

Definition 3 (The $\langle \cdot \rangle$ Sharing). *A value $s \in \mathbb{F}_p$ is said to be $\langle \cdot \rangle$-shared among a set of parties $\mathcal{X} \subseteq \mathcal{P}$, if every (honest) party $P_i \in \mathcal{X}$ holds a share s_i of s along with the opening information u_i, v_i for the commitment $\mathbf{C}_{s_i, u_i, u_i} = \mathsf{Comm}_{\mathsf{ck}}(s_i; u_i, v_i)$, such that $\sum_{P_i \in \mathcal{X}} s_i = s$. The information available to party $P_i \in \mathcal{X}$ as part of the $\langle \cdot \rangle$-sharing of s is denoted by $\langle s \rangle_i = (s_i, u_i, v_i, \{\mathbf{C}_{s_j, u_j, v_j}\}_{P_j \in \mathcal{X}})$. All parties will also have access to ck. The collection of $\langle s \rangle_i$'s corresponding to $P_i \in \mathcal{X}$ is denoted by $\langle s \rangle_{\mathcal{X}}$.*

It is easy to see that both types of secret-sharing are linear. For example, for the $\langle \cdot \rangle$ sharing, given $\langle s^{(1)} \rangle_{\mathcal{X}}, \ldots, \langle s^{(\ell)} \rangle_{\mathcal{X}}$ and publicly known constants $c_1, \ldots, c_\ell$, the parties in $\mathcal{X}$ can locally compute their information corresponding to $\langle c_1 \cdot s^{(1)} + \ldots + c_\ell \cdot s^{(\ell)} \rangle_{\mathcal{X}}$. This follows from the homomorphic property of the underlying commitment scheme and the linearity of the secret-sharing scheme. This means that the parties in $\mathcal{X}$ can locally compute $\langle c_1 \cdot s^{(1)} + \ldots + c_\ell \cdot s^{(\ell)} \rangle_{\mathcal{X}}$ from $\langle s^{(1)} \rangle_{\mathcal{X}}, \ldots, \langle s^\ell \rangle_{\mathcal{X}}$, since each party P_i in $\mathcal{X}$ can locally compute $\langle c_1 \cdot s^{(1)} + \ldots + c_\ell \cdot s^{(\ell)} \rangle_i$ from $\langle s^{(1)} \rangle_i, \ldots, \langle s^\ell \rangle_i$.

3 Main Protocol

We now present an MPC protocol implementing the standard honest-majority (meaning $\epsilon < 1/2$) MPC functionality $\mathcal{F}_f$ presented in Figure 1 which computes the function f.

Functionality $\mathcal{F}_f$

$\mathcal{F}_f$ interacts with the parties in $\mathcal{P}$ and the adversary $\mathcal{S}$ and is parametrized by an n-input function $f : \mathbb{F}_p^n \to \mathbb{F}_p$.

 – Upon receiving $(\mathsf{sid}, i, x^{(i)})$ from every $P_i \in \mathcal{P}$ where $x^{(i)} \in \mathbb{F}_p$, the functionality computes $y = f(x^{(1)}, \ldots, x^{(n)})$, sends (sid, y) to all the parties and the adversary $\mathcal{S}$ and halts.

Fig. 1. The Ideal Functionality for Computing a Given Function f

We now present the underlying idea of our protocol (outlined earlier in the introduction). The protocol is set in a variant of the *player-elimination* framework from [4]. During the computation either pairs of parties, each containing at least one actively corrupted party, or singletons of corrupted parties, are identified due to some adversarial behavior of the corrupted parties. These pairs, or singletons, are then eliminated from the set of eligible parties. To understand how we deal with the active corruptions, we need to define a dynamic set $\mathcal{L} \subseteq \mathcal{P}$ of size $\mathfrak{n}$, which will define the current set of eligible parties in our protocol, and a threshold $\mathfrak{t}$ which defines the maximum number of corrupted parties in $\mathcal{L}$. Initially $\mathcal{L}$ is set to be equal to $\mathcal{P}$ (hence $\mathfrak{n} = n$) and $\mathfrak{t}$ is set to t. We then divide the circuit ckt (representing f) to be evaluated into L levels, where each level consists of a sub-circuit of depth d/L; without loss of generality, we assume d to be a multiple of L. We denote the ith sub-circuit as ckt_i. At the beginning of the protocol, all the parties in $\mathcal{P}$ verifiably $[\cdot]$-share their inputs for the circuit ckt.

For evaluating a sub-circuit ckt_l, instead of involving all the parties in $\mathcal{L}$, we rather involve a small and random committee $\mathcal{C} \subset \mathcal{L}$ of parties of size $\mathfrak{c}$, where $\mathfrak{c}$ is the minimum value satisfying the constraint that $\epsilon^c \leq 2^{-\kappa}$; recall $\epsilon = t/n$. During the course of evaluating the sub-circuit, if any inconsistency is reported, then the (honest) parties in $\mathcal{P}$ will identify either a single corrupted party or a pair of parties from $\mathcal{L}$ where the pair contains at least one corrupted party. The identified party(ies) is(are) eliminated from $\mathcal{L}$ and the value of t is decremented by one, followed by re-evaluation of ckt_l by choosing a new committee from the *updated* set $\mathcal{L}$. This is reminiscent of the player-elimination framework from [4], however the way we apply the player-elimination framework is different from the standard one. Specifically, in the player-elimination framework, the *entire* set of eligible parties $\mathcal{L}$ is involved in the computation and the player elimination is then performed over the entire $\mathcal{L}$, thus requiring huge communication. On the contrary, in our context, only a small set of parties $\mathcal{C}$ is involved in the computation, thus significantly reducing the communication complexity. It is easy to see that after a sequence of t failed sub-circuit evaluations, $\mathcal{L}$ will be left with only honest parties and so each sub-circuit will be evaluated successfully from then onwards.

Note that the way we eliminate the parties, the fraction of corrupted parties in $\mathcal{L}$ after any un-successful attempt for sub-circuit evaluation, is upper bounded by the fraction of corrupted parties in $\mathcal{L}$ prior to the evaluation of the sub-circuit. Specifically, let $\epsilon_{\mathsf{old}} = t/n$ be the fraction of corrupted parties in $\mathcal{L}$ prior to the evaluation of a sub-circuit ckt_l and let the evaluation fail, with either a single party or a pair of parties being eliminated from $\mathcal{L}$. Moreover, let ϵ_{new} be the fraction of corrupted parties in $\mathcal{L}$ after the elimination. Then for single elimination, we have $\epsilon_{\mathsf{new}} = \frac{t-1}{n-1}$ and so $\epsilon_{\mathsf{new}} \leq \epsilon_{\mathsf{old}}$ if and only if $n \geq t$, which will always hold. On the other hand, for double elimination, we have $\epsilon_{\mathsf{new}} = \frac{t-1}{n-2}$ and so $\epsilon_{\mathsf{new}} \leq \epsilon_{\mathsf{old}}$ if and only if $n \geq 2t$, which will always hold.

Since a committee $\mathcal{C}$ (for evaluating a sub-circuit) is selected randomly, except with probability at most $\epsilon^c < 2^{-\kappa}$, the selected committee contains at least one honest party and so the sub-circuit evaluation among $\mathcal{C}$ needs to be performed via a dishonest majority MPC protocol. We choose the MPC protocol of [11], since it can be modified to identify pairs of parties consisting of at least one corrupted party in the case of the failed evaluation, without violating the privacy of the honest parties. To use the protocol of [11] for sub-circuit evaluation, we need the corresponding sub-circuit inputs (available to the parties in $\mathcal{P}$ in $[\cdot]$-shared form) to be converted and available in $\langle\cdot\rangle$-shared form to the parties in $\mathcal{C}$ and so the parties in $\mathcal{P}$ do the same. After every successful evaluation of a sub-circuit, via the dishonest majority MPC protocol, the outputs of that sub-circuit (available in $\langle\cdot\rangle$-shared form to the parties in a committee) are converted and saved in the form of $[\cdot]$-sharing among all the parties in $\mathcal{P}$. As the set $\mathcal{P}$ has a honest majority, $[\cdot]$-sharing ensures robust reconstruction implying that the shared values are recoverable. Since the inputs to a sub-circuit come either from the outputs of previous sub-circuit evaluations or the original inputs, both of which are $[\cdot]$-shared, a failed attempt for a sub-circuit evaluation does not require a re-evaluation of the entire circuit from scratch but requires a re-evaluation of that sub-circuit only.

3.1 Supporting Functionalities

We now present a number of ideal functionalities defining sub-components of our main protocol; see the full version for the UC-secure instantiations of these functionalities.

Basic Functionalities: The functionality $\mathcal{F}_{CRS}$ for generating the common reference string (CRS) for our main MPC protocol is given in Figure 2. The functionality outputs the commitment key of a double-trapdoor homomorphic commitment scheme, along with the encryption key of an IND-CCA secure encryption scheme (to be used later for UC-secure generation of completely random $\langle \cdot \rangle$-shared values as in [11]). The functionality $\mathcal{F}_{BC}$ for group broadcast is given in Figure 3. This functionality broadcasts the message sent by a sender $\text{Sen} \in \mathcal{P}$ to all the parties in a sender specified set of parties $\mathcal{X} \subseteq \mathcal{P}$; in our context, the set $\mathcal{X}$ will always contain at least one honest party. The functionality $\mathcal{F}_{COMMITTEE}$ for a random committee selection is given in Figure 4. This functionality is parameterized by a value $\mathfrak{c}$, it selects a set $\mathcal{X}$ of $\mathfrak{c}$ parties at random from a specified set $\mathcal{Y}$ and outputs the selected set $\mathcal{X}$ to the parties in $\mathcal{P}$.

Functionality $\mathcal{F}_{CRS}$

$\mathcal{F}_{CRS}$ interacts with the parties in $\mathcal{P}$ and the adversary $\mathcal{S}$ and is parameterized by κ.

- Upon receiving (sid, i) from every party $P_i \in \mathcal{P}$, the functionality computes $\text{Gen}(1^\kappa) \rightarrow (\text{ck}, \tau_0, \tau_1)$ and $G(1^\kappa) \rightarrow (\text{pk}, \text{sk})$, where G is the key-generation algorithm of an IND-CCA secure encryption scheme[a] and Gen is the key-generation algorithm of a double-trapdoor homomorphic commitment scheme. The functionality then sets $\text{CRS} = (\text{ck}, \text{pk})$ and sends $(\text{sid}, i, \text{CRS})$ to every party $P_i \in \mathcal{P}$ and the adversary $\mathcal{S}$ and halts.

---

[a] For use in the protocol of [11]

Fig. 2. The Ideal Functionality for Generating CRS

Functionality $\mathcal{F}_{BC}$

$\mathcal{F}_{BC}$ interacts with the parties in $\mathcal{P}$ and the adversary $\mathcal{S}$.

- Upon receiving $(\text{sid}, \text{Sen}, x, \mathcal{X})$ from the sender $\text{Sen} \in \mathcal{P}$ such that $\mathcal{X} \subseteq \mathcal{P}$, the functionality sends $(\text{sid}, j, \text{Sen}, x)$ to every $P_j \in \mathcal{X}$ and to the adversary $\mathcal{S}$ and halts.

Fig. 3. The Ideal Functionality for Broadcast

Functionality $\mathcal{F}_{COMMITTEE}$

$\mathcal{F}_{COMMITTEE}$, parametrized by a constant $\mathfrak{c}$, interacts with the parties in $\mathcal{P}$ and the adversary $\mathcal{S}$.

- Upon receiving $(\text{sid}, i, \mathcal{Y})$ from every $P_i \in \mathcal{P}$, the functionality selects $\mathfrak{c}$ parties at random from the set $\mathcal{Y}$ that is received from the majority of the parties and denotes the selected set as $\mathcal{X}$. The functionality then sends $(\text{sid}, i, \mathcal{X})$ to every $P_i \in \mathcal{P}$ and $\mathcal{S}$ and halts.

Fig. 4. The Ideal Functionality for Selecting a Random Committee of Given Size $\mathfrak{c}$

Functionality Related to $[\cdot]$-sharings: In Figure 5 we present the functionality $\mathcal{F}_{\mathrm{GEN}[\cdot]}$ which allows a dealer $D \in \mathcal{P}$ to verifiably $[\cdot]$-share an already committed secret among the parties in $\mathcal{P}$. The functionality is invoked when it receives three polynomials, say $f(\cdot), g(\cdot)$ and $h(\cdot)$ from the dealer D and a commitment, say $\mathbf{C}$, supposedly the commitment of $f(0)$ with randomness $g(0), h(0)$ (namely $\mathbf{C}_{f(0),g(0),h(0)}$), from the (majority of the) parties in $\mathcal{P}$. The functionality then hands $f_i = f(\alpha_i), g_i = g(\alpha_i), h_i = h(\alpha_i)$ and commitments $\{\mathbf{C}_{f_j,g_j,h_j}\}_{P_j \in \mathcal{P}}$ to $P_i \in \mathcal{P}$ after 'verifying' that **(a):** All the three polynomials are of degree at most t and **(b):** $\mathbf{C} = \mathsf{Comm}_{\mathsf{ck}}(f(0); g(0), h(0))$ i.e. the value (and the corresponding randomness) committed in $\mathbf{C}$ are embedded in the constant term of $f(\cdot), g(\cdot)$ and $h(\cdot)$ respectively. If either of the above two checks fail, then the functionality returns Failure to the parties indicating that D is corrupted.

In our MPC protocol where $\mathcal{F}_{\mathrm{GEN}[\cdot]}$ is called, the dealer will compute the commitment $\mathbf{C}$ as $\mathsf{Comm}_{\mathsf{ck}}(f(0); g(0), h(0))$ and will broadcast it prior to making a call to $\mathcal{F}_{\mathrm{GEN}[\cdot]}$. It is easy to note that $\mathcal{F}_{\mathrm{GEN}[\cdot]}$ generates $[f(0)]$ if D is honest or well-behaved. If $\mathcal{F}_{\mathrm{GEN}[\cdot]}$ returns Failure, then D is indeed corrupted.

Functionality $\mathcal{F}_{\mathrm{GEN}[\cdot]}$

$\mathcal{F}_{\mathrm{GEN}[\cdot]}$ interacts with the parties in $\mathcal{P}$, a dealer $D \in \mathcal{P}$, and the adversary $\mathcal{S}$ and is parametrized by a commitment key ck of a double-trapdoor homomorphic commitment scheme, along with t.

- On receiving $(\mathsf{sid}, D, f(\cdot), g(\cdot), h(\cdot))$ from D and $(\mathsf{sid}, i, D, \mathbf{C})$ from every $P_i \in \mathcal{P}$, the functionality verifies whether $f(\cdot), g(\cdot)$ and $h(\cdot)$ are of degree at most t and $\mathbf{C} \overset{?}{=} \mathsf{Comm}_{\mathsf{ck}}(f(0); g(0), h(0))$, where $\mathbf{C}$ is received from the majority of the parties.
- If any of the above verifications fail then the functionality sends $(\mathsf{sid}, i, D, \mathsf{Failure})$ to every $P_i \in \mathcal{P}$ and $\mathcal{S}$ and halts.
- Else for every $P_i \in \mathcal{P}$, the functionality computes the share $f_i = f(\alpha_i)$, the opening information $g_i = g(\alpha_i), h_i = h(\alpha_i)$, and the commitment $\mathbf{C}_{f_i,g_i,h_i} = \mathsf{Comm}_{\mathsf{ck}}(f_i; g_i, h_i)$. It sends $(\mathsf{sid}, i, D, [s]_i)$ to every $P_i \in \mathcal{P}$ where $[s]_i = (f_i, g_i, h_i, \{\mathbf{C}_{f_j,g_j,h_j}\}_{P_j \in \mathcal{P}})$ and halts.

Fig. 5. The Ideal Functionality for Verifiably Generating $[\cdot]$-sharing

We note that $\mathcal{F}_{\mathrm{GEN}[\cdot]}$ is slightly different from the standard ideal functionality (see e.g. [2]) of verifiable secret sharing (VSS) where the parties output *only* their shares (and not the commitment of all the shares). In most of the standard instantiations of a VSS functionality (in the computational setting), for example the Pedersen VSS [21], a public commitment of all the shares and the secret are available to the parties without violating any privacy. In order to make these commitments available to the external protocol that invokes $\mathcal{F}_{\mathrm{GEN}[\cdot]}$, we allow the functionality to compute and deliver the shares along with the commitments to the parties. We note, [1] introduced a similar functionality for "committed VSS" that outputs to the parties the commitment of the secret provided by the dealer due to the same motivation mentioned above.

3.2 Supporting Sub-protocols

Our MPC protocol also makes use of the following sub-protocols. Due to space constraints, here we only present a high level description of these protocols and state their communication complexity. The formal details of the protocols are available in the full version. Since we later show that our main MPC protocol that invokes these sub-protocols is UC-secure, it is not required to prove any form of security for these sub-protocols separately.

(A) Protocol $\Pi_{\langle \cdot \rangle \rightarrow [\cdot]}$ **:** it takes input $\langle s \rangle_{\mathcal{X}}$ for a set $\mathcal{X}$ containing at least *one* honest party and either produces a sharing $[s]$ (if all the parties in $\mathcal{X}$ behave honestly) or outputs one of the following: the identity of a single corrupted party or a pair of parties (with at least one of them being corrupted) from $\mathcal{X}$. The protocol makes use of the functionalities $\mathcal{F}_{\mathrm{GEN}[\cdot]}$ and $\mathcal{F}_{\mathrm{BC}}$.

   More specifically, let $\langle s \rangle_i$ denote the information (namely the share, opening information and the set of commitments) of party $P_i \in \mathcal{X}$ corresponding to the sharing $\langle s \rangle_{\mathcal{X}}$. To achieve the goal of our protocol, there are two clear steps to perform: *first*, the correct commitment for each share of s corresponding to its $\langle \cdot \rangle_{\mathcal{X}}$-sharing, now available to the parties in $\mathcal{X}$, is to be made available to *all* the parties in $\mathcal{P}$; *second*, each $P_i \in \mathcal{X}$ is required to act as a dealer and verifiably $[\cdot]$-share its already committed share s_i among $\mathcal{P}$. Note that the commitment to s_i is included in the set of commitments that will be already available among $\mathcal{P}$ due to the first step. Clearly, once $[s_i]$ are generated for each $P_i \in \mathcal{X}$, then $[s]$ is computed as $[s] = \sum_{P_i \in \mathcal{X}} [s_i]$; this is because $s = \sum_{P_i \in \mathcal{X}} s_i$.

   Now there are two steps that may lead to the failure of the protocol. First, $P_i \in \mathcal{X}$ may be identified as a corrupted dealer while calling $\mathcal{F}_{\mathrm{GEN}[\cdot]}$. In this case a single corrupted party is outputted by every party in $\mathcal{P}$. Second, the protocol may fail when the parties in $\mathcal{P}$ try to reach an agreement over the correct set of commitments of the shares of s. Recall that each $P_i \in \mathcal{X}$ holds a set of commitments as a part of $\langle s \rangle_{\mathcal{X}}$. We ask each $P_i \in \mathcal{X}$ to call $\mathcal{F}_{\mathrm{BC}}$ to broadcast among $\mathcal{P}$ the set of commitments held by him. It is necessary to ask each $P_i \in \mathcal{X}$ to do this as we can not trust any single party from $\mathcal{X}$, since all we know (with overwhelming probability) is that $\mathcal{X}$ contains at least one honest party. Now if the parties in $\mathcal{P}$ receive the same set of commitments from all the parties in $\mathcal{X}$, then clearly the received set is the correct set of commitments and agreement on the set is reached among $\mathcal{P}$. If this does not happen the parties in $\mathcal{P}$ can detect a pair of parties with conflicting sets and output the said pair. It is not hard to see that indeed one party in the pair must be corrupted. To ensure an agreement on the selected pair when there are multiple such conflicting pairs, we assume the existence of a predefined publicly known algorithm to select a pair from the lot (for instance consider the pair (P_a, P_b) with minimum value of $a + n \cdot b$). Intuitively the protocol is secure as the shares of honest parties in $\mathcal{X}$ remain secure.

   The communication complexity of protocol $\Pi_{\langle \cdot \rangle \rightarrow [\cdot]}$ is stated in Lemma 1, which easily follows from the fact that each party in $\mathcal{X}$ needs to broadcast $\mathcal{O}(|\mathcal{X}|\kappa)$ bits to $\mathcal{P}$.

Lemma 1. *The communication complexity of protocol* $\Pi_{\langle \cdot \rangle \rightarrow [\cdot]}$ *is* $\mathcal{BC}(|\mathcal{X}|^2\kappa, n)$ *plus the complexity of* $\mathcal{O}(|\mathcal{X}|)$ *invocations to the realization of the functionality* $\mathcal{F}_{\mathrm{GEN}[\cdot]}$.

(B) Protocol $\Pi_{\langle \cdot \rangle}$ **:** the protocol enables a designated party (dealer) $\mathsf{D} \in \mathcal{P}$ to verifiably $\langle \cdot \rangle$-share an already committed secret f among a set of parties $\mathcal{X}$ containing at least one honest party. More specifically, every $P_i \in \mathcal{P}$ holds a (publicly known) commitment $\mathbf{C}_{f,g,h}$. The dealer D holds the secret $f \in \mathbb{F}_p$ and randomness pair (g, h), such that $\mathbf{C}_{f,g,h} = \mathsf{Comm}_{\mathsf{ck}}(f; g, h)$; and the goal is to generate $\langle f \rangle_{\mathcal{X}}$. In the protocol, D first additively shares f as well as the opening information (g, h) among $\mathcal{X}$. In addition, D is also asked to publicly commit each additive-share of f, using the corresponding additive-share of (g, f). The parties can then publicly verify whether indeed D has $\langle \cdot \rangle$-shared the same f as committed in $\mathbf{C}_{f,g,h}$, via the homomorphic property of the commitments. Intuitively f remains private in the protocol for an honest D as there exists at least one honest party in $\mathcal{X}$. Moreover the binding property of the commitment ensures that a potentially corrupted D fails to $\langle \cdot \rangle$-share an incorrect value $f' \neq f$.

If we notice carefully the protocol achieves a little more than $\langle \cdot \rangle$-sharing of a secret among a set of parties $\mathcal{X}$. All the parties in $\mathcal{P}$ hold the commitments to the shares of f, while as per the definition of $\langle \cdot \rangle$-sharing the commitments to shares should be available to the parties in $\mathcal{X}$ alone. A closer look reveals that the public commitments to the shares of f among the parties in $\mathcal{P}$ enable them to publicly verify whether D has indeed $\langle \cdot \rangle$-shared the same f among $\mathcal{X}$ as committed in $\mathbf{C}_{f,g,h}$ via the homomorphic property of the commitments. The communication complexity of $\Pi_{\langle \cdot \rangle}$ is stated in Lemma 2.

Lemma 2. *The communication complexity of protocol $\Pi_{\langle \cdot \rangle}$ is $\mathcal{O}(|\mathcal{X}|\kappa)$ and $\mathcal{BC}(|\mathcal{X}|\kappa, n)$.*

(C) Protocol $\Pi_{[\cdot] \to \langle \cdot \rangle}$: the protocol takes as input $[s]$ for any secret s and outputs $\langle s \rangle_{\mathcal{X}}$ for a designated set of parties $\mathcal{X} \subset \mathcal{P}$ containing at least one honest party.

Let $f_1, \ldots, f_n$ be the Shamir-shares of s. Then the protocol is designed using the following two-stage approach: **(1)**: First each party $P_k \in \mathcal{P}$ acts as a dealer and verifiably $\langle \cdot \rangle$-share's its share f_k via protocol $\Pi_{\langle \cdot \rangle}$; **(2)** Let $\mathcal{H}$ be the set of $|\mathcal{H}| > t + 1$ parties P_k who have correctly $\langle \cdot \rangle$-shared its Shamir-share f_k; without loss of generality, let $\mathcal{H}$ be the set of first $|\mathcal{H}|$ parties in $\mathcal{P}$. Since the original sharing polynomial (for $[\cdot]$-sharing s) has degree at most t with s as its constant term, then there exists publicly known constants (namely the Lagrange's interpolation coefficients) $c_1, \ldots, c_{|\mathcal{H}|}$, such that $s = c_1 f_1 + \ldots + c_{|\mathcal{H}|} f_{|\mathcal{H}|}$. Since corresponding to each $P_k \in \mathcal{H}$ the share f_k is $\langle \cdot \rangle$-shared, it follows easily that each party $P_i \in \mathcal{X}$ can compute $\langle s \rangle_i = c_1 \langle f_1 \rangle_i + \ldots + c_{|\mathcal{H}|} \langle f_{|\mathcal{H}|} \rangle_i$. The correctness of the protocol follows from the fact that the corrupted parties in $\mathcal{P}$ will fail to $\langle \cdot \rangle$-share an incorrect Shamir-share of s, thanks to the protocol $\Pi_{\langle \cdot \rangle}$. The privacy of s follows from the fact that the Shamir shares of the honest parties in $\mathcal{P}$ remain private, which follows from the privacy of the protocol $\Pi_{\langle \cdot \rangle}$.

The communication complexity of the protocol $\Pi_{[\cdot] \to \langle \cdot \rangle}$ is stated in Lemma 3 which follows from the fact that n invocations to $\Pi_{\langle \cdot \rangle}$ are done in the protocol.

Lemma 3. *The communication complexity of $\Pi_{[\cdot] \to \langle \cdot \rangle}$ is $\mathcal{O}(n|\mathcal{X}|\kappa)$ and $\mathcal{BC}(n|\mathcal{X}|\kappa, n)$.*

(D) Protocol $\Pi_{\mathrm{RANDZERO}[\cdot]}$: the protocol is used for generating a random $[\cdot]$-sharing of 0. To design the protocol, we also require a standard Zero-knowledge (ZK) functionality $\mathcal{F}_{\mathrm{ZK.BC}}$ to publicly prove a commitment to zero. The functionality is a "prove-and-broadcast" functionality that upon receiving a commitment and witness pair $(\mathbf{C}, (u, v))$ from a designated prover P_j, verifies if $\mathbf{C} = \mathsf{Comm}_{\mathsf{ck}}(0; u, v)$ or not. If so it sends $\mathbf{C}$ to all the parties. A protocol $\Pi_{\text{ZK.BC}}$ realizing $\mathcal{F}_{\text{ZK.BC}}$ can be designed in the CRS model using standard techniques, with communication complexity $\mathcal{O}(\text{Poly}(n)\kappa)$.

Protocol $\Pi_{\text{RANDZERO}[\cdot]}$ invokes the ideal functionalities $\mathcal{F}_{\text{ZK.BC}}$ and $\mathcal{F}_{\text{GEN}[\cdot]}$. The idea is as follows: Each party $P_i \in \mathcal{P}$ first broadcasts a random commitment of 0 and proves in a zero-knowledge (ZK) fashion that it indeed committed 0. Next P_i calls $\mathcal{F}_{\text{GEN}[\cdot]}$ as a dealer D to generate $[\cdot]$-sharing of 0 that is consistent with the commitment of 0. The parties then locally add the sharings of the dealers who are successful as dealers in their corresponding calls to $\mathcal{F}_{\text{GEN}[\cdot]}$. Since there exists at least one honest party in this set of dealers, the resultant sharing will be indeed a random sharing of 0, see the full version for details. Looking ahead, we invoke $\Pi_{\text{RANDZERO}[\cdot]}$ only once in our main MPC protocol Π_f (more on this later); so we avoid giving details of the communication complexity of the protocol. However assuming standard realization of $\mathcal{F}_{\text{ZK.BC}}$, the protocol has complexity $\mathcal{O}(\text{Poly}(n)\kappa)$.

(E) Dis-honest Majority MPC Protocol : Apart from the above sub-protocols, we use a non-robust, dishonest-majority MPC protocol Π_C^{NR} with the capability of fault-detection. The protocol, allows a designated set of parties $\mathcal{X} \subset \mathcal{P}$, containing at least one honest party, to perform $\langle \cdot \rangle$-shared evaluation of a given circuit C. In case some corrupted party in $\mathcal{X}$ behaves maliciously, the parties in $\mathcal{P}$ identify a pair of parties from $\mathcal{X}$, with at least one of them being corrupted. The starting point of Π_C^{NR} is the dishonest majority MPC protocol of [11], which takes $\langle \cdot \rangle$-shared inputs of a given circuit, from a set of parties, say $\mathcal{X}$, having a dishonest majority. The protocol then achieves the following:

- If all the parties in $\mathcal{X}$ behave honestly, then the protocol outputs $\langle \cdot \rangle$-shared circuit outputs among $\mathcal{X}$.
- Else the honest parties in $\mathcal{X}$ detect misbehaviour by the corrupted parties and abort the protocol.

We observe that for an aborted execution of the protocol of [11], there exists an honest party in $\mathcal{X}$ that can *locally* identify a corrupted party from $\mathcal{X}$, who deviated from the protocol. We exploit this property in Π_C^{NR} to enable the parties in $\mathcal{P}$ identify a pair of parties from $\mathcal{X}$ with at least one of them being corrupted.

Protocol Π_C^{NR} proceeds in two stages, the *preparation stage* and the *evaluation stage*, each involving various other sub-protocols (details available in the full version). In the preparation stage, if all the parties in $\mathcal{X}$ behave honestly, then they jointly generate $C_M + C_R$ shared multiplication triples $\{(\langle \mathbf{a}^{(i)} \rangle_{\mathcal{X}}, \langle \mathbf{b}^{(i)} \rangle_{\mathcal{X}}, \langle \mathbf{c}^{(i)} \rangle_{\mathcal{X}})\}_{i=1,\ldots,C_M+C_R}$, such that $\mathbf{c}^{(i)} = \mathbf{a}^{(i)} \cdot \mathbf{b}^{(i)}$ and each $(\mathbf{a}^{(i)}, \mathbf{b}^{(i)}, \mathbf{c}^{(i)})$ is random and unknown to the adversary; here C_M and C_R are the number of multiplication and random gates in C respectively. Otherwise, the parties in $\mathcal{P}$ identify a pair of parties in $\mathcal{X}$, with at least one of them being corrupted.

Assuming that the desired $\langle \cdot \rangle$-shared multiplication triples are generated in the preparation stage, the parties in $\mathcal{X}$ start evaluating C in a shared fashion by maintaining the following standard invariant for each gate of C: *Given $\langle \cdot \rangle$-shared inputs of the gate, the parties securely compute the $\langle \cdot \rangle$-shared output of the gate.* Maintaining the invariant for the linear gates in C does not require any interaction, thanks to the linearity of $\langle \cdot \rangle$-sharing. For a multiplication gate, the parties deploy a preprocessed $\langle \cdot \rangle$-shared multiplication triple from the preparation stage (for each multiplication gate a different triple is deployed) and use the standard Beaver's trick [3]. While applying Beaver's trick, the parties in $\mathcal{X}$ need to publicly open two $\langle \cdot \rangle$-shared values using a reconstruction protocol $\Pi_{\text{REC}\langle \cdot \rangle}$ (presented in the full version). It may be possible that the opening is non-robust[5], in which case the circuit evaluation fails and the parties in $\mathcal{P}$ identify a pair of parties from $\mathcal{X}$ with at least one of them being corrupted. For a random gate, the parties consider an $\langle \cdot \rangle$-shared multiplication triple from the preparation stage (for each random gate a different triple is deployed) and the first component of the triple is considered as the output of the random gate. The protocol ends once the parties in $\mathcal{X}$ obtain $\langle \cdot \rangle$-shared circuit outputs $\langle y_1 \rangle_{\mathcal{X}}, \ldots, \langle y_{\text{out}} \rangle_{\mathcal{X}}$; so no reconstruction is required at the end.

The complete details of Π_C^{NR} is provided in the full version. The protocol invokes two ideal functionalities $\mathcal{F}_{\text{GENRAND}\langle \cdot \rangle}$ and $\mathcal{F}_{\text{BC}}$ where the functionality $\mathcal{F}_{\text{GENRAND}\langle \cdot \rangle}$ is used to generate $\langle \cdot \rangle$-sharing of random values (again see the full version). For our purpose we note that the protocol provides a statistical security of 2^{-s} and has communication complexity as stated in Lemma 4 and proved in the full version. Note that there are two types of broadcast involved: among the parties in $\mathcal{X}$ and among the parties in $\mathcal{P}$.

Lemma 4. *For a statistical security parameter s, protocol Π_C^{NR} has communication complexity of* $\mathcal{O}(|\mathcal{X}|^2(|C| + s)\kappa), \mathcal{BC}(|\mathcal{X}|^2(|C| + s)\kappa, |\mathcal{X}|)$ *and* $\mathcal{BC}(|\mathcal{X}|\kappa, n)$.

3.3   The MPC Protocol

Finally, we describe our MPC protocol. Recall that we divide the circuit ckt into sub-circuits $\text{ckt}_1, \ldots, \text{ckt}_L$ and we let in_l and out_l denote the number of input and output wires respectively for the sub-circuit ckt_l. At the beginning of the protocol, each party $[\cdot]$-share their private inputs by calling $\mathcal{F}_{\text{GEN}[\cdot]}$. The parties then select a random committee of parties by calling $\mathcal{F}_{\text{COMMITTEE}}$ for evaluating the lth sub-circuit via the dishonest majority MPC protocol of [11]. We use a Boolean flag NewCom in the protocol to indicate if a new committee has to be decided, prior to the evaluation of lth sub-circuit or the committee used for the evaluation of the $(l - 1)$th sub-circuit is to be continued. Specifically a successful evaluation of a sub-circuit is followed by setting NewCom equals to 0, implying that the current committee is to be continued for the evaluation of the subsequent sub-circuit. On the other hand, a failed evaluation of a sub-circuit is followed by setting NewCom equals to 1, implying that a fresh committee has to be decided for the re-evaluation of the same sub-circuit from the updated set of eligible parties $\mathcal{L}$, which is modified after the failed evaluation. After each successful sub-circuit evaluation, the corresponding $\langle \cdot \rangle$-shared outputs are converted into $[\cdot]$-shared outputs via protocol $\Pi_{\langle \cdot \rangle \rightarrow [\cdot]}$, while prior to each sub-circuit evaluation, the corresponding $[\cdot]$-shared inputs are converted to the required $\langle \cdot \rangle$-shared inputs via protocol $\Pi_{[\cdot] \rightarrow \langle \cdot \rangle}$. The process is repeated till the function output is $[\cdot]$-shared, after which it is robustly reconstructed (as we have honest majority in $\mathcal{P}$).

Without affecting the correctness of the above steps, but to ensure simulation security (in the UC model), we add an additional output re-randomization step before the output

---

[5] As we may not have honest majority in $\mathcal{X}$, we could not always ensure robust reconstruction during $\Pi_{\text{REC}\langle \cdot \rangle}$.

reconstruction: the parties call $\Pi_{\text{RANDZERO}[\cdot]}$ to generate a random $[0]$, which they add to the $[\cdot]$-shared output (thus keeping the same function output). Looking ahead, during the simulation in the security proof, this step allows the simulator to cheat and set the final output to be the one obtained from the functionality, even though it simulates the honest parties with 0 as the input (see the full version for the details).

Let E be the event that at least one party in each of the selected committees during sub-circuit evaluations is honest; the event E occurs except with probability at most $(t + 1) \cdot \epsilon^{\mathfrak{c}} \approx 2^{-\kappa}$. This is because at most $(t + 1)$ (random) committees need to be selected (a new committee is selected after each of the t failed sub-circuit evaluation plus an initial selection is made). It is easy to see that conditioned on E, the protocol is private: the inputs of the honest parties remain private during the input stage (due to $\mathcal{F}_{\text{GEN}[\cdot]}$), while each of the involved sub-protocols for sub-circuit evaluations does not leak any information about honest party's inputs. It also follows that conditioned on E, the protocol is correct, thanks to the binding property of the commitment and the properties of the involved sub-protocols.

The properties of the protocol Π_f are stated in Theorem 1 and the security proof is available in the full version; we only provide the proof of communication complexity here. The (circuit-dependent) communication complexity in the theorem is derived after substituting the calls to the various ideal functionalities by the corresponding protocols implementing them. The broadcast complexity has two parts: the broadcasts among the parties in $\mathcal{P}$ and the broadcasts among small committees.

Theorem 1. *Let* $f : \mathbb{F}_p^n \rightarrow \mathbb{F}_p$ *be a publicly known n-input function with circuit representation* ckt *over* $\mathbb{F}_p$, *with average width* w *and depth* d *(thus* $w = \frac{|\text{ckt}|}{d}$*). Moreover, let* ckt *be divided into sub-circuits* $\text{ckt}_1, \ldots, \text{ckt}_L$, *with* $L = t$ *and each subcircuit* ckt_l *having fan-in* in_l *and fan-out* out_l. *Furthermore, let* $\text{in}_l = \text{out}_l = \mathcal{O}(w)$. *Then conditioned on the event* E, *protocol* Π_f (κ, s)*-securely realizes the functionality* $\mathcal{F}_f$ *against* $\mathcal{A}$ *in the* $(\mathcal{F}_{\text{CRS}}, \mathcal{F}_{\text{BC}}, \mathcal{F}_{\text{COMMITTEE}}, \mathcal{F}_{\text{GEN}[\cdot]}, \mathcal{F}_{\text{GENRAND}\langle\cdot\rangle}, \mathcal{F}_{\text{ZK.BC}})$*-hybrid model in the UC security framework. The circuit-dependent communication complexity of the protocol is* $\mathcal{O}(|\text{ckt}| \cdot (\frac{n \cdot t}{d} + \kappa) \cdot \kappa^2)$, $\mathcal{BC}(|\text{ckt}| \cdot \frac{n \cdot t \cdot \kappa^2}{d}, n)$ *and* $\mathcal{BC}(|\text{ckt}| \cdot \kappa^3, \kappa)$.

PROOF (COMMUNICATION COMPLEXITY): We analyze each phase of the protocol:

1. **Input Commitment Stage:** Here each party broadcasts $\mathcal{O}(\kappa)$ bits to the parties in $\mathcal{P}$ and so the broadcast complexity of this step is $\mathcal{BC}(n\kappa, n)$.

2. $[\cdot]$-**sharing of Committed Inputs:** Here n calls to $\mathcal{F}_{\text{GEN}[\cdot]}$ are made. Realizing $\mathcal{F}_{\text{GEN}[\cdot]}$ with the protocol $\Pi_{[\cdot]}$, see the full version, this incurs a communication complexity of $\mathcal{O}(n^2\kappa)$ and $\mathcal{BC}(n^2\kappa, n)$.

3. **Sub-circuit Evaluations:** We first count the total communication cost of evaluating the sub-circuit ckt_l with in_l input gates and out_l output gates.
   - Converting the in_l $[\cdot]$-shared inputs to in_l $\langle\cdot\rangle$-shared inputs will require in_l invocations to the protocol $\Pi_{[\cdot] \rightarrow \langle\cdot\rangle}$. The communication complexity of this step is $\mathcal{O}(n \cdot \mathfrak{c} \cdot \text{in}_l \cdot \kappa)$ and $\mathcal{BC}(n \cdot \mathfrak{c} \cdot \text{in}_l \cdot \kappa, n)$; this follows from Lemma 3 by substituting $|\mathcal{X}| = \mathfrak{c}$.
   - Since the size of ckt_l is at most $\frac{|\text{ckt}|}{L}$, evaluating the same via protocol $\Pi_{\text{ckt}_l}^{\text{NR}}$ will have communication complexity $\mathcal{O}(\mathfrak{c}^2(\frac{|\text{ckt}|}{L} + s)\kappa)$, $\mathcal{BC}(\mathfrak{c}^2(\frac{|\text{ckt}|}{L} + s)\kappa, \mathfrak{c})$ and $\mathcal{BC}(\mathfrak{c} \cdot \kappa, n)$; this follows from Lemma 4 by substituting $|\mathcal{X}| = \mathfrak{c}$.

Protocol $\Pi_f(\mathcal{P}, \text{ckt})$

For session ID sid, every party $P_i \in \mathcal{P}$ does the following:

Initialization. Set $\mathcal{L} = \mathcal{P}$, $n = |\mathcal{L}|$, $t = t$ and NewCom $= 1$. Divide ckt into L sub-circuits $\text{ckt}_1, \ldots, \text{ckt}_L$, each of depth d/L.

CRS Generation. Invoke $\mathcal{F}_{\text{CRS}}$ with (sid, i) and get back $(\text{sid}, i, \text{CRS})$, where CRS $= (\text{pk}, \text{ck})$.

Input Commitment. On input $x^{(i)}$, choose random polynomials $f^{(i)}(\cdot), g^{(i)}(\cdot), h^{(i)}(\cdot)$ of degree $\leq t$, such that $f^{(i)}(0) = x^{(i)}$ and compute the commitment $\mathbf{C}_{x^{(i)}, g_0^{(i)}, h_0^{(i)}} = \text{Comm}_{\text{ck}}(x^{(i)}; g_0^{(i)}, h_0^{(i)})$ where $g_0^{(i)} = g^{(i)}(0)$, $h_0^{(i)} = h^{(i)}(0)$.

- Call $\mathcal{F}_{\text{BC}}$ with message $(\text{sid}, i, \mathbf{C}_{x^{(i)}, g_0^{(i)}, h_0^{(i)}}, \mathcal{P})$.
- Corresponding to each $P_j \in \mathcal{P}$, receive $(\text{sid}, i, j, \mathbf{C}_{x^{(j)}, g_0^{(j)}, h_0^{(j)}})$ from $\mathcal{F}_{\text{BC}}$.

$[\cdot]$-sharing of Committed Inputs.

- Act as a dealer D and call $\mathcal{F}_{\text{GEN}[\cdot]}$ with $(\text{sid}, i, f^{(i)}(\cdot), g^{(i)}(\cdot), h^{(i)}(\cdot))$.
- For every $P_j \in \mathcal{P}$, call $\mathcal{F}_{\text{GEN}[\cdot]}$ with $(\text{sid}, i, j, \mathbf{C}_{x^{(j)}, g_0^{(j)}, h_0^{(j)}})$.
- For every $P_j \in \mathcal{P}$, if $(\text{sid}, i, j, \text{Failure})$ is received from $\mathcal{F}_{\text{GEN}[\cdot]}$, substitute a default predefined public sharing $[0]$ of 0 as $[x^{(j)}]$, set $[x^{(j)}]_i = [0]_i$ and update $\mathcal{L} = \mathcal{L} \setminus \{P_j\}$, decrement t and n by one. Else receive $(\text{sid}, i, j, [x^{(j)}]_i)$ from $\mathcal{F}_{\text{GEN}[\cdot]}$.

Start of While Loop Over the Sub-circuits. Initialize $l = 1$. While $l \leq L$ do:

- **Committee Selection.** If NewCom $= 1$, then call $\mathcal{F}_{\text{COMMITTEE}}$ with $(\text{sid}, i, \mathcal{L})$ and receive $(\text{sid}, i, \mathcal{C})$ from $\mathcal{F}_{\text{COMMITTEE}}$.
- **$[\cdot]$ to $\langle \cdot \rangle_{\mathcal{C}}$ Conversion of Inputs of Sub-circuit ckt_l.** Let $[x_1], \ldots, [x_{\text{in}_l}]$ denote the $[\cdot]$-sharing of the inputs to ckt_l:
  - For $k = 1, \ldots, \text{in}_l$, participate in $\Pi_{[\cdot] \to \langle \cdot \rangle}$ with $(\text{sid}, i, [x_k]_i, \mathcal{C})$. Output $(\text{sid}, i, \langle x_k \rangle_i)$ in $\Pi_{[\cdot] \to \langle \cdot \rangle}$, if P_i belongs to $\mathcal{C}$. Else output (sid, i).
- **Evaluation of the Sub-circuit ckt_l.** If $P_i \in \mathcal{C}$ then participate in $\Pi_{\text{ckt}_l}^{\text{NR}}$ with $(\text{sid}, i, \langle x_1 \rangle_i, \ldots, \langle x_{\text{in}_l} \rangle_i, \mathcal{C})$, else participate in $\Pi_{\text{ckt}_l}^{\text{NR}}$ with $(\text{sid}, i, \mathcal{C})$.
  - If $(\text{sid}, i, \text{Failure}, P_a, P_b)$ is the output during $\Pi_{\text{ckt}_l}^{\text{NR}}$, then set $\mathcal{L} = \mathcal{L} \setminus \{P_a, P_b\}$, $t = t - 1$, $n = n - 2$, NewCom $= 1$ and go to **Committee Selection** step.
- **$\langle \cdot \rangle_{\mathcal{C}}$ to $[\cdot]$ conversion of Outputs of ckt_l.** If $(\text{sid}, i, \text{Success}, \langle y_1 \rangle_i, \ldots, \langle y_{\text{out}_l} \rangle_i)$ or $(\text{sid}, i, \text{Success})$ is obtained during $\Pi_{\text{ckt}_l}^{\text{NR}}$, then participate in $\Pi_{\langle \cdot \rangle \to [\cdot]}$ with $(\text{sid}, i, \langle y_k \rangle_i)$ or (sid, i) (respectively) for $k = 1, \ldots, \text{out}_l$.
  - If $(\text{sid}, i, \text{Success}, [y_k]_i)$ is the output in $\Pi_{\langle \cdot \rangle \to [\cdot]}$ for every $k = 1, \ldots, \text{out}_l$, then increment l and set NewCom $= 0$.
  - If $(\text{sid}, i, \text{Failure}, P_a, P_b)$ is the output in $\Pi_{\langle \cdot \rangle \to [\cdot]}$ for *some* $k \in \{1, \ldots, \text{out}_l\}$, then set $\mathcal{L} = \mathcal{L} \setminus \{P_a, P_b\}$, $t = t - 1$, $n = n - 2$, NewCom $= 1$ and go to the **Committee Selection** step.
  - If $(\text{sid}, i, \text{Failure}, P_a)$ is the output in $\Pi_{\langle \cdot \rangle \to [\cdot]}$ for *some* $k \in \{1, \ldots, \text{out}_l\}$, then set $\mathcal{L} = \mathcal{L} \setminus \{P_a\}$, $t = t - 1$, $n = n - 1$, NewCom $= 1$ and go to the **Committee Selection** step.

Output Rerandomization. Let $[y]$ denote the $[\cdot]$-sharing of the output of ckt. Participate in $\Pi_{\text{RANDZERO}[\cdot]}$ with (sid, i), obtain $(\text{sid}, i, [0]_i)$ and locally compute $[z]_i = [y]_i + [0]_i$.

Output Reconstruction. Interpret $[z]_i$ as $(f_i, g_i, h_i, \{\mathbf{C}_{f_j, g_j, h_j}\}_{P_j \in \mathcal{P}})$. Initialize a set $\mathcal{T}_i$ to $\emptyset$.

- Send $(\text{sid}, i, j, f_i, g_i, h_i)$ to every $P_j \in \mathcal{P}$. On receiving $(\text{sid}, j, i, f_j, g_j, h_j)$ from every party P_j include party P_j in $\mathcal{T}_i$ if $\mathbf{C}_{f_j, g_j, h_j} \neq \text{Comm}_{\text{ck}}(f_j; (g_j, h_j))$.
- Interpolate $f(\cdot)$ such that $f(\alpha_j) = f_j$ holds for every $P_j \in \mathcal{P} \setminus \mathcal{T}_i$. If $f(\cdot)$ has degree at most t, output $(\text{sid}, i, z = f(0))$ and halt; else output $(\text{sid}, i, \text{Failure})$ and halt.

Fig. 6. Protocol for UC-secure realizing $\mathcal{F}_f$

- Finally converting the $\text{out}_l \langle \cdot \rangle$-shared outputs to $[\cdot]$-shared outputs require out_l invocations to the protocol $\Pi_{\langle \cdot \rangle \to [\cdot]}$. This has communication complexity $\mathcal{O}(n \cdot \mathsf{c} \cdot \text{out}_l \cdot \kappa)$, $\mathcal{BC}(\text{out}_l \cdot \mathsf{c}^2 \cdot \kappa, n)$ and $\mathcal{BC}(n \cdot \mathsf{c} \cdot \kappa, n)$; this follows from Lemma 1 by substituting $|\mathcal{X}| = \mathsf{c}$.

Thus evaluating ckt_l has communication complexity $\mathcal{O}((n^2 + n \cdot \mathsf{c} \cdot \text{in}_l + n \cdot \mathsf{c} \cdot \text{out}_l + \mathsf{c}^2(\frac{|\text{ckt}|}{L} + s))\kappa)$, $\mathcal{BC}((n^2 + n \cdot \mathsf{c} \cdot \text{in}_l + \mathsf{c}^2 \cdot \text{out}_l)\kappa, n)$ and $\mathcal{BC}(\mathsf{c}^2(\frac{|\text{ckt}|}{L} + s)\kappa, \mathsf{c})$. Assuming $\text{in}_l = \mathcal{O}(w)$ and $\text{out}_l = \mathcal{O}(w)$, with $w = \frac{|\text{ckt}|}{d}$, this results in $\mathcal{O}((n^2 + n \cdot \mathsf{c} \cdot \frac{|\text{ckt}|}{d} + \mathsf{c}^2(\frac{|\text{ckt}|}{L} + s))\kappa)$, $\mathcal{BC}((n^2 + n \cdot \mathsf{c} \cdot \frac{|\text{ckt}|}{d})\kappa, n)$ and $\mathcal{BC}((\mathsf{c}^2 \cdot (\frac{|\text{ckt}|}{L} + s))\kappa, \mathsf{c})$. The total number of sub-circuit evaluations is at most $L + t$, with L successful evaluations and at most t failed evaluations. Substituting $L = t$, we get the overall communication complexity $\mathcal{O}((|\text{ckt}| \cdot (\frac{n \cdot t \cdot \mathsf{c}}{d} + \mathsf{c}^2) + n^2 t + \mathsf{c}^2 s \cdot t)\kappa)$, $\mathcal{BC}((|\text{ckt}| \cdot \frac{n \cdot t \cdot \mathsf{c}}{d} + n^2 t)\kappa, n)$ and $\mathcal{BC}((|\text{ckt}| \cdot \mathsf{c}^2 + \mathsf{c}^2 \cdot s \cdot t)\kappa, \mathsf{c})$.

4. **Output Rerandomization and Reconstruction:** The costs $\mathcal{O}(\text{Poly}(n, \kappa))$ bits.

The circuit-dependent complexity of the whole protocol comes out to be $\mathcal{O}(|\text{ckt}| \cdot (\frac{nt \cdot \mathsf{c}}{d} + \mathsf{c}^2)\kappa)$ bits of communication over the point-to-point channels and broadcast-complexity of $\mathcal{BC}(|\text{ckt}| \cdot \frac{nt \cdot \mathsf{c}}{d} \cdot \kappa, n)$ and $\mathcal{BC}(|\text{ckt}| \cdot \mathsf{c}^2 \cdot \kappa, \mathsf{c})$. Since c has to be selected so that $\epsilon^{\mathsf{c}} < 2^{-\kappa}$ holds, asymptotically we can set c to be $\mathcal{O}(\kappa)$. (For any practical purpose, $\kappa = 80$ is good enough.) It implies that the (circuit-dependent) communication complexity is $\mathcal{O}(|\text{ckt}|(\frac{nt}{d} + \kappa)\kappa^2)$, $\mathcal{BC}(|\text{ckt}| \cdot \frac{nt\kappa^2}{d}, n)$ and $\mathcal{BC}(|\text{ckt}|\kappa^3, \kappa)$. $\square$

We propose two optimizations for our MPC protocol that improves its communication complexity.

$[\cdot]$-**sharing among a Smaller Subset of** $\mathcal{P}$. While for simplicity, we involve the entire set of parties in $\mathcal{P}$ to hold $[\cdot]$-shared values in the protocol, it is enough to fix and involve a set of just z parties that guarantees a honest majority with overwhelming probability. From our analysis in Section 1, we find that $z = \mathcal{O}(\kappa)$. Indeed it is easy to note that all we require from the set involved in holding a $[\cdot]$-sharing is honest majority that can be attained by any set containing $\mathcal{O}(\kappa)$ parties. This optimization replaces n by κ in the complexity expressions mentioned in Theorem 1. It implies that the (circuit-dependent) communication complexity is $\mathcal{O}(|\text{ckt}|(\frac{\kappa t}{d} + \kappa)\kappa^2)$, $\mathcal{BC}(|\text{ckt}| \cdot \frac{t\kappa^3}{d}, \kappa)$ and $\mathcal{BC}(|\text{ckt}|\kappa^3, \kappa)$. Now instantiating the broadcast functionality in the above modified protocol with the Dolev-Strong (DS) broadcast protocol (see the full version), we obtain the following:

Corollary 1. *If $d = \omega(t)$ and if the calls to $\mathcal{F}_{\text{BC}}$ are realized via the DS broadcast protocol, then the circuit-dependent communication complexity of Π_f is $\mathcal{O}(|\text{ckt}| \cdot \kappa^7)$.*

When we restrict to widths w of the form $w = \omega(\kappa^3)$, we can instantiate all the invocations to $\mathcal{F}_{\text{BC}}$ in the protocols $\Pi_{\langle \cdot \rangle \to [\cdot]}$ and $\Pi_{[\cdot] \to \langle \cdot \rangle}$ (invoked before and after the sub-circuit evaluations) by the Fitzi-Hirt (FH) multi-valued broadcast protocol [15], see the full version. This is because, setting $w = \omega(\kappa^3)$ ensures that the combined message over all the instances of $\Pi_{\langle \cdot \rangle \to [\cdot]}$ (respectively $\Pi_{[\cdot] \to \langle \cdot \rangle}$) to be broadcast by any party satisfies the bound on the message size of the FH protocol. Incorporating the above, we obtain the following corollary with better result.

Corollary 2. *If $d = \omega(t)$ and $w = \omega(\kappa^3)$ (i.e. $|\mathsf{ckt}| = \omega(\kappa^3 t)$), then the circuit-dependent communication complexity of Π_f is $\mathcal{O}(|\mathsf{ckt}| \cdot \kappa^4)$.*

Packed Secret-Sharing. We can employ packed secret-sharing technique of [16] to checkpoint multiple outputs of the sub-circuits together in a single $[\cdot]$-sharing. Specifically, if we involve all the parties in $\mathcal{P}$ to hold a $[\cdot]$-sharing, we can pack $n - 2t$ values together in a single $[\cdot]$-sharing by setting the degree of the underlying polynomials to $n - t - 1$. It is easy to note that robust reconstruction of such a $[\cdot]$-sharing is still possible, as there are $n - t$ honest parties in the set $\mathcal{P}$ and exactly $n - t$ shares are required to reconstruct an $(n - t - 1)$ degree polynomial. For every sub-circuit ckt_l, the w_{out_l} output values are grouped so that each group contains $n - 2t$ secrets and each group is then converted to a single $[\cdot]$-sharing.

If we restrict to circuits for which any circuit wire has length at most $d/L = d/t$ (i.e. reaches upto at most d/L levels), then we ensure that the outputs of circuit ckt_l can only be the input to circuit ckt_{l+1}. With this restriction, the use of packed secret-sharing becomes applicable at all stages, and the communication complexity becomes $\mathcal{O}(|\mathsf{ckt}| \cdot (\frac{t}{d} + \kappa) \cdot \kappa^2)$, $\mathcal{BC}(|\mathsf{ckt}| \cdot \frac{t \cdot \kappa^2}{d}, n)$ and $\mathcal{BC}(|\mathsf{ckt}| \cdot \kappa^3, \kappa)$; i.e. a factor of n less in the first two terms compared to what is stated in Theorem 1. Realizing the broadcasts using DS and FH protocol respectively, we obtain the following corollaries:

Corollary 3. *If $d = \omega(\frac{n^3 \cdot t}{\kappa^4})$ and if the calls to $\mathcal{F}_{\mathsf{BC}}$ are realized via the DS broadcast protocol, then the circuit-dependent communication complexity of Π_f is $\mathcal{O}(|\mathsf{ckt}| \cdot \kappa^7)$.*

Corollary 4. *If $d = \omega(\frac{n \cdot t}{\kappa^5})$ and $w = \omega(n^2 \cdot (n + \kappa))$ (i.e. $|\mathsf{ckt}| = \omega(\frac{n^3 \cdot t}{\kappa^5}(n + \kappa)))$, then the circuit-dependent communication complexity of the protocol Π_f is $\mathcal{O}(|\mathsf{ckt}| \cdot \kappa^7)$.*

Acknowledgements. This work has been supported in part by ERC Advanced Grant ERC-2010-AdG-267188-CRIPTO, by EPSRC via grant EP/I03126X, and by Defense Advanced Research Projects Agency (DARPA) and the Air Force Research Laboratory (AFRL) under agreement number FA8750-11-2-0079[6] and the third author was supported in part by a Royal Society Wolfson Merit Award.

References

1. Abe, M., Fehr, S.: Adaptively Secure Feldman VSS and Applications to Universally-Composable Threshold Cryptography. In: Franklin, M. (ed.) CRYPTO 2004. LNCS, vol. 3152, pp. 317–334. Springer, Heidelberg (2004)
2. Asharov, G., Lindell, Y.: A Full Proof of the BGW Protocol for Perfectly-Secure Multiparty Computation. IACR Cryptology ePrint Archive 2011, 136 (2011)
3. Beaver, D.: Efficient Multiparty Protocols Using Circuit Randomization. In: Feigenbaum, J. (ed.) Advances in Cryptology - CRYPTO 1991. LNCS, vol. 576, pp. 420–432. Springer, Heidelberg (1992)

---

[6] The US Government is authorized to reproduce and distribute reprints for Government purposes notwithstanding any copyright notation thereon. The views and conclusions contained herein are those of the authors and should not be interpreted as necessarily representing the official policies or endorsements, either expressed or implied, of Defense Advanced Research Projects Agency (DARPA) or the U.S. Government.

4. Beerliová-Trubíniová, Z., Hirt, M.: Perfectly-Secure MPC with Linear Communication Complexity. In: Canetti, R. (ed.) TCC 2008. LNCS, vol. 4948, pp. 213–230. Springer, Heidelberg (2008)
5. Ben-Sasson, E., Fehr, S., Ostrovsky, R.: Near-Linear Unconditionally-Secure Multiparty Computation with a Dishonest Minority. In: Safavi-Naini, R., Canetti, R. (eds.) CRYPTO 2012. LNCS, vol. 7417, pp. 663–680. Springer, Heidelberg (2012)
6. Boyle, E., Goldwasser, S., Tessaro, S.: Communication locality in secure multi-party computation how to run sublinear algorithms in a distributed setting. In: Sahai, A. (ed.) TCC 2013. LNCS, vol. 7785, pp. 356–376. Springer, Heidelberg (2013)
7. Canetti, R., Fischlin, M.: Universally Composable Commitments. In: Kilian, J. (ed.) CRYPTO 2001. LNCS, vol. 2139, pp. 19–40. Springer, Heidelberg (2001)
8. Canny, J., Sorkin, S.: Practical large-scale distributed key generation. In: Cachin, C., Camenisch, J.L. (eds.) EUROCRYPT 2004. LNCS, vol. 3027, pp. 138–152. Springer, Heidelberg (2004)
9. Choudhury, A.: Breaking the $\mathcal{O}(n|c|)$ barrier for unconditionally secure asynchronous multiparty computation - (extended abstract). In: Paul, G., Vaudenay, S. (eds.) INDOCRYPT 2013. LNCS, vol. 8250, pp. 19–37. Springer, Heidelberg (2013)
10. Damgård, I., Ishai, Y., Krøigaard, M., Nielsen, J.B., Smith, A.: Scalable Multiparty Computation with Nearly Optimal Work and Resilience. In: Wagner, D. (ed.) CRYPTO 2008. LNCS, vol. 5157, pp. 241–261. Springer, Heidelberg (2008)
11. Damgård, I., Orlandi, C.: Multiparty Computation for Dishonest Majority: From Passive to Active Security at Low Cost. In: Rabin, T. (ed.) CRYPTO 2010. LNCS, vol. 6223, pp. 558–576. Springer, Heidelberg (2010)
12. Dani, V., King, V., Movahedi, M., Saia, J.: Brief Announcement: Breaking the $O(nm)$ Bit Barrier, Secure Multiparty Computation with a Static Adversary. In: Principles of Distributed Computing, PODC 2012, pp. 227–228 (2012)
13. Dani, V., King, V., Movahedi, M., Saia, J.: Quorums quicken queries: Efficient asynchronous secure multiparty computation. In: Chatterjee, M., Cao, J.-N., Kothapalli, K., Rajsbaum, S. (eds.) ICDCN 2014. LNCS, vol. 8314, pp. 242–256. Springer, Heidelberg (2014)
14. Feige, U.: Noncryptographic selection protocols. In: FOCS, pp. 142–153 (1999)
15. Fitzi, M., Hirt, M.: Optimally Efficient Multi-valued Byzantine Agreement. In: Principles of Distributed Computing, PODC 2006, pp. 163–168. ACM (2006)
16. Franklin, M.K., Yung, M.: Communication Complexity of Secure Computation (Extended Abstract). In: Symposium on Theory of Computing, STOC 1992, pp. 699–710. ACM (1992)
17. Kapron, B.M., Kempe, D., King, V., Saia, J., Sanwalani, V.: Fast Asynchronous Byzantine Agreement and Leader Election with Full Information. ACM Transactions on Algorithms 6(4) (2010)
18. King, V., Lonargan, S., Saia, J., Trehan, A.: Load Balanced Scalable Byzantine Agreement through Quorum Building, with Information. In: Aguilera, M.K., Yu, H., Vaidya, N.H., Srinivasan, V., Choudhury, R.R. (eds.) ICDCN 2011. LNCS, vol. 6522, pp. 203–214. Springer, Heidelberg (2011)
19. King, V., Saia, J.: Breaking the $O(n^2)$ Bit Barrier: Scalable Byzantine Agreement with an Adaptive Adversary. J. ACM 58(4), 18 (2011)
20. King, V., Saia, J., Sanwalani, V., Vee, E.: Scalable Leader Election. In: SODA, pp. 990–999 (2006)
21. Pedersen, T.P.: Non-Interactive and Information-Theoretic Secure Verifiable Secret Sharing. In: Feigenbaum, J. (ed.) Advances in Cryptology - CRYPT0 1991. LNCS, vol. 576, pp. 129–140. Springer, Heidelberg (1992)
22. Shamir, A.: How to Share a Secret. Commun. ACM 22(11), 612–613 (1979)

Statistics on Password Re-use and Adaptive Strength for Financial Accounts

Daniel V. Bailey, Markus Dürmuth, and Christof Paar

Horst Görtz Institute for IT-Security, Bochum, Germany
danbailey@sth.rub.de, {markus.duermuth,christof.paar@rub.de}

Abstract. Multiple studies have demonstrated that users select weak passwords. However, the vast majority of studies on password security uses password lists that only have passwords for one site, which means that several important questions cannot be studied. For example, how much stronger are password choices for different categories of sites? We use a dataset which we extracted from a large dump of malware records. It contains multiple accounts (and passwords) per user and thus allows us to study both password re-use and the correlation between the value of an account and the strength of the passwords for those accounts.

The first contribution of our study shows that users in our sample choose (substantially) stronger passwords for financial accounts than for low-value accounts, based on the extracted passwords as well as publicly available lists. This contribution has implications for password research, as some widely-used lists contain passwords much weaker than those used in the real world (for accounts of more than low value). In our second contribution, we measure password re-use taking account values into account. We see that although high-value passwords are stronger, they are re-used more frequently than low-value passwords – valuable passwords are identical to 21% of the remaining passwords of a user. Before our study, little was known about password re-use for different account values.

1 Introduction

Most online services rely on users to choose passwords for authentication. Conventional wisdom holds that users generally do not choose passwords that are difficult to guess. Several alternatives to passwords have been proposed, but none has found widespread use, as passwords are easy to deploy, scale to an Internet-wide user-base, and are easy to understand for the users. Alternative technologies have a number of drawbacks: hardware like *smart cards* and *security tokens* can be expensive to procure and manage for Website operators and can be perceived as an impediment to usability. *Biometric* identification systems also require extra hardware, can raise privacy issues, and many biometrics are not secret (e.g., we leave fingerprints on many surfaces we touch).

Research on password security started as early as 1979 [21], and a number of studies has been published since then. One important aspect is password re-use:

M. Abdalla and R. De Prisco (Eds.): SCN 2014, LNCS 8642, pp. 218–235, 2014.

As user accounts proliferate, users are forced to remember more and more passwords that must also remain confidential and hard to guess. In response, users often re-use the same password for multiple logins to keep the number of passwords they have to remember low [12]. When a re-used password leaks, then the security of all accounts using the same password is at risk. Even worse, a rogue service could collect login credentials (typically usernames and corresponding passwords) and test those at other sites, which is hard to detect for the user.

While it is known from leaked password lists that users choose weak passwords on average, there is some hope in the community that users choose stronger passwords for those accounts that are valuable[1] (see, e.g., [14]). However, this belief has never been justified with real-world data. Actually, there is very little data available on high-value passwords at all, which is most likely the reason why so little research has been conducted on the topic. However, this question is of importance, as a number of studies in the literature use low-value passwords as input. Arguably, research on password security is most interesting for high-value passwords, as these are most likely the target of actual attackers.

The lack of available data is one of the main problems in password research as, by their nature, passwords are meant to be confidential. For password re-use, most available studies use data collected in user surveys, where great care has to be taken to ensure ecological validity, see Section 1.1 for more details. Our data show the type of site influences the password strength chosen by a user – at least, for users of malware-infected PCs. As explained later, we feel our data provides insight into the behavior of average users as well. This work is the first, to our knowledge, studying real-world password data collected by malware.

1.1   Related Work

As early as 1979 it has been observed [21] that users tend to choose weak passwords that are susceptible to so-called *dictionary attacks*. This problem has been studied extensively since then and led to development of tools such as *John the Ripper* [7] and *HashCat* [13]. More advanced password guessers based on Markov models have been presented recently [22,30]. To increase the strength of passwords against guessing attacks, various strength measures for passwords have been developed [6]. Strength of passwords generated under different password rules were studied in [16]. However, with very few exceptions in the older literature, relevant research was conducted on passwords for low-value sites, and it is not known if users choose stronger passwords for more valuable sites.

Several studies examine password re-use. Ives et al. give an interesting high-level overview of password re-use [15], including some examples of actual damage done by password re-use. Florencio and Herley [9] present a large-scale user study

---

[1] The question which accounts have high value is another topic which is out of the scope of this text. We will use financial-related sites as high-value sites, which we believe reflects the intuition of most users. While from a security point of view, email accounts might be at least as valuable, as they are often used as fall-back security mechanism for other sites, it is unknown how many users take this into consideration.

on passwords including password re-use, where they collected their data from browsers running the Windows Live toolbar (from consenting participants). They could only test for exact re-use of passwords and get a moderate bias, both due to the study's design. They find that each user has, on average, 25 accounts and 6.5 passwords, i.e., each password is used for 3.9 accounts.

In a lab study, Gaw and Felten ask participants to conclude when groups of passwords are similar [11]. This approach is adopted to preserve confidentiality of participant passwords, but the resulting similarity measure is vague. They find between 2.2 and 3.2 accounts per password. Komanduri et al. measure the effect of password-creation rules [17]. When asked to create a new eight-character password subject to one of a set of rules, the resulting password had an entropy between 27 and 34 bits. In addition, they report on users' self-reported re-use. As rules become more complicated, the number of re-used passwords increases from 17% up to 33%. Dhamija and Perrig interviewed 30 people and reported that participants used one to seven unique passwords for ten to fifty websites [8]. Sasse et al. report that in a study of 144 employees, an average of 16 passwords was reported, but this was not limited to online activities [25]. Two other studies have based estimations of people's passwords through surveys. Brown et al. surveyed college students, finding an average of 8.18 password uses with 4.45 unique passwords [4]. Riley also used a survey to focus on online accounts, finding students had an average of 8.5 password-protected accounts [24].

Bonneau [1] used two password lists that both included usernames, allowing re-use measurement between these two sets. Both lists were hashed, so the hashes first needed to be cracked. From those accounts cracked in at least one list, 49% of users used the same password for accounts on both sites, however, this does not take into account those accounts that weren't cracked, and thus we cannot say what the actual re-use rate is. It seems plausible to assume that those passwords that weren't cracked belong to more security-savvy users and that those have a lower rate of password re-use, so 49% most likely constitutes an upper bound. Furthermore, in the same text Bonneau recognizes the need for a study on password re-use based on *account value*.

An industry advisory [28] considers password re-use by utilizing a browser plug-in intended to warn about phishing attempts against banking passwords that also detects re-use. They report that "73% of users share the online banking password with at least one nonfinancial website" [28]. However, not many details are given about the exact setup and distribution of the plug-in. In addition, to compare the results with other work we would require at least the average number of accounts per user they recorded. Forcing users to periodically change their passwords is a common technique to prevent attackers from using leaked passwords. Zhang et al. use a database of 7700 accounts to examine the difficulty in guessing the replacement password given the expired one [31]. They found in this attack model that 41% of replacement passwords could be guessed in a few seconds.

Table 1. Overview of the password lists we used

	Abbrev.	Size	Users	PWs/User	Avg. PW Length
Malware-List					
– total	MW	3531	1721	2.05	9.01
– financial	MW-Fin	177	134	1.3	9.1
– rest	MW-Btm	3354	1686	2.09	9.01
Mt. Gox (Bitcoin)	BITC	61,020	61,020	1	–
RockYou	RY	32 M	32 M	1	7.89
Carders.cc	CC	5062	5062	1	7.59

1.2 Paper Outline

In Section 2 we describe our datasets and the preprocessing steps we used. Section 3 studies the relation between password strength and account value. In Section 4 we study password re-use, concluding with some final remarks in Section 5.

2 The Datasets

This section describes our dataset along with some limitations.

2.1 The Malware Dataset

A username-password combination allows a thief to log into an online-banking account and, depending on further security measures, drain it of funds. Malware such as Trojans specifically target Web browsers and aim to capture the data entered in HTML forms. Many organizations attempt to monitor this situation, working with law enforcement, alerting affected banks, and publishing reports on emerging threats. To do so, they obtain some of this data for forensic purposes. As the malware captures all of the HTTP POST data, IP address, operating system version and so on can prove to be valuable clues on infection rates and locations. One of these organizations allowed the present authors limited access to this data. No additional malware output was collected to enable the present work. The dataset contains thousands of passwords captured by the Zeus Trojan in late 2012. We partition the Malware list (MW) into two (disjoint) subsets according to the perceived value to a user.

- **High-value accounts: Financial passwords (MW-Fin)** The first sample includes passwords for accounts at banks, insurers, brokers, and related financial services. An attacker takeover of one of these accounts has obvious financial consequences and therefore heightened risk perception on the part of the user. We selected the accounts by searching the domain names for financial-services related keywords in a variety of languages, as well as a number of known banks. In addition, we manually inspected the domain names to ensure accuracy. This yielded a set of 177 passwords from 95 different domains, however, the number of distinct entities/sites/... is smaller as a single bank may service several domains.

– **Lower-value accounts: Remaining passwords (MW-Btm)** This group includes all other passwords. This sample includes well-known email providers and social networks. This yielded a set of 3354 passwords from 1134 different sites; Facebook is the largest subset with 1163 passwords.

Perceived Value of Accounts. The perception of security risk is known to be subjective and based on several factors including dread of consequences [23]. The compromise of a user's financial account obviously carries real financial consequences for a user. Malware-promulgating attackers generally aim to take over an online account and drain it of funds – or perhaps to gather enough sensitive personal information to fraudulently apply for a credit card or loan (often called identity theft). We therefore group these financial-site passwords together (similar to [10]). This classification includes sites likely to directly enable transfer of funds including banks, credit-card issuers, stock brokers, and insurers. In addition, we include those housing sensitive information that would enable identity theft such as payroll processors and tax collectors. In fact, other accounts can be quite valuable to users as well, e.g., email accounts can be used for password recovery. However, for the overwhelming majority of users (except maybe celebrities, bloggers, and corporations) the compromise of a user email or social-networking account leads to practically no direct financial consequences. A common sentiment seems to be that "Nobody wants to read my private email."

A potential objection to this approach is that intuitively, restricting the high-value passwords to financial passwords leaves out other valuable passwords. However, we show in Section 3.2 that the passwords in MW-Fin are significantly stronger than those in MW-Btm. Even if some high-value passwords (not from financial sites) are still contained in MW-Btm, this means that the real difference is even stronger than we measured. So the error incorporated from this rather narrow interpretation would lead us to underestimate the disparity, reinforcing our main point.

Bias in the Dataset. There are two potential sources of bias in the dataset: First, we have a subset of the total set of passwords collected by the malware only, and second, this bigger set could be biased as it is collected by malware and infections are not necessarily uniform across all users. The sub-sample contains a wide variety of sites in many countries and languages, and represents a snapshot of the actual data available to criminals. Second, only those users infected by malware are included in our dataset. We feel the results will likely hold true for many other users given the widespread nature and infection methods of Zeus. According to industry reports, Zeus variants have been observed in the wild on Windows (IE, Firefox, and Chrome browsers), Android, and Blackberry, including one of every 3000 computers worldwide [27]. Most Zeus infections occur on PCs with up-to-date antivirus software. Zeus spreads through email attachments as well as "drive-by infection," where a user need only visit a Web site to become infected, thanks to a malicious JavaScript redirection. These properties to a certain extent dispel the misconception that malware afflicts only unsophisticated or careless users. The malware dataset does not include any captures from MacOS or Linux, which induces some amount of bias. However, Windows represents more than 85% of desktops accessing the Internet, so the bias due to operating system choice is expected to be small [26].

Furthermore, we expect the comparison of the strength of passwords in MW-Fin and MW-Btm (see Section 3.2) to be largely unaffected by these biases, as both lists are sampled with the same bias, and there is no indication that the bias is such that it affects both subsets in a different way.

2.2 More Password Sets

To relate our findings to previous work, we compare against several other sets.

- **RockYou (RY).** One of the largest lists publicly available is the RockYou list (RY), consisting of 32.6 million passwords that were obtained by an SQL injection attack in 2009. The passwords were leaked in plaintext, but all metadata like username was stripped from the list before it was leaked to the public. This list has two advantages: First, its large size yields precise information also about less-common passwords; second, it was collected via an SQL injection attack therefore affecting all the users of the compromised service, basically removing sample bias. These advantages have made RockYou studies quite popular in the literature, so we use it to compare our findings with previous work.
- **MtGox/Bitcoin (BITC).** Bitcoin is an emerging decentralized currency based on computation; several merchants accept these "coins" for goods and services, and researchers are studying it in terms of cryptography, privacy, and economics. Bitcoins can also be exchanged for other currencies, one of the biggest websites (at the time) providing this service was Mt.Gox. The password file containing over 61 thousand hashed passwords leaked online in 2011 [20].
- **Carders.cc (CC).** Carders.cc is an online forum where hackers would negotiate stolen assets like passwords and credit-card account numbers. In 2010, Carders.cc was itself subject to a hacking attack that exposed its database of 5,062 passwords [18]. Most interesting about this list for our purposes is the user population. Unlike general social-networking sites, this one catered to users who are (on average) both technology-savvy and security aware.

2.3 Ethical Considerations

All passwords analyzed in this paper were leaked by attacks in 2012 and collected in support of other efforts to track and remediate malware infections. No additional data was collected specifically to enable the present work. This fact means that practical attackers have already had independent access to our datasets for more than two years. It is not expected that the present work aids actual attackers.

Nevertheless, special care was taken to avoid our work leading to a new consolidated source of passwords for actual attackers. The Malware passwords themselves were stored in a private enclave away from typical corporate or academic networks. They were only available to researchers through a chain of proxies with a full complement of firewalls, network monitoring, and data-loss prevention tools meant to stop data exfiltration. Then, direct access was eschewed in favor of scripts that returned only statistics to the researchers.

3   Correlation of Password Strength and Account Value

One unique aspect of the Malware password list is that it contains passwords for multiple accounts per user, and those are sampled in the same way and with the same bias. A closer inspection reveals that it often contains passwords for accounts that are more valuable than others, which allows us to compare the strength of those passwords. These findings are relevant for several reasons: First, it allows us to test if "users choose more secure passwords for accounts of value", which is often expressed in the literature when weak passwords are discovered. Second, previous password studies are limited to the available data: collections of passwords from social networks or portals like Yahoo! [3]. By contrast, our study includes passwords directly used to protect financial transactions.

3.1   Measures for Password Strength

At a high level, we can distinguish measures that evaluate *resistance against a specific password cracker* (either by directly attacking them, or by using mathematical models to estimate their effectiveness), and approaches that consider the *distribution of passwords*. While the former are motivated by practice and model common attacks pretty well, they depend on the specific software tool and do not necessarily generalize well. The latter are based on mathematical models and thus have a clearly defined meaning and are (in some sense) optimal, but not necessarily relevant for practice.

Entropy Measures.   A number of different entropy measures have been used to measure the security of passwords. For an overview, as well as more details about the one presented here, see [2,3]. Guessing entropy [19,5] measures the average number of guesses that the optimal attack needs in order to find the correct password. However, a practical attacker is generally satisfied with breaking into a certain fraction of accounts, which guessing entropy does not take into account. *Partial guessing entropy* [2] (or α-*guesswork*) takes this into account.

For $0 \leq \alpha \leq 1$ let $\mu_\alpha = \min\{i_0 \mid \sum_{i=1}^{i_0} p_i \geq \alpha\}$ the minimal number so that the guesses cover at least a fraction α of the passwords, and let $\lambda_\alpha = \lambda_{\mu_\alpha} = \sum_{i=1}^{\mu_\alpha} p_i$ the actual sum (which is greater or equal to α). With these, partial guessing entropy is defined as

$$G_\alpha(X) = (1 - \lambda_\alpha) \cdot \mu_\alpha + \sum_{i=1}^{\mu_\alpha} i \cdot p_i \tag{1}$$

Intuitively, the first term is contributed by those passwords that weren't guessed in the allotted number of guesses, and the second term is contributed by those password that were. We want to express this in "bits of information" to be able to compare it with other measures more easily. This is done as follows:

$$\tilde{G}_\alpha(X) = \log\left(\frac{2 \cdot G_\alpha(X)}{\lambda_\alpha} - 1\right) + \log\frac{1}{2 - \lambda_\alpha} \tag{2}$$

where the "correction term" $\log\frac{1}{2-\lambda_\alpha}$ is used to make the metric constant for the uniform distribution (see [2] for a more detailed explanation).

We have two reasons to deviate from this approach. First, to approximate the distribution of X (i.e., the probabilities p_i) requires a *large sample set size* which is much larger than the Malware dataset; second, one can be interested in getting a more *comparable metric for a specific attack*. So we are interested in a combination of both, as we define in the following.

John the Ripper. A well-known and wide-spread tool for password cracking is John the Ripper (JtR) [7]. JtR uses a number of heuristics that show good performance in practice. It can be configured in a wide range, but in the standard mode of operation it performs the following steps. (i) *Single crack mode.* In a first step, JtR tries items like username and home-directory name both as-is as well as simple "mangling" modifications like appending digits or reordering letters. (ii) *Wordlist mode.* JtR comes with a dictionary of 3557 common passwords to try, along a set of mangling rules that are applied. (iii) *Incremental mode.* A mode that can try all possible combinations.

We used John the Ripper 1.7.8-jumbo-5, instrumented with an additional patch that logs the number of passwords tried. The Jumbo version supports counting of plaintext guesses as well as hashed passwords. The number of guesses by JtR is often seen as a good approximation for the practical strength of a password. As we are only interested in comparing the strength of different password lists the specific choice does not make a substantial difference. We measured the number of guesses needed for passwords in each of our lists. JtR can run for a very long time generating every possible password of a given length, so for practical considerations, we aborted JtR after a given amount of time.

For the Malware datasets, we ran JtR against every password. As the other lists contained substantially more passwords, we randomly sampled 1024 from each. The BITC list consists of salted, hashed passwords and so required substantially more computation time to check the validity of a guess. The plaintext lists required only the generation of a guess and not the hash. Experimentally, approximately the same number of hashed guesses can be checked in 10 hours of CPU time vs. one minute of CPU time for plaintext.

Experimental Entropies. We combine the theoretical entropy measure with real-world password-guessing tools to yield what we will call *experimental*

Table 2. Experimental Partial Guessing Entropy for several success probabilities, using John the Ripper as baseline as explained in Section 3.1. A dash means that fewer passwords have been cracked for the respective list, so the respective value cannot be computed from the data at hand.

	$\alpha = 5\%$	10%	15%	20%
RockYou	15.1	15.0	17.4	22.2
Malware-Btm	16.2	25.0	28.8	–
Malware-Fin	23.3	28.6	–	–
MtGox	26.1	–	–	–
Carders	14.4	13.6	13.8	14.0

guessing entropy. As discussed before, there are two main reasons why we do not use the above measures directly, namely that entropy measures require substantial knowledge about the distribution and thus a large number of samples to approximate it with sufficient precision, and second that the output of guessing tools is specific to that tool and hard to compare with other results.

To calculate the *experimental partial guessing entropy (EPGE)*, we use JtR to determine the proportion of passwords cracked for a given number of guesses (see, e.g., Figure 1). We then use these probabilities in Equations 1 and 2 instead of the optimal attack considered originally. (i.e., we replace the optimally ordered p_i's with probabilities from a realistic attack with JtR.) Note that the resulting entropy values depend on the guessing tool used, and are in general higher than the true partial guessing entropy, which assumes an optimal guesser. As our main objective is to compare different distributions, the EPGE suffices.

Statistical Significance. One potential concern about the Malware dataset is that the set is rather small (at least when compared with password lists such as the RockYou list with 32.6 million passwords), which leads to a higher variance of the results. We used an approach similar to that by Bonneau [3] to determine bounds on these effects. We sampled more than 80 uniformly chosen subsets of the RockYou password list of the appropriate size (3354 and 177, respectively), ran password guessing and entropy estimation (for both $\alpha = 0.05$ and $\alpha = 0.2$) just as for the Malware dataset, and measured the confidence interval for the level 95%. We find that the confidence intervals for a sample size of 177 passwords (as in MW-Fin) is ± 0.7 for $\alpha = 0.05$ and ± 4.4 for $\alpha = 0.2$, and for a sample size of 3354 samples (as in MW-Btm) is ± 0.35 for $\alpha = 0.05$ and ± 1.18 for $\alpha = 0.2$.

These (empirical) confidence intervals are determined from another list of passwords that might have different characteristics compared to the Malware list, and thus have to be considered carefully. However, as the differences in entropy that we will encounter later are substantially larger then these confidence intervals, they give us a reasonable level of trust.

3.2   Results: Malware Dataset

In the first experiment, we compare the strength of financial password (MW-Fin) to the remaining passwords (MW-Btm).

Running the Experiments.   We run JtR as described in Section 3.1 against the two Malware sub-lists (see Section 2), i.e., the Malware list filtered for financial passwords (MW-Fin) and the remaining (MW-Btm), the most interesting and directly comparable set of passwords. All passwords in these lists are available in plaintext, so no hash operations need to be performed and running time is no concern. Note that John the Ripper is highly customizable, with the potential for dictionaries and rules tailored for particular lists. This approach clearly gives the best performance in practice. As our purpose here is simply to *compare* guessing success among the various lists, the default settings will suffice. Our presented results do not reflect JtR's performance potential in absolute terms.

Results and Discussion.   Figure 1 shows the resulting graphs, plotting the number of password guesses on the x-axis and the fraction of accounts guessed successfully on the y-axis, Figure 2 shows a more detailed view for fewer guesses. Table 2 gives the experimental guessing entropy for $\alpha \in \{5\%, 10\%, 15\%, 20\%\}$ (along with the entropy values for other password lists we will evaluate in the following). From Figure 1 one can already see quite clearly that the different lists have different strength. This is substantiated by the entropy values in Table 2, where we see that, e.g., for $\alpha = 5\%$ we get entropies of 16.2 and 23.3, respectively. From the measurements in Section 3.1 we conclude that this difference is significant.

While this result is not surprising, prior to the present work limitations in the lists available to researchers served as a hindrance. This is because the differences may be more due to userbase, differing password policies, or other causes than a specific behavior on the part of a user population. With the Malware dataset and the two subsets MW-Fin and MW-Btm, we are finally in the situation to have several passwords sampled under comparable situations. In addition, we believe that the dataset has less bias than lists obtained by phishing. But even though the data is somewhat biased, both sublists MW-Fin and MW-Btm are biased in the same way, so the results for both are comparable.

One explanation for the difference in password strength could be that different password rules were deployed. This is hard to verify, as the passwords are from a wide variety of different accounts, and there is no efficient method to obtain the password rules that were in place at the time a password was changed. However, we are convinced that password rules do not explain the differences for two reasons: First, in general password rules are known to be a bad indicator for password strength [17,29], so we would not expect such a strong impact on password security. Other studies in the literature [10] find password rules are determined more by a site's need to be usable than the extractable financial value.

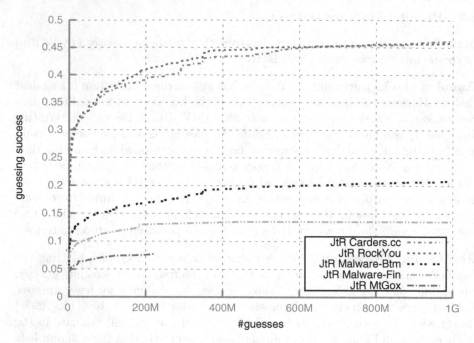

Fig. 1. Fraction of passwords successfully guessed when running JtR against various password lists

3.3   Results: Comparing with Other Datasets

More interesting insights come from comparing the results for the Malware lists MW-Fin and MW-Btm with other lists of passwords that are publicly available; this also allows us to relate our results to previous research. With the same parameters as in the previous section, we run the experiments again for other password lists: (i) the RockYou (RY) list as examples for a list of weak passwords that is regularly used in the literature that allow us to compare our results with other work, and (ii) the carders.cc (CC) list which represents a list of low-value passwords for a technology-savvy userbase (on average). Again, these lists are available in plaintext, so no hashing is required.

Results and Discussion.   We see that even the weaker passwords in MW-Btm are significantly more secure than those in the lists RY and CC (and MW-Fin is even more secure). For $\alpha = 0.1$ the entropy of MW-Btm is 25.0, whereas entropies for RY and CC are below 15.0, and similarly for $\alpha = 0.15$. (For $\alpha = 0.5$ the entropy values are still somewhat similar, which means that the weakest passwords are similarly weak in those lists.) This can also be seen in the graphs in Figures 1 and 2. (Our estimates from Section 3.1 suggest that most differences are significant.)

An additional difference between those lists of weak passwords and the MW-Btm list is that the former contain passwords from a single low-value site only,

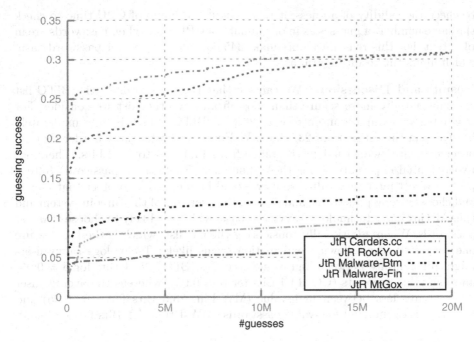

Fig. 2. Fraction of passwords successfully guessed when running JtR against various password lists (zoomed in)

whereas MW-Btm probably contains a mix of low- and medium-value (and potentially even some high-value) sites. Another factor that needs to be taken into account is that the Malware list contains data that was collected in 2012, while the RockYou list leaked in 2009. The enforced password rules as well as user's perception of password security have improved over those years, which explains the difference at least in part.

The list RY is regularly used in the literature both as example for weak passwords and as benchmark for work on password security, which might not be an optimal choice in light of our results.

3.4   Results: Comparing with MtGox

In a third experiment, we compare our results with the only other list of high-value passwords that we are aware of, the MtGox list, which is a representative for a list of high-value passwords for another technology-savvy userbase (on average). This list is, however, not available in plaintext, but in hashed form, which is a likely explanation why it has only rarely been studied in the literature. As only some passwords can be guessed in a reasonable amount of time, this results in a sample bias towards weaker passwords. In fact, this is one of the reasons why we use JtR, as we can directly compare results without additional bias. Running time for these tests is substantial. As we need to compute a hash to check the validity of a guess, it takes about ten hours of CPU time to check the same number of guesses as in one minute of CPU time when passwords are in plaintext. For this reason we only make 345,000,000 guesses per password hash, which limits the resulting graphs.

Results and Discussion. We can see that the passwords in the BITC list are substantially more secure than those from any other list we consider. For $\alpha = 0.05$, we estimate an entropy of 26.1 for BITC, which is only moderately harder than the estimate of 23.3 for MW-Fin, but substantially harder than all other estimates which fall in the range from 14.4 bits to 16.2 bits. There are two potential explanations for these difference: First, these passwords (often) protect direct monetary value, so users could be inclined to protect that money and choose strong passwords, and second, the userbase of the Bitcoin system and thus MtGox has a technology-savvy userbase, which are likely to choose stronger passwords. When additionally considering the CC list, which is the least secure one we tested, the following explanation seems likely: Technology-savvy users might differentiate between high-value accounts (BITC, 26.1 Bits for $\alpha = 0.05$) and low-value accounts (CC, 14.4 Bits for $\alpha = 0.05$), whereas the average user differentiates less between high-value (MW-Fin, 23.3 Bits for $\alpha = 0.05$) and low-value accounts and low-value passwords (MW-Btm, 16.2 Bits for $\alpha = 0.05$).

4   Password Re-use

Several studies show that users often re-use passwords for several accounts, to decrease the amount of information they need to memorize. However, re-use can be problematic, because single passwords leak quite frequently, which then puts a number of accounts at risk. Even worse, malicious website operators have direct access to a user's login credentials, and misuse will go unnoticed.

However, the studies available so far suffer from two problems: Most work uses *surveys* to answer such questions about re-use, which requires great care to avoid biased data (e.g., caused by the observer-expectancy effect). Moreover, people might not recall every site where they have registered (see Section 1.1 and Table 3). We are aware of two studies not using surveys: one [9] uses data that was collected for another purpose and was available only hashed (i.e., similarity could not be measured). The other [1] used two leaked password lists that both contained usernames, however, both were hashed and thus only those could be compared that were broken by a brute-force attack, which constitutes a bias towards weak passwords, which likely also have higher re-use.

A crucial aspect that has not been considered prior to the present work is that the security implications of re-using a password depend on the value of an account/password. (The only exception being an industry advisory [28] with unclear methodology and little explanation.) Re-using a low-value password at another low-value site can often be seen as a rational choice by the user, as creating a unique password for a large number of low-security sites is practically infeasible. What really constitutes a problem is re-using a password from a

Table 3. Comparing our results on password re-use with previous work. (A dash means that the values are not given/cannot be computed from the data.)

Source	#accts	#pwds	$\frac{\#accts}{\#pwds}$	re-use rate (RR)
Previous work				
Florencio/Herley [9]	25	6.5	3.9	12%
Gaw/Felten [11]	–	–	2.3–3.2	–
Komanduri [17]	–	–	–	27% to 52%
Dhamija/Perrig [8]	10–50	1–7	–	–
Brown et al. [4]	8.18	4.45	1.84	12%
Trusteer Inc. [28]	–	–	–	$(73\%)^2$
Our work				
RR_0^{all}	–	–	–	14%
$RR_{0.2}^{all}$	–	–	–	19%
RR_0^{fin}	–	–	–	21%
$RR_{0.2}^{fin}$	–	–	–	26%

high-value site (such as a bank) on a low-value site, as the low-value site is often easier to compromise. We will study this form of re-use in the remainder of this section.

4.1 Measuring Re-use from Random Samples

Previous work on password re-use often gives results as *average number of passwords per user* and *average number of accounts per password*. This is less than ideal, as it does not differentiate between the case where each cluster has the same size, or where the size of clusters is heavily skewed, which can make a big difference in practice. In addition, to make such a statement one needs complete knowledge of the user's accounts and passwords. This is problematic because depending on how much you press a user he will remember a different number of accounts he has, making the measure rather fragile, and when working with randomly sampled data there is no way to compare the results.

Therefore, we introduce a new measure for password re-use that we call *re-use rate*. The re-use rate gives the following probability: Choosing a user at random, and choosing two of his accounts at random, what is the probability that the two passwords for the two accounts are identical? As one would expect, a re-use rate of 0 means that no passwords are re-used, and a re-use rate of 1 means that for each user, all passwords are identical. Note that this measure can handle very well the situation when one has access to a subset of a user's passwords, provided that this sample is randomly chosen: Choosing a random password from *all* passwords or from a randomly sampled subset does not make a difference.

---

[2] This number is not directly comparable to the other numbers, as they only measured in *any* other password matched, which yields (much) higher percentages than the re-use rate.

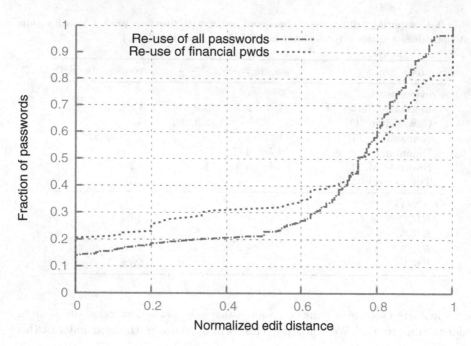

Fig. 3. Measuring the re-use of passwords for variable levels of similarity, given by their edit distance

Hence the re-use rate is a suitable measure for our dataset, where only a random sample of passwords for each user is available.

We are not only interested in exact re-use of passwords, but also in re-use of similar passwords. In practice, tools like JtR implement established concepts like *(normalized) edit distance*. The edit distance of two strings s_1 and s_2 is the minimal number of weighted edit operations required to transform s_1 to s_2. Typical edit operations are *delete/insert/substitute character* (weight 1); we add *prepend/append character* (weight 0.5) to approximate JtR's mangling rules. We normalize the resulting value by dividing by the length of the longer string.

To compare our results with previous work, we convert the numbers from previous work to re-use rate. Here, we have to make assumptions on the sizes of the clusters, which we assume to be of the same size. Writing A for the number of accounts and B for the number of accounts per password, the probability that we get the same password is $RR = \frac{B-1}{A-1}$. The results are shown in Table 3.

4.2   Results

– First, we measured *re-use across all passwords* of a user, regardless their assignment to MW-Fin or MW-Btm. These measurements allow us to compare the results with previous work.

– Second, we measured *re-use of financial passwords on other sites*, i.e., the re-use rate when, for a fixed user, selecting one password randomly from MW-Fin and one from MW-Btm. Such results have never been obtained before and are enabled by the specifics of our dataset.

For both scenarios, we considered both exact re-use as well as approximate re-use (such as "password" and "password1" for instance). For exact re-use across all passwords we got 14%, for a (normalized) edit distance of 0.2 we have 19%, and for re-use of financial passwords we got 21% and 26% percent, respectively. The results are summarized in Table 3, which also gives figures from previous work for comparison. The detailed graphs are given in Figure 3, where we plot the normalized edit distance on the x-axis, and the fraction of password pairs with normalized edit distance up to that bound on the y-axis.

4.3 Discussion

We can see that the re-use rates only increase slightly between the distance 0 and 50%, which is already larger than what is usually considered "similar". For example, the strings *"password"* and *"password-123"* have edit distance 20% while the strings *"use"* and *"re-use"* have edit distance 50%. This means that among people that re-use their password, most re-use it in the exactly same form. (Re-using with even small modifications would be a much wiser choice than exact re-use, as this would already prohibit simple forms of attack.)

Surprisingly, we find that re-use is more common for financial passwords than for all passwords, 21% vs. 14% for exact re-use and 26% vs. 19% for approximate re-use. We speculate that financial passwords are re-used more frequently because their increased strength represents a cognitive burden on the user, and this is something of a maladaptive coping strategy.

When we compare these results with the work of Florencio and Herley [9], we see that our results are very similar; because they determined a re-use rate of 12% compared with our 14%, we feel confident that these results are correct. Comparison with the study by Trusteer Inc. [28] is not easy, as they do not describe their methodology. They state that "73% of users share the online banking password with at least one nonfinancial site." How this relates to our results depends on the number of accounts they observed per user, and it is not clear how they handle the case where one user has multiple banking passwords.

5 Conclusion

In this work we studied two important aspects of password security that have received little attention previously. We used a dataset obtained by malware, which has passwords for multiple accounts for most users. This allowed us to compute meaningful statistics on two aspects of password security: first if users choose stronger passwords for accounts that are more valuable, and second on the re-use of passwords from high-value accounts on low-value accounts.

We found that password strength indeed *does* correlate with account value, a result we also were able to confirm with other lists of leaked passwords. This means that high-value real-life passwords are stronger than widely suspected, even though more work is required to see if they are actually strong enough. We were also able to show that users *do* re-use their high-value password on low-value accounts, a practice which must be considered unsafe, and we were able to confirm previous results on password re-use.

Our work also hints at further interesting research topics. First, it is interesting to find other meaningful sources for passwords that have multiple passwords for the same user, that are either larger or have a different/less bias than our present dataset. Evaluating these datasets would further increase the trust and the understanding of our results. Second, understanding the exact motives that lead to the observable differences both in password strength and password re-use is important. A reasonable method seems to be user interviews, which also might inform efforts to influence users towards better behavior, i.e., choosing strong passwords for those accounts that have high value, and to re-use only those passwords that have low value or are sufficiently protected on the server.

References

1. Bonneau, J.: Measuring password re-use empirically (February 2011), http://www.lightbluetouchpaper.org/2011/02/09/measuring-password-re-use-empirically/
2. Bonneau, J.: Guessing human-chosen secrets. PhD thesis, University of Cambridge (May 2012)
3. Bonneau, J.: The science of guessing: Analyzing an anonymized corpus of 70 million passwords. In: 2012 IEEE Symposium on Security and Privacy (2012)
4. Brown, A.S., Bracken, E., Zoccoli, S., Douglas, K.: Generating and remembering passwords. Applied Cognitive Psychology 18(6), 641–651 (2004)
5. Cachin, C.: Entropy Measures and Unconditional Security in Cryptography. PhD thesis, ETH Zürich (1997)
6. Castelluccia, C., Dürmuth, M., Perito, D.: Adaptive password-strength meters from Markov models. In: Proc. Network and Distributed Systems Security Symposium (NDSS). The Internet Society (2012)
7. Designer, S.: John the ripper, http://www.openwall.com/john
8. Dhamija, R., Perrig, A.: Deja vu: A user study using images for authentication. In: Proc. 9th USENIX Security Symposium (2000)
9. Florencio, D., Herley, C.: A large-scale study of web password habits. In: Proc. 16th International Conference on World Wide Web (WWW 2007), pp. 657–666. ACM (2007)
10. Florencio, D., Herley, C.: Where do security policies come from? In: Symposium on Usable Privacy and Security, SOUPS (2010)
11. Gaw, S., Felten, E.W.: Password management strategies for online accounts. In: Proc. Symposium on Usable Privacy and Security, SOUPS (2006)
12. Taiabul Haque, S.M., Wright, M., Scielzo, S.: A study of user password strategy for multiple accounts. In: Proc. 3rd ACM Conference on Data and Application Security and Privacy (CODASPY), pp. 173–176 (2013)
13. HashCat, http://hashcat.net/hashcat
14. Herley, C., van Oorschot, P.C., Patrick, A.S.: Passwords: If we're so smart, why are we still using them? In: Dingledine, R., Golle, P. (eds.) FC 2009. LNCS, vol. 5628, pp. 230–237. Springer, Heidelberg (2009)

15. Ives, B., Walsh, K.R., Schneider, H.: The domino effect of password reuse. Communications of the ACM 47(4), 75 (2004)
16. Kelley, P.G., Komanduri, S., Mazurek, M.L., Shay, R., Vidas, T., Bauer, L., Christin, N., Cranor, L.F., Lopez, J.: Guess Again (and Again and Again): Measuring Password Strength by Simulating Password-Cracking Algorithms. In: 2012 IEEE Symposium on Security and Privacy (2012)
17. Komanduri, S., Shay, R., Kelley, P.G., Mazurek, M.L., Bauer, L., Christin, N., Cranor, L.F., Egelman, S.: Of passwords and people: Measuring the effect of password-composition policies. In: Proc. Conference on Human Factors in Computing Systems, CHI 2011 (2011)
18. Krebs, B.: Fraud Bazaar Carders.cc Hacked (May 2010),
    http://krebsonsecurity.com/2010/05/fraud-bazaar-carders-cc-hacked/
19. Massey, J.L.: Guessing and entropy. In: IEEE International Symposium on Information Theory, p. 204 (1994)
20. Mick, J.: Inside the Mega-Hack of Bitcoin: The Full Story (June 2011),
    http://www.dailytech.com/
    Inside+the+MegaHack+of+Bitcoin+the+Full+Story/article21942.htm
21. Morris, R., Thompson, K.: Password security: A case history. Commun. ACM 22(11), 594–597 (1979)
22. Narayanan, A., Shmatikov, V.: Fast dictionary attacks on passwords using time-space tradeoff. In: Proc. 12th ACM Conference on Computer and Communications Security (CCS), pp. 364–372. ACM (2005)
23. Nurse, J.R., Creese, S., Goldsmith, M., Lamberts, K.: Trustworthy and effective communication of cybersecurity risks: A review. In: Proc. Workshop on Socio-Technical Aspects in Security and Trust (STAST), pp. 60–68. IEEE (2011)
24. Riley, S.: Password security: What users know and what they actually do. Usability News 8(1) (2006)
25. Sasse, M.A., Brostoff, S., Weirich, D.: Transforming the 'weakest link' a human/computer interaction approach to usable and effective security. BT Technology Journal 19(3), 122–132 (2001)
26. Owl, S.: Microsoft market dominance (2013),
    http://www.statowl.com/custom_microsoft_dominance.php
27. Trusteer, Inc. Detects rapid spread of new polymorphic version of zeus online banking trojan. Security Advisory (2010),
    http://www.trusteer.com/news/press-release/trusteer-detects-rapid-spread-new-polymorphic-version-zeus-online-banking-trojan
28. Trusteer, Inc. Reused login credentials. Security Advisory (2010),
    http://landing2.trusteer.com/sites/default/files/
    cross-logins-advisory.pdf
29. Weir, M., Aggarwal, S., Collins, M., Stern, H.: Testing metrics for password creation policies by attacking large sets of revealed passwords. In: Proc. 17th ACM Conference on Computer and Communications Security (CCS 2010), pp. 162–175. ACM (2010)
30. Weir, M., Aggarwal, S., de Medeiros, B., Glodek, B.: Password cracking using probabilistic context-free grammars. In: Proc. IEEE Symposium on Security and Privacy, pp. 391–405. IEEE Computer Society (2009)
31. Zhang, Y., Monrose, F., Reiter, M.K.: The security of modern password expiration: an algorithmic framework and empirical analysis. In: Proc. ACM Conference on Computer and Communications Security (CCS), pp. 176–186 (2010)

Efficient Network-Based Enforcement
of Data Access Rights

Paul Giura[1], Vladimir Kolesnikov[2], Aris Tentes[3], and Yevgeniy Vahlis[4]

[1] AT&T Security Research Center, New York, NY, USA
paulgiura@att.com
[2] Bell Labs, Murray Hill, NJ, USA
kolesnikov@research.bell-labs.com
[3] New York University, New York, USA
tentes@cs.nyu.edu
[4] Bionym, Toronto, Canada
evahlis@gmail.com

Abstract. Today, databases, especially those serving/connected to the Internet need strong protection against data leakage stemming from misconfiguration, as well as from attacks, such as SQL injection.

Other insider and Advanced Persistent Threat (APT) attacks are also increasingly common threats in the security landscape.

We introduce access control list (ACL)-based policy checking and enforcement system designed specifically to prevent unauthorized (malicious or accidental) exfiltration of database records from real-life large scale systems. At the center of our approach is a trusted *small-footprint and lightweight* policy checker (e.g., implemented as a router function) that filters all outgoing traffic. We provably guarantee that only authorized data may be sent outside, and to the right recipients.

We design and formally prove security of two access control schemes, with distinct security and performance guarantees: one based on authenticated Bloom filters, and one based on either long or *short* (e.g. 16-bits long) *aggregated* MAC codes. The use of the short codes, while providing a clear performance benefit, cannot be proven secure by a simple reduction to existing aggregated MAC tools, and required careful handling and a concrete security analysis. The advantage of our schemes is that they are both simple yet *much* more efficient than the naive MAC-based access control.

Our solution requires explicit designation of each record-attribute-user tuple as permitted or disallowed. We rely on shared secret key cryptography, and our system can scale even for use by large organizations.

We implemented and deployed our algorithms in an industrial system setup. Our tests mimic usage scenarios of medium-size DB (10M records) of telephone company call records. Our experiments show that we achieve high (scalable) efficiency both in the server and checker computation, as well as extremely low communication overhead.

Keywords: provably secure access control, aggregate MAC, Bloom filter, implementation.

M. Abdalla and R. De Prisco (Eds.): SCN 2014, LNCS 8642, pp. 236–254, 2014.
© Springer International Publishing Switzerland 2014

1   Introduction

This work presents a system for enforcement of data access policies in systems where typical volume of traffic or lack of public key infrastructure prohibits extensive use of existing trust management systems such as SD3, SDSI, PolicyMaker and KeyNote [13,5,19,4]. A central part of our system is a trusted (e.g., highly hardened) lightweight component that is present on the communication channel between the inside and outside of the protected network and verifies compliance of outgoing traffic with data access policies. The lightweight check is stateless with the exception of a long term secret key that is used in the verification process.

These features are critical in many natural deployment scenarios, such as when the verifier is executed on a router as an add-on functionality. In particular, ACL of non-trivial size *cannot* be stored on a verifier which is just a network element. We believe that none of prior work on ACL enforcement is simple and efficient enough for this type of deployment (cf. Section 1.3).

The capabilities of our system and its advantages compared to existing trust management solutions are best illustrated in a scenario where a database is accessed by a large number of users, each of which may choose to delegate partial access capabilities to untrusted and unsophisticated outsiders. An example of such a scenario can be a customer phone usage database system of a telecommunications company. The system is accessible both internally for multiple purposes such as billing, marketing, etc, and externally to the customers through an internet website.

In such a scenario, we aim to address two main threats. Firstly, the fact that the usage record database is accessible indirectly through a web server means that the web server must manage user access credentials, and make sure that queries submitted by external users do not bypass their access permissions to leverage the full permissions of the server. SQL injection exploits are an example of a situation where the web server incorrectly enforces user access control, allowing an attacker to extend his access privileges to those of the web server and gain access to private records of other users.

There is a wealth of work focused on designing access policy enforcement schemes that are as general as possible while maintaining efficiency. While some of the schemes are quite efficient and somewhat close to our model (e.g., [13]), such schemes inherently cannot take advantage of certain cryptographic techniques that can push the efficiency much further, which is needed for making the system practical for use in very high volume environments. (In particular, [13] relies on public key operations, which is inherently orders of magnitude slower than private-key primitives we rely on.) In this work, we present two protocols that take advantage of such techniques to provide an extremely efficient scheme for a set of basic database queries that are common in the scenarios described above.

More specifically, given a set of records and users, and an access control list (ACL) specified by tuples of the form (user id, record id, attribute id), we describe two methods for representing the ACL in an authenticated manner, and providing small and efficiently checkable proofs that a projection of the records is accessible by a specified user according to the ACL. A projection is a subset of records and fields within the records.

1.1   Overview of Our Methods

Our two main methods are as follows:

- **Aggregate MAC based solution.** In our first solution, the ACL is represented as a set of message authentication codes (MACs). Each MAC authenticates a single DB entry. The proof is then computed by using the MAC aggregation technique of [14,15] to combine the MACs corresponding to the projection of the records that is being returned to the user. As a result of the aggregation, the bandwidth overhead introduced by the proof is negligible – a single MAC. We further show how to use short MACs, of only a few bits of length, to highly optimize DB storage and access speed, while offering provable strong security. Computationally, our first method is as expensive as the trivial MAC based solution. The additional cost of aggregation is minimal, as we show in Section 4.
- **Bloom filter based solution.** Our second solution stores the entire set of records that is accessible by the user in a Bloom filter [6], and the Bloom filter itself is authenticated by a MAC. The proof now is simply the Bloom filter that represents the data accessible by the user. To verify the proof, the verifier checks that all records being returned are members of the set defined by the Bloom filter. This solution is applicable to settings where a small (configurable) probability of false positive is allowed.

Interestingly, the Bloom filter based solution imposes an extremely low computational overhead for the database server. This is due to the fact that, for each user, the proof is identical for all possible queries, and therefore there is no need for additional complex database searches. The price of the computational efficiency is an increase in bandwidth overhead as the Bloom filter grows with the size of the data accessible by the user, as well as the rigidity of the Bloom filter which makes changes to the ACL quite expensive. Indeed, recall that a Bloom filter is a data structure that represents a set of elements S by maintaining a bit array A such that $A(i) = 1$ if and only if there exists at least one element $s \in S$ where $h_s(i) = 1$ and h_s is a hash[1] of the element s.

Adding elements to the Bloom filter is trivially achieved by setting the appropriate bits in A to 1 and recomputing the MAC of the Bloom filter. However, if the size of the ACL for a user outgrows the capacity of the Bloom filter, the entire ACL must be available to compute a larger Bloom filter. Moreover, the authenticity of the ACL must be ascertained somehow. Requiring the database server to maintain a signed copy of the ACL is a possible solution. We do not discuss this issue further, and mention it solely to point out a practical limitation of the Bloom filter based approach.

In contrast, the aggregate MAC based solution allows efficient additions to the ACL list simply by computing MACs of the added tuples.

Revocation. We don't address revocation in this work. Rather, for the sake of completeness, we describe a possible approach. Revocation can be achieved by standard methods that are typically applied to public key certificate revocation. Suppose that the owner of

---

[1] Typically, the hash will computed by applying a cryptographic hash function, such as SHA-3, to the binary representation of s.

the data wishes to revoke some of the access privileges of a user. Clearly, just asking the database server to delete the appropriate ACL tuple or Bloom filter and MAC is insufficient in generality since there is no guarantee that a corrupted server will follow such instructions. (This simple approach would work, however, in the settings where server is not malicious and data leakage is due to misconfiguration.) It is also not clear that using Bloom filter variants, such as counting filters will help. To address access privilege revocation, we propose relying on existing techniques that are typically used in certificate revocation. In particular, if a dynamic accumulator is used, the checker will keep an up to date accumulator value, and verify for each ACL tuple or Bloom filter received that it is not present in the set defined by the accumulator. We note that, although the space requirements of most accumulator schemes are minimal, and in particular independent from the size of the ACL, checking incoming data against the accumulator will impose a significant computational overhead using current techniques. The difficulty in checking revoked access permissions is therefore a limitation of both our schemes.

1.2 Experimental Results

We tested the feasibility of our proposed solutions by using two data sets that share the same attributes as the data collected as voice call detail records (CDRs) from a large wireless carrier. We pre-processed the original data in order to encode the access policies (i.e. ACLs) using the Bloom filter representation and MACs. Then we loaded both the original data and the policy data into a MySQL database. To issue queries to the new database that include policy data, we implemented a query parser that reads the original user query statement and rewrites into a new query that includes the original query and an additional query for the policy data that will be sent to the checker. Once a query has been issued, and evaluated by the database, the results set of the original query and the policy data needed to perform the policy verification are sent to the checker, who then performs the check according to one of our two schemes.

We run two test queries against both data sets. Our tests were performed in a system setup approximating industrial deployment (with a powerful DB server and a fast network). Our results show that, with a slight storage overhead of up to 23%, both methods could be used for certain types of policy settings and query workloads. More precisely, in the cases when many users are granted access to a small set of records, the Bloom filter implementation yields better performance than the MAC approach in terms of query time and storage overhead. On the other hand, in the case when most users are granted access to a very large set of elements, the Bloom filter based solution will need much more time for checking the policy and for sending the data to the checker because of the large size of the Bloom filter, even though less time is spent for the actual query of the database. Thus, in the case of a lightweight checker that could be implemented in a portable device, such as a smart phone or tablet, with limited memory and bandwidth, the MAC solution will perform better if the users have granted access to very large number of records.

Consequently, our results show a clear trade-off between the MAC and Bloom filter based approaches. The MAC approach is more suitable for very dense access policies, while the Bloom filter based solution should be chosen for sparse policies.

1.3 Related Work

A rich body of work studies credential and trust management systems [13,17,16,2,5,19,4], but none is close in functionality/performance to this work on ACL enforcement. In most prior works, the focus is on providing an efficient way of describing trust relationships and then proving that a particular relationship holds in a specific scenario. Architecturally, the SD3 [13] system is closest to our work. In SD3, an access control policy is described using a high level language. During access, a proof is generated that the access was compliant with the policy, and is sent to an external checker, which in turn can verify the validity of the proof efficiently. Despite the similarity in architecture, the goals of the two works are very different. SD3 builds a distributed public key infrastructure, and focuses on providing an efficient proof checking mechanism for a high level policy description language. In contrast, our system assumes a shared private key setting, and does not provide the convenience of a high level policy language, but achieves very good efficiency if a policy description as an ACL tuple list is available.

Another avenue of research relates data exfiltration detection and prevention [10,18,20], and protection against related attacks, such as SQL injection [11,7].

Moreover, [1] considers the problem of misconfigurations, which is related to ours, however, the solution they provide is based on statistical analysis of past queries. Our constructions provide a stronger guarantee as we do not need to assume any statistical correlation among the queries.

Recently appearing techniques, such as searchable encryption (see e.g., Garay et al. [9]) are related to the problem we are solving, but do not apply directly. Indeed, the searchable encryption guarantees protection against corrupted server, but not against the client who is assumed to own the data in their setting. Even a recent highly scalable searchable encryption scheme [8] (and its enhanced variant [12] used in private DB search) are vastly unsuitable as a lightweight deployment. For example, the intermediate party in [8,12] is a 16-core Xeon machine with 96GB of RAM! In contrast, our system can run on just a few KB of RAM, for Aggregated MAC-based approach and a few MB for Bloom filter-based approach.

2 Preliminaries

In this section we discuss some of the required preliminaries, such as definitions and notation.

We now give the basic definition of Message Authentication Code (MAC).

Definition 1. *A* Message Authentication Code (MAC) *is a stateless deterministic algorithm* MAC $: \{0,1\}^n \times \{0,1\}^* \mapsto TAG$. *On input key* $k \in \{0,1\}^n$ *and a message* $m \in \{0,1\}^*$, MAC *outputs a tag* $\tau \in TAG$. *(Here* TAG *is the domain of tags, which depends on* n, *and is independent of the signed message length.) We will sometimes write* $\mathsf{MAC}_k(m)$ *to mean* $\mathsf{MAC}(k,m)$.

Let $k \in_R \{0,1\}^n$. *Let* $\mathcal{A}$ *be a polytime adversary with an access to the MAC oracle* $O(m) = \mathsf{MAC}_k(m)$. $\mathcal{A}$ *outputs a message* m' *and its alleged authentication tag* τ', *and must never call* $O(m')$. *We say that MAC is secure, if for every such* $\mathcal{A}$, $Prob(\tau' = \mathsf{MAC}_k(m')) < 1/n^c$ *for every* c *and sufficiently large* n.

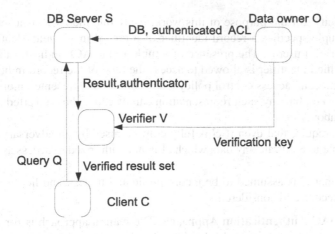

Fig. 1. Policy checking system overview

We note that MAC is a special case of the more general notion of message authentication schemes. MAC satisfies the strongest requirements of message authentication schemes [3], and is sufficient for our purposes.

An important notion of aggregate MACs was introduced by Katz and Lindell [14]. Later, Kolesnikov [15] strengthened the definition to allow aggregation of duplicate messages, which we include for reference in Appendix A.

3   Our Constructions

In this section we present all algorithmic and technical details of our underlying approaches, along with the security proofs.

3.1   Overview of Our Approach

As noted in the introduction, enforcing policy (ACL in our case) on the returned dataset is a highly desired feature in the DB management. In contrast with the traditional approach of hardening the DB server, we offer a complementary approach of employing a light-weight verifier, which is positioned on the outgoing channel and which formally ensures that only authorized data records are sent in response to the queries. This guarantee is formally proven in our system.

System Architecture. We consider the following architecture illustrated in Figure 1. The DB owner $\mathcal{O}$ owns the database $\mathcal{D}$, and wants a server $\mathcal{S}$ to operate the DB and respond to SQL queries from clients $\mathcal{C}$. However, due to the risk of compromise of a large system $\mathcal{S}$ we introduce a small machine (possibly even a small network device), verifier $\mathcal{V}$, which is responsible for checking that every record that is sent out is consistent with the ACL specified by $\mathcal{O}$ for the user that submitted the query. The ACL is too large to fit in $\mathcal{V}$, and hence ACL is encoded and authenticated in some form, and $\mathcal{V}$ verifies the authentication.

For simplicity, for the purpose of this work, we define the ACL as a set of tuples, where each tuple specifies a record identifier of a record in $\mathcal{D}$, field identifier, and a user identifier of a user $\mathcal{C}$. The presence of a tuple in the ACL indicates that the user with the specified identifier is allowed to access the field of the record indicated in the tuple. In practice, an access control policy would often be represented more concisely by the data owner, but any such representation can of course be converted to the ACL as described above.

Recall, we require that even if $\mathcal{S}$ is fully compromised by an adversary $\mathcal{A}$, he still will not be able to exfiltrate any data which $\mathcal{A}$ is not authorized to access as defined by the ACL.

We stress that $\mathcal{V}$ is assumed to be incorruptible and honest, and hence no security against $\mathcal{V}$ is needed and considered.

The Naive MAC Authentication Approach. The natural approach is for $\mathcal{O}$ to use a MAC to authenticate each authorized field-user pair, and store the entire set of MACs with $\mathcal{S}$. $\mathcal{O}$ then shares (discloses) the MAC key k with $\mathcal{V}$, so as to enable verification. The key k is not shared with $\mathcal{S}$ in order to prevent forgery of ACL tuples in case of corrupted $\mathcal{S}$. When $\mathcal{S}$ responds to a query, in addition to the result set, $\mathcal{S}$ sends to $\mathcal{V}$ the MACs of each of the corresponding fields. $\mathcal{V}$ only forwards a record to $\mathcal{C}$ if it successfully verifies MAC of each of its fields. (We do not discuss policy decisions such as what is best done in case of failed MAC).

The obvious disadvantage of the above MAC approach is the significant overhead of sending a MAC for each field of each record sent. For records with small fields consisting only of a few bytes, such as call records, the MAC transmission can result in factor $2 - 10$ overhead.

Aggregated MAC. Our first contribution is the design of the authentication scheme, which uses the recently proposed MAC aggregation schemes [14,15]. Firstly, instead of sending each MAC separately, $\mathcal{S}$ will send their sum (e.g., modulo 2^{128}), which, as shown in [15], guarantees verification and hence unforgeability of each individual MAC. Secondly, in terms of DB storage, we show that we don't need to store the entire MAC. Instead, only a few, e.g., 16 bits of the MAC are needed to achieve good security in our setting. This is because the adversary's forging attacks are "online", in the sense that $\mathcal{A}$ cannot verify forgeries other than by submitting them to $\mathcal{V}$, since only $\mathcal{V}$ has the MAC key. The online nature of the verification makes the relatively high probability of successful forgery acceptable since, once even a single forgery attempt is detected by $\mathcal{V}$, $\mathcal{S}$ can be blocked or flagged as potentially compromised. The use of short MAC also complicates our analysis, as we now cannot simply refer to [14,15] for security. Instead, we carefully re-prove the theorem of [14] for our setting, while tightening the analysis of the boundaries and probabilities.

Result set streaming. An interesting aspect of this approach is that $\mathcal{V}$ does not know whether the verification succeeded or failed until the entire result set has been processed by $\mathcal{V}$, and its aggregate MAC verified. We show how to avoid the delays and storage costs associated by buffering the result set by $\mathcal{V}$, as follows. $\mathcal{V}$ simply randomly generates a new random encryption key, and forwards the result set to the client $\mathcal{C}$ encrypted with this key. He then releases the key once the result set has been processed and aggregate MAC verified. We stress that the ability to stream the data as described above allows $\mathcal{V}$ to have extremely small footprint, suitable for deployment as a cheap network element or router functionality.

Bloom-Filter Based Approach. We also propose an alternative approach, with different security and performance properties (see our performance evaluation in Section 4). The idea here is for $\mathcal{O}$ to create a bloom filter BF per user, into which are inserted all the pieces of data (i.e. each field of each record) to which this user $\mathcal{C}$ is authorized to have access. Each BF is then authenticated with a MAC and given to $\mathcal{S}$. Now, when $\mathcal{S}$ needs to send the result set, he first sends the corresponding BF together with its authenticator, which $\mathcal{V}$ verifies and stores locally for processing of the result set. Then $\mathcal{S}$ simply sends the result set, each element of which is tested for membership in the BF by $\mathcal{V}$. If all elements are contained in the BF, the result set is forwarded to $\mathcal{C}$.

This solution is applicable to settings where a small (configurable) probability of false positive ϵ is allowed. Our analysis (Theorem 3) takes ϵ in account. We note that Bloom filter sizes/parameters are selected to reflect the acceptable ϵ; in case the DB or ACL changes, the filter might need to be updated (increased in size) to comply with ϵ.

3.2 Security Definitions

To enable formalization of the security guarantees of our system, we start with presenting the definition of security. Our definition is game-based, it describes an interaction between the players, where we say that the adversary $\mathcal{S}$ wins, if he manages to send to $\mathcal{C}$ an unauthorized record or a field of a record.

For simplicity, and without loss of generality, we will view the database $\mathcal{D}$ as a two-dimensional table, where each record (row) has several fields (columns). An Access Control List (ACL) $\mathcal{L}$ is a table which, for each record/field specifies the list of user names which are authorized to retrieve this field.

Definition 2. *Let G be the following game (experiment) played by server $\mathcal{S}$ and verifier $\mathcal{V}$. The game G generates a random secret MAC key, which is shared with $\mathcal{V}$. $\mathcal{S}$ generates a DB $\mathcal{D}$ and ACL $\mathcal{L}$ of his choice, gives $\mathcal{D}$ and $\mathcal{L}$ to G, who generates the necessary authenticators and gives them back to $\mathcal{S}$. $\mathcal{S}$ then generates a result set for a client $\mathcal{C}$, which consists of one or more records, each of which in turn consist of one or more fields.*

We say that $\mathcal{S}$ wins the game if $\mathcal{V}$ accepts the verification of a result set where at least one field value (defined as triple $\langle$row i, column j, value $v_{ij}\rangle$, with indices with respect to $\mathcal{D}$) is not authorized for retrieval by $\mathcal{C}$.

We say that the access control protocol Π *is ϵ-secure, if the probability of $\mathcal{S}$ winning the game G is at most negligibly greater than ϵ. If $\epsilon = 0$, we will simply write* secure access control protocol.

Discussion. Observe that our definition is presented with respect to one collaborating malicious client $\mathcal{C}$, while in practice there may be several such clients. We note that this is does not present a restriction in our definition, since our game is not with respect to a specific game player $\mathcal{C}$, but with respect to any (not directly named in the definition) user, who is described by the ACL generated by $\mathcal{S}$.

We note that our definition and system does not guarantee the absence of side channels, such as timing or set ordering. Indeed, a malicious C and S may agree on a system, where the intervals between the messages or the ordering of the records in the result set may encode protected information. We do not formally address these out-of-band and low-bandwidth attacks, but note that natural prevention or mitigation techniques can be employed here. For example, V can require that records are sent in the increasing order of their id, or V could introduce random delays in forwarding the messages.

3.3 Authentication by Aggregated MAC

We now formalize the Aggregated MAC-based construction, informally presented at the high level in Section 3.1. Let n be a cryptographic security parameter. Let H : $\{0,1\}^* \to \{0,1\}^n$ be a hash function modeled by random oracle.

Construction 1. *Let n be the cryptographic security parameter. Let D be the database, and L be the ACL owned by O.*

O generates MAC key $k \in_R \{0,1\}^n$. For each tuple $\langle row\ i, column\ j, value\ v_{ij} \rangle$, O generates authenticator $\tau_{i,j} = MAC_k(i,j,v_{ij})$. Further, for each client C and access right tuple $\langle row\ i, column\ j, C \rangle$, O generates authenticator $\tau_{i,j,C} = MAC_k(i,j,C)$. Finally, O sends all authenticators to S, which S stores. O sends the key k to V.

When S responds to a query by client C, S sends the entire result set to V. Further, S computes and sends to V the aggregated MAC τ of all the relevant authenticators. Namely, for each authenticator $\tau_{i,j}$ of tuple $\langle row\ i, column\ j, value\ v_{ij} \rangle$ and corresponding authenticator $\tau_{i,j,C}$ of access right tuple $\langle row\ i, column\ j, C \rangle$, S aggregates $\tau_{i,j}$ and $\tau_{i,j,C}$ into the current value of τ.

Given key k, V verifies the aggregated MAC τ and halts if the MAC is invalid. This is done by calling aggregated MAC's Vrfy function. If MAC is verified successfully, V forwards the result set to C.

Observation 1. *The verifier V in Construction 1 must receive and hold the entire result set before he can forward it to C as the verification of any part of the result set is complete only once the entire set is verified. The overhead of the storage is easily avoided as follows. When processing a query, V chooses a random key k_V, and, as he receives the result set, he forwards it to C, encrypted with k_V. Upon the verification of the validity of the result set, V sends k_V to C for decryption.*

It is easy to see that this maintains the security of the scheme, but allows V to have only small storage (a few keys and a few buffered data packets).

Theorem 1. *Construction 1 is a secure access control protocol (with negligible ϵ).*

Proof. (Sketch.) We show that an adversary S who constructs an accepted result set containing (at least one) unauthorized tuple, can be used to break security of AggregateMAC. Indeed, S is strictly weaker (i.e. asks fewer types of queries, for example, S cannot call the `Corrupt` oracle) than the adversary of the AggregateMAC game of Definition 4, and therefore, S is a valid aggregate MAC adversary. It is easy to see that an accepted result set with an unauthorized data entry generated by S represents a forged aggregate MAC (where the unauthorized data entry represents the the message on which MAC was never queried in the game of the definition of aggregate MAC). Since employed aggregate MAC can be forged only with negligible probability, it implies that the data exfiltration in such a system only possible with negligible probability.

We stress that in normal operation, we do not expect S to be corrupted, and hence it is beneficial to trade off some security against corrupted S for the performance of our scheme. It turns out that the following modification to Construction 1 achieves a very useful trade off. Consider a "truncated" MAC scheme, where only a few bits, say 16, of the output of the MAC are employed in verification. (Note that in generality, formally, any fraction, or even a majority of the bits of a secure MAC may not hold any security at all; for example they can all always be set to 0. One way of implementing the truncated MAC is to hash the entire secure MAC using random oracle, and then take the last bits of the hash. This will guarantee that these bits are as unpredictable as the entire MAC.) It turns out that using just a few bits for the MAC, for example, a 16-bit truncated MAC, gives reasonable security in our system. Intuitively, this is because the adversary is not able to see MACs of messages of his choice – only the messages corresponding to ACL-authorized entries are MAC'ed.

Remark 1. Short MAC may also be obtained directly by applying a random oracle to the pair (key,message). We chose to present our result for construction $H(\text{MAC}(m))$ to make the flow of the presentation more consistent. Further, $H(\text{MAC}(m))$ is often faster than $H(key, m)$ for longer messages. (Indeed, e.g., AES with precomputed key schedule is much faster than SHA256, especially with available CPU hardware support.)

We further remark that if MAC is based on PRF (e.g., $\tau = MAC_k(m_i) = AES_k(m_i)$), then short MAC can be obtained directly by truncating the tag τ to desired length, e.g. to 16 bits. The following theorem holds for this case as well, with an analogous proof and the same security guarantee.

Construction 2. *Let H be a hash function modeled as a random oracle. Consider Construction 1. Replace each use of MAC with that of ℓ-bit truncated MAC (denoted ℓ-MAC), implemented as the last ℓ bits of $H(MAC)$. Let the employed aggregate MAC be the additive MAC of Kolesnikov [15] or the bitwise XOR MAC of Katz and Lindell [14]. Finally, additionally require $\mathcal{V}$ to verify that no entry in the result set is submitted more than once (this is particularly relevant if the XOR aggregate MAC is used).*

For provable and efficient construction, we need to employ aggregate MAC which allows tight security reduction and provide a concrete analysis. Unfortunately, previous aggregate MAC constructions were only proven asymptotically secure, and moreover, have loose reductions. Further, we must fix the aggregate MAC scheme, since the theorem will not hold in generality for an arbitrary aggregate MAC. Indeed, in particular, a secure aggregate MAC scheme may choose to ignore the last bit of every MAC, which would affect the probability claim of our theorem. Thus, partly, our technical contribution in this section is to show that the chosen aggregate MAC schemes have no security loss (at least in our application) and provide the corresponding concrete security analysis.

Theorem 2. *Construction 2 is a $\frac{1}{2^\ell}$-secure access control protocol.*

Proof. (Sketch.)

We prove the theorem for the aggregate MAC of Katz-Lindell [14]. The case with the MAC of [15] is analogous.

While Construction 2 is based on Construction 1, the proof of security of Construction 1 does not go through as is here, since the probability of MAC forgery and MAC collisions is now non-negligible. In particular, the proof of Construction 1 reduces to the proof of security of aggregated MAC, which is not presented in concrete probability terms in either Katz-Lindell [14] or Kolesnikov [15] Another subtlety in the construction and the proof is that a malicious S can find tuples that MAC to the same value and substitute them.

We will thus present a direct and *concrete* reduction to MAC security, demonstrating a forgery of an ℓ-MAC whenever S produces an unauthorized result set which is accepted by $\mathcal{V}$.

Consider the adversary S who selects the DB $\mathcal{D}$ and ACL $\mathcal{L}$. We construct an ℓ-MAC adversary $\mathcal{A}$ as follows. Upon receipt of $\mathcal{D},\mathcal{L}$, $\mathcal{A}$ queries MAC-oracle to obtain MACs on all DB entries in $\mathcal{L}$. That is, for each DB entry $\langle i, j, v_{ij} \rangle$ and corresponding access right $\langle i, j, \mathcal{C} \rangle$, $\mathcal{A}$ asks MAC oracle for corresponding MAC. $\mathcal{A}$ then forwards all the MACs to S. In its next communication, S produces a result set and an authenticator τ. One or more entries of this result set is unauthorized according to $\mathcal{L}$. $\mathcal{A}$ then proceeds as follows.

$\mathcal{A}$ first determines the set of unauthorized entries, and considers any one of them, say $\langle i, j, v_{ij} \rangle$, and its access right $\langle i, j, \mathcal{C} \rangle$. There are two possible reasons why this entry is unauthorized: either the value v_{ij} sent is not the true value, or the access right $\langle i, j, \mathcal{C} \rangle$ is invalid (of course, both reasons can apply, as well). Note that $\mathcal{A}$ is able to determine the reason simply by inspection of submitted result set and from the knowledge of $\mathcal{L}$.

Consider the first reason, v_{ij} sent is not the true value in $\mathcal{D}$. $\mathcal{A}$ will then attempt ℓ-MAC forgery on message $m = \langle i, j, v_{ij} \rangle$. $\mathcal{A}$ will query the MAC oracle on all the remaining values corresponding to the result set (with the exception of m). $\mathcal{A}$ then computes the MAC tag $\tau' = \tau \oplus \bigoplus_i MAC(m_i)$, where XOR $\bigoplus$ is over all the authenticators used to construct the aggregate tag τ, with the exception of that of m. It is now easy to see that if the result set is accepted by $\mathcal{V}$ then τ is a valid ℓ-MAC of m. Further, τ constitutes a proper forgery in the MAC game, since $\mathcal{A}$ will not have asked the game for the MAC of m.

Considering the second reason, that the access right $\langle i, j, \mathcal{C} \rangle$ is invalid is analogous to the above. If both reasons hold, a MAC forgery attack via any one of them will work.

Finally, since the probability of forging the employed ℓ-MAC is close to $\frac{1}{2^\ell}$, it follows that the probability of success of S is close to $\frac{1}{2^\ell}$ as well, and the theorem holds. $\square$

3.4   Bloom-Filter-Based Authentication

We now formalize the Bloom filter-based construction, informally presented at the high level in Section 3.1. Let n be a cryptographic security parameter. Let $H : \{0,1\}^* \to \{0,1\}^n$ be a hash function modeled by random oracle.

Construction 3. *Let $\mathcal{D}$ be the database, and $\mathcal{L}$ be the ACL owned by $\mathcal{O}$.*

$\mathcal{O}$ *generates a MAC key $k \in_R \{0,1\}^n$. For each client $\mathcal{C} \in \mathcal{L}$, $\mathcal{O}$ generates a random Bloom filter key $k_{\mathcal{C}} \in_R \{0,1\}^n$. For each $\mathcal{C}$, $\mathcal{O}$ generates a Bloom filter $BF_{\mathcal{C}}$ by inserting, one by one, all ACL entries for $\mathcal{C}$, as follows. For tuple $\langle \mathcal{C}, row\ i, column\ j, value\ v_{ij}\rangle$, $\mathcal{O}$ inserts $H(k_{\mathcal{C}}, i, j, v_{ij})$ into the $BF_{\mathcal{C}}$, according to the BF insertion procedure. Finally, $\mathcal{O}$ authenticates $BF_{\mathcal{C}}$ and, for each $\mathcal{C}$, sends $BF_{\mathcal{C}}$ and $MAC_k(BF_{\mathcal{C}})$ to $\mathcal{S}$, which $\mathcal{S}$ stores.*

When $\mathcal{S}$ responds to a query by client $\mathcal{C}$, $\mathcal{S}$ sends $\mathcal{C}$'s name, $BF_{\mathcal{C}}$ and $MAC_k(BF_{\mathcal{C}})$ to $\mathcal{V}$. $\mathcal{V}$ verifies the MAC and halts if the MAC is invalid. For each result set entry $\langle row\ i, column\ j, value\ v_{ij}\rangle$, $\mathcal{S}$ sends $\langle i, j, v_{ij}\rangle$ to $\mathcal{V}$. $\mathcal{V}$ then computes $h = H(k_{\mathcal{C}}, i, j, v_{ij})$ and verifies that h is in $BF_{\mathcal{C}}$. $\mathcal{V}$ halts if $h \notin BF_{\mathcal{C}}$; otherwise, $\mathcal{V}$ forwards $\langle row\ i, column\ j, value\ v_{ij}\rangle$ to $\mathcal{C}$.

Observation 2. *Note that the BF function, mapping keywords to BF bit position, must be unknown to $\mathcal{S}$ (we use a hash function modeled as a random oracle keyed with a secret key, and this is sufficient). This is important as otherwise $\mathcal{S}$ may be able to verify by himself whether certain unauthorized tuples (or even arbitrary data sets) match the BF, and return them.*

Further, we need to include client-specific data, such as client's id, inside the private BF mapping function. This more subtle requirement is needed to prevent $\mathcal{S}$ from getting knowledge (or fully determining, e.g., in case where only one element is inserted in the BF) on what the BF indices corresponding to a DB entry are, and hence determine whether this DB entry will pass the BF check for an unauthorized data transfer. Such ability would violate our security definition for Bloom filters with non-negligible false positive rates.

Theorem 3. *Let ϵ be a false positive rate in the employed Bloom filter. Then construction 3 is an ϵ-secure access control protocol.*

Proof. (Sketch).

The proof follows from unforgeability of MAC of BF, generated by $\mathcal{O}$, and from the fact that there is no way for $\mathcal{S}$ to guess (other than at random) what are the BF positions corresponding to any specific unauthorized DB entry. The latter holds because of the random-oracle properties of H, and because $\mathcal{S}$ is never allowed to query H on the unauthorized DB entries.

Assume that the BF delivered to $\mathcal{V}$ is in fact not forged (probability of MAC forgery is negligible, and is hence allowed in the success rate for the attacker). Let $\langle i, j, v_{ij}\rangle$ be a data tuple, selected by $\mathcal{S}$ and unauthorized for $\mathcal{C}$. We argue that probability of its acceptance is at most negligibly greater than the false positive rate ϵ of the underlying BF. For this, it remains to show that $\mathcal{S}$ cannot predict which BF positions the entry $e = \langle k_{\mathcal{C}}, i, j, v_{ij}\rangle$ corresponds to. This, in turn, follows from the fact that the entry e was *never* queried w.r.t. H, since only $\mathcal{O}$ knows $k_{\mathcal{C}}$, and since e is not in $\mathcal{L}$, $H(e)$ was never evaluated. From the randomness of the random oracle output, it follows that the BF positions corresponding to e are unpredictable to $\mathcal{S}$.

4   System Setup and Experimental Results

In this section we show the experimental evaluation for a prototype implementation of the policy checking system. We report the results obtained by using the two methods to represent data access policy: the *aggregated MAC* and *Bloom filter* based approaches. We stress that our experiments replicate real usage scenarios of DB storage and access of a large wireless carrier.

4.1   Data

In order to protect user data privacy we used synthetic data representing voice call records with the same characteristics as real data recorded in a large wireless carrier network. Thus, we built a data generator that creates voice Call Detail Records (CDRs) using data distributions observed in real voice records, but independent of real CDR data. We generated two data sets, each with 10 million voice CDRs. One data set (Data Set 1) contains records for 500,000 users in a text file of size 484 MB, one call record (e.g. voice transaction) on each line, and approximately 20 transactions per user. This data set has the characteristics of data collected from 500,000 moderate usage voice users for a period of 1 day. By using this data set we test the overhead of the policy checking mechanisms when only few possible records have to be checked for each user. The other data set (Data Set 2) contains records for 10 users, approximately 1 million transactions per user. This data set has the characteristics of voice data collected over several months for 10 heavy users (e.g., organizations) of a voice service. By using this data set we wanted to test the overhead of policy checking for a large number of possible records. For both data sets, each record contains 6 attributes: record id (id), source number (src), timestamp (ts), destination number (dst), duration (dur), base station (bs). Table 1 summarizes data characteristics for both data sets.

Table 1. Data characteristics

	Data Set 1	Data Set 2
# of records	10,000,000	10,000,000
raw data size	484 MB	484 MB
record attributes	id, src, ts, dst, dur, bs	id, src, ts, dst, dur, bs
# of users	500,000	10
approx. # of records/user	20	1,000,000

4.2   Policy Representation

After generating the data, we generate the policy to access the data by using MACs and Bloom filter representations of the policy. Thus, we feed the original data to a policy generator that creates the policy data for both data sets. For simplicity, we assume that each user has access to only the records that list her as the source of the voice call. Thus each record can be accessed by a single user only. By making this assumption we reduce the overall experimental query runtime with policy checking enabled.

When using MACs, for each user we represent the policy by keeping a MAC value for each attribute and record id, and one MAC value for each user and record id. More precisely, we represent the policy "user A has access to record (row) $r = (id_r, src_r, ts_r, dst_r, dur_r, bs_r)$" by appending to record r the following fields: $H(id_r|src_r|key_A)$, $H(id_r|ts_r|key_A)$, $H(id_r|dst_r|key_A)$, $H(id_r|dur_r|key_A)$, $H(id_r|bs_r|key_A)$, $H(id_r|A|key_A)$, where key_A is a unique key for user A assigned by the data owner, and $H(\cdot)$ is a cryptographic hash function used to compute the MACs. In our experiments we use the first 16 bits of SHA-1 output for each MAC attribute.

When using Bloom filter representation we represent in a Bloom filter all the values of the records that the user is allowed to access. More precisely, we represent the policy "user A has access to record $r = (id_r, src_r, ts_r, dst_r, dur_r, bs_r)$" by inserting in the Bloom filter corresponding to user A, BF_A, the following items $id_r|src_r|key_A$, $id_r|ts_r|key_A$, $id_r|dst_r|key_A$, $id_r|dur_r|key_A$, $id_r|bs_r|key_A$. Additionally, for each user Bloom filter we store as the signature the value $H(BF_A, key_A)$. In order to make a fair comparison with the MAC case, for each user we select the Bloom filter size 16 times the number of elements inserted. That is, we represent each element using 16 bits in a Bloom filter and we use two hash functions, therefore each Bloom filter, for each user, yields an expected false positive rate of 0.0138.

4.3 System Setup

We set up the system as shown in Figure 1. We use a MySQL database as the "untrusted database" to store the data and the access policy hosted on MySQL server version 5.5.28 installed on a server with 16-core 2.93 GHz CPU, 86 GB RAM running openSUSE 12.2 operating system. This represents a typical hardware specification of a database system used in a production setting. We assume the user and the database are not trusted and can collude in revealing to the user more data than she is allowed to access. We created one database to store the data for all cases. We additionally created the following three tables. One table with original data $Data(src, ts, dst, dur, bs)$, one table with original and mac data $MACData(src, ts, dst, dur, bs, mac\_src, mac\_ts, mac\_dst, mac\_dur, mac\_bs, mac\_user)$ and one table with Bloom filters data for each user $BloomFilter(user, bloom\_filter, signature)$. We loaded the original data into $Data$ table, the data with MACs appended into the $MACData$ table and the Bloom filters for all users into $BloomFilter$ table. We built indexes on src attribute for $Data$ and $MACData$ tables, and on $user$ attribute for $BloomFilter$ table.

We built the Lightweight Policy Checker by implementing a *Query Parser* and a *Policy Verifier* in the Python programming language, as illustrated in Figure 2. We stress that the query parser is not a trusted component, and its corruption will not violate our security guarantee. The *Query Parser* takes as input the SQL query statement sent by the user, Q in Figure 2, and generates query Q' which additionally queries the data used in policy verification. The database processes Q' and Q and returns R' and R. R' is the auxiliary data needed to compute the policy verification and R is the result set of the initial query. If the policy verifies the result set R is forwarded to the user.

Fig. 2. Lightweight Policy checker

4.4 Experimental Results

We tested the system by running two queries with no policy checking enabled, with Bloom filter-based policy checking and with aggregate MAC-based policy checking. The first query (Query 1) retrieves all the durations of the calls for a user. This is a typical query used to calculate the billing charges for a voice customer. Second query (Query 2) returns all records for a user. This query is typically used to resolve customer service inquiries about billing or accidental service charges. Table 2 shows the data storage requirements for each policy method, and the runtime for Query 1 and Query 2 for no policy checking, policy checking using Bloom filters and using MACs.

Table 2. Experimental results. (R) = size of query result set, (R + ID) = size of query result set plus the size of record ids, B = byte, MB = megabyte

		Data Set 1 (10M records)			Data Set 2 (10M records)		
		No Policy	Bloom Filter	MAC	No Policy	Bloom Filter	MAC
Data requirements	Stored	484 MB	591 MB	598 MB	484 MB	579 MB	598 MB
	Transported	(R)	(R + ID) + 200 B	(R + ID) + 2 B	(R)	(R + ID) + 1.9 MB	(R + ID) + 2 B
Query 1 runtime	DB Query	5.34 sec	9.9 sec	12.9 sec	5.73 sec	12.3 sec	22.82 sec
	Verification	0 sec	0.03 sec	0.04 sec	0 sec	70.1 sec	8.84 sec
	Total	**5.34 sec**	**10.02 sec**	**12.94 sec**	**5.73 sec**	**82.4 sec**	**31.66 sec**
Query 2 runtime	DB Query	6.59 sec	11.09 sec	14.95 sec	7.3 sec	14.1sec	26.2 sec
	Verification	0 sec	0.03 sec	0.04 sec	0 sec	80.9 sec	16.5 sec
	Total	**6.59 sec**	**11.12 sec**	**14.99 sec**	**7.3 sec**	**95 sec**	**42.7 sec**

For Data Set 1, when using Bloom filters to store the access policy the storage overhead is about 107 MB representing that 22% more policy data is needed in addition to the original data for a total of 591 MB. Using the MAC solution requires about 598 MB in total, representing 22.5% overhead in addition to the original data. For Data Set 2, the policy data required for the MAC method has the same size as for Data Set 1, but the size of the data required to store the user Bloom filters is slightly smaller. This is the case because there are only 10 users in Data Set 2, thus 499,990 fewer user names and signatures to store than for Data Set 1.

The data required to be transported, which includes the query result set and the data needed for policy checking, is always smaller in size for the aggregate MAC-based method compared to the Bloom filter-based method. That is the case because the database will always have to send the user Bloom filter to the policy checker in addition to the results set when using the Bloom filter solution. When using MACs, the database will send only the aggregated MAC which is of size 16 bits (2 Bytes) in the experimental implementation. When using the Bloom filter solution the size of the Bloom filter sent to the verifier is approximately 200 Bytes for Data Set 1 and 1.9 Megabytes for Data Set 2.

We report the runtime of the queries for both data sets. We implement the lightweight policy checker as having two components: a query parser and a policy verifier. The query parser reads the original user query statement and rewrites into a new query that includes the original query and an additional query for the policy data that will be sent to the verifier. The time spent in reading the original query and generating the new query is negligible and we do not report it in the experiments. We consider the query runtime the time elapsed from the moment the user issues the query to the database until she receives the final result. Thus, a query execution time is composed of the time spent to query the database, DB Query in the Table 2, and the time spent to verify the access policy for the result set (which includes the time spent to transport the policy data). The policy verifier accepts as input the results set of the original query and the policy data needed to perform the policy verification for the user that issued the original query. For Data Set 1, we observe that the Bloom filter solution achieves better query runtime than the MAC solution for DB Query for both Query 1 and Query 2. This is an expected result because the database will spend more time loading the larger table MACData, that includes the MACs for the attributes, and XORing their values. Both solutions achieve almost negligible verification time because the result set is small. For Data Set 2, we observe that the Bloom filter solution allows faster execution of the BD query, because of loading less data and no need to compute XORing, but is significantly slower in policy verification, having a total runtime of Query 2 of 95 seconds, more than double the runtime of MAC solution and more than 10 times the runtime of the original query. In addition there is a possible significant unaccounted overhead for transmission of the large Bloom filter over network in cases when that is necessary. This result clearly shows that in cases when the policy is represented in a Bloom filter for a user with access to a very large set of records, the checker needs significantly more memory and data bandwidth. For all experiments the runtime of Query 2 is slightly longer than of Query 1 because there is more data to be processed for Query 2 both in the DB Query and the verification phase.

In conclusion, in the cases when many users have granted access to a small set of records, the Bloom filter implementation yields better performance in terms of query time and storage overhead. On the other hand, in the case when most users have granted access to a very large set of elements, the Bloom filter based solution will need much more time for checking the policy and for sending the data to the checker because of the large size of the Bloom filter even though less time is spent for the actual query of the database. Thus, in the case of a lightweight checker that could be implemented in a portable device, such as a smart phone or tablet, with limited memory and bandwidth, the MAC solution will perform better if the users have granted access to a very large number of records.

Acknowledgments. Vladimir Kolesnikov was supported in part by the Intelligence Advanced Research Project Activity (IARPA) via Department of Interior National Business Center (DoI/NBC) contract Number D11PC20194. The U.S. Government is authorized to reproduce and distribute reprints for Governmental purposes notwithstanding any copyright annotation thereon. Disclaimer: The views and conclusions contained herein are those of the authors and should not be interpreted as necessarily representing the official policies or endorsements, either expressed or implied, of IARPA, DoI/NBC, or the U.S. Government.

References

1. Bauer, L., Garriss, S., Reiter, M.K.: Detecting and resolving policy misconfigurations in access-control systems. In: SACMAT, pp. 185–194 (2008)
2. Becker, M.Y., Fournet, C., Gordon, A.D.: Secpal: Design and semantics of a decentralized authorization language. Journal of Computer Security 18(4), 619–665 (2010)
3. Bellare, M., Goldreich, O., Mityagin, A.: The power of verification queries in message authentication and authenticated encryption. Cryptology ePrint Archive, Report 2004/309 (2004), http://eprint.iacr.org/
4. Blaze, M., Feigenbaum, J., Keromytis, A.D.: KeyNote: Trust management for public-key infrastructures. In: Christianson, B., Crispo, B., Harbison, W.S., Roe, M. (eds.) Security Protocols 1998. LNCS, vol. 1550, pp. 59–625. Springer, Heidelberg (1999)
5. Blaze, M., Feigenbaum, J., Lacy, J.: Decentralized trust management. In: Proceedings of the 1996 IEEE Symposium on Security and Privacy, 1996, pp. 164–173. IEEE (1996)
6. Bloom, B.H.: Space/time trade-offs in hash coding with allowable errors. Commun. ACM 13, 422–426 (1970)
7. Boyd, S.W., Keromytis, A.D.: SQLrand: Preventing SQL injection attacks. In: Jakobsson, M., Yung, M., Zhou, J. (eds.) ACNS 2004. LNCS, vol. 3089, pp. 292–302. Springer, Heidelberg (2004)
8. Cash, D., Jarecki, S., Jutla, C., Krawczyk, H., Roşu, M.-C., Steiner, M.: Highly-scalable searchable symmetric encryption with support for boolean queries. In: Canetti, R., Garay, J.A. (eds.) CRYPTO 2013, Part I. LNCS, vol. 8042, pp. 353–373. Springer, Heidelberg (2013)
9. Curtmola, R., Garay, J.A., Kamara, S., Ostrovsky, R.: Searchable symmetric encryption: Improved definitions and efficient constructions. In: Juels, A., Wright, R.N., De Capitani di Vimercati, S., (eds.) ACM CCS 2006, October/November, pp. 79–88. ACM Press (2006)
10. Giani, A., Berk, V.H., Cybenko, G.V.: Data exfiltration and covert channels. In: Sensors, and Command, Control, Communications, and Intelligence (C3I) Technologies for Homeland Security and Homeland Defense (2006)
11. Halfond, W.G., Viegas, J., Orso, A.: A classification of sql-injection attacks and countermeasures. In: Proceedings of the IEEE International Symposium on Secure Software Engineering, pp. 65–81. IEEE (2006)
12. Jarecki, S., Jutla, C.S., Krawczyk, H., Rosu, M.-C., Steiner, M.: Outsourced symmetric private information retrieval. In: Sadeghi, A.-R., Gligor, V.D., Yung, M. (eds.) ACM CCS 2013, pp. 875–888. ACM Press (November 2013)
13. Jim, T.: Sd3: A trust management system with certified evaluation. In: Proceedings of the 2001 IEEE Symposium on Security and Privacy, S&P 2001, pp. 106–115. IEEE (2001)
14. Katz, J., Lindell, A.Y.: Aggregate message authentication codes. In: Malkin, T. (ed.) CT-RSA 2008. LNCS, vol. 4964, pp. 155–169. Springer, Heidelberg (2008)
15. Kolesnikov, V.: MAC aggregation with message multiplicity. In: Visconti, I., De Prisco, R. (eds.) SCN 2012. LNCS, vol. 7485, pp. 445–460. Springer, Heidelberg (2012)
16. Li, N., Mitchell, J.C.: Rt: A role-based trust-management framework. In: Proceedings of DARPA Information Survivability Conference and Exposition 2003, vol. 1, pp. 201–212. IEEE (2003)

17. Li, N., Mitchell, J.C., Winsborough, W.H.: Design of a role-based trust-management framework. In: Proceedings of the 2002 IEEE Symposium on Security and Privacy 2002, pp. 114–130. IEEE (2002)
18. Liu, Y., Corbett, C., Chiang, K., Archibald, R., Mukherjee, B., Ghosal, D.: Sidd: A framework for detecting sensitive data exfiltration by an insider attack. In: 42nd Hawaii International Conference on System Sciences, HICSS 2009, pp. 1–10. IEEE (2009)
19. Rivest, R.L., Lampson, B.: SDSI – a simple distributed security infrastructure. In: Crypto (1996)
20. Zander, S., Armitage, G., Branch, P.: A survey of covert channels and countermeasures in computer network protocols. IEEE Communications Surveys & Tutorials 9(3), 44–57 (2007)

A   Aggregate MAC

An important notion of aggregate MACs was introduced by Katz and Lindell [14]. Later, Kolesnikov [15] strengthened the definition to allow aggregation of duplicate messages, which we include for reference below.

Definition 3. *(Aggregate MAC with Message Multiplicity.) An aggregate message authentication code is a tuple of probabilistic polynomial-time algorithms* (MAC, Agg, Vrfy) *such that:*

- *Authentication algorithm* MAC: *upon input a key* $k \in \{0,1\}^n$ *and a message* $m \in \{0,1\}^*$, *algorithm* MAC *outputs a tag* τ.
- *Aggregation algorithm* Agg: *upon input two sets of message/identifier pairs* $M^1 = \{(m_1^1, \mathrm{id}_1^1), ..., (m_{i_1}^1, \mathrm{id}_{i_1}^1)\}$, $M^2 = \{(m_1^2, \mathrm{id}_1^2), ..., (m_{i_2}^2, \mathrm{id}_{i_2}^2)\}$, *and associated tags* τ^1, τ^2, *algorithm* Agg *outputs a new tag* τ. *We stress that* Agg *is unkeyed.*
- *Verification algorithm* Vrfy: *upon receiving a set of key/identifier pairs* $\{(k_1, \mathrm{id}_1), ..., (k_t, \mathrm{id}_t)\}$, *a set (possibly with multiplicity) of message/identifier pairs* $M = \{(m_1, id_1'), ..., (m_i, id_i')\}$, *and a tag* τ, *algorithm* Vrfy *outputs a single bit, with '1' denoting acceptance and '0' denoting rejection. We denote this procedure by* $\mathrm{Vrfy}_{(k_1, \mathrm{id}_1), ..., (k_n, \mathrm{id}_t)}(M, \tau)$. *(In normal usage,* $id_i' \in \{\mathrm{id}_1, ..., \mathrm{id}_t\}$ *for all* i.)

The following correctness conditions are required to hold:

- *For all* $k, \mathrm{id}, m \in \{0,1\}^*$, *it holds that* $\mathrm{Vrfy}_{k, id}(m, \mathrm{MAC}_k(m)) = 1$. *(This is essentially the correctness condition for standard MACs.)*
- *(Aggregation of MAC tags enables correct verification.) Let* M^1, M^2 *be two sets of message/identifier pairs (possibly with element multiplicity and further possibly with* $M^1 \cap M^2 \neq \emptyset$), *and let* $M = M^1 \cup M^2$, *with element multiplicity. If:*
  1. $\mathrm{Vrfy}_{(k_1, \mathrm{id}_1), ..., (k_t, \mathrm{id}_t)}(M^1, \tau^1) = 1$, *and*
  2. $\mathrm{Vrfy}_{(k_1, \mathrm{id}_1), ..., (k_t, \mathrm{id}_t)}(M^2, \tau^2) = 1$, *then*
  $\mathrm{Vrfy}_{(k_1, \mathrm{id}_1), ..., (k_n, \mathrm{id}_n)}(M, \mathrm{Agg}(M^1, M^2, \tau^1, \tau^2)) = 1$.

We now present the security part of the definition.

Definition 4. *(Security properties of Aggregate MAC with Message Multiplicity.) Let* $\mathcal{A}$ *be a non-uniform probabilistic polynomial-time adversary, and consider the following experiment involving* $\mathcal{A}$ *and parameterized by a security parameter* n:

- *Key generation: Keys $k_1, ..., k_t \in \{0,1\}^n$, for $t = poly(n)$, are generated.*
- *Attack phase: $\mathcal{A}$ may query the following oracles:*

  - *Message authentication oracle* Mac: *On input (i, m), the oracle returns* $\mathsf{MAC}_{k_i}(m)$.
  - *Corruption oracle* Corrupt: *upon input i, the oracle returns k_i.*

- *Output: The adversary $\mathcal{A}$ outputs a set of message/identifier pairs $M = \{(m_1, \mathrm{id}_1), ..., (m_i, \mathrm{id}_i)\}$ (possibly with multiplicity) and a tag τ.*
- *Success determination: We say $\mathcal{A}$ succeeds if (1) $\mathsf{Vrfy}_{k_1,...,k_t}(M, \tau) = 1$ and (2) there exists a pair $(m_{i*}, \mathrm{id}_{i*}) \in M$ such that*
  1. *$\mathcal{A}$ never queried* Corrupt(id_{i*}), *and*
  2. *$\mathcal{A}$ never queried* Mac$(\mathrm{id}_{i*}, m_{i*})$.

We say that the aggregate MAC scheme (MAC, Agg, Vrfy) is secure if for all $t = poly(n)$ and all non-uniform probabilistic polynomial-time adversaries $\mathcal{A}$, the probability that $\mathcal{A}$ succeeds in the above experiment is negligible.

EyeDecrypt —
Private Interactions in Plain Sight

Andrea G. Forte[1], Juan A. Garay[2,*], Trevor Jim[1], and Yevgeniy Vahlis[3,*]

[1] AT&T Labs, New York, NY USA
{forte,trevor}@att.com
[2] Yahoo Labs, Sunnyvale, CA USA
garay@yahoo-inc.com
[3] Byonim, Toronto, Canada
evahlis@gmail.com

Abstract. We introduce *EyeDecrypt*, a novel technology for privacy-preserving human-computer interaction. *EyeDecrypt* allows only authorized users to decipher data shown on a display, such as an electronic screen or plain printed material; in the former case, the authorized user can then interact with the system (*e.g.*, by pressing buttons on the screen), without revealing the details of the interaction to others who may be watching or to the system itself.

The user views the decrypted data on a closely-held personal device, such as a pair of smart glasses with a camera and heads-up display, or a smartphone. The data is displayed as an image overlay on the personal device, which we assume cannot be viewed by the adversary. The overlay is a form of augmented reality that not only allows the user to view the protected data, but also to securely enter input into the system by randomizing the input interface.

EyeDecrypt consists of three main components: a *visualizable encryption* scheme; a dataglyph-based visual encoding scheme for the ciphertexts generated by the encryption scheme; and a randomized input and augmented reality scheme that protects user inputs without harming usability. We describe all aspects of *EyeDecrypt*, from security definitions, constructions and analysis, to implementation details of a prototype developed on a smartphone.

1 Introduction

Nowadays personal and sensitive information can be accessed at any time, anywhere, thanks to the widespread adoption of smartphones and other wireless technologies such as LTE and IEEE 802.11 (i.e., WiFi). This always-connected paradigm, however, comes at the expense of reduced privacy. Users access sensitive information on the train, on the subway and in coffee shops, and use public computers in airports, libraries and other Internet access points. Sensitive information is at the mercy of anyone in the user's proximity and of any piece of malware running on trusted and untrusted devices such as a personal laptop or a computer in a library. This applies not just to the content displayed on a monitor but also to the interaction users have with the system (e.g., typing a password or a social security number). Someone looking at the keyboard

---

* Work done while at AT&T Labs.

M. Abdalla and R. De Prisco (Eds.): SCN 2014, LNCS 8642, pp. 255–276, 2014.

as one types in a password is as bad as showing the password in clear text on a login page.

We introduce *EyeDecrypt*, a technology aimed at protecting content displayed to the user as well as interactions the user has with the system (e.g., by typing). In particular, we do not trust the user's environment (e.g., "shoulder surfing"), nor do we trust the device the user interacts with as it may have been compromised (e.g., keyloggers).

In *EyeDecrypt*, the content provider encrypts and authenticates content and sends it to the device the user requested the content from (e.g., laptop, cellphone, ATM). Because the content arrives already encrypted to this untrusted device, any piece of malware running on it would not be able to learn anything meaningful about the content being displayed to the user; the user is then able to retrieve the content through her personal device (running the *EyeDecrypt* app). Similarly, the user interacts with the untrusted device using *EyeDecrypt* so that only the remote content provider learns the actual inputs provided by the user during the interaction (e.g., password or PIN code). A piece of malware such as a keylogger running on the untrusted device would not be able to learn what the user has typed. Figure 1 presents a basic system overview; the "untrusted device" (which we sometimes will just call the "display") represents the device the user requests content from and interacts with.

Let us now provide some intuition on how *EyeDecrypt* works at a high level. If we print a document with extremely small fonts, this will appear as a collection of dots with no meaning. If, however, we take a very powerful magnifying lens, we will be able to read the part of the document right underneath the lens; further, by moving the lens around, we will be able to read the whole document. Anyone without the magnifying lens (i.e., a shoulder-surfer) will see just dots. *EyeDecrypt* provides a similar experience.

In *EyeDecrypt* content is encrypted and visually encoded so that it appears as some pattern of dots, lines or other shape to anyone looking at it. In order to be able to decrypt such document or parts of it, users will have to use the *EyeDecrypt* app on their personal device (e.g., smartphone, Google Glass). Such app enables users to use the camera on their personal device as the "magnifying lens" described earlier. By leveraging the smartphone camera, for example, the *EyeDecrypt* app captures a part of the encrypted content, decrypts it and overlays the decrypted content on top of the camera view on the personal device—a form of augmented reality. By moving the smartphone around over the document, users will capture, decrypt and display different parts of the document. One key difference with the magnifying lens example is that the *EyeDecrypt* app will be able to decrypt a document only if it has the correct cryptographic keys for that document or that content provider. Just the *EyeDecrypt* app by itself is not enough to decrypt content.

Importantly, *EyeDecrypt* also protects users' interactions with the system. For example, in the case of a keyboard, a randomized keyboard layout can be encrypted and displayed to the user together with other encrypted content. The *EyeDecrypt* app will decrypt all content including this randomized keyboard layout and will superimpose such layout on the camera view as an overlay on the actual physical keyboard (i.e., using augmented reality). In doing so, there is now a random mapping between keys of the physical keyboard and keys of the randomized layout that the user can see. Any onlooker would see the user pressing, say, the 'A' key on the physical keyboard without

Fig. 1. System view   **Fig. 2.** Prototype view

knowing to which value it would actually map to in the randomized layout. In particular, the random mapping between physical keyboard and virtual keyboard would be known only to the user, the *EyeDecrypt* app and to the remote server that encrypted the content (see Figure 1).

The untrusted device on which the encrypted document is displayed would not be aware of such mapping. Because of this, even a keylogger running on the untrusted device the user is interacting with, would not be able to learn the actual key values inputted by the user.

As mentioned above, *EyeDecrypt* aims at protecting against attacks on content displayed to the user as well as on information sent by the user (e.g., by typing). Such attacks may be due to shoulder surfing as well as to malware. While *EyeDecrypt* can leverage any device equipped with a camera, the type of device is important as different types of devices make *EyeDecrypt* more or less effective depending on the threat scenario. Let us look at a few settings.

In the most general case of shoulder surfing, the attacker can be anywhere in the victim's surroundings. In such a case, displaying decrypted content on a device such as a smartphone does not completely remove the possibility of someone being able to glance at the smaller screen of the phone even though the smaller screen of the phone does make it harder. A better solution in this scenario would be to use *EyeDecrypt* with a device such as Google Glass where the screen is very small and close to the eyes of the user making a shoulder-surfing attack much harder.

In a different type of shoulder surfing attack, the attacker has installed a small fixed hidden camera in close proximity of an ATM keypad so as to film the hands of users as they enter their PIN code. In such a scenario, a solution based on using *EyeDecrypt* with a smartphone would be perfectly fine as the hidden camera would not be able to capture the screen of the smartphone[1]. Similarly, using *EyeDecrypt* with a smartphone would be perfectly suitable to protect against an attack involving malware such as a keylogger.

When thinking about a shoulder-surfing attack it is natural to ask, "Why not just display content in a head-mounted display without any encryption?" The answer is that this would prevent shoulder surfing, but it assumes that the device that the head-mounted display is plugged into can be trusted. It does not help in the more difficult case of a modified ATM or compromised public terminal.

---

[1] Naturally, we assume the user to be security conscious so as not to position the phone too close to the ATM keypad.

Another idea is to encrypt content at the server, send it to the untrusted device, and have the untrusted device forward it to the user's trusted personal device via wireless transmission, instead of using *EyeDecrypt*'s visual channel. This is definitely a viable solution and has its advantages, such as higher bandwidth. However, it has two significant downsides.

First, both the personal device and the untrusted device need to be equipped with the same wireless technology. It would not work, for example, with existing ATMs, which do not employ Bluetooth or WiFi. In contrast, *EyeDecrypt* works on any personal device equipped with a camera, and it makes no assumptions about the connectivity of the untrusted device; *EyeDecrypt* can work with existing ATMs, without requiring a hardware upgrade.

Fig. 3. EyeDecrypt overview

Second, wireless communication requires *secure pairing*. As in the ATM case, it may be that the user has never interacted with the public device before. Pairing is required to be sure that the personal device is communicating with the intended public device, and not some other device in the vicinity. Secure pairing by itself is a hard problem and one of the devices being untrusted (i.e., possibly misbehaving) makes it much harder. *EyeDecrypt* does not require pairing—the user knows where she is pointing her camera—making the whole process much more secure and user-friendly. Notably, most of the secure pairing solutions that have been proposed involve use of the visual channel, for exactly this reason. In other words, use of the wireless channel in these scenarios already requires some mechanism like *EyeDecrypt*. We discuss secure pairing in Section 6.

Lastly, *EyeDecrypt* also works with printed content such as passports, bank statements, medical records and any other type of sensitive material. If the human eye can see it, *EyeDecrypt* can protect it.

EyeDecrypt consists of three main components: an encryption mechanism which we term *visualizable encryption*; a suitable *visual data encoding* scheme; and a combination of augmented reality and randomization for secure input. Figure 3 shows how content is encrypted and then visually encoded.

Visualizable encryption is distinct from ordinary encryption in that information is captured incrementally, frame-by-frame, and even block-by-block within a frame, in a pan-and-zoom fashion. In addition, our notion of security refers to the security of the "*EyeDecrypt* activity" and not just to the security of the encryption scheme. As such, it must also take into account what the adversary is able to observe—not only ciphertext, but also the user's interaction (e.g., gesticulation) with the system. Thus, formally defining the security of these new applications is important, in particular since our security notion does *not* directly reduce to an encryption scheme's, and can become the basis for the development of such technologies in the future. As important is the fact that our new notion and scheme are achievable (resp., realizable) using (the practical instantiations) of basic cryptographic tools, such as a pseudorandom function generator (PRFG), a collision resistant hash function and an existentially unforgeable message authentication code (MAC) (cf. Section 3).

EyeDecrypt is symmetric key-based, and the cryptographic keys needed for decryption and authentication are provisioned and directly shared between the remote content provider and the *EyeDecrypt* app running on the user's personal device. In particular, the untrusted device *does not* have access to the keys. In the ATM scenario, for example, the keys would be shared between the bank's server, which would act as the remote content provider, and the *EyeDecrypt* app running on the user's personal device. The ATM, being untrusted, would *not* have access to the keys. Thus, the key provisioning phase is the only time at which *EyeDecrypt* requires network connectivity in order for the *EyeDecrypt* app to communicate privately with the remote content provider. For everything else, *EyeDecrypt* does not require it, making it suitable for very high-security environments where network connectivity may not be permitted.

EyeDecrypt can use any type of visual encoding (e.g., QR codes [13], Data Matrices [12], Dataglyphs [29]) as long as it satisfies some basic properties (see Section 3.3). In our proof of concept we opted for Dataglyphs as this particular encoding has very little structure such as no visual landmarks and no fixed block size. This gives us the flexibility of being able to change parameters of the underlying Visualizable Encryption scheme (e.g., cipher-block size) without affecting its visual encoding representation. In particular, we have developed a new dataglyph-based visual encoding scheme that can be decoded progressively, by zooming or moving the camera close to one part of the encoding, and panning to decode other parts. Due to our use of augmented reality this feels quite natural. At the same time, the security of panning becomes one of the central challenges in the design of a visualizable encryption scheme compatible with our visual encoding. In Section 3.3 we discuss how *EyeDecrypt* allows for the use of other visual data encodings such as QR codes.

Due to space constraints, some complementary material can be found in the full version of the paper [9].

2   Model and Definitions

In this section we present the basic model where we envision *EyeDecrypt* operating, as well as formal definitions of the different components needed for our constructions.

In its basic form, *EyeDecrypt* operates in a setting with three components, or "parties:" a user personal device U running the *EyeDecrypt* app, a server S, an a (polynomial-time) adversary Adv, controlling both the device where the information is displayed and/or entered (the "untrusted device" in Figure 1) and the shoulder-surfer(s) surrounding the user. The user device U can be any device that can capture an image, process it, and display the result to the human user. We envision the server encrypting and transmitting data to the user by visual means (e.g., rendering a visual encoding of the [encrypted] data on a computer screen), and the user receiving a (possibly noisy) version of that data. In turn, the user can transmit data back to the server by means of pressing buttons, active areas on a touch screen, etc., of the untrusted device. We expect the user and the server to engage in an interaction where the information transmitted at each "round" is dependent on all prior communication, as well as possibly other external factors.

In this paper we treat both *passive* and *active* adversaries threatening the security of the system. A passive adversary observes the visual channel as well as other available channels of information such as the user's body language, the buttons that she presses, the areas of the touch screen that she activates, the information that is transmitted through the untrusted device, etc. (This type of adversary is also called *honest-but-curious* in the literature.) An active adversary, on the other hand, can in addition *manipulate* the communication between the server and the untrusted device, mount *man-in-the-middle* attacks, etc. This could occur, for example, if the user is interacting with a terminal infected by malware that is displaying information that is transmitted by a remote trusted server. We assume, however, that the "shoulder-surfer" component of such an adversary remains passive.

Data transmitted from S to U are partitioned into *frames*, and each frame is partitioned into *blocks*. The frames represent the change of the content over time, and blocks partition the frame into logical units. The choice of what constitutes a block depends on the parameters of the system. For example, a block could be a rectangular area in an image, or a group of characters in a text document.

2.1   Security of *EyeDecrypt*

The security of *EyeDecrypt* is defined in a setting wherein the server can receive input from the user through the entry device or from another source such as a local hard drive or the Internet. A screen in the (untrusted) device is used to display information about the inputs received so far, such as outputs of a visual encoding function of the encrypted input (see below). The entry device allows the user to select values from a fixed alphabet Σ, whereas information received from other sources is viewed as arbitrary strings.

Formally, a *(stateful) EyeDecrypt scheme* is a triple of PPT (probabilistic polynomial-time) algorithms (EyeDecInit, EyeDecEntry, EyeDecRead) where EyeDecInit : $\mathbb{N} \to \mathcal{S} \times \mathcal{K}_{ED}$ takes as input a security parameter and outputs an initial state S_0 for the *EyeDecrypt* server, and a long term key for the user viewing device; here, $\mathcal{K}_{ED}$ is the space of possible keys. EyeDecEntry : $\mathcal{S} \times \Sigma \times \{0,1\}^* \to \mathcal{S}$ where $\mathcal{S}$ is the set of possible states of the scheme, and EyeDecRead : $\mathcal{K}_{ED} \times \{0,1\}^* \to \{0,1\}^*$ runs on the user device and outputs the information that is shown to the user. The expression EyeDecEntry(S, x, m) should be interpreted as the system receiving input x through the entry device, and receiving input m from another source.

For example, when considering a secure PIN entry application, $\Sigma = \{0, \dots, 9\}$ (as well as some other symbols such as '#', 'Cancel', etc., omitted here for simplicity), and corresponding to the buttons on the keypad. In our solution for the PIN entry application (see Section 3.2), S will consist of the keys of the visualizable encryption scheme, and the contents displayed on the screen

We define the security of an *EyeDecrypt* scheme in terms of the information that is "leaked" to the adversary, which may vary depending on the particular real-world application that is being modeled. Specifically, the definition of security of an *EyeDecrypt* scheme against passive adversaries is parameterized by a function Leak : $S \rightarrow \{0,1\}^*$ that specifies the information that is given to the adversary after each input. Looking ahead to our construction for the PIN entry case, Leak will reveal the current encrypted image displayed on the screen, as well as the number on the button that was most recently pressed by the user, but not the keys of the underlying visualizable encryption scheme. Active adversaries, as mentioned above, can in addition "tamper" with the information being transmitted (displayed as well as entered), adaptively and as a function of the current state and of what they observe. Thus, the definition of security of *EyeDecrypt* in this case is parameterized by a class of "tamper-leakage" functions of the form $S \times \{0,1\}^* \rightarrow S \times \{0,1\}^*$. Intuitively, these functions express in addition the ways in which the adversary is allowed to alter the information (modify the state), when communicated both to the user and to the server. Formally, the security of an *EyeDecrypt* scheme against passive and active adversaries is defined via the experiments shown in Figure 4.

Note that calls to the corresponding oracle by Adv are slightly different in each experiment, as in the case of active attacks the adversary is able to choose the tamper-leakage functions (TL_{pre}, TL_{post}) on the fly. Also, the design choice of having two functions in the active-attack case, as opposed to encoding all the tampering actions and leakage into just one, is to avoid having to specify another function for the initial leakage.

Definition 1 (Passive Attacks). *Let* EyeDec = (EyeDecInit, EyeDecEntry, EyeDecRead) *be an* EyeDecrypt *scheme, and* Leak : $S \rightarrow \{0,1\}^*$. *Then,* EyeDec *is a* Leak-secure *EyeDecrypt scheme if for all PPT adversaries* Adv, *and all* $n \in \mathbb{N}$,

$$\Pr[\mathsf{ExpEyeDec}(1^n, \mathsf{Adv}, \mathsf{EyeDec}) = 1] \leq \frac{1}{2} - \mathrm{neg}(n).$$

Definition 2 (Active Attacks). *Let* EyeDec = (EyeDecInit, EyeDecEntry, EyeDecRead) *be an* EyeDecrypt *scheme, and* TL *be a class of tamper-leakage functions. Then,* EyeDec *is* TL-secure *against active adversaries if for all PPT adversaries* Adv, *and all* $n \in \mathbb{N}$,

$$\Pr[\mathsf{ExpEyeDecNM}(1^n, \mathsf{Adv}, \mathsf{EyeDec}) = 1] \leq \frac{1}{2} - \mathrm{neg}(n),$$

as long as Adv *only queries the* TamperLeakST *oracle on inputs* $(x, m, TL_{pre}, TL_{post})$, *where* $TL_{pre}, TL_{post} \in TL$.

Note that the algorithm EyeDecRead does not play a role in the above definitions. This is because it is only used to specify the functionality of the scheme that is available to the legitimate user U (i.e., the unencrypted content from the screen). Its role is in fact similar to the role of the decryption algorithm in encryption schemes.

$\mathsf{ExpEyeDec}(1^n, \mathsf{Adv}, \mathsf{EyeDec}):$
 $S_0 \leftarrow_R \mathsf{EyeDecInit}(1^n)$
 $((x_0, m_0), (x_1, m_1), \mathsf{st}) \leftarrow \mathsf{Adv}^{\mathsf{LeakST}}(1^n, \mathsf{Leak}(S_0))$
 where $(x_0, m_0) \neq (x_1, m_1)$
 $b \leftarrow_R \{0, 1\}; \lambda \leftarrow \mathsf{LeakST}(x_b, m_b)$
 $b' \leftarrow \mathsf{Adv}^{\mathsf{LeakST}}(1^n, \lambda)$
 Output 1 if and only if $b = b'$

$\mathsf{LeakST}(x, m)$ is stateful, and works as follows:
 Initially $S \leftarrow S_0$
 Given $(x, m) \in \Sigma \times \{0, 1\}^*$ do:
  $S \leftarrow \mathsf{EyeDecEntry}(S, x, m)$
 Output $\mathsf{Leak}(S)$

$\mathsf{ExpEyeDecNM}(1^n, \mathsf{Adv}, \mathsf{EyeDec}):$
 $S_0 \leftarrow_R \mathsf{EyeDecInit}(1^n)$
 $((x_0, m_0), (x_1, m_1), \mathsf{TL}_{\mathsf{pre}}^*, \mathsf{TL}_{\mathsf{post}}^*, \mathsf{st}) \leftarrow \mathsf{Adv}^{\mathsf{TamperLeakST}}(1^n)$
 where $(x_0, m_0) \neq (x_1, m_1)$
 $b \leftarrow_R \{0, 1\}; (\lambda_{\mathsf{pre}}, \lambda_{\mathsf{post}}) \leftarrow \mathsf{TamperLeakST}(x_b, m_b, \mathsf{TL}_{\mathsf{pre}}^*, \mathsf{TL}_{\mathsf{post}}^*)$
 $b' \leftarrow \mathsf{Adv}^{\mathsf{TamperLeakST}}(1^n, \lambda_{\mathsf{pre}}, \lambda_{\mathsf{post}})$
 Output 1 if and only if $b = b'$

$\mathsf{TamperLeakST}(x, m, \mathsf{TL}_{\mathsf{pre}}, \mathsf{TL}_{\mathsf{post}})$ is stateful, and works as follows:
 Initially $S \leftarrow S_0, C^* \leftarrow \perp$
 Given $(x, m) \in \Sigma \times \{0, 1\}^*$ do:
  $S', \lambda_{\mathsf{pre}} \leftarrow \mathsf{TL}_{\mathsf{pre}}(S, C^*)$
  $S'' \leftarrow \mathsf{EyeDecEntry}(S', x, m)$
  If challenge query, set:
   $C^* \leftarrow v''$ (from S'')
  $S, \lambda_{\mathsf{post}} \leftarrow \mathsf{TL}_{\mathsf{post}}(S'', C^*)$
 Output $(\lambda_{\mathsf{pre}}, \lambda_{\mathsf{post}})$

Fig. 4. *EyeDecrypt security game definitions for both passive and active adversaries*

2.2 Defining the Building Blocks

The basic components in an *EyeDecrypt* application specify suitable ways for the information to be displayed in the rendering device and captured by the user, as well as a method for encrypting the plaintext content. We elaborate on such visual encoding schemes along with some desirable properties at the end of the section. First, we present a definition of *visualizable encryption*—a key component in our solution.

Visualizable Encryption. A *private-key visualizable encryption scheme* consists of a triple of PPT algorithms $\langle \mathsf{KeyGen}, \mathsf{Enc}, \mathsf{Dec} \rangle$, where KeyGen takes as input a security parameter $n \in \mathbb{N}$, and outputs a key; Enc takes as input a key K, a frame index f, block number i, and a plaintext m, and outputs a ciphertext; and Dec takes as input a key K, a frame index f, block number i, and a ciphertext, and outputs a plaintext.

$\mathsf{ExpVisIND\text{-}ATK}(1^n, \mathsf{Adv}, \mathsf{VisEnc}):$

$K \leftarrow_R \mathsf{KeyGen}(1^n);$

$(f_*, i_*, m_0, m_1, \mathsf{st}) \leftarrow \mathsf{Adv}^{\mathsf{EncATK}_K(\cdot,\cdot,\cdot), \mathsf{DecATK}_K(\cdot)}(1^n)$

$b \leftarrow_R \{0, 1\};\ C_* \leftarrow_R \mathsf{Enc}_K(f_*, i_*, m_b)$

$b' \leftarrow \mathsf{Adv}^{\mathsf{EncATK}_K(\cdot,\cdot,\cdot), \widehat{\mathsf{DecATK}}_K(\cdot)}(1^n)$

Let $\mathsf{view}_{\mathsf{Adv}}$ be the view of the adversary.

Output 1 if and only if $b' = b$ and $\mathsf{Check}(\mathsf{view}) = 1.$

$\mathsf{Enc}\{\mathsf{CPA}, \mathsf{CCA}\}_K(f, i, m) \overset{\text{def}}{=} \mathsf{Enc}_K(f, i, m)$

$\mathsf{DecCPA}_K(C) \overset{\text{def}}{=} \bot$

$\mathsf{DecCCA}_K(C) \overset{\text{def}}{=} \mathsf{Dec}_K(C)$

$\widehat{\mathsf{DecCCA}}_K(C) \overset{\text{def}}{=} \mathsf{Dec}_K(C)$ if $C \neq C_*$

$\qquad\qquad \bot$ if $C = C_*$

$\mathsf{Check}(\mathsf{view}):$

Let $(f_\ell, i_\ell, m_\ell)_{1 \leq \ell \leq q}$ be the queries made to EncATK. Output 1 if and only if for all ℓ, ℓ', if $f_\ell = f_{\ell'}$ and $i_\ell = i_{\ell'}$, then $m_\ell = m_{\ell'}$.

Fig. 5. *Security game definition for visualizable encryption*

Definition 3. *Let* $\mathsf{VisEnc} = \langle \mathsf{KeyGen}, \mathsf{Enc}, \mathsf{Dec} \rangle$. *Then,* VisEnc *is a* ATK-*secure visualizable encryption scheme, where* ATK $\in \{\mathsf{CPA}, \mathsf{CCA}\}$, *if for all PPT adversaries* Adv, *all* $n \in \mathbb{N}$,

$$\Pr[\mathsf{ExpVisIND\text{-}ATK}(1^n, \mathsf{Adv}, \mathsf{VisEnc}) = 1] \leq \frac{1}{2} - \mathsf{neg}(n),$$

where $\mathsf{ExpVisIND\text{-}ATK}(\cdot, \cdot, \cdot)$ *is the experiment presented in Figure 5.*

In our proofs in Section 3 we require a slightly different security property from the encryption scheme, where the adversary can receive an encryption of a sequence of blocks as a challenge instead of a single block. Namely, the adversary outputs four vectors f_*, i_*, m_0, m_1, where $m_0 \neq m_1$ and receives back a vector C_* of ciphertexts of the elements of m_b with frame and block numbers at the matching positions in f_* and i_*, respectively. Let us call this notion of security ATK-*security for multiple messages*. The following claim can be shown to be true by a standard hybrid argument:

Claim. Let $\mathcal{E}$ be an ATK-secure visualizable encryption scheme. Then, $\mathcal{E}$ is also ATK-*secure for multiple messages* with a $\frac{1}{\nu}$ loss in security, where ν is the number of messages encrypted in the challenge.

We now provide some intuition regarding the applicability of our definition to the *EyeDecrypt* setting. Recall that a main motivation for our work is to prevent "shoulder-surfing" attacks. In such a scenario, an attacker is covertly observing the content of a (supposedly) private screen or paper document; in addition, the attacker may be able to observe the activities (gesticulation, movements, etc.) of the legitimate content's owner, and infer information. For example, by measuring how long the user spends looking at a given (encrypted) document, or the sequence of buttons that the user presses, the attacker may learn a lot about the content of the document. Our definition accounts for such a scenario similarly to the way that semantic security of encryption [10] accounts for partial knowledge of the plaintext by the adversary: by allowing the adversary in the security experiment to specify all the content but a single block in a single frame, we capture any external knowledge that the adversary may have about the plaintext.

Visual Encoding. Let $d_1, d_2, t_1, t_2 \in \mathbb{N}$ (see below for an explanation of these parameters), and $\mathcal{P}$ be a finite set representing possible values that can be assigned to a pixel (e.g., RGB values[2]). A *visual encoding scheme* is a pair of functions (Encode, Decode) such that Encode : $(\{0,1\}^n)^{d_1 \times d_2} \to \mathcal{P}^{t_1 \times t_2}$, and Decode $\equiv$ Encode^{-1}.

$d_1 \times d_2$ is the size of the (ciphertext) input matrix, measured in number of blocks; the size of a block is n bits. $t_1 \times t_2$ is the size (resolution) of the output (image); e.g., 640×480 pixels. One basic but useful property of a visual encoding scheme is that it preserves the relative positioning of elements (in our case, blocks) in the source object. The following definition makes that explicit.

Definition 4. *A visual encoding scheme is said to satisfy* relative positioning *if the following conditions hold:*

1.   *Decode maps* $\mathcal{P}^{\leq t_1 \times \leq t_2}$ *to* $(\{0,1\}^n)^{\leq d_1 \times \leq d_2}$;

2.   *for all* $X \in (\{0,1\}^n)^{d_1 \times d_2}$, r_1 *and* r_2 *such that* $1 \leq r_1 < r_2 \leq d_1$, *and* c_1 *and* c_2 *such that* $1 \leq c_1 < c_2 \leq d_2$, *if* $Y \leftarrow$ Encode(X) *and* $(r_1', r_2', c_1', c_2') = (r_1 \cdot \frac{t_1}{d_1} \ldots r_2 \cdot \frac{t_1}{d_1}, c_1 \cdot \frac{t_2}{d_2} \ldots c_2 \cdot \frac{t_2}{d_2})$, *then* $X_{r_1 \ldots r_2, c_1 \ldots c_2} \leftarrow$ Decode$(Y_{r_1' \ldots r_2', c_1' \ldots c_2'})$.

3   Constructions

We start off this section with a CCA-secure construction for visualizable encryption using basic cryptographic tools, followed by an *EyeDecrypt* scheme with two flavors (secure against passive and active attacks, respectively), which are based on it. The section concludes with the dataglyphs-based visual enconding construction.

3.1   The Visualizable Encryption Scheme

Our construction of a visualizable encryption scheme uses a pseudorandom function generator (PRFG), a strongly collision resistant hash function family, and an existentially unforgeable message authentication code (MAC).

Construction 1. Let F be a PRFG with key space $\mathcal{K}_{\mathsf{PRF}}$, $\mathcal{H}$ be a family of hash functions, and MAC an existentially unforgeable MAC with key space $\mathcal{K}_{\mathsf{MAC}}$. Then we construct a visualizable encryption scheme $\mathcal{E} = \langle \mathsf{KeyGen}, \mathsf{Enc}, \mathsf{Dec} \rangle$ as follows:

– $\mathsf{KeyGen}(1^n)$: Generate $K_{\mathsf{PRF}} \in_{\mathsf{R}} \mathcal{K}_{\mathsf{PRF}}$; $K_{\mathsf{MAC}} \in_{\mathsf{R}} \mathcal{K}_{\mathsf{MAC}}$; $H \in_{\mathsf{R}} \mathcal{H}$; and output $K = (K_{\mathsf{PRF}}, K_{\mathsf{MAC}}, H)$.

– $\mathsf{Enc}_K(f, i, M)$: Compute $C_0 \leftarrow F_{K_{\mathsf{PRF}}}(H(f, i)) \oplus M$; $\tau \leftarrow \mathsf{MAC}_{K_{\mathsf{MAC}}}(C_0)$; and output $C = (C_0, \tau, i, f)$.

---

[2] The *RGB color model* is an additive color model in which red, green, and blue light are added together in various ways to reproduce a broad array of colors. The name of the model comes from the initials of the three additive primary colors.

- $\mathsf{Dec}_K(C)$: Interpret C as a tuple (C_0, τ, i, f), and compute $\tau' \leftarrow \mathsf{MAC}_{K_{\mathsf{MAC}}}(C_0)$. If $\tau' \neq \tau$, output $\perp$. Otherwise, compute and output $M \leftarrow C_0 \oplus F_{K_{\mathsf{PRF}}}(H(f, i))$.

Theorem 1. *The visualizable encryption scheme $\mathcal{E}$ in Construction 1 is CCA-secure according to Def. 3.*

Proof sketch. The proof follows by describing a sequence of hybrid arguments from the security definitions of F, $\mathcal{H}$, and MAC. We next sketch the sequence of games that gives us the proof.

- Game 0: This is the original ExpVisIND-ATK experiment.
- Game 1: Game 1 proceeds identically to Game 0, except that Check(view) is modified as follows.
  Check(view)$'$: Proceed as in Check(view), but output 1 if and only if for all ℓ, ℓ', if $H(f_\ell, i_\ell) = H(f_{\ell'}, i_{\ell'})$ then $m_\ell = m_{\ell'}$. Game 1 and Game 0 will proceed identically, unless the adversary finds a strong collision in H.
- Game 2: Game 2 proceeds as Game 1, except that $F_{K_{\mathsf{PRF}}}$ is replaced by a random function R with the same range and domain. The fact that Game 2 and Game 1 proceed identically (except with negligible probability) follows from the pseudo-randomness of F.
- Game 3: Game 3 proceeds as Game 2, except that we further modify Check(view) to output 0 if the adversary has queried the decryption oracle on two ciphertexts $C = (f, i, C_0, \tau)$ and $C' = (f, i, C_0', \tau')$ where $(C_0, \tau) \neq (C_0', \tau')$, and both queries resulted in non-$\perp$.

This concludes the proof.   □

3.2 An *EyeDecrypt* Scheme

We construct an *EyeDecrypt* scheme(s) based on our visualizable encryption scheme $\mathcal{E}$, and the dataglyphs-based visual encoding scheme described in Section 3.3, which for now can be thought of as satisfying Definition 4; let $\mathcal{V} = (\mathsf{Encode}, \mathsf{Decode})$ denote that scheme. Our construction is parameterized by a function g which specifies how an application converts inputs to a new visual frame. Here $g(x, m, \mathsf{frame}, \pi)$ outputs a sequence of blocks $\mathsf{frame}' = (t_1, \ldots, t_n)$ comprising the content of the new frame given the input from the user, an input from another source (such as a harddrive or the Internet), and the previous frame. The input π to g is a permutation over alphabet Σ, and its meaning will become clear in the discussion that follows the construction. In order to use the *EyeDecrypt* scheme for a particular application, one only has to plug in an appropriate g into the construction below.

Construction 2. The generic *EyeDecrypt* scheme secure against passive attacks works as follows:

- $\mathsf{EyeDecInit}(1^n)$: Run $\mathsf{KeyGen}(1^n)$ to obtain a key K, and generate a random permutation π over Σ. Output $S_0 = (K, \pi, \perp, \perp, 0)$ and K. The two $\perp$ values in the tuple corresponds to the current cleartext and ciphertext frames, which are initially empty, and 0 is the initial frame number.

- EyeDecEntry(S, x, m): Parse S as $(K, \pi, \text{frame}, v, j)$. Generate a random permutation π' over Σ, and compute $(t_1, \ldots, t_n) \leftarrow g(\pi(x), m, \text{frame}, \pi')$, set frame$' = (t_1, \ldots, t_n)$, and compute $c_i \leftarrow \text{Enc}_K(j, i, t_i)$ and $v' \leftarrow \text{Encode}(c_1, \ldots, c_n)$. Lastly, set $S = (K, \pi', \text{frame}', v', j+1)$.
- EyeDecRead(K, v): Compute $(c_1, \ldots, c_n) \leftarrow \text{Decode}(v)$ and $t_i \leftarrow \text{Dec}_K(c_i)$, for $1 \leq i \leq n$. Output $(t_1, \ldots, t_n)$.

The intuition behind the construction is to encrypt content as it is displayed, and to randomly permute the meaning of the possible inputs that can be received from the user input device. In the PIN entry application, for example, we envision a touchscreen in the entry device where the nine digits are randomly re-ordered each time the user enters a PIN digit; see Fig. 9b. Alternatively, the device may have a keypad with unlabeled buttons, and a random mapping of buttons to digits will be displayed to the user in encrypted form.

Theorem 2. *Let* Leak$(S) = v$. *Then, the* EyeDecrypt *scheme given in Construction 2 is* Leak-*secure according to Definition 1 if* $\mathcal{E}$ *is a* CPA-*secure visualizable encryption scheme.*

Proof sketch. We prove the theorem by reducing the security of the *EyeDecrypt* scheme to the security of $\mathcal{E}$. Let Adv be an adversary that breaks Leak-security of *EyeDecrypt*. Then, we construct Adv$'$ that breaks the CPA-security for multiple messages of $\mathcal{E}$. Then, by Claim 2.2, we obtain the security of *EyeDecrypt*.

Our adversary Adv$'$ works as follows. Initially, Adv$'$ simulates EyeDecInit(1^n) except that no encryption key is generated. Adv$'$ then simulates Adv. To answer a query (x, m) to the LeakST oracle, Adv$'$ works as follows. Adv$'$ computes $(t_1, \ldots, t_n) \leftarrow g(\pi(x), m, \text{frame}, \pi')$, and obtains $c_i = \text{Enc}_K(j, i, t_i)$ for $1 \leq i \leq n$ by querying its EncCPA oracle. All other steps are identical to EyeDecEntry. Adv$'$ then computes and returns $v' \leftarrow \text{Encode}(c_1, \ldots, c_n)$ to Adv.

When Adv submits the challenge tuple $(x_0, m_0), (x_1, m_1)$, Adv$'$ computes frame$_b \leftarrow g(\pi(x_b), m_b, \text{frame}, \pi')$ for $b \in \{0, 1\}$. If frame$_0 = $ frame$_1$, then Adv$'$ gives up, and outputs a random bit. Otherwise, Adv$'$ submits (frame$_0$, frame$_1$) as its challenge in the ExpVisIND-CPA experiment. Given a vector of ciphertexts $(c_1^*, \ldots, c_n^*)$, Adv$'$ constructs the challenge ciphertext as above, and returns the encoded version to Adv. The simulation is concluded naturally.

Given the above construction, Adv$'$ simulates Adv perfectly in the ExpEyeDec experiment, except when frame$_0 = $ frame$_1$. However, in this case, Adv obtains no information about b in the challenge. Therefore, Adv$'$ wins with the same advantage as Adv.
$\square$

Turning to active attacks, simply substituting a CCA-secure encryption scheme for the CPA-secure one in Construction 2 is not enough to achieve non-malleability of the *EyeDecrypt* scheme against an interesting class of tamper-leak functions. In addition, we must perform checks on the viewing device to see if block positions have been modified.

Construction 3. The generic *EyeDecrypt* scheme secure against active attacks works as follows: EyeDecInit(1^n) and EyeDecEntry(S, x, m) are identical to Construction 2's, except that the encryption scheme (KeyGen, Enc, Dec) must be CCA-secure according to Definition 3. The viewing function is defined as follows:

- EyeDecRead(K, v): Compute $(c_1, \ldots, c_n) \leftarrow$ Decode(v), parse each c_i as (C_0^i, τ_i, i', j') and compute $t_i \leftarrow$ Dec$_K(c_i)$ for $1 \le i \le n$. Let j be the current frame number. If $i' \ne i$ or $j' \ne j$ or $t_i = \perp$, return $\perp$; otherwise, output $(t_1, \ldots, t_n)$.

Note that the above construction requires the device to keep track of the current frame number, but this is an implementation issue. We now prove that Construction 3 is secure against active attacks where the adversary is limited to modifying the displayed contents in addition to the capabilities it is given in the passive attack setting. Specifically, let $\mathcal{TL}$ be the class of functions defined as follows:

$$\mathcal{TL} \stackrel{\text{def}}{=} \{\mathsf{TL}(\cdot) | \mathsf{TL}(K, \pi, \mathsf{frame}, v, j, C^*) = $$
$$((K, \pi, \mathsf{frame}, f(v), j), \mathsf{Leak}_{\mathsf{act}}(K, f(v), C^*))\},$$

where $f : \mathcal{P}^{t_1 \times t_2} \to \mathcal{P}^{t_1 \times t_2}$ and $\mathsf{Leak}_{\mathsf{act}} : \mathcal{K}_{\mathsf{ED}} \times \{0,1\}^* \times \{0,1\} \to \{0,1\}^*$ is defined as:

$$\mathsf{Leak}_{\mathsf{act}}(K, u, C^*) \stackrel{\text{def}}{=} \begin{cases} (\mathsf{EyeDecRead}(K, u), u) & \text{if } u_i \ne C_i^* \text{ for } 1 \le i \le n; \\ (\perp, u) & \text{otherwise.} \end{cases}$$

Note that v, the visual encoding, is the value that is tamperable and that is leaked to the adversary. Also note that in the above definition we require that the adversary does not apply any tamper-leakage functions that attempt to decrypt parts of the challenge ciphertext. Every block has to be different from the blocks of the challenge. This is so because, unlike in standard (non-visualizable) encryption, here blocks must be decryptable individually. Therefore, there is no way to determine if other blocks outside the field of view have been tampered with. We can now show the following theorem:

Theorem 3. *Let $\mathcal{TL}$ be as above. The EyeDecrypt scheme given in Construction 3 is $\mathcal{TL}$-secure according to Definition 2 if $\mathcal{E}$ is a CCA-secure visualizable encryption scheme.*

The proof proceeds by a relatively straightforward reduction to the CCA-security of the underlying visualizable encryption scheme $\mathcal{E}$. Intuitively, the decryption condition in the definition of Leak prevents the adversary from querying the challenge ciphertext, unless she is able to change the block number of a ciphertext block. However, the position of the block that is obtained by decrypting the ciphertext is verified by EyeDecRead to match the position of the block in the field of view.

Given the *EyeDecrypt* constructions above, specifying the function g defines the functionality of the application. Next, we do this to provide a complete solution to the secure PIN entry application.

Instantiating *EyeDecrypt* for Secure PIN Entry. The exact nature of g will depend on the content being protected by the PIN. However, any PIN-protected application must allocate some of the output blocks of g to display a permuted numeric keypad. Suppose that the user input device is a (fixed) numeric keypad, and suppose (wlog) that blocks $t_1, \ldots, t_i$ in the plaintext visual frame are allocated to the permuted key-pad. Let $P(\text{pin}, \text{data})$ be a program that, given the PIN and additional data, generates blocks $t_{i+1}, \ldots, t_n$. Then, $g(\text{pin}, \text{data}, \text{frame}, \pi)$ computes $(t_{i+1}, \ldots, t_n) \leftarrow P(\text{pin}, \text{data})$, and computes blocks $t_1, \ldots, t_i$ by generating an image that shows the digit d written on the physical button that has the digit label $\pi^{-1}(d)$.

Finally, as mentioned in Section 1 and made evident by the definitions and constructions above, *EyeDecrypt* is symmetric key-based. In [9] we also show how the personal device running the *EyeDecrypt* app and the content-generating server are able to share cryptographic keys in a secure manner.

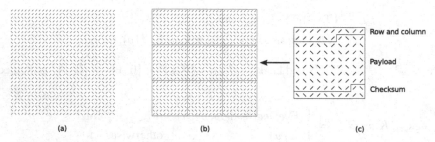

(a)   (b)   (c)

Fig. 6. (a) *Dataglyph encoding*   (b) *Blocks of the encoding*   (c) *Structure of a block*

3.3   A Dataglyphs-Based Visual Encoding Scheme

Many existing visual encoding schemes are compatible with visualizable encryption (e.g., QR codes [13], Data Matrices [12], Dataglyphs [29], High Capacity Color Barcodes (HCCB) [20]), but visualizable encryption does impose some constraints.

First, the system should be able to decrypt content when zoomed in to a single block. Our chosen visual encoder should therefore not encode more than one block per code—otherwise zooming in to a single block would present the decoder with only a portion of a code. On the other hand, we are free to encode a block using multiple codes.

Second, the system must support decoding *multiple blocks* of a frame all at once. We have found that some decoders get "confused" by images containing multiple codes (we need at least one code per block) or partial codes. Sometimes, decoders that support multiple codes per image impose constraints on their arrangement (for example, multiple QR codes require a "quiet zone" between codes).

Finally, the visual decoder must not only be able to decode multiple blocks, it must also *understand their spatial arrangement*. For any given block the decoder must understand which other block is its right neighbor, etc., so that the system can detect whether an attacker has re-arranged blocks of ciphertext (cf. Construction 3 above). This is a computer vision problem that is not solved by simply reading multiple codes independently, and existing systems using multiple codes (e.g., [6]) do not implement it. Note that simply knowing the pixel coordinates of codes within an image is not sufficient as images taken with a hand-held device exhibit rotation, skew, perspective shift, and other misalignments.

Still, within these constraints many existing visual encodings could be made to work. For our implementation we had to choose one, and we have (somewhat arbitrarily) chosen to use Dataglyphs (Figure 6(a)).

A (data)glyph is a marking with two possible angles, $+45°$ and $-45°$, indicating a 0 or 1 bit, respectively. Multiple bits are encoded by organizing multiple glyphs into a grid. Decoding multiple bits therefore means reconstructing the grid structure from the pixel coordinates of glyphs within an image. While this is not a trivial task, the great advantage in our setting is that the resulting grid structure can be used not only for decoding a single glyph, but also for understanding the spatial arrangement of multiple blocks also arranged in a grid. In fact, what is shown in Figure 6(a) is actually an encoding of a grid of blocks, with each block being encoded by a grid of glyphs, as indicated in Figure 6(b). Blocks can be arranged seamlessly into a grid of arbitrary size. This gives dataglyphs a flexibility that has proven to be very useful in experimenting with parameters of the underlying visualizable encryption scheme (e.g., cipher-block size, aspect ratio).

4   The *EyeDecrypt* Prototype

EyeDecrypt would be a natural fit for augmented-reality devices such as Google Glass [11]: the user would simply look at encrypted content and have the decrypted version displayed directly on the screen of the glasses. However, given that such devices are not yet widely available, we implemented *EyeDecrypt* on a smartphone, an iPhone 5S equipped with an 8 MP rear-facing camera.

The *EyeDecrypt* app shows a live camera view and decrypts on the fly, at a rate of 20–30 frames per second, depending on the number of blocks in view. The decrypted content is overlaid over the corresponding block of dataglyphs in the camera view itself. The only action users need to perform is to position the phone camera in front of the encrypted document they wish to decrypt and move the camera around to decrypt different parts of the document. This is illustrated in Figure 2.

Figure 7(a) shows a screenshot of the application. The encrypted message consists of ten blocks laid out in two rows. Each decrypted block is rendered independently, directly over the corresponding block of glyphs; gaps between decrypted blocks are the result of camera motion during the live capture. The decrypted blocks track the glyphs at 20–30fps, achieving a true augmented reality experience. The application verifies that adjacent blocks are correctly arranged, and displays any out-of-place blocks in red, as in Figure 7(b), making evident any rearrangement of blocks by cut-and-paste.

In the current implementation we encrypt the plaintext instantiating the PRF in the visualizable encryption scheme of Section 3.1 with AES-128, and visually-encode it using dataglyphs. Currently, no MAC is implemented and therefore our implementation is only secure against passive attacks, except for the detection of block rearrangement (Figure 7(b)).

We now list the steps that *EyeDecrypt* goes through in order to decode a visually encoded ciphertext.

Removing Moiré Patterns. *EyeDecrypt* works not only with documents printed on paper but also documents viewed on computer screens. In this second scenario,

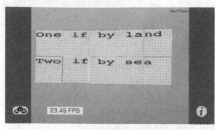

(a) A decrypted message   (b) Detecting rearranged blocks

Fig. 7. Screenshots of the *EyeDecrypt* application

additional noise is introduced to the image captured by the phone camera. In particular, Moiré patterns [31] are well-known artifacts present in digital images. In order to reduce Moiré patterns when reading a visual encoding from a screen, we apply a series of low-pass filters and high-pass filters to filter out such patterns as much as possible while, at the same time, trying to enhance the dataglyphs. In our implementation we use OpenCV [14], and, in particular, we use a Gaussian Blur as low-pass filter and a Laplacian as high-pass filter.

Contour Detection. We convert the image to gray scale, use the Scharr transform to perform edge detection, and the Suzuki-Abe algorithm to detect contours [27]. For each contour, we calculate its centroid coordinates and angle.

Reconstructing the Grid. We build a graph by Delaunay triangulation of the glyph centroids. The result is an undirected graph in which each centroid has edges to up to 8 of its nearest neighbors. We remove "diagonal" edges so that remaining edges roughly follow the rows and columns of a grid, and each centroid is connected to at most four other centroids.

Removing Noise. Camera lens deformation, non-uniform light conditions, variable distance from content and camera resolution all lead to the creation of noise and artifacts in the detection of the contours that is, in the detection of the centroids. Such artifacts are usually located at the edges of the camera field of view which translates to disconnected or missing centroids at the edges of the graph. The way users hold their phone represents another significant source of noise. In particular, given that the visual encoding we use does not have any landmark to help with alignment, if the phone is rotated by a significant amount, it may be very hard to tell left from right and top from bottom of the visually encoded content captured by the camera. Figure 8(a) shows this problem. As we can see, by just looking at the centroids of the contours we cannot tell the correct alignment of the ciphertext.

In order to solve all these issues, we apply various graph-theory algorithms that allow us to remove all the artifacts due to noise and reconstruct the graph. Figure 8(b) shows the graph reconstructed from the centroids shown in Figure 8(a). We can see that we were able to remove artifacts and infer the camera rotation which is an essential step to correctly decode the content.

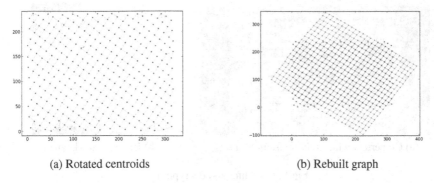

(a) Rotated centroids   (b) Rebuilt graph

Fig. 8. Rebuilding a graph from noisy centroids with unknown rotation

Decoding. The corrected graph from the previous step is next converted to a binary matrix by converting the angle information of each centroid into ones and zeros.

In the current implementation, one block of ciphertext has dimensions 10×10 bits (see Figure 6(c)). The first 16 bits of the block represent the coordinates i and j of that block in the frame, while the last 12 bits of the block represent a checksum. This checksum is the truncated output of AES-128 applied to the coordinates i, j of the block. We know we have found a valid block of ciphertext when computing AES-128 over the first 16 bits of a block, we get the same checksum found in the last 12 bits of that block. If the checksum fails, we move one column to the right in the matrix and perform the same check on the new block until we have tested all the bits of a 12x12 matrix. If a valid block is found, each block of the matrix is decrypted. Finally, the decrypted content from all the decrypted blocks is displayed as an overlay on the phone camera view.

5 Performance Evaluation

As mentioned in the previous section, each block of ciphertext has a dimension of 10×10 bits. Figure 6(c) shows the structure of the block. The first 16 bits are used to encode the coordinates i, j corresponding to the position of the block in the document, while the last 12 bits are used for the block checksum. This leaves 72 bits of encrypted payload per block. Given that the visualizable encryption scheme is length-preserving (uses a one-time pad approach; see Section 3.1), we can encrypt 72 bits of data in each block. In the case of text, this means that we can encrypt nine characters per block of ciphertext.

In general, users will hold their device so that multiple blocks will be decoded at once, that is, a multiple of nine characters will be displayed at once to the user. Increasing the ciphertext block size would reduce the overhead due to block coordinates and checksum. A larger block size, however, would also mean that users have to hold their devices at a larger distance from the encoded image in order to fit at least one block in the camera field of view. The larger distance would add additional noise, possibly leading to a higher probability of decryption failure.

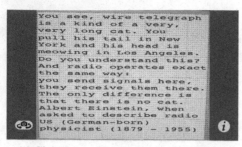

(a) Ciphertext with Moiré noise (4,800 bits)

(b) Randomized keypad

Fig. 9. Decoding and decryption

Figure 9(a) shows the correct decoding and decryption of 4,800 bits of ciphertext displayed on a computer screen, where the decoding was successful despite the presence of Moiré patterns. In such case, the decoding took an average time of 250 milliseconds (i.e., 4 frames per second). This time, however, largely depends on the camera resolution being used and the number of cipher-blocks visible in the same frame. For the decoding shown in Figure 9(a), we used a resolution of 640x480 pixels and decoded 48 cipher-blocks in a single frame. In the case of a numerical keypad, as shown in Figure 9(b), the visual encoding includes 12 cipher-blocks in a single frame which we were able to process at a rate of about 18 frames per second.

The resolution of the camera plays an important role in *EyeDecrypt*. On one hand, higher resolution means that the camera has better accuracy in reading the image, and hence a larger number of cipher blocks can be correctly decoded in a single frame. Also, decoding can happen at greater distance. On the other hand, higher resolution means that the device has to process a larger image, i.e., more information, and the decoding takes longer. Furthermore, with higher resolution Moiré noise gets amplified as well so that accuracy does not increase linearly with resolution. A consequence of this is that decrypting content in printed form is much more reliable and accurate than decrypting electronic content where Moiré noise is present. Different camera resolutions imply a tradeoff between accuracy, decryption speed and maximum decoding distance.

The visual encoding based on dataglyphs could be easily enhanced to increase the amount of information it conveys. As we mentioned in Section 3.3, we currently use only two angle values to encode ones and zeros—namely, $-45°$ for bit 1 and $+45°$ for bit 0.

Naturally, the problem in having only two possible values is that less information can be conveyed in the dataglyph encoding. In particular, by using $0°$, $+45°$, $-45°$ and $90°$, each dataglyph could encode two bits of information. This, however, would make dataglyphs less resilient to noise. Other ways to enhance dataglyphs would be by using different colors and sizes so that for each dataglyph we can now specify angle, color and size. If we assume four possible angles, four independent colors and two different sizes, one dataglyph could now convey 5 bits of information. Enhancing the visual encoding so to convey more information as described above is left for future work.

6 Related Work

Human-computer interactions almost universally involve human vision, and so *EyeDecrypt* or any other HCI technology is subject to the security limitations of vision. In particular, vision is susceptible to interception, by means as simple as shoulder surfing or as sophisticated as capturing the reflection of images from the surface of the eye [19, 1, 2]. *EyeDecrypt* protects against many interception attacks by encrypting the visual channel between the encoding and a personal device. The visual channel from the personal device to the eye remains unprotected by *EyeDecrypt* itself; it is intended for use only when the personal device remains inaccessible to adversaries. When eye reflections are a concern but it is still desirable to use the visual channel, we know no protection short of an enclosed display. *EyeDecrypt* is compatible with such a display.

On the other hand, vision has some inherent security advantages. Humans generally know with certainty what physical object they are looking at (as opposed to what device has sent them a wireless transmission), and vision is resistant to active tampering. For example, there are a few techniques to overload camera sensors but a user can detect this by comparison with their own vision. Consequently, visual encodings are widely use in security for key establishment, wireless device pairing, and trusted display establishment [17, 25, 26, 6]; *EyeDecrypt* can be used for these purposes as well.

Computer vision researchers have been studying visual encodings for decades, seeking to increase their capacity and their robustness against lens distortion, image compression, non-uniform lighting, skew, motion blur, shake, low camera resolution, poor focus, etc. [16, 30, 21]. Techniques for zooming into visual encodings include recursive grids of barcodes [22] and nested barcodes [28]. Fourier tags [24] handle the opposite case of zooming out: at close distance, they can be completely decoded, but as the camera zooms out, fewer bits can be decoded; low-order bits are lost before high-order bits.

Encrypted content is often used in single barcodes (e.g., [3]) but less often in multiple barcodes. Fang and Chang describe a method for encoding a large encrypted message in multiple barcodes [6]. All barcodes must be decoded and decrypted to view the message, and the barcodes must be presented in a known order, unlike our blocks which can be viewed independently. They are concerned with *rearrangement attacks* in which the adversary is able to rearrange the order of the barcodes so that the message cannot be decrypted. Their solution is to use a visual cue (numbers in sequence) over which each barcode is interleaved. The user can manually verify that the barcodes are in the correct order, while the device handles the decoding and decryption of the actual data. In our solution, visual clues are not necessary, as the frame and block numbers of adjacent regions are directly encoded and can be read and compared automatically by the device.

Many defenses against shoulder surfing during PIN entry have been proposed; we discuss a representative sampling here. We emphasize that unlike *EyeDecrypt*, these systems do not encrypt the device display, so they are not appropriate for *displaying* private information, only entering it.

EyePassword [15] and Cued Gaze-Points [8] are two systems that use gaze-based input for password/PIN entry. These systems require the public device (e.g., an ATM) to have a camera and they work by computing the point on the screen that the user is looking at. In the Cued Gaze-Points system PIN entry works by the user selecting gaze-points on a sequence of graphic images. In EyePassword, the user gazes at a standard onscreen keyboard. The key assumption in both cases is that the adversary does not see the input at all (the adversary does not have a view of the user's eyes). In contrast, *EyeDecrypt* assumes that the adversary can see the input but only in obfuscated form (randomized and encrypted).

Roth *et al.* [23] require users to enter PINs via *cognitive trapdoor games*, e.g., a sequence of puzzles that are easy to solve (by an unaided human) with knowledge of the PIN, but hard to solve without it. Their scheme emphasizes useability and is intended only to defend against attackers that are unaided humans (for example, with human short-term memories). Unlike gaze-entry systems, and similar to *EyeDecrypt*, it can work without modifying ATM hardware.

In the ColorPIN system [5], a user's PIN is a sequence of colored digits, and the ATM displays a ten-digit keypad where each digit appears with three colored letters. For example, the digit "1" could appear above a black "Q," a red "B," and a white "R," and the user would enter "black 1" by hitting "Q." Each letter appears with multiple digits, so that a sequence of letters is associated with multiple sequences of digits. A shoulder-surfing observer thus gets partial information about the PIN (e.g., for a four-digit pin the observer knows that it is one of $3 \times 3 \times 3 = 81$ possibilities). *EyeDecrypt*'s visual encryption protects against this sort of leakage.

MobilePIN [4], like *EyeDecrypt*, uses a trusted personal device to aid PIN entry. In MobilePIN, the ATM displays its wireless address and authentication token onscreen as a QR code, and the user reads the code using the camera of the personal device. The personal device can then establish a secure wireless connection between with the ATM (secure pairing using the visual channel). The user enters her PIN on the trusted personal device, which transmits it to the ATM over the wireless channel. MobilePIN therefore has similar assumptions as *EyeDecrypt*, except in addition it assumes that the ATM is equipped with a radio.

Most other shoulder-surfing-resistant PIN entry methods involve changing the authentication process, e.g., by using graphical passwords or security tokens, or by requiring network connectivity or device pairing.

Naturally, *EyeDecrypt* is related to the cryptographic technique known as *visual cryptography* ([18] and follow-ups), which allows visual information (pictures, text, etc.) to be encrypted in such a way that decryption becomes a *mechanical* operation that does not require a computer, such as for example over-imposing two (transparent) images in the Naor-Shamir visual secret-sharing scheme.

Finally, *EyeDecrypt* has the additional ability to ensure that only legitimate users can view the information that is openly displayed, and in that sense bears some similarity to broadcast encryption ([7] and numerous follow-ups), with closely related applications such as pay-TV. A fundamental difference in *EyeDecrypt* is the public-view nature of the rendering device.

References

[1] Backes, M., Chen, T., Drmuth, M., Lensch, H.P.A., Welk, M.: Tempest in a teapot: Compromising reflections revisited. In: IEEE Symposium on Security and Privacy, pp. 315–327 (2009)

[2] Backes, M., Drmuth, M., Unruh, D.: Compromising reflections-or-how to read LCD monitors around the corner. In: IEEE Symposium on Security and Privacy, pp. 158–169 (2008)

[3] Conde-Lagoa, D., Costa-Montenegro, E., Gonzalez-Castao, F., Gil-Castieira, F.: Secure eTickets based on QR-Codes with user-encrypted content. In: 2010 Digest of Technical Papers International Conference on Consumer Electronics (ICCE), pp. 257–258 (2010)

[4] De Luca, A., Frauendienst, B., Boring, S., Hussmann, H.: My phone is my keypad: Privacy-enhanced PIN-entry on public terminals. In: Proceedings of the 21st Annual Conference of the Australian Computer-Human Interaction Special Interest Group, pp. 401–404. ACM, New York (2009), http://doi.acm.org/10.1145/1738826.1738909

[5] De Luca, A., Hertzschuch, K., Hussmann, H.: ColorPIN: Securing PIN entry through indirect input. In: Proceedings of the SIGCHI Conference on Human Factors in Computing Systems, pp. 1103–1106. ACM, New York (2010), http://doi.acm.org/10.1145/1753326.1753490

[6] Fang, C., Chang, E.C.: Securing interactive sessions using mobile device through visual channel and visual inspection. In: Proceedings of the 26th Annual Computer Security Applications Conference, ACSAC 2010, pp. 69–78. ACM, New York (2010), http://doi.acm.org/10.1145/1920261.1920272

[7] Fiat, A., Naor, M.: Broadcast encryption. In: Stinson, D.R. (ed.) Advances in Cryptology - CRYPT0 1993. LNCS, vol. 773, pp. 480–491. Springer, Heidelberg (1994), http://dl.acm.org/citation.cfm?id=646758.705697

[8] Forget, A., Chiasson, S., Biddle, R.: Shoulder-surfing resistance with eye-gaze entry in cued-recall graphical passwords. In: Proceedings of the SIGCHI Conference on Human Factors in Computing Systems, pp. 1107–1110. ACM, New York (2010), http://doi.acm.org/10.1145/1753326.1753491

[9] Forte, A., Garay, J., Jim, T., Vahlis, Y.: Eyedecrypt – private interactions in plain sight. Cryptology ePrint Archive, Report 2013/590 (2013), http://eprint.iacr.org/

[10] Goldwasser, S., Micali, S.: Probabilistic encryption. Journal of Computer and System Sciences 28(2), 270–299 (1984), http://www.sciencedirect.com/science/article/pii/0022000084900709

[11] Google: Google Glass, http://www.google.com/glass

[12] ISO: Information technology – Automatic identification and data capture techniques – Data Matrix bar code symbology specification. ISO 16022:2006. International Organization for Standardization, Geneva, Switzerland (2006)

[13] ISO: Information technology – Automatic identification and data capture techniques – QR Code 2005 bar code symbology specification. ISO 18004:2006. International Organization for Standardization, Geneva, Switzerland (2006)

[14] Itseez: Open Source Computer Vision (OpenCV) Library, http://opencv.org

[15] Kumar, M., Garfinkel, T., Boneh, D., Winograd, T.: Reducing shoulder-surfing by using gaze-based password entry. In: Proceedings of the 3rd Symposium on Usable Privacy and Security, SOUPS 2007, pp. 13–19. ACM, New York (2007), http://doi.acm.org/10.1145/1280680.1280683

[16] Liang, J., Doermann, D., Li, H.: Camera-based analysis of text and documents: A survey. International Journal of Document Analysis and Recognition (IJDAR) 7(2-3), 84–104 (2005), http://link.springer.com/article/10.1007/s10032-004-0138-z

[17] McCune, J.M., Perrig, A., Reiter, M.K.: Seeing-is-believing: Using camera phones for human-verifiable authentication. In: IEEE Symposium on Security and Privacy, pp. 110–124. IEEE Computer Society, Los Alamitos (2005)

[18] Naor, M., Shamir, A.: Visual cryptography. In: De Santis, A. (ed.) EUROCRYPT 1994. LNCS, vol. 950, pp. 1–12. Springer, Heidelberg (1995)

[19] Nishino, K., Nayar, S.K.: Corneal imaging system: Environment from eyes. International Journal of Computer Vision 70(1), 23–40 (2006)

[20] Parikh, D., Jancke, G.: Localization and segmentation of a 2D high capacity color barcode. In: IEEE Workshop on Applications of Computer Vision, pp. 1–6. IEEE (2008)

[21] Perli, S.D., Ahmed, N., Katabi, D.: PixNet: Interference-free wireless links using LCD-camera pairs. In: Proceedings of the Sixteenth Annual International Conference on Mobile Computing and Networking, MobiCom 2010, pp. 137–148. ACM, New York (2010), http://doi.acm.org/10.1145/1859995.1860012

[22] Reilly, D., Chen, H., Smolyn, G.: Toward fluid, mobile and ubiquitous interaction with paper using recursive 2D barcodes. In: 3rd International Workshop on Pervasive Mobile Interaction Devices, PERMID 2007 (May 2007)

[23] Roth, V., Richter, K., Freidinger, R.: A PIN-entry method resilient against shoulder surfing. In: Proceedings of the 11th ACM Conference on Computer and Communications Security, pp. 236–245. ACM, New York (2004), http://doi.acm.org/10.1145/1030083.1030116

[24] Sattar, J., Bourque, E., Giguere, P., Dudek, G.: Fourier tags: Smoothly degradable fiducial markers for use in human-robot interaction. In: Fourth Canadian Conference on Computer and Robot Vision, CRV 2007, pp. 165–174 (2007)

[25] Saxena, N., Ekberg, J.E., Kostiainen, K., Asokan, N.: Secure device pairing based on a visual channel. In: IEEE Symposium on Security and Privacy, pp. 306–313. IEEE Computer Society (2006)

[26] Starnberger, G., Froihofer, L., Goeschka, K.: QR-TAN: Secure mobile transaction authentication. In: International Conference on Availability, Reliability and Security, ARES 2009, pp. 578–583 (2009)

[27] Suzuki, S., Abe, K.: Topological structural analysis of digitized binary images by border following. Computer Vision, Graphics, and Image Processing 30, 32–46 (1985)

[28] Tateno, K., Kitahara, I., Ohta, Y.: A nested marker for augmented reality. In: IEEE Virtual Reality Conference, VR 2007, pp. 259–262 (2007)

[29] Tow, R.F.: Methods and means for embedding machine readable digital data in halftone images (May 24, 1994), US Patent 5,315,098

[30] Tuytelaars, T., Mikolajczyk, K.: Local invariant feature detectors: A survey. Foundations and Trends in Computer Graphics and Vision 3(3), 177–280 (2007)

[31] Wikipedia: Moiré pattern (2013), http://en.wikipedia.org/wiki/Moir%C3%A9_pattern

Semi-adaptive Attribute-Based Encryption and Improved Delegation for Boolean Formula[*]

Jie Chen[1,**] and Hoeteck Wee[2,***]

[1] Department of Computer Science and Technology, East China Normal University
s080001@e.ntu.edu.sg
[2] École Normale Supérieure, Paris
wee@di.ens.fr

Abstract. We consider *semi-adaptive* security for attribute-based encryption, where the adversary specifies the challenge attribute vector after it sees the public parameters but before it makes any secret key queries. We present two constructions of semi-adaptive attribute-based encryption under static assumptions with *short* ciphertexts. Previous constructions with short ciphertexts either achieve the weaker notion of selective security, or require parameterized assumptions.

As an application, we obtain improved delegation schemes for Boolean formula with *semi-adaptive* soundness, where correctness of the computation is guaranteed even if the client's input is chosen adaptively depending on its public key. Previous delegation schemes for formula achieve one of adaptive soundness, constant communication complexity, or security under static assumptions; we show how to achieve semi-adaptive soundness and the last two simultaneously.

1 Introduction

Attribute-based encryption (ABE) [33, 20] is an emerging paradigm for public-key encryption which enables fine-grained control of access to encrypted data. In traditional public-key encryption, access to the encrypted data is all or nothing: given the secret key, one can decrypt and read the entire plaintext, but without it, nothing about the plaintext is revealed (other than its length). In ABE, a

---

[*] The research leading to these results has received funding from the European Research Council under the European Community's Seventh Framework Programme (FP7/2007-2013 Grant Agreement no. 339563 CryptoCloud). A longer version of this work appears in [11].

[**] Supported by Science and Technology Commission of Shanghai Municipality under Grants 14YF1404200, 13JC1403500, and the National Natural Science Foundation of China Grant No. 61172085. Part of this work was done at Nanyang Technological University, supported by the National Research Foundation of Singapore under Research Grant NRF-CRP2-2007-03.

[***] CNRS (UMR 8548) and INRIA. Supported in part by the French ANR-12-INSE-0014 SIMPATIC Project. Part of this work was done at Columbia University, supported by NSF Award CNS-1319021, and at Ruhr-Universität Bochum as a Research Fellow of the Alexander von Humboldt Foundation.

M. Abdalla and R. De Prisco (Eds.): SCN 2014, LNCS 8642, pp. 277–297, 2014.

ciphertext is labeled with an attribute vector $\mathbf{x}$, and a secret key is associated with an access policy specified as a Boolean formula, and the secret key decrypts the ciphertext if and only if $\mathbf{x}$ satisfies the access policy.[1] It is easy to see that ABE is a generalization of identity-based encryption (IBE) [34, 5, 14]. The security requirement for ABE stipulates that it resists collusion attacks, namely any group of users collectively learns nothing about the plaintext if none of them is individually authorized to decrypt the ciphertext.

Delegation. A delegation scheme allows a computationally weak client to delegate expensive computations to the cloud, with the assurance that a malicious cloud cannot convince the client to accept an incorrect computation [19, 17, 4, 15]. Recent work of Parno, Raykova and Vaikuntanathan [32] showed that any ABE with encryption time at most linear in the length of the attribute vector immediately yields a delegation scheme for Boolean formula. There is an initial pre-processing phase which fixes the formula f the client wishes to compute and produces some public key. Afterwards, to delegate computation on an input x, the client only needs to send a single message. Moreover, the ensuing delegation scheme satisfies public delegatability, namely anyone can delegate computations to the cloud; as well as public verifiability, namely anyone can check the cloud's work (given a "verification" key published by the client).

State of the Art. Since the introduction of ABE and motivated in part by the connection to delegation, there is now a large body of work providing constructions with incomparable trade-offs amongst efficiency, security guarantees and security assumptions [20, 2, 27, 31, 26]; a summary of this work is presented in Fig 1. A key measure of efficiency is the ciphertext size and the encryption time; ideally, we want this to depend at most linearly in the length of the attribute vector and independent of the size of the access structure. For security guarantees, the two primary notions are selective and adaptive security; in the more restrictive setting of selective security, the adversary must specify the challenge attribute vector prior to seeing the public parameters. Finally, the security of the schemes rely on the assumed hardness of some computational problem in bilinear groups; here, we prefer prime-order instantiations over composite-order ones, and static assumptions over parameterized ones.

1.1 Our Contributions

We introduce the notion of *semi-adaptive* security for ABE and delegation. In ABE, this means that the adversary specifies the challenge attribute vector after it sees the public parameters but before it makes any secret key queries. This

---

[1] This is typically referred to as key-policy ABE in the literature, which is the focus of this paper. A different line of works, e.g. [13, 21, 37, 27, 26], considers ciphertext-policy ABE, where the ciphertext is labeled with a formula and the secret key is associated with an attribute vector.

reference	security	Enc time	CT size	MPK size	SK size	group	assumption
GPSW06 [20]	selective	$O(n)^*$	$O(n)^*$	$O(n)$	$O(\ell)$	prime	static
ALP11 [2]		$O(n)$	$O(1)$	$O(n)$	$O(n\ell)$	prime	non-static
ALP11+LW10		$O(n)$	$O(1)$	$O(n)$	$O(n\ell)$	composite	static
T14 [35]		$O(n)$	$O(1)$	$O(n)$	$O(n\ell)$	prime	static
LOSTW10 [27]	adaptive	$O(nM)^*$	$O(nM)^*$	$O(nM)$	$O(\ell)$	composite	static
OT10 [31]		$O(nM)^*$	$O(nM)^*$	$O(nM)$	$O(\ell)$	prime	static
LW12 [26]		$O(n)^*$	$O(n)^*$	$O(n)$	$O(\ell)$	prime	non-static
A14 [1]		$O(n)$	$O(1)$	$O(n)$	$O(n\ell)$	composite	non-static
Construction 1	semi-	$O(n)$	$O(1)$	$O(n)$	$O(n\ell)$	composite	static
Construction 2	adaptive	$O(n)^*$	$O(n)^*$	$O(n)$	$O(\ell)$	prime	static

Fig. 1. Summary of existing KP-ABE schemes. Here, n denotes the universe size, M is the maximum number of times an attribute may be used, and $\ell \leq nM$ is the number of rows in the matrix $\mathbf{M}$ of the access structure. Encryption time is given in terms of group operations, and CT, PP, SK sizes are given in terms of group elements. For CT, we omit the additive overhead of n *bits* in order to transmit the attribute vector. For the quantities marked with *, n may be replaced with number of non-zero entries in the attribute vector $\mathbf{x} \in \{0,1\}^n$, which could be much smaller than n. Note that ALP11, T14 and A14 achieve large universe, we restrict the attribute universe to $[n]$ for comparison.

is stronger than selective security but weaker than adaptive security. In delegation, this means that the client's input may depend on the public key but is independent of the worker's evaluation key. In addition, we provide new constructions of efficient semi-adaptively secure ABE and delegation schemes under static assumptions.

New ABE Schemes. Our first result is a semi-adaptively secure ABE whose efficiency matches the state-of-the-art selectively secure ABE [2]:

> **(Informal Theorem)** There exists a semi-adaptively secure ABE with constant-size ciphertexts. Encryption time is linear in the length of the attribute vector and independent of the size of the access structure. The security of the scheme is based on static assumptions in composite-order groups.

We also achieve an analogous result in prime-order groups based on the SXDH Assumption; however, the ciphertext size is linear in the length of the attribute vector. Throughout this work, when we refer to ciphertext size, we measure the number of group elements, and we omit the additive overhead of n *bits* needed to transmit the attribute vector.

New Delegation Schemes. Starting from our semi-adaptively secure ABE, we obtain improved delegation schemes for Boolean formula with *semi-adaptive* soundness, where correctness of the computation is guaranteed even if the client's input is chosen adaptively depending on its public key. We note that achieving semi-adaptive soundness is important in practice, since we would like to reuse the

reference	security	$|EK_F|$	client's communication in bits	worker's complexity	groups	assumptions
GPSW06 [20]		$O(\ell)$	$O(n\lambda)$	$O(\ell)$	prime	static
ALP11 [2]	selective	$O(n\ell)$	$n + O(\lambda)$	$O(n\ell)$	prime	non-static
T14 [35]		$O(n\ell)$	$n + O(\lambda)$	$O(n\ell)$	prime	static
GGPR13 [18]		$O(\ell)$	$n + O(\lambda)$	$O(\ell)$	prime	non-static
LW12 [26]	adaptive	$O(\ell)$	$O(n\lambda)$	$O(\ell)$	prime	non-static
A14 [1]		$O(n\ell)$	$n + O(\lambda)$	$O(n\ell)$	composite	non-static
Construction 1	semi-	$O(n\ell)$	$n + O(\lambda)$	$O(n\ell)$	composite	static
Construction 2	adaptive	$O(\ell)$	$O(n\lambda)$	$O(\ell)$	prime	static

Fig. 2. Summary of existing publicly verifiable computation schemes. GGPR13 supports NC. The remaining schemes only support NC^1 and are obtained using the transformation of [32]. Here, $|EK_F|$ is the worker's evaluation key, n is the bit length of the input and ℓ is the size of the formula. In all the schemes, the public key is $O(n)$ group elements, delegation and verification complexity of client is $O(n)$ group operations, computation complexity of worker is also given in terms of group operations.

same public key across multiple inputs, which could lead to correlation between the input and the public key. Previous delegation schemes for formula achieve one of adaptive soundness [26, 18], constant communication complexity[2] [2], or security under static assumptions [20]; we achieve semi-adaptive soundness and the last two simultaneously. We compare our schemes with prior works in Fig 2. We stress that in applications such as delegating computation from mobile devices on cellular networks where bandwidth is a premium, reducing the client's communication from $O(n\lambda)$ bits to $n + O(\lambda)$ bits represents substantial savings.

1.2   Our Techniques

Following our recent works [38, 9] and inspired in part by [26], we rely on Waters' dual system encryption methodology [36, 25] to reduce the problem of building a (public-key) semi-adaptively secure ABE to that of building a private-key selectively secure ABE. Recall that dual system encryption is typically implemented by designing a "semi-functional space" where semi-functional components of keys and ciphertexts will behave like a parallel copy of the normal components of the system, except divorced from the public parameters. In particular, we will embed the private-key selectively secure ABE into the semi-functional space.

We proceed to outline the constructions of private-key ABE with short ciphertexts:

- For our composite-order scheme with constant-size ciphertext, we use a private-key variant of the selectively secure ABE scheme of Attrapadung, Libert and Panafieu (ALP) in [2]. Our main insight is that in the private-key

---

[2] Here, we refer to the client's communication overhead beyond sending the n-bit input, as measured in group elements.

setting with a single challenge ciphertext, we can replace the use of parameterized assumptions in the ALP scheme with the basic DDH assumption. Roughly speaking, fix an attribute i that does not appear in the challenge attribute. We can then rely on the DDH assumption to mask all the LSSS shares of the master secret key corresponding to attribute i (c.f. Section 3 overview and Lemma 2).[3] The formal security proof is more involved since we need to instantiate this argument within the dual system framework.

– For our prime-order scheme with $O(n)$-size ciphertext, the private-key selectively secure ABE we use is essentially that of Goyal et al. [20], which is in fact a public-key scheme and yields ciphertexts of length $O(n)$. To combine this scheme with the dual system framework, we rely on dual pairing vector spaces [29, 30, 16, 24, 12]. Here, we will also use the SXDH assumption to boost *statistical* entropy in the semi-functional key space into arbitrarily large amounts of *computational* entropy in the same space as we will need to mask an arbitrarily large number of shares corresponding to a single attribute.

For both schemes, we are able to exploit random self-reducibility to obtain security loss that do not depend on the number of secret key queries or the size of the boolean formula (but may depend on the input size n). In contrast, all known adaptively secure ABE schemes incur a loss that is at least linear in both the number of secret key queries and the size of the boolean formula (sometimes implicitly, by either making a "one-use" restriction or using a parameterized assumption).

Additional Related Work. In an independent work, Takashima [35] proposed a selectively secure KP-ABE scheme with constant-size ciphertexts under the DLIN assumption, which results in a delegation scheme with constant communication complexity and security under static assumptions but only achieving selective soundness. Upon learning of our work, Takashima showed that his scheme also achieves semi-adaptive security, thereby resolving a natural open problem from this work. Gennaro, Gentry, Parno and Raykova [18] constructed a delegation scheme achieving adaptive soundness and supporting NC but its security relies on parameterized assumptions.

Organization. We present our composite-order construction in Section 3. We provide our prime-order construction, the delegation schemes and associated definitions in the full version of this paper [11].

---

[3] In an earlier submission, an anonymous reviewer asked if it is possible to obtain the composite-order scheme by combining the Lewko-Waters ABE [26] with the ALP scheme. We clarify here that this approach (should it pan out) would inherit the parameterized assumption from [2]. In particular, none of the prior works either implicitly or explicitly build a private-key ABE with constant-size ciphertexts from static assumptions.

2   Preliminaries

Notation. We denote by $s \leftarrow_R S$ the fact that s is picked uniformly at random from a finite set S and by $x, y, z \leftarrow_R S$ that all x, y, z are picked independently and uniformly at random from S. By PPT, we denote a probabilistic polynomial-time algorithm. Throughout, we use 1^λ as the security parameter. We use $\cdot$ to denote multiplication (or group operation) as well as component-wise multiplication. We use lower case boldface to denote (column) vectors over scalars and upper case boldface to denote vectors of group elements as well as matrices. Given two vectors $\mathbf{x} = (x_1, x_2, \ldots), \mathbf{y} = (y_1, y_2, \ldots)$ over scalars, we use $\langle \mathbf{x}, \mathbf{y} \rangle$ to denote the standard dot product $\mathbf{x}^\top \mathbf{y}$. Given a group element g, we write $g^\mathbf{x}$ to denote $(g^{x_1}, g^{x_2}, \ldots)$; we define $g^\mathbf{A}$ where $\mathbf{A}$ is a matrix in an analogous way.

2.1   Access Structures

We define (monotone) access structures using the language of (monotone) span programs [22].

Definition 1 (access structure [3, 22]). *A (monotone) access structure $\mathbb{A}$ for attribute universe $[n]$ is a pair $(\mathbf{M}, \rho)$ where $\mathbf{M}$ is a $\ell \times \ell'$ matrix over $\mathbb{Z}_N$ and $\rho : [\ell] \to [n]$. Given $\mathbf{x} = (x_1, \ldots, x_n) \in \{0, 1\}^n$, we say that*

$$\mathbf{x} \text{ satisfies } \mathbb{A} \text{ iff } \mathbf{1} \in \text{span}\langle \mathbf{M_x} \rangle.$$

Here, $\mathbf{1} := (1, 0, \ldots, 0) \in \mathbb{Z}_N^{\ell'}$ is a row vector; $\mathbf{M_x}$ denotes the collection of vectors $\{\mathbf{M}_j : x_{\rho(j)} = 1\}$ where $\mathbf{M}_j$ denotes the j'th row of $\mathbf{M}$; and span refers to linear span of collection of (row) vectors over $\mathbb{Z}_N$.

That is, $\mathbf{x}$ satisfies $\mathbb{A}$ iff there exists constants $\omega_1, \ldots, \omega_\ell \in \mathbb{Z}_N$ such that

$$\sum_{j : x_{\rho(j)} = 1} \omega_j \mathbf{M}_j = \mathbf{1}.$$

Observe that the constants $\{\omega_j\}$ can be computed in time polynomial in the size of the matrix $\mathbf{M}$ via Gaussian elimination.

2.2   Key-Policy Attribute-Based Encryption

A KP-ABE scheme consists of four algorithms (Setup, Enc, KeyGen, Dec):

Setup$(1^\lambda, [n]) \to (\text{MPK}, \text{MSK})$. The setup algorithm takes in a security parameter 1^λ, and an attribute universe $[n]$. It outputs public parameters MPK and a master secret key MSK.

Enc$(\text{MPK}, \mathbf{x}, m) \to \text{CT}_\mathbf{x}$. The encryption algorithm takes in MPK, an attribute vector $\mathbf{x}$, and a message m. It outputs a ciphertext $\text{CT}_\mathbf{x}$.

KeyGen$(\text{MPK}, \text{MSK}, \mathbb{A}) \to \text{SK}_\mathbb{A}$. The key generation algorithm takes in MPK, MSK, and an access structure $\mathbb{A} := (\mathbf{M}, \rho)$. It outputs a secret key $\text{SK}_\mathbb{A}$.

Dec$(\text{MPK}, \text{SK}_\mathbb{A}, \text{CT}_\mathbf{x}) \to m$. The decryption algorithm takes in MPK, a secret key $\text{SK}_\mathbb{A}$ for an access structure $\mathbb{A}$, and a ciphertext $\text{CT}_\mathbf{x}$ encrypted under an attribute vector $\mathbf{x}$. It outputs a message m if $\mathbf{x}$ satisfies $\mathbb{A}$.

Correctness. For all $(\text{MPK}, \text{MSK}) \leftarrow \text{Setup}(1^\lambda, [n])$, all access structures $\mathbb{A}$, all decryption keys $\text{SK}_\mathbb{A}$, all messages m, all $\mathbf{x}$ satisfying $\mathbb{A}$, we have $\Pr[\text{Dec}(\text{MPK}, \text{SK}_\mathbb{A}, \text{Enc}(\text{MPK}, \mathbf{x}, m)) = m] = 1$.

2.3 Semi-adaptive Security Model

We now formalize the notation of *semi-adaptive* security for KP-ABE. Briefly, the adversary specifies the challenge attribute vector after it sees the public parameters and before it makes any secret key queries. The security game is defined by the following experiment, played by a challenger and an adversary $\mathcal{A}$.

Setup. The challenger runs the setup algorithm to generate (MPK, MSK). It gives MPK to $\mathcal{A}$.

Challenge Attribute. $\mathcal{A}$ gives the challenger a challenge $\mathbf{x}^*$.

Phase 1. $\mathcal{A}$ adaptively requests keys for access structures $\mathbb{A}$ with the constraint $\mathbf{x}^*$ does not satisfy $\mathbb{A}$. The challenger responds with the corresponding secret key $\text{SK}_\mathbb{A}$, which it generates by running the key generation algorithm.

Challenge Ciphertext. $\mathcal{A}$ submits two equal-length messages m_0 and m_1. The challenger picks $\beta \leftarrow_{\text{R}} \{0, 1\}$, and encrypts m_β under $\mathbf{x}^*$ by running the encryption algorithm. It sends the ciphertext to $\mathcal{A}$.

Phase 2. $\mathcal{A}$ continues to issue key queries as in **Phase 1**.

Guess. $\mathcal{A}$ must output a guess β' for β.

The advantage $\text{Adv}_\mathcal{A}^{\text{KP-ABE}}(\lambda)$ of an adversary $\mathcal{A}$ is defined to be $\Pr[\beta' = \beta] - 1/2$.

Definition 2. *A KP-ABE scheme is semi-adaptively secure if all PPT adversaries achieve at most a negligible advantage in the above security game.*

2.4 Composite Order Bilinear Groups

Composite order bilinear groups were first introduced in [7] and used in [23, 25, 27]. A generator $\mathcal{G}$ takes as input a security parameter 1^λ and outputs a description $\mathbb{G} := (N, G_N, G_T, e)$, where N is product of distinct primes of $\Theta(\lambda)$ bits, G_N and G_T are cyclic groups of order N, and $e : G_N \times G_N \to G_T$ is a map with the following properties:

1. (Bilinearity) $\forall g, h \in G_N, a, b \in \mathbb{Z}_N, e(g^a, h^b) = e(g, h)^{ab}$;
2. (Non-degeneracy) $\exists g \in G_N$ such that $e(g, g)$ has order N in G_T.

We require that the group operations in G_N and G_T as well the bilinear map e are computable in deterministic polynomial time with respect to λ. Furthermore, the group descriptions of G_N and G_T include generators of the respective cyclic groups. We use G_n to denote the subgroup of G_N of order n, where n divides N.

Computational Assumptions. We now state the three static assumptions that are required in our security proof. The first two assumptions are introduced in [25] and also used in [27]. The third assumption which basically asserts that the DDH problem is hard in the G_{p_2}-subgroup. This assumption is essentially implied by the composite 3-party Diffie-Hellman (3PDH) assumption in [6]. We provide more discussion and justification of this assumption in the full version of this paper [11]. All three assumptions hold in the generic group model under the assumption finding a non-trivial factor of N is hard.

Assumption 1. *Given a group generator $\mathcal{G}$, we define the following distribution:*

$$\mathbb{G} := (N = p_1p_2p_3, G_N, G_T, e) \leftarrow_R \mathcal{G},$$
$$g_1, U_1 \leftarrow_R G_{p_1}, \; U_2 \leftarrow_R G_{p_2}, \; g_3 \leftarrow_R G_{p_3},$$
$$T_0 \leftarrow_R G_{p_1}, \; T_1 \leftarrow_R G_{p_1p_2},$$
$$D := (\mathbb{G}; g_1, U_1U_2, g_3).$$

We assume that for any PPT algorithm $\mathcal{A}$,

$$\mathsf{Adv}_{\mathcal{A}}^{\mathrm{AS1}}(\lambda) := \big| \Pr[\mathcal{A}(D, T_0) = 1] - \Pr[\mathcal{A}(D, T_1) = 1] \big|$$

is negligible in the security parameter λ.

Assumption 2. *Given a group generator $\mathcal{G}$, we define the following distribution:*

$$\mathbb{G} := (N = p_1p_2p_3, G_N, G_T, e) \leftarrow_R \mathcal{G},$$
$$\alpha, s \leftarrow_R \mathbb{Z}_N,$$
$$g_1 \leftarrow_R G_{p_1}, \; g_2, X_2, Y_2 \leftarrow_R G_{p_2}, \; g_3 \leftarrow_R G_{p_3},$$
$$T_0 := e(g_1, g_1)^{\alpha s}, \; T_1 \leftarrow_R G_T,$$
$$D := (\mathbb{G}; g_1, g_1^\alpha X_2, g_1^s Y_2, g_2, g_3).$$

We assume that for any PPT algorithm $\mathcal{A}$,

$$\mathsf{Adv}_{\mathcal{A}}^{\mathrm{AS2}}(\lambda) := \big| \Pr[\mathcal{A}(D, T_0) = 1] - \Pr[\mathcal{A}(D, T_1) = 1] \big|$$

is negligible in the security parameter λ.

Assumption 3. *Given a group generator $\mathcal{G}$, we define the following distribution:*

$$\mathbb{G} := (N = p_1p_2p_3, G_N, G_T, e) \leftarrow_R \mathcal{G},$$
$$x, y, z \leftarrow_R \mathbb{Z}_N,$$
$$g_1, U_1 \leftarrow_R G_{p_1}, \; g_2, U_2 \leftarrow_R G_{p_2}, \; g_3, X_3, Y_3, U_3, W_3 \leftarrow_R G_{p_3},$$
$$T_0 := g_2^{xy} W_3, \; T_1 := g_2^{xy+z} W_3,$$
$$D := (\mathbb{G}; g_1, U_1U_2, g_2^x X_3, g_2^y Y_3, g_2 U_3, g_3).$$

We assume that for any PPT algorithm $\mathcal{A}$,

$$\mathsf{Adv}_{\mathcal{A}}^{\mathrm{AS3}}(\lambda) := \big| \Pr[\mathcal{A}(D, T_0) = 1] - \Pr[\mathcal{A}(D, T_1) = 1] \big|$$

is negligible in the security parameter λ.

3   Semi-adaptive ABE with Constant-Size Ciphertext

Overview. The starting point of our construction is the following variant of the ALP KP-ABE in [2]:

$$\text{MPK} := (g, g^{\mathbf{w}}, e(g,g)^{\alpha})$$
$$\text{CT}_{\mathbf{x}} := (g^s, g^{s\langle \mathbf{w}, \mathbf{x} \rangle}, e(g,g)^{\alpha s} \cdot m)$$
$$\text{SK}_{\mathbb{A}} := (g^{\alpha_j \mathbf{e}_{\rho(j)} + r_j \mathbf{w}}, g^{r_j} : j \in [\ell])$$

where $\alpha_1, \ldots, \alpha_\ell$ are LSSS shares of α for the access structure $\mathbb{A}$. Our construction proceeds by embedding this scheme into composite-order groups. As noted in the introduction, our main insight is to analyze this scheme in the private-key, selective setting. Fix a selective challenge $\mathbf{x}^* \in \{0,1\}^n$ and an index $k \in [n]$ and an access structure $\mathbb{A}$ not satisfied by $\mathbf{x}^*$. We proceed via a case analysis to argue that $\text{SK}_{\mathbb{A}}$ hides α computationally:

- if $x_k^* = 0$, then the shares $\{\alpha_j : \rho(j) = k\}$ reveal no information about α via the secret sharing property.
- if $x_k^* = 1$, then the ciphertext reveals no information about w_k (and since we are in the private-key setting, there is no MPK). Then, by the DDH assumption, $\{g^{\alpha_j + r_j w_k}, g^{r_j} : \rho(j) = k\}$ computationally hides α_j.

The formal security proof is more involved since we need to instantiate this argument within the dual system framework.

3.1   Construction

- Setup$(1^\lambda, [n])$: On input an attribute universe $[n]$, generate $\mathbb{G} := (N = p_1 p_2 p_3, G_N, G_T, e) \leftarrow_{\text{R}} \mathcal{G}$, pick $\alpha \leftarrow_{\text{R}} \mathbb{Z}_N, \mathbf{w} \leftarrow_{\text{R}} \mathbb{Z}_N^n$ and output

$$\text{MPK} := (\mathbb{G}, e(g_1, g_1)^\alpha, g_1, g_1^{\mathbf{w}}) \quad \text{and} \quad \text{MSK} := (\alpha, \mathbf{w}, g_2, g_3).$$

- Enc$(\text{MPK}, \mathbf{x}, m)$: On input an attribute vector $\mathbf{x} := (x_1, \ldots, x_n) \in \{0,1\}^n$ and $m \in G_T$, output

$$\text{CT}_{\mathbf{x}} := \Big(C_0 := g_1^s, \ C_1 := g_1^{s\langle \mathbf{w}, \mathbf{x} \rangle}, \ C_2 := e(g_1, g_1)^{\alpha s} \cdot m \Big),$$

where $s \leftarrow_{\text{R}} \mathbb{Z}_N$.

- KeyGen$(\text{MPK}, \text{MSK}, \mathbb{A} := (\mathbf{M}, \rho))$: On input an access structure $\mathbb{A} := (\mathbf{M}, \rho)$, where $\mathbf{M} \in \mathbb{Z}_N^{\ell \times \ell'}$ and $\rho : [\ell] \to [n]$, pick a random vector $\mathbf{u} \leftarrow_{\text{R}} \mathbb{Z}_N^{\ell'}$ such that $\mathbf{1u} = \alpha$ and set $\alpha_j := \mathbf{M}_j \mathbf{u}, j \in [\ell]$.[4] Output

$$\text{SK}_{\mathbb{A}} := \Big(D_j := g_1^{\alpha_j \mathbf{e}_{\rho(j)} + r_j \mathbf{w}} \cdot g_2^{r_j' \mathbf{w}} \cdot X_j, \ D_{0,j} := g_1^{r_j} \cdot g_2^{r_j'} \cdot Z_j \ : \ j \in [\ell] \Big),$$

where $r_1, r_1', \ldots, r_\ell, r_\ell' \leftarrow_{\text{R}} \mathbb{Z}_N; \ X_j \leftarrow_{\text{R}} G_{p_3}^n; \ Z_j \leftarrow_{\text{R}} G_{p_3}$, and $(\mathbf{e}_1, \ldots, \mathbf{e}_n)$ is the standard basis for $\mathbb{Z}_N^n$.

---

[4] The α_j's do in fact correspond to LSSS secret shares of α, distributed across n parties, where the i'th party receive $|\rho^{-1}(i)|$ shares, given by $\{\alpha_j : \rho(j) = i\}$.

– Dec(MPK, SK$_{\mathbb{A}}$, CT$_\mathbf{x}$): If $\mathbf{x}$ satisfies $\mathbb{A}$, compute $\omega_1, \ldots, \omega_\ell \in \mathbb{Z}_N$ such that

$$\sum_{j:x_{\rho(j)}=1} \omega_j \mathbf{M}_j = \mathbf{1}.$$

Then, compute[5]

$$e(g_1, g_1)^{\alpha s} \leftarrow \prod_{j:x_{\rho(j)}=1} \left(e(C_0^\mathbf{x}, \boldsymbol{D}_j) \cdot e(C_1, D_{0,j})^{-1} \right)^{\omega_j},$$

and recover the message as $m \leftarrow C_2/e(g_1, g_1)^{\alpha s} \in G_T$.

Correctness. Observe that

$$\begin{aligned}
&e(C_0^\mathbf{x}, \boldsymbol{D}_j) \cdot e(C_1, D_{0,j})^{-1} \\
&= e((g_1^s)^\mathbf{x}, g_1^{\alpha_j \mathbf{e}_{\rho(j)} + r_j \mathbf{w}} \cdot g_2^{r_j' \mathbf{w}} \cdot \boldsymbol{X}_j) \cdot e(g_1^{s\langle \mathbf{w}, \mathbf{x} \rangle}, g_1^{r_j} \cdot g_2^{r_j'} \cdot Z_j)^{-1} \\
&= e(g_1, g_1)^{\alpha_j s \langle \mathbf{e}_{\rho(j)}, \mathbf{x} \rangle} \cdot e(g_1, g_1)^{r_j s \langle \mathbf{w}, \mathbf{x} \rangle} \cdot e(g_1, g_1)^{-r_j s \langle \mathbf{w}, \mathbf{x} \rangle} \\
&= e(g_1, g_1)^{\alpha_j s}.
\end{aligned}$$

In addition, we have

$$\sum_{j:x_{\rho(j)}=1} \omega_j \alpha_j = \sum_{j:x_{\rho(j)}=1} \omega_j \mathbf{M}_j \mathbf{u} = \mathbf{1}\mathbf{u} = \alpha.$$

This means

$$\prod_{j:x_{\rho(j)}=1} \left(e(C_0^\mathbf{x}, \boldsymbol{D}_j) \cdot e(C_1, D_{0,j})^{-1} \right)^{\omega_j} = \prod_{j:x_{\rho(j)}=1} e(g_1, g_1)^{\omega_j \alpha_j s} = e(g_1, g_1)^{\alpha s}.$$

Correctness follows readily.

3.2   Proof of Security

We prove the following theorem:

Theorem 1. *Under Assumptions 1, 2 and 3 (described in Section 2.4), our KP-ABE scheme defined in Section 3.1 is semi-adaptively secure (in the sense of Definition 2). More precisely, for any adversary $\mathcal{A}$ that makes at most q key queries against the KP-ABE scheme, there exist probabilistic algorithms $\mathcal{B}_1, \mathcal{B}_2, \mathcal{B}_3$ such that*

$$\mathsf{Adv}_{\mathcal{A}}^{\text{KP-ABE}}(\lambda) \le \mathsf{Adv}_{\mathcal{B}_1}^{\text{AS1}}(\lambda) + n \cdot \mathsf{Adv}_{\mathcal{B}_2}^{\text{AS3}}(\lambda) + \mathsf{Adv}_{\mathcal{B}_3}^{\text{AS2}}(\lambda) + 1/p_1 + (n+1)/p_2,$$

and

$$\max\{\mathsf{Time}(\mathcal{B}_1), \mathsf{Time}(\mathcal{B}_2), \mathsf{Time}(\mathcal{B}_3)\} \approx \mathsf{Time}(\mathcal{A}) + q \cdot \mathrm{poly}(\lambda, n),$$

where n is the size of universe attribute set and $\mathrm{poly}(\lambda, n)$ is independent of $\mathsf{Time}(\mathcal{A})$.

---

[5] It is easy to see that $e(C_0^\mathbf{x}, \boldsymbol{D}_j)$ can in fact be computed using only a single pairing.

Overview. The proof follows via a series of games. To describe the games, we must first define semi-functional keys and ciphertexts. Fix random generators g_1, g_2, g_3, and let $\mathbf{x}^*$ denote the semi-adaptive challenge. We stress that unlike standard dual system encryption, we allow the semi-functional secret keys to depend on the semi-adaptive challenge $\mathbf{x}^*$ (this is okay because in the semi-adaptive security game, $\mathbf{x}^*$ is fixed before the adversary sees any secret keys). In the final transition (c.f. Lemma 3), we need to be able to simulate the secret keys given $g_1^\alpha X_2$ (as provided in Assumption 2) instead of g_1^α, so we define the semi-functional secret keys to have additional random G_{p_2}-components for the indices j corresponding to $x^*_{\rho(j)} = 0$ as captured by the term $\alpha'_j \mathbf{e}_{\rho(j)}$ below.

Semi-functional ciphertext.

$$\mathrm{CT}_{\mathbf{x}^*} := \left(g_1^s \cdot \boxed{g_2^{s'}}, \ g_1^{s\langle \mathbf{w}, \mathbf{x}^* \rangle} \cdot \boxed{g_2^{s' \langle \mathbf{w}, \mathbf{x}^* \rangle}}, \ e(g_1, g_1)^{\alpha s} \cdot m \right),$$

where $s' \leftarrow_{\mathrm{R}} \mathbb{Z}_N$.

Semi-functional secret key.

$$\mathrm{SK}_{\mathbb{A}} := \begin{pmatrix} g_1^{\alpha_j \mathbf{e}_{\rho(j)} + r_j \mathbf{w}} \cdot g_2^{r'_j \mathbf{w}} \cdot X_j, & g_1^{r_j} \cdot g_2^{r'_j} \cdot Z_j : x^*_{\rho(j)} = 1 \\ g_1^{\alpha_j \mathbf{e}_{\rho(j)} + r_j \mathbf{w}} \cdot g_2^{\boxed{\alpha'_j \mathbf{e}_{\rho(j)}} + r'_j \mathbf{w}} \cdot X_j, \ g_1^{r_j} \cdot g_2^{r'_j} \cdot Z_j : x^*_{\rho(j)} = 0 \end{pmatrix},$$

where fresh $\alpha'_1, \ldots, \alpha'_\ell \leftarrow_{\mathrm{R}} \mathbb{Z}_N$ are chosen for each secret key (specifically, we pick fresh $\alpha'_j \leftarrow_{\mathrm{R}} \mathbb{Z}_N$ for all j such that $x^*_{\rho(j)} = 0$).

Remark 1 (decryption capabilities). Fix $\mathbf{x}^*, \mathbb{A}$ such that $\mathbf{x}^*$ satisfies $\mathbb{A}$. Then,

- both semi-functional and normal secret key $\mathrm{SK}_{\mathbb{A}}$ can decrypt a normal ciphertext $\mathrm{CT}_{\mathbf{x}^*}$;

- a normal secret key $\mathrm{SK}_{\mathbb{A}}$ can decrypt a semi-functional ciphertext $\mathrm{CT}_{\mathbf{x}^*}$;

- a semi-functional secret key $\mathrm{SK}_{\mathbb{A}}$ *can* decrypt a semi-functional ciphertext $\mathrm{CT}_{\mathbf{x}^*}$; this is because the j'th subkey $(D_j, D_{0,j})$ corresponding to $x^*_{\rho(j)} = 0$ is not used for decryption although it has an additional semi-functional component $g_2^{\alpha'_j}$. This is different from a standard dual system encryption argument, but is okay in our setting because $\mathbf{x}^*$ is fixed semi-adaptively *before* the adversary makes secret key queries.

Game Sequence. We consider the following sequence of games:

- Game_0: is the real security game (c.f. Section 2.3).
- Game_1: is the same as Game_0 except that the challenge ciphertext is semi-functional.

- Game$_{2,k}$, $k = 1, 2, \ldots, n$: we incrementally transform each normal secret key to a semi-functional one, i.e. Game$_{2,k}$ is the same as Game$_1$ except that, for each secret key

$$\text{SK}_A := (\ D_j, D_{0,j} \quad : j \in [\ell]\ ),$$

the j'th subkey $(D_j, D_{0,j})$ is semi-functional if $\rho(j) \le k$, and normal if $\rho(j) > k$. More precisely, SK$_A$ has the distribution

$$\begin{pmatrix} g_1^{\alpha_j \mathbf{e}_{\rho(j)} + r_j \mathbf{w}} \cdot g_2^{r_j' \mathbf{w}} \cdot \boldsymbol{X}_j, & g_1^{r_j} \cdot g_2^{r_j'} \cdot Z_j : x_{\rho(j)}^* = 1 \\ g_1^{\alpha_j \mathbf{e}_{\rho(j)} + r_j \mathbf{w}} \cdot g_2^{r_j' \mathbf{w}} \cdot \boldsymbol{X}_j, & g_1^{r_j} \cdot g_2^{r_j'} \cdot Z_j : (x_{\rho(j)}^* = 0) \wedge (\rho(j) > k) \\ g_1^{\alpha_j \mathbf{e}_{\rho(j)} + r_j \mathbf{w}} \cdot g_2^{\alpha_j' \mathbf{e}_{\rho(j)} + r_j' \mathbf{w}} \cdot \boldsymbol{X}_j, & g_1^{r_j} \cdot g_2^{r_j'} \cdot Z_j : (x_{\rho(j)}^* = 0) \wedge (\rho(j) \le k) \end{pmatrix},$$

where fresh $\alpha_1', \ldots, \alpha_\ell' \leftarrow_R \mathbb{Z}_N$ are chosen for each secret key. In other words, from Game$_{2,k-1}$ to Game$_{2,k}$, we modify the first component D_j of the j'th subkey for all j such that $\rho(j) = k$ (that is, corresponds to the variable x_k) as follows:

- if $x_k^* = 1$, leave it unchanged;

- if $x_k^* = 0$, change the semi-functional component from $g_2^{r_j' \mathbf{w}}$ to $g_2^{\alpha_j' \mathbf{e}_k + r_j' \mathbf{w}}$.

Note that in Game$_{2,n}$, all keys are semi-functional.

- Game$_3$: is the same as Game$_{2,n}$ except that the challenge ciphertext is a semi-functional encryption of a random message in G_T.

Fix an adversary $\mathcal{A}$. We write $\mathsf{Adv}_{\text{xx}}(\lambda)$ to denote the advantage of $\mathcal{A}$ in Game$_{\text{xx}}$. It is easy to see that $\mathsf{Adv}_3(\lambda) = 0$, because the view of the adversary is Game$_3$ is independent of the challenge bit β. We complete the proof by establishing the following sequence of lemmas.

Lemma 1 (Normal to semi-functional ciphertext). *There exists an adversary $\mathcal{B}_1$ such that:*

$$|\mathsf{Adv}_0(\lambda) - \mathsf{Adv}_1(\lambda)| \le \mathsf{Adv}_{\mathcal{B}_1}^{\mathrm{AS1}}(\lambda) + 1/p_1 + 1/p_2$$

and $\mathsf{Time}(\mathcal{B}_1) \approx \mathsf{Time}(\mathcal{A}) + q \cdot \mathrm{poly}(\lambda, n)$ *where* $\mathrm{poly}(\lambda, n)$ *is independent of* $\mathsf{Time}(\mathcal{A})$.

Proof. We construct an adversary $\mathcal{B}_1$ for Assumption 1 using $\mathcal{A}$. Recall that in Assumption 1, the adversary is given $D := (\mathbb{G}; g_1, U_1U_2, g_3)$, along with T, where T is distributed as

$$g_1^s \quad \text{or} \quad g_1^s g_2^{s'}.$$

Here, $\mathcal{B}_1$ simulates Game$_0$ if $T := g_1^s$ and Game$_1$ if $T := g_1^s g_2^{s'}$. The quantity s, s' in the assumption will correspond the random exponents s, s' used in the ciphertext.

Specifically, $\mathcal{B}_1$ proceeds as follows:

Setup. $\mathcal{B}_1$ samples $\alpha \leftarrow_R \mathbb{Z}_n$, $\mathbf{w} \leftarrow_R \mathbb{Z}_N^n$ and outputs

$$\text{MPK} := (\ e(g_1, g_1^\alpha), g_1, g_1^{\mathbf{w}}\ ).$$

We note that

$$(\ \alpha, \mathbf{w}, g_1, U_1 U_2, g_3; T\ )$$

is known to $\mathcal{B}_1$. The adversary $\mathcal{A}$ outputs a challenge $\mathbf{x}^* := (x_1^*, \ldots, x_n^*)$.

Challenge Ciphertext. Upon receiving two equal-length messages m_0 and m_1 from $\mathcal{A}$, $\mathcal{B}_1$ picks $\beta \leftarrow_R \{0, 1\}$ and outputs the semi-functional challenge ciphertext as:

$$\text{CT}_{\mathbf{x}^*} := \left(\ T,\ T^{\langle \mathbf{w}, \mathbf{x}^* \rangle},\ e(T, g_1^\alpha) \cdot m_\beta \right).$$

Now, suppose $T = g_1^s \cdot g_2^{s'}$, then,

$$T^{\langle \mathbf{w}, \mathbf{x}^* \rangle} := (g_1^s \cdot g_2^{s'})^{\langle \mathbf{w}, \mathbf{x}^* \rangle} = g_1^{s\langle \mathbf{w}, \mathbf{x}^* \rangle} g_2^{s'\langle \mathbf{w}, \mathbf{x}^* \rangle},$$
$$e(T, g_1^\alpha) := e(g_1^s \cdot g_2^{s'}, g_1^\alpha) = e(g_1, g_1)^{\alpha s}.$$

Now, if $s' = 0$ (i.e., $T = g_1^s$), this would indeed be a normal encryption. On the other hand, if $s' \leftarrow_R \mathbb{Z}_N$ instead, this would indeed be a semi-functional encryption.

Key Queries. On input $\mathbb{A} := (\mathbf{M}, \rho)$, $\mathcal{B}_1$ needs to generate a normal key $\text{SK}_\mathbb{A}$, which has the distribution

$$\left(\ D_j := g_1^{\alpha_j \mathbf{e}_{\rho(j)}} \cdot (g_1^{r_j} \cdot g_2^{r'_j})^{\mathbf{w}} \cdot X_j,\ D_{0,j} := (g_1^{r_j} \cdot g_2^{r'_j}) \cdot Z_j\ : j \in [\ell]\ \right).$$

$\mathcal{B}_1$ picks $\tilde{r}_j \leftarrow_R \mathbb{Z}_N$ for $j \in [\ell]$ and replaces $g_1^{r_j} \cdot g_2^{r'_j}$ with $(U_1 U_2)^{\tilde{r}_j}$; then, it outputs

$$\text{SK}_\mathbb{A} := (\ g_1^{\alpha_j \mathbf{e}_{\rho(j)}} \cdot (U_1 U_2)^{\tilde{r}_j \mathbf{w}} \cdot X_j,\ (U_1 U_2)^{\tilde{r}_j} \cdot Z_j\ : j \in [\ell]\ ).$$

Observe that $(U_1 U_2)^{\tilde{r}_j}$ is properly distributed as long as $U_1 U_2$ is a generator of $G_{p_1 p_2}$ (by the Chinese Remainder Theorem), which occurs with probability $1 - 1/p_1 - 1/p_2$.

We may therefore conclude that: $|\text{Adv}_0(\lambda) - \text{Adv}_1(\lambda)| \leq \text{Adv}_{\mathcal{B}_1}^{\text{AS1}}(\lambda) + 1/p_1 + 1/p_2$.

$\square$

Lemma 2 (Normal to semi-functional keys). *For $k = 1, \ldots, n$, there exists an adversary $\mathcal{B}_2$ such that:*

$$|\text{Adv}_{2,k-1}(\lambda) - \text{Adv}_{2,k}(\lambda)| \leq \text{Adv}_{\mathcal{B}_2}^{\text{AS3}}(\lambda) + 1/p_2$$

and $\text{Time}(\mathcal{B}_2) \approx \text{Time}(\mathcal{A}) + q \cdot \text{poly}(\lambda, n)$ *where* $\text{poly}(\lambda, n)$ *is independent of* $\text{Time}(\mathcal{A})$. *(We note that* $\text{Game}_{2,0}$ *is identical to* Game_1.)

Overview of proof. Fix k. We want to modify j'th subkey $(\boldsymbol{D}_j, D_{0,j})$ for all j such that $\rho(j) = k$ (that is, corresponds to the variable x_k) as follows:

- if $x_k^* = 1$, we leave it unchanged (in this case, $\mathsf{Game}_{2,k-1}$ and $\mathsf{Game}_{2,k}$ are identical);

- if $x_k^* = 0$, we change the semi-functional component in $\boldsymbol{D}_j$ from $g_2^{r_j'\mathbf{w}}$ to $g_2^{\alpha_j'\mathbf{e}_k + r_j'\mathbf{w}}$ using Assumption 3.

In the rest of the overview, we focus on the case $x_k^* = 0$. Roughly speaking, we rely on the fact that $w_k \pmod{p_2}$ is statistically hidden given MPK to obtain computational entropy as captured by $\{g_2^{\alpha_j'} : \rho(j) = k\}$. For simplicity, we first consider a single subkey $(\boldsymbol{D}_j, D_{0,j})$ for which $\rho(j) = k$. Recall that $(\boldsymbol{D}_j, D_{0,j})$ in $\mathsf{Game}_{2,k-1}$ and $\mathsf{Game}_{2,k}$ are of the form:

$$(g_1^{\alpha_j\mathbf{e}_k + r_j\mathbf{w}} \cdot \boxed{g_2^{r_j'\mathbf{w}}} \cdot \boldsymbol{X}_j, \; g_1^{r_j} \cdot g_2^{r_j'} \cdot Z_j) \quad \text{and}$$

$$(g_1^{\alpha_j\mathbf{e}_k + r_j\mathbf{w}} \cdot \boxed{g_2^{\alpha_j'\mathbf{e}_k + r_j'\mathbf{w}}} \cdot \boldsymbol{X}_j, \; g_1^{r_j} \cdot g_2^{r_j'} \cdot Z_j)$$

Roughly speaking, it suffices to show that:

$$(g_1^{\mathbf{w}}, \; \boxed{g_2^{r_j'\mathbf{w}}} \cdot \boldsymbol{X}_j, \; g_2^{r_j'} \cdot Z_j) \quad \text{and} \quad (g_1^{\mathbf{w}}, \; \boxed{g_2^{\alpha_j'\mathbf{e}_k + r_j'\mathbf{w}}} \cdot \boldsymbol{X}_j, \; g_2^{r_j'} \cdot Z_j)$$

are computationally indistinguishable, where $g_1^{\mathbf{w}}$ is provided in MPK. We may further simplify this to show that:

$$(g_1^{w_k}, \; \boxed{g_2^{r_j'w_k}} \cdot X_j, \; g_2^{r_j'} \cdot Z_j) \quad \text{and} \quad (g_1^{w_k}, \; \boxed{g_2^{\alpha_j' + r_j'w_k}} \cdot X_j, \; g_2^{r_j'} \cdot Z_j)$$

are computationally indistinguishable, where $X_j, Z_j \leftarrow_{\text{R}} G_{p_3}$. This follows essentially from Assumption 3, which tells us that

$$(\boxed{g_2^{r_j'w_k}} \cdot X_j, \; g_2^{r_j'} \cdot Z_j, \; g_2^{w_k} \cdot Y_3) \quad \text{and} \quad (\boxed{g_2^{\alpha_j' + r_j'w_k}} \cdot X_j, \; g_2^{r_j'} \cdot Z_j, \; g_2^{w_k} \cdot Y_3)$$

are computationally indistinguishable, where $X_j, Z_j, Y_3 \leftarrow G_{p_3}$. Here, we rely crucially on the fact that $w_k \pmod{p_2}$ is completely random given $g_1^{w_k}$. To handle multiple subkeys $\{(\boldsymbol{D}_j, D_{0,j}) : j \in \rho^{-1}(k)\}$, we can proceed via a hybrid argument, but that would yield a security loss of $|\rho^{-1}(k)|$. To avoid this loss, we rely on the re-randomization trick from [28]. Finally, note that we cannot generate a semi-functional ciphertext for $\mathbf{x}^*$ such that $x_k^* = 1$ since we are only given $g_2^{w_k}Y_3$ and not $g_2^{w_k}$. (For the proof, it suffices to simulate a semi-functional ciphertext for which $x_k^* = 0$.)

Proof. We construct an adversary $\mathcal{B}_2$ (which gets as additional input $k \in [n]$) for Assumption 3 using $\mathcal{A}$. We note that the case $x_k^* = 1$ is straight-forward since $\mathsf{Game}_{2,k}$ is identical to $\mathsf{Game}_{2,k-1}$, which means

$$|\mathsf{Adv}_{2,k-1}(\lambda) - \mathsf{Adv}_{2,k}(\lambda)| = 0 \leq \mathsf{Adv}_{\mathcal{B}_2}^{\text{AS3}}(\lambda).$$

This leaves us with k such that $x_k^* = 0$. Recall that in Assumption 3, the adversary is given $D := (\mathbb{G}; g_1, U_1 U_2, g_2^x X_3, g_2^y Y_3, g_2 U_3, g_3)$, along with T, where T is distributed as

$$g_2^{xy} W_3 \quad \text{or} \quad g_2^{xy+z} W_3.$$

Here, we assume that $z \leftarrow_{\mathrm{R}} \mathbb{Z}_{p_2}^*$, which yields a $1/p_2$ negligible difference from Assumption 3 in the advantage; $\mathcal{B}_2$ simulates $\mathsf{Game}_{2,k-1}$ if $T = g_2^{xy} W_3$ and $\mathsf{Game}_{2,k}$ if $T = g_2^{xy+z} W_3$. Moreover, we use a "trick" from [28] to get a tight security reduction and avoid losing a factor of ℓ.

Specifically, $\mathcal{B}_2$ proceeds as follows:

Setup. $\mathcal{B}_2$ samples $\alpha \leftarrow_{\mathrm{R}} \mathbb{Z}_N$, $\tilde{\mathbf{w}} \leftarrow_{\mathrm{R}} \mathbb{Z}_N^n$ and implicitly sets the parameter $\mathbf{w} := \tilde{\mathbf{w}} \bmod p_1 p_3$ (whereas $\mathbf{w} \bmod p_2$ is undetermined at this point). $\mathcal{B}_2$ outputs

$$\mathrm{MPK} := (\ e(g_1, g_1^\alpha), g_1, g_1^{\tilde{\mathbf{w}}}\ ).$$

Observe that this is indeed the correct distribution since $g_1^{\mathbf{w}} = g_1^{\tilde{\mathbf{w}}}$. Moreover, we note that

$$(\ \alpha, \tilde{\mathbf{w}}, g_3; U_1 U_2, g_2^x X_3, g_2^y Y_3, g_2 U_3; T\ )$$

is known to $\mathcal{B}_2$. Upon receiving a challenge $\mathbf{x}^* := (x_1^*, \ldots, x_n^*)$ for which $x_k^* = 0$, $\mathcal{B}_2$ implicitly sets the parameter $\mathbf{w} = \tilde{\mathbf{w}} + y \cdot \mathbf{e}_k \bmod p_2$.

Challenge Ciphertext. Upon receiving two equal-length messages m_0 and m_1 from $\mathcal{A}$, $\mathcal{B}_2$ picks $\beta \leftarrow_{\mathrm{R}} \{0,1\}$ and outputs the semi-functional challenge ciphertext as:

$$\left(\ U_1 U_2,\ (U_1 U_2)^{\langle \tilde{\mathbf{w}}, \mathbf{x}^* \rangle},\ e(g_1^\alpha, U_1 U_2) \cdot m_\beta\ \right).$$

Observe that this is indeed the correct distribution since $\langle \tilde{\mathbf{w}}, \mathbf{x}^* \rangle = \langle \mathbf{w}, \mathbf{x}^* \rangle \bmod p_1 p_2$.

Key Queries. On input $\mathbb{A} := (\mathbf{M}, \rho)$, $\mathcal{B}_2$ needs to generate a secret key $\mathrm{SK}_{\mathbb{A}}$ of the form:

$$\left(\begin{array}{ll}
g_1^{\alpha_j \mathbf{e}_{\rho(j)} + r_j \mathbf{w}} \cdot g_2^{r_j' \mathbf{w}} \cdot X_j, & g_1^{r_j} \cdot g_2^{r_j'} \cdot Z_j \ : x_{\rho(j)}^* = 1 \\
g_1^{\alpha_j \mathbf{e}_{\rho(j)} + r_j \mathbf{w}} \cdot g_2^{r_j' \mathbf{w}} \cdot X_j, & g_1^{r_j} \cdot g_2^{r_j'} \cdot Z_j \ : (x_{\rho(j)}^* = 0) \wedge (\rho(j) > k) \\
g_1^{\alpha_j \mathbf{e}_{\rho(j)} + r_j \mathbf{w}} \cdot g_2^{\alpha_j' \mathbf{e}_{\rho(j)} + r_j' \mathbf{w}} \cdot X_j, & g_1^{r_j} \cdot g_2^{r_j'} \cdot Z_j \ : (x_{\rho(j)}^* = 0) \wedge (\rho(j) < k) \\
g_1^{\alpha_j \mathbf{e}_{\rho(j)} + r_j \mathbf{w}} \cdot \boxed{g_2^{r_j' \mathbf{w}}} \cdot X_j, & g_1^{r_j} \cdot g_2^{r_j'} \cdot Z_j \ : (x_{\rho(j)}^* = 0) \wedge (\rho(j) = k) \\
& \qquad\qquad \wedge (T = g_2^{xy} W_3) \\
g_1^{\alpha_j \mathbf{e}_{\rho(j)} + r_j \mathbf{w}} \cdot \boxed{g_2^{\alpha_j' \mathbf{e}_{\rho(j)} + r_j' \mathbf{w}}} \cdot X_j, & g_1^{r_j} \cdot g_2^{r_j'} \cdot Z_j \ : (x_{\rho(j)}^* = 0) \wedge (\rho(j) = k) \\
& \qquad\qquad \wedge (T = g_2^{xy+z} W_3)
\end{array} \right)$$

where $\alpha_1', \ldots, \alpha_\ell' \leftarrow_{\mathrm{R}} \mathbb{Z}_N$. Note that we know α and can therefore compute $\alpha_j := \mathbf{M}_j \mathbf{u}$ as in the normal KeyGen. We proceed via a case analysis for j. The first three cases are straight-forward, observe that

$$g_1^{\tilde{\mathbf{w}}} = g_1^{\mathbf{w}} \quad \text{and} \quad g_2^{\mathbf{w}} = g_2^{\tilde{\mathbf{w}}} \cdot (g_2^y)^{\mathbf{e}_k}.$$

We simply use $g_2 U_3$ and $g_2^y Y_3$ in place of g_2 and g_2^y respectively and pick $r_j, r_j', \alpha_j' \leftarrow_R \mathbb{Z}_N$.

This leaves us with j such that $(x_{\rho(j)}^* = 0) \wedge (\rho(j) = k)$. Here, $\mathcal{B}_2$ picks $\delta_j, \delta_j' \leftarrow_R \mathbb{Z}_N$ and implicitly sets

$$r_j' := x\delta_j + \delta_j'.$$

We can then rewrite the j'th normal subkey as:

$$\left(g_1^{\alpha_j \mathbf{e}_{\rho(j)} + r_j \tilde{\mathbf{w}}} \cdot \boxed{(g_2^{x\delta_j} \cdot g_2^{\delta_j'})^{\tilde{\mathbf{w}}} \cdot (g_2^{xy\delta_j} \cdot g_2^{y\delta_j'})^{\mathbf{e}_{\rho(j)}}} \cdot \mathbf{X}_j, \; g_1^{r_j} \cdot (g_2^{x\delta_j} \cdot g_2^{\delta_j'}) \cdot Z_j \right).$$

Here, we want to replace $g_2, g_2^x, g_2^y, g_2^{xy}$ with $g_2 U_3, g_2^x X_3, g_2^y Y_3, T$ respectively. First, $\mathcal{B}_2$ computes

$$R_j := (g_2^x X_3)^{\delta_j} \cdot (g_2 U_3)^{\delta_j'} = g_2^{r_j'} \cdot (X_3^{\delta_j} U_3^{\delta_j'}),$$

and outputs as the j'th subkey

$$\left(g_1^{\alpha_j \mathbf{e}_{\rho(j)} + r_j \tilde{\mathbf{w}}} \cdot \boxed{R_j^{\tilde{\mathbf{w}}} \cdot \left(T^{\delta_j} \cdot (g_2^y Y_3)^{\delta_j'} \right)^{\mathbf{e}_{\rho(j)}}} \cdot \mathbf{X}_j, \; g_1^{r_j} \cdot R_j \cdot Z_j \right).$$

Now, suppose $T = g_2^{xy+z} W_3$. Then,

$$R_j^{\tilde{\mathbf{w}}} \cdot \left(T^{\delta_j} \cdot (g_2^y Y_3)^{\delta_j'} \right)^{\mathbf{e}_{\rho(j)}} = g_2^{z\delta_j \mathbf{e}_{\rho(j)} + r_j' \mathbf{w}} \cdot \mathbf{X}_j'$$

for some $\mathbf{X}_j' \in G_{p_3}^n$. Now, if $z = 0$ (i.e., $T = g_2^{xy} W_3$), this would indeed be a normal subkey. On the other hand, if $z \leftarrow_R \mathbb{Z}_{p_2}^*$, this would be a semi-functional subkey, with $\alpha_j' := z\delta_j$, and where (r_j', δ_j) are pairwise-independent modulo p_2.

In summary, $\mathcal{B}_2$ outputs as SK_A:

$$
\begin{pmatrix}
\tilde{\boldsymbol{D}}_j \cdot \boldsymbol{S}_j, & \tilde{D}_{0,j} \cdot (g_2 U_3)^{r_j'} & : x_{\rho(j)}^* = 1 \\
\tilde{\boldsymbol{D}}_j \cdot \boldsymbol{S}_j, & \tilde{D}_{0,j} \cdot (g_2 U_3)^{r_j'} & : (x_{\rho(j)}^* = 0) \wedge (\rho(j) > k) \\
\tilde{\boldsymbol{D}}_j \cdot (g_2 U_3)^{\alpha_j' \mathbf{e}_{\rho(j)}} \cdot \boldsymbol{S}_j, & \tilde{D}_{0,j} \cdot (g_2 U_3)^{r_j'} & : (x_{\rho(j)}^* = 0) \wedge (\rho(j) < k) \\
\tilde{\boldsymbol{D}}_j \cdot \boxed{R_j^{\tilde{\mathbf{w}}} \cdot \left(T^{\delta_j} \cdot (g_2^y Y_3)^{\delta_j'} \right)^{\mathbf{e}_{\rho(j)}}}, & \tilde{D}_{0,j} \cdot R_j & : (x_{\rho(j)}^* = 0) \wedge (\rho(j) = k)
\end{pmatrix}
$$

where

$$\tilde{\boldsymbol{D}}_j := g_1^{\alpha_j \mathbf{e}_{\rho(j)} + r_j \tilde{\mathbf{w}}} \cdot \mathbf{X}_j \in G_{p_1 p_3}^n, \qquad \tilde{D}_{0,j} := g_1^{r_j} \cdot Z_j \in G_{p_1 p_3},$$
$$\boldsymbol{S}_j := (g_2^y Y_3)^{r_j' \mathbf{e}_k} \cdot (g_2 U_3)^{r_j' \tilde{\mathbf{w}}} \in G_{p_2 p_3}^n, \qquad R_j := (g_2^x X_3)^{\delta_j} \cdot (g_2 U_3)^{\delta_j'} \in G_{p_2 p_3}.$$

We may therefore conclude that: $|\mathsf{Adv}_{2,k-1}(\lambda) - \mathsf{Adv}_{2,k}(\lambda)| \leq \mathsf{Adv}_{\mathcal{B}_2}^{\mathrm{AS3}}(\lambda) + 1/p_2$.

$\square$

Lemma 3 (Final transition). *There exists an adversary $\mathcal{B}_3$ such that:*

$$|\mathsf{Adv}_{2,n}(\lambda) - \mathsf{Adv}_3(\lambda)| \leq \mathsf{Adv}_{\mathcal{B}_3}^{\mathrm{AS2}}(\lambda)$$

and $\mathsf{Time}(\mathcal{B}_3) \approx \mathsf{Time}(\mathcal{A}) + q \cdot \mathrm{poly}(\lambda, n)$ where $\mathrm{poly}(\lambda, n)$ is independent of $\mathsf{Time}(\mathcal{A})$.

Overview of proof. Following the final transitions in [25, 27], we use Assumption 2, in which we are given $(g_1, g_1^{\alpha} X_2, g_1^s Y_2, g_2, g_3, T)$ where T is either $e(g_1, g_1)^{\alpha s}$ or drawn uniformly from G_T to blind the challenge message m_{β}. The main challenge in our setting lies in simulating a semi-functional key $\text{SK}_{\mathbb{A}}$ given $g_1^{\alpha} X_2$ and not α itself. Recall that a semi-functional key $\text{SK}_{\mathbb{A}}$ has the same distribution

$$\left(\begin{array}{lll} \boxed{g_1^{\alpha_j \mathbf{e}_{\rho(j)}}} \cdot g_1^{r_j \mathbf{w}} \cdot g_2^{r_j' \mathbf{w}} \cdot X_j, & g_1^{r_j} \cdot g_2^{r_j'} \cdot Z_j & : x^*_{\rho(j)} = 1 \\[2mm] \boxed{g_1^{\alpha_j \mathbf{e}_{\rho(j)}}} \cdot \boxed{g_2^{\alpha_j' \mathbf{e}_{\rho(j)}}} \cdot g_1^{r_j \mathbf{w}} \cdot g_2^{r_j' \mathbf{w}} \cdot X_j, \; g_1^{r_j} \cdot g_2^{r_j'} \cdot Z_j & : x^*_{\rho(j)} = 0 \end{array} \right)$$

in both $\mathsf{Game}_{2,n}$ and Game_3. Specifically, we need to simulate (given $g_1, g_2, g_1^{\alpha} X_2$)

$$\left(\begin{array}{ll} \boxed{g_1^{\alpha_j}} & : x^*_{\rho(j)} = 1 \\[2mm] \boxed{g_1^{\alpha_j}} \cdot \boxed{g_2^{\alpha_j'}} & : x^*_{\rho(j)} = 0 \end{array} \right)$$

where $\alpha_1, \ldots, \alpha_{\ell}$ are LSSS shares of α according to $\mathbb{A} = (\mathbf{M}, \rho)$ and $\alpha_1', \ldots, \alpha_{\ell}'$ are independently random values. Roughly speaking, we proceed as follows:

- simulate the terms $(g_1^{\alpha_j} : x^*_{\rho(j)} = 1)$ by raising g_1 to the power of random LSSS shares of 0 (as determined by $\mathbf{M}\tilde{\mathbf{u}}_0$ below);

- simulate the terms $(g_1^{\alpha_j} \cdot g_2^{\alpha_j'} : x^*_{\rho(j)} = 0)$ by doing a LSSS share of $g_1^{\alpha} X_2$ "in the exponent" (as determined by $\alpha \mathbf{M}\tilde{\mathbf{u}}_1$ below), multiplying by the shares of 0 from the previous step, then re-randomizing the G_{p_2}-components.

We exploit the fact that $\mathbf{x}^*$ does not satisfy $\mathbb{A}$ to argue that we can choose $\tilde{\mathbf{u}}_1$ so that $\mathbf{M}_{\mathbf{x}^*} \cdot \tilde{\mathbf{u}}_1 = \mathbf{0}$.

Proof. We construct an adversary $\mathcal{B}_3$ for Assumption 2 using $\mathcal{A}$. Recall that in Assumption 2, the adversary is given $D := (\mathbb{G}; g_1, g_1^{\alpha} X_2, g_1^s Y_2, g_2, g_3)$, along with T, where T equals $e(g_1, g_1)^{\alpha s}$ or is drawn uniformly from G_T. Here, $\mathcal{B}_3$ simulates $\mathsf{Game}_{2,n}$ if $T := e(g_1, g_1)^{\alpha s}$ and Game_3 if $T \leftarrow_{\mathrm{R}} G_T$. The quantity α in the assumption will correspond exactly to α in MSK, and the quantity s in the assumption will correspond the random exponents s used in the (semi-functional) ciphertext.

Specifically, $\mathcal{B}_3$ proceeds as follows:

Setup. $\mathcal{B}_3$ samples $\mathbf{w} \leftarrow_{\mathrm{R}} \mathbb{Z}_N^n$ and output the public parameters

$$\text{MPK} := (\, e(g_1, g_1^{\alpha} X_2), g_1, g_1^{\mathbf{w}} \,).$$

We note that

$$(\, \mathbf{w}, g_2, g_3; g_1^{\alpha} X_2, g_1^s Y_2; T \,)$$

is known to $\mathcal{B}_3$. The adversary $\mathcal{A}$ outputs a challenge $\mathbf{x}^* := (x_1^*, \ldots, x_n^*)$.

Challenge Ciphertext. Upon receiving two equal-length messages m_0 and m_1 from $\mathcal{A}$, $\mathcal{B}_3$ picks $\beta \leftarrow_{\mathrm{R}} \{0, 1\}$ and outputs the semi-functional challenge ciphertext as:

$$\text{CT}_{\mathbf{x}^*} := \left(\, g_1^s Y_2, \; (g_1^s Y_2)^{\langle \mathbf{w}, \mathbf{x}^* \rangle}, \; T \cdot m_{\beta} \,\right).$$

Now, if T is distributed as distributed as $e(g_1, g_1)^{\alpha s}$, this would indeed be a properly distributed semi-functional encryption of m_β. On the other hand, if $T \leftarrow_R G_T$, instead, then the challenge ciphertext is a properly distributed semi-functional encryption of a random message in G_T.

Key Queries. On input $\mathbb{A} := (\mathbf{M}, \rho)$, $\mathcal{B}_3$ needs to generate a semi-functional key $\mathrm{SK}_\mathbb{A}$, which has the distribution

$$
\left(
\begin{array}{ll}
\boxed{g_1^{\alpha_j \mathbf{e}_{\rho(j)}}} \cdot g_1^{r_j \mathbf{w}} \cdot g_2^{r'_j \mathbf{w}} \cdot X_j, & g_1^{r_j} \cdot g_2^{r'_j} \cdot Z_j \quad : x^*_{\rho(j)} = 1 \\[2mm]
\boxed{g_1^{\alpha_j \mathbf{e}_{\rho(j)}}} \cdot \boxed{g_2^{\alpha'_j \mathbf{e}_{\rho(j)}}} \cdot g_1^{r_j \mathbf{w}} \cdot g_2^{r'_j \mathbf{w}} \cdot X_j, \; g_1^{r_j} \cdot g_2^{r'_j} \cdot Z_j \quad : x^*_{\rho(j)} = 0
\end{array}
\right),
$$

where $\alpha'_1, \ldots, \alpha'_\ell \leftarrow_R \mathbb{Z}_N$. The main challenge lies in simulating the terms $g_1^{\alpha_j}$ since $\mathcal{B}_3$ is only given $g_1^\alpha X_2$ and not α itself. By definition of the KP-ABE security game, $\mathbf{x}^*$ does not satisfy $\mathbb{A}$, so $\mathbf{1} \notin \mathrm{span}\langle \mathbf{M}_{\mathbf{x}^*} \rangle$. (Refer to Definition 1 for the notation.) Therefore, we can efficiently compute $\tilde{\mathbf{u}}_1 \in \mathbb{Z}_N^{\ell'}$ such that

$$
\mathbf{M}_{\mathbf{x}^*} \tilde{\mathbf{u}}_1 = 0 \quad \text{and} \quad \mathbf{1} \tilde{\mathbf{u}}_1 = 1.
$$

$\mathcal{B}_3$ samples $\tilde{\mathbf{u}}_0 \leftarrow_R \mathbb{Z}_N^{\ell'}$ such that $\mathbf{1} \tilde{\mathbf{u}}_0 = 0$, and implicitly sets

$$
\mathbf{u} := \alpha \cdot \tilde{\mathbf{u}}_1 + \tilde{\mathbf{u}}_0.
$$

Observe that $\mathbf{u}$ has indeed the correct distribution. Recall that we set $\alpha_j := \mathbf{M}_j \mathbf{u}$, which yields

$$
\alpha_j = \begin{cases} \mathbf{M}_j \tilde{\mathbf{u}}_0 & \text{if } x^*_{\rho(j)} = 1 \\ \alpha \cdot \mathbf{M}_j \tilde{\mathbf{u}}_1 + \mathbf{M}_j \tilde{\mathbf{u}}_0 & \text{if } x^*_{\rho(j)} = 0 \end{cases}
$$

where both $\tilde{\mathbf{u}}_1$ and $\tilde{\mathbf{u}}_0$ are known to $\mathcal{B}_3$. The case j such that $x^*_{\rho(j)} = 1$ is straight-forward; $\mathcal{B}_3$ simply picks $r_j, r'_j \leftarrow_R \mathbb{Z}_N$. For the case j such that $x^*_{\rho(j)} = 0$, we can then rewrite $g_1^{\alpha_j} \cdot g_2^{\alpha'_j}$ as a function of $\tilde{\mathbf{u}}_0, \tilde{\mathbf{u}}_1$, and $g_1^\alpha X_2$:

$$
g_1^{\alpha_j} \cdot g_2^{\alpha'_j} = g_1^{\alpha \cdot \mathbf{M}_j \tilde{\mathbf{u}}_1 + \mathbf{M}_j \tilde{\mathbf{u}}_0} \cdot g_2^{\alpha'_j} = (g_1^\alpha X_2)^{\mathbf{M}_j \tilde{\mathbf{u}}_1} \cdot g_1^{\mathbf{M}_j \tilde{\mathbf{u}}_0} \cdot g_2^{\tilde{\alpha}'_j},
$$

where $\mathcal{B}_3$ picks $\tilde{\alpha}'_j \leftarrow_R \mathbb{Z}_N$ and implicitly sets $g_2^{\alpha'_j} := X_2^{\mathbf{M}_j \tilde{\mathbf{u}}_1} \cdot g_2^{\tilde{\alpha}'_j}$. $\mathcal{B}_3$ then outputs

$$
\mathrm{SK}_\mathbb{A} := \left(
\begin{array}{ll}
\boxed{g_1^{\mathbf{M}_j \tilde{\mathbf{u}}_0 \mathbf{e}_{\rho(j)}}} \cdot \tilde{D}_j, & D_{0,j} \quad : x^*_{\rho(j)} = 1 \\[2mm]
\boxed{\left((g_1^\alpha X_2)^{\mathbf{M}_j \tilde{\mathbf{u}}_1} \cdot g_1^{\mathbf{M}_j \tilde{\mathbf{u}}_0} \cdot g_2^{\tilde{\alpha}'_j} \right)^{\mathbf{e}_{\rho(j)}}} \cdot \tilde{D}_j, \; D_{0,j} \quad : x^*_{\rho(j)} = 0
\end{array}
\right),
$$

where $\tilde{D}_j := g_1^{r_j \mathbf{w}} \cdot g_2^{r'_j \mathbf{w}} \cdot X_j$ and $\tilde{D}_{0,j} := g_1^{r_j} \cdot g_2^{r'_j} \cdot Z_j$.

We may therefore conclude that: $|\mathsf{Adv}_{2,n}(\lambda) - \mathsf{Adv}_3(\lambda)| \le \mathsf{Adv}_{\mathcal{B}_3}^{\mathrm{AS2}}(\lambda)$. $\qquad\square$

Acknowledgments. We thank Allison Lewko and the reviewers for helpful discussions and feedback.

References

[1] Attrapadung, N.: Dual system encryption via doubly selective security: Framework, fully secure functional encryption for regular languages, and more. In: Nguyen, P.Q., Oswald, E. (eds.) EUROCRYPT 2014. LNCS, vol. 8441, pp. 557–577. Springer, Heidelberg (2014)

[2] Attrapadung, N., Libert, B., de Panafieu, E.: Expressive key-policy attribute-based encryption with constant-size ciphertexts. In: Catalano, D., Fazio, N., Gennaro, R., Nicolosi, A. (eds.) PKC 2011. LNCS, vol. 6571, pp. 90–108. Springer, Heidelberg (2011)

[3] Beimel, A.: Secure Schemes for Secret Sharing and Key Distribution. Ph.D., Technion - Israel Institute of Technology (1996)

[4] Benabbas, S., Gennaro, R., Vahlis, Y.: Verifiable delegation of computation over large datasets. In: Rogaway, P. (ed.) CRYPTO 2011. LNCS, vol. 6841, pp. 111–131. Springer, Heidelberg (2011)

[5] Boneh, D., Franklin, M.K.: Identity-based encryption from the Weil pairing. SIAM J. Comput. 32(3), 586–615 (2003)

[6] Boneh, D., Waters, B.: Conjunctive, subset, and range queries on encrypted data. In: Vadhan, S.P. (ed.) TCC 2007. LNCS, vol. 4392, pp. 535–554. Springer, Heidelberg (2007)

[7] Boneh, D., Goh, E.-J., Nissim, K.: Evaluating 2-DNF formulas on ciphertexts. In: Kilian, J. (ed.) TCC 2005. LNCS, vol. 3378, pp. 325–341. Springer, Heidelberg (2005)

[8] Chen, J., Wee, H.: Fully (almost) tightly secure IBE and dual system groups. In: Canetti, R., Garay, J.A. (eds.) CRYPTO 2013, Part II. LNCS, vol. 8043, pp. 435–460. Springer, Heidelberg (2013)

[9] Chen, J., Wee, H.: Fully (almost) tightly secure IBE from standard assumptions. IACR Cryptology ePrint Archive, Report 2013/803, Preliminary version in [8] (2013)

[10] Chen, J., Wee, H.: Dual system groups and its applications — compact HIBE and more. IACR Cryptology ePrint Archive, Report 2014/265, Preliminary version in [8] (2014)

[11] Chen, J., Wee, H.: Semi-adaptive attribute-based encryption and improved delegation for boolean formula. IACR Cryptology ePrint Archive, Report 2014/465 (2014)

[12] Chen, J., Lim, H.W., Ling, S., Wang, H., Wee, H.: Shorter IBE and signatures via asymmetric pairings. In: Abdalla, M., Lange, T. (eds.) Pairing 2012. LNCS, vol. 7708, pp. 122–140. Springer, Heidelberg (2013)

[13] Cheung, L., Newport, C.C.: Provably secure ciphertext policy ABE. In: ACM Conference on Computer and Communications Security, pp. 456–465 (2007)

[14] Cocks, C.: An identity based encryption scheme based on quadratic residues. In: Honary, B. (ed.) Cryptography and Coding 2001. LNCS, vol. 2260, pp. 360–363. Springer, Heidelberg (2001)

[15] Fiore, D., Gennaro, R.: Publicly verifiable delegation of large polynomials and matrix computations, with applications. In: ACM Conference on Computer and Communications Security, pp. 501–512 (2012)

[16] Freeman, D.M.: Converting pairing-based cryptosystems from composite-order groups to prime-order groups. In: Gilbert, H. (ed.) EUROCRYPT 2010. LNCS, vol. 6110, pp. 44–61. Springer, Heidelberg (2010)

[17] Gennaro, R., Gentry, C., Parno, B.: Non-interactive verifiable computing: Outsourcing computation to untrusted workers. In: Rabin, T. (ed.) CRYPTO 2010. LNCS, vol. 6223, pp. 465–482. Springer, Heidelberg (2010)

[18] Gennaro, R., Gentry, C., Parno, B., Raykova, M.: Quadratic span programs and succinct NIZKs without PCPs. In: Johansson, T., Nguyen, P.Q. (eds.) EUROCRYPT 2013. LNCS, vol. 7881, pp. 626–645. Springer, Heidelberg (2013)

[19] Goldwasser, S., Kalai, Y.T., Rothblum, G.N.: Delegating computation: Interactive proofs for muggles. In: STOC, pp. 113–122 (2008)

[20] Goyal, V., Pandey, O., Sahai, A., Waters, B.: Attribute-based encryption for fine-grained access control of encrypted data. In: ACM Conference on Computer and Communications Security, pp. 89–98 (2006)

[21] Goyal, V., Jain, A., Pandey, O., Sahai, A.: Bounded ciphertext policy attribute based encryption. In: Aceto, L., Damgård, I., Goldberg, L.A., Halldórsson, M.M., Ingólfsdóttir, A., Walukiewicz, I. (eds.) ICALP 2008, Part II. LNCS, vol. 5126, pp. 579–591. Springer, Heidelberg (2008)

[22] Karchmer, M., Wigderson, A.: On span programs. In: Structure in Complexity Theory Conference, pp. 102–111 (1993)

[23] Katz, J., Sahai, A., Waters, B.: Predicate encryption supporting disjunctions, polynomial equations, and inner products. In: Smart, N. (ed.) EUROCRYPT 2008. LNCS, vol. 4965, pp. 146–162. Springer, Heidelberg (2008)

[24] Lewko, A.: Tools for simulating features of composite order bilinear groups in the prime order setting. In: Pointcheval, D., Johansson, T. (eds.) EUROCRYPT 2012. LNCS, vol. 7237, pp. 318–335. Springer, Heidelberg (2012)

[25] Lewko, A., Waters, B.: New techniques for dual system encryption and fully secure HIBE with short ciphertexts. In: Micciancio, D. (ed.) TCC 2010. LNCS, vol. 5978, pp. 455–479. Springer, Heidelberg (2010)

[26] Lewko, A., Waters, B.: New proof methods for attribute-based encryption: Achieving full security through selective techniques. In: Safavi-Naini, R., Canetti, R. (eds.) CRYPTO 2012. LNCS, vol. 7417, pp. 180–198. Springer, Heidelberg (2012)

[27] Lewko, A., Okamoto, T., Sahai, A., Takashima, K., Waters, B.: Fully secure functional encryption: Attribute-based encryption and (hierarchical) inner product encryption. In: Gilbert, H. (ed.) EUROCRYPT 2010. LNCS, vol. 6110, pp. 62–91. Springer, Heidelberg (2010)

[28] Naor, M., Reingold, O.: Number-theoretic constructions of efficient pseudo-random functions. J. ACM 51(2), 231–262 (2004)

[29] Okamoto, T., Takashima, K.: Homomorphic encryption and signatures from vector decomposition. In: Galbraith, S.D., Paterson, K.G. (eds.) Pairing 2008. LNCS, vol. 5209, pp. 57–74. Springer, Heidelberg (2008)

[30] Okamoto, T., Takashima, K.: Hierarchical predicate encryption for inner-products. In: Matsui, M. (ed.) ASIACRYPT 2009. LNCS, vol. 5912, pp. 214–231. Springer, Heidelberg (2009)

[31] Okamoto, T., Takashima, K.: Fully secure functional encryption with general relations from the decisional linear assumption. In: Rabin, T. (ed.) CRYPTO 2010. LNCS, vol. 6223, pp. 191–208. Springer, Heidelberg (2010)

[32] Parno, B., Raykova, M., Vaikuntanathan, V.: How to delegate and verify in public: Verifiable computation from attribute-based encryption. In: Cramer, R. (ed.) TCC 2012. LNCS, vol. 7194, pp. 422–439. Springer, Heidelberg (2012)

[33] Sahai, A., Waters, B.: Fuzzy identity-based encryption. In: Cramer, R. (ed.) EUROCRYPT 2005. LNCS, vol. 3494, pp. 457–473. Springer, Heidelberg (2005)

[34] Shamir, A.: Identity-based cryptosystems and signature schemes. In: Blakely, G.R., Chaum, D. (eds.) Advances in Cryptology - CRYPT0 1984. LNCS, vol. 196, pp. 47–53. Springer, Heidelberg (1985)

[35] Takashima, K.: Expressive attribute-based encryption with constant-size cipher-texts from the decisional linear assumption. In: SCN Also, Cryptology ePrint Archive, Report 2014/207 (to appear 2014)

[36] Waters, B.: Dual system encryption: Realizing fully secure IBE and HIBE under simple assumptions. In: Halevi, S. (ed.) CRYPTO 2009. LNCS, vol. 5677, pp. 619–636. Springer, Heidelberg (2009)

[37] Waters, B.: Ciphertext-policy attribute-based encryption: An expressive, efficient, and provably secure realization. In: Catalano, D., Fazio, N., Gennaro, R., Nicolosi, A. (eds.) PKC 2011. LNCS, vol. 6571, pp. 53–70. Springer, Heidelberg (2011)

[38] Wee, H.: Dual system encryption via predicate encodings. In: Lindell, Y. (ed.) TCC 2014. LNCS, vol. 8349, pp. 616–637. Springer, Heidelberg (2014)

Expressive Attribute-Based Encryption with Constant-Size Ciphertexts from the Decisional Linear Assumption

Katsuyuki Takashima

Mitsubishi Electric, 5-1-1 Ofuna, Kamakura, Kanagawa 247-8501, Japan
Takashima.Katsuyuki@aj.MitsubishiElectric.co.jp

Abstract. We propose a key-policy attribute-based encryption (KP-ABE) scheme with *constant-size ciphertexts*, whose selective security is proven under the *decisional linear (DLIN) assumption* in the standard model. The proposed scheme also has *semi-adaptively* security, which is a recently proposed notion of security. The access structure is expressive, that is given by *non-monotone span programs*. It also has fast decryption, i.e., a decryption includes only a constant number of pairing operations. As an application of our KP-ABE construction, we also propose a *fully secure* attribute-based signatures with constant-size secret (signing) keys from the DLIN. For achieving the above results, we employ a hierarchical reduction technique on dual pairing vector spaces and a modified form of pairwise independence lemma specific to our proposed schemes.

1 Introduction

1.1 Backgrounds

The notion of *attribute-based encryption* (ABE) introduced by Sahai and Waters [25] is an advanced class of encryption and provides more flexible and fine-grained functionalities in sharing and distributing sensitive data than traditional symmetric and public-key encryption as well as recent identity-based encryption. In ABE systems, either one of the parameters for encryption and secret key is a set of attributes, and the other is an access policy (structure) over a universe of attributes, e.g., a secret key for a user is associated with an access policy and a ciphertext is associated with a set of attributes. A secret key with a policy can decrypt a ciphertext associated with a set of attributes, iff the attribute set satisfies the policy. If the access policy is for a secret key, it is called key-policy ABE (KP-ABE), and if the access policy is for encryption, it is ciphertext-policy ABE (CP-ABE).

All the existing *practical* ABE schemes have been constructed by (bilinear) pairing groups, and the largest class of relations supported by the ABE schemes is (non-monotone) span programs (or (non-monotone) span programs with inner-product relations [22]). While general (polynomial size) circuits are supported [14,16] recently, they are much less efficient than the pairing-based ABE schemes

M. Abdalla and R. De Prisco (Eds.): SCN 2014, LNCS 8642, pp. 298–317, 2014.

and non-practical when the relations are limited to span programs. Since our aim is to achieve *constant-size ciphertexts* in the sizes of attribute set or access policy in expressive ABE, hereafter, we focus on pairing-based ABE with span program access structures. Here, "constant" is valid as long as the description of the attribute or policy is not considered a part of the ciphertext, which is a common assumption in the ABE application. Hence, we use "constant" in this sense hereafter.

While the expressive access control (span programs) is very attractive, it also requires additional cost in terms of ciphertext size and decryption time. Emura et al. [13], Herranz et al. [17], and Chen et al. [8] constructed ABE schemes with constant-size ciphertexts, but their access structures are very limited. Attrapadung, Libert and de Panafieu [2] first constructed a KP-ABE scheme for span programs with constant-size ciphertexts and fast decryption which needs only a constant-number of pairing operations.

While Attrapadung et al.'s KP-ABE scheme (and subsequent works [30,1]) show an interesting approach to achieving constant-size ciphertexts with expressive access structures, the security are proven only based on q-type assumptions (n-DBDHE assumption with n the maximum number of attributes per ciphertext and more complex EDHE assumptions). Previously, since the introduction by Mitsunari et al. [19] and Boneh et al. [5], various kinds of q-type assumptions have been widely used in order to achieve efficient cryptographic primitives [4,6,15,12,17]. However, the assumptions (and also the associated schemes) suffered a special attack which was presented by Cheon [10] at Eurocrypt 2006. More recently, Sakemi et al. [26] have shown that the attack can be a real threat to q-type assumption-based cryptographic primitives by executing a successful experiment. Consequently, it is very desirable that the above schemes should be replaced by an efficiency-comparable alternative scheme based on a *static* (non-q type) assumption instead of a q-type assumption. Very recently, Chen and Wee [9] introduced the notion of semi-adaptive security for ABE, where the adversary specifies the challenge attribute set after it sees the public parameters but before it makes any secret key queries, and they also constructed a small-universe KP-ABE scheme with constant-size ciphertexts on *composite-order groups*.

Hence, to construct an expressive KP-ABE scheme with constant-size ciphertexts *from a static assumption on the prime-order groups* remains an interesting open problem in terms of practical and theoretical aspects on ABE. Also, since there exist no attribute-based signatures (ABS) [18,24] with constant-size secret keys, to construct ABS with constant-size secret keys is open.

1.2 Our Results

- We propose a KP-ABE scheme with constant-size ciphertexts, whose selective security is proven from the DLIN assumption in the standard model (Section 5). It is also *semi-adaptively* secure from the same assumption (Theorem 2). The access structure is expressive, that is given by non-monotone span programs. It also has fast decryption: a decryption includes only a constant number of pairing operations, i.e., 17 pairings independently of the

Table 1. Comparison of our scheme with KP-ABE *for span programs with constant-size ciphertexts* in [2,1,9], where $|\mathbb{G}|$, $|\mathbb{G}_T|$, $|\Gamma|$, n, ℓ, r, and ν represent size of an element of a bilinear source group $\mathbb{G}$, that of a target group $\mathbb{G}_T$, the maximum number of attributes per ciphertext, and the number of rows and columns in access structure matrix for the secret key, and the maximum number of the adversary's key queries, respectively. PK, SK, and CT stand for public key, secret key, and ciphertext, respectively.

	ALdP11 [2]	A14 [1]	CW14 [9]	Proposed
Universe	large	large	small	large
Security	selective	adaptive	semi-adaptive	selective* and semi-adaptive
Order of $\mathbb{G}$	prime	composite	composite	prime
Assumption	n-DBDHE	EDHE3 & 4 parametrized by n, ℓ, r	Static assump. on composite order $\mathbb{G}$	DLIN
Access structures	Non-monotone span program	Monotone span program	Monotone span program	Non-monotone span program
PK size	$O(n)\,|\mathbb{G}|$	$O(n)\,|\mathbb{G}|$	$O(n)\,|\mathbb{G}|$	$O(n)\,|\mathbb{G}|$
SK size	$O(\ell n)\,|\mathbb{G}|$	$O(\ell n)\,|\mathbb{G}|$	$O(\ell n)\,|\mathbb{G}|$	$O(\ell n)\,|\mathbb{G}|$
CT size	$3\,|\mathbb{G}| + 1\,|\mathbb{G}_T|$**	$6\,|\mathbb{G}| + 1\,|\mathbb{G}_T|$	$2\,|\mathbb{G}| + 1\,|\mathbb{G}_T|$	$17\,|\mathbb{G}| + 1\,|\mathbb{G}_T|$

* While the reduction factor of the semi-adaptive security from DLIN is $O(\nu\ell)$, that of the selective security from DLIN is $O(n)$.
** In a subsequent work [30], CT size is reduced to $2\,|\mathbb{G}| + 1\,|\mathbb{G}_T|$.

    sizes of the used attribute set and access structure. For comparison of our scheme with previous KP-ABE for span programs with constant-size ciphertexts, see Table 1.

- As an application of our KP-ABE construction, we also propose a *fully secure* ABS scheme with constant-size secret (signing) key from the DLIN assumption (Section 7 and the full version of this paper [27]).
- For achieving the above results, we employ a hierarchical reduction technique on dual pairing vector spaces (DPVS) [21,22] and a modified form of pairwise independence lemma specific to our proposed schemes, whose original form was given in [23] for realizing constant-size ciphertexts or secret keys in inner-product encryption. For the details, see Sections 1.3 and 6.

1.3   Key Techniques

As an underlying primitive, we employ a sparse matrix key-generation on DPVS developed in [23], in which constant-size ciphertext zero/non-zero inner-product encryption are constructed from DLIN. Using the basic construction [23], to achieve short ciphertexts in our KP-ABE, attributes $\Gamma := \{x_j\}_{j=1,\dots,n'}$ are encoded in an n-dimensional (with $n \geq n' + 1$) vector $\vec{y} := (y_1, \dots, y_n)$ such that $\sum_{j=0}^{n-1} y_{n-j} z^j = z^{n-1-n'} \prod_{j=1}^{n'} (z - x_j)$ where $y_1 = 1$. Each attribute value v_i (for $i = 1, \dots, \ell$) associated with a row of access structure matrix M (in $\mathbb{S}$) is encoded as $\vec{v}_i := (v_i^{n-1}, \ldots, v_i, 1)$, so $\vec{y} \cdot \vec{v}_i = \prod_{j=1}^{n-1}(v_i - x_j)$, i.e., the value of inner product is equal to zero if and only if $v_i = x_j$ for some j. Here, the relation between $\mathbb{S}$ and Γ is determined by the multiple inner product values $\vec{y} \cdot \vec{v}_i$ for one vector $\vec{y}$ which is equivalent to Γ. Hence, a ciphertext vector element c_1 is encoded with $\omega\vec{y}$ (for random ω), which is represented by *twelve* (constant in n) group elements (as well as $\vec{y}$), and key vector elements k_i^* are encoded with $\vec{v}_i$ and shares s_i $(i = 1, \ldots, \ell)$ for a central secret s_0, respectively (see Section 5.1 for the key idea). A standard dual system encryption (DSE) approach considers a pair of vectors in the semi-functional space, $(\tau\vec{y}, r_i\vec{e}_1 + \psi_i\vec{v}_i)$ or $(\tau\vec{y}, r_i\vec{v}_i)$ with secret shares r_i of a secret r_0 and random τ, ψ_i, and then the vector pair is randomized with *preserving* the inner product values based on a *pairwise* independence argument. Since we must deal with a *common* $\tau\vec{y}$ in all the above pairs, we should modify the original argument for our scheme, which is based on a modified form of pairwise independence lemma (Lemma 4) for a specific matrix group $\mathcal{H}_{\vec{y}}(n, \mathbb{F}_q)$.

For the purpose, we prove the security in a *hierarchical* manner. First, we establish an intermediate problem (Problem 1 in Section 5.4) to prove the scheme's security, and then, the security of the problem is proven from the DLIN assumption. Problem 1 is made for proving the selective security of our KP-ABE, which takes a target vector $\vec{y}$ as input. The queried keys (and the challenge ciphertext) in the security games change to semi-functional form in DSE framework as given in Eq. (7) (in particular, w_0 is uniformly distributed in $\mathbb{F}_q$). The difference of the advantages of the adversary is bounded by the advantage gap of Problem 1 since the target attributes do not satisfy access structures for queried keys. (See [20] for a simpler example of this type argument.)

The security of the (intermediate) problem is reduced to that of DLIN through multiple reduction steps (Lemma 3). A technical challenge for the security of Problem 1 is to insert n random (sparse) matrices $\{Z_j\}_{j=1,\ldots,n}$ of size $n \times n$ which fix $\vec{y}$ i.e., $\vec{y} = \vec{y} \cdot (Z_j)^{\mathrm{T}}$ to key components $\{h_{1,j,i}^*\}$ for $j, i \in \{1, \ldots, n\}$ when the underlying matrix for the basis $\mathbb{B}_1$ is *sparse*. The randomness $\{Z_j\}_{j=1,\ldots,n}$ are sequentially inserted in a consistent manner with the security condition on the target $\vec{y}$ and key queries. It is accomplished by applying computational (*swapping*) game changes and information-theoretical (or conceptual) changes alternatingly (see Section 6.1 for the outline). For achieving the alternating changes, the above matrices Z_j are generated uniformly in an cleverly selected subgroup $\mathcal{H}_{\vec{y}}(n, \mathbb{F}_q)$ with three nice properties, which are described in Section 6.2 in detail.

1.4   Notations

When A is a random variable or distribution, $y \xleftarrow{\mathrm{R}} A$ denotes that y is randomly selected from A according to its distribution. When A is a set, $y \xleftarrow{\mathrm{U}} A$ denotes that y is uniformly selected from A. We denote the finite field of order q by $\mathbb{F}_q$, and $\mathbb{F}_q \setminus \{0\}$ by $\mathbb{F}_q^\times$. A vector symbol denotes a vector representation over $\mathbb{F}_q$, e.g., $\vec{x}$ denotes $(x_1, \ldots, x_n) \in \mathbb{F}_q^n$. For two vectors $\vec{x} = (x_1, \ldots, x_n)$ and $\vec{v} = (v_1, \ldots, v_n)$, $\vec{x} \cdot \vec{v}$ denotes the inner-product $\sum_{i=1}^n x_i v_i$. The vector $\vec{0}$ is abused as the zero vector in $\mathbb{F}_q^n$ for any n. X^{T} denotes the transpose of matrix X. A bold face letter denotes an element of vector space $\mathbb{V}$, e.g., $\boldsymbol{x} \in \mathbb{V}$. When $\boldsymbol{b}_i \in \mathbb{V}$ ($i = 1, \ldots, n$), $\text{span}\langle \boldsymbol{b}_1, \ldots, \boldsymbol{b}_n \rangle \subseteq \mathbb{V}$ (resp. $\text{span}\langle \vec{x}_1, \ldots, \vec{x}_n \rangle$) denotes the subspace generated by $\boldsymbol{b}_1, \ldots, \boldsymbol{b}_n$ (resp. $\vec{x}_1, \ldots, \vec{x}_n$). For bases $\mathbb{B} := (\boldsymbol{b}_1, \ldots, \boldsymbol{b}_N)$ and $\mathbb{B}^* := (\boldsymbol{b}_1^*, \ldots, \boldsymbol{b}_N^*)$, $(x_1, \ldots, x_N)_{\mathbb{B}} := \sum_{i=1}^{N} x_i \boldsymbol{b}_i$ and $(y_1, \ldots, y_N)_{\mathbb{B}^*} := \sum_{i=1}^{N} y_i \boldsymbol{b}_i^*$. $\vec{e}_j$ denotes the canonical basis vector $(\overset{j-1}{\overbrace{0 \cdots 0}}, 1, \overset{n-j}{\overbrace{0 \cdots 0}}) \in \mathbb{F}_q^n$. $GL(n, \mathbb{F}_q)$ denotes the general linear group of degree n over $\mathbb{F}_q$.

2 Dual Pairing Vector Spaces and Decisional Linear (DLIN) Assumption

For simplicity of description, we will present the proposed schemes on the symmetric version of dual pairing vector spaces (DPVS) [21] constructed using symmetric bilinear pairing groups. For the asymmetric version of DPVS, see Appendix A.2 of the full version of [22].

Definition 1. *"Symmetric bilinear pairing groups"* $(q, \mathbb{G}, \mathbb{G}_T, G, e)$ *are a tuple of a prime q, cyclic additive group $\mathbb{G}$ and multiplicative group $\mathbb{G}_T$ of order q, $G \neq 0 \in \mathbb{G}$, and a polynomial-time computable nondegenerate bilinear pairing $e : \mathbb{G} \times \mathbb{G} \to \mathbb{G}_T$ i.e., $e(sG, tG) = e(G, G)^{st}$ and $e(G, G) \neq 1$. Let $\mathcal{G}_{\mathsf{bpg}}$ be an algorithm that takes input 1^λ and outputs a description of bilinear pairing groups $(q, \mathbb{G}, \mathbb{G}_T, G, e)$ with security parameter λ.*

"Dual pairing vector spaces (DPVS)" of dimension N by a direct product of symmetric pairing groups $(q, \mathbb{G}, \mathbb{G}_T, G, e)$ are given by prime q, N-dimensional vector space $\mathbb{V} := \overset{N}{\overbrace{\mathbb{G} \times \cdots \times \mathbb{G}}}$ over $\mathbb{F}_q$, cyclic group $\mathbb{G}_T$ of order q, and pairing $e : \mathbb{V} \times \mathbb{V} \to \mathbb{G}_T$. The pairing is defined by $e(\boldsymbol{x}, \boldsymbol{y}) := \prod_{i=1}^{N} e(G_i, H_i) \in \mathbb{G}_T$ where $\boldsymbol{x} := (G_1, \ldots, G_N) \in \mathbb{V}$ and $\boldsymbol{y} := (H_1, \ldots, H_N) \in \mathbb{V}$. This is nondegenerate bilinear i.e., $e(s\boldsymbol{x}, t\boldsymbol{y}) = e(\boldsymbol{x}, \boldsymbol{y})^{st}$ and if $e(\boldsymbol{x}, \boldsymbol{y}) = 1$ for all $\boldsymbol{y} \in \mathbb{V}$, then $\boldsymbol{x} = \boldsymbol{0}$.

Definition 2 (DLIN: Decisional Linear Assumption [5]). *The DLIN problem is to guess $\beta \in \{0, 1\}$, given $(\mathsf{param}_{\mathbb{G}}, G, \xi G, \kappa G, \delta \xi G, \sigma \kappa G, Y_\beta) \xleftarrow{\mathsf{R}} \mathcal{G}_\beta^{\mathsf{DLIN}}(1^\lambda)$, where $\mathcal{G}_\beta^{\mathsf{DLIN}}(1^\lambda)$: $\mathsf{param}_{\mathbb{G}} := (q, \mathbb{G}, \mathbb{G}_T, G, e) \xleftarrow{\mathsf{R}} \mathcal{G}_{\mathsf{bpg}}(1^\lambda), \kappa, \delta, \xi, \sigma \xleftarrow{\mathsf{U}} \mathbb{F}_q, Y_0 := (\delta + \sigma)G, Y_1 \xleftarrow{\mathsf{U}} \mathbb{G}, \text{return } (\mathsf{param}_{\mathbb{G}}, G, \xi G, \kappa G, \delta \xi G, \sigma \kappa G, Y_\beta), \text{ for } \beta \xleftarrow{\mathsf{U}} \{0, 1\}. For a probabilistic machine $\mathcal{E}$, we define the advantage of $\mathcal{E}$ for the DLIN problem as: $\mathsf{Adv}_{\mathcal{E}}^{\mathsf{DLIN}}(\lambda) := \left| \Pr \left[\mathcal{E}(1^\lambda, \varrho) \to 1 \, \middle| \, \varrho \xleftarrow{\mathsf{R}} \mathcal{G}_0^{\mathsf{DLIN}}(1^\lambda) \right] - \Pr \left[\mathcal{E}(1^\lambda, \varrho) \to 1 \, \middle| \, \varrho \xleftarrow{\mathsf{R}} \mathcal{G}_1^{\mathsf{DLIN}}(1^\lambda) \right] \right|$. The DLIN assumption is: For any probabilistic polynomial-time adversary $\mathcal{E}$, the advantage $\mathsf{Adv}_{\mathcal{E}}^{\mathsf{DLIN}}(\lambda)$ is negligible in λ.*

3 Definition of Key-Policy Attribute-Based Encryption

3.1 Span Programs and Non-monotone Access Structures

Definition 3 (Span Programs [3]). $\mathcal{U}$ $(\subset \{0, 1\}^*)$ *is a universe, a set of attributes, which is expressed by a value of attribute, i.e., $v \in \mathbb{F}_q^\times (:= \mathbb{F}_q \setminus$*

$\{0\}$). *A span program over* $\mathbb{F}_q$ *is a labeled matrix* $\mathbb{S} := (M, \rho)$ *where* M *is a* $(\ell \times r)$ *matrix over* $\mathbb{F}_q$ *and* ρ *is a labeling of the rows of* M *by literals from* $\{v, v', \ldots, \neg v, \neg v', \ldots\}$ *(every row is labeled by one literal), i.e.,* $\rho : \{1, \ldots, \ell\} \to \{v, v', \ldots, \neg v, \neg v', \ldots\}$.

A span program accepts or rejects an input by the following criterion. Let Γ *be a set of attributes, i.e.,* $\Gamma := \{x_j\}_{1 \le j \le n'}$. *When* Γ *is given to access structure* $\mathbb{S}$, *map* $\gamma : \{1, \ldots, \ell\} \to \{0, 1\}$ *for span program* $\mathbb{S} := (M, \rho)$ *is defined as follows: For* $i = 1, \ldots, \ell$, *set* $\gamma(i) = 1$ *if* $[\rho(i) = v_i] \wedge [v_i \in \Gamma]$ *or* $[\rho(i) = \neg v_i] \wedge [v_i \notin \Gamma]$. *Set* $\gamma(i) = 0$ *otherwise.*

The span program $\mathbb{S}$ *accepts* Γ *if and only if* $\vec{1} \in \mathsf{span}\langle (M_i)_{\gamma(i)=1} \rangle$, *i.e., some linear combination of the rows* $(M_i)_{\gamma(i)=1}$ *gives the all one vector* $\vec{1}$. *(The row vector has the value 1 in eciphertextsach coordinate.)*

A span program is called monotone if the labels of the rows are only the positive literals $\{v, v', \ldots\}$. *Monotone span programs compute monotone functions. (So, a span program in general is "non"-monotone.)*

We assume that no row M_i $(i = 1, \ldots, \ell)$ of the matrix M is $\vec{0}$. We now construct a secret-sharing scheme for a non-monotone span program.

Definition 4. *A secret-sharing scheme for span program* $\mathbb{S} := (M, \rho)$ *is:*

1. *Let* M *be* $\ell \times r$ *matrix. Let column vector* $\vec{f}^{\mathrm{T}} := (f_1, \ldots, f_r)^{\mathrm{T}} \xleftarrow{\mathsf{U}} \mathbb{F}_q^r$. *Then,*
   $$s_0 := \vec{1} \cdot \vec{f}^{\mathrm{T}} = \sum_{k=1}^r f_k \text{ is the secret to be shared, and } \vec{s}^{\mathrm{T}} := (s_1, \ldots, s_\ell)^{\mathrm{T}} := M \cdot \vec{f}^{\mathrm{T}} \text{ is the } \ell \text{ shares of the secret } s_0 \text{ and the share } s_i \text{ belongs to } \rho(i).$$
2. *If span program* $\mathbb{S} := (M, \rho)$ *accepts* Γ, *i.e.,* $\vec{1} \in \mathsf{span}\langle (M_i)_{\gamma(i)=1} \rangle$ *with* $\gamma : \{1, \ldots, \ell\} \to \{0, 1\}$, *there exist constants* $\{\alpha_i \in \mathbb{F}_q \mid i \in I\}$ *such that* $I \subseteq \{i \in \{1, \ldots, \ell\} \mid \gamma(i) = 1\}$ *and* $\sum_{i \in I} \alpha_i s_i = s_0$. *Furthermore, these constants* $\{\alpha_i\}$ *can be computed in time polynomial in the size of the matrix* M.

3.2 Key-Policy Attribute-Based Encryption (KP-ABE)

In key-policy attribute-based encryption (KP-ABE), encryption (resp. a secret key) is associated with attributes Γ (resp. access structure $\mathbb{S}$). Relation R for KP-ABE is defined as $R(\mathbb{S}, \Gamma) = 1$ iff access structure $\mathbb{S}$ accepts Γ.

Definition 5 (Key-Policy Attribute-Based Encryption: KP-ABE). *A key-policy attribute-based encryption scheme consists of probabilistic polynomial-time algorithms* Setup, KeyGen, Enc *and* Dec. *They are given as follows:*

Setup *takes as input security parameter* 1^λ *and a bound on the number of attributes per ciphertext* n. *It outputs public parameters* pk *and master secret key* sk.

KeyGen *takes as input public parameters* pk, *master secret key* sk, *and access structure* $\mathbb{S} := (M, \rho)$. *It outputs a corresponding secret key* $\mathsf{sk}_{\mathbb{S}}$.

Enc *takes as input public parameters* pk, *message* m *in some associated message space* msg, *and a set of attributes,* $\Gamma := \{x_j\}_{1 \le j \le n'}$. *It outputs a ciphertext* ct_Γ.

Dec *takes as input public parameters* pk, *secret key* sk$_S$ *for access structure* S, *and ciphertext* ct$_\Gamma$ *that was encrypted under a set of attributes* Γ. *It outputs either* $m' \in$ msg *or the distinguished symbol* $\perp$.

A KP-ABE scheme should have the following correctness property: for all $(\text{pk}, \text{sk}) \xleftarrow{\text{R}} \text{Setup}(1^\lambda, n)$, all access structures S, all secret keys sk$_S \xleftarrow{\text{R}}$ KeyGen(pk, sk, S), all messages m, all attribute sets Γ, all ciphertexts ct$_\Gamma \xleftarrow{\text{R}}$ Enc(pk, m, Γ), it holds that $m = \text{Dec}(\text{pk}, \text{sk}_S, \text{ct}_\Gamma)$ if S accepts Γ. Otherwise, it holds with negligible probability.

Definition 6. *The model for defining the selectively (resp. semi-adaptively) payload-hiding security of KP-ABE under chosen plaintext attack is given by the following game:*

Setup. *In the selective security, the adversary output a challenge attribute set, Γ, the challenger runs the setup,* $(\text{pk}, \text{sk}) \xleftarrow{\text{R}} \text{Setup}(1^\lambda, n)$, *and gives public parameters* pk *to the adversary. In the semi-adaptive security, the adversary specifies the challenge attribute set after it sees the public parameters.*

Phase 1. *The adversary is allowed to adaptively issue a polynomial number of key queries, S, to the challenger provided that S does not accept Γ. The challenger gives* sk$_S \xleftarrow{\text{R}}$ KeyGen(pk, sk, S) *to the adversary.*

Challenge. *The adversary submits two messages* $m^{(0)}, m^{(1)}$. *The challenger flips a coin* $b \xleftarrow{\text{U}} \{0,1\}$, *and computes* $\text{ct}_\Gamma^{(b)} \xleftarrow{\text{R}}$ Enc(pk, $m^{(b)}$, Γ). *It gives* $\text{ct}_\Gamma^{(b)}$ *to the adversary.*

Phase 2. *Phase 1 is repeated with the restriction that no queried S accepts challenge* Γ.

Guess. *The adversary outputs a guess* b' *of* b, *and wins if* $b' = b$.

The advantage of adversary $\mathcal{A}$ in the selective (resp. semi-adaptive) game is defined as $\text{Adv}_{\mathcal{A}}^{\text{KP-ABE,Sel}}(\lambda)$ *(resp.* $\text{Adv}_{\mathcal{A}}^{\text{KP-ABE,SA}}(\lambda)$*)* $:= \Pr[\mathcal{A} \text{ wins }] - 1/2$ *for any security parameter λ. A KP-ABE scheme is selectively (resp. semi-adaptively) payload-hiding secure if all polynomial time adversaries have at most a negligible advantage in the selective (resp. semi-adaptive) game.*

4   Special Matrix Subgroups

Lemmas 1 and 2 are key lemmas for the security proof for our KP-ABE and ABS schemes. For positive integers w, n and $\vec{y} := (y_1, .., y_n) \in \mathbb{F}_q^n \setminus \text{span}\langle \vec{e}_n \rangle$, let

$$\mathcal{H}(n, \mathbb{F}_q) := \left\{ \begin{pmatrix} u & & u_1' \\ & \ddots & \vdots \\ & & u\ u_{n-1}' \\ & & u_n' \end{pmatrix} \middle| \begin{array}{l} u, u_l' \in \mathbb{F}_q \text{ for } l = 1, \ldots, n, \\ \text{a blank element in the matrix} \\ \text{denotes } 0 \in \mathbb{F}_q \end{array} \right\}, \quad (1)$$

$$\mathcal{H}_{\vec{y}}(n, \mathbb{F}_q) := \left\{ \begin{pmatrix} 1 & & u_1' \\ & \ddots & \vdots \\ & & 1\ u_{n-1}' \\ & & u_n' \end{pmatrix} \middle| \begin{array}{l} \vec{u}' := (u_l')_{l=1,\ldots,n} \in \mathbb{F}_q^n, \\ u_n' \neq 0, \quad \vec{y} \cdot \vec{u}' = y_n, \\ \text{a blank element in the matrix} \\ \text{denotes } 0 \in \mathbb{F}_q \end{array} \right\}. \quad (2)$$

Lemma 1. $\mathcal{H}_{\vec{y}}(n, \mathbb{F}_q) \subset \mathcal{H}(n, \mathbb{F}_q)$. $\mathcal{H}(n, \mathbb{F}_q) \cap GL(n, \mathbb{F}_q)$ and $\mathcal{H}_{\vec{y}}(n, \mathbb{F}_q)$ are subgroups of $GL(n, \mathbb{F}_q)$.

Lemma 1 is directly verified from the definition of groups.   □

Let

$$\mathcal{L}(w, n, \mathbb{F}_q) :=$$

$$\left\{ X := \begin{pmatrix} X_{1,1} & \cdots & X_{1,w} \\ \vdots & & \vdots \\ X_{w,1} & \cdots & X_{w,w} \end{pmatrix} \middle| X_{i,j} := \begin{pmatrix} \mu_{i,j} & & \mu'_{i,j,1} \\ & \ddots & \vdots \\ & & \mu_{i,j} \; \mu'_{i,j,n-1} \\ & & \mu'_{i,j,n} \end{pmatrix} \begin{array}{l} \in \mathcal{H}(n, \mathbb{F}_q) \\ \text{for } i, j = \\ 1, \ldots, w \end{array} \right\}$$

$$\bigcap GL(wn, \mathbb{F}_q). \tag{3}$$

Lemma 2. $\mathcal{L}(w, n, \mathbb{F}_q)$ is a subgroup of $GL(wn, \mathbb{F}_q)$.

The proof of Lemma 2 is given in Appendix A in the full version of [23].

5   Proposed KP-ABE Scheme with Constant Size Ciphertexts

5.1   Key Ideas in Constructing the Proposed KP-ABE Scheme

In this section, we will explain key ideas of constructing and proving the security of the proposed KP-ABE scheme.

First, we will show how short ciphertexts and efficient decryption can be achieved in our scheme, where the IPE scheme given in [23] is used as a building block. Here, we will use a simplified (or toy) version of the proposed KP-ABE scheme, for which the security is no more ensured in the standard model under the DLIN assumption.

A ciphertext in the simplified KP-ABE scheme consists of two vector elements, $(c_0, c_1) \in \mathbb{G}^5 \times \mathbb{G}^n$, and $c_3 \in \mathbb{G}_T$. A secret-key consists of $\ell + 1$ vector elements, $(k_0^*, k_1^*, \ldots, k_\ell^*) \in \mathbb{G}^5 \times (\mathbb{G}^n)^\ell$ for access structure $\mathbb{S} := (M, \rho)$, where the number of rows of M is ℓ and k_i^* with $i \geq 1$ corresponds to the i-th row. Therefore, to achieve constant-size ciphertexts, we have to compress $c_1 \in \mathbb{G}^n$ to a constant size in n. We now employ a special form of basis gener-

ation matrix, $X := \begin{pmatrix} \mu & & \mu'_1 \\ & \ddots & \vdots \\ & & \mu \; \mu'_{n-1} \\ & & \mu'_n \end{pmatrix} \in \mathcal{H}(n, \mathbb{F}_q)$ of Eq. (1) in Section 4, where

$\mu, \mu'_1, \ldots, \mu'_n \xleftarrow{\mathsf{U}} \mathbb{F}_q$ and a blank in the matrix denotes $0 \in \mathbb{F}_q$. The public key

(DPVS basis) is $\mathbb{B} := \begin{pmatrix} b_1 \\ \vdots \\ b_n \end{pmatrix} := \begin{pmatrix} \mu G & & \mu'_1 G \\ & \ddots & \vdots \\ & & \mu G \; \mu'_{n-1} G \\ & & \mu'_n G \end{pmatrix}$. Let a ciphertext as-

sociated with $\Gamma := \{x_1, \ldots, x_{n'}\}$ be $c_1 := (\omega \vec{y})_{\mathbb{B}} = \omega(y_1 b_1 + \cdots + y_n b_n) =$

$(y_1\omega\mu G, \ldots, y_{n-1}\omega\mu G, \ \omega(\sum_{i=1}^n y_i\mu_i')G)$, where $\omega \xleftarrow{\mathsf{U}} \mathbb{F}_q$ and $\vec{y} := (y_1, \ldots, y_n)$ such that $\sum_{j=0}^{n-1} y_{n-j}z^j = z^{n-1-n'} \cdot \prod_{j=1}^n (z - x_j)$. Then, c_1 can be compressed to only *two* group elements $(C_1 := \omega\mu G, \ C_2 := \omega(\sum_{i=1}^n y_i\mu_i')G)$ as well as $\vec{y}$, since c_1 can be obtained by $(y_1 C_1, \ldots, y_{n-1}C_1, C_2)$ (note that $y_i C_1 = y_i\omega\mu G$ for $i = 1, \ldots, n-1$). That is, a ciphertext (excluding $\vec{y}$) can be just two group elements, or the size is constant in n.

Let $\mathbb{B}^* := (b_i^*)$ be the dual orthonormal basis of $\mathbb{B} := (b_i)$, and $\mathbb{B}^*$ be the master secret key in the simplified KP-ABE scheme. We specify (c_0, k_0^*, c_3) such that $e(c_0, k_0^*) = g_T^{\zeta - \omega s_0}$ and $c_3 := g_T^\zeta m \in \mathbb{G}_T$ with s_0 is a center secret of shares $\{s_i\}_{i=1,\ldots,\ell}$ associated with access structure $\mathbb{S}$. Using $\{s_i\}_{i=1,\ldots,\ell}$, we also set a secret-key for $\mathbb{S}$ as $k_i^* := (s_i\vec{e}_1 + \theta_i\vec{v}_i)_{\mathbb{B}^*}$ if $\rho(i) = v_i$ and $k_i^* := (s_i\vec{v}_i)_{\mathbb{B}^*}$ if $\rho(i) = \neg v_i$ where $\vec{v}_i := (v_i^{n-1}, \ldots, v_i, 1)$ and $\theta_i \xleftarrow{\mathsf{U}} \mathbb{F}_q$. From the dual orthonormality of $\mathbb{B}$ and $\mathbb{B}^*$, if $\mathbb{S}$ accepts Γ, there exist a system of coefficients $\{\alpha_i\}_{i\in I}$ such that $e(c_1, \widetilde{k}^*) = g_T^{\omega s_0}$, where $\widetilde{k}^* := \sum_{i\in I \wedge \rho(i)=v_i} \alpha_i k_i^* + \sum_{i\in I \wedge \rho(i)=\neg v_i} \alpha_i(\vec{y}\cdot\vec{v}_i)^{-1}k_i^*$. Hence, a decryptor can compute $g_T^{\omega s_0}$ if and only if $\mathbb{S}$ accepts Γ, i.e., can obtain plaintext m. Since c_1 is expressed as $(y_1 C_1, \ldots, y_{n-1}C_1, C_2) \in \mathbb{G}^n$ and $\widetilde{k}^*$ is parsed as a n-tuple $(D_1^*, \ldots, D_n^*) \in \mathbb{G}^n$, the value of $e(c_1, \widetilde{k}^*)$ is $\prod_{i=1}^{n-1} e(y_i C_1, D_n^*) \cdot e(C_2, D_n^*) = \prod_{i=1}^{n-1} e(C_1, y_i D_i^*) \cdot e(C_2, D_n^*) = e(C_1, \sum_{i=1}^{n-1} y_i D_i^*) \cdot e(C_2, D_n^*)$. That is, $n-1$ scalar multiplications in $\mathbb{G}$ and *two* pairing operations are enough for computing $e(c_1, \widetilde{k}^*)$. Therefore, only a small (constant) number of pairing operations are required for decryption.

We then explain how our *full* KP-ABE scheme is constructed on the above-mentioned simplified KP-ABE scheme. The target of designing the full KP-ABE scheme is to achieve the selective (resp. semi-adaptive) security *under the DLIN assumption*. Here, we adopt and extend a strategy initiated in [22], in which the dual system encryption methodology is employed in a modular or hierarchical manner. That is, one top level assumption, the security of Problem 1, is directly used in the dual system encryption methodology and the assumption is reduced to a primitive assumption, the DLIN assumption.

To meet the requirements for applying to the dual system encryption methodology and reducing to the DLIN assumption, the underlying vector space is six times greater than that of the above-mentioned simplified scheme. For example, $k_i^* := (\ s_i\vec{e}_1 + \theta_i\vec{v}_i, \ 0^{2n}, \ \vec{\eta}_i, \ 0^n\ )_{\mathbb{B}_1^*}$ if $\rho(i) = v_i$, $k_i^* := (\ s_i\vec{v}_i, \ 0^{2n}, \ \vec{\eta}_i, \ 0^n\ )_{\mathbb{B}_1^*}$ if

$$\rho(i) = \neg v_i, c_1 = (\ \omega\vec{y}, 0^{2n}, 0^{2n}, \varphi_1\vec{y}\ )_{\mathbb{B}_1}, \text{ and } X := \begin{pmatrix} X_{1,1} \cdots X_{1,6} \\ \vdots \quad\quad \vdots \\ X_{6,1} \cdots X_{6,6} \end{pmatrix} \in \mathcal{L}(6, n, \mathbb{F}_q)$$

of Eq. (3) in Section 4, where each $X_{i,j}$ is of the form of $X \in \mathcal{H}(n, \mathbb{F}_q)$ in the simplified scheme. The vector space consists of four orthogonal subspaces, i.e., real encoding part, hidden part, secret-key randomness part, and ciphertext randomness part. The simplified KP-ABE scheme corresponds to the first real encoding part.

A key fact in the security reduction is that $\mathcal{L}(6, n, \mathbb{F}_q)$ is a *subgroup* of $GL(6n, \mathbb{F}_q)$ (Lemma 2), which enables a *random-self-reducibility* argument for reducing the intractability of Problem 1 in Definition 7 to the DLIN assumption. For the reduction, see [23]. The property that $\mathcal{H}_{\vec{y}}(n, \mathbb{F}_q)$ is a *subgroup* of $GL(n, \mathbb{F}_q)$ is also crucial for a special form of pairwise independence lemma in this paper (Lemma 4), where a super-group $\mathcal{H}(n, \mathbb{F}_q) \cap GL(n, \mathbb{F}_q)(\supset \mathcal{H}_{\vec{y}}(n, \mathbb{F}_q))$ is specified in $\mathcal{L}(6, n, \mathbb{F}_q)$ or X. Our Problem 1 employs the special form matrices $\{U_j \xleftarrow{\mathsf{U}} \mathcal{H}_{\vec{y}}(n, \mathbb{F}_q)\}$ and $\{Z_j := (U_j^{-1})^{\mathrm{T}}\}$, and makes Lemma 4 applicable in our proof. Informally, our pairwise independence lemma implies that, for all $(\vec{y}, \vec{v})$, a vector, $\vec{v}Z$, is uniformly distributed over $\mathbb{F}_q^n \setminus \mathsf{span}\langle \vec{e}_n \rangle^{\perp}$ with preserving the inner-product value, $\vec{y} \cdot \vec{v}$, i.e., $\vec{v}Z$ reveal no information but $(\vec{y}$ and$)$ $\vec{y} \cdot \vec{v}$.

5.2   Dual Orthonormal Basis Generator

We describe random dual orthonormal basis generator $\mathcal{G}_{\mathsf{ob}}^{\mathsf{KP\text{-}ABE}}$ using a sparse matrix given by Eq. (3), which is used in the proposed KP-ABE scheme.

$$\mathcal{G}_{\mathsf{ob}}^{\mathsf{KP\text{-}ABE}}(1^{\lambda}, 6, n): \; \mathsf{param}_{\mathbb{G}} := (q, \mathbb{G}, \mathbb{G}_T, G, e) \xleftarrow{\mathsf{R}} \mathcal{G}_{\mathsf{bpg}}(1^{\lambda}), \; N_0 := 5, \; N_1 := 6n,$$

$$\psi \xleftarrow{\mathsf{U}} \mathbb{F}_q^{\times}, \; g_T := e(G, G)^{\psi}, \; \mathsf{param}_n := (\mathsf{param}_{\mathbb{G}}, \{N_t\}_{t=0,1}, \; g_T),$$

$$X_0 := (\chi_{0,i,j})_{i,j=1,\dots,5} \xleftarrow{\mathsf{U}} GL(N_0, \mathbb{F}_q), \; X_1 \xleftarrow{\mathsf{U}} \mathcal{L}(6, n, \mathbb{F}_q), \; \text{hereafter,}$$

$$\{\mu_{i,j}, \mu'_{i,j,l}\}_{i,j=1,\dots,6;l=1,\dots,n} \text{ denotes non-zero entries of } X_1 \text{ as in Eq. (3)},$$

$$\boldsymbol{b}_{0,i} := (\chi_{0,i,1}G, \dots, \chi_{0,i,5}G) \text{ for } i = 1, \dots, 5, \; \mathbb{B}_0 := (\boldsymbol{b}_{0,1}, \dots, \boldsymbol{b}_{0,5}),$$

$$B_{i,j} := \mu_{i,j}G, \; B'_{i,j,l} := \mu'_{i,j,l}G \text{ for } i, j = 1, \dots, 6; l = 1, \dots, n,$$

$$\text{for } t = 0, 1, \; (\vartheta_{t,i,j})_{i,j=1,\dots,N_t} := \psi \cdot (X_t^{\mathrm{T}})^{-1},$$

$$\boldsymbol{b}_{t,i}^* := (\vartheta_{t,i,1}G, \dots, \vartheta_{t,i,N_t}G) \text{ for } i = 1, \dots, N_t, \; \mathbb{B}_t^* := (\boldsymbol{b}_{t,1}^*, \dots, \boldsymbol{b}_{t,N_t}^*),$$

$$\text{return } (\mathsf{param}_n, \mathbb{B}_0, \mathbb{B}_0^*, \{B_{i,j}, B'_{i,j,l}\}_{i,j=1,\dots,6;l=1,\dots,n}, \mathbb{B}_1^*).$$

Remark 1. Let

$$
\begin{pmatrix} \boldsymbol{b}_{1,(i-1)n+1} \\ \vdots \\ \boldsymbol{b}_{1,in} \end{pmatrix} := \left. \begin{pmatrix} B_{i,1} & & B'_{i,1,1} & B_{i,6} & & B'_{i,6,1} \\ & \ddots & \vdots & & \ddots & \vdots \\ & & B_{i,1} \; B'_{i,1,n-1} & \cdots & & B_{i,6} \; B'_{i,6,n-1} \\ & & B'_{i,1,n} & & & B'_{i,6,n} \end{pmatrix} \right\} \text{(4)}
$$

$$\text{for } i = 1, \dots, 6,$$

and $\mathbb{B}_1 := (\boldsymbol{b}_{1,1}, \dots, \boldsymbol{b}_{1,6n}),$

where a blank element in the matrix denotes $0 \in \mathbb{G}$. $\mathbb{B}_1$ is the dual orthonormal basis of $\mathbb{B}_1^*$, i.e., $e(\boldsymbol{b}_{1,i}, \boldsymbol{b}_{1,i}^*) = g_T$ and $e(\boldsymbol{b}_{1,i}, \boldsymbol{b}_{1,j}^*) = 1$ for $1 \le i \ne j \le 6n$.

5.3   Construction

We note that attributes x_j, v_i are in $\mathbb{F}_q^{\times}$, i.e., nonzero.

Setup(1^λ, n) :

$(\mathrm{param}_n, \mathbb{B}_0, \mathbb{B}_0^*, \{B_{i,j}, B'_{i,j,l}\}_{i,j=1,\ldots,6;l=1,\ldots,n}, \mathbb{B}_1^*) \xleftarrow{\mathsf{R}} \mathcal{G}_{\mathrm{ob}}^{\mathsf{KP\text{-}ABE}}(1^\lambda, 6, n))$,

$\widehat{\mathbb{B}}_0 := (\boldsymbol{b}_{0,1}, \boldsymbol{b}_{0,3}, \boldsymbol{b}_{0,5})$,

$\widehat{\mathbb{B}}_1 := (\boldsymbol{b}_{1,1}, \ldots, \boldsymbol{b}_{1,n}, \boldsymbol{b}_{1,5n+1}, \ldots, \boldsymbol{b}_{1,6n}) = \{B_{i,j}, B'_{i,j,l}\}_{i=1,6;j=1,\ldots,6;l=1,\ldots,n}$,

$\widehat{\mathbb{B}}_0^* := (\boldsymbol{b}_{0,1}^*, \boldsymbol{b}_{0,3}^*, \boldsymbol{b}_{0,4}^*)$, $\widehat{\mathbb{B}}_1^* := (\boldsymbol{b}_{1,1}^*, \ldots, \boldsymbol{b}_{1,n}^*, \boldsymbol{b}_{1,3n+1}^*, \ldots, \boldsymbol{b}_{1,5n}^*)$,

$\mathsf{pk} := (1^\lambda, \mathrm{param}_n, \{\widehat{\mathbb{B}}_t\}_{t=0,1})$, $\mathsf{sk} := \{\widehat{\mathbb{B}}_t^*\}_{t=0,1}$,   return pk, sk.

KeyGen(pk, sk, $\mathbb{S} := (M, \rho)$) :

$\vec{f} \xleftarrow{\mathsf{U}} \mathbb{F}_q^r$, $\vec{s}^{\mathrm{T}} := (s_1, \ldots, s_\ell)^{\mathrm{T}} := M \cdot \vec{f}^{\mathrm{T}}$, $s_0 := \vec{1} \cdot \vec{f}^{\mathrm{T}}$, $\eta_0 \xleftarrow{\mathsf{U}} \mathbb{F}_q$,

$\boldsymbol{k}_0^* := (-s_0,\ 0,\ 1,\ \eta_0,\ 0)_{\mathbb{B}_0^*}$,

for $i = 1, \ldots, \ell$, $\vec{v}_i := (v_i^{n-1}, \ldots, v_i, 1)$ for $\rho(i) = v_i$ or $\neg v_i$, $\vec{\eta}_i \xleftarrow{\mathsf{U}} \mathbb{F}_q^{2n}$,

if $\rho(i) = v_i$, $\theta_i \xleftarrow{\mathsf{U}} \mathbb{F}_q$, $\boldsymbol{k}_i^* := (\ \overbrace{s_i \vec{e}_1 + \theta_i \vec{v}_i}^{n},\ \overbrace{0^{2n}}^{2n},\ \overbrace{\vec{\eta}_i}^{2n},\ \overbrace{0^n}^{n}\ )_{\mathbb{B}_1^*}$,

if $\rho(i) = \neg v_i$, $\boldsymbol{k}_i^* := (\ \overbrace{s_i \vec{v}_i}^{n},\ \overbrace{0^{2n}}^{2n},\ \overbrace{\vec{\eta}_i}^{2n},\ \overbrace{0^n}^{n}\ )_{\mathbb{B}_1^*}$,

return $\mathsf{sk}_\mathbb{S} := (\mathbb{S}, \boldsymbol{k}_0^*, \boldsymbol{k}_1^*, \ldots, \boldsymbol{k}_\ell^*)$.

Enc(pk, m, $\Gamma := \{x_1, \ldots, x_{n'} \mid x_j \in \mathbb{F}_q^\times, n' \leq n-1\}$) : $\omega, \varphi_0, \varphi_1, \zeta \xleftarrow{\mathsf{U}} \mathbb{F}_q$,

$\vec{y} := (y_1, \ldots, y_n)$ such that $\sum_{j=0}^{n-1} y_{n-j} z^j = z^{n-1-n'} \cdot \prod_{j=1}^{n'}(z - x_j)$,

$\boldsymbol{c}_0 := (\omega,\ 0,\ \zeta,\ 0,\ \varphi_0)_{\mathbb{B}_0}$,

$\boldsymbol{C}_{1,j} := \omega B_{1,j} + \varphi_1 B_{6,j}$, $\boldsymbol{C}_{2,j} := \sum_{l=1}^n y_l(\omega B'_{1,j,l} + \varphi_1 B'_{6,j,l})$ for $j = 1, \ldots, 6$,

$c_3 := g_T^\zeta m$, $\mathsf{ct}_\Gamma := (\Gamma, \boldsymbol{c}_0, \{\boldsymbol{C}_{1,j}, \boldsymbol{C}_{2,j}\}_{j=1,\ldots,6}, c_3)$.   return ct_Γ.

Dec(pk, $\mathsf{sk}_\mathbb{S} := (\mathbb{S}, \boldsymbol{k}_0^*, \boldsymbol{k}_1^*, \ldots, \boldsymbol{k}_\ell^*)$, $\mathsf{ct}_\Gamma := (\Gamma, \boldsymbol{c}_0, \{\boldsymbol{C}_{1,j}, \boldsymbol{C}_{2,j}\}_{j=1,\ldots,6}, c_3)$) :

If $\mathbb{S} := (M, \rho)$ accepts $\Gamma := \{x_1, \ldots, x_{n'}\}$, then compute I and $\{\alpha_i\}_{i \in I}$

such that $\vec{1} = \sum_{i \in I} \alpha_i M_i$, where M_i is the i-th row of M, and

$I \subseteq \{i \in \{1, \ldots, \ell\} \mid [\rho(i) = v_i \wedge v_i \in \Gamma] \vee [\rho(i) = \neg v_i \wedge v_i \notin \Gamma]\}$,

$\vec{y} := (y_1, \ldots, y_n)$ such that $\sum_{j=0}^{n-1} y_{n-j} z^j = z^{n-1-n'} \cdot \prod_{j=1}^{n'}(z - x_j)$,

$(D_1^*, \ldots, D_{6n}^*) := \sum_{i \in I \ \wedge\ \rho(i) = v_i} \alpha_i \boldsymbol{k}_i^* + \sum_{i \in I \ \wedge\ \rho(i) = \neg v_i} \frac{\alpha_i}{\vec{v}_i \cdot \vec{y}} \boldsymbol{k}_i^*$,

$E_j^* := \sum_{l=1}^{n-1} y_{l-1} D_{(j-1)n+l}^*$ for $j = 1, \ldots, 6$,

$K := e(\boldsymbol{c}_0, \boldsymbol{k}_0^*) \cdot \prod_{j=1}^6 \left(e(\boldsymbol{C}_{1,j}, E_j^*) \cdot e(\boldsymbol{C}_{2,j}, D_{jn}^*)\right)$,   return $m' := c_3/K$.

Remark 2. A part of the output of Setup($1^\lambda, n$), $\{B_{i,j}, B'_{i,j,l}\}_{i=1,6;j=1,\ldots,6;l=1,\ldots,n}$, can be identified with $\widehat{\mathbb{B}}_1 := (\boldsymbol{b}_{1,1}, \ldots, \boldsymbol{b}_{1,n}, \boldsymbol{b}_{1,5n+1}, \ldots, \boldsymbol{b}_{1,6n})$ through the form of Eq. (4), while $\mathbb{B}_1 := (\boldsymbol{b}_{1,1}, \ldots, \boldsymbol{b}_{1,6n})$ is identified with $\{B_{i,j}, B'_{i,j,l}\}_{i,j=1,\ldots,6;l=1,\ldots,n}$ by Eq. (4). Decryption Dec can be alternatively described as:

$\mathsf{Dec}'(\mathsf{pk},\ \mathsf{sk_S} := (\mathbb{S}, k_0^*, k_1^*, \ldots, k_\ell^*),\ \mathsf{ct}_\Gamma := (\Gamma, c_0, \{C_{1,j}, C_{2,j}\}_{j=1,\ldots,6}, c_3)):$

If $\mathbb{S} := (M, \rho)$ accepts $\Gamma := \{x_1, \ldots, x_{n'}\}$, then compute I and $\{\alpha_i\}_{i \in I}$

such that $\vec{1} = \sum_{i \in I} \alpha_i M_i$, where M_i is the i-th row of M, and

$I \subseteq \{i \in \{1, \ldots, \ell\} \mid [\rho(i) = v_i \ \wedge \ v_i \in \Gamma] \vee [\rho(i) = \neg v_i \ \wedge \ v_i \notin \Gamma]\},$

$\vec{y} := (y_1, \ldots, y_n)$ such that $\sum_{j=0}^{n-1} y_{n-j} z^j = z^{n-1-n'} \cdot \prod_{j=1}^{n'} (z - x_j),$

$$c_1 := (\overbrace{y_1 C_{1,1}, .., y_{n-1} C_{1,1}, C_{2,1},}^{n} \overbrace{y_1 C_{1,2}, .., y_{n-1} C_{1,2}, C_{2,2},}^{n} \cdots$$
$$y_1 C_{1,5}, .., y_{n-1} C_{1,5}, C_{2,5}, \quad y_1 C_{1,6}, .., y_{n-1} C_{1,6}, C_{2,6}),$$

that is, $\quad c_1 = (\ \overbrace{\omega \vec{y}}^{n}, \quad \overbrace{0^{2n}}^{2n}, \quad \overbrace{0^{2n}}^{2n}, \quad \overbrace{\varphi_1 \vec{y}}^{n}\ )_{\mathbb{B}_1},$

$$K := e(c_0, k_0^*) \cdot e\left(c_1, \sum_{i \in I \ \wedge \ \rho(i) = v_i} \alpha_i k_i^* + \sum_{i \in I \ \wedge \ \rho(i) = \neg v_i} \frac{\alpha_i}{\vec{v}_i \cdot \vec{y}} k_i^* \right),$$

return $m' := c_3 / K.$

[**Correctness**] $e(c_0, k_0^*) \prod_{i \in I \wedge \rho(i) = v_i} e(c_1, k_i^*)^{\alpha_i} \cdot \prod_{i \in I \wedge \rho(i) = \neg v_i} e(c_1, k_i^*)^{\alpha_i / (\vec{v}_i \cdot \vec{y})}$

$= g_T^{-\omega s_0 + \zeta} \prod_{i \in I \wedge \rho(i) = v_i} g_T^{\omega \alpha_i s_i} \prod_{i \in I \wedge \rho(i) = \neg v_i} g_T^{\omega \alpha_i s_i (\vec{v}_i \cdot \vec{y}) / (\vec{v}_i \cdot \vec{y})}$

$= g_T^{\omega(-s_0 + \sum_{i \in I} \alpha_i s_i) + \zeta} = g_T^\zeta.$

5.4 Security

Theorem 1. *The proposed KP-ABE scheme is selectively payload-hiding against chosen plaintext attacks under the DLIN assumption.*

For any adversary $\mathcal{A}$, there is a probabilistic machine $\mathcal{F}$, whose running time is essentially the same as that of $\mathcal{A}$, such that for any security parameter λ, $\mathsf{Adv}_{\mathcal{A}}^{\mathsf{KP\text{-}ABE,Sel}}(\lambda) \leq \sum_{j=0}^{n} \sum_{\iota=1}^{2} \mathsf{Adv}_{\mathcal{F}_{j,\iota}}^{\mathsf{DLIN}}(\lambda) + \epsilon$, where $\mathcal{F}_{j,\iota}(\cdot) := \mathcal{F}(j, \iota, \cdot)$ for $j = 0, \ldots, n; \ \iota = 1, 2, \ \epsilon := (\nu \ell + 10n + 12)/q$, and ν is the maximum number of $\mathcal{A}$'s key queries, ℓ is the maximum number of rows in access matrices M of the key queries.

Theorem 2. *The proposed KP-ABE scheme is semi-adaptively payload-hiding against chosen plaintext attacks under the DLIN assumption.*

The reduction factor of the semi-adaptive security from the DLIN is $O(\nu \ell)$ where ν, ℓ are defined in Theorem 1. Theorem 2 is proven in the full version [27].

Proof Outline of Theorem 1. At the top level strategy of the security proof, the dual system encryption by Waters [29] is employed, where ciphertexts and secret keys have two forms, *normal* and *semi-functional*. The real system uses only normal ciphertexts and normal secret keys, and semi-functional ciphertexts and keys are used only in subsequent security games for the security proof.

To prove this theorem, we employ Game 0 (original selective-security game) through Game 2. In Game 1, the challenge ciphertext and all queried keys are changed to semi-functional form, respectively. In Game 2, the challenge cipher-text is changed to *non-functional* form. In the final game, the advantage of the adversary is zero. As usual, we prove that the advantage gaps between neigh-boring games are negligible.

A normal secret key (with access structure $\mathbb{S}$), is the correct form of the secret key of the proposed KP-ABE scheme, and is expressed by Eq. (5). Similarly, a normal ciphertext (with attributes Γ) is expressed by Eq. (6). A semi-functional ciphertext is expressed by Eq. (8). A semi-functional key is expressed by Eq. (7). A non-functional ciphertext is expressed by Eq. (9) (with c_1 in Eq. (8)).

To prove that the advantage gap between Games 0 and 1 is bounded by the advantage of Problem 1 (to guess $\beta \in \{0, 1\}$), we construct a simulator of the challenger of Game 0 (or 1) (against an adversary $\mathcal{A}$) by using an instance with $\beta \xleftarrow{\mathsf{U}} \{0, 1\}$ of Problem 1. We then show that the distribution of the secret keys and challenge ciphertext replied by the simulator is equivalent to those of Game 0 when $\beta = 0$ and those of Game 1 when $\beta = 1$. That is, the advantage of Problem 1 is equivalent to the advantage gap between Games 0 and 1 (Lemma 5). The advantage of Problem 1 is proven to be equivalent to $(2n + 2)$-times of that of the DLIN assumption (Lemma 3).

We then show that Game 1 can be conceptually changed to Game 2 (Lemma 6), by using the fact that parts of bases, $\boldsymbol{b}_{0,2}$ and $\boldsymbol{b}_{0,3}^*$, are unknown to the adversary. In the conceptual change, we use the fact that the challenge ciphertext and all queried keys are semi-functional, i.e., respective coefficients of $\boldsymbol{b}_{0,2}$ and $\boldsymbol{b}_{0,2}^*$ are random.

Key Lemmas. We will show Lemmas 3 and 4 for the proof of Theorem 1.

Definition 7 (Problem 1). *Problem 1 is to guess* β, *given* $(\mathsf{param}_n,$ $\{\widehat{\mathbb{B}}_\iota, \widehat{\mathbb{B}}_\iota^*\}_{\iota=0,1}, \boldsymbol{h}_{\beta,0}^*, \boldsymbol{e}_{\beta,0}, \{\boldsymbol{h}_{\beta,j,i}^*\}_{j=1,\dots,n;\, i=1,\dots,n}, \boldsymbol{e}_{\beta,1}) \xleftarrow{\mathsf{R}} \mathcal{G}_\beta^{\mathsf{P1}}(1^\lambda, n, \vec{y})$, *where*

$$\mathcal{G}_\beta^{\mathsf{P1}}(1^\lambda, n, \vec{y}):$$

$$(\mathsf{param}_n, \mathbb{B}_0, \mathbb{B}_0^*, \{B_{i,j}, B_{i,j,l}'\}_{i,j=1,\dots,6;\, l=1,\dots,n}, \mathbb{B}_1^*) \xleftarrow{\mathsf{R}} \mathcal{G}_{\mathsf{ob}}^{\mathsf{KP\text{-}ABE}}(1^\lambda, 6, n),$$

$$\widehat{\mathbb{B}}_0 := (\boldsymbol{b}_{0,1}, \boldsymbol{b}_{0,3}, \dots, \boldsymbol{b}_{0,5}), \qquad \widehat{\mathbb{B}}_0^* := (\boldsymbol{b}_{0,1}^*, \boldsymbol{b}_{0,3}^*, \dots, \boldsymbol{b}_{0,5}^*),$$

$$\widehat{\mathbb{B}}_1 := (\boldsymbol{b}_{1,1}, .., \boldsymbol{b}_{1,n}, \boldsymbol{b}_{1,3n+1}, .., \boldsymbol{b}_{1,6n}) \text{ is calculated as in Eq. (1)}$$

$$\text{from } \{B_{i,j}, B_{i,j,l}'\}_{i,j=1,\dots,6;\, l=1,\dots,n},$$

$$\widehat{\mathbb{B}}_1^* := (\boldsymbol{b}_{1,1}^*, .., \boldsymbol{b}_{1,n}^*, \boldsymbol{b}_{1,3n+1}^*, .., \boldsymbol{b}_{1,6n}^*), \quad \delta, \delta_0, \omega, \varphi_0, \varphi_1 \xleftarrow{\mathsf{U}} \mathbb{F}_q, \quad \tau, \rho \xleftarrow{\mathsf{U}} \mathbb{F}_q^\times,$$

$$\boldsymbol{h}_{0,0}^* := (\delta, 0, 0, \delta_0, 0)_{\mathbb{B}_0^*}, \quad \boldsymbol{h}_{1,0}^* := (\delta, \rho, 0, \delta_0, 0)_{\mathbb{B}_0^*},$$

$$\boldsymbol{e}_{0,0} := (\omega, 0, 0, 0, \varphi_0)_{\mathbb{B}_0}, \quad \boldsymbol{e}_{1,0} := (\omega, \tau, 0, 0, \varphi_0)_{\mathbb{B}_0},$$

$$\text{for } j = 1, .., n; \ i = 1, .., n; \ \vec{e}_i := (0^{i-1}, 1, 0^{n-i}) \in \mathbb{F}_q^n, \ \vec{\delta}_{j,i} \xleftarrow{\mathsf{U}} \mathbb{F}_q^{2n},$$

$$U_j \xleftarrow{\mathsf{U}} \mathcal{H}_{\vec{y}}(n, \mathbb{F}_q), \ Z_j := (U_j^{-1})^{\mathrm{T}},$$

$$\boldsymbol{h}_{0,j,i}^* := (\overbrace{\quad \delta \vec{e}_i, \quad}^{n} \overbrace{\quad 0^{2n}, \quad}^{2n} \overbrace{\quad \vec{\delta}_{j,i}, \quad}^{2n} \overbrace{\quad 0^n \quad}^{n})_{\mathbb{B}_1^*}$$

$$\overbrace{}^{n}\quad\overbrace{}^{2n}\quad\overbrace{}^{2n}\quad\overbrace{}^{n}$$

$$
\begin{aligned}
\boldsymbol{h}^*_{1,j,i} &:= (\quad \delta\vec{e}_i, \quad\quad 0^n,\ \rho\vec{e}_i\cdot Z_j, \quad\quad \vec{\delta}_{j,i}, \quad\quad 0^n \quad)_{\mathbb{B}^*_1} \\
\boldsymbol{e}_{0,1} &:= (\quad w\vec{y}, \quad\quad\quad 0^{2n}, \quad\quad\quad\quad 0^{2n}, \quad\quad \varphi_1\vec{y}\ )_{\mathbb{B}_1}, \\
\boldsymbol{e}_{1,1} &:= (\quad w\vec{y}, \quad\quad\tau\vec{y}, \quad\quad \tau\vec{y}, \quad\quad\quad 0^{2n}, \quad\quad \varphi_1\vec{y}\ )_{\mathbb{B}_1},
\end{aligned}
$$

$$\text{return } (\text{param}_n, \{\widehat{\mathbb{B}}_\iota, \widehat{\mathbb{B}}^*_\iota\}_{\iota=0,1}, \boldsymbol{h}^*_{\beta,0}, \boldsymbol{e}_{\beta,0}, \{\boldsymbol{h}^*_{\beta,j,i}\}_{j=1,\dots,n;\ i=1,\dots,n}, \boldsymbol{e}_{\beta,1}),$$

for $\beta \xleftarrow{\mathsf{U}} \{0,1\}$. *For a probabilistic adversary* $\mathcal{B}$*, we define the advantage of* $\mathcal{B}$ *as the quantity* $\mathsf{Adv}^{\mathsf{P1}}_{\mathcal{B}}(\lambda) := \left| \Pr\left[\mathcal{B}(1^\lambda, \varrho) \to 1 \,\middle|\, \varrho \xleftarrow{\mathsf{R}} \mathcal{G}^{\mathsf{P1}}_0(1^\lambda, n)\right] - \Pr\left[\mathcal{B}(1^\lambda, \varrho) \to 1 \,\middle|\right.$
$\left.\varrho \xleftarrow{\mathsf{R}} \mathcal{G}^{\mathsf{P1}}_1(1^\lambda, n)\right]\right|.$

Lemma 3. *Problem 1 is computationally intractable under the DLIN assumption.*

For any adversary $\mathcal{B}$*, there are probabilistic machines* $\mathcal{F}_{j,\iota}$ $(j = 0, \dots, n;\ \iota = 1, 2)$*, whose running times are essentially the same as that of* $\mathcal{B}$*, such that for any security parameter* λ*,* $\mathsf{Adv}^{\mathsf{P1}}_{\mathcal{B}}(\lambda) \leq \sum_{j=0}^{n}\sum_{\iota=1}^{2} \mathsf{Adv}^{\mathsf{DLIN}}_{\mathcal{F}_{j,\iota}}(\lambda) + (10n + 10)/q.$

The proof of Lemma 3 is given in the full version of this paper [27]. For an outline of the proof, see Section 6.

Next is a key lemma for applying the proof techniques in [22] to our KP-ABE and ABS schemes.

Lemma 4. *For all* $\vec{y} \in \mathbb{F}^n_q \setminus \mathsf{span}\langle\vec{e}_n\rangle$ *and* $\pi \in \mathbb{F}_q$*, let* $W_{\vec{y},\pi} := \{\vec{w} \in \mathbb{F}^n_q \setminus \mathsf{span}\langle\vec{e}_n\rangle^\perp \mid \vec{y}\cdot\vec{w} = \pi\}$*, where* $\mathsf{span}\langle\vec{e}_n\rangle^\perp := \{\vec{w} \in \mathbb{F}^n_q \mid \vec{w}\cdot\vec{e}_n = 0\}$*.*

For all $(\vec{y}, \vec{v}) \in (\mathbb{F}^n_q \setminus \mathsf{span}\langle\vec{e}_n\rangle) \times (\mathbb{F}^n_q \setminus \mathsf{span}\langle\vec{e}_n\rangle^\perp)$*, if* Z *is generated as* $U \xleftarrow{\mathsf{U}} \mathcal{H}_{\vec{y}}(n, \mathbb{F}_q)$ *and* $Z := (U^{-1})^{\mathsf{T}}$ *where* $\mathcal{H}_{\vec{y}}(n, \mathbb{F}_q)$ *is defined by Eq. (2), then* $\vec{v}Z$ *is uniformly distributed in* $W_{\vec{y},(\vec{y}\cdot\vec{v})}$*.*

The proof of Lemma 4 is given in the full version of this paper [27].

Proof of Theorem 1 : To prove Theorem 1, we consider the following 3 games. In Game 0, a part framed by a box indicates coefficients to be changed in a subsequent game. In the other games, a part framed by a box indicates coefficients which were changed in a game from the previous game.

Game 0 : Original game. That is, the reply to a key query for access structure $\mathbb{S} := (M, \rho)$ is:

$$
\left.
\begin{aligned}
&\boldsymbol{k}^*_0 := (-s_0, \boxed{0}, 1, \eta_0, 0)_{\mathbb{B}^*_0}, \\
&\text{for } i = 1, \dots, \ell; \quad \overbrace{}^{n}\quad\overbrace{}^{2n}\quad\overbrace{}^{2n}\quad\overbrace{}^{n} \\
&\text{if } \rho(i) = v_i,\ \boldsymbol{k}^*_i := (\quad s_i\vec{e}_1 + \theta_i\vec{v}_i, \quad 0^n, \boxed{0^n}, \quad \vec{\eta}_i, \quad 0^n\ )_{\mathbb{B}^*_i}, \\
&\text{if } \rho(i) = \neg v_i,\ \boldsymbol{k}^*_i := (\quad s_i\vec{v}_i, \quad\quad 0^n, \boxed{0^n}, \quad \vec{\eta}_i, \quad 0^n\ )_{\mathbb{B}^*_i},
\end{aligned}
\right\} \tag{5}
$$

where $\vec{f} \xleftarrow{\mathsf{U}} \mathbb{F}^r_q$, $\vec{s}^{\mathsf{T}} := (s_1, \dots, s_\ell)^{\mathsf{T}} := M \cdot \vec{f}^{\mathsf{T}}$, $s_0 := \vec{1} \cdot \vec{f}^{\mathsf{T}}$, $(s'_1, \dots, s'_\ell) \xleftarrow{\mathsf{U}} \mathbb{F}^\ell_q$, $\theta_i, \eta_0 \xleftarrow{\mathsf{U}} \mathbb{F}_q$, $\vec{\eta}_i \xleftarrow{\mathsf{U}} \mathbb{F}^n_q$, $\vec{e}_1 = (1, 0, \dots, 0) \in \mathbb{F}^n_q$, and $\vec{v}_i := (v^{n-1}_i, \dots, v_i, 1) \in$

$(\mathbb{F}_q^\times)^n$. The challenge ciphertext for challenge plaintexts $(m^{(0)}, m^{(1)})$ and $\Gamma :=$ $\{x_1, \ldots, x_{n'}\}$ with $n' \leq n-1$ is:

$$
\left.
\begin{aligned}
\boldsymbol{c}_0 &:= (\omega,\ \boxed{0},\ \boxed{\zeta},\ 0,\ \varphi_0)_{\mathbb{B}_0}, \qquad c_3 := g_T^\zeta m^{(b)}, \\[2mm]
& \underbrace{\phantom{\omega\vec{y},}}_{n} \qquad \underbrace{\phantom{0^{2n}}}_{2n} \qquad\quad \underbrace{\phantom{0^{2n}}}_{2n} \qquad \underbrace{\phantom{\varphi_1\vec{y}}}_{n} \\[-1mm]
\boldsymbol{c}_1 &:= (\qquad \omega\vec{y}, \qquad \boxed{0^{2n}}, \qquad 0^{2n}, \qquad \varphi_1\vec{y}\quad)_{\mathbb{B}_1},
\end{aligned}
\right\}
\tag{6}
$$

where $b \xleftarrow{\mathsf{U}} \{0,1\}; \omega, \zeta, \varphi_0, \varphi_1 \xleftarrow{\mathsf{U}} \mathbb{F}_q$, and $\vec{y} := (y_1, \ldots, y_n)$ such that $\sum_{j=0}^{n-1} y_{n-j} z^j$ $= z^{n-1-n'} \cdot \prod_{j=1}^{n'} (z - x_j)$.

Game 1 : Same as Game 0 except that the reply to a key query for access structure $\mathbb{S} := (M, \rho)$ are:

$$
\left.
\begin{aligned}
\boldsymbol{k}_0^* &:= (-s_0,\ \boxed{w_0},\ 1,\ \eta_0,\ 0)_{\mathbb{B}_0^*}, \\[1mm]
&\text{for } i = 1, \ldots, \ell; \qquad \underbrace{\phantom{s_i\vec{e}_1+\theta_i\vec{v}_i}}_{n} \quad \underbrace{\phantom{0^n,\ \vec{w}_i}}_{2n} \quad \underbrace{}_{2n} \quad \underbrace{}_{n} \\[-1mm]
&\text{if } \rho(i) = v_i,\ \boldsymbol{k}_i^* := (\ \ s_i\vec{e}_1 + \theta_i\vec{v}_i, \quad 0^n,\ \boxed{\vec{w}_i}, \quad \eta_i, \quad 0^n\ )_{\mathbb{B}_i^*}, \\[1mm]
&\text{if } \rho(i) = \neg v_i,\ \boldsymbol{k}_i^* := (\qquad s_i\vec{v}_i, \quad 0^n,\ \boxed{\overline{\vec{w}}_i}, \quad \eta_i, \quad 0^n\ )_{\mathbb{B}_i^*},
\end{aligned}
\right\}
\tag{7}
$$

where $\vec{g} \xleftarrow{\mathsf{U}} \mathbb{F}_q^r$, $\vec{r}^{\mathrm{T}} := (r_1, \ldots, r_\ell)^{\mathrm{T}} := M \cdot \vec{g}^{\mathrm{T}}$, $w_0 \xleftarrow{\mathsf{U}} \mathbb{F}_q$, $\psi_i \xleftarrow{\mathsf{U}} \mathbb{F}_q$, $\vec{w}_i \xleftarrow{\mathsf{U}} \{\vec{w}_i \in \mathbb{F}_q^n \mid \vec{w}_i \cdot \vec{y} = (r_i\vec{e}_1 + \psi_i\vec{v}_i) \cdot \vec{y}\}$, $\overline{\vec{w}}_i \xleftarrow{\mathsf{U}} \{\overline{\vec{w}}_i \in \mathbb{F}_q^n \mid \overline{\vec{w}}_i \cdot \vec{y} = r_i\vec{v}_i \cdot \vec{y}\}$, and the challenge ciphertext is:

$$
\left.
\begin{aligned}
\boldsymbol{c}_0 &:= (\omega,\ \boxed{\tau},\ \zeta,\ 0,\ \varphi_0)_{\mathbb{B}_0}, \qquad c_3 := g_T^\zeta m^{(b)}, \\[2mm]
& \underbrace{\phantom{\omega\vec{y},}}_{n} \qquad \underbrace{\phantom{\tau\vec{y},\ \tau\vec{y}}}_{2n} \qquad \underbrace{\phantom{0^{2n}}}_{2n} \qquad \underbrace{\phantom{\varphi_1\vec{y}}}_{n} \\[-1mm]
\boldsymbol{c}_1 &:= (\qquad \omega\vec{y}, \qquad \boxed{\tau\vec{y},\ \tau\vec{y}}, \qquad 0^{2n}, \qquad \varphi_1\vec{y}\quad)_{\mathbb{B}_1},
\end{aligned}
\right\}
\tag{8}
$$

where $\tau \xleftarrow{\mathsf{U}} \mathbb{F}_q$, and all the other variables are generated as in Game 0.

Game 2 : Game 2 is the same as Game 1 except $\boldsymbol{c}_0$ (and c_3) of the challenge ciphertext are

$$
\boldsymbol{c}_0 := (\omega,\ \tau,\ \boxed{\zeta'},\ 0,\ \varphi_0)_{\mathbb{B}_0}, \qquad c_3 := g_T^\zeta m^{(b)}, \tag{9}
$$

where $\zeta' \xleftarrow{\mathsf{U}} \mathbb{F}_q$ (i.e., independent from $\zeta \xleftarrow{\mathsf{U}} \mathbb{F}_q$), and all the other variables are generated as in Game 1.

Let $\mathsf{Adv}_\mathcal{A}^{(0)}(\lambda), \mathsf{Adv}_\mathcal{A}^{(1)}(\lambda)$, and $\mathsf{Adv}_\mathcal{A}^{(2)}(\lambda)$ be the advantage of $\mathcal{A}$ in Game 0,1 and 2, respectively. $\mathsf{Adv}_\mathcal{A}^{(0)}(\lambda)$ is equivalent to $\mathsf{Adv}_\mathcal{A}^{\mathsf{KP\text{-}ABE,PH}}(\lambda)$ and it is clear that $\mathsf{Adv}_\mathcal{A}^{(2)}(\lambda) = 0$ by Lemma 7. We will show Lemmas 5 and 6 that evaluate the gaps between pairs of $\mathsf{Adv}_\mathcal{A}^{(0)}(\lambda), \mathsf{Adv}_\mathcal{A}^{(1)}(\lambda), \mathsf{Adv}_\mathcal{A}^{(2)}(\lambda)$. From these lemmas and Lemma 3, we obtain $\mathsf{Adv}_\mathcal{A}^{\mathsf{KP\text{-}ABE}}(\lambda) = \mathsf{Adv}_\mathcal{A}^{(0)}(\lambda) \leq \left|\mathsf{Adv}_\mathcal{A}^{(0)}(\lambda) - \mathsf{Adv}_\mathcal{A}^{(1)}(\lambda)\right| +$ $\left|\mathsf{Adv}_\mathcal{A}^{(1)}(\lambda) - \mathsf{Adv}_\mathcal{A}^{(2)}(\lambda)\right| \leq \mathsf{Adv}_\mathcal{B}^{\mathsf{P1}}(\lambda) + (\nu\ell+2)/q \leq \sum_{j=0}^{n}\sum_{\iota=1}^{2} \mathsf{Adv}_{\mathcal{F}_{j,\iota}}^{\mathsf{DLIN}}(\lambda) + (\nu\ell + 10n + 12)/q$. This completes the proof of Theorem 1. $\qquad\square$

Lemma 5. *For any adversary $\mathcal{A}$, there exists a probabilistic machine $\mathcal{B}$, whose running time is essentially the same as that of $\mathcal{A}$, such that for any security parameter λ, $|\mathsf{Adv}_{\mathcal{A}}^{(1)}(\lambda) - \mathsf{Adv}_{\mathcal{A}}^{(0)}(\lambda)| \leq \mathsf{Adv}_{\mathcal{B}}^{\mathsf{P1}}(\lambda) + (\nu\ell + 1)/q$, where ν is the maximum number of $\mathcal{A}$'s key queries, ℓ is the maximum number of rows in access matrices M of key queries.*

The proof of Lemma 5 is given in the full version of this paper [27].

Lemma 6. *For any adversary $\mathcal{A}$, for any security parameter λ, $|\mathsf{Adv}_{\mathcal{A}}^{(2)}(\lambda) - \mathsf{Adv}_{\mathcal{A}}^{(1)}(\lambda)| \leq 1/q$.*

Lemma 6 is proven in a similar manner to Lemma 7 in the full version of [22].

Lemma 7. *For any adversary $\mathcal{A}$, for any security parameter λ, $\mathsf{Adv}_{\mathcal{A}}^{(2)}(\lambda) = 0$.*

Proof. The value of b is independent from the adversary's view in Game 2. Hence, $\mathsf{Adv}_{\mathcal{A}}^{(2)}(\lambda) = 0$.   □

6   Proof Outline of Lemma 3

6.1   Iteration of Swapping and Conceptual Change

Lemma 3 is proven by the hybrid argument through $2n+2$ experiments (given in the full version): Experiment 0 $\Rightarrow$ Experiment 1 $\Rightarrow$ for $j = 1, \ldots, n$; Experiment 2-j-1 $\Rightarrow$ Experiment 2-j-2

First, in a $\beta = 0$ instance of Problem 1 (Experiment 0), coefficients of the hidden parts of e_1 and $h_{\kappa,i}^{*}$ ($\kappa = 1, \ldots, n$) are all zero. Then, in the next Experiment 1, that of e_1 is filled with $(\tau\vec{y}, \tau\vec{y}) \in \mathbb{F}_q^{2n}$ and the first n-dim. coefficient (block) of the hidden parts of $h_{\kappa,i}^{*}$ ($\kappa = 1, \ldots, n$) are changed to $\rho\vec{e}_i \in \mathbb{F}_q^{n}$ as: (Hereafter, a blank indicates zero coefficients)

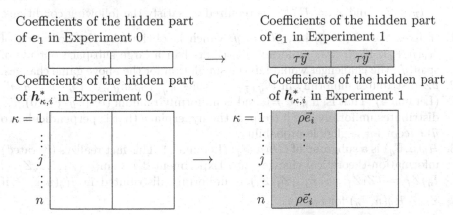

After that, in turn for $j = 1, \ldots, n$, the coefficient vector $\rho\vec{e}_i \in \mathbb{F}_q^{n}$ is *swapped* to the second block of the hidden parts of $h_{j,i}^{*}$ in Experiment 2-j-1 and the coefficient vector is *conceptually (information-theoretically) changed* to $\rho\vec{e}_i Z_j$ in Experiment 2-j-2 by a conceptual basis change. The swapping can be securely executed under the DLIN assumption. At the final Experiment 2-n-2, each $\rho\vec{e}_i Z_j$ $(j = 1, \dots, n)$ is embedded in the second block of hidden parts in $\boldsymbol{h}^*_{j,i}$, i.e., an instance of Experiment 2-n-2 is equivalent to a $\beta = 1$ instance of Problem 1.

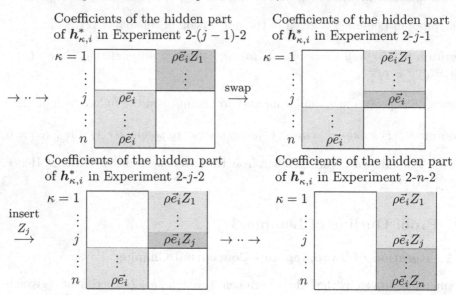

Insertion of Z_j is realized by a conceptual basis change determined by Z_j (see item 3 in Section 6.2).

6.2   Key Properties of $\mathcal{H}_{\vec{y}}(n, \mathbb{F}_q)$

In order to achieve the game transformations given above, in particular, change into Experiment 2-j-2, the transformation $(\vec{y}, \vec{v}) \mapsto (\vec{y}U, \vec{v}Z)$ by (U, Z) with $U \xleftarrow{\mathsf{U}} \mathcal{H}_{\vec{y}}(n, \mathbb{F}_q)$ and $Z := (U^{-1})^{\mathrm{T}}$ is required to satisfy the following conditions.

1. It fixes the target $\vec{y}$, i.e., $\vec{y}U = \vec{y}$, which is obvious by the definition of $\mathcal{H}_{\vec{y}}(n, \mathbb{F}_q)$. If $\vec{y}U$ was uniformly distributed in a large subspace outside of span$\langle \vec{y} \rangle$, the challenger would fail the simulation for the above game changes.
2. $\vec{v}Z$ distributes uniformly in $W_{\vec{y},(\vec{y}\cdot\vec{v})} := \{\vec{w} \in \mathbb{F}_q^n \setminus \mathsf{span}\langle \vec{e}_n \rangle^\perp \mid \vec{y}\cdot\vec{w} = \vec{y}\cdot\vec{v}\}$ (Lemma 4). That is, if $\vec{y}\cdot\vec{v} \neq 0$ and is uniformly random (resp. $\vec{y}\cdot\vec{v} = 0$), $\vec{v}Z$ distributes uniformly in $\mathbb{F}_q^n$ (resp. in the hyperplane that is perpendicular to $\vec{y}$) except for negligible probability.
3. $\mathcal{H}_{\vec{y}}(n, \mathbb{F}_q)$ is a subgroup of $GL(n, \mathbb{F}_q)$ (Lemma 1). This fact realizes (iterated) information-theoretical changes into Experiment 2-j-2 since $(Z_1, \dots, Z_{j-1}, I_n)Z_j = (Z_1 Z_j, \dots, Z_{j-1}Z_j, Z_j)$ is uniformly distributed in $\mathcal{H}_{\vec{y}}(n, \mathbb{F}_q)^j$ if $Z_i \xleftarrow{\mathsf{U}} \mathcal{H}_{\vec{y}}(n, \mathbb{F}_q)$ for $i = 1, \dots, j$.

Lemma 4 is considered to be a pairwise independence lemma specific to $\mathcal{H}_{\vec{y}}(n, \mathbb{F}_q)$. For comparison, we describe the lemma for $\mathcal{H}(n, \mathbb{F}_q)$ in [23] below.

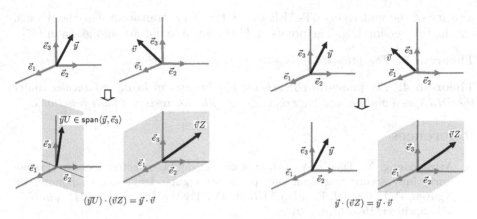

Fig. 1. Three dimensional cases of Lemma 8 on the left and Lemma 4 on the right when $\vec{y} \cdot \vec{v} \neq 0$ and is uniformly random and independent from other variables. The vectors $\vec{y}U$ and $\vec{v}Z$ are uniformly distributed in the shadowed subspaces, respectively.

Fig. 1 compares the two lemmas when $\vec{y} \cdot \vec{v}$ ($\neq 0$) is uniformly random and independent from other variables, which is an important case for the security proof of the proposed KP-ABE.

Lemma 8 (Pairwise Independence Lemma for $\mathcal{H}(n, \mathbb{F}_q)$ [23]). *Let $\vec{e}_n :=$ $(0, \ldots, 0, 1) \in \mathbb{F}_q^n$. For all $\vec{y} \in \mathbb{F}_q^n \setminus \mathrm{span}\langle \vec{e}_n \rangle$ and $\pi \in \mathbb{F}_q$, let $W'_{\vec{y}, \pi} := \{(\vec{r}, \vec{w}) \in$ $(\mathrm{span}\langle \vec{y}, \vec{e}_n \rangle \setminus \mathrm{span}\langle \vec{e}_n \rangle) \times (\mathbb{F}_q^n \setminus \mathrm{span}\langle \vec{e}_n \rangle^\perp) \mid \vec{r} \cdot \vec{w} = \pi\}$.*
For all $(\vec{y}, \vec{v}) \in \left(\mathbb{F}_q^n \setminus \mathrm{span}\langle \vec{e}_n \rangle\right) \times \left(\mathbb{F}_q^n \setminus \mathrm{span}\langle \vec{e}_n \rangle^\perp\right)$ and $(\vec{r}, \vec{w}) \in W'_{\vec{y}, (\vec{y} \cdot \vec{v})}$, $\Pr [\vec{y}U$ $= \vec{r} \wedge \vec{v}Z = \vec{w}] = 1/\sharp W'_{\vec{y}, (\vec{y} \cdot \vec{v})}$, where $U \xleftarrow{\mathsf{U}} \mathcal{H}(n, \mathbb{F}_q) \cap GL(n, \mathbb{F}_q)$ and $Z := (U^{-1})^\mathrm{T}$.

The left hand side of Fig. 1 presents the transformation $(\vec{y}, \vec{v}) \mapsto (\vec{y}U, \vec{v}Z)$ which is given in Lemma 8 using a pair of matrices (U, Z) with $U \xleftarrow{\mathsf{U}} \mathcal{H}(n, \mathbb{F}_q) \cap GL(n, \mathbb{F}_q)$ in a three-dimensional space when $\vec{y} \cdot \vec{v}$ ($\neq 0$) is uniformly random. The image $(\vec{y}U, \vec{v}Z)$ is spreading over $\mathrm{span}\langle \vec{y}, \vec{e}_n \rangle \times \mathbb{F}_q^n$ except for negligible probability since $(\vec{y}U) \cdot (\vec{v}Z) = \vec{y} \cdot \vec{v}$ is random. The right hand side of Fig. 1 presents the transformation which is given in Lemma 4 using (U, Z) with $U \xleftarrow{\mathsf{U}} \mathcal{H}_{\vec{y}}(n, \mathbb{F}_q)$ in a three-dimensional space when $\vec{y} \cdot \vec{v}$ ($\neq 0$) is uniformly random. Then, $\vec{y}$ is fixed, i.e., $\vec{y}U = \vec{y}$. Only $\vec{v}Z$ is spreading over $\mathbb{F}_q^n$ except for negligible probability since $\vec{y} \cdot (\vec{v}Z) = \vec{y} \cdot \vec{v}$ is random. Since $\vec{y}$ is fixed in this conceptual change, i.e., change to Experiment 2-j-2, we can execute the next computational change, i.e., swapping in Experiment 2-$(j + 1)$-1, in the sequence of changes given in Section 6.1.

7   Proposed Constant-Size Secret-Key ABS Scheme

We propose a *fully secure* (*adaptive*-predicate unforgeable and private) ABS scheme with constant-size secret-keys. This is because the *adaptive*-predicate unforgeability of the ABS can be guaranteed by the *non-adaptive* payload-hiding security of the underlying CP-ABE under the Naor transform. For the details, see the full version [27]. The proofs of Theorems 3 and 4 are also given in [27].

Theorem 3. *The proposed ABS scheme is perfectly private.*

Theorem 4. *The proposed ABS scheme is adaptive-predicate unforgeable under the DLIN assumption and the existence of collision resistant hash functions.*

References

1. Attrapadung, N.: Dual system encryption via doubly selective security: Framework, fully secure functional encryption for regular languages, and more. In: Nguyen, P.Q., Oswald, E. (eds.) EUROCRYPT 2014. LNCS, vol. 8441, pp. 557–577. Springer, Heidelberg (2014)
2. Attrapadung, N., Libert, B., de Panafieu, E.: Expressive key-policy attribute-based encryption with constant-size ciphertexts. In: Catalano, et al. (eds.) [7], pp. 90–108
3. Beimel, A.: Secure schemes for secret sharing and key distribution. PhD Thesis, Israel Institute of Technology, Technion, Haifa (1996)
4. Boneh, D., Boyen, X., Goh, E.J.: Hierarchical identity based encryption with constant size ciphertext. In: Cramer (ed.) [11], pp. 440–456
5. Boneh, D., Boyen, X., Shacham, H.: Short group signatures. In: Franklin, M. (ed.) CRYPTO 2004. LNCS, vol. 3152, pp. 41–55. Springer, Heidelberg (2004)
6. Boneh, D., Gentry, C., Waters, B.: Collusion resistant broadcast encryption with short ciphertexts and private keys. In: Shoup, V. (ed.) CRYPTO 2005. LNCS, vol. 3621, pp. 258–275. Springer, Heidelberg (2005)
7. Catalano, D., Fazio, N., Gennaro, R., Nicolosi, A. (eds.): PKC 2011. LNCS, vol. 6571. Springer, Heidelberg (2011)
8. Chen, C., Chen, J., Lim, H.W., Zhang, Z., Feng, D., Ling, S., Wang, H.: Fully secure attribute-based systems with short ciphertexts/signatures and threshold access structures. In: Dawson, E. (ed.) RSA 2013. LNCS, vol. 7779, pp. 50–67. Springer, Heidelberg (2013)
9. Chen, J., Wee, H.: Semi-adaptive attribute-based encryption and improved delegation for boolean formula. To appear in SCN 2014. IACR Cryptology ePrint Archive 2014, 465 (2014)
10. Cheon, J.H.: Security analysis of the strong diffie-hellman problem. In: Vaudenay (ed.) [28], pp. 1–11
11. Cramer, R. (ed.): EUROCRYPT 2005. LNCS, vol. 3494. Springer, Heidelberg (2005)
12. Delerablée, C.: Identity-based broadcast encryption with constant size ciphertexts and private keys. In: Kurosawa, K. (ed.) ASIACRYPT 2007. LNCS, vol. 4833, pp. 200–215. Springer, Heidelberg (2007)
13. Emura, K., Miyaji, A., Nomura, A., Omote, K., Soshi, M.: A ciphertext-policy attribute-based encryption scheme with constant ciphertext length. In: Bao, F., Li, H., Wang, G. (eds.) ISPEC 2009. LNCS, vol. 5451, pp. 13–23. Springer, Heidelberg (2009)
14. Garg, S., Gentry, C., Halevi, S., Sahai, A., Waters, B.: Attribute-based encryption for circuits from multilinear maps. In: Canetti, R., Garay, J.A. (eds.) CRYPTO 2013, Part II. LNCS, vol. 8043, pp. 479–499. Springer, Heidelberg (2013)
15. Gentry, C.: Practical identity-based encryption without random oracles. In: Vaudenay (ed.) [28], pp. 445–464

16. Gorbunov, S., Vaikuntanathan, V., Wee, H.: Attribute-based encryption for circuits. In: Boneh, D., Roughgarden, T., Feigenbaum, J. (eds.) STOC, pp. 545–554. ACM (2013)

17. Herranz, J., Laguillaumie, F., Ràfols, C.: Constant size ciphertexts in threshold attribute-based encryption. In: Nguyen, P.Q., Pointcheval, D. (eds.) PKC 2010. LNCS, vol. 6056, pp. 19–34. Springer, Heidelberg (2010)

18. Maji, H.K., Prabhakaran, M., Rosulek, M.: Attribute-based signatures. In: Kiayias, A. (ed.) CT-RSA 2011. LNCS, vol. 6558, pp. 376–392. Springer, Heidelberg (2011)

19. Mitsunari, S., Sakai, R., Kasahara, M.: A new traitor tracing. IEICE Trans. Fundamentals E85-A(2), 481–484 (2002)

20. Okamoto, T., Takashima, K.: Efficient (hierarchical) inner-product encryption tightly reduced from the decisional linear assumption. IEICE Trans. Fundamentals E96-A(1), 42–52 (2013)

21. Okamoto, T., Takashima, K.: Hierarchical predicate encryption for inner-products. In: Matsui, M. (ed.) ASIACRYPT 2009. LNCS, vol. 5912, pp. 214–231. Springer, Heidelberg (2009)

22. Okamoto, T., Takashima, K.: Fully secure functional encryption with general relations from the decisional linear assumption. In: Rabin, T. (ed.) CRYPTO 2010. LNCS, vol. 6223, pp. 191–208. Springer, Heidelberg (2010), full version is available at http://eprint.iacr.org/2010/563

23. Okamoto, T., Takashima, K.: Achieving short ciphertexts or short secret-keys for adaptively secure general inner-product encryption. In: Lin, D., Tsudik, G., Wang, X. (eds.) CANS 2011. LNCS, vol. 7092, pp. 138–159. Springer, Heidelberg (2011), full version is available at http://eprint.iacr.org/2011/648

24. Okamoto, T., Takashima, K.: Efficient attribute-based signatures for non-monotone predicates in the standard model. In: Catalano, et al. (eds.) [7], pp. 35–52, full version is available at http://eprint.iacr.org/2011/700

25. Sahai, A., Waters, B.: Fuzzy identity-based encryption. In: Cramer (ed.) [11], pp. 457–473

26. Sakemi, Y., Hanaoka, G., Izu, T., Takenaka, M., Yasuda, M.: Solving a discrete logarithm problem with auxiliary input on a 160-bit elliptic curve. In: Fischlin, M., Buchmann, J., Manulis, M. (eds.) PKC 2012. LNCS, vol. 7293, pp. 595–608. Springer, Heidelberg (2012)

27. Takashima, K.: Expressive attribute-based encryption with constant-size ciphertexts from the decisional linear assumption. IACR Cryptology ePrint Archive 2014, 207 (2014)

28. Vaudenay, S. (ed.): EUROCRYPT 2006. LNCS, vol. 4004. Springer, Heidelberg (2006)

29. Waters, B.: Dual system encryption: Realizing fully secure IBE and HIBE under simple assumptions. In: Halevi, S. (ed.) CRYPTO 2009. LNCS, vol. 5677, pp. 619–636. Springer, Heidelberg (2009)

30. Yamada, S., Attrapadung, N., Hanaoka, G., Kunihiro, N.: A framework and compact constructions for non-monotonic attribute-based encryption. In: Krawczyk, H. (ed.) PKC 2014. LNCS, vol. 8383, pp. 275–292. Springer, Heidelberg (2014)

Functional Encryption and Its Impact on Cryptography

Hoeteck Wee[*]

ENS, Paris, France
wee@di.ens.fr

Abstract. Functional encryption is a novel paradigm for public-key encryption that enables both fine-grained access control and selective computation on encrypted data, as is necessary to protect big, complex data in the cloud. In this article, we provide a brief introduction to functional encryption, and an overview of its overarching impact on the field of cryptography.

1 Introduction

Recent computing and technological advances such as the ubiquity of high-speed network access and the proliferation of mobile devices have had a profound impact on our society, our lives and our behavior. In the past decade, we have seen a substantial shift towards a digital and paperless society, along with a migration of data and computation to the cloud. Storing data in the cloud offers tremendous benefits: easy and convenient access to the data and reliable data storage for individuals, as well as scalability and financial savings for organizations. On the flip side, storing data remotely poses an acute security threat as these data – government, financial, medical records as well as personal information exchanged over email and social networks – are outside our control and could potentially be accessed by untrusted parties. Without taking measures to protect our data, we are at risk of devastating privacy breaches and living under digital surveillance in an Orwellian future.

However, traditional public-key encryption lacks the expressiveness needed to protect big, complex data:

(i) First, traditional encryption only provides coarse-grained access to encrypted data, namely, only a single secret key can decrypt the data. Corporate entities want to share data with groups of users based on their credentials. Similarly, individuals want to selectively grant access to their personal data on social networks and Google Docs.

(ii) Second, access to encrypted data is "all or nothing": one either decrypts the entire plaintext or learns nothing about the plaintext. In applications such as data-mining on encrypted medical records or social networks, we want to provide only partial access and selective computation on the encrypted data, for instance, restricted classes of statistical or database queries.

[*] CNRS (UMR 8548) and INRIA. Supported in part by NSF Awards CNS-1237429 and CNS-1319021 and a fellowship from the Alexander von Humboldt Foundation.

M. Abdalla and R. De Prisco (Eds.): SCN 2014, LNCS 8642, pp. 318–323, 2014.

Ideally, we want to encrypt data while enabling fine-grained access control and selective computation; that is, we want control over *who* has access to the encrypted data and *what* they can compute. Such a mechanism would reconcile the conflict between our desire to outsource and compute on data and the need to protect the data.

2 Functional Encryption

Over the past decade, cryptographers have put forth a novel paradigm for public-key encryption [30, 23, 3, 28] that addresses the above goal: (i) *attribute-based encryption* (ABE), which enables fine-grain access control, and (ii) its generalization to *functional encryption*, which enables selective computation.

- In **attribute-based encryption (ABE)**, encrypted data are associated with a set of attributes and secret keys with policies that control which ciphertexts the key can decrypt. For instance, a digital content provider can issue keys that decrypt basic and premium channel contents on weekdays and only basic ones on weekends.
- In **functional encryption**, a secret key enables a user to learn a specific function of the encrypted data and nothing else. For example, decrypting an encrypted image with a cropping key will reveal a cropped version of the image and nothing else about the image.

A salient feature of both attribute-based and functional encryption is that there are many possible secret keys with different decryption capabilities. Moreover, the keys are resilient to collusion attacks, namely any group of users holding different secret keys learns nothing about the plaintext beyond what each of them could individually learn. Together, attribute-based and functional encryption constitute a crisp generalization of several advanced notions of encryption, such as broadcast and identity-based encryption as well as searching on encrypted data; indeed, many advances in public-key encryption over the past decade can be viewed as special cases of attribute-based and functional encryption.

State of the Art. The fundamental goals in the study of attribute-based and functional encryption are two-fold: (i) to build expressive schemes that support a large class of policies and functions; and (ii) to obtain efficient instantiations based on widely-believed intractability of basic computational problems.

The simplest example of attribute-based encryption (ABE) is that of identity-based encryption (IBE), where both the ciphertext and secret key are associated with identities i.e. bit strings, and decryption is possible exactly when the identities are equal. Starting with identity-based encryption (IBE), substantial advances in ABE were made over the past decade showing how to support fairly expressive but nonetheless limited subset of policies, culminating most recently in schemes supporting any policy computable by general circuits [22, 4].

In addition, we have a wide spectrum of techniques for efficient IBE and ABE that yields various trade-offs between efficiency, expressiveness, security and intractability assumptions. The specific assumptions in use may be broadly classified into two categories: (i) pairing-based, such as variants of the Diffie-Hellman problem over bilinear groups, and (ii) lattice-based, notably the learning with errors (LWE) assumption.

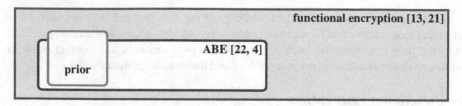

Fig. 1. Advances in attribute-based and functional encryption since 2012. The white region refers to ABE and functionalities for which we have efficient instantiations under standard assumptions; the grey region refers to functionalities beyond ABE for which our understanding is much more limited.

Beyond ABE, our understanding of functional encryption is much more limited. The only efficient schemes we have are for very simple functionalities related to computing an inner product [24]. In a recent break-through work, Garg et al. [13] gave a beautiful construction of functional encryption for general circuits; however, the construction relies on "multi-linear maps", for which we have few candidates, along with complex intractability assumptions which are presently poorly understood. In contrast, if we consider collusions of a priori *bounded* size, a weaker guarantee that is still meaningful for many applications, then it is possible to obtain functional encryption for general circuits under a large class of standard assumptions.

Along with these cryptographic advances, the community has also made a greater push towards implementation, prototypes and deployment of attribute-based and functional encryption: several IBE schemes are now standardized in RFC 5091; the CHARM project provides a Python framework for rapidly prototyping cryptosystems and includes implementations of several IBE and ABE schemes; the SHARPS project explores the use of ABE for protecting health-care data; the Mylar project presents a web application platform that uses ABE to provide fine-grained access to encrypted data.

3   Impact on Cryptography

The study of functional encryption has significantly advanced the state of the art in the field of cryptography. In particular, it motivated the development of new and powerful tools and techniques, including trapdoor and delegation techniques in lattices [16, 9] and the first candidate construction of multi-linear maps [12]. These tools and techniques have in turn found numerous applications beyond functional encryption, notably CCA-secure encryption [8], signatures schemes [5], leakage-resilient cryptography [26], delegating and verifying computation [29, 25, 11], and most recently, garbled circuits [19, 4] and program obfuscation [13, 20]. We highlight three examples, drawing upon recent developments closely related to our research in functional encryption.

Verifiable Computation. In verifiable computation, a computationally weak client with input x wishes to delegate a complex computation f to an untrusted server, with the assurance that the server cannot convince the client to accept an incorrect computation

[18, 14]. We focus on the online/offline setting, where the protocol proceeds in two phases. In the offline phase, the client sends to the server a possibly long message that may be expensive to compute. Later on, in the online phase (when the input x arrives), the client sends a short message to the server, and receives the result of the computation $f(x)$ together with a certificate for correctness. Applying an existing transformation [29] to our ABE for general circuits [22], we obtain a protocol for verifiable computation on general circuits f with a number of highly desirable properties: (i) the client's communication and computational complexity in the online phase depends only on the input/output lengths and depth of the circuit computing f but not the circuit size; (ii) anyone can check the server's work given a "verification" key published by the client; (iii) we may securely reuse the computation of the offline phase across multiple inputs in the online phase (in particular, our construction is immune to the "rejection problem" from [14]).

Short, Scalable Signatures. Many applications involving cloud computing and big data require cryptographic primitives that remain secure when used on huge data sets. In particular, we would like to design scalable signatures schemes that remain secure when used to sign a very large number of messages without any performance penalty. However, most known signature schemes are not scalable: their security guarantee degrades linearly in the number of signatures seen by an adversary; this implies a performance degradation as we need to increase key sizes to account for the security loss, which in turn increases the running time of the implementation. In a recent work [10], we presented the first scalable signature scheme in the standard model where each signature is a constant number of group elements. The signature scheme is derived from an IBE with a better security reduction that overcomes seemingly inherent limitations of prior proof techniques, via a delicate combination of techniques used for achieving full security in IBE/ABE [31, 32] and those for constructing efficient pseudo-random functions [27]. Our signature scheme has since been improved and extended to the multi-user setting in [2].

Fully Homomorphic Encryption. In 2009, Gentry [15] presented the first candidate fully homomorphic encryption (FHE) for all circuits, and substantial progress have since been made towards improving the efficiency and the underlying assumptions [6, 17]. We note that while both FHE and functional encryption support some form of computation on encrypted data, it is not known how to construct functional encryption from FHE or vice versa. Nonetheless, our lattice-based ABE for branching programs [22] has recently inspired the first FHE schemes based on the LWE assumption with a polynomial modulus-to-noise ratio [7, 1]. Roughly speaking, we propagate LWE samples across computation during decryption in ABE, and during homomorphic evaluation in FHE. If we compute on circuits, the noise accumulated in the LWE samples grows exponentially with the depth D of the circuit (the noise grows as n^D where n is the length of the LWE secret). On the other hand, by exploiting an asymmetry in computation on branching programs, it is possible to achieve noise growth that is linear in the length of the branching program. The latest FHE schemes in [7, 1] then use a branching program instead of a log-depth circuit to compute the decryption function during bootstrapping, thus incurring a polynomial as opposed to a quasi-polynomial noise growth.

Acknowledgments. I am extremely grateful to Jie Chen, Sergey Gorbunov and Vinod Vaikuntanathan for many fruitful collaborations and to Dan Boneh, Yuval Ishai, Allison Lewko and Brent Waters for many illuminating discussions. I would also like to thank Michel Abdalla and the SCN 2014 PC for inviting me as a speaker.

References

[1] Alperin-Sheriff, J., Peikert, C.: Faster bootstrapping with polynomial error. In: CRYPTO (to appear 2014)

[2] Blazy, O., Kiltz, E., Pan, J. (hierarchical) identity-based encryption from affine message authentication. In: CRYPTO (to appear 2014)

[3] Boneh, D., Sahai, A., Waters, B.: Functional encryption: Definitions and challenges. In: Ishai, Y. (ed.) TCC 2011. LNCS, vol. 6597, pp. 253–273. Springer, Heidelberg (2011)

[4] Boneh, D., Gentry, C., Gorbunov, S., Halevi, S., Nikolaenko, V., Segev, G., Vaikuntanathan, V., Vinayagamurthy, D.: Fully key-homomorphic encryption, arithmetic circuit ABE and compact garbled circuits. In: Nguyen, P.Q., Oswald, E. (eds.) EUROCRYPT 2014. LNCS, vol. 8441, pp. 533–556. Springer, Heidelberg (2014)

[5] Boyen, X.: Lattice mixing and vanishing trapdoors: A framework for fully secure short signatures and more. In: Nguyen, P.Q., Pointcheval, D. (eds.) PKC 2010. LNCS, vol. 6056, pp. 499–517. Springer, Heidelberg (2010)

[6] Brakerski, Z., Vaikuntanathan, V.: Efficient fully homomorphic encryption from (standard) LWE. In: FOCS, Cryptology ePrint Archive, Report 2011/344 (2011)

[7] Brakerski, Z., Vaikuntanathan, V.: Lattice-based FHE as secure as PKE. In: ITCS, pp. 1–12 (2014)

[8] Canetti, R., Halevi, S., Katz, J.: Chosen-ciphertext security from identity-based encryption. In: Cachin, C., Camenisch, J.L. (eds.) EUROCRYPT 2004. LNCS, vol. 3027, pp. 207–222. Springer, Heidelberg (2004)

[9] Cash, D., Hofheinz, D., Kiltz, E., Peikert, C.: Bonsai trees, or how to delegate a lattice basis. In: Gilbert, H. (ed.) EUROCRYPT 2010. LNCS, vol. 6110, pp. 523–552. Springer, Heidelberg (2010)

[10] Chen, J., Wee, H.: Fully (almost) tightly secure IBE and dual system groups. In: Canetti, R., Garay, J.A. (eds.) CRYPTO 2013, Part II. LNCS, vol. 8043, pp. 435–460. Springer, Heidelberg (2013)

[11] Chen, J., Wee, H.: Semi-adaptive attribute-based encryption and improved delegation for boolean formula. In: SCN (to appear 2014)

[12] Garg, S., Gentry, C., Halevi, S.: Candidate multilinear maps from ideal lattices. In: Johansson, T., Nguyen, P.Q. (eds.) EUROCRYPT 2013. LNCS, vol. 7881, pp. 1–17. Springer, Heidelberg (2013)

[13] Garg, S., Gentry, C., Halevi, S., Raykova, M., Sahai, A., Waters, B.: Candidate indistinguishability obfuscation and functional encryption for all circuits. In: FOCS, pp. 40–49 (2013), Also, Cryptology ePrint Archive, Report 2013/451

[14] Gennaro, R., Gentry, C., Parno, B.: Non-interactive verifiable computing: Outsourcing computation to untrusted workers. In: Rabin, T. (ed.) CRYPTO 2010. LNCS, vol. 6223, pp. 465–482. Springer, Heidelberg (2010)

[15] Gentry, C.: Fully homomorphic encryption using ideal lattices. In: STOC, pp. 169–178 (2009)

[16] Gentry, C., Peikert, C., Vaikuntanathan, V.: Trapdoors for hard lattices and new cryptographic constructions. In: STOC, pp. 197–206 (2008)

[17] Gentry, C., Sahai, A., Waters, B.: Homomorphic encryption from learning with errors: Conceptually-simpler, asymptotically-faster, attribute-based. In: Canetti, R., Garay, J.A. (eds.) CRYPTO 2013, Part I. LNCS, vol. 8042, pp. 75–92. Springer, Heidelberg (2013)

[18] Goldwasser, S., Kalai, Y.T., Rothblum, G.N.: Delegating computation: Interactive proofs for muggles. In: STOC, pp. 113–122 (2008)

[19] Goldwasser, S., Kalai, Y.T., Popa, R.A., Vaikuntanathan, V., Zeldovich, N.: Reusable garbled circuits and succinct functional encryption. In: STOC, pp. 555–564 (2013)

[20] Goldwasser, S., Gordon, S.D., Goyal, V., Jain, A., Katz, J., Liu, F.-H., Sahai, A., Shi, E., Zhou, H.-S.: Multi-input functional encryption. In: Nguyen, P.Q., Oswald, E. (eds.) EUROCRYPT 2014. LNCS, vol. 8441, pp. 578–602. Springer, Heidelberg (2014)

[21] Gorbunov, S., Vaikuntanathan, V., Wee, H.: Functional encryption with bounded collusions via multi-party computation. In: Safavi-Naini, R., Canetti, R. (eds.) CRYPTO 2012. LNCS, vol. 7417, pp. 162–179. Springer, Heidelberg (2012)

[22] Gorbunov, S., Vaikuntanathan, V., Wee, H.: Attribute-based encryption for circuits. In: STOC, pp. 545–554 (2013) Also, Cryptology ePrint Archive, Report 2013/337

[23] Goyal, V., Pandey, O., Sahai, A., Waters, B.: Attribute-based encryption for fine-grained access control of encrypted data. In: ACM Conference on Computer and Communications Security, pp. 89–98 (2006)

[24] Katz, J., Sahai, A., Waters, B.: Predicate encryption supporting disjunctions, polynomial equations, and inner products. In: Smart, N. (ed.) EUROCRYPT 2008. LNCS, vol. 4965, pp. 146–162. Springer, Heidelberg (2008)

[25] Lewko, A., Waters, B.: New proof methods for attribute-based encryption: Achieving full security through selective techniques. In: Safavi-Naini, R., Canetti, R. (eds.) CRYPTO 2012. LNCS, vol. 7417, pp. 180–198. Springer, Heidelberg (2012)

[26] Lewko, A.B., Rouselakis, Y., Waters, B.: Achieving leakage resilience through dual system encryption. In: TCC, pp. 70–88 (2010), Cryptology ePrint Archive, Report 2010/438

[27] Naor, M., Reingold, O.: Number-theoretic constructions of efficient pseudo-random functions. J. ACM 51(2), 231–262 (2004)

[28] O'Neill, A.: Definitional issues in functional encryption. Cryptology ePrint Archive, Report 2010/556 (2010)

[29] Parno, B., Raykova, M., Vaikuntanathan, V.: How to delegate and verify in public: Verifiable computation from attribute-based encryption. In: Cramer, R. (ed.) TCC 2012. LNCS, vol. 7194, pp. 422–439. Springer, Heidelberg (2012)

[30] Sahai, A., Waters, B.: Fuzzy identity-based encryption. In: Cramer, R. (ed.) EUROCRYPT 2005. LNCS, vol. 3494, pp. 457–473. Springer, Heidelberg (2005)

[31] Waters, B.: Dual system encryption: Realizing fully secure IBE and HIBE under simple assumptions. In: Halevi, S. (ed.) CRYPTO 2009. LNCS, vol. 5677, pp. 619–636. Springer, Heidelberg (2009)

[32] Wee, H.: Dual system encryption via predicate encodings. In: Lindell, Y. (ed.) TCC 2014. LNCS, vol. 8349, pp. 616–637. Springer, Heidelberg (2014)

Generic Attacks on Strengthened HMAC: n-bit Secure HMAC Requires Key in All Blocks

Yu Sasaki and Lei Wang

NTT Secure Platform Laboratories, Tokyo, Japan
sasaki.yu@lab.ntt.co.jp
Nanyang Technological University, Singapore, Singapore
Wang.Lei@ntu.edu.sg

Abstract. HMAC is the most widely used hash based MAC scheme. Recently, several generic attacks have been presented against HMAC with a complexity between $2^{n/2}$ and 2^n, where n is the output size of an underlying hash function. In this paper, we investigate the security of strengthened HMAC in which the key is used to process underlying compression functions. With such a modification, the attacker is unable to precompute the property of the compression function offline, and thus previous generic attacks are prevented. In this paper, we show that keying the compression function in all blocks is necessary to prevent a generic internal state recovery attack with a complexity less than 2^n. In other words, only with a single keyless compression function, the internal state is recovered faster than 2^n. To validate the claim, we present a generic attack against the strengthened HMAC in which only one block is keyless, thus pre-computable offline. Our attack uses the previous generic attack by Naito *et al.* as a base. We improve it so that the attack can be applied only with a single keyless compression function while the attack complexity remains unchanged from the previous work.

Keywords: HMAC, generic attack, internal state recovery, multi-collision.

1 Introduction

A message authentication code (MAC) ensures the integrity of messages transferred between two players sharing the secret key K in advance. When a sender sends a message M, he generates a tag T computed by $\mathrm{MAC}(K, M)$, and sends a pair of (M, T). A receiver computes the tag of the received message with his own key K and checks the match with received T. If they match, it turns out that no one modified the original message M during the communication.

A MAC is often built by using a hash function, e.g. a tag is produced by hashing a combination of K and M. A hash function based MAC often processes the key K first which takes a role of initialization, and then processes the message M, and finally processes the key K again which takes a role of finalization. This framework is called a hybrid MAC [1].

M. Abdalla and R. De Prisco (Eds.): SCN 2014, LNCS 8642, pp. 324–339, 2014.
© Springer International Publishing Switzerland 2014

HMAC, which was originally designed by Bellare *et al.* [2], is the most widely used hash function based MAC. HMAC is standardized by several standardization authorities such as NIST [3] and ISO [4]. Let $\mathcal{H}$ be an underlying hash function and ipad and opad be two constant values. For a message M and a key K, HMAC computes a tag T by

$$T \leftarrow \mathcal{H}(K \oplus \text{opad} \| \mathcal{H}(K \oplus \text{ipad} \| M)).$$

Let n be the output size of $\mathcal{H}$. HMAC is provably secure up to $O(2^{n/2})$ queries [5] when a narrow-pipe Merkle-Damgård hash function, e.g. NIST's hash function standard SHA-family [6], is instantiated.

On one hand, the lower-bound of the security proof of HMAC is tight. Preneel and van Oorschot showed a generic existential forgery attack with $\mathcal{O}(2^{n/2})$ queries [7] by exploiting the collision of the internal state generated by the birthday paradox. On the other hand, the internal state collisions cannot be utilized to break stronger security notions such as internal state recovery attack, universal forgery attack, key recovery attack, and so on. Security of HMAC against those notions was an open problem for a while.

Recently, several researches reported generic attacks on HMAC. Dodis *et al.* studied the indifferentiability security of HMAC in which key values are chosen by the attacker [8]. Independently, Peyrin *et al.* showed the similar weak key relation in the related key attack model [9], which can recover the internal state value with a complexity less than 2^n. Then, in 2013, two types of generic internal state recovery attacks were proposed.

The first approach was proposed by Leurent *et al.* [10]. In short, it utilizes several properties of a functional graph generated by the underlying compression function with a fixed message input. In the offline phase, the attacker precomputes the behavior of the underlying function when a long message, $\mathcal{O}(2^{n/2})$ blocks, is queried. Then, in the online phase, the attacker queries such long messages and checks if the precomputed properties are satisfied. The attack requires long queries, while the attack complexity is low, $\mathcal{O}(2^{n/2})$.

The second approach was proposed by Naito *et al.* [11]. It utilizes a multi-collision for the underlying compression function with a fixed message input. In the offline phase, the attacker precomputes the multi-collision of the compression function. In the online phase, the bias observed by the multi-collision is verified with higher probability than 2^{-n}. The attack requires queries of only 3 message blocks, while the attack complexity is high, $\mathcal{O}(2^n/n)$.

Several researches showed that by using the generic internal state recovery attack as a tool, more powerful attacks can be mounted [12–15]. It is a useful approach to strengthen the computation of HMAC so as to prevent the generic internal state recovery attack, and provide n-bit security for it. In practice, people may not expect n-bit security by using a narrow-pipe Merkle-Damgård hash function as $\mathcal{H}$ because 1) the attack complexity of $\mathcal{O}(2^n/n)$, in particular the memory usage of this size, is close to the brute force attack and 2) the generic existential forgery attack exists with $\mathcal{O}(2^{n/2})$ complexity. It seems that the simplest way to achieve the n-bit secure HMAC is using $2n$-bit hash function

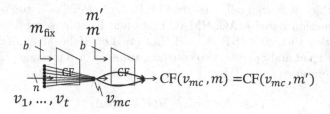

Fig. 1. Block-wise Computation Structure of HMAC

as $\mathcal{H}$. Nevertheless we believe that aiming n-bit security with an n-bit hash function contributes to make a progress in the theory of designing MACs.

Because the previous related-key attack [9] suggested an efficient countermeasure, in this paper we focus our attention on the generic internal state recovery attack in the single-key setting [10, 11]. The essence of those attacks is that the attacker can precompute the property of an underlying hash function or compression function, which holds irrespective of the key value. Thus, to prevent those attacks, we consider tweaking the compression function with key. For example, we fix n bits of each message block to the key. Then, the attacker becomes unable to perform the precomputation.

This paper is not the first one that discusses the HMAC like construction with key in all compression function invocations. An and Bellare in 1999 analyzed the NI function (Nested Iterated function) in [16], which is close to NMAC with key in all compression function invocations. A multilane variant of HMAC achieving beyond the birthday bound security was already proposed by Yasuda [17]. In this paper, we discuss how to strengthen HMAC while keeping it as a single lane, which is different from the approach in [17].

Our Contributions

We show that keying the compression function in all blocks is necessary to prevent a generic internal state recovery attack with a complexity less than 2^n. In other words, only with a single keyless compression function, the internal state is recovered faster than 2^n. We validate the claim by presenting a generic attack against the strengthened HMAC in which only one block is keyless, thus pre-computable offline. The observation can be applied for not only HMAC but also other similar type of hybrid MAC schemes such as NMAC [2] and Sandwich MAC [18]. Due to the wide usage of HMAC, we focus our attention on HMAC in this paper.

Our attack uses the previous generic attack by Naito *et al.* [11] as a base. We improve it so that the attack can be applied only with a single keyless compression function. The intuition of the attack in [11] is shown in Fig. 1. One message block m_{fix} is fixed and the attacker searches for input chaining values to the compression function which forms a multi-collision on its output. Let

$v_1, v_2, \ldots, v_t$ be input chaining values forming a t-collision[1] where $2 \leq t \leq n$. Also let v_{mc} be the colliding output. This indicates that as long as the message block is fixed to m_{fix}, the colliding value v_{mc} appears more frequently than others, which gives some advantage to the attacker. To detect the occurrence of v_{mc}, Naito et al. in the subsequent message block appended another colliding message pair m and m' which maps v_{mc} to an identical value. Then, if tags for two queries $x\|m_{\text{fix}}\|m$ and $x\|m_{\text{fix}}\|m'$ for any message block x collide, we recover that the internal state value is v_{mc} with a high probability. All in all, the attacker needs to precompute at least two blocks offline.

Because our attack model assumes that only a single block is keyless, the same approach as the previous work cannot be used. In our attack, we perform the precomputation of the multi-collision for the keyless block, and change the detecting method of the occurrence of the multi-collision.

Naito et al, evaluated that their attack complexity is $\mathcal{O}(2^n/n)$, which comes from the fact that up to n-collisions can be generated for an n-bit function with a complexity up to $\mathcal{O}(2^n)$. In the same evaluation, our attack complexity is $\mathcal{O}(2^n/n)$, which is the same as the previous work. The exact complexity depends on the output size n, and must be carefully evaluated. Considering the applications to SHA-256 and SHA-512, we evaluate the complexity for $n = 512$ and $n = 256$. For $n = 512$, the internal state is recovered with a complexity of $2^{509.52}$. For $n = 256$, the internal state is recovered with a complexity of $2^{254.27}$. Those lead to our claim that only with a single keyless block, the internal state is recovered with a complexity less than 2^n.

Paper Outline

The organization of this paper is as follows. In Section 2, HMAC with a narrow-pipe Merkle-Damgård hash function is specified. Previous generic attacks on HMAC are explained in Section 3. Our attack which requires only a single unkeyed compression function is explained in Section 4. Finally, the paper is concluded in Section 5.

2 Specification

2.1 Merkle-Damgård Hash Functions

Merkle-Damgård structure is a common approach to process the input message of arbitrary length into the fixed hash digest. Suppose that both of the internal state size and the hash digest size are n bits[2], and also suppose that the message block size is b bits. It firstly pads the input message so that its bit size becomes a multiple of the block size. In this paper, we suppose that the padding scheme only

---

[1] t-collision means t different input values which return an identical output value.

[2] If the internal state size is bigger than the hash digest size, the construction is called wide-pipe [19]. In this paper, we focus our attention on only narrow-pipe, where the internal state size and the hash digest size are identical.

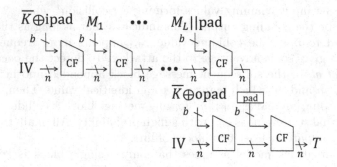

Fig. 2. Block-wise Computation Structure of HMAC

depends on the input message size, and does not depend on the message value. Note that the MD-strengthening padding, which is widely used in the current standard hash functions such as the SHA-family [6], satisfies this property. The padded message is then split into each message block $M_0, M_1, \ldots, M_{L-1}$, where the size of each M_i is b bits. Then the compression function CF : $\{0,1\}^n \times \{0,1\}^b \rightarrow \{0,1\}^n$ is iteratively applied as follows:

$$H_0 \leftarrow \text{IV},$$
$$H_i \leftarrow \text{CF}(H_{i-1}, M_{i-1}) \qquad \text{for } i = 1, 2, \ldots, L,$$

where IV stands for initial value, which is an n-bit constant defined in the specification. H_L is the hash digest of the input message.

2.2   HMAC

HMAC with a secret key K produces a MAC tag only with 2 calls of hash function $\mathcal{H}$. At first, K is processed to be b bits as follows:

- If $|K| < b$, append a necessary number of zeros, i.e. $\overline{K} \leftarrow K \| 00 \cdots 0$.
- If $|K| = b$, $\overline{K} \leftarrow K$.
- If $|K| > b$, $\overline{K} \leftarrow \mathcal{H}(K)$.

Then, the MAC tag is computed as follows.

$$\text{HMAC}_K(M) \leftarrow \mathcal{H}(\overline{K} \oplus \text{opad} \| \mathcal{H}(\overline{K} \oplus \text{ipad} \| M)),$$

where ipad and opad are b-bit constant values specified in HMAC. The block-wise representation of the HMAC construction is depicted in Fig. 2.

HMAC was firstly proven to be a secure MAC up to $\mathcal{O}(2^{n/2})$ queries under the assumption that $\mathcal{H}$ is collision resistant [2]. It was then proven to be a pseudo-random function (PRF) up to $\mathcal{O}(2^{n/2})$ queries under the assumption that $\mathcal{H}$ is weak collision resistant [5]. Finally, the proof of the exact PRF of HMAC is given by [20]. For more queries beyond the birthday bound, the proof of HMAC cannot ensure its security. Indeed, several generic attacks have already been proposed, which will be explained in Section 3.

3   Previous Work

Several generic attacks are known to HMAC with a narrow-pipe Merkle-Damgård hash function. The first generic attack was proposed by Preneel and van Oorschot which performs an existential forgery attack with $\mathcal{O}(2^{n/2})$ queries [7]. The attack utilizes a collision of the internal state value generated by the birthday paradox. Due to the iterative structure of the underlying hash function $\mathcal{H}$, it is principally hard to avoid this attack. Fortunately, application of the internal state collision is limited, namely, it cannot be used to mount more powerful attack such as universal forgery attack and key recovery attack.

In 2013, two types of the internal state recovery attack were proposed. The first approach was proposed by Leurent et al. [10] and the second approach was proposed by Naito et al. [11]. Moreover, several researches used the internal state recovery attack as a tool to mount more powerful attacks [12–15]. Hence, generic internal state recovery attacks should be prevented. This section explains more details of those two types of the internal state recovery attacks.

3.1   Long Message Attack with Functional Graph Properties

Leurent et al. proposed an efficient internal state recovery attack when an attacker can query long messages, $\mathcal{O}(2^{n/2})$ blocks [10]. The attack utilizes several properties of a functional graph generated by the underlying hash function $\mathcal{H}$. In the narrow-pipe Merkle-Damgård hashes, $\mathcal{H}$ iterates the compression function CF. The attack fixes the b-bit value of the message input to the compression function CF in all blocks, which is denoted by M. Then, the function is represented as $\mathrm{CF}_M : \{0,1\}^n \to \{0,1\}^n$. Because CF_M is a public function, the attacker can simulate the functional graph of CF_M offline.

In a functional graph, the chain of the function is computed. That is to say, a start point v_0 is determined randomly, and then $v_i \leftarrow \mathrm{CF}_M(v_{i-1})$ is computed for $i = 1, 2, 3, \cdots$ until v_i reaches the previously computed value. It is known that a functional graph satisfies several generic properties, e.g. each point will enter a cycle after $\mathcal{O}(2^{n/2})$ iterations, and the size of the largest cycle of the graph is $\mathcal{O}(2^{n/2})$.

To apply those properties to HMAC, the attack by Leurent et al. [10] works as follows.

- At offline, the attacker computes the size of the largest cycle of CF_M, which is denoted by L.
- At online, the attacker queries the following two messages of the size $\mathcal{O}(2^{n/2})$ blocks

$$M^{[2^{n/2}]} \| M_{\mathrm{rand}} \| M^{[2^{n/2}+L]},$$

$$M^{[2^{n/2}+L]} \| M_{\mathrm{rand}} \| M^{[2^{n/2}]},$$

where $M^{[x]}$ represents the x iterations of the message block M and M_{rand} represents a randomly chosen message block such that $M_{\mathrm{rand}} \neq M$. For HMAC with

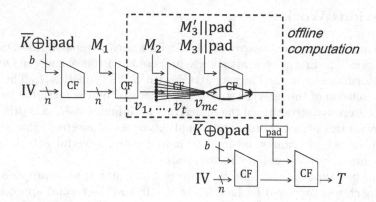

Fig. 3. Previous Internal State Recovery Attack on HMAC with Short Message Input

$\mathcal{H}$, the above two queries return the same tag with a high probability, and this gives significant information for the attacker. Leurent *et al.* pointed out that the internal state value can be recovered [10] and Peyrin and Wang [14] showed a generic universal forgery attack on HMAC by combining more properties of the functional graph.

3.2 Short Message Attack with Multi-collisions

Naito *et al.* proposed another internal state recovery attack [11]. The advantage of this attack is that it only requires queries of 3 message blocks, while the complexity of the attack is high, which is some value between 2^n and $2^n/n$. In other words, the attack efficiency is lower-bounded by $2^n/n$.

The attack fixes a b-bit message input M to the compression function to form a random function $\mathrm{CF}_M : \{0,1\}^n \to \{0,1\}^n$. The attack uses the multi-collision of CF_M which is generated by the complexity between 2^n and $2^n/n$. A t-collision is expected to be found with about $2^{(t-1)n/t}$ computations of CF_M. Thus, with a complexity up to 2^n, up to n-collision is expected. Note that this is a rough evaluation, and the exact complexity that optimizes the entire attack must be carefully calculated as was done in [11]. Let v_{mc} be the output value of the t-collision.

Naito *et al.* pointed out that v_{mc} appears more frequently than other values due to the bias confirmed by the t-collision, and this fact can be used to recover the internal state value. The entire attack procedure is as follows, which is also depicted in Fig. 3.

Offline Phase
- Fix the value of M_2.
- Choose r distinct values of the chaining variable input v_r where $2^n/n \le r \le 2^n$. Compute $\mathrm{CF}_{M_2}(v_r)$ and find t-collision where $2 \le t \le n$. For simplicity, let $v_1, v_2, \dots, v_t$ be the chaining variable inputs forming a t-collision for CF_{M_2}.

- For the later detection of the occurrence of v_{mc}, find a colliding pair $M_3\|$pad and $M_3'\|$pad such that $\text{CF}(v_{mc}, M_3\|\text{pad}) = \text{CF}(v_{mc}, M_3'\|\text{pad})$, where pad is the padding string for the online phase.

Online Phase

- Choose j distinct values of the message input M_1^j where $j = 2^n/t$. Query the following 3 block messages.

$$M_1^j\|M_2\|M_3,$$

$$M_1^j\|M_2\|M_3'.$$

One of j choices of M_1 will reach one of $v_1, \ldots, v_t$, and thus the collision is generated after $M_3\|$pad and $M_3'\|$pad. Then, the internal state value v_{mc} is recovered. The attack complexity depends on the choice of r and the corresponding j, which are between 2^n and $2^n/n$.

3.3 Preventing Internal State Recovery Attacks

Let us consider possible countermeasures against the previous internal state recovery attacks by modifying the computation of HMAC.

The essence of the previous attack is that the behavior of the compression function with a fixed message CF_M can be simulated by the attacker offline. Thus, by tweaking the compression function with a secret value derived from K the attacks are invalidated. On the contrary, the number of such a tweak should be minimized so that the bad influence to the computation efficiency is minimized.

The long message attack [10] requires the precomputation of a big functional graph. Hence, giving a key tweak in every a few blocks can prevent the attack. The short message attack [10] requires the precomputation of 2 consecutive compression functions. Hence, the attack can be prevented by giving a key tweak in every two blocks.

4 New Attack against Single Keyless Block

In this section, we show that if there exists one compression function that can be simulated by the attacker offline, the internal state recovery attack can be performed with a complexity less than 2^n. An important implication of this fact is that to ensure n-bit security against the internal state recovery attack, the compression function must depend on the key in all blocks so that the attacker cannot perform the precomputation.

4.1 Target Structure

We consider a strengthened HMAC as our attack target. That is to say, all compression function computations but for 1 block (for processing the i-th message block) are tweaked by key value and the tweak depends on the block position.

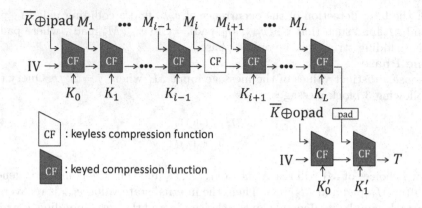

Fig. 4. Our Attack Target. Only a single block is public.

The tweak, for example, can be given by setting n bits of a b-bit message block to a value derived by the key. The modification is conservative but for the single keyless block, which will clearly indicate how the single keyless block gives a bad influence to the entire structure. The computation structure of our attack target is depicted in Fig. 4.

4.2 Attack Overview

Due to the key value in most of blocks, we use the approach of the short message attack [11] that exploits the multi-collision of the compression function.

The offline phase with the dominant complexity part is the same as the one in [11]. Namely, we fix the message input M_i and choose r distinct chaining variable inputs $v_1, v_2, \ldots, v_r$ to find a t-collision of the fixed function CF_{M_i}, where r is a some value between $2^n/n$ and 2^n. Let $v_1, v_2, \ldots, v_t$ be the obtained chaining variable inputs forming a t-collision.

Then in the online phase, we generate two messages $M_1\|M_2\|\cdots\|M_{i-1}$ which will reach one of $v_1, v_2, \ldots, v_t$. If we can detect such messages, the internal state value can take only t choices, and it is possible to recover the exact internal state value by exhaustively testing all the t choices. To generate such two messages, we fix the value of $M_1\|M_2\|\cdots\|M_{i-2}$, choose $2 \times 2^n/t$ distinct messages of M_{i-1} and query $M_1\|M_2\|\cdots\|M_{i-2}\|M_{i-1}\|M_i$ for each choice of M_{i-1}. Two messages reaching any of $v_1, v_2, \ldots, v_t$ collide after the i-th block, and thus produce an identical tag. Hence, we pick all message pairs with colliding tags. Of course this will generate a lot of noise, i.e. collisions of tags without reaching $v_1, v_2, \ldots, v_t$. We filter out those noise by using additional queries.

4.3 Offline Phase

The offline phase consists of two sub-phases which are depicted in Fig. 5.

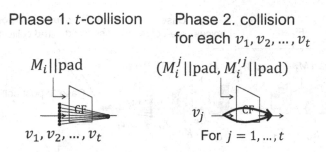

Phase 1. t-collision

$M_i\|\text{pad}$

$v_1, v_2, \ldots, v_t$

Phase 2. collision
for each $v_1, v_2, \ldots, v_t$

$(M_i^j\|\text{pad}, M_i'^j\|\text{pad})$

v_j

For $j = 1, \ldots, t$

Fig. 5. Offline Phase

Phase 1 is for constructing a t-collision of the keyless compression function CF. We fix the message input $M_i\|\text{pad}$ where pad is the padding string for the online phase. As explained later, the length of queries in the online phase is i blocks plus the size of M_i. M_i can be set to any value as long as $M_i\|\text{pad}$ fits in one block. Then, the compression function can be described as an n-bit to n-bit function $\text{CF}_{M_i}(\cdot)$. We then choose r distinct chaining variable inputs $v_1, v_2, \ldots, v_r$, and compute $\text{CF}_{M_i}(v_1), \text{CF}_{M_i}(v_2), \ldots, \text{CF}_{M_i}(v_r)$ to find a t-collision of the function's output, where r is a some value between $2^n/n$ and 2^n determined later. Let $v_1, v_2, \ldots, v_t$ be the obtained chaining variable inputs forming the t-collision.

Phase 2 is for generating a message pair $(M_i^j, M_i'^j)$ such that $\text{CF}(v_j, M_i^j) = \text{CF}(v_j, M_i'^j)$ for $1 \leq j \leq t$ for the later detection of the occurrence of $v_1, v_2, \ldots, v_t$. The idea behind is that if we later find a message $M_1\|\cdots\|M_{i-1}$ which may reach one of $v_1, v_2, \ldots, v_r$, we can confirm it by checking the tag collision of the message pair $M_1\|\cdots\|M_{i-1}\|M_i^j$ and $M_1\|\cdots\|M_{i-1}\|M_i'^j$.

The complexity of the offline phase is as follows. In phase 1, the computational cost is r compression function computations and the memory requirement is to store the r corresponding tags, where $2^n/n \leq r \leq 2^n$. The computational cost of phase 2 is $t \times 2^{n/2}$ compression function computations, which is negligible compared to phase 1. The collision search of phase 2 can be memoryless. In the end, the complexity of the offline phase is r compression function computations and a memory to store r n-bit tags. Because this is offline, the number of query is 0.

4.4   Online Phase

The online phase consists of three sub-phases called 1) *collision collection*, 2) *noise elimination*, and 3) *recovering value*. The online phase is depicted in Fig. 6. Note that the first message block of the outer function, $\overline{K} \oplus \text{opad}$, is not related to our attack. We omit its description in Fig. 4.4 by representing the first block's output as K_{OUT}.

Collision Collection. As explained in Section 4.2, we generate two messages which will reach one of $v_1, v_2, \ldots, v_t$ and collect all message pairs producing the tag collision. Because a t-collision is generated offline, we query $2 \times 2^n/t$ messages in the collision collection phase. We first fix the value of $M_1\|M_2\|\cdots\|M_{i-2}$.

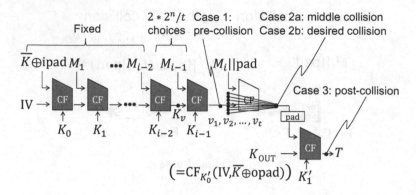

Fig. 6. Online Phase

Then for any query, the internal state value after processing M_{i-2} becomes a fixed value, denoted by K_v in Fig. 6. We then choose $2 \times 2^n/t$ distinct messages $M_{i-1}^1, M_{i-1}^2, \ldots, M_{i-1}^{2 \times 2^n/t}$ so that we can obtain two messages reaching one of $v_1, v_2, \ldots, v_t$. We query $M_1 \| \cdots \| M_{i-2} \| M_{i-1}^j \| M_i$ for $j = 1, 2, \ldots, 2 \times 2^n/t$. For those queries, HMAC pads the padding string **pad** and the last message block becomes exactly the same as the one fixed in the offline phase. Two messages reaching any of $v_1, v_2, \ldots, v_t$ collide after the last message block, and thus produce the tag collision. Here, we also obtain many collisions that do not reach $v_1, v_2, \ldots, v_t$. Those collisions are called noise. There are 3 cases that noise occurs: after processing M_{i-1} which are called pre-collisions, after processing $M_i\|$**pad** but without reaching $v_1, v_2, \ldots, v_t$ which are called middle-collisions, and after processing the outer function which are called post-collisions. Let us count the number of noise. With $2 \times 2^n/t$ queries, about $2^{2n+1}/t^2$ pairs are generated and each pair produces an identical tag value with probability 2^{-n}. In the end, we obtain the following collisions.

Case 1. $2^{n+1}/t^2$ pre-collisions
Case 2a. $2^{n+1}/t^2$ middle-collisions
Case 2b. 1 desired collision via some of $v_1, \ldots, v_t$
Case 3. $2^{n+1}/t^2$ post-collisions

In total, we obtain $3 * 2^{n+1}/t^2 + 1$ collisions.

Noise Elimination. In noise elimination, we discard all the pre-collisions and post-collisions with two more additional queries for each noise.

To eliminate pre-collisions, we query each colliding message pair by replacing M_i with another one M_i^*. Because the internal state value is already collided after processing M_{i-1}, the pair also generates a tag collision with new M_i^*. We discard all the pairs that generate another collision with new M_i^*. The probability of wrongly discarding the desired collision is 2^{-n}, which is negligible. Note that wrongly discarding other noise does not cause any problem.

To eliminate post-collisions, we query each colliding message pair by appending the padding string pad and then appending a common message block M_{i+1}. Because input value to the outer function changes, new pairs do not produce a collision with an overwhelming probability. We discard all the pairs that do not produce another collision. The probability of wrongly discarding the desired collision is 0 because the collision after processing $M_i \| $pad is preserved even after the additional common message block. A post-collision wrongly remain with probability of $2^{-n} \times 2^{n+1}/t^2 = 2/t^2$. Such a small number of post-collisions only give negligible impact to the next phase. Moreover, by iterating the noise eliminating phase twice, even such a negligible event can be avoided.

The remaining collisions are $2^{n+1}/t^2$ middle-collisions and 1 desired collision. Unfortunately, eliminating middle-collisions is hard. However, we can still recover the internal state by analyzing $2^{n+1}/t^2$ middle-collisions and 1 desired collision together.

Recovering Value. For each of $2^{n+1}/t^2 + 1$ collision pairs, we confirm that one message of the pair reaches some of $v_1, v_2, \ldots, v_t$. Thus, we replace M_i with M_i^j, and then with $M_i'^j$ for $j = 1, 2, \ldots, t$ and check if the corresponding tags collide. The desired collision always generates collision with M_i and M_i^j. Moreover, we can iterate the same test for the other message pair. Hence, the probability of the false positive is negligible. In the end, the correct internal state value is recovered.

Complexity. The complexity of the collision collecting phase is $2 \times 2^n/t$ queries, $2 \times 2^n/t$ memory accesses to deal with the obtained tags and a memory to store $2 \times 2^n/t$ tags. The complexity of the noise elimination phase is $2 * 3 * 2^{n+1}/t^2 + 1$ queries for eliminating pre-collisions and $2 * 2 * 2^{n+1}/t^2 + 1$ queries for eliminating post-collisions, which is about $20 * 2^n/t^2$ queries in total. The computational cost and memory requirement are negligible. The complexity of the recovering value phase is $2t * (2^{n+1}/t^2 + 1) \approx 4 * 2^n/t$ queries. The computational cost and memory requirement are negligible.

All in all, the total attack complexity of the online phase is as follows.

- The number of queries is $2 * 2^n/t + 20 * 2^n/t^2 + 4 * 2^n/t = 6 * 2^n/t + 20 * 2^n/t^2$.
- The computational cost is $2 * 2^n/t$.
- The memory requirement is $2 * 2^n/t$.

4.5 Choosing Optimal Parameters

The bottleneck of the offline phase is finding a t-collision with r computations of CF. Suzuki et al. showed the complexity to find a t-collision with probability 1/2 [21], which tells the exact value of r in our attack.

$$r = (t!)^{1/t} \times (2^{n \cdot \frac{t-1}{t}}) + t - 1. \tag{1}$$

Algorithm 1. Internal State Recovery on HMAC with a Single Keyless Block

---

Output: Two pairs of $i-1$ message blocks $M_1\|\cdots\|M_{i-1}$ and the internal state after the last block

Offline Phase

1: Fix M_i such that $M_i\|$pad fits in one block.
2: **for** $j \leftarrow 1, 2, \ldots, r$ **do**
3:     Choose the value of v_j, then compute $\mathrm{CF}_{M_i}(v_j)$ and store the result.
4: **end for**
5: Find a t-collision for $\mathrm{CF}_{M_i}(\cdot)$. Let t values forming a t-collision be $v_1, v_2, \ldots, v_t$.
6: **for** $j \leftarrow 1, 2, \ldots, t$ **do**
7:     Find $(M_i^j, M_i'^j)$ such that $\mathrm{CF}(v_j, M_i^j) = \mathrm{CF}(v_j, M_i'^j)$.
8: **end for**

Online Phase

9: Fix $M_1, M_2, \ldots, M_{i-2}$.
10: **for** $j \leftarrow 1, 2, \ldots, 2^n/t$ **do**
11:     Choose the value of M_{i-1}^j, then query $M_1\|\cdots\|M_{i-2}\|M_{i-1}^j\|M_i$ and store the tag.
12: **end for**
13: Pick up message pairs producing the tag collision.
14: Let $(\overline{M_z}, \overline{M_z'})$ for $z = 1, 2, \ldots, 3 * 2^n/t^2 + 1$ be pairs of $M_1\|\cdots\|M_{i-2}\|M_{i-1}$ producing the tag collision.
15: **for** $z = 1, 2, \ldots, 3 * 2^n/t^2 + 1$ **do**
16:     Choose a new value of M_i^*, then query $\overline{M_z}\|M_i^*$ and $\overline{M_z'}\|M_i^*$.
17:     **if** tags collide **then**
18:         Discard the pair.
19:     **end if**
20: **end for**
21: **for** $z = 1, 2, \ldots, 2 * 2^n/t^2 + 1$ **do**
22:     Choose a new value of M_{i+1}, then query $\overline{M_z}\|M_i\|$pad$\|M_{i+1}$ and $\overline{M_z'}\|M_i\|$pad$\|M_{i+1}$.
23:     **if** tags do not collide **then**
24:         Discard the pair.
25:     **end if**
26: **end for**
27: **for** $z = 1, 2, \ldots, 2^n/t^2 + 1$ **do**
28:     **for** $j = 1, 2, \ldots, t$ **do**
29:         Query $\overline{M_z}\|M_i^j$ and $\overline{M_z}\|M_i'^j$.
30:         **if** tags collide **then**
31:             **for** $k = 1, 2, \ldots, t$ **do**
32:                 Query $\overline{M_z'}\|M_i^k$ and $\overline{M_z'}\|M_i'^k$.
33:                 **if** tags collide **then**
34:                     **return** $(\overline{M_z}, v_j)$ and $(\overline{M_z'}, v_k)$.
35:                 **end if**
36:             **end for**
37:         **end if**
38:     **end for**
39: **end for**

The attack complexity of the online phase is $6 * 2^n/t + 20 * 2^n/t^2$ queries and $2 * 2^n/t$ computational cost and memory requirement, in which the number of queries is dominant. The data complexity is evaluated by the number of queried message blocks. Hence, the data complexity is

$$i \times (6 * 2^n/t + 20 * 2^n/t^2) \tag{2}$$

Security of the construction is evaluated in the worst case scenario. Namely, the keyless block position is chosen by the attacker to optimize the attack. Thus we evaluate the case $i = 2$. As a result, we choose the value of t which balances Eq. (1) and Eq. (2) for $i = 2$. The best choice of t depends on the tag size n. Considering the application to SHA-256 and SHA-512, the evaluation of t for $n = 512$ and $n = 256$ are summarized in Table 1.

Table 1. Attack Complexity with Optimal Parameter Choices

n	t	Offline Eq.(1)	Online Eq.(2)
512	70	$2^{509.435}$	$2^{509.523}$
256	43	$2^{254.124}$	$2^{254.266}$

4.6 Attack Procedure

We finally describe the attack procedure in Algorithm 1. The exact choices of t can be found in Table 1, and the corresponding r can be calculated by Eq. (1). As shown in Table 1, the internal state value can be recovered with a complexity less than 2^n.

5 Concluding Remarks

In this paper, we investigated the security of strengthened HMAC in which the underlying compression function is keyed to avoid the precomputation by the attacker. We improved the previous generic internal state recovery attack by Naito et al. so that it can be applied only with a single keyless compression function without increasing the attack complexity. This fact indicates that in order to avoid the generic internal state recovery attack faster than 2^n complexity, the compression function must be keyed in all blocks.

Acknowledgments. The authors would like to thank anonymous reviewers of SCN 2014 for their helpful comments. Lei Wang is supported by the Singapore National Research Foundation Fellowship 2012 (NRF-NRFF2012-06).

References

1. Tsudik, G.: Message Authentication with One-Way Hash Functions. In: ACM SIG-COMM Computer Communication Review, vol. 22(5), pp. 29–38. ACM (1992)
2. Bellare, M., Canetti, R., Krawczyk, H.: Keying Hash Functions for Message Authentication. In: Koblitz, N. (ed.) Advances in Cryptology - CRYPT0 1996. LNCS, vol. 1109, pp. 1–15. Springer, Heidelberg (1996)
3. U.S. Department of Commerce, National Institute of Standards and Technology: The Keyed-Hash Message Authentication Code (HMAC) (Federal Information Processing Standards Publication 198) (2008),
   http://csrc.nist.gov/publications/fips/fips198-1/FIPS-198-1_final.pdf
4. ISO/IEC 9797-2:2011: Information technology – Security techniques – Message Authentication Codes (MACs) – Part 2 (2011)
5. Bellare, M.: New Proofs for NMAC and HMAC: Security Without Collision-Resistance. In: Dwork, C. (ed.) CRYPTO 2006. LNCS, vol. 4117, pp. 602–619. Springer, Heidelberg (2006)
6. U.S. Department of Commerce, National Institute of Standards and Technology: Secure Hash Standard (SHS) (Federal Information Processing Standards Publication 180-3) (2008),
   http://csrc.nist.gov/publications/fips/fips180-3/fips180-3_final.pdf
7. Preneel, B., van Oorschot, P.C.: On the Security of Two MAC Algorithms. In: Maurer, U. (ed.) Advances in Cryptology - EUROCRYPT 1996. LNCS, vol. 1070, pp. 19–32. Springer, Heidelberg (1996)
8. Dodis, Y., Ristenpart, T., Steinberger, J., Tessaro, S.: To Hash or Not to Hash Again (In)differentiability Results for H^2 and HMAC. In: Safavi-Naini, R., Canetti, R. (eds.) CRYPTO 2012. LNCS, vol. 7417, pp. 348–366. Springer, Heidelberg (2012)
9. Peyrin, T., Sasaki, Y., Wang, L.: Generic Related-Key Attacks for HMAC. In: Wang, X., Sako, K. (eds.) ASIACRYPT 2012. LNCS, vol. 7658, pp. 580–597. Springer, Heidelberg (2012)
10. Leurent, G., Peyrin, T., Wang, L.: New Generic Attacks against Hash-Based MACs. In: Sako, K., Sarkar, P. (eds.) ASIACRYPT 2013, Part II. LNCS, vol. 8270, pp. 1–20. Springer, Heidelberg (2013)
11. Naito, Y., Sasaki, Y., Wang, L., Yasuda, K.: Generic State-Recovery and Forgery Attacks on ChopMD-MAC and on NMAC/HMAC. In: Sakiyama, K., Terada, M. (eds.) IWSEC 2013. LNCS, vol. 8231, pp. 83–98. Springer, Heidelberg (2013)
12. Guo, J., Sasaki, Y., Wang, L., Wang, M., Wen, L.: Equivalent Key Recovery Attacks against HMAC and NMAC with Whirlpool Reduced to 7 Rounds. In: Cid, C., Rechberger, C. (eds.) FSE. LNCS, Springer, Heidelberg (to appear 2014)
13. Guo, J., Sasaki, Y., Wang, L., Wu, S.: Cryptanalysis of HMAC/NMAC-Whirlpool. In: Sako, K., Sarkar, P. (eds.) ASIACRYPT 2013, Part II. LNCS, vol. 8270, pp. 21–40. Springer, Heidelberg (2013)
14. Peyrin, T., Wang, L.: Generic Universal Forgery Attack on Iterative Hash-based MACs. In: Nguyen, P.Q., Oswald, E. (eds.) EUROCRYPT 2014. LNCS, vol. 8441, pp. 147–164. Springer, Heidelberg (2014)
15. Sasaki, Y., Wang, L.: Improved Single-Key Distinguisher on HMAC-MD5 and Key Recovery Attacks on Sandwich-MAC-MD5. In: Lange, T., Lauter, K., Lisonek, P. (eds.) SAC 2013. LNCS, vol. 8282, pp. 493–512. Springer, Heidelberg (2013)
16. An, J.H., Bellare, M.: Construsting VIL-MACs from FIL-MACs: Message Authentication under Weakened Assumption. In: Wiener, M. (ed.) CRYPTO 1999. LNCS, vol. 1666, pp. 252–269. Springer, Heidelberg (1999)

17. Yasuda, K.: Multilane HMAC - Security beyond the Birthday Limit. In: Srinathan, K., Rangan, C.P., Yung, M. (eds.) INDOCRYPT 2007. LNCS, vol. 4859, pp. 18–32. Springer, Heidelberg (2007)
18. Yasuda, K.: "Sandwich" Is Indeed Secure: How to Authenticate a Message with Just One Hashing. In: Pieprzyk, J., Ghodosi, H., Dawson, E. (eds.) ACISP 2007. LNCS, vol. 4586, pp. 355–369. Springer, Heidelberg (2007)
19. Lucks, S.: A Failure-Friendly Design Principle for Hash Functions. In: Roy, B. (ed.) ASIACRYPT 2005. LNCS, vol. 3788, pp. 474–494. Springer, Heidelberg (2005)
20. Gazi, P., Pietrzak, K., Rybar, M.: The Exact PRF-Security of NMAC and HMAC. In: Garay, J., Gennaro, R. (eds.) CRYPTO. LNCS, Springer, Heidelberg (to appear 2014)
21. Suzuki, K., Tonien, D., Kurosawa, K., Toyota, K.: Birthday Paradox for Multi-Collisions. IEICE TRANSACTIONS on Fundamentals of Electronics, Communications and Computer Sciences E91-A(1), 39–45 (2008)

Improved Indifferentiable Security Analysis
of PHOTON

Yusuke Naito[1] and Kazuo Ohta[2]

[1] Mitsubishi Electric Corporation and The University of Electro-Communications
Naito.Yusuke@ce.MitsubishiElectric.co.jp
[2] The University of Electro-Communications
kazuo.ohta@uec.ac.jp

Abstract. In this paper, we study the indifferentiable security of the domain extension algorithm of the PHOTON hash function that was proven to be indifferentiable from a random oracle up to $\mathcal{O}(2^{\min\{c/2, c'/2\}})$ query complexity, where c is the capacity in the absorbing step of PHOTON and c' is that in the squeezing step. By reducing the size c', one can reduce the processing time spent by PHOTON, while the indifferentiable security is degraded. Note that there is no generic attack on PHOTON with $\mathcal{O}(2^{c'/2})$ query complexity. Thus it is interesting to investigate the optimality of the indifferentiable security and the size of c' ensuring the $\mathcal{O}(2^{c/2})$ security.

For these motivations, first, we prove that PHOTON is indifferentiable from a random oracle up to $\mathcal{O}(\min\{q_{\mathsf{mcoll}}(d^*, c - c'), 2^{c/2}\})$ query complexity where $q_{\mathsf{mcoll}}(d^*, c - c')$ is the query complexity to find a d^*-multi-collision of $(c - c')$ bits of hash values and d^* satisfies $q_{\mathsf{mcoll}}(d^*, c - c') = 2^{c'}/d^*$. We also show that there exists a generic attack on PHOTON with the same query complexity. Thus the indifferentiable security of our proof is *optimal*.

Second, by using this bound we study the parameter c' ensuring the $\mathcal{O}(2^{c/2})$ security. We show that the $\mathcal{O}(2^{c/2})$ security is ensured if $c' \geq c/2 + \log_2 c$, which implies that we can reduce the processing time by PHOTON with keeping the same indifferentiable security.

Finally, we propose a faster construction than PHOTON with keeping the same indifferentiable security, where the length of the first message block is modified from r bits to $r + c/2$ bits.

Keywords: Indifferentiability from a random oracle, PHOTON, optimal security.

1 Introduction

The PHOTON hash function was proposed by Guo, Peyrin, and Poschmann [10]. It is a lightweight hash function that uses a "Sponge-like" algorithm as domain extension algorithm.

The Sponge function was proposed by Bertoni, Daemen, Peeters, and Van Assche [4]. The SHA-3 hash function [3] uses it as domain extension algorithm.

M. Abdalla and R. De Prisco (Eds.): SCN 2014, LNCS 8642, pp. 340–357, 2014.
© Springer International Publishing Switzerland 2014

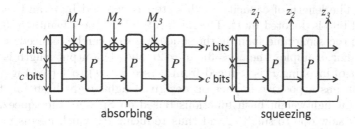

Fig. 1. Sponge

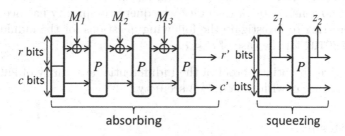

Fig. 2. PHOTON

The advantage of Sponge is that it is possible to keep the internal memory size as low as possible because it avoids any feed forward operation, and thereby it is suitable to design lightweight hash functions. For example, lightweight hash functions Quark [2] and SPONGENT [6] use Sponge as domain extension algorithm.

Sponge is a permutation based algorithm which iterates permutation P of $r + c$ bits. It can accept an input of arbitrary length and can generate an output of arbitrary length. This construction is shown in Fig. 1, which consists of two steps. The first step is called "absorbing step" which updates chaining values by absorbing message blocks of r bits. The second step is called "squeezing step" that generates the output by squeezing r-bit blocks from respective chaining values. The last c bits of each chaining value are the so-called "capacity" that keeps the security of Sponge. Bertoni et al. proved that Sponge is indifferentiable from a random oracle (denoted by $\mathcal{RO}$) up to $\mathcal{O}(2^{c/2})$ query complexity when P is ideal [5].

Indifferentiable security [11] is an important security criterion of hash functions. This framework offers an elegant composition theorem for $\mathcal{RO}$ secure cryptosystems: if a hash function H (with ideal primitives) is indifferentiable from $\mathcal{RO}$ up to q query complexity then for any single-stage security, any cryptosystem using H is at least as secure as in the $\mathcal{RO}$ model up to the same query complexity [11,13], and thereby it is ensured that there is no generic attack on H against any single-stage adversary.

The domain extension algorithm of the PHOTON hash function, denoted by PHOTON, is shown in Fig. 2, where the length of capacity in the squeezing step is flexible. The length of capacity in this step is denoted by c' and the length of squeezed bits is denoted by r'. The flexibility offers the advantage that when $c' < c$, the processing time spent in the squeezing step can be reduced, compared to Sponge. For example, when $c = 3r$, $c' = 2r$ and the output length is $3r$ bits, the number of invoking P is reduced from 2 (see Fig. 1) to 1 (see Fig. 2). This construction has a positive impact on design of lightweight hash functions. It is because for lightweight hash functions based on Sponge, the squeezing step can be very slow due to small r, and thus reducing c', which means increasing r', boosts the squeezing step. However, it was proven that PHOTON is indifferentiable from $\mathcal{RO}$ up to $\mathcal{O}(2^{\min\{c/2,c'/2\}})$ query complexity [1],[1] and thus the indifferentiable security is degraded depending on the parameter c'. Note that when $c' < c$, no generic attack with $\mathcal{O}(2^{c'/2})$ query complexity has been found.[2] So it is interesting to investigate the following questions for the indifferentiable security of PHOTON for the case of $c' < c$.

1. Can we give an optimal proof of the indifferentiable security of PHOTON?
2. Can we reduce c' with the $\mathcal{O}(2^{c/2})$ security?

1.1 Our Results

We study them by using the multi-collision based proof technique which is used in the security proofs of several hash functions such as [8,14]. So this paper considers the case of $c' < c$.

In Section 3, we improve the indifferentiable security of PHOTON: PHOTON is indifferentiable from $\mathcal{RO}$ up to $\mathcal{O}\left(\min\{q_{\mathsf{mcoll}}(d^*, c^*), 2^{c/2}\}\right)$ query complexity, where $c^* = c - c'$ and $q_{\mathsf{mcoll}}(d^*, c^*)$ is a query complexity to find a d^*-multi-collision of c^* bits of the hash outputs. Note that d^* satisfies equation $q_{\mathsf{mcoll}}(d^*, c^*) = 2^{c'}/d^*$.

In Section 4, we show the *optimality* of the indifferentiable security. To prove this, we consider a forgery attack on the hash-based message authentication code (MAC) which is the most important application of hash functions. We give a generic forgery attack on the PHOTON-MAC with this query complexity. Thus, the indifferentiable security of our proof is *optimal*.[3]

In Section 5, by using the optimal bound, we investigate the size of c' with the $\mathcal{O}(2^{c/2})$ security. We show that when $c' = c/2 + \log_2 c$ and $d^* = c/2 - \log_2 c$, the $\mathcal{O}(2^{c/2})$ security is ensured, and thereby one can improve the processing time spent in the squeezing step with keeping the indifferentiable security if $c' \geq c/2 + \log_2 c$.

---

[1] Note that [1] defined a generalized permutation-based hash function that includes PHOTON.

[2] When $c' \leq c$, the query complexity is optimal, since the collision of capacity in the absorbing step yields the differentiable attack for PHOTON, and thereby the query complexity is at most $\mathcal{O}(2^{c/2})$.

[3] While [10] gave the optimal parameter of c' for each of collision security and preimage security, our result ensures the optimal indifferentiable security which gives the optimal parameter of c' for *any* single-stage security.

Table 1. This table compares the numbers of P calls for the original PHOTON hash function, (optimized) PHOTON, and PHOTON$_m$, where the size of P is 288 bit. c_1 is the length of capacity of the first block. The third and forth columns are the numbers of P calls at absorbing and squeezing steps, respectively.

Hash Function	Capacity	Absorbing	Squeezing	Indiff. Security
PHOTON (Original) [10]	$c = c_1 = c' = 256$	9	7	2^{128}
PHOTON (Optimized)	$c = c_1 = 256, , c' = 133$	9	1	2^{128}
PHOTON$_m$	$c = 256, c_1 = 128, c' = 133$	5	1	2^{128}

In Section 6, we consider a faster construction where the length of the first message block, denoted by r_1, is flexible. We denote the modified construction by PHOTON$_m$. We show that PHOTON$_m$ has the same indifferentiable security as PHOTON if $r_1 \leq r + c/2$. Thus, one can also improve the processing time spent in the absorbing step with keeping the indifferentiable security if $r_1 \leq r + c/2$. We believe that this modification also has a positive impact on design of lightweight hash functions, especially this is effective for short messages.

Finally, in Table 1, we compare the numbers of P calls for the original PHOTON hash function, (optimized) PHOTON, and PHOTON$_m$, where the input length is 256 bit and the output length is 256 bit. We use a 288-bit permutation that is used in one of the PHOTON family called PHOTON-256/32/32 [10]. In this table, PHOTON-256/32/32 is denoted by "original PHOTON". Then, we optimize the original PHOTON by using our analysis for c'. In this table, it is denoted by "optimized PHOTON". We also optimize it by using our analysis for r_1. In this case, the numbers of P calls are 16 (original PHOTON), 10 (optimized PHOTON), and 6 (PHOTON$_m$). This example shows that the number of P calls can be reduced with keeping the indifferentiable security.

1.2 Related Works

PHOTON can be seen as the ChopMD hash function [9] shown in Fig. 3 where the compression function h is defined by $h(cv, M_i) = P((M_i \| 0^r) \oplus cv)$. Chang and Nandi [8] proved that ChopMD is indifferentiable from $\mathcal{RO}$ up to $\mathcal{O}(\min\{2^{c'}/r', 2^{r'}\})$ query complexity when h is a random oracle. Naito, Sasaki, Wang and Yasuda [12] showed that the query complexity is optimal when $r' = c'$

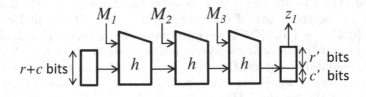

Fig. 3. ChopMD

where they gave a generic forgery attack on the ChopMD-MAC with $\mathcal{O}(2^{c'}/c')$ complexity. Thus, if the compression function $P((M_i\|0^r) \oplus cv)$ is indifferentiable from $\mathcal{RO}$, then the compression function can be used as a random oracle compression function and thereby the ChopMD result might offer the optimal security of PHOTON.

However, the compression function is not indifferentiable from $\mathcal{RO}$. One can easily find a collision of the compression function by setting $(M\|0^c) \oplus cv = (M'\|0^c) \oplus cv'$ such that $M \neq M'$. On the other hand, it is hard to find the collision of a random oracle. The difference yields the differentiable attack on the compression function. Thus the indifferentiable security of ChopMD does not ensure that of PHOTON.

Canteaut, Fuhr, Naya-Plasencia, Paillier, Reinhard, and Videau [7] defined a generalized permutation-based hash construction that includes a *fixed* output length PHOTON where the output is squeezed from a single permutation call. They proved that the generalized hash function is indifferentiable from $\mathcal{RO}$. Note that our result covers a *variable* output length PHOTON. Moreover, their query complexity is *not* optimal. For example, when $c' = c/2 + \log_2 c$ and $r' = c^2$, the query complexities are $\mathcal{O}(2^{c/2}/c)$ from [7] and $\mathcal{O}(2^{c/2})$ from our result.

2 Preliminaries

Notation. For two values x, y, $x\|y$ is the concatenated value of x and y. For some value y, $x \leftarrow y$ means assigning y to x. When X is a non-empty finite set, we write $x \xleftarrow{\$} X$ to mean that a value is sampled uniformly at random from X and assign to x. $\oplus$ is bitwise exclusive or. $|x|$ is the length (size) of binary string x. For a b-bit value x, $x[i, j]$ is the value from (left) i-th bit to (left) j-th bit where $1 \leq i \leq j \leq b$. For example, let $x = 01101001$, $x[3, 5] = 101$. $\emptyset$ is an empty set and ε is an empty string. $p_{\mathsf{mcoll}}(Q, d, c^*)$ is the probability of occurring a d-multi-collision in Q random values of r bits, which means that for Q random values $x_1, \ldots, x_Q$ of r bit, there exists d-values $x_{i_1}, \ldots, x_{i_d}$ such that $x_{i_1} = \cdots = x_{i_d}$. $q_{\mathsf{mcoll}}(d, c^*)$ is the number of random values of c^* bits wherein a d-multi-collision occurs with the probability of $1/2$. Note that the number is discussed in [15]. Please see [15] for the detail.

PHOTON Construction. Let P be a permutation of t bits. The PHOTON hash function PHOTON^P is defined in Fig. 4, which accepts a message of arbitrary length, denoted by M, and the output length denoted by n, and generates an n-bit string. Let r be the length of a message block, $c = t - r$, which is called "capacity", r' be the length of each output block, $c' = t - r'$ and $c^* = c - c'$. pad : $\{0,1\}^* \to (\{0,1\}^r)^*$ is an injective padding function such that the last r-bit value is not 0^r and its inverse unpad : $(\{0,1\}^r)^* \to \{0,1\}^* \cup \{\bot\}$ is efficiently computable. $\mathsf{unpad}(M) = M^*$ $(\neq \bot)$ if $\exists M^*$ such that $\mathsf{pad}(M^*) = M$, $\mathsf{unpad}(M) = \bot$ otherwise. For example, $\mathsf{pad}(M) = M\|1\|0^i$ where i is a smallest value such that the length of $M\|1\|0^i$ is multiples of r. IV is a constant value of n bits. $IV_1 = IV[1, r]$ and $IV_2 = IV[r + 1, t]$.

Indifferentiability [11]. Let H^P be a hash function (e.g., PHOTON) using a random permutation P. Let P^{-1} be its inverse oracle. Let $S = (S_F, S_I)$ be a simulator. The indifferentiable advantage of H^P from a random oracle $\mathcal{RO}$ is defined as follows.

$$\mathsf{Adv}^{\mathsf{indiff}, \mathcal{RO}}_{H^P, S}(\mathcal{D}) = |\Pr[\mathcal{D}^{H^P, P, P^{-1}} \Rightarrow 1] - \Pr[\mathcal{D}^{\mathcal{RO}, S^{\mathcal{RO}}_F, S^{\mathcal{RO}}_I} \Rightarrow 1]|$$

where $\mathcal{D}$ is a distinguisher has oracle access to $H^P/\mathcal{RO}, P/S_F$ and P^{-1}/S_I. S_F and S_I simulate P and P^{-1}, respectively. Since PHOTON accepts the output length n, a query to $\mathcal{RO}$ includes the output length: for query (n, M), the output is defined as $\mathcal{RO}(M)[1, n]$.

We say H^P is indifferentiable from $\mathcal{RO}$ if there exists a simulator $S = (S_F, S_I)$ such that for any distinguisher $\mathcal{D}$ the advantage is negligible.

Hereafter, we call the H world "Real World", and the $\mathcal{RO}$ world "Ideal World". We call the oracle $H^P/\mathcal{RO}$ "Left Oracle" (denoted by L) and the oracles P/S_F and P^{-1}/S_I "Right Oracles" (denoted R_F and R_I, respectively).

The indifferentiability composition theorem is as follows. It ensures that for any single-stage security such as collision security, second preimage security, and preimage security, if H^P is indifferentiable from $\mathcal{RO}$ then any cryptosystem is at least as secure in the P model via H as in the $\mathcal{RO}$ model [11,13].

Theorem 1 ([11,13](The following statement is from Theorem 3.1 of [13])). *Let G be any single-stage security game. Let S be a simulator. For any adversary $\mathcal{A}$, there exist an adversary $\mathcal{B}$ and a distinguisher $\mathcal{D}$ such that*

$$\mathbf{Pr}[\mathcal{A} \text{ wins } G \text{ under the } H^P \text{ case}] \leq \mathbf{Pr}[\mathcal{B} \text{ wins } G \text{ in } \mathcal{RO} \text{ model}]$$
$$+ \mathsf{Adv}^{\mathsf{indiff}, \mathcal{RO}}_{H^P, S}(\mathcal{D}).$$

Moreover, $t_\mathcal{B} \leq t_\mathcal{D} + q_\mathcal{A} t_S, q_\mathcal{B} \leq q_\mathcal{A} q_S, t_\mathcal{D} \leq t_G + q_G t_\mathcal{A}, q_\mathcal{D} \leq q_G + q_G t_\mathcal{A}$ where $t_\mathcal{A}, t_\mathcal{B}$, and $t_\mathcal{D}$ are the maximum running times of $\mathcal{A}, \mathcal{B}$, and $\mathcal{D}$, respectively; $q_\mathcal{A}$ and $q_\mathcal{B}$ are the maximum number of queries made by $\mathcal{A}$ and $\mathcal{B}$ in a single execution, respectively; and q_G are the maximum number of queries made by G to the left oracle and to the adversary.

3   Improving the Indifferentiable Security Bound of PHOTON

In this section, we improve the indifferentiable security of PHOTON^P where P is a random permutation and P^{-1} is its inverse oracle.

Theorem 2. *Assume that $c' \leq c$. There exists a simulator $S = (S_F, S_I)$ such that for any distinguisher $\mathcal{D}$, the following holds,*

$$\mathsf{Adv}^{\mathsf{indiff}, \mathcal{RO}}_{\mathsf{PHOTON}^P, S}(\mathcal{D}) \leq \max\left\{ N p_{\mathsf{mcoll}}(q_L, d, c^*) + \frac{(d-1)q}{2^{c'}} + \frac{q(q-1)}{2^c}, \frac{\sigma^2}{2^c} \right\}$$
$$+ \frac{\sigma(\sigma - 3)}{2^{t+1}}$$

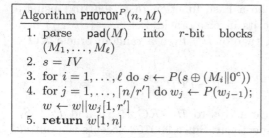

Algorithm PHOTON$^P(n, M)$

1. parse pad(M) into r-bit blocks $(M_1, \ldots, M_\ell)$
2. $s = IV$
3. for $i = 1, \ldots, \ell$ do $s \leftarrow P(s \oplus (M_i \| 0^c))$
4. for $j = 1, \ldots, \lceil n/r' \rceil$ do $w_j \leftarrow P(w_{j-1})$; $w \leftarrow w \| w_j[1, r']$
5. **return** $w[1, n]$

Fig. 4. PHOTON

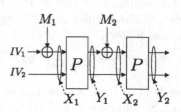

Fig. 5. PHOTON Graph

where $\mathcal{D}$ can make queries to PHOTON$^P/\mathcal{RO}$ and $(P, P^{-1})/(S_F, S_I)$ at most q_L, q times, respectively, where N is the maximum size of the sum of the input blocks of an L query and the output blocks, and d is a free parameter which can be selected such that the bound is minimum. $\sigma = Nq_L + q$. S makes at most q queries and runs in time $\mathcal{O}(q)$. ♦

3.1 PHOTON Graph

We define a PHOTON graph G_S which keeps paths constructed from query-responses of right oracles. It is initialized with the single node IV. Edges and nodes in this graph are defined by query-responses of right oracles, which follows the PHOTON structure. The nodes are chaining values and the edges are message blocks. For example, if (X_1, Y_1) and (X_2, Y_2) are query-responses of R_F or R_I such that $X_1[r + 1, t] = IV_2$ and $Y_1[r + 1, t] = X_2[r + 1, t]$ then IV, Y_1 and Y_2 are the nodes of G_S, and M_1 and M_2 are the edges where $M_1 = IV_1 \oplus X_1[1, r]$ and $M_2 = Y_1[1, r] \oplus X_2[1, r]$. We denote the path by $IV \xrightarrow{M_1} Y_1 \xrightarrow{M_2} Y_2$ or $IV \xrightarrow{M_1 \| M_2} Y_2$ (Fig. 5 may help readers to understand this graph). We say paths with a PHOTON construction "PHOTON paths". For example, $IV \xrightarrow{M} Y_1 \xrightarrow{0^r} Y_2 \xrightarrow{0^r} Y_3 \cdots$ is a PHOTON path if unpad(M) $\neq \perp$.

3.2 Simulator

We define a simulator $S = (S_F, S_I)$ in Fig. 6. S has two tables T and path that are initialized by the Initialization procedure. S keeps query-response pairs in T and the paths in path. The paths are constructed from the pairs in T.

S is defined such that S and $\mathcal{RO}$ are consistent, which means that for any path $IV \xrightarrow{M} Y_1 \xrightarrow{0^r} Y_2 \xrightarrow{0^r} \cdots \xrightarrow{0^r} Y_\ell$ in path, if unpad(M) $= M^* \neq \perp$ then $Y_1[1, r'] \| \ldots \| Y_\ell[1, r'] = \mathcal{RO}(M^*)[1, r'\ell]$.

3.3 Proof Overview

We give the outline of the indifferentiable security proof of PHOTON. In order to simplify the discussion, we fix the input lengths as r (single block) and $2r$ (two

---

$S_F(X)$

1. if $\exists (X, Y) \in T$ then return Y
2. parse X into r-bit value X_r and c-bit value X_c
3. if $\exists (IV \xrightarrow{M} u \| X_c) \in$ path then
4.   parse $M \| (u \oplus X_r)$ into M_0 and 0^{jr}

       s.t. the last block of M_0 is not 0^r

5. $Y[r' + 1, t] \xleftarrow{\$} \{0, 1\}^{c'}$
6.   if $\mathsf{unpad}(M_0) = M^* \neq \bot$ then
7. $z \leftarrow \mathcal{RO}(M^*)$
8.   assign $j + 1$-th r'-bit block of z to $Y[1, r']$
9.   else
10. $Y[1, r'] \xleftarrow{\$} \{0, 1\}^{r'}$
11.   endif
12.   insert $IV \xrightarrow{M} u \| X_c \xrightarrow{u \oplus X_a} Y$ to path
13. else
14. $Y \xleftarrow{\$} \{0, 1\}^t$
15. endif
16. insert (X, Y) to T
17. return Y

Initialization

1. $T \leftarrow \emptyset$
2. path $\leftarrow \{IV \xrightarrow{\varepsilon} IV\}$

$S_I(Y)$

1. if $\exists (X, Y) \in T$ then
    return X
2. $X \xleftarrow{\$} \{0, 1\}^t$
3. insert (X, Y) to T
4. return X

Fig. 6. Simulator

block), and the output as $n = r'$ (single block), and omit the padding function pad. The full proof is given in the next subsection.

In the real world, L makes R_F queries, where $(L, R_F, R_I) = (\text{PHOTON}^P, P, P^{-1})$. Therefore, for any PHOTON path $IV \xrightarrow{M} Y$, the relation $Y[1, r'] = L(r', M)$ is ensured. On the other hand, in the ideal world, L does not make R_F queries, where $(L, R_F, R_I) = (\mathcal{RO}, S_F, S_I)$. So S has to simulate the relation between L and R_F in the real world. If we can construct such simulator, the indifferentiable security can be ensured. In this case, we say the PHOTON consistency is ensured.

Differentiable Events. We discuss differentiable events. Consider PHOTON paths $IV \xrightarrow{M_1} Y_1$ (single block) and $IV \xrightarrow{M_1} Y_1 \xrightarrow{M_2} Y_2$ (two blocks) in the graph G_S in the ideal world. Let (X_1, Y_1) be the query-response pair corresponding with $IV \xrightarrow{M_1} Y_1$, that is, $X_1 = IV \oplus (M_1 \| 0^c)$, and similarly (X_2, Y_2) be the query-response pair corresponding with $Y_1 \xrightarrow{M_2} Y_2$. In the following discussion, we focus on the queries corresponding with (X_1, Y_1) and (X_2, Y_2).

When these pairs are defined by R_F queries and by this order, the PHOTON consistency is ensured; When $\mathcal{D}$ makes the query $R_F(X_1)$, S_F can respond the output Y_1 such that $Y_1[1, r'] = L(r', M_1)$ by making the query $L(r', M_1)$. When $\mathcal{D}$ makes the query $R_F(X_2)$, since S can know M_1 from the table path, S can respond Y_2 such that $Y_2[1, r'] = L(r', M_1 \| M_2)$.

On the other hand, the PHOTON consistency is not ensured when these pairs are defined by other patterns. These patterns can be categorized by the five events **ConnectIV**$_F$, **ConnectIV**$_I$, **Connect**$_F$, **Connect**$_I$, and **Coll**. We explain these events as follows.

- **ConnectIV**$_F$ is that for the query $R_F(X_1)$, the response Y_1 connects to IV, that is, $Y_1[r+1,t] = IV_2$. In this case, in addition to the path $IV \xrightarrow{M_1} Y_1$, other paths can be constructed, e.g., $IV \xrightarrow{M_1} Y_1 \xrightarrow{M^*} Y_1$ where $M^* = IV_1 \oplus M_1 \oplus Y_1[1,r]$. On the other hand, $Y_1 \neq L(r', M_1)$ or $Y_1 \neq L(r', M_1\|M^*)$, since $L = \mathcal{RO}$. Thus, if **ConnectIV**$_F$ occurs then the PHOTON consistency cannot be ensured.
- **ConnectIV**$_I$ is that for the query $R_I(Y_1)$, the response X_1 connects with IV, that is, $X_1[r+1,t] = IV_2$. Since $L = \mathcal{RO}$, $Y_1[1,r'] \neq \mathcal{RO}(M_1)$. Thus, if **ConnectIV**$_I$ occurs then the PHOTON consistency cannot be ensured.
- **Connect**$_F$ is that first $\mathcal{D}$ makes the query $R_F(X_2)$, and then makes the query $R_F(X_1)$. Namely, the response Y_1 connects with X_2, that is $X_2[r+1,t] = Y_1[r+1,t]$. In this case, when making the query $R_F(X_1)$, S does not know M_1. Since $L = \mathcal{RO}$, $Y_2[1,r] \neq L(r', M_1\|M_2)$. Thus if **Connect**$_F$ occurs, the PHOTON consistency cannot be ensured.
- **Connect**$_I$ is that first $\mathcal{D}$ makes the query $R_F(X_1)$, and second $\mathcal{D}$ makes the query $R_I(Y_2)$. Then the response X_2 connects with Y_1, that is $X_2[r+1,t] = Y_1[r+1,t]$. Since $L = \mathcal{RO}$ and Y_2 is chosen by $\mathcal{D}$, $Y_2[1,r'] \neq L(r', M_1\|M_2)$. Thus, if **Connect**$_I$ occurs, the PHOTON consistency cannot be ensured.
- **Coll** is that $\mathcal{D}$ makes queries $R_F(X_1^{(1)})$ and $R_F(X_1^{(2)})$, and then the responses $Y_1^{(1)}$ and $Y_1^{(2)}$ are such that $Y_1^{(1)}[r+1,t] = Y_1^{(2)}[r+1,t]$. Thus, the collision paths $IV \xrightarrow{M_1^{(1)}} Y_1^{(1)}$ and $IV \xrightarrow{M_1^{(2)}} Y_1^{(2)}$ are constructed. In this case, when the query $R_F(X_2)$ is made where $X_2[r+1,t] = Y_1^{(1)}[r+1,t]$, the response Y_2 is such that $Y_2[1,r'] \neq L(r', M_1^{(1)}\|M_2^{(1)})$ or $Y_2[1,r'] \neq L(r', M_1^{(2)}\|M_2^{(2)})$ where $M_2^{(1)} = X_2[1,r] \oplus Y_1^{(1)}[1,r]$ and $M_2^{(2)} = X_2[1,r] \oplus Y_1^{(2)}[1,r]$, since $L = \mathcal{RO}$. Thus, if **Coll** occurs, the PHOTON consistency cannot be ensured.

Note that if the PHOTON consistency cannot be ensured then one of the above events occurs. Thus, the indifferentiable advantage of PHOTON is obtained from the probabilities $\Pr[\mathbf{ConnectIV}_F]$, $\Pr[\mathbf{ConnectIV}_I]$, $\Pr[\mathbf{Connect}_F]$, $\Pr[\mathbf{Connect}_I]$, and $\Pr[\mathbf{Coll}]$.

Evaluating the Probabilities. Assume that $\mathcal{D}$ can make queries at most Q times. We give rough evaluations of these probabilities as follows.

For the probabilities $\Pr[\mathbf{ConnectIV}_F]$, $\Pr[\mathbf{ConnectIV}_I]$, $\Pr[\mathbf{Connect}_I]$, and $\Pr[\mathbf{Coll}]$, since outputs of S are chosen uniformly at random from $\{0,1\}^t$, we have

$$\mathbf{Pr}[\mathbf{ConnectIV}_F] \leq \frac{Q}{2^c}, \ \mathbf{Pr}[\mathbf{ConnectIV}_I] \leq \frac{Q}{2^c},$$

$$\mathbf{Pr}[\mathbf{Connect}_I] \leq \sum_{i=1}^{Q} \frac{i-1}{2^c} \leq \frac{Q(Q-1)}{2^{c+1}}, \ \text{and}$$

$$\mathbf{Pr}[\mathbf{Coll}] \leq \sum_{i=1}^{Q} \frac{i-1}{2^c} \leq \frac{Q(Q-1)}{2^{c+1}}.$$

Finally, we evaluate the probabilities $\mathbf{Pr}[\mathbf{Connect}_F]$. Note that [1] evaluated the probability of the event $\mathbf{Connect}_F$ as $\Pr[\mathbf{Connect}_F] \leq Q^2/2^{c'}$. The probability is from the facts that the numbers of such (X_1, Y_1) and of such (X_2, Y_2) are at most Q, respectively, and right most c' bits are uncontrollable. Hence, the probability that Y_1 connects with X_2 is at most $Q^2/2^{c'}$. On the other hand, the probability can be evaluated by using the multi-collision technique that was used in the security proofs of several hash functions such as [8,14].

Let $\mathbf{MColl}$ be a multi-collision event where for some queries $L(r', M_1^{(1)})$, $\dots$, $L(r', M_1^{(d)})$, the outputs $Z_1^{(1)}, \dots, Z_1^{(d)}$ are such that $Z_1^{(1)}[r+1, r'] = \cdots = Z_1^{(d)}[r+1, r']$ (d-multi-collision). Then the probability $\mathbf{Pr}[\mathbf{Connect}_F]$ can be bounded as

$$\mathbf{Pr}[\mathbf{Connect}_F] \leq \mathbf{Pr}[\mathbf{MColl}] + \mathbf{Pr}[\mathbf{Connect}_F | \neg \mathbf{MColl}].$$

Then,

$$\mathbf{Pr}[\mathbf{MColl}] = p_{\mathsf{mcoll}}(Q, d, c^*).$$

We evaluate the probability $\mathbf{Pr}[\mathbf{Connect}_F | \neg \mathbf{MColl}]$ as follows. In this case, we must care the two facts.

- $\mathcal{D}$ can know the left most r'-bits of some output of S by an output of L. This is from the condition that for the PHOTON path $IV \xrightarrow{M_1} Y_1$, $Y_1[1, r'] = L(r', M_1)$.
- $\mathcal{D}$ can select messages.

Thus $Y_1[1, r]$ is under the control of $\mathcal{D}$ and $Y_1[r+1, r']$ is obtained from the query $L(M_1)$. So the probability $\mathbf{Pr}[\mathbf{Connect}_F | \neg \mathbf{MColl}]$ can be evaluated from the following $\mathcal{D}$'s procedures: (1) $\mathcal{D}$ obtains $Y_1[1, r']$ by query $L(r', M_1)$, (2) makes query $S_F(X_2)$ such that $X_2[r+1, r'] = Y_1[r+1, r']$, and (3) makes query $S_F(X_1)$ such that $X_1 = IV \oplus (M_1 \| 0^r)$ where the output is Y_1. From the event $\neg \mathbf{MColl}$, the number of such $X_1[r'+1, t]$ is at most $d-1$ and $\mathcal{D}$ can make queries $S_F(X_2)$ at most Q. Thus we have

$$\mathbf{Pr}[\mathbf{Connect}_F | \neg \mathbf{MColl}] \leq \frac{(d-1)Q}{2^{c'}}.$$

Thus the query complexity to be differentiable from $\mathcal{RO}$ is

$$\mathcal{O}\left(\min\{q_{\mathsf{mcoll}}(d, c^*), 2^{c'}/d, 2^{c/2}\}\right).$$

$L(n, M)$	$L(n, M)$	$L(n, M)$
return $\mathcal{RO}(M)[1, n]$;	**return** $\mathtt{PHOTON}^{S_F}(n, M)$;	**return** $\mathtt{PHOTON}^P(n, M)$;
$R_F(x)$	$R_F(x)$	$R_F(x)$
return $S_F(x)$;	**return** $S_F(x)$;	**return** $P(x)$;
$R_I(y)$	$R_I(y)$	$R_I(y)$
return $S_I(y)$;	**return** $S_I(y)$;	**return** $P^{-1}(y)$;

Fig. 7. Game 1   **Fig. 8.** Game 2   **Fig. 9.** Game 3

We select d such that $q_{\mathsf{mcoll}}(d^*, c^*) = 2^{c'}/d^*$, and hence the query complexity is $\mathcal{O}\left(\min\{q_{\mathsf{mcoll}}(d^*, c^*), 2^{c/2}\}\right)$.

3.4   Proof of Theorem 2

This proof consists of three games, which are shown in Figs. 7, 8, and 9. In each game, the distinguisher $\mathcal{D}$ has oracle access to left oracle L and right oracles (R_F, R_I). Game 1 is the ideal world and Game 3 is the real world. Let G_i be the event that in Game i $\mathcal{D}$ outputs 1. Then

$$\mathsf{Adv}^{\mathsf{indiff}, \mathcal{RO}}_{\mathtt{PHOTON}^P, S}(\mathcal{D}) \leq |\mathbf{Pr}[G_1] - \mathbf{Pr}[G_2]| + |\mathbf{Pr}[G_2] - \mathbf{Pr}[G_3]|.$$

In the following, we evaluate each difference.

Game 1 $\Rightarrow$ Game 2. The evaluation of the difference between Game 1 and Game 2 is inspired by the proof of [9]. When considering the difference, we must care two points. The first point is that in Game 2 for a query $L(n, M)$, L makes R_F queries corresponding with $\mathtt{PHOTON}^{S_F}(n, M)$, while in Game 1 L does not makes the queries. In Game 2, $\mathcal{D}$ cannot find the additional right query-responses directly but can find them by making the corresponding right queries. So we must show that the additional right query-responses that $\mathcal{D}$ obtains don't affect the $\mathcal{D}$'s behavior. The second point is that in Game 2 $L(n, M) = \mathtt{PHOTON}^{S_F}(n, M)$, while in Game 1 $L(n, M) = \mathcal{RO}(M)[1, n]$. Thus we must ensure the following two points.

1. In Game 1, R_F and R_I consistent with L as in Game 2.
2. In Game 2, for any query $L(n, M)$, the response is equal to $\mathcal{RO}(M)[1, n]$.

Note that we assumed that n is multiple of r'. To ensure the two points, we use the following lemma.

Lemma 1. *In Game 1 and Game 2, for any* $\mathtt{PHOTON}$ *path* $IV \xrightarrow{M} y_1 \xrightarrow{0^r} y_2 \xrightarrow{0^r} \cdots \xrightarrow{0^r} y_{\ell-1} \xrightarrow{0^r} y_\ell$ *in* G_S, *unless the following bad event occurs,* $y_1[1, r']\|\ldots\|y_\ell[1, r'] = \mathcal{RO}(M^*)[1, r'\ell]$ *where* $\mathsf{unpad}(M) = M^*$.

- **Bad**$_j$: In Game j, for some i-th query $R_F(X_i)$, the response Y_i is such that $Y_i[r+1,t]$ collides with some value in $W_i \cup \{X_i[r+1,t], IV_2\}$, or for some i-th query $R_I(Y_i)$, the response X_i is such that $X_i[r+1,t]$ collides with some value in $W_i \cup \{IV_2\}$,

where W_i is a table keeping the right most c-bit values of all query-responses to R_F and R_I before the i-th query. Namely, for W_i and any $u < i$, $X_u[r+1,t], Y_u[r+1,t] \in W_i$ where (X_u, Y_u) is the u-th query-response.   ◆

Note that in Game 2, these queries include queries from L in addition to those from $\mathcal{D}$.

Proof (Proof of Lemma 1). Let $IV \xrightarrow{M} y_1 \xrightarrow{0^r} y_2 \xrightarrow{0^r} \cdots \xrightarrow{0^r} y_{\ell-1} \xrightarrow{0^r} y_\ell$ be any path. The query-response pairs corresponding with the path are denoted by $(X_1, Y_1), \ldots, (X_l, y_1), (y_1, y_2), \ldots, (y_{\ell-1}, y_\ell)$ where $X_1[r+1,t] = IV_2$, $X_i[r+1,t] = Y_{i-1}[r+1,t]$ $(i = 2, \ldots, l)$, and $M = M_1\|\ldots\|M_l$ where $M_1 = IV_1 \oplus X_1[1,r]$, $M_i = Y_{i-1}[1,r] \oplus X_i[1,r]$ $(i = 2, \ldots, l)$. We show that $y_1[1,r']\|\ldots\|y_\ell[1,r'] = \mathcal{RO}(M^*)[1,r'\ell]$ where unpad$(M) = M^*$. Assume that **Bad**$_j$ does not occur.

Since **Bad**$_j$ does not occur, $(X_1, Y_1), \ldots, (X_l, y_1), (y_1, y_2), \ldots, (y_{\ell-1}, y_\ell)$ are defined by this order and by the R_F queries. Since **Bad**$_j$ does not occur, there are no collision paths: $IV \xrightarrow{M} u_1\|X$ and $IV \xrightarrow{M} u_2\|X$. Thus, Steps 7 and 8 of S_F ensure that $y_1[1,r']\|\ldots\|y_\ell[1,r'] = \mathcal{RO}(M^*)[1,r'\ell]$.

□

Lemma 1 ensures the two points.

- In Game 1, for any PHOTON path in G_S, denoted by $IV \xrightarrow{M} y_1 \xrightarrow{0^r} y_2 \xrightarrow{0^r} \cdots y_{\ell-1} \xrightarrow{0^r} y_\ell$, $y_1[1,r']\|y_{\ell-1}[1,r']\|y_\ell[1,r'] = L(r'\ell, M^*)$ such that $M^* = $ unpad(M). Thus R_F and R_I consistent with L as in Game 2, thereby the point 1 is ensured.
- In Game 2, unless the bad event occurs, for any query $L(n, M^*)$, the response is equal to $\mathcal{RO}(M^*)[1,n]$. Thus the point 2 is ensured.

Consequently, $\mathbf{Pr}[G_1|\neg\mathbf{Bad}_1] = \mathbf{Pr}[G_2|\neg\mathbf{Bad}_2]$, and we have

$$|\mathbf{Pr}[G_1] - \mathbf{Pr}[G_2]|$$
$$\leq |\mathbf{Pr}[G_1|\mathbf{Bad}_1]\mathbf{Pr}[\mathbf{Bad}_1] + \mathbf{Pr}[G_1|\neg\mathbf{Bad}_1]\mathbf{Pr}[\neg\mathbf{Bad}_1]$$
$$- (\mathbf{Pr}[G_2|\mathbf{Bad}_2]\mathbf{Pr}[\mathbf{Bad}_2] + \mathbf{Pr}[G_2|\neg\mathbf{Bad}_2]\mathbf{Pr}[\neg\mathbf{Bad}_2])|$$
$$\leq |\mathbf{Pr}[G_1|\neg\mathbf{Bad}_1](\mathbf{Pr}[\mathbf{Bad}_2] - \mathbf{Pr}[\mathbf{Bad}_1])$$
$$+ (\mathbf{Pr}[G_1|\mathbf{Bad}_1]\mathbf{Pr}[\mathbf{Bad}_1] - \mathbf{Pr}[G_2|\mathbf{Bad}_2]\mathbf{Pr}[\mathbf{Bad}_2])|$$
$$\leq \max\{\mathbf{Pr}[\mathbf{Bad}_1], \mathbf{Pr}[\mathbf{Bad}_2]\}$$

We evaluate the bounds as follows.

First, we evaluate the probability $\mathbf{Pr}[\mathbf{Bad}_1]$. We define an event $\mathbf{MColl}_d$ in which a d-multi collision occurs for c^*-bit values of some blocks of outputs of $\mathcal{RO}$. Strictly, let $Z_1, \ldots, Z_s$ be all outputs of $\mathcal{RO}$ by L queries. Let $Z_{i,j} = Z_i[(j-1)r'+1, jr']$ (j-th block of r' bit) for $i = 1, \ldots, s$.

- **MColl$_d$**: For some j^* and some $i_1, \ldots, i_d$, $Z_{i_1,j^*}[r+1, r'] = \ldots = Z_{i_d,j^*}[r+1, r']$ (d-multi-collision).

We have

$$\Pr[\mathbf{Bad}_1] \leq \Pr[\mathbf{MColl}_d] + \Pr[\mathbf{Bad}_1 | \neg \mathbf{MColl}_d]$$
$$\leq N p_{\mathsf{mcoll}}(q_L, d, c^*) + \frac{(d-1)q}{2^{c'}} + \frac{q(q-1)}{2^c}$$

where the first term corresponds with $\Pr[\mathbf{MColl}_d]$ and the remaining terms correspond with $\Pr[\mathbf{Bad}_1 | \neg \mathbf{MColl}_d]$.

We thus justify the bound of $\Pr[\mathbf{Bad}_1 | \neg \mathbf{MColl}_d]$. Assume that $\neg \mathbf{MColl}_d$ occurs. The event $\mathbf{Bad}_1$ is triggered by some R_F query or some R_I query. Thus we consider the two cases.

- Consider the case that this event is triggered by some R_F query.
    - In this case, we must care the case that $\mathcal{D}$ can obtain left most r'-bit values of outputs of S_F by L (= $\mathcal{RO}$) queries in advance, where this case corresponds with the event $\mathbf{Connect}_F$ shown in Subsection 3.3. Since the number of queries which may connect to some block is at most $d-1$, the probability is $\leq (d-1)q/2^{c'}$.
    - On the other hand, other cases are that the r'-bit values are not obtained by L queries in advance. Fix i and assume that the i-th query triggers the event $\mathbf{Bad}_1$. The i-th query-response is denoted by (X_i, Y_i) which is defined by the R_F query. $Y_i[r+1, t]$ is chosen independent from $W_i \cup \{IV_2, X_i[r+1, t]\}$. The probability is $\leq \sum_{i=1}^{q}(2(i-1)+2)/2^c = q(q-1)/2^c$.
  Thus the probability of this case is $\leq (d-1)q/2^{c'} + q(q-1)/2^c$.
- Consider the case that this event is triggered by some R_I query. Fix i and assume that the i-th query triggers the event $\mathbf{Bad}_1$. The i-th query-response is denoted by (X_i, Y_i) which is defined by the R_I query, that is, X_i is such that $X_i[r+1, t]$ collides with some of $W_i \cup \{IV_2\}$. We note that outputs of S_I are chosen uniformly at random and independent from $\mathcal{RO}$. Thus the probability p_2 from this case is $\leq \sum_{i=1}^{q}(2(i-1)+1)/2^c = q(q-3)/2^c$.

We thus have

$$\Pr[\mathbf{Bad}_1 | \neg \mathbf{MColl}_t] \leq \max\left\{\frac{(d-1)q}{2^{c'}} + \frac{q(q-1)}{2^c}, \frac{q(q-3)}{2^c}\right\}$$
$$\leq \frac{(d-1)q}{2^{c'}} + \frac{q(q-1)}{2^c}.$$

Finally, we evaluate the probability $\Pr[\mathbf{Bad}_2]$. Fix i. Let (X_i, Y_i) be an i-th query-response to a right oracle.

- When (X_i, Y_i) is defined by the S_F query, the probability that $Y_i[r+1, t]$ collides with some of $W_i \cup \{IV_2, X_i[r+1, t]\}$ is $\leq 2(i-1)+2)/2^c$.
- When (X_i, Y_i) is defined by the S_I query, the probability that $X_i[r+1, t]$ collides with some of $W_i \cup \{IV_2\}$ is $\leq (2i-1)/2^c$.

We thus have

$$\mathbf{Pr}[\mathrm{Bad}_2] \leq \sum_{i=1}^{\sigma} \frac{2i}{2^c} = \frac{\sigma^2}{2^c}.$$

Game 2 $\Rightarrow$ Game 3. Outputs of S_F and S_I are random values, while (P, P^{-1}) is a random permutation. The difference $|\mathbf{Pr}[G2] - \mathbf{Pr}[G3]|$ is thus bounded by the collision probability in Game 2. Since S_F or S_I is called at most σ times, we thus have

$$|\mathbf{Pr}[G2] - \mathbf{Pr}[G3]| \leq \sum_{i=1}^{\sigma} \frac{i-1}{2^t} = \frac{\sigma(\sigma - 3)}{2^{t+1}}.$$

4 Optimality of Our Proof

In this section, we show that the query complexity obtained from our bound is optimal. To show this, in Subsection 4.1, we give a generic forgery attack on the PHOTON-MAC. In Subsection 4.2, we explain the optimality of the indifferentiable security.

4.1 Forgery Attack on PHOTON-MAC

For a single block size secret key K and a message M, the tag is computed by PHOTON$^P(1, K\|M)$. Thus the tag size is r' bits.

The goal of the forgery attack is to find a valid pair of message M and tag tag such that $tag = $ PHOTON$^P(1, K\|M)$ and the query corresponding the pair was not made, where K is chosen uniformly at random and a forger can make queries to PHOTON$^P(1, K\|\cdot)$.

Attack Procedure. In this attack, we shall construct a d-multi-collision of the PHOTON-MAC. We postpone determining the value of d till the next subsection.

1. Choose first message block M_1 so that the message with the padding value pad_1, denoted by $M_1\|pad_1$, fits in the first block, and make queries M_1 to obtain the corresponding tag. Iterate this $q_{\mathsf{mcoll}}(d, c^*)$ times. If no d-multi-collision occurs for the c^* bits of the tags from $r+1$ to r', then abort. Otherwise, continue the following procedures. Let $M_{1,i}$, where $i \in \{1, 2, \ldots, d\}$, be the d values forming the d-multi-collision, and let $T_{1,i}$, where $i \in \{1, 2, \ldots, d\}$, be the corresponding tags. That is, $T_{1,1}[r+1, r'] = \cdots = T_{1,d}[r+1, r']$. Let $T_1^* = T_{1,1}[r+1, r']$.
2. Choose $2^{c'}/d$ distinct c'-bit values C_j for $j = 1, \ldots, 2^{c'}/d$. For each j, $X_j = 0^r\|T_1^*\|C_j$ and $Y_j = P((pad_3\|0^c) \oplus P(X_j))$ where pad_3 is the padding value fitting in the third block.
3. For each $M_{1,i}$, set $M_2 = T_{1,i}[1, r]$, make a query $M_{1,i}\|pad_1\|M_2$ and obtain the tag $T_{3,i}$. If there exists j such that $T_{3,i} = Y_j[1, r']$ then do the following.

(a) Select distinct r-bit blocks $M_{2,1}^*$ and $M_{2,2}^*$ such that for $l = 1,2$ $M_{2,l}^* \neq M_2$.
(b) For $l = 1,2$, $X_l^* = (M_{2,l}^* \oplus T_{1,i}) \| T_1^* \| C_j$, $Y_l^* = P((pad_3\|0^r) \oplus P(X_l^*))$, and set $T_{3,l} = Y_l^*[1, r']$.
(c) Make a query $M_{1,i}\|pad_1\|M_{2,1}^*$ and obtain the tag T_3
(d) If $T_3 = T_{3,1}$, return the message $M_{1,i}\|pad_1\|M_{2,2}^*$ and the tag $T_{3,2}$.

Complexity and Success Probability. Step 1 requires to make $q_{mcoll}(d, c^*)$ queries to obtain the d-multi-collision with a probability of $1/2$. The memory requirement is $q_{mcoll}(d, c^*)$ for the internal state values on finding the d-multi-collision, and d for storing the pairs $(M_{1,i}, T_{1,i})$. Step 2 requires $2 \times \lceil 2^{c'}/d \rceil$ off-line computations of P. The memory requirement is $\lceil 2^{c'}/d \rceil$ for storing $(C_j, Y_j[1, r'])$. Step 3 requires to make d 2-block queries, which is $2d$ queries, and if $T_{3,i} = Y_j[1, r']$, requires 4-off-line computations of P and a 2-block query, which is 2 queries. Finally, we can conclude that the query complexity is $q_{mcoll}(d, c^*) + 2(d+1)$ for Steps 1 and 3, the time complexity is $2 \times \lceil 2^{c'}/d \rceil + 4$ for Steps 2 and 3, and the memory complexity is $q_{mcoll}(d, c^*) + \lceil 2^{c'}/d \rceil$ for Steps 1 and 3.

The success probability of Step 1 is roughly $1/2$ and the success probability of Step 3 is roughly $1 - 1/e$. Finally, the success probability of the entire attack is $1/2 \cdot (1 - 1/e) \approx 0.316$.

4.2   Discussion

From Theorem 2, the indifferentiable advantages of PHOTON^P is bounded by

$$\max\left\{p_{mcoll}(Nq_L, d, c^*) + \frac{(d-1)q}{2^{c'}} + \frac{q(q-1)}{2^c}, \frac{\sigma^2}{2^c}\right\} + \frac{\sigma(\sigma-3)}{2^{t+1}}.$$

We define the free parameter $d = d^*$ such that $q_{mcoll}(d^*, c^*) = 2^{c'}/d^*$. Thus the query complexity for the indifferentiable security is at least $\mathcal{O}\left(\min\{2^{c'}/d^*, 2^{c/2}\}\right)$.

On the other hand, from Theorem 1, the generic forgery attack ensures that the query complexity is at most $\mathcal{O}\left(\min\{q_{mcoll}(d, c^*) + 2^{c'}/d, 2^{c/2}\}\right)$. Note that the query complexity of $\mathcal{O}(2^{c/2})$ is from the attack based on the collision of capacity. Since for any d, $q_{mcoll}(d, c^*) + 2^{c'}/d \geq q_{mcoll}(d^*, c^*) + 2^{c'}/d^*$, the query complexity for the indifferentiable security is at most $\mathcal{O}\left(\min\{2^{c'}/d^*, 2^{c/2}\}\right)$.

Thus the query complexity of our proof is *optimal*.

5   Choosing Parameters c'

We assume that $c > c'$. Note that the indifferentiable security of PHOTON with $c \leq c'$ is ensured by the one of Sponge. We show that when $c' \geq c/2 + \log_2 c$, the query complexity to be differentiable from $\mathcal{RO}$ is $\mathcal{O}(2^{c/2})$.

The indifferentiable advantages of PHOTON^P is bounded by

$$\max\left\{p_{\text{mcoll}}(Nq_L, d, c^*) + \frac{(d-1)q}{2^{c'}} + \frac{q(q-1)}{2^c}, \frac{\sigma^2}{2^c}\right\} + \frac{\sigma(\sigma-3)}{2^{t+1}}.$$

Note that the terms $q(q-1)/2^c, \sigma^2/2^c$, and $\sigma(\sigma-3)/2^{t+1}$ ensure the complexity of $\mathcal{O}(2^{c/2})$. We thus consider remaining terms.

We consider the probability $p_{\text{mcoll}}(Nq_L, d, c^*)$.

$$p_{\text{mcoll}}(Nq_L, d, c^*) \leq \binom{Nq_L}{d}\left(\frac{1}{2^{c^*}}\right)^{d-1}.$$

We define the parameters c' and d as $c' = c/2 + \log_2 c$ and $d = c^* = c - c' = c/2 - \log_2 c$. Then,

$$\binom{Nq_L}{d}\left(\frac{1}{2^{c^*}}\right)^{d-1} \leq \frac{1}{c/2 - \log_2 c}\left(\frac{Nq_L}{2^{c/2 - \log_2 c - 1}}\right)^{c/2 - \log_2 c}$$

$$\leq \frac{1}{c/2 - \log_2 c}\left(\frac{Nq_L}{2^{c/2 - \log_2 c - 1}}\right)$$

$$\leq \frac{Nq_L}{2^{c/2 - 2}}$$

and

$$\frac{(d-1)q}{2^{c'}} = \frac{(c/2 - \log_2 c)q}{2^{c/2 + \log_2 c}} \leq \frac{q}{2^{c/2 + 1}}.$$

Thus when $c' \geq c/2 + \log_2 c$, the $\mathcal{O}(2^{c/2})$ security is ensured.

6   Modified PHOTON

In this section, we consider the faster construction than PHOTON where the length of the first block message, denoted by r_1, is flexible.

Recall the bad events discussed in Section 3.3. The query complexities to occur the bad events **ConnectIV**$_F$ and **ConnectIV**$_I$ are $\mathcal{O}(2^c)$. Thus when $r_1 \leq r + c/2$, the $\mathcal{O}(2^{c/2})$ security is ensured. Precisely, the following theorem can be proven by the same proof as Theorem 2, where the modified PHOTON, denoted by PHOTON$_m$ is indifferentiable from $\mathcal{RO}$ up to $\mathcal{O}(2^{c/2})$ query complexity.

Theorem 3. *Assume that $c' \leq c$. There exists a simulator $S = (S_F, S_I)$ such that for any distinguisher $\mathcal{D}$, the following holds,*

$$\text{Adv}^{\text{indiff}, \mathcal{RO}}_{\text{PHOTON}^P_m, S}(\mathcal{D}) \leq \max\{Np_{\text{mcoll}}(q_L, d, c^*) + \frac{(d-1)q}{2^{c'}} + \frac{q(q-2)}{2^c} + \frac{q}{2^{c/2}},$$

$$\frac{\sigma(\sigma-1)}{2^c} + \frac{\sigma}{2^{c/2}}\} + \frac{\sigma(\sigma-3)}{2^{t+1}},$$

where $\mathcal{D}$ can make queries to $\text{PHOTON}_m^P/\mathcal{RO}$ and $(P, P^{-1})/(S_F, S_I)$ at most q_L, q times, respectively, where N is the maximum size of the sum of the input blocks of an L query and the output blocks, and d is a free parameter which can be selected such that the bound is minimum. $\sigma = Nq_L + q$. S makes at most q queries and runs in time $\mathcal{O}(q)$. ◆

The probabilities $q/2^{c/2}$ and $\sigma/2^{c/2}$ are appeared due to the bad event corresponding with the initial value. Since this proof is similar to the proof of Theorem 2, we omit this proof.

References

1. Andreeva, E., Mennink, B., Preneel, B.: The Parazoa Family: Generalizing the Sponge Hash Functions. Int. J. Inf. Sec. 11 (2012)
2. Aumasson, J.-P., Henzen, L., Meier, W., Naya-Plasencia, M.: QUARK: A Lightweight Hash. In: Mangard, S., Standaert, F.-X. (eds.) CHES 2010. LNCS, vol. 6225, pp. 1–15. Springer, Heidelberg (2010)
3. Bertoni, G., Daemen, J., Peeters, M., Van Assche, G.: The Keccak sponge function family, http://keccak.noekeon.org/
4. Bertoni, G., Daemen, J., Peeters, M., Van Assche, G.: Sponge functions. In: ECRYPT Hash Workshop (2007)
5. Bertoni, G., Daemen, J., Peeters, M., Van Assche, G.: On the Indifferentiability of the Sponge Construction. In: Smart, N.P. (ed.) EUROCRYPT 2008. LNCS, vol. 4965, pp. 181–197. Springer, Heidelberg (2008)
6. Bogdanov, A., Knežević, M., Leander, G., Toz, D., Varıcı, K., Verbauwhede, I.: SPONGENT: A Lightweight Hash Function. In: Preneel, B., Takagi, T. (eds.) CHES 2011. LNCS, vol. 6917, pp. 312–325. Springer, Heidelberg (2011)
7. Canteaut, A., Fuhr, T., Naya-Plasencia, M., Paillier, P., Reinhard, J.-R., Videau, M.: A Unified Indifferentiability Proof for Permutation- or Block Cipher-Based Hash Functions. IACR Cryptology ePrint Archive, 2012/363
8. Chang, D., Nandi, M.: Improved Indifferentiability Security Analysis of chopMD Hash Function. In: Nyberg, K. (ed.) FSE 2008. LNCS, vol. 5086, pp. 429–443. Springer, Heidelberg (2008)
9. Coron, J.-S., Dodis, Y., Malinaud, C., Puniya, P.: Merkle-Damgård Revisited: How to Construct a Hash Function. In: Shoup, V. (ed.) CRYPTO 2005. LNCS, vol. 3621, pp. 430–448. Springer, Heidelberg (2005)
10. Guo, J., Peyrin, T., Poschmann, A.: The photon family of lightweight hash functions. In: Rogaway, P. (ed.) CRYPTO 2011. LNCS, vol. 6841, pp. 222–239. Springer, Heidelberg (2011)
11. Maurer, U.M., Renner, R., Holenstein, C.: Indifferentiability, Impossibility Results on Reductions, and Applications to the Random Oracle Methodology. In: Naor, M. (ed.) TCC 2004. LNCS, vol. 2951, pp. 21–39. Springer, Heidelberg (2004)
12. Naito, Y., Sasaki, Y., Wang, L., Yasuda, K.: Generic State-Recovery and Forgery Attacks on ChopMD-MAC and on NMAC/HMAC. In: Sakiyama, K., Terada, M. (eds.) IWSEC 2013. LNCS, vol. 8231, pp. 83–98. Springer, Heidelberg (2013)

13. Ristenpart, T., Shacham, H., Shrimpton, T.: Careful with Composition: Limitations of the Indifferentiability Framework. In: Paterson, K.G. (ed.) EUROCRYPT 2011. LNCS, vol. 6632, pp. 487–506. Springer, Heidelberg (2011)
14. Steinberger, J.P.: The Collision Intractability of MDC-2 in the Ideal-Cipher Model. In: Naor, M. (ed.) EUROCRYPT 2007. LNCS, vol. 4515, pp. 34–51. Springer, Heidelberg (2007)
15. Suzuki, K., Tonien, D., Kurosawa, K., Toyota, K.: Birthday paradox for multi-collisions. In: Rhee, M.S., Lee, B. (eds.) ICISC 2006. LNCS, vol. 4296, pp. 29–40. Springer, Heidelberg (2006)

Faster Maliciously Secure
Two-Party Computation Using the GPU

Tore Kasper Frederiksen, Thomas P. Jakobsen, and Jesper Buus Nielsen*

Department of Computer Science, Aarhus University, Aarhus, Denmark
{jot2re,tpj,jbn}@cs.au.dk

Abstract. We present a new protocol for maliciously secure two-party computation based on cut-and-choose of garbled circuits using the recent idea of "forge-and-loose", which eliminates around a factor 3 of garbled circuits that needs to be constructed and evaluated. Our protocol introduces a new way to realize the "forge-and-loose" approach, which avoids an auxiliary secure two-party computation protocol, does not rely on any number theoretic assumptions and parallelizes well in a same instruction, multiple data (SIMD) framework.

With this approach we prove our protocol universally composable-secure against a malicious adversary assuming access to oblivious transfer, commitment and coin-tossing functionalities in the random oracle model.

Finally, we construct, and benchmark, a SIMD implementation of this protocol using a GPU as a massive SIMD device. The findings compare favorably with all previous implementations of maliciously secure, two-party computation.

1 Introduction

Background. Secure two-party computation (2PC) is the area of cryptography concerned with two mutually distrusting parties who wish to securely compute an arbitrary function with private output based on their independent and private input. A bit more formally Alice has the input x, Bob the input y, and they wish to compute the function $f(x, y) = z$ while ensuring such properties as correctness, privacy, and input independence.[1]

2PC was introduced in 1982 by Andrew Yao [36,37], specifically for the *semi-honest* case where both parties are assumed to follow the prescribed protocol and only try to compromise security by extracting information from their own views of the protocol execution. Yao showed how to construct a semi-honestly secure protocol using a technique referred to as the *garbled circuit approach*. This approach involves having one

---

* Partially supported by the European Research Commission Starting Grant 279447 and the Danish National Research Foundation and The National Science Foundation of China (grant 61061130540) for the Sino-Danish Center for the Theory of Interactive Computation. Tore and Thomas are supported by Danish Council for Independent Research Starting Grant 10-081612.
[1] Who should learn the output z can differ and in the most general case there might be a specific output for Alice and one for Bob, i.e., $f(x, y) = z = (z_A, z_B) = (f_A(x, y), f_B(x, y))$ where Alice should only learn z_A and Bob only z_B. In this paper we only consider the case where Bob learns the entire output z. If output for Alice is also needed then any of several general approaches can be used [26,30,35].

M. Abdalla and R. De Prisco (Eds.): SCN 2014, LNCS 8642, pp. 358–379, 2014.
© Springer International Publishing Switzerland 2014

party (*the constructor*), say, Alice, encrypt, or "garble", a Boolean circuit computing the desired functionality. The "garbling" involves first choosing two random keys for each wire in the circuit, one representing a value of 0 and another representing a value of 1. Each gate in the garbled circuit is then constructed such that Bob (*the evaluator*), given only one key for each input wire, can compute only one key for the output wire, namely the key corresponding to the bit that the gate is supposed to output, for example the logical AND of the two input bits. Alice sends the garbled circuit to Bob and makes sure that for each input wire, Bob learns only one of that wire's keys. For Alice's own input, she simply sends these keys to Bob. For Bob's input, they use an oblivious transfer (OT) protocol such that Bob learns one key for each input wire corresponding to his own input, without Alice learning Bob's input. Now, given one key for each input wire, Bob can then evaluate the whole garbled circuit, gate by gate, while at the same time, he cannot learn which bits flow on the wires. Only when he reaches the output wires, he uses some auxiliary information to learn which bits the keys encode. See [27] for a thorough description of Yao's scheme.

A major reason why Yao's original protocol is only secure against a semi-honest adversary is that Bob cannot be sure that the garbled circuit he receives from a Alice has been garbled correctly. One way to ensure correct garbling is with a *cut-and-choose* approach: Instead of sending one garbled circuit, Alice sends several independently garbled versions of the circuit to Bob. Bob then randomly selects some of these, called the *check circuits*, where all the keys on the input wires are revealed to Bob, allowing him to verify that the check circuits do indeed compute the correct function f. If enough circuits are checked and all found to be correct, a large fraction of the remaining circuits, called *evaluation circuits*, will also be correct.

Doing cut-and-choose on several garbled circuits introduces some other issues that have to be dealt with in order to obtain malicious security. First, there may still be a few incorrect circuits among the evaluation circuits. Also, since there are now many circuits, some mechanisms must ensure *input consistency* amongst the circuits: Alice and Bob must give the same input to all the circuits. Information about Alice's input will leak to Bob if he gets to evaluate the circuit on different inputs. But information might also leak to Alice, depending on the function the circuit is computing, if she gives inconsistent input. Another perhaps more subtle issue that arises is a certain kind of *selective failure attack*: Since Alice will supply Bob with the keys in correspondence with his input bits through an OT Alice can simply input garbage for one of the keys, e.g, the 0-key for the first bit of his input. If Bob aborts the protocol, because he cannot evaluate a garbled circuit when one of the keys is garbage, Alice will know that the first bit of his input is 0! On the other hand, if he does not abort the protocol then his first bit must be 1!

Cut-and-choose of Garbled Circuits. In recent years several protocols have been presented which obtain malicious security by combining Yao's original protocol with cut-and-choose on the circuits [3,11,16,24–26,28,30,33–35]. They mainly differ in the way they handle the above issues and, as a consequence, in how many circuits are needed to send from Alice to Bob. We call the amount of circuits needed to be sent from Alice to Bob for the *replication factor*. Most of these approaches are based on an analysis saying that if the fraction of check circuits is high enough and if the check circuits are all found to be correct, then a *majority* of the remaining evaluation circuits will also be correct except with negligible probability. This allows Bob to compute the correct output as the majority of the outputs from the evaluation circuits.

Recent results [3, 16, 25] manage to ensure that Alice only succeeds in cheating if *all* check circuits are honestly constructed and *all* evaluation circuits are maliciously constructed. This happens with noticeably less probability than only the majority of the evaluation circuits are honestly constructed, thus making it possible to run a protocol with noticeably less garbled circuits. The main idea of [3] and [25] (called "forge-and-loose") is to make sure that if Alice cheats, that is, if two evaluation circuits yield different results, then this enables Bob to learn Alice's private input x. He can then use x to compute locally, unencrypted, the correct input $f(x, y)$. In [25] Bob learns Alice's input through an auxiliary secure protocol execution, using as input part of the transcript of the "original" protocol execution, as proof that Alice is corrupt. In [3] a special kind of commitments are used which leaks some auxiliary information if the outputs of two garbled circuits differ. This auxiliary information can then be used to learn Alice's input. The idea of [16] is to have both parties play the role of the circuit constructor *and* circuit evaluator respectively in two simultaneous executions of a cut-and-choose of garbled circuits protocol.

Other Approaches to Malicious Security. Several other approaches to maliciously secure two party computation exist, based on Yao's garbled circuits as well as other novel constructions.

In [32] Nielsen and Orlandi introduced the notion of cut-and-choose at the gate level in order to achieve malicious security for Yao's garbled circuits, popularly referred to as the LEGO approach. LEGO gave an asymptotic increase in efficiency of $O(\log(|C|))$ where $|C|$ is the amount of gates in the circuit to compute. However, their approach relied on heavy group based computations (as the protocol required homomorphic commitments) for each gate in the circuit.

In the later work [10] a new approach for constructing xor-homomorphic commitments based on error correcting codes was introduced. These xor-homomorphic commitments made it possible to use the LEGO approach without doing group operations for each gate, unfortunately at the price of large constants.

Another approach, *not* using garbled gates, was introduced in [31] where heavy usage of oblivious transfers was used to construct verified and authenticated Boolean gates. To achieve efficiency the authors constructed a highly efficient maliciously secure OT extension, which took a few random OTs as "seeds" and then used a random oracle to extend these to polynomially many random OTs.

Yet another approach, not necessarily using Yao's garbled circuits, is the idea of "MPC-in-the-head" from [19, 20] where the parties run a semi-honestly secure two-party protocol, but within this they emulate $n > 2$ parties that run a virtual second protocol secure against a malicious minority. The final protocol is then maliciously secure. Another idea is to base the protocol on preprocessed constrained randomness as in [8].

If one is willing to accept a weaker kind of "malicious" security one can get significant improvements by using the "dual execution" approach where only a single garbled circuit is constructed and evaluated by *both* parties. [17, 29, 30].

Besides all of the above approaches a whole other subfield of secure multi-party computation exists where the function to be evaluated is arithmetic (which can clearly also be used to evaluate Boolean circuits when the field for the arithmetic operations is $\mathbb{F}_2$). Some of the more recent works in this area include [1] (semi-honest security) and [6, 7] (malicious security).

Motivation. The area of 2PC and multi-party computation, MPC, (when more than two parties supply input) is very interesting as efficient solutions yield several practical applications. The first "real world" usage of MPC was described in [2] where MPC was used to decide the market clearing price of sugar beet quotas in Denmark. Still, several other applications of 2PC and MPC exists such as voting, anonymous identification, privacy preserving database queries etc. Thus we believe that it is highly relevant to find practically efficient protocols for 2PC and MPC.

Our Results. We present a new maliciously secure two-party protocol based on cut-and-choose of garbled circuits. The protocol combines previous ideas, mainly from [3, 16, 25] and [11, 34] with new optimizations to a protocol with the following benefits:

1. A small replication factor for the same reasons as [3, 25].[2] But unlike [25] our protocol eliminates the need for running an auxiliary protocol and unlike [16] we eliminate the need of both parties both constructing *and* evaluating $O(s)$ garbled circuits.
2. A very lightweight approach to ensure that Alice gives consistent input to all garbled circuits used for evaluation.
3. Reliance only on lightweight primitives (in practice a hash function) and few OTs.
4. A large degree of same instruction, multiple data (SIMD) parallelization, and therefore direct benefits from access to a large amount of computation cores.
5. A security proof in the Universally Composable (UC) model [4].[3] We also show how to realize a highly efficient version of the protocol in the Random Oracle Model (ROM) without number theoretic assumptions, only assuming access to an OT functionality.

Finally, we also provide an implementation of the protocol written in C and CUDA, using a consumer grade GPU for exploiting the inherent parallelism in the protocol.

Outline. We start by going through the overall ideas of our scheme, along with the primitives we need in Section 2. We then continue with a high level description of our protocol in Section 3. Finally a discussion of our implementation along with experimental results are given in Section 4.

Notation. We assume Alice is the constructor and Bob the evaluator and that the functionality they wish to compute is $f(x, y) = z$, where Alice gives input x, Bob gives input y and only one party, Bob, receives the output z. We denote the amount of bits of x as $|x| = m$, the amount of bits of y as $|y| = n$ and the amount of bits of z as $|z| = o$. We denote the Boolean circuit computing the functionality $f(\cdot, \cdot)$ by C and assume it

---

[2] We do not strictly obtain the same replication factor as [3,25], where the replication factor is s, when s is the statistical security parameter. Our replication factor is slightly larger as in [16]. See the full version of this paper for details [9].

[3] Specifically we provide a UC-proof of our protocol in a hybrid/random oracle model with OT, commitments and coin tossing, and a secure garbling scheme with free-xor [23].

consist of gates with fan-in 2 and fan-out 1 such as AND, XOR, OR etc. Furthermore, we say the size of C, $|C|$, is the amount of non-XOR Boolean gates. When considering a garbled version of C we add a tilde, i.e., $\tilde{C}$. In a garbled circuit we define the *semantic* value of a key to be the bit it represents. We furthermore define the *plain* values or functions to be the unencrypted, unhidden values or functionalities, e.g., the actual function $f(x, y) = z$ with inputs x and y and output z. We use s to represent a statistical security parameter, and we let κ be a computational security parameter. Technically, this means that for any fixed s and any polynomial time bounded adversary, the advantage of the adversary is $2^{-s} + \mathrm{negl}(\kappa)$ for a negligible function negl. I.e., the advantage of any adversary goes to 2^{-s} faster than any inverse polynomial in the computational security parameter. If $s = \Omega(\kappa)$ then the advantage is negligible. If $s = O(\log(\kappa))$ or $s = O(1)$ we only have covert security (see [13] for a detailed description of this concept).

Let $[n]$ denote the set of integers $\{1, 2, \ldots, n\}$ and let $\mathrm{H}(\cdot)$ denote a hash function modeled as a random oracle giving κ bits of output. We use subscript to denote index, i.e. x_i denotes the i'th bits of a vector x and $m_{i,j}$ denotes the i'th row and j'th column of the matrix m. Finally we let $x \in_R S$ denote that x is sampled uniformly at random from the set S.

2   The Big Picture

We assume the reader is familiar with free-xor Yao circuits [23] for secure computation. The overall strategy is as follows:

1. *Garbling.* Alice garbles a bunch of circuits and sends them to Bob.
2. *Oblivious Transfer.* The parties then engage in an OT protocol, secure against malicious adversaries, such that Bob, for each garbled circuit, learns the input keys corresponding to his input to the function f.
3. *Cut-and-Choose.* The parties then use a coin tossing protocol to select around half of the garbled circuits as *check* circuits and the remaining as *evaluation* circuits. Bob then verifies that the check circuits have been constructed correctly and receives from Alice the keys corresponding to her input to the evaluation circuits.
4. *Evaluation.* Bob will then use his own input keys, which he learned from the OT, along with Alice's input keys to evaluate all the evaluation circuits. Using the results from the evaluated circuits he finds the correct output.

This generic scheme leaves open how to handle the problems that arise due to the fact that the parties might act maliciously and due to multiple circuits being garbled and evaluated instead of just one circuit. These problems are (1) selective failure attacks, (2) consistency of the parties' input and (3) how to know which output is the correct one in the evaluation phase. Many different approaches exist to solve these problems with different levels of efficiency and security assumptions. In the following sections we shortly discuss various solutions and in particular, how we solve these issues.

Avoiding Selective Failure Attacks. To ensure privacy, a corrupted party should not be able to deduce anything about the other party's private input based on the other party's behavior. If care is not taken, 2PC based on cut-and-choose of circuits can easily lead to a vulnerability of this kind: If, e.g., Alice inputs another 1-key in the OT for a certain input wire than she uses when garbling the corresponding circuit, and that circuit happens to be an evaluation circuit, she can deduce that Bob's input on that wire is 1 if he aborts. Such an attack is known as a *selective failure attack* and was first pointed out by [22, 29],

Mohassel and Franklin [29] suggested thwarting the attack by means of *committing OT*'s, which makes it possible for Bob to verify Alice's input to the OT against the keys in the check-circuits. Lindell and Pinkas [26] thwarted the attack by increasing the amount of input wires of Bob, letting Bob replace his original input with constrained randomness, where certain input wires xor'ed together would give his real input. This eliminates the attack since it is hard for Alice to "guess" Bob's choice of randomness, which is needed in order for her to successfully complete her attack. Unfortunately, this also increases the size of Bob's input from n bits to $\max(4n, 8s)$ bits. Lindell and Pinkas' technique was later refined by shelat and Shen to give a smaller increase in the amount of input bits needed by Bob [34].

Another approach works by introducing a tighter coupling between the OTs and the rest of the protocol. Lindell and Pinkas [28] introduced the *single-choice batch cut-and-choose oblivious transfer* based on Diffe-Hellman pseudo-random synthesizers, which were used to "glue" together the OTs and the garbled circuits. The pseudo-random synthesizers were also used to ensure consistency of the parties' inputs to the different garbled circuits.

In our solution we handle the selective failure problem in the same manner as in [26]. The approach involves increasing the amount of input bits of the evaluator from a string y of n bits to a string $\bar{y}$ of $\bar{n} = \max(4n, 8s)$ bits. More specifically, what we do is to have Bob choose a random binary matrix $M^{\mathsf{Sec}} \in_R \{0,1\}^{\bar{n}} \times \{0,1\}^n$ and his input randomly, i.e., $\bar{y} \in_R \{0,1\}^{\bar{n}}$, but under the constraint that $M^{\mathsf{Sec}} \cdot \bar{y} = y$ where y is his "true" input. Thus the augmented functionality computes exactly the same as the original. Still, the idea is that if a selective failure attack is done, using the augmented function will not leak any useful information: as the entire vector $\bar{y}$ is random, learning a few bits of $\bar{y}$ will only give the adversary a negligible advantage in learning one of the constructor's true input bits. This follows from the fact that the other bits of $\bar{y}$ will be used to hide each of the actual bits of y. The details and a full proof of security of this approach can be found in [26].

Ensuring Consistency of Bob's Input. Making just multiple calls to a basic protocol for OT, Bob could input different choice bits for each of the circuits, which would allow him to evaluate the function on different inputs. That is, he would learn both $f(x,y)$ and $f(x,y')$ for two different inputs y and y' of his own choice, which obviously leaks too much information to Bob.

To avoid this we must make sure that for each of the bits y_i in Bob's input, he gives the same choice bit for all of the garbled circuits in the OTs. This can easily be achieved by doing fewer OTs, but of longer bit strings: For each OT Alice inputs a concatenation of the 0-, respectively 1-keys for a given input wire for all circuits, Bob inputs only one choice bit and receives the keys for all the circuits corresponding to his choice bit on that given input wire. This approach is used in most previous results [11, 25, 26, 28, 34, 35].

In the ROM this can be very efficiently realized using black box access to a one-out-of-two OT of strings of length s [11, 34].

Ensuring Consistency of Alice's Input. To see why there is also a problem if Alice is inconsistent in her inputs, assume the functionality to be computed is the inner product, that Alice inputs the strings $\langle 100 \ldots 0 \rangle$, $\langle 010 \ldots 0 \rangle, \ldots, \langle 000 \ldots 1 \rangle$ and that she is the party who is supposed to learn the output of the computation. In this case what she will learn is the majority of bits in Bob's input string, which is clearly too much information.

To ensure consistency of Alice's input Lindell and Pinkas [26] embedded a consistency check of Alice's input into the cut-and-choose step itself, resulting in $O(ms^2)$ commitments. Shelat and Shen [35] ensures input consistency using another approach based on claw-free functions.

We follow a different approach, introduced independently by Frederiksen and Nielsen [11] and shelat and Shen [34]. The idea is to augment the functionality computed by the garbled circuits such that Alice's input, apart from being used in the original computation of f, is also fed into a universal hash function decided by Bob. The output of both the original functionality f and the hash digest of Alice's input is then learned by Bob. We can now safely let Bob abort if any of these digests diverge without leaking anything to Alice about his input. Intuitively, this approach is secure if the output of the augmented functionality does not leak information about Alice's input and Alice cannot find two inputs whose digests collide. We achieve the first property by having Alice give some auxiliary random input, which one-time pads the output of the hash function. The second property will follow directly from the nature of a universal hash function if Alice is committed to her input choices before potentially learning the specific hash function used.

A specific, but simple way to construct such an augmentation is as follows [11]: Assume the functionality we wish to compute is defined by f as $f(x, y) = z$. We then define a new function f' as $f'(x', y') = f'(x\|a, y\|b) = z\|c$ where $a \in_R \{0, 1\}^s$, $b \in_R \{0, 1\}^{m+s-1}$ and $c \in \{0, 1\}^s$. To compute c we define a matrix $M^{\mathsf{ln}} \in \{0, 1\}^s \times \{0, 1\}^{|x|}$ where the i'th row is the first $m = |x|$ bits of $b << i$ where $<<$ denotes the bitwise left shift. Specifically the j'th bit of the i'th row is the $i + j$'th bit of the binary vector b, i.e., $M^{\mathsf{ln}}_{i,j} = b_{i+j-1}$. The computation of c is then defined as $c = (M^{\mathsf{ln}} \cdot x) \oplus a$, assuming all binary vectors are in column form. Now see that f computes the same function as f', but requires s extra random bits of input from Alice and $m + s - 1$ extra random bits from Bob. The s extra output bits will work as digest bits (since $(M^{\mathsf{ln}} \cdot x) \oplus a$ is actually a universal hash function) and can be used to check that Alice is consistent with her inputs to the circuits, by verifying that they are the same in all the garbled circuits which Bob evaluates.

Next, [34] observed that it is in fact not needed to have Bob specify the specific hash function as part of his input. Instead he can send Alice the vector b defining the matrix M^{ln} and have her garble the circuits to compute the hash function this vector specifies. Evaluation of the garbled universal hash function can now be done using only xor operations, which we can do for "free" with the free-xor approach. Thus the binary string $b \in \{0, 1\}^{m+s-1}$ defines a family of universal hash functions mapping m bits to s bits. In turn, a sampling of such a function is simply a random choice of the string

b. We will call a specific function from this family for $\mathbb{H}^{\mathsf{ln}}$ and call the actual circuit augmentation for $\mathbb{H}^{\mathsf{ln}} \oplus a$ where a will be Alice's auxiliary input sampled from $\{0, 1\}^s$.

A remaining problem with the construction is that Alice can now try to find a collision for the hash function before she gives her input keys to Bob. This is a significant problem as collisions for universal hash functions can be easy to find. However, if we let Alice commit to her input and *then* let Bob reveal his choice of hash function to her then she will only have negligible probability in the size of the digest of finding a collision.

It should be noted that in [34] another universal hash function was used, which required $2s + \log(s)$ auxiliary random bits of input from Alice, unlike only s in [11]. However, the authors of [11] did not observe that it was enough to send M^{ln} in plain, nor did they actually *prove* their construction secure. In the full version of this paper [9] we prove that the universal hash function used in [11] is secure in our setting when M^{ln} is sent in plain after Alice commits to her inputs.

We follow the approach of circuit augmentation outlined above. Concretely we implement the consistency check by having Alice commit to her input before the cut-and-choose phase. Then we have Bob give her the specification of the hash function. Alice then garbles the circuit with the hash function augmentation. When Bob later has evaluated the evaluation circuits, he aborts if the hash values from any two of the augmentations of these circuits differ.

Computing the Correct Output. Despite the input consistency of Alice being enforced as discussed above, Bob may still end up with more than one distinct output when he evaluates the evaluation circuits. This is due to the fact that the cut-and-choose technique does not ensure that all the remaining evaluation circuits are good. With non-negligible probability some of them may not evaluate at all and some may evaluate, but result in diverging output.

Given several different outputs, Bob cannot just abort the computation or choose a random result without becoming vulnerable to a selective failure attack. However, Lindell and Pinkas [26] showed that for a statistical security parameter s, if the number of garbled circuits, i.e., the replication factor, is greater than cs for some constant c and if half are chosen as check circuits, then, except with negligible probability, the majority of the outputs are well-defined and are in fact the correct output.

For realistic circuit sizes, the replication factor has proven to be very important for the performance of the overall protocol [11, 24, 33]. Thus recent effort has been made to reduce the replication factor. As a start, [33] claimed that [26] only requires a replication factor $\ell \geq 4s$ (to achieve failure probability at most 2^{-s}). The analysis was later improved by [28] showing that one only needed a replication factor $\ell \geq 3.22s$. Finally, [35] refined the analysis further by showing that taking 60% of the circuits to be check circuits, a replication factor $\ell \geq 3.13s$ is sufficient.

All of these results are based on taking the majority of the outputs from the evaluation circuits. As mentioned in the introduction, recently Brandão [3] and Lindell [25] independently showed how to avoid taking majority by instead enabling Bob to learn Alice's private input if the results diverge, and thereby letting Bob compute the correct result in "clear". Doing so allows for a replication factor of only s to achieve an error probability of 2^{-s}, which is a considerable improvement. Independently Huang *et al.* [16] showed the same, but with a slightly higher replication factor. In particular, doing the protocol with a replication factor ℓ gives an error probability of at most $2^{-\ell+O(\log \ell)}$. For comparison, note that for a typical application with $s = 40$, [28] and [35] need 129 and 125 circuits respectively, while [3, 25] requires only 40 circuits to be garbled.

Our protocol is based on the same idea as [3, 25] and our main theoretical contribution arrives in the way we allow Bob to find the correct output based on the evaluation of the garbled circuits. We do so without using an extra secure computation as in [25] or computationally heavy trapdoor commitments as in [3], furthermore, we do not strictly require any specific computational assumption. [4]

Let $t = \ell/2$, that is, t is the amount of check circuits. Also, let $k_{i,j}'^0$ and $k_{i,j}'^1$ be the zero and one keys for the i'th output wire on the j'th circuit. We use the free-xor technique [23] and let Alice garble each circuit with a different Δ. That is, for circuit j and all wires k Alice chooses the wire keys such that $k_{k,j}^0 \oplus k_{k,j}^1 = \Delta_j$.

We select the replication factor ℓ such that, except with probability 2^{-s}, if Alice was not caught cheating during the cut-and-choose phase, *at least one* of the evaluation circuits that remain is correct. Our strategy is then to make sure that for each pair of garbled circuit evaluations whose semantic output differ, Bob will be able to efficiently compute the Δ values for one of those circuits. Knowing the Δ value used to garble a circuit allows Bob to learn the input x that Alice submitted for that circuit.

Using Polynomials to Compute Δ's. We now explain how we let Bob compute Δs for those circuits whose outputs diverge.

As part of the garbling phase, Alice associates a polynomial of degree at most t, P_i with each output wire in the circuit, where $t = \ell/2$. Now for each garbled circuit $j \in [\ell]$ and each output wire $i \in [o]$ Alice associates a point on the corresponding polynomial, i.e., a value $P_i(j)$. Thus we have a polynomial associated with each output wire and for each of these polynomials we have a point associated with each garbled circuit. Next, for the 0-key on each output wire in each circuit $\left\{ \left\{ k_{i,j}'^0 \right\}_{i=1}^o \right\}_{j=1}^\ell$ and point $P_i(j)$ we associate the "link" $L_{i,j}$ (see the full version [9] for details). For simplicity assume that the link is realized as follows $L_{i,j} = (r_{i,j}, s_{i,j}, h_{i,j}, g_{i,j})$ where $r_{i,j}, s_{i,j} \in_R \{0,1\}^\kappa$ are uniformly random sampled elements, $h_{i,j} = \mathrm{H}\left(P_i(j), r_{i,j}\right) \oplus k_{i,j}'^0$ and $g_{i,j} = \mathrm{H}\left(k_{i,j}'^0, s_{i,j}\right) \oplus P_i(j)$. Alice sends all these links to Bob.

Next notice, that after the cut-and-choose step, Bob will learn all the 0-keys on the output wires for t garbled circuits and in turn be able to learn t points on all the polynomials (by using the output 0-keys, $k_{i,j}'^0$ along with the corresponding links $L_{i,j}$). Thus by learning just one more 0-key for a given output wire, Bob will be able to learn one more point on one of the polynomials. This will give him a total of $t + 1$ points on a polynomial of degree at most t and he will thus be able to do polynomial interpolation and learn all the points on that polynomial. Knowing all the points on a given polynomial will make it possible for Bob to

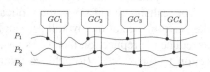

Fig. 1. Four garbled circuits with three output wires. Each 0-key on these output wires is linked to a particular point on a polynomial of degree at most 2.

---

[4] We do require access to OT, but any one-out-of-two OT can be used, including OT extensions.

learn the 0-key on a given output wire in *all* the garbled circuits (by using the points, $P_i(j)$ along with the links $L_{i,j}$).

A bit more specifically, suppose that Bob ends up with two garbled circuits where there is an output wire that outputs the 0-key in one of the circuits and the 1-key in the other. Say, w.l.o.g. that this is the case for output wire 1 in circuit 1 and circuit 2, such that Bob learns both $k_{1,1}'^0$ and $k_{1,2}'^1 = k_{1,2}'^0 \oplus \Delta_2$. Using the link $L_{1,1} = (r_{1,1}, s_{1,1}, h_{1,1}, g_{1,1})$ Bob can compute the point $P_1(1)$ as $P_1(1) = g_{1,1} \oplus H\left(k_{1,1}'^0, s_{1,1}\right)$. This gives him a total of $t + 1$ points on the polynomial P_1 (remember that he already knew t points from the check part of the cut-and-choose phase). Using these points he can then do polynomial interpolation, which in turn will make it possible for him to easily compute the point $P_1(2)$. Finally, he can then compute the following:

$$h_{1,2} \oplus H\left(P_1(2), r_{1,2}\right) \oplus k_{1,2}'^1 = k_{1,2}'^0 \oplus k_{1,2}'^1 = \Delta_2 \,.$$

Using Δ_2 he can completely degarble the second garbled circuit, and in turn, also learn Alice's plain input to circuit 2. This is so, as knowing the Δ value and one key for all wires allows to compute both keys for all wires and thus completely open up a garbled circuit.

The approach of using the links to learn the Δ values generalizes to each output wire in two circuits where one is the 0-key and other the 1-key. Thus, assuming we have enough output wires with different values it is possible to find Δ for all garbled circuits, and in turn Alice's plain input to all garbled circuits.

We want to emphasize, however, that Bob does not use the Δ values to completely open up any garbled circuit, as this would be too expensive (it would essentially count as an extra garbling towards the computational complexity). Instead Bob only opens up the input layer to learn the semantic value of the input keys of Alice to the circuit. He then evaluates the universal hash function on Alice's input in plain and compare it with the semantic meaning of the garbled evaluation of the universal hash function. Then Bob discards the circuits where the plain and semantic meaning of the output of the universal hash function is discrepant, which cannot lead to selective errors, as the correctness of the augmented part of the circuit is known by Alice already. Now, for all the remaining circuits, the inputs of Alice are the same, except with a small probability 2^{-s} that a collision for the universal hash function occurred. This is so, as the circuits computed the hash function correctly, and the hash function was chosen by Bob after Alice committed to her inputs. Hence Bob can safely abort if there are different inputs left and otherwise just evaluate f in plain on his own input and the unique input of Alice.

Ensuring Consistency of Polynomials. We made a few assumptions in the strategy described above. That is, it only works if the polynomials are consistent, that is, if they are at most degree t *and* we have enough output wires that diverge in value to make sure Bob can learn the Δ values for each of the evaluation circuits. Since Alice might be malicious, and thus can deviate from the prescribed protocol in an arbitrary manner, we cannot be sure that she constructs the polynomials of degree at most t. In particular she might construct these to be degree $2t$ and thus make it impossible for Bob to use polynomial interpolation to find the Δ values. We could use techniques like Kate *et al.* [21] to ensure consistency of the polynomials, but this would be inefficient and impose certain number theoretic assumptions. We instead introduce an additional cut-and-choose phase in which Alice prepares more polynomials than actually needed, and then Bob randomly chooses half of the polynomials as *check* polynomials, which Alice then reveals and Bob verifies to have degree at most t. We say that a polynomial of degree greater than t is *inconsistent* and if it has degree at most t we say it is *consistent*. Thus for Bob to accept the check polynomials they must all be consistent. If all the check polynomials are consistent then a large quantity of the remaining polynomials are guaranteed to be consistent. In fact, we select half of the polynomials as check polynomials, and therefore get that a majority of the remaining circuits are guaranteed to be correct except with negligible probability in the amount of challenge polynomials, for the same reasons as in the analysis of circuit cut-and-choose in [26].

Ensuring consistency of the polynomials with cut-and-choose is efficient and does not rely on any specific number theoretic assumptions. However, it leaves us with the issue that some of the polynomials that are not checked might still be inconsistent and thus not usable for interpolation in our context, along with the problem that we still need enough output wires which diverge in value to make sure Bob can learn the Δ values for each of the evaluation circuits.

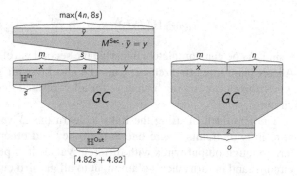

Fig. 2. Illustration comparing the original circuit (right) and the augmented circuit (left). Inputs and output are shown in light grey, whereas actual computation is shown with a darker grey.

To cope with these problems we introduce another circuit augmentation, which is a universal hash function, taking the output of the original computation as input. We then let the the wire keys used in the links be the wire keys of the output of this new universal hash function instead of the wire keys of the actual output of the garbled circuit. Intuitively, if there is any divergence on one bit in the original output then the digests of the universal hash function will diverge in many bits. Thus the hash function ensures that we have enough output wires which will differ in their keys, since the output of the hash function is uniformly distributed. Thus, if a garbled circuit is maliciously constructed then the hashed value of the malicious output will differ in many bits compared with the hashed value of the correct output. This ensures, except with negligible probability in the amount of output bits of the augmentation, that we will have enough output wires with different keys to learn Δ for all the evaluation circuits. In the full version [9] we prove that with only a majority of the polynomials guaranteed to be consistent, a hash function with at least $\lceil 4.82s + 4.82 \rceil$ output bits is sufficient in order to guarantee, except with probability 2^{-s}, that Bob will be able to learn all the Δ values of the evaluation circuits if he ends up with two or more evaluation circuits where at least one output wire diverge.

The augmentation on the output wires is done in almost the same efficient way as the augmentation to ensure input consistency of Alice. That is, we exploit the free-xor technique and let Bob send the specification of the hash function to Alice in clear. Specifically, let z be the binary output of the computation. Then we have Bob choose two random binary strings $b^{Out1} \in_R \{0,1\}^{\lceil o+4.82s+3.82 \rceil}$ and $b^{Out2} \in_R \{0,1\}^{\lceil 4.82s+4.82 \rceil}$. Using the first string we define a $\lceil 4.82s + 4.82 \rceil \times o$ binary matrix M^{Out} such that the j'th bit of the i'th row is the $i + j - 1$'th bit of b^{Out1}. That is, $M_{i,j}^{Out} = b_{i+j-1}^{Out1}$. The augmentation should then compute $\left(M^{Out} \cdot z \right) \oplus b^{Out2}$ assuming z is a binary vector in column form. Thus the binary strings $b^{Out1} \in \{0,1\}^{\lceil o+4.82s+4.82 \rceil}$ and $b^{Out2} \in \{0,1\}^{\lceil 4.82s+4.82 \rceil}$ defines a family of universal hash functions mapping o bits to $\lceil 4.82s+ 4.82 \rceil$ bits. In turn a sampling of such a function is simply a random choice of the strings b^{Out1} and b^{Out2}. We will call a specific function from this family for $\mathbb{H}^{Out}$.

An illustration of the final circuit with both augmentations is given in Fig. 2 and an informal version of the protocol itself is given in Section 3.

3   The Protocol

Assume we have access to a free-xor garbling scheme, an OT functionality, a coin-tossing functionality along with a commitment scheme supporting both computationally hiding/binding commitments and commitments where the opening to a commitment is *exactly* the message committed to. We call the last type of commitment scheme a *verifiable commitment* scheme as it allows a party to verify if a particular message is the opening of a particular commitment.

We let Alice garble ℓ versions of a Boolean circuit C using the free-xor technique [23], we call these garbled circuits $\tilde{C}_j$ where $j \in [\ell]$. For each of these garbled circuits we associate a distinct global value $\Delta_j \in \{0,1\}^\kappa$, which is used to enforce the constraint that for any wire, i, in the garbled circuit $\tilde{C}_j$, we have that $k_{i,j}^1 = k_{i,j}^0 \oplus \Delta_j$ in correspondence with a free-xor garbling scheme.

At an informal level our protocol can then be summarized with the phases *Setup, Polynomial Setup, Oblivious Transfer, Garbling, Commitment, Augmentation, Cut-and-Choose, Evaluation,* and *Reconstruction.* Of these, *Setup, Oblivious Transfer, Garbling,* and *Commitment,* are very similar to other protocol based on cut-and-choose of Yao garbled circuit, e.g., [11,26,28,34,35]. In Fig. 3 and 4 we sketch what happens in each of these steps and leave the specific details along with the proof of security against a static, malicious, computationally bounded adversary to the full version [9].

4   Implementation

As our protocol is designed to work well in the SIMD model we did our implementation in CUDA, which is a platform that supports both explicit programming of SIMD execution, along with cheap hardware, GPUs, which supports SIMD execution. More specifically we implemented our protocol in ANSI C using the CUDA extension by NVIDIA. Some parts of our implementation is based on the code from [11] which gave very efficient construction and evaluation of garbled circuits (including handling of the

1. *Setup*
   (a) Assume the function to compute is $f(x, y) = z$ where Alice inputs $x \in \{0,1\}^m$, Bob inputs $y \in \{0,1\}^n$ and Bob learns the results $z \in \{0,1\}^o$.
   (b) Bob then samples a random binary matrix $M^{Sec} \in_R \{0,1\}^{\bar{n}} \times \{0,1\}^n$ and a random input $\bar{y}$ of $\bar{n} = \max(4n, 8s)$ bits such that $M^{Sec} \cdot \bar{y} = y$. He sends M^{Sec} to Alice and they both agree on a function, f' with M^{Sec} embedded such that $f'(x, \bar{y}) = f(x, y)$. Denote the Boolean circuit computing f by C.
2. *Polynomial Setup*
   (a) Alice choses $p = 6s + 7$ random polynomials, P_i for $i \in [p]$, of degree $\leq t = \ell/2$, over a finite field with 2^κ elements.
   (b) Next Alice computes ℓ points on each of the polynomials, achieving a total of $\ell \cdot (6s + 7)$ points. Alice commits to each point j on each polynomial i using a verifiable commitment scheme and sends these commitments to Bob.
   (c) Alice and Bob complete a cut-and-choose procedure on the random polynomials to select $\lfloor 1.18s + 2.18 \rfloor$ of these for *checking* and $\lceil 4.82s + 4.82 \rceil$ for *evaluation*. For each of the check polynomials Alice sends the openings to the points committed to in the previous step. Bob then uses the points to interpolate the polynomials and verifies that they are in fact all polynomials of degree at most t. If not, he aborts.
3. *Oblivious Transfer* Alice chooses ℓ global differences for the garbling, we call these $\Delta_1, \Delta_2, ..., \Delta_\ell$. Using these values she constructs random keys for each of Bob's $\bar{n}$ input bits in correspondence with the free-xor garbling scheme for ℓ distinct garbled circuits. Alice and Bob then engage in batch OT such that Bob learns the ℓ keys in correspondence to each of his input bits y.
4. *Garbling* Alice produces ℓ garbled versions $\tilde{C}_j$ of the circuit C using the global differences and keys constructed in the previous step in the free-xor manner and sends these circuits to Bob.
5. *Commitment* Alice commits to her own choice of input keys. She also makes verifiable commitments to the concatenation of the 0- and 1-keys on each input wire in each of the garbled circuits.
6. *Augmentation*
   (a) Bob randomly samples a universal hash function $\mathbb{H}^{In}$ from a family of universal hash functions mapping $|x| = m$ bits to s bits and a universal hash function $\mathbb{H}^{Out}$ mapping $|z| = o$ bits to $\lceil 4.82s + 4.82 \rceil$ bits from another family of hash functions as described in the previous section.
   (b) Bob sends a description of these hash functions to Alice who augments all of the garbled circuits with $\mathbb{H}^{In} \oplus a$ and $\mathbb{H}^{Out}$ using only xor operations of respectively her input keys and the output keys of the garbled circuits.
   (c) Alice then sends Bob the output decryption tables of the augmentations $\mathbb{H}^{In} \oplus a$ and $\mathbb{H}^{Out}$. Alice also sends a "link" of each of the output keys of $\mathbb{H}^{Out}$ to the corresponding polynomial points. That is, for each output wire i of $\mathbb{H}^{Out}$ in each garbled circuit j she sends to Bob the link $L_{i,j}$.

Fig. 3. Protocol Overview - Part 1

possible selective failure attack on Bob's input), along with an "OT extension", using a consumer GPU. We direct the reader to [11] for details on these aspects of the implementation.

1. *Cut-and-Choose* Alice and Bob uses a coin-tossing protocol to agree on a random subset $\mathcal{C}$ of size $t = \ell/2$ of the garbled circuits, called the *check circuits*. Alice then sends both the 0- and 1-key for each input wire in the set of check circuits. Bob then verifies the keys against the commitments to the input keys and then verifies that the check circuits were correctly constructed. Using the output keys of $\mathbb{H}^{Out}$, along with the "links" from the augmentation phase, Bob computes the t points on each of the $\lceil 4.82s + 4.82 \rceil$ polynomials remaining from the set-up phase.

2. *Evaluation* Alice opens the input keys in correspondence with her input x for all the evaluation circuits to Bob. Bob then evaluates $\mathbb{H}^{In} \oplus a$. If the semantic value of any of the evaluations of $\mathbb{H}^{In} \oplus a$ are divergent, or if the output decryption table is incorrectly constructed, he aborts. Otherwise he evaluates the garbled circuits. If any of the garbled circuits fails to evaluate he discards it. If any of the semantic values on the output wires of the evaluated garbled circuits are inconsistent then he proceeds with the reconstruction phase. Otherwise he "simulates" the reconstruction phase using garbage data (to avoid timing attacks) and in the end outputs the only semantic output value he learned.

3. *Reconstruction*

   (a) Bob computes the augmented output $\mathbb{H}^{Out}$ for each of the evaluated garbled circuits. Since he now knows the semantic value on each garbled circuit's output wires, along with the specification of $\mathbb{H}^{Out}$, he can compute, in plain, the semantic values he expects to find in $\mathbb{H}^{Out}$'s output decryption table. Any augmented circuit where this is not the case he discards. From the remaining circuits he computes the points on the remaining polynomials from the *Polynomial Setup* phase using the links from the augmentation phase. He then uses the t polynomial points from the cut-and-choose phase along with the discrepant keys of an augmented output wire in two circuits to learn $t + 1$ points on a polynomial for a given wire. He then does polynomial interpolation on these points to find all the ℓ points of this wire, i.e. one for each garbled circuit. He then uses the links to find the 0-key on that wire in all of the evaluation circuits. Hence Bob can learn Δ_j for at least one garbled circuit (because the output of that wire is discrepant and thus at least one garbled circuit will have 1-key output on that wire). He continues in this manner for each discrepant output wire until he learns Δ_j for all the non-discarded evaluation circuits.

   (b) Using these Δ's along with Alice's input keys and the verifiable commitments to the keys of the input wires Bob extracts the plain values of Alice's input in all the evaluation circuits. For each input, Bob evaluates $\mathbb{H}^{In}$ on the plain input and discards the circuits where the plain output from $\mathbb{H}^{In} \oplus a$ does not match the semantic output previously computed by the garbled circuit. He then uses Alice's plain input for one of the remaining circuits and computes the function f in plain to learn the correct output. If there are no remaining circuits, Bob terminates.

Fig. 4. Protocol Overview - Part 2

It should be noted that a recent result by Husted *et al.* [18] presents another scheme for constructing and evaluation garbled circuits using the GPU. Their scheme is up to a factor 3 faster than the scheme in [11] in computation on the same hardware, but increases the size of each gate with another ciphertext (both xor and non-xor gates).

Unfortunately their result was not published until after we had completed our implementation and thus we do not know whether their scheme would be faster when used with our protocol. However, a study of this would be interesting for future work.

Trading Assumptions for Efficiency. Since the description of our protocol is given in the hybrid setting, assuming access to OTs, commitments, coin-tossing and garbling, we need to make some decisions on the security assumptions needed in order to realize the functionalities in our implementation. We have chosen to be liberal in the security assumptions in order to achieve a more efficient solution. In particular this means that our implementation assumes the existence of random oracles and SHA-1 is used to implement random oracle queries with a 160 bit output, thus we set $\kappa = 160$. We use the ROM garbling scheme of [33], which only requires 4 calls to the oracle to construct a garbled gate, and only a single call to the oracle in order to evaluate a garbled gate.

We realize a coin-tossing functionality along with a commitment scheme (that fits our needs) highly efficiently in the ROM. We also base the OTs we need on an efficient OT extension, which only assume access to $O(s)$ "seed" OTs in the ROM. See the full version [9] for details. Finally, we also implement the verification of "circuit seeds" [12] to eliminate the need of sending the garbled computation tables of the check circuits.

SIMD Implementation Optimizations. $\mathbb{H}^{\mathsf{In}}$ *and* $\mathbb{H}^{\mathsf{Out}}$. First notice that $\mathbb{H}^{\mathsf{Out}}$ is very similar to $\mathbb{H}^{\mathsf{In}} \oplus a$ and they can both be computed using only xor operations on particular keys. Furthermore, each output key of both functions can be computed independently of the other output keys, since each output key only depends on the input keys to $\mathbb{H}^{\mathsf{In}} \oplus a$, respectively $\mathbb{H}^{\mathsf{Out}}$, and the matrix M^{In}, respective M^{Out}. Thus the output of each function can clearly be done in a SIMD manner, up to the amount of outputs of $\mathbb{H}^{\mathsf{In}}$, respectively $\mathbb{H}^{\mathsf{Out}}$, i.e. s, respectively $\lceil 4.82s + 4.82 \rceil$.[5] However, the xor operation is so light that it is in general considered overkill to have a GPU thread do nothing but a few xors, because of the overhead of copying data from the RAM of the host system to the RAM of the GPU and back. Thus we simply implemented the functionalities in a sequential manner using the CPU. However, using the CPU might not always be the best case as we will discuss, based on our experiments, in Section 4.

Polynomial Representation. In the protocol description we explained that the polynomials would have points in GF (2^{160}) as they need to have the same size as the wire keys. However, we instead replace each element of GF (2^{160}) by 20 elements of GF (2^8), i.e., we use polynomials over the ring GF $(2^8)^{20}$, which is still a secure secret sharing scheme, c.f. [5]. So it is possible to implement multiplication and inversion in GF (2^8) through a lookup table instead of a quadratic time algorithm, which would otherwise be the straight forward approach for elements in GF (2^{160}).

Polynomial Construction. The $20p$ polynomials with elements from GF (2^8) are generated in a SIMD manner using the GPU based on a 160 bit seed of entropy. Specifically what we do is to have $p \times (t + 1)$ threads generate coefficients consisting of 160 bits of pseudo-randomness by hashing a seed along with a unique identifier. Using these coefficients we have $p \times 2t$ threads computing $2t$ points on each of the $20p$ polynomials.

---

[5] The computation of $\mathbb{H}^{\mathsf{In}}$ and $\mathbb{H}^{\mathsf{Out}}$ can be parallelized even further: Since xor is commutative we can use a classic reduction approach for computing each output key.

More specifically $P_i(j)$ for all $j \in [2t]$ and $i \in [20p]$. This is done by a loop of $t + 1$ iterations where an element $c_{i,j}j^d \in GF(2^8)$ is computed in the d'th iteration and then added to the result of the previous $d - 1$ iterations. Notice that the loop could also be parallelized in a SIMD manner by having a multiple of $t + 1$ more threads, each computing a single value of $c_{i,j}j^d$.

Polynomial Interpolation. Our polynomial interpolation (part of the *Polynomial Setup*) is based on Lagrange interpolation and consists of 4 subphases, *denominator, numerator, combination* and *reduction* in order to optimize the SIMD parallelization. Before we go through these phases remember that in Lagrange interpolation we assume knowledge of $t + 1$ data point pairs $\{(x_j, y_j)\}_{j=1}^{t+1}$ where all x_j are distinct. These define the interpolation polynomials in Lagrange form: $L(x) := \sum_{j=1}^{t+1} y_j l_j(x)$, where the Lagrange basis polynomials are defined as $l_j(x) := \prod_{1 \leq g \leq t+1, g \neq j} \frac{x - x_g}{x_j - x_g}$, where $1 \leq j \leq t+1$. Using $l_j(\cdot)$ an arbitrary point x can then be computed. In our case we will know $t + 1$ points from $[2t]$ and want to compute the remaining $t - 1$ points in $[2t]$.

When we verify that the $2t$ points Bob got from Alice, for each of the $\lfloor 1.18s + 2.18 \rfloor$ check polynomials, constitutes polynomials of degree at most $t + 1$, we do polynomial interpolation of the points $]t + 1; 2t]$ using the points $[1; t + 1]$ and verify that the newly interpolated points are the same as Alice sent us. Now the phases for which we interpolate these points in a SIMD manner goes as follows:

Denominator: We have $t + 1$ threads computing the denominator of each $l_j(x)$. Notice that this is enough as the choice of value of x does not come into play here, but only in the numerator. Finally, each thread computes the inverse so that each denominator can be directly multiplied onto a numerator later.

Numerator: We use $(t+1) \times (t-1)$ threads to compute the numerator of each $l_j(i)$. That is $l_j(i)$ will be computed by thread $j \cdot (t - 1) + i$ so that we compute the numerator of each of the $t + 1$ Lagrange polynomials using a different value for $i \in]t + 1; 2t]$. Finally, each thread multiply its result with the appropriate denominator from the previous step. That is, computing $l_j(i)$ for each $i \in]t + 1; 2t]$.

Combination: We use $\lfloor 1.18s + 2.18 \rfloor \times (t+1) \times (t-1)$ threads to compute each term of the $t + 1$ terms of $L(i)$ for the $20\lfloor 1.18s + 2.18 \rfloor$ polynomials for each $i \in]t + 1; 2t]$. This is simply done by having each thread multiply the appropriate values y_j for each for the $20\lfloor 1.18s + 2.18 \rfloor$ polynomials with the corresponding Lagrange basis polynomial (computed in the "Numerator" step).

Reduction: To continue with the maximal level of SIMD parallelization up to $\lfloor 1.18s + 2.18 \rfloor \times (t + 1) \times (t - 1)$ threads will complete a reduction approach, i.e. any given thread will xor together two terms of $L(i)$. A new thread will take over two of the intermediate results and xor these together. This will continue until $\lfloor 1.18s + 2.18 \rfloor \times (t - 1)$ threads remain, containing the result $L(i)$ for all $i \in]t + 1; 2t]$ and all $20\lfloor 1.18s + 2.18 \rfloor$ polynomials

All the steps are done with all generated data staying in the GPU's RAM and only at the end the final results are copied back to the host's RAM. Because all the data is on the GPU it is sensible to do the reduction step instead of a sequential computation on the host system, even though the operations done will only be xors.

Polynomial Reconstruction. The polynomial reconstruction (part of the *Reconstruction* phase) is done almost in the same manner as the polynomial interpolation. The main difference being that in the reconstruction the set of $t + 1$ points we know might be different for each of the $\lceil 4.82s + 4.82 \rceil$ sets of 20 polynomials. However, at most one of these points might be different since Bob will always learn the same t points for all the polynomials as an effect of the cut-and-choose of garbled circuits. Thus we can implement the *numerator* step in the following two substeps:

- First we use $t \times (t - 1)$ threads to compute $\prod_{1 \leq g \leq t, g \neq j} (x - x_g)$ for each point $j \in [t]$ where x_j is an index of a check circuit and for each of the $t - 1$ points, x being an index of an evaluation circuit.
- We then use $\lceil 4.82s + 4.82 \rceil \times (t + 1) \times (t - 1)$ threads to multiply the last point, which might vary from polynomial to polynomial, onto the result of the previous step. This will give us the numerator in all the $t + 1$ Lagrange basis polynomials for each of the $t - 1$ points Bob needs to learn, i.e. the $t - 1$ indices of the evaluation circuits.

The same idea applies to the computation of the *denominator* step, but with a factor $t - 1$ less, as the denominator remains the same for all possible values of x we need to learn.

    With the above approach we avoid having $\lceil 4.82s + 4.82 \rceil \times (t + 1) \times (t - 1)$ threads doing a multiplication loop of $t + 1$ iterations and instead only use $t \times (t - 1)$ threads with a loop of t iterations and $\lceil 4.82s + 4.82 \rceil \times (t + 1) \times (t - 1)$ threads with a constant amount of multiplications to achieve the same result.

A Note on Multi-threading. In order to limit the time each party is idle we employ multi-threading to the protocol in a non-SIMD manner. That is, when several distinct steps of the protocol can be carried out independently of each other we fork the host process to carry out these computations in parallel. In particular we fork when some data needs to be sent/received while other operations can be carried out with the data already known.

A Note on Parallel Complexity. The parallel complexity of cut-and-choose of garbled circuits is bounded by the depth of the circuit to compute times the garbling of a single gate along with the parallel complexity of the handling of selective failure attacks, consistency of inputs, OTs and commitments. In our case, as well as in [11], the complexity of handling selective failure attacks is bounded by $O(\log(\max(n, s)))$ as it only consists of xor'ing (because of the free-xor approach) at most $\max(4n, 8s)$ keys of κ bits with each other, $O(sn)$ times in parallel, using a reduction approach. The same argumentation goes for ensuring consistency of Alice's input, i.e. computing $\mathbb{H}^{\text{In}} \oplus a$: Using a reduction approach it is basically $O(\log(m))$ SIMD xor operations using $O(s^2 \kappa m)$ SIMD processors. Regarding handling input recovery in case of cheating, first notice that the parallel computation of $\mathbb{H}^{\text{Out}}$ is almost the same as for $\mathbb{H}^{\text{In}} \oplus a$, thus it requires $O(\log(o))$ SIMD xor operations using $O(s^2 o \kappa)$ SIMD processors.

    Considering the polynomial generation, notice that we first generate coefficients and then evaluate points based on the coefficients. Now, evaluating points can be done using a reduction approach, that is, each term of a polynomial is evaluated independently, then two terms are added together by one thread, these results are then added together two at a time, and so on until all the terms for a given point in a given polynomial has been added together. This implies that the complexity of polynomial generation is bounded by the logarithm of the degree of the polynomial, that is $O(\log(s))$ SIMD operations using $O(s^3\kappa)$ SIMD processors. Regarding polynomial interpolation, assuming we use Lagrange interpolation, the straight forward approach would be to make an evaluation of a Lagrange basis polynomial for each point we wish to interpolate. These basis polynomials will consist of $1 + s/2$ factors. Again we can compute each factor independently and combine the factors using a reduction approach. These basis polynomials will be the same for each of the polynomials we wish to interpolate, with the exception of at most one factor (depending on which augmented output wires contains 0-values for each evaluation circuits). These basis polynomials are then used to find the actual points by multiplying each of them with a known point (learned from the links) and then adding the terms together. There will be $1 + s/2$ terms and again these can be added together using a reduction approach. Thus, the interpolation complexity is also limited to $O(\log(s))$ SIMD operations using $O(s^3\kappa)$ SIMD processors.

Notice that in the above analysis we assume that addition and multiplication is constant time, which makes sense since they can be implemented through a lookup table following the implementation idea in Section 4.

Table 1. Timing in milliseconds of our protocol computing oblivious AES-128 for both Alice (A.) and Bob (B.) under different statistical security parameters (s). Column "Comp." represents wall-clock time where at least one thread does computation. Columns "IO", "Comm." and "Idle" represents wall-clock time where the protocol execution is single-threaded and does disk loading, network communication or is completely idle, respectively. Column "Total" represents the total wall-clock execution time of the entire protocol. Column "Total idle" represents the total wall-clock time when one of the parties is idle.

s		IO	Comp.	Comm.	Idle	Total	Total idle
9	A.	4.073 ± 0.036	53.19 ± 0.47	45.77 ± 0.17	81.70 ± 3.5	211.0 ± 3.6	160.1 ± 7.0
	B.	4.040 ± 0.0012	82.81 ± 0.60	45.77 ± 0.17	78.38 ± 3.5		
19	A.	4.053 ± 0.020	65.81 ± 0.89	71.97 ± 0.20	86.75 ± 4.5	260.1 ± 4.3	171.3 ± 8.7
	B.	4.039 ± 0.00097	99.49 ± 0.71	71.97 ± 0.20	84.56 ± 4.3		
30	A.	4.046 ± 0.0080	119.9 ± 0.90	108.1 ± 0.26	112.3 ± 3.8	398.1 ± 4.1	231.0 ± 7.6
	B.	4.066 ± 0.031	167.3 ± 0.70	108.1 ± 0.26	118.7 ± 3.8		
40	A.	4.055 ± 0.017	137.3 ± 0.79	132.3 ± 0.30	118.5 ± 4.1	455.7 ± 4.2	244.7 ± 8.1
	B.	4.049 ± 0.016	193.1 ± 1.0	132.3 ± 0.30	126.2 ± 4.1		
60	A.	4.043 ± 0.0069	170.1 ± 1.9	178.1 ± 0.38	130.3 ± 4.5	583.0 ± 4.3	263.7 ± 8.5
	B.	4.093 ± 0.088	266.2 ± 0.77	178.1 ± 0.38	133.4 ± 4.3		
80	A.	4.055 ± 0.017	247.1 ± 1.6	231.2 ± 0.37	168.1 ± 4.1	810.4 ± 3.5	340.2 ± 6.9
	B.	4.069 ± 0.038	398.8 ± 1.1	231.2 ± 0.37	172.0 ± 3.0		
119	A.	4.055 ± 0.020	377.9 ± 2.9	343.8 ± 0.37	215.1 ± 6.9	1220 ± 5.2	431.0 ± 12
	B.	4.040 ± 0.0026	641.5 ± 1.1	343.8 ± 0.37	215.9 ± 5.3		

Experimental Results. All of our experiments are based on the same, commonly used, circuit for oblivious 128 bit AES encryption.[6] This circuit is used as benchmark in [11, 14, 15, 28, 31], and many more implementations of 2PC for functions expressed as

---

[6] We thank Benny Pinkas, Thomas Schneider, Nigel P. Smart and Stephen C. Williams for supplying the circuit.

a Boolean circuit. We ran experiments on the circuit with several different statistical security parameters on two consumer grade desktop computers connected to Aarhus University's gigabit local area network. At the time of purchase (2012) each of these machines had a price of less than $1600. Both machines have similar specifications: an Intel Ivy Bridge i7 3.5 GHz quad-core processor, 8 GB DDR3 RAM, an Intel series-520 180 GB SSD drive, a MSI Z77 motherboard with gigabit LAN and a MSI GPU with an NVIDIA GTX 670 chip and 2 GB GDDR5 RAM. The machines ran up-to-date versions of Linux Mint 14 and CUDA 5.5. Each of the experiments was repeated 50 times and with no front end applications running on either of the machines. The timings are summarized in Table 1 and Table 2. These timings include loading circuit description and randomness along with communication between the host and device and communication between the parties. However, in the same manner as done in [31] and [11] the timings of the seed OTs have not been included as it is a computation that is needed once between two parties and thus will get amortized out in a practical context. The time it takes to initialize the GPU device (driver related overhead) has not counted either, and generally would constitute between 50 and 60 milliseconds on our test systems when the GPU is set to "persistence mode".

The timings are in milliseconds and represent "wall-clock" times. However, since some aspects of the execution are multi-threaded we have chosen to count those parts as computation time, even though one thread might not be doing computation, but rather be idle or doing communication. Thus what is counted in the communication, respectively idle columns, is the time where the party is only doing communication, respectively is completely idle.

Data Analysis. From Table 1 we see that idle time takes up a significant portion of the total execution time of the protocol, i.e. between 18% and 44% for each party and up

Table 2. Timing in miliseconds of the parts of our protocol responsible for cheating recovery. The timings are taken from the computation of oblivious AES-128 for both Alice (A.) and Bob (B.) under different statistical security parameters (s). Column "Comp." represents wall-clock time where at least one thread of a given party does computation. Columns "IO", "Comm." and "Idle" represents wall-clock time where the protocol execution is single-threaded and does disk loading, network communication or is completely idle, respectively. Column "Party total" represents the total wall-clock time of protocol execution.

s		Comp.	Comm.	Idle	Party total
9	A.	4.836 ± 0.17	1.592 ± 0.046	< 1	6.467 ± 0.17
	B.	14.04 ± 0.43	1.592 ± 0.046	4.808 ± 2.4	20.44 ± 2.5
19	A.	7.373 ± 0.93	3.885 ± 0.066	< 1	11.28 ± 0.94
	B.	20.10 ± 0.52	3.885 ± 0.066	10.49 ± 3.9	34.47 ± 3.9
30	A.	33.24 ± 1.4	8.244 ± 0.079	< 1	41.86 ± 1.4
	B.	34.56 ± 0.78	8.244 ± 0.079	12.53 ± 2.5	55.34 ± 2.7
40	A.	42.60 ± 0.46	12.64 ± 0.079	< 1	55.34 ± 0.44
	B.	51.63 ± 1.1	12.64 ± 0.079	18.40 ± 2.9	82.67 ± 3.1
60	A.	47.35 ± 0.62	24.38 ± 0.11	< 1	71.94 ± 0.58
	B.	116.1 ± 0.83	24.38 ± 0.11	23.67 ± 2.5	164.2 ± 2.7
80	A.	66.48 ± 0.40	40.91 ± 0.089	< 1	107.4 ± 0.37
	B.	185.4 ± 2.7	40.91 ± 0.089	39.13 ± 0.28	265.4 ± 2.7
119	A.	102.4 ± 0.59	84.71 ± 0.11	< 1	187.6 ± 0.51
	B.	315.1 ± 1.8	84.71 ± 0.11	71.28 ± 0.22	471.1 ± 1.7

Table 3. Timing comparison of secure two party computation protocols evaluating oblivious 128-bit AES. d is the depth of the circuit to be computed. Notice that our implementation is run on the same hardware and using the same garbling scheme as [11].

	Security	s	Model	Rounds	Time (s)	Equipment
[15]	Semi honest	-	ROM	$O(1)$	0.20	Desktop
This work	Malicious	2^{-9}	ROM	$O(1)$	0.21	Desktop w. GPU
This work	Malicious	2^{-40}	ROM	$O(1)$	0.46	Desktop w. GPU
[11]	Malicious	2^{-39}	ROM	$O(1)$	1.1	Desktop w. GPU
This work	Malicious	2^{-60}	ROM	$O(1)$	0.58	Desktop w. GPU
This work	Malicious	2^{-80}	ROM	$O(1)$	0.81	Desktop w. GPU
[31]	Malicious	2^{-58}	ROM	$O(d)$	1.6	Desktop
[24]	Malicious	2^{-80}	SM	$O(1)$	1.4	Cluster, 512 nodes
[11]	Malicious	2^{-79}	ROM	$O(1)$	2.6	Desktop w. GPU
[34]	Malicious	2^{-80}	SM	$O(1)$	40.6	Cluster, 8 nodes

to 76% of the wall-clock time one party sits idle. Taking Table 2 into account, we see that at most 30% of the overhead of recovery is idle time. The reason is probably that most messages that needs to be sent, as part of our approach to input recovery, can be batched together with messages that needs to be sent as part of the generic structure of cut-and-choose of garbled circuits.

It should be noted that we have spent quite a bit of time trying to limit the idle time of the implementation by using multi-threading, batching messages and restructuring steps within a given party's execution. Unfortunately, it remains unknown how much this has limited idle time compared to other implementations of cut-and-choose of garbled circuits, as other authors with comparable protocols have not included measurements of idle time.

Comparing the total times of Table 1 and Table 2 we see that input recovery constitutes from 10% up to 39% for of the execution time for Bob, whereas for Alice it goes from 3.5% up to 20%. Looking further into the different steps of input recovery it turns out that around half of the computation time Bob spends on *Reconstruction* is actually spent doing the "free" computation of the output keys of $\mathbb{H}^{Out}$ (since it is all xor operations on keys and we use free-xor). He spend even more time on "free" computations before we optimized the *Reconstruction* part of our implementation to limit the amount of cache-misses.

Acknowledgement. The authors would like to thank Rasmus Lauritsen for useful discussions.

References

1. Bendlin, R., Damgård, I., Orlandi, C., Zakarias, S.: Semi-homomorphic encryption and multiparty computation. In: Paterson, K.G. (ed.) EUROCRYPT 2011. LNCS, vol. 6632, pp. 169–188. Springer, Heidelberg (2011)

2. Bogetoft, P., Christensen, D.L., Damgård, I., Geisler, M., Jakobsen, T., Krøigaard, M., Nielsen, J.D., Nielsen, J.B., Nielsen, K., Pagter, J., Schwartzbach, M., Toft, T.: Secure multiparty computation goes live. In: Dingledine, R., Golle, P. (eds.) FC 2009. LNCS, vol. 5628, pp. 325–343. Springer, Heidelberg (2009)

3. Brandão, L.T.A.N.: Secure two-party computation with reusable bit-commitments, via a cut-and-choose with forge-and-lose technique - (extended abstract). In: Sako, K., Sarkar, P. (eds.) ASIACRYPT 2013, Part II. LNCS, vol. 8270, pp. 441–463. Springer, Heidelberg (2013)

4. Canetti, R.: Universally composable security: A new paradigm for cryptographic protocols. In: FOCS, pp. 136–145. IEEE Computer Society (2001)

5. Cramer, R., Fehr, S., Ishai, Y., Kushilevitz, E.: Efficient multi-party computation over rings. In: Biham, E. (ed.) EUROCRYPT 2003. LNCS, vol. 2656, pp. 596–613. Springer, Heidelberg (2003)

6. Damgård, I., Keller, M., Larraia, E., Pastro, V., Scholl, P., Smart, N.P.: Practical covertly secure MPC for dishonest majority – or: Breaking the SPDZ limits. In: Crampton, J., Jajodia, S., Mayes, K. (eds.) ESORICS 2013. LNCS, vol. 8134, pp. 1–18. Springer, Heidelberg (2013)

7. Damgård, I., Pastro, V., Smart, N., Zakarias, S.: Multiparty computation from somewhat homomorphic encryption. In: Safavi-Naini, R., Canetti, R. (eds.) CRYPTO 2012. LNCS, vol. 7417, pp. 643–662. Springer, Heidelberg (2012)

8. Damgård, I., Zakarias, S.: Constant-overhead secure computation of boolean circuits using preprocessing. In: Sahai, A. (ed.) TCC 2013. LNCS, vol. 7785, pp. 621–641. Springer, Heidelberg (2013)

9. Frederiksen, T.K., Jakobsen, T.P., Nielsen, J.B.: Faster maliciously secure two-party computation using the GPU. IACR Cryptology ePrint Archive, 2014:270 (2014)

10. Frederiksen, T.K., Jakobsen, T.P., Nielsen, J.B., Nordholt, P.S., Orlandi, C.: Minilego: Efficient secure two-party computation from general assumptions. In: Johansson, T., Nguyen, P.Q. (eds.) EUROCRYPT 2013. LNCS, vol. 7881, pp. 537–556. Springer, Heidelberg (2013)

11. Frederiksen, T.K., Nielsen, J.B.: Fast and maliciously secure two-party computation using the GPU. IACR Cryptology ePrint Archive, 2013:46 (2013)

12. Goyal, V., Mohassel, P., Smith, A.: Efficient two party and multi party computation against covert adversaries. In: Smart, N.P. (ed.) EUROCRYPT 2008. LNCS, vol. 4965, pp. 289–306. Springer, Heidelberg (2008)

13. Hazay, C., Lindell, Y.: Efficient Secure Two-party Protocols: Techniques and Constructions. Information security and cryptography. Springer, Heidelberg (2010)

14. Henecka, W., Kögl, S., Sadeghi, A.-R., Schneider, T., Wehrenberg, I.: TASTY: Tool for automating secure two-party computations. In: Al-Shaer, E., Keromytis, A.D., Shmatikov, V. (eds.) ACM Conference on Computer and Communications Security, pp. 451–462. ACM (2010)

15. Huang, Y., Evans, D., Katz, J., Malka, L.: Faster secure two-party computation using garbled circuits. In: USENIX Security Symposium. USENIX Association (2011)

16. Huang, Y., Katz, J., Evans, D.: Efficient secure two-party computation using symmetric cut-and-choose. IACR Cryptology ePrint Archive, 2013:81 (2013)

17. Huang, Y., Katz, J., Evans, D.: Quid-pro-quo-tocols: Strengthening semi-honest protocols with dual execution. In: IEEE Symposium on Security and Privacy, pp. 272–284. IEEE Computer Society (2012)

18. Husted, N., Myers, S., Shelat, A., Grubbs, P.: GPU and CPU parallelization of honest-but-curious secure two-party computation. In: Payne Jr., C.N. (ed.) ACSAC, pp. 169–178. ACM (2013)

19. Ishai, Y., Kushilevitz, E., Ostrovsky, R., Sahai, A.: Zero-knowledge from secure multiparty computation. In: Johnson, D.S., Feige, U. (eds.) STOC, pp. 21–30. ACM (2007)

20. Ishai, Y., Prabhakaran, M., Sahai, A.: Founding cryptography on oblivious transfer – efficiently. In: Wagner, D. (ed.) CRYPTO 2008. LNCS, vol. 5157, pp. 572–591. Springer, Heidelberg (2008)

21. Kate, A., Zaverucha, G.M., Goldberg, I.: Constant-size commitments to polynomials and their applications. In: Abe, M. (ed.) ASIACRYPT 2010. LNCS, vol. 6477, pp. 177–194. Springer, Heidelberg (2010)

22. Kiraz, M.S., Schoenmakers, B.: A protocol issue for the malicious case of Yao's garbled circuit construction. In: Proceedings of 27th Symposium on Information Theory in the Benelux, pp. 283–290 (2006)

23. Kolesnikov, V., Schneider, T.: Improved garbled circuit: Free XOR gates and applications. In: Aceto, L., Damgård, I., Goldberg, L.A., Halldórsson, M.M., Ingólfsdóttir, A., Walukiewicz, I. (eds.) ICALP 2008, Part II. LNCS, vol. 5126, pp. 486–498. Springer, Heidelberg (2008)

24. Kreuter, B., Shelat, A., Shen, C.-H.: Towards billion-gate secure computation with malicious adversaries. IACR Cryptology ePrint Archive, 2012:179 (2012)

25. Lindell, Y.: Fast cut-and-choose based protocols for malicious and covert adversaries. IACR Cryptology ePrint Archive, 2013:79 (2013)

26. Lindell, Y., Pinkas, B.: An efficient protocol for secure two-party computation in the presence of malicious adversaries. In: Naor, M. (ed.) EUROCRYPT 2007. LNCS, vol. 4515, pp. 52–78. Springer, Heidelberg (2007)

27. Lindell, Y., Pinkas, B.: A proof of security of Yao's protocol for two-party computation. J. Cryptology 22(2), 161–188 (2009)

28. Lindell, Y., Pinkas, B.: Secure two-party computation via cut-and-choose oblivious transfer. In: Ishai, Y. (ed.) TCC 2011. LNCS, vol. 6597, pp. 329–346. Springer, Heidelberg (2011)

29. Mohassel, P., Franklin, M.K.: Efficiency tradeoffs for malicious two-party computation. In: Yung, M., Dodis, Y., Kiayias, A., Malkin, T. (eds.) PKC 2006. LNCS, vol. 3958, pp. 458–473. Springer, Heidelberg (2006)

30. Mohassel, P., Riva, B.: Garbled circuits checking garbled circuits: More efficient and secure two-party computation. In: Canetti, R., Garay, J.A. (eds.) CRYPTO 2013, Part II. LNCS, vol. 8043, pp. 36–53. Springer, Heidelberg (2013)

31. Nielsen, J.B., Nordholt, P.S., Orlandi, C., Burra, S.S.: A new approach to practical active-secure two-party computation. In: Safavi-Naini, R., Canetti, R. (eds.) CRYPTO 2012. LNCS, vol. 7417, pp. 681–700. Springer, Heidelberg (2012)

32. Nielsen, J.B., Orlandi, C.: LEGO for two-party secure computation. In: Reingold, O. (ed.) TCC 2009. LNCS, vol. 5444, pp. 368–386. Springer, Heidelberg (2009)

33. Pinkas, B., Schneider, T., Smart, N.P., Williams, S.C.: Secure two-party computation is practical. In: Matsui, M. (ed.) ASIACRYPT 2009. LNCS, vol. 5912, pp. 250–267. Springer, Heidelberg (2009)

34. Shelat, A., Shen, C.-H.: Fast two-party secure computation with minimal assumptions. IACR Cryptology ePrint Archive, 2013:196 (2013)

35. Shelat, A., Shen, C.-H.: Two-output secure computation with malicious adversaries. In: Paterson, K.G. (ed.) EUROCRYPT 2011. LNCS, vol. 6632, pp. 386–405. Springer, Heidelberg (2011)

36. Yao, A.C.-C.: Protocols for secure computations (extended abstract). In: FOCS, pp. 160–164. IEEE Computer Society (1982)

37. Yao, A.C.-C.: How to generate and exchange secrets (extended abstract). In: FOCS, pp. 162–167. IEEE Computer Society (1986)

Systematizing Secure Computation for Research and Decision Support

Jason Perry[1], Debayan Gupta[2],
Joan Feigenbaum[2], and Rebecca N. Wright[1]

[1] Rutgers University, NJ, USA
{jason.perry,rebecca.wright}@rutgers.edu
[2] Yale University, CT, USA
{debayan.gupta,joan.feigenbaum}@yale.edu

Abstract. We propose a framework for organizing and classifying research results in the active field of secure multiparty computation (MPC). Our *systematization of secure computation* consists of (1) a set of definitions circumscribing the MPC protocols to be considered; (2) a set of quantitative axes for classifying and comparing MPC protocols; and (3) a knowledge base of propositions specifying the known relations between axis values. We have classified a large number of MPC protocols on these axes and developed an interactive tool for exploring the problem space of secure computation. We also give examples of how this systematization can be put to use to foster new research and the adoption of MPC for real-world problems.

1 Introduction

For more than 30 years, since the groundbreaking work of Yao [30,31] and Goldreich *et al.* [18], hundreds of research papers on *Secure Multiparty Computation* (MPC) have appeared, many of them proposing original protocols for carrying out general secure computation under varying sets of assumptions. In this paper, we systematically organize the main research results in this area, in order to:

- Help potential users of MPC learn which existing protocols and implementations best match the sensitive-data computations they would like to perform. This may stimulate adoption of MPC in areas where it would be beneficial.
- Help new researchers get up to speed in a complex area by providing an overview of the "lay of the land."
- Help MPC researchers explore the problem space and discover remaining openings for protocols with new combinations of requirements and security features—or for new impossibility results that preclude the existence of such protocols.

Most research papers in MPC include comparisons of their results to related work, often with tables related to the most significant protocol features, in order to provide context for understanding the paper's contributions. However,

M. Abdalla and R. De Prisco (Eds.): SCN 2014, LNCS 8642, pp. 380–397, 2014.
© Springer International Publishing Switzerland 2014

none has attempted to organize the larger problem space in order to meet the goals listed above. There are a handful of introductory surveys and textbook-like treatments of MPC [17,11,23,12]; these have (justifiably) focused on a narrower region of the problem space or specific security model, in order to present the material in a pedagogically clean way. In contrast, we do not limit ourselves to one model or set of definitions but instead provide a framework for examining their variations.

Our work shares some common goals with research meant to foster the real-world adoption of secure MPC. Such papers include the MPC-in-the-field experiments of Feigenbaum et al. and Bogetoft et al. [15,8] and the end-user survey work of Kamm et al. [7].

Since an effort such as this can never comprehensively account for every piece of research in a sprawling and active field, the framework has been deliberately designed to be extensible; it can accommodate new results and refined definitions without breaking.

In Section 2, we present the three major components that we believe are needed to systematize the main body of MPC results: (1) a set of definitions delineating the boundaries of the problem space; (2) a set of quantitative features for describing protocols; and (3) a knowledge base of propositions specifying the known relationships and dependencies among features. In Section 3, we describe the construction of a systematization database of more than 60 significant MPC protocols, and in Section 4 we present a user interface designed to aid the exploration of the database of systematized MPC protocols and show how our systematization can be put to work to facilitate new research.

2   The Systematization

As a necessary prerequisite for this work, we have carried out an extensive literature survey producing an annotated bibliography of MPC research. It contains over 180 papers from the MPC literature, as well as a sampling of important papers for related problems, including secret sharing and oblivious transfer.

In addition to a written paragraph annotating each paper, the BibTeX source of our Annotated Bibliography includes tags for each paper indicating which aspects of MPC it treats, e.g., 2party for a paper with a specifically two-party protocol, or uncond for a protocol with unconditional security. These tags make it possible to write scripts to automatically generate a bibliography for any specific sub-problem or aspect of MPC.

The bibliography continues to be updated on an ongoing basis. The most recent version is available online [27].

2.1   Definitions

In this section, we provide definitions to delimit the scope of the secure computation protocols that we are concerned with. These definitions are purposely quite broad, so that a large range of work can potentially be captured by them.

Variables that determine the fundamental nature of an MPC protocol include: (1) whether the protocol is for a fixed number of parties (most commonly, two) or is for any number $n \geq 2$ of parties, (2) whether the protocol is for computing one specific functionality (*e.g.*, set intersection) or any of a class of functionalities, and (3) whether the protocol treats exact computation only or secure computation of approximations, which is a generalization of exact MPC [14]. Our initial literature survey encompassed all of these, although not exhaustively. For the current systematization, we consider only protocols for exact computation, and thus we have four definitions, one for each setting of the two variables.

Since the way that security is defined varies from protocol to protocol, and indeed a primary purpose of our systematization is to examine such variations, our definitions necessarily cannot give any fixed definition of security. What matters is that, in the literature, protocols are proven to meet rigorous definitions of security and that our systematization indicates which definitions are actually in use for a given protocol. Therefore, for an MPC protocol to be considered as a candidate for systematization, in addition to fitting into one the definitions listed below, it must be accompanied by rigorous definitions of security, including privacy of inputs and correctness of outputs, that the protocol has been proven to meet. The nature of these security definitions is elaborated in the next subsection.

Definition 1. *A protocol for* Secure n-party Computation of a functionality f *is a specification of an interactive process by which a fixed number n of players, each holding a private input x_i, can compute a specific, possibly randomized, functionality of those inputs* $f(x_1, ..., x_n) = (y_1, ..., y_n)$.

Definition 2. *A protocol for* Secure Multiparty Computation of a functionality f *is a specification of an interactive process by which any number $n \geq 2$ of players, each holding a private input x_i, can compute a specific, possibly randomized, functionality of those inputs* $f(x_1, ..., x_n) = (y_1, ..., y_n)$.

Definition 3. *A protocol for* Secure n-party Computation of a class C of functionalities *allows a fixed number n of players, each holding a private input x_i, to compute an agreed-upon, possibly randomized, functionality of those inputs* $f(x_1, ..., x_n) = (y_1, ..., y_n)$, *where f is any member of the class C of functionalities.*

Definition 4. *A protocol for* Secure Multiparty Computation of a class C of functionalities *allows any number $n \geq 2$ of players, each holding a private input x_i, to compute an agreed-upon, possibly randomized, functionality of those inputs* $f(x_1, ..., x_n) = (y_1, ..., y_n)$, *where f is any member of the class C of functionalities.*

The class C is typically used to refer to the model of computation in which a protocol's functionalities are represented, such as circuits or RAM programs. A majority of the work in MPC has been concerned with universal (Turing-complete) computation, but there has been work exploring secure computation specifically for restricted computation classes, such as AC0 or NC1 circuits or regular or context-free languages.

All of the protocols we surveyed for the systematization fall under one of these definitions, with the majority coming under the most general definition (Definition 4). Yao-like two-party computation protocols fall under Definition 3.

2.2   Linear Axis Representation of MPC Protocol Features

The main conceptual object in our systematization is a set of linear *axes*, where each axis represents an ordering of values of a single feature of MPC protocols. Every axis has at least two labeled values, at the endpoints. Some axes are continuous and others discrete. MPC protocols can be scored on these axes, allowing them to be compared quantitatively. This is the first attempt we are aware of to factor research results in MPC into such a representation. The axes were selected based on our literature survey, using two guiding principles:

1. The axes should be as orthogonal as possible, minimizing overlap (although some logical dependencies between axes are unavoidable.)
2. The set of axes should be *complete* in the sense that they can express all distinctions of security and (asymptotic) efficiency between any two protocols.

For any discrete axis that is not inherently binary, the number of occupied intermediate values on the axis is subject to change. The diagrams below show intermediate values that are known to have been achieved by MPC protocols. However, this should not be seen as finally determining the number of points on the axis. Indeed, one of the objectives of the axis representation is to highlight the possibility of future protocols with new intermediate values. This has already happened for several axes over the history of MPC research. For example, the appearance of protocols tailored for covert adversaries, such as those of Aumann *et al.* and Goyal *et al.* [1,22], showed that there are intermediate values along the "Maliciousness" axis (Axis 7), whereas previously only the passive/malicious distinction had been considered.

We orient all the axes in the same direction, such that moving from left to right on a given axis indicates an improved protocol—*e.g.*, one that is more efficient, has a stronger security guarantee, or requires a weaker setup or computational-hardness assumption. In drawing the non-numeric axes, the points have been placed with equal spacing; the relative distances between points on these axes should not be considered significant.

Our axes do not include the model of computation in which a protocol is expressed. This is a categorical feature which is indicated by the definition (Section 2.1) under which the protocol falls. The model of computation for each protocol is included in its entry in our MPC protocol database, described in Section 3. We have not generated axes for proof techniques, because a proof technique is not a function of the protocol; a protocol's security may be proven in a number of ways.

We now proceed to describe the axes and values in detail. The axes are informally grouped into four categories, which serves to highlight the tradeoffs inherent in achieving secure multiparty computation. The axes in categories I and II, Environmental features and Assumptions, can be thought of as what one "pays" to enable secure MPC, and categories III (Security) and IV (Efficiency) can be seen as what one is "buying." A similar tradeoff structure can also be seen on a smaller scale among axes within the efficiency category. When it is helpful, our description of an axis also cites particular MPC solutions that instantiate points on the axis.

I. Environmental Features Axes

This is the category of features assumed to be provided by the execution environment. The right endpoint of these axes indicates that the feature is not required in any form.

1. Trusted setup

Common
Reference String   PKI   No trusted
●————————————————●————————————————●   setup

Protocols achieving the highest composable security levels require some type of trusted data to be shared by all the parties prior to the protocol execution. The middle point, PKI, is occupied by protocols such as that of Barak *et al.* [2], who showed how to use public-key-like assumptions instead of a polynomial-length common reference string in any case where computational security suffices.

2. Broadcast

Broadcast channel
●——● No broadcast

The broadcast-channel assumption means that each party has the ability to send a message to all other parties simultaneously, and that all parties receiving the broadcast have assurance that the same message was received by all parties.

3. Private channels

Private channels   No private channels
●——●

The private channel assumption is only significant for unconditionally secure protocols, because cryptography using basic computational-hardness assumptions can be used to emulate private and authenticated communication channels.

4. Synchronization

Synchronous   Asynchronous
communication   Limited Synchronization   model
●————————————————●————————————————————————●

A basic assumption of the early MPC protocols is that they operate on a *synchronous* network, in which all sent messages arrive on time and in order. The asynchronous case was first considered in Ben-Or *et al.* [4], where messages may be arbitrarily delayed and arrive in any order. Note that, in such a case, it is impossible to know whether a corrupted party has failed to send a message or, rather, the message is simply delayed. Later works, such as that of Damgård *et al.* [13], have staked out intermediate points on this axis by giving protocols that require a smaller number of synchronization points (typically a single one).

II. Assumption Axes

5. Assumption level

A total (linear) ordering for cryptographic assumptions is not known, and the separation of assumptions cannot currently be unconditionally proven. We therefore use broader categories of assumption type, because these are usually sufficient to distinguish protocols. If a protocol makes no such assumptions, it is said to have *unconditional* security (see Axis 10). Some work specifies protocols in a *hybrid* model, with no concrete computational assumptions, but in which some high-level cryptographic operation (such as oblivious transfer) is assumed to exist as a black box. See Section 3 for a discussion of how such protocols are treated in this systematization.

6. Specific or general assumption

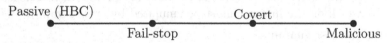

Some more efficient protocols have been designed by making use of specific number-theoretic assumptions. This axis indicates whether the protocol requires such assumptions or whether it is stated so as to use any assumption from a given class, *e.g.*, trapdoor permutations.

III. Security Axes

7. Adversary maliciousness

Passive (HBC)   Covert
            Fail-stop   Malicious

A passive, or honest-but-curious, adversary is one that follows the protocol but may use the data of corrupted parties to attempt to break the protocol's privacy. A fail-stop adversary follows the protocol except for the possibility of aborting. A malicious adversary is one whose behavior is arbitrary, and a covert adversary is like a malicious one, except that it only deviates from the protocol if the probability of being caught is low. Not present on the axis is the value "rational," since the class of rational adversaries is in fact a generalization that can encompass the entire axis, except for fully malicious, because malicious behavior can be truly arbitrary. The position of a rational adversary on the axis is determined by its utility function.

8. Adversary mobility

A static adversary must choose which parties to corrupt before the protocol begins. An adaptive adversary can choose which parties to corrupt, up to the security threshold (see Axis 9), over the course of the computation, after observing the state of previously corrupted parties. A mobile adversary is able to move corruptions from one party to another in the course of the computation.

9. Number of corrupted parties tolerated

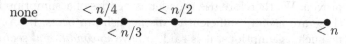

This is the maximum number of corrupted parties for which the (strongest) security guarantees of the protocol hold. The values shown are chosen merely to be representative of the most well known protocols; any value along the axis is possible.

Some protocols tolerate additional corrupted parties at a lower level of maliciousness; see axes 13 and 14.

10. Security type

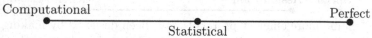

Both statistical and perfect security are unconditional, that is, not based on computational hardness assumptions. Note that true unconditional security typically cannot be achieved through the internet, even if an unconditionally-secure protocol is used, since all unconditionally secure protocols require the assumption of either private or broadcast channels, which on the internet must be emulated by cryptography.

11. Fairness guarantee

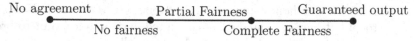

A protocol is *fair* if all honest parties receive the output if any party does. Agreement means that either all honest parties receive the output or none of them do. Protocols without agreement were introduced by Goldwasser *et al.* [20]. Some authors use the term "with abort" to refer to the no-fairness situation, in which dishonest parties can abort after receiving the correct output.

12. Composability

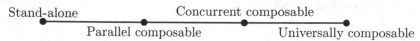

The composability guarantees of a protocol indicate whether that protocol remains secure when executed in an environment where other protocols may be executed sequentially or in parallel. The strongest guarantee, *universal composability* (UC), implies that the security properties of a protocol hold regardless of the environment in which it is executed.

13. Bound for additional passively corrupted parties tolerated

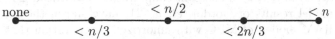

This axis applies to protocols achieving "mixed adversary" security. A protocol that tolerates a certain proportion of maliciously/covertly corrupted parties may also tolerate an additional number of passively corrupted parties, up to a certain threshold. The values on this axis represent that upper threshold. This and the following axis relate to MPC protocols with "graceful degradation", which is surveyed in Hirt *et al.* [24].

14. Corrupted parties tolerated with weakened security

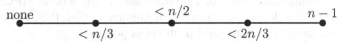

This axis applies to protocols with "hybrid security" results. A protocol that tolerates a certain proportion of corrupted parties (Axis 9) may in fact tolerate a larger number of corruptions, but with a weaker security type, *e.g.*, computational vs. unconditional security.

15. Leakage Security

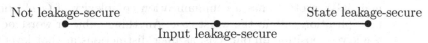

Leakage security is an additional guarantee that an adversary cannot gain an advantage even if it can force all honest players to "leak" some bits of information about their state in the course of the computation. See definitions in Bitansky *et al.* [6].

16. Auditability

Not auditable   Auditable

This axis indicates whether the protocol includes computations that allow for examining the transcript of computation after it is finished, to prove that the parties have correctly followed the protocol. This may be the most recent axis to come into existence, starting with the work of Baum *et al.* [3]

IV. Efficiency Axes

Our efficiency axes are concerned primarily with the asymptotic efficiency of the protocol in question.

17. Online computational overhead

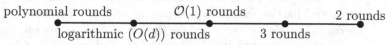

Historically, the main efficiency concern in MPC has been with communication rather than computational complexity; thus the lack of elaboration of this axis. More recently, Ishai *et al.* have notably shown how to achieve MPC with constant computational overhead [25], and the RAM-model results of Gordon *et. al* [21] have shown the possibility, in the RAM model, of MPC with amortized computation that is sublinear in the input size.

18. Online communication complexity (rounds)

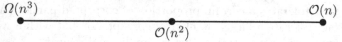

Here, d is the depth of the circuit representing the functionality. Minimizing the number of rounds of computation, independently of the total amount of bytes communicated, is crucial for efficiency in a high-latency or asynchronous network environment. Fully general MPC was shown to require at least three rounds in Gennaro *et al.* [16], although for some functionalities a 2-round protocol is possible.

19. Online communication complexity (per-gate)

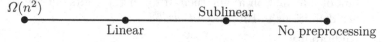

This is the most significant measure of efficiency for MPC protocols. It can represent either bits or field elements of communication. The original BGW protocol has a communication complexity of $O(n^6)$ bits per multiplication gate in the worst case. Anything cubic or worse occupies the lowest position on our axis, as finer distinctions at that level would have little value for distinguishing current, more practical protocols.

20. Preprocessing Communication complexity

$\Omega(n^2)$ Sublinear

Linear   No preprocessing

Many recent protocols achieve improved online communication efficiency by means of a preprocessing phase. In the case where the functionality is represented as an arithmetic circuit, the preprocessing phase is typically a simulation of a trusted dealer that distributes *multiplication triples*, which allow local evaluation of multiplication gates in the online phase. Sublinear preprocessing typically indicates that the preprocessing consists only of exchange of public keys, which is also indicated as a setup assumption (Axis 1).

21. Preprocessing Dependency

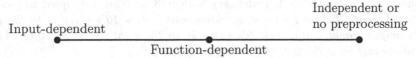

Input-dependent

Function-dependent

Independent or
no preprocessing

In some protocols, the preprocessing phase depends on the specific functionality to be computed, while in others it only depends on the upper bound of the size of the circuit. In all cases, the preprocessing is independent of the parties' inputs.

22. Preprocessing Reuse

Not Reusable   Reusable

This indicates whether the information computed in the preprocessing stage, of whatever type or amount, can be reused for multiple computations. Data of the nature of a public key typically can be reused, while *e.g.,* garbled circuits traditionally cannot be reused without breaking security. But see recent work of Goldwasser *et al.* [19].

As mentioned above, we have endeavored to make this selection of axes as complete as possible. The value of completeness in a systematization can be illustrated as follows: Suppose there are two MPC protocols whose scores along the axes are identical for every axis except one. If the set of axes is complete, then we can be confident that the protocol with the higher value on that axis is strictly better.

2.3 Dependencies between Axes

Since many MPC protocols involve essential tradeoffs in order to achieve security or efficiency, a systematization of secure computation also needs to model what is known about how features of protocols interact. In this section, we present the second major aspect of our systematization: a list of each of the theorems known to imply constraints among the axes' values, each accompanied by a statement of the constraint. References are given to the paper in which the theorem implying the constraint was proven.

Theorem 1 ([5]). *If statistical or perfect security is obtained, then either a broadcast channel or private channels must be assumed.* **Axis constraint**: *If Axis 10's value is to the right of "Computational," then either Axis 3's value is "Private channel" or Axis 2's value is "Broadcast channel".*

Theorem 2 ([29]). *No protocol with security against malicious adversaries can tolerate more than $n/2$ corrupted parties without losing the complete fairness property.* **Axis constraint**: *If Axis 7's value is "Malicious" and Axis 9's value is to the right of $n/2$, then Axis 11's value must be to the left of "Complete fairness".*

Theorem 3 ([10]). *No protocol unconditionally secure against malicious adversaries can guarantee output delivery with n/3 or more corrupted parties.* **Axis constraint**: *If Axis 7's value is "Malicious," Axis 10's value is to the right of "Computational," and Axis 9's value is to the right of "n/3," then Axis 11's value must be to the left of "Guaranteed output".*

Theorem 4 ([5]). *No protocol can have perfect security against more than n/3 maliciously corrupted adversaries.* **Axis constraint**: *If Axis 7's value is "Malicious" and Axis 9's value is to the right of n/3, then Axis 10's value must be to the left of "Perfect".*

Theorem 5 ([16]). *Any general MPC protocol with complete fairness against a malicious adversary must have at least three rounds.* **Axis constraint**: *If Axis 7's value is "Malicious" and Axis 11's value is at or to the right of "complete fairness", then Axis 18's value must be to the left of "2 rounds".*

Theorem 6 ([5]). *For unconditional security against t maliciously corrupted players, n/3 ≤ t < n/2, a broadcast channel is required.* **Axis constraint**: *If Axis 10's value is to the right of "Computational" and Axis 7's value is "Malicious" and Axis 9's value is to the right of n/3, then Axis 2's value must be "Broadcast channel".*

Theorem 7 ([18]). *For (even cryptographic) security against ≥ n/3 maliciously corrupted players, either a trusted key setup or a broadcast channel is required.* **Axis constraint**: *If axis 7's value is "Malicious" and Axis 9's value is to the right of n/3, then either Axis 2's value must be "Broadcast channel," or else Axis 1's value is to the left of "No trusted setup."*

Theorem 8 ([5]). *There can be no unconditionally secure protocol against an adversary controlling a majority of parties.* **Axis constraint**: *Axis 10's value can be to the right of "Computational" only if Axis 9's value is at or to the left of n/2.*

Theorem 9 ([9]). *There is no protocol with UC security against a dishonest majority without setup assumptions.* **Axis constraint**: *If Axis 9's value is to the right of n/2 and Axis 12's value is "Universally composable," then axis 1's value must be to the left of "No trusted setup".*

Theorem 10 ([4]). *In an asynchronous environment, there is no protocol with guaranteed output secure against a fail-stop adversary corrupting n/3 or more parties.* **Axis constraint**: *If Axis 4's value is "Asynchronous," Axis 7's value is at or to the right of "Fail-stop," and Axis 11's value is at "Guaranteed output," then Axis 9's value must be at or to the left of n/3.*

Theorem 11 ([4]). *In an asynchronous environment, there is no protocol with guaranteed output secure against a malicious adversary corrupting n/4 or more parties.* **Axis constraint**: *If Axis 4's value is "Asynchronous," Axis 7's value is "Malicious," and Axis 11's value is at "Guaranteed output," then Axis 9's value must be at or to the left of n/4.*

One validation of our choice of axes is that these theorems are directly and compactly expressible in terms of them, thus giving a unified representation of the central body of knowledge of MPC. The axis constraints can easily be represented in a programming or knowledge representation language, as Section 4 shows.

3   An Extensible Protocol Database

We scored more than 60 of the most significant protocols in secure multiparty computation on our axes, integrating information from our annotated bibliography, resulting in an extensible *MPC protocol database.*

Many papers in the area include multiple protocols. We give each protocol a separate entry in the database, which is labeled by adding a suffix to the usual "alpha"-style reference. For instance, "[GMW87]-mal" refers to the protocol of [18] that is secure against a malicious adversary. The database also indicates whether an implementation of the protocol is known to exist.

The work of constructing the database motivated many revisions of our set of axes and highlighted difficulties in systematizing MPC results, some of which we discuss here.

Efficiency. As mentioned in the axis descriptions, our efficiency axes are concerned primarily with asymptotic efficiency measurements. When we populated our database, we relied on evaluations in the literature, frequently from the paper actually introducing the protocol.

The model of computation in which a protocol's functionalities are expressed can have a large impact on concrete efficiency. Historically, MPC functionalities have been expressed as circuits. The original Yao model considers Boolean circuits, while most of the current state-of-the-art MPC protocols are in the arithmetic-circuit model. Implementing these requires performing field arithmetic, and, although the size of the field elements is a constant in the security parameter, the time taken to perform field operations can have a significant impact on efficiency. Although this difference in concrete efficiency is not captured by the axes, our protocol database notes the model of computation for each protocol.

Even in the asymptotic case, comparing the efficiency of MPC protocols is an extremely difficult problem because of multiple interacting aspects of efficiency present in MPC. In selecting an actual implementation, a concrete analysis and/or empirical efficiency measurements should also be consulted.

Substitutability. One factor that makes it nontrivial to enumerate a list of MPC protocols is that many protocols described in the literature make use of subprotocols for cryptographic operations in a black-box fashion, making it possible to substitute different protocols implementing that operation. This can alter not only the performance characteristics but also the computational and environmental assumptions and security and composability guarantees of the resultant protocol. In some cases, a new and improved subprotocol can trivially be used to improve an older MPC protocol, but no published work explicitly presents the improvement; in other cases a protocol explicitly allows for black-box substitution of subprotocols, in which case it is said to be stated in a *hybrid* model. In the case of the *OT-hybrid* model, in which oblivious transfer is a black box, recent work in *OT extension* has produced significant performance gains.

An extreme case of this "substitutability" factor is the IPS compiler of Ishai *et al.* [26], which is not only in the OT-hybrid model but also allows any of a wide of of honest-majority MPC protocols to be plugged in as an "outer protocol," with the resulting protocol inheriting some (but not all) of the security properties of the outer protocol.

To address this complex issue, we have limited our systematization to represent only concrete instantiations of hybrid protocols. The axes are such that a protocol in a hybrid model must first be "instantiated" with concrete subprotocols in order to be scored. In our database, we have sought to enumerate as many such concrete protocols as possible that are based on well-known hybrid-model protocols.

Two-Party Secure Computation. Although much research has been done specifically addressing two-party secure computation, starting from Yao's original garbled circuits idea, it can be considered as a special case of multiparty computation, in which, if security against a malicious adversary is sought, no honest majority can be assumed (Axis 9 at $n - 1$). Thus, two-party protocols can at least theoretically be compared with multiparty results in this category.

In reality, however, vast improvements in efficiency have been made for the two-party case. We note that these optimizations often come at the expense of *symmetry*: The security guarantee against cheating by one of the two parties may be weaker than for the other. For instance, one of the two parties may be able to cheat with an inverse-polynomial probability, while the other may only be able to cheat with negligible probability. Asymmetry is not included in our axis definitions, and so two-party protocols are scored by the weaker of the two sets of security guarantees. Of course, the database indicates which protocols and implementations are strictly for two parties.

4   Putting the Systematization to Work

As mentioned in Section 1, the main theorems of secure multiparty computation demonstrate essential tradeoffs involved in securely computing a functionality among distrustful parties. To leverage the information that our systematization captures about these tradeoffs and gain insight into the problem space, we experimented with visually plotting the protocol axis scores of the MPC database. However, we found that the highly categorical nature of the data makes it difficult to gain insight from a static visualization. In this section, we describe an an interactive tool we have developed for interacting with the systematization and MPC protocol database, which provides a better way of coming to grips with the multi-dimensional landscape of MPC protocols.

4.1   A Prototype Decision-Making Support Tool

We have developed a prototype GUI tool, *SysSC-UI*, which reads in a protocol database of axis values and enables the user to adjust a set of sliders and checkboxes corresponding to our axes of systematization. For the tool's interface, the axes are oriented vertically rather than horizontally as in this paper, so a higher position of a slider corresponds to a stronger result. A dynamically updated *results window* displays the protocols from the database that match the specified axis values. See the screenshot in Figure 1. The source code for the desktop version is available online https://code.google.com/p/syssc-ui/, as well as a beta web-based version http://work.debayangupta.com/ssc/.

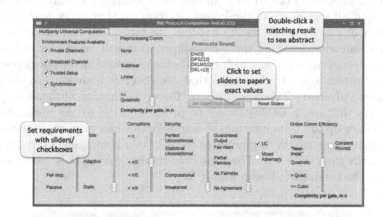

Fig. 1. Screenshot of the SysSC-UI tool for interacting with the protocol database

For a given setting of the sliders and checkboxes, the results window shows all papers whose axis values are at the same level *or higher* than the settings. Thus, the tool presents all protocols that are *at least as good* as the specified settings. When the tool is started, the sliders and checkboxes are all set to the least constraining position, such that every protocol in the database is displayed in the results window. There is also a button to reset the tool to this state. Another button sets the sliders to the exact values of the protocol in the currently highlighted protocol, allowing the precise achievements of a protocol to be examined. This has the side effect of changing the output to the results window, so that only protocols that are at least as good as the selected one are displayed.

Double-clicking on a reference in the results window will display a pop-up window giving the authors' full names and the description of the paper containing the protocol from the annotated bibliography. The GUI also indicates when the positioning of the sliders is such that a secure computation protocol is known to be impossible, by means of an encoding of the theorems in Section 2.3.

The axes and values displayed by SysSC-UI are a subset of those in the full systematization. This was done in order to simplify the interaction and avoid confusion from the visual display of too much information at once. For example, for the composability axis, there is only a single checkbox, to indicate whether the protocol is proven universally composable or not.

We now present sample use cases highlighting the features of SysSC-UI.

4.2 Sample Use Cases for SysSC-UI

Finding the Best Protocol for a Known Problem. Consider a scenario in which a technology consultant is hired by a company to find a way to compute some function of a distributed set of sensitive data residing on servers owned by different divisions of the company. We show how she can use the SysSC-UI tool to find an appropriate MPC protocol for achieving this secure computation.

In the initial state of the UI tool, all four environmental assumption boxes are checked, and all sliders are in the lowest position, so that every protocol in the database is displayed in the results window. To begin, our consultant unchecks "Private Channels", knowing that the computation will be carried out over an ordinary internet connection, which should always be assumed to be tapped. She wishes to protect against adversaries that are covertly malicious, so she moves the leftmost Adversary Type slider up to "Covert". The consultant is suspicious of protocols that use a weaker model to prove security, so she moves the first Security slider up to "Computational." Furthermore, she suspects that universal composability is necessary to guarantee security in a heterogenous environment, so she checks the "UC" box. The protocols resulting from these selections can be seen in the results window in Figure 2.

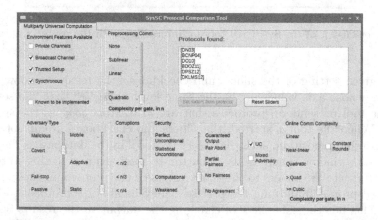

Fig. 2. Results shown by the SysSC-UI tool after selections have been made

The consultant wishes to determine the most efficient protocol that meets these requirements, so next she moves the "Online Comm Complexity" slider up to the highest level for which the results box is not empty. We would like to achieve this online complexity with the minimum preprocessing complexity, so she tries sliding the "Preprocessing comm" slider up. If it is moved up too far, the results window becomes empty. So she readjusts both this and the Online slider to find an agreeable tradeoff between online and preprocessing complexity. The results of this exploration are shown in Figure 2.

Exposing Directions for Cryptographic Research. In using the tool, one invariably stumbles upon a setting of the sliders / boxes that is not in the "known impossible" range, and yet has no papers with a matching protocol listed. Of course, one reason for this could simply be the incompleteness of the protocol database. Another possible reason is that the combination of features is not desirable from a security or efficiency standpoint. However, a third possibility exists, which is that a genuine opening for new research has been revealed. Two kinds of such "holes" may reveal new research directions: (1) Gaps between achieved and proven impossible security levels, and (2) settings in which a weakening of security parameters may allow greater efficiency. An example of the second type of advance is the case of positing composable security definitions weaker than universal composability, as in [28].

5   Ongoing Work

As it is unlikely that the authors will permanently be able to stay abreast of the growing MPC literature, we have developed a web-based survey that allows researchers to submit descriptions of new protocols and their features on the axes so that they can be integrated into the protocol database and SysSC-UI. The survey is available at http://goo.gl/T4ORzr. Author participation is vital to the continuing usefulness of this effort.

The set of theorems in Section 2.3 should also be expanded as knowledge of secure computation increases. This work has highlighted several remaining unknowns in characterizing the possibility of secure computation; for example, perhaps some of the malicious impossibility results hold for the covert case as well. A longer-term goal is to characterize the efficiency of the protocols more precisely, in terms of the number of elementary operations, to make the efficiency of all protocols directly comparable.

Systematizations of knowledge are especially needed in research fields where a large body of results have been generated in a short time, and secure multiparty computation is undoubtedly such a field. Without an effort to systematically organize results, there may be unnecessary duplication of research efforts, the barriers to entry for new researchers may be needlessly high, and results may not see useful applications as early as they could. Our systematization of secure computation is a tool that can significantly ease the task of coming to grips with this sprawling body of results, and potentially speed its adoption in fields where it would be useful.

Acknowledgments. This material is based on research sponsored by DARPA under agreement number FA8750-13-2-0058. The U.S. government is authorized to reproduce and distribute reprints for Governmental purposes notwithstanding any copyright notation thereon. The views and conclusions herein are those of the authors and should not be interpreted as necessarily representing the office policies or endorsements, either expressed or implied, of DARPA or the U.S. Government.

References

1. Aumann, Y., Lindell, Y.: Security against covert adversaries: Efficient protocols for realistic adversaries. In: Vadhan, S.P. (ed.) TCC 2007. LNCS, vol. 4392, pp. 137–156. Springer, Heidelberg (2007)
2. Barak, B., Canetti, R., Nielsen, J.B., Pass, R.: Universally composable protocols with relaxed set-up assumptions. In: Proceedings of the 45th Annual IEEE Symposium on Foundations of Computer Science (FOCS 2004), pp. 186–195. IEEE (2004)
3. Baum, C., Damgård, I., Orlandi, C.: Publicly auditable secure multi-party computation. Cryptology ePrint Archive, Report 2014/075 (2014), http://eprint.iacr.org/
4. Ben-Or, M., Canetti, R., Goldreich, O.: Asynchronous secure computation. In: Proceedings of the 25th Annual ACM Symposium on Theory of Computing (STOC 1993), pp. 52–61 (1993)
5. Ben-Or, M., Goldwasser, S., Wigderson, A.: Completeness theorems for non-cryptographic fault-tolerant distributed computation (extended abstract). In: Proceedings of the Twentieth Annual ACM Symposium on Theory of Computing (STOC 1988), pp. 1–10 (1988)
6. Bitansky, N., Canetti, R., Halevi, S.: Leakage-tolerant interactive protocols. In: Cramer, R. (ed.) TCC 2012. LNCS, vol. 7194, pp. 266–284. Springer, Heidelberg (2012)
7. Bogdanov, D., Kamm, L., Laur, S., Pruulmann-Vengerfeldt, P.: Secure multi-party data analysis: end user validation and practical experiments. Cryptology ePrint Archive, Report 2013/826 (2013), http://eprint.iacr.org/2013/826
8. Bogetoft, P., Christensen, D., Damgård, I., Geisler, M., Jakobsen, T., Krøigaard, M., Nielsen, J., Nielsen, J., Nielsen, K., Pagter, J., Schwartzbach, M., Toft, T.: Secure multiparty computation goes live. In: Dingledine, R., Golle, P. (eds.) FC 2009. LNCS, vol. 5628, pp. 325–343. Springer, Heidelberg (2009)
9. Canetti, R., Kushilevitz, E., Lindell, Y.: On the limitations of universally composable two-party computation without set-up assumptions. In: Biham, E. (ed.) EUROCRYPT 2003. LNCS, vol. 2656, pp. 68–86. Springer, Heidelberg (2003)
10. Cleve, R.: Limits on the security of coin flips when half the processors are faulty (extended abstract). In: STOC, pp. 364–369 (1986)
11. Cramer, R., Damgård, I.: Multiparty computation, an introduction. In: Contemporary Cryptology, pp. 41–87. Springer (2005)
12. Cramer, R., Damgård, I., Nielsen, J.B.: Secure Multiparty Computation and Secret Sharing: An Information Theoretic Approach. Self-published manuscript (2013), https://users-cs.au.dk/jbn/mpc-book.pdf
13. Damgård, I., Geisler, M., Krøigaard, M., Nielsen, J.B.: Asynchronous multiparty computation: Theory and implementation. In: Jarecki, S., Tsudik, G. (eds.) PKC 2009. LNCS, vol. 5443, pp. 160–179. Springer, Heidelberg (2009)
14. Feigenbaum, J., Ishai, Y., Malkin, T., Nissim, K., Strauss, M.J., Wright, R.N.: Secure multiparty computation of approximations. ACM Transactions on Algorithms 2(3), 435–472 (2006)

15. Feigenbaum, J., Pinkas, B., Ryger, R., Saint-Jean, F.: Secure computation of surveys. In: EU Workshop on Secure Multiparty Protocols. Citeseer (2004)
16. Gennaro, R., Ishai, Y., Kushilevitz, E., Rabin, T.: On 2-round secure multiparty computation. In: Yung, M. (ed.) CRYPTO 2002. LNCS, vol. 2442, pp. 178–193. Springer, Heidelberg (2002)
17. Goldreich, O.: The Foundations of Cryptography - Volume 2, Basic Applications. Cambridge University Press (2004)
18. Goldreich, O., Micali, S., Wigderson, A.: How to play any mental game or a completeness theorem for protocols with honest majority. In: Proceedings of the Nineteenth Annual ACM Symposium on Theory of Computing (STOC 1987), pp. 218–229 (1987)
19. Goldwasser, S., Kalai, Y.T., Popa, R.A., Vaikuntanathan, V., Zeldovich, N.: Reusable garbled circuits and succinct functional encryption. In: Proceedings of the 45th Annual ACM Symposium on Theory of Computing (STOC 2013), pp. 555–564 (2013)
20. Goldwasser, S., Lindell, Y.: Secure computation without agreement. In: Malkhi, D. (ed.) DISC 2002. LNCS, vol. 2508, pp. 17–32. Springer, Heidelberg (2002)
21. Gordon, S.D., Katz, J., Kolesnikov, V., Krell, F., Malkin, T., Raykova, M., Vahlis, Y.: Secure two-party computation in sublinear (amortized) time. In: ACM Conference on Computer and Communications Security (ACM CCS 2012), pp. 513–524 (2012)
22. Goyal, V., Mohassel, P., Smith, A.: Efficient two party and multi party computation against covert adversaries. In: Smart, N.P. (ed.) EUROCRYPT 2008. LNCS, vol. 4965, pp. 289–306. Springer, Heidelberg (2008)
23. Hazay, C., Lindell, Y.: Efficient Secure Two-Party Protocols – Techniques and Constructions. Information Security and Cryptography. Springer (2010)
24. Hirt, M., Lucas, C., Maurer, U., Raub, D.: Graceful degradation in multi-party computation (extended abstract). In: Fehr, S. (ed.) ICITS 2011. LNCS, vol. 6673, pp. 163–180. Springer, Heidelberg (2011)
25. Ishai, Y., Kushilevitz, E., Ostrovsky, R., Sahai, A.: Cryptography with constant computational overhead. In: Proceedings of the 40th Annual ACM Symposium on Theory of Computing (STOC 2008), pp. 433–442. ACM, New York (2008)
26. Ishai, Y., Prabhakaran, M., Sahai, A.: Founding cryptography on oblivious transfer – efficiently. In: Wagner, D. (ed.) CRYPTO 2008. LNCS, vol. 5157, pp. 572–591. Springer, Heidelberg (2008)
27. Perry, J., Gupta, D., Feigenbaum, J., Wright, R.N.: The secure computation annotated bibliography (2014), http://paul.rutgers.edu/~jasperry/ssc-annbib.pdf
28. Prabhakaran, M., Sahai, A.: New notions of security: achieving universal composability without trusted setup. In: Proceedings of the 36th Annual ACM Symposium on Theory of Computing (STOC 2004), pp. 242–251 (2004)
29. Rabin, T., Ben-Or, M.: Verifiable secret sharing and multiparty protocols with honest majority (extended abstract). In: Proceedings of the 21st Annual ACM Symposium on Theory of Computing (STOC 1989), pp. 73–85 (1989)
30. Yao, A.C.C.: Protocols for secure computations (extended abstract). In: Proceedings of the 23rd Annual IEEE Symposium on Foundations of Computer Science (FOCS 1982), pp. 160–164 (1982)
31. Yao, A.C.C.: How to generate and exchange secrets (extended abstract). In: Proceedings of the 27th Annual IEEE Symposium on Foundations of Computer Science (FOCS 1986), pp. 162–167 (1986)

An Empirical Study and Some Improvements of the MiniMac Protocol for Secure Computation

Ivan Damgård, Rasmus Lauritsen, and Tomas Toft*

Department of Computer Science, Aarhus University
{ivan,rwl,ttoft}@cs.au.dk

Abstract. Recent developments in Multi-party Computation (MPC) has resulted in very efficient protocols for dishonest majority in the pre-processing model. In particular, two very promising protocols for Boolean circuits have been proposed by Nielsen et al. (nicknamed TinyOT) and by Damgård and Zakarias (nicknamed MiniMac). While TinyOT has already been implemented, we present in this paper the first implementation of MiniMac, using the same platform as the existing TinyOT implementation. We also suggest several improvements of MiniMac, both on the protocol design and implementation level. In particular, we suggest a modification of MiniMac that achieves increased parallelism at no extra communication cost. This gives an asymptotic improvement of the original protocol as well as an 8-fold speed-up of our implementation. We compare the resulting protocol to TinyOT for the case of secure computation in parallel of a large number of AES encryptions and find that it performs better than results reported so far on TinyOT, on the same hardware.

1 Introduction

In Multi-party Computation (MPC), N players wish to compute a function securely on privately held inputs, where security means that the result must be correct, and be the only new information that is released about the inputs. This must hold even if T players are corrupted by an adversary. In this paper, we consider the case of active corruption (where the adversary takes full control over corrupted players) of up to $N - 1$ players, so-called dishonest majority. In several recent papers [2,6,5,7,9] it has been shown that we can obtain very practical MPC protocols for dishonest majority using preprocessing.

The basic idea exploited is that, while dishonest majority precludes information-theoretic (IT) constructions, the expensive and inefficient, computationally secure (public key) cryptography can be pushed to a preprocessing phase. This phase is

---

* The authors acknowledge support from the Danish National Research Foundation and The National Science Foundation of China (under the grant 61061130540) for the Sino-Danish Center for the Theory of Interactive Computation, within part of this work was performed; and from the CFEM research center, supported by the Danish Strategic Research Council. The third author was supported by European Research Council Starting Grant 279447.

M. Abdalla and R. De Prisco (Eds.): SCN 2014, LNCS 8642, pp. 398–415, 2014.
© Springer International Publishing Switzerland 2014

independent of not only the inputs, but also the function to be securely computed. The "raw-material" generated allows the use of IT-secure protocols in the online phase, i.e., protocols that are much more computationally efficient.

Two promising protocols have been proposed for the case of secure computation of Boolean circuits, namely the TinyOT protocol by Nielsen et al. [9] and the MiniMac protocol by Damgård and Zakarias [7]. [7] presents a theoretical comparison between the two: For security parameter κ, it was shown that where TinyOT requires each player to do $\Theta(\kappa)$ elementary bit operations per gate in the circuit, MiniMac requires only $O(\log \kappa)$ operations (or even $O(1)$ for some instantiations, when the number of players is large). The same overhead was found for communication and the amount of preprocessing-data each player stores.

It is, however, very unclear whether these theoretical advantages translate to greater efficiency in practice. Indeed, TinyOT has been implemented with promising results, and the $\Theta(\kappa)$ bit operations required per gate can in most cases be performed in parallel using a single or small number of CPU instructions. On the other hand, the fact that TinyOT has larger storage requirements and communication complexity remains even on a massively parallel machine.

Our Contribution. In this paper we present the first implementation of MiniMac. We compare this to a TinyOT implementation running on the same hardware with the goal of making a meaningful comparison of the two approaches in practice. As benchmark, we use parallel computation of many AES encryptions using a binary circuit; AES is often used as the de facto standard benchmark and performing multiple parallel executions has practical relevance, e.g., when encrypting data in counter mode. Additionally, we propose a new modification of MiniMac which increases the efficiency of binary circuit evaluation in both theory and practice. Our implementation is optimized for the two party case but works for any number of players.

MiniMac is based on an error correcting code of length n and dimension k over some finite field, $\mathbb{F}$, and allows k parallel evaluations of some arithmetic circuit over $\mathbb{F}$. It further uses an IT-secure authentication scheme that is based on the code; a forged message authentication code (MAC) will be accepted with probability 2^{-t} where $t = \log(|\mathbb{F}|) \cdot (n - 2k + 1)$.

Our implementation uses a Reed-Solomon code over $\mathbb{F}_{2^8}$ with $(n, k) = (256, 120)$ or $(255, 85)$, depending on the underlying implementation of operations on codewords; this implies (at least) 128-bit security. We note that [7] suggests alternative constructions of binary codes based on algebraic geometry, however, the constants involved are very large and no truly efficient encoding algorithm is known, thus, using these were not seen as a viable approach.

Using $\mathbb{F}_{2^8}$ as the underlying field is a natural choice; elements can be encoded as bytes and addressed separately, while the field is sufficiently small to allow efficient multiplication through table-lookup. Further, $\mathbb{F}_{2^8}$ has characteristic two implying that binary-XOR is simply addition.

Regarding the choice of (n, k), we strove to maximize parallel computation, i.e., maximize k. Since n is bounded by the cardinality of the field, $\mathbb{F}_{2^8}$, we have $(n, k) = (256, 120)$ when aiming for security level $t \geq 128$. However, for these parameters, our best encoding algorithm is quadratic: the naive multiplication by the generator matrix. We found this matrix multiplication to be quite costly in practice. As an alternative, we suggest to implement it using a variant of Fast Fourier Transform (FFT) – 85 divides 255 which is the order of the multiplicative group implying that roots of unity of order 255 and 85 exist in $\mathbb{F}_{2^8}$. This reduces encoding- and decoding-time, but requires that the input-size divides 255. This sets $(n, k) = (255, 85)$, however, despite the reduced parallelization we found that this still pays off.

In addition to the above implementation suggestions, we also present an improvement of the protocol when the overall goal is Boolean circuits. Taking a closer look at the choice of field, we see that using a code over $\mathbb{F}_{2^8}$ with the original MiniMac protocol to compute a Boolean circuit, implies that every bit is encoded as a byte, i.e., we "waste" a factor of 8 in terms of space. We propose an optimization that allows us to use every bit in every data byte; this increases parallelization to $8 \cdot 120 = 960$ or $8 \cdot 85 = 680$ instances. To reach this goal, we redesign the multiplication operation in MiniMac: the original protocol implements multiplication of data bytes as multiplication in $\mathbb{F}_{2^8}$. Instead, we compute bit-wise AND of two bytes. Our solution for this generalizes to other characteristic 2 fields (and even other protocols, e.g., [6]) and while it requires a small amount of extra local computation, it saves communication and storage compared to the original MiniMac. More precisely, in [7] they compute the cost per player per gate of their protocol, where the cost can be the amount of data stored from the pre-processing, the communication and the computational work. For the case of two players, these costs can be $O(1), O(1), O(\text{poly}(n))$, or all three can be $O(\text{polylog}(n))$, depending on the underlying code used. For the case of computing the same function many times in parallel, our solution obtains $O(\log(n)), O(1), O(\text{polylog}(n))$ and so is better than both previous solutions on the parameters that matter most for efficiency. This is not only a theoretical improvement: in our implementation, we obtain more than an 8-fold speedup.

Another performance boost was obtained by exploiting the structure of the AES circuit: only AND gates require communication, and we form a number of batches of gates, such that gates of one batch can all be executed in parallel. We collect the required communication in packets that each span the entire batch. This way we send fewer but larger packets and this turns out to reduce the time we wait for communication to happen. However, profiling showed that significant time was still spent waiting for communication. We therefore tried a new setup, where several instances of the program were started at slightly different times. The idea was that this would keep both CPUs busy almost all the time and give us larger throughput. Indeed, we gained a factor almost 2 from this. Finally experimenting with the best setting for compiler optimizations gave another factor of 2.

Combining all the tricks we came up with, we obtain an amortized time of about 4 ms per AES encryption with (at least) 128 bit security and about 9 seconds latency. This is almost 10 times faster than the best time reported for TinyOT evaluating the same circuit on the same hardware, where we note that this TinyOT implementation runs with only 64 bit security and much larger latency.

In [8], a different secure AES implementation is reported on, based on the SPDZ protocol [6]. It is a bit faster than ours, but is incomparable as the hardware is different and the security level lower (40 bit). Most importantly, however, the circuit used there is an arithmetic circuit over $\mathbb{F}_{2^8}$ plus some "bit-decomposition" tricks to evaluate the S-boxes. Our study should be seen primarily as targeted against at using MiniMac as efficiently as possible to evaluate a Boolean circuit. Finally, [8] reports that much of their efficiency comes from a very careful scheduling of operations and messages. We have optimized our implementation to some extent w.r.t. scheduling but based on measurements of the time we spend waiting for messages, we believe there is further potential.

2   MiniMac

The MiniMac protocol supports the operations described in Figure 1. It does this by representing values occurring in the computation in a certain format. In the original MiniMac paper this representation is optimized for the case of many players. In this paper, however, we concentrate on the two-player case and therefore we set up the representation in a way that resembles more the way it is done in the TinyOT protocol (which is inherently a two-player protocol). More precisely, whereas in the original MiniMac, each secret value, as well a Message Authentication Code (MAC), is additively secret shared among the players, we keep the additive secret sharing of the value, but add instead a MAC on each share. Whereas this is sub-optimal for the multiple player case, it makes the check of Macs simpler and adds no significant other cost for two players.

Functionality $\mathcal{F}_{\mathrm{MPC}}$

Initialize: On input $(init, k)$ from all parties, each initialize the store for block length k.

Rand: On input $(rand, P_i, vid)$ from all parties P_i, with vid a fresh identifier, pick $r \leftarrow \mathbb{F}^k$ and store (vid, r).

Input: On input $(input, P_i, vid, x)$ from P_i and $(input, P_i, vid, ?)$ from all other parties, with vid a fresh identifier, store (vid, x).

Add: On command $(add, vid_1, vid_2, vid_3)$ from all parties (if vid_1, vid_2 are present in memory and vid_3 is not), retrieve (vid_1, x), (vid_2, y) and store $(vid_3, x + y)$.

Multiply: On input $(mult, vid_1, vid_2, vid_3)$ from all parties (if vid_1, vid_2 are present in memory and vid_3 is not), retrieve (vid_1, x), (vid_2, y) and store $(vid_3, x * y)$.

Output: On input $(output, vid)$ from all honest parties (if vid is present in memory), retrieve (vid, x) and output it to the environment. If the environment returns "OK", then output (vid, x) to all players, else output $\perp$ to all players.

Fig. 1. The ideal functionality for MPC.

Representation of values. A clear text value x is k-element vector over some finite field, in our case always $\mathbb{F}_{2^8}$. We consider a systematic linear error correcting code C of length n and dimension k, and let $C(x)$ denote the encoding of x in C. We also need to consider the Schur-transform C^* of C, which is the linear span of all products of form $c_1 * c_2$, where $c_1, c_2 \in C$ and $*$ denote the coordinate-wise product of vectors.

In our set-up, players P_1 and P_2 hold random n-element vectors α_1 and α_2, serving as (parts of the) keys for the MACs. A representation of x has the following form:

$$[\![x]\!] = ((C(x_1), m_1, \beta_{x_2}), (C(x_2), m_2, \beta_{x_1}))$$

where the first component is held by P_1 and the second by P_2. It should hold that $x = x_1 + x_2$, that $m_1 = MAC(x_1) = \alpha_2 * C(x_1) + \beta_{x_1}$, and by symmetry that $m_2 = MAC(x_2) = \alpha_1 * C(x_2) + \beta_{x_2}$.

A representation can be opened if players exchange $C(x_1), m_1$ and $C(x_2), m_2$. P_1 checks that $C(x_2)$ is indeed in C, and that $m_2 = MAC(x_2) = \alpha_1 * x_2 + \beta_{x_2}$ holds; P_2 does the symmetric check on what he receives. Then both players can add the additive shares to get $C(x)$ and hence x.

This way to open a representation is secure against a corrupt P_2 if β_{x_2} is uniformly chosen, independently for each representation since then P_2 has no a priory information on α_1. From this it is easy to see, using essentially the same argument as in [7], that P_1 will accept an incorrect value of $C(x_2)$ with probability at most S^{-d} where S is the size of the field used and d is the minimum distance of C. The point is that P_2 wold have to switch to a different code word and hence change $C(x_2)$ in at least d positions. But then he could only produce the required MAC value by guessing α_1 in d positions. Of course, a similar arguments works for a corrupt P_1.

It is trivial to verify that $[\![x]\!] + [\![y]\!] = [\![x + y]\!]$ where the $+$-symbol denotes that each player locally adds corresponding components he knows from the representations.

We can easily define a similar representation $[\![x]\!]^*$, this is exactly the same as $[\![x]\!]$, except that the code C^* is used for encoding. This will mean that the MACs can now be cheated with probability S^{-d^*} where d^* is the minimum distance of C^*. This is a potential problem since in general $d^* < d$, so we need to take care when we choose C.

Now, to multiply a value on the representation with a publicly known k-vector u, u is turned into a codeword, $C(u)$ and then we define

$$C(u) * [\![x]\!] = ((C(u) * C(x_1), C(u) * m_1, C(u) * \beta_{x_2}),$$
$$(C(u) * C(x_2), C(u) * m_2, C(u) * \beta_{x_1})).$$

It is easy to see that this is indeed a well-formed representation of $u * x$, however, using the code C^*, so we can write this as $C(u) * [\![x]\!] = [\![u * x]\!]^*$.

We can also add a public constant u to a representation, namely we define

$$C(u) + [\![x]\!] = ((C(u) + C(x_1), m_1, \beta_{x_2}), (C(x_2), m_2, \beta_{x_1} - \alpha_2 * u)) = [\![u + x]\!].$$

The protocol Π_{MPC} using this representation and its linear properties is described in Figure 2. In the original protocol [7] there was also a sub-protocol for permuting entries internally in the represented vectors. However, since we only want to do several instance of one computation in parallel, we do not need this step.

Protocol Π_{MPC}

Initialize: The parties first invoke the preprocessing to get a sufficient number of multiplication triples $([\![a]\!], [\![b]\!], [\![c]\!]^*)$, random values and single values $([\![r]\!])$, $([\![s]\!], [\![s]\!]^*)$, $[\![t]\!]$.

Rand: The parties take an available single $[\![t]\!]$.

Input: To share P_i's input x_i, take an available single $[\![r]\!]$ and do the following:
1. $[\![r]\!]$ is opened privately to P_i only.
2. P_i broadcasts $\epsilon \leftarrow C(\mathbf{x_i}) - C(\mathbf{r})$.
3. The parties verify that ϵ is a codeword and if so, compute $[\![x_i]\!] \leftarrow [\![r]\!] + \epsilon$.

Add: To add representations $[\![x]\!]$, $[\![y]\!]$, parties locally compute $[\![x+y]\!] \leftarrow [\![x]\!] + [\![y]\!]$.

Multiply: To multiply $[\![x]\!]$, $[\![y]\!]$, parties take a triple $([\![a]\!], [\![b]\!], [\![c]\!]^*)$ and a pair of random values $[\![s]\!], [\![s]\!]^*$ from the set of the available ones and do:
1. Open $[\![x]\!] - [\![a]\!]$ to get ϵ and $[\![y]\!] - [\![b]\!]$ to get δ to every player (note that ϵ and δ are code words in C).
2. Compute $[\![x * y]\!]^* \leftarrow [\![c]\!]^* + \epsilon * [\![b]\!] + \delta * [\![a]\!] + \epsilon * \delta$.
3. Open $[\![x * y]\!]^* - [\![s]\!]^*$ to every player who gets $\sigma^* \in C^*$. P_1 extracts $x*y-s$ and encodes this value into a codeword $\sigma \in C$ which he broadcasts.
4. All players check that σ^*, σ are codewords for the same value and then compute $[\![x * y]\!] \leftarrow \sigma + [\![s]\!]$.

Output: This stage is entered when the players have $[\![y]\!]$. In the $[\cdot]$ MACs are checked immediately and thus the players do the following:
1. $[\![y]\!]$ is opened privately to each player P_i.

Fig. 2. The online protocol

2.1 Reed-Solomon Codes

MiniMac[7] requires that the code C and its Schur transform C^* are systematic. In this section we recall how Reed-Solomon works, what it means for a code to be systematic and how it is achieved for Reed-Solomon which is not systematic out of the box.

A Reed-Solomon code is an error correcting code described by three parameters: (n, k, d) where n is the length of the code, k is the dimension (the length of messages that can be encoded) and d the distance of the code (the amount of redundancy). There are two algorithms, one for encoding a message into a codeword and one for checking a codeword is valid.

To *encode* a message of k field elements say $a = [a_0, ..., a_{k-1}]$ as a Reed-Solomon codeword we consider the polynomial $f_a(x) = a_0 + a_1 x + \cdots + a_{k-1} x^{k-1}$ of degree $k-1$. For $n \geq k$ distinct points $v_j, j = 0, \ldots, n-1$ we define the vector

$c = (f_a(v_0), \ldots, f_a(v_{n-1}))$ to be a codeword for a. Evaluating a polynomial f_a in n distinct points is strongly connected to n by k Vandermonde matrices, $V_{n \times k}$. Encoding a polynomial f_a corresponds to multiplying such a Vandermonde matrix with the column vector $a = (a_0, \ldots, a_{k-1})^T$ as follows:

$$V_{n \times k} \cdot a = \begin{bmatrix} v_0^0 & v_0 & \cdots & v_0^{k-1} \\ v_1^0 & v_1 & \cdots & v_1^{k-1} \\ & \vdots & & \\ v_n^0 & v_n & \cdots & v_n^{k-1} \end{bmatrix} \begin{bmatrix} a_0 \\ a_1 \\ \vdots \\ a_{k-1} \end{bmatrix} =$$

$$\begin{bmatrix} a_0 + a_1 v_0 + \cdots + a_{k-1} v_0^{k-1} \\ a_0 + a_1 v_1 + \cdots + a_{k-1} v_1^{k-1} \\ \vdots \\ a_0 + a_1 + v_n + \cdots + a_{k-1} v_n^{k-1} \end{bmatrix} = \begin{bmatrix} f_a(v_0) \\ f_a(v_1) \\ \vdots \\ f_a(v_n) \end{bmatrix}$$

Observe that from k points from a codeword we can find our message a (the coefficient of f_a) again using interpolation. Thus, one naive way to *validate* a given codeword, c is to go through each of the 2^d subsets of k elements from c and check that each interpolate to the same message a.

As noted in the beginning of this section this way of encoding messages is not systematic in the following sense: A *systematic* code is a code where the encoded message directly appears in fixed positions of the codeword. In our case we will have the first k positions of a codeword to be the actual encoded message.

To encode a systematic Reed-Solomon codeword we fix an encoding matrix $V_{n \times k}$ where n is the desired codeword length and k the length of our messages. Then we take the upper $k \times k$ matrix $V_{k \times k}$ of $V_{n \times k}$ which by construction is guaranteed to be invertible and do the following:

$$V_{n \times k} (V_{k \times k})^{-1} a^T = c = \begin{bmatrix} c_0 = a_0 \\ \vdots \\ c_{k-1} = a_{k-1} \\ c_k \\ \vdots \\ c_{n-1} \end{bmatrix}$$

We take $E = V_{n \times k} (V_{k \times k})^{-1}$ to define our encoding matrix. Notice that the first k rows of E will yield the $k \times k$ identity matrix, ensuring systematic codewords as desired.

Now it is easy to check whether a vector is a codeword, namely given c we multiply E with the column vector consisting of the first k entries in c, and check the result yields c again e.g. $E[c_0, \ldots, c_{k-1}]^T \overset{?}{=} c$. If not the codeword is invalid.

As noted in the introduction, $\mathbb{F}_{2^8}$ is a natural choice as an underlying field. In particular as efficient encoding is important for MiniMac, we benefit from $\mathbb{F}_{2^8}$ being small enough that multiplication can be done by table look-up. With respect to Reed-Solomon the choice of $\mathbb{F}_{2^8}$ introduces some restrictions on the parameters (n, k, d). Namely, that as there are only 256 elements, the length of a (checkable) Reed-Solomon code can be at most 256, as we need a distinct evaluation point for each codeword position. Furthermore, the error probability for the MACs is at most 256^{-d^*}; aiming for 128-bit security implies a minimum distance of (at least) 16 field elements for C^*. We can summarize the restrictions we get on the Reed-Solomon code parameters as follows:

- $n \leq |\mathbb{F}_{2^8}| = 256$ - The length of the codewords can be at most 256.
- $d' = min(d, d^*) \geq 16$ - Altering a message to another codeword implies modifying d' positions.
- $k \leq (n - d')/2 + 1$ - If C has dimension k it is generated from polynomials of degree $k - 1$, so the Schur transform is generated from polynomials of degree $2(k - 1)$ and hence has minimum distance $d^* = n - 2(k - 1)$. For $d^* = 16$ we get $k \leq 121$ when $n = 256$. We have chosen to round this to $k = 120$ as this slightly simplifies implementation.

2.2 Preprocessing

We will not explicitly consider the preprocessing in this paper. Note, however, that since MACs are set up as in [9] and our field is characteristic 2, it is straightforward to modify the TinyOT preprocessing to obtain the one presently needed.

3 Evaluation and Comparison with TinyOT

In this section we evaluate MiniMac in practice. To put our work in perspective we wish to compare MiniMac to the previous state of the art protocol, TinyOT, in [9]. We present performance numbers for AES encryption for both protocols in our framework and their interpretation.

3.1 Empirical Setup and Performance Measurements

In the following empirical study of TinyOT and MiniMac, we use the same two computers on an Aarhus University's network. Both machines have the following specifications:

   In many of our experiments we start multiple processes on the two test machines that pair-wise execute the protocol to maximize CPU and network utilization. When more pairs of processes are executing the protocol a third machine, the *Monitor*, listens for all of them to report ready. When all processes are ready the Monitor broadcasts a "Go!" signal and records the time. When the pairs of processes running the protocol reports back to the Monitor that they are done the Monitor records the time of the *last* process. These two numbers are recorded as the start and end time of the experiment and their difference is taken to be the measured elapsed time of the experiment.

   In summary performance numbers are presented in tables with these columns:

CPU	Intel(R) Xeon(R) CPU X3430 @ 2.40 GHz
CPU op-mode(s)	32-bit, 64-bit
CPU(s)	4
Thread(s) per core	1
CPU MHz	2393.859
L1d cache	32K
L1i cache	32K
L2 cache	256K
L3 cache	8192K
RAM	32 GB
Net	Gigabit LAN with 0.215 ms avg. latency measured using the ping tool.

Fig. 3. Hardware spec

Instances. This column report how many protocol instances are run in parallel. That is, the number of processes started on each of the two test machines pair-wise carrying out the protocol.

Total (ms). This column reports on the total execution time in milliseconds. For one instance, this is also the latency, e.g. the time from initiating computation until some result is ready.

No AES. This reports the total number of single block 128-bit AES encryptions carried out.

Time per AES (ms). This column shows the amortized time in milliseconds used per AES circuit.

To even out fluctuations, every line in tables like the one below reports on the mean time from at least five runs. When appropriate, we present results with in a 95% confidence interval, indicated as 35 ± 8 ms for an experiment with mean 35 with a 95% confidence interval in $[27; 43]$ ms.

Instances	No AES	Total Time (ms)	Time per AES (ms)
8	102000	960	380 $\pm$69 ms

Fig. 4. An example performance measurement, these numbers are made up

3.2   The Benchmark - AES Circuit and Relevance

We run our experiments with a binary AES circuit encrypting one block of plaintext with a 128 bits key. The key is additively secret shared between the two test machines. The plain-text to encrypt is publicly known as well as the circuit gates. Both test machines learns the cipher-text but learns nothing new about the key. There are several practical scenarios where key material split between several servers might mitigate a potential compromise of one server.

Our concrete circuit has 6800 AND-gates and 26816 XOR-gates.

Throughout all experiments MiniMac is run with at least 128-bit security.

3.3 MiniMac Test Runs with No Optimizations

In this Section we run our implentation with all optmizations and tricks turned off to present a baseline of performance. This baseline is compared to TinyOT also implemented in our framework.

To only measure the AES circuit we exclude input and output gates. Thus when running our experiments all MiniMac processes run to the point where all parties has completed their input gates. Likewise, when the last XOR-gates of the circuit is computed the computation is recorded as complete before running any of the output gates.

Instances	No AES	Total Time (ms)	Time per AES (ms)
1	120	161651	1347 ± 1243
2	240	128283	644 ± 578
4	480	188824	393 ± 138
8	960	264596	144 ± 233
16	1920	598799	311 ± 108

Fig. 5. Running MiniMac without tricks and optimizations

3.4 Introduction to TinyOT

The protocol in [9] is nicked named TinyOT. MiniMac and TinyOT are both targeted at evaluating binary circuits. TinyOT uses Oblivious Transfer to obtain multiplication triples as described in [1].

First a short piece of history about TinyOTs implementation. A great deal of work was put in to implementing of TinyOT in Java for the publication and the performance-numbers presented in [9]. The best times achieved there were on a gigantic circuit doing 16384 AES encryptions in parallel. With this set-up, they achieved 32 ms amortised time per AES block. This circuit was not available to us here as it was custom built into a circuit generator written in Java.

Later Nielsen et. al. did experimentation with implementing TinyOT in C++. This later C++ implementation has been adapted to our set-up in plain C. This allows us to measure TinyOT performance on a single AES circuit in our framework. It is faster than the Java implementation used in [9] for one instance, probably because of the cost involved in starting up a Java process.

3.5 Empirical Results with TinyOT

The table below presents TinyOT runs on the test circuit in our setup. To get some parallelism we try to run several TinyOT processes. From the numbers it is evident that running multiple TinyOT processes in parallel actually hurts performance making each AES circuit slower. The explanation for this is that TinyOT exhausts the CPU resource on our test machines, probably in part because the administration involved in running several separate processes hurts performance.

Instances	No AES	Total Time (ms)	Time per AES (ms)
1	1	1079	1079 ± 251
2	2	1414	707 ± 183
4	4	4740	1185 ± 229
8	8	10451	1306 ± 187
16	16	41998	2624 ± 261

Fig. 6. Running TinyOT (the C version) on one instance of our AES circuit

4 MiniTrix

In this section we boost MiniMac in a number of ways.

4.1 Making the Protocol Symmetric for Multiplications

In MiniMac one player has a special role when transforming $[\![\sigma]\!]^*$ back to $[\![\sigma]\!]$ where all players wait on one player to do the re-encoding of σ as codeword in C. This happens both when multiplying with a public constant and when multiplying two secret values. This step, transforming a C^* codeword to C requires communication in the order of $2N$-codeword for N players.

With this trick we make the protocol symmetric, by opening $[\![\sigma]\!]^*$ among all players. Now each party in parallel can extract $\langle\sigma\rangle$ and reencode it in C. This increases the overall communication complexity from $2N$ to N^2, however for small N and in particular in the two party case this makes no difference, and evens out the workload for the parties. However, we did not see any significant impact of this optimization.

4.2 Use Fast Fourier Transform for Encoding

The naive MiniMac implementation spends most of its CPU-time in matrix by vector multiplications during the encoding of codewords.

Naive matrix by vector multiplication is quadratic in the length of the codeword, n, and hence there is a lot to gain by reducing this using the Fast Fourier Transform (FFT[4,3]).

In its basic form, FFT can be thought of as a recursive algorithm for multiplying a vector by an $n \times n$ Vandermonde matrix M, or its inverse. In order for this to work, the matrix must contain powers of an n'th root of unity. More specifically, starting indices from 0, the (i, j)'th entry in the matrix should be ω^{ij}, where $\omega^n = 1$. We call this matrix M_ω. If we think of a vector x as containing coefficients of a polynomial of degree (at most) $n - 1$, then computing $M_\omega x$ will evaluate the polynomial in the points $\omega^0, \omega^1, \ldots, \omega^{n-1}$, it can therefore be used for Reed-Solomon encoding.

FFT works by breaking the problem into two instance of size $n/2$ each, and in order for this to work recursively, it is usually assumed that n is a two-power. In this case, the algorithm takes time $O(n \log n)$ field multiplications. However, even if n is not a two-power but factors into smaller primes, variants of the algorithm can still be used to break the problem into smaller pieces and improve performance.

In our field $\mathbb{F}_{2^8}$, the multiplicative group has order 255, which factors into $3 \cdot 5 \cdot 17$. The field therefore contains a root of unity ω of order 255, which means that ω^3 is a root of unity of order 85. This allows us to use a Reed-Solomon code of length 255 and dimension 85, where all the required operations can be done using (a variant of) FFT:

Systematic encoding can be done by multiplying the data vector x by the 85×85 matrix $M_{\omega^3}^{-1}$ to get y containing coefficients of a polynomial that evaluates to the coordinates of x in the points $(\omega^3)^i$, $i = 0...84$. Then we compute $M_\omega y$ to get the full codeword. Note that the protocol only requires to encode in C, not in C^*. We can test if c is in C (or C^*) by computing $M_\omega^{-1} c$. This should reconstruct the polynomial underlying the purported codeword, and then we simply test if the degree is low enough.

Even using one level of recursion in FFT reduces significantly the work we need for these operations. Because 17 divides the size of both matrices, we can break both problems in 17 smaller pieces, and for multiplication by M_ω, for instance, this reduces the work from $256^2 = 65536$ field multiplications to $255 * 15 + 255 * 17 = 8160$.

Instances	No AES	Total Time (ms)	Time per AES (ms)
1	85	53699	631
2	170	59505	424
4	340	79092	207
8	680	107512	146
16	1360	257609	115

Fig. 7. Running a varying number MiniMac instances using FFT encoding

4.3 Preprocessing Dedicated for Binary Circuits

Minimac provides secure field arithmetic, and basing everything on $\mathbb{F}_2$ directly seems natural if the overall goal is secure Boolean circuit evaluation. However, constructing *binary* codes with the right properties is non-trivial as explained earlier. In this paper we solved this issue by using codes over $\mathbb{F}_{2^8}$. But this means that, although every data vector we encode will have binary entries, positions in the resulting codeword will be bytes where only the least significant position contains data; all other bit positions are identically 0. It is natural to ask if we can exploit all eight positions in each data byte. Thus, the goal here will be to evaluate not k, but $8k$ ($\log |\mathbb{F}| \cdot k$ in general) identical circuits in parallel, using the same code as before and therefore (ideally) at the same cost.

We can certainly encode a vector x that contains data in all bit positions, to get $[\![x]\!]$, and our addition $[\![x]\!] + [\![y]\!] = [\![x + y]\!]$ indeed implements $8k$ XOR operations in parallel, simply because the addition in $\mathbb{F}_{2^8}$ is the same as bit-wise XOR on bytes.

This means that we just need to redesign the multiplication protocol so that from $[\![x]\!]$, $[\![y]\!]$, we can compute $[\![x \wedge y]\!]$, where for $x = (x_1, ..., x_k)$, $y = (y_1, ..., y_k)$ we define $[\![x \wedge y]\!] = (x_1 \wedge y_1, ..., x_k \wedge y_k)$, and where $x_i \wedge y_i$ denotes bit-wise AND on bytes.

To get started, let us recall the MiniMac multiplication protocol (since we are in characteristic 2, we simplify some expressions by replacing some minus signs by plus).

To multiply $[\![x]\!]$, $[\![y]\!]$, parties take a triple $([\![a]\!], [\![b]\!], [\![c]\!]^*)$ and a pair of random values $[\![s]\!]$, $[\![s]\!]^*$ from the set of the available ones and do:

1. Open $[\![x]\!] + [\![a]\!]$ to get ϵ and $[\![y]\!] + [\![b]\!]$ to get δ to every player.
2. Compute $[\![x * y]\!]^* \leftarrow [\![c]\!]^* + \epsilon * [\![b]\!] + \delta * [\![a]\!] + \epsilon * \delta$ to every player.
3. Open $[\![x * y]\!]^* + [\![s]\!]^*$ to every player who gets $\sigma^* \in C^*$. P_1 extracts $x * y + s$ and encodes this value into a codeword $\sigma \in C$ which he broadcasts.
4. All players check that σ^*, σ are codewords for the same value and then compute $[\![x * y]\!] \leftarrow \sigma + [\![s]\!]$.

Note here that ϵ and δ are codewords. In general for $c \in C$ we will let $C^{-1}(c)$ denote the k-vector that c encodes. The reader should notice that the reason why step 2 above works is that $C^{-1}(\epsilon) = x + a$ and $C^{-1}(\delta) = y + b$.

Now, the idea is to change the computation in step 2. above. Instead we will compute:

$$[\![x \wedge y]\!]^* = [\![C^{-1}(\delta) \wedge C^{-1}(\epsilon)]\!] + [\![C^{-1}(\epsilon) \wedge a]\!]^* + [\![C^{-1}(\delta) \wedge b]\!]^* + [\![a \wedge b]\!]^*$$

It is easy to see that this equation is true, simply because the $\wedge$ operation distributes over bit-wise XOR just like the $*$-operation does. Essentially, we are simply using Beaver triples for $\mathbb{F}_2$, where the product is stored as a $\mathbb{F}_{2^8}$-element. Note that it makes sense to add $[\![]\!]$ and $[\![]\!]^*$-representations since our C is contained in C^*. Therefore $[\![C^{-1}(\delta) \wedge C^{-1}(\epsilon)]\!]$ is also a $[\![]\!]^*$-representation of the same vector (albeit not a random such representation).

Now we need to figure out how we can compute the 4 terms on the right-hand side. The last term can be obtained by requiring that the preprocessing supplies us with $[\![c]\!]^* = [\![a \wedge b]\!]^*$. Also, the first term can be computed on public values by all parties.

The "mixed terms" $[\![C^{-1}(\epsilon) \wedge a]\!]^*, [\![C^{-1}(\delta) \wedge b]\!]^*$ constitute a challenge. To compute these, the multiplication triples from the preprocessing phase are extended so that in addition to $[\![a]\!]$ and $[\![b]\!]$, the "bit decomposition" of a and b is also provided.

To explain what this means we need some notation. Say $a = (a_1, ..., a_k)$ where each $a_j \in \mathbb{F}_{2^8}$. Let $(a_j)_i$ be the byte that equals a_j in the i'th bit position and is 0 elsewhere. Furthermore, $(a_j)_{\downarrow i}$ denotes $(a_j)_i$ shifted down $i - 1$ positions, so that the "important" bit is in the least significant position. Then we define $a_i = ((a_1)_i, ..., (a_k)_i)$ and $a_{\downarrow i} = ((a_1)_{\downarrow i}...., (a_k)_{\downarrow i})$.

The assumption on the preprocessing now is that we that we are given $[\![a_i]\!], [\![b_i]\!]$ for $i = 0...7$.

One can now observe that we can compute the missing terms as follows:

$$\sum_{i=0}^{7} C(C^{-1}(\delta)_{\downarrow i}) * [\![a_i]\!] = \sum_{i=0}^{7} [\![C^{-1}(\delta)_{\downarrow i} * a_i]\!]^{*} = [\![C^{-1}(\delta) \wedge a]\!]^{*}$$

Note that we multiply by the public constant $C(C^{-1}(\delta)_{\downarrow i})$ using the normal MiniMac procedure that works over $\mathbb{F}_{2^8}$. Hence the result will indeed be a vector in the $[\![]\!]^{*}$-representation. That the vector inside the representation is indeed $C^{-1}(\delta) \wedge a$ can be seen from the fact that each byte in $C^{-1}(\delta)_{\downarrow i}$ has the value 0 or 1, depending on the value of the corresponding bits from $C^{-1}(\delta)$. It therefore acts as a "selector" that decides whether to include the bits from a_i.

A final modification concerns that last two steps in the original protocol, where the result is converted from $[\![]\!]^{*}$ to $[\![]\!]$-representation. This costs communication that we would like to avoid. To do this, consider what happens if we simply omit this conversion. This would mean that data would be passed from one gate to another using the $[\![]\!]^{*}$-representation instead. This presents no problem for doing linear computation, as the $[\![]\!]^{*}$-representation is also linear.

For the multiplication protocol to take input in the $[\![]\!]^{*}$-representation, we can just modify the preprocessing so that it would supply $[\![a]\!]^{*}, [\![b]\!]^{*}$ in stead of $[\![a]\!], [\![b]\!]$. The only effect of this is that then ϵ, δ will be C^{*}-codewords, but this has no effect on the rest of the protocol, since we anyway need to decode them and re-encode the bits in C; thus, C^{*-1} will simply denote the extraction of the first k data-entries of a C^{*} codeword.

To summarize, the multiplication triples have been replaced by a different set of data, namely

$$[\![a]\!]^{*}, \ [\![b]\!]^{*}, \ [\![a \wedge b]\!]^{*}, \ \{[\![a_i]\!]\mid i = 0...7\}, \ \{[\![b_i]\!]\mid i = 0...7\}$$

The multiplication protocol works as follows:

1. Open $[\![x]\!]^{*} + [\![a]\!]^{*}$ to get ϵ and $[\![y]\!]^{*} + [\![b]\!]^{*}$ to get δ, for every player. The following steps are then done using local operations only.
2. Compute $[\![C^{*-1}(\epsilon) \wedge C^{*-1}(\delta)]\!]$
3. Compute $\sum_{i=0}^{7} C(C^{*-1}(\delta)_{\downarrow i}) * [\![a_i]\!] = [\![C^{*-1}(\delta) \wedge a]\!]^{*}$.
4. Compute $\sum_{i=0}^{7} C(C^{*-1}(\epsilon)_{\downarrow i}) * [\![b_i]\!] = [\![C^{*-1}(\epsilon) \wedge b]\!]^{*}$.
5. Compute $[\![C^{*-1}(\delta) \wedge C^{*-1}(\epsilon)]\!] + [\![C^{*-1}(\epsilon) \wedge a]\!]^{*} + [\![C^{*-1}(\delta) \wedge b]\!]^{*} + [\![a \wedge b]\!]^{*} = [\![x \wedge y]\!]^{*}$

Theoretical Analysis of the Binary Preprocessing. It is easy to see that the above methods generalizes to any field of characteristic 2. In general the field should be of size $O(\log(n))$ to allow the use of Reed-Solomon codes and hence allow for efficient encoding using FFT.

Following [7], we compute the cost of the protocol per player per gate in the circuit we compute. By simple inspection, one sees that the storage needed from the preprocessing is $O(\log(n))$ (namely $O(1)$ field elements). The communication is $O(1)$ bits because we only do 2 openings in each multiplication protocol, and each such protocol does $\log(n)$ AND gates. Finally the computational work is $O(\text{polylog}(n))$ bit operations due to the use of FFT. As explained in the Introduction, this improves on the original MiniMac for communication and computational work. We also save one round of communication.

Experimentation and Performance Numbers. In the above we actually present two tricks. The first trick allows us to utilize all eight bits of each field element. We call this the *bit-packing trick*. In the second trick we reduce the communication complexity of the protocol by removing the down conversion from codewords in the Schur transform to codewords in C, we call this the *zero-degree constants* trick because it takes advantage of the fact that all constants in our circuit is the same value repeated many times and thus the underlying encoding polynomial must be constant.

Instances	No AES	Total Time (ms)	Time per AES (ms)
1	960	58127	60 ± 2
2	1920	104840	76 ± 6
4	3840	224146	58 ± 2
8	7680	591523	77 ± 7
16	15360	1094454	71 ± 6

Fig. 8. Running MiniMac with bit-packing-trick only, with standard matrix encoding

Instances	No AES	Total Time (ms)	Time per AES (ms)
1	680	19410	24 ± 4
2	1360	36235	26 ± 3
4	2720	71082	24 ± 8
8	5440	196322	34 ± 30
16	10880	428458	39 ± 1

Fig. 9. Running MiniMac with bit-packing-trick only, with Fast Fourier Transform encoding

4.4   Simultaneous Multiplication Gates

The present optimization is based on the observation that network utilization is much higher for large batches of data. Thus, collecting a larger amount of data before communication should give better performance.

In the previous sections our MiniMac implementation was general and works even if the circuit is streamed, e.g. without any knowledge of what is coming ahead. If our circuit description is extended with hints about which gates can be run simultaneously, then the protocol can be made to run faster. In particular, we extend our implementation to use such hints to compute blocks of multiplication (AND) gates. The hints that we allow in the circuit description describe how many of the following multiplications are independent (e.g. the number of AND gates in the following that will not read the results of each other).

Lets us recap the communication pattern in MiniMac during a multiplication from one players pointer of view:

1 The codewords for δ and ϵ are sent to every other player along with their MACs. This requires $4*n*N$ bytes of communication. Where n is the length of a codeword and N is the number of players.
2 Receive δ and ϵ with MACs from every other player.
3 Local computation, including checking the incoming MACs.

The idea is to collect say M independent AND gates before initiating communication. Then on the M'th gate the peers exchange M δ- and ϵ-values with MACs.

Instances	No AES	Total Time (ms)	Time per AES (ms)
1	960	55917	58 ± 20
2	1920	95321	70 ± 56
4	3840	205667	85 ± 148
8	7680	334529	43 ± 24
16	15360	282940	42 ± 20

Fig. 10. Running MiniMac with bit-packing-trick and simultaneous multiplication trick, with matrix encoding

Instances	No AES	Total Time (ms)	Time per AES (ms)
1	680	14313	21 ± 2
2	1360	27893	28 ± 22
4	2720	69452	25 ± 4
8	5440	140540	25 ± 6
16	10880	257556	23 ± 3

Fig. 11. Running MiniMac with bit-packing-trick and simultaneous multiplication trick, with FFT encoding

4.5   Fast Encoding of Binary Data

One should notice that in the above multiplication protocol we need to encode $C^{*-1}(\epsilon)_{\downarrow i}$ for $i = 0...7$. However, each entry in these vectors is 0 or 1, due to the shift down we did. Therefore, we can encode much faster than in general by simply XOR-ing together those rows of the generator matrix that correspond to positions in the vector that are 1. Packing bytes together in word-size chunk allows us to do this on several bytes using one CPU instruction.

Instances	No AES	Total Time (ms)	Time per AES (ms)
1	960	18060	18 ± 1
2	1920	37614	19 ± 6
4	3840	118878	28 ± 10
8	7680	252111	18 ± 10
16	15360	304846	19 ± 7

Fig. 12. Running MiniMac with bit-packing-trick, zero-degree-constants and simultaneous multiplication trick, with matrix bit encoding trick

Instances	No AES	Total Time (ms)	Time per AES (ms)
1	680	9962	14 ± 1
2	1360	17553	14 ± 5
4	2720	39886	15 ± 5
16	10880	195992	18 ± 7

Fig. 13. Running MiniMac with bit-packing-trick, zero-degree-constants and simultaneous multiplication trick, with FFT bit encoding trick

4.6 Final Optimizations

Just before the deadline for this version of the paper, we did some final experiments that greatly improved the performance. First, we observed from profiling the program that a lot of time was spent waiting for data to arrive on the communication line. In other words, both players had idle time we should be able to exploit. We therefore tried starting 8 copies of our original process with a time interval of 200ms in between them, hoping to allow some instances to compute while others were waiting. This improved the time per AES instance to about 9 ms (using 8 copies of the program seemed experimentally to be the best choice). Finally, we experimented with compiler flags and found a setting that allowed better exploitation of the CPU. This gave another factor of about 2, so that we end up with about 4 ms per AES.

5   Conclusion

We have proposed several optimisations of the MiniMac protocol, both on implementation and protocol level. In the fastest configuration of MiniMac using Fast Fourier transform and bit encoding trick with simultaneous multiplications gates we evaluate an AES circuit in 4 ms on our test setup. As far as we are aware, this is the fastest published actively secure two-party implementation of AES with 128-bit security based on a Boolean circuit.

6   Future Directions

All experiments in this paper are run on the same AES circuit. To improve performance one may try to optimize the AES circuit, for instance by reducing further the number of AND gates. Since a lot of the description of AES uses arithmetic over $\mathbb{F}_{2^8}$ it seems natural to try an arithmetic circuit over $\mathbb{F}_{2^8}$. However, the circuits of this type that we know of are all significantly larger than the binary circuit we use here. However, it is likely that adding the bit decomposition trick used in [8] could help here, so this seems an obvious direction to try in future work. However, AES leads to very specialized circuits, so it natural to broaden the scope and consider other binary circuits, for instance for hash functions such as SHA-1.

During our work with MiniMac many Operating System dependent obstacles has been identified. In particular the handling of when the TCP actually sends data. It is possible that tweaking Linux network stack parameters, and/or other strategies for better scheduling may increase throughput further.

Acknowledgements. We would like to thank Nigel Smart, Stefan Tillich and their crew at Bristol for providing a selection of excellent circuits at http://www.cs.bris.ac.uk/Research/CryptographySecurity/MPC/. Also we would like to thank Jesper Buus Nielsen for providing source code for the TinyOT C++ implementation.

References

1. Beaver, D.: Efficient multiparty protocols using circuit randomization. In: Feigenbaum, J. (ed.) CRYPTO 1991. LNCS, vol. 576, pp. 420–432. Springer, Heidelberg (1992)
2. Bendlin, R., Damgård, I., Orlandi, C., Zakarias, S.: Semi-homomorphic encryption and multiparty computation. In: Paterson, K.G. (ed.) EUROCRYPT 2011. LNCS, vol. 6632, pp. 169–188. Springer, Heidelberg (2011)
3. Conte, S.D., De Boor, C.: Elementary Numerical Analysis: An Algorithmic Approach. International series in pure and applied mathematics. McGraw-Hill (1980)
4. Cooley, J.W., Tukey, J.W.: An algorithm for the machine calculation of complex fourier series. Math. comput. 19(90), 297–301 (1965)
5. Damgård, I., Keller, M., Larraia, E., Pastro, V., Scholl, P., Smart, N.P.: Practical covertly secure MPC for dishonest majority – or: Breaking the SPDZ limits. In: Crampton, J., Jajodia, S., Mayes, K. (eds.) ESORICS 2013. LNCS, vol. 8134, pp. 1–18. Springer, Heidelberg (2013)
6. Damgård, I., Pastro, V., Smart, N., Zakarias, S.: Multiparty computation from somewhat homomorphic encryption. In: Safavi-Naini, R., Canetti, R. (eds.) CRYPTO 2012. LNCS, vol. 7417, pp. 643–662. Springer, Heidelberg (2012)
7. Damgård, I., Zakarias, S.: Constant-overhead secure computation of boolean circuits using preprocessing. In: Sahai, A. (ed.) TCC 2013. LNCS, vol. 7785, pp. 621–641. Springer, Heidelberg (2013)
8. Keller, M., Scholl, P., Smart, N.P.: An architecture for practical actively secure mpc with dishonest majority. In: Proceedings of the 2013 ACM SIGSAC Conference on Computer & Communications Security, pp. 549–560. ACM (2013)
9. Nielsen, J.B., Nordholt, P.S., Orlandi, C., Burra, S.S.: A new approach to practical active-secure two-party computation. In: Safavi-Naini, R., Canetti, R. (eds.) CRYPTO 2012. LNCS, vol. 7417, pp. 681–700. Springer, Heidelberg (2012)

Efficient NIZK Arguments via Parallel Verification of Benes Networks

Helger Lipmaa

Institute of Computer Science, University of Tartu, Estonia

Abstract. We work within the recent paradigm, started by Groth (ASI-ACRYPT 2010), of constructing short non-interactive zero knowledge arguments from a small number basic arguments in a modular fashion. The main technical result of this paper is a new permutation argument, by using product and shift arguments of Lipmaa (2014) and a parallelizable variant of the Benes network. We use it to design a short non-interactive zero knowledge argument for the **NP**-complete language CIRCUITSAT with $\Theta(n \log^2 n)$ prover's computational complexity, where n is the size of the circuit. The permutation argument can be naturally used to design direct NIZK arguments for many other **NP**-complete languages.

Keywords: Beneš networks, modular NIZK arguments, perfect zero knowledge, product argument, shift argument, shuffle.

1 Introduction

To construct a cryptographic protocol secure against malicious adversaries, one needs to employ zero-knowledge proofs [14]. To enable verifiability even in the case the prover is not online, zero-knowledge proofs must be non-interactive. Since in many applications, the proof will be verified by many independent verifiers (e.g., by many voters in an e-voting applications), then it is also desirable that the proofs be short. Finally, in several applications (like delegation of computation) one needs to construct a short non-interactive zero-knowledge (NIZK) proofs for generic **NP**-complete languages (like CIRCUITSAT).

Motivated by such applications, Groth [16] constructed a non-interactive zero knowledge and computationally sound NIZK proof (i.e., an NIZK argument) for CIRCUITSAT with communication that is a small constant number of group elements. Groth's CIRCUITSAT argument is constructed in a modular fashion from a small number of more basic arguments. More precisely, it consists of less than 10 basic Hadamard product (given three committed vectors, one of them is an entry-wise product of the other two) and permutation (given two committed vectors and a public permutation ϱ, the coefficients of one vector are ϱ-permuted coefficients of the second vector) arguments. Unfortunately, both basic arguments have CRS length (in group elements) and prover's computation (in exponentiations) quadratic in the vector dimension n, and as the result, the corresponding complexity parameters of the CIRCUITSAT argument are quadratic

M. Abdalla and R. De Prisco (Eds.): SCN 2014, LNCS 8642, pp. 416–434, 2014.

in the circuit size $|C|$. Due to this, Groth's original argument can only be used for relatively small $|C|$.

Subsequent research has improved on Groth's modular approach by both increasing the efficiency of Groth's basic arguments and studying the possibility to implement arguments for **NP**-complete languages by using different (hopefully more efficient) basic arguments. Lipmaa [19] improved Groth's basic arguments, by using progression-free sets (see Sect. 2). For vectors of length n, Lipmaa's basic arguments have CRS length of $\Theta(r_3^{-1}(n))$ group elements, while the prover's computation is dominated by $\Theta(n^2)$ scalar additions. Here, $r_3(N)$ is the size of some progression-free subset of $[N] = \{1, \ldots, N\}$. However, due to quadratic prover's computation, also Lipmaa's CIRCUITSAT argument is useful only for small $|C|$. In [12], Fauzi, Lipmaa and Zhang implemented Lipmaa's product argument in prover's computational complexity $\Theta(r_3^{-1}(n) \log r_3^{-1}(n))$ multiplications. Finally, in [21], Lipmaa used a different approach to construct a product argument with the CRS length of $\Theta(n)$ group elements and prover's computation of $\Theta(n \log n)$ non-cryptographic and $\Theta(n)$ cryptographic operations. His product argument is based on the so called *interpolating commitment scheme*.

However, none of the subsequent work improved on the asymptotic computation of the permutation argument. Instead, [12] proposed a new z-left/right shift argument (given two committed vectors, one of them is a coordinate-wise z-shift of the second vector) with linear CRS size and prover's computation. They then used the product and shift arguments to implement computationally more efficient modular NIZK arguments for the **NP**-complete languages SETPARTITION, SUBSETSUM and DECISIONKNAPSACK. (For the latter, they also need an efficient NIZK range argument, [8], which can be constructed by using product and shift arguments as shown in [12,21].) Lipmaa showed in [21] how to use the interpolating commitment scheme to efficiently implement the shift arguments, and thus also the corresponding **NP**-complete languages. Since the prover's computation in the arguments from [21] is $\Theta(n \log n)$, these arguments are usable for much larger input sizes n than the CIRCUITSAT arguments from [16,19].

On the other hand, while [12] proposed computationally efficient NIZK arguments for SETPARTITION, SUBSETSUM and DECISIONKNAPSACK, it did not propose one for CIRCUITSAT. CIRCUITSAT is a natural language to be used in various cryptographic applications, like verifiable computation. Moreover, CIRCUITSAT is often used as a benchmark to show the efficiency of new zero-knowledge techniques. Therefore, construction of a CIRCUITSAT argument with subquadratic CRS length and prover's computation and short (i.e., polylogarithmic) communication is still an important open problem.

Finally, any further advances will help one to better understand the power and limitations of the modular approach. It is likely (we will motivate this intuition later) that efficient modular arguments for other **NP**-complete languages can be constructed by using the permutation argument, and thus it is important to construct a permutation argument with better prover's computation.

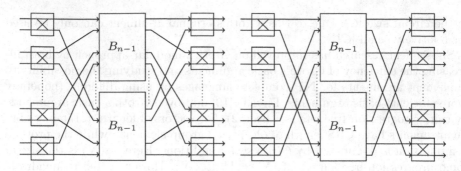

Fig. 1. The usual definition of Beneš network B_n (left), and our definition (right). The boxes with blue X denote crossbars in the input and output stage.

Our Contributions. We construct a new permutation argument for n-bit vectors, by using Beneš network [4] to combine $\Theta(\log n)$ product and shift arguments. This results in a permutation argument with $\Theta(n \log^2 n)$ prover's computation and logarithmic communication. We then plug the new permutation argument in to the NIZK arguments of [16,19] to obtain a CIRCUITSAT argument with the same asymptotic complexity. Apart from being the most efficient CIRCUITSAT argument following from the modular paradigm, the new CIRCUITSAT argument is the most complex known yet still competitively efficient NIZK argument in the modular framework. We also outline how to use the new permutation argument to construct efficient NIZK arguments for other **NP**-complete languages.

Let S_n denote the symmetric group. The Beneš network $B_{\log_2 n}$, see Fig. 1, is a multistage interconnection network [18]. Every stage consists of a number of crossbars, the outputs of which are wired to the inputs of the next stage's crossbars. The only changeable elements are the S_2-permutations implemented by each of the crossbars. Assuming that n is a power of 2, the definition of a Beneš network $B_{\log_2 n}$ is usually given recursively, from two copies of $B_{\log_2 n-1}$, an input stage (that has $n/2$ crossbars) and an output stage (that has $n/2 - 1$ crossbars; one crossbar can be fixed to implement the identity map), as in Fig. 1 (left). The network B_1 consists of a single crossbar. Each crossbar implements a permutation from S_2.

The Beneš network $B_{\log_2 n}$ implements a permutation from S_n by using nearly optimal $n \cdot \log_2 n - n + 1$ crossbars and $2 \log_2 n - 1$ stages ($\log_2 n$ input stages, followed by a single stage that implements B_1, followed by $\log_2 n$ output stages). A stage here consists of $n/2$ parallel crossbars, followed by wirings from the outputs of the crossbars of the current stage to the inputs of the next stage.

A straightforward use of Beneš networks results in a permutation (and shuffle) argument of length $\Theta(n \log n)$ [1,2]. We achieve logarithmic communication and $\Theta(n \log^2 n)$ prover's computation by verifying *in parallel* that all crossbars of the same stage of the Beneš network have been implemented correctly; this seems to be a novel use of Beneš networks. We use a small number of product and shift arguments from [21] (each of which has $\Theta(n \log n)$ prover's computation and constant communication) at every stage. Since there are $\Theta(\log n)$ stages, the resulting permutation argument consists of $\Theta(\log n)$ basic arguments.

It is not immediately clear from the standard recursive definition of Beneš networks (Fig. 1, left) how to do parallel verification. We use a slight variant (that we call a *parallelizable Beneš network*) of the usual Beneš network, see Fig. 1 (right), that is also a well-known but not the usually presented definition. In that variant, at every stage, input elements of the stage are permuted twice.

First, in crossbars, the ith input of a stage will become to the jth input of the wirings, where depending on the S_2-permutation implemented by the concrete crossbar, $j \in \{i - 1 \mod n, i, i + 1 \mod n\}$. That is, the jth output bit of the crossbars is either equal to the jth bit of the input a of the crossbars, or it is equal to the jth bit of either 1-left or 1-right shift of a. Which case happens depends on the number of the stage, the index i, and the input to the network.

Second, after the wiring, the ith output of the crossbars will go to the jth input of the next stage, where $j \in \{i - z \mod n, i, i + z \mod n\}$, where z is a stage-dependent constant. That is, the jth output bit of the wiring is either equal to jth input bit of the wiring, or to the jth bit of a z-left or z-right shift of the input of the wiring. Importantly, which case happens depends only on the number of the stage and on i, and not on the input to the network, that is, not on the concrete permutation. In the usual variant of the Beneš networks as in Fig. 1 (left), all possible z-shifts, $z \leq n/2$, are used in wirings of every stage.

These observations make it possible to verify correct implementation of one stage of the Beneš network by using a small constant number of shift and product arguments. Therefore, correct implementation of the full Beneš network can be verified by using a logarithmic number of shift and product arguments. This results in a permutation argument with related complexity parameters.

While the resulting new permutation argument, has larger communication than Groth's and Lipmaa's permutation arguments [19], it has smaller prover's computation.[1] Since quadratic prover's computation is the main obstacle in actually applying Groth's short arguments, this means that now one can use a significantly larger value of n. The relatively minor increase in the communication (from $\Theta(1)$ to $\Theta(\log n)$, where n is the circuit size) is comparatively less important.

Both the prover and the verifier have to execute an online routing algorithm that outputs the necessary shift amounts. For (the standard variant of the) Beneš network, routing can be done in time $\Theta(n \log n)$ on a single processor [28,24], or $\Theta(\log^2 n)$ on a parallel computer [23]. Clearly, routing algorithms can be modified to work with the parallelizable Beneš networks without any loss in efficiency.

We can use the methodology of Groth [16] and Lipmaa [19] to construct a CIRCUITSAT argument, given the product argument of [21] and the permutation argument of the current paper. Hence, one can construct modular

---

[1] It also has verifier's computation of $\Theta(n \log n)$ multiplications. This is larger than in [16], but smaller than in [19], where one needed $\Theta(n)$ exponentiations. (Since one exponentiation takes $\Theta(\log p)$ multiplications, and $n \ll p$.)

NIZK arguments of knowledge for **NP**-complete languages SETPARTITION [12], SUBSETSUM [12], DECISIONKNAPSACK [12] and CIRCUITSAT ([16], [19], and the current paper) that are all based on the simple "parallel programming language" consisting of two arguments, Hadamard product and (z-)shift. The fact that one can construct a CIRCUITSAT argument from the weaker set of basic primitives than in previous papers [16,19], where the programming language consisted of the product and (arbitrary) permutation arguments, can be seen as an additional contribution of the current paper. Since every shift argument is quadratically more efficient than the permutation argument of [16,19], using $\Theta(\log n)$ of them results still in a major win in efficiency.

Interestingly, the arguments for SETPARTITION, SUBSETSUM and DECISIONKNAPSACK [12,21] are more efficient than the new argument for CIRCUITSAT, and the new CIRCUITSAT argument is by far the most complex existing program in such a language. We leave it as an open question to design efficient direct (i.e., one obtained without a reduction to another **NP**-complete language) NIZK arguments for other **NP**-complete languages, and to study why some languages have more efficient arguments than others.

However, one can use the permutation argument and the product argument to construct NIZK argument for many **NP**-complete languages as follows. First, use a permutation argument (by using a *secret* permutation) to permute the inputs randomly. (See App. B for a description of how to efficiently modify the new permutation argument to handle secret permutations. The resulting argument can be seen as a *committed shuffle* argument that one committed vector is a shuffle of another vector.) Second, use a product argument to clear the bits of the inputs that are not needed to verify the witness (this can be done by checking that the permuted input a and the cleared version b satisfy $a_i \cdot c_i = b_i$, where c_i is a publicly known Boolean vector). After that, one reveals the cleared version of the inputs, from which one can — in the case of many **NP**-complete languages — directly verify the witness. This results in direct NIZK arguments for a large family of **NP**-complete languages.

As a high-level example, in the case of the HAMILTONIANPATH argument, the prover has to show that there exists a path that visits each vertex once. Here, the prover chooses a random secret permutation ϱ that permutes the input (which is usually represented as an $n \times n$ adjacency matrix), modulo the restriction that the Hamiltonian path visits vertices in the order $1 \to 2 \to 3 \ldots \to n \to 1$. The prover uses a committed shuffle argument to show that the (secret) permutation was done correctly. The prover then uses a product argument to clear $n^2 - n$ elements of the adjacency matrix, and then opens the cleared adjacency matrix. In the case that the graph had an Hamiltonian path, the opened adjacency matrix has 1-s in positions $(i, i + 1 \mod n)$. The language CLIQUE has a very similar argument, except that one verifies that the opened adjacency matrix starts with an all-1 $m \times m$ matrix for some parameter m. We leave the precise details together with bringing further examples to the future work.

We remark that the parallel programming model that consists of shift and entry-wise addition and product is well-known both in theoretical computer science [26] and parallel computing [6], but up to our knowledge it has not been applied before the current line of work (starting with [16] and made explicit in [19,12]) to verify the solutions of **NP**-complete languages — even without requiring the zero knowledge property.

Comparison to the QSP/QAP-Based Approach. In [13], Gennaro, Gentry, Parno, and Raykova showed how to construct a more efficient (linear CRS, $\Theta(n \log^3 n)$ prover's computation, constant communication, and linear verifier's computation) NIZK argument for CIRCUITSAT. The prover's computation can be improved to $\Theta(n \log^2 n)$ when one uses bilinear groups of well-chosen prime order p [13,20,21]. Their — based either on Quadratic Span Programs or Quadratic Arithmetic Programs — argument has been further improved in say [5,3,20].

First, the arguments of [13] are directly tailored for (arithmetic) CIRCUITSAT. It is unclear how to use these arguments for any **NP**-complete language $\mathcal{L}$, except via a potentially costly polynomial-time reduction. Even if this reduction takes time say $\Theta(n \log^2 n)$, the resulting argument for $\mathcal{L}$ becomes too slow (in prover's computation).

Second, our approach is completely different and therefore still interesting by itself. It is clearly beneficial to study different approaches to the same problem.

2   Preliminaries

Let $[L, H] = \{L, L + 1, \ldots, H - 1, H\}$ and $[H] = [1, H]$. By $\boldsymbol{a}$, we denote the vector $\boldsymbol{a} = (a_1, \ldots, a_n)$. For a group $\mathbb{G}$, we utilize the fact that $\mathbb{G}^2 = \mathbb{G} \times \mathbb{G}$ is a group and thus aggressively use notation like $(g, h)^a$ or $(g_1, h_1) \cdot (g_2, h_2)$. If $y = h^x$, then let $\log_h y := x$. We abbreviate probabilistic polynomial-time as PPT, and let $\mathrm{negl}(\kappa)$ be an arbitrary negligible function.

Preliminaries on Interconnection Networks. The basic components of a switching network [18] (e.g., see Fig. 1 or Fig. 2) are crossbars, and links that connect crossbars. A crossbar with n inlets and m outlets is denoted by X_{nm}. Any matching (one-to-one mapping) between the inlets and the outlets of a crossbar is considered routable, that is, a crossbar is *nonblocking*. By using different terminology, a crossbar X_{nn} can be fixed to implement any permutation from S_n. Two sets of crossbars are connected to outside world. One set of such crossbars is called input crossbars and another set output crossbars. The links on an input (output) crossbar linking to outside world are called inputs (outputs) of the network. An (N, M)-network has N inputs and M outputs, and will be called an N-network if $M = N$.

A network is (i) strict-sense nonblocking if one can, given the values of ϱ for some i together with corresponding routes in the network, always find nonintersecting routes for rest of the values of ϱ, (ii) wide-sense nonblocking if there is an algorithm for establishing paths in the network one after another, so that after each path is established, it is still possible to connect any unused input to any unused output, (iii) *rearrangeable* if it is only required that such choice of routes can be done for all i at the same time.

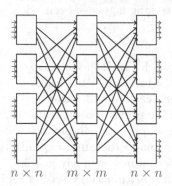

An (m, n)-Clos network [9,18] for a permutation $\varrho \in S_N$, where $N = mn$, is a three-stage network to implement ϱ, in which each stage is composed in a number of smaller crossbars. The first stage has m crossbars X_{nn}, the second stage has n crossbars X_{mm}, and the third stage has m crossbars X_{nn}. Each input crossbar is connected to each middle stage crossbar, and each middle stage crossbar is connected to each output crossbar. See Fig. 2. To implement an arbitrary permutation from S_{mn} it suffices to use a rearrangeable non-blocking network [9,4,18], for which one can choose an (m, n)-Clos network. (In fact, the Clos network is strict-sense nonblocking.) For this one just has to choose the $2m + n$ small permutations accordingly.

Fig. 2. An $(4, 4)$-Clos network for permutations from S_{16}

Beneš networks [4,18] implement an arbitrary permutation $\varrho : [N] \to [N]$ by using $2 \log_2 N - 1$ stages of X_{22} crossbars. Beneš network B_n (for permutation from S_{2^n}) is usually defined recursively by connecting an initial stage of $n/2$ X_{22} crossbars, two B_{n-1} networks and a final stage of $(n/2 - 1)$ X_{22} crossbars, as in Fig. 1, left. Clearly, the Beneš network $B_{\log_2 N}$ has $(N \log_2 N - N + 1)$ X_{22} crossbars. While the Clos network is strict-sense nonblocking, the Beneš network is only rearrangeable. Recall that X_{22} implements either an identity function id, $\mathrm{id}(x, y) = (x, y)$, or a flip flip, $\mathrm{flip}(x, y) = (y, x)$.

Waksman [28] and Opferman and Tsao-Wu [24] proposed efficient routing algorithms for the standard variant (Fig. 1, left) of the Beneš network. Their algorithm instantiates the $N \log_2 N - N + 1$ crossbars $\varrho_{i,j}$, given the input permutation ϱ, in time $\Theta(N \log N)$. Nassimi and Sahni [23] proposed a parallel routing algorithm for the Beneš network that works in time $\Theta(\log^2 N)$, given N parallel processors.

Cryptographic Preliminaries. On input 1^κ, where κ is the security parameter, a *bilinear map generator* returns $(p, \mathbb{G}_1, \mathbb{G}_2, \mathbb{G}_T, \hat{e}, g_1, g_2)$, where $\mathbb{G}_1$, $\mathbb{G}_2$ and $\mathbb{G}_T$ are three multiplicative cyclic groups of prime order p, g_z is a generator of $\mathbb{G}_z$ for $z \in \{1, 2\}$, and $\hat{e}$ is an efficient bilinear map $\hat{e} : \mathbb{G}_1 \times \mathbb{G}_2 \to \mathbb{G}_T$ that satisfies in particular the following two properties: (i) $\hat{e}(g_1, g_2) \neq 1$, and (ii) $\hat{e}(g_1^a, g_2^b) = \hat{e}(g_1, g_2)^{ab}$. Thus, if $\hat{e}(g_1^a, g_2^b) = \hat{e}(g_1^c, g_2^d)$ then $ab = cd \mod p$.

The security of the arguments of the current paper depends on the q-type computational and knowledge [10] assumptions, variants of which have been studied and used in say [15,11,16,8,19,5,12]. In fact, all known (to us) adaptive short NIZK arguments are based on q-type assumptions about genbp. We refer to [21] for a description of these assumptions.

Trapdoor commitment scheme is a randomized cryptographic primitive in the CRS model [7] that takes a message and outputs its commitment. It consists of two efficient algorithms gencom (that outputs a CRS and a trapdoor) and Com (that, given the CRS, a message and a randomizer, outputs a commitment), and must satisfy the following three security properties. **Computational binding:** without access to the trapdoor, it is intractable to open the same commitment to two different messages. **Perfect hiding:** commitments of any two messages have the same distribution. **Trapdoor:** given an access to the original message, the randomizer and the trapdoor, one can open a commitment to (say) 0 to an arbitrary message. See, e.g., [16] for formal definitions.

We use the following *interpolating commitment scheme* from [21]. Assume n is a power of 2, and assume that the group order p is such that there exist a nth primitive unit of root modulo p [21]. Let this unit be ω. Let $f_0(X) = Z(X)$ and $f_i(X) = \ell_i(X)$ be polynomials, defined as follows:

1. $Z(X) = \prod_{j=1}^{n}(X - \omega^{j-1}) = X^n - 1$, i.e., $Z(\omega^{i-1}) = 0$,
2. $\ell_i(X) = \prod_{j \neq i}(X - \omega^{j-1})/\prod_{j \neq i}(\omega^{i-1} - \omega^{j-1})$ is the ith Lagrange basic polynomial, i.e., $\ell_i(\omega^{i-1}) = 1$ and $\ell_i(\omega^{j-1}) = 0$ for $i \neq j$.

The CRS generation algorithm gencom(1^κ) first sets gk $\leftarrow$ genbp(1^κ), and then generates the trapdoor $(\sigma, \alpha) \leftarrow \mathbb{Z}_p^2$ (with $\sigma \neq 0$). It then outputs the common reference string ck $= ((g_1, g_2^\alpha)^{f(\sigma)})_{f \in \{Z, \ell_1, \ldots, \ell_n\}}$. The commmon reference string ck is made public, while the trapdoor (σ, α) is only used in security proofs. Define[2] $\mathcal{C}om_{ck}((a_1, \ldots, a_k); r) := \prod_{i=1}^{k}((g_1, g_2^\alpha)^{\ell_i(\sigma)})^{a_i} \cdot ((g_1, g_2^\alpha)^{Z(\sigma)})^r = (g_1, g_2^\alpha)^{rZ(\sigma) + \sum_{i=1}^{k} a_i \ell_i(\sigma)}$. The computation of $\mathcal{C}om$ can be sped up by using efficient multi-exponentiations algorithms [27,25]. We denote the output of the commitment either by (A_1, A_2^α) or by $(A, \hat{A})$.

As shown in [21], the interpolating commitment scheme is perfectly hiding, and computationally binding. Moreover, if a suitable knowledge assumption holds, then for any non-uniform PPT $\mathcal{A}$ that outputs a valid commitment C, there exists a non-uniform PPT extractor that, given $\mathcal{A}$'s input together with $\mathcal{A}$'s random coins, extracts a valid opening of C.

An NIZK argument for a language L consists of three algorithms, gencrs, $\mathcal{P}$ and $\mathcal{V}$. The CRS generation algorithm gencrs takes as input 1^κ (and possibly some other, public, language-dependent information) and outputs the CRS crs and the trapdoor td. The prover's algorithm $\mathcal{P}$ takes as an input crs together with a statement x and a witness w, and outputs an argument π. The verifier's algorithm $\mathcal{V}$ takes as an input crs together with a statement x and an argument π, and either accepts or rejects.

We expect the argument to be (i) perfectly complete (the honest verifier always accepts the honest prover), (ii) perfectly zero knowledge (there exists an efficient simulator who can, given x, crs and td, output an argument that comes from the same distribution as the argument produced by the prover),

---

[2] Here and in what follows, elements of the form $(g, g^\alpha)^x$, where α is a secret random key, can be thought of as a *linear-only encoding* of x, see [5] for a discussion.

and (iii) computationally sound (if $x \notin L$, then an arbitrary non-uniform PPT prover has only a negligible success in creating a satisfying argument). We refer to say [16,19] for formal definitions.

Assume that Γ is a (trapdoor) commitment scheme that commits to elements $\boldsymbol{a} = (a_1, \ldots, a_n) \in \mathbb{Z}_p^n$ for a prime p and integer $n \geq 1$. In an *Hadamard product argument* [16,19], the prover aims to convince the verifier that given commitments A, B and C, he can open them as $A = \mathcal{C}om(\mathsf{ck}; \boldsymbol{a}; r_a)$, $B = \mathcal{C}om(\mathsf{ck}; \boldsymbol{b}; r_b)$, and $C = \mathcal{C}om(\mathsf{ck}; \boldsymbol{c}; r_c)$, such that $c_i = a_i b_i$ for $i \in [n]$. In a *z-right shift argument* [12], the prover aims to convince the verifier that for two commitments A and B, he knows how to open them as $A = \mathcal{C}om(\mathsf{ck}; \boldsymbol{a}; r_a)$ and $B = \mathcal{C}om(\mathsf{ck}; \boldsymbol{b}; r_b)$, such that $a_i = b_{i+z}$ for $i \in [n-z]$, and $a_i = 0$ for $i \in [n-z+1, n]$. That is, $(a_1, \ldots, a_n) = (b_z, \ldots, b_n, 0, \ldots, 0)$. We define the z-left shift argument dually. In a *permutation argument* [16,19], the prover aims to convince the verifier that given commitments A and B and a permutation $\varrho \in S_n$, he can open them as $A = \mathcal{C}om(\mathsf{ck}; \boldsymbol{a}; r_a)$ and $B = \mathcal{C}om(\mathsf{ck}; \boldsymbol{b}; r_b)$, such that $b_i = a_{\varrho(i)}$ for $i \in [n]$.

We recall the following theorem from [21], but we only give the details that are needed in the following (for example, we state the precise security guarantees, but we leave out the description of the arguments themselves and the precise security assumptions). We do it to avoid overdependence on the concrete implementation of the basic arguments. We remark that the condition (2) in the theorem statement is called co-soundness, see [17] for an explanation.

Theorem 1 (Security of the product argument [21]). *Let $n = \mathrm{poly}(\kappa)$. Let $\mathcal{C}om$ be the interpolating commitment scheme.*

1. *The product argument from [21] is perfectly complete and perfectly witness-indistinguishable.*

2. *(CO-SOUNDNESS:) If genbp satisfies a q-type computational assumption from [21], then a non-uniform probabilistic polynomial-time adversary against the product argument from [21] has negligible chance, given $\mathsf{crs} \leftarrow \mathsf{gencrs}(1^\kappa, n)$ as an input, of outputting $\mathsf{inp}_\times = (A, \hat{A}, B, \hat{B}, C, \hat{C})$ and an accepting argument $\pi_\times$ together with a witness $w_\times = (\boldsymbol{a}, r_a, \boldsymbol{b}, r_b, \boldsymbol{c}, r_c)$, such that*

    (i) *$\boldsymbol{a}, \boldsymbol{b}, \boldsymbol{c} \in \mathbb{Z}_p^n$ and $r_a, r_b, r_c \in \mathbb{Z}_p$,*

    (ii) *$(A, \hat{A}) = \mathcal{C}om(\mathsf{ck}; \boldsymbol{a}; r_a)$, $(B, \hat{B}) = \mathcal{C}om(\mathsf{ck}; \boldsymbol{b}; r_b)$, and $(C, \hat{C}) = \mathcal{C}om(\mathsf{ck}; \boldsymbol{c}; r_c)$, and*

    (iii) *for some $i \in \{1, \ldots, n\}$, $a_i b_i \neq c_i$.*

The product argument of [21] has CRS of $\Theta(n)$ group elements, prover's computation $\Theta(n \log n)$ multiplications, verifier's computation 3 pairings, and communication of 1 group element. We denote this argument as $[\![(A, \hat{A})]\!] \circ [\![(B, \hat{B})]\!] = [\![(C, \hat{C})]\!]$.

For a vector $\boldsymbol{a} = (a_1, \ldots, a_n)$, denote $\mathsf{lsft}_1(\boldsymbol{a}) := (a_2, a_3, \ldots, a_n, 0)$ and $\mathsf{rsft}_1(\boldsymbol{a}) := (0, a_1, a_2, \ldots, a_{n-1})$. For $z > 1$, let $\mathsf{lsft}_z(\boldsymbol{a}) := \mathsf{lsft}_1(\mathsf{lsft}_{z-1}(\boldsymbol{a}))$ and $\mathsf{rsft}_z(\boldsymbol{a}) := \mathsf{rsft}_1(\mathsf{rsft}_{z-1}(\boldsymbol{a}))$. In the case of the shift argument, [21] proved an even weaker version of soundness, see [16] for explanation.

Theorem 2 (Security of the right shift argument [21]). *Let* $n = \text{poly}(\kappa)$. *Let* $\mathcal{C}om$ *be the interpolating commitment scheme.*

1. *The shift argument of [21] is perfectly complete and perfectly witness-indistinguishable.*
2. *(WEAK SOUNDNESS:) Let* Φ^z_{rsft} *be as in [21]. If* genbp *satisfies a q-type computational assumption from [21], then a non-uniform probabilistic polynomial time adversary against the shift argument of [21] has negligible chance, given* crs $\leftarrow$ gencrs$(1^\kappa, n)$ *as an input, of outputting* $\text{inp}_{\text{rsft}} \leftarrow (A, \hat{A}, B, \hat{B})$ *and an accepting argument* (π, π^β) *together with a witness* $w_{\text{rsft}} \leftarrow (a, r_a, b, r_b, (f^*_\varphi)_{\varphi \in \Phi^z_{\text{rsft}}})$, *such that*
   (i) $a, b \in \mathbb{Z}_p^n$, $r_a, r_b \in \mathbb{Z}_p$, $f^*_\varphi \in \mathbb{Z}_p$ *for* $\varphi \in \Phi^z_{\text{rsft}}$,
   (ii) $(A, \hat{A}) = \mathcal{C}om(\text{ck}; a; r_a)$, $(B, \hat{B}) = \mathcal{C}om(\text{ck}; b; r_b)$,
   (iii) $\log_{g_2} \pi = \log_{g_2^\alpha} \pi^\beta = \sum_{\varphi \in \Phi^z_{\text{rsft}}} f^*_\varphi \cdot \varphi(\sigma)$, *and*
   (iv) $(a_n, \ldots, a_1) \neq (0, \ldots, 0, b_n, \ldots, b_{z+1})$.

The communication (argument size) of the right shift argument from [21] is 2 elements from $\mathbb{G}_2$. The prover's computation is dominated by $\Theta(n)$ multiplications in $\mathbb{Z}_p$ and two $(n+2)$-wide multi-exponentiations. The verifier's computation is dominated by 4 bilinear pairings. The CRS consists of $\Theta(n)$ group elements.

The left shift argument is very similar to the right shift argument, see [12,21].

3 New Permutation Argument

We now propose a new permutation argument that has $\Theta(n \log^2 n)$ prover's computation, as compared to $\Theta(n^2)$ in previous work. The main drawback of the new argument, compared to say permutation arguments from [16,19], is increased communication.

We will use parallelizable Benes network [4] (see Sect. 2) to implement an arbitrary permutation argument. Benes networks have been used before in the context of zero knowledge, see, e.g., [1,2,16]. In App. A, we explain why the approach of [16] of using Clos networks does not give the gain in efficiency that is necessary for our purposes, even if we use Benes networks instead. Similar reasoning applies to the approach of [1,2]. To simplify the presentation, we will assume from now on that n is a power of 2.

More precisely, we show how to verify all basic permutations of the same step of the Benes network simultaneously. That is, for every step of the Benes network, we construct a short argument that this step was performed correctly by the prover. We emphasize that we use the variant of the Benes permutation from Fig. 1 (right).

In a nutshell, at every stage we show separately that the crossbars are implemented correctly and that the wiring is implemented correctly. As we explained in the introduction, at both substages, the inputs will either stay at their original position, or will be shifted up or down by a constant that only depends on the stage. Next, we will show that one can compute efficiently the indexes of elements that are not shifted at all, shifted up, or shifted down. (In the crossbar substage, the prover and the verifier have to both use a routing algorithm for this.) Given corresponding index vectors (that we call masks), one can then show — by using a small number of product and shift arguments — the correctness of each substage.

Consider the crossbar substage of the jth stage of the Beneš network, where we start counting with $j = 0$. Clearly, after the crossbar, the pair of elements indexed by $(2i, 2i + 1)$ will now be indexed by either $(2i, 2i + 1)$ or $(2i + 1, 2i)$, depending on whether the ith crossbar $C_{j,i}$ of this stage implements id or flip.

We prove the following technical lemma. As usually, for a predicate $P(X)$, let $[P(X)] = 1$ if $P(X)$ is true, and $[P(x)] = 0$ if $P(X)$ is false.

Lemma 1. *After following the crossbars, the vector $\boldsymbol{a}_j$ of intermediate values of all wires will change to a vector $\boldsymbol{b}_{j+1}$, where $\boldsymbol{b}_{j+1} := (1 - \boldsymbol{m}_{j+1}^{c,\ell} - \boldsymbol{m}_{j+1}^{c,r}) \circ \boldsymbol{a}_j + \boldsymbol{m}_{j+1}^{c,\ell} \circ \mathsf{lsft}_1(\boldsymbol{a}_j) + \boldsymbol{m}_{j+1}^{c,r} \circ \mathsf{rsft}_1(\boldsymbol{a}_j)$. Here,*

$$m_{j+1,2i}^{c,\ell} := [C_{ji} = \mathsf{flip}] \;, \quad m_{j+1,2i+1}^{c,r} := [C_{ji} = \mathsf{flip}] \;, \tag{1}$$
$$m_{j+1,2i+1}^{c,\ell} := 0 \;, \quad m_{j+1,2i}^{c,r} := 0 \;.$$

Proof. Denote $\ell_{j+1}^c \leftarrow \mathsf{lsft}_1(\boldsymbol{a}_j)$ and $r_{j+1}^c \leftarrow \mathsf{rsft}_1(\boldsymbol{a}_j)$. Clearly, the pair $(b_{j+1,2i}, b_{j+1,2i+1})$ depends only on $(a_{j,2i}, a_{j,2i+1})$ and C_{ji}. More precisely, if $C_{j+1} = \mathsf{id}$, then $(b_{j+1,2i}, b_{j+1,2i+1}) = (a_{j,2i}, a_{j,2i+1})$, and if $C_{j+1} = \mathsf{flip}$, then $(b_{j+1,2i}, b_{j+1,2i+1}) = (a_{j,2i+1}, a_{j,2i})$. Thus, $b_{j+1,2i}$ obtains the value $a_{j,2i}$ if $C_{ij} = \mathsf{id}$, and the value $\ell_{j+1,2i}^c = a_{j,2i+1}$ otherwise. Analogously, $b_{j+1,2i+1}$ obtains the value $a_{j,2i+1}$ if $C_{ij} = \mathsf{id}$, and the value $r_{j+1,2i}^c = a_{j,2i}$ otherwise. Thus,

$$b_{j+1,2i} = a_{j,2i} \cdot [C_{ij} = \mathsf{id}] + \ell_{j+1,2i}^c \cdot [C_{ij} \neq \mathsf{id}] + r_{j+1,2i}^c \cdot 0$$

and

$$b_{j+1,2i+1} = a_{j,2i+1} \cdot [C_{ij} = \mathsf{id}] + \ell_{j+1,2i+1}^c \cdot 0 + r_{j+1,2i+1}^c \cdot [C_{ij} \neq \mathsf{id}] \;.$$

Therefore, $\boldsymbol{b}_{j+1}$ can be expressed as in Eq. (1). $\qquad\square$

Here, the values $\boldsymbol{m}_{j+1}^{c,\ell}$ and $\boldsymbol{m}_{j+1}^{c,r}$ are publicly known but ϱ-dependent. Thus, they have to be computed as part of the argument. Their computation takes time $\Theta(n \log n)$, by using a standard routing algorithm.

Let $z \leftarrow n/2^j$ for $j < \log_2 n$ and $z \leftarrow 2^j/n$ for $j \geq \log_2 n$. That is, $z \leftarrow 2^{|j - \log_2 n|}$. After additionally following the wiring substage, the new value of the value vector is equal to $\boldsymbol{a}_{j+1}$, where $a_{j+1,2i+1} = b_{j+1,2i+1}$, and, letting $\oplus$ to denote the bitwise XOR, $b_{j+1,2i\oplus z}$. This follows directly from the definition of the parallelizable Beneš network as given in Fig. 1, right. Thus, for some (public) masks $\boldsymbol{m}_{j+1}^{w,\ell}$ and $\boldsymbol{m}_{j+1}^{w,r}$,

$$\boldsymbol{a}_{j+1} := (1 - \boldsymbol{m}_{j+1}^{w,\ell} - \boldsymbol{m}_{j+1}^{w,\ell}) \circ \boldsymbol{b}_{j+1} + \boldsymbol{m}_{j+1}^{w,\ell} \circ \mathsf{lsft}_z(\boldsymbol{b}_{j+1}) + \boldsymbol{m}_{j+1}^{w,r} \circ \mathsf{rsft}_z(\boldsymbol{b}_{j+1}) \;.$$

The vectors $\boldsymbol{m}_j^{w,\ell}$ and $\boldsymbol{m}_j^{w,r}$ are both publicly known and not dependent on ϱ, therefore they can be precomputed (if necessary, as a part of the CRS). We note

---

Let $\mathsf{gk} := (p, \mathbb{G}_1, \mathbb{G}_2, \mathbb{G}_T, \hat{e}) \leftarrow \mathsf{genbp}(1^\kappa, n)$, $g_1 \leftarrow \mathbb{G}_1 \setminus \{1\}$, $g_2 \leftarrow \mathbb{G}_2 \setminus \{1\}$; Let $\sigma \leftarrow \mathbb{Z}_p$; Generate the CRS of the following basic arguments separately, except that use the same values $(\mathsf{gk}, \sigma, \alpha)$ in all of them:

- (i) the product argument,
- (ii) the 2^i-left shift argument for $i < \log_2 n$,
- (iii) the 2^i-right shift argument for $i < \log_2 n$.

The CRS of the permutation argument is equal to the union of all basic arguments.

Algorithm 1. CRS generation on input $(1^\kappa, n)$

that since there are no wirings at the last stage, we will just have $a_{2 \log_2 n} = b_{2 \log_2 n}$.

Based on the explanation above, we now construct the permutation argument $\varrho([\![(B, \hat{B})]\!]) = [\![(A, \hat{A})]\!]$, where $(B, \hat{B}) = (A_0, \hat{A}_0)$ and $(A, \hat{A}) = (B_{2 \log_2 n}, \hat{B}_{2 \log_2 n})$. Note that we can remove $(B_{2 \log_2 n}, \hat{B}_{2 \log_2 n})$ from π^ϱ. See Prot. 1, Prot. 2 and Prot. 3. Here, the prover commits to all values a_j and b_j, and then shows, by using intermediate masks $m_j^{\cdot\cdot}$ and left and right shifts, that b_{j+1} is correctly computed from a_j and that a_{j+1} is correctly computed from a_{j+1}. The (weak) soundness of the argument follows directly from the (weak) soundness of the product and permutation argument. The concrete computational assumption is used to individually guarantee the (weak) soundness of the product argument and 2^i-left and 2^i-right shift arguments for $i < \log_n$.

Theorem 3. *Let $\mathcal{C}om$ be the interpolating commitment scheme.*

(1) The new permutation argument is perfectly complete and perfectly witness-indistinguishable.

(2) Let Φ_z^{rsft} be as in Thm. 2, Φ_z^{lsft} be as in Sect. 2, and $\Phi^{\mathsf{perm}} := \bigcup_{i=0}^{\log_2 n - 1} \Phi_{2^i}^{\mathsf{lsft}} \cup \bigcup_{i=0}^{\log_2 n - 1} \Phi_{2^i}^{\mathsf{rsft}}$. If genbp satisfies an appropriate computational assumption, then a non-uniform PPT adversary against the new permutation argument has negligible chance, given a correctly formed CRS crs as an input, of outputting $\mathsf{inp}^{\mathsf{perm}} \leftarrow (A, \tilde{A}, B, \tilde{B}, \varrho)$ and an accepting argument $\pi^{\mathsf{perm}} \leftarrow (\pi, \tilde{\pi})$ together with a witness $w^{\mathsf{perm}} \leftarrow (a, r_a, b, r_b, (f_\phi^*)_{\phi \in \Phi^{\mathsf{perm}}})$, such that
- *(i) $a, b \in \mathbb{Z}_p^n$, $r_a, r_b \in \mathbb{Z}_p$, and $f_\phi^* \in \mathbb{Z}_p$ for $\phi \in \Phi^{\mathsf{perm}}$,*
- *(ii) $(A, \tilde{A}) = \mathcal{C}om(\tilde{\mathsf{ck}}; a; r_a)$, $(B, \tilde{B}) = \mathcal{C}om(\tilde{\mathsf{ck}}; b; r_b)$, $\varrho \in S_n$,*
- *(iii) $\log_{g_2} \pi = \log_{\tilde{g}_2} \tilde{\pi} = \sum_{\phi \in \Phi^{\mathsf{perm}}} f_\phi^* \cdot \phi(\sigma)$, and*
- *(iv) $a_{\varrho(i)} \neq b_i$ for some $i \in [n]$.*

Proof. COMPLETENESS follows from the previous discussion. WITNESS-INDISTINGUISHABILITY follows from the fact that the argument π^{perm} is uniquely defined, given the witness.

COMPUTATIONAL SOUNDNESS. Given an adversary $\mathcal{A}$ who can break the soundness property, we construct an adversary $\mathcal{A}^*$ that either breaks either a

Let $(A_0, \hat{A}_0) = (A, \hat{A})$ be the input commitment;
Let $(B_{2\log_2 n}, \hat{B}_{2\log_2 n}) = (B, \hat{B})$ be the output commitment;
Use a routing algorithm to find out the value of C_{ij} for every crossbar;
for $i \leftarrow 0$ **to** $2\log_2 n - 1$ **do**

    /* Handling crossbars   */

    Construct a commitment $(B_{i+1}, \hat{B}_{i+1})$ to b_{i+1};

    Construct a commitment $(L^c_{i+1}, \hat{L}^c_{i+1})$ to $\ell^c_{i+1} \leftarrow \mathsf{lsft}_1(a_i)$;

    Construct a commitment $(R^c_{i+1}, \hat{R}^c_{i+1})$ to $r^c_{i+1} \leftarrow \mathsf{rsft}_1(a_i)$;

    Construct an argument $\pi_{i+1,1}$ that $\mathsf{lsft}_1([\![A_i]\!]) = [\![L^c_{i+1}]\!]$;

    Construct an argument $\pi_{i+1,2}$ that $\mathsf{rsft}_1([\![A_i]\!]) = [\![R^c_{i+1}]\!]$;

    Use Eq. (1) to construct valid masks $m^{c,\ell}_{i+1}, m^{c,r}_{i+1} \in \{0,1\}^n$;

    Construct a commitment $(D^{c,\ell}_{i+1}, \hat{D}^{c,\ell}_{i+1})$ to $d^{c,\ell}_{i+1} \leftarrow m^{c,\ell}_{i+1} \circ \ell^c_{i+1}$;

    Construct a commitment $(D^{c,r}_{i+1}, \hat{D}^{c,r}_{i+1})$ to $d^{c,\ell}_{i+1} \leftarrow m^{c,\ell}_{i+1} \circ r^c_{i+1}$;

    Construct a product argument $\pi_{i+1,3} \leftarrow [\![L^c_i]\!] \circ [\![\mathcal{C}om(\mathsf{ck}; m^{c,\ell}_{i+1}; 0)]\!] = [\![D^{c,\ell}_{i+1}]\!]$;

    Construct a product argument $\pi_{i+1,4} \leftarrow [\![R^c_i]\!] \circ [\![\mathcal{C}om(\mathsf{ck}; m^{c,r}_{i+1}; 0)]\!] = [\![D^{c,r}_{i+1}]\!]$;

    Construct a prod. arg. $\pi_{i+1,5}$ that
    $a_i \circ (1 - m^{c,\ell}_{i+1} - m^{c,r}_{i+1}) = b_{i+1} - d^{c,\ell}_{i+1} - d^{c,r}_{i+1}$;

    $\pi^c_{i+1} \leftarrow (B_{i+1}, \hat{B}_{i+1}, L^c_{i+1}, \hat{L}^c_{i+1}, R^c_{i+1}, \hat{R}^c_{i+1}, D^{c,\ell}_{i+1}, \hat{D}^{c,\ell}_{i+1}, D^{c,r}_{i+1}, \hat{D}^{c,r}_{i+1},$
        $(\pi_{i+1,j})_{j\in\{1,2\}}, (\pi_{i+1,j})_{j\in\{3,4,5\}})$;

    if $i < 2\log_2 n - 1$ **then**

        /* Handling wirings   */

        Construct a commitment $(A_{i+1}, \hat{A}_{i+1})$ to a_{i+1} ;   /* Interim values
        after the wirings */

        if $i < \log_2 n$ **then** $z \leftarrow n/2^i$ **else** $z \leftarrow 2^i/n$

        Construct a commitment $(L^w_{i+1}, \hat{L}^w_{i+1})$ of $\ell^w_{i+1} = \mathsf{lsft}_z(b_{i+1})$;

        Construct a commitment $(R^w_{i+1}, \hat{R}^w_{i+1})$ of $r^w_{i+1} = \mathsf{rsft}_z(b_{i+1})$;

        /* $m^{w,\ell}_{i+1}$ and $m^{w,r}_{i+1}$ can be part of CRS   */

        Construct valid masks $m^{w,\ell}_{i+1}, m^{w,r}_{i+1} \in \{0,1\}^n$;

        Construct a shift argument $\pi_{i+1,6}$ for $\mathsf{lsft}_z([\![B_{i+1}]\!]) = [\![L^w_{i+1}]\!]$;

        Construct a shift argument $\pi_{i+1,7}$ for $\mathsf{rsft}_z([\![B_{i+1}]\!]) = [\![R^w_{i+1}]\!]$;

        Construct a commitment $(D^{w,\ell}_{i+1}, \hat{D}^{w,\ell}_{i+1})$ to $d^{w,\ell}_{i+1} \leftarrow m^{w,\ell}_{i+1} \circ \ell^w_{i+1}$;

        Construct a commitment $(D^{r,\ell}_{i+1}, \hat{D}^{r,\ell}_{i+1})$ to $d^{w,\ell}_{i+1} \leftarrow m^{w,r}_{i+1} \circ r^w_{i+1}$;

        Construct a product argument
        $\pi_{i+1,8} \leftarrow [\![L^w_i]\!] \circ [\![\mathcal{C}om(\mathsf{ck}; m^{w,\ell}_{i+1}; 0)]\!] = [\![D^{w,\ell}_{i+1}]\!]$;

        Construct a product argument
        $\pi_{i+1,9} \leftarrow [\![R^w_i]\!] \circ [\![\mathcal{C}om(\mathsf{ck}; m^{w,r}_{i+1}; 0)]\!] = [\![D^{w,r}_{i+1}]\!]$;

        Construct a prod. arg. $\pi_{i+1,10}$ that
        $a_{i+1} - d^{w,\ell}_{i+1} - d^{w,r}_{i+1} = (1 - m^{w,\ell}_{i+1} - m^{w,r}_{i+1}) \circ b_{i+1}$;

        $\pi^w_{i+1} \leftarrow (A_{i+1}, \hat{A}_{i+1}, L^w_{i+1}, \hat{L}^w_{i+1}, R^w_{i+1}, \hat{R}^w_{i+1}, D^{w,\ell}_{i+1}, \hat{D}^{w,\ell}_{i+1}, D^{w,r}_{i+1}, \hat{D}^{w,r}_{i+1},$
            $(\pi_{i+1,6})_{j\in\{6,7\}}, (\pi_{i+1,6})_{j\in\{8,9,10\}})$;

    end

end

The argument is $\pi^\varrho \leftarrow ((\pi^c_{i+1}, \pi^w_{i+1})_{i=0}^{2\log_2 n - 2}, \pi^c_{2\log_2 n})$;

Algorithm 2. Prover's algorithm on input $(A, \hat{A}; a, r_a, b, r_b)$

Use routing algorithm to compute C_{ij} for all i, j;
for $i \leftarrow 0$ **to** $2\log_2 n - 1$ **do**
    Verify that $B_{i+1}, L_{i+1}^c, R_{i+1}^c, D_{i+1}^{c,\ell}, D_{i+1}^{c,r}$ are all group elements, and that
    their knowledge component is correctly formed;
    Construct valid masks $m_{i+1}^{c,\ell}$ and $m_{i+1}^{c,r}$ following Eq. (1);
    Compute valid masks $m_{i+1}^{w,\ell}$ and $m_{i+1}^{w,r}$;
    Verify 2 shift and 3 product arguments $\pi_{j+1,i}$ for $i \leq 5$;
    if $i < 2\log_2 n - 1$ **then**
       Verify that $A_{i+1}, L_{i+1}^w, R_{i+1}^w, D_{i+1}^{w,\ell}, D_{i+1}^{w,r}$ are all group elements, and that
       their knowledge component is correctly formed;
       Verify 2 shift and 3 product arguments $\pi_{j+1,i}$ for $i \geq 6$;
    end
end

Algorithm 3. Verifier's algorithm on input $(A, \hat{A}, B, \hat{B}; \pi^\varrho)$

computational or a knowledge assumption, as follows. For each stage, the adversary $\mathcal{A}^*$ uses the knowledge extractor to open the following commitments (the adversary also obtains the used randomizers, which we will not specify): (a) $(B_{i+1}, \hat{B}_{i+1})$ to b_{i+1}, (b) $(L_{i+1}^c, \hat{L}_{i+1}^c)$ to ℓ_{i+1}^c, (c) $(R_{i+1}^c, \hat{R}_{i+1}^c)$ to r_{i+1}^c, (d) $(D_{i+1}^{c,\ell}, \hat{D}_{i+1}^{c,\ell})$ to $d_{i+1}^{c,\ell}$, (e) $(D_{i+1}^{c,r}, \hat{D}_{i+1}^{c,r})$ to $d_{i+1}^{c,r}$, (f) $(A_{i+1}, \hat{A}_{i+1})$ to a_{i+1}, (g) $(L_{i+1}^w, \hat{L}_{i+1}^w)$ to ℓ_{i+1}^w, (h) $(R_{i+1}^w, \hat{R}_{i+1}^w)$ to r_{i+1}^w, (i) $(D_{i+1}^{w,\ell}, \hat{D}_{i+1}^{w,\ell})$ to $d_{i+1}^{w,\ell}$, (j) $(D_{i+1}^{w,r}, \hat{D}_{i+1}^{w,r})$ to $d_{i+1}^{w,r}$. $\mathcal{A}^*$ verifies that all the openings were successful. If not (that is, $\mathcal{A}$ was *not* successful), she aborts.

Now, assume that $\mathcal{A}^*$ has returned $(inp^{\mathsf{perm}}, \pi^{\mathsf{perm}}, w^{\mathsf{perm}})$ that satisfy conditions (2i–2iv). Thus, in particular, $a_{\varrho(i)} \neq b_i$ for some $i \in [n]$. Since we obtained by using the extractor the intermediate values a_i and b_i, $\mathcal{A}^*$ verifies starting from $i = 0$ and ending with $i = 2\log_2 n - 1$ where is the first point where one of those two values was computed incorrectly.

W.l.o.g., assume that for some i_0, a_i and b_i have always been computed correctly for $i < i_0$, but b_{i_0} is computed incorrectly. That is, b_{i_0} is not equal to the expression given in Lem. 1. But it must be the case that all $\pi_{i_0,3}$, $\pi_{i_0,4}$, and $\pi_{i_0,5}$ verify while b_{i_0}. Now we also have a case analysis depending on whether $d_{i_0}^{c,\ell} = m^{c,\ell}{}_{i_0} \cdot \ell_{i_0}^c$ and/or $d_{i_0}^{c,r} = m^{c,r}{}_{i_0} \cdot r_{i_0}^c$, or not. Suppose, w.l.o.g., that both equalities hold (the adversary $\mathcal{A}^*$ can check it, because due to the extractor she knows all the elements). In this case, $d_{i_0}^{c,\ell}$ and $d_{i_0}^{c,r}$ were correctly computed and $\pi_{i_0,5}$ verifies, but $(a_{i_0} - d_{i_0}^{c,\ell} - d_{i_0}^{c,r}) \neq (1 - d_{i_0}^{c,\ell} - d_{i_0}^{c,r}) \circ a_{i_0}$. But then by contradicting Thm. 1, the adversary has broken an appropriate computational assumption.

By an analogous case analysis, we obtain that the permutation argument is weakly sound, unless the weak soundness (and then the corresponding computational assumption) of one of the underlying product or shift arguments is broken. $\qquad\square$

Efficiency. As seen from Prot. 2 and Prot. 3, every step can be done by using a small number of commitments, product, and rotation arguments. Thus, the computational complexity of the whole permutation argument will be dominated by $\Theta(\log n)$ more basic product and rotation arguments. Since the product argument can be computed in $\Theta(n \log n)$ non-cryptographic operations and $\Theta(n)$ cryptographic operations, then the new permutation argument can be computed in $\Theta(n \log^2 n)$ non-cryptographic operations and $\Theta(n \log n)$ cryptographic operations. This improves on prover's computation of $\Theta(n^2)$ exponentiations in [16].

The verifier has to perform $\Theta(\log n)$ pairings in total. Moreover, the verifier has to run a routing algorithm to establish the values C_{ij}, which takes $\Theta(n \log n)$ *non-cryptographic* operations. This is fine, since in all known applications of the permutation argument, the verifier's computational complexity is $\Omega(n)$ (much more expensive) cryptographic operations.

We also note that the second component of all product arguments used in Prot. 2 is a commitment to the masks. Both the prover and the verifier know the masks, and thus the corresponding commitments do not have to be transferred. On the other hand, both parties also have to compute these commitments, and this takes $\Theta(n \log n)$ multiplications in total.

The CRS length will be $\Theta(n \log n)$ group elements because all $\Theta(\log n)$ different shift arguments have to use a linear-length (and different) CRS.

4   CircuitSAT Argument

As shown in [16], one can construct a CircuitSAT argument out of $\Theta(1)$ product and permutation arguments. Since Groth's product and permutation arguments had quadratic prover's computation complexity, so did his CircuitSAT argument. By using the product argument proposed in [21] and the permutation argument of this paper, we end up with a CircuitSAT argument with prover's computation dominated by $\Theta(n \log^2 n)$ non-cryptographic operations and $\Theta(n \log n)$ cryptographic operations. As shown in [16,19], witness-indistinguishability and (weak) soundness of the underlying arguments is sufficient to prove zero-knowledge and soundness of the CircuitSAT argument. In fact, they can also be used to prove that the CircuitSAT argument is an argument of knowledge. Again, since we do not want to introduce overdependence on concrete basic arguments, also here we omit the precise description of the underlying assumptions; they can be derived directly from the assumptions behind the product and shift arguments.

Theorem 4. *There exists a perfectly complete and zero-knowledge* CircuitSAT *argument. Under certain q-type computational and knowledge assumptions, this argument is also computationally sound and an argument of knowledge.*

Proof. The CircuitSAT argument will be exactly the same as in [19], except that it uses the new permutation argument from Sect. 3 together with the product argument from [19]. The soundness of the CircuitSAT argument follows from q-type computational and knowledge assumptions, as in [19]. We also get that the CIRCUITSAT argument is an argument of knowledge, since during the soundness proof of [19], the adversary uses the knowledge extractor to extract the whole witness. □

Acknowledgements. The author was supported by Estonian Research Council and European Union through the European Regional Development Fund.

References

1. Abe, M.: Mix-Networks on Permutation Networks. In: Lam, K.-Y., Okamoto, E., Xing, C. (eds.) ASIACRYPT 1999. LNCS, vol. 1716, pp. 258–273. Springer, Heidelberg (1999)
2. Abe, M., Hoshino, F.: Remarks on Mix-Network Based on Permutation Networks. In: Kim, K.-C. (ed.) PKC 2001. LNCS, vol. 1992, pp. 317–324. Springer, Heidelberg (2001)
3. Ben-Sasson, E., Chiesa, A., Genkin, D., Tromer, E., Virza, M.: SNARKs for C: Verifying Program Executions Succinctly and in Zero Knowledge. In: Canetti, R., Garay, J.A. (eds.) CRYPTO 2013, Part II. LNCS, vol. 8043, pp. 90–108. Springer, Heidelberg (2013)
4. Beneš, V.E.: Mathematical Theory of Connecting Networks and Telephone Traffic. Academic Press (August 28, 1965)
5. Bitansky, N., Chiesa, A., Ishai, Y., Ostrovsky, R., Paneth, O.: Succinct Noninteractive Arguments via Linear Interactive Proofs. In: Sahai, A. (ed.) TCC 2013. LNCS, vol. 7785, pp. 315–333. Springer, Heidelberg (2013)
6. Blelloch, G.: Vector Models for Data-Parallel Computing. MIT Press (1990)
7. Blum, M., Feldman, P., Micali, S.: Non-Interactive Zero-Knowledge and Its Applications. In: STOC 1988, pp. 103–112. ACM Press (1988)
8. Chaabouni, R., Lipmaa, H., Zhang, B.: A Non-Interactive Range Proof with Constant Communication. In: Keromytis, A.D. (ed.) FC 2012. LNCS, vol. 7397, pp. 179–199. Springer, Heidelberg (2012)
9. Clos, C.: A Study of Non-Blocking Switching Networks. Bell System Technical Journal 32(2), 406–424 (1953)
10. Damgård, I.: Towards Practical Public Key Systems Secure against Chosen Ciphertext Attacks. In: Feigenbaum, J. (ed.) CRYPTO 1991. LNCS, vol. 576, pp. 445–456. Springer, Heidelberg (1992)
11. Di Crescenzo, G., Lipmaa, H.: Succinct NP Proofs from an Extractability Assumption. In: Beckmann, A., Dimitracopoulos, C., Löwe, B. (eds.) CiE 2008. LNCS, vol. 5028, pp. 175–185. Springer, Heidelberg (2008)
12. Fauzi, P., Lipmaa, H., Zhang, B.: Efficient Modular NIZK Arguments from Shift and Product. In: Abdalla, M., Nita-Rotaru, C., Dahab, R. (eds.) CANS 2013. LNCS, vol. 8257, pp. 92–121. Springer, Heidelberg (2013)
13. Gennaro, R., Gentry, C., Parno, B., Raykova, M.: Quadratic Span Programs and Succinct NIZKs without PCPs. In: Johansson, T., Nguyen, P.Q. (eds.) EURO-CRYPT 2013. LNCS, vol. 7881, pp. 626–645. Springer, Heidelberg (2013)
14. Goldwasser, S., Micali, S., Rackoff, C.: The Knowledge Complexity of Interactive Proof-Systems. In: Sedgewick, R. (ed.) STOC 1985, pp. 291–304. ACM Press (1985)

15. Golle, P., Jarecki, S., Mironov, I.: Cryptographic Primitives Enforcing Communication and Storage Complexity. In: Blaze, M. (ed.) FC 2002. LNCS, vol. 2357, pp. 120–135. Springer, Heidelberg (2003)

16. Groth, J.: Short Pairing-Based Non-interactive Zero-Knowledge Arguments. In: Abe, M. (ed.) ASIACRYPT 2010. LNCS, vol. 6477, pp. 321–340. Springer, Heidelberg (2010)

17. Groth, J., Lu, S.: A Non-interactive Shuffle with Pairing Based Verifiability. In: Kurosawa, K. (ed.) ASIACRYPT 2007. LNCS, vol. 4833, pp. 51–67. Springer, Heidelberg (2007)

18. Hwang, F.K.M.: The Mathematical Theory of Nonblocking Switching Networks, 2nd edn. Series on Applied Mathematics, vol. 15. World Scientific Publishing Co Pte Ltd. (October 1, 2004)

19. Lipmaa, H.: Progression-Free Sets and Sublinear Pairing-Based Non-Interactive Zero-Knowledge Arguments. In: Cramer, R. (ed.) TCC 2012. LNCS, vol. 7194, pp. 169–189. Springer, Heidelberg (2012)

20. Lipmaa, H.: Succinct Non-Interactive Zero Knowledge Arguments from Span Programs and Linear Error-Correcting Codes. In: Sako, K., Sarkar, P. (eds.) ASIACRYPT 2013, Part I. LNCS, vol. 8269, pp. 41–60. Springer, Heidelberg (2013)

21. Lipmaa, H.: Almost Optimal Short Adaptive Non-Interactive Zero Knowledge. Tech. Rep. 2014/396, International Association for Cryptologic Research (2014), http://eprint.iacr.org/2014/396

22. Lipmaa, H., Zhang, B.: A More Efficient Computationally Sound Non-Interactive Zero-Knowledge Shuffle Argument. In: Visconti, I., De Prisco, R. (eds.) SCN 2012. LNCS, vol. 7485, pp. 477–502. Springer, Heidelberg (2012)

23. Nassimi, D., Sahni, S.: Parallel Algorithms to Set Up the Benes Permutation Network. IEEE Trans. Computers 31(2), 148–154 (1982)

24. Opferman, D.C., Tsao-Wu, N.T.: On a Class of Rearrangeable Switching Networks. Part I: Control Algorithm. Bell System Technical Journal 50(5), 1579–1600 (1971)

25. Pippenger, N.: On the Evaluation of Powers and Monomials. SIAM J. Comput. 9(2), 230–250 (1980)

26. Pratt, V.R., Stockmeyer, L.J.: A Characterization of the Power of Vector Machines. Journal of Computer and System Sciences 12(2), 198–221 (1976)

27. Straus, E.G.: Addition Chains of Vectors. American Mathematical Monthly 70, 806–808 (1964)

28. Waksman, A.: A Permutation Network. Journal of the ACM 15(1), 159–163 (1968)

A   On Groth's Use of Clos Networks

One can implement a permutation argument by constructing an efficient rearrangeable interconnection network for that permutation, and then showing in zero knowledge that both the crossbars and the wiring steps of the network are followed correctly. In particular, Groth [16] used an (m, m)-Clos network for $m \approx \sqrt{n}$, combined with permutation arguments (for permutations from S_m) to show the correctness of crossbars, and with so called dispersion arguments [16] to show the correctness of the wirings. Since Groth's dispersion argument is significantly more efficient than Groth's permutation argument (or the permutation argument that we will construct in this paper), we will only count the cost induced by the S_m-permutation arguments.

Assume that we use some multistage interconnection network that uses, w.l.o.g.[3], crossbars X_{mm} for some $m \mid n$, has n/m crossbars per stage, and k stages. To implement a single crossbar (i.e., permutation from S_m) by using Groth's permutation argument, we need a CRS of size $\Theta(m^2)$, prover's computation $\Theta(m^2)$, verifier's computation $\Theta(m)$, and communication $\Theta(1)$. Thus, when we implement all k stages of the network (and kn/m crosspoints), the prover's computation grows to $\Theta(k \cdot \frac{n}{m} \cdot m^2) = \Theta(kmn)$, the verifier's computation to $\Theta(k \cdot \frac{n}{m} \cdot m) = \Theta(kn)$, and the communication to $\Theta(kn/m)$. On the other hand, the CRS length stays at $\Theta(m^2)$.

For example, if one uses the Clos network with $m = \sqrt{n}$ as in [16], then the CRS/the communication/the prover's computation/the verifier's computation become $\Theta(n)/\Theta(n^{1.5})/\Theta(n)/\Theta(\sqrt{n})$. In the case of the Benes network, with $m = 2$ and $k = \log_2 n$, the corresponding complexities will be $\Theta(1)$, $\Theta(n \log n)$, $\Theta(n \log n)$, and $\Theta(n \log n)$. (Thus, it has the same computational and communication complexity as — interactive — shuffle by Abe [1,2], which is also based on the Benes network.) The new method (as described below) provides a significant optimization over Groth's way of using interconnection networks in a permutation argument.

B   Committed Shuffle Argument

B.1   Brief Idea

In a shuffle argument, the prover proves that two vectors of ciphertexts encrypt the same (unordered) multiset of plaintexts. Until now, only two efficient NIZK shuffle arguments have been published [17,22]. The argument of [17] is based on the Groth-Sahai proofs. The more efficient shuffle argument of [22] first uses two new basic arguments (zero argument and 1-sparsity argument), related to the techniques [16,19], to show that two commitments commit to the same (unordered) multiset of plaintexts. We call it the committed shuffle argument. After that, they use another argument to show that the same elements that were committed to were also encrypted by a ciphertext vector. We call it the commitment-ciphertext consistency argument. In [22], both arguments take linear computation and linear communication.

By using Benes networks as in the case of the permutation argument, we implement the committed shuffle argument by using quasilinear CRS, prover's computation $\Theta(r_3^{-1}(n) \log r_3^{-1}(n) \cdot \log n)$, logarithmic verifier's computation, and logarithmic communication. The main additional technical challenge here, compared to the permutation argument, is that one has to prove in zero knowledge that the committed masks are correctly formed. We show that the latter can be done efficiently. The new committed shuffle argument is, up to our knowledge, the first committed shuffle argument that requires only polylogarithmic communication. On the other hand, it requires larger prover's computation than the

---

[3] One can use crossbars of different size, but the complexity is dominated by the largest crossbar in use. Moreover, all interesting multistage interconnection networks contain crossbars of the same size.

shuffle arguments of [17,22]. Alternatively, by using Groth's balancing technique, one can achieve sublinear CRS and communication at the same time.

On top of this, we can use the commitment-ciphertext consistency argument of [22]. The resulting shuffle argument will have smaller communication and verifier's computation than the shuffle argument from [22], but at the same time it will have higher prover's computation. We note that Beneš networks have been used before to construct shuffle arguments but with significantly larger communication $\Theta(n \log n)$, see for example [1,2].

B.2   Construction

The main difference with the permutation argument is that in the committed shuffle argument, the permutation should stay unknown to the verifier. We can still use Beneš networks, but in this case the masks $m_{i+1}^{c,r}$ and $m_{i+1}^{c,\ell}$ are not public, but they are committed to. The prover has to show that both masks belong to the set of allowed masks. The rest of the argument is pretty much the same as the permutation argument.

More precisely, to show that $m_{i+1}^{c,r}$ and $m_{i+1}^{c,\ell}$ are both valid, the prover proves that $m_{i+1}^{c,r}$ and $m_{i+1}^{c,\ell}$ satisfy Eq. (1). This can be done by showing that (here, $*$ denotes an arbitrary value) (i) $m_{j+1}^{c,\ell} = (*, 0, *, 0, \ldots, *, 0)$ by using restriction argument [16], (ii) $m_{j+1}^{c,r} = (0, *, 0, *, \ldots, 0, *)$ by using restriction argument [16], (iii) $m_{j+1}^{c,\ell}$ is Boolean by using a product argument [16,19,12], (iv) $m_{j+1}^{r,\ell} = \mathsf{lsft}_1(m_{j+1}^{c,\ell})$ by using shift argument [12]. Thus, one has to do 2 restriction, 1 product and 1 shift argument. One can construct similar mask correctness arguments for any value of j. The committed shuffle argument itself takes $\Theta(\log n)$ group elements, as in the case of the permutation argument. Moreover, here the verifier does not have to execute the $\Theta(n \log n)$-time routing algorithm, and thus the verifier's computation is dominated by $\Theta(\log n)$ pairings.

Related Work. Abe and Hoshino [1,2] proposed a shuffle, where the underlying permutation is implemented by a Beneš network. Since there the correctness of every crossbar is verified individually, the resulting shuffle consists of $\Theta(n \log n)$ smaller zero-knowledge proofs and is thus less efficient than the new argument.

Non-Malleable Zero Knowledge: Black-Box Constructions and Definitional Relationships

Abhishek Jain[1] and Omkant Pandey[2]

[1] Boston University and MIT
abhishek@csail.mit.edu
[2] UIUC
omkant@uiuc.edu

Abstract. This paper deals with efficient non-malleable zero-knowledge proofs for $\mathcal{NP}$, based on general assumptions. We construct a simulation-sound zero-knowledge ($\mathcal{ZK}$) protocol for $\mathcal{NP}$, based only on the *black-box* use of *one-way functions*. Constructing such a proof system has been an open question ever since the original work of Dolev, Dwork, and Naor [18]. In addition to the feasibility result, our protocol has a *constant* number of rounds, which is asymptotically optimal.

Traditionally, the term non-malleable zero-knowledge (NMZK) refers to the original definition of [18]; but today it is used loosely to also refer to *simulation-soundness* (SimSound) [51], and *simulation-extractability* (SimExt) [47]. While SimExt implies NMZK, the common perception is that SimExt is strongest of the three notions. However, very few results about their exact relationship are known.

In the second part of this work, we provide further results about the exact relationship between these notions. We show that in the "static" case, if an NMZK protocol is also an *argument-of-knowledge*, then it is in fact SimExt. Furthermore, in the most strict sense of the definition, SimSound does not necessarily follow from SimExt. These results are somewhat surprising because they are opposite to the common perception that SimExt is the strongest of the three notions.

1 Introduction

The concept of non-malleability was introduced in the seminal work of Dolev, Dwork, and Naor [18,19]. It has proven fundamental to several developments in cryptography such as CCA2-secure encryption schemes [41,18,51], composable multiparty computation [12,45,34], privacy amplification and non-malleable extractors [17], tamper-resilience [20], hash functions [8], etc.

This paper is about non-malleability in zero-knowledge ($\mathcal{ZK}$) interactive proofs [25]. Roughly speaking, [18] define a $\mathcal{ZK}$ proof to be non-malleable, if no man-in-the-middle can improve his chances in proving a statement $\tilde{x}$ *even if* it receives a proof for a "related" statement x. An $O(\log n)$ round NMZK protocol for $\mathcal{NP}$, was given in [18] based on the existence of one-way functions (OWF). The protocol of [18] makes *non-black-box* use of one-way functions since it uses Cook-Levin

M. Abdalla and R. De Prisco (Eds.): SCN 2014, LNCS 8642, pp. 435–454, 2014.

reductions to $\mathcal{NP}$-complete problems [13,28,30]. Such reductions are usually a large source of inefficiency both in terms of computation and communication, and are highly undesirable.

Black-box Constructions. A protocol A is said to make only *black-box* use of a cryptographic primitive B if the implementation of A uses B only as an *oracle*—i.e., only refers to the input/output behavior of B. Such a black-box construction does not depend on the actual implementation details of B, and therefore precludes the use of Cook-Levin reductions in the protocol explicitly. This results in much more efficient protocols, which are more suitable for actual implementations.

Despite intensive research on non-malleable $\mathcal{ZK}$ in recent years [18,51,16,1,45,47,46,44,31,48,52,26,32], the complexity of NMZK protocols from the point of view of black-box use of cryptographic assumptions (such as OWF), is still not very well understood. And in particular, the following question has remained open thus far:

> *Do non-malleable $\mathcal{ZK}$ proofs, based only on black-box use of general assumptions, exist?*

The first part of this work resolves this question in the affirmative. Specifically, we construct a *simulation-sound $\mathcal{ZK}$* protocol for $\mathcal{NP}$, based on the existence of *one-way functions*. In fact, our result is more general and can be based on any non-malleable commitment scheme which satisfies the so called "1-1CCA security" notion [11]: it is essentially a standard non-malleable commitment except that the man-in-the-middle adversary is provided with the value it commits to on the right as soon as the right interaction finishes—even if the left interaction is still in progress. This is done by means of a non-polynomial time extraction oracle. Our protocol uses such commitment schemes only as a black-box and adds only a constant number of rounds more. Traditional schemes such as [18] satisfy 1-1CCA security; further, the recent constant round constructions of [26,27] also satisfy 1-1CCA, and [27] is based on the black-box use of (only) one-way functions.[1]

We note that black-box constructions of simulation-sound zero knowledge are important for higher-level tasks; for example, simulation-sound zero knowledge is known to be sufficient for constructing concurrently secure multiparty computation protocols [36,45].[2]

Round Complexity. Traditionally, in theory of cryptography, the round complexity of protocols has often been an important measure of efficiency. Recent implementations show that the latency of sending and receiving messages back

---

[1] Although, [18,26,27] do not explicitly claim 1-1CCA security, their security proofs implicitly achieve this property. We argue in the full version that [27] satisfies 1-1CCA and the same explanation holds for [18,26] as well.

[2] We note that in specific cases, such as when a *setup* (e.g., common random string) is available, non-malleable commitments suffice for obtaining concurrently secure multiparty computation [34]; however such a reduction is not known in general, in the plain model.

and forth can in fact be a dominating factor in running cryptographic protocols [39,4]. Unlike the "black-box use" complexity, however, the round-complexity of non-malleable $\mathcal{ZK}$ is much well understood. In a series of results, round-efficient non-malleable protocols for both $\mathcal{ZK}$ and commitments, based on general assumptions were presented in [1,47,31,48,52]. Recently, Goyal [26] and Lin-Pass [32] have constructed *constant round* non-malleable $\mathcal{ZK}$ protocols for all of $\mathcal{NP}$, assuming only one-way functions. Both of these works, however, still use the OWF in a non-black-box manner.

In light of these recent results, we can make our previous question even more strict and ask whether it is possible to construct *constant-round* simulation-sound $\mathcal{ZK}$ proofs, based only on black-box use of general assumptions. Towards this end, we note that our protocol indeed achieves constant-round complexity when it is instantiated with non-malleable commitment scheme of [27] (or even [26] which only achieves slightly weaker notion of non-malleability when OWF is used as a black-box).

Relationship between Various Notions of Non-malleability. As noted earlier, today the term non-malleable $\mathcal{ZK}$ is used loosely and can refer to any of the following three notions: NMZK as formulated by DDN [19] (see also [47]), simulation soundness (SIMSOUND) as formulated by Sahai [51] in the context of non-interactive zero-knowledge [6,7],[3] and simulation-extractability (SIMEXT) as formulated by Pass and Rosen [47] (see also [16,35]). Briefly, NMZK requires that for every man-in-the-middle M, there exists an M^* who can succeed in proving the concerned statement $\tilde{x}$ on its own with almost the same probability (in a given $\mathcal{ZK}$ protocol). SIMSOUND requires that no M can prove a false statement *even when* it can receive proofs to many false statements from the simulator. Finally, SIMEXT requires that there exist a *single* machine called the "simulator-extractor" which simulates the view of M and output witnesses for all statements that M proves successfully.

We note that while SIMEXT is *perceived* as the strongest notion of all three, an exact relationship between the three notions of non-malleability (as described above) is not known. In the non-interactive setting, Sahai demonstrated that NMZK and SIMSOUND are incomparable. Further, in the interactive setting, Pass and Rosen [47] proved that SIMEXT implies NMZK. Indeed, studying the formal relationships between various security notions is a well established line of research. For example, see the works in [2,29,3,9] for an extensive study of such relationships between security notions of encryption schemes.

In the second part of this work, we continue the study of the exact relationship between the three notions of non-malleability and obtain further results (in the interactive case), as summarized below. If a protocol satisfies a security notion A, does it also satisfy some other security notion B? If yes, then we write $A \Rightarrow B$, otherwise we write $A \nRightarrow B$. Notation $A \Leftrightarrow B$ implies that the two notions are

---

[3] We note that simulation-soundness *in the interactive case* has never been explicitly formalized in the plain model; Garay, MacKenzie, and Yang presented a formulation for the same in the CRS model [23]. We present a formulation in the plain model by building upon [51,23,47].

equivalent, i.e. $A \Rightarrow B$, and $B \Rightarrow A$. Then, roughly speaking, we arrive at the following conclusions:

$$\text{NMZK-AOK} \Leftrightarrow \text{SIMEXT} \not\Rightarrow \text{SIMSOUND}$$

Here NMZK-AOK is short for NMZK argument-of-knowledge. Pass and Rosen [47] showed that SIMEXT implies NMZK-AOK, and the folklore perception is that it is in fact stronger than the other two notions. Our conclusions are therefore somewhat surprising. We note that we only study the stand-alone and computational setting. A similar study for the more complex concurrent setting (as well as statistical notions) is an interesting future direction. Another direction is to investigate the notion of non-malleable witness indistinguishability [43] and its connection with other non-malleable primitives.

Other Related Works. In this paper, we only focus on constructions based on general assumptions, and in the plain model. If one is willing to give up on general assumptions, then under specific number-theoretical assumptions, efficient constructions are known for both non-malleable zero knowledge and commitments, e.g., see [44,42]. Likewise, if one is willing to depart from the plain model, and use setup assumptions such as a CRS, then efficient constructions are known for both non-malleable zero knowledge and commitments, e.g. see [14,23,38].

1.1 Overview of Main Ideas

The Simulation Sound Protocol. In this section, we provide key intuition behind our black-box construction of simulation-sound zero-knowledge protocol. Our protocol looks deceptively simple but in fact relies on several key ideas, as we explain below.

Intuitively, to construct NMZK, we should use a non-malleable commitment (NMCOM) to obtain some sort of "independence" between left and right execution. Consider using NMCOM in Blum's Hamiltonicity (BH) protocol. Clearly, replacing the commitment scheme in BH by NMCOM will not work since NM-COM is not necessarily *concurrent non-malleable* [18,46].[4] Another idea is to use a Feige-Shamir style construction [21,22] to establish a "trapdoor" and commit to a fake witness using NMCOM. Clearly, this approach does not suffer from the earlier issue of concurrent non-malleability. However, any such approach where NMCOM will not be later "opened" must somehow prove something about the committed value (since otherwise, intuitively, such a commitment is of no use in the protocol). Note that this will require one to use Cook-Levin reductions unless one is able to leverage some "cut-and-choose" style techniques. Unfortunately, however, there is no hope of using "cut-and-choose" style protocols to

---

[4] Indeed there is no known construction of concurrent non-malleable commitments for tags of length n that uses OWF as a black-box. Furthermore, even if there existed one, it may not be suffice here since some of the commitments sent by the prover are opened later in the third round of BH protocol.

circumvent this issue, since such protocols will run into the issues of concurrent non-malleability.

With these observations, our initial idea is to change the direction of the use of NMCOM, i.e., construct a protocol where the verifier (instead of prover) commits to some value using NMCOM, which must be opened later. One possible approach is to have the prover P and the verifier V perform coin-tossing to determine the "challenge" in the BH-protocol in the following manner: V first commits to a random string r_1 using NMCOM and then opens it after P sends a random string r_2; the BH-challenge is then set to be $r_1 \oplus r_2$.

While a-priori this sounds like a promising approach, unfortunately, we run into the following problem in the proof. Note that during the simulation, the simulator S must simulate the outcome of the above coin-tossing phase to a fixed challenge value (say) ch for which it knows how to respond successfully. Therefore, in the simulated experiment, there will be sufficient information about ch in the first message of BH. This can be exploited by the man-in-the-middle M while preparing its NMCOM, thus failing the simulation.

To this end, our next idea is to move the verifier's commitment to the "top" of the protocol. Specifically, we adopt the Goldreich-Kahan [24] approach and require V to commit its challenge ch using NMCOM *before it sees any information* from P (or S) — use of NMCOM guarantees that M's challenge will be independent of V's. However, since NMCOM used will be statistically binding[5], this approach compromises even the *stand alone* soundness of the scheme. Our *first key-idea* is to fix this stand-alone soundness. We do this by noting that the BH protocol has a special structure: once prover sends its message, then *for a false statement* x', there is at most *one* challenge ch' for which he can succeed. Therefore, to succeed, it must set $ch' = ch$. Hence, we replace the commitment scheme in BH-protocol by a special 3-round extractable commitment scheme [49,50]; this ensures that if prover sets $ch' = ch$, we can extract ch' using the extractable-commitment, without ever opening it.

When we move to the non-malleability setting, however, this approach runs into a second problem. To simulate a false proof, our simulator S will indeed rewind M and prepare the first message of BH, based on the value revealed by M, say ch_M. It is possible that M will set its value in right interaction, depending upon the message on its left. To overcome this situation, our *second key-observation* is to argue independence *without rewinding M at all*. In particular, we use the strong definition of non-malleability, which simply gives the value ch_M to S (or the distinguisher in the non-malleability experiment—see, e.g., [33,47]). Therefore, using this we can show that if M's preparation of the first BH-message on right changes as we go from real to the simulated world, we can once again extract using our first idea, while simulating in straight-line on left. A non-synchronous adversary is handled using standard scheduling arguments and known techniques.

---

[5] In case of statistical hiding, we must rely on "non-malleability w.r.t. opening", and that is a troublesome proposition since no single value is defined in the commitment. This creates several new difficulties of its own.

This essentially summarizes the high-level ideas in our protocol. We refer the reader to the technical sections for details.

Definitional Relationships. We briefly highlight here how we obtain these results. First, it is not hard to see that NMZK-AoK implies SimExt if non-malleability property uses the adversary only as a *black-box*. That is, if M^* (guaranteed by NMZK) uses M as a black-box only, then M^* and the AOK property can be (easily) combined to construct a "simulator-extractor" for SimExt property. However, in general, it is not obvious if such a simulator-extractor can be constructed at all.

We show that in the *static* case, where M declares $\tilde{x}$ (after seeing x) before any execution begins, we can in fact construct such a simulator-extractor by combining M^* with the knowledge extractor E guaranteed by AOK property. The central difficulty that arises is that the success probability of M^* may differ negligibly from that of M in the real world. Since the extraction of the witness, intuitively, must come from M^* via rewinding, this negligible difference can result in exponential time during extraction. This is a problem akin to Goldreich-Kahan [24], and we use their techniques to overcome this situation. To the best of our knowledge, this is the first time that the techniques of [24] (to ensure expected polynomial-time simulation) have been applied in the context of non-malleability. The ideal result, of course, would be to prove equivalence even for the adaptive case. We leave this as an important open question.

Finally, the result SimExt $\nRightarrow$ SimSound is obtained by exploiting the fact that SimExt does not require any security guarantee in the case when the input message is false. Since SimSound *explicitly* deals with false messages, we are able to exploit this situation to obtain a counter-example. We note that in the *bare public-key model* [10], similar ideas have been used before to separate "knowledge extraction" from "soundness," e.g., see Crescenzo and Visconti [15].

2   Basic Definitions

We assume familiarity with standard definitions such as commitment schemes, interactive proofs, zero knowledge, and arguments of knowledge. We also assume that the reader is familiar with man-in-the-middle experiments for commitments and zero-knowledge proofs. Here we recall the notation very briefly. Throughout the paper, unless stated otherwise, we will use n to denote the security parameter.

Let $\langle C, R \rangle$ be a commitment protocol where C is the algorithm for honest committer and R is the algorithm for honest receiver. We assume that $\langle C, R \rangle$ is statistically-binding and for strings of length at least n. The man-in-the-middle is denoted by A, his advice string by $z \in \{0,1\}^*$. The experiment is a random process A interacts with C receiving a commitment to v, and simultaneously interacts with R, acting as a committer. We use standard terms—left and right interactions for A's interaction with C and R respectively. At the end of A's interaction on right, let $\tilde{v}$ denote the unique value that A commits on right (possible $\perp$). As soon as A completes its interaction on right, value $\tilde{v}$ is provided to A—irrespective of the state of left interaction; the value $\tilde{v}$ is extracted by an oracle $\mathcal{O}$ which can run in exponential time.[6]

We prefer to work with *tag* based definitions; and hence every execution of $\langle C, R \rangle$ defines a tag string. We stick to the simple class of protocols where the tag string is chosen by the receiver.[7] Let the tag string on right be tag, and t$\tilde{a}$g on left (chosen by A). Without loss of generality, we assume that the length of the tag strings is the same as the security parameter n. If t$\tilde{a}$g = tag, A's interaction on right is set to the abort symbol $\perp$.

The *joint* view (of A and R) in the experiment consists of: the randomness of A, the auxiliary input z, all messages A receives in *both* interactions, the value $\tilde{v}$, *and* the randomness of R. The experiment is a random process, and hence the joint view of A is a random variable. For $v \in \{0,1\}^n, z \in \{0,1\}^*, \text{tag} \in \{0,1\}^n, n \in \mathbb{N}$, the joint view in the experiment (which includes $\tilde{v}$ given to A by the oracle $\mathcal{O}$ after the completion of right side commitment) is denoted by:

$$\text{mim}^A_{\langle C,R \rangle, \mathcal{O}}(v, z, \text{tag})$$

Definition 1 (Non-malleable (1-1CCA) Commitment). *A commitment protocol $\langle C, R \rangle$ is said to be non-malleable if there exists an oracle $\mathcal{O}$ such that for every non-uniform probabilistic polynomial time Turing machine A (man-in-the-middle), for every pair of strings $v_0, v_1 \in \{0,1\}^n$, every tag-string $\text{tag} \in \{0,1\}^n$, every (advice) string $z \in \{0,1\}^*$, the following two random variables are computationally indistinguishable,*

$$\text{mim}^A_{\langle C,R \rangle, \mathcal{O}}(v_0, z, \text{tag}) \quad \text{and} \quad \text{mim}^A_{\langle C,R \rangle, \mathcal{O}}(v_1, z, \text{tag})$$

Often we will drop the oracle $\mathcal{O}$ from the notation when it is clear from the context. In many schemes, tags of smaller length such as $O(\log n)$ are also allowed. Ideally we want schemes with longer tag length such as n. Most of the schemes in the literature, such as [18,26,27] already satisfy the notion of 1-1CCA w.r.t. tags of length n; this is implicit in their security proofs (although not claimed explicitly). The construction in [27] is based on the black-box use of one-way functions, and suffices for our result. In the full version, we argue briefly how the security proof of [27] already satisfies 1-1CCA security.

Non-malleable Interactive Proofs. Let $\langle P, V \rangle$ be an interactive proof system for an $\mathcal{NP}$ complete language L. Let $x \in L$ be a statement of length n; we assume that P is polynomial time and receives a witness $w \in R_L(x)$ as its auxiliary input. This experiment is the same as the commitment experiment except that it involves execution of proof system $\langle P, V \rangle$. The *joint* view (of A and V) in the man-in-the-middle experiment consists of: statements $x, \tilde{x}$, the randomness

---

[6] Note that this is a slight deviation from standard definition, which provide A the value $\tilde{v}$ only at the end of both interactions. Nevertheless, all non-malleable commitment schemes that we know of, are not affected by this change.

[7] Once again, this choice is in the interest of a cleaner exposition of our results, and without loss of generality. Note that A is free to choose the tag in the left session *adaptively*, after viewing the tag chosen by the receiver in the right session.

of A, the auxiliary input z, all messages A receives in *both* interactions, *and* the randomness of V. For $x \in L$, $w \in R_L(x)$, $z \in \{0,1\}^*$, $\mathsf{tag} \in \{0,1\}^n$, $n \in \mathbb{N}$, the joint view in the experiment (sometimes called the *real* experiment) is denoted by:

$$\mathsf{view}^A_{\langle P,V \rangle}(x,w,z,\mathsf{tag})$$

When a random variable representing a view, e.g., $\mathsf{view}^A_{\langle P,V \rangle}(x,w,z,\mathsf{tag})$ is *accepting*, we abuse the notation and write: "$\mathsf{view}^A_{\langle P,V \rangle}(x,w,z,\mathsf{tag}){=}1$". We now recall two formulations of non-malleability from literature: non-malleable zero-knowledge and simulation-extractability.

Let $\langle A^*, V \rangle(x,z,\mathsf{tag})$ denote the view of V in a random execution of the proof system defined by $\langle P,V \rangle$, where A^* plays the role of the prover.

Definition 2 (Non-malleable Interactive Proofs). *An interactive proof system $\langle P,V \rangle$ for a language L is said to be* non-malleable *if for every* PPT *Turing machine A (man-in-the-middle), there exists a* PPT *Turing machine A^* (stand alone prover), such that for every $x \in L$, every $w \in R_L(x)$, every tag string $\mathsf{tag} \in \{0,1\}^n$, every polynomial $q(\cdot)$, every (advice) string $z \in \{0,1\}^*$, and every sufficiently large $n \in \mathbb{N}$,*

$$\Pr\left[\mathsf{view}^A_{\langle P,V \rangle}(x,w,z,\mathsf{tag}) = 1\right] < \Pr\left[\langle A^*, V \rangle(x,z,\mathsf{tag}) = 1\right] + \frac{1}{q(n)}$$

If, in addition, $\langle P,V \rangle$ is also zero knowledge*, then $\langle P,V \rangle$ is said to be a* non-malleable zero-knowledge *interactive proof system.*

Note that, a non-malleable interactive proof is not necessarily zero knowledge. A somewhat different formulation is that of simulation-extractability (which implies non-malleable zero-knowledge). This notion requires a simulator (as in $\mathcal{ZK}$), which simulates the joint view, and also outputs a witness for the right-hand side statement if V accepts on right.

Definition 3 (Simulation Extractable Interactive Proofs). *An interactive proof system $\langle P,V \rangle$ for a language L is said to be* simulation extractable *if for every* PPT *Turing machine A (man-in-the-middle), there exists a probabilistic expected polynomial time Turing machine SE, such that for every $x \in L$, every $w \in R_L(x)$, every tag string $\mathsf{tag} \in \{0,1\}^n$, and every (advice) $z \in \{0,1\}^*$, the following properties hold:*

1. *Joint-view in the real experiment, $\mathsf{view}^A_{\langle P,V \rangle}(x,w,z,\mathsf{tag})$, is computationally indistinguishable from the first output (i.e., simulated joint-view) of SE, denoted by $SE_1(x,z,\mathsf{tag})$.*
2. *If the right execution in $SE_1(x,z,\mathsf{tag})$ is accepting for an instance $\tilde{x} \in \{0,1\}^n$, then the second output of SE is a string $\tilde{w}$ such that $\tilde{w} \in R_L(\tilde{x})$.*

3   Efficient Simulation-Sound Interactive Proofs

This section presents our first main result, a simulation-sound protocol based only on black-box use of non-malleable commitment scheme $\langle C, R \rangle$. The notion of simulation-soundness, in the interactive setting in the *plain* model, despite implicit discussions in many works, has never appeared formally. In the common reference string (CRS) model, it was introduced by Sahai [51] for non-interactive $\mathcal{ZK}$; an extension for interactive case—still in the CRS model—was considered by Garay, MacKenzie, and Yang [23]. Below we give an adaptation of the definitions of [51,23] to the plain model (in the interactive setting).

3.1   The Definition

Intuitively, simulation soundness means that in a $\mathcal{ZK}$proof, a man-in-the-middle adversary A cannot produce a convincing proof for a false statement, *even if* it can see *simulated* proofs for statements of its own choice, including *false* statements. Note that since A has to be able to access simulated proofs, in some sense, this automatically guarantees zero knowledge. This is unlike non-malleable interactive proofs, which may or may not be zero knowledge. The formal definition requires a single machine S—the simulator—which guarantees indistinguishability of the view for true statements, and the soundness for statements on *right hand side* even in the presence of simulated false proofs on *left hand side*.

Definition 4 (Simulation Sound Interactive Proofs). *An interactive proof system $\langle P, V \rangle$ for a language L is said to be* simulation sound *if for every probabilistic polynomial time Turing machine A (man-in-the-middle), there exists a probabilistic expected polynomial time machine S such that,*

1. *For every $x \in L$, every $w \in R_L(x)$, every $\mathsf{tag} \in \{0,1\}^n$, and every (advice) $z \in \{0,1\}^*$, the following distributions are computationally indistinguishable,*

$$S(x, z, \mathsf{tag}) \quad and \quad \mathrm{view}^A_{\langle P, V \rangle}(x, w, z, \mathsf{tag})$$

2. *For every $x \in \{0,1\}^n$, every $\mathsf{tag} \in \{0,1\}^n$, every (advice) $z \in \{0,1\}^*$, every polynomial $q(\cdot)$ and every sufficiently large $n \in \mathbb{N}$,*

$$\Pr\left[\nu \leftarrow S(x, z, \mathsf{tag}); \tilde{x} \notin L \wedge \tilde{b} = 1\right] < \frac{1}{q(n)}$$

where, $\tilde{x}$ represents the right hand side statement and $\tilde{b}$ denotes whether the right hand side verifier accepts, in the simulated joint view ν.

Remarks

1. The second requirement in our definition is a direct adaptation of the definition of [51,23]. This is essentially the core requirement of the definition. It also makes the definition somewhat *strict* in the sense that A can receive simulated proofs for statements that it *knows* are false. However, this is unavoidable: while A might know that a particular statement is false, it is not clear how the simulator S can access this knowledge. As a result, S must be able to simulate for all false x, irrespective of what A knows about x. This is the fact we exploit in constructing a counter-example and prove that SimExt $\nRightarrow$ SimSound. The first requirement of the definition is for capturing $\mathcal{ZK}$.

2. The strict requirement can be relaxed by considering a *distribution* based definition in which a sampler samples a statement (either true or false) but A does not know which is the case. A then receives proofs only for such sampled statements. This yields a weaker definition, denoted SIMSOUND$_D$. In this case, it is straightforward to see that SIMEXT $\Rightarrow$ SIMSOUND$_D$. We remark that this is indeed usually the situation in cryptographic settings.

3.2   Tool: Extractable Commitment

Consider the following simple challenge-response based bit commitment scheme $\langle \widehat{C}, \widehat{R} \rangle$, which can be based on top of any standard bit commitment scheme $\langle C', R' \rangle$ (e.g., [40]). The scheme has been used in several works, starting from [49,50]. The protocol $\langle \widehat{C}, \widehat{R} \rangle$ for committing to a bit b is described in Figure 1.

Commit Phase:

1. To commit to a bit b, $\widehat{C}$ chooses n independent random pairs $\{b_i^0, b_i^1\}_{i=1}^n$ of bits such that $b_i^0 \oplus b_i^1 = b$; and commits to them to $\widehat{R}$ using $\langle C', R' \rangle$. Let $c_i^0 \leftarrow C'(b_i^0)$ and $c_i^1 \leftarrow C'(b_i^1)$ for every $i \in [n]$.
2. $\widehat{R}$ sends n uniformly random bits $r_1, \ldots, r_n$.
3. For every $i \in [n]$, if $r_i = 0$, $\widehat{C}$ opens c_i^0, otherwise it opens c_i^1 to $\widehat{R}$ by sending the decommitment information (according to $\langle C', R' \rangle$).

Open Phase: $\widehat{C}$ opens all the unopened commitments by sending the decommitment information for each of them.

Fig. 1. Extractable Commitment Scheme $\langle \widehat{C}, \widehat{R} \rangle$

Some remarks about $\langle \widehat{C}, \widehat{R} \rangle$ are in order.

1. If $\langle C', R' \rangle$ is statistically binding, so is $\langle \widehat{C}, \widehat{R} \rangle$. We adopt the convention that if not all shares are such that $b_i^0 \oplus b_i^1 = b$, then the adversary has essentially aborted, setting $b = \bot$. It suffices for our application.
2. To commit to a string $s = s_1, s_2, \ldots, s_n$, execute n instances of $\langle \widehat{C}, \widehat{R} \rangle$, in *parallel*—one for each bit s_i. This is a string commitment scheme, which we shall denote by $\langle \widehat{C}_s, \widehat{R}_s \rangle$. Note that $s = \bot$ if $s_i = \bot$ for any $i \in [n]$.
3. Scheme $\langle \widehat{C}_s, \widehat{R}_s \rangle$ is a public coin protocol for $\widehat{R}_s$.
4. Finally, $\langle \widehat{C}_s, \widehat{R}_s \rangle$ admits an extractor algorithm $CExt$ which extracts a string $\mathtt{str}'$ from every C^* such that if C^* commits to a valid string $\mathtt{str}$, then $\mathtt{str}' = \mathtt{str}$. The running time of $CExt$ is inversely proportion to the probability that C^* makes a convincing commitment to R. If we increase the challenge-response rounds to $\omega(1)$, then $CExt$ runs in polynomial time.

3.3   The Simulation-Sound Protocol

We are now ready to present our simulation-sound interactive *argument* system $\langle P, V \rangle$. Our protocol uses a *non-malleable commitment scheme* $\langle C, R \rangle$, and also the *bit* commitment scheme $\langle \widehat{C}, \widehat{R} \rangle$ described above. These schemes are used in a black-box manner.

At a high level, our protocol is essentially a parallel repetition of Blum's protocol for Graph Hamiltonicity [5] with the following modifications: (a) instead of using a standard perfectly binding commitment scheme, the prover P uses the 3-round commitment scheme $\langle \widehat{C}, \widehat{R} \rangle$ described above. (b) Further, similar to [24], we require the verifier to commit to its challenge in advance. However, unlike [24] where a statistically hiding commitment scheme is used, the verifier V in our protocol uses the non-malleable commitment scheme $\langle C, R \rangle$ to commit to its challenge.

We now formally describe the protocol. Let P and V denote the prover and verifier respectively. The common input is a graph G in the form of a $n \times n$ adjacency matrix. Further, the private input to P is a Hamiltonian cycle H in G. The protocol proceeds as follows:

1. V chooses a uniformly random n bit string ch, and commits to it by using the non-malleable commitment scheme $\langle C, R \rangle$, where V acts as C and P acts as R.
2. For every $i \in [n]$:
   (a) P chooses a random permutation π_i and prepares $G_i = \pi_i(G)$. Let $\ell = n \log(n)$ denote the length of π_i.
   (b) P commits to each bit $b_{i,j}$ in matrix G_i and each bit $b'_{i,k}$ in π_i to V using the commitment scheme $\langle \widehat{C}, \widehat{R} \rangle$,[8] for every $j \in [n^2]$ and $k \in [\ell]$.

   Note that this step can be seen as running $2n$ parallel instances of $\langle \widehat{C}_s, \widehat{R}_s \rangle$, n of which commit to n^2 size bit strings $G_1, \ldots, G_n$ and and the remaining n commit to length ℓ bit strings $\pi_1, \ldots, \pi_n$. Alternatively, this step is essentially equivalent to committing a string $\mathtt{str}$ of size $n^3 + n^2 \log(n)$ using the protocol $\langle \widehat{C}_s, \widehat{R}_s \rangle$.
3. V sends ch, and decommits by sending the corresponding decommitment information.
4. For every $i \in [n]$:
   (a) If $ch_i = 0$, P reveals π_i and G_i, and decommits according to $\langle \widehat{C}, \widehat{R} \rangle$.
   (b) Otherwise, P reveals the Hamiltonian Cycle in G_i by sending the corresponding decommitment information.

Facts about $\langle P, V \rangle$

1. If graph G does *not* contain a Hamiltonian cycle, and the commitments in step 2 define a unique string (say $\mathtt{str}$), then after this step, there is *at*

---

[8] Each matrix G_i has n^2 cells, and each cell contains a single bit.

most one challenge string ch for which a cheating prover P^* can provide a convincing answer in step 4.[9]

2. Furthermore, in the above case, if there does exist a challenge ch for which a convincing answer can be produced after step 2, then given string $\mathtt{str}$, one can reconstruct the challenge ch in the following manner: for every $i \in [n]$, let π_i' denote the ith permutation and G_i' denote the ith graph in string $\mathtt{str}$. Then, if $\pi_i'(G) = G_i'$, set $ch_i = 0$, else set $ch_i = 1$.

Theorem 1. *Protocol $\langle P, V \rangle$ is a simulation-sound interactive argument system for Graph Hamiltonicity, as per definition 4.*

3.4 Proof of Security

To prove Theorem 1, we need to demonstrate an expected polynomial time machine S (simulator), satisfying both properties in definition 4. Our simulator S is almost identical to the Goldreich-Kahan simulator [24], with some obvious modifications. Before we describe our simulator, we first define a machine A' that is used later in our description.

Machine A'. We define A' as a machine that internally incorporates the adversary A and honest verifier V. A' will act as a cheating verifier and receive a proof from an honest prover. Internally, A' forwards this proof to A as the left interaction of $\langle P, V \rangle$. In addition, A' also simulates the right interaction for A, by letting it interact with the internal verifier V. At the end of the execution, A' separates the left and the right views to represent the joint-view (of the man-in-the-middle experiment for interactive proofs). A' produce such a joint-view simply by replaying the messages with fixed randomness that it used for V and A internally. The reason, we create this artificial machine A' is because we can now run Goldreich-Kahan simulator on it.

Simulator S. The description of our simulator S, for proving SIMSOUND, appears in Figure 2. Every time S rewinds A' to a previous point in execution, it provides A' with fresh randomness for the rest of the execution.

It is instructive to note that while in the NMCOM-experiment, the adversary can obtain $\tilde{v}$ as soon as it finishes the right session, no such "luxury" is available in NMZK-experiment. Therefore, A—who works in the NMZK-experiment—never asks for any such values. Note that, step (S1) represents a partial "main thread" of execution of S, which it completes in step (S4) if A' opens the challenge successfully.

---

[9] Specifically, consider the simpler case of the 3-round Blum Hamiltonicity (BH) protocol (the argument for our scheme follows in a similar manner). Recall that in BH, if the challenge bit is 0, then the prover P must open the commitments (sent in the first step) to a permutation π and a graph G' such that $\pi(G) = G'$. Otherwise, if the challenge bit is 1, P must reveal a Hamiltonian cycle in the committed graph (without decommitting to the entire committed graph). Then, if graph G does not contain a Hamiltonian cycle, and a cheating prover manages to succeed in the last step irrespective of whether the challenge bit is 0 or 1, we can contradict the binding property of the commitment scheme.

Let A' denote be a machine that internally incorporates adversary A and honest verifier V as described earlier. The simulator S first fixes a uniformly random tape for A' and then proceeds according to the following steps:

S1. S simulates the first step of the protocol by playing an honest receiver R in the execution of the non-malleable commitment scheme $\langle C, R \rangle$ with the adversary A'. Since $\langle C, R \rangle$ is statistically binding, except with negligible probability, A' is committed to a unique challenge string. Let the state of A' at the end of this step be $st_{A'}$, which S records.

S2. S now plays the next round of the protocol but commits to dummy strings (e.g., all 1s). That is, S commits by executing $2n$ parallel instances of $\langle \widehat{C}_s, \widehat{R}_s \rangle$: n instances of n^2-size strings (representing graphs) and the rest of size $2n$ (representing permutations). At the end of this step, if A' successfully opens a challenge string ch for step S1 commitment, S records ch and proceeds to the next step. Otherwise, S outputs the current view of A' and halts.

S3. S repeats step (S2) with fresh randomness until it records n^2 valid openings to ch. If t is the total number of trials, then let $\bar{p} = n^2/t$ be an estimate of $p(G, r)$. Here $p(G, r)$ is the probability that A' (when initialized with state $st_{A'}$) successfully opens ch in step (S2) over the randomness of step (S2).

S4. S now reinitializes A' with the same state $st_{A'}$, and plays step (S4) as follows. Recall that ch is the string opened in step (S2) by A. For every $i \in [n]$, S does the following: if $ch_i = 0$, S chooses a random permutation π_i and commits to π_i and $G_i = \pi_i(G)$; otherwise, S commits to a random permutation and a random n-cycle graph H_i (i.e., an $n \times n$ adjacency matrix where the cells corresponding to the cycle are set to 1 while the other cells are set to random bits). If A' replies by correctly revealing the string ch, S proceeds to complete the simulation by correctly revealing the openings to the commitments. Otherwise, the entire step (S4) is repeated for at most $\frac{\text{poly}(n)}{\bar{p}}$ times, until A' correctly reveals ch. If all the attempts fail, S outputs a special symbol indicating time-out.

Fig. 2. Simulator S for $\langle P, V \rangle$

Proving simulation-soundness. To prove that $\langle P, V \rangle$ satisfies definition 4, we show that it satisfies its two requirements. The first requirement is akin to proving that $\langle P, V \rangle$ is a $\mathcal{ZK}$ interactive argument system. The proof for this is identical to [24], barring some trivial changes, and is therefore omitted. In particular, it follows almost immediately if we show that time-out is output with negligible probability (see [24] or the proof of Claim 4.1 in section 4.1 where a similar claim is argued).

We now focus on the second requirement in definition 4, which requires that A cannot prove a false statement in the view output by S, *even if* the input to S is a false statement: i.e., an arbitrary graph $G \in \{0, 1\}^{n^2}$, which may not be Hamiltonian.[10]

---

[10] For simplicity, we are dealing with a n^2 size statement here, but this is only a syntactic change, and can be removed by scaling the number of vertices in G down to $\sqrt{n}$.

Assume that the second requirement does not hold. Then, there exists a (non-uniform) PPT man-in-the-middle adversary A, a polynomial $q(\cdot)$, an advice string $z \in \{0,1\}^*$, and infinitely many $n \in \mathbb{N}$ such that for every n there exists a graph $G \in \{0,1\}^{n^2}$, and a tag string $\mathtt{tag} \in \{0,1\}^n$ such that over the randomness of S:

$$\delta(n) \stackrel{\text{def}}{=} \Pr\left[\nu \leftarrow S(G, z, \mathtt{tag}); \tilde{G} \notin L \wedge \tilde{b} = 1\right] > \frac{1}{q(n)}$$

where, $\tilde{G}$ represents the right hand side instance and $\tilde{b}$ denotes whether the right hand side verifier accepts, in the simulated joint-view ν. Fix one such n, along with statement $G_n \in \{0,1\}^{n^2}$, and tag string $\mathtt{tag}_n \in \{0,1\}^n$, and let

$$\delta_n = \Pr\left[\nu \leftarrow S(G_n, z, \mathtt{tag}_n); \tilde{G} \notin L \wedge \tilde{b} = 1\right]$$

which is larger than $1/q(n)$. Now, recall that the man-in-the-middle A controls the scheduling of messages in the left and right executions. Figure 3 describes three representative schedules that A can choose from. Since the overall success probability of A is δ_n, A must succeed in one of the schedules with probability at least $\frac{\delta_n}{3}$. For each schedule, we will show how to break some security property of scheme $\langle C, R \rangle$.

We start by describing the three schedules, as shown in Figure 3.

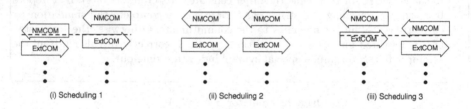

Fig. 3. Three schedules for A. NMCOM $:= \langle C, R \rangle$ and EXTCOM $:= \langle \hat{C}_s, \hat{R}_s \rangle$

Scheduling 1. A starts the right execution of extractable commitment EXTCOM $:= \langle \hat{C}_s, \hat{R}_s \rangle$ before its left execution. In particular, this means that A sends out the first message of $\langle \hat{C}_s, \hat{R}_s \rangle$ in the right execution without seeing the corresponding message in the left execution.

Scheduling 2. A schedules the left and right executions in a synchronous manner.[11]

Scheduling 3. A forces the EXTCOM protocol $\langle \hat{C}_s, \hat{R}_s \rangle$ in the left execution to be started before the NMCOM protocol $\langle C, R \rangle$ is completed in the right execution.

---

[11] This means that for every $i \in [r]$, where r is the number of rounds in $\langle P, V \rangle$, the ith message of the protocol in left and right executions is sent only after the $(i-1)^{th}$ message of the protocol has been sent in both left and right executions.

Due to space constraints, we defer the formal details of the proof for each schedule to the full version of the paper. Here, we briefly discuss the high-level intuition for each case.

In scheduling 1, we will break the hiding property of $\langle C, R \rangle$. The main observation is that in this scheduling A has already fixed the message for which he can succeed, without any help from the simulator. Therefore, we can extract this value from the ExtCOM-phase. Very briefly, the fact that simulator rewinds on left is not a problem because the extractor for ExtCOM is public-coin and S never rewinds to a point higher than ExtCOM on left.

In schedules 2 and 3, we will break the non-malleability property of $\langle C, R \rangle$. Very briefly, in schedule 2, we will demonstrate a PPT man-in-the-middle adversary A' for $\langle C, R \rangle$ and an expected PPT distinguisher D' violating the non-malleability property of $\langle C, R \rangle$. The key-idea for this schedule is that the value that A commits in NmCom, will be given as input along with the joint-view. And therefore, we do *not rewind* A at all, since we already know the trapdoor for simulation. The proof for schedule 3 is almost identical. We first observe the following: in scheduling, A ends up completing his NmCom-phase before it has received the NmCom from V. The key-observation now is that since A's commitment finishes first, it can be given the value it has committed so far during the execution. Therefore, we consider a man-in-the-middle A' for NmCom, just as before; as soon as it receives the committed value (which is the trapdoor for simulation), it internally incorporates the distinguisher D' described above and runs it with this value.

4 Relationship between Different Notions of Non-Malleable ZK

In this section, we study the definitional equivalence between the three notions of non-malleability in the context of zero knowledge, namely, NmZK, SimSound, and SimExt. We obtain two results. First, in Section 4.1, we show that NmZK with the argument of knowledge (AOK) property implies SimExt. Then, in Section 4.2, we demonstrate that SimExt does not imply SimSound. Putting these results together, we obtain the following picture regarding the equivalence of the three notions:

$$\text{NmZK-AoK} \Leftrightarrow \text{SimExt} \nRightarrow \text{SimSound}$$

4.1 NmZK versus SimExt

Simulation-extractability was formulated in [47], and it was shown that it implies non-malleable zero-knowledge. Perhaps somewhat surprisingly, we show that if the non-malleable zero-knowledge protocol is also an argument-of-knowledge, then it is actually simulation extractable.

Theorem 2. *If* $\langle P, V \rangle$ *is a* non-malleable *zero knowledge argument of knowledge for a language* $L \in \mathcal{NP}$, *it is in fact a* simulation extractable interactive argument *for* L.

This result is very generic, and applies to all types of protocols, be they computational or statistical $\mathcal{ZK}$, black-box or non-black-box $\mathcal{ZK}$, etc. This essentially shows that as far as the "moral" sense of non-malleability is concerned, the two definitions are equivalent. We note, however, that the theorem holds only for the *static* case where A must announce the theorem $\tilde{x}$ on input the theorem x, before the protocol execution begins. That is, $\tilde{x}$ depends only on x and not on the execution of the protocol. We do not consider the adaptive case (where A chooses $\tilde{x}$ based on the execution on left so far) in this paper, and leave it for future work.

Proof of Theorem 2. Let $\langle P, V \rangle$ be a non-malleable zero knowledge argument of knowledge for a language L with respect to tags of length n. This means that we have the following: (a) Since $\langle P, V \rangle$ is non-malleable, we have that $\forall$ PPT man-in-the-middle adversaries A, $\exists$ a stand-alone PPT adversary A^* such that it satisfies definition 2. Now, we can define probabilities p_a and p_{a^*} as follows: p_a is the probability that A convinces the verifier in the right session in the real execution, and p_{a^*} is the probability that A^* convinces an honest verifier. Note that by definition 2, we have that $p_{a^*} \geq p_a - \text{negl}(n)$. (b) Since $\langle P, V \rangle$ is zero knowledge, for every cheating verifier strategy, $\exists$ a simulator S satisfying the zero knowledge property. (c) Since $\langle P, V \rangle$ is an argument of knowledge, for every cheating prover P^*, $\exists$ an extractor E satisfying the argument of knowledge property.

Now, in order to prove Theorem 2, we need to construct a simulator-extractor SE satisfying Definition 3. Let V^* be a machine that internally incorporates the adversary A and verifier V and their interaction in the real execution.[12] Now, before we proceed to formally describe our simulator-extractor, let us discuss a natural approach in order to highlight the main technical challenge.

Main Issue. Consider the following natural algorithm for a simulator-extractor SE: (a) Let V^* be a machine that internally incorporates the adversary A and verifier V and their interaction in the real execution. Then, first run the simulator S with V^* to output the joint view of A. (b) Now, since we are in the static case, the instance $\tilde{x}$ in the right execution does not depend on the left view. Then, if the joint view output by S contains an accepting right execution, run the extractor E on the stand-alone adversary A^* to extract a witness for $\tilde{x}$.

Now note that the running time of the second step in the above procedure is proportional to $\frac{p_s}{p_{a^*}}$, where p_s is the probability that the joint view output by S contains an accepting right execution. Unfortunately, $\frac{p_s}{p_{a^*}}$ is not necessarily

---

[12] Note that given the view of V^* in the real execution, we can construct the joint view of A (as defined in Section 2) from the random tape of V^* and the messages that A and V exchange internally, as well as those exchanged between P and V^*. Likewise, if S is used with V^*, the joint view can still be constructed *even if* S is a non black-box simulator. This is done by first producing view$_{V^*}$, and then *replaying* the entire executions on left and right with the same V that was used to construct V^*. This yields messages corresponding to both left and right sessions of A, defining the complete joint view.

bounded by a polynomial, hence the running time of the above procedure is not expected PPT. We note that this is reminiscent of a technical problem overcome by Goldreich and Kahan in the construction of constant round zero knowledge [24]. Indeed, we overcome this problem by using ideas from [24].

The Simulator-Extractor. Given the machines defined above, we now give a detailed description of our simulator-extractor SE. The simulator-extractor SE receives statement x, advice string z, and tag-string tag as input. SE also receives access to either the code of A or black-box access to A depending upon the properties of A^* and S. SE runs the following steps:

S1. Run S with V^* on input x, z, and tag to generate a view view_{V^*}.[13] If the right execution in view_{V^*} is not accepting (i.e., A does not convince V), then output ($\text{view}_{V^*}, \bot$) and stop.

S2. Otherwise, let p_s denote the probability that simulator S in step (S1) outputs a view that contains an accepting right execution. Run S with V^* (on input x, z, and tag) repeatedly until n^2 views with accepting right execution are obtained. Let $\overline{p_s} = \frac{n^2}{t}$ be the estimate of p_s, where t is the total number of trials.

S3. Run the following two procedures in *parallel*[14] and halt as soon as one of them finishes.

(i) Run the brute force (exponential-time) search procedure to compute a witness $\tilde{w}$ for $\tilde{x}$. Output the tuple ($\text{view}_{V^*}, \tilde{w}$) and stop.

(ii) Run the following two steps: (a) First, run the (stand-alone) adversary A^* with an honest verifier V on inputs x, $\tilde{x}$ (where $\tilde{x}$ is the theorem proven by A in step S1), z, and tag repeatedly at most $\frac{\text{poly}(n)}{\overline{p_s}}$ times until an accepting view view_{A^*} is generated. If no accepting view is generated after all the trials, then output a special symbol indicating time-out and stop. (b) Next, run the argument of knowledge extractor E on A^* with input view_{A^*} to extract a witness $\tilde{w}$ for $\tilde{x}$ from A^*. Output the tuple ($\text{view}_{V^*}, \tilde{w}$) and stop.

This completes the description of our simulator extractor SE. We will now prove that it satisfies Definition 3. Here, the difficult part is to prove that the running time of SE is polynomial in expectation, as claimed below.

Claim. The simulator-extractor SE runs in expected polynomial time.

We further need to show that SE outputs a joint view indistinguishable from that in the real execution along with a valid witness for the instance in the right session. Towards that end, note that the correctness of the witness string output

---

[13] SE simply runs the man-in-the-middle adversary A such that it interacts with S and V in the "left" and "right" executions respectively. In case S is a non black-box machine, SE is non black-box as well, since it will need the code of A to construct V^*.

[14] The effect of parallel execution can be obtained by running one step of the first procedure followed by one step of the second procedure, and so on.

by SE follows directly from the correctness of the extractor machine E. Then, we only need to show that the joint view output by SE is indistinguishable from that in the real execution. To this end, we note that the proof for the same essentially follows from the zero-knowledge property guaranteed by S *provided* we can argue that SE outputs the time-out symbol with only negligible probability. In the claim below, we bound this probability. We remark that this is a standard claim, and similar claims have earlier appeared in several works before, e.g., [24,35,37].

Claim. The simulator-extractor SE outputs the *time-out* symbol with only negligible probability.

We refer the reader to the full version for the formal proofs.

4.2   SimSound versus SimExt

We show that, perhaps somewhat surprisingly, a simulation extractable protocol is not necessarily simulation sound. Intuitively, this is because the behavior of the simulator-extractor SE is not defined for *false* statements. We exploit this fact to construct a protocol which is simulation extractable, but not simulation sound.

At a high level, we consider languages $L \in \mathcal{NP} \cap co\text{-}\mathcal{NP}$, since such languages admit polynomial-size witness for both types of assertions: "$x \in L$" and "$x \notin L$". We then take any SimExt protocol and modify it so that first the man-in-the-middle A proves to P that "$x \notin L$" using a tag-string tag; if it succeeds, P proves that "$x \in L$" using a modified tag-string tag′, which A can copy on right. If x is false, it is not hard to see that A succeeds if the left interaction succeeds in proving a false statement. The concrete protocol, and its analysis, is given in the full version.

However, as we discussed in Section 3.1, in the "natural" case where S proves false statements that cannot be distinguished from true statements, it is not hard to see that simulation-extractability does imply simulation soundness (i.e., SimExt $\Rightarrow$ SimSound$_D$).

References

1. Barak, B.: Constant-round coin-tossing with a man in the middle or realizing the shared random string model. In: FOCS (2002)
2. Bellare, M., Desai, A., Pointcheval, D., Rogaway, P.: Relations among notions of security for public-key encryption schemes. In: Krawczyk, H. (ed.) CRYPTO 1998. LNCS, vol. 1462, pp. 26–45. Springer, Heidelberg (1998)
3. Bellare, M., Fischlin, M., O'Neill, A., Ristenpart, T.: Deterministic encryption: Definitional equivalences and constructions without random oracles. In: Wagner, D. (ed.) CRYPTO 2008. LNCS, vol. 5157, pp. 360–378. Springer, Heidelberg (2008)
4. Ben-David, A., Nisan, N., Pinkas, B.: Fairplaymp: a system for secure multi-party computation. In: ACM Conference on Computer and Communications Security (2008)
5. Blum, M.: How to prove a theorem so no one else can claim it. In: Proceedings of the International Congress of Mathematicians, pp. 1444–1451 (1987)
6. Blum, M., Feldman, P., Micali, S.: Non-interactive zero-knowledge and its applications (extended abstract). In: STOC, pp. 103–112 (1988)

7. Blum, M., Santis, A.D., Micali, S., Persiano, G.: Noninteractive zero-knowledge. SIAM J. Comput. 20(6), 1084–1118 (1991)
8. Boldyreva, A., Cash, D., Fischlin, M., Warinschi, B.: Foundations of non-malleable hash and one-way functions. In: Matsui, M. (ed.) ASIACRYPT 2009. LNCS, vol. 5912, pp. 524–541. Springer, Heidelberg (2009)
9. Boldyreva, A., Fehr, S., O'Neill, A.: On notions of security for deterministic encryption, and efficient constructions without random oracles. In: Wagner, D. (ed.) CRYPTO 2008. LNCS, vol. 5157, pp. 335–359. Springer, Heidelberg (2008)
10. Canetti, R., Goldreich, O., Goldwasser, S., Micali, S.: Resettable zero-knowledge
11. Canetti, R., Lin, H., Pass, R.: Adaptive hardness and composable security in the plain model from standard assumptions. In: FOCS (2010)
12. Canetti, R., Lindell, Y., Ostrovsky, R., Sahai, A.: Universally composable two-party computation. In: Proc. 34th STOC, pp. 494–503 (2002)
13. Cook, S.A.: The complexity of theorem-proving procedures. In: STOC, pp. 151–158 (1971)
14. Di Crescenzo, G., Katz, J., Ostrovsky, R., Smith, A.: Efficient and non-interactive non-malleable commitment. In: Pfitzmann, B. (ed.) EUROCRYPT 2001. LNCS, vol. 2045, p. 40. Springer, Heidelberg (2001)
15. Crescenzo, G.D., Visconti, I.: On defining proofs of knowledge in the bare public key model. In: ICTCS (2007)
16. De Santis, A., Di Crescenzo, G., Ostrovsky, R., Persiano, G., Sahai, A.: Robust non-interactive zero knowledge. In: Kilian, J. (ed.) CRYPTO 2001. LNCS, vol. 2139, pp. 566–598. Springer, Heidelberg (2001), http://link.springer.de/link/service/series/0558/papers/2139/21390566.pdf
17. Dodis, Y., Wichs, D.: Non-malleable extractors and symmetric key cryptography from weak secrets. In: STOC (2009)
18. Dolev, D., Dwork, C., Naor, M.: Non-malleable cryptography (extended abstract). In: STOC (1991)
19. Dolev, D., Dwork, C., Naor, M.: Nonmalleable cryptography. SIAM J. Comput. 30(2), 391–437 (electronic) (2000), Preliminary version in STOC 1991
20. Dziembowski, S., Pietrzak, K., Wichs, D.: Non-malleable codes. In: ICS (2010)
21. Feige, U., Shamir, A.: Zero knowledge proofs of knowledge in two rounds. In: Brassard, G. (ed.) CRYPTO 1989. LNCS, vol. 435, pp. 526–544. Springer, Heidelberg (1990)
22. Feige, U., Shamir, A.: Witness indistinguishable and witness hiding protocols. In: Proc. 22nd STOC, pp. 416–426 (1990)
23. Garay, J.A., MacKenzie, P.D., Yang, K.: Strengthening zero-knowledge protocols using signatures. J. Cryptology 19(2) (2006)
24. Goldreich, O., Kahan, A.: How to construct constant-round zero-knowledge proof systems for NP. Journal of Cryptology 9(3), 167–189 (Summer 1996)
25. Goldwasser, S., Micali, S., Rackoff, C.: The knowledge complexity of interactive proof-systems. In: Proc. 17th STOC, pp. 291–304 (1985)
26. Goyal, V.: Constant round non-malleable protocols using one way functions. In: STOC (2011)
27. Goyal, V., Lee, C.K., Ostrovsky, R., Visconti, I.: Constructing non-malleable commitments: A black-box approach. In: FOCS (2012)
28. Karp, R.M.: Reducibility among combinatorial problems. In: Complexity of Computer Computations, pp. 85–103 (1972)
29. Katz, J., Yung, M.: Complete characterization of security notions for probabilistic private-key encryption. In: STOC, pp. 245–254 (2000)
30. Levin, L.A.: Problems, complete in "average" instance. In: STOC, p. 465 (1984)

31. Lin, H., Pass, R.: Non-malleability amplification. In: STOC, pp. 189–198 (2009)
32. Lin, H., Pass, R.: Constant-round non-malleable commitments from any one-way function. In: STOC (2011)
33. Lin, H., Pass, R., Venkitasubramaniam, M.: Concurrent non-malleable commitments from any one-way function. In: Canetti, R. (ed.) TCC 2008. LNCS, vol. 4948, pp. 571–588. Springer, Heidelberg (2008)
34. Lin, H., Pass, R., Venkitasubramaniam, M.: A unified framework for concurrent security: universal composability from stand-alone non-malleability. In: STOC (2009)
35. Lindell, Y.: Parallel coin-tossing and constant-round secure two-party computation. In: Kilian, J. (ed.) CRYPTO 2001. LNCS, vol. 2139, pp. 171–189. Springer, Heidelberg (2001), http://link.springer.de/link/service/series/0558/papers/2139/21390171.pdf
36. Lindell, Y.: Bounded-concurrent secure two-party computation without setup assumptions. In: Proc. 35th STOC, pp. 683–692 (2003)
37. Lindell, Y.: Constant round zero knowledge proofs of knowledge (2010), http://eprint.iacr.org/2010/487.pdf
38. Lindell, Y.: Highly-efficient universally-composable commitments based on the DDH assumption. In: Paterson, K.G. (ed.) EUROCRYPT 2011. LNCS, vol. 6632, pp. 446–466. Springer, Heidelberg (2011)
39. Malkhi, D., Nisan, N., Pinkas, B., Sella, Y.: Fairplay - secure two-party computation system. In: USENIX Security Symposium (2004)
40. Naor, M.: Bit commitment using pseudo-randomness (extended abstract). In: Brassard, G. (ed.) CRYPTO 1989. LNCS, vol. 435, pp. 128–136. Springer, Heidelberg (1990)
41. Naor, M., Yung, M.: Public-key cryptosystems provably secure against chosen ciphertext attacks. In: STOC (1990)
42. Ostrovsky, R., Pandey, O., Visconti, I.: Efficiency preserving transformations for concurrent non-malleable zero knowledge. In: Micciancio, D. (ed.) TCC 2010. LNCS, vol. 5978, pp. 535–552. Springer, Heidelberg (2010)
43. Ostrovsky, R., Persiano, G., Visconti, I.: Constant-round concurrent non-malleable zero knowledge in the bare public-key model. In: Aceto, L., Damgård, I., Goldberg, L.A., Halldórsson, M.M., Ingólfsdóttir, A., Walukiewicz, I. (eds.) ICALP 2008, Part II. LNCS, vol. 5126, pp. 548–559. Springer, Heidelberg (2008)
44. Pandey, O., Pass, R., Vaikuntanathan, V.: Adaptive one-way functions and applications. In: Wagner, D. (ed.) CRYPTO 2008. LNCS, vol. CRYPTO, pp. 57–74. Springer, Heidelberg (2008)
45. Pass, R.: Bounded-concurrent secure multi-party computation with a dishonest majority. In: Proc. 36th STOC, pp. 232–241 (2004)
46. Pass, R., Rosen, A.: Concurrent non-malleable commitments. In: FOCS (2005)
47. Pass, R., Rosen, A.: New and improved constructions of non-malleable cryptographic protocols. In: STOC (2005)
48. Pass, R., Wee, H.: Constant-round non-malleable commitments from subexponential one-way functions. In: Gilbert, H. (ed.) EUROCRYPT 2010. LNCS, vol. 6110, pp. 638–655. Springer, Heidelberg (2010)
49. Prabhakaran, M., Rosen, A., Sahai, A.: Concurrent zero knowledge with logarithmic round-complexity. In: FOCS (2002)
50. Rosen, A.: A note on constant-round zero-knowledge proofs for NP. In: Naor, M. (ed.) TCC 2004. LNCS, vol. 2951, pp. 191–202. Springer, Heidelberg (2004)
51. Sahai, A.: Non-malleable non-interactive zero knowledge and adaptive chosen-ciphertext security. In: Proc. 40th FOCS, pp. 543–553 (1999)
52. Wee, H.: Black-box, round-efficient secure computation via non-malleability amplification. In: FOCS (2010)

On Adaptively Secure Protocols

Muthuramakrishnan Venkitasubramaniam

University of Rochester, Rochester, NY 14611, USA

Abstract. Adaptive security captures the capability of an adversary to adaptively affect a system during the course of its computation based on partial information gathered. In this work, we explore the theoretical complexity of achieving adaptive security in two settings:

1. **Adaptive UC-Secure Computation:** We provide a round-efficient compiler that transforms any stand-alone semi-honest adaptively secure multiparty computation to adaptive UC-security. Recently, Dana et. al (Asiacrypt 2013) showed how to acheive adaptive UC-security in any trusted setup under minimal assumptions. They achieve this by constructing an $O(n)$-round adaptively secure concurrent non-malleable commitment scheme. The main contribution of our work shows how to achieve the same in $O(1)$-rounds.

2. **Zero-Knowledge with Adaptive Inputs:** Lin and Pass in (TCC 2011) gave first constructions of concurrent non-malleable zero-know-ledge proofs secure w.r.t. *adaptively* chosen inputs in the plain model in a restricted setting, namely, where the adversary can only ask for proofs of *true* (adaptively-chosen) statements. We extend their definition to the fully-adaptive setting and show how to construct a protocol that satisfies this definition. As an independent contribution we provide a simple and direct compilation of any semi-honest secure protocol to a fully concurrently secure protocol under polynomial-time assumptions in the Angel-Based UC-Security.

1 Introduction

Adaptive security captures the capability of an adversary to adaptively affect a system during the course of its computation based on partial information gathered. In this work, we revisit the complexity of achieving two different notions of adaptive security: (1) Round complexity of achieving fully concurrent *adaptively* secure computation protocols, and, (2) Feasibility of concurrent non-malleable zero-knowledge protocols with *fully adaptively* chosen inputs.

Adaptive Secure Computation. The notion of *secure multi-party computation* allows m mutually distrustful parties to securely compute a functionality $f(\bar{x}) = (f_1(\bar{x}), ..., f_m(\bar{x}))$ of their corresponding private inputs $\bar{x} = x_1, ..., x_m$, such that party P_i receives the value $f_i(\bar{x})$. Loosely speaking, the security requirements are that the parties learn nothing more from the protocol than their

M. Abdalla and R. De Prisco (Eds.): SCN 2014, LNCS 8642, pp. 455–475, 2014.

prescribed output, and that the output of each party is distributed according to the prescribed functionality. This should hold even in the case that an arbitrary subset of the parties maliciously deviates from the protocol. The original setting in which secure multi-party protocols were investigated, however, only allowed the execution of a single instance of the protocol at a time; this is the so called *stand-alone setting*. A more realistic setting, is one which allows the concurrent execution of protocols. In the *concurrent setting*, many protocols are executed at the same time. This setting presents the new risk of a coordinated attack in which an adversary interleaves many different executions of a protocol and chooses its messages in each instance based on other partial executions of the protocol. The strongest (but also most realistic) setting for concurrent security—called *Universally Composable* (UC) security [Can01, PW01, DM00], or environmental-security—considers the execution of an unbounded number of protocols, running concurrently in an arbitrary, and adversarially controlled, network environment. Unfortunately, achieving UC security for most interesting functionalities is impossible unless some sort of trusted setup is assumed [CF01, CKL03, Lin03]. Previous works overcome this barrier either by using some trusted setup infrastructure or by relaxing the definition of security (we will see examples below).

When considering security in such settings, we refer to the adversary as *static* if it chooses the subset of the parties to corrupt at the beginning of the protocol and *adaptive* if it is allowed to corrupt on-the-fly. Adaptively secure multiparty computation protocols (in the non-erasure model) were first realized in Canetti, Feige, Goldreich and Naor [CFGN96] for the stand-alone case. Canetti, Lindell, Ostrovsky and Sahai [CLOS02] provided the first constructions of UC-secure protocols with adaptive security for "well-formed" functionalities in the *common reference string* model (CRS) where all parties have access to public reference string sampled from a pre-specified distribution. Subsequently, several results were obtained for both the static and adaptive case in other trusted-setup models and relaxed-security models. However, for a given functionality, realizing an adaptively secure protocol is significantly harder than realizing in the static case. In this work we focus on the round complexity of achieving adaptive security under minimal assumptions. In the static case Lin et. al [LPV08, LPV12] provide a round-efficient compiler from stand-alone semi-honest secure computation protocol to static UC-security under minimal assumptions. Since there exists $O(1)$-round protocols with static security in the semi-honest setting for most setup models, we can achieve the same with static UC-security as well. For adaptive-security, the best known semi-honest secure protocol requires $O(d_C)$-rounds for computing a circuit C, where d_C is the depth of the circuit.[1,2] When considering adaptive UC-security, for particular models such as the common-reference string (CRS) model, we know how to construct $O(d_C)$-round adaptive

---

[1] Informally, the depth of a circuit is the longest path from any input bit to the output bit.

[2] There are constant-round protocols if we assume erasures or restrict the adversary to corrupting a strict subset of the parties.

UC-secure protocols under minimal assumptions [CLOS02, DN02, CDSMW09]. For other models such as uniform reference string model [CLOS02], multi-string model [GO07], similar constructions exist with stronger assumptions (e.g., dense cryptosystems). However, when considering minimal assumptions, the work of [DSMRV13] shows how to achieve adaptive UC-security in any trusted setup in $O(nd_C)$-rounds where n is the length of the identifier of the parties. Thus the state-of-the-art shows a huge gap in the round-complexity required for achieving adaptive security under minimal assumptions in the semi-honest setting and UC-setting in most models. One of the main questions addressed in this work is

Is there a round-efficient transformation from stand-alone semi-honest adaptive security to adaptive UC-security under minimal assumptions?

In this work, we answer this question in the affirmative and show how to obtain round-efficient compilation to obtain adaptively UC-secure protocols. Concretely, our work improves the round-complexity of constructing adaptively UC-secure protocols in most setup models under "minimal assumptions" and closes the gap of round-complexity between achieving such constructions in the semi-honest and fully-malicious UC setting in any setup.

Zero-Knowledge with Adaptively Chosen Inputs.   Zero-knowledge interactive proofs [GMR89] are paradoxical constructs that allow one player (called the Prover) to convince another player (called the Verifier) of the validity of a mathematical statement $x \in L$, while providing *zero additional knowledge* to the Verifier. The notion of concurrent ZK, first introduced and achieved, by Dwork, Naor and Sahai [DNS04] considers the execution of zero-knowledge proofs in an asynchronous setting and concurrent setting. Non-malleable ZK was first introduced by Dolev, Dwork and Naor [DDN00] where they model an adversary as a man-in-the-middle participating in two executions, acting as a verifier in one execution (in the left) and as a prover in another execution (in the right). The notion of concurrent non-malleable ZK considers adversaries that participates in an unbounded number of executions as the prover and verifier. Barak, Prabharakan and Sahai [BPS06] gave the first ZK argument for **NP** that is concurrent non-malleable in the plain model (i.e. without any trusted set-up assumptions). Since then several works improve efficiency and/or construct concurrent non-malleable ZK proofs [OPV08, LPTV10, LP11b]. In all these works, the input statements for all executions on the right can be *adaptively* chosen by the adversary whereas on the left need to be selected *apriori*, i.e. at the beginning of the execution. In this work, we consider strengthening the security, by allowing the adversary to adaptively chose the statements it wishes to prove and verify. Lin and Pass [LP11b] show how to construct concurrent non-malleable ZK proofs in a restricted setting where the adversary can adaptively choose *only* true statements to receive proofs of. Furthermore, they argue that allowing the adversary to choose arbitrary statements will reveal more information and thus not be zero-knowledge (for languages in **NP**). That main question we address in this work is:

Is it possible to achieve fully adaptively chosen input concurrent non-malleable zero-knowledge protocols (CNMZK) with meaningful security?

We again answer this question in the affirmative and show that we can define ZK with meaningful security in such a setting and show how to construct such protocols in the plain model. Previous works that achieve $CNMZK$ with fully adaptive input selection have relied on some sort of trusted set-up models such as Bare-Public Key [OPV08], Common Reference String [SCO+01, CF01, DN02], etc. For the weaker case of witness indistinguishability, Ostrovksy et. al [OPV06] present a restricted version[3] of input-adaptive concurrent non-malleable witness indistinguishable argument in the plain model. As an independent contribution we show the power of our definition of ZK by showing how to achieve UC-security using super-polynomial helpers analogous to [CLP10] under polynomial-time assumptions in the angel-based security model of Prabhakaran and Sahai [PS04].

1.1   Our Results

We provide a round-efficient compilation from stand-alone adaptively secure semi-honest protocols to adaptive UC-security. We achieve this by constructing a round-efficient concurrent non-malleable equivocal commitment, a primitive defined in [DSMRV13]. From previous works [CLOS02, DN00] we know that every functionality can be compiled into a protocol in the ideal-commitment functionality hybrid model.[4] In [DSMRV13] they show (assuming the existence of simulatable public-key encryption schemes) that any t-round protocol in this hybrid model can be securely realized using an $O(t_p)$-round puzzle and $O(t_c)$ round concurrent non-malleable equivocal commitment scheme in $O(t(t_p + t_c))$ rounds. We prove the following theorem

Theorem 1 (Informal). *For any setup model T, assume the existence of a $O(t_1)$-round adaptive puzzle and one-way functions, then there exists a $O(t_1)$ round concurrent non-malleable equivocal commitment scheme.*

Since in most models, there exists $O(1)$-round puzzles, our result combined with the work of [DSMRV13] shows that in most models any t-round protocol can be realized securely with adaptive UC-security in $O(t)$-rounds, thus yielding a round-preserving transformation. Furthermore, we obtain improvements in round-complexity in several setup models. Concretely, we obtain the following corollary:

Corollary 1 (Informal). *Assuming the existence of simulatable public-key encryption, any well-formed circuit C can be realized with adaptive UC-security in $O(d_C)$-rounds in Common Reference String, Uniform Reference String, Imperfect Reference String (Sunspots), Multi-String and Bounded Concurrent model, where d_C is the depth of circuit C.*

---

[3] This definition implicitly has a similar restriction to [LP11b] where the statements in the left need to be true statements.

[4] In this hybrid model, all parties have access to the ideal commitment functionality.

We also obtain corresponding improvements for relaxed-models of security, such as quasi-polynomial simulation and non-uniform simulation, where we need to make additional assumptions on the simulatable public-key encryption. We remark, this matches previous constructions in the Common-Reference String model. For the rest of the models, to achieve an $O(d_C)$-round construction we either did not have a construction (eg, bounded-concurrent) or needed additional assumptions (uniform reference string, sunspots). Our work closes the gap in the round-complexity required to achieve adaptively-secure protocols in the semi-honest setting and the fully malicious UC setting in most setup models.

Concurrent Non-Malleable Zero-Knowledge with Adaptive Inputs: As our second contribution, we define fully adaptive concurrent non-malleable zero-knowledge (a definition inspired by [LP11b] and angel-based security model of Prabhakaran and Sahai [PS04]) and show how to construct a protocol satisfying the definition. Our definition will allow for a man-in-the-middle adversary to adaptively request proofs of arbitrary **NP** statements, may it be true or false. For true statements, it will be provided with a proof using an efficient prover P using the witness to the statement and for false statements, it will be provided with a "fake" proof by a prover that potentially runs in exponential time. To construct a protocol, we rely on the recently introduced CCA-secure commitment schemes of [CLP10]. More formally, we prove the following theorem.

Theorem 2 (Informal). *Assuming the existence of one-way functions, there exists a $\tilde{O}(\log n)$-round fully-adaptive $\mathcal{CNMZK}$ argument.*

As an independent contribution, we show that our $\mathcal{ACNMZK}$ protocol can be used to securely realize any functionality in the angel-based model introduced by Prabhakaran and Sahai [PS04]. Canetti, Lin and Pass [CLP10] were the first to show how to achieve UC-security using the CCA-secure commitments in the angel model under polynomial-time assumptions.

The high-level idea of our protocol follows previous approaches where the functionality is first compiled to a protocol in the IdealZK-hybrid model.[5] Then, in a second step, it is complied to a protocol in a slightly weaker ideal functionality called MemberZK which is the ideal zero-knowledge proof of membership protocol. Finally, a protocol realizing the MemberZK functionality is constructed assuming some setup. We show that any protocol satisfying our definition of $\mathcal{ACNMZK}$ realizes MemberZK in the angel-model. We additionally point out a subtlety that arises when compiling IdealZK into MemberZK which was not previously addressed and show how our protocol handles this. We also believe that a direct compilation, as in [GMW87], of any semi-honest protocol to full UC-security in the angel model is possible by simply requiring honest parties to provide a zero-knowledge proof using our $\mathcal{ACNMZK}$ protocol after every step.

---

[5] In the IdealZK-hybrid all parties have access to an ideal zero-knowledge proof-of-knowledge protocol.

1.2 Our Techniques

Proving UC-security essentially reduces to proving concurrent non-malleability and concurrent simulation. In [LPV09], Lin et. al inroduced the notion of a UC-puzzle that captures the concurrent simulation requirement of UC-security and showed how to achieve it using any setup under minimal assumptions. In [DSMRV13], Dana et. al extended the notion of UC-puzzle to adaptive security and showed how to achieve adaptive UC-security using an adaptive UC-puzzle and a special kind of commitment scheme known as an *equivocal non-malleable commitments*. Roughly speaking, such commitments require that no man-in-the-middle adversary participating as a sender and receiver in multiple concurrent commitments and decommitments, be able to break the binding property of the commitment scheme. Similar notions have been studied previously in the works of [CIO98, CKOS01] for the limited case of bounded concurrency and non-interactive commitments and in [OPV09, CVZ10] where they restrict the commitments and decommitments to be performed in two distinct phases that do not overlap in time.

In more detail, a tag-based commitment scheme (i.e., commitment scheme that takes an identifier—called the tag—as an additional input) is *concurrent non-malleable w.r.t opening* if for every man-in-the-middle adversary A that participates in several interactions with honest committers as a receiver (called *left* interactions) as well as several interactions with honest receivers as a committer (called *right* interactions), there exists a simulator S that can simulate the left interactions, while extracting the commitments made by the adversary in the right interactions (whose identifiers are different from all the left identifiers) before the adversary decommits.

Equivocal commitments can be constructed easily using trusted set-up. The basic idea is to provide the simulator with a trapdoor with which it can equivocate as well as extract the commitments on the right. (by e.g., relying on encryption). However, to ensure non-malleability, most constructions in literature additionally impose CCA-security or provide independent trapdoors for every interaction. In [DSMRV13], they show how to construct a concurrent non-malleable commitment scheme in any trusted set-up. More precisely, they construct a commitment scheme in any setup that admits a UC-puzzle, a formulation introduced by Lin et al [LPV08] for the case of static security that captures precisely the simulation requirement. However, the round complexity of their protocol is linear in the length of the identities. In this work we show how to construct constant-round protocols that are concurrently non-malleable. Moreover, our construction seemingly only relies on the stand-alone non-malleable commitment schemes in the static setting. In particular, using the $O(1)$-round scheme of [LP11b] we provide a $O(1)$-round concurrent non-malleable commitment w.r.t opening in any setup with a UC-puzzle.

Comparison with [DSMRV13]. The work of [DSMRV13] focused on constructing protocols with adaptive UC-security in any model under minimal assumptions. In particular their work showed how to minimize complexity assumptions and the "trust" required in the setup analogous to [LPV09] for the static setting. In this work, we focus on obtaining round-efficient protocols. The novelty in our reduction over the work in [DSMRV13] is that we are able to directly reduce the security proof to the non-malleability of the underlying non-malleable commitment scheme while [DSMRV13] rely on a particular non-malleable commitment scheme (that of [DDN00, LPV08]) and provide a security reduction that is tailored to this scheme. Our proof is modular and in our opinion simpler than that of [DSMRV13]. Although the main application of equivocal non-malleable commitments is in achieving adaptive UC-security, these commitments may also be useful for other applications such as concurrent non-malleable zero knowledge secure under adaptive corruptions or obtaining composable protocols. We believe that this notion in some sense extends the notion of security w.r.t selective opening attacks to the non-malleable setting and our protocols might be useful in such contexts as well.

$\mathcal{CNMZK}$ *with Adaptively Chosen Inputs.* Lin and Pass [LP11b] consider the scenario where a man-in-the-middle adversary participates in unbounded zero-knowledge interactions as a verifier on the left and prover on the right and can adaptively choose statements for left and right interactions with the restriction that only true statements are chosen for left interactions. They call a zero-knowledge protocol in such a setting $\mathcal{CNMZK}$ with *Adaptive Input Selection* if for every adversary A, there exists a computationally efficient simulator-extractor that can simulate both the left and right interactions for A, while outputting a witness for every statement proved by the adversary in the right interactions. As pointed out in [LP11b, OPV06], having this restriction for protocols in the plain model seems inherent in light of the impossibility result of Lindell [Lin03]. To circumvent the impossibility result one can rely on some sort of trusted setup such as the Bare-Public Key (BPK) or Common Reference String (CRS) model. Indeed there are fully input-adaptive $\mathcal{CNMZK}$ arguments in these models [SCO+01, CF01, DN02, OPV08].

In this work, we want a definition in the plain model that allows for concurrent composition. Our definition is inspired by the definitions of [LP11b] and the angel-based security model of Prabhakaran and Sahai [PS04, CLP10]. We allow the adversary to adaptively chose any statement in the left and require the existence of a simulator extractor that can achieve the same indistinguishability guarantees of [LP11b]. If we allow the adversary to choose false statements, a proof cannot be provided and hence will fall into the impossibility result of Lindell [Lin03]. Instead we will require that there be an exponential-time strategy that will provide proofs of false statements. Now for such a setting, our definition of $\mathcal{CNMZK}$ with fully adaptive input-selection requires for every adversary there be a simulator-extractor that can simulate both the left and right interactions for A, while outputting a witness for every statement proved by the adversary in the right interactions. Relying on CCA-secure commitments [CLP10, GLP+12], we show how to construct an $\tilde{O}(\log n)$-round $\mathcal{CNMZK}$ protocol with fully adaptive-inputs selection. CCA-secure commitments were introduced by Canetti, et. al [CLP10] to construct UC-secure protocol with angel-based security. We also prove that CCA-secure commitments are equivalent to $\mathcal{CNMZK}$ with fully adaptive-input selection.

2   Preliminaries

We assume familiarity with interactive protocols, commitment schemes. Some of the definitions are presented almost verbatim from [DSMRV13].

We adopt a variant of language-based commitment schemes introduced by Lindell et. al [LZ09]. Roughly speaking, in such commitments the sender and receiver share a common input, a statement x from an **NP** language L. The main difference from standard commitments is that the binding property of the commitment scheme. Informally, the binding property of the scheme asserts that any adversary violating the binding can be used to extract an **NP**-witness for the statement. We require a variant We present below the definition of a language-based equivocal commitment scheme which is a slight variant of such commitment schemes (See [DSMRV13] for the formal definition).

Definition 1 (Language-Based Equivocal Commitments). *Let L be an* **NP**-*Language and $\mathcal{R}$, the associated* **NP**-*relation. A language-based commitment scheme $\langle S, R \rangle$ for L is said to be equivocal, if there exists a tuple of algorithms $(\tilde{S}, \mathsf{Adap})$ such that the following holds:*

Special-Hiding: *For every (expected) PPT machine R^*, it holds that, the following ensembles are computationally indistinguishable over $n \in N$.*

- $\{\mathsf{sta}^{R^*}_{\langle S, R \rangle}(x, v_1, z)\}_{n \in N, x \in L \cap \{0,1\}^n, w \in \mathcal{R}(x), v_1 \in \{0,1\}^n, z \in \{0,1\}^*}$
- $\{\mathsf{sta}^{R^*}_{\langle \tilde{S}, R \rangle}(x, w, z)\}_{n \in N, x \in L \cap \{0,1\}^n, w \in \mathcal{R}(x), v_1 \in \{0,1\}^n, z \in \{0,1\}^*}$

    where $\mathsf{sta}^{R^*}_{\langle \tilde{S}, R \rangle}(x, w, z)$ denotes the random variable describing the output of $R^*(x, z)$ after receiving a commitment using $\langle \tilde{S}, R \rangle$.

Equivocability: *Let τ be the transcript of the interaction between R and $\tilde{S}$ on common input $x \in L \cap \{0,1\}^n$ and private input $w \in \mathcal{R}(x)$ and random tape $r \in \{0,1\}^*$ for $\tilde{S}$. Then for any $v \in \{0,1\}^n$, $\mathsf{Adap}(x, w, r, \tau, v)$ produces a random tape r' such that (r', v) serves as a valid decommitment for C on transcript τ.*

In [DSMRV13] (relying on the work of [LZ09]), show how to construct such schemes using one-way functions.

2.1   Definition of Equivocal Non-Malleable Commitments

Let $\langle C, R \rangle$ be a commitment scheme, and let $n \in N$ be a security parameter. Consider man-in-the-middle adversaries that are participating in left and right interactions in which $m = \mathsf{poly}(n)$ commitments take place. We compare between a *man-in-the-middle* and a *simulated* execution. In the man-in-the-middle execution, the adversary A is simultaneously participating in m left and right interactions. In the left interactions the man-in-the-middle adversary A interacts with C receiving commitments to values $v_1, \ldots, v_m$, using identities $\mathsf{id}_1, \ldots, \mathsf{id}_m$ of its choice. It must be noted here that values $v_1, \ldots, v_m$ are provided to committer on the left prior to the interaction. In the right interaction A interacts with R attempting to commit to a sequence of related values again using identities of its choice $\tilde{\mathsf{id}}_1, \ldots, \tilde{\mathsf{id}}_m$; $\tilde{v}_i$ is set to the value decommitted by A in the jth right interaction. If any of the right commitments are invalid its committed value is set to $\perp$. For any i such that $\tilde{\mathsf{id}}_i = \mathsf{id}_j$ for some j, set $\tilde{v}_i = \perp$—i.e., any commitment where the adversary uses the same identity as one of the honest committers is considered invalid. Additionally, the adversary can adaptively choose a session in the left executions that has completed the commitment phase to be *decommitted*. Let $\mathsf{mim}^A_{\langle C,R \rangle}(v_1, \ldots, v_m, z)$ denote a random variable that describes the values $\tilde{v}_1, \ldots, \tilde{v}_m$ and the view of A, in the above experiment.

In the simulated execution, a simulator S interacts only with receivers on the right as follows:

1. Whenever the commitment phase of jth interaction with a receiver on the right is completed, S outputs a value $\tilde{v}_j$ as the alleged committed value in a special-output tape.
2. During the interaction, S may output a partial view for a man-in-the-middle adversary whose right-interactions are identical to S's interaction so far. If the view contains a left interaction where the ith commitment phase is completed and the decommitment is requested, then a value v_i is provided as the decommitment.
3. Finally, S outputs a view and values $\tilde{v}_1, \ldots, \tilde{v}_m$. Let $\mathsf{sim}^S_{\langle C,R \rangle}(1^n, v_1, \ldots, v_m, z)$ denote the random variable describing the view output by the simulation and values $\tilde{v}_1, \ldots, \tilde{v}_m$.

Definition 2. *A commitment scheme $\langle C, R \rangle$ is said to be* concurrent non-malleable w.r.t. opening *if for every polynomial $p(\cdot)$, and every probabilistic polynomial-time man-in-the-middle adversary A that participates in at most $m = p(n)$ concurrent executions, there exists a probabilistic polynomial time simulator S such that the following ensembles are computationally indistinguishable over $n \in N$:*

- $\left\{ \mathsf{mim}^A_{\langle C,R \rangle}(v_1, \ldots, v_m, z) \right\}_{n \in N, v_1, \ldots, v_m \in \{0,1\}^n, z \in \{0,1\}^*}$, *and*
- $\left\{ \mathsf{sim}^S_{\langle C,R \rangle}(1^n, v_1, \ldots, v_m, z) \right\}_{n \in N, v_1, \ldots, v_m \in \{0,1\}^n, z \in \{0,1\}^*}$

We will use the slightly relaxed definition where all the values committed to the adversary in the left interaction are sampled independently from an arbitrary distribution $\mathcal{D}$ fixed *apriori*. We call a commitment scheme an *equivocal non-malleable commitment scheme* if it is both a language-based equivocal commitment scheme and is concurrent non-malleable w.r.t. opening.

2.2   Adaptive UC-Puzzles

Informally, an adaptive UC-puzzle is a protocol $\langle S, R \rangle$ between two players–a *sender* S and a *receiver* R – and a PPT computable relation $\mathcal{R}$, such that the following two properties hold:

Soundness. No efficient receiver R^* can successfully complete an interaction with S and also obtain a "trapdoor" y, such that $\mathcal{R}(\text{TRANS}, y) = 1$, where TRANS is the transcript of the interaction.

Statistical UC-simulation with adaptive corruptions. For every efficient adversary $\mathcal{A}$ participating in a polynomial number of concurrent executions with receivers R (i.e., $\mathcal{A}$ is acting as a puzzle sender in all these executions) and at the same time communicating with an environment $\mathcal{Z}$, there exists a simulator $\mathcal{S}$ that is able to statistically simulate the view of $\mathcal{A}$ for $\mathcal{Z}$, while at the same time outputting trapdoors to all successfully completed puzzles. Moreover, $\mathcal{S}$ successfully simulates the view even when $\mathcal{A}$ may adaptively corrupt the receivers.

2.3 Fully Input-Adaptive Concurrent Non-Malleable Zero-Knowledge

Our definition of fully input-adaptive concurrent non-malleable zero-knowledge is closely based on the definition of adaptive concurrent non-malleable zero-knowledge from [LP11a] (which in turn are based on [BPS06, PR05]). The main difference is that we consider adversaries that is allowed to adaptively select true and false statements to receive proofs of.

Let $\langle P, V \rangle$ be an interactive argument for a language $L \in \mathbf{NP}$ with witness relation R_L and exponential time cheating prover $\hat{P}$, and let n be the security parameter. Consider a man-in-the-middle adversary A that participates in many left and right interactions in which $m = m(n)$ proofs take place. In the left interactions, the adversary A verifies the validity of the statements $x_1, \ldots, x_m$ by interacting with a special prover $\hat{P}$, using identities $\text{id}_1, \ldots, \text{id}_m$. In the right-interactions, A proves the validity of statements $\tilde{x}_1, \ldots, \tilde{x}_m$ to an honest verifier V, using identities $\tilde{\text{id}}_1, \ldots, \tilde{\text{id}}_m$. Prior to the interactions, all parties receive as common input the security parameter in unary 1^n, and A receives as auxiliary input $z \in \{0, 1\}^*$. Furthermore, at the beginning of each left (respectively right) interaction, the adversary adaptively selects the statement x_i (respectively $\tilde{x}_i$) and the identity id_i (respectively $\tilde{\text{id}}_i$). For each left-interaction, the special-prover $\hat{P}$ behaves as follows:

1. If the statement x_i chosen by A is false, then $\hat{P}$ runs the exponential-time cheating strategy,
2. If the statement x_i chosen by A is true, then $\hat{P}$ picks a witness $w_i \in R_L(x_i)$ and runs the honest prover strategy P with private input w_i.

Let $\text{VIEW}_{A, \hat{P}}$ denote a random variable that describes the view of A in the above experiment. Informally, an interactive argument (with exponential time cheater strategy) is fully-adaptive concurrent non-malleable zero-knowledge ($\mathcal{ACNMZK}$) if for all man-in-the-middle adversary A, there exists a probabilistic polynomial time machine (called the simulator-extractor) that can simulate both the left and right interactions of A, while outputting a witness for every statement proved by the adversary in the right interactions.

Definition 3. *An interactive argument* (P, V) *for a language* L *with witness-relation* R_L *and exponential-time prover* $\hat{P}$ *is said to be fully input-adaptive concurrent non-malleable zero-knowledge if for every polynomial* m, *and every probabilistic polynomial-time man-in-the-middle adversary* A *that participates in at most* $m = m(n)$ *concurrent executions, there exists a probabilistic polynomial time machine* S, *such that,*

1. *The ensembles* $\left\{ \text{VIEW}_{A,\hat{P}}(n,z) \right\}_{n \in \mathbf{N}, z \in \{0,1\}^*}$ *and* $\{S_1(1^n, z)\}_{n \in \mathbf{N}, z \in \{0,1\}^*}$ *are computationally indistinguishable over* $n \in \mathbf{N}$

2. *Let* $z \in \{0,1\}^*$ *and* $(\text{VIEW}, \boldsymbol{w})$ *denote the output of* $S(1^n, z)$. *Let* $\tilde{x}_1, \ldots, \tilde{x}_m$ *be the statements of the right interactions in* VIEW, *and let* $\text{id}_1, \ldots, \text{id}_m$ *and* $\tilde{\text{id}}_1, \ldots, \tilde{\text{id}}_m$ *be the identities of the left-interactions and right-interactions in* VIEW. *Then for every* $i \in [m]$, *if the* i^{th} *right-interaction is accepting and* $\tilde{\text{id}}_i \neq \text{id}_j$ *for any* $j \in [m]$, $\boldsymbol{w}$ *contains* w_i *such that* $R_L(\tilde{x}_i, w_i) = 1$.

Remark 1. We remark that it would be impossible to achieve proofs according to our definition, since we allow for an exponential-time prover to convince verifiers of false statements.

3   EQNMCom Based on [LP11b]

Our starting point is any stand-alone non-malleable commitment scheme that follows that Feige-Shamir paradigm for the hiding property and the "simulation-soundness" paradigm of Sahai[Sah99] for non-malleability. More precisely, in a scheme following the Feige-Shamir paradigm, there is a trapdoor phase where, possibly through rewinding the receiver, a trapdoor can be obtained and a proof phase where the committer proves either knowledge of the value committed or knowledge of the trapdoor. To prove non-malleability, or simulation-soundness, these schemes provide a mechanism to rewind the left interaction of a man-in-the middle adversary to obtain a trapdoor while ensuring the right interactions remains "sound".

While our techniques are more generally applicable, in this work, we present a protocol based on the constant-round non-malleable commitment protocol of Lin and Pass [LP11b]. Their scheme relies on fixed-length signature scheme $\Pi = (Gen, Sign, Ver)$, zero-knowledge argument of knowledge, witness-indistinguishable special-sound proofs and we assume the readers familiarity with these primitives. Our protocol is obtained from the protocol from [LP11b] by replacing the non-interactive commitment com with the language-based equivocal commitment scheme EQCom$_x$ (see Definition 1) from [DSMRV13] and the Stage 3 protocol with the adaptively-secure witness-indistinguishable proof of knowledge (WIPOK).

In more detail, to achieve equivocability, as in [DSMRV13], we rely on a variant of Feige-Shamir's trapdoor commitment scheme. Let x be an **NP**-statement. The sender commits to bit b by running the honest-verifier simulator for Blum's Hamiltonian Circuit protocol [Blu86] on input the statement x and the verifier message b, generating the transcript (a, b, z), and finally outputting a as its commitment. In the decommitment phase, the sender reveals the bit b by providing both b, z. To achieve adaptively secure WIPOK protocol (we refer [DSMRV13] for a formal definition and construction) we rely on the protocol of Lindell-Zarosim [LZ09].

3.1   Equivocal Non-Malleable Commitment Scheme (EQNMCom) in any Setup

Given any setup $\mathcal{T}$ with an adaptive UC-Puzzle, we prove that $\Pi = \langle S, R \rangle$ described below is an equivocal non-malleable commitment scheme when combined with the adaptive UC-puzzle. In more detail, consider the following protocol: Let $(\langle S_{puz}, R_{puz} \rangle, \mathcal{R})$ be an adaptive UC-puzzle in setup $\mathcal{T}$. The protocol $\overline{\Pi}$ proceeds in two phases on common input the identity id $\in \{0, 1\}^{\ell}$ of the committer, and private-input string r for the committer and security parameter n.

Preamble Phase: An adaptive UC-Puzzle interaction $\langle S_{puz}, R_{puz} \rangle$ on input 1^n where S_{com} is the receiver and R_{com} is the sender. Let $x = \text{TRANS}$ be the transcript of the messages exchanged.

Commitment Phase: The parties run protocol $\langle S, R \rangle$ with common input x and identifier id. S plays the part of sender with input r.

Our construction relies on the equivocal commitment scheme $\langle S, R \rangle$ constructed based on the non-malleability commitment scheme of Lin and Pass [LP11b]. For the purpose of describing the simulator we will only rely on the fact that the protocol has a round where the honest committer sends a commitment to the value in its input using $EQCom_x$ and a proof phase where there are one or more adaptively secure WIPOK instantiations based on statement x from where the committer proves knowledge of the value committed using $EQCom_x$ in that interaction. We now show that the protocol $\overline{\Pi}$ is concurrent non-malleable w.r.t opening w.r.t i.i.d commitments.

Theorem 1. *Commitment scheme $\overline{\Pi}$ described above is concurrent non-malleable w.r.t. opening with independent and identically distributed (i.i.d) commitments.*

First we describe the simulator and then prove correctness. Let A be a concurrent man-in-the-middle adversary that on input 1^n participates in at most $m(n)$ left-interactions as a receiver, receiving commitments from an honest committer whose values are chosen uniformly from distribution D and at most $m(n)$ right-interactions as a committer. On a high-level, S internally incorporates A and emulates an execution with A as follows: For all puzzle interactions where A^* controls the sender, S follows the puzzle simulator's strategy to simulate the puzzle and obtains a witness which it stores. In the right puzzle interactions, Sim simply forwards the messages to an external receiver. For every left interaction, Sim internally generates the messages using the code of special committer (guaranteed by the scheme), i.e. equivocate in the commitment phase with the witness w obtained from the puzzle interactions. When a decommitment is requested by

A, Sim outputs the current partial view of the transcript of messages exchanged by A in a special-output tape. Then, it receives a value v from outside to be decommitted to in the left interaction. Internally, it runs the Adap algorithm guaranteed by the equivocal commitment scheme to generate a decommitment to v and feeds it to A.

Whenever the commitment phase is completed with a receiver on the right, Sim temporary stalls the main-execution and tries to extract the value committed to by A in this interaction. For this, Sim selects a random adaptively secure WIPOK from that interaction and *rewinds* A to the point just before which A receives the challenge-message in the WIPOK. Sim supplies a new challenge message and continues simulation. In the rewinding, the right interactions are simulated as before (i.e. honestly) while the left interactions are simulated differently. Instead of equivocating the session, Sim follows the honest committer's strategy with value v, where v is the actual value decommitted to in left interaction if one exists from the main-execution or chosen uniformly at random from $\mathcal{D}$.[6] If in the rewinding, A provides a valid response for the selected WIPOK of the right interaction, then using the special-sound property of the WIPOK, Sim extracts the witness used in the WIPOK, which contains the committed value. If the adversary fails to provide a valid response for the particular WIPOK in the right interaction, Sim cancels the current rewinding and starts a new rewinding by supplying a new challenge.

The proof of correctness of the simulator is expressed in the following lemma.

Lemma 1. *The following ensembles are computationally indistinguishable*

$$\left\{ (v_1 \ldots, v_m) \leftarrow D^n : \mathsf{mim}_{\langle S,R \rangle}^A (v_1, \ldots, v_m, z) \right\}_{n \in N, z \in \{0,1\}^*}$$

$$\left\{ (v_1 \ldots, v_m) \leftarrow D^n : \mathsf{sim}_{\langle S,R \rangle}^S (1^n, v_1, \ldots, v_m, z) \right\}_{n \in N, z \in \{0,1\}^*}$$

Proof. We consider a sequence of intermediate hybrid experiments $H_0, \ldots, H_m$. In experiment H_i, we consider a simulator Sim^i that knows all the values $(v_1, \ldots, v_n)$ being committed to in the left interactions. On input z, Sim^i proceeds as follows: It follows Sim's strategy in the first i left interactions both in the main phase and rewinding phase. For the other left interactions, i.e. $j = i+1, \ldots, n$, Sim simulates the main phase by equivocating as before, but in the rewinding phase follows the honest committers strategy using v_j. Let $\mathsf{hyb}^i(1^n, v_1, \ldots, v_m, z)$ denote the output of Sim^i in H_i. It follows from description that $\mathsf{hyb}^m(1^n, v_1, \ldots, v_m, z)$ and $\mathsf{sim}_{\langle S,R \rangle}^S(1^n, v_1, \ldots, v_m, z)$ are indistinguishable.

In hybrid experiment H_0, all puzzles are simulated and the simulator with input $(v_1, \ldots, v_m)$ proceeds exactly as the real simulator in the main execution phase, whereas in the rewindings, it uses the code of the honest committer to commit to v_i. We consider an intermediate hybrid $\overline{H_0}$ which proceeds exactly like H_0 with the exception that the simulator uses the code of the honest committer in the main execution phase as well with value v_i for left session i. Let the output

---

[6] Sim can generate such messages for any value v, since by adaptive security, Sim can obtain random coins for an honest committer and any value v that is consistent with any partial transcript generated by the equivocator.

of this experiment be $\overline{\mathsf{hyb}^0}$. The proof of the Lemma follows from the next three claims using a standard hybrid argument.

Claim. $\mathsf{mim}^A_{\langle S,R \rangle}(v_1, \ldots, v_m, z) \approx \overline{\mathsf{hyb}^0}(1^n, v_1, \ldots, v_m, z)$

Proof Sketch. The proof of this claim essentially follows from the statistical simulation of the puzzle. In fact, this step is identical to the one presented as part of the proof in [DSMRV13] (see Claim 1 in [DSMRV11]) and will be presented in the full version.

Claim. $\overline{\mathsf{hyb}^0}(1^n, v_1, \ldots, v_m, z) \approx \mathsf{hyb}^0(1^n, v_1, \ldots, v_m, z)$

Proof. Recall that in hybrid $\overline{H_0}$, the simulator follows the honest committer strategy in the main and rewinding phases for left interactions while in H_0 it equivocates in the main phase and then follows honest committer strategy in the rewindings using the random coins generated for a honest committer by the Adap algorithm of the commitment scheme. Recall that the simulator in all hybrids have all the values to be committed in the left interactions at the beginning of the experiment.

Now, assume for contradiction there exists a distinguisher that can distinguish the outputs in both the experiments with probability $\frac{1}{p(n)}$ for some polynomial $p(\cdot)$. As in the previous claim, we can conclude that in H_0 the value extracted and the value decommitted to in some right interaction by the adversary is different with probability $\frac{1}{p(n)}$. Now, we consider a truncated version of both the hybrids where both the experiments are cut-off after the simulator runs T steps. Using the same argument as in the previous claim, we can conclude that the simulator runs in expected polynomial time in both the experiments. Let $t(n)$ be an upper bound for the expected running time in both experiments. We set T to be $2t(n)p(n)$. Using Markov's inequality, it holds that the distinguisher distinguishes the truncated experiments with probability at least $\frac{1}{2p(n)}$. We will show that the adversary A can be used to violate the pseudo-randomness of the commitments under Com and thus arrive at a contradiction.

Next, following [DSMRV13], we rely on the existence of a committer strategy C^* and distributions D_0 and D_1 such that on input the witness to the puzzle-statement and a sequence of strings from distribution D_b can commit to a value v such that messages are distributed identically to the honest committer's strategy if $b = 0$ and according to the equivocating strategy if $b = 1$. In fact one of these distributions is simply commitments to the bit 0 while the other is a the uniform random string.

Now consider a simulator S^* that additionally on input T samples $s_1, \ldots, s_T$ from D_b, proceeds exactly as in $\overline{H_0}$ with the exception that for all left interactions the simulator uses the committer strategy C^* with samples $s_1, \ldots, s_T$ in the main and rewinding phase. By construction, it follows that the output of S^* with samples from D_b is identical to truncated version of $\overline{H_0}$ when $b = 0$ and H_0 when $b = 1$. Therefore, by running D on the output of S^* we can distinguish D_0 from D_1 which is a contradiction.

Claim. $\mathsf{hyb}^0(1^n, v_1, \ldots, v_m, z) \approx \mathsf{hyb}^m(1^n, v_1, \ldots, v_m, z)$

Proof. Assume for contradiction, there exists an adversary A, distinguisher D, polynomial $p(\cdot)$ such that, for infinitely many n, D distinguishes the ensembles in the claim with probability at least $\frac{1}{p(n)}$. Recall that in hyb^0, the value successfully decommitted by the adversary in every right interaction is the value extracted by the simulator. Furthermore, the view output by the simulator in both hyb^0 and hyb^m are identical since the main execution is simulated in an identical manner. Hence, if D can distinguish, it must hold that the value extracted in some right interaction in hyb^m must not be the value decommitted to by the adversary with probability at least $\frac{1}{p(n)}$. Whenever this happens in an execution in the kth right interaction, we will say that the adversary *cheats* in the kth right interaction. Therefore, given our hypothesis, there must exist an i such that the difference in probability that A cheats in the kth interaction is at least $\frac{1}{p_1(n)}$ between hyb^{i-1} and hyb^i for some polynomial $p_1(\cdot)$. Consider a random transcript truncated at the end the of kth interaction. Then, the simulation strategies of the ith left interaction according to hyb^{i-1} and hyb^i in the rewindings must yield different values extracted in k^{th} right interaction with probability at least $\frac{1}{p_1(n)}$. We can further impose the condition that the adversary has not corrupted or requested the decommitment of the left i^{th} interaction before the kth right interaction has completed.[7]

We now consider truncated experiments $\overline{\mathsf{hyb}}_A^{i-1}$ and $\overline{\mathsf{hyb}}_A^i$ where the execution is stopped after the commitment phase of the kth right interaction. We define the output of $\overline{\mathsf{hyb}}_A^{i-1}$ and $\overline{\mathsf{hyb}}_A^i$ as the partial view in the main execution and the value extracted in the kth right interaction.

Recall that the only difference between $\overline{\mathsf{hyb}}_A^{i-1}$ and $\overline{\mathsf{hyb}}_A^i$ is the simulation strategies of the ith left interaction in the rewindings. More precisely, the first $i-1$ left interactions are simulated by choosing either a random sample from D or the actual value (if it has already been decommitted to in the partial view of the main execution) in both $\overline{\mathsf{hyb}}_A^{i-1}$ and $\overline{\mathsf{hyb}}_A^i$, but the ith left interaction is simulated using a fixed commitment chosen ahead of time in $\overline{\mathsf{hyb}}_A^{i-1}$ and using a random commitment from D in $\overline{\mathsf{hyb}}_A^i$. Observe that, since the adversary cheats with small probability in $\overline{\mathsf{hyb}}_A^{i-1}$, it holds that for random samples chosen for the first $i-1$ left interactions and a fixed commitment for the ith interaction, the value extracted in the kth right interaction is the same with high probability. Hence, there must exist particular values $\boldsymbol{v}_{-i}$, v_i and $\overline{v}_i$ such that if the simulator uses the values $\boldsymbol{v}_{-i}$ and v_i for the left interactions (call this experiment E_1) and values $\boldsymbol{v}_{-i}$ and $\overline{v}_i$ in another experiment call it E_2, the probability that the values extracted in the kth right interaction is different in both the experiments with probability at least $\frac{1}{p_2(n)}$ for some polynomial $p_2(\cdot)$.

---

[7] Conditioned on the the adversary corrupting the ith left party the outputs of $\overline{\mathsf{hyb}}_A^{i-1}$ and $\overline{\mathsf{hyb}}_A^i$ are identical.

We now proceed as in the previous claim where we consider a simulator S_1^* that with T samples $s_1, \ldots, s_T$ from D_b and values v, runs the adversary until the kth right interaction and rewinds the kth right interaction with values v on the left. From the indistinguishability of D_0 and D_1, we can conclude that the value extracted by the adversary in the kth right interaction must be the same when the samples come from D_0 and D_1. By construction, when the samples $s_1, \ldots, s_T$ come from D_0 and values for left interactions are $v = v_{-i} \cup \{v_i\}$ the simulation proceeds identical to E_1 and when the samples come from D_0 and values for left interactions $v = v_{-i} \cup \{\overline{v_i}\}$ the simulation is identical to E_2. Let the corresponding experiments when the samples $s_1, \ldots, s_T$ come from D_1 and values from $v = v_{-i} \cup \{v_i\}$ and $v = v_{-i} \cup \{\overline{v_i}\}$ be E_1^* and E_2^*. In E_1^* and E_2^* all the commitments in the left are honestly generated. So we can consider corresponding experiments E_1^{**} and E_2^{**} where the puzzles are not simulated. By indistinguishability of D_0 and D_1, the values extracted from E_1^* and E_2^* will be different with non-negligible probability. By statistical-closeness of the puzzle simulation we can now conclude that values extracted in E_1^{**} and E_2^{**} are statistically close to E_1^* and E_2^* respectively and thus different with non-negligible probability. We are now ready to violate the stand-alone non-malleability of $\langle S, R \rangle$. Observe that in experiments E_1^{**} and E_2^{**} all values used in left interactions except the value in the ith left interaction are the same. We now construct a man-in-the-middle adversary that forwards the ith left interaction and k^{th} right interaction and this violates the non-malleability of $\langle S, R \rangle$.

This concludes the proof of Lemma 1 and Theorem 1.

3.2 Round-Efficient Adaptively Secure UC-Protocols

On a high-level constructing UC-secure protocol proceeds in two steps: (1) First, every functionality is compiled into a protocol in the $\mathcal{F}_{\mathsf{mcom}}$-hybrid model.[8] This step follows as corollary from previous works [CLOS02, DN00] and the round-complexity is preserved upto constant factors. (2) In the second step, assuming the existence of a UC-*puzzle* and a EQNMCom protocol, any protocol in the $\mathcal{F}_{\mathsf{mcom}}$ functionality can be securely realized in the real-model. This step was formalized and proved in [DSMRV13] and captured in the following Lemma.

Lemma 2 (Lemma 5[DSMRV13]). *Let Π' be an t_p-round protocol in the $\mathcal{F}_{\mathsf{mcom}}$-hybrid model. Assume the existence of a t_{puz}-round adaptive puzzle in a $\mathcal{G}$-hybrid model, a t_c-round EQNMCom protocol $\langle S, R \rangle$ and a simulatable PKE scheme. Then, there exists an $O(t_p(t_{puz} + t_c))$-round protocol Π in the $\mathcal{G}$-hybrid such that, for every uniform $\mathcal{PPT}$ adversary $\mathcal{A}$, there exists a simulator $\mathcal{A}'$, such that, no environment $\mathcal{Z} \in \mathcal{C}_{\mathsf{env}}$ can distinguish the real execution with $\mathcal{A}$ in $\mathcal{G}$-hybrid and the simulator $\mathcal{A}'$ in the $\mathcal{F}_{\mathsf{mcom}}$-hybrid.*

In [DSMRV13], it was shown how to construct $O(1)$-round adaptive puzzles for various models. In the previous section we showed how to construct a

---

[8] In the $\mathcal{F}_{\mathsf{mcom}}$-hybrid, all parties have access to the ideal commitment functionality called $\mathcal{F}_{\mathsf{mcom}}$ functionality.

$O(1)$-round EQNMCOM protocol based on any $O(1)$-round adaptive puzzle and one-way functions. Hence for these models, our work combined with previous Lemma yields an adaptive UC-secure protocol whose round complexity is $O(t_p)$. From previous works [DN00, CLOS02], we know that every well-formed functionality represented as a circuit C, can be realized in the $\mathcal{F}_{mcom}$-hybrid in $O(d_C)$-rounds where d_C is the depth of the circuit C. Thus, we obtain the following corollary.

Corollary 31 *Assuming the existence of simulatable public-key encryption, any well-formed circuit C with depth d_C can be realized with adaptive UC-security in $O(d_C)$-rounds*

1. *in Common Reference String, Uniform Reference String, Imperfect Reference String (Sunspots) model, and Bounded-Concurrent model, or*
2. *with Quasi-polynomial Simulation and Non-uniform Simulation*

For more details on the puzzle, we refer the reader to [DSMRV13]. We remark that in [DSMRV13], they provide puzzles for the tamper-proof model and the timing model as well. The simulators for these puzzles are not straight-line and have been excluded from this work for simplicity. However, analogous to [DSMRV13], we believe it is possible to extend our result to these models.

4   An $\mathcal{ACNMZK}$ Argument

In this section we construct a fully adaptive concurrent non-malleable zero-knowledge proof based on one-way functions. The construction is inspired by the CCA-secure commitment scheme in [GLP+12]. Let $\langle C, R \rangle$ be a tag-based commitment scheme that is $O(1)$-robust CCA − secure w.r.t decommitment oracle $\mathcal{O}$. Let NMCom be a tag-based non-malleable commitment scheme (there exists $O(1)$-round protocols for such commitments [LP11b, Goy11]). Let $\langle P_{swi}, V_{swi} \rangle$ be a public-coin strong-$\mathcal{WI}$ argument of knowledge.

We now describe $\langle P, V \rangle$, our fully input-adaptive concurrent non-malleable zero-knowledge protocol. Protocol $\mathcal{ACNMZK}$ for a language $L \in \mathbf{NP}$ proceeds in four stages given a security parameter n, a common input statement $x \in \{0,1\}^n$, an identity id, and a private input $w \in R_L(x)$ to the Prover.

Stage 1. The Prover commits to w using $\langle C, R \rangle$. Let τ_1 be the commitment-transcript.

Stage 2. The Verifier chooses a random string $r \in \{0,1\}^n$ and commits to r using $\langle C, R \rangle$.

Stage 3. The Prover commits to 0^n using the NMCom scheme. Let τ_2 be the commitment-transcript.

Stage 4. The Prover proves using $\langle P_{swi}, V_{swi} \rangle$ that either
  − $\exists y$ s.t. $y \in R_L(x)$ and τ_1 is a valid commitment to y as per $\langle C, R \rangle$, or
  − τ_2 is a valid commitment to r as per NMCom

Completeness and Soundness follows using standard techniques. On a high-level, our simulator-extractor S proceeds in two stages. First we construct an oracle hybrid-simulator $\tilde{S}$ that incorporate A internally and emulates a man-in-the-middle interaction with A. $\tilde{S}$ with oracle access to $\mathcal{O}$, will forward all the commitments made by the adversary A in Stage 1 of right-interactions and Stage 2 of left interactions to $\mathcal{O}$. To simulate left interactions $\tilde{S}$ commits to 0^n in Stage 1. Upon receiving the decommitment r from $\mathcal{O}$ of the commitment made by the adversary in Stage 2, $\tilde{S}$ will commit to r in Stage 3 using the honest-committer strategy and use r as the fake witness in Stage 4 $\mathcal{WI}$-proof. Finally $\tilde{S}$ will output the view of A from its internal emulation along with all the decommitments obtained from $\mathcal{O}$ for the Stage 1 commitments made by A in the right interactions. These will serve as the witnesses corresponding to the statements proved A in the right-interactions. Using $\tilde{S}$ we construct the actual simulator-extractor S. This essentially follows from robust CCA-security of $\langle C, R \rangle$ w.r.t $\mathcal{O}$. Recall that 0-robust CCA-security implies that for every adversary with oracle access to $\mathcal{O}$ there exists a stand-alone simulator that outputs the same. Applying this to $\tilde{S}$ we obtain S. Proving correctness of the simulator relies on standard techniques and is presented in the full version. We additionally show in the full version how to construct a CCA-secure commitment scheme using an $\mathcal{ACNMZK}$ protocol.

4.1 Achieving UC-Security with Super-Polynomial Helpers

It follows from the works of [Lin03, Pas04] that constructing UC-secure protocols for any functionality boils down to realizing the zero-knowledge proof-of-membership functionality, often referred to as the MemberZK functionality. Consider an oracle-helper $\mathcal{H}$ that will provide proof of any statement (adaptively chosen) using the $\mathcal{ACNMZK}$ protocol described above to the adversary but not allow the adversary to use it to prove false statements to honest verifiers.[9] We show how to realize MemberZK-functionality in the angel-model where all parties have access to $\mathcal{H}$. The protocol is simply requiring the prover to use the $\mathcal{ACNMZK}$ protocol to prove the statement.

A subtle issue arises when compiling a protocol in the IdealZK-hybrid to the MemberZK-hybrid. The security reduction proves that for every adversary that only sends true statements to the MemberZK-functionality (also known as non-abusing adversaries) in the MemberZK-hybrid there is a simulator in the IdealZK-hybrid. This proof inherently assumes that an adversary remains non-abusing while receiving false proofs. Previous works that follow this paradigm do not prove this additional requirement when realizing the MemberZK-functionality.[10] We remark that our compilation of the protocol in the MemberZK-hybrid using a $\mathcal{ACNMZK}$-protocol by definition achieves the additional requirement.

---

[9] This can be achieved analogous to [CLP10], by providing the helper with the identity of corrupt parties and checking the session-id of the interaction before providing the proof.

[10] The result and the constructions presented in these works are nevertheless secure, since a direct and more cumbersome proof can prove their correctness.

References

[Blu86]   Blum, M.: How to prove a theorem so no one else can claim it. In: Proceedings of the International Congress of Mathematicians, pp. 1444–1451 (1986)

[BPS06]   Barak, B., Prabhakaran, M., Sahai, A.: Concurrent non-malleable zero knowledge. In: FOCS, pp. 345–354 (2006)

[Can01]   Canetti, R.: Universally composable security: A new paradigm for cryptographic protocols. In: FOCS, pp. 136–145 (2001)

[CDSMW09]   Choi, S.G., Dachman-Soled, D., Malkin, T., Wee, H.: Simple, blackbox constructions of adaptively secure protocols. In: Reingold, O. (ed.) TCC 2009. LNCS, vol. 5444, pp. 387–402. Springer, Heidelberg (2009)

[CF01]   Canetti, R., Fischlin, M.: Universally composable commitments. In: Kilian, J. (ed.) CRYPTO 2001. LNCS, vol. 2139, pp. 19–40. Springer, Heidelberg (2001)

[CFGN96]   Canetti, R., Feige, U., Goldreich, O., Naor, M.: Adaptively secure multiparty computation. In: STOC, pp. 639–648 (1996)

[CIO98]   Di Crescenzo, G., Ishai, Y., Ostrovsky, R.: Non-interactive and non-malleable commitment. In: STOC, pp. 141–150 (1998)

[CKL03]   Canetti, R., Kushilevitz, E., Lindell, Y.: On the limitations of universally composable two-party computation without set-up assumptions. In: Biham, E. (ed.) EUROCRYPT 2003. LNCS, vol. 2656, pp. 68–86. Springer, Heidelberg (2003)

[CKOS01]   Di Crescenzo, G., Katz, J., Ostrovsky, R., Smith, A.: Efficient and non-interactive non-malleable commitment. In: Pfitzmann, B. (ed.) EUROCRYPT 2001. LNCS, vol. 2045, pp. 40–59. Springer, Heidelberg (2001)

[CLOS02]   Canetti, R., Lindell, Y., Ostrovsky, R., Sahai, A.: Universally composable two-party and multi-party secure computation. In: STOC, pp. 494–503 (2002)

[CLP10]   Canetti, R., Lin, H., Pass, R.: Adaptive hardness and composable security in the plain model from standard assumptions. In: FOCS, pp. 541–550 (2010)

[CVZ10]   Cao, Z., Visconti, I., Zhang, Z.: Constant-round concurrent non-malleable statistically binding commitments and decommitments. In: Nguyen, P.Q., Pointcheval, D. (eds.) PKC 2010. LNCS, vol. 6056, pp. 193–208. Springer, Heidelberg (2010)

[DDN00]   Dolev, D., Dwork, C., Naor, M.: Nonmalleable cryptography. SIAM J. Comput. 30(2), 391–437 (2000)

[DM00]   Dodis, Y., Micali, S.: Parallel reducibility for information-theoretically secure computation. In: Bellare, M. (ed.) CRYPTO 2000. LNCS, vol. 1880, pp. 74–92. Springer, Heidelberg (2000)

[DN00]   Damgård, I.B., Nielsen, J.B.: Improved non-committing encryption schemes based on a general complexity assumption. In: Bellare, M. (ed.) CRYPTO 2000. LNCS, vol. 1880, pp. 432–450. Springer, Heidelberg (2000)

[DN02]   Damgård, I.B., Nielsen, J.B.: Perfect hiding and perfect binding universally composable commitment schemes with constant expansion factor. In: Yung, M. (ed.) CRYPTO 2002. LNCS, vol. 2442, pp. 581–596. Springer, Heidelberg (2002)

[DNS04]   Dwork, C., Naor, M., Sahai, A.: Concurrent zero-knowledge. J.
             ACM 51(6), 851–898 (2004)
[DSMRV11]   Dachman-Soled, D., Malkin, T., Raykova, M., Venkitasubramaniam,
             M.: Adaptive and concurrent secure computation from new notions of
             non-malleability. IACR Cryptology ePrint Archive, 2011:611 (2011)
[DSMRV13]   Dachman-Soled, D., Malkin, T., Raykova, M., Venkitasubramaniam,
             M.: Adaptive and concurrent secure computation from new adap-
             tive, non-malleable commitments. In: Sako, K., Sarkar, P. (eds.) ASI-
             ACRYPT 2013, Part I. LNCS, vol. 8269, pp. 316–336. Springer,
             Heidelberg (2013)
[GLP+12]   Goyal, V., Lin, H., Pandey, O., Pass, R., Sahai, A.: Round-efficient
             concurrently composable secure computation via a robust extraction
             lemma. Cryptology ePrint Archive, Report 2012/652 (2012)
[GMR89]   Goldwasser, S., Micali, S., Rackoff, C.: The knowledge complexity of
             interactive proof systems. SIAM J. Comput. 18(1), 186–208 (1989)
[GMW87]   Goldreich, O., Micali, S., Wigderson, A.: How to play any mental
             game or a completeness theorem for protocols with honest majority.
             In: STOC, pp. 218–229 (1987)
[GO07]   Groth, J., Ostrovsky, R.: Cryptography in the multi-string model.
             In: Menezes, A. (ed.) CRYPTO 2007. LNCS, vol. 4622, pp. 323–341.
             Springer, Heidelberg (2007)
[Goy11]   Goyal, V.: Constant round non-malleable protocols using one way func-
             tions. In: STOC, pp. 695–704 (2011)
[Lin03]   Lindell, Y.: Bounded-concurrent secure two-party computation without
             setup assumptions. In: STOC, pp. 683–692 (2003)
[LP11a]   Lin, H., Pass, R.: Concurrent non-malleable zero knowledge with adap-
             tive inputs. In: Ishai, Y. (ed.) TCC 2011. LNCS, vol. 6597, pp. 274–292.
             Springer, Heidelberg (2011)
[LP11b]   Lin, H., Pass, R.: Constant-round non-malleable commitments from
             any one-way function. In: STOC, pp. 705–714 (2011)
[LPTV10]   Lin, H., Pass, R., Tseng, W.-L.D., Venkitasubramaniam, M.: Concur-
             rent non-malleable zero knowledge proofs. In: Rabin, T. (ed.) CRYPTO
             2010. LNCS, vol. 6223, pp. 429–446. Springer, Heidelberg (2010)
[LPV08]   Lin, H., Pass, R., Venkitasubramaniam, M.: Concurrent non-malleable
             commitments from any one-way function. In: Canetti, R. (ed.) TCC
             2008. LNCS, vol. 4948, pp. 571–588. Springer, Heidelberg (2008)
[LPV09]   Lin, H., Pass, R., Venkitasubramaniam, M.: A unified framework for
             concurrent security: universal composability from stand-alone non-
             malleability. In: STOC, pp. 179–188 (2009)
[LPV12]   Pass, R., Lin, H., Venkitasubramaniam, M.: A unified framework for
             UC from only OT. In: Wang, X., Sako, K. (eds.) ASIACRYPT 2012.
             LNCS, vol. 7658, pp. 699–717. Springer, Heidelberg (2012)
[LZ09]   Lindell, Y., Zarosim, H.: Adaptive zero-knowledge proofs and adap-
             tively secure oblivious transfer. In: Reingold, O. (ed.) TCC 2009. LNCS,
             vol. 5444, pp. 183–201. Springer, Heidelberg (2009)
[OPV06]   Ostrovsky, R., Persiano, G., Visconti, I.: Concurrent non-malleable wit-
             ness indistinguishability and its applications. Electronic Colloquium on
             Computational Complexity (ECCC) 13(095) (2006)

[OPV08]   Ostrovsky, R., Persiano, G., Visconti, I.: Constant-round concurrent non-malleable zero knowledge in the bare public-key model. In: Aceto, L., Damgård, I., Goldberg, L.A., Halldórsson, M.M., Ingólfsdóttir, A., Walukiewicz, I. (eds.) ICALP 2008, Part II. LNCS, vol. 5126, pp. 548–559. Springer, Heidelberg (2008)

[OPV09]   Ostrovsky, R., Persiano, G., Visconti, I.: Simulation-based concurrent non-malleable commitments and decommitments. In: Reingold, O. (ed.) TCC 2009. LNCS, vol. 5444, pp. 91–108. Springer, Heidelberg (2009)

[Pas04]   Pass, R.: Bounded-concurrent secure multi-party computation with a dishonest majority. In: STOC, pp. 232–241 (2004)

[PR05]   Pass, R., Rosen, A.: Concurrent non-malleable commitments. In: FOCS, pp. 563–572 (2005)

[PS04]   Prabhakaran, M., Sahai, A.: New notions of security: achieving universal composability without trusted setup. In: STOC, pp. 242–251 (2004)

[PW01]   Pfitzmann, B., Waidner, M.: A model for asynchronous reactive systems and its application to secure message transmission. In: IEEE Symposium on Security and Privacy, p. 184 (2001)

[Sah99]   Sahai, A.: Non-malleable non-interactive zero knowledge and adaptive chosen-ciphertext security. In: FOCS, pp. 543–553 (1999)

[SCO+01]   De Santis, A., Di Crescenzo, G., Ostrovsky, R., Persiano, G., Sahai, A.: Robust non-interactive zero knowledge. In: Kilian, J. (ed.) CRYPTO 2001. LNCS, vol. 2139, pp. 566–598. Springer, Heidelberg (2001)

Key-Indistinguishable Message Authentication Codes*

Joël Alwen[1], Martin Hirt[1], Ueli Maurer[1], Arpita Patra[2,**], and Pavel Raykov[1]

[1] Department of Computer Science, ETH Zurich, Switzerland
{alwenj,martin.hirt,ueli.maurer,pavel.raykov}@inf.ethz.ch
[2] Department of Computer Science & Automation, IISc Bangalore, India
arpita@csa.iisc.ernet.in

Abstract. While standard message authentication codes (MACs) guarantee authenticity of messages, they do not, in general, guarantee the anonymity of the sender and the recipient. For example it may be easy for an observer to determine whether or not two authenticated messages were sent by the same party even without any information about the secret key used. However preserving any uncertainty an attacker may have about the identities of honest parties engaged in authenticated communication is an important goal of many cryptographic applications. For example this is stated as an explicit goal of modern cellphone authentication protocols [rGPP12] and RFID based authentication systems [Vau10].

In this work we introduce and construct a new fundamental cryptographic primitive called *key indistinguishable* (KI) MACs. These can be used to realize many of the most important higher-level applications requiring some form of anonymity and authenticity [AHM+14a]. We show that much (though not all) of the modular MAC construction framework of [DKPW12] gives rise to several variants of KI MACs. On the one hand, we show that KI MACs can be built from hash proof systems and certain weak PRFs allowing us to base security on assumptions such as DDH, CDH and LWE. Next we show that the two direct constructions from the LPN assumption of [DKPW12] are KI, resulting in particularly efficient constructions based on structured assumptions. On the other hand, we also give a very simple and efficient construction based on a PRF which allows us to base KI MACs on some ideal primitives such as an ideal compression function (using HMAC) or block-cipher (using say CBC-MAC). In particular, by using our PRF construction, many real-world implementations of MACs can be easily and cheaply modified to obtain a KI MAC. Finally we show that the transformations of [DKPW12] for increasing the domain size of a MAC as well as for strengthening the type of unforgeability it provides also preserve (or even strengthen) the type of KI enjoyed by the MAC. All together these results provide a wide range of assumptions and construction paths for building various flavors of this new primitive.

---

* The unabridged version of this paper appears in [AHM+14b].
** Work done while the author was at ETH Zurich.

M. Abdalla and R. De Prisco (Eds.): SCN 2014, LNCS 8642, pp. 476–493, 2014.

1   Introduction

1.1   Anonymous Authenticity

In many applications preserving anonymity can conflict with other desirable security properties such as secrecy and authenticity. In [BBDP01,KMO⁺13] the authors described and analyzed cryptographic primitives providing both anonymity and secrecy. In particular [BBDP01] define and realize the notion of *Key-Private* public key encryption (PKE) which, in addition to the usual secrecy provided by PKE, also guarantees that an adversary learns nothing about the target public key under which a given ciphertext was encrypted. Intuitively this can be used to provide reciever-anonymous private communication, a concept which was formalized in [KMO⁺13].

In this work we address the dual problem of providing anonymity in tandem with authenticity. That is, we focus on the private key setting and define the notion of a *Key-Indistinguishable* Message Authentication Code (KI-MAC). These are MACs which have the added benefit that they reveal nothing about the keys used to generate the authentication tags. In [AHM⁺14a] it is shown how such schemes can be used to realize higher level applications such as anonymous authenticated or even secure message transmission and anonymous entity authentication each in strongly composable way.

1.2   Our Contributions

On the highest level we achieve our goal of constructing KI-MACs in three steps detailing a modular and flexible approach. First we formally define KI-MACs via a pair of games and describe some relevant variants thereof. In the second step we show that several constructions either based on Learning Parity with Noise (LPN) assumption or black-box primitives such as hash proof systems (HPS), certain weak pseudorandom functions (wPRF), and variable input-length PRFs are KI. From a theoretical perspective the former constructions allow us to realize KI-MACs from a wide array of number-theoretic assumptions (beyond LPN) such as the Paillier assumption, DDH, CDH and LWE. From a practical perspective the PRF construction demonstrates how to base a KI-MAC on an ideal compression function (using HMAC), an ideal block-cipher (using CBC-MAC [BPR05] and several of its variable input-length extensions such as OMAC [IK03], ECBC [BPR05]) or a fixed-input length PRF (using SS-NMAC [DS09]). In the third step we show that various transformations on MACs for strengthening their security properties also preserve or strengthen the flavour of key-indistinguishability provided by the MAC.

We remark that all MAC schemes in this work are (neccesarily) probabilistic which may be a problem for extremely light-weight computing devices. However they can easily and generically be translated into stateful but deterministic parties by using a PRG.[1]

---

[1] In particular the security proofs for the probabilistic setting then automatically carry over (at least in a computational sense) by preceding the proof with a hybrid argument replacing the output of each call to the PRG with fresh random numbers.

Exact Security. All security statements we give come with an exact security analysis (as opposed to asymptotic ones). We see at least two advantages in taking this approach. First, such results greatly facilitate comparing the quality/efficiency trade-off obtained via different constructions especially when based on the same underlying cryptographic assumptions. A somewhat less common but equally relevant advantage is that such statements make explicit the benefits obtained by enforcing constraints on the adversary through implementation choices. Take for example a protocol whose security degrades say in $q/|\mathcal{M}|$: the number of times an adversary can interact with a client divided by the size of the message space supported by a MAC. Normally such a protocol would require a MAC with at least 160-bit messages to be considered secure. However, if implemented on hardware which guarantees failure after a limited number of interactions, say $q \leq 2^{10}$ (a common assumption in the RFID setting) the MAC now need only support 100-bit messages potentially reducing the hardware costs of the resulting implementation significantly.

1.3 Related Work

MACs are one of the most fundamental, common and widely studied primitives in modern cryptography, especially in practice and a wide variety of constructions have been developed in the past. Most relevant to this work is [DKPW12] from which most of the MAC constructions and transformations analyzed in this work are taken (the notable exception being the PRF based construction of 3.1). That work focuses mainly on theoretical constructions of MACs with the aim of expanding the class of assumptions upon which we can base our security. However given practical efficiency constraints and the difficulty in designing secure symmetric key cryptographic primitives much attention has been focused on constructing secure (variable-input length) MACs from other existing (but idealized) symmetric key primitives such as block-ciphers [BPR05, IK03], compression functions [Bel06, BCK96a], and even fixed-input length PRFs [DS09]. Indeed, some of these have found wide acceptance in practice [Nat], however we stress that none of these constructions result in KI-MACs as they all result in deterministic MACs which trivially can not be key-indistinguishable.

On the other hand cryptographic applications ensuring anonymity have almost exclusively been studied in the context of interactive protocols and are therefore tailored to specific applications rather than providing a general tool with which anonymous applications can be constructed. The most relevant example to this work being [AHM+14a] which investigates how KI-MACs can be used in higher level protocols to construct various idealized multi-user anonymous functionalities. Some other notable examples are [Vau10, HPVP11, DLYZ11, BLdMT09, BM11] which primarily focus on entity authentication (often based on lite-weight RFID cards) and [AMRR11, TM12, AMR+12, LSWW13] which focus specifically on the requirements of mobile phone network communication protocols.

The most important exception to this trend is the work of [BBDP01] which investigates PKE schemes that additionally hide all information about which public key was used to encrypt a given ciphertext. This is motivated by the higher level application of receiver-anonymous private message transmission as formalized in [KMO+13].

1.4 Outline

In Section 2 we review various existing and some new security notions for MAC schemes. In Section 3 we investigate a variety of constructions of varying strengths (and their consequences) based on both black-box and number-theoretic assumptions. Finally in Section 4 we describe how to strengthen the security properties of KI-MACs via some black-box transformations.

2 Definitions

We review some variants of MACs and define the new property of KI.

A message authentication code $\mathsf{MAC} = \{\mathsf{KG}, \mathsf{TAG}, \mathsf{VRFY}\}$ is a triple of algorithms with associated key space $\mathcal{K}$, message space $\mathcal{M}$, and tag space $\mathcal{T}$.

- **Key Generation.** The probabilistic key generation algorithm $k \leftarrow \mathsf{KG}(1^\lambda)$ takes as input a security parameter $\lambda \in \mathbb{N}$ (in unary) and outputs a secret key $k \in \mathcal{K}$.
- **Tagging.** The probabilistic authentication algorithm $\tau \leftarrow \mathsf{TAG}_k(m)$ takes as input a secret key $k \in \mathcal{K}$ and a message $m \in \mathcal{M}$ and outputs an authentication tag $\tau \in \mathcal{T}$.
- **Verification.** The deterministic verification algorithm $\mathsf{VRFY}_k(m, \tau)$ takes as input a secret key $k \in \mathcal{K}$, a message $m \in \mathcal{M}$ and a tag $\tau \in \mathcal{T}$ and outputs an element of the set $\{\texttt{Accept}, \texttt{Reject}\}$.

Next we define some useful properties such a triple of algorithms can have such as completeness and unforgeability. We also discuss two further less common security notions for MACs, called message hiding and key indistinguishability which can only be achieved by *randomized* MACs. While the former notion was already introduced in [DKPW12], the latter is defined for the first time in this work.

COMPLETENESS. We say that MAC has completeness error η if for all $m \in \mathcal{M}$ and $\lambda \in \mathbb{N}$,

$$\Pr[\mathsf{VRFY}_k(m, \tau) = \texttt{Reject} : k \leftarrow \mathsf{KG}(1^\lambda), \tau \leftarrow \mathsf{TAG}_k(m)] \leq \eta.$$

UNFORGEABILITY. We recall the standard notion security for (randomized) MACs; namely unforgeability under a chosen message (and verification) attack (**uf-cmva**). We denote by $\mathbf{Adv}_{\mathsf{MAC}}^{\mathsf{uf\text{-}cmva}}(\mathsf{A}, \lambda)$, the *advantage* of the adversary A in forging the message for a random key $k \leftarrow \mathsf{KG}(1^\lambda)$. Formally it is the probability that the following experiment outputs 1.

Experiment. $\mathbf{Exp}_{MAC}^{uf\text{-}cmva}(A, \lambda)$

- $k \leftarrow KG(1^{\lambda})$
- *Invoke* $A^{TAG_k(\cdot), VRFY_k(\cdot, \cdot)}$.
- *Output* 1 *if* A *queried* (m^*, τ^*) *to* $VRFY_k(\cdot, \cdot)$ *s.t.* $VRFY_k(m^*, \tau^*) = $ Accept *and* A *did not receive* τ^* *by querying* m^* *to* $TAG_k(\cdot)$.

The above experiment can be weakened in several ways to obtain useful variants. In the *selective* unforgeability (**suf-cmva**) notion defined in [DKPW12], A has to specify the target message m^* before making any queries to the oracles in $\mathbf{Exp}_{MAC}^{uf\text{-}cmva}(A, \lambda)$. A yet weaker notion called *universal* unforgeability (**uuf-cmva**) requires the adversary to produce a fresh tag for a uniform random message $m^* \leftarrow \mathcal{M}$ given as input to the adversary. We call the modified experiments $\mathbf{Exp}_{MAC}^{suf\text{-}cmva}$ and $\mathbf{Exp}_{MAC}^{uuf\text{-}cmva}$, respectively. Another way in which the {**uuf, suf, uf**}-**cmva** security notions can be weakened is to restrict the adversary A to making only a single query to the verification oracle.[2] To denote the resulting security notions we write {**uuf, suf, uf**}-**cma** respectively.[3] Finally, if the winning condition of the experiment is to ask only those m^* that have not been previously queried to $TAG_k(\cdot)$ then we refer to the resulting notion as *weakly* unforgeable while referring to the more stringent security notions as *strong*. In particular the {**suf, uf**}-{**cma, cmva**} definitions in [DKPW12] are all weak variants. In general in this work unless stated otherwise we always mean the strong variants.

We refer to an efficient (i.e. PPT) adversary A playing a **cmva** type experiments as a (t, q_t, q_v)-adversary if it runs in time at most t, and for any pair of oracles with a fixed key A makes at most q_t tag and q_v verification queries.

Definition 1 (Unforgeability). *A* MAC *scheme is* (strongly) (t, q_t, q_v, ϵ)-**uf-cmva** *secure if for any* (t, q_t, q_v)-*adversary* A *we have:*

$$\mathbf{Adv}_{MAC}^{uf\text{-}cmva}(A, \lambda) := \Pr[\mathbf{Exp}_{MAC}^{uf\text{-}cmva}(A, \lambda) \rightarrow 1] \leq \epsilon.$$

It is (t, q_t, ϵ)-**uf-cma** *secure if it is* $(t, q_t, 1, \epsilon)$-**uf-cmva** *secure.*

We omit the analogous definitions for the **suf**, and **uuf** variants with and without verification queries detailed above. From these definitions it is immediate that for any $t, q_t, q_v \in \mathbb{N}$ and $\epsilon \geq 0$ the following relation holds for both strong and weak variants: (t, q_t, q_v, ϵ)-**uf-cmva** $\implies (t, q_t, q_v, \epsilon)$-**suf-cmva** $\implies (t, q_t, q_v, \epsilon)$-**uuf-cmva**. Further, as observed in [DKPW12], every weakly (t, q_t, ϵ)-**suf-cma** MAC is also weakly $(t, q_t, \epsilon 2^{\mu})$-**uf-cma** secure where $|\mathcal{M}| = 2^{\mu}$, since the adversary can guess in advance for which message it can mount the forgery attack. The same observation holds for strong unforgeability.

---

[2] Note that this is only a meaningful restriction for MACs with a randomized tagging algorithm since a deterministic tagging algorithm can trivially be used as a verification oracle.

[3] Equivalently we sometimes speak of the adversary simply having *no* access to the verification oracle and instead outputting an attempted forgery at the end of her execution in the **cma** type experiments.

KEY INDISTINGUISHABILITY. Intuitively, the notion of key indistinguishability (KI) ensures that tags leak no information about the secret key (or more generally the internal state of the tag algorithm). Indeed this permits the use of KI-MACs in implementing higher level anonymous authentication applications as detailed in [AHM+14a]. We note that such a property is *not* implied by even the strongest of unforgeability notions defined above.[4]

To capture the desired intuition we define a game where an adversary is given access to two sets of oracles. Its goal is to determine if the two sets use the same key or two independent random keys. To formalize this we introduce some notation. For keys $k_0, k_1 \in \mathcal{K}$ we write $[k_0, k_1]$ to denote the 4-tuple of oracles $(\text{TAG}_{k_0}, \text{VRFY}_{k_0}, \text{TAG}_{k_1}, \text{TAG}_{k_1})$. Moreover we write $[k_0, k_0]$ to denote a similar 4-tuple but where the TAG oracles share their entire internal state including secret key (and similarly for the VRFY oracles). In other words, calls to the first and third oracle of $[k_0, k_0]$ are answered by essentially the same oracle (and similarly for the second and fourth oracle).[5]

Experiment. $\mathbf{Exp}_{\text{MAC}}^{\text{ki-cmva}}(A, \lambda)$
- $k_0, k_1 \leftarrow \text{KG}(1^\lambda)$, $c \leftarrow \{0, 1\}$
- *Sample output* $c' \leftarrow A^{[k_0, k_c]}$.
- *If a tag obtained from the left oracle (namely* TAG_{k_0}*) was verified using the right verification oracle (namely* VRFY_{k_c}*) or vice versa, then output a uniform random bit.*
- *Otherwise if* $c = c'$ *output* 1 *and* 0 *otherwise.*

As usual, in the above experiment we have made a non-triviality constraint; namely that A is not allowed to make a verification query (m, τ) to the right oracle VRFY_{k_c} if τ was obtained from the left oracle TAG_{k_0} for message m (and vice versa).

As before in the following definition we say that an adversary A is a (t, q_t, q_v)-adversary if it runs in time at most t and for *each* pair of oracles with a given key makes at most q_t tag and q_v verification queries. So in total such an adversary can make up to $2q_t$ tag queries namely by making q_t queries to TAG_{k_0} and TAG_{k_c}.

---

[4] Indeed this is not difficult to see. For example we can modify any (say strongly **ufcmva**) unforgeable scheme as follows such that it is clearly not KI yet maintains its original unforgeability property. We double the key size, use the first half of the key in conjunction with the original TAG algorithm to tag the message and then append the second half of the key to the resulting tag. Clearly the scheme remains unforgeable however yet it is trivial to tell apart tags issued under different keys.

[5] For stateful MACs it is important that the full state (and not just the secret key) be shared between matching oracles in $[k_0, k_0]$. Suppose we have a secure MAC which hides all information about the secret keys. We can modify the TAG algorithm to keep a counter which is appended to each tag τ. Clearly the scheme still hides all information about the secret key. However it is unclear how such a scheme might be used to achieve anonymity. Indeed it is trivial to tell say the 10th tag issued for key k_0 from the 3rd tag issued for different key k_1.

Definition 2 (Key Indistinguishability). *A* MAC *scheme is* (t, q_t, q_v, ϵ)-**ki-cmva** secure *(informally:* key hiding*) if for any* (t, q_t, q_v)-*adversary* A *we have:*

$$\mathbf{Adv}_{\mathsf{MAC}}^{\mathsf{ki\text{-}cmva}}(\mathsf{A}, \lambda) := 2 \left| \Pr[\mathbf{Exp}_{\mathsf{MAC}}^{\mathsf{ki\text{-}cmva}}(\mathsf{A}, \lambda) \to 1] - \frac{1}{2} \right| \le \epsilon$$

Moreover if MAC *is* $(t, q_t, 0, \epsilon)$-**ki-cmva** *then we call it* (t, q_t, ϵ)-**ki-cma** *secure. In particular in the* **ki-cma** *experiment we simply omit all verification oracles.*

Multi-key KI Implies Plain KI. A possible extension of the KI notions involves giving the adversary access to n-tuples of pairs of oracles where either each of the pairs have their own states (and keys) or else all pairs share the same state. Indeed such a notion arises quite naturally in the context of a multi-user anonymous protocols as in the real world the adversary observes tags computed under many different states (one for each of the n users). Yet in the ideal and perfect anonymous world the simulator uses the same state to answer all queries.

It turns out that (just as in the case for multi-message CPA encryption) the "one-key" KI notions defined above already implies such a multi-key variant with only a minimal loss of security. (Indeed this is implicitly proved in [AHM+14a].) As has been argued for CPA security, we view this as a further justification for the format of the KI notion defined above.

Message Hiding. Finally we require the somewhat non-standard security notion for MACs called *message hiding (under chosen message attacks)* [DKPW12] which we denote by **ind-cma**. In that work it is shown how message hiding MACs with (weak) unforgeability properties can be strengthened via a generic transformation. In this work we show that the same transformation preserves any KI properties the MAC may have. The formal definition of message hiding can be found in [AHM+14b].

3   Constructing Key Indistinguishable MACs

In this section we prove that various known constructions and transformations for MACs achieve KI. These results may be viewed as analogous to [BBDP01] with the difference that we consider the symmetric key MACs instead of public-key encryption. We now provide a more detailed overview of our results and their relations in Figure 1. The letters "s" and "w" in the figure are used to denote the strong and weak unforgeability variants respectively. The figure consists of three columns. In the first column (AES, DDH, LWE, LPN) we put the underlying cryptographic assumptions upon which security is based. In the second column (HPS, PRF, weak PRF) we put common cryptographic primitives which the MAC constructions use in a black-box manner. In particular they may be implemented using the assumptions which are presented in the first column or any other computational problems. In the third column each box represents a generic MAC scheme characterized by the type of security it provides. Arrows from assumptions and primitives to such a box denote a particular construction.

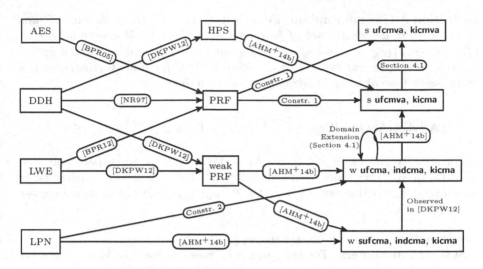

Fig. 1. Obtaining MACs from different assumptions

Additionally arrows between the generic MAC schemes represent transformations used to strengthen the security properties of MACs.

In the remainder of this section we detail two constructions (one from a PRF and one from the LPN assumption) and briefly describe three other constructions.

3.1   From PRFs

PRFs trivially give rise to deterministic MACs (simply by recasting them as the TAG algorithm). However deterministic MACs can not be key indistinguishable (even if they are only weakly universally unforgeable). Thus we now show an alternative construction called MACPRF that is {**uf**, **ki**}-**cmva**. It is very efficient in practical terms (requiring a single call to the underlying PRF) while obtaining the strongest forms of unforgeability and key indistinguishability. Thus it represents potentially the most practically relevant of the construction methods of KI MACs detailed in this paper. In particular the PRF can be instantiated based on an block cipher using say CBC-MAC [BCK96b], OMAC [IK03] or ECBC [BPR05] modes of operation or using a compresion function via the HMAC [Bel06, BCK96a] construction. Alternatively, from a theoretical standpoint the PRF can also be based on a variety of well studied number theoretic assumptions such as the DDH family of assumptions [NR97, DY05] or LWE (using PRF from [BPR12]).

Pseudorandom Function Family (PRF): A PRF is a family of functions with the property that the input-output behavior of a random instance of the family is computationally indistinguishable from that of a random function.

Definition 3 (Pseudorandom Functions). *For arbitrary domain $\mathcal{X}$ and range $\mathcal{Y}$ let $\mathcal{R}$ denote the set of functions from $\mathcal{X}$ to $\mathcal{Y}$. Moreover let* PRF $:= \{f_k : \mathcal{X} \to \mathcal{Y}\}_{k \in \mathcal{K}}$ *be a set of efficiently computable functions indexed by key space $\mathcal{K}$. Then we call* PRF *a (t, q, ϵ)-secure PRF if for any (t, q)-adversary* A *(running in time at most t making at most q queries)*

$$\mathbf{Adv}_{\mathsf{PRF}}^{\mathsf{prf}}(\mathsf{A}, \lambda) := \left| \Pr_{k \leftarrow \mathcal{K}} \left[\mathsf{A}^{f_k(\cdot)} \to 1 \right] - \Pr_{R \leftarrow \mathcal{R}} \left[\mathsf{A}^{R(\cdot)} \to 1 \right] \right| \leq \epsilon.$$

For security parameter $\lambda \in \mathbb{N}$, let $\mathcal{M} = \mathcal{M}(\lambda)$ be a message space and $\mathcal{X} = \mathcal{X}(\lambda)$ be an arbitrary space such that $|\mathcal{X}| \geq 2^\lambda$. The construction makes use of pseudorandom function PRF $= \{f_k : \mathcal{M} \times \mathcal{X} \to \mathcal{Y}\}_{k \in \mathcal{K}}$, that is, the domain of PRF is the set $\mathcal{M} \times \mathcal{X}$.

Construction 1 (MAC **from** PRF: MACPRF)
  System Parameters: *The key space is $\mathcal{K}$, message space is $\mathcal{M}$ and tag space is $\mathcal{T} = \mathcal{Y} \times \mathcal{X}$.*
  Key Generation: *The key generation algorithm* KG(1^λ) *samples $k \leftarrow \mathcal{K}$ and outputs k as the secret key.*
  Tagging: *The tagging algorithm* TAG$_k(m)$ *samples $r \leftarrow_R \mathcal{X}$, runs $z = f_k(m, r)$ and returns tag (r, z).*
  Verification: *The verification algorithm* VRFY$_k(m, (r, z))$ *outputs* Accept *if $f_k(m, r) = z$. Otherwise it outputs* Reject.

Theorem 1. *For any $t, q_t, q_v \in \mathbb{N}$, $\epsilon > 0$, if* PRF *is a $(t, q_t + q_v, \epsilon)$-secure, $(t, 2(q_t + q_v), \epsilon)$-secure and $(t, 2q_t, \epsilon)$-secure then for $t \approx t'$ we have that:*

- MACPRF *has completeness error $\eta = 0$.*
- MACPRF *is strongly $(t', q_t, q_v, \epsilon + \frac{q_v}{|\mathcal{Y}|})$-**uf**-**cmva** secure.*
- MACPRF *is $(t', q_t, q_v, 4\epsilon + \frac{4q_t^2}{|\mathcal{X}|} + \frac{2q_v}{|\mathcal{Y}|})$-**ki**-**cmva** secure.*
- MACPRF *is $(t', q_t, 4\epsilon + \frac{4q_t^2}{|\mathcal{X}|})$-**ki**-**cma** secure respectively.*

Proof. The completeness follows by inspection of the scheme and the fact that all functions in PRF are deterministic.

Strong **uf**-**cmva** *Security.* To prove this we build a reduction to the security of underlying PRF. Let A be a (t, q_t, q_v)-adversary interacting with $\mathbf{Exp}_{\mathsf{MAC}}^{\mathsf{uf}\text{-}\mathsf{cmva}}$. We give a reduction R(A) whose advantage in the **prf** experiment implies an upper bound on the advantage of A. The reduction R expects oracle $\mathcal{O}$ and emulates the experiment $\mathbf{Exp}_{\mathsf{MAC}}^{\mathsf{uf}\text{-}\mathsf{cmva}}(\mathsf{A}, \lambda)$ with the caveat that it uses $\mathcal{O}$ in place of PRF to implement the tag and verification oracles. Finally R outputs 1 if A ever makes a forgery query to the verification oracle; that is a query $(m^*, (r^*, z^*))$ such that $z^* = \mathcal{O}(m^*, r^*)$ and (r^*, z^*) was not obtained in response to a tag oracle query for message m^*. Otherwise R outputs 1. We note that R makes at most $q_t + q_v$ queries to $\mathcal{O}(\cdot)$ in order to simulate $\mathbf{Exp}_{\mathsf{MAC}}^{\mathsf{uf}\text{-}\mathsf{cmva}}$ to A. We bound the probability $\Pr[\mathsf{R} \to 1]$ for the two possible types of oracle $\mathcal{O}$.

Case $\mathcal{O} = f$: When $\mathcal{O}$ is a PRF (with random key) R perfectly simulates $\mathbf{Exp}_{MAC}^{uf\text{-}cmva}(A, \lambda)$. Therefore: $\Pr[R^f \to 1] = \mathbf{Adv}_{MAC}^{uf\text{-}cmva}(A, \lambda)$.

Case $\mathcal{O} = R$: Suppose $\mathcal{O}$ is a random function R and A makes q forgery attempts for message m^* of the form $(m^*, r^*, z_1), \ldots (m^*, r^*, z_q)$. Then the probability that for some i it holds that $z_i = R(m^*, r^*)$ is $\frac{q}{|\mathcal{Y}|}$. Moreover, if the forgery attempts involve more than one value of (m^*, r^*) then the probability of succesful forgery is even smaller. Thus after q_v verification attempts a forgery has occured with probability at most $\frac{q_v}{|\mathcal{Y}|}$. That is: $\Pr[R^R \to 1] \leq \frac{q_v}{|\mathcal{Y}|}$.

Summing up, we have $\epsilon \geq \mathbf{Adv}_{PRF}^{prf}(R, \lambda) = \left| \Pr[R^f \to 1] - \Pr[R^R \to 1] \right| \geq \mathbf{Adv}_{MAC}^{uf\text{-}cmva}(A, \lambda) - \frac{q_v}{|\mathcal{Y}|}$ or $\mathbf{Adv}_{MAC}^{uf\text{-}cmva}(A, \lambda) \leq \epsilon + \frac{q_v}{|\mathcal{Y}|}$.

ki-cmva *and* **ki-cma** *Security.* Recall that the **ki-cmva** game involves two pairs of TAG and VRFY oracles associated with key k_0 and k_1 respectively. We define two experiments closely related to $\mathbf{Exp}_{MAC}^{ki\text{-}cmva}$ incrementally replacing the responses to tag and verification queries with responses that would be outputted when PRFs are replaced with random functions (i.e. independent of key for that oracle). As a result we obtain a **ki-cmva**-like experiment where both the pairs of TAG and VRFY oracles are implemented with a pair of random functions instead of a pair of PRFs. Subsequently we introduce another hybrid experiment where the responses to any non-trivial query to any of the verification oracle is immediately replied with Reject. This results the final experiment to be same as **ki-cma** experiment where both the TAG oracles are implemented with random functions. We prove the differences of the advantages of the hybrids are negligible and also prove that (unconditionally) the advantage in the **ki-cma** using truly random functions is $\frac{2q_t^2}{|\mathcal{X}|}$.

More precisely, for parameters $\lambda \in \mathbb{N}$ and any (t, q_t, q_v)-adversary A we define the experiment $\mathbf{Exp}_0 := \mathbf{Exp}_{MAC}^{ki\text{-}cmva}(A, \lambda)$. Let experiment $\mathbf{Exp}_1$ be identical to $\mathbf{Exp}_0$ except for that any tag and verification query for the oracles associated key k_0 are responded after replacing the PRF with key k_0 with an random function R_0. Let $\mathbf{Exp}_2$ be identical to $\mathbf{Exp}_1$ except that also tag and verification queries for k_1 are responded after replacing the PRF with key k_1 with an random function R_1. Finally let $\mathbf{Exp}_3$ is identical to $\mathbf{Exp}_2$ except that all the non-trivial verification queries are immediately responded with Reject without performing any verification.

For $i \in [0, 3]$ we write $\epsilon_i := \mathbf{Adv}_{MAC}^{\mathbf{Exp}_i}(A, \lambda)$ to denote the respective advantages of A at winning these experiments. Bellow we prove that $|\epsilon_0 - \epsilon_1| \leq 2\epsilon$. An almost identical argument will apply for $|\epsilon_1 - \epsilon_2|$. We show that $|\epsilon_2 - \epsilon_3| \leq \frac{2q_v}{|\mathcal{Y}|}$ holds unconditionally. Finally, the proof that $\epsilon_3 \leq \frac{4q_t^2}{|\mathcal{X}|}$ holds implies the result, as $|\epsilon_0 - \epsilon_3| \leq 2\epsilon + \frac{2q_v}{|\mathcal{Y}|}$ implies $\epsilon_0 = 4\epsilon + \frac{4q_t^2}{|\mathcal{X}|} + \frac{2q_v}{|\mathcal{Y}|}$.

Claim 1. $|\epsilon_0 - \epsilon_1| \leq 2\epsilon$.

Proof. Given A we define reduction R interacting with the **prf** experiment with access to oracles $\mathcal{O}$ as follows. Internally it runs $\mathbf{Exp}_{MAC}^{ki\text{-}cmva}(A, \lambda)$ by sampling a random PRF f and then simulating $\mathrm{TAG}_0, \mathrm{VRFY}_0$ using $\mathcal{O}(\cdot)$ and $\mathrm{TAG}_1, \mathrm{VRFY}_1$ using f. Finally if A wins then R outputs 0, otherwise it outputs 1. We note that $\mathcal{O}(\cdot)$ might be queried $2(q_t + q_v)$ times in total when the bit c in **ki-cmva** experiment is chosen to be 0. This is the reason why we require the underlying PRF to be $(t, 2(q_t + q_v), \epsilon)$-secure.

Suppose now that $\mathcal{O} = f_k$ for a random $k \in \mathcal{K}$. Then the view of A is exactly that generated in $\mathbf{Exp}_0$. Therefore it must be that $\Pr[\mathrm{R}^{f_k} \to 0] = \frac{\epsilon_0}{2} + \frac{1}{2}$. On the other hand, if $\mathcal{O} = R$ is a random function then the view of A is identical to $\mathbf{Exp}_1$. This implies that $\Pr[\mathrm{R}^R \to 0] = \frac{\epsilon_1}{2} + \frac{1}{2}$. Together, it implies $\left| \Pr[\mathrm{R}^{f_k} \to 0] - \Pr[\mathrm{R}^R \to 0] \right| = \frac{|\epsilon_0 - \epsilon_1|}{2}$. Due to the security of PRF, it now follows that $\frac{|\epsilon_0 - \epsilon_1|}{2} \leq \epsilon$ or $|\epsilon_0 - \epsilon_1| \leq 2\epsilon$.

$\square$

Claim 2. $|\epsilon_2 - \epsilon_3| \leq \frac{2q_v}{|\mathcal{Y}|}$.

Proof. The only way A will behave differently in $\mathbf{Exp}_2$ and $\mathbf{Exp}_3$ is if she is able to produce a non-trivial query to any of the verification oracles that is accepted. I.e it makes a query $(m, (r, z))$ to a verification oracle using function f such that $f(m, r) = z$. Since both the pairs of oracles in the experiments are implemented with a pair of random functions and A has not seen the output of the random functions at point (m, r) the probability that she can produce the correct z is $\frac{1}{|\mathcal{Y}|}$. Thus via a hybrid argument over all verification queries we have that $|\epsilon_2 - \epsilon_3| \leq \frac{2q_v}{|\mathcal{Y}|}$. $\square$

Claim 3. $\epsilon_3 \leq \frac{4q_t^2}{|\mathcal{X}|}$.

Proof. Our goal is to bound the advantage ϵ_3 of any adversary A for experiment $\mathbf{Exp}_3$; that is the experiment where two random functions R_0 and R_1 are used in place of PRFs for replying TAG queries and all the non-trivial verification queries are responded with immediate Reject. We define an event for which we can show that on the one hand if the event does not occur then the adversary has little chance of winning and moreover the event occurs with only a very small probability.

First we observe that in the experiment if the bit c is chosen to be 0 then R_0 is queried up to $2q_t$ times via tag oracles (and R_1 not at all) or, when $c = 1$, then both R_0 and R_1 are queried at most q_t via the respective tag oracles. Now consider calls to R_0 and R_1 (in $\mathbf{Exp}_3$) made through the tag oracles. Each such call has the form (m, r), where A chooses m but r is sampled uniformly at random from $\mathcal{X}$. Two such calls (m, r) and (m', r') are said to *collide* if $(m, r) = (m', r')$. We define the event C to occur when A produces output in $\mathbf{Exp}_3$ and at least one pair of colliding calls was made. Then we see that conditioned on C not occurring the view of A in $\mathbf{Exp}_3$ is independent of bit c which it must guess. Consequently we have $\Pr[\mathbf{Exp}_3 = 1 | \neg C] = \frac{1}{2}$.

It remains to bound $\Pr[C]$. During each of $2q_t$ queries r is chosen independently and uniformly at random. So $\Pr[C]$ is same as the probability that an

$r \in \mathcal{X}$ is picked at least twice in these $2q_t$ queries, where there are $|\mathcal{X}|$ possibilities for r. We note that $\Pr[C] \leq \frac{\binom{2q_t}{2}}{|\mathcal{X}|} \leq \frac{2q_t^2}{|\mathcal{X}|}$. Now, we estimate the probability of A in winning $\mathbf{Exp}_3$.

$$\epsilon_3 = 2 \left| \Pr[\mathbf{Exp}_3 = 1] - \frac{1}{2} \right| =$$

$$2 \left| \underbrace{\Pr[\mathbf{Exp}_3 = 1 \mid C] \cdot \Pr[C]}_{\leq \Pr[C]} + \underbrace{\Pr[\mathbf{Exp}_3 = 1 \mid \neg C] \cdot \Pr[\neg C]}_{= \frac{1}{2}(1-\Pr[C])} - \frac{1}{2} \right| \leq \Pr[C]$$

$\square$

The proof for **ki-cma** follows from the above proof for **ki-cmva** where there is no verification oracles throughout and therefore experiments $\mathbf{Exp}_2$ and $\mathbf{Exp}_3$ become identical leading to the removal of the term $\frac{2q_v}{|\mathcal{Y}|}$ from the security parameter of **ki-cma**.

$\square$

3.2   From LPN

We now analyze the KI properties of the MAC$_{\mathsf{LPN}}$ construction based directly on the LPN assumption taken from [DKPW12] where it was shown to be **ind-cma** and wealky **uf-cma** secure. We show that aditionally it is also **ki-cma**. The resulting scheme is the most efficient of the constructions based on number-theoretic assumptions analyzed in this work.

LPN and SLPN* Assumptions: Following [Pie12], we briefly recall the LPN assumption defining it as a special case of the SLPN* assumption. Let U_n be the uniform distribution over $\mathbb{Z}_2^n$, B_τ be the Bernoulli distribution with parameter τ and B_τ^n be the n-dimensional Bernoulli distribution.[6] For a vector $\mathbf{x} \in \mathbb{Z}_2^n$ we denote by $\mathbf{x}^{\mathsf{T}}$ the transpose of $\mathbf{x}$. Moreover for a vector $\mathbf{a} \in \mathbb{Z}_2^n$ we denote by $hw(\mathbf{a})$ the hamming weight of $\mathbf{a}$. We write $\mathbf{a} \wedge \mathbf{b}$ for the component wise AND and $\mathbf{a}_{\downarrow\mathbf{b}}$ for the vector obtained from $\mathbf{a}$ by removing all components a_i of $\mathbf{a}$ where $b_i = 0$.

For $\ell \in \mathbb{N}$, $\tau \in (0, \frac{1}{2})$ and $\mathbf{s} \in \mathbb{Z}_2^\ell$ define SLPN* oracle $\Gamma_{\tau,\ell,d}(\mathbf{s}, \cdot)$ to take input vectors $\mathbf{v} \in \mathbb{Z}_2^\ell$ and return $\bot$ if $hw(\mathbf{v}) < d$. Otherwise the oracle samples fresh vector $\mathbf{r}$ according to U_ℓ and bit e according to B_τ and outputs $(\mathbf{r}^{\mathsf{T}}, \mathbf{r}^{\mathsf{T}}(\mathbf{s}\wedge\mathbf{v})+e)^{\mathsf{T}}$. On the other hand the oracle $U_{\ell+1,d}(\cdot)$, on input $\mathbf{v} \in \mathbb{Z}_2^\ell$ outputs $\bot$ if $hw(\mathbf{v}) < d$. Otherwise it outputs a fresh sample from $\mathsf{U}_{\ell+1}$.

For $t,q \in \mathbb{N}$ we call a PPT oracle machine A a (t, q)-adversary if it runs in time at most t making at most q queries and produces binary output.

The **SLPN***$_{\tau,\ell,d}$ assumption is said to be (t, q, ϵ)-*hard* if for secret $\mathbf{s}$ sampled according to $\mathsf{U}_{\ell+1}$ the distinguishing advantage between oracles $\Gamma_{\tau,\ell,d}$ and $U_{\ell+1,d}$

---

[6] That is the distribution over $\mathbb{Z}_2^n$ where each bit is chosen independently according to B_τ.

[7] The second component is same as $\mathbf{r}_{\downarrow\mathbf{v}}^{\mathsf{T}}\mathbf{s}_{\downarrow\mathbf{v}} + e$

of any (t,q)-adversaries is at most ϵ. Similarly, the $\mathbf{LPN}_{\tau,\ell}$ assumption is (t,q,ϵ)-hard if no (t,q)-adversary can distinguish oracles $\Gamma_{\tau,\ell,\ell}$ and $U_{\ell+1,\ell}$ with greater then probability ϵ.

Roughly speaking, it was shown by Pietrzak in [Pie12] that the LPN implies the SLPN*.[8]

Lemma 1 ([Pie12]). *If the* $\mathbf{LPN}_{\tau,d}$ *is* (t,q,ϵ)-*hard then for any* $\delta \in \mathbb{N}$ *the* $\mathbf{SLPN}^{*}_{\tau,\ell,d+\delta}$ *is* (t',q,ϵ')-*hard where* $t' = t - poly(q,\ell)$ *and* $\epsilon' = \epsilon + \frac{q}{2^{\delta}}$.

We now turn to the second construction from [DKPW12] which was (implicitly) shown to be **ind-cma** and weakly **uf-cma** secure in [KPC+11]. Bellow we prove it to be **ki-cma** secure.

Construction 2 (MAC from **LPN**: MAC$_{\mathsf{LPN}}$)
  System Parameters: *Parameter* $\tau \in (0,\frac{1}{2})$ *and* $\ell \in \mathbb{N}$ *which control the security quality, and parameters* $\tau' = 1/4 + \tau/2$ *and* $n \in \mathbb{N}$ *which controls the correctness error. Finally parameter* $\alpha \in \mathbb{N}$ *controls the message length. The resulting key space is* $\mathcal{K} = \mathbb{Z}_2^{(\ell+1)\times\alpha}$, *the message space is* $\mathcal{M} = \mathbb{Z}_2^{\alpha}$ *and the tag space is* $\mathcal{T} = \mathbb{Z}_2^{(\ell+1)n}$.
  Key Generation: *Algorithm* KG$(\cdot)$ *samples* $\mathbf{X} \leftarrow \mathbb{Z}_2^{\ell\times\alpha}$ *and* $\bar{\mathbf{x}} \leftarrow \mathbb{Z}_2^{\ell}$ *both uniformly and outputs secret key* $(\mathbf{X},\bar{\mathbf{x}})$.
  Tagging: *For message* $\mathbf{m}$ *and secret key* $\mathbf{s} = (\mathbf{X},\bar{\mathbf{x}})$ *the algorithm* TAG$_{\mathbf{s}}(\mathbf{m})$ *first samples* $\mathbf{R} \leftarrow \mathbb{Z}_2^{\ell\times n}$ *uniformly and* $\mathbf{e}$ *according to* B_{τ}^n. *Then it outputs tag* $\sigma = (\mathbf{R}, \mathbf{R}^{\mathsf{T}} \cdot (\mathbf{X}\cdot\mathbf{m} + \bar{\mathbf{x}}) + \mathbf{e})$.
  Verification: *To verify tag* $\sigma = (\mathbf{R},z) \in \mathbb{Z}_2^{\ell\times n} \times \mathbb{Z}_2^n$ *with secret key* $\mathbf{s} = (\mathbf{X},\bar{\mathbf{x}})$ *the algorithm* VRFY$_{\mathbf{s}}(\mathbf{m},\sigma)$ *outputs* Accept *if and only if* $hw(\mathbf{R}^{\mathsf{T}} \cdot (\mathbf{X}\cdot\mathbf{m} + \bar{\mathbf{x}}) - \mathbf{z}) \leq \tau'n$.

Theorem 2. *If* $\mathbf{LPN}_{\tau,\ell}$ *is* (t,q,ϵ)-*hard then* MAC$_{\mathsf{LPN}}$ *is* $(t,\frac{q}{2},2\epsilon)$-**ki-cma** *secure.*

Proof. At its core the proof relies on a pair of reductions to the $\mathbf{LPN}_{\tau,\ell}$ problem. In a few words the LPN assumption tells us that for a given tagging key (component) $\bar{\mathbf{x}}$ we can replace all terms of the form $\mathbf{R}^T \cdot \bar{\mathbf{x}} + \mathbf{e}$ in all tag queries with fresh uniform random elements from $\mathbb{Z}_2^n$. By doing this for both keys in the **ki-cma** game we obtain an experiment in which the bit c being guessed by adversary remains hidden from her view.

More precisely we define three experiments and show that on the one hand for any fixed adversary their outcomes are computationally indistinguishable and on the other hand all adversaries have no advantage at winning the third game. In fact we define experiments $\mathbf{Exp}_0, \mathbf{Exp}_1$ and $\mathbf{Exp}_2$ exactly as in that proof except that the construction MAC$_{\mathsf{LPN}}$ is used. For example to answer tag queries for key k_0 in $\mathbf{Exp}_1$ simply returns a fresh uniform sample from $\mathbb{Z}_2^{(\ell+1)n}$ while tag queries for key k_1 are answered using the TAG algorithm of MAC$_{\mathsf{LPN}}$.

Using the same notations of the previous proof, we observe that $\epsilon_2 = 0$ which holds unconditionally since in $\mathbf{Exp}_2$ the view of any adversary is information

---

[8] Actually a stronger result was shown, namely that the sub*space*-LPN assumption (which implies the SLPN*) is implied by the LPN.

theoretically independent of the bit c which it is trying to guess. Thus it remains only to show that $|\epsilon_0 - \epsilon_1|$ and $|\epsilon_1 - \epsilon_2|$ (defined just as before) can be at most ϵ if the $\mathbf{LPN}_{\tau,\ell}$ is (t, q, ϵ)-hard.

Claim $|\epsilon_0 - \epsilon_1| \leq \epsilon$: We reduce the the $\mathbf{LPN}_{\tau,\ell}$ assumption with the following reduction R which has access to an oracle $\mathcal{O}$ that is either and LPN oracle or a uniform oracle. The reduction emulates an experiment internally to A and outputs 1 if and only if A wins. The experiment is identical to $\mathbf{Exp}_0$ except for the following:

1. Instead of generating k_0 according to $\mathsf{KG}(1^\lambda)$ it only samples and stores $\mathbf{X} \leftarrow \mathbb{Z}_2^{\ell \times \alpha}$.
2. When a tag query $m \in \mathbb{Z}_2^\alpha$ for key k_0 is made R first obtains n fresh samples $\{(\mathbf{r}_i, b_i) \in \mathbb{Z}_2^{\ell+1}\}_{i \in [n]}$ from $\mathcal{O}$. Let $\mathbf{R} \in \mathbb{Z}_2^{\ell \times n}$ be the matrix whose i^{th} column is $\mathbf{r}_i$ and $\mathbf{b} \in \mathbb{Z}_2^n$ be the vector whose i^{th} bit is b_i. Then R returns the tag $(\mathbf{R}, \mathbf{R}^T \cdot \mathbf{X} \cdot \mathbf{m} + \mathbf{b})$.

We claim that if $\mathcal{O}$ is an $\mathbf{LPN}_{\tau,\ell}$ oracle with secret $\mathbf{x}$ then R has perfectly emulated experiment $\mathbf{Exp}_0$ with key $k_0 = (\mathbf{X}, \mathbf{x})$. This follows from the calculation:

$$\mathbf{R}^T \cdot \mathbf{X} \cdot \mathbf{m} + \mathbf{b} = \mathbf{R}^T \cdot \mathbf{X} \cdot \mathbf{m} + \mathbf{R}^T \cdot \mathbf{x} + \mathbf{e} = \mathbf{R}^T \cdot (\mathbf{X} \cdot \mathbf{m} + \mathbf{x}) + \mathbf{e}$$

which implies that $\Pr[\mathsf{R} \to 1] = \epsilon_0$ for such an oracle.

On the other hand if $\mathcal{O}$ is a uniform oracle then in particular $\mathbf{b}$ is uniformly and independently distributed for each tag query. Thus all values $\mathbf{R}^T \cdot \mathbf{X} \cdot \mathbf{m} + \mathbf{b}$ are also uniformly and independently distributed exactly as in experiment $\mathbf{Exp}_1$. It follows that $\Pr[\mathsf{R} \to 1] = \epsilon_1$ when $\mathcal{O}$ is uniform.

Taken together we can conclude that $|\epsilon_0 - \epsilon_1| \leq \epsilon$. Moreover the reduction makes at most $2q$ queries to $\mathcal{O}$.[9]

Claim $|\epsilon_1 - \epsilon_2| \leq \epsilon$: Once again an almost identical argument applied to k_1 to the previous case also proves this claim.

3.3 Further Constructions

We briefly detail three further constructions which we prove KI in the full version of this paper [AHM+14b].

From the SLPN* Assumption. We also analyze the construction $\mathsf{MAC}_{\mathsf{SLPN}^*}$ based on the SLPN* assumption of [DKPW12] which was (implicitly) shown to be **ind-cma** and weakly **suf-cma** secure in [KPC+11]. In the full version of this work [AHM+14b] we prove that it is also **ki-cma** secure based on the related Subset LPN (SLPN*) assumption which can be efficiently reduced to the more standard LPN assumption [Pie12]. The two LPN based schemes $\mathsf{MAC}_{\mathsf{LPN}}$ and $\mathsf{MAC}_{\mathsf{SLPN}^*}$

---

[9] This occurs in the case when A makes q queries to both left and right oracle and $c = 0$ in the emulated $\mathbf{Exp}_1$ experiment

are somewhat incomparable. On the one hand MAC$_{LPN}$ provides a stronger unforgeability property and comes with a tighter reduction to the LPN assumption. On the other hand MAC$_{SLPN^*}$ enjoys a smaller key size (though less efficient tagging operation) and can be instantiated with a comparatively smaller value of the security parameter to achieve the same level of security.

From Hash Proof Systems. In [AHM+14b] we also show that the MAC construction MAC$_{HPS}$ given in [DKPW12] based on any labeled hash proof systems HPS is also **ki-cma** secure. The scheme has been shown to be weakly **uf-cmva** secure. Using a slightly stronger notion of a HPS, the proof for weak **uf-cmva** goes through unchanged resulting in the same parameters for strong **uf-cmva** security. This scheme provides the most efficient KI MAC in this work based on DDH assumption.

From Key-Homomorphic Weak PRFs. We show that the MAC construction MAC$_{khwPRF}$ of [DKPW12] based on any key-homomorphic weak PRF is **ki-cma** secure. The scheme has been proven to be weakly **suf-cma** secure. In [DKPW12] an extension of the wPRF construction is provided which makes use of Waters' argument [Wat05] to achieve weak **uf-cma** (and **ind-cma**) security at the cost of a somewhat less efficient scheme. We also observe that the modified scheme is **ki-cma** secure following essentially same argument that we use for the former wPRF based construction. As observed in [DKPW12] both DDH assumption and the LWE assumptions can (for example) be used to directly instantiate efficient key-homomorphic wPRF families.

4   Transformations for Strengthening MACs

We describe several transformations for strengthening the security properties of a MAC. All but one of the transformations were originally described in [DKPW12]. In this work we show that not only do they achieve their intended goal of producing MACs with better unforgeability properties but they also preserve the underlying KI property. Moreover we show that the most important such transformation even achieves a stronger unforgeability notion (namely *strong* **uf-cmva**) then originally claimed.

4.1   Adding Support for Verification Queries

We show how to add security in the face of verification queries while preserving KI by giving a full path from any weakly {**uf, ind, ki**}-**cma** secure MAC to a strongly {**uf, ki**}-**cmva** secure one.

Verification Queries for Unforgeability. In [DKPW12] the authors present a very efficient transformation which maps any weakly {**uf, ind**}-**cma** secure scheme MAC to a weakly **uf-cmva** secure scheme $\overline{\text{MAC}}$. We show that the transformation achieves more namely the resulting MAC is even *strongly* **uf-cmva** secure. Indeed the original proof goes through unchanged also for the the stronger statement. We also show that the same transformation also preserves the **ki-cma** security of the underlying MAC.

Verification Queries for KI. The above result shows that for certain MACs we can strengthen the type of unforgeability supported while preserving the KI property. Next we show that any (strong) **uf-cmva** and **ki-cma** secure MAC is also **ki-cmva** secure. Together these results provide a full path from any weakly {**uf**, **ind**, **ki**}-**cma** secure MAC to a strongly {**uf**, **ki**}-**cmva** secure one.

Theorem 3 (uf-cmva + ki-cma $\implies$ ki-cmva). *For any $t, q_t, q_v \in \mathbb{N}$ and $\epsilon_1, \epsilon_2, \eta > 0$, if* MAC *is:*

- $(t, q_t, q_v, \epsilon_1)$-**uf-cmva** *(strongly existentially unforgeable with verification queries)*
- (t, q_t, ϵ_2)-**ki-cma** *(key indistinguishable)*
- *and has completeness error η*

then MAC *is* $(t', q_t, q_v, 4\epsilon_1 + \epsilon_2 + 4\min(q_t, q_v)\eta)$-**ki-cmva** *secure where $t' \approx t$.*

For a proof of the theorem we refer the interested reader to the full version of this work [AHM+14b].

KI Preserving Domain Extension. Recall that (for both weak and strong variants) an **suf-cma** secure MAC is also **uf-cma** secure albiet at a cost of degrading security by a multiplicative factor of $2^\mu = |\mathcal{M}|$; the size of the message space. In order to keep this 2^μ factor small, we start with (t, q_t, ϵ)-**suf-cma** MAC with very small message space and then after recasting it as **uf-cma** secure scheme we can apply the domain extension transformation of [DKPW12] to grow the message space. In the full version [AHM+14b] we show that the transformation also preserves the KI of the original scheme as long as the original MAC is also **ind-cma** secure (though not necessarily unforgeable in any sense).

References

[AHM+14a] Alwen, J., Hirt, M., Maurer, U., Patra, A., Raykov, P.: Anonymous authentication with shared secrets. Cryptology ePrint Archive, Report 2014/073 (2014), http://eprint.iacr.org/

[AHM+14b] Alwen, J., Hirt, M., Maurer, U., Patra, A., Raykov, P.: Key-indistinguishable message authentication codes. Cryptology ePrint Archive, Report 2014/107 (2014), http://eprint.iacr.org/

[AMR+12]   Arapinis, M., Mancini, L.I., Ritter, E., Ryan, M., Golde, N., Redon, K., Borgaonkar, R.: New privacy issues in mobile telephony: fix and verification. In: ACM Conference on Computer and Communications Security, pp. 205–216. ACM (2012)

[AMRR11]   Arapinis, M., Mancini, L.I., Ritter, E., Ryan, M.: Formal analysis of umts privacy, CoRR abs/1109.2066 (2011)

[BBDP01]   Bellare, M., Boldyreva, A., Desai, A., Pointcheval, D.: Key-privacy in public-key encryption. In: Boyd, C. (ed.) ASIACRYPT 2001. LNCS, vol. 2248, pp. 566–582. Springer, Heidelberg (2001)

[BCK96a]   Bellare, M., Canetti, R., Krawczyk, H.: Keying hash functions for message authentication. In: Koblitz, N. (ed.) CRYPTO 1996. LNCS, vol. 1109, pp. 1–15. Springer, Heidelberg (1996)

[BCK96b]   Bellare, M., Canetti, R., Krawczyk, H.: Pseudorandom functions revisited: The cascade construction and its concrete security. In: FOCS, pp. 514–523 (1996)

[Bel06]   Bellare, M.: New proofs for NMAC and HMAC: Security without collision-resistance. In: Dwork, C. (ed.) CRYPTO 2006. LNCS, vol. 4117, pp. 602–619. Springer, Heidelberg (2006)

[BLdMT09]   Burmester, M., Le, T.V., de Medeiros, B., Tsudik, G.: Universally composable RFID identification and authentication protocols. ACM Trans. Inf. Syst. Secur. 12(4) (2009)

[BM11]   Burmester, M., Munilla, J.: Lightweight RFID authentication with forward and backward security. ACM Trans. Inf. Syst. Secur. 14(1), 11 (2011)

[BPR05]   Bellare, M., Pietrzak, K., Rogaway, P.: Improved security analyses for CBC mACs. In: Shoup, V. (ed.) CRYPTO 2005. LNCS, vol. 3621, pp. 527–545. Springer, Heidelberg (2005)

[BPR12]   Banerjee, A., Peikert, C., Rosen, A.: Pseudorandom functions and lattices. In: Pointcheval, D., Johansson, T. (eds.) EUROCRYPT 2012. LNCS, vol. 7237, pp. 719–737. Springer, Heidelberg (2012)

[DKPW12]   Dodis, Y., Kiltz, E., Pietrzak, K., Wichs, D.: Message authentication, revisited. In: Pointcheval, D., Johansson, T. (eds.) EUROCRYPT 2012. LNCS, vol. 7237, pp. 355–374. Springer, Heidelberg (2012)

[DLYZ11]   Deng, R.H., Li, Y., Yung, M., Zhao, Y.: A zero-knowledge based framework for RFID privacy. Journal of Computer Security 19(6), 1109–1146 (2011)

[DS09]   Dodis, Y., Steinberger, J.: Message authentication codes from unpredictable block ciphers. In: Halevi, S. (ed.) CRYPTO 2009. LNCS, vol. 5677, pp. 267–285. Springer, Heidelberg (2009)

[DY05]   Dodis, Y., Yampolskiy, A.: A verifiable random function with short proofs and keys. In: Vaudenay, S. (ed.) PKC 2005. LNCS, vol. 3386, pp. 416–431. Springer, Heidelberg (2005)

[HPVP11]   Hermans, J., Pashalidis, A., Vercauteren, F., Preneel, B.: A new RFID privacy model. In: Atluri, V., Diaz, C. (eds.) ESORICS 2011. LNCS, vol. 6879, pp. 568–587. Springer, Heidelberg (2011)

[IK03]   Iwata, T., Kurosawa, K.: Omac: One-key cbc mac. In: Johansson, T. (ed.) FSE 2003. LNCS, vol. 2887, pp. 129–153. Springer, Heidelberg (2003)

[KMO+13]   Kohlweiss, M., Maurer, U., Onete, C., Tackmann, B., Venturi, D.: Anonymity-preserving public-key encryption: A constructive approach. In: De Cristofaro, E., Wright, M. (eds.) PETS 2013. LNCS, vol. 7981, pp. 19–39. Springer, Heidelberg (2013)

[KPC+11]   Kiltz, E., Pietrzak, K., Cash, D., Jain, A., Venturi, D.: Efficient authentication from hard learning problems. In: Paterson, K.G. (ed.) EUROCRYPT 2011. LNCS, vol. 6632, pp. 7–26. Springer, Heidelberg (2011)

[LSWW13]   Lee, M.-F., Smart, N.P., Warinschi, B., Watson, G.: Anonymity guarantees of the umts/lte authentication and connection protocol. Cryptology ePrint Archive, Report 2013/027 (2013), http://eprint.iacr.org/

[Nat]   National Institute of Standards and Technology, U.S. Department of Commerce, M Dworkin. Recommendation for block cipher modes of operation: the CMAC mode for authentication. NIST Special Publication 800-38B

[NR97]   Naor, M., Reingold, O.: Number-theoretic constructions of efficient pseudo-random functions. In: FOCS, pp. 458–467 (1997)

[Pie12]   Pietrzak, K.: Subspace LWE. In: Cramer, R. (ed.) TCC 2012. LNCS, vol. 7194, pp. 548–563. Springer, Heidelberg (2012)

[rGPP12]   3rd Generation Partnership Project. Ts 33.102 - 3g security; Security architecture v11.5.0 (2012)

[TM12]   Tsay, J.-K., Mjølsnes, S.F.: A vulnerability in the umts and lte authentication and key agreement protocols. In: Kotenko, I., Skormin, V. (eds.) MMM-ACNS 2012. LNCS, vol. 7531, pp. 65–76. Springer, Heidelberg (2012)

[Vau10]   Vaudenay, S.: Privacy models for RFID schemes. In: Ors Yalcin, S.B. (ed.) RFIDSec 2010. LNCS, vol. 6370, pp. 65–65. Springer, Heidelberg (2010)

[Wat05]   Waters, B.: Efficient identity-based encryption without random oracles. In: Cramer, R. (ed.) EUROCRYPT 2005. LNCS, vol. 3494, pp. 114–127. Springer, Heidelberg (2005)

Interactive Encryption and Message Authentication

Yevgeniy Dodis[1] and Dario Fiore[2,*]

[1] Department of Computer Science, New York University, USA
dodis@cs.nyu.edu
[2] IMDEA Software Institute, Spain
dario.fiore@imdea.org

Abstract. Public-Key Encryption (PKE) and Message Authentication (PKMA, aka as digital signatures) are fundamental cryptographic primitives. Traditionally, both notions are defined as non-interactive (i.e., single-message). In this work, we initiate rigorous study of (possibly) *interactive* PKE and PKMA schemes. We obtain the following results demonstrating the power of interaction to resolve questions which are either open or impossible in the non-interactive setting.

Efficiency/Assumptions. One of the most well known open questions in the area of PKE is to build, in a "black-box way", so called chosen ciphertext attack (CCA-) secure PKE from chosen plaintext attack (CPA-) secure PKE. In contrast, we show a simple 2-round CCA-secure PKE from any (non-interactive) CPA-secure PKE (in fact, these primitives turn out to be equivalent). Similarly, although non-interactive PKMA schemes can be inefficiently built from any one-way function, no efficient signature schemes are known from many popular number-theoretic assumptions, such as factoring, CDH or DDH. In contrast, we show an efficient 2-round PKMA from most popular assumptions, including factoring, CDH and DDH.

Advanced Properties. It is well known that no non-interactive signature (resp. encryption) scheme can be *deniable* (resp. *forward-secure*), since the signature (resp. ciphertext) can later "serve as an evidence of the sender's consent" (resp. "be decrypted if the receiver's key is compromised"). We also formalize a related notion of *replay-secure* (necessarily) interactive PKMA (resp. PKE) schemes, where the verifier (resp. encryptor) is assured that the "current" message can only be authenticated (resp. decrypted) by the secret key owner *now*, as opposed to some time in the past (resp. future). We observe that our 2-round PKMA scheme is both replay-secure and (passively) deniable, and our 2-round PKE scheme is both replay- and forward-secure.

1 Introduction

Digital signatures and public-key encryption (PKE) schemes are two of the most fundamental and well studied cryptographic primitives. Traditionally, both notions are defined as *non-interactive* (i.e., single message). Aside from obvious

---

* Work partially done while postdoc at NYU.

M. Abdalla and R. De Prisco (Eds.): SCN 2014, LNCS 8642, pp. 494–513, 2014.
© Springer International Publishing Switzerland 2014

convenience — both the sender and receiver need not keep any state — such non-interactive "one-and-done" philosophy is also critical in many applications. Coupled with the fact that we now have many (often efficient) candidates for both signature and encryption schemes, it might appear that there is little value in extending the syntax of signature/encryption schemes to allow for (possibly) interactive realizations.

In this work we challenge this point of view, and initiate rigorous study of (possibly) *interactive signature and public-key encryption schemes*. For the former, we will actually use the term *Public-Key Message Authentication* (PKMA) scheme, as the term "signature" often comes with expectations of "non-repudiation", which is orthogonal to the standard notion of "unforgeability" the moment interaction is allowed. First, although we agree that some applications might critically rely on the non-interactivity of PKE/PKMA schemes, we believe that many other applications, including *arguably the most basic one of sending/receiving private/authentic messages*, might not so be fixated on non-interactivity. For such applications, it appears natural to allow the sender and the receiver to interact, especially if they are involved in a conversation anyway.

Second, in this work we will show that, by allowing a single extra message (i.e., a 2-round protocol), we can "resolve" two arguably most important open problems in the area of non-interactive PKE/PKMA schemes:[1] (a) "black-box" 2-round chosen-ciphertext attack (CCA-) secure PKE from any (non-interactive) chosen-plaintext attack (CPA-) secure PKE; (b) *efficient* 2-round strongly unforgeable PKMA scheme from a variety of simple assumptions, such as factoring and DDH.

Third, we point out several useful advanced properties of PKE/PKMA schemes which are *impossible to achieve without interaction*. While some of these properties (such as *deniable* PKMA [18,20,19,15]) were already extensively studied in the past, most others (such as interactive *forward-secure* PKE, and *replay-secure* PKE/PKMA) appear to be new.

RELATED WORK. Although our work is the first to offer a detailed and comprehensive study of interactive PKE/PKMA schemes, it is certainly not the first to consider these notions. The most related prior work in this regard is the famous "DDN-paper" on non-malleable cryptography [17,18]. This seminal work had many extremely important and influential results. Among them, it also considered non-malleable, interactive encryption and authentication, and briefly sketched[2] elegant constructions for both primitives. We discuss more in detail the relation with our work in the next section, when we describe our improvements over the DDN paper.

To the best of our knowledge, the only other work providing a related definition (only for encryption) is the one of Katz [27]. However, our definition is

---

[1] Of course, we obtain this by changing the model to allow for interaction, which is the reason for the quotation marks.

[2] Due to the massive scope of [18], the DDN paper did not give formal definitions and proofs for the encryption results (saying they are "outside the scope" of their paper; see page 32), and only sketched the definition/proof for the authentication case.

stronger, as we place more restriction on the attacker to declare that the attacker 'acts as a wire'. Moreover, the solutions given in [27] use so called timing assumptions, while our constructions are in the standard model.

1.1 Our Results

We now describe our motivations and results in more detail.

DEFINITIONAL FRAMEWORK. Our first goal was to extend the short and elegant definitions of non-interactive encryption/signatures to the interactive setting, without making the definitions long and tedious. Unfortunately, in the interactive setting things *are* more complicated, as issues of concurrency and state, among others, must be dealt with. The way we managed to achieve our goal, was to split our definitions into two parts. The first (somewhat boring) part is *independent* of the particular primitive (e.g., PKE/PKMA), and simply introduces the bare minimum of notions/notation to deal with interaction. For example (see Section 2 for details), we define (a) what it means to have (concurrent) oracle access to an *interactive party* under attack; and (b) what it means to 'act as a wire' between two honest parties (for brevity, we call this trivial, but unavoidable, attack a 'ping-pong' attack). Once the notation is developed, however, our actual definitions of possibly interactive PKE/PKMA are *as short and simple as in the non-interactive setting* (see Definitions 5 and 6). E.g., in the PKMA setting (Definition 6) the attacker $\mathcal{A}$ has (concurrent) oracle access to the honest signer (as defined in (a)), and simultaneously tries to convince an honest verifier (i.e., "challenger"). $\mathcal{A}$ wins if the challenger accepts, and $\mathcal{A}$'s forgery was not a 'ping-pong' of one of its conversations with the signer (as defined in (b)).[3] Overall, the definition consists of the same couple of lines as in the non-interactive setting! And the same holds for the encryption case in Definition 5, which naturally generalizes the notion of CCA-security to the interactive setting.

BETTER EFFICIENCY/ASSUMPTIONS VIA INTERACTION. Turning from definitions to constructions, we show how a *single* extra round of interaction (i.e., a 2-round protocol) can help "solve" (in a sense explained in Footnote 1) two of the arguably toughest open problems in the areas of non-interactive PKE and PKMA, respectively.

In the area of PKE, the question is to build a CCA-secure PKE from a CPA-secure PKE. In principle, such constructions are known using an appropriately-chosen notion of non-interactive zero-knowledge proofs [18,34,35,37,29]. However, all these constructions are generally inefficient and considered somewhat unsatisfactory, since they use the code of the given CPA-secure encryption scheme. In particular, the question of finding so called *black-box* constructions of CCA-encryption from CPA-encryption remains open. In fact, although several partial progress along both positive (e.g., [12,11,30]) and negative (e.g., [23])

---

[3] This generalizes the notion of *strong* unforgeability, as opposed to regular unforgeability, as was done in DDN [18].

fronts was made, the general question remains elusive. In contrast, we show a relatively simple, black-box, 2-round CCA-secure encryption from CPA-secure encryption (in fact, the two primitives are *equivalent*). We notice that the DDN paper [18] itself already made a similar conclusion, by presenting a 3-round black-box protocol from any CPA-secure PKE.[4] Thus, aside from presenting a formal model for interactive CCA-secure encryption, our result can be viewed as improving the round efficiency of the DDN paper from 3 to 2.

In the area of PKMA, the "theory" question was settled pretty quickly, by showing that the strongest security notion for signature schemes — strong existential unforgeability against chosen message attack — can be realized assuming the mere existence of one-way functions [24,33,3,4,36]. Unfortunately, the generic constructions were primarily of theoretical interest, and did not result in practical enough signature schemes. In fact, practical signature schemes (outside of the random oracle model [7,21,38,25]) are only constructed from a handful of "not-too-standard" number-theoretic assumptions, such as 'strong RSA' [14,22] and 'Bilinear-Diffie-Hellman' [39], and even these 'practical' constructions were generally somewhat slow, requiring generation of primes, long keys or bilinear maps. In particular, one of the main open questions is to build an *efficient* digital signature scheme from a standard assumption, such as factoring, CDH or DDH.

In contrast, we show very efficient, 2-round, strongly unforgeable PKMA schemes from virtually all standard assumptions, including factoring, CDH and DDH. In fact, although we are not aware of any paper explicitly claiming this result, *it follows in a relatively simple manner by combining various prior works.*[5] Let us explain. With a different motivation in mind, the DDN paper [18] showed a simple 3-round[6] PKMA scheme from any CCA-secure encryption. At the time, CCA-secure PKE was considered a very 'advanced' primitive, so the construction was not considered 'efficient'. Over the years, though, many truly efficient CCA-secure schemes were constructed from virtually all popular assumptions, including factoring [26], CDH [40] and DDH [13] (despite the fact that no such efficient signature schemes are known from these assumptions!). Thus, these results, if combined, immediately yield an efficient 3-round PKMA from all these assumptions. Moreover, it is well known (e.g., see [28,1]) that one can reduce the number of rounds from 3 to 2 by also using a message authentication code (MAC), in addition to CCA-secure encryption. Of course, in theory, a MAC is implied by a CCA-secure PKE, albeit in an inefficient manner. Moreover, until recently, even direct efficient MAC constructions from concrete assumptions, such as DDH [31] and factoring [32], required long keys (quadratic in security parameter). Fortunately, Dodis et al. [16] recently observed an elementary

---

[4] Although they do not give a formal definition/proof, their construction is easily seen to be secure in our model.

[5] Except only establishing regular unforgeability, but the actual constructions are easily seen to be strongly unforgeable.

[6] The construction becomes 2-round if the verifier knows the authenticated message in advance.

efficient (probabilistic) MAC construction from any CCA-secure scheme. This gives an efficient 2-round PKMA scheme from any CCA-secure encryption. We also manage to further optimize the resulting construction, and obtain a really simple (new!) 2-round protocol, depicted in Figure 3. In turn, this gives efficient 2-round PKMA from a variety of standard assumptions, including factoring, CDH and DDH.[7]

DUALITY BETWEEN INTERACTIVE PKE AND PKMA. Interestingly, our 2-round CCA-secure PKE uses a *signing* key as its long-term "decryption secret" (and generates several ephemeral keys for the CPA-secure scheme), while our 2-round strongly unforgeable PKMA scheme uses a *decryption* key for a CCA-secure encryption as its long term "authentication secret". We show that this duality is not a coincidence. In fact, our 2-round results follow as corollaries of two more general schemes, depicted in Figures 1 and 2: an interactive CCA-secure scheme from any (interactive or not) strongly unforgeable PKMA scheme (plus any CPA-secure PKE[8]), and an interactive strongly unforgeable PKMA scheme from any (interactive or not) CCA-secure PKE. The 'duality' of our results (authentication using encryption and vice-versa) shows that, perhaps, the practical/theoretical distinction between *interactive* encryption and authentication is not as great as one could have guessed by looking at what is known in the *non-interactive* setting.

OVERCOMING IMPOSSIBILITY RESULTS. We also show that our simple definitional framework (one generic/reusable 'long-and-boring' part followed by many application-specific 'short-and-intuitive' parts) easily lends itself to various extensions. Examples include various notions of privacy and/or authenticity which are *impossible* in the non-interactive setting, such as forward-secure PKE and the notion of replay-secure PKE/PKMA that we introduce in this work.

1.2   Preliminaries and Notation

We denote by $\lambda \in \mathbb{N}$ the security parameter. A function $\epsilon(\lambda)$ is said *negligible* if it is a positive function that vanishes faster than the inverse of any polynomial in λ. If X is a set, let $x \xleftarrow{\$} X$ denote the process of selecting x uniformly at random in X. An algorithm $\mathcal{A}$ is called *PPT* if it is a probabilistic Turing machine whose running time is bounded by some polynomial in λ. If $\mathcal{A}$ is a PPT algorithm, then $y \xleftarrow{\$} \mathcal{A}(x)$ denotes the process of running $\mathcal{A}$ on input x and assigning its output to y.

---

[7] Of course, in practice one should not use CCA-secure encryption to build a MAC (instead, one should use practical MACs such as CBC-MAC or HMAC), but here we use it to establish *efficient feasibility results* from concrete number-theoretic assumptions.

[8] For the sake of elegance and modularity, we use a slightly stronger notion of so called "1-bounded CCA-secure PKE", but the latter can be built from any CPA-secure PKE [12].

2   Defining Message Transmission Protocols

In this section we introduce *message transmission protocols*: we define their syntax as well as suitable notions of confidentiality (called iCCA security) and authenticity (called iCMA security).

We give a generic definition of message transmission protocols involving two parties: a sender S and a receiver R, such that the goal of S is to send a message m to R while preserving certain security properties on m. In particular, in the next two sections we consider arguably the most basic security properties: the confidentiality/authenticity of the messages sent by S to R. Formally, a message transmission protocol Π consists of algorithms (Setup, S, R) defined as follows:

Setup(1^λ): on input the security parameter λ, the setup algorithm generates a pair of keys (sendk, recvk). In particular, these keys contain an implicit description of the message space $\mathcal{M}$.

S(sendk, m): is a possibly interactive algorithm that is run with the sender key sendk and a message $m \in \mathcal{M}$ as private inputs.

R(recvk): is a possibly interactive algorithm that takes as private input the receiver key recvk, and whose output is a message $m \in \mathcal{M}$ or an error $\perp$.

When S and R are jointly run, they exchange messages in a specific order, e.g., S starts by sending M_1, R sends M_2, S sends M_3, and so on and so forth until they both terminate. We say that Π is an n-round protocol if the number of messages exchanged between S and R during a run of the protocol is n. If Π is 1-round, then we say that Π is *non-interactive*. Since the sender gets no output, we assume without loss of generality that the *sender always speaks last*. Thus, in an n-round protocol, R (resp. S) speaks first if n is even (resp. odd). For compact notation, we denote with $\langle S(sendk, m), R(recvk) \rangle = m'$ the process of running S and R on inputs (sendk, m) and recvk respectively, and assigning R's output to m'. In our notation, we will use $m \in \mathcal{M}$ for messages (aka plaintexts), and capital M for protocol messages.

Definition 1 (Correctness). *A message transmission protocol* Π = (Setup, S, R) *is correct if for all honestly generated keys* (sendk, recvk) $\xleftarrow{\$}$ Setup(1^λ), *and all messages* $m \in \mathcal{M}$, *we have that* $\langle S(sendk, m), R(recvk) \rangle = m$ *holds with all but negligible probability*.

Defining Security: Man-in-the-Middle Adversaries. In our work, we assume that the sender and the receiver speak in the presence of powerful adversaries that have full control of the communication channel, i.e., the adversary can eavesdrop the content of the communication, and it can stop/delay/alter the messages passing over the channel. Roughly speaking, the goal of an adversary is to violate a given security property (say confidentiality or authenticity) in a run of the protocol that we call the *challenge session*. Formally, this session is a protocol execution $\langle S(sendk, m), \mathcal{A}^{R(recvk)} \rangle$ or $\langle \mathcal{A}^{S(sendk, \cdot)}, R(recvk) \rangle$ where the adversary runs with a honest party (S or R). By writing $\mathcal{A}^P$, we mean that the adversary has oracle access to *multiple* honest copies of party P (where P = R or P = S), i.e., $\mathcal{A}$ can start as many copies of P as it wishes, and it can run the message transmission protocol with each of these copies. This essentially formalizes the fact that the adversary can "sit in the middle of two honest parties" relaying messages between them in an active way. Sometimes, we also write $\mathcal{A}^{\mathsf{P}_k}$ to denote that the adversary can start at most k copies of party P. In our model we assume that whenever $\mathcal{A}$ sends a message to the oracle P, then $\mathcal{A}$ always obtains P's output. In particular, in the case of the receiver oracle, when $\mathcal{A}$ sends the last protocol message to R, $\mathcal{A}$ obtains the (private) output of the receiver, i.e., a message m or $\perp$.

Since all these protocol sessions can be run in a concurrent way, the adversary might entirely replay the challenge session by using its oracle. This is something that we would like to prevent in our definitions. To formalize this idea, we take an approach similar to the one introduced by Bellare and Rogaway [6] in the context of key exchange, which is based on the idea of "matching conversations". First of all, we introduce a notion of time during the execution of the security experiment. We stress that this is done for ease of analysis of the security model: there is no need to keep track of global timing in the real protocols. Let t be a global counter which is progressively incremented every time a party (including the adversary) sends a message, and assume that every message sent by a party (S, R or $\mathcal{A}$) gets timestamped with the current time t. Using this notion of time, we define the transcript of a protocol session as follows:

Definition 2 (Protocol Transcript). *The transcript of a protocol session between two parties is the timestamped sequence of messages exchanged by the parties during a run of the message transmission protocol Π. If Π is n-round, then a transcript T is of the form $T = \langle (M_1, t_1), \ldots, (M_n, t_n) \rangle$, where $M_1, \ldots, M_n$ are the exchanged messages, and $t_1, \ldots, t_n$ are the respective timestamps.*

In a protocol run $\langle \mathsf{S}(\mathsf{send}k, m), \mathcal{A}^{\mathsf{R}(\mathsf{recv}k)} \rangle$ (resp. $\langle \mathcal{A}^{\mathsf{S}(\mathsf{send}k, \cdot)}, \mathsf{R}(\mathsf{recv}k) \rangle$) we have a transcript T^* of the challenge session between S and $\mathcal{A}$ (resp. $\mathcal{A}$ and R), and Q transcripts $T_1, \ldots, T_Q$, one for each of the Q sessions established by $\mathcal{A}$ with R (resp. S) via the oracle. While we postpone to the next two sections the definition of specific security properties of message transmission (e.g., confidentiality and authenticity), our goal here is to formalize in a generic fashion which adversaries are effective for "uninteresting"/unavoidable reasons. Namely, when the challenge session is obtained by entirely replaying one of the oracle sessions: what we call a "ping-pong" attack, that we formalize via the following notion of matching transcripts.

Definition 3 (Matching Transcripts). *Let $T = \langle (M_1, t_1), \ldots, (M_n, t_n) \rangle$ and $T^* = \langle (M_1^*, t_1^*), \ldots, (M_n^*, t_n^*) \rangle$ be two protocol transcripts. We say that T matches T^* ($T \equiv T^*$, for short) if $\forall i = 1, \ldots, n$, $M_i = M_i^*$ and the two timestamp sequences are "alternating", i.e., $t_1 < t_1^* < t_2^* < t_2 < t_3 < \cdots < t_{n-1} < t_n < t_n^*$ if R speaks first, or $t_1^* < t_1 < t_2 < t_2^* < t_3^* < \cdots < t_{n-1} < t_n < t_n^*$ if S speaks first. We remark that the notion of match is not commutative.*

Given all the definitions above, we can define the notion of ping-pong adversary:

Definition 4 (Ping-pong Adversary). *Consider a run of the protocol Π involving $\mathcal{A}$ and a honest party (it can be either $\langle \mathsf{S}(\mathsf{send}k, m), \mathcal{A}^{\mathsf{R}(\mathsf{recv}k)} \rangle$ or*

$\langle \mathcal{A}^{S(\text{sendk},\cdot)}, R(\text{recvk}) \rangle$), and let T^* be the transcript of the challenge session, and $T_1, \ldots, T_Q$ be the transcripts of all the oracle sessions established by $\mathcal{A}$. Then we say that $\mathcal{A}$ is a ping-pong adversary if there is a transcript $T \in \{T_1, \ldots, T_Q\}$ such that T matches T^*, i.e., $T \equiv T^*$.

Interactive Chosen-Ciphertext-Secure Encryption. Here we propose a suitable notion of confidentiality for message transmission protocols that we call *interactive chosen ciphertext security* (iCCA). Our notion is designed as a very natural generalization of the classical notion of IND−CCA security to the interactive setting. In fact, IND−CCA security is a special case of iCCA security for 1-round (i.e., non-interactive) protocols (we leave this check to the reader). Roughly speaking, in the IND−CCA definition the adversary has to distinguish whether a given "challenge" ciphertext encrypts a message m_0 or m_1 while having access to a decryption oracle. To make the definition non-trivial, the adversary is denied to query the decryption oracle on the challenge ciphertext. Our notion of iCCA security is obtained similarly: the adversary $\mathcal{A}$ interacts with a sender which sends either m_0 or m_1 and $\mathcal{A}$ has to tell the two cases apart while having access to the receiver (instead of the decryption oracle); the restriction on the challenge ciphertext is replaced by requiring that $\mathcal{A}$ cannot be ping-pong. The formal definition follows.

Let $\Pi = (\text{Setup}, S, R)$ be a message transmission protocol and $\mathcal{A}$ be an adversary. To define iCCA security, consider the following experiment:

Experiment $\mathbf{Exp}_{\Pi,\mathcal{A}}^{\text{iCCA}}(\lambda)$

$b \xleftarrow{\$} \{0,1\}$; $(\text{sendk}, \text{recvk}) \xleftarrow{\$} \text{Setup}(1^\lambda)$
$(m_0, m_1) \leftarrow \mathcal{A}^{R(\text{recvk})}(\text{sendk})$
$b' \leftarrow \langle S(\text{sendk}, m_b), \mathcal{A}^{R(\text{recvk})}(\text{sendk}) \rangle$
If $b' = b$ and $\mathcal{A}$ is not "ping-pong", then output 1. Else output 0.

Definition 5 (iCCA security). *For any $\lambda \in \mathbb{N}$, we define the advantage of an adversary $\mathcal{A}$ in breaking iCCA security of a message transmission protocol Π as* $\mathbf{Adv}_{\Pi,\mathcal{A}}^{\text{iCCA}}(\lambda) = \Pr[\mathbf{Exp}_{\Pi,\mathcal{A}}^{\text{iCCA}}(\lambda) = 1] - \frac{1}{2}$, *and we say that Π is iCCA-secure if for any PPT $\mathcal{A}$, $\mathbf{Adv}_{\Pi,\mathcal{A}}^{\text{iCCA}}(\lambda)$ is negligible. We call a message transmission protocol satisfying this notion an* interactive encryption *scheme.*

As we mentioned in the introduction, it is worth noting that our definition is similar to the one proposed by Katz in [27]. The main difference is in the restrictions applied to the adversary in the security game. In [27] this is realized by means of a notion of "equality of transcripts" which considers only equality of messages (in the same order) and leaves any time constraint to the specific protocols realizations. Our security definition, instead, directly takes into account time constraints in the security experiment via the notion of matching transcripts. To see the difference between the two definitions with an example, consider an adversary who creates an oracle session having the same transcript as the one of the challenge session, but where the timestamps of the messages are not correctly alternating. Such an adversary would not be legal according to the definition of [27], but is legal (i.e., not ping-pong) according to ours.

EXTENSIONS. We also consider a weaker notion of iCCA security, called q-bounded-iCCA, in which the adversary is restricted to complete at most q sessions with the oracle R, i.e., in $\mathbf{Exp}_{\Pi,\mathcal{A}}^{\mathrm{iCCA}}(\lambda)$ we run $\mathcal{A}^{\mathrm{R}_q}$. This is the analogous of (non-interactive) q-bounded IND−CCA security [12].

We define an extension of interactive encryption in which both the sender and the receiver algorithms take a public string—a label—as an additional input (similarly to the non-interactive setting [8]). In the full version we provide a full formalization of *labeled* iCCA encryption and show that it can be generically constructed from 'plain' iCCA-secure encryption. Here we briefly recall that for any label L we use S^L to denote that an algorithm S takes as input L.

Interactive Chosen-Message Secure Public Key Message Authentication. Here we propose a suitable notion of authenticity for message transmission protocols that we call *interactive unforgeability under chosen message attacks* (iCMA). Our notion is designed as a very natural generalization to the interactive setting of the standard notion of strong unforgeability (suf-cma) for digital signatures. In fact, suf-cma security is a special case of iCMA security for 1-round protocols. Roughly speaking, in strong unforgeability the adversary has to produce a valid signature while having access to the signer. In order for the definition to be non-trivial, however, such signature has to be "new", i.e., not obtained from the signing oracle. Our notion of iCMA security naturally extends suf-cma as follows: the adversary $\mathcal{A}$ has to convince a receiver while having oracle access to the sender (instead of the signing oracle); the requirement that the signature must be new is replaced by requiring that $\mathcal{A}$ is not ping-pong. The formal definition follows.

Let $\Pi = (\mathsf{Setup}, \mathsf{S}, \mathsf{R})$ be a message transmission protocol and $\mathcal{A}$ be an adversary. To define iCMA security, consider the following experiment:

Experiment $\mathbf{Exp}_{\Pi,\mathcal{A}}^{\mathrm{iCMA}}(\lambda)$

   $(\mathsf{sendk}, \mathsf{recvk}) \xleftarrow{\$} \mathsf{Setup}(1^\lambda)$

   $m^* \leftarrow \langle \mathcal{A}^{\mathsf{S}(\mathsf{sendk},\cdot)}(\mathsf{recvk}), \mathsf{R}(\mathsf{recvk}) \rangle$

   If $m^* \neq \bot$ and $\mathcal{A}$ is not "ping-pong", then output 1. Else output 0.

Definition 6 (iCMA security). *For any $\lambda \in \mathbb{N}$, the advantage of $\mathcal{A}$ in breaking the* iCMA *security of a message transmission protocol Π is* $\mathbf{Adv}_{\Pi,\mathcal{A}}^{\mathrm{iCMA}}(\lambda) = \Pr[\mathbf{Exp}_{\Pi,\mathcal{A}}^{\mathrm{iCMA}}(\lambda) = 1]$, *and we say that Π is* iCMA-*secure if for any PPT $\mathcal{A}$,* $\mathbf{Adv}_{\Pi,\mathcal{A}}^{\mathrm{iCMA}}(\lambda)$ *is negligible. We call a message transmission protocol satisfying this notion a* public key message authentication *(PKMA) protocol.*

3   Basic Constructions

In this section we propose realizations of message transmission protocols satisfying our iCCA and iCMA security notions. Interestingly, our constructions show that iCCA security is implied by the iCMA and IND−CPA notions, whereas (somehow vice-versa) iCMA security is directly implied by iCCA. Our results thus show that in the interactive setting—and with a minimum level of interaction

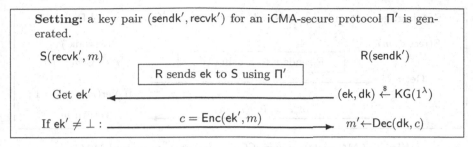

Fig. 1. iCCA protocol from iCMA-secure PKMA and *1-bounded*-IND−CCA encryption

(i.e., 2 rounds) indeed!—the notions of confidentiality and authenticity present somewhat surprising and interesting relations unknown in the non-interactive case.

iCCA Encryption from IND−CPA Encryption and iCMA PKMA. Our result is a simple interactive encryption protocol that is based on a PKMA protocol Π' and a public key encryption scheme $\mathcal{E} = (\mathsf{KG}, \mathsf{Enc}, \mathsf{Dec})$. The idea is simple and is illustrated in Figure 1: the receiver sends a "fresh" public key ek authenticated using Π', and the sender encrypts the message using ek. As we show in our theorem below, the PKMA protocol has to be iCMA-secure, while the PKE scheme $\mathcal{E}$ needs only to be *1-bounded*-IND−CCA-secure. Concretely, Π' can be a strongly unforgeable signature and $\mathcal{E}$ can be constructed using an IND−CPA-secure encryption (as shown by Cramer et al. [12]), thus yielding an *optimal* 2-round encryption protocol that is iCCA-secure based only on IND−CPA security. A more precise description follows.

Let $\Pi' = (\mathsf{Setup}', \mathsf{S}', \mathsf{R}')$ be a PKMA protocol, and $\mathcal{E} = (\mathsf{KG}, \mathsf{Enc}, \mathsf{Dec})$ be a (non-interactive) public key encryption scheme. We build protocol $\Pi = (\mathsf{Setup}, \mathsf{S}, \mathsf{R})$ as follows:

Setup(1^λ): run $(\mathsf{sendk}', \mathsf{recvk}') \xleftarrow{\$} \mathsf{Setup}'(1^\lambda)$ and output $\mathsf{sendk} = \mathsf{recvk}'$ and $\mathsf{recvk} = \mathsf{sendk}'$.

S(sendk, m): first run the PKMA protocol Π' with R by playing the role of the receiver, i.e., S runs $\mathsf{R}'(\mathsf{recvk}')$. If Π' terminates correctly with output ek, then send $c = \mathsf{Enc}(\mathsf{ek}, m)$ to R. Otherwise, stop running.

R(recvk): generate $(\mathsf{ek}, \mathsf{dk}) \xleftarrow{\$} \mathsf{KG}(1^\lambda)$, run $\mathsf{S}'(\mathsf{sendk}', \mathsf{ek})$ to send ek with authenticity to S, and keep dk as private information. After Π' terminates, on input a message c from S, the receiver algorithm computes $m \leftarrow \mathsf{Dec}(\mathsf{dk}, c)$ and returns the message m as its private output.

Theorem 1. *If $\mathcal{E}$ is 1-bounded-IND−CCA-secure and Π' is iCMA-secure, then Π is iCCA-secure.*

For lack of space, the proof of the theorem appears in the full version. As an interesting consequence of Theorem 1 we obtain an equivalence between the notions of IND−CPA and iCCA security:

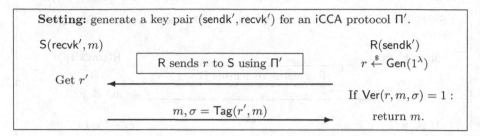

Fig. 2. iCMA protocol from iCCA-secure encryption and MACs

Corollary 1. *2-round-iCCA encryption exists if and only if (non-interactive)* IND−CPA *PKE exists.*

iCMA-secure PKMA from iCCA security. We show how to realize iCMA-secure message transmission from any message transmission protocol that is iCCA-secure, and any strongly unforgeable MAC. The protocol is based on an old idea of realizing public key authentication via CCA-secure encryption and message authentication codes. The basic idea is that the authenticator shows its ability to decrypt: the verifier encrypts a MAC key r for the authenticator, who decrypts and sends back the MAC of message m using the key r. This protocol (briefly sketched in Figure 2) implicitly appeared first in [28] and was proven secure in [1]. Here we generalize this construction in the framework of our definitions, i.e., by using (possibly interactive) iCCA-secure encryption in place of (non-interactive) IND−CCA-secure encryption. Furthermore, in the full version we generalize a 3-round protocol earlier proposed by Dolev, Dwork and Naor [18] that is based only on iCCA security.

Let MAC = (Gen, Tag, Ver) be a strongly unforgeable MAC with message space $\mathcal{M}$ and key space $\mathcal{K}$, and let $\Pi' = (\mathsf{Setup}', \mathsf{S}', \mathsf{R}')$ be an encryption protocol with message space $\mathcal{K}$. We build a PKMA protocol $\Pi = (\mathsf{Setup}, \mathsf{S}, \mathsf{R})$ as follows.

Setup(1^λ): run (sendk′, recvk′) $\xleftarrow{\$}$ Setup′(1^λ) and output recvk = sendk′ and sendk = recvk′. The message space of the protocol Π is the message space $\mathcal{M}$ of the MAC.

S(sendk, m): run the encryption protocol Π' with R with reversed roles, i.e., S runs the receiver algorithm R′ of Π' while R will run the sender algorithm S′. Let r be the output of R′ at the end of the run of protocol Π'. Then S sends ($m, \sigma = \mathsf{Tag}(r, m)$) to R as the last message.

R(recvk): generate a fresh MAC key $r \xleftarrow{\$} \mathsf{Gen}(1^\lambda)$ and send r to S using the encryption protocol Π', i.e., R runs S′(sendk′, r). Once the encryption protocol is over, R waits for a message (m, σ') from S. If $\mathsf{Ver}(r, m, \sigma') = 1$ then R outputs m. Otherwise, it outputs $\perp$.

We can now state the following theorem (its proof is in the full version).

Theorem 2. *If Π' is iCCA-secure and* MAC *is strongly-unforgeable, then Π is an iCMA-secure message transmission protocol.*

Setting: $(\mathsf{ek}, \mathsf{dk})$ a key-pair for a labeled encryption scheme $(\mathsf{KG}, \mathsf{Enc}^L, \mathsf{Dec}^L)$ is generated.

$S(\mathsf{dk}, m)$		$R(\mathsf{ek})$
$r' \leftarrow \mathsf{Dec}^{\mathsf{ek}'}(\mathsf{dk}, c)$	$\xleftarrow{\quad \mathsf{ek}',\, c = \mathsf{Enc}^{\mathsf{ek}'}(\mathsf{ek}, r) \quad}$	$(\mathsf{ek}', \mathsf{dk}') \xleftarrow{\$} \mathsf{KG}(1^\lambda)$
		$r \xleftarrow{\$} \{0,1\}^\lambda$
If $r' \neq \bot$:	$\xrightarrow{\quad m, \sigma = \mathsf{Enc}^m(\mathsf{ek}', r') \quad}$	If $\mathsf{Dec}^m(\mathsf{dk}', \sigma) = r$
		return m.

Fig. 3. 2-round iCMA protocol from labeled IND−CCA-secure encryption

Remark 1. While the protocol uses a fresh MAC key for every session, we stress that a one-time MAC (e.g., a pairwise independent hash function) is not sufficient to prove iCMA security. Intuitively, the reason is that the adversary may fully-replay the first portion of the protocol (i.e., the one related to Π′) from the challenge session to many copies of the sender, each initialized with a different plaintext $m \neq m^*$, thus obtaining several MACs under the same key.

If we instantiate the above construction with a 1-round (aka non-interactive) iCCA-secure encryption scheme, and one of the constructions of MACs from IND−CCA encryption proposed in [16] (that have the advantage of having a 'compact' secret key), we then obtain an elegant and efficient 2-round PKMA protocol based only on IND−CCA security. Moreover, by directly observing the MAC of [16] and the resulting protocol, we managed to further optimize this protocol: we notice that the ephemeral secret key dk' (which is part of the MAC key with r) is only used for verification, and there is no need to encrypt it inside c; instead, we use labels to bind ek' with c. The resulting optimized protocol is presented in Figure 3.

By instantiating the result of Theorem 2 (and our optimization above) with known constructions of CCA-secure encryption from Factoring [26], DDH [13], or CDH [40], we obtain the following corollary.

Corollary 2. *If the Factoring (resp. DDH, CDH) assumption holds, there exists an efficient 2-round PKMA.*

Secure Round Extension of Message Transmission Protocols. In the full version we discuss a generic methodology to securely increase the number of rounds of message transmission protocols. Although at a first glance this construction might not look very interesting as it decreases efficiency, it turns out to be particularly useful to achieve our stronger notions of (strong) replay security (see Section 4.1).

Theorem 3. *For any $n \geq 1$, if Π′ is an iCCA (resp. iCMA) secure n-round protocol, there exists an iCCA (resp. iCMA) secure $(n+1)$-round protocol Π.*

4   Advanced Security Properties from the Power of Interaction

We discuss three advanced security properties of message transmission protocols, each *requiring interaction*: deniability, forward security, and replay security.

While the first two properties have been already considered in previous work in the context of encryption, key exchange, and message authentication, the last one, replay security, is new and aims at obtaining more intuitive security definitions of message transmission. Interestingly, we show that replay security can be achieved only by interactive protocols, and that with enough interaction our notions of iCCA and iCMA security already provide replay-secure protocols.

Below we start with an informal discussion of these advanced security notions. Next, in Section 4.1, we formally introduce the new notion of replay-security. A formal treatment of forward security and deniability appears in the full version.

DENIABILITY.   We already mentioned that interactive PKE/PKMA might achieve advanced security properties which are impossible in the non-interactive setting. One such (well studied [18,20,19,15]) notion is that of deniable authentication, which was actually the original motivation of the DDN paper. Since this is not the main topic of this work, we only define the weakest notion of *passive deniability* (and its extension called 'passive forward deniability' [15]), and observe that our optimized 2-round variant from non-interactive CCA-secure PKE is passively forward deniable.[9]

FORWARD SECURITY.   Another example is the notion of *forward security*, which (intuitively) states that 'old' message transmissions should remain private even if the party's long term secret key is later compromised. Prior to our work, forward security has been extensively studied in the KE literature (in fact, in many cases being a mandatory part of a 'secure' KE). On the other hand, forward security is (obviously) impossible for non-interactive PKE without "changing the model"; e.g. by introducing global time periods, and periodically refreshing the secret key [9]. In contrast, no such impossibility exists for interactive PKE, and, indeed, our interactive PKE schemes are forward-secure, since all of them use ephemeral keys to actually encrypt the message.

REPLAY-SECURITY.   Yet another limitation of non-interactive PKE/PKMA schemes is that they necessarily suffer from what we informally (for now) term "replay" attacks. In the case of encryption, for example, an attacker can always record an 'old' ciphertext, and then manage to decrypt it much later. Similarly, a verifier can always pass an 'old' signature to another verifier in the future. Motivated by this impossibility, we formalize (to the best of our knowledge, for the first time) the notion of *replay-secure* (necessarily) interactive PKMA/PKE schemes. For the former, a honest verifier is assured that the "current" message is actually being authenticated by the secret key owner "now", as opposed

---

[9] The construction can be made 'actively deniable', with more rounds, using the techniques developed by [20].

to some time in the past. For the latter, a honest encryptor is similarly assured that the "current" message can only be decrypted by the secret key owner "now", as opposed to some time in the future. We then show that *any* interactive PKE/PKMA scheme which has at least 2 rounds is already replay-secure.[10] For example, we automatically get replay-secure PKE/PKMA schemes, by using the 2-round solutions in this paper.[11] We also notice that a very special case of our replay-secure PKMA, when the message space has cardinality 1, essentially corresponds to the strongest security notion for identification schemes, called impersonation security under concurrent attacks [5]. Here the attacker has concurrent oracle access to the prover (i.e., 'signer of a fixed message'), then loses this oracle access, and, finally, has to convince an honest verifier. In fact, our 2-round PKMA protocols, when specialized to this trivial case, essentially "collapse" to well-known challenge-response identification protocols from CCA-encryption and signature schemes, respectively. Of course, by having an extra "non-trivial" message, we think that replay-secure PKMA schemes should have more applications than concurrently secure identification schemes.

4.1 Replay Security

In what follows we formalize the notion of replay security, and then we show that traditional non-interactive protocols (e.g., CCA encryption and signatures) *cannot* be replay-secure. Intuitively, the reason is that a ciphertext or a digital signature can always be "replayed" after its transmission (this also explains our choice for the name of this notion).

TIME INTERVALS AND CONCURRENT SESSIONS. To formalize our definitions and argue more easily about concurrent sessions, we refine our notion of time and we introduce an intuitive terminology. If t and t' are time instants such that $t < t'$, then we denote with $[t, t']$ the *time interval* between t and t', i.e., the sequence $\langle t, t+1, t+2, \ldots, t' \rangle$. For every protocol transcript $T = \langle (M_1, t_1), \ldots, (M_n, t_n) \rangle$ (i.e., for every session) of an n-round protocol there exists a corresponding time interval $[t_1, t_n]$ in which the session starts and ends. Let $[t_1^*, t_n^*]$ and $[t_1, t_n]$ be the time intervals of two protocol sessions. We say that $[t_1^*, t_n^*]$ and $[t_1, t_n]$ *overlap* if $[t_1, t_n] \cap [t_1^*, t_n^*] \neq \emptyset$. Moreover, we say that $\mathcal{A}$ is an *overlapping* adversary if it generates an oracle session $[t_1, t_n]$ that overlaps with the challenge session $[t_1^*, t_n^*]$.

In the following lemma we show that in any protocol with at least two rounds, any ping-pong adversary is also overlapping. We use this general statement to prove that any 2-round secure message-transmission protocol is also replay-secure.

---

[10] For encryption, we also define a stronger notion of replay-security, which requires at least 3 rounds, and is realized by any 3-round CCA secure scheme.

[11] This includes already mentioned 2-round PKMA from CCA-encryption and 2-round PKE from signatures, as well as simple 2-round PKE/PKMA obtained by "extending" 1-round PKE/PKMA schemes.

Lemma 1. *Let $n \geq 2$ and Π be an n-round message transmission protocol. If $\mathcal{A}$ is a ping-pong adversary against Π, then $\mathcal{A}$ is overlapping.*

Proof. Assume by contradiction that $\mathcal{A}$ is not overlapping, then we show that $\mathcal{A}$ is not ping-pong. Let T^* and $[t_1^*, t_n^*]$ be the transcript and time interval of the challenge session. Since $\mathcal{A}$ is not overlapping, no oracle session T overlaps with T^*, i.e., for every oracle session with time interval $[t_1, t_n]$ it holds $[t_1^*, t_n^*] \cap [t_1, t_n] = \emptyset$. However, since $n \geq 2$, it is easy to see that if $[t_1^*, t_n^*] \cap [t_1, t_n] = \emptyset$ then the timestamps of these two sessions are not alternating, and thus $T \not\equiv T^*$.   □

Replay-Secure Public-Key Message Authentication. Informally speaking, a PKMA protocol is replay-secure if all oracle sessions initialized with the challenge plaintext m^* do not overlap with the challenge session. This essentially means that the adversary loses access to the legitimate signer (on message m^*) *before* starting to forge m^*.

For a more formal definition, consider the experiment $\mathbf{Exp}_{\Pi,\mathcal{A}}^{\mathsf{iCMA}}$ (defined in Section 2) and let $[t_1^*, t_n^*]$ be the time interval of the challenge session, and $\{[t_1^i, t_n^i]\}_{i=1,\ldots,Q}$ be the time intervals of all the oracle sessions established by $\mathcal{A}$. Moreover, let m^i be the plaintext used to initialize the sender oracle $\mathsf{S}(\mathsf{sendk}, m^i)$ in the i-th oracle session. Then we call $\mathcal{A}$ a *replay adversary* if there exists $i \in \{1, \ldots, Q\}$ such that $m^i = m^*$ and $[t_1^i, t_n^i] \cap [t_1^*, t_n^*] \neq \emptyset$. Replay security for PKMA is defined as as follows:

Definition 7 (Replay Secure PKMA). *Let $\mathbf{Exp}_{\Pi,\mathcal{A}}^{\mathsf{RSMA}}$ be the same experiment as $\mathbf{Exp}_{\Pi,\mathcal{A}}^{\mathsf{iCMA}}$, except that $\mathcal{A}$ is required not to be a replay adversary (instead of not being ping-pong). Then we say that an interactive protocol Π is a replay secure PKMA (RSMA for short) if for any PPT $\mathcal{A}$, its advantage $\mathbf{Adv}_{\Pi,\mathcal{A}}^{\mathsf{RSMA}}(\lambda) = \left| \Pr[\mathbf{Exp}_{\Pi,\mathcal{A}}^{\mathsf{RSMA}}(\lambda) = 1] - \frac{1}{2} \right|$ is negligible.*

First, in the following theorem we show that 1-round PKMA protocols cannot be replay-secure. Its proof is rather simple and follows from the fact that in 1-round protocols there is clearly no overlap between different sessions. Hence, the dummy adversary who replays a signature received from the legitimate signer is a valid adversary in the RSMA experiment.

Theorem 4. *Any 1-round iCMA-secure PKMA protocol is not RSMA-secure.*

It is worth noting that one can obtain 1-round replay-secure solutions in different models, e.g., by introducing global time periods and requiring the signer to always sign the message with the current timestamp. However, such a solution falls outside the pure non-interactive model considered by our work.

Therefore, while 1-round replay-secure PKMA cannot be achieved, in the following theorem we show that with at least *two* rounds of interaction any iCMA-secure protocol is a replay-secure PKMA.

Theorem 5. *For $n \geq 2$, any n-round iCMA-secure protocol Π is RSMA-secure.*

Proof. The proof follows by observing that if $\mathcal{A}$ is not a replay adversary in $\mathbf{Exp}_{\Pi,\mathcal{A}}^{\mathsf{RSMA}}$ (for Π with at least 2 rounds), then $\mathcal{A}$ is also not ping-pong in $\mathbf{Exp}_{\Pi,\mathcal{A}}^{\mathsf{iCMA}}$.

Namely, we show that for a non-replay $\mathcal{A}$ we have that for all $i = 1, \ldots, Q$, $T_i \not\equiv T^*$. For every i, there are only two possible cases: $m^i = m^*$ or $m^i \neq m^*$. If $m^i = m^*$, then $T_i \not\equiv T^*$ follows by Lemma 1. In the case of sessions i where $m^i \neq m^*$, assume by contradiction that $T_i \equiv T^*$. Then by definition of match the sessions must share the same protocol messages in the same order (i.e., $M_j^i = M_j^*$) which, by correctness, implies that $m^i = m^*$, a contradiction. $\square$

From Theorem 5 we obtain two interesting results that we summarize in the following corollary:

Corollary 3. *(1) There exists a simple 2-round replay-secure PKMA protocol based on any strongly unforgeable signature scheme (and thus on one-way functions); (2) there exists a simple 2-round replay-secure PKMA protocol based on any* IND−CCA*-secure PKE.*

The construction (1) follows by combining Theorem 5 with our round-extension result (Theorem 3) applied to any strongly unforgeable signature (aka 1-round iCMA-secure PKMA). The construction (2) from IND−CCA-secure PKE is instead obtained by applying Theorem 5 to our 2-round construction of Theorem 2 (instantiated with a non-interactive IND−CCA-secure PKE scheme).

Remark 2 (Relation to Concurrent-Secure Identification Schemes). Notice that in the special case when the message space has cardinality 1, our notion of replay-secure PKMA essentially corresponds to the strongest security notion for identification schemes, called impersonation security under concurrent attacks [5]. In this case (i.e., message space of cardinality 1), a PKMA can be indeed seen as an identification scheme. Moreover, by considering authentication with an empty message space, the 2-round PKMA protocols mentioned in Corollary 3 recover well known 2-round, signature-based and encryption-based, identification schemes (see, e.g., [2], and notice that outputting the secret key is indeed a secure MAC for an empty message space).

Replay-Secure Public-Key Encryption. Informally speaking, a PKE protocol is *replay-secure* if there is no overlap between the challenge session and all oracle sessions in which the plaintext revealed by the receiver is one of the two challenge plaintexts. In essence, this means that *during* the challenge session the adversary loses access to the legitimate decryptor, but only on the challenge plaintexts m_0 or m_1. More formally, consider the experiment $\mathbf{Exp}_{\Pi,\mathcal{A}}^{\mathsf{iCCA}}$ (defined in Section 2) and let $[t_1^*, t_n^*]$ be the time interval of the challenge session, and $\{[t_1^i, t_n^i]\}_{i=1,\ldots,Q}$ be the time intervals of all the oracle sessions established by $\mathcal{A}$. Moreover, let m^i be the plaintext revealed by the receiver in the i-th oracle session (wlog we only consider completed sessions). Then, we call $\mathcal{A}$ a *replay adversary* if there exists $i \in \{1, \ldots, Q\}$ such that $m^i = m_0$ or $m^i = m_1$, and $[t_1^i, t_n^i]$ overlaps with $[t_1^*, t_n^*]$. Replay security for PKE is defined as follows:

Definition 8 (Replay-Secure Encryption). *Let $\mathbf{Exp}_{\Pi,\mathcal{A}}^{\mathsf{RSE}}$ be the same as experiment $\mathbf{Exp}_{\Pi,\mathcal{A}}^{\mathsf{iCCA}}$, except that $\mathcal{A}$ is required not to be a replay adversary* *(instead of denying it to be ping-pong). Then we say that an interactive protocol* Π *is a* replace-secure encryption *(RSE) if for any PPT* $\mathcal{A}$, *its advantage* $\mathbf{Adv}_{\Pi,\mathcal{A}}^{\mathsf{RSE}}(\lambda) = \Pr[\mathbf{Exp}_{\Pi,\mathcal{A}}^{\mathsf{RSE}}(\lambda) = 1] - \frac{1}{2}$ *is negligible.*

It is worth mentioning that the notion of replay-secure PKE is similar to the notion of Replayable CCA-secure encryption (RCCA) introduced by Canetti, Krawczyk and Nielsen [10]. In RCCA security the adversary is allowed to submit any ciphertext c to the decryption oracle, except that if c decrypts to m_0 or m_1 the adversary gets a special string `test` as response.

Similarly to replay-secure PKMA, in the following theorems we show that replay-secure PKE requires at least 2-rounds of interaction to be achieved.

Theorem 6. *Any 1-round* iCCA-*secure PKE protocol is not* RSE-*secure.*

The proof is obtained by considering the adversary who replays the challenge ciphertext to the receiver.

Theorem 7. *For* $n \geq 2$, *any* n-round iCCA-*secure protocol* Π *is* RSE-*secure.*

The proof is similar to that of Theorem 5 and is postponed to the full version.

From Theorem 7 we obtain a collection of nice results summarized in the following Corollary:

Corollary 4. *(1)* IND−CPA-*secure PKE is sufficient to build* RSE-*secure PKE; (2) there exists an efficient 2-round* RSE-*secure PKE protocol based on 1-bounded-* IND−CCA-*secure PKE and signature schemes (see Theorem 1); (3) there exists an efficient 2-round* RSE-*secure PKE protocol based on any* IND−CCA-*secure PKE (via our round-extension transformation of Theorem 3).*

Strong Replay-Secure Encryption. We notice that our definition of replay security (for both PKMA and PKE) does not allow the adversary to suspend "critical" sessions (e.g., sessions authenticating m^*, or sessions which decrypt to m_0 or m_1) during the challenge session, and to later resume these sessions once the challenge session is over. While allowing such suspended sessions would not make sense for PKMA (indeed observe that the outcome of the security experiment is determined upon the end of the challenge session), it might be a reasonable strengthening for replay-secure PKE. Here we define strong-replay-secure PKE, and we show that two rounds of interaction are insufficient to achieve strong replay-security with suspended sessions (see Theorem 8 below), but *three* rounds are enough and indeed any (at least) 3-round iCCA-secure PKE is strong replay-secure (cf. Theorem 9).

Towards defining strong replay security more formally, let us say that $[t_1, t_n]$ is *off* during $[t_1^*, t_n^*]$ if for all $j = 1, \ldots, n$ we have that $t_j \notin [t_1^*, t_n^*]$. We call $\mathcal{A}$ a *strong replay adversary* if there exists $i \in \{1, \ldots, Q\}$ such that $m^i = m_0$ or $m^i = m_1$, and $[t_1^i, t_n^i]$ is *not off* during $[t_1^*, t_n^*]$.

Definition 9 (Strong Replay-Secure Encryption). *Let* $\mathbf{Exp}_{\Pi,\mathcal{A}}^{\mathsf{sRSE}}$ *be the same experiment as* $\mathbf{Exp}_{\Pi,\mathcal{A}}^{\mathsf{iCCA}}$, *except that* $\mathcal{A}$ *is required not to be a strong replay adversary (instead of denying it to be ping-pong). Then we say that an interactive protocol* Π *is a* strong replay secure encryption *(sRSE) if for any PPT* $\mathcal{A}$, *its advantage* $\mathbf{Adv}_{\Pi,\mathcal{A}}^{\mathsf{sRSE}}(\lambda) = \Pr[\mathbf{Exp}_{\Pi,\mathcal{A}}^{\mathsf{sRSE}}(\lambda) = 1] - \frac{1}{2}$ *is negligible.*

Theorem 8. *Any 2-round* iCCA*-secure PKE protocol is not* sRSE*-secure.*

Proof. To prove the theorem we show that there exists an adversary $\mathcal{A}$ who is not a strong replay adversary in $\mathbf{Exp}_{\Pi,\mathcal{A}}^{\mathsf{sRSE}}$ but is a ping-pong adversary. Then, being ping-pong, $\mathcal{A}$ can trivially obtain a decryption of the challenge plaintext.

First, observe that in any 2-round protocol we have the first message from R to S. So, consider the following adversary $\mathcal{A}$ that plays the role of the receiver in the challenge session:

- $\mathcal{A}$ queries R on a new session and obtains M_1 with timestamp $t_1 = t$.
- $\mathcal{A}$ sends M_1 to the honest sender S as the first protocol message in the challenge session (here M_1 gets timestamp $t_1^* = t + 1$). $\mathcal{A}$ receives back M_2 from S, where M_2 gets timestamp $t_2^* = t + 2$.
- $\mathcal{A}$ forwards M_2 to R in the session previously opened in step 1 (this message gets timestamp $t_2 = t + 3$).

While $\mathcal{A}$ is clearly ping-pong according to Definition 4, $\mathcal{A}$ is still not a strong replay adversary in $\mathbf{Exp}_{\Pi,\mathcal{A}}^{\mathsf{sRSE}}$ since $t_1, t_2 \notin [t+1, t+2]$. This is exactly a case in which the adversary suspended a session.   □

Theorem 9. *For $n \geq 3$, any n-round* iCCA*-secure protocol Π is* sRSE*-secure.*

The proof is basically the same as that of Theorem 7, except that here we use the following lemma to show that for 3-round protocols any ping-pong adversary generates an oracle session (decrypting to one of the challenge plaintexts) which is not off during the challenge session.

Lemma 2. *Let $n \geq 3$, and let T, $[t_1, t_n]$ and T^*, $[t_1^*, t_n^*]$ be the transcripts and time intervals of two sessions of an n-round protocol. If $[t_1, t_n]$ is off during $[t_1^*, t_n^*]$, then T does not match with T^*.*

Proof. Recall that $[t_1, t_n]$ is off during $[t_1^*, t_n^*]$ if for all $j = 1, \ldots, n$ we have that $t_j \notin [t_1^*, t_n^*]$. This means that either one of the following cases occurs: (1) $[t_1^*, t_n^*] \cap [t_1, t_n] = \emptyset$, (2) $[t_1^*, t_n^*] \cap [t_1, t_n] \neq \emptyset$. Case (1) is identical to that of Lemma 1. In case (2), we have that the two sessions overlap, and we also know that $t_j \notin [t_1^*, t_n^*], \forall j = 1, \ldots, n$, that is $t_1 < t_1^*$ and $t_3 > t_3^*$. Since there are at least 3 rounds, there exists at least a distinct timestamp t_2 such that $t_1 < t_2 < t_n$ and such that t_2 satisfies either one of the following conditions: $t_1 < t_2 < t_1^*$, or $t_n > t_2 > t_n^*$. However, one can again check that in neither one of these cases the timestamps are correctly alternating. Therefore, $T \not\equiv T^*$.   □

Acknowledgements. The authors would like to thank Adam O'Neill, Victor Shoup and Stefano Tessaro for valuable discussions on this work. The research of Yevgeniy Dodis is partially supported by gifts from VMware Labs and Google, and NSF grants 1319051, 1314568, 1065288, 1017471. The research of Dario Fiore is partially supported by the European Commission Seventh Framework Programme Marie Curie Cofund Action AMAROUT-II (grant no. 291803), and the Madrid Regional Government under project PROMETIDOS-CM (ref. S2009/TIC1465).

References

1. Bellare, M., Canetti, R., Krawczyk, H.: A modular approach to the design and analysis of authentication and key exchange protocols (extended abstract). In: 30th ACM STOC, pp. 419–428. ACM Press (May 1998)
2. Bellare, M., Fischlin, M., Goldwasser, S., Micali, S.: Identification protocols secure against reset attacks. In: Pfitzmann, B. (ed.) EUROCRYPT 2001. LNCS, vol. 2045, pp. 495–511. Springer, Heidelberg (2001)
3. Bellare, M., Micali, S.: How to sign given any trapdoor function (extended abstract). In: 20th ACM STOC, pp. 32–42. ACM Press (May 1988)
4. Bellare, M., Micali, S.: How to sign given any trapdoor function. Journal of the ACM 39(1), 214–233 (1992)
5. Bellare, M., Palacio, A.: GQ and schnorr identification schemes: Proofs of security against impersonation under active and concurrent attacks. In: Yung, M. (ed.) CRYPTO 2002. LNCS, vol. 2442, pp. 162–177. Springer, Heidelberg (2002)
6. Bellare, M., Rogaway, P.: Entity authentication and key distribution. In: Stinson, D.R. (ed.) CRYPTO 1993. LNCS, vol. 773, pp. 232–249. Springer, Heidelberg (1994)
7. Bellare, M., Rogaway, P.: Random oracles are practical: A paradigm for designing efficient protocols. In: Ashby, V. (ed.) ACM CCS 1993, pp. 62–73. ACM Press (November 1993)
8. Camenisch, J., Shoup, V.: Practical verifiable encryption and decryption of discrete logarithms. In: Boneh, D. (ed.) CRYPTO 2003. LNCS, vol. 2729, pp. 126–144. Springer, Heidelberg (2003)
9. Canetti, R., Halevi, S., Katz, J.: A forward-secure public-key encryption scheme. In: Biham, E. (ed.) EUROCRYPT 2003. LNCS, vol. 2656, pp. 255–271. Springer, Heidelberg (2003)
10. Canetti, R., Krawczyk, H., Nielsen, J.B.: Relaxing chosen-ciphertext security. In: Boneh, D. (ed.) CRYPTO 2003. LNCS, vol. 2729, pp. 565–582. Springer, Heidelberg (2003)
11. Choi, S.G., Dachman-Soled, D., Malkin, T., Wee, H.: Black-box construction of a non-malleable encryption scheme from any semantically secure one. In: Canetti, R. (ed.) TCC 2008. LNCS, vol. 4948, pp. 427–444. Springer, Heidelberg (2008)
12. Cramer, R., Hanaoka, G., Hofheinz, D., Imai, H., Kiltz, E., Pass, R., Shelat, A., Vaikuntanathan, V.: Bounded CCA2-secure encryption. In: Kurosawa, K. (ed.) ASIACRYPT 2007. LNCS, vol. 4833, pp. 502–518. Springer, Heidelberg (2007)
13. Cramer, R., Shoup, V.: A practical public key cryptosystem provably secure against adaptive chosen ciphertext attack. In: Krawczyk, H. (ed.) CRYPTO 1998. LNCS, vol. 1462, pp. 13–25. Springer, Heidelberg (1998)
14. Cramer, R., Shoup, V.: Signature schemes based on the strong RSA assumption. In: ACM CCS 99, pp. 46–51. ACM Press (November 1999)
15. Di Raimondo, M., Gennaro, R.: New approaches for deniable authentication. In: Atluri, V., Meadows, C., Juels, A. (eds.) ACM CCS 2005, pp. 112–121. ACM Press (November 2005)
16. Dodis, Y., Kiltz, E., Pietrzak, K., Wichs, D.: Message authentication, revisited. In: Pointcheval, D., Johansson, T. (eds.) EUROCRYPT 2012. LNCS, vol. 7237, pp. 355–374. Springer, Heidelberg (2012)
17. Dolev, D., Dwork, C., Naor, M.: Non-malleable cryptography (extended abstract). In: 23rd ACM STOC, pp. 542–552. ACM Press (May 1991)
18. Dolev, D., Dwork, C., Naor, M.: Nonmalleable cryptography. SIAM Journal on Computing 30(2), 391–437 (2000)
19. Dwork, C., Naor, M.: Zaps and their applications. In: 41st FOCS, pp. 283–293. IEEE Computer Society Press (November 2000)
20. Dwork, C., Naor, M., Sahai, A.: Concurrent zero-knowledge. In: 30th ACM STOC, pp. 409–418. ACM Press (May 1998)

21. Fiat, A., Shamir, A.: How to prove yourself: Practical solutions to identification and signature problems. In: Odlyzko, A.M. (ed.) CRYPTO 1986. LNCS, vol. 263, pp. 186–194. Springer, Heidelberg (1987)
22. Gennaro, R., Halevi, S., Rabin, T.: Secure hash-and-sign signatures without the random oracle. In: Stern, J. (ed.) EUROCRYPT 1999. LNCS, vol. 1592, pp. 123–139. Springer, Heidelberg (1999)
23. Gertner, Y., Malkin, T., Myers, S.: Towards a separation of semantic and CCA security for public key encryption. In: Vadhan, S.P. (ed.) TCC 2007. LNCS, vol. 4392, pp. 434–455. Springer, Heidelberg (2007)
24. Goldwasser, S., Micali, S., Rivest, R.L.: A "Paradoxical" solution to the signature problem. In: Blakely, G.R., Chaum, D. (eds.) CRYPTO 1984. LNCS, vol. 196, p. 467. Springer, Heidelberg (1985)
25. Guillou, L.C., Quisquater, J.-J.: A "Paradoxical" identity-based signature scheme resulting from zero-knowledge. In: Goldwasser, S. (ed.) CRYPTO 1988. LNCS, vol. 403, pp. 216–231. Springer, Heidelberg (1990)
26. Hofheinz, D., Kiltz, E.: Practical chosen ciphertext secure encryption from factoring. In: Joux, A. (ed.) EUROCRYPT 2009. LNCS, vol. 5479, pp. 313–332. Springer, Heidelberg (2009)
27. Katz, J.: Efficient and non-malleable proofs of plaintext knowledge and applications. In: Biham, E. (ed.) EUROCRYPT 2003. LNCS, vol. 2656, pp. 211–228. Springer, Heidelberg (2003)
28. Krawczyk, H.: Skeme: a versatile secure key exchange mechanism for internet. In: Proceedings of the Symposium on Network and Distributed System Security, pp. 114–127 (February 1996)
29. Lindell, Y.: A simpler construction of cca2-secure public-key encryption under general assumptions. In: Biham, E. (ed.) EUROCRYPT 2003. LNCS, vol. 2656, pp. 241–254. Springer, Heidelberg (2003)
30. Myers, S., Shelat, A.: Bit encryption is complete. In: 50th FOCS, pp. 607–616. IEEE Computer Society Press (October 2009)
31. Naor, M., Reingold, O.: Number-theoretic constructions of efficient pseudo-random functions. In: 38th FOCS, pp. 458–467. IEEE Computer Society Press (October 1997)
32. Naor, M., Reingold, O., Rosen, A.: Pseudo-random functions and factoring (extended abstract). In: 32nd ACM STOC, pp. 11–20. ACM Press (May 2000)
33. Naor, M., Yung, M.: Universal one-way hash functions and their cryptographic applications. In: 21st ACM STOC, pp. 33–43. ACM Press (May 1989)
34. Naor, M., Yung, M.: Public-key cryptosystems provably secure against chosen ciphertext attacks. In: 22nd ACM STOC, pp. 427–437. ACM Press (May 1990)
35. Rackoff, C., Simon, D.R.: Non-interactive zero-knowledge proof of knowledge and chosen ciphertext attack. In: Feigenbaum, J. (ed.) CRYPTO 1991. LNCS, vol. 576, pp. 433–444. Springer, Heidelberg (1992)
36. Rompel, J.: One-way functions are necessary and sufficient for secure signatures. In: 22nd ACM STOC, pp. 387–394. ACM Press (May 1990)
37. Sahai, A.: Non-malleable non-interactive zero knowledge and adaptive chosen-ciphertext security. In: 40th FOCS, pp. 543–553. IEEE Computer Society Press (October 1999)
38. Schnorr, C.-P.: Efficient identification and signatures for smart cards. In: Brassard, G. (ed.) CRYPTO 1989. LNCS, vol. 435, pp. 239–252. Springer, Heidelberg (1990)
39. Waters, B.R.: Efficient identity-based encryption without random oracles. In: Cramer, R. (ed.) EUROCRYPT 2005. LNCS, vol. 3494, pp. 114–127. Springer, Heidelberg (2005)
40. Wee, H.: Efficient chosen-ciphertext security via extractable hash proofs. In: Rabin, T. (ed.) CRYPTO 2010. LNCS, vol. 6223, pp. 314–332. Springer, Heidelberg (2010)

Homomorphic Signatures and Message Authentication Codes

Dario Catalano

Università di Catania, Italy
catalano@dmi.unict.it

Abstract. Homomorphic message authenticators allow to validate computation on previously signed data. The holder of a dataset $\{m_1, \ldots, m_\ell\}$ uses her secret key sk to produce corresponding tags $(\sigma_1, \ldots, \sigma_\ell)$ and stores the authenticated dataset on a remote server. Later the server can (publicly) compute $m = f(m_1, \ldots, m_\ell)$ together with a succinct tag σ certifying that m is the correct output of the computation f. A nice feature of homomorphic authenticators is that the validity of this tag can be verified *without* having to know the original dataset. This latter property makes the primitive attractive in a variety of context and applications, including, for instance, verifiable delegation of computation on outsourced data.

In this short survey, I will give an overview of the state of the art in the areas of homomorphic signatures and message authentication codes. I will (briefly) describe some of the most recent results and provide an overview of the main challenges that remain to address.

1 Introduction

Imagine that Alice wants to outsource large amounts of data to some external server (to the "cloud") so that she can later delegate the server to perform computation on this data. A natural requirement in such a situation is that the server performs the computation correctly. More precisely, the server should be able to perform the prescribed computation and also be able to convince Alice that the computation has been carried out as prescribed. What makes this task non trivial are the following additional requirements: (1) Alice does not want to keep a local copy of her data (2) the communication complexity of the protocol should not depend on the (total) size of the outsourced data. This latter restriction rules out, for instance, trivial solutions in which Alice authenticates each single message in the dataset and then receives back the same dataset to re-run the computation locally.

An elegant solution to this problem comes from the notion of homomorphic signatures (and message authentication codes, in cases were verification does not need to be publicly doable). In a preliminary phase Alice signs her dataset $\{m_i\}_{i=1,\ldots,\ell}$ and stores it on the cloud together with the corresponding signatures $\sigma_i = \mathsf{Sign}(\mathsf{sk}, m_i)$. Later the server can use a (publicly available) evaluation algorithm to compute $m = f(m_1, \ldots, m_\ell)$ together with a (succinct) valid signature

M. Abdalla and R. De Prisco (Eds.): SCN 2014, LNCS 8642, pp. 514–519, 2014.

σ on it; σ validates the computation, as homomorphic signatures are required to be unforgeable. Informally, this means that adversaries that can (adaptively) see the signatures corresponding to polynomially many messages of their own choice, cannot forge valid signature for $m^* \neq f(m_1, \ldots, m_\ell)$.

Beyond security, additional requirements of homomorphic signatures are succinctness and composability. Informally, succinctness states that both fresh and "derived" signatures should be short, meaning with this that transmitting them should require much less bandwidth than sending out the original dataset. Composability requires that derived signatures should be usable as inputs to authenticate new computations. Finally, a keynote feature of homomorphic signatures is that the validity of σ can be verified *without* needing to know the original messages $m_1, \ldots, m_\ell$.

Because of their flexibility homomorphic signatures have been investigated in several settings and flavors. Examples include homomorphic signatures for linear and polynomial functions [8,9], redactable signatures [27], transitive signatures and more [30,31].

KNOWN REALIZATIONS. The problem of realizing homomorphic message authenticators in both the symmetric (i.e. MACs) and in the publicly verifiable setting (signatures), has been the focus of many previous works. The idea of homomorphic signature was first introduced by Desmedt [17] and later refined by Johnson et al. [27]. Linearly homomorphic signatures were introduced in 2009 by Boneh et al. [8] as a tool to prevent pollution attacks in linear network coding schemes. Following this work, many results further explored this notion both in the random oracle [22,10,9,13], and in the standard model [3,14,4,15,19,5]. In the symmetric setting constructions of (linearly) homomorphic message authentication codes have been proposed by [1]. Several more recent works consider the question of supporting larger classes of functionalities. Boneh and Freeman in [9] proposed an homomorphic signature scheme for constant degree polynomials. Gennaro and Wichs [23] gave a construction of homomorphic MACs supporting arbitrary computations. This construction relies on fully homomorphic encryption and it is proved secure in a weaker security model where the adversary cannot ask verification queries. Catalano and Fiore [11] revisited this result and put forward a construction that, while capturing a less general class of functionalities (i.e. arithmetic circuits of polynomial degree), is very efficient and explicitly allows for verification queries. This latter result was further generalized by Catalano et al. in [12]. Finally, Catalano, Fiore and Warinschi [16], proposed a construction of homomorphic signatures for polynomial functions that improves over the Boneh-Freeman solution in three main aspects. First the scheme is proven secure in the standard model. Second, security is proven in a stronger fully adaptive setting[1]. Finally, signature verification is more efficient (in a amortized sense) than recomputing the function from scratch. Let us

---

[1] The solution from [9] is proven secure in a model where the adversary is required to ask all the signing queries for a given dataset at once. The scheme from [16], on the other hand, is more flexible as adversaries can ask one message at a time and even intersperse queries for messages belonging to different datasets

elaborate a bit more on this. Virtually all previous work in the area[2] proposed constructions where the cost of verifying the signature/MAC is proportional to the *description* of the function being evaluated. This means that, if one wants to check the validity of a derived signature σ for $m = f(m_1, \ldots, m_\ell)$, the cost of the verification procedure is proportional to the description of f. The solution from [16] enjoys efficient verification in the sense that verifying a signature against a function f can be done *faster* than computing f. More precisely, this holds in an amortized sense: once a first pre-computation of f is carried out locally, one can verify the evaluation of f on *any other* dataset efficiently. This feature opens the way to using homomorphic signatures for verifiable computation (e.g. [21]) and, in particular, it allows to realize simple verifiable computation schemes for outsourced data.

SNARKs. In principle one could construct (fully) homomorphic signatures using CS proofs [29] or, more in general, *succinct non interactive arguments of knowledge* (SNARKs) for NP [7]. For any given NP statement, one can use SNARKs to create a short[3] proof π that certifies knowledge of the corresponding witness. Slightly more in detail, one can create a short argument π that, given m proves knowledge of some input data set $\{m_1, \ldots, m_\ell\}$, together with corresponding signatures σ_i, such that $f(m_1, \ldots, m_\ell) = m$. The security of this construction comes from the fact that, being it an argument of knowledge, a forged signature for some function f allows to extract a (forged) signature for the underlying dataset. The main problem of (NP)-SNARKs is that they are known to require non standard assumptions [24]. In particular, known constructions either rely on random oracles [29] or on so-called "knowledge" assumptions (e.g. [25,7]).

OTHER RELATED WORK. Recently Libert *et al.* [28] introduced and realized the notion of *Linearly Homomorphic Structure Preserving signatures* (LHSPS for short). Structure Preserving cryptography provides a simple and elegant methodology to compose algebraic tools within the framework of Groth-Sahai proof systems [26]. Informally LHSPS are like ordinary Structure Preserving Signatures but they come equipped with a linearly homomorphic property that makes them interesting even beyond their usage within the Groth Sahai framework. In particular Libert *et al.* showed that LHSPS can be used to enable simple verifiable computation mechanisms on encrypted data. More surprisingly, they observed that linearly homomorphic SPS (generically) yield efficient simulation sound trapdoor commitment schemes [20], which in turn imply non malleable trapdoor commitments [18] to group elements.

Other works considered the problem of modeling notions of privacy [9,2,4]for homomorphic signatures, so to be able to compute on authenticated data in a privacy preserving way.

---

[2] A nice exception is the work of Backes *et al.* [6] that introduced the notion of homomorphic MACs with efficient verification. Their scheme, while very efficient, can only support quadratic polynomials.

[3] Here by short we mean that the length of π does not depend on the size of the statement/witness.

OPEN PROBLEMS. Currently the main open problem in the area of homomorphic authenticators is to realize fully homomorphic signatures and message authentication codes[4]. Even more ambitious goals might be to realize fully homomorphic solutions with efficient verification, as this would allow to delegate arbitrary computations on outsourced data in an efficient, verifiable way.

Acknowledgements. I would like to thank Orazio Puglisi for his comments and all my co-authors in this exciting area of research: Dario Fiore, Bogdan Warinschi, Rosario Gennaro, Luca Nizzardo and Konstantinos Vamvourellis.

References

1. Agrawal, S., Boneh, D.: Homomorphic mACs: MAC-based integrity for network coding. In: Abdalla, M., Pointcheval, D., Fouque, P.-A., Vergnaud, D. (eds.) ACNS 2009. LNCS, vol. 5536, pp. 292–305. Springer, Heidelberg (2009)
2. Ahn, J.H., Boneh, D., Camenisch, J., Hohenberger, S., Shelat, A., Waters, B.: Computing on authenticated data. In: Cramer, R. (ed.) TCC 2012. LNCS, vol. 7194, pp. 1–20. Springer, Heidelberg (2012)
3. Attrapadung, N., Libert, B.: Homomorphic network coding signatures in the standard model. In: Catalano, D., Fazio, N., Gennaro, R., Nicolosi, A. (eds.) PKC 2011. LNCS, vol. 6571, pp. 17–34. Springer, Heidelberg (2011)
4. Attrapadung, N., Libert, B., Peters, T.: Computing on authenticated data: New privacy definitions and constructions. In: Wang, X., Sako, K. (eds.) ASIACRYPT 2012. LNCS, vol. 7658, pp. 367–385. Springer, Heidelberg (2012)
5. Attrapadung, N., Libert, B., Peters, T.: Efficient completely context-hiding quotable and linearly homomorphic signatures. In: Kurosawa, K., Hanaoka, G. (eds.) PKC 2013. LNCS, vol. 7778, pp. 386–404. Springer, Heidelberg (2013)
6. Backes, M., Fiore, D., Reischuk, R.M.: Verifiable delegation of computation on outsourced data. In: Sadeghi, A.-R., Gligor, V.D., Yung, M. (eds.) ACM CCS 2013, pp. 863–874. ACM Press (November 2013)
7. Bitansky, N., Canetti, R., Chiesa, A., Tromer, E.: From extractable collision resistance to succinct non-interactive arguments of knowledge, and back again. In: Goldwasser, S. (ed.) ITCS 2012, pp. 326–349. ACM (January 2012)
8. Boneh, D., Freeman, D., Katz, J., Waters, B.: Signing a linear subspace: Signature schemes for network coding. In: Jarecki, S., Tsudik, G. (eds.) PKC 2009. LNCS, vol. 5443, pp. 68–87. Springer, Heidelberg (2009)
9. Boneh, D., Freeman, D.M.: Homomorphic signatures for polynomial functions. In: Paterson, K.G. (ed.) EUROCRYPT 2011. LNCS, vol. 6632, pp. 149–168. Springer, Heidelberg (2011)
10. Boneh, D., Freeman, D.M.: Linearly homomorphic signatures over binary fields and new tools for lattice-based signatures. In: Catalano, D., Fazio, N., Gennaro, R., Nicolosi, A. (eds.) PKC 2011. LNCS, vol. 6571, pp. 1–16. Springer, Heidelberg (2011)

---

[4] In this sense the fully homomorphic solution by Gennaro and Wichs [23] cannot be considered fully satisfactory as it does not support verification queries

11. Catalano, D., Fiore, D.: Practical homomorphic mACs for arithmetic circuits. In: Johansson, T., Nguyen, P.Q. (eds.) EUROCRYPT 2013. LNCS, vol. 7881, pp. 336–352. Springer, Heidelberg (2013)

12. Catalano, D., Fiore, D., Gennaro, R., Nizzardo, L.: Generalizing homomorphic mACs for arithmetic circuits. In: Krawczyk, H. (ed.) PKC 2014. LNCS, vol. 8383, pp. 538–555. Springer, Heidelberg (2014)

13. Catalano, D., Fiore, D., Gennaro, R., Vamvourellis, K.: Algebraic (trapdoor) one-way functions and their applications. In: Sahai, A. (ed.) TCC 2013. LNCS, vol. 7785, pp. 680–699. Springer, Heidelberg (2013)

14. Catalano, D., Fiore, D., Warinschi, B.: Adaptive pseudo-free groups and applications. In: Paterson, K.G. (ed.) EUROCRYPT 2011. LNCS, vol. 6632, pp. 207–223. Springer, Heidelberg (2011)

15. Catalano, D., Fiore, D., Warinschi, B.: Efficient network coding signatures in the standard model. In: Fischlin, M., Buchmann, J., Manulis, M. (eds.) PKC 2012. LNCS, vol. 7293, pp. 680–696. Springer, Heidelberg (2012)

16. Catalano, D., Fiore, D., Warinschi, B.: Homomorphic signatures with efficient verification for polynomial functions. In: Garay, J.A., Gennaro, R. (eds.) CRYPTO 2014, Part I. LNCS, vol. 8616, pp. 371–389. Springer, Heidelberg (2014)

17. Desmedt, Y.: Computer security by redefining what a computer is. In: NSPW (1993)

18. Dolev, D., Dwork, C., Naor, M.: Non-malleable cryptography (extended abstract). In: 23rd ACM STOC, pp. 542–552. ACM Press (May 1991)

19. Freeman, D.M.: Improved security for linearly homomorphic signatures: A generic framework. In: Fischlin, M., Buchmann, J., Manulis, M. (eds.) PKC 2012. LNCS, vol. 7293, pp. 697–714. Springer, Heidelberg (2012)

20. Garay, J.A., MacKenzie, P.D., Yang, K.: Strengthening zero-knowledge protocols using signatures. In: Biham, E. (ed.) EUROCRYPT 2003. LNCS, vol. 2656, pp. 177–194. Springer, Heidelberg (2003)

21. Gennaro, R., Gentry, C., Parno, B.: Non-interactive verifiable computing: Outsourcing computation to untrusted workers. In: Rabin, T. (ed.) CRYPTO 2010. LNCS, vol. 6223, pp. 465–482. Springer, Heidelberg (2010)

22. Gennaro, R., Katz, J., Krawczyk, H., Rabin, T.: Secure network coding over the integers. In: Nguyen, P.Q., Pointcheval, D. (eds.) PKC 2010. LNCS, vol. 6056, pp. 142–160. Springer, Heidelberg (2010)

23. Gennaro, R., Wichs, D.: Fully homomorphic message authenticators. In: Sako, K., Sarkar, P. (eds.) ASIACRYPT 2013, Part II. LNCS, vol. 8270, pp. 301–320. Springer, Heidelberg (2013)

24. Gentry, C., Wichs, D.: Separating succinct non-interactive arguments from all falsifiable assumptions. In: Fortnow, L., Vadhan, S.P. (eds.) 43rd ACM STOC, pp. 99–108. ACM Press (June 2011)

25. Groth, J.: Short pairing-based non-interactive zero-knowledge arguments. In: Abe, M. (ed.) ASIACRYPT 2010. LNCS, vol. 6477, pp. 321–340. Springer, Heidelberg (2010)

26. Groth, J., Sahai, A.: Efficient non-interactive proof systems for bilinear groups. In: Smart, N.P. (ed.) EUROCRYPT 2008. LNCS, vol. 4965, pp. 415–432. Springer, Heidelberg (2008)

27. Johnson, R., Molnar, D., Song, D.X., Wagner, D.: Homomorphic signature schemes. In: Preneel, B. (ed.) CT-RSA 2002. LNCS, vol. 2271, pp. 244–262. Springer, Heidelberg (2002)

28. Libert, B., Peters, T., Joye, M., Yung, M.: Linearly homomorphic structure-preserving signatures and their applications. In: Canetti, R., Garay, J.A. (eds.) CRYPTO 2013, Part II. LNCS, vol. 8043, pp. 289–307. Springer, Heidelberg (2013)

29. Micali, S.: CS proofs (extended abstracts). In: 35th FOCS, pp. 436–453. IEEE Computer Society Press (November 1994)

30. Micali, S., Rivest, R.L.: Transitive signature schemes. In: Preneel, B. (ed.) CT-RSA 2002. LNCS, vol. 2271, pp. 236–243. Springer, Heidelberg (2002)

31. Yi, X.: Directed transitive signature scheme. In: Abe, M. (ed.) CT-RSA 2007. LNCS, vol. 4377, pp. 129–144. Springer, Heidelberg (2006)

Efficient Proofs of Secure Erasure

Nikolaos P. Karvelas[1,*] and Aggelos Kiayias[2,*]

[1] TU Darmstadt & CASED
[2] Department of Informatics and Telecommunications,
National and Kapodistrian University of Athens, Greece

Abstract. A proof of secure erasure (PoSE) enables a space restricted prover to convince a verifier that he has erased his memory of size S. So far the only known PoSEs have linear communication complexity in S or quadratic computation complexity in S, hence their applicability is limited, since $\Theta(S)$ communication or $\Theta(S^2)$ computation can be quite impractical (e.g., for devices with S memory words when S is in the order of GB's). In this work we put forth two new PoSEs that for the first time achieve *sublinear* communication and *quasilinear* computation complexity hence they are more efficient than what was previously known. Efficiency comes at the price of slightly more relaxed security guarantees that we describe and motivate.

Keywords: Time/Space Tradeoffs, Graph Pebbling, Space-bounded adversaries.

1 Introduction

Attacks on cryptographic devices can be carried out either physically or remotely. In either case it is highly desirable that an operator (which will be also called the *verifier* in our context) is able to determine, whether the device has been compromised or not. The scenarios in which such a demand arises are many. For instance, in the case of a wireless sensor or actuator network, the verifier wants to examine which (if any at all) nodes of the network have been compromised. The suspected nodes could be asked by the verifier to erase all their memory contents and then perform an update. However it is unclear how the verifier can be convinced that this task is carried out properly without having physical access to these nodes. In another setting, the operator wishes to discard a cryptographic device. Again it is unclear, how the operator can be convinced that the device has really deleted all of its contents without physical access to the device. While problems as the ones described can be easily solved if the operator circumvents the logic of the device and accesses the hardware directly, such access can be quite cost ineffective. Therefore the question that arises is whether this problem can be solved in a *cryptographic* sense, i.e., through a protocol interaction between

* Work performed while at the National and Kapodistrian University of Athens, Research partly supported by ERC grant CODAMODA.

M. Abdalla and R. De Prisco (Eds.): SCN 2014, LNCS 8642, pp. 520–537, 2014.

the two parties, device and operator, without the need for the operator to resort to accessing the hardware of the device.

In a proof of secure erasure (PoSE) protocol, the prover (a cryptographic device with restricted memory) interacts and attempts to convince the verifier that it has erased all its memory. At an intuitive level, a PoSE is secure, if the prover cannot cheat the verifier and maintain a portion of its memory intact.

Our Results. We present a formal security model for PoSE protocols as well as two new *efficient* PoSE constructions that succeed in attaining quasilinear computational complexity and sublinear communication complexity in the prover's storage capacity, S.

The idea behind our first protocol, named iHash PoSE, is that the prover wants to invert a hash function on a given point sent to him by the verifier. This is achieved by using a time-space tradeoff, whose most computationally intensive step is an exhaustive search, performed using an algorithm inspired by Horowitz and Sahni, [10]. The security proof is based on a standard information theoretic argument (cf. Trevisan et. al. in [4] for instance).

Our second approach treads on a similar general path like the one in [7] however with the important restriction that we want to maintain quasilinear computational complexity (as opposed to quadratic achieved in [7]). To do this we construct a directed acyclic graph with constant in- and out-degree, on every node which will be used to define a function. The prover should be able to calculate this function efficiently using all his available memory, while any adversary who would use substantially less than all his memory, would either not be able at all to calculate the function or at least would have to pay in time that would be in at least quadratic. Our class of graphs results from the application of the recursive superconcentrators of Paul et al. [12] over Butterfly graphs and may be of independent interest.

Table 1. A summary of the PoSEs, with S being the prover's memory size, k the security parameter (which is lower bounded by $\log S$), q an upper bound of Adversary's running time and γ the success probability of the Adversary assuming he uses only αS space for $\alpha \in (0, 1)$

	Communication Compl.	Computation Compl.	γ	α
[13]	S	S	2^{-k}	$1 - 1/S$
[7]	$2k$	S^2	$q2^{-k}$	$1 - 1/S$
iHash	$\Theta((1-\alpha)^{-1} \log \gamma^{-1})$	$\Theta(S \log S(1-\alpha)^{-1} \log \gamma^{-1})$	any	any
graphPoSE	$2k$	$S \log S$	$q2^{-k}$	$1/32$

Our Security Guarantees. The efficiency achieved by our constructions comes at the price of more relaxed security guarantees. Specifically, in the case of iHash which achieves quasilinear computation and sublinear communication, the adversarial model in which we prove it secure assumes that the adversary acts in two distinct phases: an "offline" phase, where he is allowed to prepare a space consuming data structure without knowing the challenge and an "online" phase where he receives the challenge and he should use the results from the preparation phase as an advice, in order to invert the hash function on the given point. While this type of offline-online behavior may be enforced through timing (by having the verifier time the stages and reject when the prover takes longer) a way to formally prove full security is not apparent. GraphPoSE on the other hand is proven secure in the random oracle model (as also the previous work that provided a formal proof of security [7] did), however as evidenced by table 1, the α value we achieve is much less than the other protocols. This means that the prover is guaranteed to have to erase only a fraction of his memory. While this restricts the applicability of the protocol, its essentially optimal efficiency characteristics make it still appealing for a subset of applications (e.g., for those devices that destroying even a small percentage of the O/S would make them non-functional). The situation can be improved by devising graphs with tighter pebbling lower bounds with respect to their size which is a research direction our work can motivate.

Organization of the Paper. In Section 2.1 we present the formal security model for PoSEs. Then we present our first construction (iHash) in Section 2.2; and our second construction (graphPoSE) in Section 2.3.

Related Work. The concept of Proof of Secure Erasure (PoSE) was by Perito and Tsudik in [13] who also presented the first solution. The PoSE protocol proposed by [13] works as follows: the verifier sends to the prover random data, as large as the latter's memory capacity. The prover calculates a keyed hash function (known to both parties), using as key the last blocks of the received data and sends it back to the verifier. The verifier calculates the same function and compares the two results. Of course not any keyed hash function gives a necessarily secure instantiation e.g., when the hash function is based on the Merkle-Damgård design paradigm; on the other hand, if the function is thought to be a random oracle the security is easy to show. In any case, the protocol has very high communication complexity something that renders it impractical in many settings.

In subsequent work [7], a different solution is suggested, that minimizes the communication complexity. The idea behind this approach is that the verifier sends a small "seed" to the prover, which the latter "unravels" into a sequence of computations that in order to be carried out, the prover will have to use all its available storage. More specifically the prover has the description of a hash function and receives from the verifier an initial value. He calculates the hash function recursively in a way described by a diamond-like directed acyclic graph: Every node has constant in- and out-degrees except for the node at the top and the one at the bottom of the pyramid. The one at the top is the output value of the whole calculation and has out-degree 0 and the one in the bottom is given by the verifier and has in-degree 0. This solution reduces the communication complexity to minimum, but demands computational complexity quadratic on the size of the verifier's memory. For very small memory devices this solution can be practical, however many devices would find it extremely tolling to run a calculation proportional to the square of their memory (and in some cases, say in a 1GB memory device, the calculation becomes infeasible).

Recently and independently of our work[1] a variant of Proofs of Work (a concept introduced by Dwork and Naor in [5]) has began to receive significant attention by the community. Proofs of Space (PoS), studied independently in [2,6] address the problem where a verifier needs to be convinced that a remote prover has dedicated a specific amount of its memory, to perform a computation. PoS and PoSE's are related but also have important differences in terms of their design considerations: (i) in a PoS it is imperative that the time-complexity of the verifier is small and hence techniques like Merkle-hash trees may be used to make the verifier side computation efficient; while such requirement might be desirable in PoSE's it is not fundamental to their usefulness. In this respect a PoS imposes a stringer requirement. (ii) in a PoSE it is important that the honest prover can perform reasonably efficiently using all his memory S, however a dishonest prover with memory $S' \ll S$ should find it infeasible to convince the verifier. For a PoSE to be useful in practice the ratio $\alpha = |S'|/|S|$ should be very high (ideally very close to 1 or at least constant). For a PoS on the other hand while it is desirable to have a high α, a PoS protocol might still be quite useful even if α is, say, vanishing in the security parameter. In this respect, a PoSE imposes a somewhat stringer requirement from the point of view of security. The above remarks suggest that there may exist an "ultimate" protocol that achieves simultaneously a very high α, a very low verifier time-complexity (such protocol would thus be a PoS and a useful PoSE simultaneously), and quasilinear honest prover computation. Designing such a scheme is an interesting open question.

Finally, there is an interesting parallel between key evolution schemes for space-bounded adversaries [7,14] and proofs of space, (and in light of the above also PoSEs). In this setting the objective is to protect against a space-bounded adversary that operates from within the implementation of a cryptographic system. In key evolution schemes the adversary can be thought of as the malicious prover in a proof of space while the honest key update algorithm is following the strategy of the honest prover. The fact that the space bounded prover cannot cheat in the proof of space parallels the fact that the adversary cannot predict the evolved key after the implementation completes the update. Exploring further the formal relation between the two problems is an interesting direction.

2   PoSEs Constructions

2.1   Definitions

On a high level a (two-round) Proof of Secure Erasure (PoSE) is a protocol executed between a verifier $\mathcal{V}$ and a prover $\mathcal{P}$, who receives a challenge from $\mathcal{V}$. In order for $\mathcal{P}$ to respond to the challenge he must use all his available memory S. Otherwise (say in case he uses less that a percentage α of his memory),

---

[1] The present paper is based on the Master's thesis of the first author, titled "Proofs of Secure Erasure", supervised by the second author and submitted on Jan. 7 2013.

$\mathcal{P}$ should either not be able to respond at all or respond in time greater than the one that an honest prover would need. In order to describe the above notion more robustly we give the following definitions:

Definition 2.11. *A PoSE $(\mathcal{P}, \mathcal{V})$ is (t, s, p)−feasible if*

$$\mathrm{Prob}\left[\begin{array}{c} \mathcal{V}\ accepts \\ \mathcal{P}\ runs\ for\ time\ t\ and\ uses\ space\ at\ most\ s \end{array}\right] \geq p,$$

Similarly a PoSE $(\mathcal{P}, \mathcal{V})$ is (t, s, p)−infeasible if for all $\mathcal{P}^*$,

$$\mathrm{Prob}\left[\begin{array}{c} \mathcal{V}\ accepts \\ \mathcal{P}^*\ runs\ for\ time\ t\ and\ uses\ space\ at\ most\ s \end{array}\right] < p,$$

Definition 2.12. *For an $0 < \alpha < 1$ a PoSE is α-robust if for every $0 < \gamma < 1$, and for every s there exists a $t > 0$ such that the protocol is $(t, s, 1 - \gamma)$-feasible and $(t, \alpha s, \gamma)$-infeasible.*

Definition 2.13. *An α-robust PoSE is* efficient *if t is polynomial in the parameters $\log \gamma^{-1}$, s and $(1 - \alpha)^{-1}$.*

2.2   Invert-Hash PoSE

In this protocol, the verifier and the prover have the description of a function, which is hard to invert however it is designed in such a way that is particularly amenable to a time-space tradeoff. The verifier calculates the function on a random input and sends the output to the prover. The prover has to invert the function on the given challenge. Below we provide a formal description and analysis.

PoSE Description. Let f_1 and f_2 be two functions (to be defined later) mapping a set $[N]$ to $[N^2/2]$ (where $[N] = \{0, \ldots, N - 1\}$) and let $x_1 \in [N]$ and $x_2 \in [N]$. The prover $\mathcal{P}$ and the verifier $\mathcal{V}$ have the description of a function $f : [N^2] \to [N^2]$, which for every $x \in [N^2]$ such that $x = x_1 + x_2 N$, $f(x) = f_1(x_1) + f_2(x_2)$; note that addition here is taken over the integers. The gist of the protocol is first, the verifier chooses a challenge x and sends over to $\mathcal{P}$ the value $y = f(x)$. The prover and the verifier invert f on y. The prover sends the result to the verifier, who accepts if the result he received is the same to what he calculated.

For a given $y \in [N^2]$ such that $f(x) = y$, in order to find its pre-image x, we need to find x_1 and x_2, such that $x = x_1 + N x_2$ and satisfy the property $f(x) = f_1(x_1) + f_2(x_2)$. Note that one may search amongst all pairs (x_1, x_2) to find those that satisfy the property, however this is very inefficient as it will have complexity proportional to N^2. Instead one can use a time/space tradeoff technique like the ones described in [9] and [8]. We use the algorithm from [10] and achieve subquadratic time complexity while using the prover's all available memory. We do this by creating two tables T_1 and T_2 containing all pairs

$(x_1, f_1(x_1))$, $(x_2, f_2(x_2))$, respectively for $x_1, x_2 \in [N]$ sorted according to the second coordinate in increasing order for T_1 and decreasing order for T_2. Suppose that $(\widetilde{x}_1, \widetilde{y}_1)$, $(\widetilde{x}_2, \widetilde{y}_2)$ are the two first elements in T_1, T_2. In case $\widetilde{y}_1 + \widetilde{y}_2 = y$ we have a solution; on the other hand if $\widetilde{y}_1 + \widetilde{y}_2 > y$ we repeat by considering the next element of table T_2; finally if $\widetilde{y}_1 + \widetilde{y}_2 < y$, we repeat by considering the next element of T_1. It is easy to see that in this way we can find all solution pairs. The time complexity of this algorithm is governed by the sorting step, which will require $O(N \log N)$ time and the space complexity will be exactly N blocks.

Observe that the above computation can be naturally divided in two stages: an "off-line" stage, where the prover prepares the tables T_1, T_2 and an "online" stage where the prover receives y and uses the tables T_1, T_2 to respond to the verifier. The verifier times the prover in each stage and rejects in case the prover takes longer to respond than what he is supposed to. See Figure 1 for an overview of the protocol.

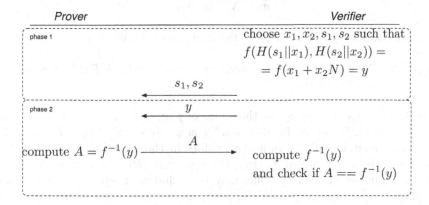

Fig. 1. Single round iHash PoSE with functions f_1 and f_2 instantiated by a hash function H with random seeds s_1 and s_2 respectively, i.e. $f_1 = H(s_1, \cdot)$, $f_2 = H(s_2, \cdot)$

In the following section we analyze the security of our PoSE, assuming adversaries that fit in the following model.

Adversarial Model. We assume that the adversary poses queries to the random oracle that are independent of the challenge y. For such an adversary it is possible to place all queries to the RO in the first stage (that is independent of the challenge y). To reflect this non-adaptivity we consider adversaries that, as it is the case of the real prover, operate on two phases: a first offline "preparation phase", during which the adversary is allowed to perform any queries he wants to the oracle function $H(\cdot)$, store the answers and perform any calculation he considers necessary. The results of this phase are stored in the adversary's memory. In the second phase the adversary receives the challenge y from the prover and uses the results stored in his memory as advice, performing computation and following any strategy he wants provided he responds within the allotted time frame (which is too short to invert the function f without the time-space tradeoff).

Security Proof. In order to prove this PoSE efficient under the definition 2.12 we will provide first some preparatory lemmas.

Lemma 1 (Fact 1). *Suppose there exists a randomized encoding procedure* $Enc : \{0,1\}^N \times \{0,1\}^r \to \{0,1\}^m$ *and a decoding procedure* $Dec : \{0,1\}^m \times \{0,1\}^r \to \{0,1\}^N$ *such that*

$$\operatorname*{Prob}_{r \in U_r}[Dec(Enc(x,r),r) = x] \geq \delta$$

Then

$$m \geq N - \log 1/\delta$$

For the lemma's proof we refer to the extended version of [4].

Lemma 2. *For* f_1, f_2 *and* f *as defined in our Invert-Hash PoSE, the expected size of* $f^{-1}(y)$ *is bounded by* 3.

Proof. Let $y = f_1(x_1) + f_2(x_2)$ be the image of f on input $x = x_1 + x_2 N$. Assume that $x_1, x_2, y, f_1, f_2(x_2)$ are fixed. Consider next the set $B = \{y - f_1(x_1^*) \mid x_1^* \in [N]\}$, which contains all the candidate values in the range of f_2 that will lead to an increase in the size of $f^{-1}(y)$. Observe that $|B| \leq N$, since this is the maximum number of elements that may be included. Then since the range of f_2 is of size $N^2/2$, the probability of assigning a value to an element $x_2^* \in [N]$ such that it belongs to B is at most $N/N^2/2 = 2/N$. The table of f_2 contains $N - 1$ elements (beyond the one that we have fixed $f_2(x_2)$) and hence the size of $f^{-1}(y)$ can be expected to be as stated. ∎

Lemma 3. *Let* $\mathcal{A}$ *be an algorithm, that succeeds in inverting* f *completely:*

$$\operatorname{Prob}[\mathcal{A}(y) = f^{-1}(y)] \geq \delta$$

Then there exist algorithms $\mathcal{A}_1, \mathcal{A}_2$ *that succeed in inverting* f_1 *and* f_2 *as follows:*

$$\operatorname{Prob}[\mathcal{A}_1(y_1) = f_1^{-1}(y_1)] \geq \delta \text{ and } \operatorname{Prob}[\mathcal{A}_2(y_2) = f_2^{-1}(y_2)] \geq \delta$$

Proof. We describe the algorithm $\mathcal{A}_1$, that inverts an element y_1 using $\mathcal{A}$ and works as follows:

1. $\mathcal{A}_1$ chooses an element $x_2 \in [N]$, forms $y = y_1 + f_2(x_2)$ and passes it to $\mathcal{A}$.
2. $\mathcal{A}$ returns all (x_1', x_2'), such that $f_1(x_1') + f_2(x_2') = y$.
3. $\mathcal{A}_1$ finds a pair (x_1', x_2') such that $x_2' = x_2$ and returns $x_1 = x_1'$.

An algorithm $\mathcal{A}_2$ can be defined in entirely symmetric fashion. We will show that $\mathcal{A}_1$ succeeds in inverting a given element y_1 with probability at least δ. Define

$$\Psi_1 = \{y_1 \in [N^2/2] : \exists y \in [N^2] \exists (x_1, x_2) \in [N]^2 : (x_1, x_2) \in \mathcal{A}(y) \wedge f_1(x_1) = y_1\},$$
$$\Psi_2 = \{y_2 \in [N^2/2] : \exists y \in [N^2] \exists (x_1, x_2) \in [N]^2 : (x_1, x_2) \in \mathcal{A}(y) \wedge f_2(x_2) = y_2\},$$
$$S = \{(x_1, x_2) \in [N]^2 : \exists y \in [N^2] : (x_1, x_2) \in \mathcal{A}(y)\},$$
$$S^{f_1, f_2} = \{(y_1, y_2) \in [N^2/2]^2 : \exists (x_1, x_2) \in S : f_1(x_1) = y_1 \wedge f_2(x_2) = y_2\}$$

Now let $(y_1, y_2) \in S^{f_1, f_2}$. Then there exists $(x_1, x_2) \in S$ such that $f_1(x_1) = y_1$ and $f_2(x_2) = y_2$. Since $(x_1, x_2) \in S$, there exists a y such that $(x_1, x_2) \in \mathcal{A}(y)$. So for this y, we have that $y_1 \in \Psi_1$ and $y_2 \in \Psi_2$, which means that $S^{f_1, f_2} \subseteq \Psi_1 \times \Psi_2$. Since $|S| \geq |S^{f_1, f_2}|$ and by the hypothesis $|S| \geq \delta N^2$, we have that $|\Psi_1 \times \Psi_2| \geq \delta N^2$.

Since $S \neq \emptyset$, we have that $S^{f_1, f_2} \neq \emptyset$ and therefore $\Psi_1 \neq \emptyset$ and $\Psi_2 \neq \emptyset$. Observe now that since $f_1^{-1}(y_1) \leq N$ (by the definition of f_1) $|\Psi_1| \leq N$ and similarly $|\Psi_2| \leq N$. Assume that $|\Psi_1| < \delta N$ and $|\Psi_2| = N$. Then $|\Psi_1 \times \Psi_2| < \delta N^2$, which is a contradiction. Therefore it must hold that $|\Psi_1| \geq \delta N$ and $|\Psi_2| \geq \delta N$.

To conclude the proof, let y_1 be a random element from $f_1([N])$. Since $\mathcal{A}_1$ inverts all the elements in Ψ_1 and $|f_1([N])| = N$, we have that $\mathsf{Prob}[\mathcal{A}_1(y_1) = f^{-1}(y_1)] \geq \frac{\delta N}{N} = \delta$ and similarly $\mathsf{Prob}[\mathcal{A}_2(y_1) = f^{-1}(y_2)] \geq \frac{\delta N}{N} = \delta$. ∎

Our security proof will hinge on the following lemma which shows how an algorithm $\mathcal{A}$ for inverting f can be used as an encoding schema for the functions f_1, f_2.

Lemma 4. *Let $\mathcal{A}$ be a probabilistic poly time algorithm that on input (σ, y), where y is the element to be inverted and σ is an advice string of length $|\sigma| = \epsilon N$, returns the set $\{(x_1^j, x_2^j) : y = f_1(x_1^j) + f_2(x_2^j), j = 1, \ldots, k, k \leq N\}$ of all the preimages of y, with the property that $(f_1(x_1^j) < f_1(x_1^{j+1}))$ and $(f_2(x_1^j) > f_2(x_1^{j+1}))$ and assume*

$$\mathsf{Prob}[\mathcal{A}(\sigma, f(x)) \text{ succeeds}] \geq \delta$$

Then using $\mathcal{A}$ we can produce a randomized encoding procedure for the function table of f_1 and f_2 that has length at most $|\sigma| + 4(1 - \delta)N \log N$.

Proof. (sketch) We begin by describing the Encoding and Decoding procedures:

Encoding. The encoding consists of the advice string σ and a table T, which contains the $2(1 - \delta)N$ elements, not inverted by $\mathcal{A}$.

Decoding.   1. Initialize a table T' that will hold the values of f_1 and f_2
      2. Fill T' with the contents of T
      3. For every element in T' that has not yet been inverted, use $\mathcal{A}$ to invert it.

Next we calculate the space needed for the encoding:

- Encode the values of $f_1 : [N] \to [N^2/2]$ that $\mathcal{A}$ cannot invert, using $\log (1 - \delta)N!$ bits.

- Encode the set $f_1((1-\delta)N)$ of the images of the elements, that cannot be inverted by $\mathcal{A}$ using $\log\binom{N^2/2}{(1-\delta)N}$ bits.

The total space needed for the encoding is:

$$|\sigma| + 2\log\left((1-\delta)N\right)! + 2\log\binom{N^2/2}{(1-\delta)N} = |\sigma| + 2\log\left((1-\delta)N\right)!\binom{N^2/2}{(1-\delta)N}$$

$$\leq |\sigma| + 4(1-\delta)N\log N$$

This completes the proof.   ∎

Proposition 2.21. *For any $\alpha > 0$, the k-round sequential composition of the Invert-Hash-PoSE is α-robust and has the performance characteristics of table 1 provided that $k = \Theta(\frac{\log\gamma^{-1}}{1-\alpha})$.*

Proof. Let S be the memory size that we want to securely erase, γ the adversary's success probability and αS the amount of memory, that the adversary will use. It is easy to see, Invert-Hash-PoSE is $(O(S\log S), S, 1-\gamma)$-feasible, since it needs $O(S\log S)$ time in order to sort the elements and needs S space to hold them. Since in order to find the inverse element, it has to go through all the table that contains f_1 and f_2, we see that

$$\mathrm{Prob}\left[\begin{array}{c}\mathcal{V}\text{ accepts}\\ \mathcal{P}\text{ ran for }O(S\log S)\text{ time and used }S\text{ space}\end{array}\right] = 1,$$

Next we show that a single round of Invert-Hash-PoSE is $(O(S\log S), \alpha S, 1-(1-\alpha)\frac{1}{3})$ infeasible. Assume that it is $(O(S\log S), \alpha S, 1-(1-\alpha)\frac{1}{3})$-feasible. Then

$$\mathrm{Prob}\left[\begin{array}{c}\mathcal{V}\text{ accepts}\\ \mathcal{P}\text{ ran for }O(S\log S)\text{ time and used }\alpha S\text{ space}\end{array}\right] \geq \delta$$

for $\delta = 1-(1-\alpha)\frac{1}{3}$. In other words there exists an algorithm $\mathcal{A}$ such that given an advice string of length αS and an element y to invert, succeeds with probability $\geq \delta$. By lemma 4 and using $\mathcal{A}$ we can construct a randomized encoding procedure that uses space $\alpha S + 4(1-\delta)S\log S$ bits. By lemma 1 we have that $\alpha S + 4(1-\delta)S\log S \geq S \cdot \log\left(\frac{S^2}{2}\right)$ which means that $4(1-\delta)\log S \geq \log\left(\frac{S^2}{2}\right) - \alpha$ from which it follows that $\delta < 1 - (1-\alpha)\frac{1}{3}$ (for S at least 3) which is a contradiction.

Recall now that the protocol is repeated k times. Then given that it holds $\left(1-(1-\alpha)\frac{1}{3}\right)^k \leq e^{-(1-\alpha)\frac{1}{3}\cdot k}$ we have that in order for the protocol to be $(O(S\log S), \alpha S, \gamma)$ infeasible it must hold that $e^{-(1-\alpha)\frac{1}{3}\cdot k} \leq \gamma$ i.e. $k \geq \frac{3\ln\gamma^{-1}}{(1-\alpha)}$. In other words the protocol is $(O(S\log S), \alpha S, \gamma)$ infeasible as long as it is iterated any k amount of times, such that $k = \Theta\left(\frac{\log\gamma^{-1}}{1-\alpha}\right)$. Based now on Lemma 2 the expected number of collisions is constant, thus achieving the communication complexity stated in table 1.   ∎

2.3   Graph Based PoSE

From the discussion in the previous sections it is reasonable to assume that for a PoSE to be efficient, a computational problem must be used, for which we know lower bounds in its space complexity while the time needed for the honest prover to solve it is less than quadratic. In this setting one comes accross the pebbling games on graphs, which have been studied extensively in the context of proving space lower bounds for calculating algebraic expressions and thus they appear to be a useful tool in the context of PoSEs, as has been previously also observed in [7]. With respect to pebbling, we refer to [11] for a detailed survey – here we provide only the necessary background for our purposes.

A PoSE based on the pebbling game is intuitevely easy to understand. Therefore we start by giving its description and stating the adversarial model. Then we provide all the necessary definitions and lemmata to describe our PoSE rigorously and prove it secure according to the definitions in 2.1.

PoSE Description. Consider a DAG with only one source and one sink (i.e. node with 0 in- and out- degree respectively). Constructing a PoSE based on this DAG is easy: The prover $\mathcal{P}$ and the verifier $\mathcal{V}$ have a hash function $H :$ $\{0,1\}^* \to \{0,1\}^k$, whose outputs we assign as labels to the various nodes of the graph. The label of every node is the hash of the labels of the node's predecessors (as well as the index of the node). In more detail we have the following protocol (which we will be calling graphPoSE):

1. $\mathcal{V}$ sends the label of the source node S_0.
2. $\mathcal{P}$ "pebbles" the graph, starting from the label of the source node and for every node uses the hash function H in order to determine the label of the descendant node. He proceeds in this manner until he pebbles the unique sink of the graph.
3. $\mathcal{P}$ sends the label of the unique sink to $\mathcal{V}$, who, having ran the same protocol, checks if the value he received is the same to the one he calculated.

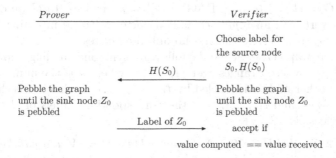

Fig. 2. The template for a graphPoSE using a DAG

Adversarial Model. We model the hash function H as a random oracle. The adversary can query it at any point during its computation.

Security Proof. The details of the protocol as well as the various definitions and lemmata needed are provided below.

Definition 2.31. *(Pebble game). Let G be a directed acyclic graph (DAG). A pebble game on G is the following one-player game. At any time t, we have a configuration $\mathbb{P}_t$ of pebbles on the vertices of G, at most one pebble per vertex. The rules of the game are as follows:*

1. *If all immediate predecessors of an empty vertex v have pebbles on them, a pebble may be placed on v. In particular, a pebble can always be placed on a source vertex.*
2. *A pebble may be removed from any vertex at any time.*

A pebbling of G, also called a pebbling strategy for G, is a sequence of pebble configurations $\mathbb{P} = \langle \mathbb{P}_0, \ldots, \mathbb{P}_\tau \rangle$. In case $\mathbb{P}_0 = X$ and $\mathbb{P}_\tau = Y$ where X, Y are the source and sink vertices of G then we call this a complete strategy. Furthermore, if for all $t \in [\tau]$, $\mathbb{P}_t$ follows from $\mathbb{P}_{t-1}$ adhering to the rules above, we call this a legal strategy. The time of a pebbling $\mathbb{P} = \{\mathbb{P}_0, \ldots, \mathbb{P}_\tau\}$ is simply $time(\mathbb{P}) = \tau$ and the space is $space(\mathbb{P}) = \max_{0 \le t \le \tau} \{|B_t|\}$ where B_t represents the set of vertices that carry a pebble in time t. The pebbling price of G, denoted $Peb(G)$, is the minimum space of any complete legal strategy for G.

Definition 2.32. *(Compact Recursive Representation) A parameterized family of Directed Acyclic Graphs $\{G_n\}_{n=1}^\infty$ will be called Compactly Recursively Representable (CRR), if for every graph $G_n = (V_n, E_n)$, there exists a circuit C of polylogarithmic size in $|V_n|$ that given a node returns its incoming edges.*

In other words, a graph that belongs in this family, will have a short (independent of the usual matrix or list) representation, which is what we need in our protocol, since for the verifier to send the whole graph in its matrix or list representation, would have to blow up the communication complexity to at least linear.

Consider $G = (V, E)$ to be a DAG of $|V| = n$ vertices. In G we distinguish some special vertices : an *input vertex* is a vertex with no incoming edges and an *output vertex* is a vertex that has no outgoing edges.

For any such graph G we define the following symbolic labeling: input vertices are labeled by x_i where i ranges over $\{1, \ldots, k\}$ where k is the number of input vertices. Any other node v is labeled by $H(v, l_1, \ldots, l_m)$ where m is the number of incoming edges and $l_1, \ldots, l_m$ are the corresponding labels of the incoming (parent) vertices.

Definition 2.33. *Let $U = \{0,1\}^s$. Given a DAG $G = (V, E)$ with k input vertices, m output vertices and bounded in-degree d, we define for a given function $H : V \times U^d \to U$ the function $G^H : U^k \to U^m$ to be the function that maps $x_1, \ldots, x_k \in U$ to the values $y_1, \ldots, y_m \in U$ that correspond to the evaluations of the symbolic labelings of the output vertices of G using the function H.*

We now fit the notion of ex-post-facto pebbling from [7] to our setting.

Definition 2.34. *Fix $U = \{0,1\}^s$ and DAG G. Given a probabilistic algorithm A utilizing an oracle $H : V \times U^s \to U$, the ex-post-facto pebbling of G corresponding to A is a pebbling strategy $\mathbb{P}$ parameterized by input $x_1, \ldots, x_k \in U$, the choice of H and the coins ρ of A that satisfies the following :*

1. *The time of the pebbling equals the number q of oracle queries of A to H.*
2. *Initially pebbles are placed on all k of the input vertices of G.*
3. *If in the i-th query A asks H for an input u and it holds that u equals the label of a node v then a pebble is placed on that vertex for the configuration $\mathbb{P}_i$.*
4. *Suppose a label l of a non-output vertex v never appears in any query j succeeding the i-th query until the sequence terminates or the label of v is recomputed. Then, no pebble is placed on v in any configuration $\mathbb{P}_{i+1}, \ldots, \mathbb{P}_j$.*

We say that an algorithm A has an execution that computes the function G^H for a given function H if it happens that the ex-post-facto pebbling of G corresponding to A on input $x_1, \ldots, x_k$ for some coins ρ of A is complete (i.e., it terminates in a configuration where all output nodes of G are pebbled). For the case where the function H behaves as a random oracle, we prove the following:

Proposition 2.31. *Fix $U = \{0,1\}^s$ and a d-bounded DAG $G = (V, E)$ with $n = |V|$ and k input vertices. Consider an algorithm A and the random variable $\mathbb{P}$ defined as the ex-post-facto pebbling of G parameterized by $x_1, \ldots, x_k$ selected uniformly at random from U and H selected uniformly at random from $(V \times U^d \to U)$. Then we have that*

$$Pr[\mathbb{P} \text{ is legal}] \geq 1 - q \cdot 2^{-s}$$

Proof. (sketch) Let $\mathbb{P} = \langle \mathbb{P}_0, \ldots, \mathbb{P}_q \rangle$ be a possible pebbling strategy of A. If $\mathbb{P}$ is not legal then there exists a smallest $i \geq 1$ such that the transition from $\mathbb{P}_{i-1}$ to $\mathbb{P}_i$ does not adhere to the rules of definition 2.31. This means that for some $i \in \{1, \ldots, q\}$, a pebble appears for vertex v in $\mathbb{P}_i$ while in $\mathbb{P}_{i-1}$ at least one of the parent nodes of v have no pebble placed in them. Translating this to our computational model, it means that the label of the parent node of v was never computed. On the other hand the fact that the ex-post-facto pebbling places a pebble on v means that the i-th query to H by A contains the label l of the node v' (where v' is one of v's parents). Then v is not an input node since all input nodes have pebbles placed on them automatically in any ex-post-facto pebbling. Let $a = (l'_1, \ldots, l'_d, v)$ be the string that defines the label $l = H(a)$. Since there was never a pebble in v' this means that a was never queried. It follows that the value l is uniformly random over U from the perspective of A, hence predicting it correctly as part of the i-th query can occur with probability at most 2^{-s}. The result follows given that i ranges in $\{1, \ldots, q\}$. ∎

Using the above proposition we conclude that any algorithm A performs a legal pebbling while computing the labels with very high probability. Next we need to establish a relation between the price of pebbling and the space required by an algorithm A. This we achieve by proving the following:

Proposition 2.32. *Fix $U = \{0,1\}^s$, a d-bounded DAG $G = (V,E)$ with $n = |V|$ and k input vertices, and $H : V \times U^d \to U$. (1) There exists an algorithm $A^{H,P}$ in the RAM model that on input $x_1, \ldots, x_k$ computes $G^H(x_1, \ldots, x_k)$ using $Peb(G)$ space and time $O(|V|)$ where $P : V \to V^d \cup \{\bot\}$ is a function that returns the d parents of a given node v or $\bot$ if it is a source node. (2) Any other algorithm A that agrees with $G^H(x_1, \ldots, x_k)$ on a fraction of inputs above α uses space $Peb(G)$.*

Proof. (sketch) (1) The proof is using P to perform a depth first search over G. Further details are omitted.

(2) Consider an execution of A for which the space complexity is less than $Peb(G)$. This means that there is a strategy that calculates $G^H(x_1, \ldots, x_k)$ but the pebbling induced by A in this execution path has price strictly smaller than $Peb(G)$ something that suggests that either it is not complete or not legal (given $Peb(G)$ is the minimum such price for complete and legal strategies). Given that there is an α fraction of complete strategies there should be at least $\alpha - q2^{-s}$ that are legal. ∎

An essential role as the building blocks of the graphs we construct is played by the superconcentrator graph family, which we describe next giving also some well known results about it, which will help us prove the security of our PoSE.

Superconcentrators are graphs that solve the problem of connecting N clients to N servers in a setting where either the clients or the servers are interchangeable and therefore it does not matter which client is connected to which server. A formal definition follows:

Definition 2.35. *A directed acyclic graph G with N input and N output nodes, will be called an $N-$ superconcentrator if for every $r \leq N$, every set of r inputs, and every set of r outputs, there exists an $r-$flow (a set of r vertex-disjoint directed paths) from the given inputs to the given outputs.*

Next we state some basic results regarding superconcentrators, which we will use for our protocol. For the proofs we refer to [11].

Lemma 5. *Suppose that $Q : u \rightsquigarrow v$ is a path in G and that $\mathbb{P} = \{\mathbb{P}_\sigma, \mathbb{P}_{\sigma+1}, ..., \mathbb{P}_t\}$ is a pebbling such that the whole path Q is completely free of pebbles at times σ and t but the endpoint v is pebbled at some point in the time interval (σ, t). Then the starting point u is pebbled during (σ, t) as well.*

Lemma 6. *Let G be an $N-$ superconcentrator, S the set of its sources and Z the set of its sinks. Then for every pebble configuration $\mathbb{P}$ with $Space(\mathbb{P}) < s$ there exist $S' \subseteq S$ and $Z' \subseteq Z$, with $|S'| \geq N - s$ and $|Z'| > s$ such that for every $s \in S'$ and $z \in Z'$ the vertex path from s to z is completely pebble free.*

Lemma 7 (Basic Lower Bound Argument). *Suppose that* $\mathcal{P} = \{\mathbb{P}_\sigma, \mathbb{P}_{\sigma_1}, \ldots,$ $\mathbb{P}_t\}$ *is a conditional (i.e.$\mathbb{P}_\sigma \neq \emptyset$) pebbling of an $N-$ superconcentrator such that* $space(\mathbb{P}_\sigma) \leq s_\sigma$, $space(\mathbb{P}_t) \leq s_t$, *and* $\mathcal{P}$ *pebbles at least* $s_\sigma + s_t + 1$ *sinks during the closed time interval* $[\sigma, t]$. *Then* $\mathcal{P}$ *pebbles and unpebbles at least* $N - s_\sigma - s_t$ *different sources during the open time interval* (σ, t).

Proposition 2.33 (Pebble lower bound). *Any complete pebbling of an $N-$ superconcentrator G in space at most s has to pebble at least $\Omega(N^2/s)$ sources.*

Paul, Tarjan and Celoni in [12] create a family of graphs for which we can find the lower bound pebbling price. This graph family construction we describe here as presented in [11]. Graphs that belong in this family we will be calling Paul-Tarjan-Celoni (PTC) graphs.

Definition 2.36. *Let $C(k) = SC_{N(k)}$ for $k = 0, 1, 2, \ldots$ denote any arbitrary but fixed family of superconcentrators with $N(k) = K \cdot 2^k$ sources and sinks for some constant $K \in \mathbb{N}^+$ and $\Theta(N(k))$ vertices of indegree 2. Then the PTC graph $\Xi(0)$ is $C(0)$, and $\Xi(i+1)$ for $i \geq 0$ is defined inductively as follows:*

The graph $\Xi(i+1)$ has sources $s_{i+1}[j]$ and sinks $z_{i+1}[j]$ for $j = 1, 2, \ldots, N(i+1)$. It contains two copies $\Xi_1(i), \Xi_2(i)$ of the PTC graph of one size smaller with sources $s_i^c[j]$ and sinks $z_i^c[j]$ for $j = 1, 2, \ldots, N(i)$ and $c = 1, 2$, and two superconcentrator copies $C_1(i), C_2(i)$ with sources $x_i^c[j]$ and sinks $y_i^c[j]$ for $j = 1, 2, \ldots, N(i)$ and $c = 1, 2$. The edges in $\Xi(i+1)$ are all internal edges within $\Xi_1(i), \Xi_2(i)$ and $C_1(i), C_2(i)$, as well as the following edges:

1. $(s_{i+1}[j], x_i^1[j])$ *and* $s_{i+1}[j+N(i)], x_i^1[j])$ *for* $j = 1, \ldots, N(i)$, *from the sources in $\Xi(i+1)$ to the sources of $C_1(i)$,*
2. $(y_i^1[j], s_i^1[j])$ *for* $j = 1, \ldots, N(i)$, *from the sinks of $C_1(i)$ to the sources of $\Xi_1(i)$,*
3. $(z_i^1[j], s_i^2[j])$ *for* $j = 1, \ldots, N(i)$, *from the sinks of $\Xi_1(i)$ to the sources of $\Xi_2(i)$,*
4. $(z_i^2[j], x_i^2[j])$ *for* $j = 1, \ldots, N(i)$, *from the sinks of $\Xi_2(i)$ to the sources of $C_2(i)$,*
5. $(y_i^2[j], z_{i+1}[j])$ *and* $(y_i^2[j], z_{i+1}[j+N(i)])$ *for* $j = 1, \ldots, N(i)$, *from the sinks of $C_2(i)$ to the sources of $\Xi_1(i+1)$,*
6. $(s_{i+1}[j], z_{i+1}[j])$ *for* $j = 1, \ldots, N(i+1)$, *directly form the sources to the sinks of $\Xi(i+1)$.*

For this family of graphs the following lemma is proved:

Lemma 8 (Lower Bound on Superconcentrator pebbling). *Let $m(i) = |S(i)| = |T(i)| = 2^i$, let $\Xi(i)$ be a DAG as in the construction of [12] and suppose that in the interval $[0, t]$ at least $c_1 m(i)$ sinks of $\Xi(i)$ are pebbled in any order for some constant c_1. Suppose also that at times 0 and t there are at most $c_2 m(i)$ pebbles on the graph for some constant c_2. Then there exist constants c_3, c_4 and a time interval $[t_1, t_2] \subseteq [0, t]$ during which at least $c_3 m(i)$ sources of $\Xi(i)$ are pebbled and at least $c_4 m(i)$ pebbles are always on the graph.*

Using the lemma, a lower bound on the pebbling price for this graph family can be found, as shown in the following:

Proposition 2.34. *There exists a family of explicitly constructible DAGs $\{G_n\}_{n=1}^{\infty}$ with $\Theta(n)$ vertices, unique sink and indegree 2, such that $Peb(G) = \Omega(n/\log n)$.*

For a detailed proof of the above we refer to [12]. In this work the constants of the lemma 8 are set to $m(i_0) = 256$, $c_1 = 14/256$, $c_2 = 3/256$, $c_3 = 34/256$ and $c_4 = 1/256$. The pebbling lower bound is actually the constant c_4, which is clearly affected by the superconcentrator family of graphs, used for the $C(i)$ graph of every recursion step. For example the superconcentrator family constructed in [1] although it is inductively constructed, its base case begins with 2^{18} sources, which clearly cannot be used in the setting that we want. On the other hand using the complete bipartite graph with N nodes again cannot be done, due its' unbounded in- and out-degree.

While the above construction provides a solution that is efficient in the asymptotic sense it is not as satisfying in terms of concrete parameters. To improve the concrete parameters we instantiate the construction with family of the butterfly graphs (where $But(n)$ denotes the butterfly graph with n sinks/sources), which actually helped us improve the hidden constants in the PTC graphs. The resulting graph we call PTC-But graph, which we further adjust by adding one extra layer of nodes (denoted as layer-$(N + 1)$ in the following) in order to fit our needs of one sink and one source. This graph clearly belongs to the CRR family of graphs and since the number of vertices is $\Theta(i2^i)^2$ (where $2^i = n$ is the number of sinks), running a BFS on the graph can pebble it in time $O(n \log n)$. Using lemma 8 makes also clear that any algorithm that pebbles it, must use $\Theta(n)$ space. It is therefore clear that this family of graphs has all the desired properties for constructing an efficient PoSE:

- It is compactly recursively representable
- It requires $\Theta(n)$ space
- It can be pebbled in $O(n \log n)$ time

Lemma 9. *Any pebbling strategy that pebbles at least 14 sinks of the butterfly graph with 64 sinks/sources ($But(64)$) and starts with a configuration of 3 pebbles, pebbles at least 34 sources, while maintaining at least one pebble throughout the whole time.*

Proof. We will prove this lemma by actually proving something stronger: namely we argue that in order to pebble 1 sink, all the sources of the graph need to be succintly pebbled. We start by observing that in order to pebble a single sink

---

[2] Solving the recursive relationship

$$V(i) = 2(2^i + 2^{i-1}2(i - 1)) + V(i - 1),$$

where $V(i)$ is the number of vertices of the PTC graph with 2^i sinks and $2^{i-1}2(i-1)$ is the number of vertices added by the $But(2^{i-1})$, proves the claim.

of the $But(4)$, any strategy would have to pebble all the 4 sources of the graph. Then since any sink of $But(8)$ needs to pebble two sinks of the two distinct $But(4)$ subgraphs and all of the latters' sources need to be pebbled, then for 1 sink of $But(8)$ to be pebbled, all the 8 sources need to be pebbled as well. The idea propagates in the next members of the butterfly graph family (easily shown by induction), thus proving that for one sink of the $But(64)$ graph to be pebbled, all its' 64 sources need to be pebbled. Then clearly the lemma holds for the case of this graph. ∎

Using then lemmata 8 and 9 we have now the following

Lemma 10. *(Main Lemma) Any algorithm that pebbles a [12] superconcentrator with 2^i sinks/sources and using the Butterfly family of superconcentrators for constructing the $C(i)$ graph of every recursion step uses at least 2^{i-6} pebbles.*

Proof. Using the butterfly superconcentrator family of graphs in every recursive call of $C(i)$, and applying Lemma 9 we can verify that the constants $c_1 = 14/64$, $c_2 = 3/64$, $c_3 = 34/64$ and $c_4 = 1/64$ satisfy the conditions required by 8, thus proving the result. ∎

We recall now the algorithm that is ran by an honest prover and prove the graphPoSE to be efficient under the definition 2.12. Assuming that each node's encoding is of the form $(index, Label, layer)$ and that for the labeling of each node a hash function $H : \{0,1\}^{2w} \rightarrow \{0,1\}^w$ is used, an honest prover pebbles a given PTC graph (with 2^i sinks/sources) in space $2^{i-1}+5$ and time $i2^i$, given the graph's structure. The main idea behind the algorithm is that using 2^{i-1} pebbles it is trivial to pebble the $PTC(2^{i-1})$ graph just by running BFS. Therefore what we really should care about is how to pebble the 2^i sources and how to "ravel" the graph after pebbling the 2^{i-1} sinks of $\Xi^2(i-1)$. For that we need a total of 5 extra pebbles, which help us maintain a "book-keeping". How the first part is done is quite easy: In order to pebble sink j of the $\Xi^1(i-1)$ graph, we place one of the extra pebbles on sink j and one more on sink $j + 2^{i-1}$ of $PTC(2^i)$. We compute the result (which is the label of pebble j of $\Xi^1(i-1)$) and store it in one of our 2^{i-1} available slots. In a similar way we use three of the extra pebbles to compute the label of sink j of $\Xi(i)$ (copying the label of sink j of $\Xi^2(i-1)$ to one of them, the label of source j of $\Xi(i)$ to the other and placing the result to the third). In a same way we compute the label of sink $j + 1$ of $\Xi(i)$ and use it to compute the label of sink j of layer-$(N+1)$ of $\Xi(i)$, "raveling" stepwise the graph, until we compute the label of the unique sink of the graph. The algorithm is stated in detail in the Appendix and using this we can now prove the main result concerning the graphPoSE in the following proposition.

Proposition 2.35. *The graphPoSE is $1/32$-robust and has the performance characteristics given in table 1 where k is the number of bits in the output of hash function H.*

Proof. The proposition follows using Lemma 10 and the space requirement of the algorithm executed by the honest prover that is described above.

References

1. Alon, N., Capalbo, M.R.: Noga Alon and Michael R. Capalbo. Smaller explicit superconcentrators. Internet Mathematics 1(2), 151–163 (2003)
2. Ateniese, G., Bonacina, I., Faonio, A., Galesi, N.: Proofs of space: When space is of the essence. Cryptology ePrint Archive, Report 2013/805 (2013), http://eprint.iacr.org/
3. Castelluccia, C., Francillon, A., Perito, D., Soriente, C.: On the difficulty of software-based attestation of embedded devices. In: ACM Conference on Computer and Communications Security, pp. 400–409 (2009)
4. De, A., Trevisan, L., Tulsiani, M.: Time Space Tradeoffs for Attacks against One-Way Functions and PRGs. In: Rabin, T. (ed.) CRYPTO 2010. LNCS, vol. 6223, pp. 649–665. Springer, Heidelberg (2010)
5. Dwork, C., Naor, M.: Pricing via Processing or Combatting Junk Mail. In: Brickell, E.F. (ed.) CRYPTO 1992. LNCS, vol. 740, pp. 139–147. Springer, Heidelberg (1993)
6. Dziembowski, S., Faust, S., Kolmogorov, V., Pietrzak, K.: Proofs of space. Cryptology ePrint Archive, Report 2013/796 (2013), http://eprint.iacr.org/
7. Dziembowski, S., Kazana, T., Wichs, D.: One-Time Computable Self-erasing Functions. In: Ishai, Y. (ed.) TCC 2011. LNCS, vol. 6597, pp. 125–143. Springer, Heidelberg (2011)
8. Fiat, A., Naor, M.: Rigorous time/space trade-offs for inverting functions. SIAM J. Comput. 29(3), 790–803 (1999)
9. Martin, E.: A cryptanalytic time-memory trade-off. IEEE Transactions on Information Theory 26(4), 401–406 (1980)
10. Horowitz, E., Sahni, S.: Computing partitions with applications to the knapsack problem. J. ACM 21(2), 277–292 (1974)
11. Nordström, J.: New wine into old wineskins: A survey of some pebbling classics with supplemental results (2011)
12. Paul, W.J., Tarjan, R.E., Celoni, J.R.: Space bounds for a game of graphs. In: Chandra, A.K., Wotschke, D., Friedman, E.P., Harrison, M.A. (eds.) STOC, pp. 149–160. ACM (1976)
13. Perito, D., Tsudik, G.: Secure Code Update for Embedded Devices via Proofs of Secure Erasure. In: Gritzalis, D., Preneel, B., Theoharidou, M. (eds.) ESORICS 2010. LNCS, vol. 6345, pp. 643–662. Springer, Heidelberg (2010)
14. Smith, A., Zhang, Y.: Near-linear time, leakage-resilient key evolution schemes from expander graphs. Cryptology ePrint Archive, Report 2013/864 (2013), http://eprint.iacr.org/

A   Appendix

Algorithm 1. HonestPebbler(S_0)

1: Input: The unique source's label, S_0
2: **for** $j = 1$ to $j = 2^i$ **do**
3:    $tmp1 \leftarrow H(j, S_0)$ {label of node j}
4:    $tmp2 \leftarrow H(2^i + j, S_0)$ {label of node $2^i + j$}
5:    $L[j] \leftarrow ((j, H(tmp1, tmp2)), 1)$ {Compute and store the labels of the sources of the first level}
6: **end for**
7: Pebble the rest of the graph using BFS until reaching the sinks of $C_2(i-1)$, updating the values in $L[]$ {now $L[]$ contains the values of the sinks of $C_2(i-1)$}
8: $tmp1 \leftarrow H(1, S_0)$ {label of node 1 at layer 0}
9: $tmp2 \leftarrow L[1]$
10: $tmp3 \leftarrow H(tmp1, tmp2)$
11: $tmp1 \leftarrow H(2, S_0)$ {label of node 2 at layer 0}
12: $tmp2 \leftarrow L[2]$
13: $tmp4 \leftarrow H(tmp1, tmp2)$
14: $tmp5 \leftarrow H(tmp3, tmp4)$
15: **for** $j = 3$ to $j = 2^i$ **do**
16:    $tmp1 \leftarrow H(j, S_0)$ {label of node j at layer 0}
17:    $tmp2 \leftarrow L[j]$
18:    $tmp3 \leftarrow H(tmp1, tmp2)$
19:    $tmp4 \leftarrow tmp5$
20:    $tmp5 \leftarrow H(tmp3, tmp4)$
21: **end for**
22: **for** $j = 2^i + 1$ to $j = 2^{i+1}$ **do**
23:    $tmp1 \leftarrow H(j, S_0)$ {label of node j at layer 0}
24:    $tmp2 \leftarrow L[j]$
25:    $tmp3 \leftarrow H(tmp1, tmp2)$
26:    $tmp4 \leftarrow tmp5$
27:    $tmp5 \leftarrow H(tmp3, tmp4)$
28: **end for**{$tmp5$ now holds the value of the unique sink}
29: Return $tmp5$

Proofs of Space: When Space Is of the Essence

Giuseppe Ateniese[1,2], Ilario Bonacina[1], Antonio Faonio[1], and Nicola Galesi[1]

[1] Sapienza - University of Rome, Italy
{ateniese,bonacina,faonio,galesi}@di.uniroma1.it
[2] Johns Hopkins University, USA

Abstract. Proofs of computational effort were devised to control denial of service attacks. Dwork and Naor (CRYPTO '92), for example, proposed to use such proofs to discourage spam. The idea is to couple each email message with a proof of work that demonstrates the sender performed some computational task. A proof of work can be either CPU-bound or memory-bound. In a CPU-bound proof, the prover must compute a CPU-intensive function that is easy to check by the verifier. A memory-bound proof, instead, forces the prover to access the main memory several times, effectively replacing CPU cycles with memory accesses.

In this paper we put forward a new concept dubbed *proof of space*. To compute such a proof, the prover must use a specified amount of space, i.e., we are not interested in the number of accesses to the main memory (as in memory-bound proof of work) but rather on the amount of actual memory the prover must employ to compute the proof. We give a complete and detailed algorithmic description of our model. We develop a full theoretical analysis which uses combinatorial tools from Complexity Theory (such as pebbling games) which are essential in studying space lower bounds.

Keywords: Space Complexity, Proof of Work, Pebbling Game, Random Oracle Model.

1 Introduction

Space has a special meaning in Computer Science. It refers to the number of cells of the working tape used by a Turing Machine (TM). While a TM computes a function, it will make several steps (relevant to time complexity) and use a certain number of tape cells (relevant to space complexity).

In [13], Dwork and Naor proposed to employ proof of work (PoW) to discourage spam and, in general, to hinder denial of service attacks. Before any action (such as sending an email), the prover must perform some work and generate a proof of it that can be efficiently verified. Proofs of work are currently being used to implement a publicly verifiable ledger for Bitcoin, where transactions are registered and verified by a community of users to avoid the double-spending problem [27]. The work performed by the prover can be CPU-bound, in which the work represents the number of steps made by a TM, or memory-bound, in which the work represents the times a TM access the working tape. The motivation

M. Abdalla and R. De Prisco (Eds.): SCN 2014, LNCS 8642, pp. 538–557, 2014.

behind memory-bound PoW is that, while CPU speed may differ significantly among distinct platforms, memory latencies vary much less across machines and may prove to be more equitable and egalitarian. We stress that memory-bound function complexity measures the number of memory accesses and does not take into account the actual amount of memory employed. That is, a TM may read and mark a single cell several times to reach a certain complexity level but it will still end up using only one cell.

In this work we define the notion of *Proof of Space* (PoSpace). PoSpace forces the prover to use at least a specified amount of memory. This means, for instance, that a TM must now use a predetermined number of distinct tape cells to be able to respond to a challenge. We will show that our PoSpace construction is also a memory-bound PoW under the definition provided in [12, 14], while in general a PoW cannot be a PoSpace under our definition. The state of the art memory-bound PoW was described in [14] by Dwork, Goldberg, and Naor. Their scheme requires both the prover and the verifier to store a large table T but they devised ways to mitigate this problem via either hash trees or public-key signatures.

We view PoSpace as a valid alternative to various flavors of PoWs. In PoSpace the spotlight is turned on the amount of space rather than on CPU cycles or memory accesses as in PoWs. In addition, PoSpace solves certain problems where PoW is not applicable. For instance, we believe PoSpace can be employed in forensic analysis or device attestation to confirm remotely that an embedded device has been successfully wiped. That is, a remote device could be instructed to respond to a wipe command with PoSpace as evidence that its functional memory is now overwritten (cf. [29]).

Straw Man Solutions. Memory-bound functions were first introduced by Abadi et al. [1]. In the main construction of memory-bound PoW given in [12], both the prover and the verifier share a large random table T. The prover must compute a function by making several memory accesses to uniformly random positions in T. Through a proper tuning of the parameters, it is also possible to force the prover to reserve a specific amount of memory. In another construction, the authors of [12] show that the verifier does not have to store T. The idea is to sign all pairs $(i, T[i])$ and then challenge the prover on ℓ positions of T. The prover will return the ℓ values $T[i]$ along with an aggregate signature that can be checked by the verifier to ensure the prover is holding the table T.

We first remark that it is possible to harness recent advances in proof of storage schemes, such as Provable Data Possession (PDP) [4] and (compact) Proof of Retrievability (POR) [31], to reduce the message complexity from $O(\ell)$ to essentially constant. This solution improves upon the one in [12] and, as long as the initialization phase is performed only once, would meet our *efficiency* requirements for PoSpace. However, proof of storage does not satisfy our definition of PoSpace since the running time of the verifier depends on the size of T. The only way to avoid linear dependency is to run a PDP-based scheme with spot checking [4], but then the prover either must use more space than required or will not access all the memory locations. Intuitively, the reason why a solution based on proof of storage will not work rests upon the interpretation of what *proof of space* really means. Proof of storage applied to our context satisfies the notion that *"the prover can* **access** *space"*. PoSpace instead captures the stronger notion that *"the prover can* **handle** *space"*, i.e., the prover possesses, controls, and manipulates space directly. In particular, we distinguish between a prover that can only read memory and a prover that can read and write memory. This is important because, among other things, write operations cannot be parallelized within classical computer architectures. We will provide a formal definition later and make this intuition rigorous.

We also remark that the adversarial model considered in [1, 12] contemplates the existence of a small but fast cache memory that must be saturated to force the prover to dispense with the cache and use traditional RAM memory. Thus, the constructions in [1, 12, 14] do provide a form of proof of space where the space coincides with the cache memory. But, as for proof-of-storage schemes, these schemes satisfy the weaker notion of PoSpace where the prover can only read memory.

Other Related Work. A proof of work is also known as a *cryptographic puzzle* in the computer security literature. Puzzles were devised to improve on the proposal by Back [6] and employed to thwart denial of service attacks. In particular, it is important to make them hard to precompute (see [22] and references therein). Waters et al. [34] suggest to outsource the creation of puzzles to an external secure entity. Abliz and Tznati [2] introduce the concept of network-bound puzzles where clients collect tokens from remote servers before querying the service provider. They argue that network latency provides a good solution to the resource disparity problem.

All solutions above deal with proof of effort and cannot be adapted to prove possession of space in the way it is meant and defined in this paper.

Litecoin (`litecoin.org`) is a variant of Bitcoin that employs *scrypt* [28] to certify a public ledger. *scrypt* is defined as a sequential memory-hard function and originally designed as a key derivation function, but it is used as a proof of effort in litecoin to hinder the use of specialized hardware. Technically, *scrypt* is not a memory-bound function as defined in [1] since no lower bound on the memory used by the function can be guaranteed. Thus, it is not even a PoSpace. We also note it requires both the prover and the verifier to dedicate a possibly large amount of memory, while ideally only the prover should reserve and use actual memory (as in our construction to be presented later).

Dziembowski et al. [18] have independently suggested a notion of proof of space. Their original construction generalizes the hash-based PoW of Cash [6] and does not employ the pebbling framework of [14] (cf. Appendix A of [15]). A major overhaul version of their paper later appeared on the IACR Crypto Eprint repository [15], along with ours [3]. Their new version does use pebbling and adopts techniques similar to ours.

However, there are two main differences between our work and [15] that make their work quite compelling:

1. The definition of proof of space in [15] is stronger in that it allows a two-stage protocol. The first stage can be executed once while the second stage can potentially be executed many times after the first. There are several applications that would benefit from this two-stage notion (see for example the Gmail scenario described in [15]). At the same time, however, this stronger notion is achieved in a more idealized model than the Random Oracle Model. To emphasize the differences between these two notions, we will often refer to ours as a one-stage PoSpace.
2. In [15] the authors provide two main constructions. The one that can be compared with our work achieves better pebbling complexity ($N/(\log(N)$ vs. $N/(\log(N) \cdot k)$). Namely, they are able to remove the extra k (a security parameter) through a clever technique.

The pebbling framework introduced in [14] has been used successfully in many other contexts (see for example [15–17, 23, 32]). Dziembowski et al. [16] built a leakage resilient key evolution scheme based on the pebbling framework. Their model allows an internal memory-bounded adversary that can control the update operation and leak bounded amounts of information. Smith and Zhang obtain a more efficient scheme [32], specifically, their update operation runs in time quasi-linear in the key length, rather than quadratic. The key-evolution scheme can be adapted to obtain a proof of space with efficient communication complexity but the space complexity of the verifier would not satisfy the efficiency constraint of PoSpace.

In a recent paper [23], Karvelas and Kiayias provide two efficient constructions for Proof of Secure Erasure (PoSE) as introduced by Perito and Tsudik [29]. Informally, in PoSE the prover must convince a verifier that a certain amount of memory has been *erased*. Both schemes in [23] are ingenious and one of them uses the pebbling framework. PoSE and PoSpace are closely related notions but have different requirements as stated in [23]. In addition, in PoSpace the prover must show that he can access (read/write) memory while in PoSE, intuitively, there should be the extra and necessary requirement that the memory contents before and after the protocol execution are uncorrelated.

General Ideas behind Our Protocol. We cast PoSpace in the context of delegation of computation, where a *delegator* outsources to a *worker* the computation of a function on a certain input. Securely delegating computation is a very active area [10,11,19,21] thanks also to the popularity of cloud computing where weak devices use the cloud to compute heavy functions. In the case of PoSpace, a function f is first selected satisfying the property that there exists a space lower bound for any TM computing it. Then, the verifier chooses a random input x and delegates to the prover the computation of $f(x)$.

Specifically, we will turn to the class of functions derived from the "*graph labeling problem*" already used in cryptography (see for example [14, 16, 17]). Important tools in delegation of computation are interactive proof (and argument) systems. The delegation problem, as described in [26], can be solved as follows: The worker computes $y := f(x)$ and proves using an interactive proof system that indeed $y = f(x)$. While interactive proofs with statistical soundness and non-trivial savings in verification time are unlikely to exist [8, 9, 20], Kilian showed [24] that proof systems for **NP** languages with only computational soundness (i.e., argument systems [7]) and *succinctness* [1] do exist. The construction in [24] relies on Merkle Trees and PCP proofs. However, in the context of PoSpace, the PCP machinery is an overkill. In fact, the prover does not have to prove the statement $f(x) = y$, but only that a space-consuming computation was carried out. Therefore, we replace the PCP verification with an ad-hoc scheme that results in a very efficient overall construction (while PCP-based constructions are notoriously impractical).

Our Contributions. We introduce a formal definition of Proof of Space (PoSpace Definition 2) capturing the intuitive idea of proving to be able to handle (read / write) at least a specified amount of space. We provide two PoSpace protocols in the ROM. In addition, we provide a weaker form of PoSpace (wPoSpace) and prove that it is indeed a separate notion. Most of previous work on proof of storage [4, 5, 31] and on memory-bound PoW, as defined in [1, 12, 14], can somehow be adapted to meet this weaker definition but we will not elaborate on this any further in this paper.

Structure of the Paper. Section 2 contains some preliminary definitions. Section 3 contains the formal definition of PoSpace and provide two PoSpace protocols. Section 5 contains the definition of a *weak* variant of PoSpace that captures read-only provers and a separation result between PoSpace and this weaker variant.

Open Problems. It is not clear whether in general PoSpace implies the standard definition of PoW in the sense of [13] (i.e., whether PoSpace is also a PoW). The main obstacle to proving a positive result consists in showing *non-amortizability*. Roughly speaking, non-amortizability means that the "price" of computing the function for l different inputs is comparable to l times the "price" of computing the same function once. In the context of PoWs, the "price" is measured in terms of computational time. A PoSpace prover for space S requires a computational time proportional to S, thus we would like to reduce an adversary for l different protocol executions to an adversary for a single execution which spends less than S computational time. The point is that in order to carry out l executions, the prover needs S space and we need to ensure that he spends $l \times S$ computational time. But space is reusable and it may well happen that something already computed for one instance is reused to compute the proof for another instance. Nevertheless, our second construction does satisfy the definition of PoW. This is simply because we resort to the Random Oracle to ensure that two instances of the protocol are uncorrelated.

---

[1] I.e., the total amount of communication and the verification time are both less than their respective values required to transmit and check the NP-witness.

2   Notations and Preliminary Definitions

Graph Notation. Given a directed acyclic graph (DAG) G, the set of successors and predecessors of v in G are respectively $\Gamma^+(v)$ and $\Gamma^-(v)$. We will implicitly assume a topological ordering on its vertex set and a boolean encoding of the vertices respecting that ordering. If $\Gamma^+(v) = \emptyset$ then v is an *output-node* and $\mathbf{T}(G)$ is the set of all output-nodes of G. Analogously if $\Gamma^-(v) = \emptyset$ then v is an *input-node* and $\mathbf{S}(G)$ is the set of all input-nodes of G.

Sampling, Interactive Execution, and Space. Let $\mathcal{A}$ be a probabilistic TM. We write $y \leftarrow \mathcal{A}(x)$ to denote y sampled from the output of $\mathcal{A}$ on input x. Moreover, given $\sigma \in \{0,1\}^*$, we write $y := \mathcal{A}(x; \sigma)$ to denote the output of $\mathcal{A}$ on input x fixing the random coins to be σ. We write PPT for the class of probabilistic polynomial time algorithms. Let $\mathcal{A}$, $\mathcal{B}$ be two probabilistic interactive TMs. An interactive joint execution between $\mathcal{A}$, $\mathcal{B}$ on common input x is specified via the next message function notation: let $b_1 \leftarrow \mathcal{B}(x)$, $a_i \leftarrow \mathcal{A}(x, b_1, \ldots, b_i)$, and $b_{i+1} \leftarrow \mathcal{B}(x, a_1, \ldots, a_i)$, then $\langle \mathcal{A}, \mathcal{B} \rangle(x)$ denotes a joint execution of $\mathcal{A}$ and $\mathcal{B}$ on common input x. If the sequence of messages exchanged is $(b_1, a_1, \ldots, b_k, a_k, b_{k+1})$ we say that k is the number of *rounds* of that joint execution and we denote with $\langle \mathcal{A}, \mathcal{B} \rangle(x) = b_{k+1}$ the last output of $\mathcal{B}$ in that joint execution of $\mathcal{A}$ and $\mathcal{B}$ on common input x.

With $\mathrm{Space}(\mathcal{A}, x)$, we denote the maximal amount of space used by the deterministic TM $\mathcal{A}$ on input x without taking into account the length of the input and output. More formally, we say that $\mathcal{A}(x)$ has space s (or $\mathrm{Space}(\mathcal{A}, x) = s$) if and only if at most s locations on $\mathcal{A}$'s work tapes (excluding the input and the output tapes) are ever written by $\mathcal{A}$'s head during its computation on x. In the case of probabilistic TM $\mathcal{A}$, the function $\mathrm{Space}(\mathcal{A}, x)$ is a random variable that depends on $\mathcal{A}$'s randomness.

Similarly, given two interactive TMs $\mathcal{A}$ and $\mathcal{B}$, we can define the space occupied by $\mathcal{A}$ during a joint execution on common input x as follows. Let $(b_1, a_1, \ldots, b_k, a_k, b_{k+1})$ the sequence of messages exchanged during $\langle \mathcal{A}, \mathcal{B} \rangle(x)$, then:

$$\mathrm{Space}_{\mathcal{A}}(\langle \mathcal{A}, \mathcal{B} \rangle, x) := \max_{i=1,\ldots,n} \{\mathrm{Space}(\mathcal{A}, x, b_1, \ldots, b_i))\}$$

As before, if $\mathcal{A}$ and $\mathcal{B}$ are probabilistic interactive TM then the function $\mathrm{Space}_{\mathcal{A}}(\langle \mathcal{A}, \mathcal{B} \rangle, x)$ is a random variable that depends on the randomness of both $\mathcal{A}$ and $\mathcal{B}$. For simplicity, when the inputs of $\mathcal{A}$ (or $\langle \mathcal{A}, \mathcal{B} \rangle$) are clear from the context, we write $\mathrm{Space}(\mathcal{A})$ (or $\mathrm{Space}_{\mathcal{A}}(\langle \mathcal{A}, \mathcal{B} \rangle)$).

Merkle Trees. Merkle Trees (MT) are classical tools in cryptography. A MT enables a party to succinctly commit itself to a string $l = (l_1, \ldots, l_n)$ with $l_i \in \{0,1\}^k$.

The term "succinctly" here means that the MT-commitment has size k which is independent with respect to the size of l. In a later stage, when a party opens the MT-commitment, it is guaranteed that the "opening" can yield only the string l committed before (the binding property). Moreover l can be succinctly opened location-by-location: the party can open l_i for any i giving the certificate attesting the value of l_i. Here we use the term succinctly to mean that the "*opening*", i.e., the certificate, has size $\log n \times k$ (sub-linear in n) with respect to the size of l.

Abstractly, we define a Merkle Tree as a tuple of three algorithms (Gen_{CRH}, MT, Open) where the first algorithm is a key generation algorithm for a collision resistance hash (CRH) function. Suppose that Gen_{CRH} outputs a key s. Then MT takes as input s and a sequence of strings l and outputs the *commitment* C for l, i.e., $C = \text{MT}_s(l)$. The algorithm Open takes as input the key s, a sequence of strings l, and an index i (it is denoted as $\text{Open}_s(l, i)$), and outputs the string l_i in l.

Usually, the term "commitment" refers to a scheme that is both *hiding* (i.e., the receiver cannot infer any knowledge on l from the commitment) and *binding*. The MT scheme that we use does not provide the *hiding* property but we still refer to it as a commitment.

A full description of the Merkle Tree is deferred to Appendix B.

Pebbling Games with Wildcards. The following definition of *pebbling game with wildcards* is a modification of the standard definition of pebbling game that can be found, for instance, in [25]. Given a DAG $G = (V, E)$, we say that a sequence $\mathcal{P} = (P_0, \ldots, P_T)$ of subsets of V is a *pebbling sequence on G with m wildcards* if and only if $P_0 = \emptyset$ and there exists a set $W \subseteq V$ of size m such that, for each $i \in \{1, \ldots, T\}$, exactly one of the following holds:

- $P_i = P_{i-1} \cup \{v\}$ if $\Gamma^-(v) \subseteq P_{i-1} \cup W$ (*pebbling*) or
- $P_i \subseteq P_{i-1}$ (*unpebbling*).

If a set of vertexes Γ is such that $\Gamma \subseteq \bigcup_{i=0}^{T} P_i$, we say that $\mathcal{P}$ *pebbles* Γ. If $\mathcal{P}$ pebbles $\mathbf{T}(G)$ then we say that $\mathcal{P}$ is a *pebbling game on G with m wildcards*. Moreover we say that the *pebbling time* of $\mathcal{P}$ is T and the *pebbling space* of $\mathcal{P}$ is $\max_i |P_i|$. Intuitively, a pebbled node is a node for which we have made some computations. Instead, W represents *complementary* nodes, for which we have made no computations.

One of the main ingredients for the correctness of our constructions is the Pebbling Theorem [25] that proves that stacks of *superconcentrators* graphs (Pippenger [30]) have an exponential pebbling space-time trade off.

Theorem 1 (Pebbling Theorem). *There exists a family of efficiently sampleable directed acyclic graphs $\{G_{N,k}\}_{k,N\in\mathbb{N}}$ with constant fan-in d, N input nodes, N output nodes and $kN \log N$ nodes in total, such that:*

1. *Any pebbling sequence that pebbles Δ output nodes has pebbling space at most S pebbles and m wildcards, where $|\Delta| \geqslant 4S + 2m + 1$, and pebbling time T such that*

$$T \geqslant |\Delta| \left(\frac{N - 2S - m}{2S + m + 1} \right)^k.$$

2. *There exists a pebbling sequence that pebbles the graph $G_{N,k}$ which has pebbling space $N+2$ and needs time $O(kN \log N)$.*
3. *For any node $v \in V(G_{N,k})$, the incoming nodes of v and the position of v in first lexicographic topologically order of $G_{N,k}$ are computable in $O(k \log N)$.*

More details about the construction and the proof of this theorem are given in Appendix A.

Graph Labeling Problem with Faults. We adopt the paradigm where the action of pebbling a node in a DAG G is made equivalent to the action of having calculated some labeling on it. This paradigm was introduced in [14] and also recently used in [16, 17]. We make use of a Random Oracle (RO) $\mathcal{H}$ to build a labeling on G according to the pebbling rules.

Definition 1 ($\mathcal{H}$-labeling with faults). *Given a DAG G with a fixed ordering of the nodes and a Random Oracle function $\mathcal{H} : \{0,1\}^* \to \{0,1\}^k$, we say that $\ell : V(G) \to \{0,1\}^k$ is a (partial) $\mathcal{H}$-labeling of G with m faults if and only if there exists a set $M \subseteq V(G)$ of size m such that for each $v \in V(G) \setminus M$*

$$\ell(v) := \mathcal{H}(v \| \ell(v_1) \| \dots \| \ell(v_d)) \text{ where } \{v_1, \dots, v_d\} = \Gamma^-(v). \tag{1}$$

Given a label ℓ and a node v, we say that ℓ well-label v if only if the equation (1) holds for ℓ and v.

Our framework generalize the paradigm of [14] by introducing the concept of "faults". As it is shown in Section 3.1, dealing with "faults" is necessary because an adversary challenged on a labeling function could cheat by providing an inconsistent label on some nodes (which, indeed, are then referred to as "faults").

The use of a Random Oracle $\mathcal{H}$ provides two important benefits to our construction: First, the incompressibility of any output given the input and the evaluation of the function in many different points. Specifically, for any x and $x_1, \dots, x_m$, the value of $\mathcal{H}(x)$ is uniformly random and independent of $\mathcal{H}(x_1), \dots, \mathcal{H}(x_m)$. Therefore, to store $\mathcal{H}(x)$, an adversary needs space equal to the minimum between the shortest description of the input and the length of the output. In particular, notice that we do not require that the *entire* function be incompressible (this holds for a Random Oracle but it is trivially false for any *real-world* instantiation of it). Second, in order to $\mathcal{H}$-label the graph, any TM must follow a pebble strategy. In particular, to label a node v, a TM must necessarily calculate and store the label values of all the predecessors $\ell(v_1), \dots, \ell(v_d)$ of the node v. If the graph G needs at least S pebbles to be pebbled efficiently in a pebbling game, then a TM needs to store at least S labels (i.e., RO outputs) to compute an $\mathcal{H}$-labeling of G. This general strategy is proven sound in [14] and referred to as the *Labeling Lemma*. In our context, however, we provide m degrees of freedom and, given a partial $\mathcal{H}$-labeling ℓ of G with m faults and a $\mathcal{H}$-labeling ℓ' of G, it will likely be the case that $\ell(v) \neq \ell'(v)$ for each node v that is a descendant of a not well-labeled node. For this reason, we must state a more general version of the Labeling Lemma in [14].

Lemma 1 (Labeling with Faults Lemma). *Consider a DAG G with degree d, a TM $\mathcal{A}$ with advice h, and a Random Oracle $\mathcal{H} : \{0,1\}^* \to \{0,1\}^k$ that computes an $\mathcal{H}$-labeling ℓ with m faults of G. If h is independent of $\mathcal{H}$, with overwhelming probability, there exists a pebbling sequence $\mathcal{P} = (P_1, \ldots, P_T)$ for the DAG G with m wildcards having pebbling space S such that:*

- $S \leqslant \frac{1}{k}\mathrm{Space}(\mathcal{A}) + d$,
- $T \leqslant (d+2)\sigma$, *where σ is the number of queries of $\mathcal{A}$ to $\mathcal{H}$.*

In particular T is a lower bound for the execution time of $\mathcal{A}$.

The proof of the Lemma above is provided in the full version of this paper [3].

3   Proof-of-Space Protocols

In this section we define the notion of PoSpace, then we provide two constructions that meet the definition. We later define a second notion of a *weak* form of PoSpace and show a separation result between the two notions. In our definition below, we allow the adversary to access extra information to model the case in which the adversary may outsource storage and computation to an external provider.

We model the write permission on the storage by providing a precomputation phase to the adversary. That is, the adversary can use as much space as needed to produce an hint. The hint, that may depend on the public parameters of PoSpace, can be read during the interactive phase (i.e., when the protocol is started). In contrast, wPoSpace does not provide the adversary with a precomputation phase.

Definition 2 (PoSpace). *Consider $\Sigma = (\mathsf{Gen}, \mathsf{P}, \mathsf{V})$, where Gen is a PPT TM, and P,V are interactive PPT TMs. Let $k \in \mathbb{N}$ be a security parameter. Suppose that the following points hold :*

(Completeness) *For all $\mathsf{pk} \in \mathsf{Gen}(1^k)$ and for all $S \in \mathbb{N}$, $S > k$ it holds $\langle \mathsf{P}, \mathsf{V} \rangle (\mathsf{pk}, 1^S) = 1$, time complexity of P is $O(\mathrm{poly}(k, S))$;*

(Succinctness) *For all $S \in \mathbb{N}$, $S > k$ the time and space complexity of V and the message complexity of $\langle \mathsf{P}, \mathsf{V} \rangle$, as functions of k and S, are $O(\mathrm{poly}(k) \cdot \mathrm{poly}\log S)$;*

(Soundness) *For any PPT adversary $\mathcal{A}$ and for any PPT TM with advice $\mathcal{A}'$ such that $\mathsf{pk} \leftarrow \mathsf{Gen}(1^k)$ and $h \leftarrow \mathcal{A}'(\mathsf{pk}, 1^S)$, the following event:*

$$\mathbf{Snd}_{\Sigma,S}^{\mathcal{A},\mathcal{A}'}(k) := \langle \mathcal{A}(h), \mathsf{V} \rangle (\mathsf{pk}, 1^S) = 1 \ \wedge \ \mathrm{Space}_{\mathcal{A}}(\langle \mathcal{A}(h), \mathsf{V} \rangle, \mathsf{pk}, 1^S) < S$$

has negligible probability (as a function of k) for all $S \in \mathbb{N}$, $S > k$.

Then, we say that $\Sigma = (\mathsf{Gen}, \mathsf{P}, \mathsf{V})$ is a (one-stage) Proof of Space (PoSpace). To be concise, we could say informally that $\mathcal{A}$ wins when the event $\exists S \in \mathbb{N}$: $\mathbf{Snd}_{\Sigma,S}^{\mathcal{A},\mathcal{A}'}(k)$ occurs.

Notice that in the completeness part we set just a very mild upper bound on the space complexity of P. This is done on purpose to allow comparison among different PoSpace protocols. In particular a useful measure on a PoSpace protocol $(\mathsf{Gen}, \mathsf{P}, \mathsf{V})$ is the following *space gap*: the ratio $\mathrm{Space}(\mathsf{P}(\mathsf{pk}, 1^S))/S$.

Notice that $\mathcal{A}'$ is a space-unbounded PPT TM that models the fact that there might be information that can be efficiently computed that the space-bounded adversary $\mathcal{A}$ can exploit somehow to compromise PoSpace.

It is easy to see that the PoSpace definition implicitly provides *sequential composability*. In fact, the adversary $\mathcal{A}'$ gives to $\mathcal{A}$ a hint which is a function of the public key, therefore the adversary $\mathcal{A}'$ can compute all the previous executions of the protocol "in his head".

We provide next a 4-messages PoSpace protocol in the Random Oracle Model (ROM) without any computational assumption. By applying the Fiat-Shamir paradigm to the scheme, we obtain a 2-message non-interactive PoSpace.

3.1   A 4-Message PoSpace Protocol

The protocol $\Sigma_4 = (\mathsf{Gen}, \mathsf{V}, \mathsf{P})$ is described in Figure 1 and it is a 4-message protocol.

The protocol follows in some way Kilian's construction of argument systems [24]. For any string $\alpha \in \{0, 1\}^*$, let $\mathcal{H}_\alpha(\cdot)$ be defined as $\mathcal{H}(\alpha \| \cdot)$. The verifier chooses a random α and asks the prover to build a $\mathcal{H}_\alpha$-labeling of graph $G_{N,k}$, where N depends on S. The purpose of α is to "reset" the Random Oracle. That is, any previous information about $\mathcal{H}$ is now useless with overwhelming probability. The labeling provides evidence that the prover has handled at least S memory cells. The prover then commits the labeling and sends the commitment to the verifier. At this point, the verifier asks the prover to open several random locations in the commitment and then it checks locally the integrity of the labeling. For a commitment C and for any node that the verifier has challenged, the prover sends what we call a *C-proof* for the node (defined next).

Definition 3 (C-proof). *Given a DAG G, a commitment C, and a Random Oracle $\mathcal{H}$, we say that a string $\pi = (\pi_0, \ldots, \pi_d)$ is a C-proof for a vertex $v \in V(G)$ w.r.t. $\mathcal{H}$ if only if given $\Gamma_G^-(v) = \{w_1, \ldots, w_d\}$ the following points hold:*

1. *π_0 is a C-opening for v, let x be the value π_0 is opening to;*
2. *for each $i = 1, \ldots, d$, π_i is a C-opening for w_i, let x_i be the value π_i is opening to;*
3. *$x = \mathcal{H}(v \| x_1 \| \ldots \| x_d)$.*

We omit C, G, and $\mathcal{H}$, when they are clear from the context, by saying that π is simply a proof.

In the definition of C-proof, the points 1 and 2 refer to the commitment C while point 3 ensures the integrity of the labeling. Note that the size of π is $O(kd \log N)$.

We remark that when TM $\mathcal{B}$ takes as input a RO $\mathcal{H}$, it is intended that $\mathcal{B}$ has oracle access to $\mathcal{H}$ and the length of the input of $\mathcal{B}$ does not take into account the (exponentially long) length of $\mathcal{H}$.

Generator Gen takes as **input** 1^k and outputs pk $:= (\{G_{N,k}\}_{N \in \mathbb{N}}, \mathcal{H}, s)$, where $\{G_{N,k}\}_{N \in \mathbb{N}}$ is a family of graphs satisfying the Pebbling Theorem (Theorem 1), equipped with the natural lexicographic topological ordering on its vertex set, $\mathcal{H}$ is a RO and s is a key for CRH H.

Common input: k, S, pk

$N := \lceil 4\gamma(d + S/k) + \gamma \rceil$, where d is the degree of $G_{N,k}$ and $\gamma \in \mathbb{R}$, $\gamma > 1$.

Verifier V		Prover P
1. Pick $\alpha \leftarrow \{0,1\}^k$	$\xrightarrow{\quad \alpha \quad}$	Let ℓ be a $\mathcal{H}_\alpha$-labeling of $G_{N,k}$, where $\mathcal{H}_\alpha(\cdot) := \mathcal{H}(\alpha \| \cdot)$.
	$\xleftarrow{\quad C \quad}$	**Commit** $C := \mathsf{MT}_s(\ell)$.
2. Pick $(v_1, \ldots, v_l) \leftarrow V^l$ uniformly at random, where $l = \lfloor k \ln^2 k \log N \rfloor$ and $V = V(G_{N,k})$	$\xrightarrow{\ (v_1, \ldots, v_l)\ }$	For any v_i, $\pi_i := \mathsf{Open}_s(\ell, v_i)$: For any $v_i^j \in \Gamma^-(v_i)$: $\pi_i^j := \mathsf{Open}_s(\ell, v_i^j)$ $\Pi_i := (\pi_i, \pi_i^1, \ldots, \pi_i^d)$
	$\xleftarrow{\ (\Pi_1, \ldots, \Pi_l)\ }$	**Send** $(\Pi_1, \ldots, \Pi_l)$
3. Check for any $i \leqslant l$ if Π_i is a C-proof for v_i wrt the $\mathcal{H}_\alpha$-labeling ℓ		

Fig. 1. The 4-message PoSpace protocol Σ_4

Theorem 2. *The protocol Σ_4 in Figure 1 is a (one-stage) PoSpace.*

We start by giving the intuition behind the proof of the Theorem. Completeness is trivial. Succinctness follows easily from point (3) of the Pebbling Theorem (Theorem 1). For Soundness, we first prove that the protocol Σ_4 is a Proof-of-Knowledge (PoK) of a partial labeling with "few" faults. By the PoK property, we can extract from a winning adversary a partial labeling with few faults. Thus, with overwhelming probability, the adversary $\mathcal{A}$ computes a partial labeling. We then exploit the binding property of the Merkle-Tree and show that the adversary has computed the labeling during the round (1) of the protocol. By appropriately fixing the randomness of the protocol, we ensure that the hint h is independent of $\mathcal{H}$, thus meeting all the hypotheses of the Labeling Lemma (Lemma 1). We obtain then a pebbling strategy that has pebbling space and pebbling time roughly upper-bounded by the respective space and time complexity of the adversary $\mathcal{A}$. Since the adversary uses strictly less space than S

and $\mathcal{A}$ is PPT then, by our choice of the parameters, there is a contradiction with the point (1) of the Pebbling Theorem (Theorem 1).

Proof. We focus on the *Soundness*. We divide the proof in two parts. First, in the PoK Lemma, we prove that the Protocol Σ_4 is a PoK for a partial labeling with "few" faults, and that the partial labeling has been computed during the round (1), i.e., after the verifier V sent the message α and before the adversary sent the commitment message C. Then we combine the PoK Lemma with the Labeling Lemma and the Pebbling Theorem to reach a contradiction assuming that there exists a winning PPT adversary.

We stress that the knowledge extractor doesn't need to be efficient since we do not rely on any computational assumption.

Lemma 2 (PoK Lemma). *Consider the protocol $\Sigma_4 = (\mathsf{Gen}, \mathsf{V}, \mathsf{P})$, a PPT adversary $\mathcal{A}$, a PPT Turing Machine with advice $\mathcal{A}'$, a space parameter S, and a security parameter k. Sample a random $\mathsf{pk} \leftarrow \mathsf{Gen}(1^k)$ and let $h \leftarrow \mathcal{A}'(\mathsf{pk}, 1^S)$. If $\Pr\left[\mathbf{Snd}_{\Sigma_4,S}^{\mathcal{A},\mathcal{A}'}(k)\right]$ is noticeable (where the probability is taken over the randomness of pk, h and all the randomness used during the protocol execution between $\mathcal{A}$ and the verifier) then, for a noticeable probability over the choice of pk, there exist a first verifier message $\tilde{\alpha}$ and an adversary's randomness $\tilde{\rho}$ such that $A(h)$ calculates an $\mathcal{H}_{\tilde{\alpha}}$-labeling ℓ of $G_{N,k}$ with m faults such that the following holds:*

- *the hint h is independent of $\mathcal{H}_{\tilde{\alpha}}$,*
- $m = O\left(\frac{N}{\ln k}\right)$ *and*
- *for any well-labeled node u in ℓ we have $(\tilde{\alpha}\|u\|\ell(u_1)\|\dots\|\ell(u_d)) \in \mathcal{Q}$,*

where $\mathcal{Q}$ is the set of queries to $\mathcal{H}$ made by $\mathcal{A}$ when fed with randomness $\tilde{\rho}$ during round (1) of the protocol Σ_4, and $\{u_1, \dots, u_d\} = \Gamma^-(u)$.

The proof of the Lemma above is provided in the full version of this paper [3].

By contradiction, suppose there exists an adversary $\mathcal{A}$ for the protocol Σ_4. By applying Lemma 2, we extract with noticeable probability a partial $\mathcal{H}_{\tilde{\alpha}}$-labeling, ensure that $\mathcal{A}(h)$ computed that labeling during round (1) and that the hint h is independent of $\mathcal{H}_{\tilde{\alpha}}$. Hence, satisfying the hypotheses of Lemma 1.

This gives us, with overwhelming probability, a pebbling sequence $\mathcal{P}$ of $G_{N,k}$ with m wildcards having pebbling space $S' = \frac{S}{k} + d$, $m = O(\frac{N}{\ln k})$. In addition, the pebbling time of $\mathcal{P}$ is a lower bound for the execution time of $\mathcal{A}$ during round (1). To apply Theorem 1, we fix N such that

$$N - l \geqslant 4S' + 2m + 1, \tag{2}$$

where l denotes the number of wildcards that are in $\mathbf{T}(G_{N,k})$.

Given $c \in (0,1)$ and $\epsilon > 0$, we have that $(2+\epsilon)m + l \leqslant cN$. If we find N such that

$$N \geqslant 4S' + cN + 1,$$

(hence $N \geqslant 4\gamma S' + \gamma$, where $\gamma = 1/(1-c)$) then the inequality (2) will follow. (This is main reason why we have set $N := \lceil 4\gamma S' + \gamma \rceil$ in the Protocol Σ_4.)

By applying Theorem 1, the execution time T of $\mathcal{A}$ is such that

$$T \geqslant (N - l) \left(\frac{N - 2S' - m}{2S' + m + 1} \right)^k \geqslant c'(1 + \epsilon)^k, \tag{3}$$

where c' is a constant that is a lower bound for $N - l$. The value $(1 + \epsilon)^k$ derives from the fact that, eventually,

$$N - 2S' - m \geqslant (1 + \epsilon)(2S' + m + 1).$$

Equation (3) shows that the execution time of $\mathcal{A}$ is exponential in k. This is not possible as, by hypothesis, $\mathcal{A}$ is PPT.

On the Space Gap of the Protocol. The prover algorithm can be implemented basically in two ways. The most natural implementation is to first build the labeling for all the nodes in the graph and then apply the Merkle Tree, while keeping in memory the labeling which is reused during the second phase of the prover algorithm. Through this algorithm, the space gap of the prover is $O(\log S)$ while the time complexity is essentially dominated by the one labeling phase. Another way to implement the prover algorithm is by computing the labeling and the Merkle Tree *simultaneously*. In this way the algorithm can reuse space resulting in a strategy with space gap $O(1)$. Note however that, in this implementation, the prover must build the labeling twice (once for the commitment and then during the challenge phase).

4   A 2-Messages PoSpace Protocol

We apply the standard *Fiat-Shamir* paradigm to the PoSpace scheme given in Section 3.1 by using two independent Random Oracles $\mathcal{H}, \mathcal{L}$:

- $\mathcal{H} : \{0,1\}^* \to \{0,1\}^k$ is used by the prover for the labeling of the graph;
- $\mathcal{L} : \{0,1\}^k \to V^l$ given the commitment C as input, it yields the second verifier's message (of the protocol Σ_4).

Let $(\Sigma_4.\text{Gen}, \Sigma_4.\text{P}, \Sigma_4.\text{V})$ the PoSpace defined in Figure 1. We define in Figure 2 a 2-messages PoSpace: we call $\Sigma_2 = (\text{Gen}, \text{P}, \text{V})$ this protocol. Furthermore, let $\mathcal{H}' : \{0,1\}^* \to \{0,1\}^k$ be a RO then the function $f(x) := \Sigma_2.\text{P}(\text{pk}, 1^S, \mathcal{H}'(x))$ is a non-interactive PoSpace that satisfies the syntactic definition of PoWs in [13].

Theorem 3. *The Protocol Σ_2 in Figure 2 is a* PoSpace.

The proof of the theorem 3 is provided in the full version of this paper [3].

5   *Weak* Proof of Space

The concept of proof of space can lead to multiple interpretations. The main interpretation formalized in the PoSpace definition requires that the prover can

Generator Gen on **input** 1^k returns pk' := (pk, $\mathcal{L}$),
where pk $\leftarrow \Sigma_4.$Gen(1^k) and $\mathcal{L}$ is a RO
Common input: $k, S, $pk

Verifier V   **Prover** P

1. **Pick** $\alpha \leftarrow \{0,1\}^k$ $\xrightarrow{\quad \alpha \quad}$ $C := \Sigma_4.$P(pk, $1^S, \alpha$)
                                                                    $v := \mathcal{L}(C)$

2. **Let** $v = \mathcal{L}(C)$ $\xleftarrow{\quad (C, \Pi) \quad}$ $\Pi := \Sigma_4.$P(pk, $1^S, \alpha, v$)
Check $\Sigma_4.$V(pk, $1^S, \alpha, C, v, \Pi) = 1$

Fig. 2. The 2-messages (one-stage) PoSpace protocol $\Sigma_2 = ($Gen, P, V$)$

handle (i.e., read/write) space. In this section we provide a definition for a weaker alternative of PoSpace we call *weak* Proof of Space (wPoSpace). This captures the property that the prover can just access space and formalizes what could effectively be achieved by properly adapting previous work on proof of storage [4, 5, 31] and on memory-bound PoW as defined in [1, 12] (where the adversary model contemplates the existence of cache memory). The definition of wPoSpace is similar to the Definition of PoSpace (Definition 2) (the only change is in the Soundness part). We will provide a protocol which is a wPoSpace but not a PoSpace, hence wPoSpace is a strictly weaker notion than PoSpace.

Definition 4 (wPoSpace). *Consider* $\Sigma = ($Gen, P, V$)$ *where* Gen *is a* PPT *TM, and* P, V *are interactive* PPT *TMs. Let* $k \in \mathbb{N}$ *be a security parameter and* pk $\leftarrow$ Gen(1^k). *Suppose that the following points hold for all* $S \in \mathbb{N}$, $S > k$:

(Completeness) and (Succinctness) *the same as in the* PoSpace *definition.*
(weak-Soundness) *For any* PPT *adversary* $\mathcal{A}$, *the following event:*

$$\mathbf{wSnd}^{\mathcal{A}}_{\Sigma, S}(k) := \langle \mathcal{A}, V \rangle \, (\text{pk}, 1^S) = 1 \wedge \text{Space}_{\mathcal{A}}(\langle \mathcal{A}, V \rangle, \text{pk}, 1^S) < S,$$

has negligible probability (as a function of k*).*

Then we say that Σ *is a (one-stage) Weak Proof of Space (wPoSpace).*

In the Soundness of PoSpace, the adversary can take advantage of an unbounded space machine which is then unavailable during the protocol execution. In the Soundness of wPoSpace, instead, this is disallowed. Notice that a wPoSpace's adversary can perform some precomputation before the execution of the protocol (i.e., before sending/receiving the first message), however, such a precomputation cannot exceed the space bound given.

Theorem 4. *There exists a protocol which is a* wPoSpace *but not a* PoSpace.

Proof. We start by providing a protocol which is not a PoSpace. Consider the protocol Σ_4 in Figure 1 where the first message α sent by V is always the same, say 0^k. We call Σ_3 this modified version of Σ_4. The protocol Σ_3 is not a PoSpace. For any k and $S \in \mathbb{N}$, consider the hint h which is the $\mathcal{H}_{0^k}$-labeling of $G_{N,k}$ plus the complete Merkle-Tree of that labeling. We define an adversary that sends the commitment C that is in h and, for any verifier's second message v, reads the right answer from h. That adversary needs to access h in *read-only* mode, hence without using any additional working space.

The protocol Σ_3 is a wPoSpace. The structure of the proof is the same as the one of Theorem 2. We provide a particular case of the PoK Lemma (Lemma 2) where the hint h is the empty string and $\tilde{\alpha}$ is 0^k. For the sake of clarity, we restate the PoK Lemma for this particular setting.

Lemma 3. *Consider the protocol* $\Sigma_3 = (\mathsf{Gen}, \mathsf{V}, \mathsf{P})$, *a* PPT *adversary* $\mathcal{A}$, *a space parameter* S *and a security parameter* k *such that* $\mathsf{pk} \leftarrow \mathsf{Gen}(1^k)$.

If $\Pr\left[\mathbf{wSnd}^{\mathcal{A}}_{\Sigma_3, S}(k)\right]$ *is noticeable, then there exists a randomness* $\tilde{\rho}$ *such that* $\mathcal{A}$ *fed with the randomness* $\tilde{\rho}$ *during the round (1) of the protocol* Σ_3 *calculates an* $\mathcal{H}_{0^k}$-*labeling* ℓ *of* $G_{N,k}$ *with* m *faults such that the following holds:*

- $m = O\left(\frac{N}{\ln k}\right)$ *and*
- *for any well-labeled node* u *in* ℓ *we have* $(\tilde{\alpha} \| u \| \ell(u_1) \| \ldots \| \ell(u_d)) \in \mathcal{Q}$,

where $\mathcal{Q}$ *is the set of queries to* $\mathcal{H}$ *made by* $\mathcal{A}$ *when fed with randomness* $\tilde{\rho}$ *until the end of round (1) and* $\{u_1, \ldots, u_d\} = \Gamma^-(u)$.

By contradiction, suppose there exists an adversary $\mathcal{A}$ for the protocol Σ_3. By applying Lemma 3, we extract a partial $\mathcal{H}_{0^k}$-labeling, ensuring that $\mathcal{A}$ computed that labeling during round (1) (hence satisfying the hypotheses of Lemma 1).

This gives us, with overwhelming probability, a pebbling sequence $\mathcal{P}$ of $G_{N,k}$ with m wildcards and with pebbling space $S' = \frac{S}{k} + d$, $m = O(\frac{N}{\ln k})$. The pebbling time of $\mathcal{P}$ is a lower bound for the execution time of $\mathcal{A}$ before round (2). The rest of the proof follows exactly the same structure of the proof of Theorem 2 and it is therefore omitted. □

Acknowledgements. We are grateful to Krzysztof Pietrzak for his insightful comments and suggestions.

References

1. Abadi, M., Burrows, M., Manasse, M., Wobber, T.: Moderately hard, memory-bound functions. ACM Trans. Internet Technol. 5(2), 299–327 (2005)
2. Abliz, M., Znati, T.: A guided tour puzzle for denial of service prevention. In: ACSAC, pp. 279–288. IEEE Computer Society (2009)
3. Ateniese, G., Bonacina, I., Faonio, A., Galesi, N.: Proofs of space: When space is of the essence. Cryptology ePrint Archive, Report 2013/805 (2013), http://eprint.iacr.org/

4. Ateniese, G., Burns, R., Curtmola, R., Herring, J., Kissner, L., Peterson, Z., Song, D.: Provable data possession at untrusted stores. In: Proceedings of the 14th ACM Conference on Computer and Communications Security, CCS 2007, pp. 598–609. ACM, New York (2007)
5. Ateniese, G., Kamara, S., Katz, J.: Proofs of storage from homomorphic identification protocols. In: Matsui, M. (ed.) ASIACRYPT 2009. LNCS, vol. 5912, pp. 319–333. Springer, Heidelberg (2009)
6. Back, A.: Hashcash - a denial of service counter-measure. Technical report (2002)
7. Barak, B., Goldreich, O.: Universal arguments and their applications. In: IEEE Conference on Computational Complexity, pp. 194–203. IEEE Computer Society (2002)
8. Boppana, R.B., Hastad, J., Zachos, S.: Does co-np have short interactive proofs? Inf. Process. Lett. 25(2), 127–132 (1987)
9. Caires, L., Italiano, G.F., Monteiro, L., Palamidessi, C., Yung, M. (eds.): ICALP 2005. LNCS, vol. 3580. Springer, Heidelberg (2005)
10. Canetti, R., Riva, B., Rothblum, G.N.: Refereed delegation of computation. Information and Computation 226, 16–36 (2013)
11. Chung, K.-M., Kalai, Y., Vadhan, S.: Improved Delegation of Computation Using Fully Homomorphic Encryption. In: Rabin, T. (ed.) CRYPTO 2010. LNCS, vol. 6223, pp. 483–501. Springer, Heidelberg (2010)
12. Dwork, C., Goldberg, A.V., Naor, M.: On memory-bound functions for fighting spam. In: Boneh, D. (ed.) CRYPTO 2003. LNCS, vol. 2729, pp. 426–444. Springer, Heidelberg (2003)
13. Dwork, C., Naor, M.: Pricing via processing or combatting junk mail. In: Brickell, E.F. (ed.) CRYPTO 1992. LNCS, vol. 740, pp. 139–147. Springer, Heidelberg (1993)
14. Dwork, C., Naor, M., Wee, H.: Pebbling and proofs of work. In: Shoup, V. (ed.) CRYPTO 2005. LNCS, vol. 3621, pp. 37–54. Springer, Heidelberg (2005)
15. Dziembowski, S., Faust, S., Kolmogorov, V., Pietrzak, K.: Proofs of space. Cryptology ePrint Archive, Report 2013/796 (2013), http://eprint.iacr.org/
16. Dziembowski, S., Kazana, T., Wichs, D.: Key-evolution schemes resilient to space-bounded leakage. In: Rogaway, P. (ed.) CRYPTO 2011. LNCS, vol. 6841, pp. 335–353. Springer, Heidelberg (2011)
17. Dziembowski, S., Kazana, T., Wichs, D.: One-time computable self-erasing functions. In: Ishai, Y. (ed.) TCC 2011. LNCS, vol. 6597, pp. 125–143. Springer, Heidelberg (2011)
18. Dziembowski, S., Pietrzak, K., Faust, S.: Proofs of space and a greener bitcoin. Talk presented at Workshop on Leakage, Tampering and Viruses, Warsaw 2013 (2013)
19. Fiore, D., Gennaro, R.: Publicly verifiable delegation of large polynomials and matrix computations, with applications. In: Proceedings of the 2012 ACM Conference on Computer and Communications Security, CCS 2012, p. 501 (2012)
20. Goldreich, O., Hastad, J.: On the complexity of interactive proofs with bounded communication. Information Processing Letters (1998)
21. Goldwasser, S., Kalai, Y.T., Rothblum, G.N.: Delegating computation: interactive proofs for muggles. In: Proceedings of the 40th Annual ACM Symposium on Theory of Computing, STOC 2008, pp. 113–122. ACM, New York (2008)
22. Juels, A., Brainard, J.G.: Client puzzles: A cryptographic countermeasure against connection depletion attacks. In: NDSS. The Internet Society (1999)

23. Karvelas, N.P., Kiayias, A.: Efficient Proofs of Secure Erasure. In: Abdalla, M., De Prisco, R. (eds.) SCN 2014. LNCS, vol. 8642, pp. 526–543. Springer, Heidelberg (2014)

24. Kilian, J.: A note on efficient zero-knowledge proofs and arguments (extended abstract). In: Proceedings of the Twenty-Fourth Annual ACM Symposium on Theory of Computing, STOC 1992, pp. 723–732. ACM, New York (1992)

25. Lengauer, T., Tarjan, R.E.: Asymptotically tight bounds on time-space trade-offs in a pebble game. Journal of the ACM (JACM) 29(4), 1087–1130 (1982)

26. Micali, S.: Computationally sound proofs. SIAM Journal on Computing 30(4), 1253–1298 (2000)

27. Nakamoto, S.: Bitcoin: A peer-to-peer electronic cash system (May 2009)

28. Percival, C.: Stronger key derivation via sequential memory-hard functions. Presented at BSDCan 2009 (2009)

29. Perito, D., Tsudik, G.: Secure code update for embedded devices via proofs of secure erasure. In: Gritzalis, D., Preneel, B., Theoharidou, M. (eds.) ESORICS 2010. LNCS, vol. 6345, pp. 643–662. Springer, Heidelberg (2010)

30. Pippenger, N.: Superconcentrators. SIAM J. Comput. 6(2), 298–304 (1977)

31. Shacham, H., Waters, B.: Compact proofs of retrievability. In: Pieprzyk, J. (ed.) ASIACRYPT 2008. LNCS, vol. 5350, pp. 90–107. Springer, Heidelberg (2008)

32. Smith, A., Zhang, Y.: Near-linear time, leakage-resilient key evolution schemes from expander graphs. IACR Cryptology ePrint Archive, 2013:864 (2013)

33. Tompa, M.: Time-space tradeoffs for computing functions, using connectivity properties of their circuits. In: Proceedings of the Tenth Annual ACM Symposium on Theory of Computing, STOC 1978, pp. 196–204. ACM, New York (1978)

34. Waters, B., Juels, A., Alex Halderman, J., Felten, E.W.: New client puzzle outsourcing techniques for dos resistance. In: Proceedings of the 11th ACM Conference on Computer and Communications Security, CCS 2004, pp. 246–256. ACM, New York (2004)

A Proof of the Pebbling Theorem (Theorem 1)

For the sake of convenience we re-write the statement of that theorem here. For the definitions of pebbling games, pebbling space and pebbling time we refer the reader to Section 2.

Pebbling Theorem (Theorem 1). *There exists a family of efficiently sampleable directed acyclic graphs $\{G_{N,k}\}_{k,N\in\mathbb{N}}$ with constant fan-in d, N input nodes, N output nodes and $kN\log N$ nodes in total, such that:*

1. *Any pebbling sequence that pebbles Δ output nodes has pebbling space at most S pebbles and m wildcards, where $|\Delta| \geqslant 4S + 2m + 1$, and pebbling time T such that*

$$T \geqslant |\Delta| \left(\frac{N - 2S - m}{2S + m + 1} \right)^k.$$

2. *There exists a pebbling sequence that pebbles the graph $G_{N,k}$ which has pebbling space $N + 2$ and needs time $O(kN\log N)$.*

3. *For any node $v \in V(G_{N,k})$, the incoming nodes of v and the position of v in first lexicographic topologically order of $G_{N,k}$ are computable in $O(k \log N)$.*

The family of graphs $G_{N,k}$ we build is made from DAGs that are k layered stack of superconcentrators [30] with N inputs and N outputs.

Definition 5 (superconcentrator). *We say that a directed acyclic graph $G = (V, E)$ is an N-superconcentrator if and only if*

1. *$|\mathbf{S}(G)| = |\mathbf{T}(G)| = N$,*
2. *for each $S \subseteq \mathbf{S}(G)$ and for each $T \subseteq \mathbf{T}(G)$ such that $|S| = |T| = \ell$ there exist ℓ vertex-disjoint paths from S to T, i.e. paths such that no vertex in V is in two of them.*

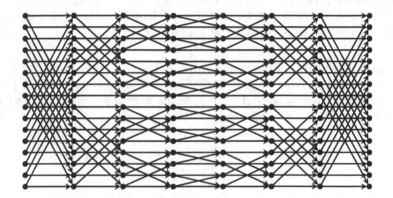

Fig. 3. An example of 16-superconcentrator: the Butterfly Graph

Definition 6 (stack of superconcentrators). *Given an N-superconcentrator G we define the graph $G^{\times k}$, the stack of k copies of G, inductively as follows: $G^{\times 1} = G$ and $G^{\times k}$ is obtained from $G^{\times (k-1)}$ and G by first renaming the vertexes of G so that they do not appear in the vertexes of $G^{\times (k-1)}$, obtaining a graph G', and then by identifying $\mathbf{T}(G^{\times (k-1)})$ with $\mathbf{S}(G')$.*

Not any k layered stack of superconcentrators satisfies points 2 and 3 of the Pebbling Theorem. To obtain those properties we use the following well-known superconcentrator: the *Butterfly Graph* B_N built by putting together two FFT graphs with N inputs and outputs [33]. An example of such construction (for $N = 16$) is given in Figure 3.

It is easy to see that the family of graphs $G_{N,k} := B_N^{\times k}$ satisfies points 2 and 3 of the Pebbling Theorem and it is a k layered stack of N-superconcentrators. It remains to prove only point 1.

For superconcentrator graphs we can prove a tradeoff between pebbling space and pebbling time, even for pebbling games with wildcards. This result is based on a generalization of the *"Basic Lower Bound Argument"* (BLBA) by Tompa [33].

Lemma 4 (BLBA with wildcards). *Consider an N-superconcentrator G, a set $M \subseteq \mathbf{T}(G)$, and a pebbling sequence $\mathcal{P} = (P_0, \ldots, P_\ell)$ with m wildcards that pebbles M. Let A be the set of all elements of $\mathbf{S}(G)$ pebbled and unpebbled at some point in $\mathcal{P}$. If $|M| \geqslant |P_0| + |P_\ell| + m + 1$ then $|A| \geqslant N - |P_0| - |P_\ell| - m$.*

Proof. By contradiction suppose that $|A| < N - |P_0| - |P_\ell| - m$, this means that $|A^c| \geqslant |P_0| + |P_\ell| + m + 1$ and every element in A^c, by definition, is not pebbled and unpebbled. Take any $B \subseteq A^c$ such that $|B| = |M|$ then, as G is an N-superconcentrator, we have $\pi_1, \ldots, \pi_{|M|}$ vertex disjoint paths from B to M. Let W be a set of m faults for $\mathcal{P}$. By construction $|M| > |P_0 \cup P_\ell \cup W|$ thus we have some path π from some element v of B to some element w of M such that $\pi \cap (P_0 \cup P_\ell \cup W) = \emptyset$. By definition of A^c, and hence of B, v is not pebbled and unpebbled and $v \notin P_0 \cup P_\ell \cup W$, thus $v \notin P_i$ for each $i \in [\ell]$. As $\pi \cap (P_0 \cap W) = \emptyset$, we must have that $\pi \cap P_i = \emptyset$ for each $i \in [\ell]$. But then the vertex w is not in $\bigcup_{i \in [\ell]} P_i$ contradicting the fact that $\mathcal{P}$ pebbles M. $\qquad\square$

Theorem 5 (Pebbling Theorem (point 1)). *Let $G^{\times k}$ be a stack of k copies of an N-superconcentrator G, $\Delta \subseteq \mathbf{T}(G^{\times k})$ and $\mathcal{P}$ a pebbling sequence for $G^{\times k}$ with m wildcards that pebbles Δ. Let S be the pebbling space of $\mathcal{P}$ and T the pebbling time of $\mathcal{P}$. If $|\Delta| \geqslant 4S + 2m + 1$ then*

$$T \geqslant |\Delta| \left(\frac{N - 2S - m}{2S + m + 1} \right)^k.$$

Proof. Let $G_1, \ldots, G_k$ be the k copies of G that form $G^{\times k}$. Suppose we want to pebble a set $M \subseteq \mathbf{T}(G_i)$ such that $|M| \geqslant 2S + m + 1$ and let $A_1, \ldots, A_n$ be disjoint subsetes of M such that A_1 are the first $2S + m + 1$ elements of M to be pebbled in $\mathcal{P}$, A_2 are the second $2S + m + 1$ elements of M to be pebbled in $\mathcal{P}$ and so on. Clearly we have that the number of these sets is $n = \left\lfloor \frac{|M|}{2S+m+1} \right\rfloor$. By Lemma 4 we have that for each A_j there exists a set $\beta(A_j)$ in $\mathbf{S}(G_i)$, whose elements are pebbled and unpebbled, of size at least $N - 2S - m$. Thus we have that the total number of elements in $\mathbf{S}(G_i)$ that have been pebbled and unpebbled is at least $(N - 2S - m) \left\lfloor \frac{|M|}{2S+m+1} \right\rfloor$. Notice now that each $\beta(A_j) \in \mathbf{T}(G_{i-1})$ hence we can reapply the argument above to it provided that for each j, $|\beta(A_j)| \geqslant N - 2S - m \geqslant 2S + m + 1$ (and this is implied by the fact that $N \geqslant |\Delta| \geqslant 4S + 2m + 1$). Thus starting from $\mathbf{T}(G_k) = \mathbf{T}(G^{\times k})$ we can prove by induction, going back to G_1, that at least

$$|\Delta| \left(\frac{N - 2S - m}{2S + m + 1} \right)^k$$

actions of pebbling and unpebbling take place on $\mathbf{S}(G_1) = \mathbf{S}(G^{\times k})$. As each action is an elementary step in the pebbling game $\mathcal{P}$ we have that the result follows. $\qquad\square$

B   Merkle Tree

Consider the complete binary tree T over n leaves. Without loss of generality we can assume that n is a power of 2 by using padding if necessary. Label the i-th leaf with l_i, then, use a collision resistant hash (CRH) function $H_s : \{0,1\}^{2k} \to \{0,1\}^k$ with random seed s to propagate the labeling l of the leaves to a labeling ϕ along the tree T up to the root according to the following rules:

1. $\phi(v) := l_i$ if v is the i-th leaf of T,
2. $\phi(v) := H_s(\phi(v_1)\|\phi(v_2))$ where v_1, v_2 are the two children of v.

Then the *commitment* for a string l is the label $\phi(r)$ of the root of the tree: we denote it with $MT_s(l)$. The commitment is succinct in fact it has size k which is independent of n.

An *opening for the i-th element in the sequence l* is an ordered sequence formed by elements of $\{0,1\}^k$ that are intended to be the label l_i of the i-th leaf of T together with the labels $\phi(v_j)$ for each v_j that is a sibling of vertices in the path from the root of the tree to the i-th leaf. An example of opening is shown in Figure 4.

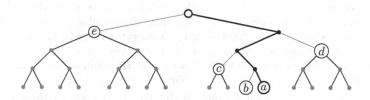

Fig. 4. An example of opening: $c = (a, b, c, d, e)$

We denote with $\text{Open}_s(l, i)$ the opening formed by l_i together with all the $\phi(v_j)$. Notice that from $\text{Open}_s(l, i)$ it is possible to compute $\phi(w)$ for each vertex w in the path from the root to the leaf at the i-th position. In particular it is efficient to compute $MT_s(l)$. The opening is succinct in fact it has size $k \cdot \log n$ which is (almost) independent of n. In general, given an opening $c = (c_1, \ldots, c_{\log n})$ for some position i we can think of it as equivalent to $\text{Open}_s(l, i)$ and compute the label of the root according to the given c and position i. If this value is equal to $MT_s(l)$, we say that c *opens the i-th position to c_1*. As H is a CRH function, then for any i, it is guaranteed that $MT_s(l)$ can open the i-th position only to l_i.

Chosen Ciphertext Security on Hard Membership Decision Groups: The Case of Semi-smooth Subgroups of Quadratic Residues*

Takashi Yamakawa[1,2], Shota Yamada[2], Koji Nuida[2],
Goichiro Hanaoka[2], and Noboru Kunihiro[1]

[1] The University of Tokyo, Japan
yamakawa@it.k.u-tokyo.ac.jp, kunihiro@k.u-tokyo.ac.jp
[2] National Institute of Advanced Industrial Science and Technology (AIST), Japan
{yamada-shota,k.nuida,hanaoka-goichiro}@aist.go.jp

Abstract. Nowadays, the chosen ciphertext (CCA) security is considered as the de facto standard security notion for public key encryption (PKE). CCA secure PKE schemes are often constructed on efficiently recognizable groups i.e., groups where the corresponding membership decision problem is easy. On the other hand, when we prove the CCA security of PKE schemes on not efficiently recognizable groups, much care are required. For example, even if a decryption query involves an unexpected element out of the group which causes a problem, the challenger cannot detect it due to the hardness of the membership decision for the group. However, such a possibility is often overlooked.

As an example of such a group, in this paper, we consider the *semi-smooth subgroup* which was proposed by Groth (TCC 2005) for enhancing efficiency of factoring-based cryptographic primitives. Specifically, we propose a general technique to guarantee the CCA security of PKE schemes on the semi-smooth subgroup. Roughly speaking, we prove that for almost all natural "verification equations," it is impossible to generate a query which does not consist of elements in the group and satisfies the equation if the factoring problem is hard. Hence, queries whose components are not in the group will be automatically rejected even though the simulator cannot recognize whether these components are in the group or not. By the same technique, we also prove that the strong Diffie-Hellman assumption holds on the "signed" semi-smooth subgroup under the factoring assumption, and improve the efficiency of a factoring-based non-interactive key exchange scheme by instantiating it on the semi-smooth subgroup.

Keywords: key encapsulation mechanism, chosen ciphertext security, non-interactive key exchange, factoring assumption, semi-smooth subgroup.

---

* The first and second authors are supported by a JSPS Fellowship for Young Scientists.

M. Abdalla and R. De Prisco (Eds.): SCN 2014, LNCS 8642, pp. 558–577, 2014.

1   Introduction

1.1   Background

Factoring-based Cryptographic Primitives. In the modern cryptography, constructing provably secure cryptographic primitives based on reliable assumptions is considered one of the most important research topics. Among such assumptions, the *factoring* assumption is considered the most reliable in the sense that it has been intensively analyzed for a long time and is also implied by many other popular assumptions, e.g., the quadratic residuosity and RSA assumptions. And hence, there have been proposed various cryptographic primitives based on the factoring assumption.

In contrast to its reliable security, cryptographic primitives based on the factoring assumption is not computationally very efficient in general as there exist sub-exponential algorithms for solving the factoring problem and therefore, relatively large order group is required to provide sufficient level of security. For example, for providing 128-bit security, 3072 bits is required for the order of the underlying groups of the (conventional) factoring-based constructions while 256 bits is sufficient for that in the elliptic-curve-based constructions [29].

Semi-smooth Subgroup over $\mathbb{Z}_N^*$. For improving computational costs in factoring-based schemes, there have been attempts to utilize small order subgroups over $\mathbb{Z}_N^*$ and construct cryptographic schemes on them. Especially, Groth [15] introduced the notion of a *semi-smooth RSA modulus* which is a special class of composite integers, and showed that for a semi-smooth RSA modulus N, it is possible to extract a subgroup of $\mathbb{Z}_N^*$ on which we can construct computationally efficient variants of various existing factoring-based schemes, e.g., the Cramer-Shoup signature [6] and additive homomorphic encryption [23]. This subgroup is called the *semi-smooth subgroup.*

It is also likely that the semi-smooth subgroup can be applied to the Hofheinz-Kiltz cryptosystem [17] which is the first practical chosen-ciphertext (CCA) secure public key encryption (PKE) from the factoring assumption, and actually, following [15], Mei, Li, Lu, and Jia [22] constructed its variants based on the semi-smooth subgroup. However, we point out that their security proofs are not precise and thus incomplete. In brief, in the security proof in [22], it seems that they implicitly assume that the adversary submits only decryption queries which consists of elements in the semi-smooth subgroup. This will be explained in the next paragraph in more detail.

Difficulty of Handling CCA security over Semi-smooth Subgroup. As mentioned above, the security proofs of the variants of [17] over the semi-smooth subgroup which are given in [22] are incomplete. We stress that the missing part of the proof is *crucial* as it is the most complicated part in the security proof when introducing the semi-smooth subgroup while it does not arise when we do not introduce the semi-smooth subgroup. Furthermore, this issue is not unique to the scheme in [22] but should be carefully treated in the case that the adversary is allowed to adaptively submit some queries, e.g., decryption queries.

Specifically, when applying the semi-smooth subgroup to a factoring-based scheme (which does not originally depend on the semi-smooth subgroup), there newly arises the following non-trivial issue. Since for a given semi-smooth subgroup G over $\mathbb{Z}_N^*$, it is generally hard to distinguish an element in G from that in $\mathbb{Z}_N^*$ without knowing the factorization of N, in the security proof, the simulator cannot distinguish a decryption query which consists of elements in G from that consists of random elements in $\mathbb{Z}_N^*$.[1] Consequently, if the simulator can correctly respond only for elements in G, then its behavior becomes significantly different from the real world, and thus, intuitively, the simulation would fail. (Actually, for example, in an earlier version of [26], a similar problem arose but was not properly addressed. Later, this was pointed out in [19], and a concrete attack was also shown.)

In summary, in the security proofs of cryptographic primitives based on the semi-smooth subgroup, it is generally required to somehow handle queries which consists of random elements in $\mathbb{Z}_N^*$. This issue is considered significantly sensitive, but have never been rigorously discussed so far.

IMPORTANT REMARK. Actually, the group that we consider in this paper is not a semi-smooth subgroup G, but G^+ which consists of absolute values of elements of G. We call G^+ signed semi-smooth subgroup. A merit of considering signed groups is that the membership in $\mathbb{QR}_N^+$ can be decided efficiently [16] but that in $\mathbb{QR}_N$ cannot (under the quadratic residuosity assumption). Note that the above membership decision algorithm for $\mathbb{QR}_N^+$ cannot be extended to the case for G^+ since it uses the specific structure of $\mathbb{QR}_N^+$ (See [16] for more details). The results in Sec. 3 and 4 hold if G^+ is replaced with G. However, those in Sec. 5, 6 and 7 do not hold for G since they essentially use the fact that the membership in $\mathbb{QR}_N^+$ can be decided efficiently.

1.2   Our Main Theorem

In this paper, we resolve the issue which is posed in the previous subsection, and show how to handle decryption (and other similar kinds of) queries which may be out of G^+. Specifically, we point out that it is still hard to distinguish an element of the semi-smooth subgroup and a random one, but we also demonstrate that under the factoring assumption, in various constructions, no effective attack utilizing the hardness of membership decision is possible. We first state our result in a general manner as our main theorem, and then, show its concrete applications. Here, we briefly explain the main theorem which is informally stated as follows:

Our Main Theorem (informal). Let g be a random element in G^+ and $X :=$ g^x where x is chosen from sufficiently large domain. If the factoring assumption holds, then any efficient adversary that is given N, g and X and allowed to

---

[1] There is no proof that the membership decision problem in G is hard. However, no efficient algorithm for this problem is known, and [15] used it even as an assumption.

access "decryption oracle" with secret key x, cannot generate (A, B) such that $A^x = B$ and $A \notin G^+$.

In the context of the CCA security, x and X correspond to a secret key and a public key respectively and the equation $A^x = B$ corresponds to a "verification equation" by the decryption oracle. Roughly speaking, the above theorem implies that for almost all natural "verification equations," it is impossible to generate a query which does not consist of elements in G^+ and satisfies the equation if the factoring problem is hard. Hence, queries whose components are not in G^+ will be automatically rejected even though the simulator cannot recognize whether these components are in G^+ or not.

The above theorem is formally stated in Sec. 3, and its formal description (Theorem 1) and proof are significantly more complicated than the above. This means that it is not trivial at all and must be carefully treated in the security proofs of cryptographic primitives which depend on the semi-smooth subgroup, e.g., Mei et al.'s variant of the Hofheinz-Kiltz cryptosystem.

1.3   Applications of the Main Theorem

Here, we give an overview of applications of our main theorem. These are originally factoring-based cryptographic primitives, and by introducing the semi-smooth subgroup, their computational costs can be significantly improved. We note that due to the issues which are mentioned in Sec. 1.1, it becomes difficult to prove their security (without using our main theorem). Our main theorem is crucial for proving them.

Hofheinz-Kiltz Scheme and Its Variants. The Hofheinz-Kiltz scheme [17,18] is an efficient CCA secure KEM on $\mathbb{QR}_N$ or $\mathbb{QR}_N^+$ which is CCA secure in the standard model under the factoring assumption. We consider instantiating the original Hofheinz-Kiltz scheme on G^+ and show that it is CCA secure in the standard model under the factoring assumption. As a result, we obtain a much more efficient scheme than the Hofheinz-Kiltz scheme. Note that the construction has been already proposed by Mei et al. [22] and they also showed a security proof. However, their proof is incomplete as mentioned above. Our contribution is to make the proof complete. Moreover, our technique can be applied to variants of the Hofheinz-Kiltz scheme [22,20,21] and we can improve the efficiency of them. Note that it is already mentioned that these schemes can be instantiated on the semi-smooth subgroup in the same papers. However, they lack the security proof.

The Strong Diffie-Hellman Assumption. The SDH assumption informally says that any efficient algorithm cannot solve the CDH problem even with a fixed base DDH oracle. We show that the factoring assumption implies the strong Diffie-Hellman (SDH) assumption on G^+. Moreover, we can show a more strong assumption called the double strong Diffie-Hellman (DSDH) assumption [10] on G^+. It is already shown that these assumptions hold on a group of signed quadratic residue $\mathbb{QR}_N^+$ [16,10]. However, these proofs rely on the fact that the group is efficiently recognizable and cannot be simply extended to the case of G^+ which is not efficiently recognizable, and our main theorem is required.

Hashed ElGamal KEM. Hashed ElGamal KEM (also called DHIES) [1] is a natural variant of the ElGamal encryption scheme and it is proven CCA secure in the random oracle model under the SDH assumption. We consider the hashed ElGamal KEM instantiated on G^+ and show that the scheme is CCA secure in the random oracle model under the factoring assumption by using the fact that the factoring assumption implies the SDH assumption on G^+ as mentioned above. Note that it has been already shown that the hashed ElGamal KEM on QR_N^+ is CCA secure in the random oracle model under the factoring assumption. However, our scheme achieves much better efficiency than it since the order of G^+ is significantly smaller than that of QR_N^+.

Non-interactive Key Exchange. Freire et al. [10] proposed a secure non-interactive key exchange scheme on QR_N^+ in the random oracle model under the factoring assumption. We consider a variant of this scheme instantiated on G^+ and prove its security in the random oracle model under the factoring assumption by using the above mentioned result that the factoring assumption implies the DSDH assumption. As a result, we obtain a much more efficient scheme than Freire et al.'s scheme since the order of G^+ is significantly smaller than that of QR_N^+.

1.4   Related Work

The first PKE scheme that is shown to be secure (in the sense of one-wayness) under the factoring assumption is proposed by Rabin [28], and its semantically secure variant (under the quadratic residuosity assumption) was later proposed by Goldwasser and Micali [13]. However, these schemes only achieve chosen-plaintext (CPA) security.

Naor and Yung [25] presented a generic construction of a (non-adaptively) CCA secure PKE scheme from any CPA secure PKE scheme and non-interactive zero-knowledge (NIZK) proof. Since it is known that NIZK proofs can be constructed from the factoring assumption [12], we can also construct a (non-adaptively) CCA secure PKE scheme from only the factoring assumption by using CPA secure PKE and NIZK proofs which are secure under the factoring assumption. Sahai [27] and Dolev, Dwork, and Naor [9] later extended the Naor-Yung construction to have adaptive CCA security. However, all of these constructions require NIZK proofs, which are very inefficient, and therefore resulting schemes are not practical.

Cramer and Shoup proposed a framework for constructing CCA secure PKE schemes which is called the hash proof system [7]. By this framework, we can obtain PKE schemes that are CCA secure under the quadratic residuosity assumption or decisional composite residuosity assumptions that are implied by the factoring assumption. However, there was no known practical PKE scheme which is CCA secure solely under the factoring assumption for a long time.

Hofheinz and Kiltz [17] finally proposed the first CCA secure PKE scheme from the factoring assumption and broke through the situation. Following this work, Mei et al. [22] further presented that the efficiency of the Hofheinz-Kiltz scheme can be improved if it is instantiated on the semi-smooth subgroup [15]. However, as mentioned above, its security proof is considered incomplete. There exists some other variants of the Hofheinz-Kiltz scheme that achieve better efficiency than the original scheme [20,21]. [20,21] also claimed that these schemes can be made more efficient by instantiating them on the semi-smooth subgroup. However, they gave no security proof though careful treatments are required in the security proof as is done in this paper.

In a different line of research, Bellare and Rogaway [2] proposed the random oracle model, and in this model, various practical CCA secure PKE schemes have been proposed such as [2,11], though the random oracle model is known to be somehow problematic [4].

2 Preliminaries

2.1 Notation

We use $\mathbb{N}$ to denote the set of all natural numbers, and $[n]$ to denote the set $\{1, \ldots n\}$ for $n \in \mathbb{N}$. If S is a finite set, then we use $x \xleftarrow{\$} S$ to denote that x is chosen uniformly at random from S. If $\mathcal{A}$ is an algorithm, we use $x \leftarrow \mathcal{A}(y)$ to denote that x is output by $\mathcal{A}$ whose input is y. We say that a function $f(\cdot) : \mathbb{N} \to [0,1]$ is negligible if for all positive polynomials $p(\cdot)$ and all sufficiently large $\lambda \in \mathbb{N}$, we have $f(\lambda) < 1/p(\lambda)$. We say f is overwhelming if $1 - f$ is negligible. We say that an algorithm $\mathcal{A}$ is efficient if there exists a polynomial p such that execution time of $\mathcal{A}$ with input length λ is less than $p(\lambda)$. We use $a|b$ to mean that a is a divisor of b. We use $a \equiv b \mod n$ to mean $n|(a-b)$. We use $(a \mod n)$ to denote a unique integer $x \in \{0, \ldots, n-1\}$ such that $x \equiv a \mod n$. We use λ to denote a security parameter. For random variables X and Y, we define the statistical distance between them as $\Delta(X, Y) := \frac{1}{2} \Sigma_a |\Pr[X = a] - \Pr[Y = a]|$. We say that X and Y are exponentially close if $\Delta(X, Y) = O(2^{-\lambda})$.

2.2 Basic definitions

Key Encapsulation Mechanism. It is shown that a CCA secure PKE scheme is obtained by combining a CCA secure key encapsulation mechanism (KEM) and a CCA secure symmetric cipher (DEM) [8]. A KEM consists of three algorithms (Gen, Enc, Dec). Gen takes a security parameter 1^λ as input and outputs (PK, SK), where PK is a public key and SK is a secret key. Enc takes a public key PK as input and outputs (C, K), where C is a ciphertext and K is a symmetric key. Dec takes a secret key SK and a ciphertext C as input and outputs a key K with length ℓ_K or $\bot$. We require that for all (PK, SK) output by Gen and all (C, K) output by Enc(PK), we have Dec$(SK, C) = K$.

To define the CCA security of KEM, we consider the following game for an adversary $\mathcal{A}$ and a KEM KEM $=$ (Gen, Enc, Dec). In the game, a public key and a secret key are generated as $(PK, SK) \leftarrow$ Gen(1^λ) and a challenge ciphertext C^* is generated as $(C^*, K) \leftarrow$ Enc(PK) as well as random bit $b \xleftarrow{\$} \{0,1\}$. Then a challenge key is set as $K^* := K$ if $b = 1$, and otherwise $K^* \xleftarrow{\$} \{0,1\}^{\ell_K}$. Then (PK, C^*, K^*) is given to the adversary $\mathcal{A}$. In the game, $\mathcal{A}$ has access to an oracle $\mathcal{O}(SK, \cdot)$ that returns Dec(SK, C) if $C \neq C^*$, and otherwise $\perp$. Finally, $\mathcal{A}$ outputs a bit b'. We define the CCA advantage of $\mathcal{A}$ as $\mathsf{Adv}^{cca}_{\mathcal{A},\mathsf{KEM}}(\lambda) := |\Pr[b' = b] - 1/2|$. We say that $\mathcal{A}$ (t, q, ϵ)-breaks KEM if $\mathcal{A}$ runs in time at most t, makes queries at most q times and we have $\mathsf{Adv}^{cca}_{\mathcal{A},\mathsf{KEM}}(\lambda) \geq \epsilon$. We say that KEM is CCA secure if $\mathsf{Adv}^{cca}_{\mathcal{A},\mathsf{KEM}}(\lambda)$ is negligible for any efficient adversary $\mathcal{A}$.

Non-interactive Key Exchange. Here, we review the definition of non-interactive key exchange (NIKE). A NIKE scheme consists of three algorithms CommonSetup, NIKE.KeyGen and SharedKey together with identity space $\mathcal{IDS}$ and a shared key space $\mathcal{SHK}$. CommonSetup takes a security parameter 1^λ as input and outputs a set of system parameters $params$. We assume, without loss of generality, that $params$ is included in pk. NIKE.KeyGen takes $params$ and an identity ID $\in \mathcal{IDS}$ and outputs a public key/ secret key pair (pk, sk). SharedKey takes an identity $\mathsf{ID}_1 \in \mathcal{IDS}$ and a public key pk_1 along with another identity ID_2 and a secret key sk_2 as input and outputs a shared key in $\mathcal{SHK}$ for the two identities, or a failure symbol $\perp$. This algorithm is assumed to always output $\perp$ if $\mathsf{ID}_1 = \mathsf{ID}_2$. For correctness, we require that for any pair of identities ID_1, ID_2 and corresponding key pairs (pk_1, sk_1) and (pk_2, sk_2), SharedKey$(\mathsf{ID}_1, pk_1, \mathsf{ID}_2, sk_2) =$ SharedKey$(\mathsf{ID}_2, pk_2, \mathsf{ID}_1, sk_1)$ holds.

There exists some security notions of NIKE that are called CKS-light, CKS, CKS-heavy and m-CKS-heavy security. However, it is shown in [10] that they are polynomially equivalent. Therefore we simply say that an NIKE scheme is *secure* if the scheme satisfies these security notions. Since we do not need concrete definitions of these security notions in this paper, we omit them here and they can be found in the full version.

Target Collision Resistant Hash Functions. Here, we review the definition of a target collision resistant hash function (also called universal one-way hash function [24]). Let $H_\kappa : \{0,1\}^* \rightarrow \{0,1\}^{\ell_H}$ be an efficiently computable keyed function, indexed by a key $\kappa \in \{0,1\}^k$. For any adversary $\mathcal{A} = (\mathcal{A}_1, \mathcal{A}_2)$, we define the advantage of $\mathcal{A}$ with respect to H as $\mathsf{Adv}^{tcr}_{H,\mathcal{A}}(\lambda) = \Pr[(x, \mathsf{st}) \leftarrow \mathcal{A}_1(1^\lambda); \kappa \leftarrow \{0,1\}^k; x' \leftarrow \mathcal{A}_2(\kappa, \mathsf{st}) : x' \neq x \wedge H_\kappa(x') = H_\kappa(x)]$. We say that H is a target collision resistant hash function if $\mathsf{Adv}^{tcr}_{H,\mathcal{A}}(\lambda)$ is negligible for any efficient adversary $\mathcal{A}$. We say that $\mathcal{A}$ (t, ϵ)-breaks te target collision resistance of H if $\mathcal{A}$ runs in time at most t and we have $\mathsf{Adv}^{tcr}_{H,\mathcal{A}}(\lambda) \geq \epsilon$. For notational convenience, in this paper we make the index κ of a hash function implicit.

2.3 Semi-smooth Subgroups and Signed Groups

Semi-smooth Subgroups [15,22]. An integer $N = PQ$ is called a semi-smooth RSA modulus if $P = 2p'p+1$ and $Q = 2q'q+1$ are distinct odd primes with the same length, where p' and q' are distinct odd primes and p and q are products of some distinct odd primes smaller than a polynomially bounded integer B which satisfy $\gcd(p, q) = 1$. Let P_B be the product of all odd primes smaller than B. We can efficiently compute x^{P_B} for $x \in \mathbb{Z}_N^*$. Let $\mathsf{IGen}(1^\lambda)$ be an efficient algorithm which outputs a random semi-smooth RSA modulus such that N is $\ell_N(\lambda)$-bit, p' is $\ell_{p'}(\lambda)$-bit and q' is $\ell_{q'}(\lambda)$-bit. For simplicity, we often omit λ and simply denote them as ℓ_N, $\ell_{p'}$ and $\ell_{q'}$. For any adversary $\mathcal{A}$ and IGen, we define the factoring advantage of $\mathcal{A}$ with respect to IGen as $\mathsf{Adv}_{\mathcal{A},\mathsf{IGen}}^{fact}(\lambda) := \Pr[N \leftarrow \mathsf{IGen}(1^\lambda); x \leftarrow \mathcal{A}(1^\lambda, N) : x \in \{P, Q\}]$. $\mathcal{A}$ (t, ϵ)-breaks the factoring assumption if $\mathcal{A}$ runs in time at most t and we have $\mathsf{Adv}_{\mathcal{A},\mathsf{IGen}}^{fact}(\lambda) \geq \epsilon$. We say that the factoring assumption holds with respect to IGen if $\mathsf{Adv}_{\mathcal{A},\mathsf{IGen}}^{fact}(\lambda)$ is negligible for any efficient adversary $\mathcal{A}$. For 80-bit security, [15] proposed to set $\ell_{p'} = \ell_{q'} = 160, \ell_N = 1024, B = 2^{15}$ as a sample parameter. We note that by this parameter setting, N is resilient to the attack described in [5] since the attack takes time $O(\min\{\sqrt{p'}, \sqrt{q'}\})$

We consider the structure of multiplicative group $\mathbb{Z}_N^*$ for a semi-smooth RSA modulus $N = PQ = (2p'p + 1)(2q'q + 1)$. We define the group of quadratic residues as $\mathbb{QR}_N := \{u^2 : u \in \mathbb{Z}_N^*\}$. Since N is a Blum integer, $\mathbb{QR}_N$ is a cyclic group with order $(P - 1)(Q - 1)/4 = p'q'pq$ and we have $-1 \notin \mathbb{QR}_N$. It follows that there exists a unique subgroup of $\mathbb{QR}_N$ with order $p'q'$, which we call the semi-smooth subgroup and denote by G. The following properties are shown in [22].

- A random element in G is a generator of G with overwhelming probability.
- If we set $u \xleftarrow{\$} \mathbb{Z}_N^*$ and $h := u^{P_B}$, then h is distributed uniformly in G.
- For any $x \in \mathbb{Z}$ and a generator g of G, the distribution of $g^{\mu+x}$ where $\mu \xleftarrow{\$} [2^{\ell_{p'}+\ell_{q'}+\lambda}]$ is exponentially close to the uniform distribution in G.
- If there exists an adversary $\mathcal{A}$ that computes the square root of a randomly chosen element of G, then there exists an adversary $\mathcal{B}$ that factorizes N with almost the same time as $\mathcal{A}$.

Remark 1. *In general, we say that an integer n is B-semi-smooth if all prime factors of n except one are smaller than B. In this meaning, a semi-smooth RSA modulus $N = PQ$ is not semi-smooth. Rather, $P - 1$ and $Q - 1$ are B-semi-smooth. Similarly, the order of the semi-smooth subgroup is not semi-smooth. Though this may be somehow confusing, we use this terminology for consistency to [22].*

Signed Groups. [16]. Let $N = PQ = (2p'p + 1)(2q'q + 1)$ be a semi-smooth RSA modulus. For any subgroup $H \subset \mathbb{Z}_N^*$, we define its signed group as $H^+ := \{|x| : x \in H\}$ where $|x|$ is the absolute value of x when it is represented as an element of $\{-(N - 1)/2, \ldots, (N - 1)/2\}$. This is certainly a group by defining a multiplication as $x \circ y := |(xy \mod N)|$ for $x, y \in H^+$. For simplicity, we often denote multiplications on H^+ as usual multiplication when it is clear that we are working over a signed group. If H is a subgroup of $\mathbb{QR}_N$, then $H \cong H^+$ by the natural projection since $-1 \notin \mathbb{QR}_N$. In particular, $\mathbb{QR}_N^+$ is a cyclic group with order $p'q'pq$ and G^+ is a cyclic group with order $p'q'$. We call $\mathbb{QR}_N^+$ as a group of signed quadratic residues and G^+ as a signed semi-smooth subgroup. A remarkable property of $\mathbb{QR}_N^+$ is that it is efficiently recognizable, that is, there exists an efficient algorithm that determine whether given string is an element of $\mathbb{QR}_N^+$ or not [16]. Note that such an algorithm is not known for G^+.

Blum-Blum-Shub Pseudorandom Number Generator. Here, we recall the Blum-Blum-Shub (BBS) pseudorandom number generator [3]; more precisely, its signed variant appeared in [22]. It is defined on $\mathbb{QR}_N^+$ and uses the Goldreich-Levin predicate [14]. For $u \in \mathbb{QR}_N^+$, $r \in \{0,1\}^{\ell_N}$ and $\ell_K \in \mathbb{N}$, we define $\mathsf{BBS}_{r,\ell_K}(u) := (\mathsf{GL}_r(u), \mathsf{GL}_r(u^2), \ldots, \mathsf{GL}_r(u^{2^{\ell_K-1}}))$ where $\mathsf{GL}_r(u)$ denotes the bitwise inner product of r and u.

We define the BBS advantage of an adversary $\mathcal{A}$ with respect to IGen on a signed semi-smooth subgroup G^+ as $\mathsf{Adv}_{\mathcal{A},\mathsf{IGen}}^{bbs,\ell_K,G^+}(\lambda) :=$ $|\Pr[\mathcal{A}(N, z, r, \mathsf{BBS}_{r,\ell_K}(u)) = 1] - \Pr[\mathcal{A}(N, z, r, U_{\{0,1\}^{\ell_K}}) = 1]|$ where $N \xleftarrow{\$}$ $\mathsf{IGen}(1^\lambda)$, $u \xleftarrow{\$} G^+$, $z := u^{2^{\ell_K}}$, $r \xleftarrow{\$} \{0,1\}^{\ell_N}$, $U_{\{0,1\}^{\ell_K}} \xleftarrow{\$} \{0,1\}^{\ell_K}$.[2] $\mathcal{A}$ (t,ϵ)-breaks the BBS generator if $\mathcal{A}$ runs in time at most t and we have $\mathsf{Adv}_{\mathcal{A},\mathsf{IGen}}^{bbs,\ell_K,G^+}(\lambda) \geq \epsilon$. Similarly as in [22], we can show that if the factoring assumption holds for IGen and ℓ_K is polynomially bounded in the security parameter, then for any efficient adversary $\mathcal{A}$, $\mathsf{Adv}_{\mathcal{A},\mathsf{IGen}}^{bbs,\ell_K,G^+}(\lambda)$ is negligible.[3]

3 Our Main Theorem

In this section, we show our main theorem. Our main theorem abstracts the technique to prove the CCA security of a PKE scheme on a signed semi-smooth subgroup. In the following, we prepare some properties about a semi-smooth subgroup to prove our main theorem in Sec. 3.1 and state and prove our main theorem in Sec. 3.2.

3.1 Preparation for Our Main Theorem

Here, we define subgroup $G^\perp$ in $\mathbb{QR}_N$ and show its properties to prove our main theorem. For a semi-smooth RSA modulus $N = PQ = (2p'p + 1)(2q'q + 1)$, we denote the unique subgroup of $\mathbb{QR}_N$ with order pq by $G^\perp$. Then we have $\mathbb{QR}_N = G \times G^\perp$ and therefore we have $\mathbb{QR}_N^+ = G^+ \times (G^\perp)^+$. In the following, we show some easy propositions, whose proofs are given in the full version.

---

[2] Note that the BBS generator is defined on $\mathbb{QR}_N^+$. However, we consider its advantage on G^+.

[3] The only difference from [22] is that we are working over G^+ whereas [22] considered on G. However, it is easily checked that we can prove the pseudorandomness of the BBS generator similarly.

Proposition 1. *If* $u \in \mathrm{QR}_N^+$, *then* $u^{p'q'} \in (G^\perp)^+$. *In particular, if* $u \in G^+$, *then we have* $u^{p'q'} = 1$.

Proposition 2. *For* $x \in \mathrm{QR}_N^+$, $x \in (G^\perp)^+$ *is equivalent to* $x^{P_B} = 1$. *In particular,* $(G^\perp)^+$ *is efficiently recognizable.*

The following lemma claims that if given any element of $(G^\perp)^+$ which is not equal to 1, then N is factorized efficiently. The idea behind the proof of this lemma is used in [15]. The proof of this lemma can be found in the full version.

Lemma 1 *Let* $N = PQ = (2p'p+1)(2q'q+1)$ *be a semi-smooth RSA modulus. There exists an efficient algorithm* $\mathcal{A}$ *that factorizes* N *if* N *and any element* $h \in (G^\perp)^+ \setminus \{1\}$ *are given.*

3.2   Our Main Theorem

Here, we state and prove our main theorem. Our main theorem is abstract formalization of our technique to prove the CCA security of a scheme on G^+. In particular, this is the technique to deal with an *invalid* query by an adversary, where invalid query means that it is out of G^+. Briefly, our main theorem states that any efficient CCA adversary cannot make an invalid query that satisfies a verification equation in a decryption algorithm with non-negligible probability. By using this theorem, we can simulate a decryption oracle for both valid and invalid queries though we still cannot tell whether that is valid or not. Thus we can overcome the difficulty of an invalid query.

Then we prepare some definitions to state the formal description of our theorem. First, as an abstraction of decryption oracles in CCA secure schemes on G^+, we consider a family of (deterministic) oracles $\mathcal{D} = \{\mathcal{D}_{N,x}\}$ where $N = (2p'p+1)(2q'q+1)$ is a semi-smooth RSA modulus and $x \in [2^{\ell_{p'}+\ell_{q'}+\lambda}]$ that satisfies the following properties.

- Input of $\mathcal{D}_{N,x}$ consists of two elements in QR_N^+.[4]
- $\mathcal{D}_{N,x}$ can be efficiently simulated if N and x are known. That is, there exists an efficient algorithm Sim such that $\mathrm{Sim}(N, x, A, B) = \mathcal{D}_{N,x}(A, B)$ for all integers N, x and $(A, B) \in \mathrm{QR}_N^+ \times \mathrm{QR}_N^+$
- $\mathcal{D}_{N,x}(A, B)$ returns $\perp$ if $f_1(A, B)^x \neq f_2(A, B)$ where $f_1 : \mathrm{QR}_N^+ \times \mathrm{QR}_N^+ \to \mathrm{QR}_N^+$ and $f_2 : \mathrm{QR}_N^+ \times \mathrm{QR}_N^+ \to \mathrm{QR}_N^+$ are efficiently computable functions which do not depend on x.
- For $(A, B) \in \mathrm{QR}_N^+ \times \mathrm{QR}_N^+$, if $f_1(A, B) \in G^+$ holds, then $\mathcal{D}_{N,x}(A, B)$ is completely determined by $(x \bmod p'q')$. That is, if $x \equiv x' \bmod p'q'$, then $\mathcal{D}_{N,x}(A, B) = \mathcal{D}_{N,x'}(A, B)$ for all $(A, B) \in \mathrm{QR}_N^+ \times \mathrm{QR}_N^+$ such that $f_1(A, B) \in G^+$.

---

[4] We define input of $\mathcal{D}_{N,x}$ as two group elements in QR_N^+ since ciphertexts of most factoring-based CCA secure KEM consist of two group elements. We can easily extend our main theorem to more general cases (i.e., cases that the ciphertext consists of more than two group elements.).

We say that $\mathcal{D}$ is *compatible* for our main theorem if the above conditions are satisfied. Note that decryption algorithms of most CCA secure KEMs from the factoring assumption in the standard model [17,22,20,21] satisfy the above conditions by defining f and g properly when they are instantiated on G^+. For example, as seen in Sec. 4, the decryption algorithm of the Hofheinz-Kiltz scheme [17,18] on G^+ is compatible for our main theorem by defining $f_1(A,B) := A^{2^\nu}$ and $f_2(A,B) = A^{2^\nu} B^{-H(B)}$ where H is a hash function contained in a public key and ν is a constant which depends on a security parameter. We say that a query $(A,B) \in \mathbb{QR}_N^+ \times \mathbb{QR}_N^+$ to $\mathcal{D}_{N,x}$ is *effective* if $f_1(A,B)^{x+np'q'} = f_2(A,B)$ for some $n \in \mathbb{Z}$ and $f_1(A,B) \notin G^+$. Then, we define an experiment for an adversary $\mathcal{A}$ which we call Main with respect to an oracle $\mathcal{D}$ as follows.

Experiment $\mathsf{Main}_{\mathcal{A},\mathsf{IGen},\mathcal{D}}(\lambda)$
$N \leftarrow \mathsf{IGen}(1^\lambda)$, $g \xleftarrow{\$} G^+$, $x \xleftarrow{\$} [2^{\ell_{p'}+\ell_{q'}+\lambda}]$, $X := g^x$
Run $\mathcal{A}^{\mathcal{D}_{N,x}}(N,g,X)$
If $\mathcal{A}$ made at least one *effective* query (A,B), then return 1, and otherwise return 0.

We define the advantage $\mathsf{Adv}^{main}_{\mathcal{A},\mathsf{IGen},\mathcal{D}}(\lambda)$ of an adversary $\mathcal{A}$ in $\mathsf{Main}_{\mathcal{A},\mathsf{IGen},\mathcal{D}}(\lambda)$ as the probability that the experiment returns 1. We say that $\mathcal{A}$ (t,q,ϵ)-wins $\mathsf{Main}_{\mathcal{A},\mathsf{IGen},\mathcal{D}}(\lambda)$ if $\mathcal{A}$ runs in time at most t, makes queries at most q times and $\mathsf{Adv}^{main}_{\mathcal{A},\mathsf{IGen},\mathcal{D}}(\lambda) \geq \epsilon$. Now we are ready to state our main theorem.

Theorem 1. *If the factoring assumption holds and $\mathcal{D}$ is compatible with our main theorem, then $\mathsf{Adv}^{main}_{\mathcal{A},\mathsf{IGen},\mathcal{D}}(\lambda)$ is negligible for any efficient algorithm $\mathcal{A}$. More precisely, If there exists $\mathcal{A}$ which $(t_{main}, q_{main}, \epsilon_{main})$-wins $\mathsf{Main}_{\mathcal{A},\mathsf{IGen},\mathcal{D}}(\lambda)$, then there exists $\mathcal{B}$ which $(t_{fact}, \epsilon_{fact})$-breaks the factoring assumption, where $t_{fact} \approx t_{main}$ and $\epsilon_{fact} + O(2^{-\lambda}) \geq \epsilon_{main}/2$.*

Proof. We consider a slightly modified experiment $\mathsf{Main}'_{\mathcal{A},\mathsf{IGen},\mathcal{D}}(\lambda)$. $\mathsf{Main}'_{\mathcal{A},\mathsf{IGen},\mathcal{D}}(\lambda)$ is the same as $\mathsf{Main}_{\mathcal{A},\mathsf{IGen},\mathcal{D}}(\lambda)$ except that x is chosen uniformly from $[M]$ instead of $[2^{\ell_{p'}+\ell_{q'}+\lambda}]$, where M is the smallest multiple of $p'q'$ larger than $2^{\ell_{p'}+\ell_{q'}+\lambda}$. It is easy to see that the statistical distance between the uniform distribution on $[2^{\ell_{p'}+\ell_{q'}+\lambda}]$ and the uniform distribution on $[M]$ are exponentially small, and therefore we consider the experiment $\mathsf{Main}'_{\mathcal{A},\mathsf{IGen},\mathcal{D}}(\lambda)$ in the following.

For $x \in [M]$, we can uniquely define $r \in [p'q']$ and $m \in \mathbb{Z}$ such that $x = r + mp'q'$. Then r is uniformly distributed in $[p'q']$ and m is uniformly distributed in $\{0, 1, \ldots, \lfloor \frac{2^{\ell_{p'}+\ell_{q'}+\lambda}}{p'q'} \rfloor\}$ when $x \xleftarrow{\$} [M]$. Then we can restate the condition that $(A,B) \in \mathbb{QR}_N^+ \times \mathbb{QR}_N^+$ is effective as that $f_1(A,B)^{r+n'p'q'} = f_2(A,B)$ holds for some $n' \in \mathbb{Z}$ and $f_1(A,B) \notin G^+$.

In the following, we consider how much information about m $\mathcal{A}$ can obtain in the experiment. We can see that the distribution of X is completely determined by r and independent from m, and therefore $\mathcal{A}$ cannot obtain any information about m from X in the experiment. Moreover, we can prove the following claim.

Claim 1. *If* $(A, B) \in QR_N^+ \times QR_N^+$ *is not an effective query, then the response by the oracle* $\mathcal{D}_{N,x}$ *to this query does not leak any information about* m.

Proof of Claim 1. Assume that (A, B) is not an effective query. If $f_1(A, B) \in G^+$, then $\mathcal{D}_x(A, B)$ does not reveal any information about m by the assumption that $\mathcal{D}$ is compatible with our main theorem. If $f_1(A, B) \notin G^+$, then $\mathcal{D}_x(A, B)$ returns $\bot$ since (A, B) is not effective and therefore $f_1(A, B)^x \neq f_2(A, B)$. We show that this reveals no information about m. This is because even if m is replaced by any integer m' (that is, if $x = r + mp'q'$ is replaced by $x' = r + m'p'q'$), the response by $\mathcal{D}$ is always $\bot$. This is because if there exists m' such that $\mathcal{D}$ does not return $\bot$, then there exists $n' \in \mathbb{Z}$ such that $f_1(A, B)^{x'+n'p'q'} = f_2(A, B)$, and it contradicts to that (A, B) is not effective.   □

Then we return to the proof of Theorem 1. Assume that there exists an efficient algorithm $\mathcal{A}$ which makes an effective query in $\mathsf{Main}'_{\mathcal{A},\mathsf{IGen},\mathcal{D}}(\lambda)$ with non-negligible probability. Then we construct an efficient algorithm $\mathcal{C}$ that outputs an element of $(G^\bot)^+ \setminus \{1\}$ with non-negligible probability. If such $\mathcal{C}$ exists, then we can construct an efficient algorithm $\mathcal{B}$ that factorizes N by Lemma 1 and it contradicts to the factoring assumption. The construction of $\mathcal{C}$ is as follows.

$\mathcal{C}(N):$ $\mathcal{C}$ chooses $g \xleftarrow{\$} G^+$, $x \xleftarrow{\$} [2^{\ell_{p'}+\ell_{q'}+\lambda}]$, sets $X := g^x$ and gives (N, g, X) to $\mathcal{A}$ as input. Whenever $\mathcal{A}$ queries $(A, B) \in QR_N^+$, $\mathcal{C}$ returns $\mathcal{D}_{N,x}(A, B)$ to $\mathcal{A}$ by using N and x. $\mathcal{C}$ also calculates $f_2(A, B)f_1(A, B)^{-x}$ and if $f_2(A, B)f_1(A, B)^{-x} \in (G^\bot)^+ \setminus \{1\}$ then $\mathcal{C}$ outputs it and halts. If $\mathcal{A}$ halts before $\mathcal{C}$ outputs any value, then $\mathcal{C}$ aborts.

It is easy to see that the distribution of the input (N, g, X) of $\mathcal{A}$ is exponentially close to that in $\mathsf{Main}'_{\mathcal{A},\mathsf{IGen}}(\lambda)$ and $\mathcal{C}$ correctly simulates $\mathcal{D}_{N,x}$ for $\mathcal{A}$. Let (A, B) be the first effective query by $\mathcal{A}$. It suffices to show that $f_2(A, B)f_1(A, B)^{-x} \in (G^\bot)^+ \setminus \{1\}$ with non-negligible probability. Since (A, B) is effective, we have $f_1(A, B)^{r+n'p'q'} = f_2(A, B)$ for some $n' \in \mathbb{Z}$ and $f_1(A, B) \in QR_N^+ \setminus G^+$. Then we have $f_2(A, B)f_1(A, B)^{-x} = (f_1(A, B)^{p'q'})^{n'-m}$. We can see $(f_1(A, B)^{p'q'})^{n'-m} \in (G^\bot)^+$ from Proposition 1. What is remained to prove is $(f_1(A, B)^{p'q'})^{n'-m} \neq 1$ with non-negligible probability. Let e be the order of $f_1(A, B)^{p'q'}$. Since $f_1(A, B) \in QR_N^+ \setminus G^+$, we have $f_1(A, B)^{p'q'} \neq 1$ and $e \geq 3$. What we should prove is $e \not| n' - m$ with non-negligible probability. We can see from Claim 1 that $\mathcal{A}$ have no information about m more than that is distributed uniformly in $\{0, 1, \ldots, \lfloor \frac{2^{\ell_{p'}+\ell_{q'}+\lambda}}{p'q'} \rfloor\}$ before $\mathcal{A}$ makes the first effective query. Therefore it is clear that the probability that $e \not| n' - m$ is larger than $1/2$.[5] This completes the proof of Theorem 1.

4   Variants of Hofheinz-Kiltz Scheme

Hofheinz and Kiltz [17] proposed a practical CCA secure PKE scheme in the standard model under the factoring assumption. Following the work, Mei et al.

---

[5] Here, we implicitly assume $\lfloor \frac{2^{\ell_{p'}+\ell_{q'}+\lambda}}{p'q'} \rfloor \geq 3$. Note that this is always true if $\lambda \geq 2$.

[22] showed that the efficiency of the Hofheinz-Kiltz scheme can be improved if it is instantiated on the semi-smooth subgroup. Specifically, in 80-bit security, the encryption and decryption become 2.5 and 1.5 times faster than those of the original Hofheinz-Kiltz scheme, respectively. However, the security proof in [22] disregarded the fact that the semi-smooth subgroup is not efficiently recognizable and therefore the proof is incomplete. In this section, we present how to overcome the difficulty and give a complete proof for the Hofheinz-Kiltz scheme instantiated on the (signed) semi-smooth subgroup.

4.1 Description of Hofheinz-Kiltz Scheme on Signed Subgroups

The construction of the Hofheinz-Kiltz scheme on G^+ is as follows. We call this scheme as HK_{sss}. This is the same scheme as Mei et al.'s scheme [22] except that we are working over G^+ instead of G.[6] In the following, ℓ_H is the length of hash value, ℓ_K is the symmetric key length and $\nu := \ell_H + \ell_K$.

Keygeneration : $\mathsf{Gen}(1^\lambda)$ chooses $N \leftarrow \mathsf{IGen}(1^\lambda)$, a target-collision resistant function $H : \mathbb{QR}_N^+ \to [2^{\ell_H} - 1]$, $g \xleftarrow{\$} G^+$, $r \xleftarrow{\$} \{0,1\}^{\ell_N}$, and $\rho \xleftarrow{\$} [2^{\ell_{p'} + \ell_{q'} + \lambda}]$. Then it sets $X := g^{\rho 2^\nu}$. It outputs the public key $PK := (N, g, X, r, H)$ and the secret key $SK := (\rho)$.

Encapsulation : $\mathsf{Enc}(PK)$ chooses $\mu \xleftarrow{\$} [2^{\ell_{p'} + \ell_{q'} + \lambda}]$ and sets $R := g^{\mu 2^\nu}$, $t := H(R)$, $S := (g^t X)^\mu$, $T := g^{\mu 2^{\ell_H}}$ and $K := \mathsf{BBS}_r(T)$. Then it outputs the ciphertext $C := (R, S)$ and the key K.

Decapsulation : $\mathsf{Dec}(SK, (R, S))$ verifies $(R, S) \in \mathbb{QR}_N^+ \times \mathbb{QR}_N^+$ and rejects if not. Then it computes $t := H(R)$ and verifies $S^{2^\nu} = R^{t + \rho 2^\nu}$, and rejects if not. Next it computes $a, b, c \in \mathbb{Z}$ such that $2^c = \gcd(t, 2^\nu) = at + b2^\nu$. Finally, it computes $T := (S^a R^{b - a\rho})^{2^{\ell_H - c}}$, $K := \mathsf{BBS}_r(T)$ and outputs K.

The proof of the correctness of this scheme can be found in the full version.

4.2 Security

We prove that the scheme is CCA secure under the factoring assumption. Note that Mei et al.' [22] also claimed to prove it. However their proof does not care about the fact that the (signed) semi-smooth subgroup is not efficiently recognizable, and therefore their proof is not sufficient. Formally, the security of HK_{sss} is stated as follows.

Theorem 2. *If the factoring assumption holds for IGen and H is a target collision resistant hash function, then HK_{sss} is CCA secure. More precisely, if there exists an adversary $\mathcal{A}$ which (t, q, ϵ)-breaks the CCA security of the above scheme, then there exists an adversary $\mathcal{B}$ that $(t_{tcr}, \epsilon_{tcr})$-breaks the target collision resistance of H, an adversary $\mathcal{C}$ that $(t_{fact}, \epsilon_{fact})$-breaks the factoring assumption with respect to IGen and an adversary $\mathcal{D}$ that $(t_{bbs}, \epsilon_{bbs})$-breaks the BBS generator, where $t_{tcr} \approx t$, $t_{fact} \approx t$, $t_{bbs} \approx t$ and $2\epsilon_{fact} + \epsilon_{tcr} + \epsilon_{bbs} + O(2^{-\lambda}) \geq \epsilon$.*

---

[6] In this paper, we only consider the scheme on G^+. However, the situation is almost the same for the scheme on G (i.e., Mei et al.'s scheme), and we can prove the CCA security of the scheme on G almost similarly.

Proof.(sketch) Here, we give only an intuitive explanation. The full proof can be found in the full version. First, we try to prove the security in the same way as the original Hofheinz-Kiltz scheme [17] (as discussed in [22]). Assume that there exists an adversary $\mathcal{A}$ that breaks the CCA security of HK_{sss}. We construct an adversary $\mathcal{B}$ that breaks the security of the BBS generator by using $\mathcal{A}$. The construction of $\mathcal{B}$ is as follows.

$\mathcal{B}(N, z, r, V)$: $\mathcal{B}$ chooses H and g as in HK_{sss}, and sets $R^* := z$, $t^* := H(R^*)$, $\beta \xleftarrow{\$} [2^{\ell_{p'}+\ell_{q'}+\lambda}]$, $X := g^{-t^*+\beta 2^{\nu}}$ (This implicitly defines ρ as a value such that $\rho \equiv \beta - t^*/2^{\nu} \bmod p'q'$.), $S^* := (R^*)^{\beta}$ and $K^* := V$. Then $\mathcal{B}$ gives (N, g, X, r, H) as a public key, (R^*, S^*) as a challenge ciphertext and K^* as a challenge key to $\mathcal{A}$. When $\mathcal{A}$ makes a query $(R, S) \in \mathbb{QR}_N^+ \times \mathbb{QR}_N^+$ to the decryption oracle, $\mathcal{B}$ does as follows. If $S^{2^{\nu}} \neq R^{t-t^*+\beta 2^{\nu}}$ or $t = t^*$ where $t := H(R)$, then $\mathcal{B}$ returns $\bot$ to $\mathcal{A}$, and otherwise $\mathcal{B}$ can simulate the decryption oracle by the standard "all-but-one extraction", and return the decryption result to $\mathcal{A}$. Finally, when $\mathcal{A}$ outputs b', $\mathcal{B}$ also outputs b'.

It seems that $\mathcal{B}$ correctly simulates the CCA game for $\mathcal{A}$ and therefore has the same BBS advantage as $\mathcal{A}$'s CCA advantage. However, this is not true. More precisely, the verification equation $S^{2^{\nu}} = R^{t-t^*+\beta 2^{\nu}}$ in the simulation by $\mathcal{B}$ is not always equivalent to the real verification equation $S^{2^{\nu}} = R^{t+\rho 2^{\nu}}$. That is, if $R \in G^+$, then these equations are equivalent since we have $\mathrm{ord}(R)|p'q'$ and $\rho \equiv \beta - t^*/2^{\nu} \bmod p'q'$. However, otherwise $\mathrm{ord}(R)$ may not be a divisor of $p'q'$ and therefore these equations are not equivalent. More precisely, $S^{2^{\nu}} = R^{t-t^*+\beta 2^{\nu}}$ is equivalent to $S^{2^{\nu}} = R^{t+\rho 2^{\nu}+np'q'}$ for some $n \in \mathbb{Z}$

To overcome this difficulty, we prove that if $R \notin G^+$, then (R, S) does not satisfy $S^{2^{\nu}} = R^{t-t^*+\beta 2^{\nu}}$ nor $S^{2^{\nu}} = R^{t+\rho 2^{\nu}}$ with overwhelming probability. If this is proven, then the simulation of the decryption oracle by $\mathcal{B}$ is correct with overwhelming probability even if $R \notin G^+$ since both real and simulated decryption oracle return $\bot$ with overwhelming probability, and therefore we can prove that $\mathcal{B}$ breaks the BBS generator with almost the same advantage as $\mathcal{A}$ breaks the CCA security of the scheme. To prove it, we use our main theorem (Theorem 1). To do so, we check that the decryption oracle in the scheme is compatible with our main theorem by defining $f_1(R, S) = R^{2^{\nu}}$, $f_2(R, S) = S^{2^{\nu}} R^{-t}$ where $t = H(R)$. This is because $f_1(R, S)^{\rho} = f_2(R, S)$ is equivalent to $S^{2^{\nu}} = R^{t+\rho 2^{\nu}}$, and if $f_1(R, S) = R^{2^{\nu}} \in G^+$ and $S^{2^{\nu}} = R^{t+\rho 2^{\nu}}$ hold, then we have $R \in G^+$ and $S \in G^+$, and therefore the output of the decryption oracle is completely determined by $(\rho \bmod p'q')$. Therefore by our main theorem, we can prove that $\mathcal{A}$'s query (R, S) is not effective with overwhelming probability, i.e., if $R \notin G^+$, then $S^{2^{\nu}} \neq R^{t+\rho 2^{\nu}+np'q'}$ for all $n \in \mathbb{Z}$. Then our claim follows from it immediately, and the proof is completed. $\qquad\square$

4.3 Other CCA Secure Schemes on (Signed) Semi-smooth Subgroup

There is the same problem in the security proof of the second scheme in [22] and we can fix it by the same technique. Moreover, we can apply our technique to prove the security of other variants of the Hofheinz-Kiltz scheme [20,21] instantiated on (signed) semi-smooth subgroup. Note that it was mentioned by the authors of [20,21] that these schemes can be instantiated on a semi-smooth subgroup and enjoy high efficiency. However, they did not take care about the fact that a semi-smooth subgroup is not efficiently recognizable. Therefore, more careful argument is required to prove the security of these schemes as seen in this paper.

5   The Strong Diffie-Hellman Assumption

In this section, we present that our main theorem can be also used for proving the SDH assumption on a signed semi-smooth subgroup is implied by the factoring assumption. It is shown that the SDH assumption holds on $\mathbb{QR}_N^+$ under the factoring assumption in [16]. However, the proof relies on the fact that $\mathbb{QR}_N^+$ is efficiently recognizable and cannot be applied on G^+ since it is not known to be efficiently recognizable. We use our main theorem (Theorem 1) to overcome this difficulty.

The SDH assumption is first proposed in [1]. The SDH assumption informally says that any efficient algorithm cannot solve the CDH problem even with a fixed base DDH oracle. To define the SDH assumption on G^+, we consider the following game for an adversary $\mathcal{A}$. At first, semi-smooth RSA modulus N is generated by $N \xleftarrow{\$} \mathsf{IGen}(1^\lambda)$ as well as $x, y \xleftarrow{\$} [2^{\ell_{p'} + \ell_{q'} + \lambda}]$ and $g \xleftarrow{\$} G^+$.[7] Then, X and Y are set as $X = g^x$ and $Y = g^y$. The adversary $\mathcal{A}$ is given (N, g, X, Y) as input, and finally $\mathcal{A}$ outputs Z. In the game, $\mathcal{A}$ has access to an oracle DDH_x which returns 1 if $A^x = B$, and otherwise 0 for a query $(A, B) \in \mathbb{QR}_N^+ \times \mathbb{QR}_N^+$. Let T be the event that $Z = g^{xy}$ holds. We define the SDH advantage of $\mathcal{A}$ as $\mathsf{Adv}_{\mathcal{A}, \mathsf{IGen}}^{sdh}(\lambda) := \Pr[T]$. We say that $\mathcal{A}$ (t, q, ϵ)-breaks the SDH assumption if $\mathcal{A}$ runs in time at most t, makes queries at most q times and $\mathsf{Adv}_{\mathcal{A}, \mathsf{IGen}}^{sdh}(\lambda) \geq \epsilon$. We say that the SDH assumption holds on G^+ with respect to IGen if $\mathsf{Adv}_{\mathcal{A}, \mathsf{IGen}}^{sdh}(\lambda)$ is negligible for any efficient adversary $\mathcal{A}$.

There are two differences between the SDH assumption on G^+ defined above and the original SDH assumption on a prime order group. They are to make it useful for the security proof of cryptographic protocols. The first difference is that x and y are chosen from exponentially larger domain than the order of G^+. This is because we cannot know the order of G^+ without knowing factorization of N. The second difference is that an adversary is allowed to query not only elements of G^+ but also elements of $\mathbb{QR}_N^+$. This is because G^+ is not efficiently recognizable and the adversary (and even a simulator in security proofs which does not know the factorization) cannot tell whether its query is elements of G^+ or not.

Then we state our theorem formally.

Theorem 3. *If the factoring assumption holds with respect to* IGen, *then the SDH assumption holds on* G^+ *with respect to* IGen. *More precisely, if there exists*

---

[7] Then g is a generator of G^+ with overwhelming probability.

an adversary $\mathcal{A}$ which $(t_{sdh}, q_{sdh}, \epsilon_{sdh})$ breaks the SDH assumption on G^+ with respect to IGen, then there exists an adversary $\mathcal{B}$ which $(t_{fact}, \epsilon_{fact})$-breaks the factoring assumption with respect to IGen and $\mathcal{C}$ which $(t'_{fact}, \epsilon'_{fact})$-breaks the factoring assumption with respect to IGen, where $t_{fact} \approx t_{sdh}$, $t'_{fact} \approx t_{sdh}$ and $2\epsilon_{fact} + \epsilon'_{fact} + O(2^{-\lambda}) \geq \epsilon_{sdh}$.

Proof (sketch). Here, we give only an intuitive explanation. The full proof can be found in the full version. First, we try to prove the theorem similarly as [16, Theorem 2] which states that the factoring assumption implies the SDH assumption on $\mathbb{QR}_N^+$. Assume that there exists an adversary $\mathcal{A}$ that breaks the SDH assumption on G^+. We construct an adversary $\mathcal{B}$ that breaks the factoring assumption by using $\mathcal{A}$. To do so, we construct an algorithm $\mathcal{C}$ that is given N and $h \xleftarrow{\$} G^+$ and computes $h^{1/2}$. If such $\mathcal{C}$ exists, a factoring adversary $\mathcal{B}$ is easily constructed. The construction of $\mathcal{C}$ is as follows.

$\mathcal{C}(N, h)$: $\mathcal{C}$ sets $g := h^2$, $a, b \xleftarrow{\$} [2^{\ell_{p'} + \ell_{q'} + \lambda}]$, $X := hg^a$ and $Y := hg^b$. This implicitly defines x and y as a value such that $x \equiv a + 1/2 \bmod p'q'$ and $y \equiv b + 1/2 \bmod p'q'$. For DDH query $(A, B) \in \mathbb{QR}_N^+ \times \mathbb{QR}_N^+$ by $\mathcal{A}$, $\mathcal{C}$ verifies $A^{2a+1} = B^2$ and returns 1 if the equation holds, and otherwise 0 to $\mathcal{A}$. Finally, if $\mathcal{A}$ outputs Z, then $\mathcal{C}$ outputs $Zh^{-(2ab+a+b)}$.

We consider the success probability of $\mathcal{C}$. If $Z = g^{xy}$, then $Zh^{-(2ab+a+b)} = g^{xy}h^{-(2ab+a+b)} = (h^2)^{(a+1/2)(b+1/2)}h^{-(2ab+a+b)} = h^{1/2}$. Therefore, if $\mathcal{C}$ correctly simulates the SDH game for $\mathcal{A}$, then $\mathcal{C}$ succeed to compute $h^{1/2}$ with the probability larger than $\mathcal{A}$ wins in the SDH game, and the theorem follows. However, one can see that the simulation of DDH oracle by $\mathcal{C}$ is not always correct when $A \notin G^+$. More precisely, $A^{2a+1} = B^2$ is equivalent to $A^{x+np'q'} = B$ for some $n \in \mathbb{Z}$.

To overcome this difficulty, we prove that if $A \notin G^+$, then (A, B) does not satisfy $A^{2a+1} = B^2$ nor $A^x = B$ with overwhelming probability. If this is proven, then the simulation of the decryption oracle by $\mathcal{C}$ is correct with overwhelming probability even if $A \notin G^+$ since both real and simulated oracle returns 0 with overwhelming probability, and therefore we can prove that $\mathcal{C}$ succeeds in computing $h^{1/2}$ with almost the same probability as $\mathcal{A}$'s SDH advantage. To prove it, we use our main theorem. One can see that the DDH oracle is compatible with our main theorem if we interpret that the DDH oracle outputs 0 as that it outputs $\perp$ by defining $f_1(A, B) = A$ and $f_2(A, B) = B$. Therefore by our main theorem, we can prove that $\mathcal{A}$'s query (A, B) is not effective with overwhelming probability i.e., if $A \notin G^+$, then $A^{x+np'q'} \neq B$ for all $n \in \mathbb{Z}$ with overwhelming probability. Then our claim follows immediately and the proof is completed. $\square$

Moreover, we can prove the following more strong assumption called the double strong Diffie-Hellman (DSDH) assumption [10] on G^+. The DSDH assumption is defined as the same as the SDH assumption except an adversary is allowed to access a DDH oracle with base y adding to that with base x. Then the following theorem holds.

Theorem 4. *If the factoring assumption holds with respect to IGen, then the DSDH assumption holds on G^+ with respect to IGen.*

This theorem can be proven similarly as Theorem 3 except that we require "double" version of our main theorem. The details can be found in the full version.

6   Hashed ElGamal KEM

Hashed ElGamal KEM (DHIES) [1] is a natural variant of the ElGamal KEM in which the DEM key is replaced by output of a hash function. It is well known that the Strong Diffie-Hellman (SDH) assumption on the underlying group implies the CCA security of hashed ElGamal KEM is CCA in the random oracle model [1,8]. Moreover, [16] showed that the factoring assumption implies the SDH assumption on the group of signed quadratic residues $\mathbb{QR}_N^+$ and therefore Hashed ElGamal KEM on $\mathbb{QR}_N^+$ is CCA secure in the random oracle model under the factoring assumption.

In this section, we show that the hashed ElGamal KEM on G^+ is also CCA secure in the random oracle model under the factoring assumption. This follows from Theorem 3. Since the order of G^+ is smaller than that of $\mathbb{QR}_N^+$, our construction is more efficient than the scheme on $\mathbb{QR}_N^+$ with regard to the secret key size, encryption cost and decryption cost. (See Sec. 6.3.)

6.1   Construction

The proposed scheme $\mathsf{HEG}_{sss} = (\mathsf{Gen}, \mathsf{Enc}, \mathsf{Dec})$ is described as follows. We denote a DEM key length by ℓ_K.

Keygeneration: $\mathsf{Gen}(1^\lambda)$ sets $N \leftarrow \mathsf{IGen}(1^\lambda)$, chooses a hash function $H :$ $\{0,1\}^{2\ell_N} \rightarrow \{0,1\}^{\ell_K}$, a generator $g \xleftarrow{\$} G^+$, $x \xleftarrow{\$} [2^{\ell_{p'}+\ell_{q'}+\lambda}]$ and sets $X :=$ g^x. Then $\mathsf{Gen}(1^\lambda)$ outputs the public key $PK := (N, g, X, H)$ and the secret key $SK := (x)$.
Encapsulation: $\mathsf{Enc}(PK)$ chooses $y \xleftarrow{\$} [2^{\ell_{p'}+\ell_{q'}+\lambda}]$ and sets $Y := g^y$ and $K :=$ $H(Y, X^y)$. Then $\mathsf{Enc}(PK)$ outputs the ciphertext Y and the DEM key K.
Decapsulation: $\mathsf{Dec}(SK, Y)$ verifies $Y \in \mathbb{QR}_N^+$ and rejects if not. Then $\mathsf{Dec}(SK, Y)$ sets $K := H(Y, Y^x)$ and outputs K.

6.2   Security

The security of HEG_{sss} is stated as the following theorem.

Theorem 5. *If the factoring assumption holds with respect to* IGen, *then* HEG_{sss} *is CCA secure in the random oracle model where* H *is modeled as a random oracle. More precisely, if there exists an adversary* $\mathcal{A}$ *which* (t, q, ϵ)-*breaks the CCA security of* HEG_{sss}, *then there exists an adversary* $\mathcal{B}$ *which* $(t_{fact}, \epsilon_{fact})$-*breaks the factoring assumption and* $\mathcal{C}$ *which* $(t'_{fact}, \epsilon'_{fact})$-*breaks the factoring assumption, where* $t_{fact} \approx t_{sdh}$, $t'_{fact} \approx t_{sdh}$ *and* $2\epsilon_{fact} + \epsilon'_{fact} + O(2^{-\lambda}) \geq \epsilon_{sdh}$.

This is proven by combining Theorem 3 and the following theorem.

Theorem 6. *If the SDH assumption holds on* G^+ *with respect to* IGen, *then* HEG_{sss} *is CCA secure in the random oracle model where* H *is modeled as a random* *oracle. More precisely, if there exists an adversary $\mathcal{A}$ which (t, q, ϵ)-breaks the CCA security of* HEG_{sss}, *then there exists an adversary $\mathcal{B}$ which $(t_{sdh}, q_{sdh}, \epsilon_{sdh})$-breaks the SDH assumption, where $t_{sdh} \approx t$, $q_{sdh} = q$ and $\epsilon_{sdh} = \epsilon$.*

Theorem 6 can be proven similarly as [16, Theorem 9] which claims that the SDH assumption implies the CCA security of Hashed ElGamal KEM on $\mathbb{QR}_N^+$.

6.3   Efficiency

Here, we compare HEG_{sss} with the the original HEG (that is the scheme on $\mathbb{QR}_N^+$ proposed in [16]). To estimate the efficiency of schemes, we use a parameter given in [15]. They propose for security parameter $\lambda = 80$, $\ell_N = 1024$, $\ell_{p'} = \ell_{q'} = 160$. The ciphertext size and the public key size of our scheme are 1024-bit and 3072-bit respectively, which is the same as that of HEG. Ignoring the cost to calculate H, HEG_{sss} needs about $3(\ell_{p'} + \ell_{q'} + \lambda) = 1200$ multiplications in the encapsulation algorithm whereas HEG needs about $3\ell_N = 3072$ multiplications. The decapsulation algorithm of our algorithm needs about $1.5(\ell_{p'} + \ell_{q'} + \lambda) = 600$ multiplications whereas HEG needs about $1.5\ell_N = 1536$ multiplications. Here we assume that an exponent of length ℓ requires 1.5 modular multiplications. To sum up, the encapsulation and the decapsulation algorithm of HEG_{sss} is about 2.5 times faster than that of HEG.

7   Non-interactive Key Exchange

Here, we instantiate the NIKE scheme in [10] on G^+. We prove that the proposed scheme is secure in the random oracle model under the factoring assumption as same as the scheme in [10] by using Theorem 4, which states that tha factoring assumption implies the DSDH assumption on G^+. Our proposed scheme is more efficient than the original scheme in [10].

7.1   Construction

The proposed scheme $\mathsf{NIKE}_{sss} = (\mathsf{CommonSetup}, \mathsf{NIKE.KeyGen}, \mathsf{SharedKey})$ is described as follows.

CommonSetup(1^λ): This computes $N \leftarrow \mathsf{IGen}(1^\lambda)$, sets $g \xleftarrow{\$} G^+$ and $params \leftarrow (H, N, g)$ and outputs $params$.

NIKE.KeyGen$(params, \mathsf{ID})$: This sets $sk \xleftarrow{\$} [2^{\ell_{p'} + \ell_{q'} + \lambda}]$ and $pk := g^{sk}$ and outputs (pk, sk).

SharedKey$(\mathsf{ID}_1, pk_1, \mathsf{ID}_2, sk_2)$: If $\mathsf{ID}_1 = \mathsf{ID}_2$ or $pk_1 \notin \mathbb{QR}_N^+$ or $pk_2 \notin \mathbb{QR}_N^+$, then this outputs $\bot$. Otherwise it outputs

$$\begin{cases} H(\mathsf{ID}_1, \mathsf{ID}_2, pk_1^{sk_2}) & (\text{If } \mathsf{ID}_1 > \mathsf{ID}_2.) \\ H(\mathsf{ID}_2, \mathsf{ID}_1, pk_1^{sk_2}) & (\text{If } \mathsf{ID}_2 > \mathsf{ID}_1.) \end{cases}.$$

7.2   Security

We show that NIKE_{sss} is secure in the random oracle model under the factoring assumption. More precisely, it is as follows.

Theorem 7. *If the factoring assumption holds with respect to IGen, then* NIKE$_{sss}$ *is secure in the random oracle model where H is modeled as a random oracle.*

This is easily proven by using Theorem 4 since [10] shows that the DSDH assumption implies the security of the NIKE scheme. Though [10] only considers the scheme on $\mathbb{QR}_N^+$, the situation is similar if we consider the scheme on G^+.

7.3 Efficiency

Here, we compare NIKE$_{sss}$ with the the original NIKE (that is the scheme on $\mathbb{QR}_N^+$ proposed in [10]). To estimate the efficiency of schemes, we use a parameter given in [15]. They propose for security parameter $\lambda = 80$, $\ell_N = 1024$, $\ell_{p'} = \ell_{q'} = 160$. The ciphertext size and the public key size of our scheme are 1024-bit and 3072-bit respectively, which is the same as that of NIKE. Ignoring the cost to calculate H, NIKE$_{sss}$ needs about $1.5(\ell_{p'} + \ell_{q'} + \lambda) = 600$ multiplications in SharedKey whereas NIKE needs about $1.5\ell_N = 1536$ multiplications. Here we assume that an exponent of length ℓ requires 1.5 modular multiplications. To sum up, SharedKey of NIKE$_{sss}$ is about 2.5 times faster than that of NIKE.

Acknowledgment. We would like to thank the anonymous reviewers and members of the study group "Shin-Akarui-Angou-Benkyou-Kai" for their helpful comments. Especially, we would like to thank the reviewer who pointed out our improper use of the term "semi-smooth" in the submitted manuscript.

References

1. Abdalla, M., Bellare, M., Rogaway, P.: The oracle diffie-hellman assumptions and an analysis of DHIES. In: Naccache, D. (ed.) CT-RSA 2001. LNCS, vol. 2020, pp. 143–158. Springer, Heidelberg (2001)
2. Bellare, M., Rogaway, P.: Random oracles are practical: A paradigm for designing efficient protocols. In: ACM Conference on Computer and Communications Security, pp. 62–73 (1993)
3. Blum, L., Blum, M., Shub, M.: A simple unpredictable pseudo-random number generator. SIAM J. Comput. 15(2), 364–383 (1986)
4. Canetti, R., Goldreich, O., Halevip, S.: The random oracle methodology, revisited (preliminary version). In: STOC, pp. 209–218 (1998)
5. Coron, J.-S., Joux, A., Mandal, A., Naccache, D., Tibouchi, M.: Cryptanalysis of the RSA subgroup assumption from TCC 2005. In: Catalano, D., Fazio, N., Gennaro, R., Nicolosi, A. (eds.) PKC 2011. LNCS, vol. 6571, pp. 147–155. Springer, Heidelberg (2011)
6. Cramer, R., Shoup, V.: Signature schemes based on the strong RSA assumption. ACM Trans. Inf. Syst. Secur. 3(3), 161–185 (2000)
7. Cramer, R., Shoup, V.: Universal hash proofs and a paradigm for adaptive chosen ciphertext secure public-key encryption. In: Knudsen, L.R. (ed.) EUROCRYPT 2002. LNCS, vol. 2332, pp. 45–64. Springer, Heidelberg (2002)
8. Cramer, R., Shoup, V.: Design and analysis of practical public-key encryption schemes. SIAM Journal on Computing 33(1), 167–226 (2003)
9. Dolev, D., Dwork, C., Naor, M.: Non-malleable cryptography (extended abstract). In: STOC, pp. 542–552 (1991)

10. Freire, E.S.V., Hofheinz, D., Kiltz, E., Paterson, K.G.: Non-interactive key exchange. In: Kurosawa, K., Hanaoka, G. (eds.) PKC 2013. LNCS, vol. 7778, pp. 254–271. Springer, Heidelberg (2013)
11. Fujisaki, E., Okamoto, T.: Secure integration of asymmetric and symmetric encryption schemes. In: Wiener, M. (ed.) CRYPTO 1999. LNCS, vol. 1666, pp. 537–554. Springer, Heidelberg (1999)
12. Goldreich, O.: Basing non-interactive zero-knowledge on (Enhanced) trapdoor permutations: The state of the art. In: Goldreich, O. (ed.) Studies in Complexity and Cryptography. LNCS, vol. 6650, pp. 406–421. Springer, Heidelberg (2011)
13. Goldwasser, S., Micali, S.: Probabilistic encryption. J. Comput. Syst. Sci. 28(2), 270–299 (1984)
14. Goldreich, O., Levin, L.A.: A hard-core predicate for all one-way functions. In: STOC, pp. 25–32 (1989)
15. Groth, J.: Cryptography in subgroups of Z_n^*. In: Kilian, J. (ed.) TCC 2005. LNCS, vol. 3378, pp. 50–65. Springer, Heidelberg (2005)
16. Hofheinz, D., Kiltz, E.: The group of signed quadratic residues and applications. In: Halevi, S. (ed.) CRYPTO 2009. LNCS, vol. 5677, pp. 637–653. Springer, Heidelberg (2009)
17. Hofheinz, D., Kiltz, E.: Practical chosen ciphertext secure encryption from factoring. In: Joux, A. (ed.) EUROCRYPT 2009. LNCS, vol. 5479, pp. 313–332. Springer, Heidelberg (2009)
18. Hofheinz, D., Kiltz, E., Shoup, V.: Practical chosen ciphertext secure encryption from factoring. J. Cryptology 26(1), 102–118 (2013)
19. Joye, M., Quisquater, J.-J., Yung, M.: On the power of misbehaving adversaries and security analysis of the original EPOC. In: Naccache, D. (ed.) CT-RSA 2001. LNCS, vol. 2020, pp. 208–222. Springer, Heidelberg (2001)
20. Lu, X., Li, B., Mei, Q., Liu, Y.: Improved tradeoff between encapsulation and decapsulation of HK09. In: Wu, C.-K., Yung, M., Lin, D. (eds.) Inscrypt 2011. LNCS, vol. 7537, pp. 131–141. Springer, Heidelberg (2012)
21. Lu, X., Li, B., Mei, Q., Liu, Y.: Improved efficiency of chosen ciphertext secure encryption from factoring. In: Ryan, M.D., Smyth, B., Wang, G. (eds.) ISPEC 2012. LNCS, vol. 7232, pp. 34–45. Springer, Heidelberg (2012)
22. Mei, Q., Li, B., Lu, X., Jia, D.: Chosen ciphertext secure encryption under factoring assumption revisited. In: Catalano, D., Fazio, N., Gennaro, R., Nicolosi, A. (eds.) PKC 2011. LNCS, vol. 6571, pp. 210–227. Springer, Heidelberg (2011)
23. Naccache, D., Stern, J.: A new public key cryptosystem based on higher residues. In: ACM Conference on Computer and Communications Security, pp. 59–66 (1998)
24. Naor, M., Yung, M.: Universal one-way hash functions and their cryptographic applications. In: STOC, pp. 33–43 (1989)
25. Naor, M., Yung, M.: Public-key cryptosystems provably secure against chosen ciphertext attacks. In: STOC, pp. 427–437 (1990)
26. Okamoto, T., Uchiyama, S.: A new public-key cryptosystem as secure as factoring. In: Nyberg, K. (ed.) EUROCRYPT 1998. LNCS, vol. 1403, pp. 308–318. Springer, Heidelberg (1998)
27. Sahai, A.: Non-malleable non-interactive zero knowledge and adaptive chosen-ciphertext security. In: FOCS, pp. 543–553 (1999)
28. Rabin, M.O.: Digital signatures and public key functions as intractable as factorization. Technical Report MIT/LCS/TR-212, Massachusetts Institute of Technology (January 1979)
29. Yasuda, M., Shimoyama, T., Kogure, J., Izu, T.: On the strength comparison of the ECDLP and the IFP. In: Visconti, I., De Prisco, R. (eds.) SCN 2012. LNCS, vol. 7485, pp. 302–325. Springer, Heidelberg (2012)

On Selective-Opening Attacks against Encryption Schemes

Rafail Ostrovsky[1,2], Vanishree Rao[1], and Ivan Visconti[3,*]

[1] Department of Computer Science, UCLA, USA
[2] Department of Mathematics, UCLA, USA
{rafail,vanishri}@cs.ucla.edu
[3] Dipartimento di Informatica, University of Salerno, Italy
visconti@unisa.it

Abstract. At FOCS'99, Dwork et al. put forth the notion of 'selective-
-opening attacks' (SOAs, for short). In the literature, security against
such attacks has been formalized via indistinguishability-based and
simulation-based notions, respectively called IND-SO-CPA security and
SIM-SO-CPA security. Furthermore, the IND-SO-CPA notion has been
studied under two flavors – weak-IND-SO-CPA and full-IND-SO-CPA
security. At Eurocrypt'09, Bellare et al. showed the first positive results
on SOA security of encryption schemes: 1) any lossy encryption scheme is
weak-IND-SO-CPA secure; 2) any lossy encryption scheme with efficient
openability is SIM-SO--CPA secure.

Despite rich further work on SOA security, the (un)feasibility of
full--IND-SO-CPA remains a major open problem in the area of SOA
security. The elusive nature of the full-IND-SO-CPA notion of security
is attributed to a specific aspect of the security game, namely, the
challenger requiring to perform a super-polynomial time task. Not only
do we not know whether there exists a scheme that is full-IND-SO-CPA
secure, but we also do not know concrete attacks against popular
schemes such as the ElGamal and Cramer-Shoup schemes in the
full-IND-SO-CPA model.

The contribution of our work is three-fold.

1. Motivated by the difficulty in understanding (un)feasibility of the
   full-IND-SO-CPA notion, we study a variant of this notion that is
   closer in spirit to the IND-CPA notion but still embodies the security
   captured by the full-IND-SO-CPA notion. We observe that the *weak*
   form of our variation does not introduce any significant change to
   the weak-IND-SO-CPA notion; that is, the *weak* form of our notion
   is equivalent to the weak-IND-SO-CPA notion.
2. Interestingly, we can show that a large class of encryption schemes can
   be proven insecure for the *full* form of our notion. The large class
   includes most known constructions of weak-IND-SO-CPA secure
   schemes and SIM-SO-CPA secure schemes and also popular schemes
   like the ElGamal and Cramer-Shoup schemes.
3. Our third contribution studies the complexity of SIM-SO-CPA security.
   Complementing the result of Bellare et al., we show that lossiness is

---

* Work partially done while visiting UCLA.

M. Abdalla and R. De Prisco (Eds.): SCN 2014, LNCS 8642, pp. 578–597, 2014.

not necessary to achieve SIM-SO-CPA security. More specifically, we present a SIM-SO-CPA scheme that is not a lossy encryption scheme (regardless of efficient openability). Since SIM-SO-CPA security implies weak-IND-SO-CPA security, it follows as a corollary that the converses of both the implications proved by Bellare et al. do not hold. Furthermore, as a corollary of our techniques, on a slightly unrelated but useful note, we obtain that lossiness is not required to obtain non-committing encryption. Previously, at Eurocrypt'09, Fehr et al. showed a construction of a non-committing encryption scheme from trapdoor permutations and this scheme was, as noted by the authors, possibly not lossy. Our scheme amounts to the first construction of a non-committing encryption scheme that is provably not lossy.

1 Introduction

Public-key encryption (PKE, for short) notion forms one of the most principal cryptographic notions. For PKE schemes, indistinguishability of ciphertexts under chosen-plaintext attacks (IND-CPA) and chosen-ciphertext attacks (IND-CCA) are usually viewed as strong notions of security both conceptually and in practical applications. However, there is a natural setting where these standard notions do not necessarily imply security. Namely, note that on one hand it is easy to see that a PKE scheme continues to be IND-CPA secure even if an adversary is given multiple ciphertexts of multiple plaintexts; however, on the other hand, if the adversary sees *openings* (that is, not only the plaintexts but also the coins used) of some subset of the ciphertexts of its choice, then, somewhat surprisingly, it is not known whether IND-CPA security is sufficient to ensure privacy of the unopened plaintexts. This subtlety was first pointed out by Dwork et al. in [DNRS99], and such an adversarial attack is called a selective-opening attack (SOA, for short).

Dwork et al. [DNRS99], besides bringing to light the subtlety of SOA, also investigated SOA security of commitment schemes. SOA security of PKE schemes was studied by Bellare et al. in [BHY09].

The three flavors of SOA security. SOA security of PKE schemes has been studied under various notions in the literature. The simulation-based security notion is dubbed SIM-SO-CPA security. The two indistinguishability-based notions are dubbed weak-IND-SO-CPA security and full-IND-SO-CPA security; the two indistinguishability-based notions are together dubbed IND-SO-CPA security. In this work, we study certain aspects of both the simulation-based and the indistinguishability-based security notions. Below, we provide a quick and pertinent glimpse on the state-of-the-art for these notions to keep in mind; then we explain these notions informally.

Bellare et al. [BHY09] solved a longstanding open problem by showing how to construct SIM-SO-SOA schemes. In fact, they showed that every lossy encryption scheme is SIM-SO-SOA secure and that SIM-SO-SOA security implies weak-IND--SO-CPA security. However, despite much work in the area, *we still do not know whether or not full-IND-SO-CPA security is feasible and, in particular, if existing techniques to build weak-IND-SO-CPA schemes and SIM-SO-CPA schemes can be useful to achieve full-IND-SO-CPA security. It is also not known whether lossiness is necessary for SOA security.* Thus, SOA notion still houses many more challenging open questions.

IND-SO-CPA security. Let us review the structure of IND-SO-CPA security. At a high level, the adversary gets a vector of ciphertexts. Then, the adversary chooses a subset of ciphertexts of which it receives openings. For the rest of the ciphertexts, the adversary gets either the actual plaintexts or randomly chosen messages (conditioned on the revealed plaintexts), and he is challenged to tell them apart. More specifically, the IND-SO-CPA challenger first chooses a public-key/secret-key pair and gives the adversary the public key. Then the adversary presents a description of a joint distribution over message vectors. Then the challenger would sample a message vector from this distribution, encrypt each message component, and give the adversary the resulting vector of ciphertexts. Next, the adversary chooses a subset of the ciphertexts to be opened (where, 'opening' corresponds to revealing both the plaintext and the random coins used in generating the ciphertext). The adversary, then, besides the openings to the chosen subset of ciphertexts, is given *either* the plaintexts of the remaining ciphertexts *or* a message vector that is freshly sampled from the specified (joint) message distribution, conditioned on the message components already opened to. The objective of the adversary is to tell them apart.

Note that depending on the message distribution, sampling conditioned on an arbitrary subset of messages can be an inefficient process that could render the IND-SO-CPA security experiment inefficient. It is easily conceivable that achieving IND-SO-CPA security when the message distribution does not have an efficient resampling algorithm can be challenging: in its proof of security, the reduction to some underlying hardness assumption might have the onus of providing resampled message vectors, a computationally inefficient task. This gives rise to two flavors of IND-SO-SOA-security: one, where it is required that the message distribution specified by the adversary has efficient resampling algorithm this flavor of security is called *weak*-IND-SO-CPA security; the other, where there is no such requirement on message distributions this flavor of security is called *full*-IND-SO-CPA security[1].

SIM-SO-CPA security. The aforementioned technicality in the definition of the indistinguishability based notion of IND-SO-CPA security (namely, the full-IND -SO-CPA notion), and the fact that there is no known full-IND-SO-CPA secure PKE scheme, motivated continuation of the study of the alternative formulation of SOA security: the simulation-based SOA security notion by Bellare et al. [BHY09].

---

[1] The nomenclature 'weak' and 'full' were already used in earlier works such as [BHK12].

State-of-the-art. With multiple flavors of SOA security taking shape in the literature, Böhl et al. pursued an important and useful question, in this line of research, of relationship between the many flavors of SOA security [BHK12]. In detail, they showed that SIM-SO-CPA security and full-IND-SO-CPA security are isolated. In other words, they showed a SIM-SO-CPA secure scheme that is not full-IND-SO-CPA secure, and (under the assumption that a full-IND-SO-CPA secure scheme exists) a full-IND-SO-CPA secure scheme that is not SIM-SO--CPA secure. On the positive side, as mentioned above, after many years for which achieving SOA security eluded researchers, Bellare et al. showed that SIM-SO-CPA security is already enjoyed by every lossy encryption scheme with efficient openability [BHY09]. Furthermore, they also showed that weak-IND-SO--CPA security (which is trivially implied by SIM-SO-CPA security) is enjoyed by every lossy encryption scheme.

Discussion. Owing to the complex state-of-the-art of full-IND-SO-CPA security, SIM-SO-CPA seems to be better understood, achievable, and thus preferable to use in practice. However, on the other hand, there exists no proof of unfeasibility of full-IND-SO-CPA security. Thus, there is no concrete reason to forgo this notion entirely, and it thus becomes an important and intriguing open problem to either construct a full-IND-SO-CPA secure scheme if one exists, or to discover further evidences of unfeasibility of full-IND-SO-CPA security.

The above discussion pertains to the motivation of our first result that we will discuss in Section 1.1. For the second question that we pursue, we continue to study the complexity of SOA security, now in relation to the perhaps most related primitive, lossy encryption [Hof12]. Towards better understanding the complexity of SOA security, a natural question is whether the 'lossiness' is necessary for SOA security. In particular, we question whether the converses of the implications proved by Bellare et al. hold.

1.1 Our Contributions

Result 1. Variant of full-IND-SO-CPA closer in spirit to IND-CPA. Motivated by the elusive nature of full-IND-SO-CPA notion, we study a variant notion that is closer in spirit to the IND-CPA notion but still embodies the security captured by the IND-SO-CPA notion. We observe that the *weak* form of our variation does not introduce any significant change to the weak-IND-SO-CPA notion; that is, the *weak* form of our notion is equivalent to the weak- IND-SO-CPA notion.

Result 2. Insecurity of standard schemes like ElGamal and Cramer-Shoup and of known weak-IND-SO-CPA secure and SIM-SO-CPA secure schemes w.r.t. variant full-IND-SO-CPA notion. Surprisingly, although the variation on the weak-IND-SO-CPA notion showed no significant change, we show that a large class of PKE schemes, namely the class of PKE schemes with public-key space having a Σ-protocol (formalized later), can be proven insecure for the *full* form of our variant of IND-SO-CPA notion. This class subsumes many popular PKE schemes such as the ElGamal [Gam84] and the Cramer-Shoup [CS98] schemes and most known constructions of weak-IND-SO-CPA secure and SIM-SO-CPA [BHY09, HLOV09, PVW08, Hof12] secure schemes.

Details on Result 2. In the IND-CPA notion due to Goldwasser and Micali [GM84], the adversary is challenged upon two messages; then it gets a ciphertext encrypting one of the messages chosen at random; the adversary's objective is to guess the plaintext from that known set of two messages. On the other hand, in the IND-SO-CPA notion recalled earlier in the Section, the challenger first chooses a vector of messages from an adversary-specified distribution, and gives the adversary their encryptions; the adversary then gets to see openings of a subset of the ciphertexts it chooses; for the remaining ones, he is given *only one of the following two: either* the plaintexts of all the unopened ciphertexts *or* a freshly resampled messages conditioned on the opened plaintexts.

Observe here that the message distribution specified from the adversary is possibly of 'high' min-entropy. Hence, in the event that an adversary against full-IND-SO-CPA security is given a resampled message vector, *the vector of actual plaintexts is 'hidden'.* This is in contrast with the IND-CPA game where the adversary gets both messages (including the actual plaintext) that it is challenged upon.

In this work, we study an alternative formulation of IND-SO-CPA security notion that is a more natural extension of the IND-CPA game, and study the new notion, more specifically in relation to the existing notions. To distinguish between the new and the existing notions, we rename the existing weak and full notions as '*weak single-vector-given IND-SO-CPA*' and '*full single-vector-given IND-SO-CPA*' games, respectively. We present the corresponding two new notions as '*weak both-vectors-given IND-SO-CPA*' and '*full both-vectors-given IND-SO- -CPA*' games.

To corroborate the already acquired intuition that the variation is not drastic, we also observe that, just like full single-vector-given IND-SO-CPA and SIM-SO- -CPA security notions are separated [BHK12], the new full both-vectors-given IND-SO-CPA and SIM-SO-CPA security notions are also separated. We provide a detailed note on the separation in the full version.

[BHK12] offers an informative inference that, given the separation result in [BHK12] combined with the positive state-of-the-art on SIM-SO-CPA security [BHY09], simulation-based notion is perhaps the 'more appropriate' formulation. From the separation between full both-vectors-given IND-SO-CPA security and SIM-SO-CPA security and our evidence of unfeasibility of full both-vectors-given IND-SO-CPA security further corroborates the above inference in [BHK12].

Result 3. Lossiness vs. SOA security. For our final result, we continue the study of complexity of SOA security, now in relation to perhaps the most related and better studied primitive, lossy encryption [BHY09, HLOV09, PVW08, Hof12]. As mentioned earlier, Bellare et al. showed that

1. every lossy encryption scheme is weak-IND-SO-CPA secure;
2. every lossy encryption scheme with efficient openability is SIM-SO-CPA secure.

Thus, towards understanding the complexity of SOA security, a natural question is whether lossiness is *necessary* to achieve SOA-security; that is, do the converses, stated below, of the implications proved by [BHY09] hold:

1. "Is every weak-IND-SO-CPA secure scheme also a lossy encryption scheme?"
2. "Is every SIM-SO-CPA secure scheme also a lossy encryption scheme with efficient openability?"

We answer both the questions in the negative.

Details on Result 3. Most existing constructions of weak-IND-SO-CPA secure and SIM-SO-CPA secure schemes follow the general paradigm of lossy encryption [BHY09, HLOV09] (except for the constructions that aim to achieve special additional features such as CCA, identity-based encryption (IBE, for short), etc. [FHKW10, BWY11], since some of the instantiations of the generic solutions provided in [FHKW10, BWY11] may not be known to be lossy; we shall expand on this later in the full version).

While at the face value of the definitions of SOA security and lossy encryption it seems that the answers to the above questions are affirmative, as mentioned above, we prove otherwise. In fact we prove a stronger result: we show a SIM-SO--CPA secure scheme that is not a lossy encryption scheme (even without efficient openability). Since simulation-based security implies weak-IND-SO-CPA security, the negative result proves that the converses of both the implications proven by [BHY09] do not hold.

Furthermore, as a corollary of our techniques, on a slightly unrelated but useful note, we obtain that lossiness is not required to obtain non-committing encryption. We remark that [FHKW10] gave a generic construction of NC-CPA secure scheme from trapdoor permutations; as remarked by the authors, this construction is possibly not lossy. We give a first construction of NC-CPA secure scheme that is *provably* not lossy.

1.2 Our Techniques

We now present at a high level our technical approach in achieving the aforementioned results (ignoring some of the subtleties that are handled in the proofs).

Equivalence of the existing and new notions for weak-IND-SO-CPA security. The fact that weak both-vectors-given IND-SO-CPA notion is equivalent to weak single-vector-given IND-SO-CPA notion follows trivially from their definitions.

(Un)feasibility of new notion of full-IND-SO-CPA security. We show that if a PKE scheme has a public-key space {pk} for which there exists a Σ-protocol, then the scheme is not full both-vectors-given IND-SO-CPA. To prove this, we construct an adversary which specifies the following particular distribution: Given the public key pk, the adversary specifies the distribution as a uniform distribution over the Σ-protocol transcripts for the statement pk $\in$ {pk}. Then,

once the adversary receives a vector of three ciphertexts (corresponding to the three messages of a Σ-protocol transcript), it opens only the first ciphertext. Later upon given the actual plaintext and resampled message vectors, the adversary runs the special-soundness extractor of the Σ-protocol to recover the witness, namely, the secret-key. The adversary consequently will be able to decrypt every ciphertext, thus breaking full both-vectors-given IND-SO-CPA security of the scheme in question. All known schemes achieving (the existing notion of) IND-SO-CPA security [BHY09, HLOV09, Hof12, PVW08, FHKW10, BWY11], which are based on the general theme of lossiness, (except for the schemes that aim to achieve additional features such as CCA, IBE, etc. [FHKW10, BWY11], since some instantiations of the generic solutions provided in [FHKW10, BWY11] may not be known to be lossy) are subsumed by our negative result.

Complexity of SIM-SO-CPA security with respect to lossy encryption. For the second result, we first give a very simple counterexample. Namely, we construct an ElGamal-like SIM-SO-CPA scheme that is not a lossy encryption scheme. However, one can argue here that this scheme satisfies some sort of 'computational lossiness' (which shall formally define later) and, for all practical purposes, this computational lossiness is all that is required of a lossy encryption scheme. In light of this argument, we present another, but more technically involved counterexample. The core idea for this construction stems from the following observation. For a PKE scheme to be a lossy encryption scheme, the following condition, called 'lossiness of ciphertexts', needs to hold: there exist special public keys (called lossy public keys) such that for any such public key, and any message, a ciphertext – called 'lossy ciphertext' – generated to encrypt that message is lossy. That is, such a ciphertext can be opened to any plaintext message. The crucial point here is that lossiness needs to hold even for the ciphertexts that are honestly generated using the encryption algorithm (but with a lossy public key). On the other hand, in the SIM-SO-CPA security definition, the simulator is required to be able to open the ciphertexts to any given plaintext message; however, the simulator needs to be able to do so only for the ciphertexts that are generated by the simulator himself. Thus, it is conceivable that there could exist a simulator that generates malicious ciphertexts and that it is able to equivocate only those ciphertexts. This is the subtlety we build upon to construct a SIM-SO-CPA secure scheme with a simulator that works by building malicious ciphertexts. Furthermore, we show for this scheme that for honestly generated ciphertexts, for any malicious public key, there does not exist an opening for at least one message, with some non-negligible probability thus disqualifying the scheme from being a lossy encryption scheme.

Other related works. In [BDWY12], Bellare et al. studied the complexity of SIM-SO-CPA security with respect to IND-CPA security of PKE schemes. They showed that a large class of IND-CPA secure PKE schemes, including ElGamal, do not achieve SIM-SO-CPA security. In [HR14], Hofheinz et al. studied the relationship between IND-CPA security (resp., IND-CCA security) and IND-SO--CPA (respectively, IND-SO-CCA security); they showed that while IND-CPA and IND-SO-CPA notions are equivalent in a generic model of computation, IND-CCA security does not suffice to achieve IND-SO-CCA security. It has also been shown how to achieve SOA-secure encryption with additional features such as IND-CCA security [HLOV09, FHKW10] and IBE [BWY11]. SOA security for commitments is also an active area of research and there had been many advancements in understanding the complexity of this primitive in terms of feasibility and impossibility results [BHY09, DNRS03, ORSV13, Xia11].

2 Background

Notations. In this paper, we usually consider vectors of length N, for $N \in \mathbb{N}$, and we point at the components of such vectors at indices i with the set of indices in question, called the '*index-set*'. Also, we denote the set $[N] \setminus \mathcal{I}$ as $\overline{\mathcal{I}}$. If a vector of messages $\mathbf{m} = (m[1], \ldots, m[N])$ is specified only at indices specified by an index-set $\mathcal{I} \subseteq [N]$, then we call such a partially specified message vector as a '*partial vector*' and denote it by $\mathbf{m}_{\mathcal{I}} = (m[i])_{i \in \mathcal{I}} \in (\{0,1\}^{\lambda})^{|\mathcal{I}|}$. For any $\mathcal{I} \in [N]$, let $\mathbf{m}^0{}_{\mathcal{I}}$ and $\mathbf{m}^1{}_{\overline{\mathcal{I}}}$ be two partial vectors. Then the (whole) vector resulting by placing $m^0[i]$ at the ith index if $i \in \mathcal{I}$ and by placing $m^1[j]$ at the jth index if $j \in \overline{\mathcal{I}}$, is denoted by $\mathbf{m}^0{}_{\mathcal{I}} \| \mathbf{m}^1{}_{\overline{\mathcal{I}}}$. Let $\mathcal{M}$ be a distribution over $(\{0,1\}^{\lambda})^N$. We say that a partial vector $\mathbf{m}^0{}_{\mathcal{I}} \in \mathrm{Supp}(\mathcal{M})$ iff $\exists\, \mathbf{m}^1{}_{\overline{\mathcal{I}}} := (m^1[i])_{i \in \overline{\mathcal{I}}}$ such that $\mathbf{m}^0{}_{\mathcal{I}} \| \mathbf{m}^1{}_{\overline{\mathcal{I}}} \in \mathrm{Supp}(\mathcal{M})$.

Below we recall the definition of efficiently resamplable distributions. At a high level, these are joint distributions $\mathcal{M}$ over components of message vectors with the following property: Conditioned on any subset of the components, the rest of the components are efficiently samplable as per $\mathcal{M}$. More precisely:

Definition 1 (Efficiently resamplable distribution). *Let $N = N(\lambda) > 0$, and let $\mathcal{M}$ be a joint distribution over $(\{0,1\}^{\lambda})^N$. We say that $\mathcal{M}$ is efficiently resamplable if there exists a PPT algorithm $\mathrm{ReSamp}_{\mathcal{M}}$ such that, for any $\mathcal{I} \subseteq [N]$ and any partial vector $\mathbf{m}_{\mathcal{I}} := (m[i])_{i \in \mathcal{I}} \in \mathrm{Supp}(\mathcal{M})$, $\mathrm{ReSamp}_{\mathcal{M}}(\mathbf{m}_{\mathcal{I}})$ samples from $\mathcal{M}|_{\mathbf{m}_{\mathcal{I}}}$ (i.e., from the distribution $\mathcal{M}$ conditioned on the ith component being $m[i]$ for all $i \in \mathcal{I}$).*

Opening oracles. In our definitions, like in [BHK12], upon providing the adversary with a public key and a vector of ciphertexts, we provide him with an opening oracle to allow adaptive queries. Such an oracle is a stateful functionality that takes one argument. When queried with a set of indices, it responds via the corresponding openings of the ciphertexts (i.e., the plaintexts encrypted in the ciphertexts at the specified indices and the randomnesses used in generating these ciphertexts). When queried with the string 'get queries', it returns the set of all indices it has provided openings for since its instantiation.

Plaintext vector, Resampled message vector. Let $\mathcal{M}$ be a joint distribution over vectors of messages. Let $\mathbf{m}^0 := (m^0[i])_{i \in [N]} \leftarrow \mathcal{M}$ and let $\mathbf{c} := (c[i])_{i \in [N]}$ be such that $c[i]$ is and n encryption of $m^0[i]$ (under some public key). Under this notation:

1. we call $\mathbf{m^0}$ as the *plaintext vector*.
2. Let $\mathcal{I} \subseteq [N]$ be a subset of the indices. Consider a message vector $\mathbf{m^1}$ such that $\mathbf{m^1}_{\mathcal{I}} = (m^0[i])_{i \in \mathcal{I}}$; let the rest of the components of $\mathbf{m^1}$ be sampled according to $\mathcal{M}$ conditioned on the components at $i \in \mathcal{I}$ being $\mathbf{m^1}_{\mathcal{I}}$. We denote the way $\mathbf{m^1}$ is sampled via $\mathbf{m^1} \leftarrow \mathcal{M}|_{\mathbf{m^0}_{\mathcal{I}}}$ and we call $\mathbf{m^1}$ as the *resampled message vector*.

2.1   Existing SOA Definitions

We now recall the existing definitions for various flavors of IND-SO-CPA security. All the definitions here below are taken almost verbatim from [BHK12]. However, the definitions have been slightly renamed in order to emphasize the difference between the existing and the new notions. The new definitions are described below[2].

Definition 2 (Weak   Single-vector-given   Indistinguishability-based SOA Security). *For a PKE scheme* $\mathsf{PKE} = (\mathsf{KeyGen}, \mathsf{Enc}, \mathsf{Dec})$, *a polynomially bounded function* $N = N(\lambda) > 0$, *an opening oracle* $\mathcal{O}$, *and a stateful PPT adversary* $\mathcal{A}$, *consider the following experiment:*

Experiment $\mathbf{Expt}_{\mathsf{PKE},\mathcal{A},b}^{\mathsf{weak-singleVect-ind-so}}$:
  1. $(\mathrm{pk}, \mathrm{sk}) \leftarrow \mathsf{KeyGen}$
  2. $(\mathcal{M}, \mathsf{ReSamp}_{\mathcal{M}}) \leftarrow \mathcal{A}(\mathrm{pk})$
  3. $\mathbf{m^0} := (m^0[i])_{i \in [N]} \leftarrow \mathcal{M}$
  4. $(r[i])_{i \in [N]} \leftarrow (\mathsf{Coins}_{\mathsf{Enc}})^N$
  5. $\mathbf{c} := (\mathsf{Enc}(\mathrm{pk}, m^0[i]; r[i]))_{i \in [N]}$
  6. $\mathbf{O} := (m^0[i], r[i])_{i \in [N]}$
  7. $\mathcal{A}^{\mathcal{O}(\cdot)}(\mathsf{select}, \mathbf{c})$
  8. $\mathcal{I} := \mathcal{O}(\mathsf{get\ queries})$
  9. $\mathbf{m^1} \leftarrow \mathcal{M}|_{\mathbf{m^0}_{\mathcal{I}}}$
  10. $out_{\mathcal{A}} \leftarrow \mathcal{A}(\mathsf{output}, \mathbf{m}^b)$
  11. *if* $out_{\mathcal{A}} = b$, *then return* 1; *otherwise return* 0

---

where, the oracle $\mathcal{O}$ *uses* $\mathbf{O}$ *to answer the queries of* $\mathcal{A}$. *We say that* PKE *is weak single-vector-given IND-SO-CPA secure if, for any* $\mathcal{A}$ *that always outputs an efficiently resamplable distribution* $\mathcal{M}$ *over* $(\{0,1\}^{\lambda})^N$ *with corresponding efficient resampling algorithm* $\mathsf{ReSamp}_{\mathcal{M}}$, *the following is negligible:*

$$\mathbf{Adv}_{\mathsf{PKE},\mathcal{A}}^{\mathsf{weak-singleVect-ind-so}} \tag{1}$$

$$:= \left| \Pr[\mathbf{Expt}_{\mathsf{PKE},\mathcal{A},1}^{\mathsf{weak-singleVect-ind-so}} = 1] - \Pr[\mathbf{Expt}_{\mathsf{PKE},\mathcal{A},0}^{\mathsf{weak-singleVect-ind-so}} = 1] \right|. \tag{2}$$

---

[2] We recall that Coins_A denotes the space of randomness of an algorithm A.

Definition 3 (Full Single-vector-given Indistinguishability-based SOA Security). *For a PKE scheme* PKE = (KeyGen, Enc, Dec), *polynomially bounded* $N = N(\lambda) > 0$, *an opening oracle* $\mathcal{O}$, *and a stateful PPT adversary* $\mathcal{A}$, *we define experiment* $\mathbf{Expt}_{PKE,\mathcal{A},b}^{full-singleVect-ind-so}(\lambda)$ *analogously to* $\mathbf{Expt}_{PKE,\mathcal{A},b}^{weak-singleVect-ind-so}(\lambda)$ *with the only change the adversary is not required to provide a resampling algorithm; i.e.,* $\mathcal{A}(pk)$ *just outputs a message distribution* $\mathcal{M}$. *We say that* PKE *is full single-vector-given IND-SO-CPA if, for any such* $\mathcal{A}$, *the following is negligible.*

$$\mathbf{Adv}_{PKE,\mathcal{A}}^{full-singleVect-ind-so} \tag{3}$$

$$:= \left| \Pr[\mathbf{Expt}_{PKE,\mathcal{A},1}^{full-singleVect-ind-so} = 1] - \Pr[\mathbf{Expt}_{PKE,\mathcal{A},0}^{full-singleVect-ind-so} = 1] \right|. \tag{4}$$

Definition 4 (Simulation-based SOA Security). *For a PKE scheme* PKE_2^{soa} = (KeyGen$_2^{soa}$, Enc$_2^{soa}$, Dec$_2^{soa}$), *a polynomially bounded function* $N = N(\lambda) > 0$, *an opening oracle* $\mathcal{O}$, *and a stateful PPT adversary* $\mathcal{A}$, *a PPT distinguisher* $\mathcal{D}$ *with a boolean output, consider the following experiments:*

Experiment $\mathbf{Expt}_{PKE,\mathcal{A},\mathcal{D}}^{sim-so-real}$:	Experiment $\mathbf{Expt}_{PKE,\mathcal{A},\mathcal{D}}^{sim-so-ideal}$:
1. (pk, sk) $\leftarrow$ KeyGen	1. $\mathcal{M} \leftarrow$ Sim;
2. $\mathcal{M} \leftarrow \mathcal{A}(pk)$	2. $\mathbf{m} := (m[i])_{i \in [N]} \leftarrow \mathcal{M}$
3. $\mathbf{m} := (m[i])_{i \in [N]} \leftarrow \mathcal{M}$	3. $out_{Sim} \leftarrow Sim^{\mathcal{O}(\cdot)}(select)$
4. $(r[i])_{i \in [N]} \leftarrow (Coins_{Enc})^N$	4. $\mathcal{I} := \mathcal{O}(get\ queries)$
5. $\mathbf{c} := (Enc(pk, m[i]; r[i]))_{i \in [N]}$	5. $return\ \mathcal{D}(\mathbf{m}, \mathcal{M}, \mathcal{I}, out_{Sim})$
6. $\mathbf{O} := (m[i], r[i])_{i \in [N]}$	
7. $out_{\mathcal{A}} \leftarrow \mathcal{A}^{\mathcal{O}(\cdot)}(select, \mathbf{c})$	
8. $\mathcal{I} := \mathcal{O}(get\ queries)$	
9. $return\ \mathcal{D}(\mathbf{m}, \mathcal{M}, \mathcal{I}, out_{\mathcal{A}})$	

where, the oracle $\mathcal{O}$ uses $\mathbf{O}$ to answer the queries of $\mathcal{A}$ in $\mathbf{Expt}_{PKE,\mathcal{A},\mathcal{D}}^{sim-so-real}$ and uses only $\mathbf{m}$ in $\mathbf{Expt}_{PKE,\mathcal{A},\mathcal{D}}^{sim-so-ideal}$. We say that the scheme is SIM-SO-CPA secure if for every adversary $\mathcal{A}$ there is a PPT algorithm called the simulator Sim such that, for all PPT distinguishers $\mathcal{D}$, the distributions induced by the experiments $\mathbf{Expt}_{PKE,\mathcal{A},\mathcal{D}}^{sim-so-real}$ and $\mathbf{Expt}_{PKE,\mathcal{A},\mathcal{D}}^{sim-so-ideal}$ are statistically close. That is,

$$\mathbf{Adv}_{PKE,\mathcal{A},\mathcal{D}}^{sim-so-cpa} := |\Pr[\mathbf{Expt}_{PKE,\mathcal{A},\mathcal{D}}^{sim-so-real} \to 1] - \Pr[\mathbf{Expt}_{PKE,\mathcal{A},\mathcal{D}}^{sim-so-ideal} \to 1]| \le negl(\lambda).$$

Assuming knowledge of the standard definition of lossy encryption (the definition is recalled in the full version), we provide here a new definition of lossiness, called 'computational lossiness', that we informally define below. A formal definition appears in the full version.

Definition 5 (Computational lossy encryption (Informal)). *A scheme* PKE^{losPKE} = (KeyGen^{losPKE}, FakeKeyGen^{losPKE}, Enc^{losPKE}, Dec^{losPKE}, Opener) *is said to be a computational lossy encryption scheme if it satisfies all the* *properties of a lossy encryption scheme except for the following: for every 'lossy cddertext', the randomness output by the opening algorithm* Opener *needs to be only computationally indistinguishable from the actual distribution of the random coins for ciphertext.*

2.2 PKE with Pseudorandom Ciphertexts

We now define PKE schemes with pseudorandom ciphertexts [CLOS02, BC05]. Roughly, these are the schemes with a property that for any plaintext message a randomly generated ciphertext is computationally indistinguishable from a uniform random string of the same length.

Definition 6 (PKE with pseudorandom ciphertexts). *A PKE scheme* $\mathsf{PKE}^\$ = (\mathsf{KeyGen}^\$, \mathsf{Enc}^\$, \mathsf{Dec}^\$)$ *is said to have pseudorandom ciphertexts if, for* $(\mathrm{pk}^\$, \cdot) \leftarrow \mathsf{KeyGen}^\$$, *for any plaintext message m, the distribution ensembles* $\mathsf{Enc}^\$(\mathrm{pk}^\$, m)$ *and* $U_{\mathrm{cipherLen}}$ *are all computationally indistinguishable, where the ciphertexts of* $\mathsf{PKE}^\$$ *are of length* cipherLen.

In [CLOS02], Canetti et al. also provide a simple construction of such schemes based on trapdoor permutations. Briefly, the construction in [CLOS02] is as follows. With the public key as the description f of a trapdoor function, encryption of a bit b is: $f(x), b \oplus HC(x)$, where x is chosen at random from the domain of f and $HC(\cdot)$ is a hard-core predicate of f. Notice that for this scheme, the distribution of encryption of a random bit b is itself a uniform distribution over strings of the same length as the ciphertexts.

We now define PKE schemes with decidable public-key space. Roughly, for such schemes, it is easy to verify whether a given string is a 'valid' public key; i.e., whether a given string lies in the public-key space or not.

Definition 7 (PKE with decidable public-key space). *A PKE scheme* $\mathsf{PKE}^{\mathrm{deci}}$ *is said to be public-key decidable if there exists a PPT algorithm that given a string* $\mathrm{pk}^{\mathrm{deci}}$ *outputs 1 if there exists some randomness with which the key-generation algorithm outputs* $\mathrm{pk}^{\mathrm{deci}}$ *as a public key, and outputs 0 otherwise (that is, the public-key space is efficiently decidable).*

We will be interested in PKE schemes with decidable public-key space and pseudorandom ciphertexts. We shall denote such a PKE scheme by $\mathsf{PKE}^{\$,\mathrm{deci}}$. Note that if we use certified[3] trapdoor permutations instead of any permutations in the construction of [CLOS02] discussed above, we get a scheme that enjoys both – decidable public-key space and pseudorandom ciphertexts.

3 New IND-SO-CPA Definitions

In this section, we propose our new definitions for indistinguishability-based SOA security. In comparison with the existing definitions, the new ones differ from the

---

[3] A trapdoor permutation [BY96] is certified if one can verify from its description that it is indeed a permutation.

existing ones in the following respect: in the existing definitions, corresponding to the ciphertext vector given to the adversary, the adversary is given only either the actual plaintext vector or the resampled message vector; on the other hand, in the new definitions the adversary is given both the vectors that it is challenged upon, thus being closer in spirit to the IND-CPA notion as discussed earlier.

Definition 8 (Weak Both-vectors-given Indistinguishability-based SOA Security). *For a PKE scheme* PKE $=$ (KeyGen, Enc, Dec), *a polynomially bounded function* $N = N(\lambda) > 0$, *an opening oracle* $\mathcal{O}$, *and a stateful PPT adversary* $\mathcal{A}$, *consider the experiment that is identical to* $\mathbf{Expt}_{\mathsf{PKE},\mathcal{A},b}^{\mathsf{weak-bothVect-ind-so}}$ *except for the following modification in* $\mathbf{Expt}_{\mathsf{PKE},\mathcal{A},b}^{\mathsf{weak-bothVect-ind-so}}$: *1. out*$_\mathcal{A}$ $\leftarrow$ $\mathcal{A}(\text{output}, \mathbf{m}^b, \mathbf{m}^{\bar{b}})$.

We say that PKE *is* weak both-vectors-given IND-SO-CPA *secure if, for any* $\mathcal{A}$ *that always outputs efficiently resamplable* $\mathcal{M}$ *over* $(\{0,1\}^\lambda)^N$ *with corresponding efficient re-sampling algorithm* $\mathsf{ReSamp}_\mathcal{M}$, *the following is negligible:*

$$\mathbf{Adv}_{\mathsf{PKE},\mathcal{A}}^{\mathsf{weak-bothVect-ind-so}}$$
$$:= \left| \Pr[\mathbf{Expt}_{\mathsf{PKE},\mathcal{A},1}^{\mathsf{weak-bothVect-ind-so}} = 1] - \Pr[\mathbf{Expt}_{\mathsf{PKE},\mathcal{A},0}^{\mathsf{weak-bothVect-ind-so}} = 1] \right|.$$

Definition 9 (Full Both-vectors-given Indistinguishability-based SOA Security). *Given PKE scheme* PKE $=$ (KeyGen, Enc, Dec), *a polynomially bounded function* $N = N(\lambda) > 0$, *an opening oracle* $\mathcal{O}$, *and a stateful PPT adversary* $\mathcal{A}$, *the experiment* $\mathbf{Expt}_{\mathsf{PKE},\mathcal{A}}^{\mathsf{full-bothVect-ind-so}}(\lambda)$ *is defined as* $\mathbf{Expt}_{\mathsf{PKE},\mathcal{A}}^{\mathsf{weak-bothVect-ind-so}}(\lambda)$ *with the only change that we do not require the adversary to provide an algorithm for re-sampling; i.e.,* $\mathcal{A}(\text{pk})$ *just outputs a message distribution* $\mathcal{M}$. *We say that* PKE *is* full both-vectors-given *if, for any PPT adversary* $\mathcal{A}$, *the following is negligible:*

$$\mathbf{Adv}_{\mathsf{PKE},\mathcal{A}}^{\mathsf{full-bothVect-ind-so}}$$
$$:= \left| \Pr[\mathbf{Expt}_{\mathsf{PKE},\mathcal{A},1}^{\mathsf{full-bothVect-ind-so}} = 1] - \Pr[\mathbf{Expt}_{\mathsf{PKE},\mathcal{A},0}^{\mathsf{full-bothVect-ind-so}} = 1] \right|.$$

4 Equivalence of Weak Notions and (Im)possibility of Full Notion

In this section we give a strong evidence of (un)feasibility of the new notion. Namely, we show that every PKE scheme that has public-key space that has a Σ-protocol is not fully secure under the new notion. Thus, our tweak on the security definition has made it easier to prove (un)feasibility for full security. On the other hand, for weak security, we show that the new notion is in fact equivalent to the old notion.

4.1 Equivalence Between Old And New (Weak) Notions

Theorem 1 (weak-bothVect-IND-SO-CPA ⇒ weak-singleVect-IND-SO-CPA). *If* PKE *is* weak both-vectors- given IND-SO-CPA *secure then it is also* weak single-vector-given IND-SO-CPA *secure.*

This implication is almost trivial and the proof appears in the full version.

Theorem 2 (weak-singleVect-IND-SO-CPA ⇒ weak-bothVect-IND-SO-CPA). *If* PKE *is* weak single-vector- given IND-SO-CPA *secure then it is also* weak both-vectors-given IND-SO-CPA *secure.*

Proof Sketch: This implication also almost immediately follows from the definitions. However, for completeness, we present a proof. Briefly, the implication is derived from the following two facts about the experiments in question. Firstly, since both the experiments concern the weak model, in each of the experiments, an adversary also presents an efficient algorithm for resampling. Secondly, the only difference in the two experiments is the following. An adversary in the singleVect experiment receives only one message vector (namely, either the actual plaintext vector or the resampled message vector); on the other hand, an adversary in the bothVect experiment receives both the message vectors (in a random order). Thus, in our reduction, an adversary in the weak-singleVect-IND-SO-CPA experiment, who gets only one vector of messages, can sample the other vector of messages by itself. However, note that the reduction cannot identically simulate the bothVect experiment since among the two message vectors an adversary receives in the bothVect experiment one is definitely the actual message vector, and in the event that the only message vector received by our reduction is the resampled message vector (from its own experiment), it can never give the adversary in the bothVect experiment the actual message vector. This difficulty can however be easily overcome via a hybrid argument using two more hybrid games. A more detailed proof appears in the full version.   □

Theorem 3 (full-bothVect-IND-SO-CPA ⇒ full-singleVect-IND-SO-CPA). *If* PKE *is a* weak both-vectors- given IND-SO-CPA *secure then it is also* weak single-vector-given IND-SO-CPA *secure.*

Proof Sketch: The proof is similar to the proof of (Theorem 1).   □

4.2 Impossibility of Full Security

We show that any public key encryption scheme for which the public-key space has a Σ-protocol is *not* full-bothVect-IND-SO-CPA secure.

If {pk} *has a Σ-protocol, then the PKE scheme is* **not** *full-bothVect-IND-SO-CPA secure.* At a high level, we prove this negative result by showing an explicit full-bothVect-IND-SO-CPA attack on any PKE scheme with a public-key space that has a Σ-protocol. The attack stems from the idea that upon receiving the public key pk from the challenger, the adversary can specify the message distribution to be a distribution that is statistically close to uniform proof-of-knowledge (via the Σ-protocol) of a secret key *corresponding to the public key* pk. It specifies this distribution simply as the output distribution of the simulator of the Σ-protocol. Now, the core idea crucially relies on the special-soundness property of the Σ-protocol. (Recall that special-soundness implies existence of an efficient extractor that, for any theorem statement, given two proof transcripts with the same first-round message but with distinct second-round messages and corresponding third-round messages, the extractor computes a valid witness to the theorem statement.) The rest of the idea then is for the adversary to ask to open the ciphertext corresponding to only the first-round message. Then the two vectors of messages given by the challenger would be two random Σ-protocol proof-of-knowledge transcripts with the same first-round message, and, with all but negligible probability, with distinct second-round messages and corresponding third-round messages. Then the adversary can run the Σ-protocol extractor to compute the witness, which in fact is a secret key corresponding to the pk in question. Then the adversary can decrypt any ciphertext and break full-bothVect-IND-SO-CPA of the PKE scheme with probability negligibly close to 1. The full formal proof of the following theorem appears in the full version.

Theorem 4. *Let* PKE *be a PKE scheme such that* {pk} *has a Σ-protocol. Then* PKE *is* not full both *-vectors-given* IND-SO-CPA *secure.*

5 Relationship between SOA Security and Lossy Encryption

[BHY09] presented the first positive results for SOA security of encryption schemes. The constructions presented crucially used lossiness of encryption. More specifically, they proved the following implications.

Implication 1. Every lossy encryption scheme is weak-singleVect-IND-SO-CPA secure.

Implication 2. Every lossy encryption scheme with efficient openability is SIM-SO-CPA secure.

In the study of complexity of SOA-security, a natural question then is whether the converses of these implications hold too. Namely:

Question 1. "Is every weak-singleVect-IND-SO-CPA secure scheme a lossy encryption scheme?"

Question 2. "Is every SIM-SO-CPA secure scheme a lossy encryption scheme with efficient openability?"

These are the questions that we investigate in this Section. We answer these questions in the *negative*. In fact, we prove a *stronger result*. Namely, we give a concrete construction of a SIM-SO-CPA secure scheme that is not a lossy encryption (even without efficient openability). Since every SIM-SO-CPA security trivially implies weak-singleVect-IND-SO-CPA security, it follows as a corollary of our result that none of the converses of the implications proved by [BHY09] hold.

The road-map for the rest of the section is as follows. We shall first give a very simple construction for a SIM-SO-CPA secure scheme that is not a lossy scheme. However, although this scheme is not lossy in the traditional sense, it satisfies 'computational lossiness' defined in Definition 5. Arguably, this for most practical purposes, computational lossiness suffices, and thus it seems that this counterexample does not give a clear answer to our question of whether lossiness is necessary for SOA security. This brings us to our next counterexample; although technically involved, this counterexample gives a convincing answer to our question of whether lossiness is necessary for SOA security.

Construction 1. Our first construction of a SIM-SO-CPA secure scheme that is not lossy follows. Let $\mathbb{G}$ be a group of prime order p. Let g be a generator of $\mathbb{G}$. We shall denote the scheme as $\mathsf{PKE}_1^{\mathrm{soa}} = (\mathsf{KeyGen}_1^{\mathrm{soa}}, \mathsf{Enc}_1^{\mathrm{soa}}, \mathsf{Dec}_1^{\mathrm{soa}})$.

$\mathsf{KeyGen}_1^{\mathrm{soa}}$: Choose $x \leftarrow \mathbb{Z}_p$. Set $\mathrm{sk} := x$ and $\mathrm{pk} := g^x$.

$\mathsf{Enc}_1^{\mathrm{soa}}$: On input a message $m \in \{0, 1\}$, sample random coins $(r, R_1, R_2) \leftarrow \mathbb{Z}_p \times \mathbb{G}^2$, and proceed as follows. If $m = 0$, then output (g^r, pk^r); otherwise, output (R_1, R_2).

$\mathsf{Dec}_1^{\mathrm{soa}}$: On input a ciphertext (c_1, c_2), check if $c_2 = (c_1)^{\mathrm{sk}}$. If so, then output 0; otherwise, output 1.

Fig. 1. A SIM-SO-CPA secure scheme that is not a lossy encryption scheme

We shall first show that $\mathsf{PKE}_1^{\mathrm{soa}}$ is a SIM-SO-CPA secure scheme but not a lossy encryption scheme.

Theorem 5 ($\mathsf{PKE}_1^{\mathrm{soa}}$ is SIM-SO-CPA secure). *Assuming DDH assumption holds in $\mathbb{G}$, $\mathsf{PKE}_1^{\mathrm{soa}}$ is SIM-SO-CPA secure.*

The full proof appears in the full version. We give a proof sketch here below.
Proof Sketch: Recall from Definition 4 that in order to show that a PKE scheme is SIM-SO-CPA secure, we need to show existence of a PPT simulator such that, for every adversary $\mathcal{A}$, the output of the simulator is computationally indistinguishable from the output of the $\mathcal{A}$ in the real world. We shall construct such a simulator $\mathsf{Sim}^{\mathsf{PKE}_1^{\mathrm{soa}}}$ for $\mathsf{PKE}_1^{\mathrm{soa}}$.

Recall that in the real world $\mathcal{A}$, upon receiving a vector of ciphertexts, chooses a subset $\mathcal{I}$ of ciphertexts and sees their openings. On the other hand, in the ideal world, the simulator first needs to output $\mathcal{I}$; then it receives the plaintext messages to which it needs to show openings to of the ciphertexts.

The idea for simulation is that $\mathsf{Sim}^{\mathsf{PKE}_1^{\mathrm{soa}}}$ would run $\mathcal{A}$ by providing a tuple of ciphertexts $(c_1, \ldots, c_N)$ where every c_i is an encryption of 0. That is c_i is computed as (g^{r_i}, pk^{r_i}). Then, upon $\mathcal{A}$ choosing the subset of the ciphertexts, $\mathsf{Sim}^{\mathsf{PKE}_1^{\mathrm{soa}}}$ would receive the plaintext values for which it needs to provide openings to. If for any ciphertext c_i, the plaintext value to which it needs to be opened to is 0, then set the opening (randomness) of c_i as $(r_i, R_i^{(1)}, R_i^{(2)})$ for some random $R_i^{(1)}, R_i^{(2)} \in \mathbb{G}$. Otherwise, to provide opening to 1, claim that the randomness used was $(r_i', g^{r_i}, pk^{r_i})$ for some random $r_i' \leftarrow \mathbb{Z}_p$.

Note that the only differing factor in the outputs of the real and simulated worlds is that while an encryption of 1 is $(r_i', R_i^{(1)}, R_i^{(2)})$ for independently random $R_i^{(1)}, R_i^{(2)}$ in the real world, in the simulated world, encryption of 1 is $(r_i', g^{r_i}, pk^{r_i})$. Note that this difference directly corresponds to being given a non-DDH tuple and a DDH tuple, resp.: $(g, pk, R_i^{(1)}, R_i^{(2)})$ and $(g, pk, g^{r_i}, pk^{r_i})$. Thus, from the DDH assumption, the scheme $\mathsf{PKE}_1^{\mathrm{soa}}$ is SIM-SO-CPA secure.   □

Theorem 6 ($\mathsf{PKE}_1^{\mathrm{soa}}$ is not lossy). $\mathsf{PKE}_1^{\mathrm{soa}}$ *is not a lossy encryption scheme.*

Proof. The proof is straight-forward. Note that every $g' \in \mathbb{G}$ belongs to the public-key space of $\mathsf{PKE}_1^{\mathrm{soa}}$. Also for any public key pk, a ciphertext (c_1, c_2) can either be of the form $c_2 = c_1^{\mathrm{sk}}$ or not; hence, a ciphertext decrypts to either 0 or 1 and not both. Thus, $\mathsf{PKE}_1^{\mathrm{soa}}$ is not a lossy encryption scheme.

Our scheme is described below. The two ingredients we use to construct this scheme are a lossy encryption scheme with efficient openability and a CPA secure PKE scheme with decidable public-key space and pseudorandom ciphertexts. Note that the assumption that lossy encryption scheme with efficient openability exists is without loss of generality while considering Question 1, since if no lossy encryption scheme exists then the answer to Question 1 is trivially negative. For Question 2, however, we only need to assume any lossy encryption the reason being the following: looking ahead, our approach is to take any lossy scheme, that is already known to be weak-IND-SO-CPA secure, and modify it such that the modified scheme is still weak-IND-SO-CPA secure but not a lossy encryption scheme. The approach for constructing such a weak-IND-SO-CPA secure scheme is the same as the approach below for constructing a SIM-SO-CPA secure scheme and we omit the details). For the same reason as for Question 1, this assumption too is without loss of generality when we consider Question 2.

Let $\mathsf{PKE}^{\mathrm{losPKE}} = (\mathsf{KeyGen}^{\mathrm{losPKE}}, \mathsf{FakeKeyGen}^{\mathrm{losPKE}}, \mathsf{Enc}^{\mathrm{losPKE}}, \mathsf{Dec}^{\mathrm{losPKE}})$ be a lossy encryption scheme. Let $\mathsf{PKE}^{\$, \mathrm{deci}} = (\mathsf{KeyGen}^{\$, \mathrm{deci}}, \mathsf{Enc}^{\$, \mathrm{deci}}, \mathsf{Dec}^{\$, \mathrm{deci}})$ be a CPA-secure public key encryption scheme with decidable public-key space $\{pk^{\$, \mathrm{deci}}\}$ and with pseudorandom ciphertexts. We construct a scheme $\mathsf{PKE}_2^{\mathrm{soa}} = (\mathsf{KeyGen}_2^{\mathrm{soa}}, \mathsf{Enc}_2^{\mathrm{soa}}, \mathsf{Dec}_2^{\mathrm{soa}})$ as follows.

Theorem 7 ($\mathsf{PKE}_2^{\mathrm{soa}}$ is SIM-SO-CPA secure). *Let $\mathsf{PKE}^{\mathrm{losPKE}}$ be a lossy encryption scheme and $\mathsf{PKE}^{\$, \mathrm{deci}}$ be a public-key-decidable CPA-secure encryption scheme with pseudorandom ciphertexts. Then $\mathsf{PKE}_2^{\mathrm{soa}}$ is SIM-SO-CPA secure.*

The full proof appears in the full version. We give a proof sketch here below.
Proof Sketch: We construct such a simulator $\mathsf{Sim}^{\mathsf{PKE}_2^{\mathrm{soa}}}$ for our $\mathsf{PKE}_2^{\mathrm{soa}}$ scheme.

$\mathsf{KeyGen}_2^{\mathrm{soa}}$:

- Run $(\mathrm{pk}^{\mathrm{real}}, \mathrm{sk}^{\mathrm{real}}) \leftarrow \mathsf{KeyGen}^{\mathrm{losPKE}}$.
- Run $(\mathrm{pk}^{\$,\mathrm{deci}}, \mathrm{sk}^{\$,\mathrm{deci}}) \leftarrow \mathsf{KeyGen}^{\$,\mathrm{deci}}$.
- Set soa-pk $:= (\mathrm{pk}^{\mathrm{real}}, \mathrm{pk}^{\$,\mathrm{deci}})$ and soa-sk $:= (\mathrm{sk}^{\mathrm{real}}, \mathrm{sk}^{\$,\mathrm{deci}})$.

$\mathsf{Enc}_2^{\mathrm{soa}}$: On input a message m, proceed as follows.

- Sample $r \leftarrow \mathsf{Coins}_{\mathsf{Enc}^{\mathrm{losPKE}}}$ and compute $c^{\mathrm{real}} \leftarrow \mathsf{Enc}^{\mathrm{losPKE}}(\mathrm{pk}^{\mathrm{real}}, m; r)$.
- Sample a random bit $b \leftarrow \{0,1\}$.
- Compute $c_b^{\$,\mathrm{deci}} \leftarrow \mathsf{Enc}^{\$,\mathrm{deci}}(\mathrm{pk}^{\$,\mathrm{deci}}, r)$ and sample $c_{\bar{b}}^{\$,\mathrm{deci}} \leftarrow \{0,1\}^{\mathrm{cipherLen}}$.
- Output $(c^{\mathrm{real}}, c_0^{\$,\mathrm{deci}}, c_1^{\$,\mathrm{deci}})$.

$\mathsf{Dec}_2^{\mathrm{soa}}$: On input a ciphertext $(c^{\mathrm{real}}, c_0^{\$,\mathrm{deci}}, c_1^{\$,\mathrm{deci}})$, proceed as follows.

- Compute $m \leftarrow \mathsf{Dec}^{\mathrm{losPKE}}(\mathrm{sk}^{\mathrm{real}}, c^{\mathrm{real}})$.
- If there exists $b \in \{0,1\}$ such that $r := \mathsf{Dec}^{\$,\mathrm{deci}}(\mathrm{sk}^{\$,\mathrm{deci}}, c_b^{\$,\mathrm{deci}})$ *and* $c^{\mathrm{real}} = \mathsf{Enc}^{\mathrm{losPKE}}(\mathrm{pk}^{\mathrm{real}}, m; r)$, then output m; otherwise, output $\bot$.

Fig. 2. A SIM-SO-CPA secure scheme that is not a lossy encryption scheme

We begin by providing a high-level sketch of $\mathsf{Sim}^{\mathsf{PKE}_2^{\mathrm{soa}}}$. Recall that the underlying primitives in our construction of $\mathsf{PKE}_2^{\mathrm{soa}}$ are a lossy encryption scheme with efficient openability and a public-key-decidable encryption scheme. Also recall that we know from [BHY09] that every lossy encryption scheme with efficient openability is a SIM-SO-CPA secure scheme. Thus every lossy encryption scheme with efficient openability has a SIM-SO-CPA simulator associated with it. With this, to build the SIM-SO-CPA simulator $\mathsf{Sim}^{\mathsf{PKE}_2^{\mathrm{soa}}}$ for our $\mathsf{PKE}_2^{\mathrm{soa}}$ scheme (which is built by using a lossy encryption scheme with efficient openability and public-key-decidable CPA-secure encryption scheme) we naturally extend the SIM-SO-CPA simulator of the underlying lossy encryption scheme.

It is helpful to first recall at a high-level the SIM-SO-CPA simulator of the underlying lossy encryption scheme. Let $\mathsf{Sim}^{\mathsf{PKE}^{\mathrm{losPKE}}}$ be the SIM-SO-CPA simulator of the underlying lossy encryption scheme with efficient openability $\mathsf{PKE}^{\mathrm{losPKE}}$. $\mathsf{Sim}^{\mathsf{PKE}^{\mathrm{losPKE}}}$ first samples a lossy public key. Then it encrypts a tuple of dummy messages and gives the ciphertext tuple to the adversary. Upon receiving an index-set $\mathcal{I}$ from the adversary and the values to be opened to at these indices from the opening oracle, it runs the PPT algorithm Opener ensured by the lossy encryption scheme to open the lossy ciphertexts at these indices to the requested values. Finally, it simply outputs the output of the adversary. With this, indistinguishability of the simulated output from the output of the adversary in the real experiment follows from indistinguishability of real keys from lossy keys of the lossy encryption scheme.

Now, having recalled the structure of $\mathsf{Sim}^{\mathsf{PKE}^{\mathrm{losPKE}}}$, our simulator $\mathsf{Sim}^{\mathsf{PKE}_2^{\mathrm{soa}}}$ is a slight modification of $\mathsf{Sim}^{\mathsf{PKE}^{\mathrm{losPKE}}}$. Roughly speaking, this modification directly corresponds to the modification to the underlying lossy scheme $\mathsf{PKE}^{\mathrm{losPKE}}$ introduced in our $\mathsf{PKE}_2^{\mathrm{soa}}$. Recall that the modifications to $\mathsf{PKE}^{\mathrm{losPKE}}$ were basically two-fold: one was to append the public key $\mathrm{pk}^{\mathrm{lossy}}$ with the public key $\mathrm{pk}^{\$,\mathrm{deci}}$ of the public-key-decidable encryption scheme $\mathsf{PKE}^{\$,\mathrm{deci}}$; the other modification was that, while encrypting, besides encrypting the plaintext with the (real) public key of the lossy encryption scheme to get a ciphertext c^{real}, append two more components to this ciphertext – namely, an encryption of the randomness used in generating c^{real} and a random value from $\{0,1\}^{\text{cipherLen}}$, in random order. The corresponding modification to the simulator $\text{Sim}^{\text{PKE}^{\text{losPKE}}}$ would be the following: $\text{Sim}^{\text{PKE}_2^{\text{soa}}}$ also appends the lossy public key with a uniformly sampled public key $\text{pk}^{\$,\text{deci}}$ of the $\text{PKE}^{\$,\text{deci}}$ scheme. Then, to construct a ciphertext, it would first construct a lossy ciphertext c^{lossy} (with some dummy plaintext); then it would compute openings r_0 and r_1 of this lossy ciphertext to 0 and 1, respectively, encrypt both r_0 and r_1 in a random order using $\text{pk}^{\$,\text{deci}}$ to get $c_0^{\$,\text{deci}}, c_1^{\$,\text{deci}}$. The resulting ciphertext is thus $(c^{\text{lossy}}, c_0^{\$,\text{deci}}, c_1^{\$,\text{deci}})$.

With this, the simulator can open each ciphertext to both 0 and 1 as follows. To open to $m \in \{0,1\}$, it would output the pre-computed opening, r_m, of c^{lossy} to m and also an opening of the one between $c_0^{\$,\text{deci}}$ and $c_1^{\$,\text{deci}}$) that encrypts r_m (with a pretense that the other ciphertext component was randomly chosen from $\{0,1\}^{\text{cipherLen}}$. With this, from the indistinguishability of real keys from lossy keys of the lossy encryption scheme and from the pseudorandomness of the ciphertexts of the $\text{PKE}^{\$,\text{deci}}$ scheme, indistinguishability of the simulated output from the output of the adversary in the real experiment follows.   □

Theorem 8. $\text{PKE}_2^{\text{soa}}$ *is not a lossy encryption scheme.*

The full proof appears in the full version. We give a proof sketch here below.
Proof Sketch: We begin by providing some intuition to the proof. Recall that for $\text{PKE}_2^{\text{soa}}$ to be a lossy encryption scheme, there must exist algorithms $\text{FakeKeyGen}^{\text{soa}}$ and (possibly inefficient) $\text{Opener}^{\text{soa}}$ such that the following holds:

1. public keys, called lossy public keys, sampled using $\text{FakeKeyGen}^{\text{soa}}$ are computationally indistinguishable from those sampled using $\text{KeyGen}_2^{\text{soa}}$, and,
2. for a ciphertext, called a lossy ciphertext, generated using any lossy public key can be opened to any bit value using $\text{Opener}^{\text{soa}}$.

The idea would be to show that no pair of algorithms $(\text{FakeKeyGen}^{\text{soa}}, \text{Opener}^{\text{soa}})$ can satisfy these properties for our scheme. Assume for contradiction that there exist such a pair of algorithms $(\text{FakeKeyGen}^{\text{soa}}, \text{Opener}^{\text{soa}})$.

We rely on the following facts about our scheme.

1. A public key soa-pk of our scheme consists of two components soa-pk $=$ $(\text{pk}^{\text{real}}, \text{pk}^{\$,\text{deci}})$, where the second component is easily decidable. Thus:
   - A lossy public-key output by $\text{FakeKeyGen}^{\text{soa}}$ is such that its second part is still within the public-key space of $\text{PKE}^{\$,\text{deci}}$.
   - Any ciphertext generated using the second component of soa-pk (regardless of soa-pk being real or lossy) cannot be opened to two distinct plaintexts.
2. Consider soa-pk$^{\text{lossy}} = (\text{pk}^{\text{lossy}}, \text{pk}^{\$,\text{deci}})$ sampled using $\text{FakeKeyGen}^{\text{soa}}$. As per our scheme a ciphertext generated using soa-pk^{lossy} consists of three components: $(c^{\text{lossy}}, c_0^{\$,\text{deci}}, c_1^{\$,\text{deci}})$, where c^{lossy} is an encryption using pk^{lossy} of the plaintext with randomness r and one of the other two components, say $c_b^{\$,\text{deci}}$, is an encryption of r using $\text{pk}^{\$,\text{deci}}$. This has the following implication.

- In order for the $\mathsf{Opener}^{\mathsf{soa}}$ algorithm to open such a ciphertext to both 0 and 1, it has to be the case that $c_0^{\$,\mathsf{deci}}$ and $c_1^{\$,\mathsf{deci}}$ are encryptions of openings of c^{lossy} to 0 and 1 (in some random order).

From the above observations on your $\mathsf{PKE}_2^{\mathsf{soa}}$, we have the following. Let $c = (c^{\mathsf{lossy}}, c_0^{\$,\mathsf{deci}}, c_1^{\$,\mathsf{deci}}) \leftarrow \mathsf{Enc}_2^{\mathsf{soa}}(\mathsf{soa\text{-}pk}^{\mathsf{lossy}}, m)$ for $m \in \{0,1\}$. Recall that our encryption algorithm works by choosing one of $c_0^{\$,\mathsf{deci}}$ and $c_1^{\$,\mathsf{deci}}$ uniformly from $\{0,1\}^{\mathsf{cipherLen}}$ (and by computing the other as an encryption of the randomness r used in generating c^{lossy}). For concreteness of discussion, let the random string be $c_0^{\$,\mathsf{deci}}$. From the above observations, for (any) algorithm, and in particular for $\mathsf{Opener}^{\mathsf{soa}}$, to open c to $1 - m$, the following condition must hold:
- there must exist an opening r' of c^{lossy} to $1 - m$ such that there exists an opening of $c_0^{\$,\mathsf{deci}}$ to r'.

We can show that this condition does not hold with non-negligible probability over the choice of $c_0^{\$,\mathsf{deci}}$. The subtlety however to make this argument work is the following. It is possible that, for $\mathsf{PKE}^{\mathsf{losPKE}}$ there are multiple openings of a lossy ciphertext to either 0 or 1. Furthermore, for $\mathsf{PKE}^{\$,\mathsf{deci}}$, the number of ciphertexts encrypting one message could be different than the number of ciphertexts encrypting another message. We shall discuss the subtlety in detail and get around it to still make the argument work in the full proof.   □

Furthermore, as a corollary of our techniques, on a slightly unrelated but useful note, we obtain that lossiness is not required to obtain non-committing encryption. Details are given in the full version.

Acknowledgments. Work supported in part by NSF grants 09165174, 1065276, 1118126 and 1136174, US-Israel BSF grant 2008411, OKAWA Foundation Research Award, IBM Faculty Research Award, Xerox Faculty Research Award, B. John Garrick Foundation Award, Teradata Research Award, and Lockheed-Martin Corporation Research Award. This material is based upon work supported by the Defense Advanced Research Projects Agency through the U.S. Office of Naval Research under Contract N00014 -11 -1-0392. The views expressed are those of the author and do not reflect the official policy or position of the Department of Defense or the U.S. Government.

References

[BC05]   Backes, M., Cachin, C.: Public-key steganography with active attacks. In: Kilian, J. (ed.) TCC 2005. LNCS, vol. 3378, pp. 210–226. Springer, Heidelberg (2005)

[BDWY12]   Bellare, M., Dowsley, R., Waters, B., Yilek, S.: Standard security does not imply security against selective-opening. In: Pointcheval, Johansson (eds.) [PJ12], pp. 645–662

[BHK12]   Böhl, F., Hofheinz, D., Kraschewski, D.: On definitions of selective opening security. In: Fischlin, M., Buchmann, J., Manulis, M. (eds.) PKC 2012. LNCS, vol. 7293, pp. 522–539. Springer, Heidelberg (2012)

[BHY09]   Bellare, M., Hofheinz, D., Yilek, S.: Possibility and impossibility results
           for encryption and commitment secure under selective opening. In: Joux,
           A. (ed.) EUROCRYPT 2009. LNCS, vol. 5479, pp. 1–35. Springer,
           Heidelberg (2009)

[BWY11]   Bellare, M., Waters, B., Yilek, S.: Identity-based encryption secure
           against selective opening attack. In: Ishai, Y. (ed.) TCC 2011. LNCS,
           vol. 6597, pp. 235–252. Springer, Heidelberg (2011)

[BY96]   Bellare, M., Yung, M.: Certifying permutations: Noninteractive
           zero-knowledge based on any trapdoor permutation. J. Cryptology 9(3),
           149–166 (1996)

[CLOS02]   Canetti, R., Lindell, Y., Ostrovsky, R., Sahai, A.: Universally composable
           two-party and multi-party secure computation. In: Reif, J.H. (ed.) STOC,
           pp. 494–503. ACM (2002)

[CS98]   Cramer, R., Shoup, V.: A practical public key cryptosystem provably
           secure against adaptive chosen ciphertext attack. In: Krawczyk, H. (ed.)
           CRYPTO 1998. LNCS, vol. 1462, pp. 13–25. Springer, Heidelberg (1998)

[DNRS99]   Dwork, C., Naor, M., Reingold, O., Stockmeyer, L.: Magic functions. In:
           Foundations of Computer Science (FOCS 1999), pp. 523–534 (1999)

[DNRS03]   Dwork, C., Naor, M., Reingold, O., Stockmeyer, L.: Magic functions. J.
           ACM 50(6), 852–921 (2003)

[FHKW10]   Fehr, S., Hofheinz, D., Kiltz, E., Wee, H.: Encryption schemes secure
           against chosen-ciphertext selective opening attacks. In: Gilbert, H. (ed.)
           EUROCRYPT 2010. LNCS, vol. 6110, pp. 381–402. Springer, Heidelberg
           (2010)

[Gam84]   El Gamal, T.: A public key cryptosystem and a signature scheme based
           on discrete logarithms. In: Blakely, G.R., Chaum, D. (eds.) CRYPTO
           1984. LNCS, vol. 196, pp. 10–18. Springer, Heidelberg (1985)

[HLOV09]   Hemenway, B., Libert, B., Ostrovsky, R., Vergnaud, D.: Lossy encryption:
           Constructions from general assumptions and efficient selective opening
           chosen ciphertext security. Cryptology ePrint Archive, Report 2009/088
           (2009), http://eprint.iacr.org/

[Hof12]   Hofheinz, D.: All-but-many lossy trapdoor functions. In: Pointcheval,
           Johansson (eds.) [PJ12], pp. 209–227

[HR14]   Hofheinz, D., Rupp, A.: Standard versus selective opening security:
           Separation and equivalence results. In: Lindell, Y. (ed.) TCC 2014. LNCS,
           vol. 8349, pp. 591–615. Springer, Heidelberg (2014)

[ORSV13]   Ostrovsky, R., Rao, V., Scafuro, A., Visconti, I.: Revisiting lower and
           upper bounds for selective decommitments. In: Sahai, A. (ed.) TCC 2013.
           LNCS, vol. 7785, pp. 559–578. Springer, Heidelberg (2013)

[PJ12]   Pointcheval, D., Johansson, T. (eds.): EUROCRYPT 2012. LNCS,
           vol. 7237. Springer, Heidelberg (2012)

[PVW08]   Peikert, C., Vaikuntanathan, V., Waters, B.: A framework for efficient
           and composable oblivious transfer. In: Wagner, D. (ed.) CRYPTO 2008.
           LNCS, vol. 5157, pp. 554–571. Springer, Heidelberg (2008)

[Xia11]   Xiao, D. (Nearly) round-optimal black-box constructions of commitments
           secure against selective opening attacks. In: Ishai, Y. (ed.) TCC 2011.
           LNCS, vol. 6597, pp. 541–558. Springer, Heidelberg (2011)

Narrow Bandwidth Is Not Inherent in Reverse Public-Key Encryption

David Naccache[1], Rainer Steinwandt[2*],
Adriana Suárez Corona[3,**], and Moti Yung[4]

[1] École Normale Supérieure, Paris CEDEX 05, F-75230, France
david.naccache@ens.fr
[2] Florida Atlantic University, Boca Raton, FL 33431, USA
rsteinwa@fau.edu
[3] Universidad de León, 24004 León, Spain
adrixsua@gmail.com
[4] Google Inc. and Columbia University, New York, NY, USA
moti@cs.columbia.edu

Abstract. Reverse Public-Key Encryption (RPKE) is a mode of operation exploiting a weak form of key privacy to provide message privacy. In principle, RPKE offers a fallback mode, if the underlying encryption scheme's message secrecy fails while a weak form of key privacy survives. To date, all published RPKE constructions suffer from a low bandwidth, and low bandwidth seems naturally inherent to reverse encryption. We show how reverse encryption can, in connection with and as a novel application of anonymous broadcast encryption, achieve high-bandwidth. We point out that by using traditional and reverse encryption simultaneously, a form of crypto-steganographic channel inside a cryptosystem can be provided.

Keywords: public-key encryption, mode of operation, reverse public-key encryption, broadcast encryption.

1 Introduction

Reverse Public-Key Encryption (RPKE) is generally thought to be a low bandwidth mode of operation. In fact, even the *Encyclopedia of Cryptographic Security* [vTJ11] defines RPKE as *"a low-bandwidth public key encryption mode of operation [that] turns a weak form of key privacy into message privacy ..."*; a detailed discussion of RPKE can be found in [NSY09] which introduces the concept and explains how to use it to obtain message privacy from key privacy. What is important to note here, is that the security of the reverse mode

---

[*] RS was supported by the Spanish Ministerio de Economía y Competitividad through the project grant MTM-2012-15167.
[**] ASC was supported by the Spanish Ministerio de Economía y Competitividad through the project grant MTM-2010-18370-C04-01. This work was performed while ASC was in University of Denver.

M. Abdalla and R. De Prisco (Eds.): SCN 2014, LNCS 8642, pp. 598–607, 2014.

of operation does in no way depend on the security of the traditional mode of operation—any guarentees offered in reverse mode derive from key privacy (alone). Straightforward RPKE requires the transmission of $O(k)$ ciphertexts to encode a k-bit plaintext, e.g., to RPKE transmit a 128-bit AES key using 200-bit EC-ElGamal, several KBytes of data must be sent. This is highly inefficient, even for a fallback mode of operation. A natural problem left open in [NSY09] is the existence of *"broadband RPKE"*; it is interesting theoretically and may have implication in cases where the notion applies.

Our contribution. We investigate the use of anonymous broadcast encryption for achieving RPKE. Building on work by Fazio and Perera [FP12] we show how in this setting RPKE can be made broadband—a single ciphertext and a small overhead typically suffice to transmit a complete session key in reverse mode. As technical tool we introduce a notion of robustness for anonymous broadcast encryption which may be of independent interest. Combining traditional and reverse encryption for an anonymous broadcast encryption scheme enables a conceptually interesting dual use, where two independent meaningful plaintexts are packed into one ciphertext. This can serve as a plausible deniability measure against censorship. We also note, on the way to our result, a technicality in the definition of RPKE and argue that for enabling security of the reverse mode of operation, key privacy should come with a form of robustness.

2   Preliminaries

To show how broadband RPKE can be realized, we first review the definition of RPKE and the relevant terminology for anonymous broadcast encryption. The expression *random* will always refer to a uniform distribution.

2.1   Reverse Public-Key Encryption

To emphasize the difference between what is known and what we achieve regarding the reverse mode of operation we adopt the terminology of [NSY09]:

Definition 1 (Traditional Public-Key Encryption). *A (traditional) public-key encryption scheme $\mathcal{P} = (\mathcal{G}, \mathcal{K}, \mathcal{E}, \mathcal{D})$ consists of four polynomial time algorithms:*

- *A randomized common-key generation algorithm $\mathcal{G}$ which given the security parameter 1^k, outputs a common key ck.*
- *A randomized key generation algorithm $\mathcal{K}$, which given ck outputs a (public key, secret key)-pair (pk, sk).*
- *A randomized encryption algorithm $\mathcal{E}$, which given pk and a plaintext $m \in \mathfrak{M}(pk)$ outputs a ciphertext c. Here $\mathfrak{M}(pk)$ denotes the message space associated with pk.*
- *A deterministic decryption algorithm $\mathcal{D}$ which given (sk, c) either returns m or an error symbol $\bot \notin \mathfrak{M}(pk)$.*

For all $m \in \mathfrak{M}(pk)$ we impose $\mathcal{D}(sk, \mathcal{E}(pk, m)) = m$.

Complementing the above definition, we assume the existence of a sampling algorithm $\mathcal{M}$ which on input a public key pk samples plaintexts in $\mathfrak{M}(pk)$. This algorithm can be very simple and may even have constant output. As in [NSY09], we denote by $\text{Im}(\mathcal{M}(pk)) \subseteq \mathfrak{M}(pk)$ the set of $\mathcal{M}(pk)$'s possible outputs and assume that membership in $\text{Im}(\mathcal{M}(pk))$ can be tested in polynomial time.

Definition 2. *Given a public-key encryption scheme $\mathcal{P} := (\mathcal{G}, \mathcal{K}, \mathcal{E}, \mathcal{D})$, [NSY09] construct a "reverse public-key encryption scheme" $\mathcal{P}^{\mathrm{R}} := (\mathcal{G}^{\mathrm{R}}, \mathcal{K}^{\mathrm{R}}, \mathcal{E}^{\mathrm{R}}, \mathcal{D}^{\mathrm{R}})$ allowing to encrypt a single bit. $\mathcal{P}^{\mathrm{R}}$ and $\mathcal{P}$ share the same key generation algorithm $\mathcal{G}^{\mathrm{R}} := \mathcal{G}$, but $\mathcal{P}^{\mathrm{R}}$'s remaining algorithms differ as follows:*

Key Generation: *$\mathcal{K}^{\mathrm{R}}$ runs $\mathcal{K}$ twice to generate independent key-pairs (pk_0, sk_0) and (pk_1, sk_1). The public key output by $\mathcal{K}^{\mathrm{R}}$ is the pair (pk_0, pk_1) and the secret key is (sk_0, sk_1).*

Encryption: *to encrypt a plaintext $b \in \{0, 1\}$, we set $\mathcal{E}^{\mathrm{R}}(pk, b) := \mathcal{E}(pk_b, m_b)$, where $m_b \xleftarrow{\$} \mathcal{M}(pk_b)$. So the plaintext selects which of the two public keys pk_0 and pk_1 is applied to (the possibly public!) m_b.*

Decryption: *to decrypt a ciphertext $c = \mathcal{E}(pk_b, m_b)$, the algorithm $\mathcal{D}^{\mathrm{R}}$ computes*

$$\tilde{m}_0 \leftarrow \mathcal{D}(sk_0, c)$$
$$\tilde{m}_1 \leftarrow \mathcal{D}(sk_1, c)$$

and then determines the output as

$$\mathcal{D}^{\mathrm{R}}(sk, c) := \begin{cases} 0 & \text{if } \tilde{m}_0 \in \text{Im}(\mathcal{M}(pk_0)) \text{ and } \tilde{m}_1 \notin \text{Im}(\mathcal{M}(pk_1)) \\ 1 & \text{if } \tilde{m}_1 \in \text{Im}(\mathcal{M}(pk_1)) \text{ and } \tilde{m}_0 \notin \text{Im}(\mathcal{M}(pk_0)) \\ \bot & \text{else.} \end{cases}$$

The intuition behind the proposed construction is already visible here: the case $\tilde{m}_1 \in \text{Im}(\mathcal{M}(pk_1))$ and $\tilde{m}_0 \in \text{Im}(\mathcal{M}(pk_0))$ is left unexploited.

In [NSY09] the correctness of $\mathcal{P}^{\mathrm{R}}$ is taken for granted, although this is not an evidence in itself: Consider a (degenerate) public-key encryption scheme $\mathcal{P}$ where the plaintext space is identical for all public keys and $\mathcal{E}$ simply implements, for all keys, the identity map on the plaintext space. Obviously this scheme must be regarded as completely insecure in the traditional mode of operation, but at the same time offers an extreme form of key privacy. Given a ciphertext, it is information-theoretically impossible to identify the public key that was invoked for encryption. As security of the reverse mode of operation is supposed to stem from key privacy alone, one might have high hopes for the security of $\mathcal{P}^{\mathrm{R}}$. However, $\mathcal{D}^{\mathrm{R}}$ consistently fails and outputs $\bot$.

The problem for this failure is a lack of *robustness*, and to remedy this problem it is in principle sufficient to impose that $\mathcal{P}$ is *weakly robust* as defined by Abdalla et al. in [ABN10] (WROB-CPA) which essentially defines a cryptosystem where it is of negligible probability to find a message which is valid under two different keys. Abdalla et al. also offer a general transformation to make (semantically secure and anonymous) public-key encryption schemes robust. Weak robustness is a guarantee that holds with overwhelming probability only, and to take care of this technicality we slightly weaken the correctness requirement in Definition 1:

Definition 3 (Overwhelming Correctness). *Let $\mathcal{P}$ be as in Definition 1. Then $\mathcal{P}$ is an overwhelmingly correct public-key encryption scheme if for all $m \in \mathfrak{M}(pk)$ the equality $\mathcal{D}(sk, \mathcal{E}(pk, m)) = m$ holds with overwhelming probability. Here the probability is taken over the random choices of $\mathcal{E}$.*

Having addressed this technical issue, RPKE can be used as described in [NSY09].

Proposition 1. *Let $\mathcal{P}$ be an overwhelmingly correct and weakly robust traditional public-key encryption scheme. If the sampling algorithm $\mathcal{M}(pk)$ has a constant output $m_0 \in \mathfrak{M}(pk)$ for all public keys pk, then $\mathcal{P}^\mathrm{R}$ as described in [NSY09] is overwhelmingly correct.*

Proof. If $\mathcal{P}$ is overwhelmingly correct, the case $\tilde{m}_0 \notin \mathrm{Im}(\mathcal{M}(pk_0))$ and $\tilde{m}_1 \notin \mathrm{Im}(\mathcal{M}(pk_1))$ can only happen with negligible probability.

The case $\tilde{m}_0 \in \mathrm{Im}(\mathcal{M}(pk_0))$ and $\tilde{m}_1 \in \mathrm{Im}(\mathcal{M}(pk_1))$ also leads to a $\bot$ output, but if $\mathcal{P}$ is weakly robust, this can only happen with negligible probability. Hence, overwhelming correctness is guaranteed. □

This clarifies the conditions for reversibility of encryption, and to overcome the narrow-band restriction implicit in RPKE, we next transfer the reverse mode of operation to anonymous broadcast encryption.

2.2 Anonymous Broadcast Encryption

The main tool to implement a broadcast variant of RPKE is an (outsider) anonymous broadcast encryption scheme. We consider a general enough setting to include both the public-key case and the identity-based case [LPQ12, FP12]. For specific constructions we refer the reader to the latter works by Libert *et al.* and by Fazio and Perera.

Definition 4 (Anonymous Broadcast Encryption). *Let $U = \{1, \dots, n\}$ with $n \in \mathbb{N}$ be a fixed set of users, let $\mathfrak{M}$ be a message space and $\mathfrak{C}$ a ciphertext space. An anonymous broadcast encryption scheme (ANOBES) is a tuple of polynomial time algorithms $(\mathcal{S}^\mathrm{B}, \mathcal{G}^\mathrm{B}, \mathcal{E}^\mathrm{B}, \mathcal{D}^\mathrm{B})$ defined as follows:*

– *$\mathcal{S}^\mathrm{B}$ is probabilistic. Given the security parameter 1^k and n, the setup algorithm $\mathcal{S}^\mathrm{B}$ outputs a (master public key, master secret key)-pair (mpk, msk).*
– *$\mathcal{G}^\mathrm{B}$ is probabilistic. Given msk, mpk and an index $i \in U$, $\mathcal{G}^\mathrm{B}$ generates the private key sk_i of user i.*
– *$\mathcal{E}^\mathrm{B}$ is probabilistic. Given mpk and $m \in \mathfrak{M}$ and a subset $S \subseteq U$, $\mathcal{E}^\mathrm{B}$ outputs a ciphertext c.*
– *$\mathcal{D}^\mathrm{B}$ is deterministic. Given mpk, sk_i and $c \in \mathfrak{C}$, $\mathcal{D}^\mathrm{B}$ outputs a message m or a special error symbol $\bot$.*

We require that for all $S \subseteq U$ and for all $i \in U$, if:

- $c = \mathcal{E}^{\mathrm{B}}(mpk, m, S)$
- *and sk_i was generated by $\mathcal{G}^{\mathrm{B}}$*

then $\mathcal{D}^{\mathrm{B}}(mpk, sk_i, c) = m$ with overwhelming probability.

To characterize the security of an (outsider) ANOBES, anonymity and indistinguishability are simultaneously captured in a single definition by [LPQ12, FP12]. We adopt the security model of [FP12]:

- **Setup:** The challenger $\mathcal{C}$ runs $\mathcal{S}^{\mathrm{B}}$ to obtain (mpk, msk) and hands mpk to $\mathcal{A}$.
- **Phase 1:** $\mathcal{A}$ can query a private key extraction oracle for any index $i \in U$: given an index $i \in U$, $\mathcal{C}$ computes $\mathcal{G}^{\mathrm{B}}(mpk, msk, i)$.
- **Challenge:** $\mathcal{A}$ chooses two equal length messages $m_0, m_1 \in \mathfrak{M}$ and two sets $S_0, S_1 \subseteq U$ with the restriction $i \notin S_0 \cup S_1$ for every index i queried before. $\mathcal{A}$ hands (m_0, m_1, S_0, S_1) to $\mathcal{C}$.[a] Then $\mathcal{C}$ selects a random bit $b \in \{0, 1\}$, computes $c^* = \mathcal{E}^{\mathrm{B}}(mpk, m_b, S_b)$ and hands c^* to $\mathcal{A}$.
- **Phase 2:** $\mathcal{A}$ can issue private key queries as in Phase 1, subject to the condition that $i \notin S_0 \cup S_1$.
- **Guess:** The adversary outputs $b' \in \{0, 1\}$ and wins if $b = b'$.

---

[a] In some instantiations, we may require that $\#S_0 = \#S_1$.

Fig. 1. Security in the sense of oABE-IND-CPA for an anonymous broadcast encryption scheme

Definition 5 (oABE-IND-CPA security). *An anonymous broadcast encryption scheme is oABE-IND-CPA-secure if the advantage of any probabilistic polynomial time adversary $\mathcal{A}$ in the game described in Figure 1 is negligible. Here $\mathcal{A}$'s advantage is defined as the function $\mathrm{Adv}_{\mathcal{A}}^{\mathrm{oABE\text{-}IND\text{-}CPA}}(k) = \left| \Pr[b = b'] - \frac{1}{2} \right|$.*

[LPQ12] proposes a stronger security model, where the adversary can be an insider. Also, both definitions can be adapted to chosen ciphertext scenarios. For our purposes, we require outsider CPA-security as captured by Definition 5.

3   Robust Anonymous Broadcast Encryption

As for key private encryption, *robustness* is a desirable feature for anonymous broadcast encryption: robustness ensures that when a user decrypts a ciphertext without error, she can be sure to be an intended recipient. This guarantee will enable us to construct a broadband RPKE variant. Note that independently of our specific application such a property seems desirable to have. For anonymous broadcast encryption, no formalization of robustness seems to be available in the literature, so we start by proposing one:

Definition 6 (WROB-CPA security). *An ANOBES is* WROB-CPA-*secure (or weakly robust) if the advantage of any probabilistic polynomial time adversary $\mathcal{A}$ in the game described in Figure 2 is negligible. Here the advantage of $\mathcal{A}$ is*

$$\text{Adv}_{\mathcal{A}}^{\text{WROB-CPA}}(k) = \Pr[\text{Succ}_{\mathcal{A}}^{\text{WROB-CPA}}]$$

with $\text{Succ}_{\mathcal{A}}^{\text{WROB-CPA}}$ *denoting the event that $\mathcal{A}$ wins.*

- **Setup:** The challenger $\mathcal{C}$ runs $\mathcal{S}^{\text{B}}$ to obtain (mpk, msk) and hands mpk to $\mathcal{A}$.
- **Phase 1:** $\mathcal{A}$ can query a private key extraction oracle for any index $i \in U$: given an index $i \in U$, $\mathcal{C}$ computes $\mathcal{G}^{\text{B}}(mpk, msk, i)$. Let I be the set of all indices i queried by $\mathcal{A}$ during this phase.
- **Challenge:** $\mathcal{A}$ outputs a message m, a set $S \subseteq U \setminus I$ and an index $id \notin S$. $\mathcal{A}$ wins if and only if $\mathcal{D}^{\text{B}}(mpk, \mathcal{E}^{\text{B}}(mpk, m, S), sk_{id}) \neq \bot$.

Fig. 2. Security in the sense of WROB-CPA for an anonymous broadcast encryption scheme

If an ANOBES is not weakly robust, a transformation similar to the one proposed in [ABN10] can be applied. Namely, let $(\mathcal{S}^{\text{B}}, \mathcal{G}^{\text{B}}, \mathcal{E}^{\text{B}}, \mathcal{D}^{\text{B}})$ be an anonymous broadcast encryption scheme. Then (for a message size reduced by k bits,) the transformed scheme is as follows:

- $\overline{\mathcal{S}^{\text{B}}}$ runs $\mathcal{S}^{\text{B}}$ to obtain a master public key mpk and a master secret key msk. Next, $\overline{\mathcal{S}^{\text{B}}}$ randomly selects $K \xleftarrow{\$} \{0,1\}^k$ and outputs (mpk, K) as master public key and msk as master secret key.
- $\overline{\mathcal{G}^{\text{B}}}$ runs $\mathcal{G}^{\text{B}}$ to generate the private key sk_i for user i.
- $\overline{\mathcal{E}^{\text{B}}}$: to encrypt a message $\overline{m}$ to a set of recipients S, $\overline{\mathcal{E}^{\text{B}}}$ executes $\mathcal{E}^{\text{B}}$ on input mpk, message $\overline{m}\|K$ and $S \subseteq U$ to obtain a ciphertext c.
- $\overline{\mathcal{D}^{\text{B}}}$ runs $\mathcal{D}^{\text{B}}$ on mpk, an sk_i and a ciphertext $c \in \mathcal{C}$. If $\mathcal{D}^{\text{B}}$ returns $m = \overline{m}\|K$, then $\overline{\mathcal{D}^{\text{B}}}$ returns $\overline{m}$. Otherwise $\bot$ is returned.

Proposition 2. *Denote by $\mathcal{BE} = (\mathcal{S}^{\text{B}}, \mathcal{G}^{\text{B}}, \mathcal{E}^{\text{B}}, \mathcal{D}^{\text{B}})$ an ANOBES with a set of users $U = \{1, \ldots, n\}$ with $n \in \mathbb{N}$ and let $\overline{\mathcal{BE}}$ be the anonymous broadcast encryption scheme resulting from applying the weak robustness transform described above. If $\mathcal{BE}$ is* oABE-IND-CPA-*secure, then $\overline{\mathcal{BE}}$ is* oABE-IND-CPA-*secure and weakly robust.*

Proof (sketch). Proving the oABE-IND-CPA security of $\overline{\mathcal{BE}}$ if $\mathcal{BE}$ is oABE-IND-CPA-secure is straightforward. We only prove that the resulting scheme $\overline{\mathcal{BE}}$ is weakly robust. For this we use a short game hopping proof: Let $\mathcal{A}$ be an adversary against the robustness of $\overline{\mathcal{BE}}$. We let $\mathcal{A}$ interact with a simulator and denote $\mathcal{A}$'s success probability (in this case equal to the advantage of $\mathcal{A}$) in Game i by $\text{Adv}_{\mathcal{A}}^{\text{Game } i}$.

Game 0: This game is identical to the original attack game and the success probability is the same as in the original game. Therefore

$$\mathrm{Adv}_{\mathcal{A}}^{\mathrm{Game\ 0}}(k) = \mathrm{Adv}_{\mathcal{A}}^{\mathrm{WROB\text{-}CPA}}.$$

Game 1: This game is identical to Game 0, but the adversary $\mathcal{A}$ is only considered successful if he outputs a message m, a set S, and an identity id satisfying $\mathcal{D}^{\mathrm{B}}(mpk, \mathcal{E}^{\mathrm{B}}(mpk, 0^{|m|}||0^k, S), sk_{id}) = m^*||K$, with $m^* \neq \bot$. To show that $\mathcal{A}$'s advantage in Game 1 and in Game 0 differs by no more than a negligible function, consider the following adversary $\mathcal{B}$ against the oABE-IND-CPA security of $\mathcal{BE}$:

The adversary $\mathcal{B}$ acts as challenger for $\mathcal{A}$, initializing $\mathcal{A}$ with the public parameters mpk that $\mathcal{B}$ receives from its own challenger and a randomly selected $K \xleftarrow{\$} \{0,1\}^k$. To answer $\mathcal{A}$'s queries on private keys, $\mathcal{B}$ queries its own oracle. Once $\mathcal{A}$ outputs a message m, a set $S \subseteq U \setminus I$ and identity $id \notin S$, the algorithm $\mathcal{B}$ sends to its challenger the two messages $0^{|m|}||0^k$ and $m||K$ and the (identical) sets S and S. Now, after receiving the challenge c^*, $\mathcal{B}$ queries the private key corresponding to id—this is an allowed query, as $id \notin S$. Next, $\mathcal{B}$ computes $\mathcal{D}^{\mathrm{B}}(mpk, sk_{id}, c^*)$. If this algorithm returns $\bot$, then $\mathcal{B}$ returns the guess $b' = 0$ for the random bit b of $\mathcal{B}$'s challenger. If $\mathcal{D}^{\mathrm{B}}(mpk, sk_{id}, c^*) = \overline{m}||K^*$, where $K^* \neq K$, then $\mathcal{B}$ returns $b' = 0$. Otherwise, $\mathcal{B}$ returns $b' = 1$. Therefore

$$|\mathrm{Adv}_{\mathcal{A}}^{\mathrm{Game\ 0}} - \mathrm{Adv}_{\mathcal{A}}^{\mathrm{Game\ 1}}| \leq |\Pr[b' = 1|b = 1] - \Pr[b' = 1|b = 0]|$$

and the latter is upper-bounded by $2 \cdot \mathrm{Adv}_{\mathcal{B}}^{\mathrm{oABE\text{-}IND\text{-}CPA}}$, which by assumption on $\mathcal{BE}$ is negligible.

To conclude the proof, it suffices to recognize $\mathrm{Adv}_{\mathcal{A}}^{\mathrm{Game\ 1}}$ as negligible. To do so, we show that $\Pr[\mathrm{Succ}_{\mathcal{A}}^{\mathrm{Game\ 1}}]$—the probability that

$$\mathcal{D}^{\mathrm{B}}(mpk, \mathcal{E}^{\mathrm{B}}(mpk, 0^{|M|}||0^k, S), sk_{id}) = M^*||K$$

with $M^* \neq \bot$—is at most $2^{2n+\log_2(t)-k}$. Here $t = t(k)$ is $\mathcal{A}$'s running time, which by assumption is polynomial in k. So with n being constant, $2^{2n+\log_2(t)-k}$ is indeed negligible for properly chosen large enough k.

If none of the inputs mpk, $\mathcal{E}^{\mathrm{B}}(mpk, 0^{|M|}||0^k, S)$, $|M|$, S, sk_{id} depends on K, then the probability of getting the last k bits of the decryption result to be equal to K would be 2^{-k} and therefore $\Pr[\mathrm{Succ}_{\mathcal{A}}^{\mathrm{Game\ 1}}] = 2^{-k}$. The choice of the set of users we extract the private keys from can depend on K. As the set of users $U = \{1, \ldots, n\}$ has size n, we have 2^n possibilities, so this choice can carry no more than n bits of information. The choice of the set S can also potentially carry information about K. Again, as the set of users has size n, at most n bits of information about K can be obtained in this way. Consequently,

$$\Pr[\mathrm{Succ}_{\mathcal{A}}^{\mathrm{Game\ 1}}] \leq 2^{2n+\log_2(t)-k},$$

as claimed. □

Remark 1. The general transformations we invoke to ensure the weak robustness prerequisite in Proposition 1 and Proposition 2 are formulated in a scenario where both key anonymity and message security are given; we indeed employ oABE-IND-CPA-security as a single security notion assuring both as our starting point.

4 Realizing Broadband Reverse Encryption

Let $\mathcal{BE} = (\mathcal{S}^B, \mathcal{G}^B, \mathcal{E}^B, \mathcal{D}^B)$ be an ANOBES with set of users $U = \{1, \ldots, n\}$, message space $\mathfrak{M}$ and ciphertext space $\mathfrak{C}$. We can run $\mathcal{BE}$ in *reverse mode* by deriving the following *reverse encryption scheme* $\mathcal{BE}^R$ to encrypt messages in $\{0, 1\}^n$ (*i.e.*, for encrypting an 128-bit AES key, a set of $n = 128$ users is needed):

- $\mathcal{S}^{RB}$: This algorithm runs $\mathcal{S}^B(k, n)$.
- $\mathcal{G}^{RB}$: Runs $\mathcal{G}^B(mpk, msk, i)$ for all $i \in U$ to obtain the private key sk_i for all users $i \in U$. The private key is $sk = (sk_1, \ldots, sk_n)$, and the public key is mpk.
- $\mathcal{E}^{RB}$: To encrypt a message $M = (b_1, \ldots, b_n) \in \{0, 1\}^n$, the set $S_M :=$ $\{i \in U | b_i = 1\}$ is constructed, reflecting the positions of non-zero bits. An arbitrary $m \in \mathfrak{M}$ is selected and $\mathcal{E}^B(mpk, m, S_M)$ is returned.
- $\mathcal{D}^{RB}$: To decrypt a ciphertext $C \in \mathfrak{C}$ using the private key $sk = (sk_1, \ldots, sk_n)$, this algorithm evaluates $\mathcal{D}^B(mpk, sk_i, C)$ for all $i \in U$. If $\mathcal{D}^B(mpk, sk_i, C) = \bot$, then $b_i = 0$, otherwise $b_i = 1$. Finally, $M = (b_1, \ldots, b_n)$ is reconstructed.

One could consider a different formulation where the encrypted message m is published as a public parameter, and the decryption procedure not only checks validity, but also the exact value obtained from $\mathcal{D}^B$. We think that the above formulation better reflects the intuition behind reverse encryption, and, as explained below, enables an interesting double use of an ANOBES.

Remark 2. If the underlying anonymous broadcast encryption scheme requires the sets S_0 and S_1 in the oABE-IND-CCA game to have the same size (so that the adversary cannot trivially win), in reverse mode we have to restrict ourselves to plaintexts of a fixed Hamming weight. Encoding bitstrings as bitstrings of a fixed Hamming weight is a well-known problem, and we refer to, *e.g.*, [OS09] for a possible realization of such an encoding. Similarly, if the underlying broadcast encryption scheme does not support the empty recipient set, the plaintext space has to be adjusted accordingly.

Proposition 3. *Let $\mathcal{BE}$ be a weakly robust ANOBES. Then $\mathcal{BE}^R$ as described above is overwhelmingly correct.*

Proof. The correctness of $\mathcal{BE}$ guarantees that if the plaintext bit b_i is set ($i \in S_M$), then the reverse broadcast decryption will recover a 1 in that position with overwhelming probability. Moreover, if $\mathcal{BE}$ is weakly robust, we correctly obtain a 0 from the reverse broadcast decryption algorithm for the plaintext bit b_i ($i \notin S_M$) with overwhelming probability. This argument applies to all n bits comprising a plaintext. So $\mathcal{BE}^R$ is indeed overwhelmingly correct.   □

$\mathcal{BE}^{\mathrm{R}} = (\mathcal{S}^{\mathrm{RB}}, \mathcal{G}^{\mathrm{RB}}, \mathcal{E}^{\mathrm{RB}}, \mathcal{D}^{\mathrm{RB}})$ forms a public-key scheme in the sense of Definition 1, and if the underlying ANOBES is suitable, $\mathcal{BE}^{\mathrm{R}}$ comes with a strong security guarantee.

Proposition 4. *Let $\mathcal{BE}$ be an* oABE-IND-CPA-*secure ANOBES. Then $\mathcal{BE}^{\mathrm{R}}$ as defined above is* IND-CPA-*secure*.

Proof. Let $\mathcal{A}$ be an adversary against the IND-CPA security of $\mathcal{BE}^{\mathrm{R}}$. From $\mathcal{A}$ we derive an adversary $\mathcal{B}$ that serves as challenger for $\mathcal{A}$ and attacks the oABE-IND-CPA security of $\mathcal{BE}$. First, $\mathcal{B}$ initializes $\mathcal{A}$ with its own master public key—note that $\mathcal{S}^{\mathrm{B}} = \mathcal{S}^{\mathrm{RB}}$. When $\mathcal{A}$ outputs two (challenge) messages $M_0, M_1 \in \{0,1\}^n$, the algorithm $\mathcal{B}$ computes the corresponding sets S_{M_0}, S_{M_1} and submits them along with an arbitrary plaintext message m. Upon receiving its challenge ciphertext, $\mathcal{B}$ forwards it to $\mathcal{A}$. When $\mathcal{A}$ outputs a guess $b' \in \{0,1\}$ which message $M_{b'}$ has been encrypted, $\mathcal{B}$ outputs the same bit. By construction, $\mathcal{B}$ wins whenever $\mathcal{A}$ wins. Therefore

$$\mathrm{Adv}_{\mathcal{A}}^{\text{IND-CPA}} \leq \mathrm{Adv}_{\mathcal{B}}^{\text{oABE-IND-CPA}},$$

and the latter is by assumption negligible.   □

To summarize:

Theorem 1. *Assume the existence of an anonymous broadcast encryption scheme $\mathcal{BE}$ which is* oABE-IND-CPA-*secure. Then there exists $\mathcal{BE}^{\mathrm{R}}$ as defined above which is a public-key encryption scheme that is correct,* IND-CPA-*secure, and supports broadband messages whose size is proportional to n, the size of the group of receivers*.

5   Discussion: Cryptosteganographic Encryption

It is interesting to note that the reverse mode of operation is oblivious to the plaintext message m that is encrypted using $\mathcal{E}^{\mathrm{B}}$—m could even be public. However, one could also use traditional anonymous broadcast encryption in combination with the reverse mode that we have just described: the full plaintext space could be used, and at the same time the reverse mode can be employed to transmit additional information—with a set of only 128 users a full AES-key can be "piggybacked" in that way.

In view of typical constructions for anonymous broadcast encryption, it is fair to say that the public-key encryption scheme obtained from the reverse mode is not extremely efficient, but it is compatible with the traditional mode of operation. We can exploit the latter to design a public-key system where the sender can encrypt a hidden message (in the reverse mode) and an alternative decoy message in the usual (traditional) mode. This provides the receiver with deniability against authorities that later demand the user's private key.

Given the first receiver, Alice, the sender sends it a message M, and at the same time it sends it to a group which includes User 1. The group encodes the hidden message (by the other members of the receiver group except User 1). The receiver who has the master secret key, can learn both the decoy message M and the real message (the subset). To deny, the receiver will erase the master secret key and will keep only the private user key sk_1, which is given to the authority, which can compute M, the decoy, but not the actual message encoded as the receiving group. This is an interesting deniable cryptographic steganography (as there is no proof whether the receiver has kept or did not keep the original master secret key).

6   Conclusion

The above shows how a weakly robust ANOBES can be used to overcome the narrow-bandwidth limitation of reverse public-key encryption. In fact, the suggested realization of reverse encryption allows the simultaneous use of the traditional mode of operation of an anonymous broadcast encryption scheme and the reverse mode. For a weakly robust ANOBES the full plaintext space remains usable[1] while (additional) information is transmitted in reverse mode, allowing for cryptographic steganographic applications. Defining deniable cryptographic steganography and investigating it in depth is an interesting open issue.

Acknowledgment. The authors thank the anonymous referees for constructive feedback.

References

[ABN10]   Abdalla, M., Bellare, M., Neven, G.: Robust encryption. In: Micciancio, D. (ed.) TCC 2010. LNCS, vol. 5978, pp. 480–497. Springer, Heidelberg (2010), http://eprint.iacr.org/2008/440

[FP12]   Fazio, N., Perera, I.M.: Outsider-Anonymous Broadcast Encryption with Sublinear Ciphertexts. In: Fischlin, M., Buchmann, J., Manulis, M. (eds.) PKC 2012. LNCS, vol. 7293, pp. 225–242. Springer, Heidelberg (2012), http://eprint.iacr.org/2012/129

[LPQ12]   Libert, B., Paterson, K.G., Quaglia, E.A.: Anonymous Broadcast Encryption: Adaptive Security and Efficient Constructions in the Standard Model. In: Fischlin, M., Buchmann, J., Manulis, M. (eds.) PKC 2012. LNCS, vol. 7293, pp. 206–224. Springer, Heidelberg (2012), http://eprint.iacr.org/2011/476

[NSY09]   Naccache, D., Steinwandt, R., Yung, M.: Reverse Public Key Encryption. In: BIOSIG 2009 Proceedings. Lecture Notes in Informatics, pp. 155–169. GI, Springer (2009)

[OS09]   Overbeck, R., Sendrier, N.: Code-based cryptography. In: Post-Quantum Cryptography, pp. 95–145. Springer (2009)

[vTJ11]   Naccache, D.: Reverse Public Key Encryption. In: van Tilborg, H.C.A., Jajodia, S. (eds.) Encyclopedia of Cryptography and Security, 2nd edn., p. 1044. Springer (2011)

---

[1] If the transformation from Section 3 needs to be applied first to establish weak robustness, we lose k bits from the plaintext space.

Author Index